WORLD LITERATURE CRITICISM

1500 to the Present

WORLD LITERATURE CRITICISM
Advisory Board

WORLD LITERATURE CRITICISM

1500 to the Present

*A Selection of
Major Authors from
Gale's Literary
Criticism Series*

5

Pope-Stevenson

JAMES P. DRAPER, Editor

Gale Research Inc. · *DETROIT · LONDON*

STAFF

James P. Draper, *Editor*

Laurie DiMauro, Tina Grant, Paula Kepos, Jelena Krstović, Daniel G. Marowski, Roger Matuz, James E. Person, Jr., Joann Prosyniuk, David Segal, Joseph C. Tardiff, Bridget Travers, Lawrence Trudeau, Thomas Votteler, Sandra L. Williamson, Robyn V. Young, *Contributing Editors*

Catherine Falk, Grace Jeromski, Michael W. Jones, Andrew M. Kalasky, David Kmenta, Marie Lazzari, Zoran Minderović, Sean René Pollock, Mark Swartz, *Contributing Associate Editors*

Jennifer Brostrom, David J. Engelman, Andrea Gacki, Judith Galens, Christopher Giroux, Ian A. Goodhall, Alan Hedblad, Elizabeth P. Henry, Christopher K. King, Kyung-Sun Lim, Elisabeth Morrison, Kristin Palm, Susan M. Peters, James Poniewozik, Eric Priehs, Bruce Walker, Debra A. Wells, Janet Witalec, Allyson J. Wylie, *Contributing Assistant Editors*

Jeanne A. Gough, *Permissions & Production Manager*

Linda M. Pugliese, *Production Supervisor*
Paul Lewon, Lorna Mabunda, Maureen Puhl, Camille Robinson, Jennifer VanSickle, *Editorial Associates*
Donna Craft, Brandy C. Johnson, Sheila Walencewicz, *Editorial Assistants*

Victoria B. Cariappa, *Research Manager*

Maureen Richards, *Research Supervisor*
Mary Beth McElmeel, Tamara C. Nott, *Editorial Associates*
Andrea B. Ghorai, Daniel J. Jankowski, Julie K. Karmazin, Robert S. Lazich, *Editorial Assistants*

Sandra C. Davis, *Permissions Supervisor (Text)*
Maria L. Franklin, Josephine M. Keene, Michele M. Lonoconus, Denise M. Singleton, Kimberly F. Smilay, *Permissions Associates*
Rebecca A. Hartford, Shalice Shah, Nancy K. Sheridan, *Permissions Assistants*

Margaret A. Chamberlain, *Permissions Supervisor (Pictures)*
Pamela A. Hayes, *Permissions Associate*
Amy Lynn Emrich, Karla Kulkis, Nancy M. Rattenbury, Keith Reed, *Permissions Assistants*

Mary Beth Trimper, *Production Manager*
Mary Winterhalter, *Production Assistant*

Arthur Chartow, *Art Director*
C. J. Jonik, *Keyliner*
Kathleen A. Hourdakis, Mary Krzewinski, *Graphic Designers*

This book is printed on acid-free paper that meets the minimum requirements of American National Standard for Information Sciences— Permanence Paper for Printed Library Materials, ANSI Z39.48-1984.

ISBN 0-8103-8361-6 (6-volume set)
A CIP catalogue record for this book is available from the British Library

Printed in the United States of America

Published simultaneously in the United Kingdom
by Gale Research International Limited
(An affiliated company of Gale Research Inc.)

Table of Contents

xxi

Introduction

A Comprehensive Information Source
on World Literature

Worid Literature Criticism, 1500 to the Present (WLC) presents a broad selection of the best criticism of works by major writers of the past five hundred years. Among the authors included in WLC are sixteenth-century Spanish novelist Miguel de Cervantes and English dramatist William Shakespeare; seventeenth-century English poet John Milton and dramatist Aphra Behn; eighteenth-century Anglo-Irish novelist Jonathan Swift, English essayist Samuel Johnson, and French Enlightenment masters Jean-Jacques Rousseau and Voltaire; acclaimed nineteenth-century writers Jane Austen, William Blake, Emily Brontë, Lewis Carroll, Charles Dickens, Fyodor Dostoyevsky, Frederick Douglass, Gustave Flaubert, Edgar Allan Poe, Mary Shelley, Robert Louis Stevenson, William Wordsworth, and Emile Zola; and major twentieth-century authors W. H. Auden, James Baldwin, Albert Camus, Arthur Conan Doyle, Ralph Ellison, F. Scott Fitzgerald, Ernest Hemingway, James Joyce, Franz Kafka, Toni Morrison, Sylvia Plath, J. D. Salinger, Gertrude Stein, John Steinbeck, Virginia Woolf, and Richard Wright. The scope of WLC is wide: more than 225 writers representing dozens of nations, cultures, and time periods.

Coverage

This six-volume set is designed for high school, college, and university students, as well as for the general reader who wants to learn more about literature. WLC was developed in response to strong demand by students, librarians, and other readers for a one-stop, authoritative guide to the whole spectrum of world literature. No other compendium like it exists in the marketplace. About 95% of the entries in WLC were selected from Gale's acclaimed Literary Criticism Series and completely updated for publication here. Typically, the revisions are extensive, ranging from new author introductions to wide changes in the selection of criticism. A few entries—about 5%— were prepared especially for WLC in order to furnish the most comprehensive coverage possible.

Inclusion Criteria

Authors were selected for inclusion in WLC based on the advice of leading experts on world literature as well as on the recommendation of a specially formed advisory panel made up of high school teachers and high school and public librarians from throughout the United States. Additionally, the most recent major curriculum studies were closely examined, notably Arthur N. Applebee, A Study of Book-Length Works Taught in High School English Courses (1989); Arthur N. Applebee, A Study of High School Literature Anthologies (1991); and Doug Estel, Michele L. Satchwell, and Patricia S. Wright, Reading Lists for College-Bound Students (1990). All of these resources were collated and compared to produce a reference product that is strongly curriculum driven. To ensure that WLC will continue to meet the needs of students and general readers alike, an effort was made to identify a group of important new writers in addition to the most studied authors.

Scope

Each author entry in *WLC* presents a historical survey of critical response to the author's works. Typically, early criticism is offered to indicate initial responses, later selections document any rise or decline in literary reputations, and retrospective analyses provide modern views. Every endeavor has been made to include seminal essays on each author's work along with commentary providing current perspectives. Interviews and author statements are also included in many entries. Thus, *WLC* is both timely and comprehensive.

Organization of Author Entries

Information about authors and their works is presented through ten key access points:

- The **Descriptive Table of Contents** guides readers through the range of world literature, offering summary sketches of authors' careers and achievements.

- In each author entry, the **Author Heading** cites the name under which the author most commonly wrote, followed by birth and, where appropriate, death dates. Uncertain birth or death dates are indicated by question marks. Name variations, including full birth names when available, are given in parentheses in the caption below the **Author Portrait**.

- The **Biographical and Critical Introduction** contains background information about the life and works of the author. Emphasis is given to four main areas: 1) biographical details that help reveal the life, character, and personality of the author; 2) overviews of the major literary interests of the author—for example, novel writing, autobiography, poetry, social reform, documentary, etc.; 3) descriptions and summaries of the author's best-known works; and 4) critical commentary about the author's achievement, stature, and importance. The concluding paragraph of the **Biographical and Critical Introduction** directs readers to other Gale series containing information about the author.

- Every *WLC* entry includes an **Author Portrait**. Many entries also contain **Illustrations**—including holographs, title pages of works, letters, or pictures of important people, places, and events in the author's life—that document the author's career.

- The **List of Principal Works** is chronological by date of first book publication and identifies the genre of each work. For non-English-language authors whose works have been translated into English, the title and date of the first English-language edition are given in brackets beneath the foreign-language listing. Unless otherwise indicated, dramas are dated by first performance rather than first publication.

- **Criticism** is arranged chronologically in each author entry to provide a useful perspective on changes in critical evaluation over the years. Most entries contain a detailed, comprehensive study of the author's career as well as book reviews, studies of individual works, and comparative examinations. To ensure timeliness, current views are most often presented, but not to the exclusion of important early pieces. For the purpose of easy identification, the critic's name and the date of the critical work are given at the beginning of each piece of criticism. Unsigned criticism is preceded by the title of the source in which it appeared. Within the criticism, titles of works by the author are printed in boldface type. Publication information (such as publisher names and book prices) and certain numerical references (such as footnotes or page and line references to specific editions of works) have been deleted at the editor's discretion to provide smoother reading of the text.

■ Critical essays are prefaced by **Explanatory Notes** as an additional aid to readers of *WLC*. These notes may provide several types of valuable information, including: 1) the reputation of the critic; 2) the importance of the work of criticism; 3) the commentator's approach to the author's work; 4) the purpose of the criticism; and 5) changes in critical trends regarding the author. In some cases, **Explanatory Notes** cross-reference the work of critics within an entry who agree or disagree with each other.

■ A complete **Bibliographical Citation** of the original essay or book follows each piece of criticism.

■ An annotated list of **Sources for Further Study** appears at the end of each entry and suggests resources for additional study. These lists were specially compiled to meet the needs of high school and college students. Additionally, most of the sources cited are available in typical small and medium-size libraries.

■ Many entries contain a **Major Media Adaptations** section listing important non-print treatments and adaptations of the author's works, including feature films, TV mini-series, and radio broadcasts. This feature was specially conceived for *WLC* to meet strong demand from students for this type of information.

Other Features

WLC contains three distinct indexes to help readers find information quickly and easily:

■ The **Author Index** lists all the authors appearing in *WLC*. To ensure easy access, name variations and changes are fully cross-indexed.

■ The **Nationality Index** lists all authors featured in *WLC* by nationality. For expatriate authors and authors identified with more than one nation, multiple listings are offered.

■ The **Title Index** lists in alphabetical order all individual works by the authors appearing in *WLC*. English-language translations of original foreign-language titles are cross-referenced to the foreign titles so that all references to a work are combined in one listing.

Citing *World Literature Criticism*

When writing papers, students who quote directly from *WLC* may use the following general forms to footnote reprinted criticism. The first example is for material drawn from periodicals, the second for material reprinted from books:

Gary Smith, "Gwendolyn Brooks's 'A Street in Bronzeville,' the Harlem Renaissance and the Mythologies of Black Women," *MELUS*, Vol. 10, No. 3 (Fall 1983), 33-46; excerpted and reprinted in *World Literature Criticism, 1500 to the Present*, ed. James P. Draper (Detroit: Gale Research, 1992), pp. 459-61.

Frederick R. Karl, *American Fictions, 1940/1980: A Comprehensive History and Critical Evaluation* (Harper & Row, 1983); excerpted and reprinted in *World Literature Criticism, 1500 to the Present*, ed. James P. Draper (Detroit: Gale Research, 1992), pp. 541-46.

Acknowledgments

The editor wishes to acknowledge the valuable contributions of the many librarians, authors, and scholars who assisted in the compilation of *WLC* with their responses to telephone and mail inquiries. Special thanks are offered to the members of *WLC*'s advisory board, whose names are listed opposite the title page.

Comments Are Welcome

The editor hopes that readers will find *WLC* to be a useful reference tool and welcomes comments about the work. Send comments and suggestions to: Editor, *World Literature Criticism, 1500 to the Present*, Gale Research Inc., Penobscot Building, Detroit, MI 48226-4094.

WORLD LITERATURE CRITICISM

1500 to the Present

Alexander Pope

1688-1744

English poet, critic, translator, and essayist.

INTRODUCTION

*D*eemed the perfecter of the English heroic couplet, Pope is considered the foremost writer of the Augustan Age and one of the most forceful poetic satirists of all time. His verse, described as both epigrammatic and magisterial, is viewed as the ultimate embodiment of eighteenth-century neoclassical ideals. These ideals, such as order, beauty, sophisticated wit, and refined moral sentiment, are exemplified throughout his poetry, particularly in such works as *An Essay on Criticism* (1711), which is at once a treatise of literary theory and a working manual of versification, and the mock-heroic poem *The Rape of the Lock* (1712), a charming, slightly irreverent depiction of English high society. However, Pope's most controversial work and the one most often considered his masterpiece is *The Dunciad* (1728). Also concerned with the moral, social, and intellectual state of humanity, this poem severely satirizes London writers whom Pope believed had unjustly maligned him or whom he considered contributors to the dissolution of Augustan ideals in England. Although Pope's reputation has suffered from adverse critical reactions to the relentless, occasionally overzealous invective of *The Dunciad*, most twentieth-century scholars regard it as the cornerstone of his canon.

Pope was the only child of a moderately wealthy London linen merchant. Under the Anglican rule of William of Orange and Mary Stuart (who ousted the Catholic monarch James II in the year of Pope's birth), Pope's family, like all Roman Catholics living in England at the time, faced numerous restrictions; they were, for example, forbidden by law to practice their religion openly, hold public office, or attend public schools and universities. Also enacted at this time was a law prohibiting Catholics from residing within ten miles of London; and so the Popes relocated in nearby

Windsor Forest, beside the Thames. Under these circumstances, Pope received his education irregularly through private tutors and Catholic priests, but was largely self-taught. By the age of twelve, he was already well versed in Greek, Roman, and English literature and diligently emulated the works of his favorite poets. At this time, Pope contracted a tubercular condition from infected milk, which caused permanent curvature of the spine and severely stunted growth; as a result, he attained a maximum height of only four feet, six inches, and throughout adulthood was so physically debilitated that he required daily care. Yet, this did not deter him from the literary life he sought. By his teens, after voluminous reading of the classics, he had come to regard the heroic couplets of John Dryden as the highest, most sustained form of English poetry yet produced, and he decided to pattern verse after this Restoration master. During periodic visits to London at this time, Pope met three of Dryden's contemporaries: the poet William Walsh, and dramatists William Wycherley and William Congreve. Each encouraged Pope in his aspirations, particularly upon reading the manuscript version of his early bucolic poems, "Pastorals." Walsh, in fact, confided in Pope that he believed there had not yet been an entirely "correct" English poet and urged Pope to make this his goal: to achieve in his work an uncompromising precision of rhythm, rhyme, and language. Through the influence of these writers, Pope's manuscript captured the attention of Jacob Tonson, then Britain's leading publisher, and in 1709 the "Pastorals" appeared in Tonson's *Poetical Miscellanies.* Consciously affined with the verse of Virgil, Edmund Spenser, John Milton, and Dryden, the "Pastorals" demonstrated Pope's veneration for established literary figures and traditions. Pope then went on to commend the theory and practice of such critics as Horace and Nicolas Boileau, publishing the poem *An Essay on Criticism* in 1711. Composed by Pope at the age of twenty-three, this work rendered literary London society awestruck, for it displayed not only a precocious mastery of the couplet form but originated a wealth of impeccably expressed eighteenth-century sentiments ("To err is human, to forgive divine," "A little learning is a dangerous thing") that have since become firmly embedded in English and American culture.

Following the *Essay*'s appearance, Pope contributed poems and articles to the Whig journal the *Spectator.* His *Rape of the Lock,* published in two cantos in 1712, and later expanded to five in 1714, was influenced by the fusion of high humor and moralization characteristic of this publication. The poem quickly became popular, and Pope, wishing to capitalize on his rising fame, issued a multi-volume translation of Homer's *Iliad* (1715-20). An attestation both to his growing understanding of the commercial aspects of publishing and to his quickly established position as a prominent poet of the age, it enabled Pope to obtain enough money through subscriptions to render him the first independently wealthy, full-time writer in English history. During this time, Pope also edited Shakespeare's plays, published a series of miscellanies with Jonathan Swift, and collaborated on a translation of Homer's *Odyssey.* He closely oversaw the publication of everything he wrote, often editing and reissuing his works in updated and collected volumes. Not surprisingly, Pope's huge financial and literary successes enraged less-fortunate London writers and critics. Due to his success, as well as his Catholic religion and unpopular Tory politics, Pope attracted abusive critical and personal attack with nearly every new literary venture he began. Until the publication of *The Dunciad* in 1728, he refrained from wholesale refutation of these attacks, but pent-up anger at being caricatured as an ape, a madman, and a literary scoundrel, as well as growing impatience with what he saw as a widespread profanation of the writer's responsibility to society, provoked him to formulate a scathing satirical response. Thereafter, in the various editions of *The Dunciad* as well as in such works as *Epistles to Several Persons* (1731-35), *Satires and Epistles of Horace, Imitated* (1733-37), and *An Essay on Man* (1734), the moral, social, and political decay in England under the Hanoverian kings George I and II became his primary focus. Pope's last years were spent revising the body of his writings in preparation for a complete, edited edition of his works; he died in 1744 of acute asthma and dropsy before this task was completed.

Undoubtedly Pope's most conceptually imaginative and publicly cherished work is *The Rape of the Lock.* Celebrated as a masterstroke of English originality in his lifetime and scrutinized as an ethereal curiosity in the nineteenth century, it has, in the twentieth century, attracted profuse, diverse interpretation, from character analyses to examinations of Pope's political motivations and extensive literary allusions to the *Iliad,* the *Aeneid,* and *Paradise Lost.* Perhaps the approach that has most illuminated this work in relation to Pope's others is the one that focuses on his concurrent acceptance and satirization of high English society. While his central purpose in *The Rape of the Lock* is believed to have been the production of an amusing piece of entertainment rather than a curative satire, the case is different with *The Dunciad,* the *Satires and Epistles of Horace, Imitated,* and *An Epistle from Mr. Pope, to Dr. Arbuthnot* (1735).

The Dunciad, given its cutting, relentlessly abusive tone, is the obverse of *The Rape of the Lock.* In the first edition of *The Dunciad,* Pope designated as his chief victim Lewis Theobald, a writer who had heavily criticized him for his emendations and modernizations of Shakespeare. The following year Pope published *The Dunciad, Variorum,* which included mock-pedantic footnotes intensifying his attack on the reputations and abilities of a host of London critics and writers. In 1742 Pope expanded *The Dunciad* to four books and broadened its satirical scope to encompass the whole of English society, which he believed by then to be dangerously near moral collapse. Pope reconstructs London literary society as a chaotic kingdom ruled by "Dulness" and populated by Dunces: literary contemporaries of Pope whom he had singled out for blistering indictment for professional ineptitude, malice, and idiocy. Since the work's original conception, Pope had witnessed what he perceived as a progressive deterioration of morals under the crass, egoistic rule of George II and his First Minister, Robert Walpole. Consequently, he dramatized in epic terms the dangerously corrupt political, social, and moral status of England. In his eleven *Satires and Epistles of Horace, Imitated* and *An Epistle from Mr. Pope, to Dr. Arbuthnot*, Pope contrasted the frivolous, materialistic values of the ruling Whig party with the Horatian standards of reason and temperance while suggesting that widespread moral reform might yet be effected.

As commentators note, Pope's stance between the first and last publications of *The Dunciad* shifted dramatically from that of a detached, angry, yet bemused observer of the London scene to one of an empowered social critic, devoutly aware, as was Horace, of his weighty responsibilities as a satirist. The gradual dissipation of Augustan ideals in both the structure and imagery of his later verse suggests his realization of England's precarious moral state. The circumstances about which Pope wrote during this period compelled him to seek new forms of expression, forms which would both mirror England's disorder and express his dissatisfaction with it. Consequently, Pope produced, in the parody and invective of *The Dunciad,* in the self-revelations of *Epistle to Dr. Arbuthnot,* and in the dialogic summary of *Epilogue to the Satires* (1738), a gamut of daring rhythmic, visual, and linguistic invention within the couplet form—an achievement which many critics hold to be his greatest.

At present, Pope's literary reputation is exceedingly high. He ranks as the unquestioned master of the heroic couplet, and this, combined with his keen satiric and moral sensibility, affords Pope an exalted position as one of the most proficient and powerful versifiers of all time.

(For further information about Pope's life and works, See *Dictionary of Literary Biography*, Vols. 95, 101 and *Literature Criticism from 1400 to 1800*, Vol. 3.)

CRITICAL COMMENTARY

SAMUEL JOHNSON

(essay date 1779)

[A remarkably versatile and distinguished man of letters, Johnson was the major English literary figure of the second half of the eighteenth century. His monumental *Dictionary of the English Language* (1755) standardized English spelling and pronunciation for the first time, while his moralistic criticism strongly influenced contemporary tastes. In the following excerpt from his *Lives of the English Poets* (1779), he assesses Pope's achievement in verse.]

Pope was not content to satisfy; he desired to excel, and therefore always endeavoured to do his best: he did not court the candour, but dared the judgement of his reader, and, expecting no indulgence from others, he shewed none to himself. He examined lines and words with minute and punctilious observation, and retouched every part with indefatigable diligence, till he had left nothing to be forgiven. (p. 307)

His declaration, that his care for his works ceased at their publication, was not strictly true. His parental attention never abandoned them; what he found amiss in the first edition, he silently corrected in those that followed. He appears to have revised the *Iliad,* and freed it from some of its imperfections; and the *Essay on Criticism* received many improvements after its first appearance. It will seldom be found that he altered without adding clearness, elegance, or vigour. Pope had perhaps the judgement of Dryden; but Dryden certainly wanted the diligence of Pope.

In acquired knowledge, the superiority must be allowed to Dryden, whose education was more scholastick, and who before he became an author had been allowed more time for study, with better means of information. His mind has a larger range, and he collects his images and illustrations from a more extensive circumference of science. Dryden knew more of man in his general nature, and Pope in his local manners. The notions of Dryden were formed by comprehensive speculation, and those of Pope by minute attention. There is more dignity in the knowledge of Dryden, and more certainty in that of Pope.

Principal Works

"Pastorals" (poetry) 1709; published in Poetical Miscellanies, vol. 6

An Essay on Criticism (poetry) 1711

"The Messiah" (poetry) 1712; published in journal The Spectator

The Rape of the Lock (poetry) 1712; also published as The Rape of the Lock [enlarged edition], 1714

Windsor Forest (poetry) 1713

The Iliad of Homer. 6 vols. [translator] (poetry) 1715-20

"A Discourse on Pastoral Poetry" (criticism) 1717; published in The Works of Mr. Alexander Pope

"Eloisa to Abelard" (poetry) 1717; published in The Works of Mr. Alexander Pope

* "Verses to the Memory of an Unfortunate Lady" (poetry) 1717; published in The Works of Mr. Alexander Pope

The Works of Mr. Alexander Pope (poetry and criticism) 1717

The Works of Shakspear. 6 vols. [adapter] (poetry) 1725

The Odyssey of Homer. 5 vols. [translator; with William Broome and Elijah Fenton] (poetry) 1725-26

The Dunciad (poetry) 1728

"Peri Bathous; or, The Art of Sinking in Poetry" (criticism) 1728; published in Miscellanies, vol. 3

The Dunciad, Variorum. With the Prolegomena of Scriblerus. (poetry) 1729

Epistles to Several Persons (poetry) 1731-35

Satires and Epistles of Horace, Imitated (poetry) 1733-37

An Essay on Man, Being the First Book of Ethic Epistles. To Henry St. John L. Bolingbroke (poetry) 1734

An Epistle from Mr. Pope, to Dr. Arbuthnot (poetry) 1735

Mr. Pope's Literary Correspondence for Thirty Years; from 1704 to 1734 (letters) 1735

Letters of Mr. Alexander Pope and Several of His Friends [authorized edition] (letters) 1737

Epilogue to the Satires (poetry) 1738

Memoirs of the Extraordinary Life, Works, and Discoveries of Martinus Scriblerus [with John Arbuthnot, John Gay, Thomas Parnell, and Jonathan Swift] (satires) 1741

The New Dunciad: As It Was Found in the Year 1741. With the Illustrations of Scriblerus, and Notes Variorum (poetry) 1742

The Dunciad, in Four Books (poetry) 1743

Satires of Dr. Donne Versified (poetry) 1751; published in The Works of Alexander Pope

The Works of Alexander Pope. 9 vols. (poetry and criticism) 1751

The Correspondence of Alexander Pope (letters) 1956

*This work is also referred to as "Elegy to the Memory of an Unfortunate Lady."

Poetry was not the sole praise of either; for both excelled likewise in prose; but Pope did not borrow his prose from his predecessor. The style of Dryden is capricious and varied, that of Pope is cautious and uniform; Dryden obeys the motions of his own mind, Pope constrains his mind to his own rules of composition. Dryden is sometimes vehement and rapid; Pope is always smooth, uniform, and gentle. Dryden's page is a natural field, rising into inequalities, and diversified by the varied exuberance of abundant vegetation; Pope's is a velvet lawn, shaven by the scythe, and levelled by the roller.

Of genius, that power which constitutes a poet; that quality without which judgement is cold and knowledge is inert; that energy which collects, combines, amplifies, and animates; the superiority must, with some hesitation, be allowed to Dryden. It is not to be inferred that of this poetical vigour Pope had only a little, because Dryden had more; for every other writer since Milton must give place to Pope; and even of Dryden it must be said, that if he has brighter paragraphs, he has not better poems. Dryden's performances were always hasty, either excited by some external occasion, or extorted by domestick necessity; he composed without consideration, and published without correction. What his mind could supply at call, or gather in one excursion, was all that he sought, and all that he gave. The dilatory caution of Pope enabled him to condense his sentiments, to multiply his images, and to accumulate all that study might produce, or chance might supply. If the flights of Dryden therefore are higher, Pope continues longer on the wing. If of Dryden's fire the blaze is brighter, of Pope's the heat is more regular and constant. Dryden often surpasses expectation, and Pope never falls below it. Dryden is read with frequent astonishment, and Pope with perpetual delight.

This parallel will, I hope, when it is well considered, be found just; and if the reader should suspect me, as I suspect myself, of some partial fondness for the memory of Dryden, let him not too hastily condemn me; for meditation and enquiry may, perhaps, shew him the reasonableness of my determination. (pp. 307-09)

It seems natural for a young poet to initiate himself by Pastorals, which, not professing to imitate real life, require no experience, and, exhibiting only the simple operation of unmingled passions, admit no subtle reasoning or deep enquiry. Pope's *Pastorals* are not however composed but with close thought; they have reference to the time of the day, the seasons of the year, and the periods of human life. The last, that which turns the attention upon age and death, was the author's favourite. To tell of disappointment and misery, to thicken the darkness of futurity, and perplex the labyrinth of uncertainty, has been always a delicious employment of the poets. His preference was probably just. I wish, however, that his fondness had not overlooked a line in which the *Zephyrs* are made *to lament in silence.*

To charge these *Pastorals* with want of invention, is to require what was never intended. The imitations are so ambitiously frequent, that the writer evidently means rather to shew his literature than his wit. It is surely sufficient for an author of sixteen not only to be able to copy the poems of antiquity with judicious selection, but to have obtained sufficient power of language, and skill in metre, to exhibit a series of versification, which had in English poetry no precedent, nor has since had an imitation.

The design of *Windsor Forest* is evidently derived from *Cooper's Hill,* with some attention to Waller's poem on *The Park;* but Pope cannot be denied to excel his masters in variety and elegance, and the art of interchanging description, narrative, and morality. The objection made by Dennis is the want of plan, of a regular subordination of parts terminating in the principal and original design. There is this want in most descriptive poems, because as the scenes, which they must exhibit successively, are all subsisting at the same time, the order in which they are shewn must by necessity be arbitrary, and more is not to be expected from the last part than from the first. The attention, therefore, which cannot be detained by suspense, must be excited by diversity, such as his poem offers to its reader.

But the desire of diversity may be too much indulged; the parts of *Windsor Forest* which deserve least praise, are those which were added to enliven the stillness of the scene, the appearance of Father Thames, and the transformation of *Lodona.* Addison had in his *Campaign* derided the *Rivers* that *rise from their oozy beds* to tell stories of heroes, and it is therefore strange that Pope should adopt a fiction not only unnatural but lately censured. The story of *Lodona* is told with sweetness; but a new metamorphosis is a ready and puerile expedient; nothing is easier than to tell how a flower was once a blooming virgin, or a rock an obdurate tyrant.

The *Temple of Fame* has, as Steele warmly declared, *a thousand beauties.* Every part is splendid; there is great luxuriance of ornaments; the original vision of Chaucer was never denied to be much improved; the allegory is very skilfully continued, the imagery is properly selected, and learnedly displayed: yet, with all this comprehension of excellence, as its scene is laid in remote ages, and its sentiments, if the concluding paragraph be excepted, have little relation to general manners or common life, it never obtained much notice, but is turned silently over, and seldom quoted or mentioned with either praise or blame.

That the *Messiah* excels the *Pollio* is no great praise, if it be considered from what original the improvements are derived.

The *Verses to the Memory of an Unfortunate Lady* have drawn much attention by the illaudable singularity of treating suicide with respect; and they must be allowed to be written in some parts with vigorous animation, and in others with gentle tenderness; nor has Pope produced any poem in which the sense predominates more over the diction. But the tale is not skilfully told; it is not easy to discover the character of either the Lady or her Guardian. History relates that she was about to disparage herself by a marriage with an inferior; Pope praises her for the dignity of ambition, and yet condemns the unkle to detestation for his pride; the ambitious love of a niece may be opposed by the interest, malice, or envy of an unkle, but never by his pride. On such an occasion a poet may be allowed to be obscure, but inconsistency never can be right.

The *Ode for St. Cecilia's Day* was undertaken at the desire of Steele: in this the author is generally confessed to have miscarried, yet he has miscarried only as compared with Dryden; for he has far outgone other competitors. Dryden's plan is better chosen; history will always take stronger hold of the attention than fable: the passions excited by Dryden are the pleasures and pains of real life, the scene of Pope is laid in imaginary existence; Pope is read with calm acquiescence, Dryden with turbulent delight; Pope hangs upon the ear, and Dryden finds the passes of the mind. (pp. 309-11)

One of his greatest though of his earliest works is the *Essay on Criticism,* which, if he had written nothing else, would have placed him among the first criticks and the first poets, as it exhibits every mode of excellence that can embellish or dignify didactick composition, selection of matter, novelty of arrangement, justness of precept, splendour of illustration, and propriety of digression. I know not whether it be pleasing to consider that he produced this piece at twenty, and never afterwards excelled it: he that delights himself with observing that such powers may be so soon attained, cannot but grieve to think that life was ever after at a stand. (pp. 312-13)

To the praises which have been accumulated on *The Rape of the Lock* by readers of every class, from the critick to the waiting-maid, it is difficult to make any addition. Of that which is universally allowed to be the most attractive of all ludicrous compositions, let it rather be now enquired from what sources the power of pleasing is derived.

Dr. Warburton, who excelled in critical perspicacity, has remarked that the preternatural agents are very happily adapted to the purposes of the poem. The heathen deities can no longer gain attention: we should have turned away from a contest between Venus and Diana. The employment of allegorical persons always excites conviction of its own absurdity; they may produce effects, but cannot conduct actions; when the phantom is put in motion, it dissolves; thus *Discord* may raise a mutiny, but *Discord* cannot conduct a march, nor besiege a town. Pope brought into view a new race of Beings, with powers and passions proportionate to their operation. The sylphs and gnomes act at the toilet and the tea-table, what more terrifick and more powerful phantoms perform on the stormy ocean, or the field of battle; they give their proper help, and do their proper mischief.

Pope is said, by an objector, not to have been the inventor of this petty nation; a charge which might with more justice have been brought against the author of the *Iliad,* who doubtless adopted the religious system of his country; for what is there but the names of his agents which Pope has not invented? Has he not assigned them characters and operations never heard of before? Has he not, at least, given them their first poetical existence? If this is not sufficient to denominate his work original, nothing original ever can be written.

In this work are exhibited, in a very high degree, the two most engaging powers of an author. New things are made familiar, and familiar things are made new. A race of aerial people, never heard of before, is presented to us in a manner so clear and easy, that the reader seeks for no further information, but immediately mingles with his new acquaintance, adopts their interests, and attends their pursuits, loves a sylph, and detests a gnome.

That familiar things are made new, every paragraph will prove. The subject of the poem is an event below the common incidents of common life; nothing real is introduced that is not seen so often as to be no longer regarded, yet the whole detail of a female-day is here brought before us invested with so much art of decoration, that, though nothing is disguised, every thing is striking, and we feel all the appetite of curiosity for that from which we have a thousand times turned fastidiously away.

The purpose of the Poet is, as he tells us, to laugh at *the little unguarded follies of the female sex.* It is therefore without justice that Dennis charges the **Rape of the Lock** with the want of a moral, and for that reason sets it below the *Lutrin,* which exposes the pride and discord of the clergy. Perhaps neither Pope nor Boileau has made the world much better than he found it; but if they had both succeeded, it were easy to tell who would have deserved most from publick gratitude. The freaks, and humours, and spleen, and vanity of women, as they embroil families in discord, and fill houses with

disquiet, do more to obstruct the happiness of life in a year than the ambition of the clergy in many centuries. It has been well observed, that the misery of man proceeds not from any single crush of overwhelming evil, but from small vexations continually repeated.

It is remarked by Dennis likewise, that the machinery is superfluous; that, by all the bustle of preternatural operation, the main event is neither hastened nor retarded. To this charge an efficacious answer is not easily made. The sylphs cannot be said to help or to oppose, and it must be allowed to imply some want of art, that their power has not been sufficiently intermingled with the action. Other parts may likewise be charged with want of connection; the game at *ombre* might be spared, but if the Lady had lost her hair while she was intent upon her cards, it might have been inferred that those who are too fond of play will be in danger of neglecting more important interests. Those perhaps are faults; but what are such faults to so much excellence!

The Epistle of *Eloisa to Abelard* is one of the most happy productions of human wit: the subject is so judiciously chosen, that it would be difficult, in turning over the annals of the world, to find another which so many circumstances concur to recommend. We regularly interest ourselves most in the fortune of those who most deserve our notice. Abelard and Eloisa were conspicuous in their days for eminence of merit. The heart naturally loves truth. The adventures and misfortunes of this illustrious pair are known from undisputed history. Their fate does not leave the mind in hopeless dejection; for they both found quiet and consolation in retirement and piety. So new and so affecting is their story, that it supersedes invention, and imagination ranges at full liberty without straggling into scenes of fable.

The story, thus skilfully adopted, has been diligently improved. Pope has left nothing behind him, which seems more the effect of studious perseverance and laborious revisal. Here is particularly observable the *curiosa felicitas,* a fruitful soil, and careful cultivation. Here is no crudeness of sense, nor asperity of language.

The sources from which sentiments, which have so much vigour and efficacy, have been drawn, are shewn to be the mystick writers by the learned author [Joseph Warton] of the *Essay on the Life and Writings of Pope:* a book which teaches how the brow of Criticism may be smoothed, and how she may be enabled, with all her severity, to attract and to delight.

The train of my disquisition has now conducted me to that poetical wonder, the translation of the *Iliad;* a performance which no age or nation can pretend to equal. (pp. 315-18)

The chief help of Pope in this arduous undertaking was drawn from the versions of Dryden. Virgil had borrowed much of his imagery from Homer, and part of the debt was now paid by his translator. Pope searched the pages of Dryden for happy combinations of heroick diction; but it will not be denied that he added much to what he found. He cultivated our language with so much diligence and art, that he has left in his *Homer* a treasure of poetical elegances to posterity. His version may be said to have tuned the English tongue; for since its appearance no writer, however deficient in other powers, has wanted melody. Such a series of lines so elaborately corrected, and so sweetly modulated, took possession of the publick ear; the vulgar was enamoured of the poem, and the learned wondered at the translation.

But in the most general applause discordant voices will always be heard. It has been objected by some, who wish to be numbered among the sons of learning, that Pope's version of Homer is not Homerical; that it exhibits no resemblance of the original characteristick manner of the Father of Poetry, as it wants his awful simplicity, his artless grandeur, his unaffected majesty. This cannot be totally denied; but it must be remembered that *necessitas quod cogit defendit;* that may be lawfully done which cannot be forborn. Time and place will always enforce regard. In estimating this translation, consideration must be had of the nature of our language, the form of our metre, and, above all, of the change which two thousand years have made in the modes of life and the habits of thought. Virgil wrote in a language of the same general fabrick with that of Homer, in verses of the same measure, and in an age nearer to Homer's time by eighteen hundred years; yet he found, even then, the state of the world so much altered, and the demand for elegance so much increased, that mere nature would be endured no longer; and perhaps, in the multitude of borrowed passages, very few can be shewn which he has not embellished.

There is a time when nations emerging from barbarity, and falling into regular subordination, gain leisure to grow wise, and feel the shame of ignorance and the craving pain of unsatisfied curiosity. To this hunger of the mind plain sense is grateful; that which fills the void removes uneasiness, and to be free from pain for a while is pleasure; but repletion generates fastidiousness; a saturated intellect soon becomes luxurious, and knowledge finds no willing reception till it is recommended by artificial diction. Thus it will be found, in the progress of learning, that in all nations the first writers are simple, and that every age improves in elegance. One refinement always makes way for another, and what was expedient to Virgil was necessary to Pope.

I suppose many readers of the English *Iliad,* when they have been touched with some unexpected beauty of the lighter kind, have tried to enjoy it in the original, where, alas! it was not to be found. Homer doubtless owes to his translator many *Ovidian* graces not exactly

suitable to his character; but to have added can be no great crime, if nothing be taken away. Elegance is surely to be desired, if it be not gained at the expence of dignity. A hero would wish to be loved, as well as to be reverenced.

To a thousand cavils one answer is sufficient; the purpose of a writer is to be read, and the criticism which would destroy the power of pleasing must be blown aside. Pope wrote for his own age and his own nation: he knew that it was necessary to colour the images and point the sentiments of his author; he therefore made him graceful, but lost him some of his sublimity. (pp. 319-20)

Of the *Odyssey* nothing remains to be observed: the same general praise may be given to both translations, and a particular examination of either would require a large volume. . . . Of the *Dunciad* the hint is confessedly taken from Dryden's *Mac Flecknoe;* but the plan is so enlarged and diversified as justly to claim the praise of an original, and affords perhaps the best specimen that has yet appeared of personal satire ludicrously pompous.

That the design was moral, whatever the author might tell either his readers or himself, I am not convinced. The first motive was the desire of revenging the contempt with which Theobald had treated his *Shakespeare,* and regaining the honour which he had lost, by crushing his opponent. Theobald was not of bulk enough to fill a poem, and therefore it was necessary to find other enemies with other names, at whose expence he might divert the publick.

In this design there was petulance and malignity enough; but I cannot think it very criminal. An author places himself uncalled before the tribunal of criticism, and solicits fame at the hazard of disgrace. (p. 321)

The beauties of this poem are well known; its chief fault is the grossness of its images. Pope and Swift had an unnatural delight in ideas physically impure, such as every other tongue utters with unwillingness, and of which every ear shrinks from the mention.

But even this fault, offensive as it is, may be forgiven for the excellence of other passages; such as the formation and dissolution of Moore, the account of the Traveller, the misfortune of the Florist, and the crowded thoughts and stately numbers which dignify the concluding paragraph.

The alterations which have been made in the *Dunciad,* not always for the better, require that it should be published, as in the last collection, with all its variations.

The *Essay on Man* was a work of great labour and long consideration, but certainly not the happiest of Pope's performances. The subject is perhaps not very proper for poetry, and the poet was not sufficiently master of his subject; metaphysical morality was to him a new study, he was proud of his acquisitions, and, supposing himself master of great secrets, was in haste to teach what he had not learned. Thus he tells us, in the first Epistle, that from the nature of the Supreme Being may be deduced an order of beings such as mankind, because Infinite Excellence can do only what is best. He finds out that these beings must be *somewhere* and that *all the question is whether man be in a wrong place.* Surely if, according to the poet's Leibnitian reasoning, we may infer that man ought to be, only because he is, we may allow that his place is the right place, because he has it. Supreme Wisdom is not less infallible in disposing than in creating. But what is meant by *somewhere* and *place,* and *wrong place,* it had been vain to ask Pope, who probably had never asked himself.

Having exalted himself into the chair of wisdom, he tells us much that every man knows, and much that he does not know himself; that we see but little, and that the order of the universe is beyond our comprehension; an opinion not very uncommon; and that there is a chain of subordinate beings *from infinite to nothing,* of which himself and his readers are equally ignorant. But he gives us one comfort, which, without his help, he supposes unattainable, in the position *that though we are fools, yet God is wise.*

This *Essay* affords an egregious instance of the predominance of genius, the dazzling splendour of imagery, and the seductive powers of eloquence. Never was penury of knowledge and vulgarity of sentiment so happily disguised. The reader feels his mind full, though he learns nothing; and when he meets it in its new array, no longer knows the talk of his mother and his nurse. When these wonder-working sounds sink into sense, and the doctrine of the *Essay,* disrobed of its ornaments, is left to the powers of its naked excellence, what shall we discover? That we are, in comparison with our Creator, very weak and ignorant; that we do not uphold the chain of existence, and that we could not make one another with more skill than we are made. We may learn yet more; that the arts of human life were copied from the instinctive operations of other animals; that if the world be made for man, it may be said that man was made for geese. To these profound principles of natural knowledge are added some moral instructions equally new; that self-interest, well understood, will produce social concord; that men are mutual gainers by mutual benefits; that evil is sometimes balanced by good; that human advantages are unstable and fallacious, of uncertain duration, and doubtful effect; that our true honour is, not to have a great part, but to act it well: that virtue only is our own; and that happiness is always in our power.

Surely a man of no very comprehensive search may venture to say that he has heard all this before; but it was never till now recommended by such a blaze of embellishment, or such sweetness of melody. The vig-

orous contraction of some thoughts, the luxuriant amplification of others, the incidental illustrations, and sometimes the dignity, sometimes the softness of the verses, enchain philosophy, suspend criticism, and oppress judgement by overpowering pleasure.

This is true of many paragraphs; yet if I had undertaken to exemplify Pope's felicity of composition before a rigid critick, I should not select the *Essay on Man;* for it contains more lines unsuccessfully laboured, more harshness of diction, more thoughts imperfectly expressed, more levity without elegance, and more heaviness without strength, than will easily be found in all his other works.

The *Characters of Men and Women* are the product of diligent speculation upon human life; much labour has been bestowed upon them, and Pope very seldom laboured in vain. That his excellence may be properly estimated, I recommend a comparison of his *Characters of Women* with Boileau's *Satire;* it will then be seen with how much more perspicacity female nature is investigated, and female excellence selected; and he surely is no mean writer to whom Boileau shall be found inferior. The *Characters of Men,* however, are written with more, if not with deeper, thought, and exhibit many passages exquisitely beautiful. The *Gem and the Flower* will not easily be equalled. In the women's part are some defects; the character of *Atossa* is not so neatly finished as that of *Clodio;* and some of the female characters may be found perhaps more frequently among men; what is said of *Philomede* was true of *Prior.*

In the *Epistles* to Lord Bathurst and Lord Burlington, Dr. Warburton has endeavoured to find a train of thought which was never in the writer's head, and, to support his hypothesis, has printed that first which was published last. In one, the most valuable passage is perhaps the elogy on *Good Sense;* and the other the *End of the Duke of Buckingham.*

The [*Epistle to Dr. Arbuthnot*], now arbitrarily called the *Prologue to the Satires,* is a performance consisting, as it seems, of many fragments wrought into one design, which by this union of scattered beauties contains more striking paragraphs than could probably have been brought together into an occasional work. As there is no stronger motive to exertion than self-defence, no part has more elegance, spirit, or dignity, than the poet's vindication of his own character. The meanest passage is the satire upon *Sporus.*

Of the two poems which derived their names from the year, and which are called the *Epilogue to the Satires,* it was very justly remarked by Savage, that the second was in the whole more strongly conceived, and more equally supported, but that it had no single passages equal to the contention in the first for the dignity of Vice, and the celebration of the triumph of Corruption.

The *Imitations of Horace* seem to have been written as relaxations of his genius. This employment became his favourite by its facility; the plan was ready to his hand, and nothing was required but to accommodate as he could the sentiments of an old author to recent facts or familiar images; but what is easy is seldom excellent; such imitations cannot give pleasure to common readers. The man of learning may be sometimes surprised and delighted by an unexpected parallel; but the comparison requires knowledge of the original, which will likewise often detect strained applications. Between Roman images and English manners there will be an irreconcilable dissimilitude, and the work will be generally uncouth and party-coloured; neither original nor translated, neither ancient nor modern.

Pope had, in proportions very nicely adjusted to each other, all the qualities that constitute genius. He had *Invention,* by which new trains of events are formed, and new scenes of imagery displayed, as in the *Rape of the Lock;* and by which extrinsick and adventitious embellishments and illustrations are connected with a known subject, as in the *Essay on Criticism.* He had *Imagination,* which strongly impresses on the writer's mind, and enables him to convey to the reader, the various forms of nature, incidents of life, and energies of passion, as in his *Eloisa, Windsor Forest,* and the *Ethick Epistles.* He had *Judgement* which selects from life or nature what the present purpose requires, and, by separating the essence of things from its concomitants, often makes the representation more powerful than the reality: and he had colours of language always before him, ready to decorate his matter with every grace of elegant expression, as when he accommodates his diction to the wonderful multiplicity of Homer's sentiments and descriptions. (pp. 322-26)

It is remarked by Watts, that there is scarcely a happy combination of words, or a phrase poetically elegant in the English language, which Pope has not inserted into his version of Homer. How he obtained possession of so many beauties of speech, it were desirable to know. That he gleaned from authors, obscure as well as eminent, what he thought brilliant or useful, and preserved it all in a regular collection, is not unlikely. When, in his last years, Hall's *Satires* were shewn him, he wished that he had seen them sooner.

New sentiments and new images others may produce; but to attempt any further improvement of versification will be dangerous. Art and diligence have now done their best, and what shall be added will be the effort of tedious toil and needless curiosity. (p. 327)

Samuel Johnson, "Pope," in his *Lives of the English Poets, Vol. II,* Oxford University Press, London, 1967, pp. 223-344.

PAUL ELMER MORE
(essay date 1910)

[More was an American critic who, along with Irving Babbitt, formulated the doctrines of New Humanism in early twentieth-century American thought. In the following excerpt from an essay that first appeared in the *Nation* in 1910, he upholds Pope's satiric verse, especially *An Epistle to Dr. Arbuthnot.*]

"After all this, it is surely superfluous to answer the question that has once been asked, whether Pope was a poet, otherwise than by asking in return, If Pope be not a poet, where is poetry to be found? To circumscribe poetry by a definition will only show the narrowness of the definer, though a definition which shall exclude Pope will not easily be made."

When Dr. Johnson handed down that famous decision he had no means of foreseeing, and indeed would not have cared to see, the great romantic revival which was to ask a good many times whether Pope was a poet, and was to circumscribe poetry with innumerable definitions. Even so cautious and classical a critic as Matthew Arnold was reduced by his Wordsworthian fervour into saying that, "though they may write in verse, though they may in a certain sense be masters of the art of versification, Dryden and Pope are not classics of our poetry, they are classics of our prose." Probably the majority of readers of verse to-day, certainly the lagging "official critics," still talk of Pope in an offhand way as a great writer, perhaps, but as at bottom scarcely a poet at all. Yet there are signs that the sounder taste of the present, grown a little weary of the old romantic presumptions, borrowed from Germany, is tending rather to a truer estimate of the neo-classic school. (pp. 125-26)

No one, I think, would be so narrow-minded as to rank Chamberlain or Katherine Philips or Thomas Tickell above Pope, yet to reach a fair estimate of Pope's greatness we must begin by admitting that even in these minor writers there is an occasional glimpse of divine mysteries of whose existence Pope seems not even to have dreamed. If this were all there could be no gainsaying those who deny him the title of poet altogether. But it is by no means all, and there are other large fields of the imagination which the romantic poets closed to us. Pope, as a matter of fact, has been dethroned as much for his great positive qualities as for his deficiencies. Admirers of Pope, therefore, are likely to feel a touch of impatience at the extravagant praise so often bestowed upon *The Rape of the Lock,* as if his consummate success in this filagree of the mock-heroic should be held up as an excuse for his failure in the more serious style. There is only one honest way to deal with him; we must treat him squarely as the poet of satire, and, unfortunately for his fame, the world has come to regard satire as scarcely poetry at all. If it is not poetry, then, indeed, Pope was but the fragment of a poet. There are, of course, special reasons why such a satire as the *Dunciad,* which by reason of its size and scope comes first to mind, should find few and painful readers. All great poems, even those most universal in their human appeal, require a fairly high-developed historic sense for their appreciation, and it is idle to suppose that the *AEneid* will mean much to those who have not trained themselves to live in the Latin world, or that *Paradise Lost* can ever be interesting except to the scholar. No long poem of the past is really popular; but the *Dunciad* demands for its comprehension an altogether exorbitant acquaintance with men and manners of a brief particular period. (pp. 133-34)

And even after the necessary minute knowledge has been acquired—and to the scholar this local habitation and name of the *Dunciad* may have a special though somewhat artificial attraction—there remains the fact that the current of historic sympathy has set strongly away from Pope, and that most of us in our hearts are stung by his ridicule as were his living enemies. For that battle of the wits was no causeless or merely bookish event, but was part of the great political war of the land. It grew inevitably out of the ruinous divisions, as it echoed the drums and tramplings, of the previous century; and if ink now flowed instead of blood, the contest was hardly the less venomous for that, or the consequences less serious. (pp. 134-35)

There is personal spite aplenty in the *Dunciad,* innumerable strokes of vicious retaliation and wanton offence—these faults cannot be severed from the character of the author; but beneath these motives of personal satire we shall miss the whole meaning of the poem if we fail to see the passionate warfare of the losing party of wit against the triumphant party of practical common-sense. (pp. 136-37)

But there is still a deeper cause of our distaste than the old echoes of faction and our political incompatibility. A great change has come upon us in our attitude towards human nature itself, and, curiously enough, Pope himself is one of the prime movers of this revolution which has carried us away from the very comprehension of his own principal works. For there is this strange paradox in the philosophy of Pope. On the one hand, we have his contemptuous treatment of mankind, as if his satires were no more than a long development of the text of Machiavelli that "all men are caitive [*cattivi,* captive to the base impulses of egotism], and are ever ready to use the malignity of their spirit, when they have free opportunity." On the other hand,

in his *Essay on Man,* inspired by the dubious optimism of his friend Bolingbroke, we have the deistic conception of the world as the best possible creation and of men as naturally altruistic in desire and as needing only liberty from restraint to develop into unselfishness of action. . . . (pp. 138-39)

And deism, which, be it noted, was the express theme of the philosophers and divines who hung upon the court of Caroline, won the day, altering our whole conception of society and our manner of judging the individual. We have in the course of the last two hundred years acquired a kind of tenderness for humanity, which causes us to shrink from the old theological notion of absolute evil in the world, and also from the literature of the moralists which was based on the same belief. With this tenderness, if it be not the source of the feeling, our individual sensitiveness has increased enormously, so that we take in a quite personal way the attacks of moralist and satirist on mankind in general. We can listen to the singing of the still sad music of humanity with a delicate self-pity, but from the philosophy of a Rochefoucauld or a Machiavelli we start back as if a hand were laid on a concealed sore. It is certainly true that he who has imbibed deeply this modern humanitarianism with its fashion of mutual flattery, will be repelled from the literature of which Pope's satires are so perfect an example; in those attacks on the meanness and folly and dulness and venality of the world he will suffer a kind of uneasiness, and, taking his revenge by decrying them as a base form of art, will turn for consolation to what Cowper calls the

> charity that soothes a lie,
> And thrusts the truth with scorn and
> anger by.

I would not say that Machiavelli expressed the whole truth, any more than did the deists, but it may as well be recognized that, without some lingering suspicion of the eternal deceitfulness of the heart and some malicious glee in the unveiling of the deceit, no man shall feel at home in the old battle of the wits. Only the absence of that suspicion and glee can account, I think, for the common apathy towards Pope's masterpiece, the *Epistle to Dr. Arbuthnot,* which is at once the prologue and the consummation of his satires.

For myself I will admit frankly that I have read the *Epistle* oftener, perhaps, than any other English poem except *Lycidas,* and that long familiarity with its lines has given me always a deepening admiration for its art. If it is not poetry, I do not know where poetry is to be found. That Pope's inspiration moves on a lower plane than Milton's—though his art is as flawless—I should be the last to deny. Yet in a way their themes, despite the great difference of their age and faith, have unexpected points of contact. Milton, like the poet of Queen Anne, wrote in the heat of battle, and with him, too, *fecit indignatio versus* ["made a verse of indignation"]. He was moved by a sublime rage against those who, as he believed, were degrading the Church and fattening on her spiritual poverty, against the blind mouths who, for their bellies' sake, were creeping into the fold, and against their lean and flashy songs. In contrast to this contagion he draws in a picture the true beauty and peace of the shepherd's trade, and the sweet companionship of those who walk therein, singing together their eager Doric lays, as it were an image and foretaste of the heavenly societies and of the unexpressive nuptial song.

The gap from Milton's theme to Pope's may seem complete, yet in reality one is the true successor of the other, and nothing can better show the mischievous confusion resulting from the division in the Stuart days than the fact that the practical party which Milton represented—so far as he can be said to have represented anybody but himself—was now the people of Dulness, while the party of the imagination, as we see it in the writings of Swift and Pope, was divested of all the magnificences of morality. Yet if the *Epistle to Dr. Arbuthnot* lacks Milton's mighty impulse of religion and

draws from lower springs of Helicon, it still has its great compensations. The indignation is as terrible, if its causes are more mixed. Here, even more ruinously than in the *Dunciad,* and without the longer poem's tediousness of obscure detail, the dreaded secret is revealed—

That secret to each fool, that he's an ass.

We may doubt what was the exact nature of that two-handed engine which Milton suspended against the enemies of Puritanism, but there is nothing ambiguous about the revenge of Pope, whether with one blade he hews down his open enemies or with the other attacks his pretended friends. (pp. 139-42)

To understand the *Epistle* we must read it as Pope's *apologia pro vita sua,* at once an excuse for the warfare in which his days had passed and an acknowledgement of their waste and bitter fruit. With a kind of childlike and, I think, utterly sincere regret he compares the quiet tenor of his father's life with the discordant ambitions of literature, and counts as the one indisputable blessing to himself the homely respect for that life

"The Distressed Poet," a 1736 engraving by William Hogarth, captioned with a quotation
from *The Dunciad.*

2777

which he had preserved against all the inroads of the world's malice. . . . (p. 147)

It may seem that the beauty of these contrasted notes in Pope's greatest poem is lost to the world today, because one of them at least, the warfare of the wits, was a temporary thing, now long forgotten and of interest only to the special student. To a certain degree and in the matter of form, this is no doubt the case. Yet the warfare substantially is not ended, and shall not end while the differences of human nature remain unreconciled. Men in this living age, always a few, are still fighting for the rights of the mind against a dull and delusive materialism, for the freedom of the imagination against a prosaic tyranny, for a pure and patient ambition against the quick successes of vanity and pliant cleverness, for the reality of human nature against a fatuous self-complacency. To these the triumphant satire of Pope is a perpetual encouragement, while his pathetic apology expresses for them the relief needed when success appears far away, or, even if near, not worth the cost in the humiliating wager of soul against soul. Nor is the theme of the *Epistle* without its more universal aspect. For after all life itself, not for the wit only, but for each man in his place, is a contest, and poetry, from the time when Homer portrayed his heroes battling with sword and fire on the banks of the Simois, and longing for the peace of hearth and kindred and friends across the seas, has been the expression, varying in form and instruments, of that inevitable fate. The presentation of this truth may in Pope be narrowed to a particular manner and time, it may assume ignoble images and speak too often in reprehensible language, nevertheless he who does not respond to the deep emotion and humanity underlying the *Satires* has travelled but a short way into the realm of letters; he has even, I dare assert, felt but a little of the great realities of man's life. (pp. 148-49)

Paul Elmer More, "Pope," in his *With the Wits: Shelburne Essays, Tenth Series,* Houghton Mifflin Company, 1919, pp. 123-49.

F. R. LEAVIS
(essay date 1936)

[Leavis is an influential contemporary English critic. In the following excerpt from a work that first appeared in 1936, he suggests paths toward a judicious comprehensive assessment of Pope's achievement.]

Pope has had bad luck. Dryden, fortunate in the timeliness of Mr. Mark Van Doren's book, was enlisted in the argument against the nineteenth century. It was an op-

portunity; the cause was admirable and *Homage to John Dryden* admirably served it (though Mr. Eliot, who—or so it seems to me—has always tended to do Dryden something more than justice, was incidentally, perhaps accidentally, unfair to Pope). The homage announcing, on the other hand, Pope's rehabilitation was left to Bloomsbury, and Pope, though he has more to offer the modern reader than Dryden and might have been enlisted in the argument with certainly not less effect, was taken over, an obvious property, by the post-war cult of the *dix-huitième*—an opportunity for Lyton Strachey and Miss Sitwell.

Such attention as he has received from critics qualified to appreciate him—an aside from Mr. Middleton Murry, a note by Mr. Edgell Rickword, a paragraph or two of Empsonian analysis—has been casual. It is true that what is offered by these three critics (and there is not a great deal more to record) would, if considered, be enough to establish an intelligent orientation to Pope. And Pope's achievement being so varied, I can hardly pretend to attempt more than this. Keeping in view . . . the necessary limits of space, I can aim at little more than to suggest coercively the re-orientation from which a revaluation follows; if more, to indicate something of Pope's range and variety.

'Re-orientation,' here, envisages in particular the classification 'satirist.' It may be no longer necessary to discuss whether satire can be poetry, and we may have entirely disposed of Matthew Arnold; nevertheless, when Pope is classed under 'Satire' it is still with a limiting effect, as if he did only one kind of thing, and that involving definite bounds and a restricted interest. So there is point in considering to begin with a poem of an excellence that is obviously not satiric.

The rare fineness of the *Elegy to the Memory of an Unfortunate Lady* has not had the recognition it deserves. It is praised commonly (when praised) for a 'pathetic' power distinguishing it from the body of Pope's work, but this does not appear to recommend it even to Miss Sitwell. In fact, though to condemn the manner as declamatory is no longer the thing, there is something about it that is found unengagingly outmoded. I remember to have heard, incredulously, a theory, purporting to come from a critic of high repute, that is worth mentioning because it calls attention to certain essential characteristics of the poem. The theory was that Pope opened in all solemnity, but finding it impossible to continue in so high-flown a strain without smiling at himself (he had, after all, a sense of humour), slipped in a qualifying element of burlesque and achieved a subtle total effect analogous to that of *Prufrock.* The evidence? Well, for example, this:

> As into air the purer spirits flow,
> And sep'rate from their kindred dregs below;
> So flew the soul to its congenial place,
> Nor left one virtue to redeem her Race.

The percipient reader, one gathered, smiled here, and, if it were pointed out that 'dregs' turned 'the purer spirits' into a ludicrous metaphor, the less percipient would smile also.

Nevertheless, the reader who sees the relevance here of remarking that Pope was born in the seventeenth century will not be inclined to smile any more than at

> But ah! my soul with too much stay
> Is drunk, and staggers in the way

in Vaughan's *The Retreat.* If it had never even occurred to one that the image could strike any reader as funny, it is not because of the lulling effect of Pope's orotund resonances, but because, by the time one comes to the lines in question, one has been so potently reminded of Pope's Metaphysical descent. The preceding lines are actually those quoted by Mr. Middleton Murry as illustrating the Metaphysical element in Pope:

> Most souls, 'tis true, but peep out once an age,
> Dull sullen pris'ners in the body's cage:
> Dim lights of life, that burn a length of years
> Useless, unseen, as lamps in sepulchres;
> Like Eastern Kings a lazy state they keep,
> And close confin'd to their own palace, sleep.

Mr. Murry's observation is just. Pope is as much the last poet of the seventeenth century as the first of the eighteenth. His relationship to the Metaphysical tradition is aptly suggested by his *Satires of Dr. Donne Versified:* bent as he was (with Dryden behind him) on being the first 'correct' poet, Metaphysical 'wit'—the essential spirit of it—was at the same time congenial to him, more so than to Dryden; and what is suggested in the undertaking to 'versify' Donne he achieved in his best work. In it subtle complexity is reconciled with 'correctness,' his wit is Metaphysical as well as Augustan, and he can be at once polite and profound.

In the passage first quoted one is not merely solemnly impressed by the striking images; their unexpectedness and variety—the 'heterogeneous ideas' that are 'yoked together'—involve (on an adequate reading) a play of mind and a flexibility of attitude that make such effects as that of 'dregs' acceptable when they come: there is an element of surprise, but not the shock that means rejection (complete or ironically qualified) of the inappropriate. Seriousness for Pope, for the Metaphysicals, for Shakespeare, was not the sustained, simple solemnity it tended to be identified with in the nineteenth century; it might include among its varied and disparate tones the ludicrous, and demand, as essential to the total effect, an accompanying play of the critical intelligence. So in these lines of Pope: the associations of 'peep' are not dignified, and one's feelings towards the 'souls' vary, with the changing imagery, from pitying contempt for the timorous peepers, through a shared sense (still qualified with critical con-

tempt, for one is not oneself dull and sullen) of the prisoners' hopeless plight, and a solemn contemplation in the sepulchral couplet of life wasted among shrivelled husks, to that contempt mixed with humour and a sense of opulence that is appropriate to the Kings lazing in their palaces.

The Kings are at least dignified, and they make the transition to the complete dignity of the Lady, who enters again in the next couplet:

> From these perhaps (ere nature bade her die)
> Fate snatch'd her early to the pitying sky.
> As into air the purer spirits flow,*etc.*

But her dignity is not a precarious one, to be sedulously guarded from all possibly risible associations. The 'mean' element in the texture of the previous passage can be safely carried on in 'dregs.' The very violence of this, directed as it is upon her contemptible family ('her Race'), draws the attention away from the value it gives, retrospectively, to 'spirits,' though enough of this value is felt to salt a little, as it were, the sympathetically tender nobility that is opposed to 'dregs.'

Indeed, the successful reconciliation of so formally exalted a manner with such daring shifts and blends is conditioned by this presence of a qualifying, seasoning element. This presence is wit. We have a clear sense of its being generated (to take the process at its most observable) in the play of thought and image glanced at above, from 'Most souls' to 'sleep.' The changes of tone and attitude imposed on the reader (consider, for instance, that involved in passing from 'souls' to 'peep' in the first line) result in an alertness; a certain velleity of critical reserve in responding; a readiness for surprise that amounts in the end to an implicit recognition, at any point, in accepting what is given, of other and complementary possibilities. It becomes plain, in the light of such an account, why we should find ourselves describing as 'mature' the sensibility exhibited by verse in which wit is an element, and also why, in such verse, a completely serious poetic effect should be able to contain suggestions of the ludicrous such as for Gray, Shelley or Matthew Arnold would have meant disaster. (pp. 68-73)

The commentary called for by the exalted decorum of the *Elegy* is . . . implicitly provided by Pope himself:

> 'Tis Use alone that sanctifies Expense,
> And Splendour borrows all her rays from Sense.

Pope was at one with a society to which these were obvious but important truths. So supported, he could sustain a formal dignity such as, pretended to, would make a modern ridiculous. 'Use' represents robust moral certitudes sufficiently endorsed by the way of the world, and 'Sense' was a light clear and unquestionable as the sun. (pp. 80-1)

After various tones of declamation, we pass through . . . to the deeply moving final paragraph, in which the strong personal emotion, so firmly subdued throughout to the 'artificial' form and manner, insists more and more on its immediately personal intensity.

It is time now to turn to the satirist. What in the foregoing page or two may have appeared excessively elementary will be recognized, perhaps, in its bearing on the satire, to serve at least some purpose. For, granting Pope to be pre-eminently a satirist and to enjoy as such what favour he does enjoy, one cannot easily find good reasons for believing that an intelligent appreciation of satiric poetry is much commoner to-day than it was among the contemporaries of Matthew Arnold. Elementary things still need saying. Such terms as 'venom,' 'envy,' 'malice' and 'spite' are, among modern connoisseurs, the staple of appreciation (it is, at any rate, difficult to find anything on Pope in other terms): '. . . we are in the happy position of being able, quite imperturbably, to enjoy the fun. . . . We sit at our ease, reading those *Satires* and *Epistles,* in which the verses, when they were written, resembled nothing so much as spoonfuls of boiling oil, ladled out by a fiendish monkey at an upstairs window upon such of the passers-by whom the wretch had a grudge against—and we are delighted.' The Victorians disapproved; Bloomsbury approves: that is the revolution of taste.

It is, in some ways, a pity that we know so much about Pope's life. If nothing had been known but the works, would 'envy,' 'venom,' 'malice,' 'spite' and the rest have played so large a part in the commentary? There is, indeed, evidence in the satires of strong personal feelings, but even—or, rather, especially—where these appear strongest, what (if we are literate) we should find most striking is an intensity of art. To say, with Leslie Stephen and Lytton Strachey, that in the character of Sporus Pope 'seems to be actually screaming with malignant fury' is to betray an essential inability to read Pope.

But one has to conclude from published criticism that the nature of Pope's art is very little understood. Just as I reach this point there comes to hand the following, by an American critic: 'A familiar charge often brought against Shelley is lack of discipline, but in such charges one must always know what the poet is trying to control. If, as in the case of Pope, it is the mere perfection of a regulated line of verse, the problem becomes one of craftsmanship.' A 'mere perfection of a regulated line of verse' is not anything as clearly and precisely indicated as the critic, perhaps, supposes; but that he supposes Pope's technique ('craftsmanship' being plainly depreciatory) to be something superficial, some mere skill of arranging a verbal surface, is confirmed by what he goes on to say: Pope's 'recitation of the dogmas of his day is hollow,' and 'in his day as in ours it is a relatively simple matter to accept a ritual of

devotion as a substitute for an understanding of basic moral values.'

An 'understanding of basic moral values' is not a claim one need be concerned to make for a poet, but that Pope's relation to the 'basic moral values' of the civilization he belonged to was no mere matter of formal salute and outward deference has been sufficiently shown above, in the discussion of the close of *Epistle IV.* When Pope contemplates the bases and essential conditions of Augustan culture his imagination fires to a creative glow that produces what is poetry even by Romantic standards. His contemplation is religious in its seriousness. The note is that of these lines, which come in *Epistle III* not long after a vigorous satiric passage and immediately before another:

> Ask we what makes one keep and one bestow?
> That Pow'r who bids the Ocean ebb and flow,
> Bids seed-time, harvest, equal course maintain,
> Thro' reconcil'd extremes of drought and rain,
> Builds life on Death, on Change Duration founds,
> And gives th' eternal wheels to know their rounds.

The order of Augustan civilization evokes characteristically in Pope, its poet, when he is moved by the vision of it, a profound sense of it as dependent on and harmonious with an ultimate and inclusive order. The sense of order expressed in his art when he is at his best (and he is at his best more than most poets) is nothing merely conventional or superficial, explicable in terms of social elegance and a pattern of verse. His technique, concerned as it is with arranging words and 'regulating' movements, is the instrument of a fine organization, and it brings to bear pressures and potencies that can turn intense personal feelings into something else. 'His "poetic criticism of life," ' says Lytton Strachey, gibbeting solemn fatuity, 'was simply and solely the heroic couplet.' Pope would have found it hard to determine what precisely this means, but her certainly would not have found the fatuity Arnold's, and if the Augustan idiom in which he expressed much the same commonplaces as Arnold's differed from the Victorian, it was not in being less solemn.

> Ask you what Provocation I have had?
> The strong Antipathy of Good to Bad

—we may not accept this as suggesting adequately the moral basis of Pope's satire, but it is significant that Pope could offer such an account: his strength as a satirist was that he lived in an age when such an account could be offered.

The passages of solemnly exalted imagination like those adduced above come without incongruity in the midst of the satire—the significance of this needs no further insisting on. What does need insisting on is that with this capacity for poised and subtle variety goes a remarkable command of varied satiric tones. The politeness of the Atticus portrait is very different from that of the *Rape of the Lock* (a work that, in my opinion, has enjoyed more than justice); the intense destructive vivacity of the Sporus portrait is different from that of the attack on Timon; the following (which is very far from an exception) is enough to dispose of the judgment that 'Pope was witty but not humorous'—the theme is Paper Credit:

> Had Colepepper's whole wealth been hops and
>   hogs,
> Could he himself have sent it to the dogs?
> His Grace will game: to White's a Bull be led,
> With spurning heels and with a butting head.
> To White's be carry'd, as to ancient games,
> Fair Coursers, Vases, and alluring Dames.
> Shall then Uxurio, if the stakes he sweep,
> Bear home six Whores, and make his Lady weep?

The story of Sir Balaam at the end of *Epistle III* is, again, quite different—but one cannot by enumerating, even if there were room, do justice to Pope's variety. Indeed, to call attention to the satiric variety as such is to risk a misleading stress. (pp. 81-5)

A representative selection of passages would fill a great many pages. A selection of all Pope that one would wish to have by one for habitual re-reading would fill a great many more. Is it necessary to disclaim the suggestion that he is fairly represented in short extracts? No one, I imagine, willingly reads through the *Essay on Man* (Pope piquing himself on philosophical or theological profundity and acumen is intolerable, and he cannot, as Dryden can, argue interestingly in verse); but to do justice to him one must read through not merely the *Epistles,* but, also as a unit, the fourth book of the *Dunciad,* which I am inclined to think the most striking manifestation of his genius. It is certainly satire, and I know of nothing that demonstrates more irresistibly that satire can be great poetry.

An adequate estimate of Pope would go on to describe the extraordinary key-position he holds, the senses in which he stands between the seventeenth and the eighteenth centuries. Communications from the Metaphysicals do not pass beyond him; he communicates forward, not only with Johnson, but also (consider, for instance, *Eloisa to Abelard*) with Thomson and Gray. It was not for nothing that he was so interested in Milton. (pp. 90-1)

F. R. Leavis, "Pope," in his *Revaluation: Tradition & Development in English Poetry,* George Stewart Publishers, Inc., 1947, pp. 68-100.

DAVID B. MORRIS
(essay date 1984)

[In the following excerpt, Morris demonstrates Pope's changing aesthetic through a comparison of the "Pastorals" and *Epilogue to the Satires*, one of the author's last major works.]

"There's no fooling with Life, when it is once turn'd beyond Forty," wrote the seventeenth-century poet and essayist Abraham Cowley, whom Pope admired for his heartfelt truths even though Cowley's labored pindarics and metaphysical style had passed from favor. Pope had turned forty in 1728, the year that signaled his transition to satire with the appearance of *The Dunciad* in its initial three-book format. Pope was fifty when he published the equally transitional *Epilogue to the Satires . . .* , which closed a decade of ethical writing unparalleled in English poetry. Pope was acutely conscious of the sense of closure. He concluded the epistolary satire that had occupied him steadily during the 1730s with a firm resolution—later printed as a final annotation to the *Epilogue*—"to publish no more." We should understand Pope's five-year silence after publishing the *Epilogue* not as an evasion or disclaimer of his responsibilities as satirist, but as a steadfast refusal. He called it "a sort of PROTEST." The corruption of the times had grown so insuperable, he explained, that satire was not both "unsafe" and "ineffectual." Yet, the decade of Pope's forties was also a time of personal changes which in some sense predicted his refusal to publish. Repeatedly his letters express versions of his statement to Bolingbroke, after a period of severe illness, that he had left behind a former stage of life: "I am already arriv'd to an Age which more awakens my diligence to live Satisfactorily, than to write unsatisfactorily." Art for Pope in the 1730s finds its justification almost wholly as an instrument of the ethical life.

His forties especially sharpened Pope's sense of change by forcing upon him an intensified experience of illness and loss. At age thirty-nine he could write, in reference to his own weakness and the condition of friends: "I see and hear of nothing but sickness and death." (pp. 241-42)

The changes around him were inevitably accompanied by internal changes. With the steady loss of friends Pope also grew more conscious of the toll time exacted from his own character. In imitating a passage from Horace, he altered the meaning slightly but decisively in describing the loss of his companions as a form of self-diminishment:

Years foll'wing Years, steal something ev'ry day,
At last they steal us from our selves away;
In one our Frolicks, one Amusements end,
In one a Mistress drops, in one a Friend:
This subtle Thief of Life, this paltry Time,
What will it leave me, if it snatch my Rhime?
If ev'ry Wheel of that unweary'd Mill
That turn'd ten thousand Verses, now stand still.

The tone of this passage is so mixed—compounded of meditative pathos, irony, and self-deprecating humor—that we cannot know quite how to understand Pope's attitude toward his art, which seems all that stands between self and nothingness, all that (in its unwearied motion) remains constant amid his growing sense of departure and change. The farewell or leave-taking is a repeated gesture in his later verse. Pope had once described the poet's life as leaving father and mother to cleave unto the Muse. Now even the Muses are included in a half-joking, half-serious valediction. As he tells his old friend John Caryll: "It is high time after the fumbling age of forty is past, to abandon those ladies, who else will quickly abandon us."

Pope is among the first English poets who considered poetry his vocation, his life's work, and who understood his literary acts as constituting a developing career or oeuvre. The *Epilogue to the Satires,* closing the decade of his forties and his series of Horatian imitations, thus offers an appropriate occasion for examining several important changes in Pope's career. He began, of course, committed to the Virgilian paradigm of poetic development, leading from pastoral to georgic to epic. After *Windsor Forest,* the Virgilian schema began to wobble and finally collapsed. Instead of the original epic he had planned—on the subject of Brutus, legendary founder of Britain—Pope turned to the mock-heroic, to translations of Homer, and to Horatian epistles and satires. One reason for his failure or refusal to create an original epic poem was doubtless Pope's unshakable distrust of heroism. *An Essay on Man* casts a cold eye on traditions of heroic conduct, present and past:

Heroes are much the same, the point's agreed,
From Macedonia's madman to the Swede;
The whole strange purpose of their lives, to find
Or make, an enemy of all mankind! . . .

From Alexander to Charles XII, Pope saw only a procession of lunatics and bullies, and even Homer's world, where poetry made large amends for a chronicle of bloodshed, clearly began to exhaust and to disspirit him. Achilles and Brutus were simply too ponderous, despite their virtues, to carry Pope's concern for the quality of individual lives. After Homer, he longed for a change. "I mean no more Translations," he wrote, "but something domestic, fit for my own country, and for my own time." The immediate present, in his occa-

sional poems, had always offered Pope an appealing diversion from the demands of timeless themes and historical significance. In his forties, with each day stealing something irreplaceable, Pope made his "own time"—including his character as poet and the events of each new year—the explicit subject of his works.

The original titles of the two related "dialogues" which comprise the *Epilogue to the Satires* offer a vivid illustration of how he uses temporality as a theme in his later poetry. The full titles are *One Thousand Seven Hundred and Thirty Eight. A Dialogue Something like Horace* and *One Thousand Seven Hundred and Thirty Eight. Dialogue II.* A title consisting almost entirely of digits is more than a curiosity, more than a deliberate violation of strictures against numbering the streaks of the tulip. It represents a complete reversal of the course of Pope's poetic career. Just as *An Epistle to Dr. Arbuthnot* contains an explicit critique of his own early writings, the *Epilogue to the Satires* insists on its corrective relation to other aspects of Pope's oeuvre. As "epilogue" to the imitations of Horace which Pope published throughout the 1730s, it continues and comments upon the work which it implies is now at an end, much as the epilogue to a neoclassical play serves as both commentary and coda. But the numerical explicitness of the original titles also looks back to the very beginning of Pope's career and in a sense brings it full circle. The power of Pope's speech in the *Epilogue* depends in part on our recognition of how much has changed in his life and art.

Pope's changing attitudes toward time and literary form are most evident if we compare the *Epilogue* with his first published poems, known today under the collective name of the *Pastorals.* They were published originally in 1709, when Pope was little more than twenty, and appeared under the individual titles **"Spring," "Summer," "Autumn,"** and **"Winter."** Such self-explanatory titles invite little commentary, but it is significant (in marking the change from Renaissance to neoclassical poetics) that Pope has reduced and simplified Spenser's twelve monthly pastorals in *The Shepheardes Calender* (1579)—a work to which Pope openly alludes—to the trim symmetry of four seasons. Significant, too, is the (limited) choice of sequence, because a series beginning in winter and ending in fall, for example, would convey quite different impressions. Pope chooses to begin the Pastorals in **"Spring,"** which he depicts as a dewy and dawn-filled space, where there is no chronology, no history, only (as in Milton's Eden) an endless cycle of delight. Change in **"Spring"** exists simply to add the pleasures of variety to what is already perfect. Such changeless variety is appropriate, because a pastoral, according to Pope, is by definition uninvolved with time. It presents a picture of the *"Golden Age"* (*The Guardian* no. 40). Loving and singing are its chief actions, leisure pursuits devoid of genuine conflict; and, where conflict does not exist, coyness is welcome and seduction unnecessary. . . . The succeeding pastorals—**"Summer," "Autumn,"** and **"Winter"**—introduce increasingly disharmonious elements. Love changes from erotic play to anxiety, betrayal, and loss. The songs grow strained. The final poem, **"Winter,"** closes with the first of Pope's literary farewells, as Thyrsis stands at the point where pastoral dissolves irrevocably into the landscape of time:

> Sharp *Boreas* blows, and Nature feels Decay,
> Time conquers All, and We must Time obey.
> Adieu ye *Vales*, ye *Mountains, Streams* and *Groves*,
> Adieu ye Shepherd's rural *Lays* and *Loves*,
> Adieu my Flocks, farewell ye *Sylvan* Crew,
> *Daphne* farewell, and all the World adieu!

The change that converts the Virgilian *omnia vincit amor* into Pope's elegiac and pessimistic "Time conquers All" suggests how thoroughly pastoral is being left behind. Pope would write no more eclogues. Despite its finality, however, there is nothing hasty or haphazard about Thyrsis' departure, for his valediction is highly stylized and recapitulates in the final four lines the distinctive subjects and scenes of each of the preceding poems. Pope's *Pastorals*, even in acknowledging the nonpastoral world of time and loss, manages to contain it within the composing and consoling patterns of art.

Art in the *Epilogue to the Satires* has renounced its power to oppose change with aesthetic order. Change has darkened to corruption, form too decomposes as we plunge into the unpatterned disorder brought on by history. Damon, Thyrsis, Lycidas, and Strephon—names timeless and euphonic—give way to the cacophonous register of modern knavery: Selkirk, Bond, Walter, Wild, Chartres, Walpole. The luxuriousness of pastoral lament yields to the abruptness and sharpness of satirical innuendo mingled with humiliating abuse. The couplet, which begins as an artificial language that calls attention to its own fictive contrivances, now yields its balance to asymmetry, violation, and disfigurement. Aesthetic order now seems so minimal and makeshift that it is always on the edge of a collapse into formlessness. Interruption and confusion are among the most conspicuous features in Pope's later poems. Here, for example, are the opening three lines from Dialogue II of the *Epilogue:*

> *Fr.* Tis all a Libel—*Paxton* (Sir) will say.
> *P.* Not yet, my Friend! to-morrow 'faith it may;
> And for that very cause I print to day.

No [major] poem by Pope—[and only one negligible minor poem]—*begins* with a triplet rhyme. Indeed, Pope normally avoided triplet rhymes [everywhere in his work]. The effect of this beginning is thus to interrupt or to violate the expectations his practice had helped to establish. The disruptive beginning also creates potential confusion by introducing the name

Paxton. Swift had protested vigorously that Pope's allusions to specific people and events were too obscure. . . . Nicholas Paxton, Walpole's private watchdog for antiministerial publications, was hardly a household word. (Pope's only other reference to him occurs in this same dialogue.) Yet, Paxton and the triplet rhyme are symptomatic of a deepening confusion. *What* is all a libel? (Using a strategy borrowed from Donne, Pope plunges the reader instantly into a conversation that precedes the poem, making the text merely a fragment of a longer discourse.) And what *is* libel if it can change its meaning from day to day?

The confusion, fragmentation, and disruption Pope embraces in the *Epilogue* reflect not simply the inevitable differences between a satire and a pastoral but the changed perspective of the poet. In his *Pastorals* Pope had assigned himself, as poet, a place outside of history. He arranged time in the poem as if he were immune to it, ordering Spenser's bulky calendar so that each of the four seasonal pastorals has its distinguishing location and time of day. Like the contrived symmetries which characterize his revisions of *The Rape of the Lock,* such aesthetic ordering implies a theory of art in which form represents the poet's attempt to resist or control time and the disorder it brings. In the *Epilogue* Pope, as speaker and as author, no longer stands apart from the disorders that surround him. Unlike the poet of the *Pastorals,* he speaks from *inside* history.

This new position within history is noticeable in all of the Horatian satires and epistles Pope imitated during the 1730s, but, like Horace, Pope nevertheless maintained some distance from the disorders he was attacking—a distance he emphasized by printing Horace's Latin text directly opposite his imitation. Indeed, Pope found it convenient to suggest at times that he was merely modernizing Horace's examples, illustrating in resemblances between Rome and England the timelessness of folly. In the *Epilogue,* however, Pope takes pains to dissociate himself from Horace. His words are no longer shadowed by a Latin text across the page, and English corruption no longer takes its model from Rome. In establishing such distance, the *Epilogue* does not repudiate its debt to Horace, but the most immediate influence upon the form and technique of the poem is Pope's immersion in a temporal world of conflict where the imitative and composing harmonies of art are inappropriate—and perhaps unavailable. Conflict is not merely the subject of the poem but its shaping force as well.

A poet writing within history has no alternative but to open his verse to the disordering interruptions of time. Unlike the decorous antiphonal speeches in the *Pastorals* in which each shepherd completely finishes speaking before his partner responds in (most often) an equal number of lines, the principal exchanges in the *Epilogue* are hasty, unbalanced, and incomplete:

P. Ye Rev'rend Atheists!—*F.* Scandal! name them, Who?
P. Why that's the thing you bid me not to do.
Who starv'd a Sister, who forswore a Debt,
I never nam'd—the Town's enquiring yet.
The pois'ning Dame—*Fr.* You mean—*P.* I don't.—*Fr.* You do.
P. See! now I keep the Secret, and not you. . . .

Secrecy and innuendo are to meaning what interruption is to form. Although Pope had labored to make his *Pastorals* "musical" (as he said) to a degree unprecedented in English, especially by maintaining the caesura at what he considered the natural pause after the fourth, fifth, or sixth syllable, he seemed to abandon this goal in the *Epilogue,* where caesuras fall almost anywhere—once, incredibly, before the very last syllable of the line. . . . The meter returns to its iambic base only to depart from it, repeatedly and eccentrically, making regular scansion impossible. Immersed with history, the poet cannot use his leisure for corrections and cannot afford the time to deliberate over revisions. Writing at high speed, he rushes to publish—"I print to day"—before vice can transform today's truths into tomorrow's lies.

A sense of Pope's developing career helps us to recognize how far he has moved toward a purposeful disfigurement of his art. The "Freedom" he granted to epistolary verse cannot alone account for the conscious deformities of the *Epilogue to the Satires.* The *Epilogue* is extreme even among Pope's earlier Horatian imitations. In the *Epilogue* points of debate are not resolved or developed but hastily put aside to explore adjacent (but not necessarily related) topics. No subtle design holds the various parts together in a pleasing unity. Instead, we experience an *illusory* movement which leads nowhere. Neither speaker truly responds to the other but simply asserts a position. Pope, of course, contrived such a fruitless exchange to emphasize the inflexible knavery of his temporizing, self-serving opponents. No true dialogue is possible, it seems, when virtuous poet and worldly courtier enter into conversation. Yet, the contrivance also attributes to virtue an unfortunately strained and inflexible self-righteousness, creating a curiously static poem, as if it were meant to dramatize a state of impasse, a condition in which poetry, as we normally understand it, cannot be written.

The two dialogues could be said to exist mainly for the sake of their conclusions, which abruptly shift the poems to a new level of discourse, elevated and visionary (in its Augustan sense). We enter something like an allegorical moment in which time, in all its particularity, is both acknowledged and abruptly transcended. Dialogue I closes with the vivid picture of the Triumph of Vice, while Dialogue II shows us the Muse, as Priestess of Virtue, opening the Temple of Eternity. These concluding passages resemble nothing that has preceded them and are certainly among the most noble lines Pope ever wrote. (pp. 242-48)

The Triumph of Vice is among the most powerful denunciations of contemporary manners and morals in the history of satire, yet Pope represents himself finally as a mere witness. Powerless to deter or to reform, the satirist in his attacks on vice has become more than ineffectual. He appears almost ludicrous in his futility. Lashing out is now an absurd mission, like sweeping back the tide. Even his status as witness is contingent upon the survival of his verse, which he represents as uncertain. In effect, the satirist seems doomed to a life of contradiction. He continues to lash out at individuals, though under the cover of innuendo. . . . Yet, his attack, at its moment of intensest rhetorical power, has also betrayed his weakness, his inefficacy, his isolated absurdity. Further, by exaggerating the satirist's isolation and defiance, Pope risks transforming him into an unwitting self-parody—a Jeremiah, whose prophetic gloom would be too weighty for a modern man of sense, however virtuous. . . . In Dialogue II Pope . . . complicates and modifies his earlier conclusion with a second, less solitary, less ambiguous version of the poet's role.

In the conclusion to Dialogue II the poet turns from passive witness to active guardian. Instead of ambiguous attack or solitary disdain, he celebrates the constructive power of communal praise. Although still isolated within the world of history and politics, he relieves his solitude by including the satirist within the larger, timeless circle of virtuous men. No longer is the survival of his protest conditional—"*if* such a verse remain"—but the poet is instead assured, defiant, and resolved to assert his lapsed powers:

Let Envy howl while Heav'n's whole Chorus sings,
And bark at Honour not confer'd by Kings;
Let Flatt'ry sickening see the Incense rise,
Sweet to the World, and grateful to the Skies:
Truth guards the Poet, sanctifies the line,
And makes Immortal, Verse as mean as mine. . . .

This bold claim of immortality for verse so choked with the debris of time and history is linked directly with a defense of satire as a "sacred Weapon." . . . If literary force proves ineffective in attacking Vice, it is still useful in defending Virtue. As an active guardian of Virtue, the poet can work constructively despite the howls of envy or triumph of corruption. (pp. 256-57)

Pope's vision of the Temple of Eternity does not magically transform the time-bound world. Vice still rules; the poet is still embattled and solitary. "Yes, the last Pen for Freedom let me draw," he affirms in the next to last paragraph, but, despite his isolation, he speaks now with a confident authority that conceals no passiveness or resignation. The new qualities of affirmation and confidence in Dialogue II were evident to Pope's perhaps most tiresome correspondent, the indefatigable Aaron Hill. "I find in this satire," he wrote, "something inexpressibly daring and generous . . . It places the *Poet* in a light for which *nature* and *reason* designed him; and attones all the pitiful *sins* of the *trade,* for to a *trade,* and a *vile* one, poetry is irrecoverably sunk in this kingdom." This is intelligent commentary that Pope would appreciate. Poetry as a trade implies none of the rich exchange between present and past that Pope evoked in his metaphors of commerce. Trade is mere day-labor, common journeyman's work, like the hack writing and Grub Street propaganda which Walpole so heavily subsidized. In restoring to the poet an

ancient alliance with truth and virtue, Pope thus also implicitly insists that poetry can serve an elevated and affirmative purpose *within* the corrupt world of politics and time, even if it will surely be deformed in the process. Pope's renunciation of satire at the conclusion of the *Epilogue to the Satires* depends for its full significance on our sense that it is one change in a poetic career that continues to unfold. The tradesmen-poets of Pope's day could have ceased to publish for five years without anyone's noticing. Only Pope could transform even silence into an eloquent and continuing, if desperate, speech. (p. 258)

David B. Morris, in his *Alexander Pope: The Genius of Sense,* Cambridge, Mass.: Harvard University Press, 1984, 370 p.

SOURCES FOR FURTHER STUDY

Bateson, F. W., and Joukousky, N. A., eds. *Alexander Pope: A Critical Anthology.* Middlesex, England: Penguin Books, 1971, 512 p.

Excerpts of representative criticism by and about Pope from 1706 to 1968.

Brower, Reuben Arthur. *Alexander Pope: The Poetry of Allusion.* Oxford: Clarendon Press, 1959, 368 p.

Highly regarded study of Pope's attention to form and recurrent use of literary allusion in his works.

Clark, Donald B. *Alexander Pope.* New York: Twayne Publishers, 1967, 180 p.

Presents "a coherent, unified interpretation of Pope's major poems. It argues that the poet's vision of harmony through variety—the friendly strife—is a guiding philosophy which runs from the first work to the final version of *The Dunciad.*"

Guerinot, J. V., ed. *Pope: A Collection of Critical Essays.* Englewood Cliffs, N.J.: Prentice-Hall, 1972, 184 p.

Includes "Rhetoric and Poems," by William K. Wimsatt, Jr.; "The Cistern and the Fountain: Art and Reality in Pope," by Irvin Ehrenpreis; and "The Satiric Adversary" by John M. Aden.

Mack, Maynard, ed. *Essential Articles for the Study of Alexander Pope.* Hamden, Conn.: Shoe String Press, 1968, 844 p.

Collection of forty-nine articles covering the most salient aspects of Pope's work.

Wimsatt, William Kurtz. *The Portraits of Alexander Pope.* New Haven and London: Yale University Press, 1965, 391 p.

Biography of Pope and guide to the numerous portraits of him.

Ezra Pound

1885-1972

(Full name Ezra Loomis Pound; also wrote under pseudonyms B. H. Dias, Abel Saunders, and William Atheling) American poet, translator, critic, essayist, editor, and librettist.

INTRODUCTION

Among the foremost literary figures of the twentieth century, Pound is credited with creating some of modern poetry's most enduring and inventive verse. In such volumes as *Ripostes* (1912) *Cathay* (1915), and *Hugh Selwyn Mauberley* (1920), he expedited the modern period in English and American letters by introducing and elucidating Imagist and Vorticist theories. These works display Pound's efforts to "resuscitate the dead art" and "make it new" by combining stylistic elements from the verse of Provençal and Tuscan troubadours, French and Oriental poets, and the Pre-Raphaelites with Imagistic principles expounded by T. E. Hulme, Ernest Fenellosa, and Ford Madox Ford. Eschewing verbosity and enjambment, Pound sought to employ *le mot juste*—the precise word—which often took the form of foreign phrases, archaic dialects, or technical diction, and he revived the end-stopped line to create self-contained measures of poetry that resonate with independent significance. In addition, Pound's experiments with rhythm are often considered the first substantial twentieth-century efforts to liberate poetry from iambic patterns.

Born in Hailey, Idaho, and raised in Philadelphia, Pound made his first visits to Europe with his family in 1898 and 1902. After receiving a philosophy degree from Hamilton College, Pennsylvania, in 1905, Pound pursued graduate work in Romance languages at the University of Pennsylvania and was awarded a fellowship to study the plays of Lope de Vega in London and Madrid. For a short while in 1907, Pound taught Romance languages at Wabash College, Indiana, until relieved of his duties for reputedly sheltering a woman overnight in his rooms. Disgusted with American provincialism, Pound returned to Europe and privately published his first volume, *A lume spento* (1908), in Venice. From there he traveled to London and initiated a period of intense productivity in literary and artistic endeavors. His association with *New Age* magazine over the next several years introduced him to important artists, economists, and politicians and contributed to the development of ideas he would expound upon in his later works. In 1921, having been the key agent in the publication of some of the previous decade's most influential works, Pound moved to Paris, where he continued to assert his literary tastes. Pound left Paris in 1924 to live in Rapallo, Italy, where he endorsed the Fascist government of Benito Mussolini and declared his political beliefs in a series of radio broadcasts during World War II. Arrested by American allies and charged with treason, Pound was briefly imprisoned in Pisa before being found mentally unfit to stand trial and was committed to St. Elizabeths Hospital for the insane in Washington, D.C., in 1946. He returned to Italy upon his release in 1958 and died in Venice.

Pound's early poetry is considered by many critics to emulate the verse of Robert Browning, Charles Algernon Swinburne, and William Butler Yeats. *A lume spento* and the volumes published during his first years in London, *A Quinzaine for This Yule* (1908), *Personae* (1909), *Exultations* (1909), *Provença* (1910), and *Canzoni* (1911), contain such frequently anthologized pieces as "The Goodly Fere" and "Sestina: Altaforte," in which Pound adopts the voice of a historical persona to narrate the poem. While these books earned him a reputation as a man of letters, they were faulted for Pound's use of archaic diction and medieval allusions, a frequent criticism of his early verse.

By 1911, Pound was immersed in London's intellectual milieu as a critic and poet. The editor of *New Age,* A. R. Orage, regularly published Pound's writings and introduced him to some of the era's most influential and challenging thinkers. Pound's response to this intellectual and aesthetic stimuli was to found Imagism, which involved a group of artists who assimilated techniques of the French Symbolists and Oriental writers. Impelled by essays published in *New Age* by F. S. Flint and T. E. Hulme on modern French poets, as well as the notebooks of Ernest Fenellosa, an American scholar preoccupied with Chinese and Japanese literature, and the work of Provençal poet Arnaut Daniel, Pound developed a verse style noted for encouraging rhythmical variation. He emphasized the "direct treatment of the 'thing' whether subjective or objective" and "the language of common speech, but always the exact word." Pound's poems "The Return," in *Ripostes,* and "In a Station of the Metro" exemplify his Imagist ideal of "an intellectual and emotional complex in an instant of time."

In these pieces, the reader intuits meaning through images, while emotion is conveyed through sound. The impact of Imagism is evident in *Des imagistes,* an anthology edited by Pound which contains works by such other notable twentieth-century authors as Hilda Doolittle, Richard Aldington, James Joyce, and William Butler Yeats. By 1914, Pound perceived limitations inherent within Imagism and disparagingly termed it "Amygism" after Amy Lowell, the poet who edited several subsequent Imagist anthologies and whom he believed devalued the term to connote free verse. With sculptor, painter, and writer Wyndham Lewis and sculptor Henri Gaudier-Brzeska, Pound created Vorticism, a dynamic amalgamation of visual and literary arts. These artists believed the image to be "a VORTEX, from which, through which, and into which, ideas are constantly rushing." While the outbreak of World War I and the enlistment of Lewis and Gaudier-Brzeska ended the movement, much of Pound's later writing displays Vorticism's intolerance, gregariousness, and didacticism.

Pound's remaining years in England were marked by the publication of some of his most renowned work. The poems in *Cathay* (1915) rework Ernest Fenellosa's translations of Chinese verse. Such frequently anthologized pieces as "The River Merchant's Wife: A Letter" and "The River Song" are admired by critics for their refined style and austere beauty. Pound's other volumes from this period are heavily indebted to his readings of such French authors as Theophile Gautier, Jules Laforgue, and Remy de Gourmont, all of whom he admired for their use of formal structures and intellectual content. "Homage to Sextus Propertius," contained in *Quia pauper amavi* (1919), is noted for its stylistic similarities to the heavily ironic verse of Laforgue. In this poem, Pound loosely translated and embellished the work of Roman poet Sextus Propertius with modern references, latinate puns and malapropisms, and scatological language to display his love and knowledge of history as well as his commitment to the endurance of great art in the modern world. He further explored these themes in *Hugh Selwyn Mauberley,* which is considered his masterpiece by many critics. More reliant on traditional metrical patterns and stanzaic forms, this long poem details Pound's attitudes toward art, public philistinism, World War I, and his earlier poetic affinities. Pound's affiliation with Vorticism is evident in his vituperative description of the destruction of earlier cultural achievements during World War I and his proclamation that the West is "an old bitch gone in the teeth / . . . a botched civilization." Donald Davie asserted: "*Hugh Selwyn Mauberley* remains a very important poem; apart from anything else, it has proved to be the most insidiously and aptly quotable of Pound's poems, and it has very great merit as an Englishing of Gautier."

Before *Hugh Selwyn Mauberley* was published, Pound had already begun work on the *Cantos,* a discursive, multilingual, heavily allusive sequence of poems on which he endeavored for more than forty years.

While his concept of the *Cantos* continuously changed, he initially described it as a "cyselephantine poem of immeasurable length." Pound later indicated his epic intentions for the *Cantos* by referring to them as his *"commedia agnostica"*—an allusion to Dante's *Divine Comedy.* In the *Cantos,* Pound draws from the historical and artistic wealth of the ages to depict a cultural and political odyssey through time. While inevitably obscure in parts, these verses reveal Pound's vast and eclectic knowledge and his determination to use the past to explicate the present. The first three pieces, often referred to as the "Ur-Cantos," appeared in 1917 in *Poetry* magazine and were subsequently revised or deleted from the main corpus of the poem. Later installments, including *A Draft of XVI Cantos* (1925), *A Draft of XXX Cantos* (1930), and *Drafts and Fragments of Cantos CX to CXVII* (1968), were published in unfinished form.

Pound continued to work on the *Cantos* after leaving England in 1921 to live in Paris, where he associated with Dadaists Tristan Tzara and Louis Aragon. Essentially a Europeanization of Vorticism's polemical content and irreverence toward contemporary literary trends, Dadaism actively ignored logic and grammar in favor of random associations. Elements of Dadaism, as well as the influences of Chinese ideograms and James Joyce's seminal novel *Ulysses,* are prominent in *A Draft of XVI Cantos.* By 1924, Pound had left Paris and settled in Rapallo, Italy. Removed from the barrage of cultural stimuli he experienced in England and Paris, Pound composed poetry during this period in a myriad of styles and was unaffiliated with any single literary movement. *A Draft of XXX Cantos, Eleven New Cantos, XXX-XLI* (1934), *The Fifth Decad of Cantos* (1937), and *Cantos, LII-LXXI* (1940) render Pound's impressions of Confucius, American presidents and political theorists John Quincy Adams and Thomas Jefferson, economist Major C. H. Douglas, and Fascist dictator Benito Mussolini.

Following his imprisonment for broadcasting treasonous messages and his confinement at St. Elizabeths Hospital, Pound published *The Pisan Cantos* (1948), his most controversial volume of poetry. The awarding of the Bollingen Prize to *The Pisan Cantos* polarized the American literary community. The Library of Congress panel, which awarded the prize, stated: "To permit other considerations than that of poetic achievement [to sway the decision] would destroy the significance of the award and would in principle deny the validity of that objective perception of value on which any civilized society must rest." The editors of the *Saturday Review* argued: "[Even] if all political aspects, pro and con, are brushed aside, the fact remains that *The Pisan Cantos,* for the most part, seem to us to be less poetry than a series of word games and hidden allusions which, however they may delight certain

of Pound's followers, are hardly deserving of an award bearing the name of the United States Library of Congress." The interpretation of several of these verses is also the subject of critical debate. The famous line "Pull down thy vanity," repeated throughout "Canto LXXXI," for example, is perceived by some critics as Pound's condemnation of his captors and by others as a recantation of his earlier beliefs. Nevertheless, *The Pisan Cantos* marks a transition toward a more personal and elegiac poetry. *Section: Rock Drill de los cantares* (1955), *Thrones de los cantares* (1959), and *Drafts and Fragments of Cantos CX-CXVII* document Pound's resignation to the impossibility of his ideal of a cultural paradise. Although Pound never completed his enterprise and wrote in "Canto CXVI," "But the beauty is not the madness / Tho' my errors and wrecks lie about me. / And I am not a demigod, / I cannot make it cohere," *The Cantos* are generally acknowledged by critics as a fascinating display of poetic styles and ideas as well as one of the most ambitious verse projects of the twentieth century. Affirming the importance of the sequence, Archibald MacLeish stated: "The nearest thing we have . . . to a moral history of our tragic age is the *Cantos* of Ezra Pound, that descent, not into Dante's hell, but into our own."

In addition to his poetic accomplishments, Pound is recognized as a formidable literary critic. Along with his essays outlining Imagist tenets and Chinese poetic techniques, Pound contributed three important concepts to literary criticism: melopoeia, phanopoeia, and logopoeia. Each of these terms isolates a method by which poetry imbues language with significance. In melopoeia, meaning is conveyed by the musical qualities of words: phanopoeia is the "casting of images upon the visual imagination"; and logopoeia is described by Pound as the "dance of intellect among words." Pound is likewise acknowledged as a selfless purveyor of other writers' works. His most significant contributions involved securing publication of Ernest Hemingway's *In Our Time* and T. S. Eliot's poem "The Love Song of J. Alfred Prufrock" and editing *The Waste Land,* which Eliot acknowledged in his dedication to Pound as *"il miglior fabbro,"* "the greater craftsman." Pound also partially financed the publication of Joyce's *Ulysses,* and he assisted Yeats in developing the style of his later poetry. The numerous periodicals with which Pound was associated in an editorial capacity include *Poetry,* the *Egoist, New Age,* the *Little Review,* the *Dial,* the *transatlantic review,* and the *Exile.*

While much of Pound's work has been charged with obscurity verging on meaninglessness, his verse has often been acknowledged for its technical ingenuity and for evidencing his knowledge of a wide range of esoteric subjects. Among contemporary scholars, Pound remains one of the most provocative figures in modern literature, and his importance and influence as a poet have been the subject of constant debate. Summarizing Pound's contributions to literature, Cyril Connolly noted: "Ezra Pound had two very remarkable qualities: he was a poet and, despite his passion for the past, a deeply original one. He was also something rarer than a poet—a catalyst, an impresario, a person who both instinctively understood what the age was about to bring forth and who helped it to be born."

(For further information about Pound's life and works, see *Contemporary Authors*, Vols. 5-8, 37-40 [obituary]; *Concise Dictionary of American Literary Biography, 1917-1929*; *Contemporary Literary Criticism*, Vols. 1, 2, 3, 4, 5, 7, 10, 13, 18, 34, 48, 50; *Dictionary of Literary Biography*, Vols. 4, 45, 63; and *Major 20th-Century Writers*.)

CRITICAL COMMENTARY

F. R. LEAVIS

(essay date 1932)

(Leavis is an influential contemporary English critic whose methodology combines close textual criticism with predominantly moral and social concerns. In the following excerpt from a 1932 study, he registers Pound's *Hugh Selwyn Mauberley* as the single example of great poetry in Pound's oeuvre.)

In *Mauberley* we feel a pressure of experience, an impulsion from deep within. The verse is extraordinarily subtle, and its subtlety is the subtlety of the sensibility that it expresses. No one would think here of distinguishing the way of saying from the thing said. It is significant that the pressure seems to derive (we are reminded of Mr. Yeats) from a recognition of bankruptcy, of a devoted life summed up in futility. A study of the earlier work, then, does at least help the commentary on *Mauberley*: it helps to bring out the significance of the poem for the inquiry in hand.

Mauberley is in the first place (the description suggests itself readily) the summing-up of an individual life. It has also a representative value, reflecting as it does the miscellaneousness of modern culture, the absence of direction, of an alphabet of forms or of any one predominant idiom; the uncongeniality of the modern world to the artist; and his dubious status there. It offers, more particularly, a representative experience of the phase of English poetry in which it became plain that the Romantic tradition was exhausted. One might, at the risk of impertinence, call it quintessential autobiography, taking care, however, to add that it has the impersonality of great poetry: its technical perfection means a complete detachment and control. (p. 29)

Mr. Pound's main concern has always been art: he is, in the most serious sense of the word, an aesthete. It is this that makes the peculiar nature of Mr. Eliot's plea for the earlier work necessary. But here, in *Mauberley*, there is the pressure of personal experience. The title of the first poem, with its ironical allusion to Ronsard—"E. P. Ode Pour L'Election de son Sepulchre"—is explicitly personal: it indicates what is to follow. The poet is looking back on a life devoted to the cultivation of aesthetic fastidiousness, technical perfection, exquisite eclecticism. He is no longer trying to resuscitate the dead art of poetry, or observing the elegance of Circe's hair; he is taking stock, and what has it all amounted to? What is the outcome? He touches various notes, plays on various themes, and recalls various representative memories in the different constituent poems. The poems together form one poem, a representative experience of life—tragedy, comedy, pathos, and irony. And throughout there is a subtlety of tone, a complexity of attitude, such as we associate with seventeenth-century wit.

In this first poem he conveys, with masterly compression, the nature of the interests and attitudes that have occupied his life. The ironically sublime comparison of himself to Capaneus, the hero who defied the gods and paid the penalty, has its comment in the contemptuous contrasting image: "trout for factitious bait"—the stake a mere gaudy fly, and a faked one at that. The Homeric quotation suggests his romantic addiction to the classics and the past: his ear has been unstopped to too many Sirens.

His true Penelope was Flaubert

—In all his romantic excursions he has remained constant to one faith, the aesthetic: his main concern has been art, art as represented by Flaubert, saint and martyr of the artistic conscience.

He fished by obstinate isles

suggests his inveterate eclecticism, his interest in various periods and cultures, Provençal, Italian, Chinese, classical, and so on. He has always

Observed the elegance of Circe's hair
Rather than the mottoes on sun-dials.

Principal Works

A lume spento (poetry) 1908

Exultations (poetry) 1909

Personae (poetry) 1909

A Quinzaine for this Yule (poetry) 1909

The Spirit of Romance (criticism) 1910

Canzoni (poetry) 1911

Ripostes (poetry) 1912

Lustra (poetry) 1916

Pavannes and Divisions (criticism) 1918; also published as Pavannes and Divigations, 1958

Quia pauper amavi (poetry) 1919

Instigations of Ezra Pound Together with an Essay on the Chinese Written Character by Ernest Fennollosa (criticism) 1920

Hugh Selwyn Mauberley (poetry) 1920

Poems, 1918-21 (poetry) 1922

Indiscretions (criticism) 1923

A Draft of XVI Cantos (poetry) 1925

Personae: The Collected Poems (poetry) 1926

A Draft of XXX Cantos (poetry) 1930

How to Read (criticism) 1931

ABC of Reading (criticism) 1934

Eleven New Cantos, XXX-XLI (poetry) 1934

Make It New (criticism) 1934

Jefferson and/or Mussolini (history) 1935

The Fifth Decad of Cantos (poetry) 1937

Guide to Kulchur (criticism) 1938

Cantos, LII-LXXI (poetry) 1940

The Cantos (poetry) 1948

The Pisan Cantos (poetry) 1948

Literary Essays (criticism) 1954

Section: Rock-Drill de los cantares (poetry) 1955

Thrones de los cantares (poetry) 1959

Drafts and Fragments of Cantos CX-CXVII (poetry) 1968

Selected Prose, 1909-1965 (criticism) 1973

Collected Early Poems (poetry) 1976

He has devoted his life to aesthetic discrimination and technical perfection while life slipped by. Life now has, it seems, slipped by, and what has come of it all? The last stanza answers with an oblique reference to Villon, the unfastidious blackguard whose "wasted" life produced so rich a harvest of poetry. His own industrious career, on the contrary, our poet sees as yielding

No adjunct to the Muses' diadem.

Nevertheless, this disillusioned summing-up is itself great poetry, "criticism of life" in the best sense of the phrase, as Mr. Eliot says. For Mr. Pound has not been unaffected by the march of all events. However uncongenial one may find his eclectic aestheticism, his devotion to the elegance of Circe's hair, it has been accompanied by intense seriousness: Mr. Pound is not an American for nothing. What we have in *Mauberley* is a representative sensibility, that of a poet who found his starting point in the Nineties, lived through the heavy late-Victorian years of Edward VII, saw his friends disappear in the war, and now knows that the past holds more for him than the future.

His technical skill is now a matter of bringing to precise definition a mature and complex sensibility. The rhythms, in their apparent looseness and carelessness, are marvels of subtlety: "out of key with his time" is being said everywhere by strict rhythmic means. What looks like the free run of contemporary speech achieves effects of a greater precision than can be found very often in *The Oxford Book*. And the verse has extraor-

dinary variety. The subtlety of movement is associated with subtlety of mood and attitude. "Wit" is present. Critical activity accompanies feeling and remembering. Mr. Pound can be, as the seventeenth century poets were, serious and light at the same time, sardonic and poignant, flippant and intense.

Devices that might easily degenerate into tricks ("stunts") remain under perfect control. Take, for example, the use of inverted commas:

Unaffected by "the march of events,"

   . . . .

The "age demanded" chiefly a mould in plaster,
Made with no loss of time,
A prose kinema, not, not assuredly, alabaster
Or the "sculpture" of rhyme.

   . . . .

The tea-rose tea-gown, etc.
Supplants the mousseline of Cos,
The pianola "replaces"
Sappho's barbitos.

   . . . .

Incapable of the least utterance or composition,
Emendation, conservation of the "better tradition,"
Refinement of medium, elimination of superfluities,
August attraction or concentration.

To be able to use such a device as freely as Mr. Pound does without prejudice to subtlety of tone and emphasis is to pass a severe test. His poise, though so varied, and for all his audacities, is sure; how sure, nothing can show better than the pun in the last stanza of the third poem. . . . In what poet, after the seventeenth century, can we find anything like this contributing to a completely serious effect (the poem is not only tragically serious but solemn).

The second and third poems introduce the modern world of mass-production and levelling-down, a world that has destroyed the traditions and is hostile, not only to the artist, but to all distinction of spirit. The fourth and fifth poems bring in the war. They are a more remarkable achievement than they may perhaps at first appear to be.

> Died some, pro patria,
> non "dulce" non "et decor" . . .
> walked eye-deep in hell
> believing in old men's lies, then unbelieving
> came home, home to a lie,
> home to many deceits,
> home to old lies and new infamy;
> usury age-old and age-thick
> and liars in public places.

—That is a dangerous note, and only the completest integrity and the surest touch could safely venture it. But we have no uneasiness. The poet has realized the war with the completely adult (and very uncommon) awareness that makes it impossible to nurse indignation and horror. *Mauberley* came out in 1920. The presence of the war in it, we feel, is not confined to these two small poems: they are not mere detachable items. They represent a criterion of seriousness and purity of intention that is implicit in the whole. To say this is to indicate the gulf between any of the earlier work, archaizing or modernizing, and *Mauberley.*

In **"Yeux Glauques,"** the next piece, we hark back to the age of peace and prosperity that prepared the war; the phase of English culture out of which the poets of the Nineties started. Pre-Raphaelite art with, for setting, Gladstone, Ruskin, and Victorian morality on the one hand, and Swinburne, Rossetti, and Victorian immorality on the other. Next, in *"Siena mi fe'; disfecemi Maremma,"* we have the Nineties themselves with their blend of religion, religiosity, aestheticism, and dissipation:

> For two hours he talked of Gallifet;
> Of Dowson; of the Rhymers' Club;
> Told me how Johnson (Lionel) died
> By falling from a high stool in a pub . . .
> But showed no trace of alcohol
> At the autopsy, privately performed—
> Tissue preserved—the pure mind
> Arose toward Newman as the whiskey warmed.

The irony of this might be called flippant: if so, it is a flippancy that subserves a tragic effect. Nothing could illustrate more forcibly Mr. Pound's sureness of touch, his subtle mastery of tone and accent. The poem is one of the most daring things in the sequence— though "daring" might suggest a possible qualm about it: it is justified by complete success. Rhythmically it is

consummate; but that must be said of *Mauberley* as a whole, in all its rich variety. Mr. Pound's rhythmic suppleness continually surprises.

In **"Mr. Nixon"** he gets new effects out of colloquial speech. It is sardonic comedy; the theme, Success in modern letters. Mr. Pound's earlier satiric verse is always technically adroit and often amusing; but no one would have thought the author capable of a satiric note that should be in keeping with tragic seriousness. **"Mr. Nixon"** is. That is enough to say by way of emphasizing the distinction of the achievement.

Numbers X and XI might have appeared in *Lustra,* though they have their place here in the context of the whole. But XII exhibits again technical mastery functioning at the highest level. It is another marvel of tone and poise. The movement is extraordinarily varied, and the tempo and modulation are exquisitely controlled. The theme is another aspect of modern letters: elegant patronage, modish dilettantism.—

> . . . . .
> Conduct, on the other hand, the soul
> "Which the highest cultures have nourished"
> To Fleet St. where
> Dr. Johnson flourished;
>
> Beside this thoroughfare
> The sale of half-hose has
> Long since superseded the cultivation
> Of Pierian roses.

—For the author, what is the actuality, what does it all come to, but journalism, the all-absorbing, which hardly any talent nowadays escapes? The trade of writing could once support a Johnson. It is now commercial in senses and at levels inconceivable in Johnson's time.

The **"Envoi"** that follows sets off the subtlety of Mr. Pound's rhythmic inventions by a masterly handling of canorous lyric measures that can be chanted at sight. This lovely little poem, which will hardly escape the anthologist when he discovers it, I have found useful in convincing the classically trained that Mr. Pound's metrical irregularities are not the result of incompetence.

The section called **"Mauberley,"** which occupies the remaining five pages of the fifteen, brings the personal focus of the whole to sharp definition. . . . The habit of disinterested aesthetic contemplation, of observing the elegance of Circe's hair rather than the mottoes on sun-dials, takes on a tragic significance. The poem is poignantly personal, and yet, in its technical perfection, its ironical economy, impersonal and detached. Consider, for instance, the consummate reserve of this:

> Unable in the supervening blankness
> To sift TO AGATHON from the chaff
> Until he found his sieve . . .

Ultimately, his seismograph:

—With what subtle force the shift of image in the last line registers the realization that the "orchid" was something more, the impact more than aesthetic! And with what inevitability the "seismograph" and the scientific terminology and manner of what follows convey the bitter irony of realization in retrospect! Mr. Pound's regeneration of poetic idiom is more than a matter of using modern colloquial speech. . . .

It is a contemporary sensibility that expresses the futile bitterness of this recognition in this air of scientific detachment, of disinterested scrutiny. (pp. 30-5)

The next poem, **"The Age Demanded,"** has much the same theme, more generalized: the penalty for absorption in aesthetic contemplation, for too much concern with fineness of living; the unfitness for survival of the artist in the modern world, the world of Lady Valentine, and the world which follows

The discouraging doctrine of chances

preached by Mr. Nixon. The poem is not difficult, unless rhythmically (the state of education in poetry being what it is), and comment will serve no purpose. Along with the preceding one it represents the summit of Mr. Pound's superbly supple and varied art.

But *Hugh Selwyn Mauberley,* it must be repeated, is a whole. The whole is great poetry, at once traditional and original. Mr. Pound's standing as a poet rests upon it, and rests securely. The earlier poems have a minor kind of interest, and (to revert to the first person of modesty) I do not think that it is a service to the poet or the reader to insist upon them. They have the kind of bearing upon *Mauberley* that has been indicated: they help the commentator. And in them, clearly, Mr. Pound developed his technique. It is interesting to follow this development, but not in the least necessary. If the earlier poems are read at all with profit it is likely to be because of *Mauberley,* which will convince, if at all, by itself, and is in itself capable of being a decisive influence.

Since *Mauberley* the *Cantos* have, at various times, appeared, the latest collection being *A Draft of XXX Cantos.* Again I find myself embarrassed by the necessity of disagreeing with Mr. Eliot. One gathers from the *Introduction* to *Selected Poems* that he regards the *Cantos* as being an advance upon *Mauberley.* . . . (p. 36)

When Mr. Eliot in *The Waste Land* has recourse to allusion, the intrinsic power of his verse is commonly such as to affect even a reader who does not recognize what is being alluded to. But even when one is fully informed about Mr. Pound's allusions one's recognition has no significant effect: the value remains private to the author. The methods of association and contrast employed in *The Waste Land* subserve an urgency pressing from below: only an austere and deep seriousness could have controlled them into significance. But the *Cantos* appear to be little more than a game—a game serious with the seriousness of pedantry. We may recognize what Mr. Pound's counters stand for, but they remain counters; and his patterns are not very interesting, even as schematic design, since, in the nature of the game, which hasn't much in the way of rules ("without reference to a philosophy or to any system of teleological principles"), they lack definition and salience.

The radical criticism is made, oddly enough, by [Dudley Fitts in *The Hound and Horn,* Winter 1931] in the end of his review, as a kind of unimportant afterthought:

. . . But he has failed to convey these associations to the reader. For the moment he is indulging in pure pedantry—and not very accurate pedantry at that. Again he has ceased to assert; he has substituted something unconvincingly dead for something convincingly alive. And I would suggest that this tendency is fundamental. Mr. Pound's attitude *is* the pedantic, unreal attitude. Throughout the book he has substituted book-living for actual living.

The judgment seems to me just and damning. The *Cantos* are the kind of "poem of some length" to which, looking back, we can see that the early work (apart from *Mauberley*) points. They are Mr. Pound's *The Ring and the Book.* In so far as they have a representative significance it is as reflecting the contemporary plight that has already been discussed—the lack of form, grammar, principle, and direction. To compel significant art out of that plight needed the seriousness, the spiritual and moral intensity, and the resolute intelligence that are behind *The Waste Land.* Mr. Pound's kind of seriousness is not enough. The very nature of the recognition that (deepened by the war) turned him into a major poet in *Mauberley* seems to constitute a presumption against success in such an undertaking as the *Cantos.*

All this insistence must appear ungracious. But it seems to me the only way of being just to Mr. Pound— to put the stress in a still more important place, the most hopeful way of getting *Mauberley* recognized for the great poem it is.

Of the major figures dealt with in the book, Pound, though he has written much since (and is still writing), is the one of whom my general sense has been least modified. Of *Hugh Selwyn Mauberley* I think as highly as ever: it seems to me a great poem, and a weightier achievement than any single thing—for *Mauberley* does form a whole—to be found in Yeats. As for the *Cantos,* there are more of them than there were when I first wrote about Pound, and the more of them there are, the plainer does it become that they tend to obscure rather than to strengthen Pound's real claims. I am not at all impressed when I am told by enthusiasts that I ought in consistency to admire them, since they merely employ on a larger scale the methods of *Mauberley.*

I think that Mr. Eliot did Pound and criticism an ill service when he threw out that tip about the superiority of the *Cantos* and their great technical value; a value he defined for himself by saying that he was not interested in what Pound had to say, but only in his way of saying it. Today it is assumed that if one withholds one's admiration from the *Pisan Cantos,* it must be because one's dislike of the Fascism and anti-Semitism in what Pound says (and my own dislike is intense) prevents one from recognizing the beauty and genius of the saying. But how boring that famous versification actually is—boring with the emptiness of the egotism it thrusts on us. A poet's creativity can hardly be a matter of mere versification; there is no profound creative impulse at all for Pound's technical skill to serve. He has no real creative theme. His versification and his *procédés* are servants of wilful ideas and platform vehemences. His moral attitudes and absolutisms are bullying assertions, and have the uncreative blatancy of one whose Social Credit consorts naturally with Fascism and anti-Semitism. It still remains true that only in *Mauberley* has he achieved the impersonality, substance, and depth of great poetry. The classical status of *Mauberley,* however, hasn't anything like general recognition—a fact that throws a depressing light on the supposed liveliness of current interest in contemporary verse. (pp. 38-40)

F. R. Leavis, "Ezra Pound," in *Ezra Pound: A Collection of Critical Essays,* edited by Walter Sutton, Prentice-Hall, Inc., 1963, pp. 26-40.

M. L. ROSENTHAL

(essay date 1960)

(Rosenthal has written several books on Pound's verse. In the following excerpt from a work first published in 1960, he briefly discusses *The Cantos,* finding that they expand upon the themes and structural methods of *Hugh Selwyn Mauberley.*)

Space forbids our going into the *Cantos* in even as much detail as we have into *Mauberley.* We have already, however, noted some of the leading ideas behind this more involved and ambitious work, and though we cannot here trace their handling throughout its winding, Gargantuan progress, a few suggestions concerning its character as a poetic sequence may be useful. First of all, we may take as our point of departure the fact that in motivation and outlook the *Cantos* are a vast proliferation from the same conceptions which underlie *Mauberley.* The difference lies partly in the multiplicity of "voices" and "cross-sections," partly in the vastly greater inclusiveness of historical and cultural scope, and partly in the unique formal quality of the longer sequence; it is by the very nature of its growth over the years a work-in-progress. Even when the author at last brings it to conclusion, reorganizing it, supplying the withheld Cantos 72 and 73, completing his revisions, and even giving his book a definitive title, it will remain such a work. Each group of cantos will be what it is now—a new *phase* of the poem, like each of the annual rings of a living tree. The poet has put his whole creative effort into a mobilization of all levels of his consciousness into the service of the *Cantos;* there has been a driving central continuity, and around it new clusters of knowledge and association linked with the others by interweavings, repetitions, and overall perspective. Pound has staked most of his adult career as a poet on this most daring of poetic enterprises; literary history gives us few other examples of comparable commitment.

The *Cantos* has been called Pound's "intellectual diary since 1915," and so it is. But the materials of this diary have been so arranged as to subserve the aims of the poem itself. Passage by passage there *is* the fascination of listening in on a learned, passionate, now rowdy, now delicate intelligence, an intelligence peopled by the figures of living tradition but not so possessed by them that it cannot order their appearances and relationships. Beyond the fascination of the surface snatches of song, dialogue, and description, always stimulating and rhythmically suggestive though not always intelligible upon first reading, there is the essential overriding drive of the poem, and the large pattern of its overlapping layers of thought. The way in which the elements of this pattern swim into the reader's line of vision is well suggested by Hugh Kenner, one of Pound's most able and enthusiastic interpreters:

The word "periplum," which recurs continually throughout the *Pisan Cantos* [74-84], is glossed in **"Canto LIX:"**

periplum, not as land looks on a map
but as sea bord seen by men sailing.

Victor Brerard discovered that the geography of the *Odyssey,* grotesque when referred to a map, was minutely accurate according to the Phoenician voyagers' *periploi.* The image of successive discoveries breaking upon the consciousness of the voyager is one of Pound's central themes. . . . The voyage of Odysseus to hell is the matter of **"Canto I."** The first half of **"Canto XL"** is a periplum through the financial press; "out of which things seeking an exit," we take up in the second half of the Canto the narrative of the Carthagenian Hanno's voyage of discovery. Atlantic flights in the same way raise the world of epileptic maggots in **"Canto XXVIII"** into a sphere of swift firm-hearted discovery. . . . The periplum, the voyage of discovery among facts, . . . is everywhere contrasted with the conventions and artificialities of the bird's eye view afforded by the map. . . .

Thus, the successive cantos and layers of cantos must be viewed not so much schematically as experientially. Here we see how the early Pound's developing idealization of the concrete image, the precise phrase, the organically accurate rhythm are now brought to bear on this vast later task. The many voices, varied scenes and *personae,* and echoes of other languages and literatures than English reflect this emphasis on experience itself: something mysterious, untranslatable, the embodied meaning of life which we generalize only at peril of losing touch with it. So also with Pound's emphatic use of Chinese ideograms, whose picture-origins still are visible enough, he believes, so that to "read" them is to think in images rather than in abstractions. His use of them is accounted for by the same desire to present "successive discoveries breaking upon the consciousness of the voyager." The first effect of all these successive, varied breakings is not intended to be total intellectual understanding, any more than in real experience we "understand" situations upon first coming into them. But by and by the pattern shapes up and the relationships clarify themselves, though always there remains an unresolved residue of potentiality for change, intractable and baffling.

Pound's "voyager," upon whose consciousness the discoveries break, is, we have several times observed, a composite figure derived first of all from the poet-speaker's identification with Odysseus. A hero of myth and epic, he is yet very much of this world. He is both the result of creative imagination and its embodiment. He explores the worlds of the living, of the dead, and of the mythic beings of Hades and Paradise. Lover of mortal women as of female deities, he is like Zagreus a symbol of the life-bringing male force whose mission does not end even with his return to his homeland. Gradually he becomes all poets and all heroes who have somehow vigorously impregnated the culture. He undergoes (as do the female partners of his procreation and the *personae* and locales in time and space of the whole sequence) many metamorphoses. Hence the importance of the Ovidian metamorphosis involving the god Dionysus, the sea (the female element and symbol of change), and the intermingling of contemporary colloquial idiom and the high style of ancient poetry in **"Canto 2."** The first canto had ended with a burst of praise for Aphrodite, goddess of love and beauty, and in language suggesting the multiple allusiveness of the sequence: to the Latin and Renaissance traditions, as well as the Grecian-Homeric, and to the cross-cultural implications suggested by the phrase "golden bough." The second canto takes us

swiftly backward in the poetic tradition, through Browning, then Sordello and the other troubadours, and then to the classical poets and the Chinese tradition. All poets are one, as Helen and Eleanor of Aquitaine and Tyro (beloved of Poseidon) and all femininity are one and all heroes are one.

In the first two cantos, then, the "periplum" of the sequence emerges into view. Three main value-referents are established: a sexually and aesthetically creative world-view, in which artistic and mythical tradition provides the main axes; the worship of Bacchus-Dionysus-Zagreus as the best symbol of creativity in action; and the multiple hero—poet, voyager, prophet, observer, thinker. The next four cantos expand the range of allusiveness, introducing for instance the figure of the Cid, a chivalric hero, to add his dimension to the voyager-protagonist's consciousness. Also, various tragic tales are brought to mind, extending the initial horror of Odysseus' vision of the dead and thus contributing to the larger scheme of the poet in the modern wasteland. In absolute contrast, pagan beatitudes are clearly projected in **"Canto"** in the pictures of Poseidon and Tyro:

> Twisted arms of the sea-god,
> Lithe sinews of water, gripping her, cross-hold,
> And the blue-gray glass of the wave tents
>   them. . . .

and, at the scene's close, in the phallic "tower like a one-eyed great goose" craning up above the olive grove while the fauns are heard "chiding Proteus" and the frogs "singing against the fauns." This pagan ideal comes in again and again, sharp and stabbing against bleak backgrounds like the "petals on the wet, black bough" of the **"Metro"** poem. Thus, in **"Canto 3:"**

> Gods float in the azure air,
> Bright gods and Tuscan, back before dew was shed.

In **"Canto 4:"**

> Choros nympharum, goat-foot, with the pale foot
>   alternate;
> Crescent of blue-shot waters, green-gold in the
>   shallows,
> A black cock crows in the sea-foam. . . .

In **"4"** and **"5"** both there are deliberate echoes of such poets as have a kindred vision (Catullus, Sappho, and others), set against the notes of evil and damnation. The lines from Sordello in **"6"** serve the same purpose:

> "Winter and Summer I sing of her grace,
> As the rose is fair, so fair is her face,
> Both Summer and Winter I sing of her,
> The snow makyth me to remember her."

The Lady of the troubadours, whose "grace" is a secularized transposition from that of Deity, is another manifestation of "the body of nymphs, of nymphs, and Diana" which Actaeon saw, as well as of what Catullus meant: " 'Nuces!' praise, and Hymenaeus 'Brings the girl to her man. . . .' "

After these archetypal and literary points of reference have been established, Cantos 8-19 move swiftly into a close-up of the origins of the modern world in the Renaissance, and of the victory of the anticreative over the active, humanistic values represented by Sigismundo Malatesta and a few others. ("**Canto 7**" is transitional; in any case we can note only the larger groupings here.) The relation between the "Renaissance Cantos" (8-11) and the "Hell Cantos" (14-16), with their scatological picturings of the contemporary Inferno, is organic: the beginning and the end of the same process of social corruption. The beautiful dialogue on order in "**13**" provides a calm, contrasting center for this portion of the sequence, and is supported by the paradisic glow and serenity of Elysium, revealed in "**16**" and "**17**." The earlier cantos had given momentary attention to Oriental poetry and myth and, as we have seen, Elysian glimpses also. Now these motifs are expanded and related to a new context, bringing the sequence into revised focus but carrying all its earlier associations along. This leaping, reshuffling, and reordering is the organizational principle behind the growth, the "annual rings," of the **Cantos**.

The next ten cantos interweave the motifs of these first two groups and prepare us for the next leap (in Cantos 30-41) of perspective. There are various preparations for this leap, even as early as "**Canto 20**," in which there is a moment of comment from the "outside" as if to take stock before hurtling onward. From their remote "shelf," "aerial, cut in the aether," the disdainful lotus-eaters question all purposeful effort:

"What gain with Odysseus,
"They that died in the whirlpool
"And after many vain labours,
"Living by stolen meat, chained to the rowingbench,
"That he should have a great fame
"And lie by night with the goddess? . . ."

Is the question wisdom or cynicism? No matter. The poem, given the human condition and the epic tasks that grow out of it, is held in check but an instant before again plunging ahead. The *Cantos* accepts the moral meaning and the moral responsibility of human consciousness. The heroic ideal remains, as on the other hand the evil of our days remains even after the goddess' song against pity is heard at the beginning of "**30**."

The new group (30-41) is, like the later Adams cantos (62-71), in the main a vigorous attempt to present the fundamental social and economic principles of the Founding Fathers as identical with Pound's own. Adams and Jefferson are his particular heroes, and there is an effort to show that Mussolini's program is intended to carry these basic principles, imbedded in the Constitution but perverted by banking interests, into action. Pound works letters and other documents, as well as conversations real and imagined, into his blocks of verse, usually fragmentarily, and gives modern close-ups of business manipulations. The method has the effect of a powerful exposé, particularly of the glimpsed operations of munitions-profiteers. The cantos of the early 1930's have, indeed, a direct connection with the interest in social and historical documentation and rhetoric that marks much other work of the same period, and at the end of Canto 41 (in which Mussolini is seen) we should not be surprised to find an oratorical climax similar in effect to that of Poem IV in *Mauberley* (1919). As in the earlier groups, however, we are again given contrasting centers of value, especially in "**Canto 36**" (which renders Cavalcanti's *A lady asks me*) and in "**Canto 39**," whose sexually charged interpretation of the spell cast over Odysseus and his men on Circe's isle is one of Pound's purest successes.

The Chinese cantos (53-61) and the Pisan group (74-84) are the two most important remaining unified clusters within the larger scheme. Again, the practical idealism of Confucianism, like that of Jefferson and Adams, becomes an analogue for Pound's own ideas of order and of secular aestheticism. "**Canto 13**" was a clear precursor, setting the poetic stage for this later extension. "Order" and "brotherly deference" are key words in Confucius' teachings; both princes and ordinary men must have order *within* them, each in his own way, if dominion and family alike are to thrive. These thoughts are not clichés as Pound presents them. We hear a colloquy that has passion, humor, and depth, and what our society would certainly consider unorthodoxy. . . . The development of Pound's interest in Chinese poetry and thought, as well as his varied translations from the Chinese, is in itself an important subject. This interest, like every other to which he has seriously turned his attention, he has brought directly to bear on his own poetic practice and on his highly activistic thinking in general.

With the *Pisan Cantos* and *Rock-Drill* we are brought, first, into the immediately contemporary world of the poet himself, in Fascist Italy toward the close of World War II, in a concentration camp at Pisa, during the last days of Mussolini; and second, into a great, summarizing recapitulation of root-attitudes developed in all the preceding cantos: in particular the view of the banking system as a scavenger and breeder of corruption, and of ancient Chinese history as an illuminating, often wholesomely contrasting analogue to that of the post-medieval West. Even more than before, we see now how the *Cantos* descend, with some bastardies along the line, from the Enlightenment. They conceive of a world creatively ordered to serve human needs, a largely rationalist conception. Hence the stress on the sanity of Chinese thought, the immediacy of the

The opening of the Jockey Club in Paris, ca. 1923. Kneeling: Man Ray, Mina Loy, Tristan Tzara, Jean Cocteau; second row: far right, Ezra Pound, third from right, Jean Heap; others unidentified.

Chinese ideogram, and the hardheaded realism of a certain strain of economic theory. The *Pisan Cantos* show Pound's vivid responsiveness as he approached and passed his sixtieth birthday: his aliveness to people, his Rabelaisian humor, his compassion. The lotus-eaters of **"Canto 20,"** aloof and disdainful, have missed out on the main chances. **"Canto 81"** contains the famous "Pull down thy vanity" passage in which the poet, though rebuking his own egotism, yet staunchly insists on the meaningfulness of his accomplishment and ideals. As the sequence approaches conclusion, the fragments are shored together for the moral summing-up. In the *Rock-Drill* section, Cantos 85-95, the stock-taking continues and we are promised, particularly in **"Canto 90,"** an even fuller revelation than has yet been vouchsafed us of the Earthly Paradise.

Cantos 96-109 begin to carry out this promise, though after so many complexities, overlappings, and interlocking voices it must be nearly impossible to bring the work to an end. It is essentially a self-renewing process rather than a classical structure, and

there is no limit to the aspects of history and thought the poet has wished to bring to bear on the poem. **"Canto 96,"** for instance, touches on certain developments after the fall of Rome, especially two decrees in the Eastern Empire by Justinian and Leo VI concerning standards of trade, workmanship, and coinage. The special emphasis in this canto on Byzantine civilization is particularly appropriate because of Byzantium's historical and geographical uniting of East and West as well as its mystical associations pointing to a new and dramatic paradisic vision. Although the memory of earlier glimpses of "paradise" and the recapitulative, self-interrupting method militate against an effect of a revelation overwhelmingly new, the pacing of the whole sequence has made this difficulty at the end inevitable. Pound's conclusion must be introduced as emergent from the midst of things, still struggling from all in life and consciousness that makes for disorder. (pp. 57-63)

M. L. Rosenthal, "The Cantos," in *Ezra Pound: A Collection of*

Critical Essays, edited by Walter Sutton, Prentice-Hall, Inc., 1963, pp. 57-63.

J. P. SULLIVAN
(essay date 1963)

[Sullivan is editor of *Critical Essays on Roman Literature* and author of a book-length study on Pound's *Homage to Sextus Propertius*. In the following excerpt, he describes Pound's work on the *Homage* as his most important contribution to twentieth-century literature.]

Creative translation is important to Ezra Pound because of the very nature of his poetry. Pound is a profoundly original poet inasmuch as he largely created the poetry of our time, and revolutionized its poetic diction and verse-forms. There are more *perfect* poets, but none responsible for more innovations. And the stress laid by critics on Pound's use of translation is important; his poetry is not to be separated from his translation, for the latter is part of it. This has led R. P. Blackmur, for example, to say that Pound is at his best when he is using what another poet has said to express his own feelings and ideas. But it would be more just to say that Pound often realized that what he wanted to express could *only* be expressed in that particular way.

The *Homage to Sextus Propertius* may be considered as translation, as part of a live tradition of an important art-form. But the *Homage,* like all similar examples of the genre, is also a poem in its own right, and one of the tasks of the critic is to explain why the poem is what it is and not any other thing. To understand the genesis of the *Homage* it is necessary to glance briefly at Pound's poetic theories.

Pound, like T. S. Eliot, sees literature, not as a succession of isolated, self-contained works of art, whose genesis is obscure and whose efficient cause is simple genius, but rather as the result of an interaction between the individual talent and tradition. (p. 142)

Pound's interest in such a wide range of literature, his critical "tipping" of such a diverse variety of merit, is partly why he has so affected twentieth century poetry. The influence of Pound on Eliot and Yeats, which enabled them to find their own individual voices, is well known; but less obvious effects are everywhere for the discerning: a poem like Robert Lowell's *The Ghost (After Sextus Propertius)* would have been impossible but for the *Homage.* If Pound's influence on twentieth century poetry had to be summed up it would be that he had taught poets how to use other poets.

This belief in the whole range of literature as the source of poetic material underlies Pound's use of *personae,* masks of his poetic personality. The theory behind this has been explained by Pound himself. Pound uses other poets to widen the range and deepen the effects of his own poetic personality. The method allows almost infinite nuances and shades of feeling, of irony and ambiguity, but above all an accuracy and a conciseness of expression for certain things he felt.

Although Pound has tried other ways of writing, he has given us a brief sketch of this poetic development into which the *Homage* fits:

> In the "search for oneself," in the search for "sincere self-expression," one gropes, one finds, for some seeming verity. One says "I am" this, that or the other, and with the words scarcely uttered one ceases to be that thing. . . . I began this search for the real in a book called *Personae,* casting off, as it were complete masks of the self in each poem. I continued in long series of translations, which were but more elaborate masks.

And he has fortunately given us a description of the mood, the self, which in 1917 made Propertius his mask; in a letter he said in defence of his poem:

> . . . I may perhaps avoid charges of further mystification and obscurity by saying that it [the *Homage*] presents certain emotions as vital to men faced with the infinite and ineffable imbecility of the British Empire as they were to Propertius some centuries earlier, when faced with the infinite and ineffable imbecility of the Roman Empire. These emotions are given largely, but not entirely, in Propertius' own terms. If the reader does not find relation to life defined in the poem, he may conclude that I have been unsuccessful in my endeavour. . . .

It is hard to imagine now the atmosphere of those days, when the military stupidity of generals was equalled only by the militant stupidity of jingoists, when cultural internationalists like Pound were pressed to betray (in the national interest) values which had no connection with the aims of the warring powers. Pound's state of mind in a milieu which hysterically sentimentalized one of the most idiotic and tragic of human affairs, and which looked to Kipling for a new Tyrtaeus, is more clearly seen in *Mauberley* (in this sense at least *Mauberley* is a popularization of the *Homage*). However, it was the Roman poet who first became the mask through which Pound registered his protest at the monstrous state of society and culture in which he found himself living.

The general implications of this Pound *felt* as strongly as, say, Eliot, but his perception was not so sharp, nor could he realize its implications so broadly (*Mauberley's* merits are more parochial than those of the *Waste Land*). It was entirely a matter of thinking and feeling, and not simply one of expression. Pound could express anything he felt and his expression of things seen is equally adequate, but neither his visual nor his mental conceptions are in general superlative. Herein lay the importance of Propertius: Pound's literary flair made him see in Propertius a structure from which he could evolve for his own feelings at the time an artistic *credo* and an expression of that creed. It was in the ability to absorb that part of Propertius' work and by means of some novel techniques make the Roman elegist his *persona* that Pound's originality in writing the *Homage* consists. *Mauberley* is a more complex expression of his feelings and it is more intensely charged with emotion, but it is a continuation of the Propertian themes, a clarification of their attitudes—in particular a change from an attitude of resignation and isolation to despair and disgust.

The change did not come entirely from within:

Died some, pro patria,
non "dulce" non "et decor" . . .
walked eye-deep in hell
believing in old men's lies, then unbelieving
came home, home to a lie,
home to many deceits,
home to old lies and new infamy;
usury age-old and age-thick
and liars in public places.

All of this naturally affected Pound's view of Propertius. Once he had seen in Propertius (rightly or wrongly) a kindred spirit, his aim was to enlist him as his mouthpiece. The whole structure and articulation of the *Homage* as a poem depends on Pound's view of Propertius as an *alter ego.*

Propertius for us is a love poet. Pound's choice of the opening of Propertius Book III to begin the *Homage* is therefore a critical one: Section I of the *Homage* discusses the nature of the art of Propertius and the expectations of the artist in a given society. "His true Penelope was Flaubert" is a mere modernization of:

Shades of Callimachus, Coan ghosts of Philetas
It is in your grove I would walk. . . .

This is the avowal of the artist's devotion to art and not to public propaganda, even though his audience is thereby limited to "young ladies of indeterminate character" and posterity. *Mauberley* puts it more savagely:

The age demanded an image
Of its accelerated grimace . . .
Not, not certainly, the obscure reveries
Of the inward gaze . . .

This is also the subject of Sections II and V in a rather different form. In Section II the poet seems about to attempt the very themes he has declared himself unwilling to attempt, but he is recalled from them by Apollo:

Alba, your kings, and the realm your folk

have constructed with such industry
Shall be yawned out on my lyre—with such industry. . . .
And Phoebus looking upon me from the Castalian tree,
Said then "You idiot! What are you doing with that water:
"Who has ordered a book about heroes? . . ."

Here Propertius himself serves the function of those characters in *Mauberley* such as Brennbaum or Mr. Nixon, who wished to conform to what "the age demanded." But Apollo, Propertius' conception of his own art and limitations, recalls him: like Pound himself or the minor poet Mauberley, Propertius, with the aid of Apollo, here finally makes the great refusal. In Section V he makes another assault on these themes, but the irony and doubt which pervade the first part of his section "If I have not the faculty, 'The bare attempt would be praiseworthy . . .' " is underlined by the juxtaposition of Part 2:

Yet you ask on what account I write so many love-lyrics . . .
my ventricles do not palpitate to Caesarial *ore rotundos.*

This stress on the relation of the artist to society, the vindication of private poetic morality against public compulsions, whether these be the demands of a government or promises of fame and fortune, is what Pound saw as the important element in Propertius and this is the critical burden of the *Homage.* It is interesting that Pound's choice of themes to represent Propertius' half-hearted attempts to conform, to write national epic, represents clearly certain elements in Propertius' work which reveal Propertius' own ambivalence towards the Augustan requirements. In the end Propertius made more concessions than did Pound or Mauberley.

Propertius' private themes, the centre of his art, are love, passion, and his mistress Cynthia; this was *his* "cultivation of Pierian roses." Here he differs from Pound in the *Homage:* Pound's prime concern is art and artistic freedom. Pound however offers a selection, reworked in a sophisticated manner, of some of the best of the Propertian love elegies. Although there are important other themes, these largely take up Sections III, VI, XI and part of XII, for the subject Propertius has chosen and vindicated against external grosser claims for his poetic allegiance is his love of Cynthia. Pound's allegiances which his *persona* in *Mauberley* vindicates against the temptations of Mr. Nixon are different, but he is at one with Propertius in the determination to cling to his chosen art. Consequently, although page for page we have more of Propertius' love poetry than his poetic *credo,* the significance of Propertius for Pound (which he clearly brings out in the ordering of the *Homage*) is the latter. It is for this that he serves Pound as a *persona,* not in his capacity as love poet. The two themes are woven together to produce variety, but the choice of theme for the opening and the close of the sequence makes Pound's critical intention clear.

Once the outline of the sequence is stated, one may turn to the subsidiary motifs present in the *Homage.* An attempt is made to define the society (and thus the societies) from which the protest emerges. The censor to which Harriet Monroe alluded in her letter to the Editor of the *English Journal* (XX [1931], 86-87) was not a censor of sexual morals, but a censor of thought. There is nothing lewd in the *Homage,* but there are elements which might be regarded as productive of "alarm and despondency" in the political and cultural climate of the times. Although in the *Homage* there is nothing like the bitterness and disillusion of *Mauberley,* the general philosophy of the poem has much in common with the later work. The recognition of failure, of the futile end of endeavour, most clearly represented in the person of Mauberley himself, is also present in the *Homage.* Propertius envisages a vindication by time, Pound in *Mauberley* only a response in the sensitive reader:

> And I also among the later nephews of this city
> shall have my dog's day. . . .

is to be contrasted with

> . . . the case presents
> No adjunct to the Muses' diadem.

The hopelessness of poetic endeavour and the impossibility of contemporary recognition is brought out clearly in the *Homage's* concern with death, which reduces all things to one level:

> One raft on the veiled flood of Acheron.
> Marius and Jugurtha together.
> Nor at my funeral either will there be any long trail,
> bearing ancestral lares and images; . . .
> A small plebeian procession.
> Enough, enough and in plenty
> There will be three books at my obsequies
> Which I take, my not unworthy gift, to Persephone.

Yet even this note, the hope of posthumous recognition, has behind it the tones of despair:

> In vain, you call back the shade,
> In vain, Cynthia. Vain call to unanswering shadow,
> Small talk comes from small bones.

There is a failure implicit, "wrong from the start," which is deepened in *Mauberley.* Yet this is extracted from Propertius not by choosing elements which correspond to Pound's feeling of artistic futility and cultural death—for Propertius although fighting against the contemporary current of literature has a characteristic Roman confidence of his ultimate fame—but by utilizing Propertius' horror of death (which Pound himself does not have) to symbolize the artistic death for which

Pound wrote in *Mauberley* the impressive poem—**"E.P. Ode pour l'Election de son Sepulchre."** This feeling of horror, most clearly seen in Propertius IV.7 *(Sunt aliquid Manes)* is used by Pound to express his disgust at the passing of a cultural climate.

So although the bitterness of *Mauberley* is lacking (partly through the limitations of Propertius as a *persona,* partly through the conditions of the time, and partly because Pound could not see into the post-war future), the sequence springs from the same mood as *Mauberley.* Here and there, through the insistence on the claims of art itself, through the confidence of final vindication, a note of disillusioned indifference, almost of emptiness, shows itself. . . . Pound, as always when he is infusing the verse with his deepest convictions, departs radically from the sense of the original. And the final passage of the poem does not alter this pessimism; the end is still a dying fall.

It should be clear then that the *Homage* emerges from and expresses the same attitudes and circumstances as *Mauberley.* It is less complex, of course, and lacks the range of that great poem; but *Mauberley* yields its secrets to the inspection it patently invites. The *Homage* is simpler in conception and feeling, but the local difficulties (which are many) and the constant misunderstanding of its aims as translation and as original poem, have stood in the way of a close study of the individual sections where much of the poetic action takes place. The whole sequence tends even now to be skimmed through for the striking themes, which are more obvious, limited, and repetitious than the subjects of the individual poems in *Mauberley,* which have always received due critical attention. Because of this too easy acceptance by the sympathetic and the too obtuse rejection by hostile critics, Pound felt obliged to call *Mauberley* a "popularization" of the *Homage,* even though it was also a deeper and subtler treatment of the whole subject. It was too easy and too hard for the understanding Pound had hoped for, and it attracted to itself too much irrelevant criticism.

Mauberley and the *Homage* are important documents for insight into Pound and a whole literary generation, indeed it would not be too much to say into a crisis of our time. They express much the same discontent as does *The Waste Land.* The difference between that poem and the two poems under discussions is significant. Pound and Eliot were in different ways immensely concerned for their civilization and its discontents. In Pound the concern is evinced by a care for intelligence, literature, and art and thus for the society from which these emerge. Eliot's temperament and insight, on the other hand, is other-worldly; he is a greater *thinker* (in poetic terms) and is less interested in technique than Pound is. Content and form are not separable and this comment is not to deny Eliot's technical gifts, but to indicate the difference of his poetic interests and his conception of his art. Eliot's diagnosis in *The Waste Land* implies a more universal criticism; it is concerned with spiritual and only then social malaise; art is not mentioned. Eliot's implied remedy is therefore a spiritual one.

This distinction makes it easier to understand Pound's movement further and further towards Fascism and such things as monetary reform. Pound is not concerned with any deeper spiritual reality; his roots strike only into this world and this society and it is here he wishes reform to begin. The death of art in the modern world is attributable to social causes, to the venal vulgarities of the Arnold Bennetts, to certain classes and conspiracies, and ultimately to a certain form of government which brought about the betrayal, cultural and social, of a civilization.

All men, in law, are equals.
Free of Pisistratus,
We choose a knave or an eunuch
To rule over us.

In turn of course Pound insisted that when the work of the "damned and despised *literati*" goes bad, "when their very medium, the very essence of their work, the application of word to thing goes rotten . . . the whole machinery of social and individual thought and order goes to pot."

The emphasis on art and intellect, the contempt for "a tawdry cheapness," the anti-democratic bias (not unreminiscent of an attitude to be found in some Latin poets—*Odi profanum vulgus et arceo*) produced, as we know and must deplore, a different personal solution from Eliot's, and the strong contrast between the poems each of them wrote after this period makes this plain. Their different roads led to strangely different places, but their ultimate destinations may be discerned in the earlier poems.

Nevertheless between the *Homage* and *Mauberley* important distinctions may be made. And although *Mauberley* is for me the greater poem, not all of its poetic attitudes are an advance on the *Homage*. There is one way at least in which the *Homage* because of the nature of its source is preferable to *Mauberley* as a criticism of life. The single-minded devotion of Pound to his craft is sometimes reminiscent of the art fancier's attitude to culture. Culture is seen as something *out there*. This externality perhaps springs from certain peculiar American conditions, the divorce of culture from a native tradition and from any solid grounding in the national life. It is the tourist's attitude to art, and it is not without significance that Ezra Pound himself is an American expatriate. One result of this is a simple-minded contrast between the idyllic past and the vulgar present, a mistake which the greater spiritual insight of Eliot did not allow him to make. *The Waste Land* offers a more timeless view of spiritual disease; its diagnosis

is made *sub specie aeternitatis*. In "A Game of Chess" all vulgarity, Cleopatra's, Elizabeth's, and the modern lady's, is brought before us. Eliot is here subtler and more perceptive than Pound. Pound idealizes the past in *Mauberley*:

Conduct, on the other hand, the soul
"Which the highest cultures have nourished"
To Fleet St. where
Dr. Johnson flourished;
Beside this thoroughfare
The sale of half-hose has
Long since superseded the cultivation
Of Pierian Roses.

But Dr. Johnson himself can effectively "place" this idealization (and by implication the idealization of *"the mousseline of Cos"* and *"Sappho's barbitos"*). In *The Vanity of Human Wishes* we are told:

Mark then what ills the scholar's life assail,
Toil, envy, want, the patron and the jail.

In the *Homage* Pound is forced, despite himself, to adopt an historical view; the sentimentalization of the past becomes impossible because Propertius *is* the past. It is for this reason perhaps that the *Homage* has found at least one critic who rates it as a poem above *Mauberley*. (pp. 143-51)

J. P. Sullivan, "Pound's 'Homage to Propertius': The Structure of a Mask," in *Ezra Pound: A Collection of Critical Essays,* edited by Walter Sutton, Prentice-Hall, Inc., 1963, pp. 142-51.

MICHAEL ALEXANDER

(essay date 1979)

(In the excerpt below, Alexander examines the bulk of Pound's poetic output and argues that while Pound's work frequently exhibits evidence of great literature, the author was unable to create one poem of sustained quality.)

The vitality of Pound's contribution to the arts before the Great War, and the redirection he gave to poetry during his years in Kensington, are acknowledged. His own poetry, however, has received less unanimous recognition, and is commonly not much considered, in Britain at least. It seems that the active English poetic tradition has still to come to terms with Pound's poetic output as a whole. While in America scholars are establishing the detailed references of the remoter Cantos, in Britain a wider appreciation even of his more accessible poetry has not yet arrived. (p. 15)

Indifference and bafflement are today more common than hostility, though for some Pound was simply a Fascist and an anti-Semite, not a poet at all. Academic appreciation has made progress with the studies that followed in the wake of Hugh Kenner. More generally, an opening-up of British poetry to America, to verse in translation, and to its own history in this century make it easier for us to see Pound's poetry. Yet to be ushered into posterity as the greatest literary influence since Wordsworth suggests that Pound's chief interest is to literary historians. Though Pound is said to have altered the course of poetry in this century, most, even among the interested parties, still do not know quite what to make of him. (p. 17)

The anti-Semitic and Fascist sympathies expressed in the middle Cantos cannot be overlooked; these delusions had a destructive effect on the poetry. Pound's treatment at Pisa, the treason charge, the twelve years of 'mental care' and the legal disabilities and press-ganging which he suffered for the fifteen years that remained to him, were, however, nemesis enough. The strife stirred up has deflected readers from poetry which rewards attention in ways that no other poetry of our time can do.

The poetic output of Ezra Pound is very large. Between 1907 and 1920 he published several small volumes, now collected. During the War he began on 'that great forty-year epic' which he had proposed to himself before 1908 and which was to occupy him to the end. The earlier verse is marked by a change from 'romance' to a concern with contemporary manners which culminates in the two sequences, **"Homage to Sextus Propertius"** and *Mauberley*. The *Cantos* themselves divide into the first thirty (chiefly about the Renaissance); the Cantos of the Thirties (Italian, American and Chinese history); the *Pisan Cantos*, partly autobiographical; and the three last volumes, *Rock-Drill, Thrones* and *Drafts and Fragments*. There are also translations and imitations, most of which are stations on the main line of progress, for example *Cathay* and **"Propertius."** The *Cantos* themselves contain translations, for example from Homer in **"Canto I"** and from Cavalcanti in **"Canto 36."** It is often remarked that Pound's poems are translations and his translations are original poems. But most of the later translations appeared outside the *Cantos*, notably *The Classic Anthology Defined by Confucius*, and his version of Sophocles' *Women of Trachis*. Such was the sequence of Ezra Pound's poetic output, revolving from 'romance' to politics and back again to a splintered realization of 'romance'.

A single approach to such a gargantuan body or work cannot be entirely satisfactory. But Pound's true achievement will benefit from an attempt to define it and to discriminate within it; and such an attempt may also help to make Pound's work more accessible to a famished British tradition in need of 'scaled invention' and 'true artistry', of a larger world of ideas and objective reference, and of a more profound self-dedication

in her poets. America too, though she has recently paid Pound a more honourable and extensive attention, may need to see him more critically.

As for the Muses, it might be said without anticipating too far, that though one cannot without preamble claim for Pound a major work of unflawed greatness, yet he repeatedly achieved the rarest standards of poetic excellence and invention. Indeed his imaginative writing is so frequently touched with greatness that only Yeats and Eliot seem of a clearly superior order of magnitude among contemporaries. 'Greatness'—even if, as Pound noted, it is a Victorian word—is not an easy one to do without. But poetic courage and largeness, sustained creative enterprise, integrity in his art, the intense reflection of the light vouch-safed, these are not qualities lightly to be despised.

Pound's original sensibility and poetic character preserved a remarkable constancy throughout his career, in spite of the equally constant developments of technique, and in spite also of his changes of fortune, of manner and of subject-matter. (pp. 17-18)

Pound was himself a learned man, though a virtuoso rather than an exact scholar; he did not work in a field. He was, however, very widely, intensely and curiously read in literature and history. 'Curiosity' is perhaps the key word. He was an enthusiastic popularizer as well as savant, and is held in some suspicion by specialists in each of the ten languages that he translated from. Pound was a passionate amateur of literature, a dilettante in scholarship, in old senses of these words, although lacking in the indolence associated with them, and dedicated to the profession of poetry. This pattern used to be common among men of letters—Ford was an example—and even among dons in the days when the Arts at university meant 'humaner letters' and literature meant poetry. An acquaintance with the quotable in European poetry and cultural history could then more confidently have been relied on among the educated than it can in a graduate seminar. Pound's obscurity is thus partly due to changes in what is thought to be worth knowing; he was not, for the lettered reader of his young day, a particularly arcane poet. It must be granted, however, that in old age the poet's allusive obliqueness developed into an elliptical and idiosyncratic manner of reference. Yet, when all the missing information has been supplied, the essence of his poetry remains visionary, mythical or archetypal, and for an appreciation of this kind of poetry, popular in the last century, not so very much learning is initially required, though some literary education is certainly presupposed.

Pound had Donne's 'hydroptic, immoderate desire of human learning and languages', and his version of history is heterodox, but an understanding of his poetic truth relies more on a lively capacity for aesthetic experience and a gift for imaginative affinities than on breadth or depth of learning—he relies rather on quickness, and a willingness to learn. Pound communicates a Rabelaisian enjoyment of literacy and a passionate care for the evolution and direction of Western culture: in this crucial sense he is certainly a poet for the educated reader. (pp. 19-20)

For all their polish, Pound's poems are unfinished; the parts are highly finished, but they require the reader to compose and complete them. The particular instances are so stated that, when taken in conjunction with each other, they project unspoken corollaries, and it is the relation between these unspoken corollaries—in the reader's mind—that brings out the counterpoint. The contemplation of the parts is an aesthetic process; the unfolding of their implications a detective one; the result is catalytic, emotional. Thus a Pound poem is static and may be blank until it is understood, when it becomes dynamic and delivers its charge. There is a tension between the parts, initially palpable, ultimately meaningful. (pp. 42-3)

Pound's condensation undoubtedly makes him cryptic at times, and his ruthless cutting-out of rhetoric leaves the new reader of the *Cantos* without a handrail; but the enigmatic face of his work, seized on early by anthologists of such poems as **"In a Station of the Metro"** and **"The Return"**, is not merely the result of modern technique (or modernized Nineties-ism). Pound's obliquity, though it has to do with his dislike for obvious conceptualization, is the semi-dramatic strategy natural to a sensibility inwardly in awe of life, and the product of a temperament possessed of deep instincts, though normally reticent in their expression. The mysteriousness and refinement in Pound is not an affectation, in spite of his striking of attitudes; it is rather that his inner life was not for direct export. In this he resembles the other 'men of 1914'—Joyce and Eliot, and Wyndham Lewis—if not D. H. Lawrence. As the reader comes to know Pound's poetry, he will increasingly recognize and go beyond the multifarious objects of knowledge that at first dominate the landscape of each poem, and he will become more interested in the poetic character of the presence, seer, protagonist who presents the data. The data are variously instructive, diverting, beautiful or awe-inspiring, and the patterns of emotion and moral value that they create are fascinating or rewarding. Eventually, however, it is the richness and quality of the mind, rather than the *virtù* of the objects it contains and which it salutes, that continue to fascinate and to instruct. It is only at first that Pound's purism of surface and form seem clinically to exclude the presence of a known human speaker. Not that Pound is often predictable; but he becomes easier to locate. The reader of Pound is forced to develop his senses and his antennae. The art of reading him is, in a phrase he applied to Henry James in **"Canto 7"**, 'drinking the tone of things'. (p. 43)

What to say of a dedicated life? In seeking to make an estimate of Pound's poetic achievements, Pound's own career is itself a warning not to rush to conclusions. To take only the last of its transformations for example, *Drafts and Fragments* significantly softens the impression left by *Rock-Drill* and *Thrones,* and by the *Cantos* as a whole; it has a reintegrative effect on the reader's experience of the poem. The shape the *Cantos* will assume in the minds of poets and readers of the future cannot be predicted, though it is already clear that whereas in the past it has been asked to stand as sponsor at many an unlikely font, in the future it risks becoming a semi-academic institution, at least in the U.S.A. The account given here does not do justice to the overall design of the poem, especially in the later stages, for which much evidence is being produced. It will remain true, however, that this plan is often lost to view, and that for many readers it will be the variety of the *Cantos,* its picaresque explorations and reclamations, that strike and hold the mind. (p. 225)

Certainly his residence in Rapallo and his devotion to the *Cantos* took Pound away from the English language and from the modern world, possibly to his (and their) detriment. Who is to say, however, that the *Cantos*—though a long way round—were a misuse of his gifts, since they clearly remain 'the most important long poem of the century'? For all their wrong-headed politics and confusing form, they present simultaneously an heroic imaginative openness to actual living and to nature, and also to cultural and ideal worlds more various, larger and deeper. This double vision may prove a precious legacy in an age when our own historical culture is becoming alien to us; already, the London, Paris and Provence he knew have gone, and with them certain cultural possibilities that cannot be reproduced. The distinctness and concentration of Pound's mind will not be easily emulated; nor his skills of free-verse composition. (pp. 227-28)

The tendentiousness and unevenness of some of Pound's achievement make it difficult to settle squarely on a tolerable generalization about his place among the poets; he is perhaps the greatest of the moderns, since that term does not exactly fit Yeats, nor the Eliot of *Four Quartets.* However, his Promethean gifts are so original that the process of comparison with others does not seem very productive; perhaps he should not be placed among others. Eliot entitled his first article on Pound "Isolated Superiority."

Unlike many of his readers, I do not exclude any period of Pound's work as without good poetry, from **"The Tree"** to the last sybilline leaf of the *Cantos;* nor do I see significant and decisive developments which lead to radical positive or negative judgements about his career, either in its modernization in *Lustra,* its sophistication in *Mauberley,* its grandiose epic ambitions or its later fragmentation. Like many readers, I do not find the Chinese history fruitful, and find that many of the fragments of politics and history stick in my throat, just as other fragments stick in my head. I share Pound's 'coherent idea'—the idea around which, he said in 1962, his 'muddles accumulated'—that 'European culture ought to survive'; in this enterprise the *Cantos* are perhaps the biggest single effort made by an individual of this century; and may well prove the most valuable. Unlike many readers, I cannot discard the idea that the *Cantos* do form a unity and do record a moral progress both in their content (by design) and in the author. It follows too that I see Pound's whole poetic output as a unity.

Leaving aside the translations, themselves a fresh and distinct adjunct to any bouquet for the Muses, the best of the original work seems to come from six periods: *Lustra* and *Cathay; Propertius* and *Mauberley;* the first seventeen *Cantos;* the *Fifth Decad of Cantos;* the *Pisan Cantos;* and *Drafts and Fragments. Cathay* seems to me the most underrated of his volumes, and I would repeat the suggestion that if the British want to make a fresh start on Pound (and it is about time they did) they could begin with the disciplined free verse of *Lustra* and *Cathay.* 'We will leave it as a test: when anyone has studied Mr. Pound's poems in *chronological* order, and has mastered *Lustra* and *Cathay,* he is prepared for the *Cantos*—but not till then. If the reader then fails to like them, he has probably omitted some step in his progress, and had better go back and retrace the journey. (p. 228)

Michael Alexander, in his *The Poetic Achievement of Ezra Pound,* University of California Press, 1979, 247 p.

SOURCES FOR FURTHER STUDY

Davie, Donald. *Studies in Ezra Pound.* Manchester, England: Carcanet Press Limited, 1991, 388 p.

Reprints Davie's respected book *Ezra Pound: Poet as Sculptor* (1964) as well as Davie's essays on Pound from 1972 to 1990.

Hesse, Eva, ed. *New Approaches to Ezra Pound.* Berkeley: University of California Press, 1969, 406 p.

Includes essays by such noted Pound scholars as Donald Davie, Richard Ellman, Forrest Read, J. P. Sullivan, John Espey, and George Dekker.

Kenner, Hugh. *The Poetry of Ezra Pound.* Norfolk, Conn.: New Directions, 1951, 342 p.

Early and appreciative book on Pound's verse.

——. *The Pound Era.* Berkeley: University of California Press, 1971, 606 p.

Widely acknowledged study of Pound's life and the cultural and historical sources documented in Pound's poetry.

Norman, Charles. *Ezra Pound.* New York: The Macmillan Company, 1960, 493 p.

Biography of Pound interspersed with interesting anecdotal accounts concerning many of Pound's works.

Quinn, Sister Bernetta, O.S.F. *Ezra Pound: An Introduction to the Poetry.* New York: Columbia University Press, 1972, 191 p.

Concise introduction to the life and poetical works of Pound, from his earliest lyrics to the last drafts of the *Cantos.*

Marcel Proust

1871-1922

French novelist, critic, essayist, translator, short story writer, and poet.

INTRODUCTION

*P*roust is primarily known for his multivolume novel *A la recherche du temps perdu* (1954; *Remembrance of Things Past*, 1981), regarded as one of the most important works of twentieth-century literature. Highly esteemed for its exquisite formal construction, Proust's novel transcends the narrative linearity of the traditional novel, creating a fictional space in which themes, motifs, and images blend, dissolve, and reappear as in the circular development of a musical composition. A philosophical meditation on the nature of time and consciousness, Proust's masterpiece also offers profound psychological insights into the labyrinthine world of the human soul, particularly the changes it undergoes as it struggles in the stream of time. In addition, the novel provides a social chronicle of turn-of-the-century Parisian society. An acute observer of the mores and inner lives of the French bourgeoisie and aristocracy, Proust, as critics have observed, conveys a profound and universal view of human existence.

Proust was born at Autueil, which in part served as a model for Combray in *Remembrance of Things Past*. His early childhood was sheltered and for the most part comfortable. In 1880, however, he suffered his first attack of asthma, one of the chronic maladies that affected the acutely sensitive writer's view of life. Nevertheless, his uncertain health did not interrupt Proust's formal education at the Lycée Condorcet, where he contributed to the class magazine, or his attendance at the Ecole des Sciences Politiques, where he took *licences* in law and literature. Proust complemented his regular studies by reading the works of France's leading intellectuals, such as the philosopher Henri Bergson, whose insights into the nature of time would influence the novelist. Nor did his frail physical condition keep him from a year of military service, which he recalled as one of the happiest periods of his life. As a young man Proust moved in the circles of salon matrons, aristocrats, artists, and literati, distinguishing himself as an entertaining wit with a talent for mimicking speech and mannerisms. Particularly applauded were his imitations of Count Robert de Montesquiou, whose flamboyant personality provided some of the character traits for Baron de Charlus in *Remembrance of Things Past.*

In the mid-1890s Proust was chiefly known as a contributor of short prose to various Paris reviews. These pieces, collected in *Les plaisirs et les jours* (1896; *Pleasures and Days,* 1957), are often described as precious, though in retrospect they have gained value as examples of Proust's earliest experiments leading to the composition of his major work. Likewise, *Jean Santeuil* (1952), Proust's first attempt at a longer work of fiction, served as a rehearsal for many of the characters and scenes in *Remembrance of Things Past,* though lacking, in Martin Turnell's phrase, the "richness and complexity" of the later novel. Critics have also noted that in *Jean Santeuil* Proust did not utilize the perspective of first-person narration, which in *Remembrance of Things Past* becomes a unifying device for a vast and complicated scenario.

In an important work of criticism, *Contre Sainte-Beuve* (1954; *By Way of Sainte-Beuve,* 1958), Proust presented his conception of literature. As opposed to C. A. Saint-Beuve, a traditionalist who made no distinction between a writer's life and his work, Proust contended that a work of literature discloses a perspective unique to itself, independent of its author's biography. Walter A. Strass explains that Proust was a critic who looked "deeply into the writer's creative personality, discerning the writer's special vision and his method of recreating this vision in terms of literature." Proust's own vision of life informed his massive novel.

Started in 1909, *Remembrance of Things Past* originally appeared in seven volumes, three of which were not published until after Proust's death. The novelist never finished revising these final volumes, and they retain certain narrative inconsistencies and abridgments that, as critics maintain, require further revision. *Du côté de chez Swann* (*Swann's Way,* 1922), the first volume of *Remembrance of Things Past,* was published in 1913. Like the other volumes in the series, it is a complete novel in itself. However, it also introduces the many themes and motifs—such as memory, jealous love, social ambition, sexual inversion, and the importance of art—that are developed at length in later volumes. In the second volume, *A l'ombre des jeunes filles en fleurs* (1919; *Within a Budding Grove,* 1924), the narrator Marcel describes his youthful love for Gilberte Swann. This love, as Wallace Fowlie has observed, is not based on "the satisfaction of the senses," but entirely on "the proliferation of the lover's imagination," with the result that Marcel is utterly de-

ceived regarding Gilberte's wanton nature. Such unresolvable and often tragic conflicts between imagination and reality are characteristic of Proustian love.

The third volume of *Remembrance of Things Past, Le côté de Guermantes* (1920; *The Guermantes Way,* 1924), won the Prix Goncourt, a national literary prize for young authors, in 1920, and brought Proust international recognition. In *The Guermantes Way,* Proust introduced his most masterfully drawn character, the Baron de Charlus. The elegant Baron is the apotheosis of the French aristocracy as portrayed by Proust in *Remembrance of Things Past;* Charlus's moral corruption and eventual fall parallel the degeneracy and decline of his class. Proust also ironically examined the phenomenon of social ambition, and the disillusionment that often accompanies the achievement of one's social goals. *Sodome et Gommorrhe* (1922; *Cities of the Plain,* 1927) explores the theme of homosexuality and corruption. In the novel, sexual inversion, as it is revealed in such unlikely individuals as Charlus and Robert de Saint-Loup, becomes a symbol for the hidden but pervasive evils that afflict society, rendering it shallow, ineffectual, and decadent. Proust also discusses his theory of memory in an important prelude to the second half of this volume, entitled "Les intermittances du coeur" ("The Intermittances of the Heart"). *La prisonnière* (1923; *The Captive,* 1929) and *La fugitive* (1925; *The Sweet Cheat Gone,* 1930), the fifth and sixth volumes of the series, were not included in Proust's original plan for *Remembrance of Things Past,* and some critics now believe that events in Proust's personal life led him to expand the scheme of his novel to include the story of Albertine with the themes of jealous love and deception. *Le temps retrouvé* (1927; *Time Regained,* 1930), the final volume of the work, successfully ties together all of the novel's recurrent themes and motifs. In *Time Regained,* Marcel realizes that memory is the key to the meaning of the past that he has been seeking, and that art has the ability to redeem experience from disillusionment, deception, and the decay of time. The themes which were touched upon throughout the novel are here given full expression. *Remembrance of Things Past* concludes with Marcel's discovery of his own artistic vocation, and his determination to recover his past by writing a novel based on his life.

The title of *A la recherche du temps perdu* is often rendered more literally as *In Search of Lost Time* to emphasize the conscious pursuit by the narrator of past selves which have been altered over the years, and for the original qualities of experiences which are effaced by normal memory. For the narrator there are two means of recapturing a former stage of one's life: either through the consciously willed effort of "voluntary memory," or through the unwilled and unexpected outpouring of "involuntary memory." The first yields only limited and deceptive impressions of the past, while the second creates a vivid and faithful recollection. In the absence of religion, memory becomes a vehicle of transcending the annihilation by time and death of all things known in one's life. Sensation, sensibility, and intuition are the keys to the world of lost time, and as such supercede the laws of reason, in Proust's view of experience. Another source of triumph over the frustrations of human existence is that of art, which allows viewpoints not possible in mundane experience. Among life's major frustrations are the unstable nature of personal identity and the deceptive quality of private truths subsequently revealed as illusion. Proust used various devices to convey his sense of confusion and disillusionment to the reader of *Remembrance of Things Past.* Most notable among them was his deliberate misrepresentation of certain characters, such as Albertine and Monsieur Vinteuil. Proust allowed Marcel, and consequently the reader, to perceive these characters in a way that is ultimately shown to be false, and contrary to their true natures. Albertine, in particular, dramatically embodies Proust's ideas about the confusing and elusive nature of identity. Critics have long regarded her as one of the most enigmatic characters in all of literature. Although the narrator's relationship with her provides the subject matter for two volumes of *Remembrance of Things Past,* the mystery that surrounds her is never penetrated by Marcel or by the reader. For this reason, she perfectly illustrates Proust's theory that the experience of love is utterly subjective—based entirely in the imagination of the lover, and not, as is commonly thought, on the character of the beloved. Thus, in Proust's view, even romantic love is subject to the "intermittances of the heart," which transform seemingly durable emotions into occasional phenomena without continuity.

Although today the brilliance of Proust's achievement is seldom disputed, in the past his novel was frequently the subject of critical controversy. Its almost overwhelming length and sprawling structure, combined with Proust's reticular and highly original prose style has occasionally led critics to assert that Proust's aesthetic was actually a rationalization of his artistic weakness: his inability to select and reject material. Proust constantly disputed such statements, maintaining that the novel had to be considered as a whole in order for its structure, which is based on the musical leit-motif, to become apparent. One of the most important issues in Proust criticism is the role of Marcel as protagonist and narrator of *Remembrance of Things Past,* and his relationship to Proust himself. There is strong evidence for both identifying Proust with Marcel and for isolating the two, and some critics' readings of the novel are more autobiographical than those of others. Perhaps the firmest ground for likening Proust with Marcel is their mutual struggle to realize themselves as artists, with each making art the highest value in their lives. For both, the search for lost time ends in the disillusioned abandonment of life and in the affirmative re-creation of life as a work of art.

(For further information about Proust's life and works, see *Contemporary Authors,* Vols. 104, 120; *Dictionary of Literary Biography,* Vol. 65: *French Novelists, 1900-1930;* and *Twentieth-Century Literary Criticism,* Vols. 7, 13, 33.)

CRITICAL COMMENTARY

MARCEL PROUST

(letter date 1912)

[In the following excerpt, Proust discusses the themes of *Swann's Way* and briefly explains his theory of voluntary and involuntary memory.]

Du côté de chez Swann is the fragment of a novel, which will have as general title *A la recherche du temps perdu.* I should have liked to have published it as a single whole, but it would have been too long. They no longer publish works in several volumes. There are novelists, on the other hand, who envisage a brief plot with few characters. That is not my conception of the novel. There is a plane geometry and a geometry of space. And so for me the novel is not only plane psychology but psychology in space and time. That invisible substance, time, I try to isolate. But in order to do this it was essential that the experience be continuous. I hope that by the end of my book what I have tried to do will be understandable; some unimportant little event will show that time has passed and it will take on that beauty certain pictures have, enhanced by the passage of the years.

Then, like a city which, while the train pursues its winding course, seems to be first on our right, then on our left, the varying aspects the same character will have assumed to such a degree that they will have made him seem like successive and different characters, will project—but only in that one way—the sensation of

Principal Works

Les plaisirs et les jours (short stories, sketches, poetry, and criticism) 1896

   [Pleasures and Regrets, 1948; also translated as Pleasures and Days, and Other Writings, 1957]

Portraits de peintres (poetry) 1896

*Du côté de chez Swann (novel) 1913

   [Swann's Way, 1922]

*A l'ombre des jeunes filles en fleurs (novel) 1919

   [Within a Budding Grove, 1924]

Pastiches et mélanges (parodies and essays) 1919

*Le côté de Guermantes (novel) 1920

   [The Guermantes Way, 1924]

*Sodome et Gomorrhe (novel) 1922

   [Cities of the Plain, 1927]

*La prisonnière (novel) 1923

   [The Captive, 1929]

*La fugitive (novel) 1925

   [The Sweet Cheat Gone, 1930; also published as The Fugitive in Remembrance of Things Past, 1981]

*Le temps retrouvé (novel) 1927

   [The Past Recaptured, 1931; also published as Time Regained, 1970]

Oeuvres complètes de Marcel Proust. 10 vols. (novels, criticism, short stories, sketches, poetry, parodies, and essays) 1929-36

Correspondance générale de Marcel Proust (letters) 1930

Letters of Marcel Proust (letters) 1949

Jean Santeuil (unfinished novel) 1952

   [Jean Santeuil, 1955]

†A la recherche du temps perdu. 3 vols. (novel) 1954

   [Remembrance of Things Past. 3 vols., 1981]

Contre Sainte-Beuve (criticism) 1954

   [By Way of Sainte-Beuve, 1958]

Marcel Proust: Selected Letters 1880-1903 (letters) 1983

*These works comprise the multivolume novel A la recherche du temps perdu and were first collected in Oeuvres complètes de Marcel Proust.

†This edition of A la recherche du temps perdu, compiled by Pierre Clarac and André Ferré for Bibliothèque de la Pléiade, is a corrected edition based on Proust's own notes and galley corrections. It is now considered the standard edition and is the text on which Terence Kilmartin's 1981 revised translation of the novel is based.

---

time passed. Such characters will later reveal themselves as different from what they were in the present, different from what one believes them to be, a circumstance which, indeed, occurs frequently enough in life.

But not only the same characters who reappear under varying aspects, in the course of this work as in certain of Balzac's cycles, but there is one continuous character. From that point of view my book will perhaps be like an attempt at a sequence of novels of the unconscious. They are not Bergsonian novels, for my work is dominated by a distinction which not only doesn't figure in Bergson's philosophy but which is even contradicted by it.

Voluntary memory, which is above all the memory of the intelligence end of the eyes, gives us only the surface of the past without the truth; but when an odor, a taste, rediscovered under entirely different circumstances evoke for us, in spite of ourselves, the past, we sense how different is this past from the one we thought we remembered and which our voluntary memory was painting like a bad painter using false colors. Even in this first volume the character who narrates, who calls himself "I" (and who is not I) will suddenly rediscover forgotten years, gardens, people in the taste of a sip of tea in which he found a piece of a *madeleine;* doubtless he remembers them anyway, but without color and shapes. I have been able to make him tell how as in the little Japanese game of dipping into water compressed bits of paper which, as soon as they are immersed in the bowl, open up, twist around and become flowers and people, so all the flowers of his garden, the good folk of the village, their little houses and the church and all of Combray and its environs—everything that takes on form and solidity has come, city and garden, out of his cup of tea.

I believe that it is involuntary memories practically altogether that the artist should call for the primary subject matter of his work. First, just because they are involuntary, because they take shape of their own accord, inspired by the resemblance to an identical minute, they alone have the stamp of authenticity. Then they bring things back to us in an exact proportion of memory and of forgetting. And finally, as they make us savor the same sensation under wholly different circumstances, they free it from all context, they give us the extratemporal essence. Moreover, Chateaubriand and Baudelaire practised this method. My novel is not a work of ratiocination; its least elements have been supplied by my sensibility; first I perceived them in my own depths without understanding them, and I had as much trouble converting them into something intelligible as if they had been as foreign to the sphere of the intelligence as a motif in music.

Style is in no way an embellishment, as certain

people think, it is not even a question of technique; it is, like color with certain painters, a quality of vision, a revelation of a private universe which each one of us sees and which is not seen by others. The pleasure an artist gives us is to make us know an additional universe. How, under these conditions, do certain writers declare that they try not to have a style? I don't understand it. (pp. 225-28)

Marcel Proust, in a letter to Antoine Bibesco in November? 1912, in his *Letters of Marcel Proust,* edited and translated by Mina Curtiss, Random House, 1949, pp. 225-28.

JOSEPH CONRAD
(letter date 1923)

[The Polish-born Conrad was a noted English novelist and short story writer known for his insights into the sinister aspects of human nature. His writings include *Lord Jim* (1900), *Nostromo* (1904), and *Under Western Eyes* (1911). In the following excerpt, he praises Proust's artistry, pointing to the French novelist's unparalleled power of analysis.]

As to Marcel Proust, *créateur*, I don't think he has been written about much in English, and what I have seen of it was rather superficial. I have seen him praised for his "wonderful" pictures of Paris life and provincial life. But that has been done admirably before, for us, either in love, or in hatred, or in mere irony. One critic goes so far as to say that Proust's great art reaches the universal, and that in depicting his own past he reproduces for us the general experience of mankind. But I doubt it. I admire him rather for disclosing a past like nobody else's, for enlarging, as it were, the general experience of mankind by bringing to it something that has not been recorded before. However, all that is not of much importance. The important thing is that whereas before we had analysis allied to creative art, great in poetic conception, in observation, or in style, his is a creative art absolutely based on analysis. It is really more than that. He is a writer who has pushed analysis to the point when it becomes creative. All that crowd of personages in their infinite variety through all the gradations of the social scale are rendered visible to us by the force of analysis alone. I don't say Proust has no gift of description or characterisation; but, to take an example from each end of the scale: Françoise, the devoted servant, and the Baron de Charlus, a consummate portrait—how many descriptive lines have they got to themselves in the whole body of that immense work? Perhaps, counting the lines, half a page each. And yet no intelligent person can doubt for a moment their plastic and coloured existence. One would think

that this method (and Proust has no other, because his method is the expression of his temperament) may be carried too far, but as a matter of fact it is never wearisome. There may be here and there amongst those thousands of pages a paragraph that one might think over-subtle, a bit of analysis pushed so far as to vanish into nothingness. But those are very few, and all minor instances. The intellectual pleasure never flags, because one has the feeling that the last word is being said upon a subject much studied, much written about, and of human interest—the last word of its time. Those that have found beauty in Proust's work are perfectly right. It is there. What amazes one is its inexplicable character. In that prose so full of life there is no reverie, no emotion, no marked irony, no warmth of conviction, not even a marked rhythm to charm our ear. It appeals to our sense of wonder and gains our homage by its veiled greatness. I don't think there ever has been in the whole of literature such an example of the power of analysis, and I feel pretty safe in saying that there will never be another. (pp. 126-28)

Joseph Conrad, in a letter to C. K. Moncrieff in 1923, in *Marcel Proust: An English Tribute,* edited by C. K. Moncrieff, Thomas Seltzer, 1923, pp. 126-28.

ANDRÉ MAUROIS
(essay date 1949)

[Maurois was a French novelist, biographer, and historian. In the following excerpt from a work first published in French in 1949, he discusses the comical elements of Proust's characterizations in *Remembrance of Things Past*, asserting that "it is important to note how ill-defined is the dividing line between the comic and the monstrous."]

Stendhal said that the novelist, having constructed his novel, must add to it an element of the ridiculous. Proust uses an even stronger word. It was his opinion that there must, in every great work of art, be something of the grotesque. A short book, whether prose narrative or stage play, can be uniformly emotional and moving—though on this point Shakespeare would not have agreed with him. But in a long novel, as in life itself, there must be comic moments, the purpose of which is to restore the balance of the whole and to relieve the tension. . . . Proust, although, and perhaps because, he was one of the great analysts of misery, could note the oddities and futilities of mankind. The human comedy fascinated and amused him. (p. 225)

Proust's comic themes are of two kinds: those that are a permanent part of human nature, that have frightened and consequently amused mankind from the beginning of recorded history, and those that were peculiar to his period, his world, and his temperament.

First and foremost among the permanent themes is what we may call *"La Danse Macabre."* From time immemorial the comic writer has always exploited the contrast between the panic engendered by the idea of death, and the mechanical routine of living which compels us, when faced by the most terrifying of all dramas, to continue acting and talking as we have always done. (p. 228)

In one of the saddest passages of [*Remembrance of Things Past*], the scene in which the grandmother dies, Proust, the humorist with the implacable eye, gives a subtle, balanced, but profoundly comic sketch of Professor Dieulafoy, the usher of Death and master of the funeral ceremonies. (pp. 229-30)

From the days of Molière to those of Jules Romains, doctors have been among the favorite butts of comic writers, because their power and their learning inspire all mankind with a secret terror. Proust, the son and the brother of doctors, is, at one moment, full of respect for medicine, at another, severe in his criticism of medical men. He created in Dr. Cottard a man who was almost half-witted, and yet, at the same time, a great practitioner. He wrote that "medicine knows nothing of the secret of curing, but has mastered the art of prolonging illness"; that "medicine is a compendium of the successive and contradictory mistakes of doctors." But he could also give it as his opinion that "to believe in medicine would be the greatest folly, were it not that refusal to believe in it would be a greater." (p. 231)

Proust becomes harsher when he touches on his favorite theme of snobbery. That Proust himself, in the days of his youth, manifested certain symptoms of snobbery is of small importance. Not only is the perfect lucidity of the comic writer not incompatible with personal experience, but actually presupposes it. The "sense of humor" consists of mocking in oneself what deserves mockery. (pp. 231-32)

Snobbery, in Proust's novel, appears in many different forms. There is the snobbery of the man (or the woman) who, wishing to belong to a certain coterie, and having succeeded in getting a foot over the threshold, feels so little sure of himself that, rather than run the risk of compromising himself in the eyes of his new friends he is prepared to deny his old ones. This is the case of Legrandin, who, with his flowing, spotted tie, his candid glance, and his charming utterances, has the appearance of a poet though, in fact, he is obsessed by a violent and unsatisfied desire to be on terms of intimacy with the Duchesse de Guermantes and the local bigwigs. So long as no countess or marchioness is in sight, he is extremely affable to the Narrator's grandfather, but when walking with one of the neighboring

great ladies, he pretends not to know his Commoner friend. (p. 232)

Second specimen: the snobbery of genuine aristocrats, belonging to a noble family, but to a junior branch of it, who, as the result of constant snubs, are like "trees which, springing from a bad position on the edge of a precipice, are compelled to grow with a backward slant in order to maintain their equilibrium." Of this type is Madame Gallardon. . . . (pp. 233-34)

Third specimen: the snobbery of the Guermantes themselves, who are so sure of their own social superiority that they regard the whole of humanity with an undiscriminating good will born of an undiscriminating contempt. They attach very little importance to having aristocratic relations, because all their relations are aristocratic: they are severe in their judgment on those who want to move in high society, but, at the same time, find an odd sort of pleasure in entertaining a "Highness," of speaking of their royal connections, and also, or at least this was so in the case of the Duchess, of appraising intellectual achievements with an air of knowledgeable authority which had no real justification. The Guermantes, who had once been, for the Narrator, figures in a fairy tale, quickly become a group of comic characters as a result of that artless self-assurance which led the Duke to quote and to provoke his Duchess's "witticisms," and her to live up to the part for which she had thus been cast.

Finally, at the very top of the social ladder are perched those Royal Highnesses—such as the Princesse de Parme and the Princesse de Luxembourg—who want to be kindly, but behave in so remote and condescending a fashion that they give the impression of being barely able to distinguish a human being from an animal, as when one of them offers a cake to the Narrator's grandmother much in the same way as a visitor to the zoo might feed one of the exhibits. (pp. 234-35)

The culminating point of Proust's satirical treatment of snobbery is to be found in the "Marquise" episode. "Marquise" was the nickname given by the Narrator's grandmother to the lessee of the small shabby pavilion, masked by a green trellis, which did duty in the Champs-Elysées for a public lavatory. The "Marquise" was the possessor of an enormous face, smothered in a sort of rough cast of powder, and wore, on her red wig, a small black lace bonnet. She was of a friendly disposition, but inclined to be haughty, and was ruthless in the contempt with which she refused admission to such visitors as she happened to dislike. "I choose my customers," she said; "I don't let just anybody into what I call my parlors. Don't they just look like parlors with all them flowers? Some of my customers are very nice people, and not a day passes but one or another of them brings me some lilac or jasmine or roses—the which is my favorite blooms. . . ." The Narrator's grandmother, who has overheard the conversation, makes the following comment: "No one could be more Guermantes or more Verdurin-little-nucleus."

That single short phrase pricks the bubble of snobbery more effectively than any diatribe by a moralist could do, because it shows that vanity and disdain are universal sentiments, and that there exists no man or woman so completely disinherited but can find someone to exclude from his or her own particular circle.

The comic writer's favorite method is limitation. Dickens, when he wants to hold the barristers of his day up to ridicule, introduces into *Pickwick* a prosecuting counsel's speech which is *almost* genuine, but sufficiently distorted to underline the point of the mockery. Proust was a perfect imitator. Imitation is a difficult art, because it demands not only that the imitator should be able to reproduce the very voice, the very gestures of his victim, but also that he should have mastered his tricks of speech and ways of thinking. To be able to talk like Charlus or Norpois is nothing if one cannot think, and arrange one's thoughts, like Charlus or Norpois. Therein lay Proust's supreme gift. Not content with analyzing a character in abstract phrases, he delighted in bringing him on to the stage and letting him speak for himself.

Take, for instance, the astonishing figure of the old diplomat. Proust never just says, "This was what Monsieur de Norpois was thinking"; but the long speeches which he puts into his mouth enable us to grasp the mechanism of his thought. The essence, the mainspring, of the Norpois style is this, that the diplomat will never allow himself to say anything that might possibly commit him irrevocably to any statement whatever. So precisely does he balance his sentences that they cancel one another out. At the end of any of his speeches we discover that he has said precisely nothing at all which could possibly be interpreted as a definite expression of opinion. Add to this his use of a number of professional formulas, his habit of referring to the Great Powers in terms of the buildings associated with the practice of diplomacy—the Quai d'Orsay, Downing Street, the Wilhelmstrasse, the Pont aux Chantres—or reveling in subtleties and discovering in the use of an adjective the key to a national policy, and we are in a position to establish the true Norpois "tone." This particular character who, on his first appearance may deceive the reader just as he deceived the Narrator, is comic because, behind the imposing façade, there is nothing but utter emptiness, a sham subtlety, and a few elementary emotions—an ambition that does not lessen with increasing age, and a rather touching desire to please Madame de Villeparisis. (pp. 235-37)

Another method common to Proust and Dickens, which partially confirms Bergson's theory of the significance of the comic, is that by which amusing effects are produced from the mechanical aspects of the human creature, or from his occasional resemblance to members of the animal, vegetable, or mineral worlds. The passage in which Proust describes the auditorium of the Opera as being an immense aquarium, a sort of marine cave, where white Nereids float in the recesses of their boxes, is followed by this:

> The Marquis de Palancy, his face bent downwards at the end of his long neck, his round, bulging eye glued to the glass of his monocle, was moving with a leisurely displacement through the transparent shade and appeared no more to see the public in the stalls than a fish that drifts past, unconscious of the press of curious gazers, behind the glass walls of an aquarium.
>
> (p. 242)

This transformation of man into fish is as productive of laughter as might be the successful completion of a conjuring trick.

For a third method he was indebted to [Anatole] France, rather than to Dickens—for the method, that is—which consists in achieving a comic contrast between the nature of the thing described and the solemn tone of a description conceived in terms of Homer or of Bossuet. To write with gravity about frivolous subjects, or with magnificence about trivial objects or mediocre people, produces just that sense of shocked surprise which is the very essence of the comic. Proust (like Aristophanes) loves to spin out a long lyric line, and then end it by a sudden drop into bathos. (pp. 242-43)

If we are fully to explore this whole great subject, it is important to note how ill-defined is the dividing line between the comic and the monstrous. I have already pointed out that men laugh whenever the shock of surprise, provoked by extraordinary actions or words, is followed by a feeling of safety, born of the fact either that the oddities to which their attention has been drawn are harmless, or that they decide, as a result of their amused scrutiny, that such things are only a part of that same human nature which can be seen at work in ourselves. This feeling of safety ceases to exist when the actions (or the words) in question overstep the normal limits of human fatuity, and we find ourselves in the presence of a strange and antisocial phenomenon which, by its very nature, produces a sense of terror. This overstepping is what happens in the case of Monsieur de Charlus who, when he first appears upon the scene, merely provokes us to laugh at his inordinate pride, but who, later in the book, turns into a monster.

It is a fact of importance that in all the greatest works of fiction, there is almost always a monster, and sometimes more than one. The characters thus designated are at once superhuman and inhuman, and they dominate the works in which they appear, giving them unity in a way that nothing else could do. This is true of Balzac's Vautrin, and it is true of Proust's Charlus. The monster opens windows on to mysterious depths just because it is beyond our power to understand him completely. He passes beyond our range of vision, if only by the horror he inspires; but he does, nevertheless, contain elements of a kind that are in us as well. Had the circumstances been different, we might have become what he is, and this thought at once terrifies and fascinates us. Monsters provide the story with unexplored and secret depths which reveal the sublime.

Before Proust, Shakespeare alone had succeeded in orchestrating the magic dissonances amidst which these monsters move. The humor which expresses itself in lovely lines, the earthbound bodies which can loose spirits on the world, the allegories and the ravishing images which end in horseplay, the flicker of fairy lights, all these things bring the world of Shakespeare to our minds. Proust, like Shakespeare, had plumbed the extremes of human misery, but, like Shakespeare, found in humor a saving grace, and again like Shakespeare, serenity in Time Regained. The end of *A la Recherche du temps perdu* is not unlike the end of Shakespeare's *Tempest*. The play is ended; the Enchanter has surrendered his secret. Back into their box he has put the marionnettes whom he has shown us for the last time, touched with hoarfrost, at the Prince de Guermantes' great reception. Now he says, like Prospero: "We are such stuff as dreams are made on, and our little life is rounded with a sleep. . . . " The Guermantes and the Verdurins vanish in smoke: Swann's bell tinkles for the last time at the garden gate and, while the final cadences on the nature of Time are drawing to a close, we seem to hear, in the moon-drenched trees, far away and barely audible, Marcel's laughter, the laughter of a schoolboy spluttering behind his hand, but softened now, and become the laughter of a very old child to whom life has taught the lesson not only of pain but of pity. (pp. 245-47)

André Maurois, in his *Proust: Portrait of a Genius,* translated by Gerard Hopkins, Harper & Brothers, 1950, 332 p.

JOSÉ ORTEGA Y GASSET
(essay date 1958-59)

[Ortega y Gasset was an eminent Spanish philosopher and essayist. In the following excerpt, he analyzes *Remembrance of Things Past,* noting a certain static, oppressive quality in Proust's meticulous reconstruction of evanescent memories.]

In the midst of contemporary production, which is so capricious, so lacking in necessity, [Proust's] work presents itself with the stamp of something ordained. If it had never come into being, there would have remained, in the literary evolution of the nineteenth century, a specific gap with a clearly defined outline. One might even say, in order to point up its inevitability, that it was created a little late, that analysis would disclose a slight anachronism in its physiognomy. (pp. 504-05)

The narrative themes that come and go on the surface of [Proust's] work have only a tangential and secondary interest; they are like buoys adrift on the bottomless flood of his memories. Before Proust, writers had commonly taken memory as the material with which to reconstruct the past. Since the data of memory are incomplete and retain of the prior reality only an arbitrary extract, the traditional novelist fills them out with observations drawn from the present, together with chance hypotheses and conventional ideas. In other words, he unites fraudulent elements with the authentic materials of memory.

This method makes sense as long as the intention is, as it formerly was, to *restore* things of the past, i.e. to feign a new presence and actuality for them. The intention of Proust is the very opposite. He does not wish to use his memories as materials for reconstructing former realities; on the contrary, by using all conceivable methods—observations of the present, introspective analyses, psychological generalizations—he wants literally to reconstruct the very memories themselves. Thus, it is not things that are remembered, but the memory of things, which is the central theme of Proust. Here for the first time memory ceases to be treated as the means of describing other things and becomes itself the very thing described. For this reason Proust does not generally add to what is remembered those parts of reality which have eluded memory. Instead, he leaves memory intact, just as he finds it, objectively incomplete, occasionally mutilated and agitating in its spectral remoteness the truncated stumps that still remain to it. There is a very suggestive page in which Proust speaks of three trees on a ridge. He remembers that behind them there was something of great importance, something which has been effaced by time, abolished from memory. In vain the author struggles to recapture what has escaped him, to integrate it with that bit of decimated landscape—those three trees, sole survivors of the mental catastrophe which is forgetting.

The narrative themes in Proust are, then, mere pretexts and, as it were, *spiracula,* air-holes, tiny portals of the hive through which the winged and shuddering swarm of reminiscences succeed in liberating themselves. It is not for nothing that Proust gave his work the general title of *A la recherche du temps perdu.* Proust is an investigator of lost time as such. With utter scrupulousness he refuses to impose upon the past the anatomy of the present; he practices a rigorous non-intervention guided by an unshakable will to avoid reconstruction of any sort. From the nocturnal depths of the soul a memory surges upwards, excitingly, like a constellation in the night which ascends above the horizon. Proust represses all interest in restoration and limits himself to describing what he sees as it arises out of his memory. Instead of reconstructing lost time, he contents himself with making an edifice of its ruins. You might say that in Proust the genre of Memoirs attains the distinction of a pure literary method.

So much for his treatment of time. But even more elemental and stupefying is the nature of his invention with regard to space.

Various people have counted the number of pages that Proust employs in telling us that his grandmother is taking her temperature. Indeed, one cannot talk about Proust without noting his prolixity and concern for minutiae. In his case, prolixity and minute analysis cease to be literary vices and become two sources of inspiration, two muses that might well be added to the other nine. It is necessary for Proust to be prolix and minute for the simple reason that he gets much closer to objects than people are accustomed to. He is the inventor of a new distance between us and things. This fundamental revolution has had such tremendous consequences—as I have said—that almost all previous literature appears to be grossly panoramic, written from a bird's-eye point of view, as compared with the work of this delectably myopic genius. (pp. 505-07)

The monograph on Swann's love is an example of psychological pointillism. For the medieval author of *Tristan and Iseult* love is a sentiment that possesses a clear and definite outline of its own: for him, a primitive psychological novelist, love is love and nothing other than love. As opposed to this, Proust describes Swann's love as something that has nothing like the form of love. All kinds of things can be found in it: touches of flaming sensuality, purple pigments of distrust, browns of habitual life, grays of vital fatigue. The only thing *not* to be found is love. It comes out just as the figure in a tapestry does, by the intersection of various threads, no one of which contains the form of the figure. Without Proust there would have remained unwritten a literature that must be read in the way that the paintings of Monet are looked at, with the eyes half-shut.

It is for this reason that when Proust is compared to Stendhal one must proceed with caution. In many respects they represent two opposite poles, and are antagonistic one toward the other. Above all else, Stendhal is a man of imagination: he imagines the plots, the situations, and the characters. He copies nothing: everything in him resolves to fantasy, into clear and concentrated fantasy. His characters are as much "designed" as are the features of a madonna in the paintings of Raphael. Stendhal believes firmly in the reality of his characters and makes every effort to draw a sharp

and unequivocal outline of them. The characters of Proust, on the other hand, have no silhouette; rather, they are changeable atmospheric condensations, spiritual cloud-formations that varying wind and light transform from one hour to the next. Certainly Proust belongs in the company of Stendhal, "investigator of the human heart." But while Stendhal takes the human heart as a solid with a definite though plastic shape, it is for Proust a diffuse and gaseous volume that varies from moment to moment with a kind of meteorological versatility. (p. 509)

[In the volumes of Proust], nothing happens, there is no dramatic action, there is no process. They are composed of a series of pictures extremely rich in content, but static. We mortals, however, by our very nature, are dynamic; we are interested in nothing but movement.

When Proust tells us that the little bell jangles in the gateway of the garden in Combray and that one can hear the voice of Swann who has just arrived, our attention lights upon this event and gathering up its forces prepares to leap to another event which doubtless is going to follow and for which the first one is preparatory. We do not inertly install ourselves in the first event; once we have summarily understood it, we feel ourselves dispatched towards another one still to come. In life, we believe, each event announces its successor and is the point of transition towards it, and so on until a trajectory has been traced, just as one mathematical point succeeds another until a line has been formed. Proust ruthlessly ignores our dynamic nature. He constantly forces it to remain in the first event, sometimes for a hundred pages and more. Nothing follows the arrival of Swann; no other point links up with this one. On the contrary, the arrival of Swann in the garden, that simple momentary event, that point of reality, expands without progressing, stretches without changing into another, increases in volume and for page after page we do not depart from it: we only see it grow elastically, swell up with new details and new significance, enlarge like a soap-bubble embroidering itself with rainbows and images.

We experience, thus, a kind of torture in reading Proust. His art works upon our hunger for action, movement, progression as a continual restraint that holds us back; we suffer like the quail that, taking flight within his cage, strikes against the wire vault in which his prison terminates. The muse of Proust could well be called "Morosidad" (Sloth), his style consisting in the literary exploitation of that *delectatio morosa* which the Councils of the Church punished so severely. (pp. 511-12)

José Ortega y Gasset, "Time, Distance, and Form in Proust," in *The Hudson Review*, Vol. XI, No. 4, Winter, 1958-59, pp. 504-13.

GEORGES POULET

(essay date 1963)

[A distinguished Belgian critic, Poulet is known for his efforts to interpret a literary work as a struggle of the human consciousness to grasp the meaning of existence and individuality. In the following excerpt from a 1963 study, he addresses the question of Proust's conception of time, arguing that, in contradistinction to Henri Bergson's pure duration, Proust's time is always spatialized.]

"We juxtapose," says Bergson, "our states of consciousness in such a way as to perceive them simultaneously: Not one following the other, but one alongside the other; in brief, we project time into space."

This is perhaps the most serious piece of criticism addressed by Bergsonism to the intellect. Intellect would tend to annihilate the true continuity of our being, by substituting for it a sort of mental space in which the moments would align themselves without ever interpenetrating themselves. Hence, there is for Bergson the necessity of destroying this "space" in order to come back by intuition to pure duration, to the modulated murmur by which existence reveals its inexhaustibly changing nature to the mind. It is singular that one who had so often been taken for a disciple of Bergson should have assumed, probably without knowing it, a position diametrically opposite. If the thought of Bergson denounces and rejects the metamorphosis of time into space, Proust not only accommodates himself to it, but installs himself in it, carries it to extremes, and makes of it finally one of the principles of his art. . . . To the bad juxtaposition, to the intellectual space condemned by Bergson, there is opposed a good juxtaposition, an aesthetic space, where, in ordering themselves, moments and places form the work of art, altogether memorable and admirable. (pp. 3-4)

In terms of the title it bears, one knows that the Proustian novel is very exactly a "search for lost time." A being sets out in quest of his past, makes every effort to rediscover his preceding existence. Thus one sees the hero awakening in the middle of the night and asking himself to what epoch of his life there is attached this moment in which he recovers consciousness. This is a moment totally deprived of any connection with the rest of duration, a moment suspended in itself, and profoundly anguished, because the one who lives it does not literally know *when* he lives. Lost in time, he is reduced to an entirely momentary life.

But the ignorance of this awakened sleeper is much graver than it seems. If he does not know *when* he lives, he no longer knows *where* he lives. His ignorance is no less important as to his position in space than as to his position in duration: "And when I awakened in the middle of the night, as I was *ignorant as to where I found myself,* I did not know in the first instant who I was." (pp. 7-8)

[With] Proust, there is a diversity of places, unmingled with others, which seem to live within their frontiers an absolutely independent life. Such is their essential characteristic. From the external world to themselves, there is not this natural topographical continuity that is found everywhere between one place and other places. From the moment one perceives them, on the contrary, one gets the clear idea that they do not extend into the surrounding universe, that they are separate from it. There is, for example, not far from Raspelière a certain landscape of forest and shingles: "One instant, the denuded rocks by which I was surrounded, the sea, which one perceived through their clefts, *floated before my eyes like the fragments of another universe."* (pp. 19-20)

[There is nothing less objective] than genuine Proustian places; genuine places, those which are invariably connected with certain human presences. There is never, in fact, with Proust, a place described without in the foreground, the profile of such or such a figure; in the same way that there never appears in Proust a figure without the presence of a framework ready to insert and support it. Invariably it is in a landscape minutely circumscribed that the Proustian personage shows itself for the first time.

From the moment it appears, this place, associating itself with him, gives him a note as distinct and recognizable as a Wagnerian *leitmotiv.* Yes, no doubt, in what follows the personage will reappear elsewhere. But he will not cease to be bound to the primitive site in our memory. It is of this that we are reminded from the very first moment; it is this that we see unfold, unfold promptly, in whatever spot the personage finds himself; as if he had been fixed in a painting more revealing than anything else, where he will always be showing up against the same background.

It is thus with all Proustian personages. How to recall, for example, Gilberte, or rather the image the hero has formed of her, if not under the aspect of a little girl, accompanied by an old gentleman, and silhouetting herself with him against the background of the cathedrals they visit by turn. (pp. 23-4)

Thus, for Proust, human beings appear located in certain places that give them support and outline, and that determine the perspective according to which one is allowed to see them. A singular thing, this novelist of interiority invariably obliges himself to present his personages (except for one central consciousness) under the aspect of exteriority. (p. 25)

Infallibly, then, with Proust, in reality as in dream, persons and places are united. The Proustian imagination would not know how to conceive beings otherwise than in placing them against a local background that plays for them the part of foil and mirror. To evoke a human being, this act so simple, which is the first act of the novelist composing his work, is tantamount with Proust to rendering a form visible and putting it in a framework. It is a trick of mind veritably essential, and which, with Proust, can be noticed not only in his novels, but in his critical writings and ideological essays, and even in his correspondence. (pp. 27-8)

Like works by the same painter on display at different museums of Europe, a whole series of Proustian sites seem . . . to proclaim their belonging to a single universe. But these sites or pictures have been spearated, the ones from the others, by great neutral distances, in such a way that the first aspect suggested by the work of Proust is that of a very incomplete ensemble, where the number of subsisting traces is largely sur-

Proust in military service (1890).

passed by the number of gaps. Rarely does the representation of things there appear total or panoramic. It is nearly always fragmentary, now larger, now narrower, but most often reduced, whether it be by some obstruction, or more often, by some "fracture" in the field of vision—to a section of the real, strictly limited, beyond which it is hopeless to try to see anything. In brief, the most exact image of the Proustian universe is no different from that image of Combray which appears at the beginning of Proust's tale: "*a sort of luminous wall looming up on the midst of indistinct shadows* like those that the flaming up of a Bengal light or some electrical projection brightens up and *divides into sections* in an edifice of which all other parts remain immersed in night." (pp. 37-8)

But what is it, to juxtapose?

It is to place one thing *beside* another.

Beside, and not above! In fact it is necessary carefully to distinguish juxtaposition from its analogue, superposition. (p. 91)

The experience of Proust is not at all the burial of the past under the present; quite the contrary, it is a resurrection of the past in spite of the present. Proust dreams of a kind of superposition periodically or irregularly broken by an inverse phenomenon of upheaval. He conceives of a superposition of a geological and Plutonian type, a sort of unstable stratification, where, from time to time, "the upheavals bring to the level of the surface old strata." Or he imagines an arrangement similar to that of the magic lantern. Of course, as to what concerns its internal functioning, the magic lantern offers a process that one should not confound with superposition. It does not conceal; it supersedes. To the previous moment, through a mixed movement, interrupted and abrupt, which, besides, is bound to please Proust more than the fluid and uninterrupted gliding of cinematographic images, it substitutes a subsequent moment that involves the total annihilation of the one preceding it. The Proustian universe is not, therefore, that of the magic lantern; or, if one wishes, it is just that, but on the condition of imagining the painted plates not in the motion that projects the ones *after* the others, but arranged, the ones *beside* the others, in a simultaneous order. (pp. 92-3)

Do not let us be deceived then by the declaration so often reported of Proust, according to which, in his novel, he had wanted to render palpable a fourth dimension, the dimension of time. For the dimension of time is, in his mind, only a dimension entirely similar to all three others, a dimension, itself also, purely spatial. *"Time for him is like space,"* he writes of one of his characters, Jean Santeuil. And in the same way, one can say of his novel what he himself said of a certain place called Guermantes, which like the church of Combray, was full of memories: *"Time has taken there the form of space."*

Now if Proustian time *always* takes the form of space, it is because it is of a nature that is directly opposed to Bergsonian time. Nothing resembles less the melodic continuity of pure duration; but nothing, in return, more resembles what Bergson denounced as being a false duration, a duration the elements of which would be exteriorized, the ones relatively to the others, and aligned, the ones beside the others. Proustian time is time spatialized, juxtaposed. . . .

It could not happen differently, from the moment when Proust had conceived the temporality of his universe under the form of a series of pictures, which, successively presented in the course of the work, would finally reappear all together, simultaneously, to be sure, outside of time, but not outside of space. Proustian space is this final space, made of the order in which there are distributed, the ones in harmony with the others, the different episodes of the Proustian novel. The order is not different from that which binds between them the predellas, and the predellas to the reredos. A plurality of episodes makes way for and constructs its own space, which is the space of the work of art. (pp. 105-06)

Georges Poulet, in his *Proustian Space,* translated by Elliott Coleman, The Johns Hopkins University Press, 1977, 113 p.

WALLACE FOWLIE
(essay date 1964)

[An American literary scholar, critic, novelist, poet, and translator, Fowlie is known for his studies of French literature. In the following excerpt, he comments on each of the seven parts of Proust's *Remembrance of Things Past,* analyzing the novelist's perceptions of time and reality and concluding that Proustian time is an inner record of subjective memory, "removed from the dangerous contingencies of the present."]

The first of the seven parts of Proust's novel, *Du Côté de chez Swann* [(*Swann's Way*)], serves as an introduction to the long work, but it is far more than that. It is itself a novel, with a beginning, a middle, and an end. It is true that these three demarcations, as they occur in *Du Côté de chez Swann,* are not typical of the usual novel. The beginning of the book, *Combray,* is the introduction to characters and the announcement of themes to be continued throughout the entire work. The themes of *Combray* will be explored with the ever-deepening sensibility of the protagonist, and the characters will evolve and change with the passing of time.

The ending of *Du Côté de chez Swann,* which is given the special title: *Noms de Pays: le Nom (Place Names),* is both an end and a rebeginning, a recapitulation of *Combray,* the child's world which constantly returns in that circular movement we call memory with no absolute beginning and no absolute ending. The middle section, *Un Amour de Swann (Swann in love),* is a flashback, but so elaborate and so unified a flashback, that it is a novel in itself, a love story, the first of a series of love stories. But it is also quite literally the middle of *Du Côté de chez Swann,* because it initiates the boy of *Combray* to the world. It is Marcel's introduction to the world in a general sense, that is, to everything that is not his parents' home, as well as to the three specific worlds or experiences that form the substance of *A la recherche du temps perdu:* the world of passion, the world of society, and the world of art.

With the very first word of the novel, *Longtemps* (which will reappear capitalized, as if it had become one of the characters, as the very last word of the novel: *dans le Temps*), Proust offers the key to his work. It is the phenomenon of the time during which the novel was written, because of which the novel was conceived, and which the novelist hopes to defeat in the successful completion of the novel.

A preoccupation with time and its irrevocability is a familiar human experience. With Marcel Proust it became a veritable obsession. The changes brought about in nature, in human beings, in society, by the passing of time are sung by him almost as a lament. Time is the relentless force that attacks the beauty of the human body, the stability of human personality, the freshness and the completeness of works of art—a painting, for example, or a cathedral. Proust grew to look upon life itself as a constant struggle against time. Much of the so-called pessimism of his book comes from the hopelessness of this struggle, from the inevitable failure of life to preserve itself intact from the encroachments of time.

He analyzes one after the other those major experiences of life that are the most hallowed efforts of man to reach some absolute within time, some stable value that will oppose the flow of time: the loyalty of friendship, for example, the passions of love, the steadfastness of convictions, either theological or philosophical or political. Proust the novelist discovers that even such experiences, which, when they are real, seem absolute, are, in time, subjected to change and even oblivion. The human self, immersed in time, is never exactly the same two days in succession. All the elements of personality are constantly being affected by time: they are either being weakened or strengthened. They are receding or in the ascendant. Even the self which is in love, deeply, jealously and passionately, will change, according to Proust, and become disillusioned.

The self is never one but a succession of selves.

If this is true—and the substance of the book as well as the method of writing are based upon this Bergsonian assumption—what happens to the selves we once were? Do these selves, which were once real, sink into oblivion? Proust answers this question with a vigorous no! They are not lost. They do not disappear. They are in us, in that part of us that is often called the subconscious. They live in our dreams and indeed at times in our states of consciousness. The opening theme of Proust's novel is the protagonist's literal awakening. This is a familiar experience for everyone every morning when we leave the state of sleep for the state of consciousness. Proust looks upon this emergence as an effort to recover our identity, to find out who we are, where we are, and what particular self we are inhabiting. (pp. 51-3)

Proust explains early in his novel that there are for him two ways in particular by which the past can be recalled. The first, on which he will rely a great deal, and which he acknowledges to be, of the two, less sure and less sound, is the willful memory of the intelligence. *La Mémoire volontaire,* as he calls it, seems to be the rationalistic, the deductive method which is based on documents, testimonials, and ratiocination. When Marcel evokes a typical summer evening at Combray, when the family spends the last hours of daylight in the garden, we have a good example of willful memory. (p. 55)

[The narrator] indicates the limitations of *la mémoire volontaire.* He realizes that this kind of memory is able to recall only a small part of his past, and he asks whether all the rest of Combray has been forgotten. The answer again is no. Another kind of memory—involuntary—*la mémoire involontaire* is able to evoke the real past. But the operation of this kind of memory depends on chance. To illustrate, the narrator now relates the episode of the madeleine cake, *la petite madeleine.* Once when dipping a madeleine into a cup of tea, he remembers his tante Léonie at Combray who used to give him a madeleine and a cup of linden tea (*tilleul*). Through the sensation of taste, he recalls, without effort, a similar experience (of *déjà vu*), and the complete picture of the past returns to him: his aunt, his room in her house, the garden, the town, the square where the church is, the streets and the paths. All of Combray, in fact, as if by magic, came out of his cup of tea. (p. 56)

After the announcement of the two principles of voluntary and involuntary memory, the narrator describes the past he associates with Combray. (p. 57)

Marcel's life in Combray was very much related to two walks he describes. . . . After the brief analysis of past time, and the possibilities of bringing it back, he reconstructs the past by means of another dimension: space. Swann's Way (*le côté de chez Swann*), or, as it is sometimes called, Méséglise, is a long walk that leads past the park of Tansonville, the estate of M. Swann.

Guermantes' Way (*le côté de Guermantes*) is an even longer walk which leads in the direction of the Guermantes', the aristocratic family that resides at least part of the year at Combray. (p. 58)

To Marcel, both Swann's Way and Guermantes', are remote. Both represent a vague geographical distance. Swann's Way is far off, a point somewhere on the horizon. Guermantes' Way is even farther off, and more removed from reality. It has the remote unreality of the equator, or the North Pole, or the Orient. Each "way" is related to an aspect of Marcel's initiation to life. Méséglise (or Swann's Way) is the hawthorn-lined park of Tansonville where he first sees Gilberte and hears someone call her name. It is also the way to Montjouvain where he observes the scandalous scene of sexuality. Swann's Way is Marcel's introduction to pure and impure love. Guermantes' Way, from which he can see the water lilies of the Vivonne and the steeples of Martinville, is associated not only with all the Guermantes' prestige, but also with Marcel's concern with his own literary talent and his vocation.

The two ways lead Marcel away from his family and initiate him into the three orders of experience which are to dominate his life: love, society and art. At Combray the two ways seemed to the boy to lead in opposite directions, toward opposite goals, totally cut off one from the other. But one of the principal actions of the entire novel is to demonstrate that time, in its fluidity and its power to effect metamorphosis, will join the two ways and fuse them in an extraordinary fashion. (pp. 59-60)

Un Amour de Swann, the second section of *Du Côté de chez Swann,* has been often looked upon as a separate novel that interrupts the life story of the protagonist. In reality, this episode has innumerable bonds with all parts of the work, and the significance of Swann's role becomes more evident the closer we read the novel.

The importance of Charles Swann, at least in the three divisions of *Du Côté de chez Swann,* is clear. In *Combray* he is the refined and rather mysterious friend who visits the boy's parents. We are made aware of his intelligence, his erudition, his elegance of manner and dress. We even learn some things about him that Marcel's family does not know: his cordial relations with the highest society, with the aristocratic Guermantes, even with the Prince of Wales. For the boy Marcel, M. Swann is a gentleman of sympathetic kindness, endowed with great prestige, who stands out as an almost godlike figure in Combray. In the second division, *Un Amour de Swann,* Swann is the protagonist and the story is centered on his love for Odette: the origin of his love, the experience of suffering and jealousy, and love's end. In the third division, *Noms de Pays: le Nom,* Swann plays a more effaced, a more subtle role. Marcel's dreams about Balbec and Italy have been somewhat induced by Swann's conversations and allusions. The boy's dreams about Gilberte, and his love for her in the Champs-Elysées scenes, are also dreams about the name of Swann and the strong attraction the boy feels for the glamorous Mme Swann. One always feels behind the sentimental boyish love of Marcel for Gilberte, the stronger, more violent and more deeply analyzed love of Swann for Odette.

Un Amour de Swann is far more than a separate monograph on passion. Swann, as Marcel's precursor, is related to the two "ways"; his own way, first, which leads us to Odette, and the Verdurin clan where Swann sees Odette, and to Elstir (or rather, M. Biche), the painter, and the work of the composer Vinteuil. But Swann is also a close friend of Oriane, duchesse de Guermantes, and of the baron de Charlus, both of whom represent Guermantes' Way. Swann's daughter, Gilberte, will finally marry a Guermantes, Robert de Saint-Loup. With this marriage, at the end of the novel, in Mlle de Saint-Loup, the two ways are joined. Thus, *Un Amour de Swann* is the indirect but indispensable prelude to the great social upheaval which will be described in *Le Temps retrouvé.* (pp. 67-8)

Swann's liaison with Odette before their marriage is the first full illustration in the novel—prelude to the rest—of the dual experience with which man is involved every moment of life, consciously or unconsciously: the duality of destruction and preservation. Time is the force that slowly and inexorably destroys everything. But memory is time's only deterrent, the one staying factor, the one force for permanence. The scene where by chance Swann hears again Vinteuil's sonata at Mme de Saint-Euverte's concert is Swann's most exalted moment. At this point in the liaison, he senses that Odette is unfaithful and has become Forcheville's mistress. But before the scene closes, he relives the past: he recaptures what is lost to time. The musical phrase of the sonata, which his sentimentality identified with Odette, forces him, without his willing it, to feel once again the sensations and the gestures and the loving kindnesses that he shared with Odette. These memories are so precisely real as to be almost intolerable. This moment of total recall transcends the mere story of the liaison: its slow beginning, its passion, and its decline. (p. 72)

In the third section of *Du Côté de chez Swann*, *Noms de Pays: le Nom*, we leave Swann's world of passion and disillusionment, and return to Marcel and a boy's world of mystery. It is not Combray now but Paris. And throughout the meditations on names (Balbec, Venice, Florence especially, and the towns through which the train passes: Bayeux, Coutances, Vitré, Lannion, Lamballe, Pont-Aven), and on the afternoons spent in the Champs-Elysées where Gilberte, known at first only as a cipher, comes to life, and in the Bois de Boulogne, where Mme Swann passes in her carriage

along the Avenue des Acacias, the theme of love is never lost: it is only momentarily subdued in Marcel's thoughts of Balbec and La Berma. (p. 75)

This section of the novel, which completes *Du Côté de chez Swann*, returns to Marcel's principal narrative by its allusion to the moment back at Combray when he had first heard the name of Gilberte in the garden of Tansonville. The first elaboration of the major philosophical theme of the disparity between the imagination and reality, the section is also an analysis of an initial phase in Proustian love, which will be more lengthily treated in the case of Marcel than in the case of Swann.

Marcel's love for Gilberte has little or nothing to do with the satisfaction of the senses (which was of vital importance in Swann's love for Odette). It is predominantly the proliferation of the lover's imagination. Marcel forms an elaborate mental world in which Gilberte is the center. Exalted by the slightest attention she manifests, he is equally depressed by her slightest indifference. The fits of despondency are forms of suffering which have the strange perverse power of attaching Marcel to Gilberte even more firmly than in moments of happiness. (p. 79)

The third section of Proust's novel, *Le Côté de Guermantes*, [*Guermantes' Way*], is divided into two parts, both dominated by a vast social fresco, the setting of French society: the first at the Paris home of Mme de Villeparisis, and the second a dinner party at the Paris residence of Mme de Guermantes. (p. 114)

The prevailing emphasis in *Le Côté de Guermantes* is on society's forms and the false perceptions we constantly cultivate because of our limited knowledge and our misconceptions of human relationships. We are led to these scenes by individuals whom Marcel knows. There is, in reality, only one character—Marcel—in *A la recherche du temps perdu* in the triple role of protagonist, narrator, and novelist, but he succeeds, despite the staggering subjectivity of the work, in bringing countless characters to life outside himself, yet formed by his perceptions and seen through his rich and tolerant sensitivity.

One of the most fully developed of these Proustian characters is the duchesse de Guermantes, Oriane, who presides over the beginning and the ending of *Le Côté de Guermantes* and who introduces us, more dramatically than any other character, to the complexities and the cruelties of society. (p. 115)

The originality of Proust's art as novelist lies in the extraordinary skill with which he is able to present so many themes simultaneously: the personal dramas of individual characters (the adaptation of Françoise to a new house, Marcel's infatuation with Mme de Guermantes, Saint-Loup's stormy liaison with his actress-mistress); the large social settings, the tableaux of characters involved in a comedy of manners and class distinctions (the Opéra where the *baignoire* of the princesse de Guermantes is the center of attention, the descriptions of the life in a garrison town, the matinée at Mme de Villeparisis', the first very detailed social fresco in *A la recherche du temps perdu*). Other novelists, Stendhal, for example, emphasize either society or the individual. At no point in the closely woven texture of Proust's writing is any demarcation visible between society and the individuals interacting within the society.

In accordance with the usual preoccupation of the novelist, Proust shows us what is actually seen in such a town as Doncières: streets, shops, hotel rooms, military men. But he is constantly adding to what can be seen by everyone, an artist's personal subjective vision. In other words, he is interested in telling us in what way he was led to see what he does see. For example, in describing a tawdry secondhand novelty shop in Doncières (*un petit magasin de bric-à-brac* . . .), the light of a candle and the light of a lamp fall in such a way on various odd objects that, for Marcel, the drabness of the scene is momentarily transformed into a Rembrandt painting.

In addition to these two kinds of writing—the description of what can be seen and the peculiarly subjective way in which Marcel Proust sees it—there is a theoretical kind of writing far more occasional than the other two, in which the writer tells his reader why he has chosen to describe his society and the customs of his time. This is the function of the memorialist who, more than the historian, seeks to understand the meaning of individual and social behavior, to derive general theories concerning the relationship between man and man, and man and society. The writing of a novel would never be sufficient for Marcel Proust. Consciously, and at times unconsciously, he makes the novel a justification for writing, and, more than that, a justification for his own life. The protagonist in *A la recherche du temps perdu* is never seen alone: he is portrayed in conjunction with some object (such as the porch of a church), or with some human being, or with some social group. In the same way, Marcel Proust is never solely the novelist. He is the novelist who is at the same time aesthetician and memorialist. (p. 120)

By instinct and by habit, Proust is an observer never satisfied until he has divided any phenomenon he is studying into as many elements as possible. The worlds he knows and observes are the worlds in his novel. A futile criticism often levelled against Marcel Proust is the narrowness of the world he chose to depict. This criticism is not accurate because, in the first place, Proust did not limit himself to one world in Paris. Several different, interacting classes are present in his novel. But wisely, in keeping with the most permanent tradition of art, he focused his attention on those worlds he knew the most intimately: the aristocracy,

the upper bourgeoisie, and the servant class. The universality of genius lies in the profundity of its understanding, and not in the mere multiplicity of its themes. The major novelists have quite consistently sought that historical moment and that social world most favorable to their talent. Dickens, Balzac, Henry James carefully chose a world they knew or could easily document: they recreated these worlds into what is recognizable today as a Dickensian, a Balzacian, a Jamesian world. Proust belongs to this category of novelists whose power of observation is coupled with an imaginative visionary power which exaggerates and deepens and clarifies the observable and the documented elements of their writing. (pp. 122-23)

Most of the observations Marcel makes on the Guermantes and their *esprit* are fairly objective analyses, but in a few very important instances in the narrative of the dinner, he relates this study to himself and thus attaches it firmly to the leading theme of the novel—Marcel's initiation to the great concepts of time and eternity. In his description of the attractive suppleness in the ceremonial physical movements of the Guermantes, we are led to feel that this is a special attribute which separates them from Marcel whose own physical movements are somewhat bourgeois. He realizes that Oriane's mind was formed long before his own and he realizes in particular that Oriane, being a Guermantes, possibly the highest representative of her family, cannot understand what he had first looked for in her, in Combray, when he was a boy, and what he is now looking for in Paris: the magical spell (*le charme*) of the Guermantes name. In a sense, their relationship is between a highly imaginative young man and a highly sophisticated lady of the world. Oriane de Guermantes creates for Marcel a magic spell that exerts a strong attraction over him. She incarnates it every day so naturally, so unthinkingly, that she could not possibly understand what it is to be someone else.

Marcel sees in the Guermantes the persistence of the past. Geography, history, trees, and Gothic spires are in their name. All of these elements, and many others, have shaped their faces, the characteristics of their minds and attitudes, their prejudices. Their history is of far more interest to Marcel than to the Guermantes (despite their endless discussion of genealogies). Marcel, in this regard, compares himself to an anticlerical archaeologist who knows far more about the history of a church than the curé who celebrates his daily mass in the church. . . . (pp. 140-41)

The title of the fourth section of *A la recherche du temps perdu* [*Sodome et Gomorrhe* (Cities of the Plain)] calls attention to a new theme which the section is to be concerned with—a theme only briefly and intermittently referred to previously in the novel. By using the biblical title, with its implicit disapproval of sexual inversion, Proust announces an attitude that would seem moralistic. And yet he is hostile to the moralizing novelist. The drama of inversion is an important part of his novel. By "drama" is meant the suffering and the social ostracism inversion entails. All the vices exist to some degree in Proust's work, but they are not condemned as vices. Proust affirms them, and he studies in particular the subconscious role they play in the moral and spiritual and social make-up of his characters. Proust is far more fully conscious of the vice of inversion in Charlus than Charlus himself. According to Proust's canon, only the artist, when functioning as artist, is fully conscious.

Inversion is only one reflection, however strong and dramatic, of the entire moral problem of the protagonist, and hence of the entire novel. Almost as if he were the protagonist of a mediaeval morality play, Marcel faces two sets of alternatives throughout the history of his life: the virtues of Combray, on the one hand, and the vices of society, on the other. The novel asks the question: Which will win Marcel's heart? The answer to this leading question is saved for the very end of the work. (p. 147)

Charlus will be the major representative of Sodom in the novel, but he is also one of the major representatives of the Guermantes, and his personal anomaly will designate metaphorically the decadence of the French aristocracy and, beyond that, a point in the cyclical movement of history when the weaknesses and defects of man suddenly show themselves under the hard carapace of continuous tradition. In fact, it would be difficult to find a major theme in Proust's novel that Charlus does not incarnate.

Everything Proust says about personality is exemplified in Charlus. He is both changeable and unchanging. He is one man, and he is all men. This dual aspect of human character, in one man, Charlus, means that everything that can be said about personality is true. Truth is, for Proust, the container of contradictions. And this is one aspect of Proust's concept of the absolute. Charlus' impeccable good taste, his knowledge and love of the arts, his magnanimity and kindness, revealed on many occasions, his understanding of history and politics and the ways of man, have been acquired during his conscious life as a highly privileged French aristocrat. When sexual desire transforms him into a reprobate, he is the same man, responding to a bestial trait inherited from some distant ancestor. No part of past human conduct is ever completely lost. Our instincts and our feelings are predetermined, even if our will is free to carry out or repress these instincts, to submerge or express these feelings. The love Charlus has doubtless already felt for Marcel in the first part of the novel—not exactly the same attraction he demonstrates for Jupien in the courtyard scene—is the adventure of a stranger alienated from himself. This is the persistent Proustian formula for the experience of love.

Its full analysis comes in time, with Marcel himself, in his love for Albertine. But in Charlus, more than in Marcel, we are able to follow a conscience, actually a consciousness in perpetual motion, traversing all the levels of an awareness of the past, an awareness implicit in the living conscience, and able, under certain conditions, to take hold and direct the present. (pp. 150-51)

In the classical sense of the tragic hero, Charlus qualifies far more easily than Marcel Proust.

At this stage in the novel, the opening of *Sodome et Gomorrhe*, the Guermantes, including not only Charlus but the others as well, have triumphed over time. They have resisted its power of change more successfully than others. They form a bastion of prestige and strength and invincibility. But the revelation of Charlus' character, made to Marcel as he watches the courtyard and the fertilization of the flower, marks the beginning of change, the first crack in the bastion wall. The depiction of Charlus' moral defect is the sinister sign of change and evil which will spread, in similar and other manifestations, to an entire family, a caste, and even, it can be argued, a civilization. With the Charlus-Jupien pantomime scene, a new epoch begins; one characterized by disenchantment, decadence, and vanity.

After the incisiveness, the glaring crudity of the action, the sinister quasi-comic, quasi-tragic quality of the prelude comes the opening chapter of *Sodome et Gomorrhe*, one of the most elaborate in the novel: the reception at the princesse de Guermantes' which Proust sees as dominated by the position of M. Charlus in society. There are so many characters, so many dramas—trivial and significant—that begin or continue during the soirée, so much falseness and wit are exhibited and so much humor at the expense of human feelings, that no theme, no character is given the stage for long. (p. 154)

Following the reception at the princesse de Guermantes', there is a brief preparatory passage for Marcel's return to Balbec (his second and last visit to the beach resort), and before the narrative in *Sodome et Gomorrhe* is devoted to a spring-summer visit in Balbec and the environs. The figure of Marcel becomes more important in the narrative. Now definitely the protagonist, he is extremely concerned with his fluctuating erotic thoughts. (p. 163)

Sodome et Gomorrhe, after the prelude with Charlus and Jupien and the reception chez la princesse de Guermantes, is Balbec, seen now not as the romantic setting for a youth's reverie, where Marcel was awed and even terrified by much that he saw, but seen as a kind of hell, a city of the plain. The revelation of Balbec as Sodom and Gomorrah is gradual.

However, in contrast to the preoccupation in the first part with inversion, Balbec is reintroduced by a remarkable prelude that has nothing to do with inversion. The prelude has a title: *Les Intermittences du Coeur.* This passage on "the intermittences of the heart" (a title Proust once thought of giving to the entire novel) contains an episode of involuntary memory which is as important for the second half of the novel, as the madeleine-tea episode is for the first half. It is one of Marcel's sobering and deeply felt experiences, and one not to be recaptured throughout the rest of *Sodome et Gomorrhe.* Its poignancy, despite its brevity, is strong enough to counteract the continual erotic preoccupations which occupy so much of this section of the novel. (pp. 163-64)

The intermittences of the heart, with which the novel henceforth is going to be increasingly concerned, are what controls the accumulation of our memories. Proust believes that this accumulation is at all times present within us, but not always accessible to our conscious mind. As he lives in the present, Marcel is going to testify over and over again to the disappearance of strong sentiments in him, to the cessation of loves that at one time dominated his existence. Even those individuals whom he loved dearly, such as his grandmother, are destined to die a second time. There is first the

physical death, and then there is the death in the conscious mind of the one who lives. But the experience of deep love or strong sentiment never dies in the subconscious memory of a man. Although it is, of course, possible that no sensation in the present will ever bring back the love that once existed.

In the prelude scene to the new Balbec, we reach a high level of meditation on Marcel's meaning of the word *real.* It is true that he is held only briefly by this overwhelming experience of recall, and soon plunges into the "unreal" world of Balbec society. But the long narrative rests on these rare intuitions of time and the reality of the objective world. We have just learned once again, with Marcel, that things are not what they are. They are what we make them, they are the record of our subjective memory and totally present within us, although removed from the dangerous contingencies of the present. In other words, time is a form that beings and objects take within us. It is not, therefore, solely the chronological force that destroys sentiments and beings and things. (pp. 165-66)

Wallace Fowlie, in his *A Reading of Proust,* Anchor Books, 1964, 307 p.

SOURCES FOR FURTHER STUDY

Auchincloss, Louis. "Proust's Picture of Society." *The Partisan Review* 27, No. 4 (1960): 690-701.

Discussion of Proust's characterizations of French aristocrats.

Girard, René, ed. *Proust: A Collection of Critical essays.* Englewood Cliffs, N.J.: Prentice-Hall, 1962, 182 p.

Includes essays by Henri Peyre, Jacques Riviere, Albert Thibaudet, Leo Spitzer, Charles Du Bos, and Georges Poulet. The critics cover various aspects of Proust's writing, including imagery, style, and the meaning of style in *Remembrance of Things Past.*

Kilmartin, Terence. *A Reader's Guide to "Remembrance of Things Past."* New York: Random House, 1983, 256 p.

Introduction to the plot, themes, and characters of the novel.

Linder, Gladys Dudley, ed. *Marcel Proust: Reviews and Estimates.* Stanford, Cal.: Stanford University Press, 1942, 314 p.

Essays and appreciations by prominent English critics and authors, including J. Middleton Murry, Clive Bell, Arnold Bennett, Edith Warton, Wyndham Lewis, and John Cowper Powys.

Strauss, Walter. *Proust and Literature: The Novelist as Critic.* Cambridge, Mass.: Harvard University Press, 1957, 263 p.

Comments on Proust's critical writings, asserting that his "great achievement as a literary critic lies in the fact that he attempted to elucidate the mystery, without dispelling it—because for him art, like religion, needs its mysteries."

Turnell, Martin. "Proust's Early Novel." *The Commenweal* 63, No. 13 (30 December 1955): 333-35.

Concludes that *Jean Santeuil* "does not possess the richness and complexity of *Remembrance of Things Past.*"

Alexander Pushkin

1799-1837

(Full name Alexander Sergeyevich Pushkin; Also trans-literated as Aleksandr, Alexandre, Aleksanndr; also Pushchkin, Púshkin, Pouchkin, Poushkin, Púskin, Pùshkin, Puškin) Russian poet, dramatist, short story writer, novelist, essayist, and critic.

INTRODUCTION

*P*ushkin is regarded as one of the most significant writers to influence Russian literature and culture. Emphasizing the simplicity and beauty of his native tongue, he transformed the Russian literary language and helped Russian literature to escape from the domination of eighteenth-century European classicism. Pushkin absorbed many of the structural and stylistic characteristics of European authors (notably François Voltaire, Lord Byron, Shakespeare, and Sir Walter Scott), recasting them in a uniquely Russian mold.

Pushkin was proud of his aristocratic ancestors, particularly his maternal great-grandfather, Abram Petrovich Hannibal, a Moorish noble who was kidnapped, taken to Russia, and made a ward of Peter the Great. As a child, Pushkin was closest to his grandmother and to his nurse, Arina, who told him fairy tales and folk legends which he later incorporated into his writings. At twelve he was sent to the government lycée at Tsarskoe Selo, where he read voraciously—especially French literature—and wrote prolifically. After graduation Pushkin obtained a sinecure in St. Petersburg. There he alternately engaged in periods of dissipation and intense writing and finished his first full-length piece, *Ruslan i Lyudmila* (*Ruslan and Lyudmila*), in 1820. This *poema*, or verse narrative, was based on folklore and stylistically influenced by Voltaire, Evariste Parny, and André Chenier, as was much of his early work. Just before its publication, Alexander I exiled Pushkin to southern Russia for his allegedly "revolutionary" verse. Censorship remained a lifelong problem for Pushkin; after Nicholas I appointed himself his personal censor, he was under strict observation, forbidden to travel freely or leave Russia. Pushkin despaired: "The devil prompted my being born in Russia with a soul and with talent."

Pushkin was productive during his four-year southern exile, however, writing, among other works, *Kavkazski plennik* (1822; *The Captive of the Caucasus*), *Bakhchisaraiski fontan* (1824; *The Bak-chesarian Fountain: A Tale of the Tauride*), and *Tsygany* (1827; *The Gipsies*). These are romantic *poemas* which reflect the influence of Byron, whom Pushkin read during this period. Byronism is evident, too, in *Yevgeny Onegin* (1833; *Eugene Onegin*), which Pushkin began in 1823 and completed in 1831. Critics agree that this "novel-in-verse" is Pushkin's masterpiece, representing, according to V. G. Belinsky, "an encyclopedia of Russian life." In addition to its pure, expressive language, which is the hallmark of Pushkin's style, the work features character types that appear frequently in later Russian fiction: the "superfluous man," represented by Onegin, and the idealized Russian woman, characterized by Tatiana.

Eugene Onegin inaugurated a new Russian genre, as did *Boris Godunov* (1831; *Boris Godunoff*), a historical drama which Pushkin hoped would break the influence of the French classical style that had long dominated Russian theater. Although *Boris Godunoff* was completed in 1825, censors prevented it from being published until 1831, and it was not performed until 1870. A further innovation in Russian theater is represented by Pushkin's "little tragedies," four one-act plays in blank verse which emphasize character development. *Pir vo vremya chumy* (1832; *A Feast in the City of the Plague*), for example, which was adapted from John Wilson's *The City of the Plague*, is considered one of the first Russian dramas of psychological realism. *Medny vsadnik* (1837; *The Bronze Horseman*), a later poem, was inspired partially by the poetry of Adam Mickiewicz, the Polish nationalist whom Pushkin met while in exile. In this work, Pushkin juxtaposes the omnipotence of Peter the Great with the helplessness of the character Eugene, who is symbolic of the masses sacrificed for the construction of St. Petersburg and the glory of imperial Russia.

Later in his career, Pushkin devoted himself to writing short stories and novellas. These reflect his belief that prose should be simple and unembellished. Ivan Belkin, the narrator and central character of a series of loosely related short stories titled *Povesti Belkina* (1831; *The Tales of Ivan Belkin*), was a prototype for the realistically depicted Russian character, and his matter-of-fact style of narration became a model for Russian fictional prose. The influence of Scott is obvious in Pushkin's fiction, particularly in *Kapitanskaya dochka* (1836; *The Captain's Daughter; or, The Generosity of the Russian Usurper Pugatscheff*), but his own pure style transcends imitation. Here, as in all of his writing, Pushkin exemplifies George Saintsbury's comment: "When a man of genius steals, he always makes the thefts his own."

Pushkin was killed in 1837 by a French officer in a duel over Nathalia Pushkin, the author's young wife. Mourned then as Russia's national poet, Pushkin remains in the minds of many critics the greatest and most influential of Russian authors. Yet Pushkin is rarely read in foreign countries. Critics attribute this to the fact that his superlative style is difficult to translate. Although foreign readers may not be directly acquainted with Pushkin's works, his influence is evident in the more widely-known books of Fedor Dostoevski, Leo Tolstoy, Ivan Turgenev, and Nikolai Gogol, each of whom acknowledged his debt to Pushkin. Pushkin has also influenced Russian music: both the operas *Boris Godunov* by Modest Mussorgsky and *Eugene Onegin* by Peter Illyich Tchaikovsky are based on his works. His impact on Russian culture is immense. Alexander Herzen said of him: "As soon as he appeared he became necessary; as though Russian literature could never again dispense with him. The other Russian poets are read and admired; Pushkin is in the hands of every civilized Russian, who reads him again and again all his life long."

(For further information about Pushkin's life and works, see *Nineteenth-Century Literature Criticism*, Vols. 3, 27.)

CRITICAL COMMENTARY

D. S. MIRSKY

(essay date 1926)

[Mirsky, a Russian prince, wrote widely on literary issues, both during his exile after the Bolshevik Revolution and after his return to the newly formed Soviet regime. Below, he surveys Pushkin's works, praising the drama *Eugene Onegin* and the four short plays known collectively as the "*Little Tragedies*."]

In the life-work of Pushkin *Evgeni Onegin* occupies a central place. . . . No other single poem of his contains such an abundance of beautiful poetry. This poetry is in his freest and most spontaneous manner. It is genial and hospitable, entirely devoid of what in much of his

Principal Works

Ruslan i Lyudmila (poetry) 1820

   [Ruslan and Lyudmila published in Tales and Legends
   of Old Russia, 1926]

Kavkazski plennik (poetry) 1822

   [The Captive of the Caucasus, 1890]

Bakhchisaraiski fontan (poetry) 1824

   [The Bak-chesarian Fountain: A Tale of the Tauride,
   1849]

Stansy (poetry) 1826

Bratya razboiniki (poetry) 1827

Graf Nulin (poetry) 1827

   [Count Nulin published in Three Comic Poems: Alexander Pushkin, 1974]

Tsygany (poetry) 1827

   [The Gipsies published in Translations from Pushkin in
   Memory of the Hundredth Anniversary of the Poet's
   Birthday, 1899]

Poltava (poetry) 1829

   [Poltava published in Russian Lyrics in English Verse,
   1887]

Boris Godunov [first publication] (drama) 1831

   [Boris Godunoff published in Translations from Pushkin
   in Memory of the Hundredth Anniversary of the Poet's
   Birthday, 1899]

*Motsart i Saleri [first publication] (drama) 1831

   [Mozart and Salieri published in Translations from Pushkin in Memory of the Hundredth Anniversary of the
   Poet's Birthday, 1899]

Povesti Belkina (short stories) 1831

   [The Tales of Ivan Belkin, 1954]

*Pir vo vremya chumy [first publication] (drama) 1832

   [A Feast in the City of the Plague, 1927; also published
   as A Feast during the Plague in Little Tragedies, 1965]

Yevgeny Onegin (novel) 1833

   [Eugene Onéguine, 1881; also published as Eugene
   Onegin, 1937]

Pikovaya dama (novella) 1834

[The Queen of Spades, 1850]

Skazi (fairy tales) 1834

Istoriya Pugacheva (history) 1835

Kapitanskaya dochka (novella) 1836

   [The Captain's Daughter; or, The Generosity of the Russian Usurper Pugatscheff, 1846]

Puteshestvie v Arzrum (travel essay) 1836

   [A Journey to Arzrum, 1974]

*Skupoi rytsar [first publication] (drama) 1836

   [The Avaricious Knight, 1933; also published as The
   Covetous Knight in The Poems, Prose and Plays of Alexander Pushkin, 1936]

Arap Petra Velikogo (unfinished novel) 1837

   [The Moor of Peter the Great published in Russian Romance, 1875; also published as The Negro of Peter the
   Great, 1924]

Istoriya sela Goryukhina (unfinished novel) 1837

   [History of the Village of Goryukhina published in The
   Queen of Spades and Other Stories, 1892]

Medny vsadnik (unfinished poetry) 1837

   [The Bronze Cavalier published in Translations from
   Pushkin in Honor of the Hundredth Anniversary of the
   Poet's Birthday, 1899; also published as The Bronze
   Horseman in Russian Poems, 1929]

*Kammeny gost [first publication] (drama) 1839

   [The Statue Guest published in Translations from Pushkin in Honor of the Hundredth Anniversary of the Poet's
   Birthday, 1899; also published as The Stone Guest in
   The Poems, Prose and Plays of Alexander Pushkin,
   1936]

Rusalka (unfinished drama) 1841

   [The Water Nymph, 192?]

Table Talk (essays) 1857

*These works are collectively referred to as "Little Trage-
dies."

---

later work seemed to his contemporaries, and may still seem to us, a defiant *odi profanum vulgus,* a jealous wall erected against the reader's ecstasies. Even more than his lyrics *Evgeni Onegin* produces the impression of admitting the reader into the poet's innermost intimacy. (p. 137)

[In *Onegin*] the apparent freedom and expansiveness of the style is kept in control by the unapparent but ubiquitous forces of discipline. The two great elements of Poetry—the fertility of the creative impulse and the steadiness of critical inhibition—were united in Pushkin in a perfect harmony, and this harmony is perhaps nowhere more happily balanced than in *Evgeni Onegin.* (p. 138)

The novel is written in octosyllabics, in a peculiar 14-line stanza, the rhyming pattern of which is a b a b c c d d e f f e h h, a, c and e being double and b, d, f and h single rhymes. The Letters of Tatiana to Onegin in the third and of Onegin to Tatiana in the eighth chapter are in unstanzaed octosyllabics. The third chapter contains a short story (eighteen lines) in a folklore measure. A few of the stanzas are incomplete. (p. 140)

Evgeni Onegin, then, is a "novel in verse." It proceeds from *Don Juan* avowedly and candidly. The idea of writing a loosely constructed tale of modern life in stanzaed verse, in a mixed style of grave and gay, and admitting sentimental or humorous digressions ad libitum, with a free use made of Sternian ways of toying with the plot and playing with the narrative illusion, was suggested to Pushkin by Byron. The direct influence of Sterne (of whom Pushkin was a great admirer) is also indubitable. But the differences between Pushkin's novel and its models is far greater than the resemblance, and, when all is said and done, *Evgeni Onegin* is the most original of all Pushkin's writings (except *The Bronze Horseman*). The principal differences between *Onegin* and *Don Juan* are three: firstly, it is not satirical; secondly, it is the picture of contemporary Russian life in the exact frames of a given time and place, free from all semi-romantic Sevilles and Harems; thirdly, it is a complete whole with a beginning, a middle, and an end, and the ultimate impression produced by it is not conditioned by the cumulative effect of the individual parts, but by the thread of plot that holds them together. (pp. 140-41).

Evgeni Onegin is like a living growth: the same throughout, and yet different. We recognize in the eighth chapter the style of the first as we recognize a familiar face, changed by age. The difference is great and yet the essential proportions are the same. It is a face of unique beauty.

The genealogy of Pushkin's manner in *Evgeni Onegin* is complicated and includes many foreign ancestors. The initial French groundwork is always recognizable. It is thoroughly Russian, so Russian as even to be incapable of reproduction in any other tongue. But it is the Russian of an age that spoke French as well as and oftener than Russian. Pushkin never disclaimed this French flavour of his Russian. He alludes to it often, humorously and affectionately. He does not omit to mention, before quoting it, that Tatiana's letter to Onegin was written in French, and that his translation of the "original" is only "the pale copy of a living picture" or Weber's *Freischütz* "played by the fingers of timid schoolgirls." It is amusing to retranslate it: it can easily be done word for word. (p. 147)

But the triumph, the pure quintessence of the style, is in the first chapter. Here it reaches its greatest freedom and expansive force. It bubbles and plays like a fountain in the sun. Its sparkling lightness has been compared to a newly uncorked champagne bottle, and its exhilarating effect can be likened to nothing but champagne. The lyrical digressions especially, so spontaneous, so effortless, so divinely light, give that effect of creation out of the void which is not elsewhere to be found in Pushkin. The flawless perfection of the craftsmanship is all the more striking as it is quite concealed and can produce nothing but the effect of absolutely spontaneous improvisation on the lay reader. The

youthful exuberance of this first unfettered flight is somewhat sobered down in the later chapters. But the essential lightness and spontaneity of the style remains. The story is told spaciously and freely. It moves in an atmosphere of pure yet earthly and unromantic poetry, where humour and feeling form a blend of exquisite mellowness. The scene is laid with detailed and perfect realism, which is only sublimated by the light touch of the poetic wand. There are scenes almost verging on broad comedy; as the picture of the provincial ball at the Larins'; but humorously transfused sentiment is the main tone of the central chapters (from the second to the sixth). The note of tragedy is first sounded in the sixth chapter when Onegin, instead of showing himself a "man of honour and understanding," proves to be a "playball of prejudice," and with incredible but inevitable levity accepts Lensky's challenge. In the closing scene of the chapter—the death of Lensky—the style rises to the intense pathos and high moral earnestness of tragedy, but never for a moment does this make the lightness and transparency of the poetical atmosphere heavier or dimmer. In the eighth chapter the style is still the same, but the note of tragedy and of retaliation grows. It extends even over the sad smile of the closing stanzas. There is no emphasis, no underlining; understatement is always the trusty instrument of Pushkin. And yet the sentiment of the inevitable, of the operation of Karma, of Paradise missed, makes this last chapter of the boisterously begun poem one of the most tragically coloured of all his works. It is a discreet and homely sort of tragedy, a tragedy in the minor key. The eighth chapter of *Onegin* left a profound impress on the subsequent destinies of Russian literature. Of all Pushkin's situations the parting of Onegin and Tatiana is the one that bore the most abundant posthumous fruit. It is the egg out of which Turgenev hatched all his endings, and its progeny can be traced through the whole of Russian narrative literature of the nineteenth century, from its first born, the great novel of Lermontov, to its distant collateral descendants, the tales of Chekhov.

Altogether the influence of *Evgeni Onegin* on Russian literature was greater than that of all the rest of Pushkin's works put together. It is the real ancestor of the main line of Russian fiction. For it was as a novel not as a poem that it was most fruitful. Its poetic manner was often imitated, without fruitful originality if not without success. But the setting, the "argument," and the characters of *Evgeni Onegin* are as authentic a "source" as can be discovered in the History of Literature. Pushkin's picture of Russian provincial life laid its impress on all the main line of Russian novelists from Lermontov to Chekhov. The characters of Onegin and Tatiana were the direct ancestors, the authentic Adam and Eve of the Mankind that inhabits Russian fiction. And the muffled, unhappy ending, as I have already said, became the standard ending of all Russian novels.

Turgenev in particular is saturated with the fable, though not with the manner, of Pushkin's great novel in verse. (pp. 148-50)

The characters of *Evgeni Onegin* are the least classical productions of Pushkin's workshop. They are very largely achieved by "suggestion" and "atmosphere." They are essentially lyrical. They are irreducibly individual, but this individuality of theirs is not achieved by the objective methods of Tolstoy, Dostoyevsky, or Proust, not by the actions or words that are ascribed to them, but by what the poet himself says of them and by the way he says it. Their unity is one of atmosphere, and in this respect it is again Turgenev who is the truest disciple of Pushkin (or rather of the author of *Onegin*). It is essentially irrelevant to look for psychological consistency in the personalities of Onegin or of Tatiana, for their portraits are not achieved by objective psychological methods. Contemporary criticism, for instance, not without good grounds noticed an inconsistency between the Tatiana of the eighth and of the previous chapters. We do not, as a rule, remark this, however familiar we may be with the poem, and even the more familiar we are the less we see the inconsistency. Our Tatiana is the rural Tatiana of the early chapters plus the married Tatiana, and we see each half-Tatiana in terms of the whole Tatiana. Still, psychologically and logically speaking, the gulf between the two is very real, and it is bridged by no psychological bridgework, only by a poet's arbitrary *sic iubeo*. We have obeyed the poet, but we have done so because we have been fascinated by his lyrical power, not because we have weighed the objective evidence as we have been allowed to do in the case of a very similar transformation, that of Tolstoy's Natasha. In this sense *Evgeni Onegin* is evidently lyrical and subjective and to return to what we began with, it is the ripest and fullest expression of Pushkin's early, lyrical, and subjective manner. This manner, by the time the Novel was being finished, had long given way, in all his other works, to a new manner, impersonal and objective, which had already brought and was yet to bring to light, other and very different sides of his multiform genius. (pp. 150-52)

The first expression on a larger scale of Pushkin's turn towards objectivity and self-restriction is the tragedy of *Boris Godunov*. . . . *Boris Godunov* is a premeditated and experimental work, written not so much for the subject as for the literary form. (p. 153)

During his first year at Mikhaylovskoye Pushkin, we know from his letters, gave much of his time to the reading of history, in particular of Karamzin, and of Shakespeare. *Boris Godunov* is the result of these readings. The subject is taken from the *History* of Karamzin and the treatment from the histories of Shakespeare. "I tried to imitate Shakespeare in his broad painting of character," said Pushkin, but he imitated him in more than that: in the choice of blank verse, in the occasional

introduction of prose dialogue, in the mixture of grave and gay, in the decided contempt for at least two of the unities: the scene changes very often (twenty-five times during the whole play) and the time stretches out over a space of seven years, from 1598 to 1605. Only the unity of action is fully preserved. (p. 156)

[*Boris Godunov* is] a drama of expiation, and the thread of "crime and punishment" is kept up from beginning to end of the play. The idea of Boris's guilt is taken bodily from Karamzin, and the treatment of it, as in Karamzin, is mainly melodramatic and rhetorical. The idea of tragic poetic justice was a main idea of Pushkin's, and no one more than he felt those secret forces that move the moral universe. But in his really original and free-born works the idea is treated differently, more tragically, more impersonally, and less sentimentally. In the *Gypsies,* in *Onegin,* in *Mozart and Salieri,* it is just touched on in a climax of infinite pregnancy. In the *Stone Guest* it is treated with a rapid concision and terseness which leave no place for sentimental moralizing. In *Boris Godunov* it is not free-born, it is imposed by a preconceived idea of foreign origin (Karamzin), and this sentimental treatment of the tragic situation is the original sin of the play.

It must be confessed that, apart from this original sin, we are in a singularly bad position to be as enthusiastic about *Boris Godunov* as its first hearers were. The play loses if compared with Shakespeare, it loses if compared with Pushkin's own little tragedies of 1830, it loses (it must be confessed) when compared with the great musical drama Musorgsky built up with its partial help. It is on the other hand too closely connected with its posthumous progeny, the numerous historical dramas written since 1860. The consistent mediocrity of these plays casts a disagreeable reflection on their common ancestor. Another point which is more evident now than it was in 1826 is that the great poet of Petrine Russia (for all his genealogical sympathies) could not assimilate the spirit of Old Muscovy. This is especially apparent in the conventional diction of the metrical dialogue; and all the more apparent since in his later (European) dramas he succeeded in creating a style of dramatic diction infinitely superior and more vigorous, and also because it was precisely this conventional and inadequate diction that the later dramatists perpetuated when they did not debase it. The metre is also inadequate, monotonous and stiff, and again the comparison with the Little Tragedies is not to the advantage of the earlier play—a slight change of the metrical pattern (absence of compulsory caesura after the second foot) made the stiff and lifeless verse of *Godunov* one of the richest and most pregnant metres of the Russian language. It is like the change from *Gorboduc* to *Anthony and Cleopatra*. (pp. 158-59)

But though we cannot share the enthusiasm of the first hearers of *Boris Godunov*, . . . it is still a work by Pushkin and abounds in merits of the highest order. The construction, though not strictly dramatic, is masterly, and gives signal proof of that artistic economy which was gradually becoming his most outstanding characteristic: there is not a scene too much. . . . If the tone of the metrical dialogue and the poet's view of the high classes of Muscovite society do to a certain extent jar on our excessively developed sense of historical colour—for after all it was through the sentimentally magnificent rhetoric of Karamzin that Pushkin saw old Muscovy—the popular scenes still retain their original charm, and the prose dialogue, always verging on the comic, is wonderful without reserve. The mass-scenes are admirably managed, and it is no wonder that Musorgsky chose the play for the material of his "popular drama" (though the last scene of his opera—the lynching of Khrushchov—is an addition of his own). The comic parts are on the whole best, and the scene in the tavern near the Lithuanian frontier with the two vagabond monks (the broadest and the best of Pushkin's hints to Musorgsky) is a glorious masterpiece. The scene between the Patriarch and the Abbot who comes to report to him the escape of an obscure novice, who is to become the Impostor, is marked by a fine, incisive, Swiftean irony. The scene where the news of the appearance of a Pseudo-Demetrius is broken to the criminal Tsar Boris is remarkable for an irony of a sterner and grimmer kind, and the scene at the fountain between the Impostor and his Polish fiancée, Marina Mniszek, is an excellent piece of dramatized emotional reasoning. Finally the climax of the play, the death of Boris, with its paradoxical and transient katharsis, followed in the next scene by the tragic end of his innocent family, is a conception of rare and audacious originality, dictated though it may have been by historical tradition. The closing scene of the massacre (behind the scenes—no blood flows on the stage; here at least Racine had the better of Shakespeare) of the boy Tsar Theodore and of his mother moves the reader (perhaps for the only time in the play) to "pity and terror." (pp. 160-61)

[What] Pushkin did not achieve in *Boris Godunov*, he achieved in the four miniature plays written in Boldino in the autumn of 1830, *The Covetous Knight, Mozart and Salieri, The Stone Guest*, and *The Feast during the Plague*. They are known as the Little Tragedies, a name given to them by Pushkin himself. . . . The form of the miniature drama seems to have been suggested to Pushkin by the "diminutive dramas" of Barry Cornwall, an author for whom, like Pushkin, so many of his contemporaries had an admiration that we have not inherited. But unlike *Boris Godunov*, the Little Tragedies are not primarily experiments in form. They are "dramatic investigations" of character and situation. They were not intended to revolutionize the Russian stage, but just to embody certain dramatic situations that had occurred to their author. They belong to a more intimate and "esoteric" category than the earlier tragedy. Only two of them (*Mozart and Salieri* and *The Feast during the Plague*) were published immediately after their completion. *The Covetous Knight* appeared (anonymously) in 1836; *The Stone Guest* only after the poet's death.

The Tragedies are associated with English influences. The hint came from Barry Cornwall; *The Covetous Knight* bears the subheading "from Chenstone's tragi-comedy *The Cavetous* (sic) *Knight* " . . . ; *The Feast during the Plague* is a (fairly exact) translation of a scene from John Wilson's *The City of the Plague,* to which are only added two original songs. The metre of the Tragedies is blank verse of a kind much more akin to the English dramatic variety as represented in Shakespeare's later plays, and entirely free from the stiffness and monotony of the same metre as used in *Boris Godunov*. (pp. 162-63)

[The longest of the *Little Tragedies*] is *The Stone Guest,* a variation on the eternal theme of Don Juan. Pushkin probably did not know Tirso de Molina's play, and his only "sources" were Molière and the libretto of Mozart's *Don Giovanni. The Stone Guest* has more than once been proclaimed Pushkin's masterpiece, and it is certainly one of the serious candidates for that title. It is admirable and perfect from what ever standpoint it be viewed. The style and the diction solve the seemingly insoluble problem of writing realistic and humorous Russian dialogue representative of foreign speech. It is the only Russian work of imaginative literature where the realistic dialogue of foreign rogues and adventurers has not the intolerable taste of translated vulgarity. This problem, I believe, is peculiar to the Russian language, but it is none the less real. It has never been solved since Pushkin. The construction of the play is a marvel of nicety, economy, and inevitable logic. The situation is borrowed, but it is treated with a sureness of touch and a skill that do not belong to the originals. It is constructed with the precision of a mathematical formula, and the combination of this mathematical terseness with the live and vibrating flexibility of the dialogue produces a unique effect. It is also one of the most impressive and ultimate expressions of Pushkin's fundamental idea of inherent Nemesis. The romantic conceit of the original legend becomes in Pushkin's hands the inevitable working of a moral law. (pp. 163-64)

[*Mozart and Salieri*] is founded on a tradition which charges the composer Salieri with having poisoned Mozart out of envy. Another anecdote reports that at the first night of *Don Giovanni* Salieri, alone in the audience, hissed and walked out of the theatre. Pushkin remarked of these two traditions that the man who was capable of hissing *Don Giovanni* was fully capable of poisoning the author. The play originally bore the name of *Envy*. But Pushkin does not make Salieri a vulgar envier. He has devoted all his life to the service of music and achieved much, but now Mozart has come who, without trouble, without labour, merely by the unjust gift of the gods, has created music that casts into the outer darkness all Salieri's achievement. . . . The play is largely a monologue and once again the exposition is so packed and condensed that it is impossible to give a résumé of it. For passionate reasoning Pushkin never surpassed the monologues of Salieri, and the tragedy, like *The Guest*, has claims to be considered his masterpiece. (pp. 165-66)

The Covetous Knight is less severely constructed: it consists of three almost loosely connected scenes. In the first and the third, where the principal person is the Covetous Baron's thriftless son, the dialogue rivals that of *The Stone Guest*. . . . It is the most *magnificent*, the most poetically saturated, the most "Elizabethan" creation of Pushkin, and this magnificence and this saturation are arrived at without his for a moment departing from the fundamental characteristics of his style—the absence of metaphor and imagery. They are arrived at by the mere concrete, emotional, and logical value of the words, by the pregnant flexibility of the blank verse, and by the perfect distribution of the vowels and consonants. (pp. 166-67)

The Feast during the Plague is on the face of it the least original of the Little Tragedies. It is merely a translation of a scene from Wilson's play. It is the custom with Russian critics to expand on the infinite superiority of the translation to the original. This is nonsense. Wilson's play and the special scene are by no means contemptible. Pushkin's translation is almost word for word; the conscious alterations are very few; there are, on the other hand, several obvious misunderstandings of the English text. And still *The Feast during the Plague* is one of the great masterpieces of Pushkin and takes an infinitely greater place in Russian Literature than that held by Wilson's play in English Literature. There is of course the terrible handicap of perfection in verse and diction. At the time he wrote *The Feast* Pushkin was simply incapable of writing a line without imparting to it the absolute perfection he had attained. Then there is the choice of the scene, where to begin and where to end it. But even this would not make *The Feast* a great masterpiece were it not for the two songs, which, though vaguely suggested by *The City of the Plague*, are in substance quite original. They give to the Little Tragedy that magical touch which lifts it above mere efficient craftsmanship. The first of them has an English (or rather Lowland Scottish setting) and English names (Jenny and Edmund). It is the song of a girl awaiting death from the plague and imploring her lover not to approach her body when she dies, and to pay her grave a visit when the pestilence is over. It is one of Pushkin's sweetest and most piercing lyrics. . . . The

other song is very different. It is a *Hymn in Honour of the Plague*, a grim and haunting poem, one of the most highly strung in the whole of Pushkin's poetry. It was particularly popular and frequently quoted in the days . . . when Symbolism, the cult of the Dark and Nietzschean individualism, were the order of the day. (pp. 167-69)

One is apt to abuse the adjective "unique" in speaking of Pushkin, but *Rusalka* [Pushkin's unfinished drama] is unique in a stricter sense than any other of Pushkin's works. Of course, it has "sources," the principal of which is *Das Donauweibchen,* a Viennese romantic *opéra-comique.* But its uniqueness is not so much in its originality (which however is perhaps greater than that of any other poem of Pushkin's) as in its inimitability. In it is created a world which did not survive, a world of Russian Romance which, however incompatible these two words may seem, is both unmistakably Russian and undoubtedly Romantic. It is at the same time distinctly Realistic and, in so far as we can judge of the potential whole from the torso we have, it would have been as genuine a tragedy as Pushkin ever attempted. (pp. 169-70)

In *Rusalka* Pushkin certainly reaches one of his highest summits, for, whatever he may have made of the continuation, the existing part is saturated with a poetry where Romance, tragic truth, and Russian raciness appear in a blend of infinitely complex *bouquet* and which opens infinitely receding vistas of suggestiveness. The blank verse is, if possible, of an even higher quality than in the other tragedies. It is all transfused with a mellow maturity and softness, without the slightest trace of debility or laxity. But such descriptive terms convey no impression to the reader. And one can only feel a tantalizing pity for those who are prevented from tasting of it. . . .

After the comic scenes in *Boris Godunov* Pushkin never returned to prose comedy. But there exists a little sketch, *The Almanach-Monger* which shows that he might have achieved great things in this direction. *The Almanach-Monger* is an incisive and unkind skit of a type of Grub Street parasite that was one of the pests of the time. (p. 171)

[As a prose writer Pushkin is, to a certain extent,] the pupil of Karamzin; he inherited most of his vocabulary and his mannerism of ending sentences with an adjective—an obvious Gallicism. He has a great concern for the good balance of a sentence, but he is careful to make its rhythm always strictly prosaic. His prose is curiously free from rhetorical cadence. His real masters were the French. In that which has always been regarded by them as the crowning virtue of prose, a neat exactness of expression, Pushkin's prose has never been equalled by any subsequent Russian writer. But Pushkin's literary prose (as distinct from that of his letters) has not that appearance of ease and freedom which his verse has in *Onegin* and in the dialogue of the *Little Tragedies.* It is obviously canalized. It produces the effect of being premeditated, of following an external rule, in short, of being what in our modern literary jargon we call "stylized," that is, drawn to a foreign pattern. In reading Pushkin's prose one always feels its form, one is always conscious of "the resistance of the material" and though the spectacle, at which one unintermittently assists, of the material being victoriously applied to the writer's purpose, is one of the highest artistic enjoyments obtainable, the higher level is never reached (as it always is in Pushkin's verse) where all awareness of effort and resistance disappears and perfection seems to be the result of a natural, unpremeditated growth. (p. 174)

Recent students of Pushkin's prose have discovered in it unmistakable traces of his familiarity with verse. It appears to be articulated into short cola approximately of the length of an octosyllabic line. But these cola, though due to the constant practice of that line, are organized along lines not only entirely different, but studiously obliterative of every trace of their metrical origin. Pushkin was very careful to avoid all similarity between the movement of prose and verse, and in his work the two are as distinct as were Latin verse and Latin (pre-Livian) prose. In this respect Pushkin went counter to the general tendencies of his, and of the following age which found expression in the rhythmical and ornamental prose of Bestuzhev, Weltmann, Odoevsky, and above all of Gogol. To contemporaries his prose seemed reactionary, as it was in certain respects (persistent structural Gallicisms and certain details of vocabulary). But the practice of later Russian prose is allied to Pushkin, through the intermediary of Lermontov and not to Gogol. Pushkin's mannerisms and idiosyncrasies were not inherited by his successors but the general will to keep prose as far as possible from poetry dominates all the second half of the nineteenth century. (p. 175)

[*The Nigger of Peter the Great*] owes its existence to Pushkin's desire to write a historical novel, and its subject to the romantic interest he took in the person of his black great-grandfather. However, he was imperfectly acquainted with the details of "Hannibal's" life and the novel is not founded on facts. The first chapter which deals with the Nigger's life in Paris, his success in French society, and his love affair with a French Countess, is admirable and displays almost all the best qualities of Pushkin's prose. The story of the Countess's giving birth to a black child on the eve of Hannibal's departure for Russia and of the way it was replaced by a white one in order not to disturb the unsuspecting Count is particularly good. It is reminiscent of the French novelists of the eighteenth century rather than of Scott. But the following chapters are overencumbered with historical colour and all the antiquar-

ianism dear to the heart of Sir Walter. There is good reason to believe that it was precisely this that caused Pushkin to leave off in the beginning, for in his later work he never revived the manner.

Tales by Belkin are five short and rapidly told stories—*The Shot, The Snowstorm, The Stationmaster, The Undertaker* and *The Peasant Gentlewoman.* They are ascribed by the author to one Ivan Petrovich Belkin. . . . This mask was necessary to Pushkin for two reasons. The *Tales* were an experimental work; he was not quite sure of its good reception by the public, and wanted an *alias.* On the other hand the simplicity and naïvety of their alleged narrator was a justification of the self-effacement and studied naïvety of their real author, which Pushkin thought essential to the good story-teller. (pp. 177-78)

Pushkin attached a great importance to the *Tales.* . . . They were meant as "exemplary novels," as models for the future story-teller of the right way to tell a story. They are absolutely barren of all ornament. Their style is studiously simple. They contain no psychology, no reflections, no irrelevant descriptions, and very little conversation. They are all action—real stories. At the same time they are free from the nervous concentration of *The Queen of Spades.* The narrative is leisurely and moves on without haste, without omission. . . . [Pushkin] had deliberately eliminated from [the stories] every element of interest except that of sheer narrative. The subjects were mere anecdotes, sometimes disturbingly naïve and openly puerile. Their conscious triviality embarrassed the critics of the Thirties who had not yet freed themselves from the grand style of French Classicism and were already infected by the pretensions of German Idealism. They continued to embarrass the critics through the nineteenth century, and only by degrees (partly owing to a growing spirit of idolatry) did they come to be acknowledged as masterpieces. This they certainly are, and not because of the deep hidden meanings which imaginative criticism has of late discovered in them, but because they show a perfect adaptation of means to end and a highly developed art of narrative. As perfect narrative constructions they are unsurpassed (except by Pushkin himself and by Leskov) in the whole range of Russian literature. They are anecdotes. (pp. 178-79)

The *Tales* were evidently written originally without any idea of Belkin, who came as an afterthought. But when he came, Pushkin was not satisfied with the silhouette of him given in the preface, and Ivan Petrovich soon expanded into a living and pathetically humourous figure. This happened in the *History of the Manor of Goryukhino.* . . . [Belkin decides] to write a history of his estate the Manor of Goryukhino. The preface (together with the earlier preface) presents Ivan Petrovich Belkin as one of the most delightfully humourous figures in Russian literature. His portrait by

Pushkin is perhaps the first in date to display that blend of fun and sympathy which is characteristic of modern humour. The *History* itself is at once a parody of the *Russian History* of Polevoy (Pushkin's journalistic enemy and in history an unintelligent, self-confident, and ignorant imitator of Niebuhr), and a keen and concentrated Swiftian satire on the social system based on serfdom. (pp. 179-80)

[Pushkin left] numerous fragments and unfinished stories in various stages of completion, from *A Russian Pelham,* of which only the plan and a few opening lines survive, to *Dubrovsky,* consisting of eighteen complete chapters and a detailed summary of what was to follow. This last story which occupied Pushkin in the winter of 1832-1833 is closely allied in manner to *Tales by Belkin.* It is melodramatic in subject and exceedingly simple in style. . . . The story is perfectly thrilling and, were it not for its unfinished state, it would be the best story of incident in the language. But unlike *Tales by Belkin* it has more besides. It has a very definite social background and gives a forcible and ruthless picture of Russian rural conditions under Catherine II. The two great noblemen, Troekurov and Vereysky, both bullies, but the one an uncouth country lord, the other covered with a Parisian veneer, are evocative of the medieval environment. They are both, and especially Troekurov, powerful creations of character and important figures in Pushkin's portrait gallery. The hero Dubrovsky is of course conventional; he is the noble brigand of romantic tradition. There is in him a noble and bracing "theatricality", often found in French and English novelists and absent from later Russian literature. But that Pushkin was capable of grimmer effects is proved by the terrible and ruthless scene of the burning of Dubrovsky's house with the drunken law-officers in it, which might have been conceived by a contemporary novelist writing of the Civil War.

The remaining fragments are of very varied nature. *A Russian Pelham* was planned as a vast biographical and social novel. *Roslavlev,* the story of an heroic girl during Napoleon's invasion, and the beginning of a novel in letters, were to be novels *à thèse* abounding in discussions on social, political, and moral subjects. The novel in letters especially stands halfway between Pushkin's imaginative and journalistic prose.

The most interesting *membra disjecta* of Pushkin's prose are those which he intended to form the framework of the epic fragment on *Cleopatra,* originally written in 1825. The picturesquely horrible theme of that poem needed a pretext to be introduced into a novel, and Pushkin attempted numerous ways of doing so. One of his plans was to introduce it into a story of Roman life. He began what is perhaps the piece of prose that is most frequently known by heart to his admirers. It begins "Caesar was travelling", and shows

him in his most "Latin" and Caesar-like aspect. Finally Pushkin adopted the device of introducing the poem as the performance of a wandering Italian improvisatore given at an artistic house in St Petersburg. These three chapters (entitled *The Egyptian Nights*) are very remarkable, particularly for the figure of Charsky, the aristocrat-poet, who is ashamed of his genius because it makes him a ridiculous figure in society. It is a striking study of the psychology of the Snob, or to use a less offensive and more contemporary word, of the Dandy. It would have pleased Stendhal. There is good ground to believe, as is currently assumed, that Charsky is a projection of Pushkin himself, though emphasized and accentuated for purposes of "psychic cure."

The only stories completed by Pushkin after *Tales by Belkin* were *Kirjali, The Queen of Spades,* and *The Captain's Daughter.* They are unequal in length and importance. *Kirjali* is merely a well-told anecdote of the life of a famous Moldavian brigand—a reminiscence of Bessarabian days. *The Queen of Spades* and *The Captain's Daughter* are, together, Pushkin's most important achievement in prose. They are mutually complementary and representative of two opposed tendencies in his developed prose manner. The former is a short story, pointing towards E. T. A. Hoffmann and Edgar Allan Poe—the latter an almost Waverley novel of broad narrative painting. Both display that compact terseness which is the essence of Pushkin's prose, but they display it in very different ways. *The Queen of Spades* is nervously compact like a compressed spring. *The Captain's Daughter* in an ever greater degree than *Tales by Belkin* progresses in a calm and homely manner, leisurely epical even when it dwells on the horrors of the great Jacquerie that is its historical setting. (pp. 181-83)

The *Queen of Spades* is beyond doubt Pushkin's masterpiece in prose. Its cold and concentrated glamour has exercised a most powerful effect on romantic readers, among others on Dostoyevsky. But it is essentially a glorified anecdote, or *novella,* and the "glamour" is everywhere tempered by a no less cold and essentially "classical" irony.

The Queen of Spades contains a little over 10,000 words; *The Captain's Daughter* about 45,000, and there is more elbowroom in it and less tension. . . . It is avowedly due to the influence of Scott, and the last chapter has a rather close parallel in the Kew Gardens scene of [Lodovico Ariosto's] *The Heart of Midlothian.* But the story is far more concise and compact than any one of the Northern Ariosto's. It is quite free from all antiquarianism, description, and bric-a-brac. Pushkin's customary virtues of under-statement and economy of means are displayed fully. The story is told in the first person, and its tone in many cases is reminiscent rather of Fielding or the Abbé Prevost than of Scott, whose influence amounts to the manner of treating the past as if it were the present and to a scrupulous regard for historical truth. The story is neatly constructed but without too great an elaboration of plot, and combines the elements of a novel of adventure and of a family novel. As in *Dubrovsky* and unlike *Tales by Belkin* the interest is divided between the narrative development, the painting of manners, and the drawing of character. Captain Mironov himself and his wife are masterpieces of the very highest order. Comical and seemingly trivial, though honest and kind-hearted in time of peace, the Mironovs rise to a noble courage in the face of emergency and meet death at the hands of the rebels with calm and simple heroism. This unpretending heroism was a new and novel departure in portrait painting and, together with the figure of Belkin, those of the Mironovs are among the most decisive fountainheads of subsequent Russian realism. Another very notable character is the hero's servant, Savelyich, at once servile and despotic with his master and heroic when emergency claims him. The rebel leader, Pugachev, is surrounded with a romantic glamour in the true tradition of the Russian robber folk-songs, and in spite of his lack of historical truth he is one of the most popular and national of Pushkin's creations.

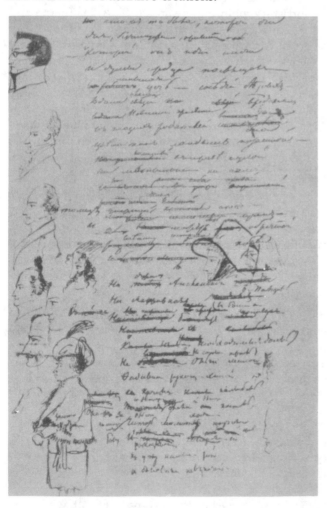

Manuscript page of the novel *Eugene Onegin.*

The Captain's Daughter was not, like *Boris Godunov* and *Tales by Belkin,* a premeditated experiment in form. It was almost the chance by-product of the historical studies the author had entered on since 1832. The direct product of these stories, of which the novel was an offshoot, was Pushkin's only completed, historical work *The History of the Pugachev Rebellion.* . . . *The History* is, all said and done, a masterpiece and, though modern historians have tried to discredit it as insufficiently attentive to social conditions, such disparagement only proves a lack of historical perspective in these historians. All Pushkin's training and literary past conditioned his exposition of history as the history of individuals and individual actions. But he by no means loses sight of the social background and social mainsprings of the Rebellion, though his classicism prevented him from presenting it in the generalized and abstract terms of "mass movement" and "class struggle". If *The History* has a fault, it is a fault of information: owing to the lack of material Pushkin did not give the right proportions to the various individual movements constituting the rebellion and concentrated too much on the army of Pugachev himself, at the expense of the numerous armies that operated under less conspicuous leaders. But he does not idealize Pugachev in *The History* as he does in the novel, and he clearly sees him as the plaything of his environment. But whatever it may be as history, as literature *The History of the Pugachev Rebellion* is a masterpiece. . . . In this respect Pushkin approaches Voltaire, though his outlook is far wider and more "modern" than Voltaire's.

The other historical *opus magnum* of Pushkin, *The History of Peter the Great,* remained practically uncommenced. The notes intended for it often reveal to us the depth of Pushkin's historical insight, but they do not allow us to guess what form it would have taken had it been written.

Closely allied to *The History of Pugachev* is Pushkin's only work of travel, *A Voyage to Arzrum.* . . . It shows his prose style at its tersest and nudest, and considered in this light is one of his most characteristic productions. But apart from these formal works, Pushkin has left us another very different kind of historical writing. These are the anecdotes collected by him under the title of *Table Talk* (the title is in English). . . . [Pushkin] was a true child of the eighteenth century in his love of pointed stories and of every kind of anecdote. The most interesting series of these are those told him by Mlle Zagryazhsky, a grand aunt of his wife's, who was the daughter of Elizabeth's favorite Razumovsky and was young in 1760. These stories are particularly admirable for the way in which the speech and very accent of the old lady are reproduced—a considerably less "literary" and schoolmastered language than Pushkin's formal prose—and with close affinities to his letters.

Pushkin's letters, quite apart from their importance for the biographer, are as admirable as literature and as worth reading as anything he wrote. (pp. 186-89)

D. S. Mirsky, in his *Pushkin,* G. Routledge & Sons, Ltd., 1926, 266 p.

EDMUND WILSON

(essay date 1943)

[Wilson wrote widely on cultural, historical, and literary matters. In the excerpt below from a 1943 essay, he offers an appreciation of Pushkin's career and works.]

[The] great fountainhead of Russian literature is Pushkin. From him [Turgenev, Chekhov, Tolstoy, and Dostoevsky] in more or less degree derive. . . .

The Russians are in the habit of comparing Pushkin with Mozart, and this is perhaps the nearest one can come to a simple comparison. Pushkin does, through both his career and his qualities, somewhat recall Mozart: he is able to express through an art that is felicitous and formal a feeling that is passionate and exquisite; he has a wide range of moods and emotions, yet he handles them all with precision; and . . . he achieved in the poetry of his time a similar preëminence to Mozart's in music. (p. 16)

The poets that overlapped the [eighteenth and nineteenth centuries] or were born in the early eighteen hundreds, who lived in the stimulating disturbing time between the old world and the new, tend, in the very disorder of their lives, to repeat the same evolution. They are precocious, they soon make themselves masters of their art; they do personal and original work, and they are likely to try their hands at several genres: they die before their time, of disease or dissipation or the results of reckless living. . . . Byron, Keats, Shelley, Heine, Poe, Musset—here the earliest date (Byron's birth) is 1788 and the latest (Musset's death) 1857, with all these writers except the tough Heine dying in their twenties or thirties or forties (as Mozart died at thirty-five). (pp. 16-17)

Now, though Goethe is of course the figure who dominates the perilous swing out of the past into the modern world, Pushkin . . . is the great figure of this short-lived group. Unlikely though it may seem, he had something in common with every one of the writers named above. He is the universal poet of that moment. Pushkin's cultural roots and branches reach out about him in every direction; he studied Latin and Greek, and he made a beginning with Hebrew; he digested the age

of Voltaire and derived from it all that he needed; he tried his hand at translating Wordsworth, exploited Barry Cornwall by borrowing the form of the Englishman's *Dramatic Scenes,* and he achieved a perspective on Byron which few of the European romantics had, by a careful reading of Shakespeare, from whom he learned what he required for his chronicle play, **Boris Godunov,** he established with the Polish poet Mickiewicz one of those intimate literary relationships, half-competitive, half-coöperative, that are likely to be so profitable to both parties, and he exchanged, for Prosper Mérimée's pioneer work in learning Russian and translating him and Gogol into French, translations which improved the originals, of Mérimée's forged Slavic folk-songs: and in the field of Russian culture itself, he retold the Russian fairy stories as perhaps the fairy stories of no other nation have ever been retold; he acted as literary godfather to Gogol, giving him the cues to his artistic development and supplying him with the themes of *Dead Souls* and *The Inspector General;* bequeathed to the Russian composers enough subjects for ballets and operas to last all the rest of the century, and sowed the seeds of a Russian realism united with a fine sensibility that has been flourishing ever since. Pushkin had a mastery of language as remarkable certainly as that of any other nineteenth-century poet; and, with this, a kind of genius which none of the other poets had, and few of the novelists to the same degree: the genius for dramatic projection.

In this rare combination of qualities, it seems to me that Pushkin is the only modern poet in the class of Shakespeare and Dante. . . . The scale of Pushkin's work is different because his life-span is different. Just as the subject of Shakespeare is the full experience of a man who is young and passes through middle age and finally grows old, and as Dante's whole project depends for its force on a discipline in organizing experience through self-discipline and an ultimate aloof contemplation hardly attainable before late middle age (Dante died at fifty-six, as soon as his poem was finished); so Pushkin, incongruously situated in the Russia of the Decembrist uprising, where he had felt all his life at the back of his neck the pressure of a remorseless paw, found a way to make his fate itself both the measure and the theme of his work, with a dignity, an objectivity, a clear and pure vision of human situations which remove him completely from the category of the self-dramatizing romantic poets. (pp. 17-19)

[Pushkin] is one of the few writers who never seem to fall—from the point where he has outgrown his early models—into formulas of expression. He finds a special shape and a special style for every successive subject; and, even without looking for the moment at his dramatic and narrative poems, one is amazed at the variety of his range. You have lyrics in regular quatrains that are as pointed and spare as Greek epigrams or as forceful and repercussive as the *Concord Hymn,* and you have lyrics in broken accents: soliloquies that rise out of sleep or trail off in unspoken longings—where the modulated meter follows the thought; you have the balladry and jingling of folksongs, and you have set-pieces like *To a Magnate* . . . (in the meter and rhyme scheme of Boileau's epistles) of a rhetorical solidity and brilliance that equals anything in Pope or the Romans; you have droll little ribaldries like the *Tsar Nikita,* informal discursive poems like *Autumn* that are like going to visit Pushkin for a week-end in the country, and forgings of fierce energetic language, now metallic and unmalleable, now molten and flowing, like *The Upas Tree* and *The Prophet.* You have, finally, dramatic lyrics like *The Fiends* and *Winter Evening,* for which it is hard to find phrases or comparisons because they are as purely and intensely Pushkin as *Furi et Aureli, comites Catulli* is purely and intensely Catullus or *Sweeney among the Nightingales* Eliot.

As for the texture of Pushkin's language and its marvelous adaptation to whatever it describes, one is helpless to give any idea of it without direct quotation from his poetry; but a passage . . . may be mentioned in which the patterns and motifs must be obvious even to readers who do not know Russian. (pp. 19-20)

[A] charming example is in *The Tale of the Tsar Saltan,* when the brave little prince, adrift with his mother, begins his appeal to the sea: . . .

"O thou, my sea, my sea!
So indolent and free" . . .

[In Russian,] the v's alternate with *l's,* and the soft *l's* alternate with hard *l's.* The rhyme words—*sea* and *free*—are identical except for this difference in the *l's.* Pushkin here uses metonymically the word for *wave* for *sea;* and the whole effect is smooth and undulating like the movement of a gentle swell. (pp. 21-2)

It is characteristic of Pushkin that [this passage should owe its] vividness primarily to the representation of *movement.* Movement is a specialty of Pushkin's. He can do sounds, landscapes, personalities, and all the other things, too; but there is probably no other poet since Virgil, with his serpents, his limping Cyclops, his wheel of Ixion, and his armies moving off, who has this sense so completely developed as Pushkin; and the control of the consistency and pace of the hexameter can never give the freedom for such effects that Pushkin finds in his rapider meters. The flood in *The Bronze Horseman,* the ballet-girl in *Evgeni Onegin,* the hawk that drops on the chicken-yard in *Ruslan and Lyudmila,* the cat in *Count Nulin* creeping up and pouncing on a mouse—Pushkin is full of such pictures of actions that seem as we read to take place before our eyes without the intervention of language.

This natural instinct for movement is shown in another way in the poet's command of the movement of his verse and the movement of his play or his story. . . . The timing in Pushkin is perfect. He never for a moment bores you, yet—touching on nothing, however briefly, without some telling descriptive stroke—he covers an immense amount of ground. The one hundred and seventy pages of *Onegin* take us through as much of life as many Victorian novels, and give us the feeling of having lived it more intimately. (pp. 22-3)

The events that resulted in Pushkin's death make one of the queerest and most disquieting stories in the whole of literary history—a story perhaps more dramatic than anything Pushkin ever invented; and it would provide one of the most fascinating problems for which literature affords the opportunity, to try to explain Pushkin's writing and these happenings in terms of one another. I am by no means prepared to undertake the explanation, but I am certain that, as Pushkin perfects his art, as he sharpens the profile of his style and intensifies his concentration on human personalities and relations, he is reflecting ever more clearly the internal and external conflicts in which he finds his spirit involved. Aleko [in *The Gypsies*], who flees to the gypsies from the organized social world, but finds himself eventually driven to commit among them the same kind of crime that has originally made him an outlaw, and so becomes outlawed by the gypsies themselves; the clerk of *The Bronze Horseman,* who loses all he has in the flood and yet pays for his rebellion with madness; the young guardsman in *The Little House in Kolomna* who dresses as a woman and works as a cook . . .—all are the images of Pushkin's false position between the old nobility and the new, between the life of society and the life of art, between the tsardom and the instincts of modern thought, between marriage and the man for himself.

Yet in these dramas the whole situation is usually seen so much in the round, the presentation of opposing forces is so little obscured by animus, that it becomes almost impossible to say that the poet is on either side. In *Onegin* the clever but sterile Evgeni envies the stupid Lensky for his idealism, his poetic aspirations and his capacity for love, and manages to kill him in a duel; in *Mozart and Salieri* the academic composer envies the genius and poisons him. Both themes are plainly the reflections of something that has been deeply experienced by Pushkin and on which he might have brooded with bitterness; yet he handles them in such a way that there is never any melodrama involved: Lensky is extremely sincere, but foolish and perhaps a bad poet; Salieri is a villain, but he states his point of view with so much conviction and dignity that we almost come to respect him. The emotion that we get from reading Pushkin is something outside the picture: it is an emotion, half-comic, half-poignant, at contemplating the nature of things. He gives us the picture created by art—and this is to a considerable extent true even of his personal poetry—and refrains from other comment. . . . (pp. 25-6)

We always feel, thus, in reading Pushkin, that there is something behind and beyond, something we can only guess at; and this makes his peculiar fascination—a fascination which has something in common with the inexhaustible interest of Shakespeare, who seems to be giving us his sonnets and *Hamlet* and *Lear* and the rest as the moods and dreams of some drama the actuality of which we never touch.

> Others abide our question. Thou art free.
> We ask and ask: Thou smilest and art still . . .

Pushkin smiles, but he is never free in the sense that Shakespeare in the end is free, and he has always in relation to his art a seriousness and an anxiety of one who knows the night is coming. As his mind grows in clarity and power, the prison of the world grips him tighter; and his final involvement and defiance and defeat are themselves a projection of the drama which is always still behind and beyond. (pp. 26-7)

Edmund Wilson, "Pushkin," in his *A Window on Russia: For the Use of Foreign Readers,* Farrar, Straus and Giroux, 1972, pp. 15-27.

MARC SLONIM

(essay date 1950)

[Slonim was a Russian-born American critic who wrote extensively on Russian literature. In the excerpt below, he discusses Pushkin's political convictions as reflected in his poetry and prose.]

[No convincing proof for Pushkin's poetic genius] can be offered in English, French, or German translations, for, with a few rare exceptions, they are rather disappointing and to non-Russians do not justify the reputation Pushkin enjoys in Russia. Hardly anything in these translations is striking or particularly beautiful, and the European or American reader has to take for granted that Pushkin was a marvelous poet. (p. 81)

To the general difficulties inherent in translating poetry, Pushkin adds some special ones. One of the main characteristics of his poetry is its perfect marriage of sound and meaning. Pushkin's poems do not merely follow Arnold's definition in presenting the best words in the best order. They endow the plainest, almost trivial words with poetic meaning. The simplicity and naturalness of Pushkin's lines turn into platitudes in translations, because the latter fail to convey their musical lucidity, their freshness and melodious quality. Push-

kin had the magic power of extracting poetic resonance from colloquialisms, of instilling emotional intensity into the simplest sentences, of expressing profound thought in easy and concise statements. What is called the perfection of Pushkin's form is the complete coalescence of sound, rhythm, image, and meaning. Another aspect is Pushkin's clarity and directness of style, as well as his ability to obtain unobtrusive enduring effects—with economy, sober directness, and a sense of measure and balance; these do not exclude subtlety and a wide range of technical devices, which the poet—an astonishing master of versification—used with superb craftsmanship. He also had the gift of giving the same word—placing it in another context or qualifying it by varying the epithets or enhancing it by a diversified rhythmic and melodical movement—a solemn, an intimate, or a pensive value, according to the inner spirit of the individual poem. A poem by Pushkin in Russian creates the impression that what he says could never be said otherwise, that each word fits perfectly, serving as a necessary part of a whole, and that no other words could ever assume a similar function. And still these words are, for the most part, the plain words we use in our daily talk.

With Pushkin the Russian modern literary style was born, which was undoubtedly a phenomenon of national importance. He liberated Russian literature from the heavy legacy of Church-Slavonic, as well as from the artificial mannerisms prevailing at the beginning of the nineteenth century. His was not the language of any particular class (although he knew how to employ the linguistic mannerisms of each social group and was fully aware of the differences between them) but that of contemporary Russia—alive, rich, expressive, blending popular colloquialisms with the achievements of literary evolution. The entire development of Russian letters in the eighteenth century and at the beginning of the nineteenth was in the direction of a fusion of folklore and literary tradition, but only Pushkin succeeded in accomplishing this task. (pp. 81-2)

The role played by Pushkin in this process explains the importance of one of his first (but not best) poems, *Russlan and Liudmila*. . . . Despite all its weaknesses, *Russlan and Liudmila* marked the beginning of a new way of writing—free, lively, and colloquial. At the same time by its opposition to the remnants of Classicism and its distinct avoidance of sentimentality or the Romantic 'poetry of horror,' it inaugurated a new literary and stylistic movement. (p. 83)

[Pushkin's lyrical, subjective poetry has] two distinct features that give it its inimitable character. First of all, these intensely emotional lines are never vague or misty. The imagery, the rhythm, and the melodious movement of each stanza are perfectly amalgamated with the actual idea, reflecting the activity of a lucid and penetrating mind. Whether they capture a fleeting mood, unfold an image, or express a thought, they are plastic, precise, unmistakably clear even in their conciseness, and all this without sacrificing the slightest nuance or relapsing into academic aloofness. Secondly, whatever the actual theme of these lyrics may be, even the most despairing ones, they are filled with potent vitality, with a sense of life that accepts reality and masters it. . . . [Even the] pensive lyrics never stress despair and are balanced by a positive attitude toward reality. But Pushkin's 'healthy optimism' is no mere acceptance of reality. He does not shut his eyes to the horrors and contradictions of life; he is extremely conscious of death, pain, injustice; and he does not attempt to hide anything or to play with illusions—but his attachment to the earth and his desire of experiencing everything, of living life fully in every way, give his poems intensity and power. . . . Pushkin also wrote a score of sensual and erotic poems in a pagan and Epicurean tone. But sensuality and eroticism are no more than a facet of his Apollonian genius. His delight in life embraces the subtle joys of the mind, the exaltation of spirituality, the simple pleasures of nature, as well as the raptures of the flesh and the voluptuousness of love. A coined phrase labels Pushkin's poetry as 'sunny,' and a bright and warm light as of midday does illumine his poems. However, such a definition is too constrained, for Pushkin also knew how to explore and present the nocturnal and ambiguous side of life. (p. 84)

Pushkin's poetry in its emphasis on the dignity of

man is profoundly humanistic. It extols man—in all his aspects. Man, freedom, action, love, art, are for Pushkin the true values.

This supreme poet reveals himself as both human and humane, not only in his serious works but also in his light ones. Abhorring anything flat, stilted, and dull, he attacked pretentiousness, academic solemnity, and artificiality, in both life and literature. He wrote biting epigrams, which made him many enemies; blasphemous facetiae (such as his **"Gabrieliad,"** . . . in which the Virgin Mary is seduced by the Serpent, the Archangel Gabriel, and the Holy Ghost, all in one day), rather indecent but decidedly droll; erotic poems (such as **'Czar Nikita'** and **'Count Nulin'** . . . , the latter a version of *The Rape of Lucrece*). . . . These poems had a definite literary and psychological importance. They were weapons with which Pushkin fought against the rigidity of established forms and canons, demolishing the restrictions of Classicism and effecting a reunion of life and literature. This was one of his main aims—to bring art down to earth, to make poetry realistic, alive, capable equally of creating laughter or treating serious problems. . . .

It was with precisely [the intent] of bringing realism to art that Pushkin began his long novel in verse, *Eugene Oneghin*. . . . (p. 85)

Eugene Oneghin, like all of Pushkin's poems, has a diversity of elements, a peculiar structure: the narrative is interrupted by long lyrical passages devoted to the poet's personal feelings or memories; the author converses with the reader, discusses his own work, indulges in intimate confessions or jests, and, in general, creates an atmosphere of ease and intimacy. While the lyrical passages of the poem are subtle and suggestive, the pictures of Russian autumn and winter, the countryside, or Moscow society are among the highest achievements of Russian descriptive art. . . .

Begun as a mere fanciful imitation of the Romantic pattern, this light novel turned out to be a serious and realistic representation of Russian life, with social and psychological portraits of Pushkin's contemporaries which assumed the proportions of all-Russian types. (p. 86)

[Reading *Eugene Oneghin*, Pushkin's contemporaries] were most impressed by two things: that a simple plot taken from every-day life and deliberately devoid of exciting adventures could provide enough material for a long poem, and that the author's purpose had been fulfilled through the great variety of poetic devices, with such clarity, freshness, *brio*, humor, and feeling. (p. 88)

When Pushkin was twenty-two he wrote a few poems 'under the sign of Byron.' The influence of the English poet was, however, superficial and evanescent. Pushkin was too lucid, too fond of reason, logic, and reality, and far too fond of balance and measure in art to become a true disciple of the author of 'The Corsair' and 'Manfred.' Nevertheless Byron's influence, mitigated by these tendencies of Pushkin, is apparent in certain early poems, such as *The Caucasian Captive*. . . . And in *The Gypsies* . . . [a] Byronic hero, Aleko, while fleeing the 'thralldom of the stifling city,' joins a band of wandering gypsies and falls in love with Zemphira—a beautiful daughter of the 'prophetic tribe'—but fails in his attempts to lead a romantically free life. After Aleko kills Zemphira, who has betrayed him, and her lover, he is rejected by the chief of the gypsies. 'Leave us, proud man,' the old man tells him. 'You are not born for a free life; you look but for your own fancy, you are wicked and bold—whereas we are kind and peaceful; no need have we of bloodshed and groans.' This juxtaposition of the 'noble savage' to the forceful intellectual is far from the Byronic idealization of the 'dark hero.' The simplicity and kindness of the gypsies (somewhat in the Russian tradition) triumph over the evil sophistication of the city dweller.

In his fragmentary **'The Brigand Brothers'** . . . and the delightful **'Fountain of Bahchisarai'** . . . , which evokes a vision of Tartar khans and their harems and wives captured in battle, the Byronic influence has been assimilated to such an extent as to appear completely transformed. Despite the ardor and tempestuousness of his own temperament, Pushkin disliked exaggeration in art and carefully avoided the unbelievable or supernatural in his non-folkloristic poems. The protagonists of his most Romantic works are far from being mysterious or wild: they are simply disenchanted souls like the Caucasian captive whose aloofness from life is the result of precocious experiences that have seared his heart. Pushkin's attitude to this sort of hero changes rapidly: at first he treats him seriously (the Caucasian captive, or Aleko in *The Gypsies*), then, more critical of this representative of a prematurely aged generation, he makes him the target of satire and parody (Eugene Oneghin).

Pushkin's departure from the Romantic pattern marks his liberation from Byronic influence. By 1825, when he was fully aware of Byron's affectations and other faults, he reproaches the English poet for making each of his heroes merely the personification of some one trait of his own personality: one of his pride, a second of his scorn, a third of his melancholy—'thus out of a sombre, energetic and full character Byron has created several insignificant ones.' (pp. 88-9)

Pushkin's chief debt to Romanticism was the idea of freedom. He wrote in the forms adopted by the school—the novel, the short story, historical chronicle, drama, light verse—and he evinced a certain interest in dramatic situations and in the clash of strong emotions. He utilized freely the Romantic blend of diverse elements—serious, comic, sublime, ironic—in the same work. He also voiced repeatedly that supreme longing for things beyond reality that is the essence of Romanticism, but he could never accept the Romantic lack of proportion and haphazard, whimsical, and fantastic way of writing. His style, therefore, scarcely touched by Romanticism, is pure, sober, classically perfect; its richness never lapses into luxuriance, its originality never becomes a prose. (pp. 89-90)

Pushkin was convinced that a true poet was a sounding board responsible to the voices of contemporary life. He wanted the poet to be actively interested in the ideas and events of his time. A series of his poems on political themes proves that he put this theory into practice. He was also of the opinion that a free, independent writer was bound to produce works of social and moral significance. In his justly proud poem **'A Monument I Reared'** . . . , he foretells his future fame and explains why his name will be cherished by the people, over all of great Russia: 'Because I awakened kind feeling with my lyre, because in my ruthless age I glorified freedom and called for mercy for the vanquished.' These lines are no mere generalities. Pushkin had a definite political stand and he was the poet of freedom. . . . Throughout his life Pushkin remained a Westernizer and a liberal. He belonged to the progressive tradition of the educated nobility, which owed its beginnings to Peter the Great, and he therefore attached prime importance to the reforms initiated by the Great Czar. (pp. 91-2)

Pushkin condones the oppression and violence Peter had used in order to lead Russia toward the West, and he hails his will power, indomitable energy, and grandiose vision. . . . Pushkin was the first Russian poet who consciously accepted the Empire and the St. Petersburg period of Russian history. And he was also the first rhapsodist of the new capital, of that beautiful and fantastic metropolis. . . . (p. 92)

Pushkin knew the price the common man had to pay for the splendor of this artificial and proud capital. It was a price paid by the Russian people for the consolidation and expansion of the Empire, for its military conquests, and for its glorious position among other nations. He was fully aware of the fundamental conflict between the fate of an individual and the destiny of the State: the individual longings for peace and happiness were crushed by the merciless progress of the nation. This tragic and universal paradox is the theme of *The Bronze Horseman*, which, in my opinion, is the most beautiful and haunting of Pushkin's poems, written in vigorous, sweeping, and supple verse. (p. 93)

The prologue of the poem is a miniature epic of the city's creation. The narrative shifts to a later day and describes the flood of 1824—hostile nature in elemental revolt against the works of man. During the flood the hero of the poem, Eugene, a minor official, loses all his dreams of happiness—his betrothed, his home, and all his belongings. Overwhelmed by the horror of the catastrophe, his mind becomes unhinged. In a fit of frenzy he threatens Peter, the Bronze Horseman, the cause of all his ills, the cruel builder of this unreal city that defies God and nature. The Bronze Horseman and horse leap down from the pedestal and pursue the offender through the empty streets of a silent city. Wherever Eugene turns he hears at his heels hoofs thundering over the reverberating pavement.

The symbolism of the poem is all too obvious. The Bronze Horseman 'on the height, at the very edge of the abyss, with his bridle of iron, has made Russia rear'—and none can tell which way he will go. In his flight over cliffs and precipices many lives will inevitably be sacrificed. But the acceptance, and even the justification, of this historic necessity does not prevent Pushkin from feeling sympathy and compassion for the victims. The Eugene of this poem is portrayed as a lonely 'little man' whose misfortune, misery, and madness affect us deeply. The lot of the 'little man' was to become one of the main themes of Russian literature, from Gogol (directly influenced by Pushkin) and Dostoevsky to Chekhov and the Soviet writers.

One of the most striking features of *The Bronze Horseman* is the portrayal of Eugene's madness, which is so vivid that the grim pursuit of the minor official by an equestrian statue becomes a reality. In this romantic fusion of realism and fantasy, devoid of exaggeration, Pushkin is again a forerunner of Gogol and Dostoevsky. The delirium of his hero is depicted by Pushkin in a simple, succinct, matter-of-fact manner.

He used the same device in his prose. His short stories, told in an efficient, brisk style free of adornment or grandiloquence (they are on a par with those of Mérimée and Stendhal), often treat romantic or fantastic situations in a soberly rational way (*The Coffin-Maker* has a ghastly nightmare after a celebration, the *Queen of Spades* brings about the ruin of Hermann, a gambler with *Übermensch* notions, and so on). The economy of artistic devices and the directness of the style make alive and concrete the episodes and characters in Pushkin's short stories and novelettes. They were the most important phenomenon in Russian prose since Karamzin, but they are far removed from the affected sentimentality and artificiality of the author of *Poor Liza.* Here again he is a pioneer, leaving the posterity perfect specimens of the short story (*The Shot, The Blizzard*), the novelette (*The Queen of Spades*), and the short historical novel (*The Captain's Daughter*). (pp. 93-4)

In *Boris Godunov,* that romantic tragedy in which the Byronic influence is definitely supplanted by the Shakespearean, the reader is engrossed not only by the masterful characterization, the swiftly moving plot, and the suspense, but also by the vision of the hidden springs of Russian history and by the interpretation of the national psychology. The true hero of the tragedy is the people, but they are silent when the boyars, after their murders and uprisings, announce their new Czar—none other than Dimitri, the mock pretender. It is a silence pregnant with symbolic significance: sooner or later the people will make themselves heard—at first clamorously, as during the Pugachev rebellion, but the day will inevitably come when it will be in an articulate voice. Pushkin dreamt of education through freedom and tolerance, enabling the Russian people to take the place that was rightly theirs. He well knew the merits and deficiencies of the Russian national character; he nurtured no illusions, admitting that a Russian revolt was always senseless and cruel, but at the same time he could not help but feel and think as a typical representative of Russia. (pp. 94-5)

Pushkin's national awareness, his feeling for Russia as a unit, did not affect his fundamental liberalism. He suffered from political oppression and exposed the evils of the autocratic regime. What was more, he never lapsed into chauvinism, and combined his national pride and patriotism with a strong leaning towards Western Europe. This combination formed one of the many complexities of the Pushkin phenomenon in Russian culture. His self-assertion as a Russian was coincident with his acceptance and assimilation of the Western legacy. (p. 95)

'I love Europe with all my heart,' said Pushkin, and he displayed his love and his intuitive understanding of Europe in his poems and dramatic pieces, which involve Scotland (*A Feast during the Plague*), Spain (*The Stone Guest,* dealing with Don Juan), Italy (*Angelo* and numerous lyrics), the Balkans (*Songs of the Western Slavs*), and which range in time from the Middle Ages (*The Covetous Knight*) to the eighteenth century (*Mozart and Salieri*) and Pushkin's own day (his lyrical poems). In his translations or 'imitations' he rendered the spirit of various periods and countries in the most striking fashion. He so absorbed the spirit of various forms of European civilization that he was right in proclaiming himself as much a Westerner as a Russian. He was at once a national and a European writer without ever being inconsistent, for in this, as in so many other things, Pushkin presented a oneness, an organic unity seldom found among great poets. According to Dostoevsky, his universality was not only the main feature of Pushkin's work and mentality, but it made him the most typical representative of the Russian spirit in so far as the latter always tends to transform the national into the universal.

Whatever this universality may be, one fact remains certain: Pushkin's work, for all its unmistakably national flavor, is part and parcel of world literature. It was Pushkin who won for Russian letters a place in European art, and this came about at the very moment Russian literature acquired, also through Pushkin, an awareness of its national peculiarities and asserted its formal and spiritual individuality. The whole importance of Pushkin's role is contained in this statement. The curious part of it is that Pushkin himself was conscious of what he was doing and had set precise objectives for himself and for his fellow writers. Despite all the romantic aura about his conception of the poet as the beloved child of the Muses and the inspired disciple of the gods, Pushkin acted as a man of great intellectual power and understanding. (pp. 96-7)

Pushkin was one of the few great writers who won true fame during their lives. His contemporaries acclaimed his genius. The 'School' of Pushkin included practically all the poets of his period, and even such original writers as Lermontov could not entirely escape his influence. The national significance of Pushkin's work, however, became fully apparent only after his death, when the growth of his popularity assumed extraordinary proportions; he became the symbol of national and artistic perfection. 'He is an astounding and perhaps a unique phenomenon of the Russian spirit,' proclaimed Gogol, 'He embodies what the Russian may become two hundred years hence.'

The founder of the modern Russian literary language, who fulfilled the hopes of the past and opened the roads for further development, Pushkin appealed equally to realists like Nekrassov, to idealistic esthetes like Fet, to the symbolists of the 'nineties like Bruissov, or to the Soviet poets who still strive to imitate his clarity, directness, and simplicity and willingly employ his metric forms. Although anti-Pushkin revolts took place in the 'sixties and in 1920, it is safe to say that all Russian poetry of the last hundred years advanced under the aegis of Pushkin and can never shed his spell. He determined its development, established its standards, formulated its idiom, and even shaped its main forms.

His influence upon Russian prose was no less profound. He laid the foundations of Russian realism in the short story, in the novel, in the historical narrative, and in the drama, not counting his contributions to the essay and literary criticism. Gogol considered himself his disciple; Dostoevsky worshiped him with a kind of superstitious awe; Leo Tolstoy advised young writers to take Pushkin's short stories as models and spoke of their lasting and beneficial effect on his own prose; Chekhov and Gorky placed Pushkin above all other Russian writers—even as Soviet poets and novelists do today. (pp. 106-07)

Marc Slonim, "Pushkin," in his *The Epic of Russian Literature: From Its Origins through Tolstoy,* Oxford University Press, 1950, pp. 81-107.

SOURCES FOR FURTHER STUDY

Bayley, John. *Pushkin: A Comparative Commentary.* Cambridge, England: Cambridge University Press, 1971, 369 p.
> Offers an in-depth comparative analysis of thematic and stylistic concerns in Pushkin's poetry and prose.

Lavrin, Janko. *Pushkin and Russian Literature.* London: Hodder & Stoughton, 1947, 226 p.
> Examines the influence of Pushkin's works on Russian literature, observing that Pushkin "was destined to play a double role as a poet: while completing the eighteenth-century currents, he at the same time led the way to modern Russian literature."

Pritchett, V. S. "Alexander Pushkin: Founding Father." In his *The Myth Makers: Literary Essays,* pp. 77-88. New York: Random House, 1979.
> Appreciative overview characterizing Pushkin's work as vital and innovative.

Simmons, Ernest J. "Pushkin—The Poet as Novelist." In his *Introduction to Russian Realism,* pp. 3-43. Bloomington: Indiana University Press, 1965.
> Traces the development of Pushkin's narrative technique, arguing that Pushkin "tremendously advanced the whole conception of Russian realism."

Troyat, Henri. *Pushkin.* Translated by Nancy Amphoux. Garden City, N.Y.: Doubleday & Company, 1970, 655 p.
> Well-illustrated and annotated biography.

Wreath, Patrick J., and Wreath, April I. "Alexander Pushkin: A Bibliography of Criticism in English." *Canadian-American Slavic Studies* 10, No. 2 (Summer 1976): 279-304.
> Lists essays and books published in English between 1920 and 1975, in addition to selected reviews of books about Pushkin.

Thomas Pynchon

1937-

(Full name Thomas Ruggles Pynchon, Jr.) American novelist and short story writer. This photograph, taken in 1953, is one of only a few photographs of Pynchon known to exist. The most recent photo dates from 1955.

INTRODUCTION

Pynchon is widely regarded as one of the most eminent literary stylists in contemporary American fiction. His novels, often described as labyrinthine or encyclopedic in scope, are characterized by an aura of great mystery and reveal a knowledge of many disciplines in the natural and social sciences. Pynchon's use of sophisticated ideas is balanced by his verbal playfulness with such elements as black humor, outlandish puns, slapstick, running gags, parody, and ridiculous names. Through this blend of serious themes and comic invention and combination of documented fact and imaginative fantasy, Pynchon paradoxically affirms and denies the notion that mundane reality may possess hidden meaning. Living amidst the chaos of modern existence that is mirrored in the fragmented structures of his novels, Pynchon's protagonists typically undertake vague yet elaborate quests to discover their identities and to find meaning and order in their lives. Although critics often describe Pynchon's novels as labored or incomprehensible, they continue to be widely popular.

Perhaps the most significant biographical fact about Thomas Pynchon is his anonymity. Pynchon is so reticent about himself and so wary of publicity that it is unclear even what he looks like: the most recent published photographs of him come from his high school annual. For a time it was commonplace to compare him with J. D. Salinger, another famous American novelist who evades public scrutiny, but the comparison proved inadequate: Salinger, at least, can be located, while Pynchon keeps even his whereabouts a secret from everyone but his closest and most loyal friends. A former Cornell classmate, Jules Siegel, hinted in 1977 that this reclusiveness stems from the kind of paranoia that characteristically informs Pynchon's fiction (and has been termed "Pynchonesque"), but other evidence suggests that in his personal life this daring and iconoclastic writer is merely intensely private and intensely shy.

Two short occasional pieces that Pynchon wrote in the 1980s provide some information about his development as a writer. The first of these, an introduction to the 1983 reissue of Richard Farina's novel, *Been Down So Long It Looks Like Up to Me,* is largely made up of reminiscences about the days when Pynchon and Farina were undergraduates at Cornell University. Pynchon pictures himself as an admirer and to some extent a follower of the late poet, songwriter, folksinger, and fiction writer, who knew not only the best parties but also "coeds I had lusted after across deep lecture halls." Some of Pynchon's former professors construe the relationship rather differently, however. "Farina was the performer," Walter Slatoff, professor of English at Cornell, recalled. "Pynchon watched. He was always on the sidelines, but that was because he was taking everything in."

If Pynchon spent a great deal of time watching during those years, he was also listening. In the introduction to his collection of early short stories, *Slow Learner* (1984), he refers to his most serious youthful fault as "Bad Ear" and lists the writers—Jack Kerouac and the Beats generally, Saul Bellow, Herb Gold, and Philip Roth—who helped him develop his perception of voices by showing him "how at least two very distinct kinds of English could be allowed in fiction to exist." He also confirms thematic influences that various critics have noted as consistently important in his work: Niccolo Machiavelli's *The Prince,* Norbert Wiener's expositions of information theory, *The Education of Henry Adams,* and Karl Baedeker's guides. And he asserts his preoccupation with mortality, perhaps the single most resonant theme in his fiction. "When we speak of 'seriousness' in fiction," he observes, "ultimately we are talking about an attitude toward death—how characters may act in its presence, for example, or how they handle it when it isn't so immediate." This concern with mortality underlies Pynchon's fascination with the apparently abstract notion of entropy: the tendency for any system to move from a state of order to one of disorder. "Certain processes, not only thermodynamic ones but also those of a medical nature, can often not be reversed," he notes dryly, and adds, "Sooner or later we all find this out, from the inside."

Pynchon's literary career began with the publication of several short stories, five of which are included in *Slow Learner.* Although Pynchon's short fiction is regarded as less accomplished than his later novels, many reviewers maintain that his early stories offer insight into his stylistic development. Pynchon's initial novel, *V.* (1963), was compared to works by such authors as Joseph Heller, William Burroughs, Kurt Vonnegut, and John Barth for its experimental format and use of black and absurdist humor. Among other events, the book relates the obsessive quest of Herbert Stencil to discover the identity of a person or thing referred to as "V." in his father's diary. Stencil's quest is complicated by a superabundance of clues that he feels obliged to follow. During his travels, Stencil encounters a group of people known as the "Whole Sick Crew," whose decadence and aimlessness are widely regarded as representative of the moral, social, and cultural decline of Western civilization. Pynchon contrasts the energetic Stencil with the moribund state of the Whole Sick Crew as part of an intensive investigation into the nature of the animate and inanimate. While some critics consider Pynchon to have overelaborated essentially simple themes, others were impressed by the vast historical scale of *V.,* particularly its multiple perspectives on twentieth-century events and the intricate network of referents that serve to expand the implications of Stencil's quest.

The Crying of Lot 49 (1966), is widely regarded as Pynchon's most accessible work due to its concise development. In this work, he employs the second law of thermodynamics a rule of physics that describes entropy—as a metaphor for the forces that contribute to social decline. *The Crying of Lot 49* centers on Oedipa Maas, who is named the executrix of the will of Pierce Inverarity, a California real-estate mogul and her former lover. In executing Inverarity's will, Oedipa stumbles upon clues suggesting that a centuries-old communications system is secretly competing with the United States Postal Service. Like many of Pynchon's characters, Oedipa is uncertain whether her perception is valid or a result of either her own paranoia or the manipulation of her thoughts by others. Throughout his fiction, Pynchon alludes to paranoia, through which his characters often assign an organizing principle to a world that would otherwise be random and meaningless. Frank Kermode stated: "The shortest of [Pynchon's] novels, *The Crying of Lot 49* most perfectly expresses, as a kind of riddle, the question whether evidence that seems amply to support a theory of universal correspondence, secret networks of significance, covert modes of oppression, is really to be found out there in the world or only in the crazed mind of the person who discerns it." Like many of Pynchon's works, *The Crying of Lot 49* ends before the protagonist's quest is resolved. Critics have offered many interpretations of the novel but have generally praised Pynchon's metaphorical use of the concept of entropy.

Pynchon's third novel, *Gravity's Rainbow* (1973), received a National Book Award and was also nominated for the Pulitzer Prize. While Pynchon's detractors have variously faulted this controversial novel as obscene, nihilistic, or incomprehensible, many designate *Gravity's Rainbow* a masterpiece, contending that Pynchon has fashioned a work of profound implications by connecting a wide variety of human activities and ideas with the mass destruction of World War II. Described as an extended meditation on death, *Gravity's Rainbow* blends factual details and fantastic events, includes scenes of comedy and brutality, develops extensive symbolic implications, and offers several perspectives of historical events. In addition to suggesting that Western society actively promotes a culture of death by perfecting such weapons as the German V-2 rocket, Pynchon links advances in science and technology with historical patterns, political, economic, and social values, and international cartels in their contributions to the war effort.

Nearly seventeen years elapsed between the publication of *Gravity's Rainbow* and Pynchon's next novel, *Vineland* (1990). On one level, the title of this work alludes to America as it was discovered by Leif Ericson prior to Christopher Columbus; on another, Vineland refers to a fictitious county near the coast of northern California, the state's last uncharted wilderness. In the 1980s, Vineland serves as a refuge for middle-aged veterans of the 1960s counterculture who have sought refuge from government repression. The novel focuses primarily upon Prairie Wheeler's search for her long-lost mother, Frenesi Gates, a beautiful for-

mer member of a defunct radical group dedicated to exposing the corruption and hypocrisy of the Nixon administration. Although the novel contains many subplots and characters, combining elements of soap opera and political thriller, *Vineland* is generally considered less ambitious in scope, thematic complexity, and historical range than Pynchon's previous works. Terrence Rafferty commented: "*Vineland*, for all its wild, abrupt turnings, is the clearest novel Thomas Pynchon has written. . . . This novel is as funny, as smart, as lyrical, and as subversive as any American fiction of the past decade, but the most remarkable thing about it is the purity of its desire to get through to us. These days, Pynchon seems to be writing out of the deepest, most uncontrollable motive for speech: the need to pass along what he has learned before it's lost forever."

(For further information about Pynchon's life and works, see *Contemporary Authors*, Vols. 17-20; *Contemporary Authors New Revision Series*, Vol. 22; *Contemporary Literary Criticism*, Vols. 2, 3, 6, 9, 11, 18, 33, 62; *Dictionary of Literary Biography*, Vol. 2: *American Novelists Since World War II*; and *Major 20th-Century Writers*.)

CRITICAL COMMENTARY

ROBERT SKLAR

(essay date 1967)

[In the following essay, Sklar places Pynchon at the forefront of modern American literature for "absorbing and transforming new scientific and philosophical perspectives within his art."]

If fiction has not completely lost its relevance as an art form to creative young people, then it languishes in a period of biding time; since fiction is tied more closely to events and ideas than other arts, perhaps it stands in a fallow period, assimilating new configurations, as happened in the mid-19th century after Darwin and the early 20th after Freud. In this perspective, Thomas Pynchon is far more than, dutifully recognized, the only known and therefore leading writer of the under-30s; for more than any other contemporary American novelist he has succeeded, in two interesting, intelligent and serious novels, in absorbing and transforming new scientific and philosophical perspectives within his art. (p. 277)

The critical point in Pynchon's career so far lies

in the radical shift in literary focus he undertook to make from *V.* to *The Crying of Lot 49.* To say that the second novel is a better and more important novel than the first is not simply a way of scoring an easy victory over dull reviewers or doggedly insisting on a principle of growth. To grasp the nature of Pynchon's shift, for its artistic and intellectual value, and as a liberating gesture in its own right, is to take the measure of his wider significance for contemporary American fiction.

As a liberating gesture, Pynchon's shift from *V.* to *The Crying of Lot 49* broke him free from the constricting limitations of belonging to a "school" and writing in a genre. One reason the second novel proved disappointing to some admirers of the first, in fact, was its failure to fulfill the stereotyped expectations they had held for him. Yet even if *V.* wears a "black-humor" label, and stands as one of the most intricate and elaborate novels in that genre, it accomplishes a good deal more than that. One who rereads *V.* in the light of *The Crying of Lot 49* may come to feel that *V.* is itself a liberating gesture, a gesture of liberation from nearly all the styles and forms of fiction that have preceded it.

Principal Works

V. (novel) 1963

The Crying of Lot 49 (novel) 1966

Gravity's Rainbow (novel) 1973

Slow Learner: Early Stories (stories) 1984

Vineland (novel) 1990

As *Catch-22* may be the first American novel truly to have attained a Cubist form in its treatment of space and time, so *V.* may be the first American novel of collage, an abstract composition put together with parodies of spy novels, political novels, adventure novels, decadent novels, romances, utopias and whatever other category the ingenious mind can find. . . . [The] attentive explicator will find that one of the principal subjects of parody in *V.* is the "black-humor" style itself.

Read in the light of *The Crying of Lot 49*, then, *V.* does not appear as a launching platform for a style or a subject but rather as an isolated object or as an ending. That novel published in 1963 seems in 1967 not so much a contemporary work as a historical work, a novel that reflects the moods of the late fifties in America and the style of the early sixties. Part of this feeling, if it is an accurate one, may be attributed to a stylistic trait of the novel common to many works in the "black-humor" genre, a style deliberately constructed to put a distance between the reader and the work, as if the novel were a game drawing on the reader's mental faculties but deliberately excluding his emotions. (pp. 277-78)

V. is like a riddle that once correctly answered never taxes the mind again; *The Crying of Lot 49* is founded in an emotion of mystery, an emotion which remains, inviolate and mysterious, even when the outward mystery is solved. *V.* is a complex novel that gets simpler with each rereading, *The Crying of Lot 49* a simple novel that reread grows more complex.

V. is chiefly memorable for what its earlier admirers called its vast warehouses of information, its immense knowledgeability, its prodigies of research. If one function of the novel, as Mary McCarthy once suggested, has been to provide facts, to let the reader know how to catch a whale or cut a field of hay, Pynchon's *V.* may rank as one of the most encyclopedic founts of facts in the history of the novel. In *V.* the reader may find out how to perform a nose operation; how the Germans wiped out the native population of South West Africa before the First World War; how British espionage agents operated in the Middle East since the time of Kitchener; a good part of the history of Malta in this century, and much more. How much one may care to

rely on Pynchon's facts is another matter. . . . [Given] Pynchon's propensity to parody the fictional styles which have conveyed this sort of subject in the past, it might be wise not to make any bets on the basis of what one reads in *V.* In any case the truth of Pynchon's details, or even their significance, is not a matter that deeply engages the reader's concern.

Form and style in *The Crying of Lot 49* combine to give a far greater resonance to facts. . . .

Nevertheless, Pynchon has created in *V.* an aura of formidable intellectual competence, and nowhere more significantly than in his mastery of scientific and technical subjects, particularly physics and electronic technology. It may be that no American novelist before Pynchon—science-fiction writers not excepted—has brought so thorough and so prepared a scientific intelligence to bear on modern life, and this capacity to include in the novel the pervasive scientific and technological aspects of our day-to-day lives rather than to neglect them through ignorance, may make *V.* a landmark of the novel in yet another sense.

It is true, though, that Pynchon dissipates this competence by expending it on a theme beloved of science-fiction writers and their cousins among black humorists, the battle between men and machines, between the power of animation and the power of the inanimate. . . . At the heart of Pynchon's imagination lies not science and technology, nor the parody and wild humor which are so much a part of his style but a sense of mystery, a vision of fantasy, that expresses itself in dualisms, in images of surface and depth, of mirrors, of secret societies and hidden worlds.

The prime mystery of *V.*, of course, is the mystery of V. herself, as a woman in many guises—Victoria Wren, Hedwig Vogelsang, Veronica Manganese, a mysterious woman in Paris, the Bad Priest killed in Malta—as a bald cipher that is charged with greater resonance with every repetition, until the eye responds to every capital letter V as if it were inked in red. . . . Who is V.? The British espionage agent, Sidney Stencil, one of her lovers, in 1899 had written in his journal: "There is more behind and inside V. than any of us had suspected. Not who, but what: what is she? God grant that I may never be called upon to write the answer, either here or in any official report."

Pynchon, however, does feel called upon to write the answer, and he raises few mysteries in *V.* for which he does not quite openly and obviously provide the solution. But to answer who she is in her many masks is not to answer Sidney Stencil's question, what she is, and that question Pynchon leaves to his exegetes. (p. 278)

Pynchon's radical shift in literary focus from *V.* to *The Crying of Lot 49* took the shape not of new themes and images but rather changes in form and tone that significantly altered the value of old themes and images. His verbal playfulness, puns and jokes are reduced in quantity rather than intensity, and are made to serve the movement of the novel. Factual materials remain as important to the second novel as to the first, but where in *V.* the facts seemed to have been real but not necessarily true, Pynchon quite obviously invented the "historical facts" in *The Crying of Lot 49* for the purpose of the novel and thereby made them more plausible, artistically more true. The form of *V.*, moreover, exaggerated the sense of mystery and the aura of an exotic unknown, though Pynchon too often broke in and disengaged the mystery by providing explanations. In *The Crying of Lot 49,* the form of the novel centers on the normal and the everyday: strange events are explained earnestly and straightforwardly, yet the aura of mystery obstinately grows. And finally, whatever sense of mystery remained in *V.* was focused and contained by the past, where in *The Crying of Lot 49* the feeling of mystery that will not down comes inexorably to rest in the present and the future.

The Crying of Lot 49 is the story of how Mrs. Oedipa Maas discovers a world within her world, an anti-world, an adversary world—or invents one in her imagination. (pp. 278-79)

Oedipa comes upon her new magic—to adopt language which Pynchon's reference to religion validates—in an immanent world which gradually becomes more and more imminent.

The adversary world reveals itself to Oedipa through the symbol of a muted post horn and also by signs bearing the initials WASTE or w.a.s.t.e. These signs and symbols represent an underground postal system which operates parallel to or in direct subversion (through forged stamps and cancellations) of the U.S. Post Office. Oedipa pursues the long history of this secret system through investigations into the arcane byways of bibliography—a good part of the novel centers on the performance of a mock Jacobean revenge play, *The Courier's Tragedy,* and the tracing of its various texts and editions—and philately, giving Pynchon an opportunity to display his intellectual ingenuity in two fields he neglected to cover in *V.*

But the backbone of Pynchon's intellectual structure in *The Crying of Lot 49* as in *V.* is science, and in the second novel he develops a scientific metaphor far more rich and more original than the animate-inanimate dichotomy he borrowed or parodied in *V.* . . . Pynchon set down the new theme even more precisely in a preliminary short story, **"Entropy,"** of which however, only the theme carried over to the novel. In physics the term entropy applies to the second law of thermodynamics. It describes loss of energy, or the amount of energy unavailable for use in a thermodynamic system. Henry Adams borrowed this idea for his essay, "The Rule of Phase Applied to History," in

which he calculated the running down of intellectual energy on earth—Thought would reach the limits of its possibilities, he postulated, in the year 1921.

Henry Adams' concept of entropy lies at the core of Pynchon's story of that title, but the concept of entropy most important for *The Crying of Lot 49* derives from communications and information theory, particularly as that term was discussed by the mathematician Norbert Wiener. In *The Human Use of Human Beings* and in *Cybernetics,* Wiener argued against the pessimism which the second law of thermodynamics had engendered in Henry Adams and others. He agreed that the universe's energy would surely run down some day, but at a given moment in a given part of the system there were forces powerful enough to decrease entropy, to increase the amount of available energy in that part. "We may well regard living organisms," Wiener wrote, "such as Man himself, in this light." In *The Crying of Lot 49* Pynchon takes up not only the scientific significance of Wiener's viewpoint but its obvious social and political significance as well. The w.a.s.t.e. system puts to use moral and human energies that the surface system—the United States Government and the dominant American mode of life, as Pynchon makes explicit—lets go to waste.

The Crying of Lot 49 is a radical political novel. Where in *V.* . . . . Pynchon tossed out an idea of political apocalypse with bravado and as if to scare the liberals, in *The Crying of Lot 49* he never uses the word "apocalypse" but rather builds a concept and a structure of revolution right into the form of the novel. Unexpectedly Oedipa runs across a Mexican anarchist she and Pierce had once argued with in Mexico. The anarchist says to her:

> You know what a miracle is. Not what Bakunin said. But another world's intrusion into this one. . . . Like the church we hate, anarchists also believe in another world. Where revolutions break out spontaneous and leaderless, and the soul's talent for consensus allows the masses to work together without effort, automatic as the body itself. And yet, señá, if any of it should ever really happen that perfectly, I would also have to cry miracle. An anarchist miracle.

The Crying of Lot 49, too, in this sense, is an anarchist miracle, a novel which not only postulates another world but creates with the truth of art another world's intrusion into this one.

It is perhaps idle to talk of American tradition in the novel, but one of the unmistakable virtues of *The Crying of Lot 49* is its success in making new and contemporary a traditional concern of the great American novelists—the creation, through the style and form of their fiction, of a social system more true to their national ideals than the existing political and social system. *The Crying of Lot 49* ends with Oedipa Maas awaiting the auctioning of the lot of postage stamps which will prove whether the muted post horn symbol and the w.a.s.t.e. signs form only a web to snare her paranoia or, in truth, the communication network of another world.

For all his philosophical and scientific competence, for all his revolutionary political inclinations, Pynchon is above all an artist; and the ending of *The Crying of Lot 49* makes clear what the Argentine Jorge Luis Borges meant when he wrote in an essay, "that imminence of a revelation that is not yet produced is, perhaps, the aesthetic reality." One would like to say of *The Crying of Lot 49* what T. S. Eliot said of *The Great Gatsby,* that it represents the first step forward for American fiction in some time; for if the road ahead for fiction lies in the direction Borges in his stories has pointed, toward greater philosophical and metaphysical sophistication, Pynchon surely ranks as the most intelligent, most audacious and most accomplished American novelist writing today. (pp. 279-80)

Robert Sklar, "The New Novel, USA: Thomas Pynchon," in *The Nation,* New York, Vol. 205, No. 9, September 25, 1967, pp. 277-80.

EDWARD MENDELSON
(essay date 1978)

[Mendelson is an American critic, editor, and educator. In the excerpt below, he presents Pynchon as a rare modern author who avoids placing the self-conscious at the center of his works.]

Pynchon's anonymity—like his books—calls into question the familiar modes of modern writing and the styles of modern authorship. Just as his books take little interest in the interior psychological labyrinths and the narrow domestic landscapes which are the fields of this century's fiction, so his minimal personal presence in the literary world, the vacancy he offers to the eye of the camera and the interviewer, deliberately rejects all the varieties of artistic heroism which the romantic and modernist traditions have created. Pynchon's books try to be seriously *there;* while he himself is somewhere else entirely.

The aggrandizement of the self-conscious artist, the conflation (as in Joyce) of his person into his work—or, conversely, the cultivation (as in Beckett) of a detachment so complete and serene that it lifts the artist entirely away from the world of his subjects—are both consequences of the change in sensibility which marked the end of the eighteenth century, whose ef-

fects are still with us. That change established self-consciousness (or its corollary, the self's consciousness of a world important only to the extent that it is perceived) as the central fact of human existence and as the central subject of art. It transferred the significant aspects of history from the stable generalities of the human race to the dynamic particularity of individual nations and individual minds. The romantic era hardly invented self-consciousness, but until then it had been a *problem* only for the exceptional—only for the rare Oedipus or Hamlet whose self-conscious isolation could be watched with pity and fear by audiences who were secure in the knowledge that they would never share it. (pp. 1-2)

Pynchon is one of a few, as yet a very few, major writers for whom self-consciousness is a central problem only in their early work, a problem they eventually manage to put aside. In these writers' maturity, self-consciousness becomes only one of many possible channels of perception, and not the most important one. (Brecht is another such writer; Auden is a third.) To the methods of reading and criticism which the past two centuries have developed in order to domesticate romantic and modernist literature, the work of these writers is almost opaque and impermeable. But those methods of reading have reached the point of diminishing returns. Pynchon suggests this in *Gravity's Rainbow.* The one character whom the book presents through the techniques of self-conscious modernism ends in disintegration and dissolution. He literally falls apart, diffuses. This character is Tyrone Slothrop, the reflexive, isolated, mysteriously inspired charismatic who attempts a quest for an understanding of his own uniqueness. His literary modes of being, the means through which he exists on the printed page, are private perspective and interior monologue—the central literary modes of the great Moderns. Slothrop's failure and disappearance dramatize Pynchon's conviction that these modes are no longer sufficient to the tasks of literature. The work of self-discovery which they were designed to perform has now been done. For Pynchon there are other tasks, and other methods. . . . (pp. 2-3)

In its attention to the interior landscape, recent fiction has forgotten the density of the exterior one. Modernism prefers to speak of the world of politics and ethics in personal and aesthetic terms. Pynchon does the opposite. In his books, character is less important than the network of relations existing either between characters, or between characters and social and historical patterns of meaning. Pynchon also tries to attend to the force with which history, politics, economics, and the necessities of science and language shape personal choices and are in turn shaped by those choices. To see in this a deliberate turning away from novelistic realism, as some readers have done, is to confuse certain mediating literary conventions with unmediated reality. For most of this century, fiction has located the origins of human action in the depths of personal psychology. Pynchon comes up for air and looks elsewhere. What he finds seems cold and abstract only to the extent that it remains unfamiliar in literature and art (if nowhere else).

Pynchon's realism, in short, is built on an attention to realities ignored by the fiction that we have come to accept as "realistic." That is, Pynchon has begun to develop or revive a repertory of conventions that can render aspects of non-literary experience that Modernist conventions are unable to comprehend. To choose a small but significant example: the characters in *Gravity's Rainbow* are among the very few fictional characters whose thoughts and actions are affected by the work they do. In the world outside fiction, anyone can recognize that there is a connection between one's work and one's idea of the world, but Modernism never found—and necessarily could never have found—a way of making use of this recognition. In part, this is because Modernism itself had no work to do, no *use* or *occasion* that demanded its existence, no function in the world beyond its self-declared claims to significance.

In *Gravity's Rainbow* Pynchon begins to find work for his fiction. He tries to respond to an occasion created for his book by the conditions of recent history; that is, he recognizes the changes in modern culture that have created, as other changes have done in the past, a felt need for an encyclopedic fictional survey of the new conditions. Pynchon's book tries to fulfill a public function. From the perspective of *Gravity's Rainbow,* his earlier books, *V.* and *The Crying of Lot 49,* have the appearance of preparatory exercises for this public work; but they have their own importance as well. *V.* served in part as a preliminary essay in organizing vast quantities of data into a coherent literary form. As a piece of apprentice-work it is already mature in technique, but it also has clear signs of the later depths and range. *The Crying of Lot 49,* Pynchon's most attractive and accessible book, was his first effort, in a narrow field, at detailing the kinds of relationships and responsibilities he would explore massively in his third book. (pp. 4-6)

The problem of responsibility, which arises mostly by indirection in *V.,* makes a direct appearance in *The Crying of Lot 49.* This may be why the second book, although much shorter than the first, is far more substantial. . . . There is generally no doubt, in the world of *V.,* that a process of decline is universal, but it is the reader—and not any of the characters—who is in the privileged position of having no doubt about the matter. In *The Crying of Lot 49,* the status of reader and character is altered. Again there is a universal historical process, but now the reader and the book's central character, Oedipa Maas, have equal knowledge of it—and not only equal knowledge, but equal doubt, and

comparable responsibility for its existence or nonexistence. There is no certainty in *Lot 49* (as there is in *V.*) that the book's historical process is "really" (by which, in speaking of fiction, I mean "virtually") there: the book ends with both the reader and Oedipa in doubt. The reader is left not with a puzzle to be solved, as in *V.* or *Ulysses,* but with a radical and insoluble problem of interpretation. *V.* leaves its reader secure in his superiority, once he has found the key to all its mysteries of detail. *Lot 49* leaves its reader caught in an irreconcilable ambiguity, one which takes on a disturbing moral weight. The book ends with Oedipa left alone to decide whether the events she has witnessed do in fact cluster together to point to a "reason that mattered to the world" or whether they simply amount to a chaos which her own paranoia has set into a spurious, projected order. The book offers an analogue of this choice to its reader as well: Is the book in part an ethically disturbing parable of the choices he must make in interpreting the world, or is it merely an aesthetic structure? The book challenges its readers to choose their relation to experience. Either, like the romantics and Modernists, they will project their private aesthetic order onto what they perceive as the malleable or ultimately inaccessible objects of the world, or else they will accept responsibility for and to the order which exists already in the world of which they are an active part. This choice is one that everyone confronts at every moment; but great works of art, those works which both rebuke and console, can make the issues vivid and memorable.

By the time Pynchon wrote *Gravity's Rainbow,* there was no longer any doubt about the difficulty of this choice. Responsibility was now real. Everyone in the book is inextricably implicated in complex patterns of meaning, in large historical processes which at once limit freedom and are themselves established by individual acquiescence and choice. In direct addresses to his readers, Pynchon tries to implicate them also in the choices the book itself includes—either passive acceptance and impersonal detachment, or ethical resistance and personal love. *Gravity's Rainbow* is in part a second-person novel which periodically addresses "you." When a question of interpretation—and its ethical consequences—arises, like the question Oedipa must face at the end of *Lot 49,* Pynchon poses the alternative responses and asks, "Which do you want it to be?"

This is more than a rhetorical stance, more than an artist's self-important pose. Pynchon's questions and challenges to his readers have force—in part because in *Gravity's Rainbow* he himself has changed his literary status from *author* to *institution.* Few authors ever undergo this transition; only one or two who achieve it have ever desired it; and some have endured it who wished it had never happened. But when an author becomes a monument in his own lifetime, the history of his work becomes entangled with the history of his readers and his culture. (pp. 7-9)

Critical industries tend to organize themselves around a special variety of book (or author) which is encountered only rarely in literary history. A useful term for such a book is *encyclopedic narrative;* and one can speak also of an *encyclopedic author.* Not all books that establish industries are authentic narratives of this kind . . . , but all encyclopedic narratives are eventually recognized not only as books which have industries attached to them, but also as *national* books that stand as written signs of the culture of which they are a part. The industries devoted to Dante, Shakespeare, Cervantes, and Goethe are not restricted to the academy; they are national industries as well.

All encyclopedic narratives . . . are metonymic compendia of the *data,* both scientific and aesthetic, valued by their culture. They attempt to incorporate representative elements of all the varieties of knowledge their societies put to use. . . . All encyclopedic narratives contain, *inter alia,* theoretical accounts of statecraft, histories of language, and images of their own enormous scale in the form of giants or gigantism. They are generally set a decade or two before publication, so that they can include prophecies of events that actually occurred in history. All are polyglot books, and all are so determined to achieve encyclopedic range that they exclude from their plots the single centripetal focus that develops when a narrative records a completed relation of sexual love. These books usually appear at the moment when a national culture begins to recognize its uniqueness—at that cusp (to use a word from Pynchon) dividing the pre-history of a national culture from its history, its potential from its actual achievements and failures. At least six such books are familiar to literary history: Dante's *Commedia,* Rabelais' five books of Gargantua and Pantagruel, Cervantes' *Don Quixote,* Goethe's *Faust,* Melville's *Moby-Dick,* and (a special case) Joyce's *Ulysses.* Shakespeare's plays . . . hold a comparable place in English culture, as do Pushkin's works in Russia. (pp. 9-10)

The genre of national encyclopedic narrative is severely exclusive in its numbers but massively inclusive in the contents of its individual members. *Gravity's Rainbow* offers itself as the latest member of the genre. The book proposes itself as the encyclopedia of a new international culture of electronic communication and multi-national cartels. Whether or not Pynchon's historical conceptions will eventually correspond to our culture's perception of itself, at least those conceptions have an urgent plausibility. *Gravity's Rainbow* is a book which hopes to be active in the world, not a detached observer of it. It warns and exhorts in matters ranging from the ways in which the book itself will be read, to the way in which its whole surrounding culture operates.

With some exceptions, critics seem uncomfortable with *Gravity's Rainbow*'s efforts at *agency.* Like generals who are ready to fight the last war but not the next one, critics who dislike *Gravity's Rainbow* try to read it as if it were another *Ulysses.* But to read it this way is to mistake its purpose and its role. (pp. 10-11)

[Joyce] acknowledged that his book focuses on its own structure, and that an understanding of the world outside *Ulysses* is of little use in understanding the world within it. No other major work of art is at the same time so extreme in its factuality and yet so tenuous in its relation to its historical setting.

The inward turn of *Ulysses,* the circularity of its narrative, is among the late consequences of the romantic and modernist sensibility whose triumphant achievement is a literature which exists finally only for itself. Such literature may claim a public function or an unacknowledged legislative role, but these are claims best honored when left untested. (p. 11)

In short, the romantic quest is the image of romantic literature's own condition: purposeless, aspiring to a goal it can never achieve or define. And in *Ulysses,* the circular journey of Bloom, turning in an endless and purposeless repetition, is the culminating disillusioned image of that same condition.

It is different in Pynchon. There is a quest-without-object in *Gravity's Rainbow*—the journey of Tyrone Slothrop—but Pynchon knows that it must lead only to disintegration and dissociation. Pynchon faces, possibly for the first time, the consequences of the romantic quest. Outside the disintegrating Slothrop, the book insists on calling attention to real tasks and purposive choices that cannot be evaded. In *Ulysses,* all ends in resigned forgiveness; from its vast final perspectives, no single event in human history matters very much. But as *Gravity's Rainbow* nears its end, Roger Mexico finds himself approaching a dilemma which he must somehow resolve, a decision from which he cannot turn aside, one which will have irreversible consequences. "It is not a question he has ever imagined himself asking seriously," Pynchon writes. "It has come by surprise, but there's no sending it away now, he really does have to decide, and soon enough. . . . He has to choose between his life and his death. Letting it sit for a while is no compromise." And in raising problems like this one, Pynchon never suggests any comforting possibility that the solutions can be simple or painless.

The ethical problems in *Gravity's Rainbow* have analogues in the linguistic and interpretive problems it raises as well. Language for Pynchon is not a system complete in itself but an ethically and socially performative (his word is "operative") system, one which can be altered by deliberate acts. The model of language in *Ulysses,* on the other hand, is characteristically self-enclosed. For Joyce, the history of language is, in effect, an embryological history (in the chapter known as "Oxen of the Sun"), a version of an unconscious cycle unaffected by personal or social choice. *Gravity's Rainbow*'s history of language (in the episode set in the Kirghiz) is instead political, "less unaware of itself," determined by conscious decisions. Consistently, *Gravity's Rainbow* refers outside itself to the cluster of problems raised by political and ethical conditions, and insists that "letting it sit for a while is no compromise."

In Pynchon, unlike Joyce, the surface details are often incredible and baroque, while the underlying organization is all too plausible and disquieting. Beneath the fantasies and the paranoia, Pynchon organizes his book according to historical and scientific theory—according, that is, to an order independent of *literary* imagination, an order derived more from the realms of politics and physics than from the self-conscious Modernist reflexivities of language and literature. *Gravity's Rainbow*'s large vision of political connectedness has domestic analogues in its vision of sexuality perverted by local varieties of compulsion and control. And, similarly, the book's vision of Slothrop's personal *discon*nectedness (what the book calls "anti-paranoia") has its correspondences in the political chaos of the postwar German Zone—a chaos that is about to be ordered once again into bureaucracies, just as the vacancy left by Slothrop's disintegration will be filled with comforting explanations and organized memorialists.

Serene in its vision of unalterable cycles, *Ulysses* ends just before its beginnings, and closes with its tail in its mouth. *Gravity's Rainbow* devotes its final hundred pages not to a return on itself, but to an effort at finding ultimate beginnings and endings. *Ulysses* ends in an eternal return, *Gravity's Rainbow* in the dangerous facts of a moment of crisis—which is, always, our present moment. (pp. 13-14)

[The] special challenge that Pynchon offers to critics and readers is the challenge to become aware—and publicly aware—of their motives and, in the political sense, of their *interests.* This challenge is never made by modernist literature, which, like romanticism, imagines that it establishes its own value, and uses only its own terms to question itself. . . . *Gravity's Rainbow,* when intelligently read, gives little comfort to the interpretive legions who would rationalize and restrain. And the book has no tolerance for their unacknowledged social motives. (pp. 14-15)

It would be satisfying if one could report that Pynchon's challenge has been met by his critics, but for the most part this has not been the case. There is, of course, nothing that requires a critic to think as his author does—literary history would be in chaos if there were—but when an author questions the basis of a critic's enterprise, then that critic ought at least to acknowledge that the question has been raised.

Pynchon's challenge to confront the motives of criticism, his insistence that readers consider the *effects* of interpretation in the world of ethics, is precisely the challenge that criticism must face if it is to escape at last from the centripetal, reflexive momentum of romantic and Modernist writing and of the literary theory that such writing has engendered. Recent critical theory, especially in its philosophical branches, merely extends the hermetic self-referentiality that his already brought literary Modernism to its unmourned dead end.

Pynchon's challenge to literary studies offers one means of turning away from this dead end—there are other means available as well, of course—and to turn instead to methods of reading that have (as Oedipa Maas imagines in a similar context) "a reason that mattered to the world." As with criticism, so with the act of reading itself: Pynchon challenges his readers to participate, not merely in the linguistic and philosophical puzzles of his books' interpretation, but in the choices that those books make plain. It is a challenge with special urgency, for it is offered by a writer who—in the judgement of this reader, and of many others—is the greatest living writer in the English-speaking world. (p. 15)

Edward Mendelson, in an introduction to *Pynchon: A Collection of Critical Essays,* edited by Edward Mendelson, Prentice-Hall, Inc., 1978, pp. 1-15.

ALFRED MAC ADAM
(essay date 1978)

[In the excerpt below, Mac Adam discusses Pynchon's use of satire.]

When we read a Pynchon text we may be disconcerted by it, but we usually find ourselves comfortable with at least one of its elements: setting. In fact, Pynchon's *mise en scène* may be the only reason for calling his books novels. He is as archeologically precise about places and things as Flaubert, although he should probably be compared to the Flaubert of *Salammbô.* In that text, Flaubert transports Emma Bovary's problems back to Carthage, rendering both Emma and the setting abstract. Pynchon, on the other hand, creates a false familiarity in the mind of the reader which makes him forget that what he is reading is not a study of people in a historical setting but the clash of personified ideas surrounded by the things of the twentieth century. Flaubert and Pynchon are opposites that converge: Flaubert makes the alien familiar by recreating the problems of the nineteenth-century bourgeoisie in Carthage and

Pynchon makes the familiar strange by having his personifications collide in a setting we know only too well.

This disjunction between character and setting is the first indication that Pynchon is a satirist, that he is reworking satire as a modern-day disciple of Petronius, Apuleius, or Voltaire might. In addition to this use of a pasteboard, *trompe-l'oeil* setting, there are three other aspects of his work that support a reading of them as satires: his characters are associated with ideas or *idées fixes,* his scenes take precedence over his plots, and his characters' psychological development is reduced to a minimum. The difference between satire and, for example, novel may be seen in two areas: character and plot. Novelistic plots, as Fielding suggests in *Tom Jones,* both echoing and modifying Cervantes, tend toward history writing, and it would not be unreasonable to suggest that the particular form of history used as the model for novelistic plots is the developmental sort we associate with Hegel. (pp. 555-56)

We cannot become "intimate" with characters in either satire or romance because they never acquire psychological depth. In both genres, character is subordinated to some greater concept, either ideas, in the case of satire, or archetypes, especially those associated with fertility, death, regeneration, or sterility in the case of romance. In both genres, characters are impenetrable, not human, and this alien quality is only mitigated by occasional outpourings of sentiment or flashes of wit. The relationship between satire and romance, with regard to character, is interesting because of the antithetical nature of the two genres: romance tends toward the noble, the heroic, and the superhuman, while satire tends toward the roguish or ordinary. (pp. 556-57)

The juxtaposition of romance and satire is also important for understanding Pynchon's esthetic enterprise because he appropriates one of romance's principal plots, the quest, and uses it for satiric purposes. . . .

All three of Pynchon's texts are ironic quests, but *V,* his first, is the most mysterious. It is a search for something or someone, V, but what V is is never made clear. The search ends in mystery and death, and all the reader knows at the end is that the enigma concerns the existence or nonexistence of something "out there," something that either possesses meaning or not. But whatever it is it must be at all costs ascertained, and this idea of a mystery-to-be-resolved is what defines the reader's situation in all three of Pynchon's satires. *V* is arranged in such a way that, as a totality, it seems to be defying the reader to find a system of meaning. This dare, this either/or crux, is in fact the result of yet another juxtaposition, that of faith and paranoia, and it is through this juxtaposition that Pynchon makes his readers participate in his texts as though they were characters. (p. 557)

The reader of *V,* or so it would seem, cannot help but create meaning as he reads. Despite what may be warnings to the contrary, the reader will inevitably forge both meaning and unity, a plot that signifies, out of a series of chapters from disparate but related stories. The fact that the text is bound as a volume virtually guarantees this creation of meaning, although this very act is one of the pitfalls the author is preparing for his meaning-bound readers. The book begins in 1955 and ends in 1919, a reversal which suggests that time in the text does not have the same relationship to space and meaning it has in romance, where plots are often, as in *Parzifal,* linked to the changes of the seasons. . . .

There are, naturally, other texts that resemble *V,* other texts in which episodes are heaped together in such a way that it is the decision of the reader to determine the presence or absence of meaning. Huxley's *Eyeless in Gaza,* Marc Saporta's *Composition Number 1,* Julio Cortázar's *Hopscotch,* or Guillermo Cabrera Infante's *Three Trapped Tigers* might be examples. In all of these books, as in *V,* the reader is the most important character, whose principal problem is the invention or discovery of meaning in the text. Whether he will exist in doubt and disregard the problem of meaning completely, or whether he will postulate a meaning for the text, is his dilemma. (p. 558)

The clash of faith and paranoia, grace and fulmination is the subject of *The Crying of Lot 49. Gravity's Rainbow* takes an element present in both *V* and *The Crying of Lot 49,* the international corporation, and identifies it as the occult, meaningful system "out there," although while the system is supposed to possess meaning, it is never made clear just what its meaning is, as if meaning could be divorced from intentionality. All we learn in the three books is that the corporation, the Yoyodyne corporation which appears first in *V* and reappears in the other two texts, stands on both sides of all political, social, and ethical fences. In *Gravity's Rainbow,* the protagonist discovers he is actually the "product" of the company, and in *The Crying of Lot 49* we learn that Pierce Inverarity, the dead man who may be the invisible force behind Oedipa Maas's quest, is an owner of Yoyodyne Inc. . . .

The Crying of Lot 49 reveals both Pynchon's sense of literary genres and his attitude toward meaning in literature. This slim volume mediates between two very large-scale enterprises, *V* and *Gravity's Rainbow,* and may be taken as the ironic rewriting of the romance plot of enlightenment (a parody of either *The Golden Ass* or perhaps *La Nausée*) or as a detective fiction in which the detective, like Oedipus, is both the investigator and the object of investigation. Whether by chance or by design, *The Crying of Lot 49* stands as a pivotal text in Pynchon's oeuvre: it restates the central issue of *V,* to make order of confusion or remain in doubt, in the shape of a classical satire, a narrative interspersed with verse interludes, here in the form of songs. This model provides the structure for *Gravity's Rainbow,* the spectacular difference being that of scale. (p. 559)

The most typical of all the devices in Pynchon's repertoire is his use of trick names: how are readers supposed to react to a woman named Oedipa? The Sophoclean or Freudian association is inevitable, and baffling, but an understanding of the device as a device and not as the knot which, once unraveled, opens the way to some deeper meaning, may make Pynchon's esthetics more comprehensible. Our task is to understand the device, not to decipher it. Pynchon's onomastic punning produces a kind of Brechtian "alienation effect," reminding the reader that what he is reading is a fiction, that the words here are only words. (pp. 559-60)

Pynchon seems to have modeled his text on a short story by Jorge Luis Borges, "The Approach to Al-Mu'tasim" (1935) from the *Ficciones* (1944) collection. . . . Borges's story is a bogus book review in which Borges, or his narrator, pretends to be writing about *The Approach to Al–Mu'tasim,* by one Mir Bahadur Alí, "the first detective novel written by a native of Bombay City," a text damned (apocryphally) by the English essayist Philip Guedalla as "a rather uncomfortable combination of those allegorical poems of Islam which rarely fail to interest their translators and those crime fictions which inevitably baffle John H. Watson and refine the horror of human life in the most irreproachable hotels of Brighton" (translations mine). The copy Borges reviews also bears a spurious prologue by yet another English literary figure, Dorothy Sayers, just to make its credentials all the more "irreproachable."

The plot is simple: an Islamic Indian kills a Hindu in a riot. He flees and while hiding finds a horrible man who mentions in passing a few mysterious names. The next day the unnamed protagonist sets out to investigate those names. The search, the quest for whatever lies behind those names, which would seem to be the "good," leads the protagonist, like Kim, over all of India, to all levels of life. In the last scene he approaches the final name, Al-Mu'tasim, an encounter Borges does not describe. He does note that in the second, revised edition, the one he reviews, the text is rendered allegorical: Al-Mu'tasim becomes a symbol of God, the search a search for Him. Pynchon appropriates this story or plot summary and fleshes it out, although it seems he prefers the earlier, less obviously allegorical version, where Al-Mu'tasim's identity is still ambiguous. (pp. 560-61)

Unless we revise *The Crying of Lot 49* and make it too into an allegorical quest for God, we must be content with uncertainty. We can never, if we eschew allegorization, know if Tristero and the W.A.S.T.E. system are good or evil, and we accept the fact that we will never know who is bidding for lot 49 at the end of the narrative. We agree that there is nothing more to the story than unresolved mystery.

Borges resolves the "lady or the tiger" crux Pynchon leaves undecided because he wants to maintain the pose of the book reviewer and because he wants to show the *disponibilité* of any literary plot, its susceptibility to interpretation. Both Pynchon and Borges deploy their material in their own way, but both are rewriting the same plot, the quest. (p. 561)

One way, then, of approaching *The Crying of Lot 49* is to dismiss the reader's quest for meaning from the inquiry. Instead of dispelling ambiguity for the sake of coherence or intellectual security, the reader would focus his attention on how the text deploys its devices and how it translates the satiric tradition. We might begin with character: Mucho Maas, Metzger, Hilarius, and the others stand as foils for Oedipa Maas; she is chosen to be Pierce Inverarity's executrix, they are not. None of them is meant to be the *pharmakos.* . . . These characters are only updated types. For the Panglossian pedant of traditional satire, Pynchon substitutes the mad psychoanalyst. The rest of Oedipa's male companions embody one or another profession, from lawyer to disc jockey, each in his way caricaturing all members of his profession. The rock groups and the Yoyodyne chorus stand as ironic commentators on the action, their traditional role in satire.

Another fixture of satire reworked here is the relentless outpouring of information. Pynchon includes an inordinate amount of scientific knowledge about such matters as entropy and the calculus theorem abbreviated as "dt" or "delta-t." Entropy, divorced both from physics and communication theory and translated into literary speculation, defines the relationship between a text and a tradition. A text may simply reiterate the given patterns of a literature as long as there is enough energy in the system, the complex relationship between readers and writers, to sustain it. But somewhere in the business of literary production the system begins to lose energy—epics, for example, are today only sporadically written and even more rarely read. In order to revitalize the process, some agency recombines elements present in the tradition so that work may go on. This would seem to be the role of the individual author: he cannot contribute new elements to the process, but he certainly can recombine them in a new way, or, more importantly, infuse new power into the system by means of irony. (pp. 562-63)

The importance of irony in this revitalization cannot be overemphasized. And Pynchon's irony is derived primarily from juxtaposition: he wants romance and satire to clash and to create a situation in which the reader will realize that both genres are nothing more than fictions, not mirrors of the age or imitations of life. . . .

In this sense, Oedipa Maas is a metaphor for the reader, just as Pierce Inverarity may be understood to represent the artist. His name, as suggestive as hers, renders both roles sexual, the artist being the masculine, the reader feminine. His given name, Pierce, complements this sexual division of labor by evoking the phallic stylus violating the white purity of the page, while his last name, Inverarity, hints at such concepts as inveracity and inversion, the illusory or lying aspect of writing. The text constitutes the communion of these two archetypes, the writer who leaves of himself only the misleading traces of his will . . . , and the reader who executes it, seeing it in an extraordinarily dark glass. Oedipa follows Pierce's map, and it is through this act that the calculus concept becomes a literary metaphor: she charts his course as if it were the trajectory of a projectile instead of a literary plot. . . . She sacrifices her life in order to carry out his ambiguous will, but without her sacrifice, entropy would once again threaten the system. Without the participation of the reader, the text would cease to exist. (p. 563)

Oedipa's role as reader and interpreter is alluded to throughout *The Crying of Lot 49*, but perhaps the most significant instance occurs at the beginning of chapter 2, when she first comes to San Narciso, Pierce Inverarity's city in southern California. She associates Pierce's realm, as she observes it from above, with a printed circuit: "there were to both [San Narciso and the printed circuit] outward patterns a hieroglyphic sense of concealed meaning, of an intent to communicate." . . . What the actual message is, what the meaning is of the circuit or city, which both stand as signs in an unknown script, is the plot she sees spread out before her. Just as in one version of Borges's story the search is its own justification and not the outcome of the search, the searcher, in this case, the reader, would seem to be the real object of the quest. Oedipa, in the same passage, senses the adumbration, the shadow of Pierce . . . , and the narrator calls it "an odd, religious instant," vaguely horrifying yet wonderful. Suddenly the geometry of the scene changes: instead of looking down on San Narciso, Oedipa is in the middle of things, the eye of a hurricane. . . . Oedipa is variously looking down at a man-made landscape, an artifact as artificial as a literary plot, or standing at the center of a silent whirl, excluded from communication, divorced from the Word, yet tantalized by the possibility both may exist. Fixtures taken from a literary tradition concerned with producing awe through language are here made grotesque: if there is a divinity in this text, it is Pierce Inverarity, proteus, wearing one more disguise.

Another romance device revitalized through irony here is the interpolated tale. Here it is Richard Wharfinger's Jacobean drama *The Courier's Tragedy*, a bogus text worthy of comparison with Mir Bahadur Ali's *The Approach to Al–Mu'tasim*. We notice that the play constitutes a gathering point for two of *The Crying of Lot 49*'s principal themes, the Echo and Narcissus relationship between Oedipa and Pierce (which is a motif: San Narciso, the Saint Narcissus of Wharfinger's play, and Echo Courts, the motel in San Narcisco where Oedipa stays), and the concept of language as a failed system of communication, one which has only a shadow existence, an "intent to communicate" (just as road systems, printed circuits, urban design all seem to be attempts to say something, although what that may be is unknown), while true communication can only take place between those linked by bonds other than language, those who have been initiated into secret societies. Of course, what is communicated among the initiates is not a message but the fact of communality, which would make them like circuits through which an electric current would flow. Wharfinger, much sicker than his namesake "Sick Dick," member of yet another rock group, wrote, according to Driblette, his twentieth-century director, another "reworker" analogous to Borges and Pynchon, only to entertain. . . . The interpolated play, like its traditional counterparts, reflects and comments on the major action: *The Crying of Lot 49* is entertainment and it entertains, like Gothic romance, by posing mysteries, enigmas not to be resolved but to be enjoyed for their own sake.

It is perhaps as entertainment that all satires should be read instead of being defined, as they have been, as literature's commentary on society's foibles. Satire may use its didacticism as an *apologia pro vita sua*, but to reduce Swift, Pope, and Peacock to the level of censor is to trivialize their texts as esthetic enterprises. What Pynchon attempts to do in his writings is to create a literature that destroys the concept that art must mirror life. His texts constantly point out their own artificiality, their identity as literature, and consistent with this mockery of the dictates of literary realism is a turn toward intellect, to the mind as creator of unreal systems, especially philosophy and theology. (pp. 564-66)

The ideology of satire, as Pynchon writes it, is not to reform the reader, who would then, presumably, reform the world, but to reclaim for literature one of the purposes essential to all rhetorical exercises: to delight. (p. 566)

Alfred Mac Adam, "Pynchon as Satirist: To Write, to Mean," in *The Yale Review*, Vol. LXVII, No. 4, Summer, 1978, pp. 555-66.

CHARLES CLERC
(essay date 1983)

[Clerc is an American novelist, short story writer, and critic. In the excerpt below, he discusses various aspects of *Gravity's Rainbow*.]

The word *classic* is bandied so freely these days that it has become virtually meaningless. It is a favorite in the bloated repertoire of hype, and hype, as we all know of contemporary culture, almost never delivers the goods promised. Nevertheless, the word still must be taken seriously when the genuine article comes along. The important criterion for a novel, beyond its own aesthetic accomplishments, is that it will have enduring significance and worth, a work of art to be read and discussed and analyzed with ever renewing enjoyment, understanding, and enrichment by generations of readers.

In these respects, Thomas Pynchon's *Gravity's Rainbow* is destined to become a classic of literature. (p. 3)

It would be unreasonable to expect that any single novel could provide sufficient materials for a liberal education, but certainly *Gravity's Rainbow* comes closer to that goal than any other work of fiction produced in America. It is a dazzling pioneer work in its utilization of manifold subject matter: history, war, mythology, literature, film, culture (whether canonical or pop), religion, philosophy, the military-industrial complex (whether in peace or war), psychology, politics, geography, cybernetics, sex, death, comedy, scatology, music, international cartels, engineering, ballistics, mysticism, plastics, and many more. Further, some of these areas have their own subdivisions; for instance, science, which includes specific uses of chemistry, mathematics, biology, physics, and cosmology. As a multitopic novel, it thus makes many demands of its readership. . . .

Gravity's Rainbow should be experienced, in the best sense of the word. It is a novel to be enjoyed and endured, fought with and agonized over in the zone of intimacy between reader and page. (p. 9)

Whatever interpretations are brought to bear, there is no mistaking the historical foundations upon which the novel is built. Although wonderfully inventive and imaginative, it pays scrupulous attention to verifiable factual details. As historical fiction, one of its chief intentions is to reflect inheritance of the past in the present. The major historical symbol that unifies the four parts of the novel and many of its seventy-three unnumbered chapters and that also resonates into

multiple meanings for our own time is the German A-4 rocket, known more commonly as the V-2. The terrible reign of these flying bombs shattered Britain during the latter stage of the war. The Rocket is a symbol that betokens modern civilization's obsession with technology, whether devising, building, or launching the weapon, or pursuing the secrets of its mysterious potency. As a gigantic destructive phallus, it couples sex and death and links to other related obsessions. (p. 11)

Gravity's Rainbow is the kind of artistic work that needs to be read slowly, thoughtfully, and persistently in small chunks, without distraction, and then read again and again. Many of its passages are so extraordinary that they ought to be read aloud. Such suggestions may seem unwarranted, perhaps pointless, because the same can be said of any challenging literature. But in this case the advice is emphatically necessary because the reader must surmount obstacles that grow fiercer along the way. To complicate matters, the author puts on an intellectual light show of such erudition that its beams bedazzle rather than clarify. Thus the reader may often be prevented from knowing where he or she is going. . . .

First, the novel's enormous cast is difficult to keep track of, especially in the moiling rush of their entries and exits. Some of the principal characters do not appear until the middle third of the novel. The unsuspecting reader may be thrown off by the initial twenty pages devoted to minor characters. Some incidental characters occupy long later passages; others will merely trip in and out of a paragraph or even a sentence. Furthermore, an important character may be dropped, not to reappear for hundreds of pages, or simply dissolve. (p. 12)

Besides the difficulty of keeping all the characters straight, the reader encounters difficulty following the lines of action. Just as Pynchon abandoned some traditional notions of characterization, he also dispenses with some of the standard and familiar guidelines for constructing plots. In a novel filled with schemes, conspiracies, spying, networks, conglomerates, the plotting cannot be disentangled with any ease, nor should it be. The same holds true for the intricate path-crossings of individuals, all in search of something or other: a rocket, relatives, lovers, power, secrets, drugs, kicks, or their own identity. (p. 15)

Although treatment of characters and plot may seem initially overwhelming, like a parody of an internationalized soap opera . . . , the two problems can be surmounted. Many novels of the past—typical social novels or family sagas from Russia, Britain, Scandinavia—have had huge casts and multiple story lines. But Pynchon's ways of telling his story require some readjustment by even the most practiced readers. His narrative methodology confirms that the timeworn critical tactic of affixing convenient plot, characterization, motives, and so on may be in large measure an inappropriate enterprise. The episodic, discontinuous structure manages to work effectively for conveying varied modes of experience, and, in turn, for reflecting the chaos of fragmenting cultures. The swift movie-cutting, the mixture of styles, the picaresque movement, the sporadic pacing, the emphasis on poetic evocation, the crazy quilt of subject matter, historicity, and the outright subversion of that same historicity by comedy and surrealism, amply reveal that the reader who is used to the staples of consistency, causality, credibility, and unity of effect is in for many surprises.

One of them is digressiveness, which allows Pynchon to pursue any tangent, whether a scientific discourse or the history of generations behind a character. . . . Unquestionably, some of the detours are long and self-indulgent. Creative genius may on occasion give way to excess, particularly when the artist is a put-inner, like Pynchon, rather than a take-outer. Once begun, the putting-in process becomes difficult to stop, a problem clearly evident in, say, Joyce's later fiction, in Jean-Luc Godard films, in the music of Stravinsky. Although this novel might have profited from greater selectivity in places, the detours eventually come to be regarded as within the itinerary. In fact, upon reflection most are found to be integral, and a few are positively brilliant. . . . Overall, the digressions contribute rather than detract, so that in the end—to use Pynchon's words from another context—"It was worth the trip, just to see this shining. . . ."

The narrative voice is extremely flexible. Of indeterminate gender, it often stays detached to maintain an objective third-person point of view, but it also rises in protean ways to become involved, intimate, even paranoid. It speaks pointedly to the reader ("You will want cause and effect. All right."), makes frequent other uses of second person ("You have to be on your toes for this: you trade four-line stanzas. . . ."), and on rare occasions gives parenthetic advice, like its recommendation that the reader check out Ishmael Reed. . . . Whenever objectivity is set aside, the flexibility of the voice makes possible various uses. Among examples, it can be didactic to settle a score (although Pynchon almost never delivers overt messages); it can be lyrical to convey emotions; it can be deeply concerned, in which case Pynchon may skirt character to address the reader directly, sometimes seeming to embrace humanity as he does so; it can be ambiguous, provoking diverse streams of thought in the reader. In these shifts the voice may give the impression of being many and haphazard, but it is singular and quite in control. Even punctuation becomes a manipulative instrument. Ellipses are liberally used to suspend action, to pause, to suggest prolonged continuance or repetition, to trail off, to interpolate, and conversely to join,

ideas. And undercutting is achieved by glibly nimble phonetic shortenings, such as *sez* for *says*.

Like the mercurial voice, the tone also refuses categorization. It can be tender and compassionate, hard and ruthless, witty, sensitive, jolly, obscene. It can dynamically shift from straight-forward scholarly data to jaunty hyperbolic cartooning, from graphic realism to sophomoric tomfoolery to elegiac beauty. (pp. 16-18)

Additional proof that Pynchon loves to play with mood, as he loves to play with language and ideas, may be seen in his use of interruptive-supportive songs and poems, which number close to a hundred and range in length from a couplet to some fifty lines. They cover a wide diversity of types: from macaronic to limerick to haiku, from cadenza to Broadway show tune; they come in varied languages, mostly English, but also German, Latin, Middle Dutch, Spanish, Japanese; their rhythms change from beguine to fox-trot to sea chanty, from rumba to jazz to Hawaiian beat. One beguine, "Pavlovia," is sung by laboratory rats and mice doing a Busby Berkeley dance routine. A few more are equally as silly. . . . They work in a manner equivalent to songs in musical comedy, except that often their presence is oxymoronic. They are used to change mood and focus, to spoof, to extrapolate, to underscore action while at the same time achieving distance from it, to show a lighter underside to horror or ugliness or futility, to hint at the illusion behind the reality or vice versa. Notably, the songs, as if in spite of themselves, also lend support to an ironic affirmation. (p. 18)

This juxtaposition of the apocalyptic and the comic is a sure sign of Pynchon's ambivalence. For all the novel's forbidding concerns with waste, fragmentation, destructiveness, victimization, and death, life is sustained. Much of that very sustenance derives from humor, the unquenchable human capacity to laugh at ourselves. *Gravity's Rainbow* is a very funny book, laden with sight gags, practical jokes, zany chases, and pratfalls. Its puns are deliberately egregious: "I Ching feet," "Unto thee I pledge my trough," "For DeMille, young fur-henchmen can't be rowing." (p. 19)

Although one of the most serious novels ever written persistently attempts not to take itself too seriously, its seriousness is magnified—for the same reason that an image of giving the finger can be inverted and overblown to become an atomic bomb blast. So we are never able only to laugh, not with a book as concomitantly visceral and discomforting as this one. There is no way to avoid being moved by the homages to nature, by sadness for the passed-over Preterite, by pain of loss, especially of the young like Ilse or Bianca, because the author's sympathy for children comes through so genuinely. Nor is there any escape from the squirm of shock brought on by vivid details of sado-masochism and coprophilia. On the comic side of the spectrum, Slothrop falls naked through a tree using a purple bedsheet as a parachute; on the tragic side, Blicero sends Gottfried hurtling off to a fiery ritual suicide in the Rocket. It is not always easy to reconcile these disparities of low comedy and high tragedy. By the same token, Pynchon's narrative methodology is often so indirect and tortuous that the reader may be uncertain of what is going on. (pp. 19-20)

Beams flashing the brightest in *Gravity's Rainbow* generate from Pynchon's own erudition. They cause us to blink and squint and grope because he knows so many subjects we may know little about: quantum mechanics, the Beveridge Proposal, the five positions on the launching switch of an A-4 rocket. His reconditeness encompasses tarot cards, the Cabala, mandala, Qlippoth, the Wheel of Fortune, delta-t, double integral, yin-yang, a mathematical equation for motion under yaw control. He dips into Orphic, Norse, and Teutonic myths, and divines with ease necessary detritus of pop culture: Wonderwoman, German movies, zoot suits, Plasticman, King Kong, the Wizard of Oz, Carmen Miranda's hats.

By authentic quotations and paraphrasing, Pynchon makes serious use of mathematicians, scientists, philosophers, socio-political thinkers like Leibniz, Kekulé and Heisenberg, Max Weber, Wernher von Braun, and Teilhard de Chardin. He dredges up Patrick Maynard Stuart Blackett's buried remark that "the scientist can encourage numerical thinking on operational matters, and so can help to avoid running the war on gusts of emotion," which appeared in the obscure *Scientists at the Operational Level,* published in 1941. . . . As is Pynchon's customary playfulness, these authoritative citations are counterbalanced by imaginative flights: his Proverbs for Paranoids, his excerpt from *Neil Nosepicker's Book of 50,000 Insults,* his fragment from the Gospel of Thomas: "Dear Mom, I put a couple of people in Hell today." A plethora of allusions from literature, art, opera, film, science, music, and scripture beckon the cataloger to Gilbert and Sullivan, Käthe Kollwitz, Conrad, *Moby Dick,* Tannhäuser, Prometheus, *The Waste Land,* Hänsel and Gretel and the Witch, Fritz Lang, the Bible, Elena Petrovna Blavatsky, the Niebelungen Saga, Jakob Ackeret. He authentically quotes Emily Dickinson on decay and death and parodically injects a monosyllabic "What?" from Richard Nixon. A mournful dirge is played by Rainer Maria Rilke's *Duino Elegies,* which recurs again and again.

The allusions have a way of reinforcing their new context and enlarging the situation. Moreover, they can be symbolic or analytical, and, most importantly, they can contribute by enriching thematic meaning. (pp. 20-1)

The keenest probe among the beams of erudition is historical: it emanates from Pynchon's sound knowledge of the organization of international cartels, life in London during the Blitz, inner workings of Peenemün-

de and Nordhausen, intricacies of the German black market. Down to the trivia of prison camp jargon, an American B movie, comic book action, radio shows, including who played what on the organ for BBC, it is a brilliantly researched novel (overlooking a few minor errors), all the more remarkable because, as a child during World War II, Pynchon could bring no firsthand knowledge of the period to his book.

These ramifications of esoterica and research suggest that the reader be sufficiently literary and intellectual to want to pursue the references, the puzzles, the allusions, the concatenations. However, the appeal is not meant to be strictly elitist. A sensuous, unschooled vulnerability may be just as important as trained critical faculties. Put another way, the reader ought to be quite nonliterary too—open, responsive, amenable to radical form and diverse content. In either case, some powers of discernment are needed because Pynchon has a way of writing history as if it didn't happen, when it did—or vice versa. The reader is probably better off for knowing the difference. . . . Pynchon makes no concession to an audience to whom a more readable, clear-cut novel might otherwise appeal. Here, then, is a writer determined to go his own way, to present the universe as he sees it.

What is the nature of his vision in *Gravity's Rainbow*? The reader is forewarned on the very first page of "a progressive *knotting into*—." That entanglement becomes a cultural and historical emblem of Western traditions. The culmination of "knotting into" is the massive gargoyle of modern society malformed by war and political-industrial-technological chicaneries, all extensions of past malaise. Although authorial reach is necessarily vast, it is also selective in its fixations upon origins, values, hierarchies, upon superficialities, fantasies, and endings. Furthermore, the novel is tenaciously concerned with a mysterious supernatural world beyond the empirical ordinary one we know. (pp. 21-2)

The complexity of Pynchon's vision is spun out by webs of motifs, images, and symbols each identifying with some theme or fragment of theme. (p. 22)

These and other thematic subjects emerge out of the brilliant conceptual stroke of creating a war novel that is less about war than it is about how a world was and is wrought. It fixes upon a moment in history when the world was poised at apparent teeter-totter balance—the past on one side, the future, including of course our own time, on the other. At a barely distinguishable fulcrum, a chaotic war ends, a chaotic peace begins, Europe is divided up, new allegiances are formed, and the dark, age-old magnetism points the weapons across the deadly playground all over again. Their firing must perforce follow the rainbow of gravity—if they fire. That basic tension is subjected to a series of interrelated dialectical tensions. . . . Some are dramatic contrasts that do not necessarily provoke any authorial judgement: like German-American (or Russian-American, etc.), mind-body, cause-effect, war-peace.

The last duality reminds us again of the consistent unusualness of Pynchon's vision. In his view, there is virtually no difference in conditions of our existence in either peace or war. The teeter-totter hardly moved; nothing much happened at the fulcrum. Put another way, the same forces remain at work upon humanity when a war is over. This is one reason why almost no significance is attached in the novel to the ending of World War II.

Other tensions represent decidedly negative and positive poles: control-freedom, rationality-fantasy, determinism-randomness, mundaneness-magic, supernature-nature, stasis-flux, repression-uninhibitedness, "modern analysis-savage innocences," frigid north-tropical climes, fragmentation-connectedness, white-black, Elect-Preterite, They-We. Pynchon's attraction to the positive poles in all these instances is clearly discernible. His sympathies go out to little people, clowns, rebels, children, endangered species (man or animals), victims, rapscallions who are endearing because they either resist the System or disdain it by their carefree attitudes. (pp. 23-4)

The resolution of one dispute will probably continue to remain tantalizing: ascertaining whether Pynchon is ultimately a diabolic prophet of doom or a humanistic visionary. At first, critical response to the novel seemed to favor the former, but in recent years the pendulum has swung toward more humanistic readings. Which is probably as it should be, since even in an apparent dead heat optimism will win out over pessimism. The writer, after all, is on hand to give alarm signals, not death knells. Otherwise, if the decline of civilization were irreversible, one must wonder the point of even writing about it. The issue merits continued debate. Meanwhile, artistry always matters more than polemics anyway, and we can be indebted to Pynchon for the richness of his created worlds and, we must hope, others to come. (p. 24)

Charles Clerc, in an introduction to *Approaches to "Gravity's Rainbow"*, edited by Charles Clerc, Ohio State University Press, 1983, pp. 3-30.

MICHAEL WOOD
(essay date 1984)

[In the excerpt below, Wood discusses Pynchon's early stories collected in *Slow Learner*.]

It's always an occasion when the invisible man comes to dinner. Thomas Pynchon, like J. D. Salinger, is a writer who has been hiding away for years, and in *Slow Learner* he cautiously paints himself back into the public view. Indeed, he makes more of an appearance than he has ever done, since the volume not only collects five early works but offers an easygoing, seemingly vulnerable 20-page introduction by the vanishing author himself. . . .

This introduction had me worried for a while. Was this man of such patient discretion about to crumble and cry, to spill his soul on the confessional page? It would be like the Scarlet Pimpernel having a breakdown. Why was Mr. Pynchon presenting these pieces if he didn't like them? But my worry soon subsided. There is no confession, only the reflections of a writer looking back over ground traveled, and a very engaging, informal history of an odd American time, the tag end of the 50's, too late for bop and beat, too early for the hippies. (p. 1)

In his introduction to *Slow Learner* Mr. Pynchon . . . says of his generation: "There were no more primary choices for us to make. We were onlookers: the parade had gone by and we were already getting everything secondhand, consumers of what the media of the time were supplying us." It was the generation of students Lionel Trilling became very worried about; they were receiving Kafka's despair and Conrad's anguish as commodities, dished out in literature courses among other requirements.

What is admirable about Mr. Pynchon is that, knowing this, he doesn't give up or set out to become a lumberjack, searching for fabulous, untainted writerly experience. He writes with the resources that writers always have, but will not always use: memory, imagination, curiosity, access to accumulated funds of knowledge. This approach paid off particularly in *Gravity's Rainbow* (1973), where Mr. Pynchon impeccably describes details of life in wartime England—and speculates, amid a densely imagined postwar Europe, not on the personal quests and panics of his earlier novels, but on the possible master connections of modern history: the links between rocketry and Puritanism, for instance, or between language and death; between race and sex, and sex and class; between the anonymous cruelties of economics and the things we are now (but were not always) prepared to do to each other. . . . We may quarrel with or fail to comprehend whole chunks of this difficult book but there can be no doubt that it is here to stay, a major work whose local liveliness is such that its parts make us want to bet on the whole.

The faults of his early stories are just what Mr. Pynchon says they are—"bad habits, dumb theories," purple prose and a portentousness that crops up in all his writing. What he doesn't talk about, although it is a perfect answer to our question about why he is publishing this book, is how extremely good the stories are for all their faults, how quickly they carry us into their scruffy, variegated, wonderfully imagined worlds. . . .

"The Small Rain" centers on one Nathan "Lardass" Levine, a sort of ancestor of Benny Profane in *V.*, and an enlisted man who is sleeping his days away at Fort Roach, La. He is a college grad who takes the army as a refuge from feeling and thought, from what a character in *V.* calls "the acquired sense of animateness." He is sent out on a detail helping to clear up after a hurricane, and one day, without being ordered to and without knowing why, he joins a group collecting corpses from the flood. . . .

Does Levine find his way back to life because of this encounter with death? Perhaps. At the end of the story he is asleep again. The hovering presence of T. S. Eliot's "The Waste Land" in this text is a little tiresome, to use Mr. Pynchon's word. All these characters are waiting for rain, see, rootless soldiers in a dry and then soaked land. (p. 28)

The landscape of **"Low-lands"** moves steadily toward fantasy. The scene changes from a Long Island house full of sewers and cellars and "innumerable tunnels, which writhed away radically like the tentacles of a spastic octopus" to a nearby dump . . . ; beneath its blasted surface the dump is honeycombed with tunnels and secret rooms, the work of a 30's terrorist group. Dennis Flange, a well-off ex-navy man, is thrown out of his home by his wife and finds in the dump a romantic, diminutive rescuer in the shape of a lovely girl called Nerissa, only three and a half feet tall. . . .

Flange, like Levine, is hiding in various ways from life's entanglements, and perhaps little Nerissa, as Mr. Pynchon suggests in his introduction, is a picture of what Flange thinks he can manage. . . . What Flange fears is "eventual convexity," the rising wave, the dump filled in so that the plain becomes a hill, "so that he would be left sticking out like a projected radius, unsheltered and reeling." These moral landscapes are metaphors for his need, and the impossibility of his position is part of Mr. Pynchon's implied argument.

Flange meets Nerissa at "a desolate hour somehow not intended for human perception," and this, in many ways, is Mr. Pynchon's hour. Amid a shuffling, funny, amiable life, the 50's behaving as if they would last forever, someone sees what he was not supposed to see, as if the heart of darkness were to open up in Nassau County. The story brings us very close to *V.*, which has the same mixture of austere thought and broad but enjoyable bad jokes. By the time of *Gravity's Rainbow,* of course, the ordinary world is not so amiable or funny to start with; it has fallen into war and its aftermath, and is mined with conspiracies, like the dump in **"Low-lands."**

"Entropy" is the best known of Mr. Pynchon's stories, much anthologized and commented on. It gains from being placed in the company of the other early pieces, because its characters, like those in the other stories, can be seen searching for images, means of arranging their lives in their minds. Thus Callisto in **"Entropy"** seals himself in his room, "a tiny enclave of regularity in the city's chaos," thinks about entropy and awaits the end of the world, the moment when all temperatures, inside and out and everywhere, will be the same, and so no heat of any kind will be transferred. (pp. 28-9)

Critics are fond of this story, with its neat antitheses—the death wish in one place, the disorder of life in another. . . . But I find that **"Entropy"**'s abstraction makes it rather pale in comparison with the other pieces in *Slow Learner.* Still, I treasure the crazy communion of those silent musicians. What difference does it make, if there is nothing to hear, whether one of them is playing the wrong tune, or no tune? How could they even know? It makes all the difference, I would say, and that is how we know a lot of what we know—like whether we are loved, and when people are lying to us. It's all a matter of "inference," of "imaginative anxiety," as Mr. Pynchon says in **"V."** We can get all sorts of things right by those means. Wrong too, of course, but nobody's perfect. . . .

Thomas Pynchon was a cult figure in the mid-60's. Copies of *V.* were passed around and annotated amid the Dylan records and the beginning of the end of the Beatles. He was then taken up in a big way by the academy and must be now among the most written about of contemporary authors. I have the highest opinion of Mr. Pynchon's work myself, but what I miss in the figure he has become for scholarly critics, in the difficult, meditative writer who is thought to put all merely lucid or entertaining practitioners to shame, is the sense of a man in a particular time and place, and of a living author whose faults as a writer are not to be extricated from his great virtues. This is just what *Slow Learner* helps to restore. (p. 29)

Michael Wood, "The Apprenticeship of Thomas Pynchon," in *The New York Times Book Review,* April 15, 1984, pp. 1, 28-9.

SOURCES FOR FURTHER STUDY

Cowart, David. *Thomas Pynchon: The Art of Allusion.* Carbondale: Southern Illinois University Press, and London: Feffer & Simons, 1980, 154 p.

> Analyzes Pynchon's use of such media forms as painting, film, music, and literature in his fiction.

Hite, Molly. *Ideas of Order in the Novels of Thomas Pynchon.* Columbus: Ohio State University Press, 1983, 183 p.

> Study of form, structure, plot, and other elements in Pynchon's novels.

Schaub, Thomas H. *Pynchon: The Voice of Ambiguity.* Urbana: University of Illinois Press, 1981, 165 p.

> Explores indefinite aspects of Pynchon's fiction.

Seed, David. *The Fictional Labyrinths of Thomas Pynchon.* Iowa City: University of Iowa Press, 1988, 260 p.

> Close reading of *V., The Crying of Lot 49, Gravity's Rainbow,* and the short stories. Seed stresses Pynchon's concern with crafting a fictional counter-history of Western depredations against nature and against the indigenous people of conquered empires.

Stark, John O. *Pynchon's Fictions: Thomas Pynchon and the Literature of Information.* Athens: Ohio University Press, 1980, 183 p.

> Analyzes Pynchon's unusual method of attaining coherency through the use of scientific information and theories in his work.

Tanner, Tony. *Thomas Pynchon.* London: Methuen, 1982, 95 p.

> Concise biographical and critical analysis.

François Rabelais

1494?-1553

(Also wrote under pseudonyms Alcofribas Nasier and *L'abstracteur de quinte essence*) French satirist, editor, and translator.

INTRODUCTION

A Renaissance monk, physician, and scholar, Rabelais has for centuries following his death received resounding acclaim for his *Gargantua and Pantagruel* (1532–64), a multivolume narrative comprising comedy, satire, myth, and humanist philosophy and detailing the epic stories of two giants' upbringing, ribald adventures, and journeys towards self-discovery. Throughout this massive work shine the language and wit of a profound thinker possessing a remarkably original voice and vivacious literary style. A prominent influence on writers from Laurence Sterne to James Joyce, Rabelais ranks as one of the greatest figures in European literature for his dazzling verbal experimentation and corresponding exploitation of the prose narrative form.

Although important dates and biographical events of his life remain uncertain, it is believed that Rabelais was born around 1494 into a wealthy family in Chinon and was tutored at home as a child. He received a formal education at a Franciscan monastery in Poitou. Despite imposition of a severely confined curriculum there, Rabelais and a fellow monk began to independently study many of the Latin, Greek, and Hebrew classics prohibited by the Church. Acquiring in a short time considerable knowledge of secular history, myth, and humanist thought, Rabelais began composing letters in a mixture of Latin and Greek to Guillaume Budé and Desiderius Erasmus, Christian humanists whom he admired for their forthright views and unwillingness to bow to Church dogmatism. He also completed at this time Latin translations of the Greek satires of Lucian, a writer whose style and imagination markedly influenced Rabelais's later prose. Yet, with the monastery's discovery and confiscation of his secretly acquired Classical texts, Rabelais's pursuit of scholarly interests as well as his monastic career were seriously threatened. Fortunately, he received the patronage and protection of a high-ranking friend, Bishop Geoffroy d'Estissac, who accepted Rabelais into the Benedictine order at Saint-Pierre-de-Maillzeais in 1524.

As d'Estissac's secretary, Rabelais travelled with the bishop throughout his diocese and became intimately acquainted with rural peoples, acquiring a keen ear for rustic dialects, popular tales, and an appreciation of simple existence—all of which heavily imbued his fictional world. Following two years under d'Estissac, Rabelais set out on his own as a secular priest and aspiring physician who travelled about France teaching and studying. In 1530 he entered the widely esteemed University of Montpellier, where he obtained a medical degree. He soon gained renown as a talented lecturer, doctor, and editor-translator of works by the Greek physicians Hippocrates and Galen, proving instrumental in reviving and incorporating their theories into contemporary medical practice. Because of his reputation and accomplishments in the field, Rabelais was appointed chief physician in 1532 to the well-known Hôtel Dieu in Lyon.

After editing further Latin and Greek texts that year, Rabelais surprised his colleagues by composing and publishing an apparently frivolous narrative in French, a language which at the time was considered undignified, even vulgar, by the Latin-oriented Church and aristocracy. Explanations for this abrupt literary endeavor include the supposition that Rabelais fixed upon a lucrative publishing scheme because of personal financial problems, and the belief that he had yearned for some time to unleash his convivial wit, cherished by patients, students, and friends, in order to entertain as well as edify a wider audience. In any event, *Les horribles et espouvantables faictz et prouesses du tres renommé Pantagruel Roy des Dipsodes, filz du gran géant Gargantua* (1532; *Pantagruel, King of the Dipsodes, with His Heroic Acts and Prowesses*) proved a huge, instantaneous success. First appearing at the annual Lyons fair, and modeled after a recently published, popular chapbook tale of Arthurian giants (*Les grandes et inestimables chroniques du grand et énorme géant Gargantua*), Rabelais's work met with a captive readership, particularly as *Pantagruel,* unlike its predecessor, contained allusions to current events and more vividly portrayed human life under the humorous guise of gianthood—a fantastic realm then in vogue with French readers. This work was soon revised and expanded and accompanied by two shorter works: ludicrous astronomical predictions by Rabelais's narrator Alcofribas Nasier (an anagram of the author's name) for 1533 and 1534.

In October 1533, *Pantagruel* was denounced by the Sorbonne for excessive obscenity; however, no immediate restrictions were placed on Rabelais. Early the next year Rabelais left Lyons for Rome as companion and personal physician to bishop and diplomat Jean du Bellay. For the next decade Rabelais periodically assisted du Bellay and his brother Guillaume, governor of the Piedmont region of Italy, in various capacities. Primarily, he served as family physician and intermediary in attempts to reconcile Catholic and Protestant factions, who had been at odds since Martin Luther's revolutionary pronouncements against the Church in 1517. Between his travels and official service Rabelais continued to practice and study medicine. He also honed and expanded his literary skills, publishing sequels to *Pantagruel* in 1534, 1546, and 1552. The first of these, *La vie inestimable du grand Gargantua, père de Pantagruel,* represents Rabelais's attempt to recreate the myth of Gargantua, father of his first fictive hero. Due to the chronological precedence of its story *Gargantua* has been placed first in sequence by editors of Rabelais's work. Next came the *Third* and *Fourth Books,* the last to be positively attributed to Rabelais; in these works, the giant element is downplayed and a greater emphasis is placed on the quest for truth and meaning in life. More complex in structure, more copious in allusion and ambiguity, these later books greatly contributed to Rabelais's posthumous reputation as a profound thinker and allegorist. All four books, at the time, were condemned by the Sorbonne, whose members thought Rabelais an immoral, Lutheran sympathizer. Rabelais was also censured by the extreme Protestant wing of the Calvinists, who deemed him a dangerous spokesman for atheistic values. Despite such religious opposition, *Gargantua and Pantagruel* remained immensely popular with a wide cross-section of people, from liberal intelligentsia to marginally educated laboring classes. Due to Rabelais's several influential acquaintances, the publication and sale of his books were protected by royal edict; however, it is believed that Rabelais was occasionally plagued by various religious authorities because of his works and was forced, from time to time, to leave the country.

In his last years Rabelais received the curacies of Meudon and Saint-Christophe-du-Jambet through the patronage of Jean du Bellay. He resigned these offices for unknown reasons in 1553 and died shortly thereafter. Nine years later *L'isle sonante* (1562; *The Ringing Island*) appeared in print under Rabelais's name. The majority of scholars recognize this work as a largely authentic continuation of the Pantagruel story. This publication was followed by *Le cinquième et dernier livre des faictz et dictz heroiques du bon Pantagruel* (1564; *The Fifth and Last Book of the Heroic Deeds and Sayings of the Good Pantagruel*), which included *L'isle sonante* as its first sixteen chapters. The authenticity of the latter portion of this work, given its predominantly unrelieved didactic, moralistic tenor, has been seriously questioned and the issue remains unresolved.

The difficulty of interpreting Rabelais's masterpiece is made apparent by the wide-ranging, conflicting analyses it has received. Some critics perceive a dominant comic element, others a decidedly satiric, and still others a comprehensive fictional plan which incorporates these and other elements in a highly individual, joyful affirmation of humanity. What can be agreed upon by most scholars is that *Gargantua and Pantagruel* is an overwhelmingly rich and complex narrative mosaic which comprises Socratic doctrine, Platonic philosophy, Bacchanalian and biblical allusion, relentless linguistic experimentation, Christian humanism, and an underlying, Renaissance concern with the spiritual and intellectual perfection of the individual.

The unwieldy size and scope of *Gargantua and Pantagruel* prevents simple summary of its circuitous plot and numerous themes. The first two books are closely allied in that both center around the birth, education, and maturity of the hero-giants Gargantua and Pantagruel, who demonstrate remarkable physical prowess and wisdom, yet often find themselves, or their friends, caught in a series of ridiculous predicaments. There results a central dichotomy in Rabelais's work between sagacious, occasionally profound, prose and superficial, rollicking entertainment. Through modern analyses, scholars have shown that despite several ribald episodes and seemingly aimless, digressive language, *Gargantua* does move gradually toward higher concerns. In the closing chapter to Book II, Gargantua builds an archetypal religious abbey (Thélème) for his aide and confidante Friar Jean. The abbey, for its egalitarian tenets and adoption of Renaissance principles of education and open-mindedness, is regarded as Rabelais's idealized conception of a new world order. The inscription on one of its cornerstones, "Fay ce que vouldras" ("Do what you will"), combined with an emphasis on responsible, active participation in God's community on earth, represent ideals which Rabelais iterates throughout the novel in various ways, often cloaking his humanist beliefs in irony, humor, and allegory.

Central to Rabelais's artistic world, and to his humanist conception of life, was the potency, magic, and unlimited appeal of human language itself. Often compared to prose experimentalist James Joyce, Rabelais released in his books a pyrotechnical display of verbal constructs and linguistic games widely considered excelled only by those of *Finnegans Wake* (1939). Yet, such inventiveness, and a purported inattention to contiguous plot and relevant detail, have provoked some harsh criticism of his work. Many sixteenth- and seventeenth-century scholars took his ribald, seemingly amoral humor and madcap verbiage at face value, and labelled the author a drunken fool with a prolific, profane pen rather than a serious writer with a uniquely organized and effectively expressed message for the world. However, most later critics acknowledge the serious intent of *Gargantua and Pantagruel* and accept the wordplay, circuitous narrative, and occasional grossness as the natural outpourings of a literary genius artistically intoxicated with life at its fullest, language at its richest.

Many twentieth-century critical pioneers, from Mikhail Bakhtin, who has studied Rabelais's work as a reflection of medieval folk culture, language, and belief, to Thomas M. Greene, who recognizes Rabelais as a comic writer made complex by his purposeful fictional grounding in paradox and ambiguity, concede that Rabelaisian scholarship is far from complete. Yet, virtually all scholars of European letters affirm his immense importance to the development of European literature and thought. As Bakhtin has declared: "His place in history among the creators of modern European writing, such as Dante, Boccaccio, Shakespeare, and Cervantes, is not subject to doubt. Rabelais not only determined the fate of French literature and of the French literary tongue, but influenced the fate of world literature as well (probably no less than Cervantes)."

(For further information about Rabelais's life and works, see *Literature Criticism from 1400 to 1800,* Vol. 5.)

CRITICAL COMMENTARY

A. F. CHAPPELL
(essay date 1924)

[In the following excerpt, Chappell traces the development of Rabelais's personal philosophy.]

Rabelais was a philosopher. He was not a mere mocker of his fellows. Nor was he always one whose views on life encouraged and urged men to a joyous abandonment to all pleasures. He was, moreover, a philosopher whose school was life, or possibly whose life enabled him to criticize traditional views, and his thoughts were affected no more by his natural buoyant optimism than by the saddest of convictions. Amidst the most boister-

---

Principal Works

*Les horribles et espouvantables faictz et prouesses du tres renommé Pantagruel Roy des Dipsodes, filz du grand géant Gargantua [as Alcofrybas Nasier] (satire) 1532

[Pantagruel, King of the Dipsodes, with His Heroic Acts and Prowesses, 1653]

*La vie inestimable du grand Gargantua, père de Pantagruel [as *l'abstracteur de quinte essence*] (satire) 1534

[The Inestimable Life of the Great Gargantua, Father of Pantagruel, 1653]

†Epistre de Maistre François Rabelais, homme de grans lettres grecques et latines à Jehan Bouchet, traictant des ymaginations qu'on peut avoir touchant la chose désirée (letter) 1545; published in Épîtres morales et familières du traverseur

*Le tiers livre des faictz et dictz heroiques du noble Pantagruel (satire) 1546

[Third Book of the Heroic Deeds and Sayings of the Good Pantagruel, 1693]

*Le quart livre des faictz et dictz heroiques du noble Pantagruel (satire) 1552

[Fourth Book of the Heroic Deeds and Sayings of the Good Pantagruel, 1693-94]

L'isle sonante (satire) 1562

‡Le cinquième et dernier livre des faictz et dictz heroiques du noble Pantagruel (satire) 1564

[The Fifth and Last Book of the Heroic Deeds and Sayings of the Good Pantagruel, 1693-94]

Oeuvres. 9 vols. [variorum edition] (satires) 1823-26

Oeuvres. 7 vols. (satires) 1912-65

*These works are commonly referred to together as Gargantua and Pantagruel.

†This work was written between 1524 and 1527.

‡The authenticity of this work has been debated and remains uncertain.

---

ous pages our attention is arrested by some sad phrase. It may indeed hardly be doubted that his definition of Pantagruelism hides the bitter, patient smile of a disappointed man. It was the same man who spoke of the climax and end of the comedy approaching . . . , when he thought of life and death. And surely something of the same disillusionment explains the sobriety in Bacbuc's rhapsody on natural philosophy compared with the exuberant hopes of the Pantagruelion passage. That is easily comprehended. But if there be a development in Rabelais' views, and if the conclusion be actually of a much later date, it is obvious that other more subtle *differentiae* ["differences"] should be traceable.

The search for Rabelais' philosophy is difficult. His whole romance is so extensive, his wilfully enigmatic utterances so abundant and his appeal to humanity so powerful that there has been always a temptation for his readers to treat Rabelais as Shakespeare and others have been treated. Yet there is hardly the same difficulty to account for the certain failures which come from reading into sundry portions of the romance the most widely divergent systems of philosophy. Unlike Shakespeare, Rabelais probably never succeeded in curbing his personal likes and dislikes; he never wholly succeeded in taking an objective view of his creation. Even the discussions of the *Tiers Livre* are faulty in this, for they each and every one protrude upon us the simple truth which the author would have us grasp. In every part of the romance we never shake off the author's guiding hand, and we may therefore hope to cut through the windings of his labyrinth and so escape into the light of day. The main difficulty is not one of

deciding Rabelais' personal relation to his creatures and their utterances, as it is in Shakespeare; it is one of chronology and of probable development. Most human revaluations time and a changed life will explain; and the change that overtook Rabelais was far greater than any of which we have knowledge from Shakespeare's biography—unless the *Sonnets* hide it. Little, however, as the author of the great tragedies can be recognized in the early worker on still earlier plays, an even wider gap separates the *Tiers* and *Quart Livres* from the two early books. Narrative told for its own sake preceded narrative of a different kind in which from time to time we notice an underlying motive; and we cannot doubt that the fruits of his active life must weigh more heavily than those of his semi-cloistered years. Indeed, contrary to the general practice, we might almost exclude the first two books, so opposed to them is the thought of the mature work; and that would be perhaps justifiable, though it would deprive us of glimpses of the true Rabelais beneath his unnatural trappings. (pp. 160-62)

[His] age seems to have assumed that only in the philosophies of Greece and Rome could the slightest basis of thought be found; and indeed in many instances the real substance of ancient literature was forgotten in fashionable raptures over language and style. In that early period, too, and up to a comparatively late stage in Rabelais' career, everything written in the Greek tongue received equal attention from students. Every man, it has been doubtfully said, is born a Platonist or an Aristotelian, with a mind subjective or objective, though the records of that age hardly confirm the view. Certainly the realist author of *Pantagruel* glided readily into the transcendental author of *Gargantua;* and neither the one nor the other wrote the attack upon the Ramus-Galland controversy. The fact is that when he trusted the ancient wisdom he assumed impartially the doctrines of all; when, however, his eyes were opened, he saw clearly how unreal his contemporaries' learning was, and how vainly mankind could look for help to ancient philosophy. Rabelais was not unaffected by either Platonism or Aristotelianism. It is beyond doubt that he savagely attacked all who clung helplessly to the latter, and that he ridiculed the languorous worshippers at the former shrine; but this rather proves his reasoned or instinctive hatred of the past than definite disagreement with the ancient systems. He was prepared to accept their teachings in so far as they could be proved. In his study of Nature he preferred to follow Pliny rather than Aristotle, and thence resulted a certain resemblance to the philosopher whom he attacked. In his general thought, however, he more clearly inclined towards Platonism. At one time the *Republic,* at another the *Laws,* attracted him; but at all times the *Dialogues* centring round Socrates, and specially the *Memorabilia* of Socrates, were what he delighted in recalling. But—and this is important—these books always charmed his mind because, in the same measure as his experience, they gave him a sense of reality. With little world-knowledge he was satisfied with the *Republic;* greater experience pricked that bubble, and he turned to the *Laws;* but always Socrates seems to have satisfied his greatest needs. And one proof of this lies in his constant rejection of the *Symposium* in spite of his certain acquaintance with it. The gross realism of *Pantagruel,* as well as the Platonism of *Gargantua,* affords the clearest demonstration of Rabelais' sincerity. He appears to have been always sensitively responsive to outside influences, and until he had laid down a course for himself the predominant creed among his immediate associates would always induce belief in him. It is not therefore surprising that having left in turn his vagabond student's life which gave him his first book, and the cultured society of Lyons (Thelema) to enter the world of statesmen and practical men, who are of necessity least bound by academic views, he should have responded in like manner to worldly influences. His mature work was no more Platonistic than the people among whom he spent his days. In the same way his gross egotism, purified by Platonism, almost loses itself in the humble student of man and the world, of the later books. His choice of a profession had somewhat contributed to this change: it had forced upon him interests which, as we can trace in his writings, corrected his unwholesome passion for self-approving display; but it was his delight in all that seemed real to him that had governed his actions from first to last. We can trace that from book to book, under all its disguises. That is the source of his vitality, of his charm, and of his sordid imaginings. His later moderated self-revelation made

of Pantagruel a truly notable character, and commended his work to the most varied types of mind. Surely the man who conceived such a hero, and who combined in him an extensive knowledge of ancient philosophy, introspective insights, and strong interest in the world about him,—surely such a man cannot truly be styled a follower of Aristotle or of Plato. He united the best elements of his race with the most vital energy of Renaissance learning, and he left the past on a voyage of discovery.

The tumultuous movement of the later books, instinct with life and development, clearly demonstrates a more satisfactory freedom than the much boasted dream of Thelema. Without demanding conformity with a preconceived ideal, mankind shall henceforth pursue truth, and find freedom in their search. Not selfish gratification but freedom of the mind to seek and ensure real human welfare became his later ideal. He himself made the journey to the source of truth, and mankind must do likewise. Characteristically his search began with an actual problem, or rather with several urgent questions of the day. Characteristically too, in his enquiries into marriage and prognostication, he ransacked learning and commonplace stories; and he mingled with his spoils his personal convictions and the results of personal observation. Truth, he would seem to say, must be human truth; it is of no advantage to raise questions of the Absolute. Our truths must be of the earth and must shed light upon practical matters, and so philosophers and theologians could not be of much service. And if the avowed purpose of the *Tiers Livre*—the discussion of Panurge's marriage—became almost hopelessly confused, it was because in his quest other equally pressing problems rose in his mind and overflowed into his writing. The one positive subject had led him on to revise all his former values. To compress into such a book all that he had considered, Rabelais would have needed, nay he had probably discovered in the process of composing it that he needed, all the moderation that he later urged upon his readers. For beside the two main topics, there is much in the repeated statement that decision and will-power must be cultivated. Not only Panurge, but the author and human kind also must be trained to decide and act decisively, putting aside the delusive fancy that they may forecast the future. And then too there is the question of death and human destiny, which for the first time rose in the author's written thoughts, but which became more and more insistent. On that question he appears already to have taken up the stand of his maturity in that he combined a sense of mystery with a passionate love of earth. . . . To what he could be sure of he clung with pathetic violence, to earth and worldly interests; and almost with horror he began to reject Platonist abstractions.

He was convinced that only a comprehensive

study of human nature could quiet doubts on the marriage institution and could reveal the truth about it; he asserted time and again that human needs alone may adequately explain human inventions. For him no other conceivable explanation existed, and Pantagruelism could do no more than carry further what physical need (Messer Gaster) had already originated. He revered that mythical being in consequence, but he became enthusiastic over humanity's future triumphs. And in spite of Rabelais' supposed delight in the things of the body, the physical really occupied no more than a subordinate place in his thoughts. (pp. 162-68)

Interest in reality and consequently some neglect of supramundane matters had given him dreams of a system of natural philosophy. And although his work marked little positive advance because, despite his closest scrutiny of ancient scientific lore, he always demanded scientific learning from the Ancients, he compared most satisfactorily in point of achievement with his contemporaries and many of his immediate successors, who claimed to be men of science, and who were actually more favourably placed for scientific study. He was more independent than they of Hearsay ("Ouy-dire"); and even his strong faith in Nature did not run to such extremes as that of lesser men. To him the natural world seemed far from perfect, yet it is that of which man can obtain the most certain knowledge. Indeed Pantagruelion had inspired him with enthusiasm for possible progress; it had appeared to him to be the only means whereby mankind might be newly tempered for its search for truth, and through which the new spirit, undaunted by burnings and persecutions, should cause the old gods to tremble at mankind's power. The vision of man scaling heaven and spreading dismay among "celestial minds" ("intelligences celestes") provokes comparison with Bacbuc's exhortation to the returning pilgrims; but the visionary's study of nature had, long before the arrival at the Oracle, considerably moderated his enthusiasm. No longer did he hope for superhuman powers from scientific knowledge, but all that he dreamed of was to ameliorate mankind's lot on earth. In the later account there is disillusionment and disappointment. His task had proved not so simple as he had believed, but it had become more definite and less fantastic. . . . [Although] with his old zeal he still maintained that all possible recesses of knowledge should be explored, he manifestly felt that the main stumbling block—as it was the strongest support of superstition—was the servile worship of antiquity. True he did not present in its proper relation with this theme the suggestion, made elsewhere, that this reverence for authority sprang from a desire for quiet in an unresting world; nor did he, as elsewhere, proclaim the limitations of the human intellect. Those facts would perhaps have injured the intended effect of this passage. But he did assert that a new spirit, which should not let men

shrink from the unknown as Panurge did from the Frozen Words, must come upon mankind; and in addition to the material progress with which (in the *Tiers Livre*) he had been concerned, he did propose to make intellectual and moral progress. In short Rabelais' life had taught him that scientific and moral advance must be one, and that consequently neither he nor his fellows could hope to realize their high ambitions. The travellers in search of truth must return, not empty-handed, but possessed of the certainty that truth is relative to the hearts and minds of the searchers.

Yet this moral emphasis was no new element in Rabelais' thought. The Olympians say to one another that

Pantagruel will marry; and he will have children by whom a herb will be discovered that shall conduct them to the springs of hail, the channels of rain and the workshop of thunder. They will invade the regions of the moon and, entering the territory of the constellations, they will be able to sit at table with us and take to wife our goddesses, which is the only way to be deified. . . .

Now this final reference to the marriage question was necessary only in so far as it may connect the vision of progress with the discussions of a practical problem. No doubt in the *Tiers Livre* some mention of marriage was to be expected even in the Pantagruelion section; but the peculiar phrasing would suggest that Rabelais was convinced that human problems depend for their solution upon a wider knowledge of Nature, or even that those problems were the chief reason for his scientific curiosity. In the absence of the deeper comprehension of existence there may be certain phenomena to trouble man's basal principles, those principles across and upon which his existence is laid; and the enthusiastic student of science realized that until a moral reformation came to pass those phenomena could not even be analyzed. Rabelais was, it seems, more deeply interested in man than in pure scientific knowledge, hence, no doubt, his reliance upon ancient writers in this respect; and by urging his fellows to press onwards to a full knowledge of Nature's most mysterious retreats, he tried to confine the supernatural and the incomprehensible to a much smaller area. To that task, the real work of the future, he had been permitted to set his hand. And though he had obtained only a hazy view of the promised land, Bacbuc's vision, thus interpreted, would become a worthy conclusion to his whole work. Not purely scientific, that passage would in fact represent the purpose about which he was wholly in earnest.

To dwell too much upon his supposed system of natural philosophy would necessitate the neglect of the more important incidental discoveries that he had made. Certainly the discoverer more dearly prized the insights into life and human nature than his fairly obvious plan which they threw into confusion. From the beginning his main attention had been engrossed by the lives of his fellows, and though his learning and the fulfilment of immediate purposes had obscured this characteristic yet, as we have seen, this living interest pierced repeatedly through the deadening covering. Apparently nothing had been too trivial to arouse his inquisitive nature; and it is therefore an important sign that his love for Plutarch survived and even became more fervid in after life, in spite of much material that he could not help disputing. In Plutarch first the interest in living beings and then the strong ethical interest gripped him; and his reading fostered in him a taste for depicting the manifold strange peoples, each of which represents some moral distinction. From the beginning also mankind's obsession with the question whether they might foretell events had fascinated him. At first, no doubt, the subject had made him scornfully angry or contemptuous; it was unworthy of an enlightened age. Later, however, he had seriously weighed the evidence and had rejected most of it as false; indeed, it may be half in mockery he had assumed the seer's rôle himself. Nevertheless, in spite of his reasoned rejection of dreams and other divinatory methods, he seems to have retained a secret feeling that, though undemonstrable, forecasting events may be possible; perhaps indeed the process of mocking prophets and their prophecies in the *Tiers Livre* vision had in part converted the sceptic. Perhaps he had felt that in so outlining mankind's future he was actually prophesying; but certainly Guillaume du Bellay's conversation just before his death, in which he foretold things "part of which we have seen come to pass and part we expect to do so," however naïve it may seem, had troubled his mind and forced him to admit that there were "more things in heaven and earth than were dreamt of in his philosophy." He treasured up the words of dying men, for they were more human than a witch's or a conjuror's gesticulations, and so more reliable. Before he had made a real advance in story-telling he had needed a personal interest in the story; and before he could make a real advance in knowledge and thought he needed a personal mystery, an inference that we are justified in making by the only instances in the *Tiers Livre* which show him yielding to a belief rejected by him. Yet the circumstances of that death scene, at which he was present, and which prompted his visit to the Macreons, must have been in keeping with previous examples of his patron's foresight; and surely in their intimacy he must have noted those too. What made the difference was that not only respect for his patron's greatness, but more probably and to a greater extent his consciousness of "prophetic power" and his passionate human feeling had overcome and pushed aside his pronounced dislike for the mysterious. The mystery of the supernatural, in which he still refused to believe, had paled beside the more profound mystery of the natural and the human.

And in pondering on these questions he could not help discovering much about human character. (pp. 171-78)

[The] central facts of Rabelais' philosophy are traceable in the contrast between Panurge and his leader. The former, dreaming of a static world of selfish delight, unable apparently to profit by his experiences and his reading, is completely opposed to the unresting inquisitive spirit and the benevolence and humanity of Pantagruel; but still more are they contrasted on all occasions when resolution becomes necessary. They are united by common human feelings; they are separated by the gulf between the noblest progressive character and the commonplace retrospective being, between the future and the past, between the possible and the actual. It is indeed difficult to express the difference between them because in each of them the personality must be seen in action to be understood. Each of them lives by his deeds. Yet surely Panurge's beliefs about the universe were generally accepted not only by medieval Christianity, but for the most part by ancient paganism. They were merely a crude form of that old-world spirit which sought the Absolute in everything. And Pantagruel's noble nature proves that Rabelais denied that spirit. Relative truth is all that mankind can hope for, and man must be himself the interpreter of observed facts ("Soyez vous mesmes interpretes de vostre entreprinse," said Bacbuc). Not even man's surest interests stand firm from one period of his life to another: the author's own life must have taught him that, and, therefore, the necessity for adopting Pantagruel's attitude. Rabelais, we feel assured, saw life and movement in every part, and specially in man himself; and if, to judge by the above conclusion, his romance appears to be an extraordinary hoax, it can only be so on the most improbable supposition that at a certain time he had planned the whole sequel. Bacbuc's vision at the end of the *Quint Livre* certainly seems to be a memory of the last chapters of the *Tiers Livre;* but while the resemblance is slight, the differences alone would tend to prove that in the meantime Rabelais' views had changed, and that he had abandoned even the disruptive interests of science for the less definite but more fundamental questions of behaviour. Possibly just as he had remodelled Pantagruel's settlement of his conquered territory . . . he had set himself to modify his former vision. We cannot tell, but in spite of his last book being a posthumous publication there is enough evidence in Bacbuc's speech to confirm the teaching of the two central books. The action in them turns upon the idea that a selfish dreamer, whose environment must be arranged so as to satisfy his every desire, will inevitably feel dissatisfaction and discomfort when he has to act on his own initiative in the everyday world. That was one of the prime discoveries which accounted for Rabelais' transformation, for at the beginning of the

Tiers Livre Panurge and Pantagruel were contrasted in respect of it.

According to the later writings, although most men are unaware of their powers and true purposes, the individual combines legitimate personal rights and duties as a social being whose impulses society's demands must restrain or crush. The conflict between individual liberty and social duty was fought out in Panurge; and it is one of Rabelais' claims to distinction that he offered us no cut-and-dried solution of an age-old problem. His lack of system and his vague views are what we should expect of a sincere man. The difficulty he had grasped, but, perhaps because he realized more and more the vastness of the province that he had undertaken and his own insufficiency, he honestly refrained from adopting one or other of the various philosophies which would have included those broad expanses that he had not explored. His conviction that mankind was not governed by reason, though of slow growth, was constantly strengthened by his observation and supported by his growing personal sympathy with inward religion. He held back from theorizing on man's social relations; he refused to discuss man's relation to God. But whereas, in the early Education Scheme, it had seemed to him reasonable to regard mankind as God's vassals who must pay tribute and service to Him, Rabelais' latest beliefs were that, in aiming at human development, each individual may and must be doing the will of God. In this as in all other respects, even in his dreams of scientific progress, he had left definite views behind him. Like his fellows of all time, he had fashioned his idea of the Creator according to his conceptions of humanity; and his sense of the inexplicable in human nature led him to imagine a nonpersonal deity, a vague living force, "whose centre is everywhere and whose circumference nowhere." (pp. 181-84)

A. F. Chappell, in his *The Enigma of Rabelais: An Essay in Interpretation,* Cambridge at the University Press, 1924, 196 p.

LEO SPITZER

(essay date 1953)

[In the following excerpt, Spitzer discusses *Gargantua and Pantagruel* as evidence of the Renaissance evolution in social and philosophical thinking.]

[Rabelais' five-book,] lengthy and incoherent, formless and rambling tale, crammed as it is with ancient learning and a popular farcical spirit of Gauloiserie—what does it ultimately mean? In the prologue to the first book Rabelais admonishes his prospective reader to follow the example of the dog, the most philosophical animal as Plato says in Book II of the *Republic,* of the dog who worries a bone until he has found a little marrow: similarly the reader will find in Rabelais' book a *substantifique moelle,* a substance hidden behind the allegorical surface, indeed the most glorious doctrines and dreadful mysteries, religious, political, and economic. On the other hand he tells us that he has written his book, at odd moments, while eating and drinking, for the benefit of the "most illustrious drinkers and you thrice-precious syphilitics." Consequently, the allusion to the philosophical marrow cannot be taken too seriously; it is only a humanistic taunt directed against the medieval habit of allegorical explanation of literature.

Since we cannot derive any clarification of the meaning of the books from the author, let us, in the fashion of Panurge, consult the authorities, in this case the literary historians. These generally tell you that Rabelais is a propagandist of Renaissance ideas and that the *substantifique moelle* is the doctrine of the emancipation of man's mind and senses from the coercion of the other worldly and ascetic dogma of the Church. Thus Rabelais would be, along with the freethinking Montaigne, one of the ancestors of eighteenth century enlightenment and deism, of Locke, Voltaire, Rousseau, and Goethe. You will find in the current monographs about Rabelais separate chapters, full of excerpts from Rabelais' work torn from their context, dealing with Rabelais' educational theories, his philosophy, religion, and politics. Accordingly, the Abbey of Thélème would represent a model of modern education as seen by Rabelais and the oracle *Trink* of the Pristess Bacbuc an exhortation to increasing intellectual thirst, in line with the intellectual thirst expressed by a Giordano Bruno. The program of Thélème might be accepted in this light were it not for the personality of the director of this program, the debauched and comic monk Jean des Entommures, and in the chapters on the oracle of Bacbuc we cannot forget the farcical allusions to drinking and fornication. The word *Trink,* taken from the lowly language of the guzzling Swiss mercenaries, carries connotations of vulgarity. And what shall we think of a Chinese priestess bearing a Hebrew name whose oracle speaks the German of the *Landsknechte?* It is precisely when Rabelais is expounding the ideas most dear to him that he indulges in the utmost of whimsicality and buffoonery. How is this to be explained? As a device to disarm the ecclesiastical authorities by pretending that his ideas are only jests? If so, his biography has shown us that he did not succeed with his strategy since his books incurred ecclesiastical condemnation and his life always skirted danger. Perhaps, then, this spirit of the farce was no secondary thing, but is a primary element of his creative mind. For we should note that also in his direct satire Rabelais is moved not only by hatred, but by an enjoyment of the fantastical shapes his satire helps him create. For example, who can read his allegorical presentation of the figure *Anti-physie* (Counter-Nature), whose children walk on their heads, with the feet upward, because the Creator has shown by the example of the trees that the roots (equivalent to man's hair) should be below, the branches (corresponding to man's legs) above—who can read this satirical allegory which caricatures medieval nature symbolism—who can read this *myth* of Rabelais' without the feeling that he must have experienced true artistic enjoyment in visualizing human beings walking on their heads, just as much as Dante enjoyed the visual picture of the punishment of the Pope, who in his life had been guilty of simony, of reversing divine values, and now in Hell is buried head downward, while his feet, continually singed by flames, protrude from holes in the marble slab. Such scenes, apart from any didactic intention, represent the play of free imagination and appeal to the artistic sense of the reader precisely because they transcend any model in reality—a type of art, incidentally, which we moderns are perhaps better able to understand than were our ancestors, given the development of modern art away from precise models in reality. Rabelais is then deliberately seeking for what is not real, and neither in his didactic nor in his satirical tales should we look only for his serious intention. The Rabelaisian in Rabelais is his capacity for comic visualization of what has never been seen.

Let us study in detail some of those semi-serious conclusions Rabelais is fond of extracting from a fantastic context: for example, the famous eulogy of the debtors and creditors delivered by Panurge. Pantagruel has asked this improvident fellow, always out of pocket, when he would finally stop making debts. Panurge answers: on Saint Never-Never's day. To make debts is something creative—to make *something* out of *nothing* is what the Creator did. And indeed the debtor when he circulates among his creditors, who watch his movements to see whether he shows any inclination of settling up that day, moves like a god among human beings. Moreover, debts are the general principle which holds the universe together: what would the cosmos be if the stars did not borrow their light from each other (the moon from the sun), if the elements did not borrow and lend among each other (by transformation of water into air, of air into fire), if one man did borrow and lend to his fellow man, if the body of man, that microcosm, were not based on debt and credit (the blood-circulation being nothing but such a business transaction). Consequently, Nature has created man in order that he may borrow and lend. And now comes this significant exclamation of Panurge: "*Vertugoy, je me noye, je me perds, je m'esgare on ce profond abisme du monde*—By God, I sink, I drown, I perish when I enter into the consideration of the profound abyss of this world, thus lending,

thus owing. Believe me, it is a divine thing to lend; to owe, an heroic virtue."

This last paradox is proclaimed by the most unheroic and unvirtuous Panurge who a moment ago had only intended somehow to justify his personal weakness, but suddenly creates before us a vision of the well-ordered universe that functions harmoniously thanks to the sympathy and generosity of the elements. Inspired as he becomes by a pantheistic, religious and poetic frenzy, he comes to experience the Dionysiac fever of the priest in Greek mysteries: at the climax of his vision he feels his own absorption by the God he has evoked; he is swallowed up into the abysmal richness of the world which he himself had opened up before us. Out of this hypocritical ne'er-do-well and debtmaker Panurge, there has developed a seer who divines the mysteries of the universe, an *artist,* a *demiurge,* a *Panurgos* who recreates the universe and its processes—his transformation anticipates the visions of *le Neveu de Rameau,* that nephew of the famous composer whom, two centuries later, Diderot shows us as he experiences the cosmic exaltations and trances of a genius—without ever becoming one, as Diderot makes it clear. Rabelais, less disillusioned than Diderot, fails to distinguish between real and sham genius. His Panurge becomes a visionary genius before our eyes. He develops out of poor material, no better than the *Neveu de Rameau,* out of a type of Frenchman whom we know so well from French literature (Sganarelle, Mascarille, Gil Blas, Figaro) and whom we see appear with Panurge for the first time: the self-satisfied, sensuous and cynical *blagueur* who, disillusioned with the world as he is, never allows things to be what they are, but either takes important things lightly or blows up small things to sham importance, and in any case provides for himself an ideological alibi with which to live with the feeling of his personal superiority. Could it perhaps be that the curve described between Panurge the *blagueur* and Panurgos the visionary, between the prankster and the singer of World-Harmony, is perhaps Rabelais' own artistic path—did he . . . find in himself a perpetual clown who was able, on the spur of the moment, to transform himself into a prophet of the mystery and harmony of life? And it is indeed very difficult with Rabelais to tell where the clown leaves off and the mystic begins. Rabelais may at any moment engender gratuitous visions out of the fullness of his imagination, with no limit set to his Homeric fabulating mind.

As we watch Panurge, the true protagonist of Rabelais' work, moving through four of the books, we will discover that his whole character is built on gratuitous mental freedom—that is mental freedom for its own sake. His is the mind that frees itself from outward reality by building up a world of fancy for its own pleasure. We see him first on his return from Turkey, covered with wounds, his clothes in rags, fainting from hunger and thirst. He does not begin his conversation, however, with references to his condition and to his need for help; instead he has the leisure to answer Pantagruel's questions with lengthy, rhetorical speeches in a dozen languages (including Hebrew and Basque), only at the end to ask for help in plain French. He allows himself the sly pleasure of showing off his linguistic superiority, in a nonsensical postponement of his real and truly urgent purpose. This is self-enjoyment of resourcefulness in the abstract, quite detached from reality.

Later we learn that Panurge never carries weapons with him—obviously he knows that the weapon of his mind cuts more sharply than a sword. His pockets are instead filled with gadgets or trinkets which may serve for tricks he performs on innocent victims: a sharp little knife for cutting purses, little horns full of fleas and lice which he borrowed from the beggars of St. Innocent to cast into the necks of the daintiest gentlewomen he could find, plus needles and thread the better to sew people together—in short the apparatus of a rogue who enjoys the gratuitous act, not of charity, but of amorality. That Panurge is indifferent to his own practical advantage is illustrated also by the scene of the consultation of Pantagruel about the marriage question, a scene in which he seems less interested in a solution than in the dialectical play of his mind with which he provokes now a yes, now a no, *just for the hell of it,* priding himself on his own mental freedom and power of analysis. In fact, Rabelais never tells us whether or not Panurge ever does marry although the problem of this marriage provides the plot for three books—as though Rabelais wished to intimate that neither this problem nor this plot are of any importance.

Panurge's relationship toward money is also quite idealistic: though he knows sixty-three ways to procure money, he knows many more ways to get rid of it. He steals coins from indulgence boxes, to spend them in order to procure an hour of sensuous love for frustrated women. His most famous prank, cruel and criminal as it is, has become proverbial in France *(les moutons de Panurge):* in order to humiliate the bourgeois pride in possessions of the sheepraiser Dindenault, he decides to destroy his flock by throwing the bellwether into the water, whereupon the whole flock follows, dragging with it its owner (who happens to have in his pocket a sum of money he owes to Panurge). Thus our sixteenth century figure represents an ancestor of those protagonists of twentieth century French novels (by André Gide, Valéry Larbaud, *et al.*) who perpetrate gratuitous crimes out of boredom in order to assert their moral autonomy. Only the *actes gratuits* of Panurge are relatively more gratuitous than those of the rich *blasés* of our day: they are performed by a social outcast.

Panurge is not the only character who embodies that particular Rabelaisian quality of gratuitous reality. The stories of the giants are similarly situated on the border-line between phantasmagoria and realistic description. We hear, for example, that Pantagruel with his tongue only half extended is able to protect a whole army from rain as a hen does her chickens. And "I who relate to you these so veritable stories," says Rabelais, "went along full two leagues upon his tongue, and so long marched, that at last I came into his mouth. But, oh gods and goddesses, what did I see there! [I] saw there great rocks like the mountains of Denmark—I believe that those were his teeth. I saw also fair meadows, large forests, great and strong cities, not a jot less than Lyons or Poictiers" and finally Rabelais saw a fellow who was raising cabbages in order to sell them "in the city which is here behind."

"Jesus!" said I, "is there here a new world?"

"Sure," said he, "it is never a jot new, but it is commonly reported that without this, there is an earth, whereof the inhabitants enjoy the light of a sun and moon, and that it is full of very good commodities; but yet this is more ancient than that." And another fellow found there was a bird catcher who tended his nets to catch the pigeons which fly from that other world into Pantagruel's mouth everytime he yawns; and in his throat there are two cities called Larynx and Pharynx; at this time they are being laid waste by a plague which has killed in one week "more than 280,016 people"—a plague caused by the stinking breath of the giant after he had eaten garlic.

The literary historian will not fail to point out that Rabelais here combines two sources, the popular tale of good-hearted giants and the facetious account by the Greek satirist Lucian of a journey through the throat of a whale. But who does not sense that to these literary sources Rabelais has added that particular feeling of bewildered elation which his contemporaries must have felt when faced, no longer with the hermetically closed, boxed-in cosmology of the Middle Ages, but with the discovery of new worlds and ever widening perspective? They must have asked themselves, like Rabelais walking on the tongue of the giant, with their confidence in the existence of only one world shaken, "Which of the two worlds is the old, which the new one? And which of them is real?" Once it is granted that a new world is possible, man, proudly, if not too assuredly, may strike forward into the infinite, the unreal, the utopia, the nowhere.

The feeling of relativity newly gained in the sixteenth century, the feeling of "all coherence gone" which will inspire Pascal's theo-philosophy in the seventeenth and which will be exploited much more timidly in the eighteenth century in *Gulliver's Travels* and *Micromégas,* was not nearly as frightening to the first Renaissance thinkers as it is to our modern so-called "one world" which again tends to become a boxed-in world, the finite world of Einstein which also includes "one death," atomic death. The sixteenth century felt the infinite to be life-giving and friendly, a realm where man will be eternally able to drink at the inexhaustible springs of Nature. The generous Pantagruel, like the generous priestess Bacbuc, represents a universe that is good and cheerful and works for the good and for gaiety. The medieval giant Pantagruel who has become a Platonic philosopher-king suggests, by his name, also *pan,* the universe; and the gigantic dimensions of his body which he uses for the good represent the gigantic dimensions of the goodness of this earth. We modern readers are astonished at the carnality of such an imaginary figure and at the precise realism with which it is presented. But for Rabelais to imagine a figure is to incarnate him. His is a flesh-giving imagination in a period which resuscitated the flesh.

We have just spoken of the vistas of new worlds which Rabelais, like his contemporaries, saw with delight opened up before him. But there is still another new world which existed for the humanist Rabelais and which he felt to be as palpable as the flesh of his imaginary characters, and this is, to use the title of a famous dictionary of the sixteenth century, *The World of Words,* a world emancipated from the tutelage of pure logic and of every-day reality, a world with its own laws over which Rabelais ruled as a king. (pp. 133-40)

Rabelais must have recognized the paradox which haunted him in his whole artistic activity: his fiction creates *unreal reality*—so does language in general. In an episode of the fourth book, the episode of the "unfrozen words," Rabelais has created a myth which centers precisely on the intangible, but at the same time tangible, aspect of language. As they are sailing in the Arctic regions, the party of Pantagruel suddenly becomes aware of sounds in the air, without being able to discover their source. They hear voices of men, women, horses, sounds of trumpets and drums. Panurge is afraid as usual and advises them to flee, but the humanist Pantagruel, by way of explanation, is immediately ready with ancient literary parallels referring to the possibility of sounds becoming frozen. And the skipper confirms Pantagruel's suggestion: "Be not afraid, my lord, we are on the confines of the Frozen Sea, on which, about the beginning of the last winter, happened a great and bloody fight between the Arimaspians and the Nephelobates. Then the words and cries of men and women, the striking of battle-axes, the striking of armors and harnesses, the neighing of horses, and all other martial din and noise froze in the air, and now, the rigor of the winter being over, by the warmth of the weather, they melt and are heard." Panurge the skeptic asks to see some such not yet melted words, whereupon Pantagruel throws handfuls of them on the deck of the ship, here throaty insults and bloody words, there golden and green and azure words. No

passage could show better how for Rabelais language has become an atmospheric element which now coagulates, now evaporates, now is a reality, now is not. And here modern linguistic science cannot but acknowledge the rightness of Rabelais' poetic view: do our linguists not speak of "petrified expressions?" It remained for the dadaistic and surrealistic poetry of our century to capitalize on the automatic and petrified in the language of our age of mechanism and social standardization. The automatic writing of Rabelais is inspired by his happiness over the possibilities given to human expressivity—that of James Joyce, on the contrary, is overhung with his pessimism about a civilization felt to be on the verge of disintegration.

Summing up our analysis of the historical significance of Rabelais, we may say that he came at that moment of the Renaissance movement when man had learnt to realize the power and potentialities given to man. And Rabelais, like his character Panurge, used this power gratuitously, "for the hell of it." His epic which includes all the tremendous knowledge of which humanism was capable is obviously . . . conceived as an epic of human cognizance, a glorification of cognizant man, but the goal ultimately arrived at is mainly the cognizance of his cognitive power without any practical results of his cognizing activities being shown to us. We only learn that man can and should drink at the springs of knowledge for the sake of drinking. Rabelais' Argonauts bring home from their voyage no golden fleece, only the enigmatic word *Trink.* Neither have they reached at the end of their expedition a higher stage of development: Pantagruel and Panurge are in the fifth book what they were in the second, in this inferior to medieval protagonists such as Parzival or the traveler to the beyond, Dante. While we are reminded in the case of Rabelais' heroes of Goethe's maxim: "One does not travel in order to arrive, one travels in order to travel," we must remember that Goethe himself allows his protagonists (Wilhelm Meister, Faust) to reach new stages of development. In his static conception of characters whose categorical imperative we would think it should be to develop, Rabelais is quite isolated: his characters seem in truth to be only pretexts for the free play given through them to ideas: in the story of the unfrozen words Pantagruel and Panurge have no other function but to help a myth, emancipated from reality, into being. Never after Rabelais will we find thought playing with life and man so freely and so joyfully.

Similarly his vitality which exists only for the sake of vitality accepts no limits. We should not be astonished at his failure to arrive at formal beauty, at serene and balanced composition, at true imitation of Greek art: had he been an Ariosto, a Camoens, a Ronsard, he would have been limited by artistic form. But Rabelais' art is life untamed, it lives in the moment, the law of its being is freedom from law, improvisation, the dart and the spurt, the drive towards the unlimited, the unreal, the colossal, the grotesque, the macabre (his hypervividness sometimes comes close to the cramp of death). From classical civilization he, proceeding quantitatively, appropriated only the enormous arsenal of facts and those innumerable possibilities of life which fascinated his encyclopedic mind, and he mixes with the ancient elements, without scruple or sophistication, the gross monkish satire, the medieval slapstick farce and the spirit of fleshly French *gauloiserie* ["coarse joking"]. He represents for us that unique moment in Occidental literature when Renaissance man, become conscious of the boundless resources of the life of this world, experienced the rapture of this very discovery without yet having achieved the new style of life and art which should have been the necessary consequence of this discovery. Outside of Italy, works of art of the Renaissance serenity of Raphael or Ariosto are rare. Very soon after Rabelais, the spirit of the Counter-Reformation will set in to curtail the boundless aspirations of man; in French literature it is Malherbe who is said by Boileau to have set a more limited task for the Muse *(et la Muse réduisit au devoir)*—in other words, it was Malherbe who ushered in that French neo-classical literature which is a literature of the Counter-Reformation, of rules and canons, of what historians of art call the baroque age. The seventeenth century satirist Labruyère will find in Rabelais the taste of the rabble *(le goût de la canaille),* and Rabelais' *gauloiserie* will remain only as an undercurrent in French literature, chastened by classical taste, with Molière, La Fontaine and Voltaire.

From the seventeenth century on what is not refined is not worthy of literary expression in France, and Rabelais, apart from nineteenth century Romantic lovers of the colossal and the grotesque such as Balzac, V. Hugo, Th. Gautier, Flaubert, will generally figure as a writer more praised by manuals of literary history then actually read. It is the classic or baroque age that has categorically opposed the bold rejection of the limits of the finite world of reality that was characteristic of Rabelais. It will insist again, as had the Middle Ages, on the distinction between this world of appearances and the reality which is behind it, which may be either transcendental as in Calderon (life a dream from which the Christian should awake), or disillusioned to the point of nihilism as in Shakespeare's well-known lines: "Life's but a walking shadow, a poor player that struts and frets his hour on the stage . . . it is a tale told by an idiot, full of sound and fury, signifying nothing."

A spurious legend has it that Rabelais died with the words on his lips: "Draw the curtain, the farce is ended." This sentence Rabelais cannot have said: he is no baroque writer of disillusionment. For him, as you know him now, this world was a deep ocean into whose

A rendering of Panurge, by Gustave Doré.

treasure-containing waves he was ready to dissolve: *"je me noye, je me perds, je m'esgare on profond abisme de ce monde,"*—a universe seen not in its clear contours and finite limitations, but as an infinity of creative possibilities which enraptured that dionysiac mind. (pp. 144-47)

Leo Spitzer, "The Works of Rabelais," in *Literary Masterpieces of the Western World,* edited by Francis H. Horn, The Johns Hopkins University Press, 1953, pp. 126-47.

THOMAS M. GREENE

(essay date 1970)

[In the excerpt below, Greene summarizes Rabelais's thought, fictional technique, and literary significance.]

The book without a title written by François Rabelais is a work of immensities—vast energies, towering presences, gigantic laughter, monstrous appetites, Olympian wisdom. It is a shocking, irreverent book, subversive and rowdy, laced with unseemly and malodorous profanity, an embarrassing, genially disturbing book, but it is also an instrument of healing, reassuring and therapeutic in its profound gaiety, robust and sane in the contagion of its vital joy. It is a difficult book, shadowy, enigmatic, exasperating, inconsistent, a book of many meanings and of none, of grotesque disproportions and hideous fantasies, elusive, perverse, capricious, superbly and enticingly obscure. It is a book of words, lovingly and prodigally dispensed, lists and collections of words, piles, mountains, inundations. It is a book of knowledge, of generosity, of faith—"foy formée de charité"—of high courage and magisterial serenity. (p. 1)

The episodic and uneven narrative formed compositely by [the] five volumes has been called a novel, but the word is seriously misleading. For *The Books of Pantagruel* (to approximate their missing title) cannot in their sprawling irregularity be contained by any convenient generic term. Rabelais has been called "realistic," but the adjective is meaningless in his presence; his book has been called a "satire," but the label shrivels up before him. The first obstacle to apprehending him lies in his inconsistencies and contradictions: his giants, who tend progressively to conduct themselves like men of normal stature; his setting, which is capable of shifting without acknowledgement from Utopia to France; his characters, who alter their personalities from volume to volume; his laws of life and death, so disconcertingly flexible as to allow the late Gargantua, laid to rest in *Pantagruel,* to return inexplicably to life in the succeeding volumes; his sense of time, liberated of its conventional limitations. His imagination was not enclosed by one of those little Aristotelian minds for which consistency is a hobgoblin. The amplitude of his work contains multitudes, and to seize it we must accept its endless paradoxicality.

A kind of fruitful perversity lies in fact at the basis of his art. The comic sense of Rabelais, unlike Molière's, unlike most comic writers', does not repose on a judicious common sense, observing from the solid center of experience the eccentricities of deviation. He does not command the assurance of the moderate sage, fortified by rational wisdom and an authorized ethic. He writes rather from the fringe of nonsense. He knew the secret folly at the heart of the universe, the wild uncertainty, the abyss of lunacy that underlies our rational constructions. He embraces that lunacy, both within and without us, and builds his comedy upon it. Beyond the immediate object of his laughter, in any given episode, lies that night of hilarious mystery which encloses his world. The greatest of his comic characters, Panurge, is precisely the incarnation of the universal perversity in things. Rabelais is so powerful and so dis-

turbing a comic writer because he portrays human life as radically irrational, vitally unhinged, sublimely grotesque. He knows that to be alive is to be paradoxical and finally incomprehensible. Thus his moral instinct, which is strong and healthy, recognizes the factitious element in the authorized morality based only on reason, and reaches for an unauthorized alternative.

But balancing the intuition of comic perversity there is an opposing intuition of moral and religious seriousness. The conflict of these intuitions never finds, fortunately, an explicit resolution, but it leads to a running dialogue of distinct narrative voices a little below the surface of the fiction. Mingled with the demonic voice, the voice of comic darkness and grotesquerie, is an angelic voice, gentle, grave, affirming a radiant and serene wisdom. Mingled with the comic indignities of Rabelais's world, and with the malicious and vicious, is a strain of heavenly music for him who can hear it:

. . . céleste, divine, angélique, plus absconse et de plus loing apportée. . . .

. . . celestial, divine, angelic, more abstruse and brought from greater distances.

This angelic voice gains resonance from a faith in the value of knowledge, and although the concept of knowledge extends far beyond the kind of learning to be found in books, although it embraces implicitly the whole range of experience, nonetheless Rabelais shares the profound humanist belief in the potential power and goodness of books in themselves. The book appears as the complementary image to the bottle, and both meet in the recurrent image of the flask shaped to resemble a breviary. The reader who thinks that this image is merely and trivially slanted to the praise of alcohol has read superficially.

This case in fact is a good example of the difficulty which the reading of Rabelais involves. The mind behind the *Books of Pantagruel* is not only learned and curious but deeply engaged, wrestling with the profound issues which disturbed its time and which are more or less perennial. The guarantee of this moral seriousness lies not so much in the passages of reflective "eloquence" which punctuate the prose, as in the very restless and shifting persistence with which certain questions recur. This "angelic" seriousness is beyond cavil, and yet it is often disguised or entangled with its opposite. When we are laughing, we do not precisely distinguish between that which we believe or disbelieve, and not even, always, that which we love or scorn. The solvent of laughter disregards the conventional psychic categories, and if it is unscrupulous, it is also tolerant. There exists a certain state of consciousness in which this essential tolerance of laughter remains as a permanent acquisition, in which the objective perceptions of the intelligence are humanized but not blurred by comic magnanimity. That this enduring state of consciousness can maintain its equilibrium, the book of Rabelais is the most impressive proof. It directs genuine anger or contempt only against those who deny experience itself, those who suppress the freedom implicit in the act of laughter, those who in any of a hundred ways choose to say no. For the rest of the world, it reserves a kind of complicitous bonhomie, which will not be too quick to make hard distinctions and which must not be too quickly understood.

It is this equilibrium of Rabelais which saves him as a comic artist. That vision of the irresolvable paradoxes and mad improbabilities which beset our mortal state might have led to the nightmares of Hieronymus Bosch, closer to hell than to tragedy. The true evidence of Rabelais's spiritual strength, as Christian and humanist, lies in his capacity to entertain that vision with more than equanimity—with joy, just as Pantagruel maintains his instantaneous love for Panurge. Although his book reflects continuously the contingent and the problematic, he remains a tower of spiritual force.

There has been considerable doubt over the precise content of Rabelais's faith, a debate justified by the ambiguities of his own comments. He is difficult to interpret because he may have changed his position, because his humorous indirection extended to religious matters, and possibly—though not certainly—because he wanted to conceal his beliefs out of prudence. But the legend which once prevailed of his religious skepticism has happily been allowed to die. The joking liberty he takes with the most sacred subjects is not the liberty of a mythical Renaissance "paganism" but of medieval belief—and specifically, it would appear, of the Franciscan order. When in *Gargantua* one of the tipplers (*bien-ivres*) pronounces as he drinks the word of the crucified Christ—*Sitio* (I thirst)—the humor may be shocking to a Christian but it is not blasphemous. It points to a belief in the goodness of physical pleasure, a belief which is itself, in this context, religious, rather than to a sarcastic levity with the Passion. It represents the kind of harmless blasphemy which only the believer can permit himself.

Having reached this point with assurance, one must proceed to further affirmations cautiously. It is at least safe to say that the first two of Rabelais's volumes show strong and explicit sympathy with the Evangelical (pre-Calvinist Protestant) party, with the Protestant stress on scripture as preeminent authority, and with the Protestant reliance on Saint Paul. There is the same opposition common to Erasmus, the early Evangelicals, and the full-blown Reform, to certain "abuses" or "superstitions"—pilgrimages, the cult of saints, the sale of indulgences, above all, monasticism. There is, in the abbey of Thélème, the notable absence of a chapel, but an oratory is provided for private worship in each chamber. There is, in the *Quart Livre,* a bitter attack on the decretals as instruments of papal authority, written at a moment when King Henri II was at odds with the pope. The *Isle Sonante* contains a powerful denunciation of ecclesiastical greed, idleness, and celibacy. On the other hand, there is no firm support for the doctrine of justification by faith alone, and there is a jibe, added to later editions of *Pantagruel,* at "prestinateurs," those who believed with Luther and Calvin in predestination. There is certainly an evident incompatibility with the Calvinist doctrine of human depravity. And there is praise (sincere or insincere) in the *Tiers Livre* for those who work to

> extirper les erreurs et haerésies . . . et planter profondément ès cueurs humains la vraye et vive foy catholicque. . . .

> extirpate all errors and heresies and implant deep in the hearts of men the true and living Catholic faith.

Perhaps it is least risky to conclude that the book testifies to a sympathy with the limited reformism of an Erasmus, to an unwillingness to break unambiguously with the established church, and to its author's slowness to recognize his own growing isolation in the disappearing center.

These doctrinal perplexities, however knotty, do not in any case compose the highest obstacle to apprehending the book. Its most remarkable quality doubtless lies in its imaginative reality, its absolutely firm and marvelously fecund invention. But this created reality adheres less faithfully than does most fiction to what we commonly call reality, and in particular Rabelais's treatment of character does violence to our conventional expectations. In the modern sense there are no characters; there is no psychology, no deliberate and motivated development, no dawning insight into progressively deeper feelings. Instead there are presences with names: Grandgousier, Gargantua, Frère Jean, Pantagruel, Panurge. We come to associate a set of traits with a given presence, but the traits may abruptly undergo a mutation. We come to know the voices of the respective figures, but the voice may alter its timbre and accent. Grandgousier's voice so alters, and Panurge's. That alteration is not, in the experience of this particular work, of great importance. What matters is the poetic quality, in any given episode, of the figure's presence. For the figures are almost mythic; they loom out of the flickering narrative darkness with the imaginative substance of legend, and to apprehend them involves more than the simple and cheap process of understanding. It is surprising that they retain this quality of massive but shadowy presence even when their conduct is funny or undignified. Panurge, the most perverse, in a sense the least imposing of Rabelais's heroes, never loses this enveloping aura of folk-memory, the curious unpierceable density of the naïve popular fancy.

As with character, so with narrative structure. There is a line in the history of fiction that runs from Madame de Lafayette through Laclos and Jane Austen to Flaubert, the line of the classical novel which is basically French. This line depends on Flaubert's view of fiction as the art of sacrifice; it is exclusive, and its products are chiseled, symmetrical, and pure. But there is another line that runs from Petronius through Chaucer to Cervantes, Sterne, Zola, and Joyce, a line of asymmetrical structure and a cluttered story line, impure, rough-hewn, and inclusive. This is the line in which the *Books of Pantagruel* occupy a prominent place. The principle of unity found in this line depends in large part on the coherence of the author's imagination. One must not require of it the classical modes of continuity, momentum, or suspense. It may be that Rabelais imitated in this respect those debased popular stories he professed to be following. The *Grandes Chroniques* remain essentially shapeless, to be added to or subtracted from at will. The *Books of Pantagruel* are not shapeless in that sense, and with familiarity they reveal unifying threads of action, image, and motif. But they ask us to contemplate the page we are reading primarily for itself. The chapter titles echo the naïveté of the *Grandes Chroniques* by opening with a *comment*:

Comment Gargantua nasquit en façon bien estrange. Comment le nom fut imposé à Gargantua et comment il humoit le piot.

How Gargantua was born in a very odd manner. How Gargantua was named, and how he swallowed liquor.

This *comment*, this "how," is of course not only concerned with the how in the proper sense—that is to say, with the manner in which an event occurs. In the language of children and popular tales, the "how" introduces the event itself, the verb more than the adverb. In his consciously archaic chapter titles, which contribute to the consciously archaic technique throughout, Rabelais underscores the distinct separation between chapters. But the chapters cluster nonetheless into small groups to form episodes, isolated subsections of the action which constitute its basic narrative element. It is a structure which allows a minimum of narrative stress or relief or impetus, and a maximum of eclectic heterogeneity. There seems to be room for everything.

There is certainly room for what we are accustomed to call obscenity. There are three ways not to respond to Rabelais's coarseness. The first is the schoolboy's titillation at hearing the forbidden mentioned. The second is the prude's mechanical shock at the offense to trivial proprieties. The third is the intellectual's abstract, condescending pleasure in whatever challenges respectability. All three responses are irritating because they are undiscriminating. To read the book well, one must unfortunately discriminate. One must overcome his squeamishness, silence the inner voices of schoolboy and prude, pass beyond the abstract thrill, to decide as fairly as possible where the coarseness is effective as literature and where it is tiresome. There really are no rules to follow. One reader may feel that Rabelais's inclusiveness, his tolerance, his affection for the body, his comic genius, all depend upon his disregard for the polite taboos. Another reader may feel that the most memorable and even the funniest pages of his book happen not to be the coarsest. Both readers might well be right.

Rabelais's freedom with the indecorous has debased the adjective made from his name. When Gargantua is newly arrived in Paris and fresh from his theft of the bells of Notre Dame, he is visited by a grotesque parade of clerics, filthy, red-nosed, bizarrely garbed—emissaries of the Sorbonne to request the bells' return. Their leader delivers himself of an harangue, exquisitely garbled, which provokes Gargantua and his friends to delighted laughter. The bells in fact have been returned, but when the discourse is concluded, they load their clumsy, pompous visitor with gifts, and having given him drink, send him on his way bowed by the tokens of their liberality. That impulse of generosity, informed with laughter, intelligence, and tolerance as well as pride—that is *Rabelaisian*.

The world of Pantagruel owes part of its vitality to the words that give it being, words which insist upon their own color and texture and their mediating position between the fiction and the reader. Rabelais lived too soon to know the ideal of the word as self-effacing, discreet, transparent; he insisted rather on its assertive, quirky presence. If his pages have been difficult to read, not only for modern Frenchmen but for his own contemporaries, it is because he chose to make them so, heightening in his revisions the archaic turn of a phrase, and importing into his prose many hundreds of foreign words. He coined them not only from Greek and Latin, nor only from Italian, English, and German, but also from Arab, Hebrew, Turkish, and Basque, to say nothing of the French patois and dialects he drew upon. No other French writer has been responsible for so many coinages which caught on. No other writer has felt called upon to supply a glossary for his story, of the kind appended to the *Quart Livre.* No one else before Joyce seems to have felt words so sensitively as lively, explosive objects, opaque, malleable, and volatile.

For the word in Rabelais is an expression of both those voices we have distinguished in him, the comic and the angelic. It is a plaything of demonic gaiety, to be destroyed and refashioned with effervescent zest. Rabelais is incessantly assaulting and belaboring his language, twisting it out of shape, mincing it, sending it up in smoke. Nothing is perfunctory, nothing is insipid; no sentence quite follows the course one foresees for it. The word, so close to our conventional systems of apprehension, becomes in his restless hands the weapon that undermines those systems and exposes our unconscious servitudes. Nobody says "to make love" (faire l'amour) in his book; they say "gimbretile-tolleter," or "franfrelucher," or "fretinfretailler," or "rataconniculer," or "bouttepoussenjamber," or two dozen other things, any given verb never more than once, most of them untranslatable because created ad hoc by a tireless verbal imagination. They almost become miniature works of art themselves, these verbs, because they do more than convey the abstract notion of the act; they convey its joy, its atmosphere of physical freedom, in the process of naming it. Thus Rabelais calls upon language to enforce his celebration of the unauthorized, and to evoke that shadowy opacity of his artistic universe. Yet even in the midst of all the antirational verbal generosity, the word remains as well the instrument of intellectual research and of lucid reflection.

His experiments with language were made against the background of a linguistic crisis. Those of his contemporaries who aspired to be serious writers were faced, before setting pen to paper, with the crucial question of the language they were to write in. There were several alternatives; each stamped the writer who chose it, and each carried a risk. The risk was great because Renaissance humanism had made the discovery of style. That is to say, the humanists had seen, more clearly than anyone for over a millennium, that rhetori-

cal manipulation can be beautiful, that it can reflect a personality, and that it deeply affects "content." The rediscovery of these things, reinforced by the discovery of ancient authors like Quintilian who had also seen them, led to an extraordinary, doubtless an excessive preoccupation with style among educated men. (pp. 10-17)

The quest for a new language was *ipso facto* a quest for a fresh human style, capable of that poise, urbanity and irony which are found in the writers of antiquity. To read Rabelais aright, one has to understand this composite unity of moral style.

His own solution to the linguistic problem was audacious. He insisted, as no other humanist chose or dared to do, upon the colloquial substratum of the written word. He exploited the pungent fertility of popular speech, gave literary status to the folk phrases and rhythms he lovingly rehearsed, jumbled the stylistic levels, and defied decorum. He did this even as he enriched the capacity of his language for "serious" discourse by raising it occasionally to unprecedented loftiness, by multiplying the wealth of its vocabulary, and by loosening its syntactic rigor. Not all his paragraphs are free from awkward turns or a too intricate sentence structure. But his book as a whole constitutes an impressive demonstration of the French language's immense resources, its color, its breadth, and its potential eloquence.

The dazzling and wearying prodigality of Rabelais's verbal pyrotechnics suggests a faith in language which we can only begin to sound. The length of certain catalogues which pile up nouns or adjectives for pages on end betrays an intoxication with words for themselves which few readers have been able to match. Not only is the joyous exhibitionism a token of spiritual *allegresse,* ["liveliness"], but, vice versa, the *allegresse* may have gathered buoyancy from a *copia* ["abundance"] which is godlike in its creative amplitude. Rabelais would have found a peculiar propriety in the religious authority assigned by the Reform to a book. The inscription over the gate of Thélème banishes from the abbey the enemies of the holy word and it enjoins the residents:

Chascun en soit ceinct;
Chascune ayt enceincte
La parolle saincte. . . .

Each wears it on his heart,
Each wears it as a sword,
Our Holy Writ and Word.

These lines mean that each should be immersed in scripture. But the banal metonymy of "parolle saincte" (holy word) acquires particular force from Rabelais's pen. When the quest of the latter books leads finally to the oracle who is to conclude it, the resolution comes in the form of a single word, which the priestess calls divine. There is a link between the sacred word of the *Gargantua* and the divine "Trinch" of the *Cinquième Livre*. The link could easily be overstressed or oversimplified, but it can at least bear witness to the power and mystery invested in the "parolle," awesome talisman and instrument of fellowship, prayer, knowledge, and revelation. The embryon of meaning contains in itself a potential mysterious *yes* in response to the continuous comic *maybe*. (pp. 18-19)

The very last symphonic sentence of Rabelais's book is one of his most beautiful. It praises the land of the oracle in terms that evoke all the exotic majesty of the great earth itself, turning back away from fantasy to regard the immense wonder of the actual globe. But that panoramic vastness in turn gives way to home, to Touraine, and if this fanciful land is said to surpass all the others, it is merely equal to that most familiar province.

> Par ung païs plain de toutes délices, plaisant, tempéré plus que Tempé en Thessalye, salubre plus que celle partie d'Egipte, laquelle a son aspect vers Libye, irrigu et verdoyant plus que Thermischrie, fertile plus que celle partie du mont Thaure, laquelle a son aspect vers Aquillon, plus que l'isle Hiperborrée en la mer judaïque, plus que Caligès on mont Caspit, flairant, serain et gratieulx aultant qu'est le païs de Touraine, enfin trouvasmes noz navires au port. . . .

> And so we passed through a country full of all delights, pleasanter and more temperate than Tempe in Thessaly, healthier than that part of Egypt which faces towards Libya, better watered and greener than Themischyra, more fertile than that part of Mount Taurus which faces towards the North, or than the Hyperborean Island in the Judaic Sea, or than Caliges on Mount Caspius, sweet-smelling, smiling and delightful as the country of Touraine; and at last we found our ships in the harbor.

The port that awaits the voyagers is an image of conclusion and repose, and yet, as the final punctuation mark of *this* book, how can it fail to be as well an image of the opposite? The ships are waiting in the harbor for another setting out, and in this end lies a new beginning. Nothing represents the book better than this final symbol of opening and renewal. For the writing of the book itself produced a renewed picture of man and his adventure on the planet. Bound as it was by countless ties to the past, it sketched nonetheless an original design of human potentiality, a new liberty and courage, a new laughter, a new pride, a new interrogation of the universe.

M. De Diéguez is right when he remarks that the Pantagruelist quest is unique because it is interrogative. So in a larger sense is the whole book. In the history of the human imagination, Rabelais's profoundest originality lies doubtless in that insidious capacity he first incarnated to *question*, to entertain in his head a character, a situation, a thought both with potential respect and potential irony. He does that . . . in his climactic episode just as he does from the opening, when the murder of Abel marks a fall into hilarious and irrational monstrosity. At the center of Rabelais's comedy lies this irony neither classical nor medieval, which lies open alike to affection and skepticism, which scrutinizes equally wisdom and folly. This magisterial distance even from the things he cares for most, this fondness for toying with the sublime and the commonplace together, this comic withdrawal from a lovably intractable world, betoken his uniqueness and his genius. His relish for abysmal absurdity altered with time to a bleaker inquisition. But his book never drops its unsettling play with perspectives and its juggling with moral focus. It never ceases to be difficult to read, of a difficulty radical and salutary, and if we know we laugh, the tone and the drift of our laughter often elude us. Rabelais was almost the first of the great creators to unearth the duplicitous darkness of the word. The very universe his art creates we cannot help but accept, but it transforms its shapes and aspects by random laws that are never codified.

Rabelais's mind is perpetually surprising because of its overwhelming generosity toward a world in disorder. Perhaps his liberality is the product of this supple wideness which holds in one intuition the world's unsortable perplexities. The opening of the last chapter employs a characteristic verb: *eslargir*, which meant "to bestow" and "to widen." Today it also means "to set free." "We place the supreme good," Bacbuc says, "not in taking or receiving, but in giving and bestowing."

> Nous establissons le bien souverain non en prendre et recepvoir, mais en eslargir et donner. . . .

She means among other things that she disapproves the Calvinist doctrine of grace as an arbitrary gift from God. But we will not wrench her meaning much if we take it in a less specific sense. The story she concludes in all its gigantic dimension is really designed to draw together all the meanings of *élargissement*. The liberating breadth of Rabelais's comic toleration underlies his stupendous largesse. Olympian irony is of a piece with Olympian munificence. (pp. 113-15)

Thomas M. Greene, in his *Rabelais: A Study in Comic Courage*, Prentice-Hall, Inc., 1970, 119 p.

SOURCES FOR FURTHER STUDY

Bakhtin, Mikhail. *Rabelais and His World.* Boston: The MIT Press, 1968, 484 p.

> In-depth critical analysis of Rabelais's works as a reflection of medieval folk culture, language, and belief.

Chesney, Elizabeth A. *The Countervoyage of Rabelais and Ariosto: A Comparative Reading of Two Renaissance Mock Epics.* Durham, N.C.: Duke University Press, 1982, 232 p.

> Extensive comparison of Ludovico Ariosto's *Orlando furioso* and Rabelais's *Gargantua and Pantagruel.* The discussion centers on the works' "humanistic voyages of discovery" and each author's "propensity for exploring the opposite of every truth and the other side of every argument."

Coleman, Dorothy Gabe. *Rabelais: A Critical Study in Prose Fiction.* Cambridge: University Press, 1971, 241 p.

> Critical study of Rabelais's works with particular attention to the role of the narrator.

Frame, Donald M. *François Rabelais: A Study.* New York: Harcourt Brace Jovanovich, 1977, 238 p.

> Comprehensive examination of *Gargantua and Pantagruel.*

Kinser, Samuel. *Rabelais's Carnival.* Berkeley: University of California Press, 1990, 293 p.

> Analyzes carnivalesque elements of *Gargantua and Pantagruel* in relation to the rise of the printed word.

Lewis, D. B. Wyndham. *Doctor Rabelais.* New York: Sheed and Ward, 1957, 274 p.

> Enthusiastic, illustrated biography.

Ayn Rand

1905-1982

(Born Alice Rosenbaum) Russian-born American novelist, nonfiction writer, dramatist, scriptwriter, and editor.

INTRODUCTION

Rand occupies a unique position in the history of American literature. In many ways she was a paradox: a writer of popular romances whose ideas were taken seriously as well as a fierce individualist who collected many followers. Politically and aesthetically, she defied the cultural currents of her times. She is chiefly remembered for her controversial novels *The Fountainhead* (1943) and *Atlas Shrugged* (1957), which promote her philosophy of "objectivism." This extreme form of individualism has been defined by Rand as "the concept of man as a heroic being, with his own happiness as the moral purpose of his life, with productive achievement as his noblest activity, and reason as his only absolute."

Rand's lifelong enmity to collectivist political systems was engendered by her personal experiences growing up in Russia and living through the Bolshevik Revolution and the beginnings of the Soviet system. In 1979, when talk-show host Phil Donahue asked her about her feelings for Russia, she described them as "complete loathing." Russia, she said, is "the ugliest, and incidentally, most mystical country on earth." Rand was an American patriot in the manner that only one who has emigrated from a totalitarian regime can be, and capitalism was the system she championed; *Atlas Shrugged* is described as, among other things, a theodicy of capitalism. Rand was a proponent of laissez-faire capitalism, a system she defined as the only social system based on the recognition of individual rights, the only system that bans force from social relationship, and the only system that fundamentally opposes war. Rand's defense of capitalism on moral grounds is unique. She based this defense on her view that only capitalism is consonant with man's rational nature, protective of his survival as man, and fundamentally just.

Rand's firsthand experience of Communism shaped her politics for life. Her family lived through the privations of World War I and then struggled to adapt itself to the new Communist regime. For Rand herself, life in Russia at that time was dreary, and the future held little hope, particularly for one who rejected the system in power. Rand wanted to write about the world as it could be, to show life as she felt it was meant to be lived. As a young girl, she decided to become a writer. Still, she chose to major in history at the University of Petrograd. She dismissed literature and philosophy, the fields in which she would later make her mark, because she abhorred what the majority of the academic world valued in both of those fields. Aristotle is the only philosopher to whom she acknowledges any intellectual debt; early in her life, she was attracted to the theories of Friedrich Wilhelm Nietzsche, but she discarded his writing when she encountered his *The Birth of Tragedy* with its antirational stance. Her favorite novelists were Victor Hugo and Fyodor Dostoevsky, her favorite playwrights, Friedrich Schiller and Edmond Rostand.

Rand emigrated to the United States in 1926. There, Alice Rosenbaum became Ayn Rand. (Her unique personality and insistent individuality are reflected in her name choice. Her first name should be pronounced to sound like the German number one, "ein." The last name she adopted from the Remington-Rand typewriter she used to write her first movie scenarios in America.) Despite her raw language skills, she soon headed for Hollywood, where she hoped to make her living writing for the movies. On her second day in town she was befriended by her favorite American director, Cecil B. DeMille, who took her to watch the shooting of "The King of Kings"; he gave her work first as an extra and then as a junior writer. Rand's 1929 marriage to Charles Francis "Frank" O'Connor, also an extra in "The King of Kings," insured that she would be allowed to stay in America. Shortly after her marriage, Rand got a job in the wardrobe department of RKO Studios. She hated the work, but it supported her financially while she improved her English and perfected her writing craft. Her progress was remarkable: She was to become one of a very few writers to attain artistic success in a language nonnative to them.

Rand's first novel was written in order to keep a promise she had made to a family friend at a farewell party given for her before she left Russia. Her friend had begged her to tell Americans that Russia was a huge cemetery and that its citizens were slowly dying; and in *We the Living* (1936) Rand detailed the deterioration of spirit and body under the Communist system. In particular, she wanted to show that Communism wreaks special havoc on the brightest, most creative thinkers. All three of the major characters are destroyed. The heroine loses her life; the anti-Communist hero loses his spirit; and the Communist hero's faith and life are so undermined by the excesses he sees in the system that he takes his own life. By making one of her major characters a hero of the revolution, one who had believed fervently in the Communist cause, Rand was able to communicate basic flaws in the system. Rand continually emphasized that her opposition to Communism was based on the evil of its essential principle, that Man should exist for the sake of the state. She warned Americans against accepting the myth that the Communist ideal was noble, although its methods might be evil.

Rand's primary reputation is as a novelist, but her first professional success was as a playwright. In all, Rand wrote four plays, two of which were produced on Broadway. Her best–known play, *Night of January 16th* (1936), is significant for dramatic ingenuity as well as for historical sidelights. Rand developed the innovative theatrical device of using audience members at each performance to serve as the jury in this courtroom drama, and she wrote alternative endings for the cast to use in response to either the guilty or the not guilty verdict.

Anthem (1938), a novella, is Rand's shortest work. A parable-like dystopian tale, it portrays a totally collectivized world after some great war or holocaust. Originally titled "Ego," the work illustrates the negative effects on society of the suppression of individual ego and talent for the supposed good of all: When, in the name of all, no individual is allowed to stand above the others, then all stand in darkness.

Rand had done extensive research before she began writing her next novel, *The Fountainhead,* which was originally titled "Secondhand Lives." Although she worked for some time in the office of Eli Jacques Kahn, a famous New York architect, Rand's main purpose in the novel was not, as some critics have alleged, to extol the profession of architecture. Rather, the central purpose of the work, as in the ones before it, is to champion individualism versus collectivism. But in *The Fountainhead* the focus is not on the political system, as it was in *We the Living,* but on what Rand called collectivism in the soul. *The Fountainhead* is a defense of egoism, a positive rational egoism. Protagonist Howard Roark explains to Dominique Francon at one point in the book, "To say 'I love you' one must know first how to say the 'I.' " The egoism Rand defined in this novel is an integral part of the individualism she championed, just as the selfishness she described is a virtue as opposed to the selflessness she abhorred.

Positive reviewers appreciated the powerful writing, intensity, and dramatic plot of *The Fountainhead.* Rand's favorite review, by Lorine Pruette, appeared in the *New York Times Book Review* in May 1943. Pruette correctly identified *The Fountainhead* as a novel of ideas, pointing out that such a work by an American woman was a rarity. She lauded the quality of Rand's intellect, calling her "a writer of great power" with "a subtle and ingenious mind and the capacity of writing brilliantly, beautifully, bitterly." The success of *The Fountainhead* brought Rand to the attention of individuals who shared her perception of life. It also precipitated a lucrative movie sale.

In *Atlas Shrugged* Rand accomplished her goal of creating the ideal man. His name is John Galt, and in the work he and a number of like-minded followers succeed in stopping the motor of the world by removing themselves and their productive capacities from exploitation by forces they regard as looters and leeches. All of Rand's novels dramatize the primacy of the individual, but this is particularly evident in *Atlas Shrugged,* where the unique and precious individual human life is the standard by which good is judged. If something nourishes and sustains life, it is good; if it negates or impoverishes the individual's pursuit of happiness, it is evil. The secondary themes in Rand's fiction unfold as the logical consequence of her major theme, but it was not until *Atlas Shrugged,* the fullest explication in fiction of her philosophy, that Rand worked out all the political, economic, and metaphysical implications of that theme.

Critical calumny greeted the publication of *Atlas Shrugged,* especially from the battlements of the conservative establishment. Whittaker Chambers called it "remarkably silly," "bumptious," and "preposterous." He remarked: "Out of a lifetime of reading, I can recall no other book in which a tone of overriding arrogance was so implacably sustained. Its shrillness is without reprieve. Its dogmatism is without appeal." In the *Saturday Review,* Helen Beal Woodward, who conceded that "Ayn Rand is a writer of dazzling virtuosity," reacted negatively to the "stylized vice-and-virtue characters" and "prolixity." Woodward found *Atlas Shrugged* a book "shot through with hatred." Such critical attacks had no effect on the reading public, who have made *Atlas Shrugged* a multi-million selling phenomenon. *Atlas Shrugged* truly fueled a movement. Its publication established Rand as a thinker whose influence extended to such diverse locales as Parliament (Margaret Thatcher is an admirer); tennis courts (Billie Jean King acknowledges Rand's effect on her); the Federal Reserve System (Alan Greenspan calls her instrumental in forming his thinking); and the Alaskan legislature (it issued a memorial citation in honor of Rand at the request of Dick Randolph, a Libertarian legislator).

Rand was fifty-two when she published her last novel, but the end of her career as a fiction writer launched the beginning of her career as a public philosopher, speaker, and cult figure. The publication of *For the New Intellectual: The Philosophy of Ayn Rand* in 1961 began a series of nonfiction books that anthologized her essays on such diverse subjects as the American public school system, Romanticism, and racism. In her nonfiction writings as well as in her fiction, she characterized the main areas of conflict in the field of human rights: (1) individualism versus collectivism, (2) egoism versus altruism, (3) reason versus mysticism. In Rand's philosophy, all of these areas are interconnected. Reason is the tool by which the individual discerns what is life-sustaining and ego-nourishing. Collectivism, altruism, and mysticism work against individual freedom, a healthy ego, and rationality.

"Ayn Rand is dead. So, incidentally, is the philosophy she sought to launch dead; it was in fact stillborn." William F. Buckley's derogatory obituary in the *National Review* sounded a note of wishful thinking on the part of Rand's persistent critics. More objective observers of the contemporary political and publishing scenes, however, might be moved to remark, as Mark Twain did upon hearing rumors of his own demise, that the news of that death was greatly exaggerated. Rather than quelling interest in her or her philosophy, Rand's death, in March of 1982, initiated a new era of academic interest and fueled the continued promotion of her philosophies by her followers. In the five years following her death there were as many books published about Rand as there were during all the years of her life. Some of her writing is also being published posthumously: *Philosophy: Who Needs It* (1971), a volume of essays she had planned but did not complete, came out the year of her death, and *The Early Ayn Rand: A Selection from Her Unpublished Fiction* was issued in 1984. Her novels continue to sell well, as do some of her nonfiction works, and further publishing ventures are planned by her literary executor, Leonard Peikoff.

(For further information about Rand's life and works, see *Contemporary Authors,* Vols. 105, 15–16; *Contemporary Authors New Revision Series,* Vol. 27; *Contemporary Literary Criticism,* Vols. 3, 30, 44; and *Major Twentieth-Century Writers.*)

CRITICAL COMMENTARY

NATHANIEL BRANDEN

(essay date 1962)

[Branden, a Canadian-born American psychologist, was a close friend and colleague of Rand for nearly twenty years. In the following excerpt, he argues that Rand is a "Romantic Realist" and that she presents humanity's true potential in her novels.]

The projection of "things as they might be and ought to be" names the essence of Ayn Rand's concept of literature. In the wave of Naturalism that has engulfed the literature of the twentieth century, her novels are an outstanding exception. They are at once a continuation of the Romantic tradition and a significant departure from the mainstream of that tradition: she is a *Romantic Realist.* "Romantic"—because her work is concerned with *values,* with the essential, the abstract, the universal in human life, and with the projection of man as a heroic being. "Realist"—because the values she selects pertain to this earth and to man's actual nature, and because the issues with which she deals are the crucial and fundamental ones of our age. Her novels do not represent a flight into mystical fantasy or the historical past or into concerns that have little if any bearing on man's actual existence. Her heroes are not knights, gladiators or adventurers in some impossible kingdom, but engineers, scientists, industrialists, men who belong on earth, men who function in modern society. As a philosopher, she has brought ethics into the context of reason, reality and man's life on earth; as a novelist, she has brought the dramatic, the exciting, the heroic, the stylized into the same context.

Just as in philosophy she rejects every version of the mystics' soul-body dichotomy: theory versus practice, thought versus action, morality versus happiness—so in literature she rejects the expression of this same dichotomy: the belief that a profound novel cannot be entertaining, and that an entertaining novel cannot be profound, that a serious, philosophical novel cannot have a dramatic plot, and that a dramatic plot-novel cannot possibly be serious or philosophical.

Atlas Shrugged—the greatest of her novels—is an action story on a grand scale, but it is a consciously philosophical action story, just as its heroes are consciously philosophical men of action. To those who subscribe to the soul-body dichotomy in literature, *Atlas Shrugged* is a mystifying anomaly that defies classification by conventional standards. It moves ef-

fortlessly and ingeniously from economics to epistemology to morality to metaphysics to psychology to the theory of sex, on the one hand—and, on the other, it has a chapter that ends with the heroine hurtling toward the earth in an airplane with a dead motor, it has playboy crusader who blows up a multi-billion-dollar industry, a philosopher-turned-pirate who attacks government relief ships, and a climax that involves the rescue of the hero from a torture chamber. Notwithstanding the austere solemnity of its abstract theme, her novel—as a work of art—projects the laughing, extravagantly imaginative virtuosity of a mind who has never heard that "one is not supposed" to combine such elements as these in a single book. (pp. 88-9)

[Each of Rand's four novels] has a major philosophical theme. Yet they are not "propaganda novels." The primary purpose for which these books were written was not the philosophical conversion of their readers. The primary purpose was to project and make real the characters who are the books' heroes. *This* is the motive that unites the artist and the moralist. The desire to project the ideal man, led to the writing of novels. The necessity of defining the premises that make an ideal man possible, led to the formulating of the philosophical content of those novels. (p. 89)

In the novels of Ayn Rand, the sense of life projected is conscious, deliberate, explicit and philosophically implemented. It is as unique and unprecedented in literature as the premises from which it proceeds. It is a sense of life untouched by tragedy, untouched by any implication of metaphysical catastrophe or doom. Its essence is an unclouded and exaltedly benevolent view of existence, the sense of a universe in which man *belongs,* a universe in which triumph, enjoyment and fulfillment are possible—although not guaranteed—to man, and are to be achieved by the efficacy of his own effort.

No matter how terrible their struggle, no matter how difficult the obstacles they encounter, the basic sense of life of Ayn Rand's heroes—as of the novels—is indestructibly affirmative and triumphant. Whether the characters achieve victory or, as in *We the Living,* suffer defeat, they do not regard pain and disaster as the normal, as the inevitable, but always as the abnormal, the exceptional, the *unnatural.*

Ayn Rand shares with the Romantic novelists of the nineteenth century the view of man as a being of free will, a being who is moved and whose course is de-

Principal Works

*Night of January 16th (play) 1936

We the Living (novel) 1936

Anthem (novella) 1938

The Fountainhead (novel) 1943

The Fountainhead (screenplay) 1949

Atlas Shrugged (novel) 1957

For the New Intellectual: The Philosophy of Ayn Rand (philosophy) 1961

The Virtue of Selfishness (essays) 1964

Capitalism: The Unknown Ideal (essays) 1966

Introduction to Objectivist Epistemology (philosophy) 1967

The Romantic Manifesto: A Philosophy of Literature (philosophy) 1969

Philosophy: Who Needs It (philosophy) 1971

The New Left: The Anti-Industrial Revolution (essay) 1982

The Ayn Rand Lexicon: Objectivism from A to Z (philosophy) 1984

The Early Ayn Rand: A Selection from Her Unpublished Fiction (fiction) 1984

*First produced as Woman on Trial, 1934.

termined, not by fate or the gods or the irresistible power of "tragic flaws," but by the *values* he has *chosen.* (pp. 92-3)

Romanticism was a literary school whose authors discarded the role of transcriber and assumed the role of creator. For the first time in literary history, a sharp line was drawn between fiction and journalism, between artistic creation and historical reporting. The Romantic novelists did not make it their goal to record that which *had* happened, but to project that which *ought* to happen. They did not take the things man had done as the given, as the unalterable material of existence, like facts of physical nature, but undertook to project the things that men should *choose* to do. (p. 94)

Naturalism—the literary counter-revolution against Romanticism—was a regression to a pre-Romantic view of man, to a view lower than that against which the Romanticists had rebelled. It was Naturalism that reintroduced the "fate" motif into literature, and once more presented man as the helpless plaything of irresistible forces. (p. 95)

Today, the Romantic method of writing has been all but forgotten. Many commentators speak as if it were an axiom that all fiction is to be judged by the canons of Naturalism, as if no other school had ever existed. In their view—and by their sense of life—to project man as a being moved by his chosen values, and to

show him at his heroic potential, is "unrealistic." Only the helpless, the passive, the sordid, the depraved are "real."

If Romanticism was defeated by the fact that its values were removed from this world, the alternative offered by Naturalism was to remove values from literature. The result today is an esthetic vacuum, left by the historical implication that men's only choice is between artistic projections of near-fantasy—or Sunday supplement exposés, gossip columns and psychological case-histories parading as novels.

It is against the background of the despair, the exhausted cynicism and the unremitting drabness that have settled over contemporary literature, that the novels of Ayn Rand have appeared.

Ayn Rand has brought values back to literature—and back *to this earth.* She has chosen to write about the most fundamental and urgent issues of our age, and to use them as the material of Romantic art. In her novels, the ruling values *are* applicable to reality, they *can* be practiced, they *can* serve as man's guide to success and happiness. As a result, her heroes predominantly *win* their battles, they *achieve* their goals, they succeed *practically* and in their own lives. **Anthem, The Fountainhead** and **Atlas Shrugged** do not end with heroic death, but with heroic victory. (p. 97)

[Ayn Rand] does not face man with the camera of a photographer as her tool, but with the chisel of a sculptor. Howard Roark, Hank Rearden, Francisco d'Anconia and John Galt are not statistical composites of men "as they are." They are projections of man as he might be and ought to be; they are projections of the human *potential.* (p. 98)

Whether she is presenting a Howard Roark or a Peter Keating, a John Galt or a Wesley Mouch, the principle of characterization is the same: to present a character by means of essentials, that is, to focus on the actions and attributes which reflect the character's basic values and premises—the values and premises that motivate him and direct his crucial choices. A successful characterization is one which makes a man distinguishable from all other men, and makes the causes of his actions intelligible. To characterize by essentials is to focus on the universal—to omit the accidental, the irrelevant, the trivial, the contingent. . . . (pp. 98-9)

To write and to characterize by means of essentials requires that one know what *is* essential and what is derivative, what is a cause and what is a consequence. It is by identifying causes that one arrives at basic principles. No such understanding is required by the Naturalist method of characterization. (p. 101)

Once, after having delivered an address to members of the publishing profession, Ayn Rand was asked: "What are the three most important elements in a novel?" She answered: "Plot—plot—and plot." The most beautifully written novel that lacks a plot, she has remarked, is like a superbly outfitted automobile that lacks a motor.

Plot . . . is central and basic to the Romantic novel; it proceeds from the concept of man as a being of free will who must choose his values and struggle to achieve them. . . . Either a man achieves his values and goals or he is defeated; in a novel, the manner in which this issue is resolved constitutes the *climax.* Thus, plot is not, as the Naturalists have contended, an "artificial contrivance" that belies the actual facts of reality and the nature of human life. Plot is *the abstraction of man's relation to existence.* (pp. 105-06)

Purpose is the ruling principle in [Ayn Rand's] novels, in two basic respects. First, all the characters are motivated by their purposes, by the goals they are seeking to achieve, and the events of the novel dramatize the conflicts of these purposes. Second, the *author* is purposeful, that is, every event, every character and every adjective is selected by the standard of the logical requirements of the novel; nothing is accidental and nothing is included for reasons extrinsic to the needs of the plot and the theme. (p. 106)

In contradistinction to the typical philosophical novel, such as, for instance, Thomas Mann's *The Magic Mountain,* the characters in Ayn Rand's books who hold opposing views do not merely sit on verandas or on mountain tops and debate or argue their theoretical convictions, while all action is suspended. Every idea, every issue and every intellectual conflict in these novels is *dramatized*—that is, presented in terms of *action,* in terms of the practical consequences to which it leads. (p. 107)

The ingenuity and artistry of Ayn Rand as a plot-writer lie in the nature of the situations she creates, in her sense of drama and conflict, and in her matchless integration of philosophy and action.

Consider the basic plot-situation in *We the Living.* In order to obtain money to send Leo Kovalensky, the man she loves, to a tuberculosis sanitarium, Kira Argounova becomes the mistress of Andrei Taganov, an idealistic communist. Neither man knows of Kira's relationship with the other; and both men hate each other; Leo is an aristocrat—Andrei, a member of the Soviet secret police.

Now, the situation of a woman forced to sleep with a man she does not love, in order to save the life of the man she does love, is not new. . . . The originality of Ayn Rand's treatment of the subject—from the point of view of plot—is in the way she intensifies the conflict and makes it more complex. . . . [In] *We the Living,* Andrei is *not* a villain; he is profoundly in love with Kira and believes that she is in love with him; he does not know of her love for Leo. And Kira does *not* despise him; increasingly she comes to respect him. At

the start of their affair, she had acted in desperation, knowing this was her only chance to save Leo and knowing that Andrei had helped to establish the system that forced such an action upon her; but as their relationship progresses, as Andrei finds the first happiness he has ever known, he begins to understand the importance of an individual life—and begins to doubt the ideals for which he has fought. And thus the conflicts involved—and the suspense about what will happen when the two men find out about each other—are brought to the highest intensity. (pp. 108-09)

In presenting the evil of dictatorship, Ayn Rand does not focus primarily on the aspect of physical brutality and horror—on the concentration camps, the executions without trial, the firing squads and the torture chambers. These elements are present in *We the Living* only in the background. Had these horrors been the *primary* focus, the impact would be less profound—because violence and bloodshed necessarily suggest a state of *emergency,* of the *temporary.* Ayn Rand achieves a far more devastating indictment of dictatorship by focusing on the "normal" *daily* conditions of existence. (p. 109)

Another crucial element contributing to the power of Ayn Rand's indictment of collectivism is the fact that she presents Andrei *sympathetically;* he is not the worst representative of the system, but the best—the most idealistic and sincere. And that is why—as the events of the novel demonstrate with inexorable logic—he is as inevitably doomed to destruction as Kira and Leo. It is his *virtues* that make his survival impossible. (p. 110)

One of the most impressive examples of Ayn Rand's power as a plot-writer is the climax of *The Fountainhead.* (p. 113)

Roark's dynamiting of Cortlandt, and the events to which this leads, integrate the conflicts of the leading characters into a final focus of violent intensity, maximizing the philosophical values and issues at stake. The climax involves each of these characters intimately and, in accordance with the logic of the basic course the characters have chosen, brings each of them to victory or defeat.

Philosophically, the climax dramatizes the central theme of the book: individualism versus collectivism—the rights of the individual versus the claims of the collective. It dramatizes the role of the creator in human society and the manner in which the morality of altruism victimizes him. It dramatizes the fact that human survival is made possible by the men who think and produce, not by those who imitate and borrow—by the creators, not the second-handers—by the Roarks, not the Keatings. (p. 116)

When one reads Ayn Rand's novels in the order in which they were written, one is struck by the enormous artistic and philosophical growth from novel to novel. All the basic elements of her literary method are present from the beginning in *We the Living,* as are, implicitly, the basic elements of her philosophy. But each work is a richer and fuller expression of those elements, a more accomplished implementation, in a startlingly new and different form.

Just as, within each novel, the climax sums up and dramatizes the meaning of all the preceding events, raised to the highest peak of emotional and intellectual intensity—so, as a total work, *Atlas Shrugged* is the artistic and philosophical climax of *all* of Ayn Rand's novels, bringing the full of her dramatic, stylistic and intellectual power to its most consummate expression.

Ayn Rand has proudly referred to *Atlas Shrugged* as a "stunt novel"—proudly, because she has made the word "stunt" applicable on so high a level. By the standard of sheer originality, the idea of a novel about the minds of the world going on strike is as magnificent a plot-theme as any that could be conceived. If Ayn Rand has scorned the Naturalists who write about the people and events next door, if she has declared that the purpose of art is to project, not the usual, but the *unusual,* not the boring and the conventional, but the exciting, the dramatic, the unexpected, the rationally desirable yet the astonishingly new—then she is, preeminently, a writer who practices what she preaches.

Atlas Shrugged is a mystery story, "not about the murder of a man's body, but about the murder—and rebirth—of man's spirit." The reader is presented with a series of events that, in the beginning, appear incomprehensible: the world seems to be moving toward destruction, in a manner no one can identify, and for reasons no one can understand. (pp. 118-19)

There are no "red herrings" in the story, no false clues. But the mystery is to be solved by *philosophical* detection—by identifying the philosophical implications of the evidence that is presented. When the reader is finally led to the solution, the meaning and inescapable necessity of all the things he has been shown seems, in retrospect, simple and self-evident.

It is epistemologically significant that *Atlas Shrugged* is written in the form of a mystery. This is consistent with the philosophy it propounds. The reader is not given arbitrary assertions to be taken on faith. He is given the facts and the evidence; his own mind is challenged to interpret that evidence; he is placed, in effect, in the position of the people in the novel, who observe the events around them, struggle to understand their cause and meaning, and are told the full truth only when they have seen sufficient evidence to form a reasoned judgment.

The most impressive feature of *Atlas Shrugged* is its integration. The novel presents the essentials of an entire philosophical system: epistemology, metaphys-

ics, ethics, politics (and psychology). It shows the interrelation of these subjects in business, in a man's attitude toward his work, in love, in family relationships, in the press, in the universities, in economics, in art, in foreign relations, in science, in government, in sex. It presents a unified and comprehensive view of man and of man's relationship to existence. If one were to consider the ideas alone, apart from the novel in which they appear, the integration of so complex a philosophical system would be an extraordinarily impressive achievement. But when one considers that all of these philosophical issues are dramatized through a logically connected series of events involving a whole society, the feat of integration is breathtaking.

If one were told that an author proposed to dramatize, in a novel, the importance of recognizing the ontological status of the law of identity—one could not be blamed for being skeptical. But it is of such startling dramatizations that the virtuosity of *Atlas Shrugged* is made. (pp. 119-20)

Tremendously complex in its structure, presenting the collapse of an entire society, the novel involves the lives, actions and goals of dozens of characters. . . . Yet every character, action and event has a dramatic and philosophical purpose; all are tied to the central situation and all are integrated with one another; nothing is superfluous, nothing is arbitrary and nothing is accidental; as the story moves forward, it projects, above all, the quality of the implacably, the irresistibly logical. (p. 121)

The climax of *Atlas Shrugged* is singularly typical of the spirit of the novel as a whole: the integration of the unexpected and the utterly logical—of that which starts by appearing shocking and ends by appearing self-evident. One reader has described *Atlas Shrugged* as having the quality of "cosmic humor." It is written from the perspective of a mind that has discarded the conventional categories, standards and frame of reference—and has looked at reality with a fresh glance. (p. 126)

No other climax could sum up so eloquently the thesis and the meaning of *Atlas Shrugged.* The men of ability have all gone on strike, the world is in ruins, and the government officials make a last grotesque effort to preserve their system: they torture Galt to force him to join them and save their system *somehow.* They order him to *think.* They *command* him to take control. Naked force—seeking to compel a mind to function. And then the ultimate absurdity of their position is thrown in the torturers' faces: they are using an electric machine to torture Galt, and its generator breaks down; the brute who is operating the machine does not know how to repair it; neither do the officials; Galt lifts his head and contemptuously tells them how to repair it.

The brute runs away in horror—at the realization

that they need Galt's help even to torture him. The officials flee the cellar also—"the cellar where the living generator was left tied by the side of the dead one." (pp. 126-27)

There are persons to whom clarity and precision are the enemies of poetry and emotion; they equate the artistic with the fuzzy, the vague and the diffuse. Seeking in art the reflection and confirmation of their sense of life, they are psychologically and esthetically at home only with the blurred and the indeterminate: that which is sharply in focus, clashes with their own mental state. In such persons, Ayn Rand's literary style will invoke a feeling of disquietude and resentment; Ayn Rand's use of language is best characterized by a line concerning Dagny Taggart: "she had regarded language as a tool of honor, always to be used as if one were under oath—an oath of allegiance to reality and to respect for human beings." Because her writing is lucid, such persons will tell themselves that it is crude; because her writing conveys an unequivocal meaning, and does not suggest a "mobile" to be interpreted by the subjective whim of any reader, they will tell themselves that it lacks poetry; because her writing demands that they be conscious when they read it, they will tell themselves that it is not art.

But the specific trademark of her literary style is its power vividly to re-create sensory reality and inner psychological states, to induce the most intense emotions—and to accomplish this by means of the most calculated selection of words, images and events, giving to logic a poetry it had never had before, and to poetry a logic it had never had before. (p. 129)

In *Atlas Shrugged,* Ayn Rand has created more than a great novel. By any rational, objective literary standard—from the standpoint of plot-structure, suspense, drama, imaginativeness, characterization, evocative and communicative use of language, originality, scope of theme and subject, psychological profundity and philosophical richness—*Atlas Shrugged* is the climax of the novel form, carrying that form to unprecedented heights of intellectual and artistic power. (p. 140)

Just as in philosophy Ayn Rand has challenged the modern doctrines of neo-mysticism and epistemological agnosticism, so in literature she has challenged the view of man as an impotent zombie without intellect, efficacy or self-esteem. Just as she has opposed the fashionable philosophical dogmas of fatalism, determinism and man's metaphysical passivity, so she has opposed the fashionable literary projections of man as a stuporous puppet manipulated by instinct and socioeconomic status. Just as she has rejected the mystics' theories of Original Sin, of man's depravity and the misery of life on earth, so she has rejected the presentations of unfocused, whim-worshipping neurotics staggering along a trail of hysterical destruction to the abyss of whimpering defeat. Just as she has rescued philosophy from the cult of the anti-mind and the anti-man, so she has rescued literature from the cult of the anti-novel and the anti-hero. As an artist, she has brought men a new sense of life. As a philosopher, she has brought them the intellectual implementation of that sense of life: she has shown what it depends upon and how it is to be earned.

When one considers the quality of enraptured idealism that dominates her work, and the affirmative view of the human potential that she projects, the most morally corrupt of the attacks leveled against her—and the most psychologically revealing—is the assertion that she is "motivated by a hatred of humanity."

It is culturally significant that writers who present dope addicts and psychopaths as their image of human nature, are *not* accused of "hatred for humanity"—but a writer who presents men of integrity and genius as her image of human nature, *is.*

In Ayn Rand's novels, the heroes, the men of outstanding moral character and intellectual ability, are exalted; the men of conscientious honesty and average ability are treated with respect and sympathy—a far more profound respect and sympathy, it is worth adding, than they have ever been accorded in any "humanitarian" novel. There is only one class of men who receive moral condemnation: the men who demand any form of the unearned, in matter or in spirit; who propose to treat other men as sacrificial animals; who claim the right to rule others by physical force. Is it her implacable sense of justice—her loyalty to those who are *not* evil—her concern for the morally innocent and her contempt for the morally guilty—that makes Ayn Rand a "hater of humanity?" If those who charge Ayn Rand with "hatred," feeling themselves to be its object, choose to identify and classify themselves with the men she condemns—doubtless they know best. But then it is not Ayn Rand—or humanity—whom they have damned. (pp. 141-42)

The most tragic victims of the man-degrading nature of contemporary literature are the young. They have watched the progression from the boredom of conventional Naturalism to the horror of nightmare Symbolism—the progression from stories about the folks next door to stories about the dipsomaniac next door, the crippled dwarf next door, the axe-murderer next door, the psychotic next door. *This,* they are now informed, is what life is *"really"* like.

In projecting the artist's view of man's metaphysical relationship to existence, art explicitly or implicitly holds up to man the value-goals of life: it shows him what is possible and what is worth striving for. It can tell him that he is doomed and that *nothing* is worth striving for—or it can show him the life of a Howard Roark or a John Galt. It is particularly when one is young, when one is still forming one's soul, that one desperately needs—as example, as inspiration, as fuel, as antidote to the sight of the world around one—the vision of life as it might and ought to be, the vision of heroes fighting for values worth achieving in a universe where achievement is possible. It is not *descriptions* of the people next door that a young person requires, but an *escape* from the people next door—to a wider view of the human potentiality. This is what the young have found in the novels of Ayn Rand—and that is the key to the enormous popularity of her novels. (pp. 143-44)

Nathaniel Branden, in his *Who Is Ayn Rand? An Analysis of the Novels of Ayn Rand,* Random House, 1962, 239 p.

JERRY H. BRYANT
(essay date 1970)

[Bryant is an American educator and critic. In the excerpt below, he discusses basic themes in *Atlas Shrugged.*]

[For] Ayn Rand in *Atlas Shrugged* there can be no satisfaction, properly defined, outside of the true business world, that world which is based upon unconditional free enterprise, and a full-blown *laissez-faire* individualism. And Miss Rand has a carefully constructed philosophy to support her position, which is a curious blend of the values of the "open decision" and their outright denial. The highest good for her is the life of the individual, and the virtuous man will not surrender that life without a fight. As with Jaspers and Heidegger, Miss Rand suggests that human death is not simply physical; it may occur with the submergence of the self in the apparatus, the values of the "they." The man who wants to live must guard against humanitarianism, often passed off as a virtue but, in Miss Rand's view, a vicious softness which requires one to sacrifice his life for another. The greatest wealth that one can own is the outright title to his own life, unentailed by other claims or debts. The moral purpose of one's life, says Miss Rand, is "the achievement of happiness," but that happiness is not assured simply by possession of title. It comes from growth: "Every living thing must grow . . . or perish." Life is growth—not biological growth, but intellectual. The form of that growth is familiar. It is conceiving an aim and then shaping matter to the purpose of that aim. Thus created objects like motors have life "because they are the physical shape of the action of a living power—of the mind that had been able to grasp the whole of this complexity, to set its purpose, to give it form." The function of life is action, and action is the harnessing of thought to the production of goods. There is more, however, to happiness than mere

action in Miss Rand's world. Part of the moral purpose of life—that is, happiness—is payment for services rendered. *Giving* is a pernicious word in her vocabulary. The more one produces the more wealth one ought to have; the contrary also holds true. (p. 169)

The society organized on these values is not simply auspicious for individual satisfaction, as Miss Rand sees it; it is virtuous in what approaches a religious sense. Those who reject such a society are represented as wicked and evil, malevolently bent upon destroying life itself simply because they are too weak to live it and would spite everyone who is strong. In *Atlas Shrugged* such men appear within the very business world which is presented as carrying our salvation. Their presence is corrosive, and one of the duties of the good is to rid the world of this corrosiveness. These men, together with those in government gradually strangle the country's practitioners of free enterprise, professing patriotism and concern for the social good. Frustrated and enraged that, in their weakness, they cannot compete with the truly good and the truly strong, they pass laws controlling what and how much is produced in the country, how much is sold, and to whom it is sold. These evil men preach a vicious social ethic: obedience rather than argument, belief rather than understanding, adjustment rather than rebellion, compromise rather than struggle. They speak hypocritically of brotherhood and the common good, and of the conviction that all must share each other's burdens. They are the "enemy," and they scorn reason as illusion, have a "leering hatred of the human mind." The "moderation" and the ambiguities of the "open decision" are here represented by Miss Rand as sinister threats to her conception of reality. Men who live by these antivalues (as Tom Rath does) ride ungratefully upon the backs of the capable, demanding what they neither earn nor deserve, and declaring that the deserving rich need them more than they need the rich.

Miss Rand has created a world composed of all that she most vehemently resents. This she represents as a true assessment of the present structure of reality, and she proceeds to attack that structure with strong vindictiveness. The weaklings must be taught a lesson; they must be punished for their ungratefulness. (pp. 170-71)

Atlas Shrugged is more myth than novel. Miss Rand's heroes and heroines are god-like creatures who, in their leviathan strength, resist the wickedness of the pernicious weaklings around them and achieve their ends at will, though not without devoted and gigantic effort. Their tool is reason, their aim is individual satisfaction. While the enemy collapses of his own evil, the godlike producers retire to reap the harvest of the world. For Miss Rand there are no contradictions inherent in the human condition between man's image of himself and the ability to actualize that image. The notions of moderation and absurdity she flatly rejects. The for-itself *can* become an in-itself. One *can* achieve full identity. The real and the ideal *can* merge under the direction of the human mind. And . . . a sense of human solidarity is represented as an obstacle to the achievement of the highest good, for it smacks of humanitarianism. (p. 171)

Jerry H. Bryant, "The Business Novel: The Tycoon and the Tortured Thinker," in his *The Open Decision: The Contemporary American Novel and Its Intellectual Background,* The Free Press, 1970, pp. 165-98.

PHILIP GORDON
(essay date 1977)

[In the excerpt below, Gordon attempts to explain the enormous appeal of Rand's works.]

Throughout her long career as popular author and philosophizer, Ayn Rand has concentrated on her individualist-heroes to formulate from their absolute dedication to their own self-interests the model for all mankind. In contrast to those who have seen in the economic crisis of the twentieth century the waste of capitalism, Rand, obsessed with the fear of collectivist association, has seen universal salvation possible only through even more intensive laissez-faire capitalism. In so far as exposing Rand's politics to a more enlightened historical awareness would be like smashing a pea with a hammer, this brief study suggests instead some intersections of Rand's fiction-tracts and popular culture in an attempt to explain the nature of her enormous appeal. While providing an ever-increasing audience with the soothing rationalization of self-primacy, all of Rand's works, but particularly *The Fountainhead* (1943) expose the sharpness of the familiar line drawn between *self* and *other;* and thus she challenges us to recognize that the society which does not encourage individualism invites a tyranny of bland mediocrity. (p. 701)

In the thirties, when American capitalism's breakdown was so conspicuous and its breakup so urgent, Rand's overwhelming fear of anything collective harmonized with the American myth of rugged individualism, and her fiction assumed a prophetic air. In her second novel, *Anthem* (1938), Rand created a science-fictional scenario of "total collectivism with all of its ultimate consequences; men have relapsed into primitive savagery and stagnation; the word *I* has vanished from the human language, there are no singular pronouns, a man refers to himself as *we* and to another man as *they*." To combat that absolute lack of individuality, Rand's new heroes operate with an absolute lack

of flexibility. Crucial discoveries, of man and nature, can only be made by "a man of intransigent mind," whose theme, to be sung in Rand's subsequent novels of "rational self-interest," is typically simplistic: "Many words have been granted to me," *Anthem's* hero proclaims, "and some are wise, and some are false, but only three are holy: 'I will it.' " Rand's sacred word is unmistakably "EGO." (pp. 701-02)

Rand has steadfastly avoided psychological terminology and formulations, offering instead the "philosophy of rational self-interest" as a prescription for the individualist in twentieth-century America. . . . Rand argues for a purely competitive world in which the best would always rise to the top. Indeed, it seems un-American to doubt the notion, "why not the best?" But, of course, under every individual capitalist's success lies the exploited working class—a state of relations which can only increase mutual hostility, even if sublimated in liberal rhetoric and rationalistic narcissism falsely promising equal opportunity. Not coincidentally, in constructing her idealized heroes, Rand has tapped the traditional justification of bourgeois individualism and, hence, of hostility toward all others: *they're out to get you.* (p. 702)

Rand's reductive, linear absolutism taps the popular mind anxious to live mythically, in black and white polarities, ignorant of the contradictions inherent in the worship of old possibilities and ahistorical directions.

In her major work, *The Fountainhead,* Rand dramatizes the struggle of an individual to maintain his integrity and not to give in to others' interests. . . . Beginning with her early works, Rand has been consistent in her commitment to the primacy of self, "that man exists for his own sake, that the pursuit of his own happiness is his highest moral purpose, that he must not sacrifice himself to others, nor others to himself." Rand makes Howard Roark, protagonist of *The Fountainhead,* an architect whose profession perfectly blends individual artistic creation with social utilization. To be constructed and used, Roark's buildings must depend on others besides himself. Although he acknowledges the importance of the ultimate occupation of his buildings, his exclusive concern is with his individual creative act and its product. . . . Roark does not mention the needs of the occupier, nor does his sense of aesthetics involve taking notice of the shape of the community. In addition to organizing the building materials, the architect organizes the inhabitants' lives within the structures, as well as organizing their perspectives on the world outside.

These are very definitely not the concerns of Rand when she isolates Roark in a shell of introverted self-expression, and provides him with a rationalization called "integrity." . . . Rand's use of "integrity" is surely based on the second definition in the *Oxford En-*

glish Dictionary: unimpaired or uncorrupted state, original perfect condition; and perhaps even the obsolete usage meaning sinlessness. No wonder the boundaries must be fenced, reinforced, and patrolled. If the behemoth's condition is threatened by the corrupt "hordes of envious mediocrities"—then Rand condones Any protective action, whatever the cost. When his own housing project is about to be completed with some modifications he does not approve, Roark destroys his creation—better purity in others' homelessness than corruption of his aesthetics.

Violence, as *strong* action, finds ample rationalization. Never mind that a basic principle of Rand's Objectivist philosophy is the prohibition of the initial use of physical force against others: to the ideal man, any attempt to thwart his will justifies any response. (pp. 703-04)

[Rather] than conceive of reason as a historical tool, one which helps clarify the intricate relationships between individuals and society, Rand emphasizes reason as the justification and expression of the pure pursuit of individualist domination. Like many other moral systematists, Rand believes arrogantly in her own infallibility. Is it a surprise that her favorite modern novelist is Mickey Spillane, whose hero, Mike Hammer, never requiring proof beyond his own personal judgment, metes out justice immediately, lethally and illegally?

In creating her psychically stiff heroes, Rand presents nothing new with which to penetrate the legitimate and salient deliberation regarding connections of self to others. She has neither come to terms with Freud's tripartite scheme of id, ego, and super-ego (which might have helped in making a "rational" case of Roark) nor operated on the previous conflict-construct of conscious and unconscious mind. . . . Rand concedes that "man is born with certain physical and psychological needs, but he can neither discover them nor satisfy them without the use of his mind. . . . His so-called urges will not tell him what to do." (pp. 707-08)

Rand proposes that we need to create a society which will foster individualists of the Howard Roark strength and type. . . . Erecting starkly simplistic frameworks highly antagonistic to her own views, Rand winds the key in her heroes' backs, and then commands them in rigid opposition. In *Anthem* the futuristic world of self-denial prevails, and in *The Fountainhead* a collectivist rat-race locks everyone's focus into conformity with each other's image of each other. In either situation, Rand's solution is an amalgamation of a new capitalism and a new intellectualism, a program she develops more fully in her later novel, *Atlas Shrugged* (1957). (pp. 708-09)

Finally, let us consider how Rand occasionally tries to humanize her heroes, for example when Roark admits how difficult it is to be so great. Unintentionally, Rand has divulged here the essential flaw of her ideal, rational man: that to consider oneself so great, to be obsessed with one's individual substance, *must* entail being against others, and thus invites the conceit that, alas, no one else can be his equal. Self means division, and division means superiority-inferiority hierarchies. This is the junction at which all of Rand's roads—the reality principle, the violent interpersonal domination, the extroflection, and the "objective rationalization"— converge and lead to exactly what her hated *collectivists* propose as their final solution, a ruling elite. Seemingly antagonistic, Toohey, *The Fountainhead*'s collectivist, and Roark, the individualist, in fact imply the same social, political, and intellectual control, just as the Soviet Union (increasingly) and the United States are both monopoly capitalistic societies, one through state collectivism and the other through private enterprise. These, among other glaring ironies, Ayn Rand does not seem to recognize. (p. 709)

Philip Gordon, "The Extroflective Hero: A Look at Ayn Rand," in *Journal of Popular Culture,* Vol. X, No. 4, Spring, 1977, pp. 701-10.

MIMI R. GLADSTEIN
(essay date 1978)

[Gladstein is an American educator and critic. In the excerpt below, she approaches Dagny Taggart, the protagonist of *Atlas Shrugged*, as a positive feminist character.]

[*Atlas Shrugged*] is not generally considered to be philosophically feminist. In fact, it may not be on anyone's reading list for Women's Courses, except mine. But close analysis of the book's themes and theories will provide that it should be. Much that Rand says is relevant to feminist issues. Best of all, the novel has a protagonist who is a good example of a woman who is active, assertive, successful, and still retains the love and sexual admiration of three heroic men. Though the situation is highly romantic, and science fiction to boot, how refreshing it is to find a female protagonist in American Fiction who emerges triumphant. (p. 681)

The refrain of *Atlas Shrugged* is John Galt's oath, "I swear by my life and my love of it that I will never live for the sake of another man [person] nor ask another man [person] to live for mine." (For purposes of this paper I will feminize or neuter all masculine nouns and pronouns. Though Ms. Rand refers to men and mankind, she obviously means humankind as evidenced in the rest of this study.) While the context of the oath is economic, the message is the same one advanced by feminists that no woman should live her life for or through others, as women have traditionally been encouraged to do. Typical of the studies that touch upon this issue is Edith de Rham's *The Love Fraud.* In her attack on "the staggering waste of education and talent among American Women," de Rham argues that by persuading women to concentrate their lives on men who in turn concentrate on work "Women become victims of a kind of fraud in which their love is exploited and in which they are somehow persuaded that they are involved in legitimate action." It is just this kind of exploitation that Ayn Rand deplores.

Whereas de Rham calls it *The Love Fraud,* Rand calls it self-sacrifice or altruism. Rand's attack on altruism, which is defined as an ethical principle that "holds that one must make the welfare of others one's primary moral concern and must place their interests above one's own . . . that service to others is the moral justification of one's existence, that self-sacrifice is one's foremost duty and highest virtue" is especially relevant to women because they have been the chief internalizers of this concept. This concept of self-sacrifice has encouraged women to view themselves as sacrificial animals whose desires and talents are forfeited for the good of children, family and society. This negative behavior produces looters, moochers, leeches, and parasites in Rand's vernacular. Women have been socialized to feel guilty if they fail to carry out the practice of sacrificing their careers for the advancement of others, whether it be husband, family or simply a matter of vacating a position to a more needy male. And this sacrificing of a woman's abilities and potential is not viewed with horror or outrage, but rather with acceptance, while a similar male sacrifice is seen as a great tragedy or waste. Of course, Rand rejects any sacrifice as negative because she sees it as the surrender of a greater value for the sake of a lesser one or for the sake of a nonvalue. (pp. 682-83)

Galt, Rand's spokesperson, does not believe happiness is to be achieved through the sacrifice of one's values; he believes instead that "Woman has to be woman, she has to hold her life as a value, she has to learn to sustain it, she has to discover the values it requires and practice her virtues. . . . Happiness is that state of consciousness which proceeds from the achievement of one's values." What could be more relevant to feminism?

The nature of male/female relationships is another important area of philosophical exploration for Rand. Through Dagny's associations with Francisco D'Anconia, Hank Rearden and John Galt, Rand illustrates what a relationship between two self-actualized, equal human beings can be. In such relationships, Rand denies the existence of a split between the physical and the mental, the desires of the flesh and the longings of the spirit. (pp. 683-84)

According to [Rand's] philosophy, the object of a person's desires is a reflection of one's image of self. In the novel, Dagny—our positive protagonist—uses this fact as a standard of measuring others. Since Hank Rearden is capable of wanting her, he must be worthy of her. As she puts it, "I feel that others live up to me, if they want me." . . . In this context, also, if one desires a person, one also prizes everything that person is and stands for. . . . Within this framework, the act of sexual intercourse possesses special meaning. It is a joyous affirmation of one's life, of one's beliefs, of all that one is. Dagny realizes this after her first sexual encounter with Francisco. . . . Dagny picks sexual partners who affirm her and affirm life. (p. 684)

Though Rand stresses the primacy of individual action and responsibility, she does not exclude the importance of sisterhood. It is simply that Rand sees the development of *individual* strength as primary. When Cherryl Taggart, in desperation, turns to Dagny for help, Dagny's response to Cherryl's uncertain approach is the affirmative, "We're sisters, aren't we?" . . . Dagny stresses the fact that her offer of help is not a charitable act, but a recognition of Cherryl's essential worth. She invites Cherryl to stay with her and even elicits a promise that Cherryl will return. Still, though the sisterhood is warming, it is not enough to save Cherryl, for she has not developed enough strength to cope with the horror of her situation.

The Utopia of the novel, Galt's Gulch, is inhabited by people whose behavior and ideals Ayn Rand admires. They are people who are engaged in positive and productive endeavors and the woman who chooses motherhood is deliberately included. Dagny reflects on the joyous results of such choice, two eager and friendly children.

But domestic duties are not solely the realm of women in Galt's Gulch. Various of the male inhabitants are seen cooking, cleaning, and serving. When Dagny does housework, she is paid for her contribution.

In full honesty, there are attitudes toward women and femininity in the novel that are offensive, but they are few and are heavily outweighed by the positive aspects. Most significantly, for our purposes, Dagny Taggart is an affirmative role model. She is the head of a railroad. She has sexual relationships with three men and retains their love and respect. She is not demeaned or punished for her emancipation, sexual or professional. She has no intention of giving up her railroad for the man she loves. She retains them both. She behaves according to her code of ethics and is not punished by God or society. She is that rarity in American fiction—a heroine who not only survives, but prevails. (p. 685)

Mimi R. Gladstein, "Ayn Rand and Feminism: An Unlikely Alliance," in *College English*, Vol. 39, No. 6, February, 1978, pp. 680-85.

KEVIN MCGANN

(essay date 1978)

[In the following excerpt, McGann critiques *The Fountainhead*.]

The Fountainhead (1943) railed against the dragon forces of boorish "collectivism" and conventional aesthetic standards in *this* country as concerned citizen Rand determined to save America from "dying." . . . (p. 325)

Howard Roark, an architect-genius, persists in designing great buildings without sacrificing an inch of his integrity to the inevitably compromising demands of professional peers, opinion-makers, the public taste, and his clients. . . . Throughout the book he is implicitly compared with pusillanimous Peter Keating, college roommate and then fellow architect, whose overriding desire for commercial success makes him willing to accommodate anyone who promises to further his career.

The general principle upon which the book is based—that the mass of mankind is talentless, without creativity or originality, and bitterly jealous of those few who are different—is manifested most strongly in the character of Ellsworth Toohey . . . , an architectural critic for a mammoth newspaper chain. Through his highly influential intellectual position, Toohey hypocritically manipulates public opinion in the direction of "selflessness," which, through Ayn Rand's inverted rhetoric, becomes a kind of meek mindless drift toward that ideological archvillain, "collectivism." (pp. 325-26)

The first premise of Rand's philosophy—that everyone is ultimately selfish—is demonstrated in all three figures (Toohey, Keating, and Roark); but only one, Roark, also has "character," and the author's endorsement of his values places him far from the middling crowd, separating him from the spineless Keating and pitting him against the traitorous Toohey. The dialectic battle between a fantasy version of individualism—Roark—and a satanic version of the cooperative spirit—Toohey—culminates when Roark purposely dynamites a public-works housing project he designed because its architectural "integrity" has been compromised by the Toohey clique.

Between these forces are two other characters in *The Fountainhead* who, because they lack the courage to defend Roark's brilliant architecture before the rabble, masochistically bend their efforts to ruin it. Gail Wynand, the powerful Hearst-like publisher of Toohey's column, is an isolated cynic who at first tries to corrupt Roark to validate his own pessimism about human nature. Failing at that, and smitten finally by a glimpse of Roark's moral determination and idealistic faith . . . , Wynand throws his whole reputation into defending the young architect in his newspapers. The attempt at a personally redemptive crusade comes too late. Rand presents Wynand as a case study of the potentially enlightened capitalist-entrepreneur, but she makes him pay for his tardy patronage. Toohey subverts his organization and Wynand is stripped of his wealth [and] his wife. . . . (p. 326)

Like Wynand whom she married, Dominique Francon is a bitter example of approach-avoidance ambivalence. She is the daughter of a "successful" architect, but she despises her father's conventional mediocrity and secretly loves Roark. Her characterization is perhaps the most interesting aspect of the book. . . . She is by turns the destroyer, the seducer, the disciple, and finally an ally. The passionate relationship is in reality a struggle for dominance; when she realizes she cannot win the struggle over Roark, she is compelled to love him. (p. 327)

Although it has all the characteristics of pulp fiction, including flood-tide length and watery content, *The Fountainhead* is, of course, much more than a potboiler about the personal traumas behind the lives of busy architects. It is actually an "idea" novel, however crude or obvious, about fiercely opposing political ideologies. It is an overheard version of an internal American cultural debate between individualism and collectivism. . . . In articulating this struggle, Rand speaks simultaneously to the highest aspirations and the deepest suspicions of the culture, precipitating the broadly based, though mostly unspoken, acceptance of her work.

Part of *The Fountainhead*'s success is due to the way in which it includes its reader in a disenfranchised "elect." It appeals to the romantic sense of alienation and superiority, asking the reader to identify with an elite still sensitive to aesthetic "integrity" and tortured by the low-brow conventional mediocrity of a small-minded society. It has the bitterness of the "outsider" and offers a hero who is determined enough to overcome these obstacles. . . . This country, *The Fountainhead* seems to say, does not lack True Believers but rather something or someone to believe in: a Howard Roark, a moral absolutist and fervent crusader amidst the ugly spiritual malaise. Perceived by some as "radical" because its values—the emphasis on individualism, the romantic faith in the efficacy of an idea over all practical obstacles, grim moral purity—belong to an earlier, pioneer stage of economic development in a capitalist culture, it is ultimately an attack on present society from the regressive Right Wing. (pp. 328-29)

Kevin McGann, "Ayn Rand in the Stockyard of the Spirit," in *The Modern American Novel and the Movies,* edited by Gerald Peary and Roger Shatzkin, Frederick Ungar Publishing Co., 1978, pp. 325-35.

DOUGLAS DEN UYL AND DOUGLAS B. RASMUSSEN

(essay date 1983)

[Den Uyl and Rasmussen are American educators and philosophers. In the excerpt below, they examine Rand's basic philosophical theses.]

Perhaps it is fair to say that if there is one message Ayn Rand the theorist would have wanted to leave us it is, philosophy matters! The recent death of Ayn Rand provides the occasion for us to recall the importance of this message. In the heat of contemporary social and political debates we often forget to consider basic principles. The writings of Ayn Rand will always be with us as a reminder that pragmatism and expediency are ultimately self-defeating. And it is in this spirit of a concern for basic questions that we wish to briefly outline some of Rand's basic theses here.

We see three central themes in the philosophy of Ayn Rand: 1) The major metaphysical and epistemological tenets of Aristotelian realism are true—viz., reality exists and is what it is independent of our awareness of it, and yet it can be known by the human mind. 2) Self-actualization is the correct approach to ethics. There are appropriate goals for human beings to pursue, and these goals (with the appropriate means) are grounded in human nature. Values can be found in "facts" or the nature of things, thus making a doctrine of natural rights possible, and 3) The conflict between ancient and modern political philosophy over whether the state should promote freedom or virtue need not be a source of conflict. Virtue and liberty are inherently related, and laissez-faire capitalism is the only economic and political system that recognizes this intimate connection.

Rand argues for the first thesis in her *Introduction to Objectivist Epistemology.* Her basic purpose is to show that though knowledge requires that the content of our mind answer to what is actually "out there," the manner in which we come to know things (i.e., form concepts) may depend on certain cognitive processes peculiar to human nature. For example, concepts are "universals." My concept of "dog" (if correct) will apply universally to an indefinite number of dogs. Thus

while only individual dogs exist in nature, the mind may hold the concept of "dog" as a universal. This view of knowledge and concepts is a version of what philosophers call the "moderate realist" tradition—a tradition initiated by Aristotle and perhaps most fully developed by Thomas Aquinas. (p. 67)

The main non-fiction work in which Rand argues for the second thesis is *The Virtue of Selfishness.* In that work, especially the essay **"The Objectivist Ethics,"** Rand seeks to move ethics from the Kantian view in which ethics is a matter of duties to others to the Greek view of promoting well-being or self-actualization. She specifically rejects the tendency among ethicists to consider actions done for self as amoral. But Rand is just as insistent that self-interest is not a matter of what one feels like doing. Human nature sets the standards for what is in one's self-interest, and thus it is possible to do what one "wants" to do and still not act in one's own interest. This view of ethics places Rand squarely within the Aristotelian natural law tradition. (pp. 67-8)

But perhaps the most unique contribution Rand has made concerns showing the relationship between what we have called thesis two and thesis three. Rand argues that human excellence cannot be achieved without giving central importance to freedom of choice. . . . This is why liberty is the most important social/political value—it keeps the possibility of excellence open. Indeed Rand's theory of rights is simply a way to insure that freedom is protected. And her theory is a *natural* rights theory because the justification for these rights depends upon her naturalistic ethics. Thus moral excellence is achieved only through political freedom, making the dichotomy between freedom and virtue a false one.

Since the free market is not paternalistic, it allows for the achievement of human excellence. This is not utopianism, since freedom cannot, by the very fact that it is freedom, guarantee that all will act to achieve their fullest potential. But the free market society does provide some incentives to this end, since the individual himself suffers most from his errors. Moreover, known and yet to be discovered possibilities for achievement are not forcibly closed off. In this connection it is vitally important to realize a point made in her essay **"What is Capitalism"** contained in *Capitalism: The Unknown Ideal*—the book in which much of this third thesis can be found. Rand's theory of excellence is thoroughly individualistic. Excellence should not be viewed in terms of what is excellent for some class or group, e.g., intellectuals, businessmen, artists, or whomever. The achievement of excellence must be considered in the context of an individual's own circumstances and conditions. Freedom guarantees that the possibility of excellence will be open to all as they are respectively able to understand and achieve it. (pp. 68-9)

The foregoing remarks indicate why Rand does

not excessively exaggerate when she gives herself credit for understanding the moral basis for capitalism better than anyone else. Previous moral arguments were of the "necessary evil" variety. We tolerate the "selfishness" of individuals under capitalism to gain all the economic benefits that would result. Apart from the fact that this view implies that there is no moral basis for capitalism, it shows an ignorance both of human nature and the complex motives people have when they consider alternatives. . . .

In conclusion, it is worth noting that Rand is a thinker but not a professional academic. This has both advantages and disadvantages. One of the primary advantages is that she has not been held captive by many of the intellectual fashions that have swept philosophy during the twentieth century. It also means her writings are not jargonistic. One of the primary disadvantages is that she has not always bothered to work out all the details of her ideas in a way necessary to solidify her position. It is for this very reason that her thought needs professional attention. Nevertheless, Rand's philosophizing can be a source of knowledge as well as inspiration. Thus even though Rand is often rejected by professional academics and goes in and out of fashion among libertarians, it just might be that the very "stone which the builders rejected" could well be the "one to become the head of the corner." (p. 69)

Douglas Den Uyl and Douglas B. Rasmussen, "The Philosophical Importance of Ayn Rand," in *Modern Age,* Vol. 27, No. 1, Winter, 1983, pp. 67-9.

SOURCES FOR FURTHER STUDY

Baker, James T. *Ayn Rand.* Boston: Twayne Publishers, 1987, 159 p.
    Concise analysis of Rand as creative writer and philosopher.

Branden, Barbara. *The Passion of Ayn Rand.* Garden City, N. Y.: Doubleday.
    Critical biography.

Branden, Nathaniel. *Judgment Days: My Years with Ayn Rand.* Boston: Houghton Mifflin, 1989, 436 p.
    Memoirs by Rand's close friend and colleague.

Den Uyl, Douglas J. and Douglas B. Rasmussen. *The Philosophic Thought of Ayn Rand.* Urbana: University of Illinois Press, 1984, 235 p.
    Collection of essays on Rand and objectivism.

Gladstein, Mimi Reisel. *The Ayn Rand Companion.* Westport, Conn.: Greenwood Press, 1984, 130 p.
    Explication of Rand's works, characters, and criticism.

Teachout, Terry. "Farewell, Dagny Taggart." *National Review* XXXIV, No. 9 (14 May 1982): 566-67.
    Labels *Atlas Shrugged* "a preposterous book," but concludes: "No novel of comparable quality has ever been so tenacious in its hold on the public, give or take *Gone with the Wind.*"

Samuel Richardson

1689-1761

English novelist and moralist.

INTRODUCTION

Richardson is considered the originator of the modern English novel. He has also been called the first dramatic novelist, as well as the first of the eighteenth-century "sentimental" writers. In his masterpiece, *Clarissa; or, The History of a Young Lady* (1747–48), he introduced tragedy to the novel form; and in *The History of Sir Charles Grandison* (1753–54) he substituted social embarrassment for tragic conflict, thus developing the first novel of manners. Most significantly, Richardson's detailed exploration of his characters' motives and feelings, accomplished through his subtle use of the epistolary method, added a new dimension to the art of fiction. Similarly, his experiments with point-of-view narration profoundly influenced the development of the novel and helped establish the genre as an intimate record of inner experience. Richardson also developed the novel from its previously single-level structure, consisting primarily of the experiences of a sole protagonist, to a multilevel rendering of the complexity of life with his use of subordinate and parallel plots. His combination of tragedy and comedy, irony and melodrama, metaphysical and social morality, have led some critics to call him the Shakespeare of the Neoclassical Age. Although most feel that this is an exaggeration, few scholars doubt the impact Richardson had on the novel form. Arnold Kettle explains that Richardson "got deeper into the subtle, wayward and contradictory feelings of human beings than any previous novelist had managed."

Little is known of Richardson's early life. He was born in Derbyshire, England, the son of a cabinetmaker and his wife. Although his parents had hoped to educate him for the ministry, poverty thwarted their plans, and the young Richardson received only a modest education. In 1706, after the family had moved to London, he was apprenticed to a printer, John Wilde, and soon became a freeman to the Stationers' Company in 1715. In 1718 or 1719 Richardson began his own printing business, quickly becoming one of the leading merchants in London. Through his business, he became a friend and patron of many writers, including Samuel Johnson, Sarah Fielding, and Edward Young. Although his career continued to prosper, Richardson's outward success concealed the impact of much private tragedy. He was married twice, in 1721 and 1732. All six children by his first marriage died by the age of four. Another son, born to his second wife, died while still an infant. These and other bereavements helped to bring on a nervous condition that plagued his later life. Richardson died at Parson's Green, London, in 1761.

Richardson began writing what would become his first novel, *Pamela; or, Virtue Rewarded* (1740-41), at the age of fifty-one. This work was the result of a commission he undertook at the request of two booksellers, Charles Rivington and John Osborn. Both Rivington and Osborn felt that a collection of model letters to be used by people with little formal education would be a prosperous venture, and they proposed the idea to Richardson, who enthusiastically accepted. Two years later the volume was published under the title *Letters Written to and for Particular Friends, on the Most Important Occasions* (1741). While he was writing this work, Richardson recollected a story he had heard concerning the attempted seduction of a servant girl by her master and decided to develop this incident into a series of letters from the girl to her parents. Thus arose *Pamela,* and so began Richardson's second career, as a novelist. Perhaps the most popular novel of the eighteenth century, *Pamela* and its sequel crystalized the aspirations of the growing middle class in England. The story of a virtuous servant girl who consistently refuses the sexual advances of her aristocratic master and is eventually rewarded with his offer of marriage, *Pamela* symbolized the supremacy of the Puritan ethic over the licentiousness and immorality of the wealthy class. It also demonstrated quite clearly the ambivalent nature of the Puritan psyche, for while the novel champions the virtues of the middle-class way of life, it also depicts the middle-class fascination with the aristocracy. *Pamela's* lasting significance, however, lies in its dramatic and exploratory use of the epistolary form. Richardson depicted his heroine through her daily explorations into her own identity, rather than through an omniscient narrator or a first-person narrator speaking in retrospect.

Richardson's second novel, *Clarissa,* can be read on a number of levels. At one level, it is a sombre indictment of bourgeois materialism and family tyranny, as well as an attack on the aristocratic notion of class supremacy. Both the bourgeois Harlowes and the aristocratic Lovelace suffer because they fail to realize the most important values in life. It is also a revealing portrait of a consciousness doomed to enact its life under the continuous threat of destruction. Clarissa's death is a direct result of those qualities which both the characters in the novel and the reader consider saintly, namely her purity of body and soul. Clarissa's ultimate moral strength resides in her refusal to compromise these qualities to the physical world of violence, materialism, and sin. Instead, she chooses negation and death as her final salvation. Clearly, Richardson saw Clarissa's death as a mark of divine grace, releasing her from a world in which human beings torture one another and themselves. Structurally, *Clarissa* represents a great advance over *Pamela.* Although Richardson utilizes the epistolary method once again, he also uses three other points of view—Anna Howe's, Lovelace's, and Belford's—to explore the various implications of the events. Most critics consider the central dilemma of the novel more genuinely moral than that of *Pamela.* The problem is not whether Clarissa will be seduced, but how she chooses to structure her life once that seduction has been accomplished.

Critics generally believe that Richardson wrote his last novel, *Sir Charles Grandison,* as a response to Henry Fielding's *Tom Jones.* He wanted to demonstrate, after the great success of Fielding's work, what he believed a "good man" was really like. Although *Sir Charles Grandison* exhibits deeply held beliefs, it is often considered inferior to Richardson's two previous novels. The hero, Charles Grandison, illustrates the author's conviction that the foundation of all morality is goodness of heart, and that the truest human pleasure flows from virtue and benevolence; however, Sir Charles comes across as priggish rather than virtuous. Unlike Pamela and Clarissa, he never explores the recesses of his being or struggles with the nature of his identity. Yet some critics, such as Alan Dugald McKillop and R. F. Brissenden, consider the novel the most influential of Richardson's canon, and the great novelist of manners Jane Austen regarded it as his best. Perhaps the best features of the novel result from Richardson's ability to introduce conflict to the social arena and to move the novel from the English countryside to the tea-rooms and parlors of fashionable London.

From the very beginning of his writing career, Richardson was blessed with readers and critics who sympathized with his aims in art. His contemporaries focused almost exclusively on his moral teachings, and many praised the author for his "judgment" and "honesty." Most importantly, the reading public immediately sensed the magnitude of the social concerns Richardson was trying to depict in his novels, such as the growing pressure during the 1700s for financially secure marriages, the conflict between individuals and society, and the conflicts between a developing middle class and the old aristocracy. Richardson's response to these problems, couched in the language of Puritan morality but actually individualistic and democratic, won the approval of a middle-class reading public torn between its sense of virtue and its desire for the luxuries of the aristocracy.

Richardson is still regarded as the originator of the modern English novel and the first writer to fully explore the individual psychology of his characters. His influence can be seen in the works of Henry James, Jane Austen, Jean-Jacques Rousseau, Gotthold Lessing, Johann Wolfgang von Goethe, and Carlo Goldoni. Along with Henry Fielding, he remains one of the most important figures in the history of the novel.

(For further information about Richardson's life and works, see *Dictionary of Literary Biography*, Vol. 39: *British Novelists, 1660-1800* and *Literature Criticism from 1400 to 1800*, Vol. 1.)

CRITICAL COMMENTARY

SIR WALTER SCOTT
(essay date 1824)

[Scott was a novelist and literary critic. In the following excerpt from his preface to an 1824 edition of Richardson's novels, he discusses Richardson's aptitude for circumstantial description, focusing on the author's characters, technique, and insight into human passions.]

It was by mere accident that Richardson appears to have struck out the line of composition so peculiarly adapted to his genius. He had at all times the pen of a ready correspondent, and from his early age had . . . been accustomed to lend it to others, and to write, of course, under different characters from his own. There can be no doubt that, in the service of the young women who employed him as their amanuensis and confidant, this natural talent must have been considerably improved; and as little that the exercise of such a power was pleasing to the possessor. Chance at length occasioned its being employed in the service of the public. (p. 222)

Pamela . . . made a most powerful sensation on the public. Hitherto romances had been written, generally speaking, in the old French taste, containing the protracted amours of Princes and Princesses, told in language coldly extravagant and metaphysically absurd. In these wearisome performances there appeared not the most distant allusion to the ordinary tone of feeling, the slightest attempt to paint mankind as it exists in the ordinary walks of life—all was rant and bombast, stilt and buskin. It will be Richardson's eternal praise, did he merit no more, that he tore from his personages those painted vizards, which concealed, under a clumsy and affected disguise, everything like the natural lineaments of the human countenance, and placed them before us barefaced, in all the actual changes of feature and complexion, and all the light and shade of human passion. (pp. 225-26)

The simplicity of Richardson's tale aided the effect of surprise. An innocent young woman, whose virtue a dissolute master assails by violence, as well as all the milder means of seduction, conquers him at last by persevering in the paths of rectitude, and is rewarded by being raised to the station of his wife, the lawful participator in his rank and fortune. Such is the simple story by which the world was so much surprised and affected. (p. 226)

[The] character of Pamela is far from attaining an heroic cast of virtue. On the contrary, there is a strain of cold-blooded prudence which runs through all the latter part of the novel, to which we are obliged almost to deny the name of virtue. She appears originally to have had no love for Mr. B., no passion to combat in her own bosom, no treachery to subdue in the garrison while the enemy was before the walls. Richardson voluntarily evaded giving this colouring to his tale, because it was intended more for edification than for effect, and because the example of a *soubrette* falling desperately in love with a handsome young master might have been imitated by many in that rank of life who could not have defended themselves exactly like Pamela against the object of so dangerous a passion. Besides, Richardson was upon principle unwilling to exhibit his favoured characters as greatly subject to violent passion of any kind, and was much disposed to dethrone Cupid, whom romance-writers had installed as the literal sovereign of gods and men. Still the character of Pamela is somewhat sunk by the eager gratitude with which she accepts the hand of a tyrannical and cruel master, when he could not at a cheaper rate make himself master of her person. There is a parade of generosity on his side, and of creeping submission on hers, which the case by no means calls for; and unless, like her namesake in Pope's satire, she can console herself with the 'gilt chariot and the Flanders mares,' we should have thought her more likely to be happy had

Principal Works

she become the wife of poor Mr. Williams, of whose honest affection she makes somewhat too politic a use in the course of her trials, and whom she discards too coolly when better prospects seem to open upon her.

It is perhaps invidious to enter too closely upon the general tendency of a work of entertainment. But when the admirers of *Pamela* challenged for that work the merit of doing more good than twenty sermons, we demur to the motion. (pp. 226-27)

[The] direct and obvious moral to be deduced from a fictitious narrative is of much less consequence to the public than the mode in which the story is treated in the course of its details. If the author introduces scenes which excite evil passions, if he familiarises the mind of the readers with impure ideas, or sophisticates their understanding with false views of morality, it will be an unavailing defence that, in the end of his book, he has represented virtue as triumphant. In the same manner, although some objections may be made to the deductions which the author desired and expected should be drawn from the story of *Pamela,* yet the pure

and modest character of the English maiden is so well maintained during the work; her sorrows and afflictions are borne with so much meekness; her little intervals of hope or comparative tranquillity break in on her troubles so much like the specks of blue sky through a cloudy atmosphere, that the whole recollection is soothing, tranquillising, and, doubtless, edifying. We think little of Mr. B.—, his character, or his motives, and are only delighted with the preferment of our favourite, because it seems to give so much satisfaction to herself. The pathetic passage in which she describes her ineffectual attempt to escape may be selected, among many, as an example of the beautiful propriety and truth with which the author was able to throw himself into the character of his heroine, and to think and reason, and express those thoughts and reasons, exactly as she must have done, had the fictitious incident really befallen such a person.

The inferior persons are sketched with great truth, and may be considered as a group of English portraits of the period. In particular, the characters of the father and mother, old Andrews and his wife, are, like that of Pamela herself, in the very best style of drawing and colouring. . . . (pp. 227-28)

Eight years after the appearance of *Pamela,* Richardson published *Clarissa,* the work on which his fame as a classic of England will rest for ever. The tale, like that of its predecessor, is very simple, but the scene is laid in a higher rank of life, the characters are drawn with a bolder pencil, and the whole accompaniments are of a far loftier mood.

Clarissa, a character as nearly approaching to perfection as the pencil of the author could draw, is persecuted by a tyrannical father and brother, an envious sister, and the other members of a family who devoted everything to its aggrandisement in order to compel her to marry a very disagreeable suitor. These intrigues and distresses she communicates, in a series of letters, to her friend Miss Howe, a young lady of an ardent, impetuous disposition, and an enthusiast in friendship. After a series of sufferings, rising almost beyond endurance, Clarissa is tempted to throw herself upon the protection of her admirer Lovelace, a character in painting whom Richardson has exerted his utmost skill, until he has attained the very difficult and critical point of rendering every reader pleased with his wit and abilities, even while detesting the villainy of his conduct. Lovelace is represented as having devoted his life and talents to the subversion of female virtue; and not even the charms of Clarissa, or her unprotected situation, can reconcile him to the idea of marriage. (p. 230)

The conduct of the injured Clarissa through the subsequent scenes, which are perhaps among the most affecting and sublime in the English school of romance, raise her, in her calamitous condition, so far above all around her, that her character beams on the reader with something like superhuman splendour. Our eyes weep, our hearts ache, yet our feelings triumph with the triumph of virtue, as it rises over all the odds which the deepest misfortune, and even degradation, have thrown into the scale. . . . It was reserved to Richardson to show that there is a chastity of the soul, which can beam out spotless and unsullied, even after that of the person has been violated; and the dignity of Clarissa, under her disgrace and her misfortunes, reminds us of the saying of the ancient poet, that a good man, struggling with the tide of adversity, and surmounting it, was a sight which the immortal gods might look down upon with pleasure. (pp. 232-33)

The greatness of Clarissa is shown by her separating herself from her lover as soon as she perceives his dishonourable views; in her choosing death rather than a repetition of the outrage; in her rejection of those overtures of marriage, which a common mind might have accepted of, as a refuge against worldly dishonour; in her firm indignant carriage, mixed with calm patience and Christian resignation; and in the greatness of mind with which she views and enjoys the approaches of death, and her meek forgiveness of her unfeeling relations. (pp. 233-34)

[Richardson] knew, that to bestow Clarissa upon the repentant Lovelace, would have been to undermine the fabric he had built. This was the very purpose which the criminal had proposed to himself, in the atrocious crime he had committed, and it was to dismiss him from the scene rewarded, not punished. The sublimity of the moral would have been altogether destroyed, since vice would have been no longer rendered hateful and miserable through its very success, nor virtue honoured and triumphant even by its degradation. The death of Clarissa alone could draw down on the guilty head of her betrayer the just and necessary retribution, and his guilt was of far too deep a dye to be otherwise expiated. Besides, the author felt, and forcibly pointed out, the degradation which the fervent creation of his fancy must have sustained, could she, with all her wrongs forgotten, and with the duty imposed on her by matrimony, to love, honour, and obey her betrayer, have sat down the commonplace good wife of her reformed rake. Indeed, those who peruse the work with attention, will perceive that the author has been careful, in the earlier stages of his narrative, to bar out every prospect of such a union. Notwithstanding the levities and constitutional good humour of Lovelace, his mind is too much perverted, his imagination too much inflamed by his own perverted Quixotism, and, above all, his heart is too much hardened, to render it possible for any one seriously to think of his conversion as sincere, or his union with Clarissa as happy. He had committed a crime for which he deserved death by the law of the country; and notwithstanding those good qualities with which the author has invested him,

that he may not seem an actual incarnate fiend, there is no reader but feels vindictive pleasure when Morden passes the sword through his body.

On the other hand, Clarissa, reconciled to her violator, must have lost, in the eye of the reader, that dignity, with which the refusal of his hand, the only poor reparation he could offer, at present invests her; and it was right and fitting that a creature, every way so excellent, should, as is fabled of the ermine, pine to death on account of the stain with which she had been so injuriously sullied. We cannot, consistently with the high idea which we have previously entertained of her purity of character, imagine her surviving the contamination. On the whole, as Richardson himself pleaded, Clarissa has, as the narrative presently stands, the greatest of triumphs, even in this world—the greatest even in and after the outrage, and because of the outrage, that any woman ever had.

It has often been observed that the extreme severity of the parents and relatives in this celebrated novel does not belong to our day, or, perhaps, even to Richardson's; and that Clarissa's dutiful scruples at assuming her own estate, or extricating herself by Miss Howe's means, are driven to extremity. Something no doubt must be allowed for the licence of an author, who must necessarily, in order to command interest and attention, extend his incidents to the extreme verge of probability; but besides, it is well known, that at least within the century, the notions of the *patria potestas* were of a much severer nature than those now entertained; that forced marriages have actually taken place, and that in houses of considerable rank; that the voice of public opinion had then comparatively little effect upon great and opulent families, inhabiting their country seats, and living amid their own dependants, where strange violences were sometimes committed, under the specious pretext of enforcing domestic discipline. . . . But whether we consider Richardson as exhibiting a state of manners which may have lingered in the remote parts of England down to his own time, or suppose that he coloured them according to his own invention, and particularly according to his high notions of the 'awful rule and right supremacy,' lodged in the head of a family, there can be no doubt of the spirit with which the picture is executed; and particularly of the various gradations in which the Harlowe spirit exhibits itself, in the insolent and conceited brother, the mean and envious sister, the stern and unrelenting father, softened down in the elder brother James, and again roughened and exaggerated in the old seaman Anthony, each of whom, in various modifications, exhibits the same family features of pride, avarice, and ambition.

Miss Howe is an admirably sketched character, drawn in strong contrast to that of Clarissa, yet worthy of being her friend—with more of worldly perspicacity, though less of abstracted principle, and who, when they argue upon points of doubt and delicacy, is often able, by going directly to the question at issue, to start the game, while her more gifted correspondent does but beat the bush. Her high spirit and disinterested devotion for her friend, acknowledging, as she does on all occasions, her own inferiority, show her in a noble point of view; and though we are afraid she must have given honest Hickman (notwithstanding her resolutions to the contrary) rather an uneasy time of it after marriage, yet it is impossible not to think that she was a prize worth suffering for.

The publication of *Clarissa* raised the fame of the author to the height. No work had appeared before, perhaps none has appeared since, containing so many direct appeals to the passions, stated too in a manner so irresistible. And high as his reputation stood in his own country, it was even more exalted in those of France and Germany, whose imaginations are more easily excited, and their passions more easily moved by tales of fictitious distress, than are the cold-blooded English. Foreigners of distinction have been known to visit Hampstead, and to inquire for the Flask Walk, distinguished as a scene in Clarissa's history, just as travellers visit the rocks of Meillerie, to view the localities of Rousseau's tale of passion. (pp. 235-38)

The subject of the third and last novel of this eminent author seems to have been in a great degree dictated by the criticism which *Clarissa* had undergone. To his own surprise, as he assured his correspondents, he found that the gaiety, bravery, and, occasionally, generosity of Lovelace, joined to his courage and ingenuity, had, in spite of his crimes, made him find too much grace in the eyes of his fair readers. He had been so studious to prevent this, that when he perceived his rake was rising into an undue and dangerous degree of favour with some of the young ladies of his own school, he threw in some darker shades of character. (p. 238)

With this view, the author tasked his talents to embody the *beau idéal* of a virtuous character, who should have all the title to admiration which he could receive from wit, rank, figure, accomplishment, and fashion, yet compounded inseparably with the still higher qualifications which form the virtuous citizen and the faithful votary of religion. It was with this view that Richardson produced the work originally denominated *The Good Man,* a title which, before publication, he judiciously exchanged for that of *Sir Charles Grandison.*

It must be acknowledged that, although the author exerted his utmost ability to succeed in the task which he had assumed, and, so far as detached parts of the work are considered, has given the same marks of genius which he employed in his former novels, yet this last production has neither the simplicity of the

first two volumes of *Pamela,* nor the deep and overwhelming interest of the inimitable *Clarissa,* and must, considering it as a whole, be ranked considerably beneath both these works. (p. 239)

Sir Charles Grandison is a man of large fortune, of rank, and of family, high in the opinion of all who know him, and discharging with the most punctilious accuracy his duties in every relation of life. But, in order to his doing so, he is accommodated with all those exterior advantages which command awe and attract respect, although entirely adventitious to excellence of principle. . . . Sir Charles encounters no misfortunes, and can hardly be said to undergo any trials. (p. 240)

The only dilemma to which he is exposed in the course of the seven volumes is the doubt which of two beautiful and accomplished women, excellent in disposition, and high in rank, sister excellencies, as it were, both being devotedly attached to him, he shall be pleased to select for his bride; and this with so small a shade of partiality towards either, that we cannot conceive his happiness to be endangered where-ever his lot may fall, except by a generous compassion for her whom he must necessarily relinquish. Whatever other difficulties surround him occasionally vanish before his courage and address; and he is almost secure to make friends, and even converts, of those whose machinations may for a moment annoy him. In a word, Sir Charles Grandison 'walks the course' without competition or rivalry.

All this does well enough in a funeral sermon or monumental inscription, where, by privilege of suppressing the worst qualities and exaggerating the better, such images of perfection are sometimes presented. But, in the living world, a state of trial and a valley of tears, such unspotted worth, such unvarying perfection, is not to be met with and, what is still more important, it could not, if we suppose it to have existence, be attended by all those favours of fortune which are accumulated upon Richardson's hero. (pp. 240-41)

It is not the moral and religious excellence of Sir Charles which the reader is so much disposed to quarrel with, as that, while Richardson designs to give a high moral lesson by the success of his hero, he has failed through resting that success on circumstances which have nothing to do either with morality or religion, but might have been, if indeed they are not, depicted as the properties of Lovelace himself. It is impossible that any very deep lesson can be derived from contemplating a character, at once of unattainable excellence, and which is placed in circumstances of worldly ease and prosperity that render him entirely superior to temptation. (p. 241)

To take the matter less gravely, and consider *Sir Charles Grandison* as a work of amusement, it must be allowed, that the interest is destroyed in a great measure by the unceasing ascendency given to the fortune as well as the character of the hero. We feel he is too much under the special protection of the author to need any sympathy of ours, and that he has nothing to dread from all the Pollexfens, O'Haras, and so forth, in the world, so long as Richardson is decidedly his friend. Neither are our feelings much interested about him, when his fate is undetermined. He evinces too little passion, and certainly no preference, being clearly ready, with heart and goodwill, to marry either Clementina or Harriet Byron, as circumstances may render most proper, and to bow gracefully upon the hand of the rejected lady, and bid her adieu. (p. 242)

The real heroine of the work, and the only one in whose fortunes we take a deep and decided interest, is the unhappy Clementina, whose madness, and indeed her whole conduct, is sketched with the same exquisite pencil which drew the distresses of Clarissa. There are in those passages relating to her, upon which we do not dwell, familiar as they must be to all our readers, scenes which equal any thing that Richardson ever wrote, and which would alone be sufficient to rank him with the highest name in his line of composition. These, with other detached passages in the work, serve to show that it was no diminution in Richardson's powers, but solely the adoption of an inferior plan, which renders his two earlier works preferable to *Sir Charles Grandison.* (p. 244)

Richardson was well qualified to be the discoverer of a new style of writing, for he was a cautious, deep, and minute examinator of the human heart, and, like Cook or Parry, left neither head, bay, nor inlet behind him until he had traced its soundings and laid it down in his chart, with all its minute sinuosities, its depths, and its shallows. (p. 249)

It is impossible to tell whether Richardson's peculiar and circumstantial mode of narrative arose entirely out of the mode in which he evolves his story, by the letters of the actors, or whether his early partiality for letter-writing was not rather founded upon his innate love of detail. But these talents and propensities must have borne upon and fortified each other. To the letter-writer every event is recent, and is painted immediately while under the eye, with reference to its relative importance to what has past and what has to come. All is, so to speak, painted in the foreground, and nothing in the distance. A game at whist, if the subject of a letter, must be detailed as much at length as a debate in the House of Commons upon a subject of great national interest; and hence, perhaps, that tendency to prolixity, of which the readers of Richardson frequently complain.

There is this additional disadvantage, tending to the same disagreeable impression, that incidents are, in many instances, detailed again and again by the various actors to their different correspondents. If this has the advantage of placing the characters each in their own peculiar light, and contrasting their thoughts, plans, and sentiments, it is at least partly balanced by arresting the progress of the story, which stands still while the characters show all their paces, like horses in the manège, without advancing a yard. But then it gives the reader . . . the advantage of being thoroughly acquainted with those in whose fate he is to be interested. (p. 251)

It must not be overlooked that, by the circumstantial detail of minute, trivial, and even uninteresting circumstances, the author gives to his fiction an air of reality that can scarcely otherwise be obtained. In every real narrative, he who tells it dwells upon slight and inconsiderable circumstances, no otherwise interesting than because they are associated in his mind with the more important events which he desires to communicate. De Foe, who understood and availed himself on all occasions of this mode of garnishing an imaginary history with all the minute accompaniments which distinguish a true one, was scarce a greater master of this peculiar art than was our author Richardson.

Still, with all these advantages, which so peculiarly adapted the mode of carrying on the story by epistolary correspondence to Richardson's peculiar genius, it has its corresponding defects. In order that all may be written which must be known for the purpose of the narrative, the characters must frequently write, when it would be more natural for them to be acting—must frequently write what it is not natural to write at all,—and must at all times write a great deal oftener, and a great deal more than one would now think human life has time for. (pp. 252-53)

Richardson was himself aware of the luxuriance of his imagination, and that he was sometimes apt to exceed the patience of the reader. He indulged his own vein by writing without any fixed plan, and at great length, which he afterwards curtailed and compressed; so that, strange as it may seem, his compositions were reduced almost one half in point of size before they were committed to the press. In his first two novels also he showed much attention to the plot, and, though diffuse and prolix in narration, can never be said to be rambling or desultory. No characters are introduced but for the purpose of advancing the plot; and there are but few of those digressive dialogues and dissertations with which *Sir Charles Grandison* abounds. The story keeps the direct road, though it moves slowly. But in his last work the author is much more excursive. There is indeed little in the plot to require attention; the various events which are successively narrated, being no otherwise connected together than as they place the character of the hero in some new and peculiar point of view. (p. 253)

The style of Richardson was of that pliable and facile kind, which could, with slight variety, be adapted to what best befitted his various personages. When he wrote in his higher characters, it was copious, expressive, and appropriate; but, through the imperfection of his education, not always strictly elegant, or even accurate. (p. 254)

The power of Richardson's painting in his deeper scenes of tragedy never has been, and probably never will be, excelled. Those of distressed innocence, as in the history of Clarissa and Clementina, rend the very heart; and few, jealous of manly equanimity, should read them for the first time in the presence of others. In others, where the same heroines, and particularly Clarissa, display a noble elevation of soul, rising above earthly considerations and earthly oppression, the reader is perhaps as much elevated towards a pure sympathy with virtue and religion as uninspired composition can raise him. His scenes of unmixed horror, as the deaths of Belton and of the infamous Sinclair, are as dreadful as the former are elevating; and they are directed to the same noble purpose, increasing our fear and hatred of vice, as the former are qualified to augment our love and veneration of virtue. The lighter qualities of the novelist were less proper to this distinguished author than those which are allied to tragedy. Yet, not even in these was Richardson deficient; and his sketches of this kind display the same accurate knowledge of humanity manifested in his higher efforts. His comedy is not overstrained, and never steps beyond the bounds of nature, and he never sacrifices truth and probability to brilliancy of effect. Without what is properly termed wit, the author possessed liveliness and gaiety sufficient to colour those scenes; and though he is never, like his rival Fielding, irresistibly ludicrous, nor indeed, ever essays to be so, there is a fund of quaint drollery pervades his lighter sketches, which renders them very agreeable to the reader. (p. 255)

Sir Walter Scott, "Richardson," in his *Lives of the Novelists*, Oxford University Press, London, 1906, pp. 206-56.

SIR LESLIE STEPHEN
(essay date 1894)

[Stephen was an English literary critic. In the following excerpt, he criticizes Richardson's "device for inculcating morality" but claims that it was the moral issues themselves that ignited the author's imagination.]

Richardson's sympathy with women gives a remarkable power to his works. Nothing is more rare than to find a great novelist who can satisfactorily describe the opposite sex. . . . [The] heroines of male writers are for the most part unnaturally strained or quite colourless; male hands are too heavy for the delicate work required. Milton could draw a majestic Satan, but his Eve is no better than a good-managing housekeeper who knows her place. It is, therefore, remarkable that Richardson's greatest triumph should be in describing a woman, and that most of his feminine characters are more life-like and more delicately discriminated than his men. Unluckily, his conspicuous faults result from the same cause. His moral prosings savour of the endless gossip over a dish of chocolate in which his heroines delight; we can imagine the applause with which his admiring feminine circle would receive his demonstration of the fact, that adversity is harder to bear than prosperity, or the sentiment that 'a man of principle whose love is founded in reason, and whose object is mind rather than person, must make a worthy woman happy.' These are admirable sentiments, but they savour of the serious tea-party. If *Tom Jones* has about it an occasional suspicion of beer and pipes at the bar, *Sir Charles Grandison* recalls an indefinite consumption of tea and small-talk. . . . [Richardson's] device for inculcating morality is of course ineffectual, and produces some artistic blemishes. The direct exhortations to his readers to be good are still more annoying; no human being can long endure a mixture of preaching and storytelling. For Heaven's sake, we exclaim, tell us what happens to Clarissa, and don't stop to prove that honesty is the best policy! In a wider sense, however, the seriousness of Richardson's purpose is of high value. He is so keenly in earnest, so profoundly interested about his characters, so determined to make us enter into their motives, that we cannot help being carried away; if he never spares an opportunity of giving us a lecture, at least his zeal in setting forth an example never flags for an instant. The effort to give us an ideally perfect character seems to stimulate his imagination, and leads to a certain intensity of realisation which we are apt to miss in the purposeless school of novelists. He is always, as it were, writing at high-pressure and under a sense of responsibility.

The method which he adopts lends itself very conveniently to heighten this effect. Richardson's feminine delight in letter-writing was, as we have seen, the immediate cause of his plunge into authorship. Richardson's novels, indeed, are not so much novels put for convenience under the form of letters, as letters expanded till they become novels. A genuine novelist who should put his work into the unnatural shape of a correspondence would probably find it a very awkward expedient; but Richardson gradually worked up to the novel from the conception of a collection of letters; and his method, therefore, came spontaneously to him. (pp. 60-3)

The result of [this method] is a sort of Dutch painting of extraordinary minuteness. The art reminds

CLARISSA.

OR, THE

HISTORY

OF A

YOUNG LADY:

Comprehending

The most Important Concerns *of* Private LIFE.

And particularly shewing,

The DISTRESSES that may attend the Misconduct
Both of PARENTS and CHILDREN,

In Relation to MARRIAGE.

Published by the EDITOR *of* PAMELA.

VOL. I.

LONDON:
Printed for S. Richardson:
And Sold by A. MILLAR, over-against *Catharine-street* in the *Strand:*
J. and JA. RIVINGTON, in *St. Paul's Church-yard:*
JOHN OSBORN, in *Pater-noster Row;*
And by J. LEAKE, at *Bath.*

M.DCC.XLVIII.

Title page of the first edition of Richardson's *Clarissa.*

us of the patient labour of a line-engraver, who works for days at making out one little bit of minute stippling and cross-hatching. The characters are displayed to us step by step and line by line. We are gradually forced into familiarity with them by a process resembling that by which we learn to know people in real life. We are treated to few set analyses or summary descriptions, but by constantly reading their letters and listening to their talk we gradually form an opinion of the actors. We see them, too, all round; instead of, as is usual in modern novels, regarding them steadily from one point of view; we know what each person thinks of everyone else, and what everyone else thinks of him; they are brought into a stereoscopic distinctness by combining the different aspects of their character. Of course, a method of this kind involves much labour on the part both of writer and reader. . . . Richardson's own interest in his actors never flags. The distinct style of every correspondent is faithfully preserved with singular vivacity. When we have read a few letters we are never at a loss to tell, from the style alone of any short passage, who is the imaginary author. Consequently, readers who can bear to have their amusement diluted, who

are content with an imperceptibly slow development of plot, and can watch without impatience the approach of a foreseen incident through a couple of volumes, may find the prolixity less intolerable than might be expected. If they will be content to skip when they are bored, even less patient students may be entertained with a series of pictures of character and manners skilfully contrasted and brilliantly coloured, though with a limited allowance of incident. Within his own sphere, no writer exceeds him in clearness and delicacy of conception.

In another way, the machinery of a fictitious correspondence is rather troublesome. As the author never appears in his own person, he is often obliged to trust his characters with trumpeting their own virtues. Sir Charles Grandison has to tell us himself of his own virtuous deeds; how he disarms ruffians who attack him in overwhelming numbers, and converts evil-doers by impressive advice; and, still more awkwardly, he has to repeat the amazing compliments which everybody is always paying him. Richardson does his best to evade the necessity; he couples all his virtuous heroes with friendly confidants, who relieve the virtuous heroes of the tiresome task of self-adulation; he supplies the heroes themselves with elaborate reasons for overcoming their modesty, and makes them apologise profusely for the unwelcome task. Still, ingenious as his expedients may be, and willing as we are to make allowance for the necessities of his task, we cannot quite free ourselves from an unpleasant suspicion as to the simplicity of his characters. *Clarissa* is comparatively free from this fault, though Clarissa takes a questionable pleasure in uttering the finest sentiments and posing herself as a model of virtue. But in *Sir Charles Grandison* the fulsome interchange of flattery becomes offensive even in fiction. The virtuous characters give and receive an amount of eulogy enough to turn the strongest stomachs. (pp. 68-70)

Richardson's defects are, of course, obvious enough. He cares nothing, for example, for what we call the beauties of nature. There is scarcely throughout his books one description showing the power of appealing to emotions through scenery claimed by every modern scribbler. In passing the Alps, the only remark which one of his characters has to make, beyond describing the horrible dangers of the Mont Cenis, is that 'every object which here presents itself is excessively miserable.' His ideal scenery is a 'large and convenient country-house, situated in a spacious park,' with plenty of 'fine prospects,' which you are expected to view from a 'neat but plain villa, built in the rustic taste.' And his views of morality are as contracted as his taste in landscapes. The most distinctive article of his creed is that children should have a reverence for their parents which would be exaggerated in the slave of an Eastern despot. (p. 90)

But narrow as his vision might be in some directions, his genius is not the less real. He is a curious example of the power which a real artistic insight may exhibit under the most disadvantageous forms. To realise his characteristic power, we should take one of the great French novelists whom we admire for the exquisite proportions of his story, the unity of the interest and the skill—so unlike our common English clumsiness—with which all details are duly subordinated. He should have, too, the comparative weakness of French novelists, a defective perception of character, a certain unwillingness in art as in politics to allow individual peculiarities to interfere with the main flow of events; for, admitting the great excellence of his minor performers, Richardson's most elaborately designed characters are so artificial that they derive their interest from the events in which they play their parts, rather than give interest to them—little as he may have intended it. Then we must cause our imaginary Frenchman to transmigrate into the body of a small, plump, weakly printer of the eighteenth century. We may leave him a fair share of his vivacity, though considerably narrowing his views of life and morality; but we must surround him with a court of silly women whose incessant flatteries must generate in him an unnatural propensity to twaddle. It is curious, indeed, that he describes himself as writing without a plan. He compares himself to a poor woman lying down upon the hearth to blow up a wretched little fire of green sticks. He had to live from hand to mouth. But the absence of an elaborate scheme is not fatal to the unity of design. He watches, rather than designs, the development of his plot. He has so lively a faith in his characters that, instead of laying down their course of action, he simply watches them to see how they will act. This makes him deliberate a little too much; they move less by impulse than from careful reflection upon all the circumstances. Yet it also implies an evolution of the story from the necessity of the characters in a given situation, and gives an air of necessary deduction to the whole scheme of his stories. All the gossiping propensities of his nature will grow to unhealthy luxuriance, and the fine edge of his wit will be somewhat dulled in the process. He will thus become capable of being a bore—a thing which is impossible to any unsophisticated Frenchman. In this way we might obtain a literary product so anomalous in appearance as *Clarissa*—a story in which a most affecting situation is drawn with extreme power, and yet so overlaid with twaddle, so unmercifully protracted and spun out as to be almost unreadable to the present generation. But to complete Richardson, we must inoculate him with the propensities of another school: we must give him a liberal share of the feminine sensitiveness and closeness of observation of which Miss Austen is the great example. And perhaps, to fill in the last details, he ought, in addition, to have a dash of the more unctuous and offensive variety of the dissenting preacher—for we know not where else to look for the astonishing and often ungrammatical fluency by which he is possessed, and which makes his best passages remind us of the marvellous malleability of some precious metals.

Anyone who will take the trouble to work himself fairly into the story will end by admitting Richardson's power. . . . Probably, a person eager to enjoy Richardson's novels now would do well to take them as his only recreation for a long holiday in a remote place and pray for steady rain. On these conditions, he may enter into the whole spirit. And the remark may suggest one moral, for one ought not to conclude an article upon Richardson without a moral. It is that a purpose may be a very dangerous thing for a novelist in so far as it leads him to try means of persuasion not appropriate to his art; but when, as with Richardson, it implies a keen interest in an imaginary world, a desire to set forth in the most forcible way what are the great springs of action of human beings by showing them under appropriate situations, then it may be a source of such power of fascination as is exercised by the greatest writers alone. (pp. 91-3)

Sir Leslie Stephen, "Richardson's Novel," in his *Hours in a Library, Vol. I,* revised edition, 1894. Reprint by Putnam's, 1899, pp. 47-93.

GEORGE SAINTSBURY
(essay date 1913)

[Saintsbury was an English literary historian and critic. In the excerpt below, he discusses Richardson's novels, focusing on characterization, plot, description, and dialogue.]

[There is in *Pamela*] not very much plot, in the martinet sense of that word: there never was in Richardson, despite his immense apparatus and elaboration. The story is not knotted and unknotted; the wheel does nto come full circle on itself; it merely runs along pleasantly till it is time for it to stop, and it stops rather abruptly. The siege of Pamela's virtue ends merely because the besieger is tired of assaults which fail, and of offering dishonourable terms of capitulation which are rejected: because he prefers peace and alliance. But such as it is, it is told with a spirit which must have been surprising enough to its readers, and which makes it, I confess, seem to me now much the best *story* in Richardson. The various alarums and excursions of the siege itself go off smartly and briskly: there may be more sequence than connection—there is *some* connection, as in the case of that most unlucky and ill-treated person the Rev. Mr. Williams—but the sequence is rapid and unbroken, and the constituents of it as it were jostle each other—not in any unfavourable sense, but in a sort of rapid dance, "cross hands and down the middle," which is inspiriting and contagious. He lost this faculty later: or rather he allowed it to be diluted and slackened into the interminable episodes of the not dissimilar though worse-starred plot against Clarissa, and the *massacrant* trivialities of the Italian part of *Grandison.* But he had it here: and it is not a fair argument to say (as even in these days I have known it said) that Pamela's honour is a commodity of too little importance to justify such a pother about it.

This may bring us to the characters. They also are not of the absolutely first class—excepting . . . the great attempt of Lovelace, Richardson's never are. But they are an immense advance on the personages that did duty as persons in preceding novels, even in Defoe. "Mr. B." himself is indeed not very capital. One does not quite see why a man who went on as long as he did and used the means which he permitted himself to use, did not go on longer or use them more thoroughly. But Richardson has at least vindicated his much-praised "knowledge of the human heart" by recognising two truths: first, that there are many natures (perhaps most) who are constantly tempted to "over-bid"—to give more and more for something that they want and cannot get; and, secondly, that there are others (again, perhaps, the majority, if not always the same individuals) who, when they are peremptorily told *not* to do a thing, at once determine to do it. . . . As for the minor characters, at least the lower examples are more than sufficient: and Mrs. Jewkes wants very little of being a masterpiece. But of course Pamela herself is the cynosure, such as there is. She has had rather hard measure with critics for the last century and a little more. The questions to ask now are, "Is she a probable human being?" and then, "Where are we to find a probable human being, worked out to the same degree, before?" I say unhesitatingly that the answer to the first is "Yes," and the answer to the second "Nowhere." The last triumph of originality and individuality she does not indeed reach. Richardson had, even more than other men of his century in England, a strong Gallic touch: and he always tends to the type rather than the individual. . . . There might be fifty or five hundred Pamelas. . . . She is the pretty, good-natured, well-principled, and rather well-educated menial, whose prudence comes to the aid of her principles, whose pride does not interfere with either, and who has a certain—it is hardly unfair to call it—slyness which is of the sex rather than of the individual. But, as such, she is quite admirably worked out—a heroine of Racine in more detail and different circumstances, a triumph of art, and at the same time with so much nature that it is impossible to dismiss her as merely artificial. The nearest thing to her in English prose fiction before (Marianne, of course, is closer in

French) is Moll Flanders: and good as Moll is, she is flat and lifeless in comparison with Pamela. (pp. 85-7)

As for description and dialogue, there is not very much of the former in *Pamela,* though it might not be unfair to include under the head those details, after the manner of Defoe (such as Pamela's list of purchases when she thinks she is going home), which supply their own measure of verisimilitude to the story. But there are some things of the kind which Defoe never would have thought of—such as the touches of the "tufts of grass" and the "pretty sort of wildflower that grows yonder near the elm, the fifth from us on the left," which occur in the gipsy scene. The dialogue plays a much more important part. . . . It is "reported" of course, instead of being directly delivered, in accordance with the letter-scheme of which more presently, but that makes very little difference; to the first readers it probably made no difference at all. Here again that process of "vivification," which has been so often dwelt on, makes an astonishing progress—the blood and colour of the novel, which distinguish it from the more statuesque narrative, are supplied, if indirectly yet sufficiently and, in comparison with previous examples, amply. Here you get, almost or quite for the first time in the English novel, those spurts and sparks of animation which only the living voice can supply. Richardson is a humorist but indirectly; yet only the greatest humorists have strokes much better than that admirable touch in which, when the "reconciliations and forgivenesses of injuries" are being arranged, and Mr. B. (quite in the manner of the time) suggests marrying Mrs. Jewkes to the treacherous footman John and giving them an inn to keep—Pamela, the mild and semi-angelic but exceedingly feminine Pamela, timidly inquires whether, "This would not look like very heavy punishment to poor John?" She forgives Mrs. Jewkes of course, but only "as a Christian"—as a greater than Richardson put it afterwards and commented on it in the mouth of a personage whom Richardson could never have drawn, though Fielding most certainly could.

The original admirers of *Pamela,* then, were certainly justified: and even the rather fatuous eulogies which the author prefixed to it from his own and (let us hope) other pens (and which probably provoked Fielding himself more than even the substance of the piece) could be transposed into a reasonable key. But we ought nowadays to consider this first complete English novel from a rather higher point of view, and ask ourselves, not merely what its comparative merits were in regard to its predecessors, and as presented to its first readers, but what its positive character is and what, as far as it goes, are the positive merits or defects which it shows in its author.

The first thing to strike one in this connection is, almost of course, the letter-form. More agreement has been reached about this, perhaps, than about some other points in the inquiry. The initial difficulty of fiction which does not borrow the glamour of verse or of the stage is the question, "What does all this mean?" "What is the authority?" "How does the author know it all?" And a hundred critics have pointed out that there are practically only three ways of meeting this. The boldest and the best by far is to follow the poet and the dramatist themselves; to treat it like one of the magic lions of romance, ignore it, and pass on, secure of safety, to tell your story "from the blue," as if it were an actual history or revelation, or something passing before the eyes of the reader. . . . Then there is the alternative of recounting it by the mouth of one of the actors in, or spectators of, the events—a plan obvious, early, presenting some advantages, still very commonly followed, but always full of little traps and pits of improbability, and peculiarly trying in respect to the character (if he is made to have any) of the narrator himself. Thirdly, there is the again easy resource of the "document" in its various forms. Of these, letters and diaries possess some prerogative advantages; and were likely to suggest themselves very particularly at this time when the actual letter and diary (long rather strangely rare in English) had for some generations appeared, and were beginning to be common. In the first place the information thus obtained looks natural and plausible: and there is a subsidiary advantage—on which Richardson does not draw very much in *Pamela,* but which he employs to the full later—that by varying your correspondents you can get different views of the same event, and first-hand manifestations of extremely different characters.

Its disadvantages, on the other hand, are equally obvious: but there are two or three of them of especial importance. In the first place, it is essentially an artificial rather than an artful plan—its want of verisimilitude, as soon as you begin to think of it, is as great as that of either of the others if not greater. In the second, without immense pains, it must be "gappy and scrappy," while the more these pains are taken the more artificial it will become. In the third, the book is extremely likely, in the taking of these pains and even without them, to become intolerably lengthy and verbose. In the first part . . . of *Pamela,* Richardson avoided these dangers fairly if not fully; in the second part he succumbed to them; in his two later novels, though more elaborate and important plots to some extent bore up the expansion, he succumbed to them almost more. (pp. 88-91)

There is no doubt that one main attraction of this letter-plan (whether consciously experienced or not does not matter) was its ready adaptation to Richardson's own special and peculiar gift of minute analysis of mood, temper, and motive. The diary avowedly, and the letter in reality, even though it may be addressed to somebody else, is a continuous soliloquy: and the novelist can use it with a frequency and to a length which would be intolerable and impossible on the stage. Now soliloquy is the great engine for self-revelation and analysis. It is of course to a great extent in consequence of this analysis that Richardson owes his pride of place in the general judgment. . . . Now this minute analysis and exhibition, though it is one way of drawing or constructing character, is not the only, nor even a necessary, one. It can be done without: but it has impressed the vulgar, and even some who are not the vulgar, from Dr. Johnson to persons whom it is unnecessary to mention. They cannot believe that there is "no deception"—that the time is correctly told—unless the works of the watch are bared to them: and this Richardson most undoubtedly does. . . . [No] one had risen (or descended) to anything like the minuteness and fullness of Richardson. As was before pointed out in regard to the letter-system generally, this method of treatment is exposed to special dangers, particularly those of verbosity and "overdoing"—not to mention the greater one of missing the mark. Richardson can hardly be charged with error, though he may be with excess, in regard to Pamela herself in the earlier part of the book—perhaps even not in regard to Mr. B.'s intricacies of courtship, matrimonial compliment, and arbitrary temper later. But he certainly succumbs to them in the long and monstrous scene in which Lady Davers bullies, storms at, and positively assaults her unfortunate sister-in-law before she is forced to allow that she *is* her sister-in-law. Part of course of his error here comes from the mistake with which Lady Mary afterwards most justly reproached him—that he talked about fine ladies and gentlemen without knowing anything about them. It was quite natural for Lady Davers to be disgusted, to be incredulous, to be tyrannical, to be in a certain sense violent. But it is improbable that she would in any case have spoken and behaved like a drunken fishfag quarrelling with another in the street: and the extreme prolongation of the scene brings its impropriety more forcibly into view. Here, as elsewhere . . . Richardson follows out, with extraordinary minuteness and confidence, a wrong course: and his very expertness in the process betrays him and brings him to grief. If he had run the false scent for a few yards only it would not matter: in a chase prolonged to something like "Hartleap Well" extension there is less excuse for his not finding it out. Nevertheless it would of course be absurd not to rank this "knowledge of the human heart" among the claims which not only gave him but have kept his reputation. I do not know that he shows it much less in the later part of the first two volumes (Pamela's recurrent tortures of jealous curiosity about Sally Godfrey are admirable) or even in the dreary sequel. But analysis for analysis' sake can have few real, though it may have some pretended, devotees. (pp. 91-3)

Clarissa . . . is a sort of enlarged, diversified, and transposed *Pamela,* in which the attempts of a libertine of more resolution and higher gifts than Mr. B. upon a young lady of much more than proportionately higher station and qualities than Pamela's, are—as such success goes—successful at last: but only to result in the death of the victim and the punishment of the criminal. The book is far longer than even the extended *Pamela;* has a much wider range; admits of episodes and minor plots, and is altogether much more ambitious; but still—though the part of the seducer Lovelace is much more important than that of Mr. B.—it is chiefly occupied with the heroine. (p. 94)

It is a disagreeable thing to have to say: but Clarissa's purity strikes one as having at once too much questionable prudery in it and too little honest prudence: while her later resolution has as much false pride as real principle. Even some of her admirers admit a want of straightforwardness in her; she has no passion, which rather derogates from the merit of her conduct in any case; and though she is abominably ill-treated by almost everybody, one's pity for her never comes very near to love.

Towards Lovelace, on the other hand, the orthodox attitude, with even greater uniformity, has been shocked, or sometimes even unshocked, admiration. Hazlitt went into frequently quoted raptures over the "regality" of his character: and though to approve of him as a man would only be the pretence of a cheap paradoxer, general opinion seems to have gone various lengths in the same direction. There have, however, been a few dissenters: and I venture to join myself to them in the very dissidence of their dissent. Lovelace, it is true, is a most astonishingly "succeeded" blend of a snob's fine gentleman and of the fine gentleman of a silly and rather unhealthy-minded schoolgirl. He is . . . handsome, haughty, arbitrary, as well as rich, generous after a fashion, well descended, well dressed, well mannered—except when he is insolent. He is also—which certainly stands to his credit in the bank which is not that of the snob or the schoolgirl—no fool in a general way. But he is not in the least a gentleman except in externals: and there is nothing really "great" about him at all. Even his scoundrelism is mostly, if not wholly, *pose.* . . . Now if Richardson had *meant* this, it might be granted at once that Lovelace is one of the greatest characters of fiction: and I do not deny that *taken as this,* meant or not meant, he is great. But Richardson obviously did *not* mean it; and Hazlitt did not mean it; and none of the admirers mean it. *They* all thought and think that Lovelace is something like what Milton's Satan was, and what my Lord Byron would have liked to be. This is very unfair to the Prince of Darkness: and it is even not quite just to "the noble poet."

At the same time, the acute reader will have no-

ticed, the acknowledgment that the fact that Richardson—even not knowing it and intending to do something else—did hit off perfectly and consummately the ideal of such a "prevailing party" (to quote Lord Foppington) as snobs and schoolgirls, is a serious and splendid tribute to his merits: as is also the fact that his two chief characters are characters still interesting and worth arguing about. Those merits, indeed, are absolutely incontestable. (pp. 95-7)

[Richardson] did very great things—first by gathering up the scattered means and methods which had been half ignorantly hit on by others, and coordinating them into the production of the finished and complete novel; secondly (though less) by that infusion of elaborate "minor psychology" as it may be called, which is his great characteristic; and, thirdly, by means of it and of other things, in raising the pitch of interest in his readers to an infinitely higher degree than had ever been known before. . . . On the comic side he was weak: and he made a most unfortunate mistake by throwing this part of the business on young ladies of position and (as he thought) of charm—Miss Darnford, Miss Howe, Charlotte Grandison—who are by no means particularly comic and who are sometimes very particularly vulgar. But of tragedy positive, in the *bourgeois* kind, he had no small command, and in the middle business—in affairs neither definitely comic nor definitely tragic—he was wonderfully prolific and facile. His immense and heartbreaking lengthiness is not *mere* verbosity: it comes partly from the artist's natural delight in a true and newly found method, partly from a still more respectably artistic desire not to do the work negligently. (pp. 97-8)

George Saintsbury, "The Four Wheels of the Novel Wain," in his *The English Novel,* E. P. Dutton & Co., 1913, pp. 77-132.

WILLIAM M. SALE, JR.
(essay date 1949)

[In the following excerpt, Sale argues that Richardson was the first English novelist to depict his society's concern with "the interpenetration of the emergent middle class and surviving aristocracy."]

Richardson, whether or not he was the father of the novel, was certainly the first novelist deliberately to show in his fiction an awareness of the disturbing forces at work in his society, for he was, both as man and novelist, acutely sensitive to class differences. During the two hundred years since he wrote *Pamela,* and especially during the last hundred years, many men, feeling somewhat as Richardson felt, have turned to the novel as a particularly effective form for the expression of this feeling. (p. 127)

If we can see more clearly how his fiction rendered the conflicts he saw in his own society, we may see more clearly the meaning that his fiction had for his century and that it may have for ours. (pp. 128-29)

Literature is not a transcript of life but life rendered at the remove of form. To secure this remove the novelist must, among other things, create the images, the symbols, by which he can indirectly communicate his ideas and emotions. With the passing of time a wider and wider gap may open up between the image and the idea it is designed to communicate. To the extent—and only to the extent—that we can close this gap can the literature of the past become available for us. . . . It is not always easy to close this gap in the fiction of Richardson, but if the imagination does not fail us we may perhaps be able to recover his novels for our century. ·

We know that Richardson's characters and incidents were effective symbols for his contemporaries; this fact is attested by the avidity with which they were seized upon. He was providing new insights. He was realizing for his generation the emotions engendered by the conditions of life that defined his generation's hopes and that set limitations upon the fulfillment of those hopes. Before his novels appeared, however, eighteenth-century Englishmen were sufficiently aware of the fact that their vital social problem was the interpenetration of the emergent middle class and the surviving aristocracy. . . . Richardson caught the attention of his readers not by introducing a novel subject but by defining the subject in a new way and by rendering it in a different spirit.

Before the appearance of *Pamela,* fiction of two sorts existed. The eighteenth century kept the romances alive after a fashion, but by their flickering light the aristocrat and his world seemed little more than an artifact. Defoe introduced a fiction which, by contrast with the romances, was vigorously alive, but his characters, like their creator, lived outside the social pale. . . . With the romances dead and with Defoe's pirates and prostitutes living outside the pale, it remained with Richardson to bring the heirs of a seventeenth-century Church of England piety into the world of the fatally attractive and profligate aristocrat.

Like James and like Meredith he preferred women for his central characters—the new women, products of a time when a new freedom seemed attainable but was certainly not attained. Richardson brought his heroines into the orbit of the aristocrat, just as Henry James brought the morally sensitive products of a new American civilization into the ancient and enchantedly evil gardens of Europe. He chose, as central symbolic incident, the real or threatened seduction of his heroines,

just as Meredith chose the curious psychological violation of his heroine for the central incident of *Diana of the Crossways,* and just as James again and again exposed his heroines to a violation of the spirit, a deflowering of the human soul. Like James's heroines, Richardson's sought union with, not opposition to, those aristocrats who threatened their integrity. In the exploration of this subject lay the novelty of his fiction for his generation. In this respect his fiction shows an affinity with the modern novel. (pp. 129-31)

It is obvious that Richardson knew little at first hand of the life of the English aristocracy. But this lack of knowledge is not fatal. His taste for aristocracy, like that of his heroines, is an index of his need to make common cause with a superior social class. This need of the author is no more apparent in Richardson than it is in Shakespeare or in James.

But the need to make some sort of common cause with the English aristocracy did not mean that a complete absorption within its world was possible, however desirable in some respects such an absorption might seem. This was what Richardson learned between the writing of *Pamela* and *Clarissa.* The subject of the two novels is not radically different, but for many reasons he was unable to realize this subject in *Pamela,* whereas in *Clarissa* it had taken full shape. Had he come to the writing of *Clarissa* without the experience provided by the earlier novel, he might well have failed to preserve the sharp outlines of his subject and might indeed have never discovered its real importance. It is in the importance of the subject, fully grasped in *Clarissa,* that Richardson differentiates himself from Fielding. *Tom Jones,* for all its display of talent and for all the ingenuity of its construction, has a subject which is not fully worth the care and attention that Fielding lavished on it. It is Fielding himself and not the subject of his novel that continues to win our admiration, whereas all the irritation that we may feel with the author of *Clarissa* should not prevent our seeing that its subject is of the first importance.

In both *Pamela* and *Clarissa* Richardson chose to see his world in the microcosm of the family. Families were, as he said, but "so many miniatures" of the great community of the world. Tyranny, treachery, loyalty—duty and responsibility, right and prerogative—all these aspects of life he sought to comprehend within the world of the family. His concept of the family was never quite broad enough for the uses to which he wanted it put, but this constricted vision is more apparent in *Pamela* than in *Clarissa.* The master-servant relationship in the household is not so flexible as the father-daughter relationship which he uses in *Clarissa.* In order to maintain the conflict in the earlier novel, Richardson had in some degree to sacrifice the character both of Pamela and of her master. In eighteenth-century England a servant is not bound to her master as Pamela seems at times to feel that she is bound; nor do we find it easy to accept the highhanded fashion in which Mr. B. abrogates the laws of his country in carrying through an abduction. In the earlier sections of *Pamela* the heroine seems to be trumping up excuses in order to keep Richardson's novel going; in later sections, she is a prisoner with her freedom of choice so restricted that the novel becomes in large part an adventure story. The dual role of master and of lover which Mr. B. has to play clouds the main issue of the novel. Were he cast solely as lover, we could see more clearly that his dilemma arises because he falls in love with the girl he should seduce. Were he not Pamela's master as well as the man she wants to marry, Pamela would seem far less the schemer than she too often shows herself to be.

Richardson encountered these difficulties . . . because the main outlines of his story were determined before he started to tell it. He chose to follow a story from real life in which a master finally married the serving girl he tried to seduce. When Richardson turned to the reworking of his theme in *Clarissa,* he created his own story and held to it in spite of the advice and entreaty of his friends who sought to reshape it for him. Again he chose the microcosm of the family, but he wisely placed Lovelace outside the domestic orbit of the Harlowes. Furthermore, he idealized the Harlowes just as he idealized Lovelace. The Harlowes, if you will, are essentially London middle-class tradesmen with the tradesman's narrowness of soul and smallness of mind. . . . But Richardson moves them from the city to the country; he wants us to see not the fact but the essence of their materialism, of their penny pinching, their selfishness. If we compare the idealized treatment of the Harlowes with the more direct transcription that Richardson employs for the middle-class Danbys of *Grandison* or for the tradesmen's daughters, Sally Martin and Polly Horton, of *Clarissa,* we can see clearly that the Harlowes are larger than life. The stultifying atmosphere of Harlowe Place is so pervasive that even the kindly instincts of some of the clan prove abortive. Clarissa alone is a free spirit, struggling desperately to preserve her integrity and her independence of mind and soul. She is set apart from the Harlowes more significantly than Pamela is set apart from her parents or from her companions belowstairs.

To make this distinction between Clarissa and her family a sharp one is only part of the task that Richardson had to accomplish in the first two volumes of his novel. Though her father's inhumanity seems intolerable, we must see that Clarissa can never escape from the fact of his fatherhood. She cannot, as Pamela could, quit her master. Though she finds it imperative to incur her father's curse in following the law of her own being, this curse lies upon her like a leaden weight, and Richardson takes pains to make clear that she cannot

free herself from its weight until her soul speeds its way to heaven. Pamela's power of choice was removed, but choice is given to Clarissa. To make us see that she cannot escape from the consequence of her choice is a responsibility that the novel accepts and which it continuously makes clear. . . . Clarissa, despite the clarity of her mind, is the victim of the curse incurred when she defies her father and elopes with Lovelace. This aspect of the situation, so dimly grasped in *Pamela,* is clearly realized in *Clarissa.*

It is her fate to defy her father; it is also her fate to be attracted by the free spirit of Lovelace, who stands in such marked contrast to the Harlowes. Lovelace moves in a world of larger freedoms, of wider spaces. His values, however reprehensible, are not the countinghouse values of the Harlowes. Clarissa allows herself to hope that in union with him she will in some way complete her life. She knows and tells us in so many words that in marriage with Solmes, her family's choice, her life will stop. . . . In our century the slackening of family ties has perhaps resulted in making less effective Richardson's symbol of the parental curse. In like manner, the steady democratization of modern society may make it difficult for us to accept an aristocratic rake at Richardson's evaluation, equivocal though that evaluation may be. Aristocracy meant to Richardson a distinction of personal existence. That he should have seen this distinction only in the acts of the attractive libertine is a commentary on his age. In their pursuit of women these energetic sons of the older families perpetuated a mode of life which had flourished during the Restoration. With political action frequently denied them, they flagrantly asserted the *droit de seigneur,* flinging their tattered banners from the falling walls. These gestures both attracted and repelled the creator of Lovelace. He caught fleeting glimpses of them outside his windows, and he idealized them as he did the Harlowes; he heightened the qualities that made them both attractive and repellent. But with them he had to make some kind of common cause if his vision of human potentialities was to extend beyond the narrow confines of his own middle-class world.

The degree to which he could make such cause and the success which could attend the attempt were matters that Richardson had not clearly thought through when he wrote *Pamela.* When he allowed the marriage to take place between Pamela and Mr. B. he did not really resolve his conflict. He merely put an end to it. It is true that he postponed marriage as long as his inventive genius would permit; he even borrowed all the antiquated machinery of romance to keep his story going through the long Lincolnshire episode. But, following his story from real life, he had eventually to bring his characters to the altar. It is difficult to see how Richardson might have avoided the marriage, but to include it is to suggest that a large part of the antecedent

---

Richardson on the intent of *Clarissa*:

What will be found to be more particularly aimed at in [*Clarissa; or, The History of a Young Lady*] is—to warn the inconsiderate and thoughtless of the one sex, against the base arts and designs of specious contrivers of the other—to caution parents against the undue exercise of their natural authority over their children in the great article of marriage—to warn children against preferring a man of pleasure to a man of probity upon that dangerous but too commonly received notion, *that a reformed rake makes the best husband*—but above all, to investigate the highest and most important doctrines not only of morality, but of Christianity, by showing them thrown into action in the conduct of the *worthy* characters; while the *unworthy*, set those doctrines at defiance, are condignly, and, as may be said, consequentially punished.

Richardson, in a preface to his *Clarissa; or The History of a Young Lady*, 1747.

---

action is much ado about nothing. Richardson, of course, recognized the specious optimism implied in the marriage and tried to recover his subject. He devoted his second volume to the conflicts experienced by Pamela because she was the maid who had become the mistress. But the mood of the second volume is that of social comedy, and despite all his efforts the effect is that of anticlimax. To ignore the second volume, as so many critics of Richardson seem to do, is to fail to see, however, the efforts that Richardson made to preserve Pamela's integrity.

Richardson saw clearly what both Pamela and Mr. B. had lost when he turned to Clarissa's story. He would not allow his friends to persuade him to close her story with a wedding. . . . There are moments when both Clarissa and Lovelace are tempted by the thought of their union; and marriage, as a symbolic act, is kept constantly in the forefront of the novel. But this story is no "love" story. It is not love for which Clarissa's old pious world is well lost; it is for a chance to live life more completely in conformity with an ideal of conduct. Clarissa is no more a girl in search of a husband than is Isabel Archer. She is—if I may risk a dangerous abstraction—humanity desperately if futilely seeking freedom in a world where duty and responsibility are constant limitations upon that search. (pp. 132-37)

It is [Clarissa's] dependence on heaven that is the final cause for the disturbance of many modern readers. The central irony in *Clarissa* is easily recognized, but her faith in heaven is felt to mitigate the sharpness of this irony. And indeed it does. We accept more readily James's secularized versions of a similar theme in which at the end the heroine receives the kiss of death. His heroines have fulfilled their tragic fate as inevitably as has Clarissa, but they have not her hope of heaven. In the closing sections of James's novels his heroines are frequently above or beyond life, even as Clarissa is during the last two volumes of her story. They are beyond earthly considerations; they live in an atmosphere as rarefied as that of heaven itself. The secularized version may be more acceptable to some modern readers, but the intent of the two novelists is not markedly different. Certainly in the charity of our imagination we should be able to understand Richardson's intent, despite his pious vocabulary and his pious symbols. He wants us to see that Clarissa is a child of heaven, finally removed alike from the world of the Harlowes and of the Lovelaces. The need of heaven was imperative. In this world Richardson could not, as did many of his contemporaries, find room in which to fit everything and a place in which everything might fit. (pp. 137-38)

William M. Sale, Jr., "From 'Pamela' to 'Clarissa'," in *The Age of Johnson: Essays Presented to Chauncey Brewster Tinker*, edited by F. W. Hilles, Yale University Press, 1949, pp. 127-38.

SOURCES FOR FURTHER STUDY

Brophy, Elizabeth Bergen. *Samuel Richardson: The Triumph of Craft.* Knoxville: University of Tennessee Press, 1974, 131 p.

    Study of Richardson's artistic method.

Carroll, John, ed. *Samuel Richardson: A Collection of Critical Essays.* Englewood Cliffs, N. J.: Prentice-Hall, 1969, 185 p.

    Collection of critical essays, including studies by A. M. Kearney, Ian Watt, A. D. McKillop, George Sherburn, and others.

Eaves, T. C. Duncan, and Kimpel, Ben D. *Samuel Richardson: A Biography.* Oxford: Clarendon Press, 1971, 728 p.

    Standard biography, noted for its comprehensive treatment of Richardson's life, work, and reputation.

Flynn, Carol Houlihan. *Samuel Richardson: A Man of Letters.* Princeton, N.J.: Princeton University Press, 1982, 342 p.

    Thorough study of Richardson's novels.

Golden, Morris. *Richardson's Characters.* Ann Arbor: University of Michigan Press, 1963, 202 p.

    Detailed study of the development of character and social milieu in Richardson's novels.

Wolff, Cynthia Griffin. *Samuel Richardson and the Eighteenth-Century Puritan Character.* Hamden, Conn.: Archon Books, 1972, 259 p.

    Important study of the development of Richardson's characters.

Arthur Rimbaud

1854-1891

(Full name Jean Nicolas Arthur Rimbaud) French poet.

INTRODUCTION

Rimbaud is considered one of the most influential poets in the history of French letters. Although his writing career was brief and his output small, Rimbaud's development of the prose poem and innovative use of the unconscious as a source of literary inspiration influenced the Symbolist movement and anticipated the freedom of form characteristic of much contemporary poetry. Rimbaud's most celebrated works, *Une saison en enfer* (1873; *A Season in Hell,* 1932) and *Les illuminations* (1886; *Illuminations,* 1932), demonstrate his belief that the poet must reject conventional notions of ego, beauty, and art in order to penetrate the unknown and liberate the mind from the constraints of logic. Scholars have speculated that Rimbaud's elliptic style, mysterious imagery, and metaphysical language were influenced by his interest in magic and alchemy. Believing that the poet possesses supernatural powers, Rimbaud attempted to create a new poetic language by which he could control nature and attain moral and intellectual perfection. Although he eventually abandoned alchemy and its spiritual doctrine, Rimbaud's metaphysical preoccupations had a powerful influence on the scope and tone of his verse.

Rimbaud was raised in Charleville, a small town near the Belgian border. His parents separated when he was six years old, and Rimbaud was thereafter raised by his mother in a strict religious environment. A very overprotective woman, she accompanied her child to and from school, supervised his homework, and would not allow him to associate with other boys. While enrolled at the Collège de Charleville, Rimbaud excelled in all his subjects and was considered a brilliant student. His rhetoric professor, Georges Izambard, befriended the boy, and under his tutelage Rimbaud avidly read the Romantic and Parnassian poets and strove to emulate their work. His literary apprenticeship was abruptly halted when Izambard left Charleville at the outbreak of the Franco-Prussian War in 1870. Rimbaud fled to Paris by train in desperate search of his mentor, but was arrested and jailed for traveling without a ticket. Although Izambard eventually rescued the youth and brought him home, Rimbaud's growing disgust with provincial life drove him away again a few months later. Scholars believe that his experiences as a runaway may have included a brutal incident which strongly altered both his personality and the tone of his work. Allusions to the event are cited in his poem "Le coeur volé," but what actually transpired is unknown; some biographers suggest that Rimbaud may have been sexually abused by soldiers. After the incident, Rimbaud renounced his sentimental early verse and wrote poems in which he expressed disgust with life and a desire to escape from reality.

In 1871 Rimbaud created an aesthetic doctrine, which he articulated in several letters, two to Izambard and another to a friend, Paul Démeny. The letter, now known as the "lettre du voyant" or "letter of the seer," explicates Rimbaud's concept of poetry and of his own role as a poet. After tracing the history of the genre, Rimbaud concluded that only the ancient Greeks and the French poets Louis Racine and Charles Baudelaire had created verse of any value. Castigating such authors as Alfred de Musset and Victor Hugo for their rigid and archaic writing, Rimbaud declared that the poet must "derange" his senses and delve into his unconscious in order to create a language accessible to all the senses. Rimbaud acknowledged that while this painful process involved much suffering and introspection, it was necessary to the development of vital and progressive poetry: "If all the old fools had not stuck to the false conception of the *ego* we should not now have to sweep away these millions of skeletons." Soon after writing the "lettre du voyant," Rimbaud returned again to Charleville. Feeling stifled and depressed, he sent several poems to the renowned poet Paul Verlaine, whose works Rimbaud admired. Verlaine responded with praise and an invitation to visit him in Paris. Before he left, Rimbaud composed *Le bateau ivre* (1920; *The Drunken Boat*, 1941), a visual and verbal evocation of a savage universe in which a drifting boat serves to symbolize Rimbaud's fate as a poet. Although the versification in *The Drunken Boat* is traditional, Rimbaud's daring images and complex metaphors portended the philosophical concerns of his later works and his fascination with alchemy.

In Paris, Rimbaud was warmly received by Verlaine's family, but the young poet found them representative of the bourgeois values he disdained and quickly alienated them with his flagrantly anti-social behavior. However, Verlaine himself was strongly drawn to Rimbaud, and the two writers began a notorious and stormy homosexual relationship. They drank absinthe heavily, claiming that the liquor was "an enlightened nectar from God." At first, Rimbaud was admired by the Parisian writers who gathered in the city's cafés—Victor Hugo called him "a young Shakespeare"—but the youthful poet left Paris when his consistently drunken and rude behavior made him increasingly unpopular. Verlaine, after unsuccessfully attempting a reconciliation with his wife, pleaded for Rimbaud to return, declaring that he could not live without him. Rimbaud complied, and the two poets traveled through England and Belgium from 1872 to 1873. Rimbaud believed that his dissipated lifestyle was a form of artistic stimulation, and his creativity flourished during this period. He studied Eastern religion and alchemy, denied himself sleep, and took hallucinogenic drugs. During this time he also wrote *La chasse spirituelle,* a work speculated to have later been destroyed by Verlaine's wife. According to Verlaine, this work was Rimbaud's intended masterpiece.

As his literary output increased, Rimbaud began to find his relationship with Verlaine tiresome. After a series of quarrels and separations, Rimbaud, overwhelmed by Verlaine's suffocating affection, demanded an end to the relationship. In desperation, Verlaine shot Rimbaud, wounding him in the wrist. Verlaine was imprisoned in Brussels for two years and Rimbaud returned to his family's new home in Roche, a small village near Charleville. There he finished *A Season in Hell,* a volume comprised of nine prose poems of various lengths. Although some commentators have characterized *A Season in Hell* as a chronicle of Rimbaud's tumultuous relationship with Verlaine, others contend that the work conveys Rimbaud's admission that his early theory of poetry was false and unattainable. Despite controversy concerning whether the book was written before or after *Illuminations, A Season in Hell* is often considered Rimbaud's "farewell to poetry."

In 1873, Rimbaud returned to Paris, where he completed *Illuminations,* a work thought to have been written over the course of two years. In this collection of prose poems, Rimbaud abandoned the rules of syntax, language, and rhythm, and sought to express the chaos of his poetic vision. While several critics have interpreted the childlike awe and wonder exhibited in these poems as an expression of Rimbaud's Catholic faith, most contend that Rimbaud was attempting to recapture the innocent exuberance of youth. Enid Starkie has asserted: "[We] find in *Illuminations* all the things which had filled [Rimbaud's] imaginative life as a child—all the characters and stage properties of the fairy-tales and novels of adventure which had been his chief reading. These now mingled with his recent study of alchemy and magic, the subject matter of which . . . was of the same legendary and mythical nature." Upon completing these poems Rimbaud gave the manuscript to Verlaine and ceased to write. After ending his literary career, Rimbaud decided to become "a real adventurer instead of a mystic vagabond" and traveled throughout Europe and Africa. He finally settled in Abyssinia, Ethiopia, where he was believed to have worked as a gunrunner and slave trader. In 1886, Verlaine, assuming his friend to be dead, published the manuscript Rimbaud had given him as "*Les illuminations* by the late Arthur Rimbaud." Though Rimbaud later learned of its popular reception and of the Rimbaud "cult" that was developing in Paris, he expressed no interest in returning to his former life. Instead, in an abrupt change from his earlier beliefs and practice, Rimbaud spoke enthusiastically of marrying and having a son. These dreams went unrealized, however, for he developed cancer in his right knee and was forced to return to France for medical treatment. Rimbaud's leg was amputated, but the cancer continued to spread and he died soon after.

Rimbaud continues to be one of the most widely studied poets in world literature. Although he himself abandoned poetry after a literary career of less than five years, Rimbaud's influence on Verlaine and the subsequent Symbolist and Surrealist movements is considered to be lasting and profound. Starkie has underscored Rimbaud's importance to the thematic development of modern poetry: "Rimbaud's poetry has proved—even if this was not his aim—how much rich material there is for art in the [unconscious] mind, in the half-remembered sensations of childhood, in these sensations which have been registered without our realizing their full meaning. This has opened up a rich field to literature and it can be claimed that Rimbaud started . . . the literature of the [unconscious] depths of human nature."

(For further information about Rimbaud's life and works, see *Nineteenth-Century Literature Criticism*, Vol. 4 and *Poetry Criticism*, Vol. 3.)

CRITICAL COMMENTARY

MATTHEW JOSEPHSON

(essay date 1931)

[Josephson was an American editor, essayist, and biographer who wrote numerous works on nineteenth-century French literature. In the following excerpt from an essay that first appeared in *The New Republic* in 1931, he provides an overview of Rimbaud's poetry.]

Genius of poetry that he undoubtedly was, the most beautiful and enigmatic thing of all Rimbaud did was certainly his own life. It has the aspects of profound interior drama and extravagant physical adventure. He was precocious; for two or three years, after the age of sixteen, he wrote verses and prose stamped with greatness. Yet at nineteen he abandoned literature for good and all; he also put behind him completely European civilization itself, to embark upon fabulous adventures in the Orient and lose himself in its more primitive life currents. That he was fully aware of all his own powers and of the meaning of every step he took—such as the attempted destruction of his manuscripts—makes his case all the more haunting. His life has a dreadful beauty. (p. 397)

His own sparse writings, little known during his violent and brief artistic career, seem to prophesy and record his personal fate. Beyond the immediate brilliance of device and literary effect, his work has the refulgence of his strange destiny as a seeker of the "primitive," as a kind of superman—so the French have always believed—contemporary to the still unknown Nietzsche. The fantastic and sonorous lines of *The Drunken Boat*, the hallucinations of his **"Nigger Book,"** the spiritual drama of a Lucifer in his *Season in Hell* . . . , which was his last testament to posterity— all this is a consistent and inconceivably bitter repudiation of his age, an age outwardly mercenary and spiritually defeated; and all of it exercises a perpetual invitation to uneasy little men of letters to abandon their hollow arts and advance with Rimbaud into the unknown, the nameless and the vertiginous.

Yet his writings, which he himself spurned, seem also to beckon one back, reviving, illuminating, as one disciple declares, "all the ways of art, of religion and life." . . . [There] was expressed in Rimbaud at one stage a religion of art, a religion of pure literature. He himself, after long vigils, was to learn something that made him curse art and flee it; but he left certain secrets or clues which men seized upon, under the temptation to become alchemists in their turn. (pp. 397-98)

An early letter of 1871, called the "letter of the Seer," reveals his theories and plans which were soon to be fulfilled in *The Drunken Boat* and in the *Illuminations*. . . .

"Je est un autre," he writes; which may be translated: "The *I* is another self." One part of the poet, the *I*, gives himself up to the vigilant study of the other self.

Principal Works

Une saison en enfer (poetry) 1873
    [A Season in Hell, 1932]
Les illuminations (poetry) 1886
    [Prose Poems from Les Illuminations, 1932]
Reliquaire, Poésies (poetry) 1891
Poésies complètes (collected works) 1895
    [Rimbaud: Complete Works, Selected Letters 1966]
Oeuvres (poetry) 1898
Oeuvres (vers et proses) (poetry and prose) 1912
*Le bateau ivre (poetry) 1920
    [The Drunken Boat, 1941]
Lettres de la vie littéraire d'Arthur Rimbaud (letters and
    prose) 1931

*This work was written in 1871.

"He searches for his soul, inspects it, tests it, knows it." He is present at "the unfolding of his own thought"; hangs upon it, poised; gives a stroke of his baton, and lo, the full orchestra sounds for him. But this mastery, this "cultivation of the self," must become something dangerous. (p. 399)

The formula of genius, as it came to Rimbaud so early in life, implied the fierce, single-minded development of the self at all costs; it implied, above all, the abandonment of known landmarks. Life was to be a perpetual inventing of new experiences, an eternal exploration, a supreme trial of the soul. . . . He tried, as if by a great wager, to bring about some "monstrous" change in himself, so that he might once more extend human expression and human values. (One remembers that he was for a moment one of the *communards* of '71; he was an infidel of the Church, a rebel against his mother and society.) But he was quite alone, with his visions, like Blake; he had no common currency of speech that might bring him the companionship of his fellows.

"The poet comes to the *unknown*," his letter continues; "and when maddened, he ends by losing all understanding of his visions, still he has seen them, hasn't he? Let him burst with his palpitations—with the unheard of, nameless things he has seen. Then let other horrible workers come after him; they will begin at the horizons where he expired!"

It is as if in his absolute revolt the poet turns to Nature, "pure and free," augments, sharpens, all his senses, seeking at one stroke to penetrate universal mysteries. That Rimbaud had taken the path of the mystic we perceive from the closing lines of his letter which refer to the "language" of the future poet. *"All language being idea,"* he ends, "the day of the universal language will come."

Baudelaire, too, had taken this path of the mysticism of poetry; Baudelaire, whom Rimbaud termed "the first of the seers, king of poets, a real god," had suggested garnering the occult symbols of the Universal. In his mysterious sonnet, "Correspondences," the elder poet had called Nature a "temple of living columns," "a forest of symbols, through which man passed, observing and observed, listening to the long echoes that mingled always in a profound and shadowy unity, to the perfumes, colors and sounds replying to each other." . . . Rimbaud, too, would find his medium in the forest of symbols. He declares almost in identical words: "This language, the *new* or *universal,* will speak from soul to soul, summing up all perfumes, sounds, colors, linking together all thought."

By "symbolism" in Rimbaud, one means not the parable or allegory of a Maeterlinck, but that technique which transforms or sublimates the material of life, using symbols of it, rather than its substance. He attempted by a formula—if I may define it in another way—that poetic magic, that blended music of image and tone which Coleridge, in "Kubla Khan," achieved by opiates! (pp. 399-401)

The "alchemist of the word," as he liked to style himself in youth, was committed to experiments of all sorts. One can scarcely explain what a full bag of tricks he seemed to have, and with what gayety he played them. He was one of the first to employ distortions and dissociations systematically. He used verbs, instead of adjectives, to lend violence to his page; he used adjectives chiefly to summon up precise colors; he sought a great variety of meters: ranging from that of the quick, nervous lyric to that of pompous oration; and where Hugo had freed the Alexandrine from the *caesura,* he broke from regular meter to experiment with free verse. (His prose is really free verse, of the most precise intervals, having nothing in common with that mongrel product, "prose poetry.") He would use now the tones of direct vulgar speech, or now drawing upon technical language, similes suggestive of laboratories, even of the magnifying motion picture, which of course did not exist in his time. And significantly he would use repetition or "recapitulation," of phrases or images, in the way of a sonata or a symphony, scorning the sequence of common-sense, informative literature, as no one had dared before him. "His form was musical," Claudel observes.

To be sure, these innovations were in the air. Rimbaud seized upon them, exploited them in the extreme degree. When he had left, literature was full of a dangerous confusion. Rimbaud's very *tours de force,* his excesses, were to create traditions for the too-cultured people whom he detested. But his motives were entirely different from theirs of playing the polite parlor game of literature.

The poems that he wrote, it has been said, are largely visions, revolts, valedictions. In the prose and verse of the *Illuminations,* there is continuous, oblique reference to his life drama; there are also premonitions that we begin to understand now of colossal machines, industrialized chimeras and unthinkable wars. These poems, though Rimbaud scorned them at the last, are at the farthest remove from literary exercises.

The very intensity, the very primitive violence of his writing, at this stage (1871-1873) seem to forecast his early exile from letters. The livid beauty of *The Drunken Boat,* whose careenings in unknown seas prophesy his own course, that of the orphic *Illuminations,* is not to be found in the emulative devotees of literature; it is the fruit of Rimbaud's deliberate disordering of his senses, of his effort to bring a "monstrous" change upon himself, and of his submission to overpowering visions. He himself explains mockingly in the autobiographical *Season in Hell* how he would dream "crusades, voyages, republics without histories, dislodgments of continents," believing in "all the spells of magic"; how, playing with the "inexpressible," with the vertiginous, he sought still to control the color, the form, the movement of each continent. (pp. 401-02)

[Rimbaud's *Season in Hell* was] designed not as a work of art, but as the testament of a unique religious struggle from which he emerged apparently without church and without hope. He breathes a lasting hatred of Christianity. "No more hymns! Hold all gains!" he cries at the end.

For all its cryptic and dissociated style, the *Season in Hell* indicates to us clearly that Rimbaud regrets finally having "fed himself with lies." . . . Cycles of art are rapidly compressed within two or three years of his life, and seem to forecast all that will come to those who follow him—the retreat from "unbreathable" zones! Indeed, literature ever since Rimbaud has been engaged in the struggle to circumvent him. In the first place he makes poetry too dangerous. And in the end he exhorts us to abandon it. For then he knew how to honor beauty. "By running away." His example and his appeal for us is endlessly disturbing. No answer may be made; save perhaps at the end of a life which, by most of us, is to be known and plumbed far more slowly. And shall we dare to "begin at the horizons where he expired"?

He turns himself toward the East. "I see that my unhappiness comes from not having realized soon enough that we are in the Occident. The Occidental swamps!" With the artist in him effaced, he goes to lose his identity, beyond the tropical seas, in the African deserts, among the tides of black men. Yet he seems in-credulous, even departing for the Orient, as if doubting at bottom the wisdom and purity of the ancient races.

One suspects that Rimbaud, having sung all songs, having exhausted all the esthetic poisons of Europe, quit the civilization of white men with immense hopes of some sort of self-renewal. But on this adventure, in the East and in Africa, the whole second half of his life, he is forever enigmatic. Did he see something of that which he used to conjure up out of school atlases? Did he become truly a "child of the sun" as he led caravans across the desert? Or should we mind only his intermittent cries of pain, at inhuman suffering, at the defeat of flesh and bone, and his incredible, final reversion to inherited character? The tragic last act, which resembles that of no other play one has read, seems to leave for each one his own lesson. Most of us might not have followed Rimbaud; nor would we have changed anything in him, if we could. (pp. 403-04)

Matthew Josephson, "Rimbaud: The Flight from Literature," in *The New Republic Anthology: 1915-1935,* edited by Groff Conklin, Dodge Publishing Company, 1936, pp. 397-404.

ENID STARKIE
(essay date 1938)

[An Irish critic, educator, and editor, Starkie wrote numerous works on nineteenth-century French literature. In the following excerpt from her *Arthur Rimbaud* (1938), she explores the poet's mysticism, his yearning for transcendent experience, and his efforts to escape reality.]

Rimbaud, at the time of his greatest creative power, believed that he had become God. . . . Rimbaud thought that poetry was the means of penetrating into the unknown and of becoming identified with God. Later he came to realize that this had only been a dream, that he was not in fact God, but merely an insignificant unit in a long line of ignorant peasants; that everything on which he had built his life had been a delusion, that poetry was not a means of discovery, that it had been with him what it was for every one else, that despised thing, a vehicle for self-expression. *Une saison en enfer* sets forth the agony of that discovery and his effort to return to normal human life. It is probable that he intended to continue to write, but works like those of other writers; he discovered, however, that having tasted higher and rarer joys, this humbler form of art had no savour for him. How be satisfied with being a mere human writer when one has been God? (pp. 2-3)

Baudelaire had said that it was through dreaming that man entered into communication with the rich dark world which surrounds him and Rimbaud used all known means to induce in himself this state of perpetual dreaming. Drugs, alcohol, even hunger, thirst and fatigue, all served to loosen the cramping grip of conscious thought and they quickly brought on the state of semi-hallucination which he found most fruitful for composition. Then he could no longer distinguish, and no longer wished to distinguish, what was true vision and what was mere hallucination, what was dream or what was reality, since everything possessed the same blended solidity and vagueness. He could not distinguish, and neither can we now, between what was real, although transposed and transfigured by his imagination, and what had no existence at all. This state of hallucination eventually became so frequent with him that he came to regard the world around him as a shifting spectacle whose solidity and truth must not too seriously be relied upon. Then he saw nothing strange in blending with these material objects those he had invented, and he refused to be bound by the ordinary rules of verisimilitude and reality. He was God, and reality was merely the raw material for his creative vision with which he could take complete liberty. In this he reached, but in a manner unforeseen by him, 'le dérèglement de tous les sens', each sense being obliged to receive impression normally only experienced by another. In *Les illuminations* we find associated together images we do not usually connect. (pp. 179-80)

It was, however, not always easy for Rimbaud to achieve this magic state of receptivity, for he knew that he was still bound by what he considered his besetting inhibition, a consciousness of sin. He was unable yet to accept everything simply and naturally, for he had not completely uprooted the effects of his early training; and he constantly felt that he was being submitted to temptation and that he was yielding to it. He was not yet able to achieve the instinctive certainty he wished to possess that he was verily above the reach of sin and condemnation. He knew that only when he had shaken himself free from what seemed to him no more than a foolish inhibition could he achieve full creative power. (p. 181)

It is not surprising to find that many of *Les illuminations* are the expression of Rimbaud's transcendental experience of God. There can be no doubt of the certainty of his vision of God, though one would not be so bold as to claim that it was Catholic or in any way fundamentally Christian. Many conflicting claims have been put forward for Rimbaud, but out of all these claims the conviction emerges that when a man has reached the ultimate heights of mystical, transcendental experience and union with God, creeds and dogmas are of no more account, and the experience will be precisely the same for the members of the different religions, whether of the East or of the West. Rimbaud, moreover, never showed, by any positive expression of

belief, that he subscribed to the dogmas and tenets of any religion; he seemed, indeed, to feel no need of these or of any ritual. It is, however, not astonishing that members of different sects should have found conversion to their own religious beliefs after a reading of *Les illuminations,* for Rimbaud's experience of God was so intense and genuine as to seem to others to transcend his own rational beliefs, and, moreover, those who seek God seek him normally along the same spiritual paths they trod when they were children. (pp. 183-84)

Rimbaud's mystical poems are the manifestation of a transcendental experience trying to find expression in concrete, logical and therefore ineffective speech. The spirit tries to incarnate itself in images incapable of containing it entirely and adequately and the only possible way of suggesting the experience is to do so symbolically, not by description but by evoking in the reader the poet's emotional state and spiritual intuition. Each little group of words is then intended to suggest not the full experience, but one single flash of intuition. We do not receive the whole vision at once, but in a series of illuminations, of flashes, which in the end force the impression into our mind. We can feel that Rimbaud is groping after his experience, trying to express a sensation too deep to be rendered in mere words, and that these words will always remain somewhat inadequate. *Les illuminations* are often mere exclamations of superhuman joy in which the words mean little in themselves and their only value lies in their spontaneous power of suggestion. They are in the nature of an incantation, words strung together, without logical order, just as we used, as children, to string odd words together in an endeavour to express the overwhelming ecstasy we experienced but did not yet comprehend, beautiful words which we used to repeat over and over again, words whose meaning we did not fully know, because they seemed to exteriorize our rapture. (pp. 186-87)

In *Les illuminations* we find the expression of Rimbaud's growing hatred of life, a hatred that has gone on increasing since his experience in Paris the previous year and which his present life has done nothing to diminish, a hatred of the material world made by man and so-called civilization in which we are called to live. He considered that the first purity of the Garden of Eden had been replaced by our ugly modern world which is contrary to all nature, and in the prose poem "Après le déluge" he described what had taken place. After the fall of Adam the world had become a sorry place of vice, and God then sent the deluge to wipe away all traces of decadence and to give man a second chance of starting again from the very beginning, in a world washed clean from all stain and corruption. For a short time everything was beautiful once more, for a time everything was pure. . . . Very soon, however, the same old squalor and vice sprang up again, just as if the world had never been washed clean; the same old towns with their old sordidness, their vulgar boulevards, their monstrous hotels; all their same old errors. The only hope now left for the world was to raze everything to the ground once more and to carry everything away in a new destruction. In **"Vertige"** Rimbaud calls, in wild enthusiasm, on destruction to arise with blood and fire and to sweep away great powers, manufacturers and capitalists. (pp. 188-89)

Rimbaud's own secret for escaping the modern world which he did not feel capable of accepting was to return, in memory, to the days of his childhood, to the time of his vivid impressions when his mind had not yet been vitiated by education. Now in retrospect, since his sensitive nature had been bruised by the ugliness and coarseness of life, it seemed to him a fairyland of peace and beauty. (p. 189)

Une saison en enfer is the key to *Les illuminations;* it is the most merciless indictment of all his previous hopes and beliefs, the most cruel criticism of his former life. From beginning to end of its burning pages he looks back, through his blinding tears, on his plan to change the world, to invent a new language, a new form of art, to become God, and realizes how fantastic has been his previous arrogance, and how guilty he has been of spiritual pride, one of the seven deadly sins.

He had staked everything on this one card, of forcing himself into eternity and identifying himself with the Eternal; he had tried to enter into Heaven before his appointed time. He had imagined that poetry was the magic key to that kingdom, that he had acquired supernatural powers, that his poetry was God's voice speaking through him. But his card had been worthless. Now when everything broke down, he discovered that he had done only what all the poets whom he despised had done, he had only been able to draw on what was in himself. Poetry had been for him, with all his fine hopes, merely what it had always been for the wretched Verlaine, a vehicle of self-expression. What he had considered *illuminations* were only, after all, *hallucinations.* (pp. 223-24)

In the days of his belief in his art, he had hoped that poetry would bring him 'la vraie vie' and what he called thus real life was mystical union with God. But he discovered now that, after all, 'la vraie vie' was absent from his work. (p. 224)

The three important *leitmotiven* in *Une Saison en Enfer* are the problem of sin, the problem of God, or rather his personal need of believing in God, and the problem of life, the acceptance or endurance of life. These thread their way backwards and forwards through the texture of the work, never, even at the end, brought to a full conclusion.

Rimbaud had previously imagined that with his art he had soared into the beyond, but he discovered

now that it was not Heaven into which he had penetrated, but Hell; it had verily been a season in Hell. It was his pride and arrogance which had brought him to such a pass and had led him into the deepest state of sin. This brought him face to face with the problem of evil. What was sin and did it really exist? At the time of *Les illuminations* he had thought that the tree of Good and Evil could be cut down. . . .

But this had been an illusion like all his other illusions, for the tree had sent out sucker shoots that had grown big enough to destroy him. (p. 245)

One of his main reasons for beginning to write *Une saison en enfer* was to solve, once and for all, the problem of this conflict between Good and Evil. He had meant by his first title, *Livre Païen ou Livre Négre,* to indicate that his intention was to return to the days before the advent of Christianity, before there had existed our tragic dilemma of right and wrong. Pagans and Negroes can still live in blissful primitive ignorance, knowing nothing of the problem of good and evil; the tree of knowledge, with its heavy sickly shade, does not yet darken their lives. Rimbaud intended to refuse to accept the ideals of Christianity and to return to the real kingdom of the children of Ham. (pp. 245-46)

The characteristic sign of Westerners, of Christians, is their consciousness of sin. Baudelaire's poetry had been the expression of the conflict between *Spleen* and *Idéal.* Rimbaud's work now becomes the expression of a similar conflict, between God and Satan, between good and evil. The two voices rise one after the other, sometimes in unison, sometimes mingling in a strange duet. With Baudelaire we have no doubt on which side he would wish to weight the scales; but with Rimbaud we do not know which voice is stronger, nor which voice is divine, that of God or of Satan, and even he himself is uncertain.

The second *leitmotiv* is that of Rimbaud's longing for God, for a belief in God. His need of God was one of the fundamental needs of his nature and when he found that he could no longer accept the God of his Catholic teaching he could not rest until he had found a God that satisfied his spiritual aspirations. He had staked everything on expressing God and the infinite, on becoming himself God. When this conviction failed he was left bewildered and lost; his problem was now whether he could return to the humble Christian position in front of God. From the beginning to the end of *Une saison en enfer* we find expressed his burning longing for a religion in which to lose himself, but this longing is damped down by his inability to accept the loss of personality and liberty, by his desire to keep *la liberté dans le salut.* He was incapable of the simple trusting faith of Verlaine; he would not be God's humble servant, nor the patient little donkey of the Lord. (pp. 246-47)

In spite of what Catholic critics allege, Rimbaud came out of his season in Hell determined to leave God's love behind him and to keep his personal freedom at all costs. That is the victory on which, at the end, he prided himself; he had not given in in spite of his longing to yield; God fought with him using against him all His powers of persuasion, all the weight of His arm, but Rimbaud stood out till the end and kept himself intact. Nevertheless his later career was to prove that his victory left him mutilated and that by stifling the voice of God in himself he condemned himself to live out his life spiritually maimed and crippled.

The third big problem is that of the acceptance or endurance of life as we have to live it in the world. The manner in which Rimbaud approached this problem and tried to solve it reveals his fundamental inability to accept life as it is and to live like all those ordinary human beings whom he so deeply despised. *Une saison en enfer* is the acutest expression of the idealism of youth hurt by all the ugliness which it encounters and which it cannot explain, since it has not yet learnt the bitterest of all the lessons which we have to learn, to make compromises with our ideals and principles, and to accept the second best. Rimbaud never learned to make compromises and since he could not possess what he believed was *la vraie vie* he would have nothing. In the days of his pride and his belief in his powers he refused life as it was given to him; he intended to make his own life on his own conditions. He would destroy everything that existed, naturally, in himself; he would build everything again and transform life. And so he spurned and refused all the things which made life sweet for ordinary simple human beings; work, love and hope. . . . But this martyrdom eventually led him only to the dead end of the acceptance of the inevitable. The struggle with this problem which we find expressed in *Une saison en enfer* led, finally, to the sad end of the grudging acceptance of reality, of perpetual slavery. 'Esclaves, ne maudissons pas la vie!'

Rimbaud's *bateau ivre,* instead of bearing him into the centre of the ocean of Infinity, or as Baudelaire's boat had carried him to the shores of that endless sea, had merely described a complete circle, bringing him back to the reality from which he had fled, from which he had imagined he had escaped, to revolting reality. That was the final port into which his boat sailed after all the storms, and the return was not easy. Whatever he might say or think, reality was what Rimbaud was never able, and never would be able, to accept. (pp. 247-48)

When he started writing Rimbaud had reached no point whatsoever; his only certainty was his state of anguish and distress, and his conviction that all his past life and art had been a delusion. Thus in *Une saison en enfer* we live the struggle with the poet, with him we contemplate the problems, dropping them partially solved, only to take them up later, casting aside the early abortive solutions. *Une saison en enfer* is a moment of Rimbaud's life with all the burning intensity of a struggle whose end is not known to the writer. (pp. 248-49)

Rimbaud increased the evocative power of poetry, independently of the sense it conveyed; words with him are no longer intended to bear their dictionary meaning; they are no longer to express a logical content, or to describe; they are intended to evoke a state of mind and soul. Poetry is no longer to consist in the words or in the images, however beautiful these might be, poetry is the very sensation itself, and this sensation is to be allowed to find its own best expression, just as the lava stream burns out its own bed. In his desire to express what cannot be expressed, Rimbaud left out all unnecessary words, all the connecting links, leaving only the essential vision itself, and this vision is not always easily seen by others. Inspiration had come to him, first in a boiling torrent, but he had sifted out what was the essence of his vision, casting away what was not absolutely necessary, all the explanatory relative clauses. In endeavouring to reach the unknown, Rimbaud did in fact give poetry an evocative power that has been equalled by no other poet.

Rimbaud's poetry has proved—even if this was not his aim—how much rich material there is for art in the subconscious mind, in the half-remembered sensations of childhood, in these sensations which have been registered without our realizing their full meaning. (pp. 382-83)

In poetry Rimbaud dug many new roads, and cleared large sections of the bush, and when he fell by the wayside, others were able to continue along the new road towards the unknown, beyond the horizon. . . . Without Rimbaud it is doubtful whether there would ever have been the Surrealist school of art. (p. 384)

The Surrealist artistic programme has many similarities to Rimbaud's theory of poetry. It aims at discovery of the precise relations existing between metaphysics and poetry, to remove all moral ban from literature and art. Poetry, like the poet, must be beyond good and evil. And finally it seeks to bring about a fuller acknowledgement of the supreme poetic quality of ballads and anonymous literature. A great many of the verse poems of *Les illuminations* were written on the model of simple and naïve folk-songs. It was as if Rimbaud felt that the soul of a people unconsciously wrote itself in its folk-literature, that this was a form of unconscious folk symbolism.

Rimbaud is, however, for us to-day, not merely a poet who is important in the history of poetry, important because he symbolizes his own time, or because he opened the gates of another kingdom for us. He is significant also in his own right, because the collected edition of his writings is the bedside book of many who do not concern themselves with the history of literature, or with the craft of poetry. These read him for the direct message he has for them.

Rimbaud's work has, perhaps, not the depth of the work of Baudelaire; it does not reveal the same adult experience and reflection on the eternal problems that rack the souls of men. Through Baudelaire we reach a fuller conscious knowledge of ourselves, of human nature and of the problem of human weakness faced with right and wrong. Rimbaud felt acutely, had violent intuitions, but he rarely reflected. (pp. 384-85)

There is with Rimbaud the paradoxical situation that he who in his writings was, in spite of what any one may say, an unbeliever—a mystical unbeliever—he who at the end of *Une saison en enfer* refused belief for himself, should have led others back to faith. . . . In his experience of God Rimbaud reached, without orthodox beliefs, the stage that all mystics seek to attain, where there is no longer possibility for belief or disbelief, for doubt or reflection, but only pure sensation, mystic ecstasy and union with the Eternal. (pp. 385-86)

In *Les illuminations* is found expressed, as no where else, except perhaps in the poems of Saint John of the Cross, man's eternal longing for spiritual beauty; *Une saison en enfer* is the hell of doubt which is always with us, the age-long struggle between the angel and the beast in us, and few writers have expressed, in so poignant and moving a manner, the bitterness of the cry that bursts from us; while in *Le bateau ivre,* perhaps, intrinsically, his greatest work, we find all the nostalgic longing of human nature, its aspiration and its passionate desire to escape from outworn values and to sail towards new hopes. *Le bateau ivre* is freighted with the suffering of a stricken world, with its infinite weariness with all that surrounds it; it carries on board the world's ardent longing for escape to the open sea away from the stifling stench of the port, there to wash itself clean from all that has soiled and defiled it and to find a newer and cleaner self. The ship speeds along far out at sea sailing, as it were, between two skies, two infinities, but may it not prove to be, like Rimbaud's craft, . . . a fragile paper boat which a child launches on a cruel sea only to be swallowed up by its devouring waves! (pp. 386-87)

Enid Starkie, in her *Arthur Rimbaud,* Faber and Faber, 1938, 425 p.

ALBERT CAMUS
(essay date 1954)

[An Algerian-born French novelist, essayist, dramatist, and short story writer, Camus was one of the most important literary figures of the twentieth century. In the following excerpt from an essay originally published in the English translation of *The Rebel*, he examines the nihilism he believes stems from conflicts in Rimbaud's life and work.]

This is not the place to deal at length with Rimbaud. Everything that can be said about him—and even more, unfortunately—has already been said. It is worth pointing out, however, for it concerns our subject, that only in his work was Rimbaud the poet of rebellion. His life, far from justifying the myth it created, only illustrates (an objective perusal of the letters from Harrar suffices to prove this) the fact that he surrendered to the worst form of nihilism imaginable. Rimbaud has been deified for renouncing his genius, as if his renunciation implied superhuman virtue. It must be pointed out, however, despite the fact that by doing so we disqualify the alibis of our contemporaries, that genius alone— and not the renunciation of genius—implies virtue. Rimbaud's greatness does not lie in the first poems from Charleville nor in his trading at Harrar. It shines forth at the moment when, in giving the most peculiarly appropriate expression to rebellion that it has ever received, he simultaneously proclaims his triumph and his agony, his conception of a life beyond the confines of this world and the inescapability of the world, the yearning for the unattainable and reality brutally determined on restraint, the rejection of morality and the irresistible compulsion to duty. At the moment when he carries in his breast both illumination and the darkness of hell, when he hails and insults beauty, and creates, from an insoluble conflict, the intricate counterpoint of an exquisite song, he is the poet of rebellion—the greatest of all. The order in which he wrote his two great works [*Les illuminations* and *Une saison en enfer*] is of no importance. In any case there was very little time between the conception of the two books, and any artist knows, with the certainty born of experience, that Rimbaud simultaneously carried the seeds of the *Season in Hell* (*Une saison en enfer*) and the *Illuminations* within him. Though he wrote them one after the other, there is no doubt that he experienced the suffering of both of them at the same time. This contradiction, which killed him, was the real source of his genius.

But where, then, is the virtue of someone who re-

fuses to face the contradiction and betrays his own genius before having drunk it to the last bitter drop? Rimbaud's silence is not a new method of rebelling; at least,
we can no longer say so after the publication of . . .
[his] letters. His metamorphosis is undoubtedly mysterious. But there is also a mystery attached to the banality achieved by brilliant young girls whom marriage
transforms into adding or knitting machines. The myth
woven around Rimbaud supposes and affirms that
nothing was possible after the *Season in Hell.* But what
is impossible for the supremely gifted poet or for the
inexhaustibly creative writer? How can we imagine
anything to follow *Moby Dick, The Trial, Zarathustra, The
Possessed?* Nevertheless, they were followed by great
works, which instruct, implement, and bear witness to
what is finest in the writer, and which only come to an
end at his death. Who can fail to regret the work that
would have been greater than the *Season in Hell* and
of which we have been deprived by Rimbaud's abdication?

Can Abyssinia be considered as a monastery; is it
Christ who shut Rimbaud's mouth? Such a Christ
would be the kind of man who nowadays lords it over
the cashier's desk in a bank, to judge by the letters in
which the unhappy poet talks only about his money
which he wants to see "wisely invested" and "bringing
in regular dividends." (It is only fair to note that the
tone of these letters might be explained by the people
to whom they are written. But they do not suggest that
Rimbaud is making a great effort to lie. Not one word
betrays the Rimbaud of former times.) The man who
exulted under torture, who hurled curses at God and at
beauty, who hardened himself in the harsh atmosphere
of crime, now only wants to marry someone "with a future." The mage, the seer, the convict who lived perpetually in the shadow of the penal colony, the man-king
on a godless earth, always carried seventeen pounds of
gold in a belt worn uncomfortably round his stomach,
which he complained gave him dysentery. Is this the
mythical hero, worshipped by so many young men
who, though they do not spit in the face of the world,
would die of shame at the mere idea of such a belt? To
maintain the myth, those decisive letters must be ignored. It is easy to see why they have been so little
commented upon. They are a sacrilege, as truth sometimes is. A great and praise-worthy poet, the greatest
of his time, a dazzling oracle—Rimbaud is all of these
things. But he is not the man-god, the burning inspiration, the monk of poetry as he is often presented. The
man only recaptured his greatness in the hospital bed
in which, at the hour of his painful end, even his mediocrity becomes moving: "How unlucky I am, how very
unlucky I am . . . and I've money on me that I can't
even keep an eye on!" The defiant cry of those last
wretched moments: "No, no, now I rebel against
death!" happily restores Rimbaud to that part of com-

mon human experience which involuntarily coincides
with greatness. The young Rimbaud comes to life again
on the brink of the abyss and with him revives the rebellion of the times when his imprecations against life
were only expressions of despair at the thought of
death. It is at this point that the bourgeois trader once
more rejoins the tortured adolescent whom we so much
admired. He recaptures his youth in the terror and bitter pain finally experienced by those who do not know
how to attain happiness. Only at this point does his
passion, and with it his truth, begin. (pp. 209-11)

The apocalypse of crime—as conceived by Rimbaud in the person of the prince who insatiably slaughters his subjects—and endless licentiousness are rebellious themes that will be taken up again by the surrealists. But finally, even with Rimbaud, nihilist dejection
prevailed; the struggle, the crime itself, proved too exacting for his exhausted mind. The seer who drank, if
we may venture to say so, in order not to forget ended
by finding in drunkenness the heavy sleep so well
known to our contemporaries. One can sleep on the
beach, or at Aden. And one consents, no longer actively, but passively, to accept the order of the world, even
if the order is degrading. Rimbaud's silence is also a
preparation for the silence of authority, which hovers
over minds resigned to everything save to the necessity
of putting up a fight. Rimbaud's great intellect, suddenly subordinated to money, proclaims the advent of
other demands, which are at first excessive and which
will later be put to use by the police. To be nothing—
that is the cry of the mind exhausted by its own rebellion. This leads to the problem of suicide of the mind,
which, after all, is less respectable than the surrealists'
suicide, and more fraught with consequences. Surrealism itself, coming at the end of this great act of rebellion, is only significant because it attempted to perpetuate that aspect of Rimbaud which alone evokes our
sympathy. Deriving the rules for a rebellious asceticism
from the letter about the seer and the system it implies,
he illustrates the struggle between the will to be and
the desire for annihilation, between the yes and the no,
which we have discovered again and again at every
stage of rebellion. (pp. 211-12)

Albert Camus, "Surrealism and Revolution," in *The Idea of the
Modern in Literature and the Arts,* edited by Irving Howe, Horizon
Press, 1968, pp. 209-19.

C. A. HACKETT
(essay date 1957)

[Hackett, an English educator and critic, has written
numerous studies on Rimbaud. In the following ex-

cerpt from his *Rimbaud* (1957), he states that while the poet's vision was fundamentally childlike, his verse is uniquely dynamic, omnipotent, and mystical.]

It is customary, and in a sense fitting, to place Rimbaud in the line of those writers who, since Baudelaire, have sought to endow words with a magical power, and to view poetry not simply as a means of expression but as a—or rather *the*—means of knowledge and truth. Yet, with the utmost lucidity, Rimbaud came to see what those who approach his work so often fail to see: that literature can never be a way of life, and that even the purest of 'pure poetry' is but one of the manifestations of our human condition and adventure. (p. 11)

The most obvious fact about Rimbaud's work is that, both as regards its chronological place in his life and its emotional content, it is the work of an adolescent. (p. 14)

[In his] early poems, Rimbaud is possessed by feelings so violent that they erupt through the orthodox verse forms and find expression in the most direct and primitive manner—in words (so numerous as to be termed obsessional) that describe the body, its gestures, attitudes, and functions; and in a fierce, muscular rhythm that informs his work as a whole. At times he seems to delight in aggression for its own sake; but his attacks are never gratuitous. Their very ferocity implies the ideal that he later formulates as 'changer la vie'. (p. 20)

Like so much of Rimbaud's work, the "Lettre du voyant" seems to suggest that he was striving to defy the inevitable slowness of growth—and indeed the whole of the natural order—and to induce by exceptional, self-inflicted means a 'mutation' in himself and in the literary tradition. Sudden and radical changes, though rare and very infrequent, have occurred in the organic world, but at random. Rimbaud, intoxicated by an overwhelming sense of power, sees no reason why they should not be produced by him, in the mind, and be transmitted as the inheritance of all future poets; the raw material for a completely new poetic evolution. If he could achieve that he would enable the poet to be not only a creator with words but also a *'multiplier of progress'*; he would both have 'found a language' and 'changed life'.

The "Lettre du voyant" has been given many interpretations and has been the source of numerous Rimbaud myths. This is not surprising when one reflects that the letter itself is the expression of a universal myth: a child's dream of omnipotence. That is the myth to which Rimbaud sacrificed himself, first as a poet in the *Illuminations,* an imaginary world in which the illusion of omnipotence could momentarily be captured; and then in the world of practical living, as a trader and explorer in Abyssinia. What are sometimes referred to as his 'victory' and his 'defeat' are complementary aspects—the one poetic, the other prosaic—of the same myth. (pp. 27-8)

["**Les poètes de sept ans**" has] so many structural defects (emphasised by the repeated 'et') that one is tempted to describe it as inartistic. But it is intentionally inartistic; for Rimbaud is concerned less with giving his experience a satisfying aesthetic form than with expressing, and *seeing,* it as completely and as accurately as possible. In some of his earlier poems, such as "**Première soirée**" and "**Les reparties de nina,**" he was, as it were, looking at the world through the eyes of the adults; but in "**Les poètes de sept ans**" there is no false air of sophistication. The vision is entirely personal. . . . "**Les poètes de sept ans**" is a sharply particularised, and essentially un-Romantic evocation, in which the poet is unmistakably Rimbaud, and the mother Madame Rimbaud. . . . [In this poem], there are none of the elements of caricature so pronounced in earlier poems such as "**Le châtiment de Tartufe**" and "**Vénus anadyomène.**" The figures are drawn to scale and, though a past tense is used throughout, they are—with all their physical and mental characteristics—vividly and concretely present. But they are present only to be

Sketches of Rimbaud in Paris by Paul Verlaine.

dismissed. **"Les poètes de sept ans"** . . . marks the end both of a certain way of looking at life and of writing about it . . . **"Les poètes de sept ans"** is the culmination of a series of portraits that are unique in French literature—portraits of children, of adults, of the poet himself. It is also something more: a critical survey of Rimbaud's own childhood, of a 'real' world, which is evoked in order to be rejected. (pp. 31-3)

[**"Ce qu'on dit au poète à propos de fleurs"**] is both a parody of Banville and a semi-serious application of the new poetic theory. Rimbaud ridicules with irony, impudent humour, and an exuberance of mordant fancy the outmoded properties of Parnassian poetry—its lilacs, lilies, violets, and roses. . . . [In] **"Ce qu'on dit au poète à propos de fleurs,"** he sarcastically repudiates both nineteenth-century materialism and Parnassian idealism as he formulates some amusing counter-propositions. . . . (pp. 34-5)

In **"Ce qu'on dit au poète,"** Rimbaud was addressing the poet; in **"Voyelles"** he addresses language—the poet's material. This sonnet is the artist's palette, his raw material of sounds and colours, language itself. It is like an experiment in which Rimbaud says: 'Let A be black, E white, I red, U green, O blue, then let us see what the possibilities are'. Critics have suggested that **"Voyelles"** is a commentary on the coloured letters of an alphabet which Rimbaud had used as a child. But if, as we read the opening line, 'A noir, E blanc, I rouge, U vert, O bleu: voyelles', we seem to hear a child reciting a lesson, we also hear the *voyant* announcing a new faith in the power of language—which he is using not to describe but to create. As we pass through a sequence of visual and dynamic images, from the dark source 'A', 'golfes d'ombre', to the radiant 'O', child-like symbols are transformed into a cosmic vision. . . . Yet while affirming his mastery over the elements of language, [**"Voyelles"**] foreshadows his ultimate failure, the failure to coordinate the separate colours of his universe into a clear vision, to be in the full sense of the word a *voyant*. Like the contrasted colours of this sonnet, his vision is rich and vivid but it lacks the nuances and the fine gradations; and, though illuminating, it is always fragmentary. (pp. 35-6)

[*Le bateau ivre*] is a more extended application of the *voyant* theory. Having shown his power over the vowels, Rimbaud now displays his ability to orchestrate all the resources of language. . . . *Le bateau ivre*, like nearly all Rimbaud's poems, is fundamentally childlike, that is, a-moral. It springs from a belief that not only art but life itself is, or should be, 'innocent'; and that consequently the possibilities of human as well as of artistic fulfilment are infinite. . . . Rimbaud has, in fact, attempted to show that, in order to enrich our experience of the world, we do not need to travel to distant lands—or even to travel at all; we need new sight, new eyes. (pp. 37-8)

[The **"Dernier vers,"** written during his first months in Paris,] may well be what in fact they appear to be, namely, Rimbaud's first 'illuminations'. (p. 40)

In poems which seem by their form as artless and as anonymous as nursery-rhymes or folk-songs, Rimbaud has expressed feelings that are complex and intensely personal. Here is all the frustration, the disillusionment, and the solitude he felt on his return from Paris, as well as a primitive and childlike ecstasy. Although he passes abruptly from extreme suffering to extreme joy, Rimbaud's tone remains assured and the expression transparently clear; and it is this contrast between the content and the form that gives to these last verse poems their unusual poignancy. . . . Even in his most lyrical, child-like poems he is invariably unsentimental, alert, and self-critical. He realises how futile his experience in Paris has been; that till now his youth had been 'enslaved to everything' except to what was essential—his own original vision; and he is fully aware that the poems he is now writing are, as he says of them in *Une saison en enfer*, his 'farewell to the world'.

Rimbaud turns for consolation to familiar landscapes and themes and, at a deeper level, to Nature herself—though never in the manner of a Lamartine. His attitude is strikingly different; and the unusual warmth and tenderness of these lyrics are accompanied by an equally marked coldness and defiance. Although Nature was clearly a maternal symbol for Rimbaud, he does not treat her as his confidante, and he rarely attributes to her precise human characteristics. He seeks rather to divest her of all those qualities and feelings with which the Romantics and other poets had endowed her. Nature is for him not a person but an elemental force to which he returns in order to renew and purify his poetic vision. (pp. 41-2)

[In these poems], the stress falls more on the poet's volition and his desire for freedom than on his adversity; and it has none of those qualities that mar so much of the Romantics' nature poetry: inert self-pity and posturing before a personified Nature. The 'thirst' and the 'hunger' which Rimbaud brings to Nature are his inspiration in its most instinctive and dynamic form. (p. 43)

[In **"Fêtes de la faim"**], Rimbaud drives his insatiable hunger through the whole realm of nature to seek nourishment from her hardest features—rocks and iron—as well as from her most ethereal elements—air and the vibrant sky. . . . [The theme of this poem and **"Comédie de la soif "**] is frustration, but it is also that of a search for other, and purer, poetic satisfactions than the stale symbols in which generations of poets had presented, or rather hidden, Nature. (pp. 43-4)

This 'return to Nature' is profoundly child-like, but at the same time it is virile and supremely creative.

In "**Larme,**" for example, Rimbaud appears to be the child who, 'far from the birds, the flocks, the village girls', seeks refuge in the tenderness of nature (represented here by the woods, the 'tendres bois de noisetiers'; and the river, the 'jeune Oise'), but he is also the *voyant* whose senses are so acute and receptive that every variation in the atmosphere and the landscape produces new visions for his poetry. (p. 45)

The *Illuminations* are at once a sustained application of Rimbaud's *voyant* theory and a spontaneous expression of his inner drama. They form the most original and the most important part of his work. Even the least comprehensible of these revolutionary prose poems force a response from the reader, quicken the sensibility and, at least momentarily, illumine the mind. More complex in substance than the *Poésies* or *Une saison en enfer,* they evoke a new yet strangely familiar world—primitive and barbaric, yet essentially modern and human; hard and resistant, yet fluid and mobile; jumbled and chaotic, yet marked by an almost obsessional precision and order; silent and desolate, yet charged with the music of spiritual resonances; savage, yet tender and ecstatic; unreal and phantasmagoric, yet full of echoes from a childhood rooted in Charleville and the Ardennes. The *Illuminations* express with unexampled sureness and intensity the innumerable contrasts and oppositions that give Rimbaud's work its peculiar richness. Whatever the exact nature of the experience which he underwent at the time of writing the *Illuminations,* its expression in these 'superb fragments' is at once so profound and so condensed that it is impossible to translate or to paraphrase it, or even to comment on it adequately. (pp. 54-5)

"**Après le déluge**" is strikingly different from any of the *Poésies.* Whereas they were like a spontaneous, physical assault upon the objective world, here aggression is the necessary preliminary to the creation of a new poetic vision. What before was only attacked must now be annihilated so that Rimbaud can re-create his own world—a world where poetry is no longer discursive or anecdotic, as to some extent it still is in "**Après le déluge,**" but pure vision, as it is in the complementary poem, "**Barbare,**" "**Après le déluge**" marks an end and a fresh beginning—an end of the 'inspired' poetry (repudiated in the "Lettre du voyant") and the beginning of the visionary poetry which is a result of the technique formulated in the phrase 'un long, immense et raissoné *dérèglement* de *tous les sens'.*

The five short pieces, entitled "**Enfance,**" which follow "**Après le déluge,**" form the threshold to this new world. Here we must not seek to identify objects and people, nor ask why they are where they are, nor what they mean. We have only to see them as material for, and in, poetry. (pp. 58-9)

In "**Après le déluge,**" people, animals, and things were doing what we might expect them to do—the children were looking at pictures, the beavers were building, the flowers were opening, the blood was flowing in the slaughter houses. Everything was doing what it normally does in real life; which is why Rimbaud invoked the floods to destroy them. But in "**Enfance**" people and objects have no utilitarian function. They exist simply as elements in a skilfully constructed and coherent pattern. It is precisely because they are now devoid of any practical purpose, and have no obvious reference to our ordinary existence, that they become alive in a different way—poetically alive. The undeniable vitality of this particular passage is conveyed by the clusters of plural, concrete nouns and active verbs; through the stresses and rhythms, the movement of the whole passage, and by the suggestion that Rimbaud's imaginary world is so near—'at the edge of the forest', 'close to the sea'—if we will only look. (p. 60)

There have been many 'il y a' poems since this one [from "**Enfance**"], but most of them are artificial and diffuse, and none combines, as Rimbaud's does, the vision of a child and a *voyant.* Its *vaivete* is, for example, markedly different from that of Verlaine. There is no nostalgic lament and the attitude is completely unsentimental. Even if we take the last line to be a reference to the child, thwarted and driven away, it is expressed as a sharp, objective statement. It is impersonal, yet aggressively personal too; for the 'quelqu' un' is Rimbaud. He has deliberately frustrated our normal appetites and expectations; and through a poem which is an illumination in its simplest form he is forcing us to enter a world emancipated from reason, logic, and habit. But before we can enjoy its spiritual satisfactions we must—as Rimbaud has already done in "**Comédie de la soif**" and "**Fêtes de la faim**"—say 'farewell to the world' and reject its 'thirst' and 'hunger'.

Rimbaud's intention is clearly seen not only in the prose poems entitled "**Enfance**" and "**Ieunesse**" but also in the series entitled "**Villes,**" which resemble jig-saw pictures spilled from a box in miraculous disorder. In some of them past, present, and future exist simultaneously; in others, bits of London, Paris, and Charleville form part of the same town. The disorder is intentional. Rimbaud is altering, or destroying, conventional perspectives—spatial, temporal, and human—so that our thoughts and feelings, forced from their habitual rut, will be free to follow the 'thousand swift furrows' ("**Ornières**") of his vision. (pp. 61-2)

We experience an intense exhilaration as we move through Rimbaud's imaginary world where objects and people are seen as poetic essences, and the elements themselves—earth, air, fire, water—appear to be transformed and made new. And we participate in the poet's irresistible sense of power; for this is a world in which Rimbaud (and the reader) feels omnipotent. (pp. 63-4)

"**Conte**" expresses with ferocious clarity the creative and destructive impulses that are so closely related in all Rimbaud's work. This prose poem has a special force because it appeals simultaneously on the objective and the subjective levels. Its narrative style and its two characters, the Prince and the Genie, are reminiscent of a fairy story; but this story is also an illumination about Rimbaud himself and the equivocal, self-destructive nature of his genius. In his search for 'the truth, the hour of essential desire and satisfaction', the Prince—like Rimbaud in **"Après le déluge"**—endeavours to renew the source of life by destroying what are to him its imperfect manifestations. But the women he assassinates, the animals he slaughters, the followers he kills, the people he massacres, the palaces he burns—all continue to exist. (pp. 66-7)

"Conte" is a paradox. With supreme artistry, Rimbaud demonstrates the ultimate futility of his art and, at the same time, expresses by the most inhuman means a human aim: the liberation of his spirit. For him, this liberation is never something to be achieved gradually, through continual gropings and adjustments, but—as here—immediately, with overwhelming suddenness and finality. This paradoxical victory (is it perhaps Rimbaud's 'secret' for 'changing life'?) is possible, however, only in dreams and phantasy, where all is 'as simple as a musical phrase' (**"Guerre"**). In the real world, to which the poem abruptly returns with the words '*ce* Prince', there is no 'musique savante'; and the Prince's revolt is vain. Life, resisting all his efforts to destroy it, has killed his genius; and forces him to live out his own human personality. He dies, in his palace, at an 'ordinary age'.

This ending, an anti-climax, where what has been created and what has been destroyed are recorded with apparent detachment, and then brusquely repudiated, is typical of many of the *Illuminations.* Here, as in **"Après le déluge,"** it is more than a literary device used in order to mystify the reader and to give the poem extra point (both of which it does); it is an inevitable and, as it were, an organic conclusion, a sudden relaxation of tension accompanied by weariness and disillusionment, after the expression of extreme and 'guilty' feelings. It is a necessary return to the ordinary world, both for reassurance that everything still exists and for 'real', if mediocre, achievement. (pp. 67-8)

[The] *Illuminations* are not merely a series of 'coloured plates' to be contemplated for their aesthetic enjoyment. They are an 'opéra fabuleux' where Rimbaud is at once producer, stage-manager, and all the actors. The clash of conflicting emotional forces has reached its highest pitch; but because they are projected into imaginary figures moving in an imaginary world they can be endured. By this device—no doubt an unconscious one—and by brilliant technical skill, Rimbaud achieves a marvellous, if precarious, equilibrium. The *Illuminations* mark the highest point of his poetic

evolution. They are the climax to a drama of which *Une saison en enfer* is the *dénouement.* (p. 69)

Like the *Illuminations, Une saison en enfer* can be interpreted in many different ways ranging from what critics have termed a 'return to reality' to a 'return to God'. Rather it is a fierce, sardonic commentary on Rimbaud's own experience, on his human and literary ambitions; and a violent attack on all those who, like him, are the product of Western civilisation. It is also, to use his own words, a 'bataille spirituelle', in which the protagonists are good and evil, guilt and innocence, God and Satan—the varying forms of a dualism which Western man accepts but which Rimbaud seeks vehemently to reject. The sincerity of the work is not often, if ever, questioned. Yet it contains numerous declamatory and would-be oracular utterances in which Rimbaud is striving after an effect; and others in which he is striking a pose as dated and outmoded as Baudelaire's satanism. Occasionally, his experience even seems to be derivative; for example, in the prologue and in the section **"Nuit de L'enfer,"** where certain words and sentences, as well as the tone and general feeling, are strongly reminiscent of the concluding pages of Balzac's *Le Père Goriot.* But where he writes from first-hand experience—that of a boy of eighteen—*Une saison en enfer* is, by virtue of its intensity and immediacy, both convincing and original. (pp. 71-2)

In *Une saison en enfer,* guilt and innocence are complementary themes that give the work an underlying unity. With his talent for self-dramatisation, Rimbaud goes on to imagine scenes in which he can enact at one and the same time his sense of guilt and his sense of innocence. (p. 74)

The virile, dynamic force which, alternating with nostalgic child-like laments, persists right through *Une saison en enfer* is no longer creative. The energy, which in *Poésies* was a primitive means of self-expression, and in the *Illuminations* a source of disciplined artistic vision, becomes in *Une saison en enfer* a destructive force which Rimbaud directs against his work and against himself. When he exclaims 'Si la damnation est éternelle! Un homme qui veut se mutiler est bien damné, n'est-ce pas?' [Suppose damnation is eternal! A man who wants to mutilate himself is certainly damned, isn't he?] his suffering is very different from the 'ineffable torture' which the *voyant* had endured and welcomed in his search for the unknown. In *Une saison en enfer,* Rimbaud has moved uncompromisingly from the artistic to the human plane; and the words on which it ends—'*une âme et un corps*'—refer to a soul and a body whose energies are henceforth to be used not to produce visions but to grapple with reality. (pp. 83-4)

Rimbaud's work is so fragmentary, elliptical, ambiguous, and paradoxical that it permits, if it does not justify, almost any and every interpretation. And it seems natural enough that these interpretations should be as violent, as conflicting, and often as contradictory, as the emotions that are expressed in the work itself. It is as if this poetry, essentially dynamic in itself and in its effect, represents an unfinished phase in human growth, which many writers have sought to continue and complete—some theoretically, in literature; some practically, in actual living. (p. 92)

In some ways, Rimbaud's work (like that of Baudelaire, too) is 'dated'. It is rooted in a fundamentally Romantic conception of the poet and his role which, as poets writing in a different and rapidly changing social context are finding, is no longer valid or appropriate. Today, poets—and critics—are discovering what Rimbaud discovered before them, namely, that poetry has no superhuman, omnipotent power; and while they seek to preserve the fresh qualities which Baudelaire and his successors introduced into the literary tradition, they are searching for a new and less ambitious *art poétique.* But if time, social changes, and new literary doctrines are modifying some aspects of Rimbaud's work, they will leave untouched, and further reveal, its deep and underlying theme: a child's belief in his omnipotence. That, from the first poems to the last letters, is the unifying theme of Rimbaud's work. It is as ephemeral, and as timeless, as childhood itself. As children we share, in fact live, Rimbaud's theme; and it is then that (if we respond to poetry at all) our response to his work is most vivid and extreme. Inevitably, as adults, our reaction is more critical; or rather, one must add, it should be more critical. The striking fact is that Rimbaud's fierce lyricism, which appeals not to our reason but to the tumultuous and undisciplined emotions of our childhood, continues to provoke extreme reactions. The cliché about being 'too near' an author to understand him properly applies in a special way to Rimbaud. It is not chronologically that we are too near him, but emotionally. It is perhaps only in so far as we can develop beyond our own immaturity, and are unafraid to recall the ecstasies and the terrors of a time when we too were omnipotent children, that we shall really be able to *see* and to understand Rimbaud's work.

In retrospect, his work may appear slight—but it is unique. In the brief space of four or five years, his **"Matinée d'ivresse"** (to quote the title of one of his *Illuminations*), Rimbaud used brilliantly most of the devices of modern poetry, and announced nearly all its themes. His poetry admittedly lacks some of the qualities one finds in the greatest art—notably, maturity; a quality we find, for example, in Racine, whom Rimbaud in his youthful arrogance called the 'Divine Idiot', and in Baudelaire, whom in his youthful enthusiasm he acclaimed as 'a true God' and then condemned for the poverty of his artistic form. But whereas Racine, and even Baudelaire, could draw strength from a stable heritage—literary, social, and religious—Rimbaud no longer could. For him, their kind of maturity was not pos-

sible. His poetry *is* immature, and fragmentary: it reflects his own age, his adolescence, and the civilisation into which he was born—our civilisation of materialism and spiritual confusion. Yet he is the greatest French poet since Baudelaire, and in saying this one does not forget that the line includes Mallarmé, Claudel, and Valéry. Rimbaud's work has a range, a penetration, and a quickening power we do not find in theirs; for in expressing the conflicts of his own development he also expressed the conflicts of our civilisation, and with a permanently disturbing force he has challenged all its values. (pp. 93-5)

C. A. Hackett, in his *Rimbaud,* Bowes & Bowes Publishers Limited, 1957, 109 p.

HENRI PEYRE
(essay date 1974)

[Peyre was a French essayist, editor, and critic who wrote numerous works on French literature. In the following excerpt from a work that first appeared in French in 1974, he discusses the symbolic elements in Rimbaud's verse.]

All our notions about Rimbaud are obscured with very little gain in seeking to make him fit some preconceived idea or in labeling him with some epithet by which we think he can be summed up: "Rimbaud the child," "Rimbaud the voyant," "Rimbaud the hooligan" . . . , Rimbaud the mystic or the masochist, seeing himself as unhappy and "a great invalid, a great criminal, suffering under a great curse." He was all that and much more.

But before everything else, for posterity and among European writers of the second half of the twentieth century, Rimbaud represents the rebel. "I am he who suffers and who rebelled," he cried out in the most ferociously anti-Christian of his early poems, **"The Just Man."** He rises like the Cain that Byron and Leconte de Lisle had already taken as their spokesman, against the false innocent (Christ) before whom his mother had thought she could make him kneel. "Eternal thief of vitality," he calls Him in another blasphemous line. Even earlier, a schoolboy impassioned by carnal, pagan goddesses in **"Sunlight and Flesh,"** he had cried out in a burst of joy: "No more gods! Man / Man is God!" The new literature demanded above all the scornful rejection of worn-out beliefs that had only served to reduce man to a slave state. . . . Rimbaud seeks to leap without the slightest remorse into a fall from grace, to demean himself, to become as hideously monstrous as the hero of **"The Man Who Laughs,"** to make himself the scapegoat of his fellowmen and of all humanity. Out of this inclination rises the heartrending cry of sincerity in the "Letter from the Voyant". . . . In the famous **"Alchemy of the Word,"** from *A Season in Hell,* Rimbaud makes allusion to "worn-out poetic forms," while confessing that they had not been excluded from the alchemist's experiments by the young destroyer. In barely one or two years he succeeded in sweeping away all the tinsel of his predecessors' poetic diction and in passing beyond personal poetry whose era he declared henceforth to have passed away. (pp. 34-5)

Too often people have sought to present Rimbaud as a Communard or even make of him a communist, which amounts to only slightly less a deformation than to caricature him as a pious Catholic. He knew moments of anarchist revolt against every established order; the poem **"What for Us, My Heart, Are Pools of Blood"** cries it out forcefully. More regularly, he felt himself spontaneously in revolt against maternal tyranny and the prison of the family. His poems of early adolescence say this with brutality and verve. (p. 36)

Rimbaud right at the outset surpasses everything that the end-of-the-century poets and theoreticians of symbolism were to attempt. Although most of them were to be content with a vague philosophical idealism, with Platonic declarations of devotion to beauty, and with technical discussions of the means and the rules to achieve renewed verse form, Rimbaud in his rebellion invades the domains of psychology and philosophy. With him, dreams do not merely flow into our waking lives, they blend with half-conscious reveries, with thoughts, impulses, desires. Rimbaud dips with both hands into what is most confused, sometimes the most pure and most deeply buried within himself and within us. The stars dance in his sentences like flowers; they emit the sounds of bells or of joyous fanfares; sounds and colors blend together, fused into a single poetic vision. (p. 37)

Rimbaud's poetry becomes a means of exploring the depths that lie beyond clear consciousness and that the magician, with his omnipotent wand, causes to jet forth like geysers. It becomes equally a way to knowledge and invades domains before which science was abdicating. The adolescent Rimbaud wanted to reinvent love and perhaps reject the mutual incomprehension of the two sexes, unite the strength of the one and the other in a complete androgyny. He had doubtless been disappointed by woman, after his rebellion against a mother with whom he knew secretly he had many affinities. He had dreamed of finding in woman patience, gentleness, comprehension, consolation, as in the "domestic dream" that Verlaine sketched before meeting Rimbaud and even before his marriage. The lines of prose from **"Deserts of Love"** reveal how vulnerable the adolescent was in his avid need for tender-

ness and in the awkward brutality that badly concealed his appeal for sentiment. (pp. 37-8)

Symbols that reveal the workings of the Rimbaldian imagination can be easily garnered in the poems written before his seventeenth year. Several already evince a rare beauty: **"The Poets of Seven Years"** in a sarcastic mode, **"Ophélie,"** less original and more descriptive, but already marking the appearance in Rimbaud's poetry of the victim of drowning, and that admirable, mocking, and joyous reverse *art poétique,* **"What One Says to the Poet on the Subject of Flowers."** *The Drunken Boat* is, among all of them, the symbolic poem par excellence. The virtuosity that the seventeen-year-old adolescent displays therein, his verbal mastery, the breadth of its development, have aroused many admiring commentaries. The most diverse sources have, of course, been assigned to it, most of them without any real relationship to the lines and phrasings of the text. Rimbaud doubtless had not yet seen the sea, but he had contemplated or seen images of it in books; he dreamed of liberation and flight. . . . He embodies in this symbol of the boat adrift and the unleashed universe all his romantic fury. Throughout twenty-five stanzas of four alexandrines each, he unfolds a power of inspriation and animated rhythm that Vigny or Baudelaire might have envied. The drunkenness of the boat and of the adolescent dreaming of his freedom becomes, thanks to the sounds, to the broken and sometimes abrupt rhythm of the lines, to the clash of images, the reader's own. Hugo himself rarely succeeded in orchestrating his eloquence to this point. (pp. 38-9)

The Drunken Boat, colored, leaping, intoxicated with its verbal richness, imperious in its near Hugoesque eloquence, is still turned towards the past. Émile Verhaeren, Claudel at times, Pierre Emmanuel, and Jean Grosjean will know moments of impetuous inspiration and sometimes biblical anger that will render their works akin to the adolescent's romantic masterpiece. Rimbaud's true technical innovations and his art of rendering mystery and shadows unfolds with more secret intensity in his other long poem, a masterpiece of symbolic poetry, **"Memory,"** probably written the following year. There, the oratorical tone is broken; unity no longer lies in that flight that blows like a tempest across the conquering stanzas; the lines are often segmented with virtuosity and run insolently into one another. The stanzas within each of the five sections, clearly differentiated by their tone and visual arrangement on the page, do not enclose impressions and regrets in a rigid mold of four alexandrines; they, too, flow into one another and carry with them, like the river that is at one and the same time the setting and the actor in the poem, the flow of memories and regrets. To emphasize better that gentleness in the continuity of a dream or reverie charged with mystery, the poet did away with capital letters at the beginning of each line; his use of exclamation points was even more sober than in his preceding masterpiece. We no longer have the seer whose eye deforms reality in order to enlarge it and make it whirl about furiously. (pp. 40-1)

Henri Peyre, "Rimbaud, or the Symbolism of Revolt," in his *What Is Symbolism?* translated by Emmett Parker, The University of Alabama Press, 1980, pp. 33-47.

JOESPH BIANCO

(essay date 1990)

[In the essay excerpted below, Bianco traces Rimbaud's poetic development.]

The letter that Rimbaud wrote to his friend Paul Demeny on May 15, 1871, is . . . a capital poetic statement. Much can still be said about this letter: for all the glossing it has received we still do not know how to read it. It can and has been interpreted well enough as to the ideas that its various parts contain, and their wealth or dearth of originality. But as it is most often quoted in bits and pieces, and with a reverence that it perhaps does not deserve, this letter, brief as it is, has not yet disclosed the proportions in which its parts must be viewed in relation to each other. Beginning with an overview of the writings that preceded it, we would like to take it up again here, in an attempt to find the just intensity of the light in which to see the letter, within a career that will not be governed by it.

At the time of the Second Empire in France, the poet's isolation was something normal and generally unquestioned, and interplay between the poet and society as a whole was by then what it is today: an ideal as impossible as the "wholeness" of life itself. The only exception to this state of affairs, besides the journalists, and the ephemeral poets and *chansonniers* who were preparing the euphoric Paris of the Commune, was Victor Hugo, who was living a long and conspicuous exile. But the fall of the Second Empire, in September 1870, and the circumstances attendant to it, may be said, for at least one obscure poet, to represent a partial renewal of the visionary atmosphere of the first decade or so of Romantic activity in France. Rimbaud had been writing poems seriously for perhaps a year. In May he had sent his long poem **"Credo in unam" ("Soleil et chair")**, along with **"Ophélie"** and **"Sensation,"** to Théodore de Banville, in the hope of "finding a place" in the forthcoming *Parnasse contemporain.* By October of 1870 Rimbaud completed what may safely be considered his first volume of poetry: I am speaking of that collection of twenty-two poems, all fair-copied for publication,

that he left with Paul Demeny at Douai that October. (p. 31)

What the poems of this first phase convey, when we consider them together as a volume, is youth, freedom, and a tremendous sense of release. The collection must be seen as a whole in order to perceive the powerful modulation that is its ordering principle. The swing is wide, from the exuberant proclamations of a desire for experience (**"Sensation"** and **"Ma bohème,"** which open and close the volume, and **"Au cabaret-vert"**), to dark premonitions of adulthood and death (**"Ophélie,"** **"Bal des pendus"**). There are expressions of the radical ideal in politics that, under Victor Hugo, survived in exile as a central aspect of Romantic poetry. Among these politically inspired poems, we may cite **"Le châtiment de Tartuffe," "Le forgeron," "Morts de quatre-vingt-douze et de quatrevingt-treize," "Le mal," "Rages de Césars,"** and **"L'eclatante victoire de Sarrebruck."** There are adolescent love poems (**"Première soirée," "Rêvé pour l'hiver"**), satirical pieces (**"A la musique,"** for example), and genrepieces (**"Le buffet," "La maline"**). And, in the best Romantic tradition, the "volume" includes a major poetic statement in which all of its diverse tendencies are summed up: the important long poem, **"Soleil et chair,"** which had already been sent to Banville the previous spring (to no known result). (pp. 31-2)

The interstellar voyage is a Romantic theme that can be traced back through Hugo, Nerval and Vigny, to Jean-Paul Richter's famous "dream," the *Rede des Todten Christus;* we need not limit ourselves to Hugo, but his is the immediate influence here. Rimbaud is now taking up the theme with great success in **"Soleil et chair."** But we can see how close these lines are to Hugo. More than that, the Rimbaud of **"Soleil et chair"** was imitating—admiringly, consciously, we are inclined to say, because he has captured exactly the Hugolian idiom and rhythms, and has not appended a single note of irony—the poet of astral contemplation; and his own originality (which Rimbaud's admirers constantly insist upon) was not even a concern for Rimbaud while he was writing these lines, because he was writing an anthem to humanity, and to confound himself with the universal song was his ideal. . . . "Originality," for the Rimbaud of this moment, consists in orchestrating, for his poems, models and themes from an existing tradition. When we look deeper into **"Soleil et chair,"** we also find, for example, Musset's "Rolla," Théodore de Banville's "L'Exil des Dieux" (which Rimbaud would have read in the 1866 *Parnasse contemporain*), as well as later manifestations of these themes in Baudelaire (the poem "J'aime le souvenir de ces époques nues") and in Verlaine (the "Prolouge" to the *Poèmes saturniens*).

Everything leads us to consider this first (unpublished) collection of Rimbaud's poems as a true first volume, an apprentice volume. The influences are

---

Rimbaud on how a poet becomes a "Seer":

The poet becomes a *seer* through a long, immense, and reasoned *derangement of all the senses*. All shapes of love, suffering, madness. He searches himself, he exhausts all poisons in himself, to keep only the quintessences. Ineffable torture where he needs all his faith, all his superhuman strength, where he becomes among all men the great patient, the great criminal, the great accursed one—and the supreme Scholar! For he reaches the *unknown!* Since he cultivated his soul, rich already, more than anyone else! He reaches the unknown, and when, demented, he would end by losing the intelligence of his visions, he has seen them! Let him die in his leaps among unheard-of and unnamable things; other horrible workers will come: they will begin from the horizons where the other one has collapsed!

Rimbaud, in his "Lettre du voyant," 1871.

---

many, as the scholarship devoted to these poems has in part, but not sufficiently, shown. Yet the effect is one of pure creative vitality.

Rimbaud's private revolt in the fall of 1870 may represent his own independence and poetic birth, but it is not fanciful to connect it with the overwhelming sense of relief and escape that was sweeping through republican sections of the population after the capitulation of the Empire. With the ardent rebellious idealism characteristic of him at this time, Rimbaud shared in this mood—which is why many of the subjects upon which he exerted his newfound skill were political. . . . The mood of the country—or, more properly, of Paris—after twenty years of despotism also found its expression in the return, from his equally long exile, of the bard of republicanism, Victor Hugo himself. The historical period of the siege of Paris and of the Commune corresponds to a critically formative period in Rimbaud's writing life. But though this is one of the most obscure periods in the life of the poet, it furnishes the major document for the ideas of the critic.

"Voyant"—"Seer"—seemed to him the most appropriate definition of the task of the future Poet because it was sufficiently general, not to say ambiguous, to suggest the full, exalted comprehensiveness of this most essential of functions. If Rimbaud was in fact disposed to accept for himself, in this exceptionally new sense, the ancient title of Seer (which rejoins prior conceptions such as Michelet's proto-creative Sorceress), it was only because it conveyed some impression of his unique relation, as he saw it, with poetry. In fact, the term, as Rimbaud uses it, acquires very little meaning when aligned with occult or mystical tradition. "Seer" portrays, more than anything else, a victim of extravagant temperament and impossible ideals: it denotes the

presence of the Romantic ideal of living poetically. The "lettre du Voyant" was written by someone who claimed to know poetry in a way that no one else ever did, this is clear. And the letter prompts us to conclude, as it was meant to do, that right or wrong, fool or genius, poetry is the supreme reality in this person's existence.

But although the famous letter of May 15, 1871, to Paul Demeny (along with its first draft, the May 13 letter . . .) has come to be called the "letter from the Seer," it is not completely clear that he saw himself in this role. He implied, of course, that he wanted to be one, but even here it is not certain that this pronouncement is devoid of irony. The irony is inherent mostly in the choice of poems that illustrate the new esthetic—**"Chant de guerre parisien," "Mes petites amoureuses,"** and **"Accroupissements"**—as well as in the tone of bravado characteristic of the letter as a whole.

In our view, the letter of May 15, 1871, is above all a declaration of faith in modern creativity, just as Hugo's *William Shakespeare* was seven years before, and the Preface to *Cromwell* was forty-four years before, and just as Du Bellay's *Defense et Illustration de la langue françoyse* was, over three hundred years before. And this declaration is deeply related, as I have said, to the political events and revolutionary and poetic possibilities of the period 1870-1871.

In Rimbaud's letter, poetic epochs and makers of poetic epochs are sharply characterized and subjected to a somewhat comical and yet urgent evaluation. It is this urgent character of Rimbaud's letter that must be above all retained. It has almost the quality of a military dispatch from the battlefield. Indeed, it is a new literary battle that Rimbaud is proposing. . . . (pp. 32-4)

But if, in his letter, Rimbaud's interest in poetry from the time of the Greeks to the Romantic age is not literary-historical in the conventional sense, he is still concerned to ask one question of paramount importance to any literary historian and theorist: what is the overall shape of French poetry, and then world poetry, up to now? What is its future? It is in order to emphasize the urgency of these questions, more than to answer them, that Rimbaud offers us his vaguely diagrammatic map of the history of poetry. . . . (p. 35)

Rimbaud completes his map by bringing it up to date:

[The second romantics are very much *seers:* Théophile Gautier, Leconte de Lisle, Théodore de Banville. But inspecting the invisible and hearing the unheard of being something other than recapturing the Spirit of dead things, Baudelaire is the first seer, king of poets, *a real God.* Still, he lived within too artistic a circle, and the form so much praised in him is mean. Inventing the unknown claims for new forms . . . The new school, called Parnassian, has two seers, Albert Mérat and Paul Verlaine, a true poet.]

It is clear that Rimbaud saw himself as arriving in something like a fourth wave of *voyants,* after the "first" and "second" Romantics, and after the "new school." Of course, it is his marvelous faith in the nineteenth century—that is, faith in the possibilities of his own time—that shows through all the arbitrariness of his pronouncements, as it certainly must for any Romantic poet. But how, for all its weak points and even absurdity, has Rimbaud's candidly evaluative elucidation of the stages in the history of poetry attained something of a classic status? It would certainly have no importance had its author not written the great texts it remained for him to write. It is true, of course, that the twentieth century sees Rimbaud as a continuation of the poetic revolution begun by Baudelaire: Rimbaud's own self-evaluation betrays, then, excellent judgment on his part, an almost oracular vision of how he himself would come to be judged. But his summary account of world literary history would certainly be meaningless if we did not include its counterweight, the thing that it really means and points to: that the poet's eyes are fixed intrepidly on the future, not on the past which he so preposterously sums up. Like Du Bellay in 1549, and like Hugo in 1831, Rimbaud sees himself as announcing a new era, as representing a rising generation of poets that will someday spawn The Poet. The Rimbaud of the "Seer" letter is speaking, in fact, not for himself, but for a generation, for a future that, in his eyes, *has already begun.* He sees himself, in fact, as not alone—an idea to which his metaphor of the symphony gives expression: " . . . j'assiste à l'éclosion de ma pensée: je la regarde, je l'écoute: je lance un coup d'archet: la symphonie fait son remuement dans les profondeurs, ou vient d'un bond sur la scène."

The symphony of poets is there, or is forming, and Rimbaud by no means sees himself as alone in opening a path to the future. The poet who was capable of saying, in his letter to Izambard two days before, that it is false to say "I think," and that one should rather say "Others think me," or perhaps "I am thought" ("C'est faux de dire: Je pense: on devrait dire on me pense"), no longer erects barriers between the symphony in his own mind and the symphony he feels is out there forming—other, as yet unknown "voyants" just like himself, selflessly working to usher in the new poetry that will in turn usher in the new world. In the present letter to Demeny the theme finds a degree of amplification: Rimbaud here writes of the "false meaning" of the "self," for example, and uses the collective "we" several times. At one moment he even discounts himself in order to evoke what really interests him, the future. . . . (pp. 37-8)

But in the true Romantic spirit, nothing can be considered without also envisaging its origins, however remote or obscure. And here, in Rimbaud's letter, Greece is the necessary counterweight to the poet's restless inclinations toward the future. This is why he feels it necessary to write, in connection with the poetry of the future, that "au fond, ce serait encore un peu la Poésie grecque." The ideal of Greece functions as a symbol, first of all, of a superior alternative to the contemporary world, at a time when the almost contrary ideal of Rome, and the concept of Empire, meant a great deal. Which is to say that criticism of conservative France is largely implicit in the evocation of Greece, that cultural star so revered by the alienated artists and progressive thinkers of late nineteenth-century Europe. And Greece implies the city-states of enlightened Athens and heroic Sparta: one need only read *Les Châtiments* and *L'Année terrible* to realize the extent to which these eternal ideals could be applied to the mythical Paris of 1848 and 1870-1871, and the criticism of Bonaparte's and then Thiers's France that they implied. This is reflected throughout Rimbaud's letter in the distinction he draws between Paris and the rest of France—the very distinction that had come to a head in the Commune: " . . . tout est français, c'est-à-dire haïssable au suprême degré; français, pas parisien!"

In addition, then, to expressing the desire to relate his feelings to something outside of himself, to this lost Golden Age, to the wider issues of life and its problems, to a rising generation that had yet to take account of itself, and to the future that this invisible generation was working to bring about, Rimbaud's Greece is also, and above all, an expression of the timeless *present.* We can see in the letter Rimbaud's aspirations toward a total philosophy of life. His letter is the starting point in an urgent appeal to the timeless here and now. He is making his first serious attempt to put into practice the "wholeness" to which he had been aspiring and of which the main document had been, up to that time, the important **"Soleil et chair."** In any case, we must note in the letter the relating of the artistic to the existential, characteristic of the whole line of French Romantic poets. Greece implies the quest for perfection, but certainly not in the traditional sense. Functioning ostensibly as a reference point for thoughts on the history of poetry, the ideal of Greece as employed here allows Rimbaud—and us—to conceive of this history as the development of a series of careers and works toward the full realization of the place that poetry must occupy at the center of life ("vie harmonieuse") and gives to these works the character of experiments, within the framework of the Promethean quest, and therefore necessarily imperfect. Art, society, progress, and the perfection of the individual, as Rimbaud conceived it, are simply inseparable, and the Greek ideal functions as an emblem for this conception. And it is clear that this conception is accompanied, in the "Seer" letter, by a growing resentment of the way in which this essential ideal was being practiced by the recognized and accepted poets of his day. The final paragraph of the letter contains an indictment of more than twenty of these poets, and the epithets used—"innocents," "schoolboys," "dead," "imbeciles," "bohemians"—serve to accentuate their divorce from what Rimbaud saw as reality in all of its ramifications and fullness.

On the other side of the coin, it must be noted that the decline of this poetry-culture, Greece—the abstract repository of Rimbaud's hopes and aspirations up to May and perhaps June of 1871—can also be related to the intellectual vulnerability of his poetic ideal. Linked to a lost state of plenitude, Rimbaud is proposing a poetics that carries with it its own denial. The "Voyant" is fated—to failure, to extinction. (pp. 38-40)

As dark as [his] pronouncement seems to be, it is essentially optimistic. It is, first, Romantic in its acceptation of the myth of progress, and in its affirmation that the individual's work lives on *unaltered* in others after his own destruction. This is, then, a picture of unobstructed poetic progress: no ground that is gained can be lost, literary history marches on through a process of accumulation of knowledge—or rather, each runner passes the baton on to the next. Which is to say that Rimbaud's letter, in its envisionment of the poet's individual destruction in the service of humanity—and this vision outweighs by far all of the letter's comical and ironic elements—is meant as heroic. And cast as it is in the heroic mode, the letter carries its own denial. However, it stops just short of recognizing this. It insists upon announcing something new; and yet, it seems more representative of Rimbauds's progression as a poet up to and including the time of writing, rather than after. Poetry for him still retains an element of transcendence. It is not pure expenditure, because it can purchase—at an admittedly terrible price—progress, time, respite from death for future generations. He has still to watch the Commune in its final week, and with it some of the original hopes and aspirations he had brought to bear upon his poetic vocation come to a crushing and bloody end.

By the spring of 1872—one year later—Rimbaud will have turned away from the concentration upon the extreme urgency of the poet's function in society, and begun to reflect more and more upon the personal artistic experience. How can we begin to understand this apparent deflection from his original poetic goals, and the undeniable disillusion that will be recorded in the poems of the spring of 1872—the **"Derniers vers"** or **"Vers nouveaux et chansons"**? Only through an understanding of the original hopes and beliefs with which Rimbaud began to write poetry, and which pro-

pelled him up through the summer of 1871. The exalted notions of his poetic project, as outlined in the "Seer" letter, served only to make the inevitable fall all the harder.

But in addition to the radical ideal, another of the illusions his ambitions may have aggravated, and one closer to poetical interests, was the belief that a great poem must be a long poem—for only thus may one dominate *à la Hugo*. He had precedents for this, of course: Hugo's *Le Satyre* and Leconte de Lisle's *Qaïn* were two of his favorite and most formative poems. There were also his own two early attempts we mentioned at the outset. These were **"Soleil et chair"** and **"Le forgeron"**—each a good deal longer than almost anything that was being produced under the "Parnassian" label. In the "Seer" letter to Demeny he boasts—probably only half jokingly—of two long poems: " . . . je vous livrerais encore mes *Amants de Paris,* cent hexamètres, Monsieur, et ma *Mort de Paris,* deux cent hexamètres!" And then in a letter to Verlaine in September of 1871, searching perhaps a bit too frantically for a "sponsor" after his failure to interest Théodore de Banville, he wrote: "J'ai fait le projet de faire un grand poème, et je ne peux travailler à Charleville." But then it is probable that Rimbaud wrote no poetry between September of 1871 and the spring of 1872 (—except for the poems written into the *Album Zutique* in the fall of 1871, which are not considered within Rimbaud's work proper). This would leave a long fallow period of many months. Can this be explained without recourse to the tired themes of social, literary, and adolescent revolt? It may very well be that, after having shown so much promise to Verlaine, Rimbaud felt that he was in the impossible position of having to write an acknowledged masterpiece. It must have been with something of this spirit that he had handed to Verlaine, upon his arrival in Paris in September, his great production of May 1871, *Le bateau ivre.*

But only the following month he would emit a statement that, for all its brevity, should be accorded an importance at least equal to that of the "Seer" letter, if one is to understand Rimbaud the theorist. Writing to Demeny on June 10, he will ask him to "burn, absolutely," the entire manuscript of his first collection of poems. "Il faut être absolument moderne," he would later write, at the end of *Une saison en enfer.* A process of resolute bridge-burning and radical self-revision, *à l'instant preès,* more than any of the precepts outlined in the vehement "Seer" letter, is what governs Rimbaud's writing life. (pp. 40-1)

Joseph Bianco, "Rimbaud from Apprentice to Seer," in *Romance Quarterly,* Vol. 37, No. 1, February, 1990, pp. 31-42.

SOURCES FOR FURTHER STUDY

Bonnefoy, Yves. *Rimbaud.* Translated by Paul Schmidt. New York: Harper Colophon, 1973, 145 p.

>Biographical and critical study. Bonnefoy attempts to fashion a sensitive, intimate portrait of Rimbaud during the poet's greatest period of creativity.

Fowlie, Wallace. *Rimbaud.* Chicago: The University of Chicago Press, 1966, 280 p.

>Translation and analysis of *Les illuminations.* Maintains that the work was Rimbaud's effort to resolve the problems of his childhood and to "recover and repair his earliest experience in the world."

Frohock, W. M. *Rimbaud's Poetic Practice: Image and Theme in the Major Poems.* Cambridge, Mass: Harvard University Press, 1963, 250 p.

>Thematic and structural analysis of Rimbaud's poetry. Includes brief bibliography.

Hare, Humphrey. *Sketch for a Portrait of Rimbaud.* New York: Haskell House, 1974, 127 p.

>Biographical study in which Hare maintains that the dominant force in Rimbaud's life was his lust for power.

MacLeish, Archibald. "The Anti-World: Poems of Rimbaud." In his *Poetry and Experience,* pp. 149-72. Boston: Houghton Mifflin Company, 1961.

>Discusses the poetic theory contained in Rimbaud's "lettre du voyant."

Miller, Henry. *The Time of the Assassins: A Study of Rimbaud.* New York: New Directions, 1946, 162 p.

>Praises Rimbaud's poetic genius and asserts that his significance lies in his attempt to bridge the schism between art and life.

Christina Rossetti

1830-1894

(Full name Christina Georgina Rossetti) English poet, short story writer, and prose writer.

INTRODUCTION

Rossetti is ranked among the finest English poets of the nineteenth century. Closely associated with Pre-Raphaelitism, an artistic and literary movement that aspired to recapture the aesthetics of Italian religious painting before Raphael, Rossetti was equally influenced by the religious conservatism and asceticism of the Oxford Movement. Scholars find in her poetry an enduring conflict between these opposing forces, as well as an adeptness with a variety of poetic forms.

Rossetti's father was an Italian exile who settled in London four years before the birth of his daughter. Although Rossetti grew up in England, her Italian heritage remained an important influence throughout her life and provides an interesting contrast to the predominantly English sensibility found in her work. She demonstrated her poetic gifts early, writing sonnets in competition with her brothers William Michael and Dante Gabriel, a practice that undoubtedly developed her command of metrical forms. Always an avid reader, Rossetti began at age eighteen studying Dante, whose works became a major and lasting influence. Among English poets, she favored Samuel Taylor Coleridge, John Keats, Percy Bysshe Shelley, and William Blake.

Rossetti's first published poem appeared in the *Athenaeum* when she was eighteen. Her brother Dante Gabriel founded the Pre-Raphaelite journal *The Germ* in 1852, and Rossetti became a frequent contributor. Her first collection of poetry, *Goblin Market and Other Poems* (1862), gained her immediate recognition as a skilled and original poet. *Goblin Market* was also the first great success for the Pre-Raphaelites and shows their influence in its symbolism, allegory, and rich, sensual imagery. Its title poem, narrating two sisters' encounter with the goblins and their tantalizing fruits, has been variously interpreted as a moral fable for children, an erotic fantasy, and an experiment in meter and rhyme. This volume and her next collection, *The Prince's Progress and Other Poems* (1866), contains much of her finest work and established Rossetti's reputation as an important poet.

Rossetti's poetic production diminished as she grew older and became increasingly committed to writing religious works. A succession of serious illnesses strongly influenced her temperament and outlook on life. Because she often believed herself close to death, religious devotion and mortality became persistent themes in both her poetry and prose. In 1871 she developed Graves' disease and though she published *A Pageant and Other Poems* in 1881, following this illness she concentrated primarily on works of religious prose, such as *The Face of the Deep: A Devotional Commentary on the Apocalypse* (1892). Critics often remark on the inferior quality of the later prose works, but Rossetti's extreme religious devotion was not entirely detrimental to her poetic output. Much of her finest verse was obviously inspired by her all-consuming faith.

Rossetti's religious convictions dominated her personal life as well as her work. As a young woman, she declined two marriage proposals because her suitors' beliefs failed to conform to the tenets of the Anglican Church. Rather than marry, she chose to remain with her mother, an equally devout Anglican. The beautiful sonnet sequence "Monna Innominata," included in *A Pageant and Other Poems*, celebrates Rossetti's denial of human love for the sake of religious purity.

The contradictions and complexities of Rossetti's intellect and experience served as her richest subject matter. Rather than grapple with the social problems that preoccupied such other nineteenth-century literary figures as Thomas Carlyle, John Ruskin, and William Morris, Rossetti chose to explore the themes of love and death. Faulted by some critics for an alleged indifference to social issues, she is praised by most for her simple diction, moral vision, and consummate stylistic technique.

(For further information about Rossetti's life and works, see *Dictionary of Literary Biography*, Vol. 35: *Victorian Poets after 1850; Nineteenth-Century Literature Criticism*, Vol. 2; and *Something about the Author*, Vol. 20. For related criticism, see the entry on the Pre-Raphaelite Movement in *Nineteenth-Century Literature Criticism*, Vol. 20.)

CRITICAL COMMENTARY

EDMUND GOSSE

(essay date 1896)

[Gosse was a prominent turn-of-the-century English man of letters. In the following excerpt from an 1896 revision of an essay that first appeared in print in 1893, he extols Rossetti as a skillful and moral poet.]

Severely true to herself, an artist of conscientiousness as high as her skill is exquisite, [Rossetti] has never swept her fame to sea in a flood of her own outpourings. In the following [essay] I desire to pay no more than a just tribute of respect to one of the most perfect poets of the age—not one of the most powerful, of course, nor one of the most epoch-making, but to one of the most perfect—to a writer toward whom we may not unreasonably expect that students of English literature in the twenty-fourth century may look back as the critics of Alexandria did toward Sappho and toward Erinna. (p. 138)

What is very interesting in her poetry is the union of this fixed religious faith with a hold upon physical beauty and the richer parts of Nature which allies her with her brother and with their younger friends. She does not shrink from strong delineation of the pleasures of life even when she is denouncing them. In one of the most austere of her sacred pieces, she describes the Children of the World in these glowing verses:

Milk-white, wine-flushed, among the vines,
Up and down leaping, to and fro,
Most glad, most full, made strong with wines,
Blooming as peaches pearled with dew,
Their golden windy hair afloat,
Love-music warbling in their throat,
Young men and women come and go.

There is no literary hypocrisy here, no pretence that the apple of life is full of ashes; and this gives a startling beauty, the beauty of artistic contrast, to the poet's studies in morality. Miss Rossetti, indeed, is so didactic in the undercurrent of her mind, so anxious to adorn her tale with a religious moral, that she needs all her art, all her vigorous estimate of physical loveliness, to make her poetry delightful as poetry. That she does make it eminently delightful merely proves her extraordinary native gift. The two long pieces she has written, her two efforts at a long breath, are sustained so well as to make us regret that she has not put out her

---

Principal Works

Goblin Market and Other Poems (poetry) 1862

The Prince's Progress and Other Poems (poetry) 1866

Commonplace and Other Short Stories (short stories) 1870

Sing-Song (children's verse) 1872

A Pageant and Other Poems (poetry) 1881

Poems (poetry) 1882

Time Flies: A Reading Diary (religious prose) 1885

The Face of the Deep: A Devotional Commentary on the Apocalypse (religious prose) 1892

Verses (poetry) 1893

New Poems (poetry) 1896

The Poetical Works of Christina Georgina Rossetti (poetry) 1904

---

powers in the creation of a still more complete and elaborated composition. Of these two poems **"Goblin Market"** is by far the more popular; the other, **"The Prince's Progress,"** which appeared in 1866, has never attracted such attention as it deserves.

It is not necessary to describe a poem so well known to every lover of verse as **"Goblin Market."** It is one of the very few purely fantastic poems of recent times which have really kept up the old tradition of humoresque literature. Its witty and fantastic conception is embroidered with fancies, descriptions, peals of laughing music, which clothe it as a queer Japanese figure may be clothed with brocade, so that the entire effect at last is beautiful and harmonious without ever having ceased to be grotesque. I confess that while I dimly perceive the underlying theme to be a didactic one, and nothing less than the sacrifice of self by a sister to recuperate a sister's virtue, I cannot follow the parable through all its delicious episodes. Like a Japanese work of art, again, one perceives the general intention, and one is satisfied with the beauty of all the detail, without comprehending or wishing to comprehend every part of the execution. For instance, the wonderful scene in which Lizzie sits beleaguered by the goblins, and receives with hard-shut mouth all the syrups that they squeeze against her skin—this from the point of view of poetry is perfect, and needs no apology or commentary; but its place in the parable it would, surely, be extremely hard to find. It is therefore, astonishing to me that the general public, that strange and unaccountable entity, has chosen to prefer **"Goblin Market,"** which we might conceive to be written for poets alone, to **"The Prince's Progress,"** where the parable and the teaching are as clear as noonday. The prince is a handsome, lazy fellow, who sets out late upon his pilgrimage, loiters in bad company by the way, is decoyed by

light loves, and the hope of life, and the desire of wealth, and reaches his destined bride at last, only to find her dead. This has an obvious moral, but it is adorned with verse of the very highest romantic beauty. Every claim which criticism has to make for the singular merit of Miss Rossetti might be substantiated from this little-known romance, from which I must resist the pleasure of quoting more than a couple of stanzas descriptive of daybreak:

> At the death of night and the birth of day,
> When the owl left off his sober play,
> And the bat hung himself out of the way,—
>   Woke the song of mavis and merle,
> And heaven put off its hodden grey
>   For mother-o'-pearl.
>
> Peeped up daisies here and there,
> Here, there, and everywhere;
> Rose a hopeful lark in the air,
>   Spreading out towards the sun his breast;
> While the moon set solemn and fair
>   Away in the West.

With the apparent exceptions of **"Goblin Market"** and **"The Prince's Progress,"** both of which indeed are of a lyrical nature, Miss Rossetti has written only lyrics. All poets are unequal, except the bad ones, who are uniformly bad. Miss Rossetti indulges in the privilege which Wordsworth, Burns, and so many great masters have enjoyed, of writing extremely flat and dull poems at certain moments, and of not perceiving that they are dull or flat. She does not err in being mediocre; her lyrics are bad or good, and the ensuing remarks deal with that portion only of her poems with which criticism is occupied in surveying work so admirably original as hers, namely, that which is worthy of her reputation. Her lyrics, then, are eminent for their glow of colouring, their vivid and novel diction, and for a certain penetrating accent, whether in joy or pain, which rivets the attention. Her habitual tone is one of melancholy reverie, the pathos of which is strangely intensified by her appreciation of beauty and pleasure. There is not a chord of the minor key in **"A Birthday,"** and yet the impression which its cumulative ecstasy leaves upon the nerves is almost pathetic:

> My heart is like a singing-bird
>   Whose nest is in a watered shoot;
> My heart is like an apple-tree
>   Whose boughs are bent with thick-set fruit;
> My heart is like a rainbow-shell
>   That paddles in a halcyon sea;
> My heart is gladder than all these
>   Because my love is come to me.
>
> Raise me a dais of silk and down;
>   Hang it with vair and purple dyes;
> Carve it in doves and pomegranates,
>   And peacocks with a hundred eyes;

Work it in gold and silver grapes,
  In leaves and silver fleurs-de-lys;
Because the birthday of my life
  Is come, my love is come to me.

It is very rarely, indeed, that the poet strikes so jubilant a note as this. Her customary music is said, often poignantly sad. Her lyrics have that *desiderium,* that obstinate longing for something lost out of life, which Shelley's have, although her Christian faith gives her regret a more resigned and sedate character than his possesses. In the extremely rare gift of song-writing Miss Rossetti has been singularly successful. Of the poets of our time she stands next to Lord Tennyson in this branch of the art, in the spontaneous and complete quality of her *lieder,* and in their propriety for the purpose of being sung. At various times this art has flourished in our race; eighty years ago, most of the poets could write songs, but it is almost a lost art in our generation. The songs of our living poets are apt to be over-polished or under-polished, so simple as to be bald, or else so elaborate as to be wholly unsuitable for singing. But such a song as this is not unworthy to be classed with the melodies of Shakespeare, of Burns, of Shelley:

Oh, roses for the flush of youth,
  And laurel for the perfect prime;
But pluck an ivy-branch for me
  Grown old before my time.

Oh, violets for the grave of youth,
  And bay for those dead in their prime;
Give me the withered leaves I chose
  Before in the old time.

Her music is very delicate, and it is no small praise to her that she it is who, of living verse-writers, has left the strongest mark on the metrical nature of that miraculous artificer of verse, Mr. Swinburne. In his *Poems and Ballads,* as other critics have long ago pointed out, as was shown when that volume first appeared, several of Miss Rossetti's discoveries were transferred to his more scientific and elaborate system of harmonies, and adapted to more brilliant effects. The reader of Mr. Swinburne would judge that of all his immediate contemporaries Miss Rossetti and the late Mr. FitzGerald, the translator of *Omar Khayyám,* had been those who had influenced his style the most. Miss Rossetti, however, makes no pretence to elaborate metrical effects; she is even sometimes a little naïve, a little careless, in her rough, rhymeless endings, and metrically her work was better in her youth than it has been since.

The sonnets present points of noticeable interest. They are few, but they are of singular excellence. They have this peculiarity, that many of them are objective. Now the great bulk of good sonnets is purely subjective—occupied with reverie, with regret, with moral or religious enthusiasm. Even the celebrated sonnets of Gabriel Rossetti will be found to be mainly subjective.

On the question of the relative merit of the sonnets of the brother and the sister, I hold a view in which I believe that few will at present coincide; I am certain Miss Rossetti herself will not. If she honours me by reading these pages, she may possibly recollect a conversation, far more important to me of course than to her, which we held in 1870, soon after I had first the privilege of becoming known to her. I was venturing to praise her sonnets, when she said, with the sincerity of evident conviction, that they "could only be admired before Gabriel, by printing his in the *Fortnightly Review,* showed the source of their inspiration." I was sure then, and I am certain now, that she was wrong. The sonnets are not the product of, they do not even bear any relation to those of, her brother.

Well do I recollect the publication of these sonnets of Gabriel Rossetti, in 1869, when, at a moment when curiosity regarding the mysterious painter-poet was at its height, they suddenly blossomed forth in a certain number of the *Fortnightly Review,* in whose solemn pages we were wont to see nothing lighter or more literary than esoteric politics and the prose mysteries of positivism. We were dazzled by their Italian splendour of phraseology, amazed that such sonorous anapests, that such a burst of sound, should be caged within the sober limits of the sonnets, fascinated by the tenderness of the long-drawn amorous rhetoric; but there were some of us who soon recovered an equilibrium of taste, in which it seemed that the tradition of the English sonnet, its elegance of phrase, its decorum of movement, were too rudely displaced by this brilliant Italian intruder, and that underneath the melody and the glowing diction, the actual thought, the valuable and intelligible residue of poetry, was too often much more thin than Rossetti allowed it to be in the best of his other poems. As to Gabriel Rossetti's sonnets being his own best work, as has been asserted, I for one must entirely and finally disagree. I believe that of all his poetry they form the section which will be the first to tarnish. Quite otherwise is it with Miss Christina Rossetti. It is in certain of her objective sonnets that her touch is most firm and picturesque, her intelligence most weighty, and her style most completely characteristic. The reader need but turn to **"After Death," "On the Wing," "Venus's Looking-Glass"** (in the volume of 1875), and the marvellous **"A Triad"** to concede the truth of this; while in the more obvious subjective manner of sonnet-writing she is one of the most successful poets of our time. In **"The World,"** where she may be held to come closest to her brother as a sonneteer, she seems to me to surpass him.

From the first a large section of Miss Rossetti's work has been occupied with sacred and devotional themes. Through this most rare and difficult department of the art, which so few essay without breaking on the Scylla of doctrine on the one hand, or being whirled in the Charybdis of commonplace dulness on the other, she has steered with extraordinary success. Her sacred poems are truly sacred, and yet not unpoetical. As a religious poet of our time she has no rival but Cardinal Newman, and it could only be schismatic prejudice or absence of critical faculty which should deny her a place, as a poet, higher than that of our exquisite master of prose. To find her exact parallel it is at once her strength and her snare that we must go back to the middle of the seventeenth century. She is the sister of George Herbert; she is of the family of Crashaw, of Vaughan, of Wither. The metrical address of Herbert has been perilously attractive to her; the broken stanzas of **"Consider"** or of **"Long Barren"** remind us of the age when pious aspirations took the form of wings, or hour-glasses, or lamps of the temple. The most thrilling and spirited of her sacred poems have been free from these Marini-like subtleties. There is only what is best in the quaint and fervent school of Herbert visible in such pieces as **"The Three Enemies," "A Rose Plant in Jericho," "Passing Away, Saith the World,"** and **"Up Hill."** Still more completely satisfactory, perhaps, is **"Amor Mundi,"** first included in the *Poems* of 1875, which takes rank as one of the most solemn, imaginative, and powerful lyrics on a purely religious subject ever printed in England. (pp. 148-57)

Edmund Gosse, "Christina Rossetti," in his *Critical Kit-Kats,* 1913. Reprint by Scholarly Press, 1971, pp. 135-62.

VIRGINIA WOOLF

(essay date 1930)

[Woolf was an English novelist, essayist, and critic. In the following essay, written in 1930 to celebrate the one-hundredth anniversary of Rossetti's birth, she offers an enthusiastic assessment of Rossetti's poetry, perceiving her as an instinctive talent.]

On the fifth of this December [1930] Christina Rossetti will celebrate her centenary, or, more properly speaking, we shall celebrate it for her, and perhaps not a little to her distress, for she was one of the shyest of women, and to be spoken of, as we shall certainly speak of her, would have caused her acute discomfort. Nevertheless, it is inevitable; centenaries are inexorable; talk of her we must. We shall read her life; we shall read her letters; we shall study her portraits, speculate about her diseases—of which she had a great variety; and rattle the drawers of her writing-table, which are for the most part empty. Let us begin with the biography—for what could be more amusing? As everybody knows, the fascination of reading biographies is irresistible. No sooner have we opened the pages of Miss Sandars's careful

and competent book (*Life of Christina Rossetti,* by Mary F. Sandars) than the old illusion comes over us. Here is the past and all its inhabitants miraculously sealed as in a magic tank; all we have to do is to look and to listen and to listen and to look and soon the little figures—for they are rather under life size—will begin to move and to speak, and as they move we shall arrange them in all sorts of patterns of which they were ignorant, for they thought when they were alive that they could go where they liked; and as they speak we shall read into their sayings all kinds of meanings which never struck them, for they believed when they were alive that they said straight off whatever came into their heads. But once you are in a biography all is different.

Here, then, is Hallam Street, Portland Place, about the year 1830; and here are the Rossettis, an Italian family consisting of father and mother and four small children. The street was unfashionable and the home rather poverty-stricken; but the poverty did not matter, for, being foreigners, the Rossettis did not care much about the customs and conventions of the usual middle-class British family. They kept themselves to themselves, dressed as they liked, entertained Italian exiles, among them organ-grinders and other distressed compatriots, and made ends meet by teaching and writing and other odd jobs. By degrees Christina detached herself from the family group. It is plain that she was a quiet and observant child, with her own way of life already fixed in her head—she was to write—but all the more did she admire the superior competence of her elders. Soon we begin to surround her with a few friends and to endow her with a few characteristics. She detested parties. She dressed anyhow. She liked her brother's friends and little gatherings of young artists and poets who were to reform the world, rather to her amusement, for although so sedate, she was also whimsical and freakish, and liked making fun of people who took themselves with egotistic solemnity. And though she meant to be a poet she had very little of the vanity and stress of young poets; her verses seem to have formed themselves whole and entire in her head, and she did not worry very much what was said of them because in her own mind she knew that they were good. She had also immense powers of admiration—for her mother, for example, who was so quiet, and so sagacious, so simple and so sincere; and for her elder sister Maria, who had no taste for painting or for poetry, but was, for that very reason, perhaps more vigorous and effective in daily life. For example, Maria always refused to visit the Mummy Room at the British Museum because, she said, the Day of Resurrection might suddenly dawn and it would be very unseemly if the corpses had to put on immortality under the gaze of mere sightseers—a reflection which had not struck Christina, but seemed to her admirable. Here, of course, we, who are outside the tank, enjoy a hearty laugh, but

Christina, who is inside the tank and exposed to all its heats and currents, thought her sister's conduct worthy of the highest respect. Indeed, if we look at her a little more closely we shall see that something dark and hard, like a kernel, had already formed in the centre of Christina Rossetti's being.

It was religion, of course. Even when she was quite a girl her life-long absorption in the relation of the soul with God had taken possession of her. Her sixty-four years might seem outwardly spent in Hallam Street and Endsleigh Gardens and Torrington Square, but in reality she dwelt in some curious region where the spirit strives towards an unseen God—in her case, a dark God, a harsh God—a God who decreed that all the pleasures of the world were hateful to Him. The theatre was hateful, the opera was hateful, nakedness was hateful—when her friend Miss Thompson painted naked figures in her pictures she had to tell Christina that they were fairies, but Christina saw through the imposture—everything in Christina's life radiated from that knot of agony and intensity in the centre. Her belief regulated her life in the smallest particulars. It taught her that chess was wrong, but that whist and cribbage did not matter. But also it interfered in the most tremendous questions of her heart. There was a young painter called James Collinson, and she loved James Collinson and he loved her, but he was a Roman Catholic and so she refused him. Obligingly he became a member of the Church of England, and she accepted him. Vacillating, however, for he was a slippery man, he wobbled back to Rome, and Christina, though it broke her heart and for ever shadowed her life, cancelled the engagement. Years afterwards another, and it seems better-founded, prospect of happiness presented itself. Charles Cayley proposed to her. But alas, this abstract and erudite man who shuffled about the world in a state of absent-minded dishabille, and translated the gospel into Iroquois, and asked smart ladies at a party 'whether they were interested in the Gulf Stream', and for a present gave Christina a sea mouse preserved in spirits, was, not unnaturally, a freethinker. Him, too, Christina put from her. Though 'no woman ever loved a man more deeply', she would not be the wife of a sceptic. She who loved the 'obtuse and furry'—the wombats, toads, and mice of the earth—and called Charles Cayley 'my blindest buzzard, my special mole', admitted no moles, wombats, buzzards, or Cayleys to her heaven.

So one might go on looking and listening for ever. There is no limit to the strangeness, amusement, and oddity of the past sealed in a tank. But just as we are wondering which cranny of this extraordinary territory to explore next, the principal figure intervenes. It is as if a fish, whose unconscious gyrations we had been watching in and out of reeds, round and round rocks, suddenly dashed at the glass and broke it. A tea-party is the occasion. For some reason Christina went to a party given by Mrs. Virtue Tebbs. What happened there is unknown—perhaps something was said in a casual, frivolous, tea-party way about poetry. At any rate,

> suddenly there uprose from a chair and paced forward into the centre of the room a little woman dressed in black, who announced solemnly, 'I am Christina Rossetti!' and having so said, returned to her chair.

With those words the glass is broken. Yes [she seems to say], I am a poet. You who pretend to honour my centenary are no better than the idle people at Mrs. Tebbs's tea-party. Here you are rambling among unimportant trifles, rattling my writing-table drawers, making fun of the Mummies and Maria and my love affairs when all I care for you to know is here. Behold this green volume. It is a copy of my collected works. It costs four shillings and sixpence. Read that. And so she returns to her chair.

How absolute and unaccommodating these poets are! Poetry, they say, has nothing to do with life. Mummies and wombats, Hallam Street and omnibuses, James Collinson and Charles Cayley, sea mice and Mrs. Virtue Tebbs, Torrington Square and Endsleigh Gardens, even the vagaries of religious belief, are irrelevant, extraneous, superfluous, unreal. It is poetry that matters. The only question of any interest is whether that poetry is good or bad. But this question of poetry, one might point out if only to gain time, is one of the greatest difficulty. Very little of value has been said about poetry since the world began. The judgment of contemporaries is almost always wrong. For example, most of the poems which figure in Christina Rossetti's complete works were rejected by editors. Her annual income from her poetry was for many years about ten pounds. On the other hand, the works of Jean Ingelow, as she noted sardonically, went into eight editions. There were, of course, among her contemporaries one or two poets and one or two critics whose judgment must be respectfully consulted. But what very different impressions they seem to gather from the same works—by what different standards they judge! For instance, when Swinburne read her poetry he exclaimed: 'I have always thought that nothing more glorious in poetry has ever been written', and went on to say of her New Year Hymn

> that it was touched as with the fire and bathed as in the light of sunbeams, tuned as to chords and cadences of refluent sea-music beyond reach of harp and organ, large echoes of the serene and sonorous tides of heaven.

Then Professor Saintsbury comes with his vast learning, and examines **'Goblin Market,'** and reports that

The metre of the principal poem ['Goblin Market'] may be best described as a dedoggerelised Skeltonic, with the gathered music of the various metrical progress since Spenser, utilised in the place of the wooden rattling of the followers of Chaucer. There may be discerned in it the same inclination towards line irregularity which has broken out, at different times, in the Pindaric of the late seventeenth and earlier eighteenth centuries, and in the rhymelessness of Sayers earlier and of Mr. Arnold later.

And then there is Sir Walter Raleigh:

I think she is the best poet alive. . . . The worst of it is you cannot lecture on really pure poetry any more than you can talk about the ingredients of pure water—it is adulterated, methylated, sanded poetry that makes the best lectures. The only thing that Christina makes me want to do, is cry, not lecture.

It would appear, then, that there are at least three schools of criticism: the refluent sea-music school, the line-irregularity school, and the school that bids one not criticize but cry. This is confusing; if we follow them all we shall only come to grief. Better perhaps read for oneself, expose the mind bare to the poem, and transcribe in all its haste and imperfection whatever may be the result of the impact. In this case it might run something as follows: O Christina Rossetti, I have humbly to confess that though I know many of your poems by heart, I have not read your works from cover to cover. I have not followed your course and traced your development. I doubt indeed that you developed very much. You were an instinctive poet. You saw the world from the same angle always. Years and the traffic of the mind with men and books did not affect you in the least. You carefully ignored any book that could shake your faith or any human being who could trouble your instincts. You were wise perhaps. Your instinct was so sure, so direct, so intense that it produced poems that sing like music in one's ears—like a melody by Mozart or an air by Gluck. Yet for all its symmetry, yours was a complex song. When you struck your harp many strings sounded together. Like all instinctives you had a keen sense of the visual beauty of the world. Your poems are full of gold dust and 'sweet geraniums' varied brightness'; your eye noted incessantly how rushes are 'velvet-headed', and lizards have a 'strange metallic mail'—your eye, indeed, observed with a sensual Pre-Raphaelite intensity that must have surprised Christina the Anglo-Catholic. But to her you owed perhaps the fixity and sadness of your muse. The pressure of a tremendous faith circles and clamps together these little songs. Perhaps they owe to it their solidity. Certainly they owe to it their sadness—your God was a harsh God, your heavenly crown was set with thorns. No sooner have you feasted on beauty with your eyes than your mind tells you that beauty is vain and beauty passes. Death, oblivion, and rest lap round your songs

with their dark wave. And then, incongruously, a sound of scurrying and laughter is heard. There is the patter of animals' feet and the odd guttural notes of rooks and the snufflings of obtuse furry animals grunting and nosing. For you were not a pure saint by any means. You pulled legs; you tweaked noses. You were at war with all humbug and pretence. Modest as you were, still you were drastic, sure of your gift, convinced of your vision. A firm hand pruned your lines; a sharp ear tested their music. Nothing soft, otiose, irrelevant cumbered your pages. In a word, you were an artist. And thus was kept open, even when you wrote idly, tinkling bells for your own diversion, a pathway for the descent of that fiery visitant who came now and then and fused your lines into that indissoluble connexion which no hand can put asunder:

But bring me poppies brimmed with sleepy death
And ivy choking what it garlandeth
    And primroses that open to the moon.

Indeed so strange is the constitution of things, and so great the miracle of poetry, that some of the poems you wrote in your little back room will be found adhering in perfect symmetry when the Albert Memorial is dust and tinsel. Our remote posterity will be singing:

When I am dead, my dearest,

or:

My heart is like a singing bird,

when Torrington Square is a reef of coral perhaps and the fishes shoot in and out where your bedroom window used to be; or perhaps the forest will have reclaimed those pavements and the wombat and the ratel will be shuffling on soft, uncertain feet among the green undergrowth that will then tangle the area railings. In view of all this, and to return to your biography, had I been present when Mrs. Virtue Tebbs gave her party, and had a short elderly woman in black risen to her feet and advanced to the middle of the room, I should certainly have committed some indiscretion—have broken a paper-knife or smashed a tea-cup in the awkward ardour of my admiration when she said, 'I am Christina Rossetti'. (pp. 54-60)

Virginia Woolf, "I Am Christina Rossetti," in her *Collected Essays, Vol. IV*, Harcourt, Brace & World, Inc., 1967, pp. 54-60.

GEORGINA BATTISCOMBE
(essay date 1981)

[Battiscombe is an English biographer whose studies of nineteenth-century figures have been praised as sympathetic and perceptive. In the following excerpt from her *Christina Rossetti: A Divided Life*, she discusses the collection *Goblin Market*, providing biographical background and offering both Christian and sexual interpretations of the poems.]

Eighteen sixty-one was, on the whole, a happy year for Christina. For the first time she achieved a measure of real success as a writer, and though she could tell Mrs Heimann, an old family friend, that of necessity she was 'husbanding my not exuberant strength' she was nevertheless enjoying what was for her a period of good health. 'Perhaps the least unhealthy years of her womanhood were towards 1861,' William [Michael Rossetti] was to write. Then, in June, she had the treat of a first holiday abroad, when she went with William and her mother to France, visiting Paris, and from there going on to Rouen, Saint Lô, Avranches, Coutances (where they stayed for nearly three weeks) and home by way of Jersey.

In the autumn came what must always be one of the most thrilling moments in an author's life, the acceptance of her first book for publication. Alexander Macmillan planned to bring out her poems in 'an exceedingly pretty little volume', but he did not appear to be particularly enthusiastic about this project. 'I quite think a selection of them would have a chance—or to put it more truly that with some omissions they might do', he wrote to Dante Gabriel. 'At least I would run the risk of a small edition.' The book was to be called *Goblin Market* and was to include a selection of lyrics as well as the title-poem. Dante Gabriel was to supply two woodcuts as illustrations. So speedy was the publishing process in 1861 that *Goblin Market* was planned as a Christmas book for that year, but in the event it did not appear until March 1862, less than a month after Lizzie Rossetti had died of an overdose of laudanum.

Of Christina's reaction to this tragedy we know nothing. As so often at a crucial moment in her life no letters survive, no scrap of notes or diary, no word of oral tradition to tell us something of her thoughts and feelings. She had few intimate friends and no regular correspondents apart from the members of her own family, who were all at home at the time of Lizzie's death; no need, therefore, for letter-writing. Unable to face the house at Chatham Place with its memories of Lizzie, Dante Gabriel came back to the family home and remained there until he could find rooms for himself in Lincoln's Inn Fields. In October he moved to Tudor House, Cheyne Walk, an old house overlooking the river which he had loved so well at Chatham Place. At the back of the house was a large garden where he could keep a menagerie of strange birds and animals, peacocks, racoons, an armadillo, a zebra, and a furry wombat which was Christina's favourite. (It was she, and not Dante Gabriel, who had first discovered one of these charming little creatures at the zoo.)

Like the good brother that he was Dante Gabriel took real pleasure in the success of Christina's book, sending her copies of reviews, which were on the whole enthusiastic although the sales were at first slightly disappointing. Reading these poems the first impression is one of freshness. Here is a new and very individual voice. Christina has two gifts invaluable to any singer whether poet or musician, a clear, pure tone, and a very acute ear. 'Your instinct was so clear, so direct, so intense,' Virginia Woolf wrote of her, 'that it produced poems that sing like music in one's ears—like a melody by Mozart or an air by Gluck' [see excerpt dated 1930]. The irregularity which so much displeased Ruskin is one of the greatest charms of her poetry; in her verse 'it is this quality of the unexpected, the avoidance of the *cliché* in metre, the fact that here and there you must beat time in a rest of the melody, that gives it its fascination and its music,' said Ford Madox Ford.

Nowhere is her technical skill more apparent than in the title poem, **'Goblin Market.'** Maurice Bowra speaks of 'her command of a rippling metre'; but sometimes she ripples so much that she approaches perilously near to a Gilbert and Sullivan patter-song:

> It suffices. What suffices?
> All suffices, reckoned rightly;
> Spring shall bloom where now the ice is.

In **'Goblin Market,'** however, this short, tripping metre exactly suits the fairy-tale subject, and here Christina varies it with a skill that amounts almost to genius:

> Come buy, come buy:
> Our grapes fresh from the vine,
> Pomegranates full and fine,
> Dates and sharp bullaces,
> Rare pears and greengages,
> Damsons and bilberries,
> Taste them and try:
> Currants and gooseberries,
> Bright-fire-like barberries,
> Figs to fill your mouth,
> Citrons from the South,
> Sweet to tongue and sound to eye;
> Come buy, come buy.

'Goblin Market' is perhaps the best known and most admired of Christina's poems, and with good reason, for **'Goblin Market'** is that rare thing, a wholly satisfactory narrative poem. Christina's poetic invention never flags; she manages to hold our attention from beginning to end. The story is a fairy-tale with overtones. Day after day two sisters, Laura and Lizzie, hear the goblins crying their wares. Lizzie flees from temptation but Laura is less prudent. One evening she buys the goblin fruit with a curl from her golden head and eats her fill. When she returns home Lizzie gently upbraids her:

> Dear, you should not stay so late,
> Twilight is not good for maidens;
> Should not loiter in the glen
> In the haunts of goblin men.
> Do you not remember Jeanie,
> How she met them in the moonlight,
> Took their gifts both choice and many,
> Ate their fruits and wore their flowers
> Plucked from bowers
> Where summer ripens at all hours?
> But ever in the moonlight
> She pined and pined away;
> Sought them by night and day,
> Found them no more, but dwindled and grew grey;
> Then fell with the first snow.

Laura now begins to pine away as Jeanie had pined, craving the magic fruit which no one may taste twice. Those who have fallen victim to the goblins' wiles can never again hear them calling, never again buy their wares. But Lizzie hears them:

> Beside the brook, along the glen,
> She heard the tramp of goblin men,
> The voice and stir
> Poor Laura could not hear;
> Longed to buy fruit to comfort her,
> But feared to pay too dear.

At length Lizzie masters her fear and seeks out the goblins, begging them to **sell** her their fruit so that she can take it back to Laura. This they will not do unless she first tastes it herself and when she refuses they set upon her:

> Their tones waxed loud,
> Their looks were evil.
> Lashing their tails
> They trod and hustled her,
> Clawed with their nails,
> Barking, mewing, hissing, mocking,
> Tore her gown and soiled her stocking,
> Twitched her hair out by the roots,
> Stamped upon her tender feet,
> Held her hands and squeezed their fruits
> Against her mouth to make her eat.

But she is not to be moved: and at last the goblins tire of tormenting her and vanish. With her face covered with fruit pulp and running with juice she hurries home to Laura and cries to her to make haste:

> Hug me, kiss me, suck my juices

> Squeezed from goblin fruits for you,
> Goblin pulp and goblin dew.
> Eat me, drink me, love me:
> Laura, make much of me;
> For your sake I have braved the glen
> And had to do with goblin merchant men.

Laura is saved by Lizzie's self-sacrifice; she will never forget 'how her sister stood, In deadly peril to do her good. And win the fiery antidote'. Some readers may feel that the poem falls away at the end and that the last six lines sound a note of bathos:

> For there is no friend like a sister
> In calm or stormy weather;
> To cheer one on the tedious way,
> To fetch one if one goes astray,
> To lift one if one totters down,
> To strengthen whilst one stands.

Others may be reminded of the last scene of *Don Giovanni* when after the statue of the Commendatore has dragged the Don down to hell the remaining characters step forward and in a brief finale bid the audience consider the all-too-evident moral of the tale. Perhaps both Christina Rossetti and Mozart thought some drop in tension was advisable before the return to everyday life; or perhaps they feared that, left to ourselves, our sympathies would be with the reprehensible Laura and Don Giovanni rather than with the virtuous but slightly boring Lizzie and Don Ottavio.

The moral of Christina's fable must not be pressed too hard since she herself said that in her own intention **'Goblin Market'** was no allegory at all. The poem can be read at many levels of meaning, as a straightforward fairy-story, as a parable of temptation, sin and redemption, as a hymn in praise of sisterly devotion, or as a sexual fantasy. The sexual interpretation has been applied ribaldly in an article in the magazine *Playboy,* and in all seriousness by [Lona Mosk Packer, in her *Christina Rossetti,* 1963] and by Maureen Duffy in *The Erotic World of Faery* (1974). Mrs Packer provides 'an analysis of the poem in the light of the emotional facts of Christina's life,' that is to say, in the light of the 'fact' of her 'outlawed love' for [William Bell] Scott.

A month before Christina finished **'Goblin Market'** Scott, while painting at Wallington, met Alice Boyd, a handsome woman in her thirties and herself something of an artist. From this meeting sprang what Scott himself described as 'friendship at first sight', a friendship which soon developed into a thoroughgoing and lifelong love-affair. 'That Scott could have "turned from one love to another" with such apparent ease must have been a serious shock to Christina,' Mrs Packer writes. 'His behaviour would have shown her the unstable nature of his earlier attachment to her, would have revealed the depth of the abyss into which she had almost plunged, the peril of the temptation from which, like Laura, she had been saved.' (Laura, by the way, had not been saved from temptation but had yielded to it.)

Maureen Duffy does not connect the poem with any actual love of Christina's but instead sees it as an erotic fantasy, a collection of sexual symbols. Thus the goblins 'are mostly in phallic bird and fish forms' and the two sisters, Laura and Lizzie, are an example of 'the double female image' which is 'an interesting component of the period's eroticism'. Dante Gabriel's woodcut of the sisters folded in each other's arms certainly bears out this theory. According to Maureen Duffy 'two girls entwined 'cheek to cheek and breast to breast Locked together in one nest" are no longer individuals but duplicate images ripe for polygamy'. Christina herself, however, did not see them thus; whatever notions may have been floating about in her subconscious mind, consciously she may well have remembered her father's description of herself and Maria as 'lovely turtle-doves in the nest of love', a description which of course can have been itself an unconscious piece of eroticism.

The sexual undertones in **'Goblin Market'** are fairly obvious. Even small children, too young to be aware of sex, sometimes find themselves, for no reason that they can understand or explain, obscurely puzzled and embarrassed by the poem. A sexual interpretation is a legitimate and convincing one, but it must not be

Title page of *Goblin Market, and Other Poems,* designed by Rossetti's brother Dante Gabriel Rossetti.

pushed too far nor must it be regarded as the only permissible meaning. Readers instinctively equate the goblin fruit with illicit sexual experience and, because this fruit can only be enjoyed once, they connect it, though less definitely, with the loss of virginity. Almost certainly this is what Christina herself understood and intended; but further than this she did not go, nor did she, consciously at least, read any sexual significance into the details of her parable. Of course she was interested in love and sex, and of course she was strongly affected by the fact that her own sexual desires had not been satisfied; she would have been less than human otherwise. But if she was preoccupied with *eros* she was far more deeply preoccupied with *agape.* The religion to which she sacrificed her hopes of sexual love was the very core and centre of her life; and although it has been almost wholly neglected by the critics, the religious interpretation of **'Goblin Market'** is much nearer to her own way of thought than the sexual one.

'Goblin Market' has obvious connections with the story of Eve, a theme which occurs frequently in Christina's poetry, in **'An Afterthought'** for instance, and in **'Bird and Beast.'** One of her most quoted poems is actually entitled **'Eve'**—a poem like **'Goblin Market'** written in the short irregular metre which is particularly her own:

> How have Eden bowers grown
> Without Adam to bend them?
> How have Eden flowers blown,
> Squandering their sweet breath,
> Without me to tend them?
> The Tree of Life was ours,
> Tree twelvefold-fruited,
> Most lofty tree that flowers,
> Most deeply rooted:
> I chose the Tree of Death.

Laura cannot resist temptation; she eats the goblin fruit, dwindles and pines, apparently 'knocking at Death's door'. So the human race, in the person of Eve, is tempted by the serpent and eats 'the fruit of that forbidden tree whose mortal taste Brought death into the world and all our woe'. Laura is saved by the self-sacrifice of her sister, who deliberately faces temptation but does not yield to it. Lizzie stands up to the vicious attacks of the goblins, braving mockery and terror and pain, and through her suffering she wins 'the fiery antidote' which alone can save Laura. According to the Christian faith, Christ, the brother of us all, of his own will chose to face temptation, to suffer and to die, and by his sacrifice to win salvation for mankind. The parallel is obvious. Again, details must not be pressed too hard nor must this explanation be regarded as excluding all others; but if the sexual interpretation throws some light on Christina's subconscious mind the Christian one is closer to her conscious thought.

The shorter poems in the *Goblin Market* volume

are divided into two sections, religious and secular. The secular section is a well-chosen and comprehensive selection from the poems she was writing from about 1848 to 1861. Here are two of the best of her sonnets, **'Remember Me'** and **'After Death';** here are poems reminiscent of Border ballads; and here too is **'In the Round Tower at Jhansi,'** a successful experiment in the manner of Browning, its subject an actual incident during the Indian Mutiny. Significantly, the book contains no less than four poems listed simply as 'Song'; and many more might be so described, for the general tone is lyrical in the strict sense of that word.

Not all the poems, however, fall into this category. Two ballads, **'Sister Maude'** and **'Noble Sisters,'** tell of the treachery of a sister in contradiction of the moral so carefully explained at the end of **'Goblin Market.'** That sinister little colloquy, **'The Hour and the Ghost,'** is a good example of Christina's preoccupation with the occult and the macabre. (The still more sinister poem, **'A Nightmare,'** was written about this time but not published till after her death.) One longer poem is in a class by itself. William describes **'My Dream'** as an example of 'the odd freakishness which flecked the extreme and almost excessive seriousness of her thought'.

Mrs Packer treats this poem simply as a sex fantasy. She will have it that the magnificent and terrifying crocodile of Christina's dream represents Scott, her supposed lover, because 'beauty inspires terror only in a love relationship', a statement of doubtful validity, to say the least. She quotes the horrifying lines describing how the crowned crocodile devours all the other crocodiles:

> An execrable appetite arose,
> He battened on them, crunched, and sucked them in.
> He knew no law, he feared no binding law,
> But ground them with inexorable jaw.
> The luscious fat distilled upon his chin,
> While still like hungry death he fed his maw;
> Till, every minor crocodile being dead
> And buried too, himself gorged to the full,
> He slept with breath oppressed and unstrung claw.

'Read symbolically,' Mrs Packer comments, 'the lines reveal their sexual significance, for what Christina is doing here is substituting one sort of sensuous appetite for another, a common form of displacement in dreams.' This may make sense; but nevertheless there is no ground for identifying Christina's love, and therefore the crocodile, with Bell Scott. To put either James Collinson or Charles Cayley in the place of this regal monster is palpably absurd. If **'My Dream'** is to be interpreted sexually—and such an interpretation may well be the correct one—the crocodile must be taken as representing the Male in general, not any particular man.

The poem has all the nightmare inconsequence of a real dream. Standing by the river Euphrates the dreamer sees a host of young crocodiles:

> Each crocodile was girt with massive gold
> And polished stones that with their wearers grew

After this typical dream fantasy of growing jewels she describes how one crocodile grew larger and more powerful than the rest:

> But special burnishment adorned his mail
> And special terror weighed upon his frown

This crocodile devours all the other crocodiles and, satiated, falls asleep. Now comes, as in a real dream, a totally inconsequent development:

> In sleep he dwindled to the common size,
> And all the empire faded from his coat.
> Then from far off a wingèd vessel came,
> Swift as a swallow, subtle as a flame;
> I know not what it bore of freight or host,
> But white it was as an avenging ghost.

The crocodile's reaction to this strange craft is surprising:

> Lo, as the purple shadow swept the sands,
> The prudent crocodile rose on his feet
> And shed appropriate tears and wrung his hands.

The picture of a crocodile wringing his hands suggests a conceit out of *Alice in Wonderland,* another dream fantasy which the pundits regard as sexual in origin. Oddest of all is the epithet 'prudent'. Dante Gabriel, for no apparent reason, borrowed this term as a nickname for William Morris, a man who bore no resemblance to a crocodile and who was certainly not prudent.

In the poem itself Christina emphatically declares that the dream was a real one—'Hear now a curious dream I dreamed last night. Each word whereof is weighed and sifted truth'—but against her own copy she wrote the words 'Not a real dream'. What then is the origin of this astonishing fancy? The obvious comparison is with De Quincey's opium-induced visions of the horrible, ubiquitous crocodile: 'All the feet of the tables, sofas etc. soon became instinct with life: the abominable head of the crocodile and his leering eyes looked out at me multiplied into a thousand repetitions; and I stood loathing and fascinated.' There is no evidence, however, to prove that Christina ever read that particular passage from *The Confessions of an English Opium-Eater,* much less that it was in her mind when writing **'My Dream.'** Apart from De Quincey, the nearest literary parallel is to be found in the Bible, in the Old Testament prophets and in particular the Book of Daniel—is this the explanation of the reference to the Euphrates?—and in the New Testament Apocalypse or Book of Revelation. Christina was a great student of the Bible with a special liking for the Apocalypse (in later life she was to write a devotional commentary on that book). She had a remarkably vivid visual imagination and plenty of time for day-dreaming. Some of these day-dreams may have taken the form of quasi-visions akin to the biblical visions which were so much in her mind. So Christina may have 'seen' her crocodile fantasy, but realising that most readers would have no experience of such waking dreams or visions, she transposed it into a sleeping dream. It was for a later generation, reared on modern psychology rather than on Bible stories, to interpret her vision as an emanation from her subconscious mind, probably sexual in origin. Christina herself was at a loss as to its meaning. (Significantly enough, biblical visions were often incomprehensible to the visionary until they were interpreted.)

> What can it mean? you ask. I answer not
> For meaning, but myself must echo, What?

The puzzled reader can only re-echo that query.

The third section of the *Goblin Market* volume is headed 'Devotional Pieces'. On the whole it is disappointing, though it contains a few remarkable poems. Christina herself chose the verses to be included, with help from Dante Gabriel and from Macmillan, and therefore it is she who is herself responsible for placing **'Sleep at Sea'** in this section. If this haunting poem is a religious poem so too is **'The Ancient Mariner.'** Here also is **'A Better Resurrection,'** one of the most notable of her religious poems:

> I have no wit, no words, no tears;
>   My heart within me like a stone
> Is numbed too much for hopes or fears.
>   Look right, look left, I dwell alone;
> I lift mine eyes, but dimmed with grief
>   No everlasting hills I see;
> My life is in the falling leaf;
>   O Jesus, quicken me.

The cry is one of such purely human anguish that the last line strikes on the reader with a sense of shock. For Christina there was no deep division between *eros* and *agape,* love human and love divine; she saw the two as very closely akin. There is a curious and touching purity in her *eros* feeling; there is passion in her conception of *agape.*

One of the very last poems in the volume is a *tour de force.* Christina, who was never particularly happy in her choice of titles, incongruously lists it as an **'Old and New Year Ditty'.** In it she performs the astonishing feat of writing twenty-six lines of verse, all with the same rhyme, and not one of them either false or far-fetched:

> Passing away, saith the World, passing away:
> Chances, beauty, and youth, sapp'd day by day:
> Thy life never continueth in one stay.
> Is the eye waxed dim, is the dark hair changing to grey
> That hath won neither laurel nor bay?
> I shall clothe myself in Spring and bud in May:

> Thou, root-stricken, shall not rebuild thy decay
> On my bosom for aye.
> Then I answer'd: Yea.

> Passing away, saith my Soul, passing away:
> With its burden of fear and hope, of labour and play,
> Hearken what the past doth witness and say:
> Rust in thy gold, a moth is in thine array,
> A canker is in thy bud, thy leaf must decay.
> At midnight, at cockcrow, at morning, one certain day
> Lo the Bridegroom shall come and shall not delay;
> Watch thou and pray.
> Then I answer'd: Yea.
> Passing away, saith my God, passing away:
> Winter passeth after the long delay:
> New grapes on the vine, new figs on the tender spray,
> Turtle calleth turtle in Heaven's May.
> Though I tarry, wait for Me, trust Me, watch and pray:
> Arise, come away, night is past and lo it is day,
> My love, My sister, My spouse, thou shalt hear Me say.
> Then I answer'd: Yea.

Many years later Swinburne was to write, 'The poem I put at the head of all her work and of all the religious poetry I know in any language is . . . the matchless and transcendental third of the *Old and New Year Ditties* "Passing away, saith the World, passing away". I have always thought that nothing more glorious in poetry has ever been written.' Maybe this praise is an exaggerated piece of hyperbole; the poem is nevertheless a remarkable achievement. (pp. 101-13)

Georgina Battiscombe, in her *Christina Rossetti: A Divided Life,* Holt, Rinehart and Winston, 1981, 233 p.

ANTONY H. HARRISON

(essay date 1988)

[Harrison is an English-born American educator and critic whose writings focus on issues of gender and sexuality. In the following excerpt from his *Christina Rossetti in Context,* he delineates Rossetti's aesthetic beliefs.]

To William Edmonston Aytoun, the satirist of Spasmodicism and contributing editor of *Blackwood's Magazine,* Christina Rossetti on 1 August 1854 forwarded six new poems, along with what most students of her work today would perceive as a startlingly self-assertive cover letter. In it she disingenuously describes herself as an "unknown and unpublished" writer, a "nameless rhymester." But speaking, as she says, "to a poet," she takes the liberty of insisting that Aytoun consider her works seriously. She stresses her own true identity as a poet, explaining: "I hope that I shall not be misunderstood as guilty of egotism or foolish vanity, when I say that my love for what is good in the works of others teaches one that there is something above the despicable in mine; that poetry is with me, not a mechanism, but an impulse and a reality; and that I know my aims in writing to be pure, and directed to that which is true and right."

Despite Rossetti's deliberate assertions that a commitment to the poetic vocation was of primary importance in her life, critics until very recently have been reluctant to view her as a writer fully devoted to her craft. She was, in fact, a determined and careful artist whose unremitting ambition was to fulfill her potential to generate perfected poetic artifacts, "pure" creative works "directed to that which is true and right." This passage further points to what emerges as *the* pivotal tension of her existence, arising from a conflict, not always easily resolved for Rossetti, between aesthetic and moral (indeed, often ascetic or even prophetic) impulses. Evidence from this letter written when she was twenty-three, and also from earlier and later letters, confirms Rossetti's unrelenting belief in her own vocation as an artist. Yet critics still have not fully acknowledged her drive for aesthetic fulfillment, and, as a result, they have frequently been misguided in evaluating the precise aesthetic qualities, effects, and implications of her work. With . . . Rebecca Crump's . . . three-volume variorum edition of Rossetti's poetry . . . , however, we can begin a decades-overdue revaluation of Rossetti's methods of composition, her aesthetics, the value of her poems, and her true position in relation to the other major Victorian poets. But first, we must establish the proper sociohistorical and literary contexts in which to view her work.

Easy access to the previously scattered manuscript texts of Rossetti's poems, and to the emendations of those texts after their initial publication, at last provides an opportunity to scrutinize the artistic procedure of an enigmatic poet. For almost a century Rossetti has suffered severely from the critical approaches of biographical scholars who have frequently read her verse to lay bare the nature of her unfulfilled passions or to discover the identity of her innominate lover. Readings of Christina Rossetti's works by such critics have depended on the fallacious assumption that her poetry is written for the most part in a confessional poetic mode, as that mode was reinforced by the atmosphere of earnestness inescapable for middle-class Victorians. Such, however, is by no means predictably the case with Rossetti's often experimental verse. Her poems are exploratory, presenting notably different views—from poem to poem and even from one version of a poem to another—of a given set of social, psychological, amatory, and artistic issues. Moreover, as only the most recent commentators have begun to indicate, her aesthetic values often derive from extremely diverse and sometimes ostensibly incompatible literary sources.

In light of the misplaced emphases of past scholarship (as well as the dearth of genuinely useful criticism), a full reassessment of Christina Rossetti is in order. Such a reassessment has profound implications that may well force us to revise currently accepted approaches to Pre-Raphaelite poetry as a whole and to see more clearly than ever the Pre-Raphaelites' importance in providing aesthetic documents that constitute the transition between Romantic and modern literary modes.

The most important piece of work to propagate the myth of Rossetti's "romantic" sincerity and her artistic innocence is William Michael Rossetti's "Memoir," which appears in his collected edition of her *Poetical Works,* published ten years after Christina's death. There he promotes and extends a previously generated image of her poetic practice. He explains that

> her habits of composition were entirely of the casual and spontaneous kind, from her earliest to her latest years. If something came into her head which she found suggestive of verse, she put it into verse. It came to her (I take it) very easily, without her meditating a possible subject, and without her making any great difference in the first from the latest form of the verses which embodied it. . . . What she wrote was pretty well known in the family as soon as her impeccably neat manuscript of it appeared . . . but she did not show it about as an achievement, and still less had she, in the course of her work, invited any hint, counsel, or co-operation.

William Michael was simply wrong—or at least significantly misguided—on both of the major points he introduces here. His sister revised in very important ways and, during her mature years, consistently sought criticism of her manuscripts from Dante Gabriel. In his memoir William Michael is, however, in part transmitting an image of his sister—as a pious and ascetic woman unconcerned with worldly achievements—that she herself had been at some pains to cultivate, especially after 1870. This image suppresses half the truth of Christina Rossetti's values and aspirations. Once dislodged, assumptions of her artistic innocence—that is, of the spontaneity and therefore craftlessness of her poetic production and the selflessness of her pursuits in general—must be radically qualified. We may then begin to discover the kind of values—emotional, social, and psychological, but especially literary—that inspire and inform Rossetti's poetry. (pp. 1-3)

In William Michael's memoir of his sister, he remarks, this time without any mistake,

It may be asked—Did Christina Rossetti consider herself truly a poetess, and a good one? Truly a poetess, most decidedly yes; and, within the range of her subject and thought, and the limits of her executive endeavour, a good one. This did not make her in the least conceited or arrogant as regards herself, nor captious as to the work of others; but it did render her very resolute in setting a line of demarcation between a person who is a poet and another person who is a versifier. Pleadings of *in misericordiam* were of no use with her, and she never could see any good reason why one who is not a poet should write verse in meter.

The extent to which Christina Rossetti did insist upon the unique capabilities of the artist, as well as the autonomy of the artist's imagination and creative powers, is clear from her commentaries on her own poems. Paradigmatic is a passage from a letter written by her on 13 March 1865 to Dante Rossetti, who was at the time supervising her revisions of poems that would appear in *The Prince's Progress* (1866). Her comments in the passage concern the poem **"Under the Rose"** (in 1875 retitled **" 'The Iniquity of the Fathers upon the Children' "**). Some readers might incorrectly assert that this is a surprisingly worldly poem for Christina Rossetti. It is a 545-line monologue spoken by a young woman, Margaret, who, in recalling events of her past life, has concluded that she is the illegitimate daughter of a kindly, unmarried aristocratic woman. In order to retain her reputation, Margaret deduces, this eminent lady was forced to repudiate Margaret at her birth. At the end of **"Under the Rose,"** Margaret, now ostensibly her mother's servant but virtually an adopted child, determines to lead a life of resignation and renunciation, keeping her mother's secret but thereby also fully retaining her own autonomy.

Judging from Christina Rossetti's response to him, her brother was dismayed by the "unpleasant-sided subject" of this poem, but more especially by the fact that it came from a *woman's* pen. Rossetti's reaction to Dante's critique of **"Under the Rose"** is as illuminating as anything she wrote about her own art, or, indeed, about any other author's work. Not only does it reveal her perceptions of the relationship between art and the commonly accepted sexual roles of men and women, but it also makes explicit her understanding of the relations between poetry and the personal experience of the author. Although she begins the passage with the self-effacing rhetoric typical of her, she concludes on a strongly assertive note. To Dante Gabriel she writes,

"U. the R." herewith . . . I meekly return to you, pruned and rewritten to order. As regards the unpleasant-sided subject I freely admit it: and if you think the performance coarse or what-not, pray eject it . . . though I thought **"U. the R."** might read its own lesson, but very likely I misjudge. But do you know, even if we throw **"U. the R."** overboard,

and whilst I endorse your opinion of the unavoidable and indeed much-to-be-desired unreality of women's work on many social matters, I yet incline to include within female range such an attempt as this: where the certainly possible circumstances are merely indicated as it were in skeleton, where the subordinate characters perform (and no more) their accessory parts, where the field is occupied by a single female figure whose internal portrait is set forth in her own words. Moreover the sketch only gives the girl's own deductions, feelings, semiresolutions; granted such premises as hers, and right or wrong it seems to me she might easily arrive at such conclusions: and whilst it may truly be urged that unless white could be black and Heaven Hell my experience (thank God) precludes me from hers, I yet don't see why "the Poet mind" should be less able to construct her from its own inner consciousness than a hundred other unknown quantities.

The keynote of this passage appears in its final sentence, where her description of "the Poet mind" is reminiscent of Keats's ideals of the chameleon poet and of "negative capability." But Rossetti's full commentary is fascinating in several respects. For one thing, her rhetorical strategy is cunning; more significantly, the strategy contributes to our understanding of Christina Rossetti's patterns of behavior in life as well as the values that inexorably support those patterns. Her apparent indifference to the publication of this poem is genuine and reflects her relentless quest for autonomy and self-sufficiency. This quest at last resulted in her virtually complete withdrawal from active life, as well as her reliance upon "the Poet mind"—the creative imagination that *generates* experience—to sustain her, to enrich her, and to serve as both a buffer and a mechanism for mediation between her and the external world that threatened always to encroach upon her independence.

Like her friend A. C. Swinburne in the second half of his career, Christina Rossetti became an ascetic aesthete, whose spheres of experience, both secular and religious, were largely internal and imaginative. Both modes of experience were grounded, however, in external—socially and historically "real"—institutions, those of artistic tradition and the church. Her creative impulse oscillated between two ideal passions, whose respective objects were man and God. Both passions were intense and involved suffering, but the experience of them made her always accessible to exquisite, ethereal sensations of the spirit and emotions, sensations akin to the "wakeful anguish of the soul" memorialized by Keats. For Rossetti, only thralldom to art and to religion could generate ideal experiences of this sort that transform and transcend experience in the "real" world. Because of the capacities of the "Poet mind," Christina Rossetti could (unlike Keats) happily renounce life in the world for the superior life of the imagination. Such a life, of course, allows for the sublimation of physical ills and the manipulation of moral values, while ensuring freedom from censure, oppression, and responsibility. The religious aesthete, in life, enjoys the "paradise within" while preparing for the more permanent Paradise of the afterlife. For Christina Rossetti art and prayer became the primary modes, not merely of self-expression, but of *existence.* Rather than attempting to mirror reality, they subsumed it.

Much of Rossetti's poetry, therefore, abjures both didacticism and sincerity, actively resisting autobiographical readings. Many of her poems are self-reflexive, directing our interest to a fictive personality (as in **"Under the Rose"** and **"Maude Clare"**); to the process of creation; to specific literary works and general literary traditions that provide the enabling conditions for her own work; or to the created artifact itself, rather than to any external reality or extrinsic concerns. Such poems sometimes appropriately reveal her ability to be playful and ironically detached, to parody the kinds of issues her poetry raises. Such is the case in a poem like **"Winter: My Secret."** In it the speaker confesses to wearing masks:

> I tell my secret? No indeed, not I.
>
> . . . . .
>
> I cannot ope to everyone who taps.
> And let the draughts come whistling thro' my hall;
> Come bounding and surrounding me,
> Come buffeting, astounding me,
> Nipping and clipping thro' my wraps and all.
> I wear my mask for warmth.

And we are taunted in the last stanza:

> Perhaps some languid summer day,
> When drowsy birds sing less and less,
> And golden fruit is ripening to excess,
> If there's not too much sun or too much cloud,
> And the warm wind is neither still nor loud,
> Perhaps my secret I may say,
> Or you may guess.

We find the clue to understanding this enigmatic poem in its self-parodic tone. The extraordinary fact here is that the work builds a thoroughly engaging relationship between the speaker and reader out of nothing substantial. No events transpire or are described, and even the "secret" has no extrinsic reference. The reader's curiosity and affection for the speaker are generated entirely by means of a fictive enigma that compels our interest. The poem thus becomes a commentary upon itself, upon the "secret" power of art. It also becomes, on an admittedly small scale, an exemplification of artistic perfection, a self-sufficing artifact. That such may be its design is indicated by the clear allusions, in the first three lines of the last stanza, to Keats's odes "To a Nightingale" and "To Autumn," both of which are concerned with acts of poetic creativity and the acceptance of created beauty (whether imaginative or natural) for its own sake.

Like many of Rossetti's poems, **"Winter: My Secret"** skillfully indulges in linguistic, formal, and metaphorical play. Such works by her are often unsettling because of their self-conscious experimentation and their aesthetic as well as substantive challenges to convention. Yet, unlike **"Winter: My Secret,"** these works frequently close in conventionally settled ways—with the thematic, dramatic, or psychological tensions resolved. Closure, however, very often embodies a literal resignation of the rebelliousness of language, themes, and characterization within the works, a giving over of the potential evoked in the poems for destabilizing the conventional world (of language, social expectations, literary conventions) in which the poems are usually set.

The much-discussed dualisms, contraries, and oppositions in Rossetti's poems open up a space for decoding the world as we know it or expect it to be, and for encoding a new world, or a new apprehension of the old world's genuine truths or possibilities for change. But this potential is often abruptly truncated in the end by a deliberate reintroduction of the conventional world and expectations associated with it. Such a pattern of development enables varied and opposed reader-responses, including relief that conventional "order" or reality is restored; disappointment that a promised new order remains unrealized; or a synthesis of both of these responses, in which emotional, psychological, and aesthetic dissatisfactions evoked by the conclusion refocus reader attention on the generative space that the poem has made visible. The pattern even of Rossetti's nondevotional poems is thus eschatological: by drawing attention to the open-endedness of language, of literary traditions, of social or amatory possibility, she thrusts the reader into a new world that is at first disorienting. But he or she is finally delivered back into the old world that was briefly deconstructed or subverted. Some of Rossetti's best-known and most ambitious poems, including **"Goblin Market," "Monna Innominata,"** and **"The Lowest Room"** operate in this way, as does her early novella, **Maude.** Even the larger structure of her volumes of poetry usually reflects this dialectical mindset, which insistently evokes a concern with purely aesthetic matters by means of the tensions it generates. The counterpoint between the "secular" and devotional poems in her three major volumes of verse (published in 1862, 1866, and 1881), for instance, effectively directs a reader's attention to the distance between the adventurous and the conventional, and finally to the issues of aesthetic modes and motives—of beauty and rhetoric—that displace other potential critical issues, such as thematics, biography, or history.

Even a wholly undisguised ideal of self-sufficing and self-reflexive artistry is clear in a number of Christina Rossetti's poems, though sometimes that ideal is equated with a more conventional ideal of beauty, as it is in **"A Summer Wish"**:

> Live all thy sweet life thro',
>   Sweet Rose, dew-sprent,
> Drop down thine evening dew
> To gather it anew
> When day is bright:
>   I fancy thou wast meant
> Chiefly to give delight.
>
> Sing in the silent sky,
>   Glad soaring bird,
> Sing out thy notes on high
> To sunbeam straying by
> Or passing cloud;
>   Heedless if thou art heard
> Sing thy full song aloud.
>
> Oh that it were with me
>   As with the flower;
> Blooming on its own tree
> For butterfly and bee
> Its summer morns:
>   That I might bloom mine hour
> A rose in spite of thorns.
>
> Oh that my work were done
>   As birds that soar
> Rejoicing in the sun:
> That when my time is run
> And daylight too,
>   I so might rest once more
> Cool with refreshing dew.

The symbols in this poem are open ended, of course, but the work might easily be seen to advocate the value of beauty created "chiefly to give delight," and its language insists on the exuberance, the "rejoicing," that accompanies the act of (poetic) creation: "Heedless if thou art heard / Sing thy full song aloud."

"A Summer Wish" also manifests a pervasive characteristic in Rossetti's poetry, both secular and religious: her use of what Ruskin in her own day designated "the pathetic fallacy." The projection by a speaker of a state of mind and emotion upon what would normally be seen as external, objective, and nonfeeling is clearly a solipsistic poetic strategy that reconstitutes "the world" and empirical conceptions of it. (Ruskin saw the practice as originating with the Romantics.) In this way intellectual and emotional responses displace "the world" and regenerate it as artifact or aesthetic object, "a thing of beauty." Ruskin described poets who in this way anthropomorphically impute life to the object-world as "Reflective or Perceptive." In that category he included Wordsworth, Keats, and Tennyson, poets whose work was necessarily limited by its very modes of generation and operation. As Harold Bloom has observed, Ruskin's "Perceptive" poets were later termed "Aesthetic" poets by Walter Pater. They com-prise "not a second order but the only poets possible in the universe of death, the Romantic world" in which Rossetti lived. Pater's description of aesthetic poets appeared first in his 1868 review, "Poems by William Morris," and became famous when published as part of the conclusion to *The Renaissance.*

Analysis of the body of Christina Rossetti's poetry in its proper literary-historical contexts demonstrates that, like Morris's work, hers embodies important characteristics of "aesthetic poetry," as Pater describes them, and it does so precisely by means of the dominant tensions upon which it is constructed: between beauty and death; between love of man and love of God; between the ephemeral and the eternal; between the sensory and the transcendent. It "projects above the realities of its time a world in which the forms of things are transfigured. Of that world [it] takes possession, and sublimates beyond it another still fainter and more spectral, which is, literally an artificial or 'earthly paradise.' It is a finer ideal, extracted from what in relation to any actual world is already an ideal."

What of course distinguishes Rossetti's work from that of Morris and other "aesthetic" poets is that her "finer ideal" is extrapolated largely from Christian texts and doctrine, especially from Neoplatonic reifications of Christian orthodoxy. Indeed, Plato's most distinctive characteristic according to Pater is equally Rossetti's: an "aptitude for things visible, with the gift of words, empowers [her] to express, as if for the eyes, what except to the eye of the mind is strictly invisible, what an acquired asceticism induces [her] to rank above, and sometimes, in terms of harshest dualism, opposite to, the sensible world." For Pater, Plato is "a seer who has a sort of sensuous love of the unseen."

Rossetti's amatory poetry, also like that of "aesthetic" poets, often returns in setting, or merely in theme, to a "profound medievalism," in which "religion shades into sensuous love, and sensuous love into religion." Dominated by a frequently dreamlike atmosphere, poems from **"The Convent Threshold," "Three Nuns,"** and **"The Prince's Progress"** to **"An Old World Thicket," "Paradise,"** and **"Monna Innominata"** seem to operate largely in "a Kingdom of reverie": "Of religion this poetry learns the art of directing towards an imaginary object sentiments whose natural direction is towards objects of sense. Hence a love defined by the absence of the beloved, choosing to be without hope, protesting against all lower uses of love, barren, extravagant, antinomian. It is the love which is incompatible with marriage." In the great bulk of the poems, too, there appears "the continual suggestion, pensive or passionate, of the shortness of life . . . the sense of death and the desire of beauty; the desire of beauty quickened by the sense of death." Rossetti's poetry can sometimes even appear to assume "artistic beauty of form to be an end in itself."

In these Paterian terms, then, we can perceive aestheticism as a fundamental impulse in a large number of Rossetti's works. Her poetry does, of course, embody several major "thematic" concerns. These include the agonizing conflicts between erotic passion and love of God; the manifold beauties of nature; the need to renounce earthly love and all the world's vanities to await death and salvation. Yet these concerns are often subordinated to her interest in attaining an ideally beautiful world—a beatific paradise—or, equally often, to the process of generating such a world in beautiful poetry (or, self-reflexively, to beauty's multifarious powers and its historical precedents). Thus Rossetti is manifestly self-conscious about form in her poems, about the literary origins of her subject matter, and about language, the processes and effects of signification in reconstituting reality. (pp. 15-22)

Antony H. Harrison, in his *Christina Rossetti in Context,* University of North Carolina Press, 1988, 231 p.

SOURCES FOR FURTHER STUDY

Bell, Mackenzie. *Christina Rossetti: A Biographical and Critical Study.* 1898. Reprint. New York: Haskell House Publishers, 1971, 405 p.

> The earliest critical biography of Rossetti. Bell's account is enhanced by his acquaintance with Rossetti and other Pre-Raphaelites and serves as a good introduction to her life and works.

Kent, David A., ed. *The Achievement of Christina Rossetti.* Ithaca, N.Y.: Cornell University Press, 1987, 367 p.

> Collection of essays, including works by Kent, Betty S. Flowers, and Jerome Bump.

Mayberry, Katherine J. *Christina Rossetti and the Poetry of Discovery.* Baton Rouge: Louisiana State University Press, 1989, 141 p.

> Critical study of Rossetti exploring "the contrast between the luxuriance of the poetry and the asceticism of the life."

Packer, Lona Mosk. *Christina Rossetti.* Berkeley, Los Angeles: University of California Press, 1963, 459 p.

> A biography which concentrates on Rossetti's emotional life, "for it is in these subterranean depths that the source and mainspring of Christina's poetic energy may be found." Packer hypothesizes that the clue to Rossetti's poetry can be found in a secret love relationship with the Pre-Raphaelite poet and painter William Bell Scott.

Thomas, Eleanor Walter. *Christina Georgina Rossetti.* New York: Columbia University Press, 1931, 229 p.

> A critical biography in which the critic endeavours to "call attention to the relation of Christina Rossetti's work to the literature of her time, to study her prose books for the light which they throw upon her poetry, and to indicate the association of some of her poems with the experiences of her life."

Winwar, Frances. *Poor Splendid Wings: The Rossettis and Their Circle.* Boston: Little, Brown, and Co., 1933, 413 p.

> A detailed account of the private lives and personal relationships of the Pre-Raphaelite artists and writers.

Dante Gabriel Rossetti

1828-1882

(Born Gabriel Charles Dante Rossetti) English poet, translator, and short story writer.

INTRODUCTION

*E*qually renowned as a painter and poet, Rossetti was the leader of the Pre-Raphaelite Brotherhood, a group of artists and writers who sought to emulate the purity and simplicity of the Italian Proto-Renaissance school of art. His greatest distinction as a painter was as a colorist, and the best-known of his paintings include *Beata Beatrix* and *Monna Vanna*. His sister, the poet Christina Rossetti, is the central figure in many of his early paintings. Although the subjects of his verse are often considered narrow, Rossetti is an acknowledged master of the ballad and sonnet forms. His poetry is characterized by its mysticism, its rich and sensuous imagery, and its vivid detail. "The Blessed Damozel" (1850), "Sister Helen" (1870), and the sonnet-sequence "The House of Life" (1881), are often noted as his finest poems.

An exiled Italian patriot, Rossetti's father came to England four years before Rossetti's birth. Rossetti received his early education at home and was particularly influenced by Thomas Percy's *Reliques,* the works of Sir Walter Scott, and the medieval romances. He later attended King's College School and studied art at the Royal Academy. Unhappy with the conventional methods of painting taught at the Academy, Rossetti left in 1848 to study with Ford Madox Brown. After a short time, however, he joined John Everett Millais and William Holman Hunt in founding the Pre-Raphaelite Brotherhood. Rossetti quickly became the leader of the group and later inspired William Morris, Edward Burne-Jones, and Algernon Charles Swinburne to become members.

Rossetti first received recognition as a poet in 1850, when he published "The Blessed Damozel" in the Pre-Raphaelite journal *The Germ.* Written when he was only eighteen, this poem is characteristic of much of Rossetti's later poetry, with its sensuous detail and theme of lovers, parted by death, who long for reunion. Many other early poems appeared in *The Germ,* as well as his only completed short story, "Hand and Soul." In 1861 he published *The Early Italian Poets from Ciullo to Dante Alighieri (1100-1200-1300) in the Original Metres, Together with Dante's "Vita Nuova,"* a distinguished volume praised for its meticulous translations.

In 1860, after a nine-year engagement, Rossetti married Elizabeth Siddal, the subject of many of his paintings and sketches. By the time of their wedding, however, she was obviously consumptive, and after two unhappy years of marriage she died from an overdose of laudanum, which she had been taking regularly for her illness. The question of whether her death was an accident or a suicide remained unanswered and plagued Rossetti for the rest of his life. In a fit of remorse and guilt, Rossetti buried the only manuscript of his poems with his wife. At the urging of friends, he allowed the manuscript to be exhumed in 1869.

The following year Rossetti published *Poems,* which established his reputation as a leading poet. Containing much of Rossetti's finest work, *Poems* includes "Eden Bower," "The Stream's Secret," and "Sister Helen," which is regarded by many as one of the finest Victorian literary ballads. The influence of Rossetti's painting is felt throughout *Poems.* Just as his literary background influenced his choice of mythological, allegorical, and literary subjects for his paintings, his Pre-Raphaelite love of detail, color, and mysticism shaped much of his poetry. Another collection, titled *Ballads and Sonnets,* appeared in 1881. This volume contains the completed version of Rossetti's sonnet-sequence, "The House of Life," which many critics praise as evidence of Rossetti's mastery of the sonnet form. Rossetti's biographers continue to debate his source of inspiration for the anguished love lyrics included in the sequence. Although his early biographers assumed that his wife was the sole subject of his love poetry, many now maintain that Rossetti's frustrated passion for William Morris's wife, Jane, inspired much of his finest work.

Following the publication of *Poems,* numerous reviews appeared praising Rossetti as the greatest poet since Shakespeare. In 1871, Robert Buchanan pseudonymously published a venomous attack against Rossetti called "The Fleshly School of Poetry," in which he claimed that Rossetti's only artistic aim was "to extol fleshliness as the distinct and supreme end of poetic and pictorial art; to aver that poetic expression is greater than poetic thought, and by inference that the body is greater than the soul, and sound superior to sense." When Buchanan's identity was revealed, Rossetti published a convincing reply called "The Stealthy School of Criticism." Rossetti was devastated by Buchanan's criticism and he became convinced that he was the object of an undeserved and insidious campaign. His subsequent dependence upon whiskey and chloral to alleviate his anxiety and insomnia precipitated a gradual decline in health which ended with his death at age fifty-four.

Following his death, Rossetti's works suffered somewhat from critical neglect. However, with the renewed interest in Pre-Raphaelitism, numerous studies have appeared. Rossetti is now recognized as a distinguished artist and verbal craftsman whose work greatly influenced such notable contemporaries as Morris and Swinburne, as well as the Aesthetes and Decadents of the later nineteenth century.

(For further information about Rossetti's life and works, see *Dictionary of Literary Biography,* Vol. 35: *Victorian Poets After 1850* and *Nineteenth-Century Literature Criticism,* Vol. 4.)

CRITICAL COMMENTARY

THOMAS MAITLAND [PSEUDONYM OF ROBERT BUCHANAN]
(essay date 1871)

[In the following excerpt from his notorious attack on Rossetti and the Pre-Raphaelites, Buchanan insists that their sole aim is "to extol fleshliness as the distinct and supreme end of poetic and pictorial art." He concedes, however, that some of Rossetti's poems do exhibit such qualities as "delicacy of touch" and descriptive beauty, and under the guise of a pseudonym he cites himself as the inspiration for "Jenny," which he considers the finest poem in *Poems.*]

If, on the occasion of any public performance of Shakespere's great tragedy, the actors who perform the parts of Rosencranz and Guildenstern were, by a preconcerted arrangement and by means of what is technically known as "gagging," to make themselves fully as prominent as the leading character, and to indulge in soliloquies and business strictly belonging to Hamlet

Principal Works

"The Blessed Damozel" (poetry) 1850; published in journal The Germ

"Hand and Soul" (short story) 1850; published in journal The Germ

The Early Italian Poets from Ciullo to Dante Alighieri (1100-1200-1300) in the Original Metres, Together with Dante's "Vita Nuova" [translator] (poetry) 1861

Poems (poetry) 1870

Dante and His Circle: With the Italian Poets Preceding Him (1100-1200-1300) [translator] (poetry) 1874

Ballads and Sonnets (poetry) 1881

The Complete Poetical Works of Dante Gabriel Rossetti (poetry) 1903

himself, the result would be, to say the least of it, astonishing; yet a very similar effect is produced on the unprejudiced mind when the "walking gentlemen" of the fleshy school of poetry, who bear precisely the same relation to Mr. Tennyson as Rosencranz and Guildenstern do to the Prince of Denmark in the play, obtrude their lesser identities and parade their smaller idiosyncrasies in the front rank of leading performers. In their own place, the gentlemen are interesting and useful. Pursuing still the theatrical analogy, the present drama of poetry might be cast as follows: Mr. Tennyson supporting the part of Hamlet, Mr. Matthew Arnold that of Horatio, Mr. Bailey that of Voltimand, Mr. Buchanan that of Cornelius, Messrs. Swinburne and Morris the parts of Rosencranz and Guildenstern, Mr. Rossetti that of Osric, and Mr. Robert Lytton that of "A Gentleman." It will be seen that we have left no place for Mr. Browning, who may be said, however, to play the leading character in his own peculiar fashion on alternate nights.

This may seem a frivolous and inadequate way of opening our remarks on a school of verse-writers which some people regard as possessing great merits; but in good truth, it is scarcely possible to discuss with any seriousness the pretensions with which foolish friends and small critics have surrounded the fleshly school, which, in spite of its spasmodic ramifications in the erotic direction, is merely one of the many sub-Tennysonian schools expanded to supernatural dimensions, and endeavouring by affectations all its own to overshadow its connection with the great original. In the sweep of one single poem, the weird and doubtful "Vivien," Mr. Tennyson has concentrated all the epicene force which, wearisomely expanded, constitutes the characteristic of the writers at present under consideration; and if in "Vivien" he has indicated for them the bounds of sensualism in art, he has in "Maud," in

the dramatic person of the hero, afforded distinct precedent for the hysteric tone and overloaded style which is now so familiar to readers of Mr. Swinburne. The fleshiness of "Vivien" may indeed be described as the distinct quality held in common by all the members of the last sub-Tennysonian school, and it is a quality which becomes unwholesome when there is no moral or intellectual quality to temper and control it. Fully conscious of this themselves, the fleshly gentlemen have bound themselves by solemn league and covenant to extol fleshliness as the distinct and supreme end of poetic and pictorial art; to aver that poetic expression is greater than poetic thought, and by inference that the body is greater than the soul, and sound superior to sense; and that the poet, properly to develop his poetic faculty, must be an intellectual hermaphrodite, to whom the very facts of day and night are lost in a whirl of aesthetic terminology. . . . [The] fleshly school of verse-writers are, so to speak, public offenders, because they are dilligently spreading the seeds of disease broadcast wherever they are read and understood. Their complaint too is catching, and carries off many young persons. What the complaint is, and how it works, may be seen on a very slight examination of the works of Mr. Dante Gabriel Rossetti. . . . (pp. 334-36)

[Mr. Rossetti] belongs, or is said to belong, to the so-called Pre-Raphaelite school, a school which is generally considered to exhibit much genius for colour, and great indifference to perspective. . . . Judged by the photographs [of his paintings], he is an artist who conceives unpleasantly, and draws ill. . . . [[He] is distinctively a colourist, and of his capabilities in colour we cannot speak, though we should guess that they are great; for if there is any good quality by which his poems are specially marked, it is a great sensitiveness to hues and tints as conveyed in poetic epithet. These qualities, which impress the casual spectator of the photographs from his pictures, are to be found abundantly among his verses. There is the same thinness and transparence of design, the same combination of the simple and the grotesque, the same morbid deviation from healthy forms of life, the same sense of weary, wasting, yet exquisite sensuality; nothing virile, nothing tender, nothing completely sane; a superfluity of extreme sensibility, of delight in beautiful forms, hues, and tints, and a deep-seated indifference to all agitating forces and agencies, all tumultuous griefs and sorrows, all the thunderous stress of life, and all the straining storm of speculation. . . . [The] mind of Mr. Rossetti is like a glassy mere, broken only by the dive of some water-bird or the hum of winged insects, and brooded over by an atmosphere of insufferable closeness, with a light blue sky above it, sultry depths mirrored within it, and a surface so thickly sown with water-lilies that it retains its glassy smoothness even in the strongest wind. (pp. 336-37)

[In **"Nuptial Sleep,"** Rossetti puts] on record for other fullgrown men to read, the most secret mysteries of sexual connection, and that with so sickening a desire to reproduce the sensual mood, so careful a choice of epithet to convey mere animal sensations, that we merely shudder at the shameless nakedness. We are no purists in such matters. We hold the sensual part of our nature to be as holy as the spiritual or intellectual part, and we believe that such things must find their equivalent in all; but it is neither poetic, nor manly, nor even human, to obtrude such things as the themes of whole poems. It is simply nasty. (p. 338)

It must not be supposed that all Mr. Rossetti's poems are made up of trash like this. Some of them are as noteworthy for delicacy of touch as others are for shamelessness of exposition. They contain some exquisite pictures of nature, occasional passages of real meaning, much beautiful phraseology, lines of peculiar sweetness, and epithets chosen with true literary cunning. But the fleshly feeling is everywhere. Sometimes, as in **"The Stream's Secret,"** it is deliciously modulated, and adds greatly to our emotion of pleasure at perusing a finely-wrought poem; at other times, as in the **"Last Confession,"** it is fiercely held in check by the exigencies of a powerful situation and the strength of a dramatic speaker; but it is generally in the foreground, flushing the whole poem with unhealthy rose-colour, stifling the senses with overpowering sickliness, as of too much civet. Mr. Rossetti is never dramatic, never impersonal—always attitudinizing, posturing, and describing his own exquisite emotions. . . . In petticoats or pantaloons, in modern times or in the middle ages, he is just Mr. Rossetti, a fleshly person, with nothing particular to tell us or teach us, with extreme self-control, a strong sense of colour, and a careful choice of diction. Amid all his "affluence of jewel-coloured words," he has not given us one rounded and noteworthy piece of art, though his verses are all art; not one poem which is memorable for its own sake, and quite separable from the displeasing identity of the composer. The nearest approach to a perfect whole is the **"Blessed Damozel,"** a peculiar poem. . . . In spite of its affected title, and of numberless affectations throughout the text, the **"Blessed Damozel"** has great merits of its own, and a few lines of real genius. . . . The steadiness of hand lessens as the poem proceeds, and although there are several passages of considerable power . . . , the general effect is that of a queer old painting in a missal, very affected and very odd. What moved a British critic to ecstasy in this poem seems to us very sad nonsense indeed, or, if not sad nonsense, very meretricious affectation. . . . On the whole, one feels disheartened and amazed at the poet who, in the nineteenth century, talks about "damozels," "citherns," and "citoles," and addresses the mother of Christ as the "Lady Mary." . . . A suspicion is awakened that

the writer is laughing at us. We hover uncertainly between picturesqueness and namby-pamby, and the effect, as Artemus Ward would express it, is "weakening to the intellect." The thing would have been almost too much in the shape of a picture, though the workmanship might have made amends. (pp. 339-41)

We would rather believe that Mr. Rossetti lacks comprehension than that he is deficient in sincerity; yet really, to paraphrase the words which Johnson applied to Thomas Sheridan, Mr. Rossetti is affected, naturally affected, but it must have taken him a great deal of trouble to become what we now see him—such an excess of affectation is not in nature. There is very little writing in [*Poems*] spontaneous in the sense that some of Swinburne's verses are spontaneous; the poems all look as if they had taken a great deal of trouble. . . . Mr. Rossetti is a poet possessing great powers of assimilation and some faculty for concealing the nutriment on which he feeds. . . . [He] may be described as a writer who has yielded to an unusual extent to the complex influences of the literature surrounding him at the present moment. He has the painter's imitative power developed in proportion to his lack of the poet's conceiving imagination. He reproduces to a nicety the manner of an old ballad, a trick in which Mr. Swinburne is also an adept. Cultivated readers, moreover, will recognise in every one of these poems the tone of Mr. Tennyson broken up by the style of Mr. and Mrs. Browning, and disguised here and there by the eccentricities of the Pre-Raphaelites. . . . [That] the sonnets have been largely moulded and inspired by Mrs. Browning can be ascertained by any critic who will compare them with the "Sonnets from the Portuguese." Much remains, nevertheless, that is Mr. Rossetti's own. We at once recognise as his own property such passages as this:—

> I looked up
> And saw where a brown-shouldered harlot leaned
> Half through a tavern window thick with vine.
> Some man had come behind her in the room
> And caught her by her arms, and she had turned
> With that coarse empty laugh on him, as now
> He *munched her neck with kisses, while the vine*
> *Crawled in her back.*

Or this:—

> As I stooped, her own lips rising there
> *Bubbled with brimming kisses* at my mouth.

Or this:—

> What more prize than love to impel thee,
> *Grip* and *lip* my limbs as I tell thee.

Passages like these are the common stock of the walking gentlemen of the fleshly school. We cannot forbear expressing our wonder, by the way, at the kind of women whom it seems the unhappy lot of these gentlemen to encounter. We have lived as long in the world as they have, but never yet came across persons of the other sex who conduct themselves in the manner described. Females who bite, scratch, scream, bubble, munch, sweat, writhe, twist, wriggle, foam, and in a general way slaver over their lovers, must surely possess some extraordinary qualities to counteract their otherwise most offensive mode of conducting themselves. It appears, however, on examination that their poet-lovers conduct themselves in a similar manner. They, too, bite, scratch, scream, bubble, munch, sweat, writhe, twist, wriggle, foam, and slaver, in a style frightful to hear of. . . . We get very weary of this protracted hankering after a person of the other sex; it seems meat, drink, thought, sinew, religion for the fleshly school. There is no limit to the fleshliness, and Mr. Rossetti finds in it its own religious justification. . . . Whether he is writing of the holy Damozel, or of the Virgin herself, or of Lilith, or Helen, or of Dante, or of Jenny the streetwalker, he is fleshly all over, from the roots of his hair to the tip of his toes; never a true lover merging his identity into that of the beloved one; never spiritual, never tender; always self-conscious and aesthetic. . . . **"Jenny"** [is] in some respects the finest poem in the volume, and in all respects the poem best indicative of the true quality of the writer's humanity. It is a production which bears signs of having been suggested by Mr. Buchanan's quasi-lyrical poems, which it copies in the style of title, and particularly by "Artist and Model." . . . (pp. 341-43)

What we object to in this poem is not the subject, which any writer may be fairly left to choose for himself; nor anything particularly vicious in the poetic treatment of it; nor any bad blood bursting through in special passages. But the whole tone, without being more than usually coarse, seems heartless. There is not a drop of piteousness in Mr. Rossetti. He is just to the outcast, even generous; severe to the seducer; sad even at the spectacle of lust in dimity and fine ribbons. Notwithstanding all this, and a certain delicacy and refinement of treatment unusual with this poet, the poem repels and revolts us, and we like Mr. Rossetti least after its perusal. We are angry with the fleshly person at last. The **"Blessed Damozel"** puzzled us, the **"Song of the Bower"** amused us, the love-sonnet depressed and sickened us, but **"Jenny,"** though distinguished by less special viciousness of thought and style than any of these, fairly makes us lose patience. We detect its fleshliness at a glance; we perceive that the scene was fascinating less through its human tenderness than because it, like all the others, possessed an inherent quality of animalism. (p. 344)

Thomas Maitland [pseudonym of Robert Buchanan], "The Fleshly School of Poetry: Mr. D. G. Rossetti," in *Contemporary Review,* Vol. XVIII, No. III, October, 1871, pp. 334-50.

LAFCADIO HEARN
(lecture date 1902)

[In the following excerpt from a lecture delivered at the University of Tokyo in 1902, Hearn surveys the themes and subjects of Rossetti's poetry.]

We must rank Dante Gabriel Rossetti as not inferior to Tennyson in workmanship—therefore as occupying the very first rank in nineteenth century poetry. He was not inferior to Tennyson either as a thinker, but his thinking was in totally different directions. He had no sympathy with the ideas of his own century; he lived and thought in the Middle Ages; and while one of our very greatest English poets, he takes a place apart, for he does not reflect the century at all. He had the dramatic gift, but it was a gift in his case much more limited than that of Browning. Altogether we can safely give him a place in the first rank as a maker of poetry, but in all other respects we cannot classify him in any way. He remains a unique figure in the Victorian age, a figure such as may not reappear for hundreds of years to come. It was as if a man of the thirteenth century had been reborn into the nineteenth century, and, in spite of modern culture, had continued to think and to feel very much as men felt and thought in the time of the great Italian poet Dante. (pp. 1-2)

To the cultivated the very highest quality of emotional poetry is that given by blending the artistically sensuous with the mystic. This very rare quality colours the greater part of Rossetti's work. Perhaps one may even say that it is never entirely absent. Only, the proportions of the blending vary, like those mixtures of red and blue, crimson and azure, which may give us either purple or violet of different shades according to the wish of the dyer. The quality of mysticism dominates in the symbolic poems; we might call those deep purple. The sensuous element dominates in most of the ballads and narrative poems; we might say that these have rather the tone of bright violet. But even in the ballads there is a very great difference in the proportions of the two qualities. The highest tone is in the **"Blessed Damozel,"** and in the beautiful narrative poem of the **"Staff and Scrip";** while the lowest tone is perhaps that of the ballad of **"Eden Bower,"** which describes the two passions of lust and hate at their greatest intensity. But everything is beautifully finished as work, and unapproachably exquisite in feeling. I think the best example of what I have called the violet style is the ballad of **"Troy Town."** (pp. 15-16)

This wonderful ballad, with its single and its double refrains, represents Rossetti's nearest approach to earth, except the ballad of **"Eden Bower."** Usually he seldom touches the ground, but moves at some distance above it, just as one flies in dreams. But you will observe that the mysticism here has almost vanished. There is just a little ghostliness to remind you that the writer is no common singer, but a poet able to give a thrill. The ghostliness is chiefly in the fact of the supernatural elements involved; Helen with her warm breast we feel to be a real woman, but Venus and love are phantoms, who speak and act as figures in sleep. This is true art under the circumstances. We feel nothing more human until we come to the last stanza; then we hear it in the cry of Paris. But why do I say that this is high art to make the gods as they are made here? The Greeks would have made Venus and Cupid purely human. But Rossetti is not taking the Greek view of the subject at all. . . . [Even] in a Greek subject of the sensuous kind Rossetti always keeps the tone of the Middle Ages; and that tone was mystical. (pp. 19-20)

[**"The Blessed Damozel"**] and a lovely narrative poem entitled **"Staff and Scrip"** form the most exquisite examples of the poet's treatment of mystical love. (p. 20)

[**"The Blessed Damozel"**] is very wonderful in its sweetness of simple pathos, and in a peculiar, indescribable quaintness which is not of the nineteenth century at all. It is of the Middle Ages, the Italian Middle Ages before the time of Raphael. The heaven painted here is not the heaven of modern Christianity—if modern Christianity can be said to have a heaven; it is the heaven of Dante, a heaven almost as sharply defined as if it were on earth. (pp. 20-1)

We have here a picture of heaven, with all its mysteries and splendours, suspended over an ocean of ether, through which souls are passing like an upward showering of fire; and all this is spiritual enough. But the Damozel, with her yellow hair, and her bosom making warm what she leans upon, is very human; and her thoughts are not of the immaterial kind. The suggestions about bathing together, about embracing, cheek against cheek, and about being able to love in heaven as on earth, have all the delightful innocence of the Middle Ages, when the soul was thought of only as another body of finer substance. Now it is altogether the human warmth of the poem that makes its intense attraction. (p. 34)

Outside of the sonnets . . . , I do not know any more beautiful example of the mystical feeling of love in Rossetti than [**"The Portrait"**]. . . . [This poem demonstrates] one of the peculiar qualities distinguishing Rossetti from all the other Victorian poets—the mingling of religious with amatory emotion in the highest form of which the language is capable. (p. 51)

[Let] us now consider Rossetti simply as a story-teller, and see how wonderful he is in some of those lighter productions in which he brought the art of the refrain to a perfection which nobody else, except perhaps Swinburne, has equalled. Among the ballads there is but one, **"Stratton Water,"** conceived altogether after the old English fashion; and this has no refrain. I do not know that any higher praise can be given to it than the simple statement that it is a perfect imitation of the old ballad—at least so far as a perfect imitation is possible in the nineteenth century. Should there be any criticism allowable, it could be only this, that the tenderness and pathos are somewhat deeper, and somewhat less rough in utterance, than we expect in a ballad of the fourteenth or fifteenth century. Yet there is no stanza in it for which some parallel might not be found in ballads of the old time. . . . [No] narrative could be more simple. But as the great pains and great joys of life are really in simple things, the simplest is capable of almost infinite expansion when handled by a true artist. Certainly in English poetry there is no ballad more beautiful than this; nor can we imagine it possible to do anything more with so slight a theme. (pp. 52-3)

Perhaps [**"Sister Helen"**] is the best example of story telling in the shorter pieces of Rossetti—not because its pictures are more objectively vivid than the themes of the **"White Ship,"** but because it is more subjectively vivid, dealing with the extremes of human passion, hate, love, revenge, and religious despair. All these are passions peculiarly coloured by the age in which the story is supposed to happen, the age of belief in magic, in ghosts, and in hell-fire. (p. 53)

I know of nothing more terrible in literature than this poem, as expressing certain phases of human feeling, and nothing more intensely true. The probability or improbability of the incidents is of no more consequence than is the unreality of the witch-belief. It is enough that such beliefs once existed to make us know that the rest is not only possible but certain. For a time we are really subjected to the spell of a mediaeval nightmare. (p. 69)

[**"Sister Helen"**] is mainly a subjective study. As an objective study, **"The White Ship"** shows us an equal degree of power, appealing to the visual faculty. . . . The story is founded upon historical fact. The son and heir of the English king Henry I, together with his sister and many knights and ladies, was drowned on a voyage from France to England, and it is said that the king was never again seen to smile after he had heard the news. Rossetti imagines the story told by a survivor—a butcher employed on the ship, the lowest menial on board. . . . It is a simple mind of this sort that can best tell a tragical story; and the butcher's story is about the most perfect thing imaginable of its kind. Here also we have one admirable bit of subjective work, the narration of the butcher's experience in the moment of drowning. (pp. 69-71)

Both in its realism and in its emotion this ballad is a great masterpiece. It is much superior to **"The King's Tragedy,"** also founded upon history. **"The King's Tragedy"** seems to us a little strained; perhaps the poet attempted too much. (pp. 72-3)

["**Lilith**"] is an expression of passion—but not passion merely human; rather superhuman and evil. For she who speaks in this poem is not a woman like **"Sister Helen";** she is a demon.

Not a drop of her blood was human,
But she was made like a soft sweet woman.

Perhaps the poet desired to show us here the extremest imaginative force of hate and cruelty—not in a mortal being, because that would repel us, but in an immortal being, in whom such emotion can only inspire fear. (p. 73)

The ideas are in one way extremely interesting; they represent the most tragical and terrible form of jealousy—that jealousy written of in the Bible as being like the very fires of Hell. We might say that in Victorian verse this is the unique poem of jealousy, in a female personification. (p. 74)

But there is a masterly phase of jealousy described in one of Rossetti's modern poems, **"A Last Confession."** Here, however, the jealousy is of the kind with which we can humanly sympathise; there is nothing monstrous or distorted about it. The man has reason to suspect unchastity, and he kills the woman on the instant. I should, therefore, consider this poem rather as a simple and natural tragedy than as a study of jealousy. . . . Rossetti did not confine himself to mediaeval or supernatural subjects. Three of his very best poems are purely modern, belonging to the nineteenth century. This **"Last Confession,"** appropriately placed in Italy, is not the most remarkable of the three, but it is very fine. . . . The other two poems of modern life to which I have referred are **"The Card-Dealer"** and **"Jenny." "The Card-Dealer"** represents a singular faculty on the poet's part of seeing ordinary facts in their largest relations. (pp. 74-6)

Much more modern is **"Jenny."** . . . [It is a] wonderful psychological study, which no other poet of the nineteenth century, except perhaps Browning, could have attempted. (p. 77)

The extraordinary charm of the story [of **"Rose Mary"**] is in its vividness—a vividness perhaps without equal even in the best work of Tennyson (certainly much finer than similar work in Coleridge), and in the attractive characterisation of mother and daughter. There is this great difference between the mediaeval poems of Coleridge or Scott, and those of Rossetti, that when you are reading "The Lay of the Last Minstrel" or the wonderful "Christabel," you feel that you are reading a fairy-tale, but when you read Rossetti you are

looking at life and feeling human passion. It is a great puzzle to critics how any man could make the Middle Ages live as Rossetti did. (p. 87)

Lafcadio Hearn, "Studies in Rossetti," in his *Appreciations of Poetry,* edited by John Erskine, Dodd Mead & Company, Inc. 1916, pp. 37-125.

HAROLD L. WEATHERBY
(essay date 1964)

[In the following excerpt, Weatherby studies Rossetti's use of realistic and allegorical details in his poetry.]

The most significant problem . . . in coming to an accurate estimate of Rossetti's poetry is that of the relationship between form and content. . . . Rossetti often failed to work-out a proper relationship between what he had to say and the way he went about saying it. This failure may be a private one—a weakness in Rossetti's poetic sensibility, but I doubt if that is the whole of it. To be sure he lacks the general stature of Tennyson, Browning, and Arnold, but so does a poet like Gerard Manley Hopkins whose work is no less complete on account of its limitations. Rossetti's difficulty is more profound and hence more interesting than any weakness of his own. It is essentially the difficulty that beset the Victorian art for art's sake movement—the failure of content, the failure of meaning, the failure of traditional symbols to function properly when they were cut loose from the belief in spiritual realities which originally produced them.

One of the most peculiar qualities of Pre-Raphaelite art is the way in which highly realistic and deliberately allegorical details are combined. (p. 11)

The same problem confronts us in much of Rossetti's early poetry. In **"My Sister's Sleep,"** for instance, the sharp details of the death scene—the firelight reflected in the mirror, the click of needles and rustle of a skirt—contribute to an impression of Zola-esque precision in the recording of life. Yet these details are set in a quasi-supernatural frame—the scraping of chairs in the room above and the peculiarly appropriate hour of the death. We are left wondering whether the poem is supposed to be a realistic portrayal of a young girl's death or whether it is a symbolic study having something vaguely to do with "Christ's blessing on the newly born!" . . . [The] poem blurs upon our vision because it lacks an integrity of focus, and yet . . . it represents an attempt at a highly formalized sort of art. Consider for a moment the last line of **"My Sister's Sleep,"** "Christ's blessing on the newly born!" In terms of the poem itself this is precisely the right ending. It fills out the pattern, places the last thread in the tapestry, and points up very neatly the suggested parallel between the death of the sister (by implication her rebirth) and the birth of Christ. However, as soon as any sort of experience foreign to the immediate text of the poem intrudes itself, and whenever we are confronted with a symbol as rich in allusion as the birth of Christ, external experience will perforce intrude, the threads unravel. In fact the heightening of meaning which the Christmas morning setting could provide, either directly or ironically, in a thoroughly unified poem would be an immeasurable asset. However, in **"My Sister's Sleep"** it breaks the fabric into shreds because it is never clear exactly where the poem stands. The sharp realism of detail renders a willing suspension of disbelief impossible, but on the other hand Rossetti makes no attempt whatever to use his religious effects for an ironic purpose. . . . Dismissing for a moment the questions of whether or what Rossetti believed, the reality of the Christian allusion in **"My Sister's Sleep"** is highly questionable. What we believe in here is the firelight and the rustling skirt; the Christmas morning setting looks suspiciously like decoration, like an embellishment which Rossetti adds to otherwise photographic realism in order to qualify the representation for the name of "poem"—in short, to give it a form. (pp. 12-13)

[It] is tempting to suggest . . . that [Rossetti's] failure is as much a religious or metaphysical as it is a poetic problem. In short, to create a symbolic representation of a mystical reality which is not really believed to be real is difficult: and the problem confronts Rossetti again and again. In **"The Blessed Damozel,"** for instance, once we attempt to transcend its purely formal attributes, it becomes very difficult to speak intelligently about the supposedly supernatural machinery of the piece. For one thing Rossetti's cosmology is hopelessly jumbled, and it becomes readily apparent that far from attempting a serious symbolic representation of heaven and earth he is using the whole scheme for something very close to the purposes of decoration. Not that he necessarily should be endeavoring to justify the ways of God to man, but cosmologies, like Christmas eves, refuse to be used indiscriminately. Traditional meanings attach themselves and demand more serious consideration than can ever be implicit in a warm breast and a few artistic tears.

All of this points to the central weakness in **"The Blessed Damozel"**—the problem of meaning in relationship to the reality or unreality of the supernatural. Whether we are to take the portrait literally or not (the woman, lilies, and stars comprise a portrait within the poem) is never clear. The passages in parenthesis, the lover's, presumably the poet's, thoughts, ought to provide a key for our understanding but they are contra-

dictory. . . . It is impossible to tell exactly what Rossetti expects us to believe or disbelieve, for the poem is neither fully committed to the supernatural . . . , nor ironically detached. . . . The structure of the piece is very neat, and in so far as there is a kind of abstract geometric beauty in well-constructed rhetorical and metaphoric patterns it is beautiful. But it will not sustain analysis because it has, finally, no center—no commitment to any single conception of values. . . . [It] is never quite clear whether we have to do with anything real at all—even the falling leaves, even the grief, are artistic constructs, matters of form.

It is this weakness of meaning, this lack of faith in the reality of his material, which is responsible for many of our current objections to [Rossetti's] work. His surfaces seem overwrought, not because they are, comparatively speaking, exceedingly ornate but because there is often no solid fabric beneath them; and his love poetry seems unhealthily sensuous because the physical fact is not always redeemed by the idea. . . . In a sonnet like **"Through Death to Love"** . . . , with its highly ornate imagery and virtually intolerable syntax . . . one feels again that Rossetti is simply decorating, as if he were unable . . . to maintain for any extended period the mystical understanding of the relationship between body and soul which is absolutely necessary for the kind of love poetry which **"The House of Life"** attempts to be.

Rossetti's successes, like his failures, are not, however, limited to his sonnets or even to his love poetry. When he has a subject in which he either thoroughly believes or believes enough to engage with a thorough aesthetic commitment, he is apt to succeed admirably. In a poem like **"Jenny,"** for instance, all Victorian objections notwithstanding, there is little trace of cloying, overwrought sensuousness. To be sure we have a realistic, even a sordid scene, rendered at times in elaborate images. . . . But there is no attempt to confuse the real and the ideal, no sentimentalizing about whoredom. . . . One feels that Rossetti is deeply and honestly involved in his subject—the ugliness of prostitution in contrast with the beauty of the woman—"Poor shameful Jenny, full of grace," and it is revealing, in light of Rossetti's success in this poem, that **"Jenny"** does not commit him to the specific use of any sort of spiritual machinery. Consequently he is never drawn into the trap of decorating his design with symbols which fail to convince.

This withdrawal from religion as poetic artifice is carried still further in **"The Burden of Ninevah"** where, in fact, the very rudiments of religious thought are questioned. . . . Ninevah's pagan burden has become London's—a thoroughly sceptical sort of idea. The poem probes at doubt . . . , and though the result of thorough scepticism is likely to be a very limited kind of poetry, and though we can always hope for better, it may be the only kind possible in an age like Rossetti's. Certainly it is preferable to a poetry of spiritual ornament without spiritual content. (pp. 14-17)

The peculiar and perhaps unfortunate thing about Rossetti . . . is that he had a strong predilection for the supernatural, as strong indeed as his predilection for the flesh (and the two go hand in hand). The critical detachment of an Arnold or a Browning was not native to him, and though their type of poetry is probably the most successful which the last half of the century produced, it is very doubtful that Rossetti could have sustained their ironic, critical vein for any prolonged endeavor. He is far more at home with a mysteriously voluptuous woman or a legion of devils than he is with an archeological specimen or even a reasonably domesticated prostitute like Jenny. . . . If he was not sure enough about the reality of medieval hierarchies to write convincingly of a Christian heaven, he was nevertheless capable of treating physical and spiritual disintegration with great conviction. Even in his love poetry, perhaps we should say *especially* in his love poetry, even while he strives toward the idea of a perfect union and fulfillment, there is likely to be a reversion to the opposite extreme of perfect evil. In fact the figure that fascinated him most is *la belle dame sans merci.* She is scarcely hidden by "the swift heat / And soft subsidence of the spirit's wing," and she rises to full view in a poem like **"The Card Dealer"** in which Rossetti's propensity for juxtaposing realistic detail with supernatural machinery works to good advantage. The atmosphere of a gaming house lends itself quite well to this vision of death whose "eyes unravel the coiled night / And know the stars at noon," but the success of the poem does not depend so much upon the technique of correlating realistic with supernatural detail as upon the fact that the reality of death and hence the validity of Rossetti's symbol, is assumed from the outset—just as the heavenly, redemptive reality of Dante's Beatrice is assumed. Rossetti believed in the horror which the card dealer symbolizes; the blessed damozel and her heaven are artifice. (p. 18)

Rossetti was capable both of variety and intensity, genuinely a poet, capable of rendering feeling as language. It is too often, though, exactly that and no more—just good *poetry;* he wrote only a few good *poems.* For despite his conscious efforts at the creation of poetic forms, his content, which in the final analysis is the only thing that can validate form, often failed him. Or he failed it. (p. 19)

Harold L. Weatherby, "Problems of Form and Content in the Poetry of Dante Gabriel Rossetti," in *Victorian Poetry,* Vol. II, December, 1964, pp. 11-19.

FLORENCE SAUNDERS BOOS
(essay date 1976)

[In the following excerpt, Boos explores the stylistic and thematic development of "The House of Life" sonnet-sequence and comments on the evolution of Rossetti's narrative ballad style.]

The most ambitious Victorian sonnet sequence and Rossetti's most formal and extended treatment of his idealisms is **"The House of Life"**, a Victorian meditation on work, will, art, metaphysics and time as well as stylized erotic love. (p. 18)

[The poem presents] a sequence from love to loss, but all is foreboded, foreknown, and fore-announced. [The] early portion of the sequence is presumably devoted to satisfied love, yet it is difficult to find a sonnet unqualified by fear, weariness, painful memories, and thoughts of death. Even possession of the beloved is a ritualistic, heavy, solemn easing of pain. Emphasis is on that from which the beloved must rescue the lover as much as on their affection or passion; nothing is unselfconscious or lighthearted. (p. 19)

"Love" in Rossetti, as in almost all nineteenth-century poets, is a metaphor for all that is best and most concentrated in life—memory, sensuousness, idealism, the aesthetic and the intense. Whereas in Keats' poetry the knowledge of warm human love seemed of greater significance even than death, and to Pater and certain Decadents aesthetic experience or love was the self-expression of a private identity perpetually verging on extinction, Rossetti offered a middle view; private experience must involve some other human being or be a response, even if purely subjective and internal, to a minimally social relation. Yet he considered the possibility that even this experience might be nullified by death or error, or might only be able to exist in painfully uncertain and attenuated forms.

An ambiguity pervades ["**The House of Life**"], however, as the result of Rossetti's unclarified and perhaps inconsistent attitude toward sexual love. In his narratives and ballads sexuality is more frequently and overtly associated with moral guilt, although considered inevitable. **"The House of Life"**, by contrast, has virtually no moral context; whether the love it celebrates is socially appropriate or "caused" is not explained. . . . However one of the sequence's principal obsessions is guilt. The cause of this guilt is never stated, but I feel it is some combination of regret for lost time or opportunity and diffused suggestions of an inevitable taint imposed upon all sexual emotion. (p. 88)

In my opinion death is covertly associated with guilt throughout the entire sequence. The many shadowed veils, dim reflections, and frail screens could well be coverings for an irrational, nebulous, contextless guilt. Love and the beloved seem always to suggest time passing, death, separation, the highest intensities of a doomed life. Even though only a few sonnets directly interweave the sense of guilt for lost time, death, and romantic love, to Rossetti erotic love is consistently, among other things, the concentrated symbol of the obscenely hastening hour.

In **"The House of Life"** Rossetti has associated, in the shifting way in which possibly they were experienced, several of the most recurrent Victorian preoccupations and perceptions—the fragmentation of the self through temporality, guilt-in-isolation, and the strangulation of all sex, art, love, and pleasant nature, not only by bourgeois convention, but by the great gray blankness of the cold and faceless world. . . . (pp. 88-9)

Rossetti's balladic style fuses narrative, ballad, Victorian contemplativeness and Romantic literary mannerisms. . . . Within [the] general category [of the literary ballad] appear some of Rossetti's best and some of his most idiosyncratic poems, and in experimenting with romantic ballad forms he showed his greatest variation and progression in style and preoccupation. This development parallels his shifts within the sonnet

Pencil and chalk self-portrait by Rossetti, March 1847.

and other non-balladic forms, and its extent belies both the charge that he altered technically while presenting identical themes or, on the other hand, that he was able to vary his themes but never improved on his early techniques. (p. 102)

Rossetti's several early romantic ballads [including **"The Bride's Prelude"** and **"The Staff and Scrip"**] illustrate sexual idealism, sublimation, and repression; his later lengthy narratives are increasingly obsessed with revenge and violent death. The early narratives espouse a metaphysic of heavenly reunion for virtuous lovers as reparation for the sufferings of earth; by the late **"The King's Tragedy"** the specific injustices of earth are more fully documented, but the only reparation possible for murder is a bloody revenge; retribution falls alike on the guilty and innocent. The later narratives are simultaneously more complex and unified in form, contain fewer Keatsian and ornamental mannerisms, and exchange the earlier languishing female figures for more aggressively active heroines.

The category of sexual revenge ballad [which includes **"Sister Helen"**, **"Eden Bower"**, and **"Troy Town"**] is roughly intermediate in chronology between the early and late romantic narratives. . . . These concentrated ballad narratives of sexual vengeance constitute Rossetti's most unusual achievement; there is nothing quite so cheerfully or aggressively horrible in Victorian literature. Sex emerges from its romanticized disguises, not to render mankind happy but to extinguish totally the human ego. In most early poems he had moralized over seduction, thus preserving conceptions of human will and choice. Here destruction seems both externally inevitable and internally willed; man is fated to destroy himself, as well as to be destroyed by woman from without, and evilly wills his own overthrow. Rossetti preserves considerable impartiality concerning the natures of man and woman, however; neither agent seems the more blameable, although woman is subjectively the more psychologically threatening. (pp. 102-03)

All of these ballads are concerned with the psychological responses of one person, whether protagonist or observer; narrative plot is significant only as it rationalizes or precipitates this response. In the use of color and detail Rossetti is only minimally a painter-in-words; instead he records the psychology of intense suspension in the presence of an event, image, or tableau. The long narratives seem extensions of his short poems and sonnets on pictures; in the longer poems he reacts to a changing tableau rather than a single picture, but the psychology is not greatly altered. **"The Bride's Prelude"**, for example, is a lengthy tableau/narrative which reenacts a single psychic state.

"The Bride's Prelude" expresses so many Victorian romance mannerisms that it is virtually a parody of that genre. The elaborated narrative romance form is used to portray a situation simultaneously attractive and repellent, sensuous and painful. Since it is both a tableau and narrative, one might expect narrative action to relieve the tableau's static quality, but in fact these reinforce one another. The tableau concentrates on the heroine's ingrown psychology of shame and stagnation, while the narrative interprets and reinforces her misery by listing, simplistically and oppressively, the past and present sensations which cause it. (p. 104)

Rossetti seldom again used the extensive detail of this early poem; it here functions . . . not to create movement but to curtail it, to intensify emotion by holding the mind fixed on certain objects. Rossetti's early poetic style is not inconsistent with his late, less consciously descriptive manner, although he learns to produce the same effects of doomed elegance and psychological brooding more briefly and less circularly; his elaborations, ironically, become more direct. Here as in **"The House of Life"**, sensuousness is sedate, uncertain, allied with latent guilts.

Stasis within **"The Bride's Prelude"** is emphasized by the point in time at which the narrative begins—all is almost ended, the narration is painful memory. The bride awaits with complete passivity what to her is ultimate shame and horror, marriage to the murderer of her former betrothed, also previously the father by her of an illegitimate child. The poem focuses intently on repression—the repression of nature, the repression of her past life, her suppressed pain as she narrates the story, and even her sister's effortful self-strangulation of mirroring responses.

One of the oppressive external restraints is time, which both passes inexorably and yet refuses to pass. Thus the great emphasis on stillness, pause, hesitation. . . . (pp. 105-06)

[An] all-absorbing silence is intensified by the constant stifling presence of heat and glare, culminating towards the poem's end in a destructive fire. . . . Even when shade and water are permitted to occur, they fail to provide relief; sometimes they suggest further ominous associations. . . . [Other] manifestations of nature are uniformly unpleasant or destructive: famine, storm, harsh noises, or the choked and restrained song of a caged bird. . . . The juxtaposition of heat, drouth, beating sensations, and isolated passive misery suggests the purgative journey of Coleridge's Ancient Mariner, now domesticized, sexualized, and transposed into a Victorian narrative frame. (pp. 106-08)

In **"The House of Life"** fire, light, closeness, and stillness are psychic accompaniments of sensuality; it is not surprising that other Rossettian properties of sensuousness found there are found also in **"The Bride's Prelude"**—elaborate dress, music, jewels, incense, gold and silver, swans, religious suggestions, female companions to the central lady, preoccupation with female lips, eyes, neck, forehead, hands, even allusions to magic spells, winds, the elements, mirrors, hovering wings.

The sensuousness of **"The Bride's Prelude"** is not only sick and oppressive, but its dull insistent monotony is identified with shame and sexual guilt. In **"The House of Life"** the association of guilt and sensuality is more ambiguous; in **"The Bride's Chamber"**, however, sexuality, dizziness, fainting, sexual gratification, and guilt form recurring associations in Rossetti's mind. (pp. 108-09)

In the light of this identification of discomfort, weakness, and sexuality, the character of Rossetti's heroine is interesting. She is incapable of action and her entire experience is consistent in its weakness, passivity, pain, and fear. Even her responses to her sister are governed, not by her own will, but by what she projects as divine causation. . . . (p. 109)

Aloÿse is the ultimate embodiment of a particular early Victorian stereotype of the heroine—swooning, hypochondriac, self-pitying, creatress of an intense, circular emotionality. (p. 110)

Every event is carefully described to avoid expressions of her own activity or will; instead of "I fell down from my palfrey", she says, "My palfrey threw me", instead of "I escaped to the postern", "I was led down to the postern". Much of her suffering, symbolically, occurs when she is physically prostrate, in bed, drawn on a litter, *et cetera*. . . . Her internal sufferings also mirror passively the heat and cold, water and drouth, of the outside elements; she is alternately flushed and chilled, states associated with her weariness, dizziness, and disease. . . .

Even a limited narcissism, the last refuge of the totally repressed and apathetic, seems barely able to creep out of her. . . . (p. 111)

Aloÿse's passivity is further emphasized by contrast with her sister Amelotte, who exhibits at once greater violence of response and more self-control. The sisters form an interesting antiphony of unhappiness. . . . (p. 112)

In **"The House of Life"** Rossetti's persona and mistress are often represented by a few disjoint portions of their bodies, even by mere breathings and emanations; here also hands, eyes, breath, tears, hair, arms, and necks of his heroines function independently. . . . (p. 113)

Frequently in the poem Rossetti mentions unexpectedly an object or part of the body distant from those he has described—the effect is jerky, brittle, sudden, artificial, and eccentric.

This sense of disjoint objects around a blurred center may be a part of what is considered a Pre-

Raphaelite manner. . . . Further, the sense that images are broken up into pieces, that different parts of a body or situation are at any time liable to express emotion independently, gives an effect of automation, of forces popping up mysteriously, emphasising again both the external passivity and the deep obsessive roots of the emotions expressed. (pp. 113-14)

The atmosphere of hot breath and faintness throughout **"The Bride's Prelude"** is not merely physical. Here as in **"The House of Life"** the reader is told carefully what are the emotions he should see within the situation—shame, luxuriousness, and passion. The definitions are partially Aloÿse's, while nothing in the poem indicates that they should be interpreted with reservations or irony. . . . [Within] the repetitions and closed atmosphere of her tale, grief, despair, and anguish come to define one another, so that her pain is self-diagnosed, then intensified by circular restatement. We are expected to feel many of the sister's subjective emotions and guilts vicariously, but since the dramatic situation fails to explain or justify them further on rational or objective grounds, Aloÿse's narration remains solely a confession. (p. 115)

"The Staff and Scrip" is Rossetti's closest approximation to a cheerful and romanticized idealization of sexual love, as well as his only poem mentioning chivalric combat. . . . The poem openly expresses the metaphysic of a heaven for true lovers which in varying forms underlies all the early romance narratives, although some cases, such as **"The Bride's Prelude"** or **"Sister Helen"**, embody the inverse, that faithless lovers do not unite in heaven.

Rossetti's early romantic writings tended to idealize the passive, beautiful, golden-haired woman, often an inspiration to male virtue; the Queen of **"The Staff and Scrip"** exhibits all of these characteristics. Of such early heroines only the Blessed Damozel survives this stereotyping process with any individual traits. Rossetti's other heroines divide roughly into three categories: the virtuous but wronged heroines Aloÿse and Rose Mary are also "fallen" women, the aggressive and interesting Helen and Lilith are evil, and Beatrice and King James' wife are noble and beautiful but totally without character or distinctiveness. The Queen in **"The Staff and Scrip"** most resembles the flaccid ladies of the last category. (pp. 130-31)

"The Staff and Scrip" is useful for comparisons with other early Rossetti poems. As the imagery and situation of the early **"The Bride's Prelude"** faintly echoes the purgative journey of Coleridge's mariner, several elements of **"The Staff and Scrip"** seem to recombine or suggest that journey—the hill, heat, fire, setting and rising sun, tribulations, and verbal echoes. . . . This is not to argue that Rossetti consciously had Coleridge in mind when writing **"The Staff and Scrip"**, merely that for several decades after "The Rime" it was difficult to write a poem concerning an extended and painful moral/redemptive process without some memories of Coleridge.

While **"The Bride's Prelude"** had suppressed most water-images, **"The Staff and Scrip"** has a healthy impartiality of water, fire, sun, air, dust, wasteland, and flower references. . . . In **"The Staff and Scrip"**, as in **"The Blessed Damozel"**, Rossetti emphasizes the lovers' reunion in heaven, while the mention of courtly games and sport in **"The Staff and Scrip"** suggests Aloÿse's experiences. The use of a conventional pseudo-medieval religious framework is common to much of Rossetti's earlier poetry, but here **"The Blessed Damozel"**'s ambiguities of faith and evil are absent, as well as **"The Bride's Prelude"**'s theme of treacherous love. Another romantic motif which Rossetti will later rework appears briefly here, that of the beloved known in the unconscious before first seen with physical eyes. . . . (pp. 132-34)

"The Staff and Scrip" is seldom considered one of Rossetti's more skillful or original poems. . . . However it is interesting as an early romantic literary ballad with few metaphysical complexities, faithful if separated lovers, and a partially happy ending. Also, with a certain evenhanded monotony and unambiguity it collects usefully Rossettian mannerisms and preoccupations expressed elsewhere, especially in other early ballads.

"Dante at Verona" is Rossetti's only early narrative ballad which combines political and love themes; it is similar to **"The King's Tragedy"**, his last lengthy narrative, in its definitions of political and personal virtue and its assumption that corruption inevitably prevails in high places. (p. 134)

The poem reveals its kinship with the other early narratives, however, in its imagery, piety, moralizing tone, its long-suffering, passive protagonist, and its idealized golden-haired woman figures. (p. 135)

"Dante at Verona" is noticeably consistent in moral tone with other early Rossetti poems. Sexual license is condemned . . . , the nobly aspiring leave sordid, worldly details and affairs for the pursuit of art, and the greedy and unjust dominate and ostracize the worthy. In **" 'Retro Me, Sathana!' "** . . . , for example, the righteous walk lowly ways while Satan's minions travel broad highways; in **"The Choice"** sexual hedonism and total asceticism must be renounced for aspiration, reflection, and work; in **"Old and New Art"** the desire for artistic achievement, external fame, and the reestablishment of morality are assumed synonymous. In all cases outward neglect and inward melancholy or hesitation retard the artist's progress. (pp. 138-39)

Not surprisingly for a sexual moralist, Rossetti used rape as a metaphor for aggression throughout his early political sonnets, and **"Dante at Verona"** parallels political corruption with harlotry. . . . In **"Jenny"** the siren-figure, tamed and rendered pathetic, represents one individual of the aggregate social problem created by male sexual license. In **"The Burden of Nineveh"** civilizations decay because individual men reject Christ's "lowly ways" for vanity and material gain. Dante and King James are both men of personal honor; King James redresses the wronged poor and leads a blameless domestic life, while Dante faithfully mourns his early love and desires to rescue his city from moneychangers. In general, the presence or absence of social justice depends on the self-control and rectitude of individual persons. Yet there is some shift between the two political narratives; the moralistically aggrieved tone of **"Dante at Verona"** differs from the more laconic pathos with which the king's murder is described. Rossetti's early instinctive, vaguely documented pessimism and his fear that the noble must suffer is replaced by a more concrete imagination of political evil. There is less need to exaggerate or plead the malicious intent of what is self-evidently horrible.

Rossetti's early ballads manifest several common characteristics of his early style, belief, and expectations. Several narratives describe the trials of unhappy protagonists, ending in death or emotional deprivation. Both male and female personae possess intense emotions; to attain happiness women must divorce these from sexuality and embrace love and religion, while men must channel them into romantic, chivalric, or patriotic behavior. They must deserve their ideal love in order to unite with her in heaven; for the early lovers, then, the real world is of little direct significance except as a place within which they must suffer to earn love. (pp. 139-40)

Throughout the early ballads earthly sexuality is invariably frustrated; the actively sexual are evil. Each ballad contains at least one idealized heroine, who is pious, restrained, and totally lacking in aggressiveness or vigor. Society invariably defeats or victimizes the worthy individual—the rejected poet and statesman, the virtuous if violated heroine, the chivalrous pilgrim. The only female protagonist [Aloÿse] is identified with sexual transgression, a consistent pattern in Rossetti's narratives, while male protagonists are associated with political and poetic as well as romantic endeavor.

The early ballads are generally somewhat anecdotal. Only **"The Blessed Damozel"** avoids the effect of running incidents and images arranged without climax, and even the shortest, **"The Staff and Scrip"**, is marred by sudden gaps and pauses in narrative. Yet in spite of these traits, which suggest the rough transitions, disparate images and disconnected moralizing of Rossetti's early sonnets, the early diffuse, romantic ballads have an attractive freshness of open statement and self-revelatory emotion. Although in these early ballads Rossetti is not as skilled as he later will become in

altering or embodying point of view, the early poems are at least important in considering his private emotions and poetic development, and some of his early images are bright and memorable in a manner interestingly variant from his later more shrouded, dark effects. Two of the early ballads, **"The Blessed Damozel"** and **"Dante at Verona"**, are excellent, unusual works, and both reveal qualities characteristic of their early period of composition.

The sexual vengeance ballads are a tiny, significant category, consisting of **"Sister Helen"**, **"Eden Bower"**, and **"Troy Town"**. . . . These ballads are the extreme and idiosyncratic expression of one of [Rossetti's] chief interests, maleficent sexuality. In the early romantic narratives fatality and women are loosely related, but here he conjoins them suddenly with fierce concentration. The female becomes a more active force, sexual, vengeful; in contrast to the quietist, masochistic Aloÿse, she responds to rejection with destructive rage. The lovers' heaven disappears, and evil is simultaneously contemplated and dramatized. (pp. 140-41)

Although in these ballads human sexuality has become a completely destructive force, unproductive of ultimate good or happiness, man and woman are mutually enchained. As inhuman abstractions the destructive women may seem repellent, but they illustrate a certain psychological truth, sex viewed in a state of ter-

Rossetti's tombstone at Birchington-on-Sea, designed by Ford Madox Brown.

ror, a puritanised libido arising to protest its discomfort. (p. 142)

["**Sister Helen**"] contains another one of Rossetti's domestic situations, sister conversing with little brother, used with great irony; amusingly this poem also parallels the other narratives in which a young woman confides a sin to a member of her immediate family. The sister-younger brother situation is not common in poetry, and the religious connotations of "**Sister Helen**" weirdly belie her actual witch nature.

The meter and rhythm of the poem are intricately appropriate to the subject, with four of seven lines designed as echo or refrain to comment mournfully on the brother's questions and Helen's answers. (pp. 145-46)

The images are simple, starkly presented, and repeated. Frequently occurring are the moon, wind, chill (cold, ice), and fire. . . .

Sounds also are important; there are the loud wind, the cries of the first three supplicants, the crying of Keith of Ewern, the "heavy sound" of the knell, the "woe's dumb cry" of the bride and her weeping. (p. 147)

The final picture left by "**Sister Helen**" is admirably stark—the red fire glowing in the black night, the pale faces, hair, and plumes of the visitants, the "white" soul crossing the door. More than is usual in Rossetti's poems, this one both narrates a story and yet conveys a pictorial effect. (p. 148)

"**Sister Helen**" is certainly no poem of detailed description; all is known by the presence of elemental forces, shapes, contrasts of color, voices, and sounds of pain. In place of description are direct interpretations of the emotions felt by the characters. . . . Yet the action has given sufficient cause for [the characters'] reactions; they seem an obvious response rather than an intrusion on the reader's judgment. (p. 149)

The strong colors, emphatic rhythms, and lurid scenes of "**Sister Helen**" . . . create an eccentrically humorous and self-parodying effect, incongruous but interesting. . . . "**Sister Helen**" has perhaps appropriately become a Rossettian set-piece, since it is original and direct in stanza form, imagery, and theme. To the extent that "originality" can mean the crafted use of the ballad's potentiality for combining the passionate, symbolic, incantatory, and parodic, this is one of Rossetti's most individualistic and carefully wrought poems. (p. 150)

The metrics, refrain, and sound effects of "**Eden Bower**" seem as consciously and tightly constructed as in any Rossetti work, and perhaps more so than in any other ballad. . . . As in "**Sister Helen**" the artifice can seem humorous and self-mocking, but here I think it undercuts Rossetti's intention severely and produces lugubriousness instead of horror. Perhaps Lilith is too

simple-mindedly malicious to create much interest or sympathy. (p. 152)

Adam and Eve are also presented too externally to reinforce sympathy, so that neither aggressor nor victims are as appealing as their counterparts in "**Sister Helen**". With the reader's interest alienated from the central characters, the poem becomes as much a contrived set-piece of allegorical effects as a dramatic narrative. . . .

Unlike Rossetti's other lovers, [Lilith] seeks no reunion with her former lover either in heaven or earth, only simple revenge. The biblical cosmology places her in context; she is more limited in character than the humans she affects, yet able to pervert their destiny and happiness. Trivial in her motives, she is the Rossettian evil/seductive life force—amoral sexuality—both less human and closer to abstraction than Sister Helen. (p. 154)

Like "The Rime of the Ancient Mariner", "**Eden Bower**" ostensibly expresses the theme of the temptation of archetypal man; Rossetti sexualizes the temptation, however, minimizes the Adam figure, and concerns himself with the psychology of the temptress, a female who opposes the poem's cosmological order.

Whatever the repellent qualities of Sister Helen and Lilith, they are vigorous and passionate women. When in "**Jenny**" Rossetti transfers the pattern of destructive sexuality and the sexually free or "wronged" woman to contemporary England, he becomes noticeably more squeamish, sentimental, and indirect in treating female character. His lengthy pieties on man as the cause of sexual evil might seem to refute this. . . . However Rossetti is unable to ascribe to Jenny any of the positive emotions or strength of will which he postulates for his exotically distant or extra-natural heroines, in most cases also "fallen". Jenny is a weak, trivial person, attracted solely to money, personal finery, and gaudy luxuries, at best innocent of her own deeds and oblivious to her sordid future. . . . (p. 156)

Although Rossetti differed from contemporary poets in his somewhat more overt discussions of a self-conscious and intelligent sexuality, his assumptions were not especially deviant. For all his pieties concerning fallen women, the ironies of causation, and so forth, it does not occur to him that acts which the prostitute commits may be morally neutral, or the result of economic coercion rather than choice. He argues for pity, perhaps, or interest in the prostitute's condition, but never for unjudging neutrality or practical aid. (p. 158)

In "**Jenny**", as in the revenge ballads, human sexuality and attendant jealousy destroy life. Yet the narrator of "**Jenny**" avoids expressing his own emotional responses directly and severely condescends to those of Jenny. Ironically, in his exotic, supernatural ballads Rossetti represents more clearly his age's preoccupation with sublimation, its conception of women as passive yet secretly demanding.

Rossetti's evil or partially evil heroines are attractive not so much because they incarnate evil passion but because they are assumed to be at least to some degree active agents in their fate. However revengeful Sister Helen may be, she is presented as suffering a long mental trial. She is one of Rossetti's heroines who is simultaneously active and passive, the inflicting force and the afflicted. Lilith is more vicious, less comprehensible, but also vigorous, strikingly colorful, passionate, and peripheral to human moral judgments.

Rossetti's sexual vengeance ballads show great improvement over former works in dramatic concentration, starkness of imagery, and contrived verbal effects. For the revenge ballads he creates his idiosyncratic refrains, and their fusion of narrative and psychological allegory seems as congenial to Rossetti's temperament as any poetic form which he attempted. They parallel the increasingly dramatic, condensed, and consciously rhetorical later sonnets, and their virtues of concentration, symbolic vividness, diminished prudery, and dramatic impartiality were in lessened form transferable to Rossetti's later lengthy narratives.

In his last narratives Rossetti experienced a partial return to the early extended ballad, creating his most complex poems and some of the finest examples of a very strange genre, the Victorian tragic narrative ballad. His later narratives reveal increased concentration of form, less emphasis on romantic love and more on death and revenge. What had always been a dark view of the world alters its focus and deepens; the sexual impulse still leads to sin and death, although its victims may be good people, and the external world can only neglect and crucify its noble men. As Rossetti ages, he becomes less eager to condemn human sexual behavior, less preoccupied with the inequities of artistic fame, but more pessimistic concerning the eventual results of sexuality and artistic endeavor. (pp. 159-60)

["**Rose Mary**"] is Rossetti's most elaborate ballad and romantic narrative, and his longest poem aside from **"The House of Life"** and **"The Bride's Prelude"**. Also it is one of his most ornately exotic, consisting of a trilogy of situations each surrounding a reflecting image, combining narration, mystery-symbology, and Coleridgean rhythms into an artfully dissonant music. (p. 160)

"Rose Mary" is superior to Rossetti's earlier romantic narrative **"The Bride's Prelude"**, and his simple ballad **"The Staff and Scrip"**; it combines ballad directness with the elaborate plotting and imagery of romantic narrative. Like **"The Bride's Prelude"** it begins near the end of the action and is presented in tableau; also like **"The Bride's Prelude"** it contains the gradual uncovering of past treachery and error, and is the unhap-

py story of a "sinning" woman and faithless lover narrated in a domestic context—here to Rose Mary's mother. Rossetti has managed several improvements since **"The Bride's Prelude"**, however; he conveys weariness and pain without producing those same effects in the reader. . . . [Rose Mary] turns more swiftly to action than Aloÿse; the narrative is climaxed by her resolute breaking of the beryl stone, knowing that she and the spirits will be destroyed. Her emotions shift also from fear to hope to fear throughout the poem, creating suspense; **"The Bride's Prelude"** has all the suspense of a clock winding down, from slow predictability to slower predictability. (pp. 160-61)

The beryl stone is the ultimate form of Rossetti's preoccupation with reflective images. In **"The Bride's Prelude"** the reflecting jewels and mirror are fortuitous except for their addition to the sense of circularly oppressive heat and narcissism; here the beryl reflects the theme and action and is therefore less extraneous and decorative. (p. 162)

The beryl is an image of Rose Mary, a beautiful object destroyed by sin, yet since Rose Mary is also the agent of destruction she is granted a final apotheosis. Unlike Aloÿse she possesses an active moral self which can destroy another portion of herself of which she disapproves. (p. 164)

[Rose Mary] embodies Rossetti's ideal of the singlemindedly passionate person (almost invariably female) who will die for love. Rose Mary's story, like Aloÿse's, could be read as a gloss on the theme "sin brings punishment", but since her sin is merely stated rather than elaborated, it becomes less a Victorian disgrace than a mysterious psychological fact with which she must reckon.

There is direct paradox in Rossetti's interpenetration of piety and occultism throughout the poem. . . . [The] sense of mundane reality is lessened by the presence of both world and antiworld; all is mystery, sacred and profane. The identification of the traditional extremes of religion and sorcery divorces the poem's imagery and plot from expected standards of judgment, and responses become personal, arbitrary, and preordained. . . . The combination of mystery and religion carries conviction, but one is not quite sure of what— the deep, the unfathomable, sudden shocks of "good" and "evil". States of mind and body, such as the trance and swoon, are used not only to convey emotion but to express a relationship to strange cosmic forces. . . . (pp. 165-66)

"Rose Mary" differs from earlier poems in its complexly interrelated symbology of mysteries, ordering themes which otherwise might seem vague and emotive. The swirling-together of objects reduced nearly to abstractions produces mystical impressions, redeemed from imprecision only by the careful use of a mystic symbology. For example, the rose combines associations of nature, religion, and passion; the sword those of antiquity, time, metallic, flashing qualities, and pain; the crystal, associations of water, clouds, air, light, moon-and-sun shapes, mysticism, gems, reflections, and purity. The snake associates with the mythology of both sorcery and orthodox religion; the architectural projections suggest both the unpleasant tomb and attractive ritual. Virtually all these symbols gather into one description, that of the altar which Rose Mary approaches to confront the beryl stone and to destroy and be destroyed by its evil. . . . (pp. 174-75)

["**The White Ship**"] presents something as close to a just world as occurs in Rossetti's canon. (p. 178)

Both of Rossetti's late medieval ballads, "**The White Ship**" and "**The King's Tragedy**" notice in passing whether the governance of their medieval kingdoms is for good or evil. . . . The king and son of "**The White Ship**" are notorious exploiters, so their mutual fate is an earned retribution. . . . But the emphasis on the victims' evil character is partially counterbalanced by the Prince's self-sacrifice in attempting to save his sister and the king's own death at the shock of hearing of his son's. If cruel to outsiders, they at least show nobility in caring for each other. Once again a Rossettian poem reduces largely to domestic melodrama. (pp. 179-80)

In relation to the number of ballads Rossetti produced, he did experiment with a fairly wide range of themes and mannerisms. The later ballads show improvement over their predecessors in heightened incidents, imagery, and subtlety of point of view. In his late narratives Rossetti was more careful to define and qual-

ify perceptions of sexual and political evil, and his early moralistic romantic pessimism became more somberly dramatic. Simultaneously he improved his mixture of the parodic and the simple, the artificial and direct, to produce the incongruous grim cheerfulness of "**The White Ship**" and "**Jan Van Hunks**". Since Rossetti's final narratives were his psychological counterpart to Coleridge's mystery poems, it is appropriate that these show more direct use of Coleridge's rhythm and imagery, especially to emphasize descriptions of the weird and inscrutable, than had most of his previous ballads. (p. 192)

Rossetti's romantic narratives seem almost an historical anomaly, successors of Keatsian romance and Tennysonian domestic sentiment but less prophetic of what was to come. "**Rose Mary**", the final example, seems virtually the last appearance of a contrived and complex literary form. . . . "**Rose Mary**" approaches a baroque parody of both ballad and narrative, yet ironically Rossetti's romantic narratives are also among his most eclectic and careful works, fusing lushness and mystery in a way he never quite achieved elsewhere. While "**The Bride's Prelude**", an early romance, looks backward to Keats, Coleridge, Patmore, and Tennyson, "**Rose Mary**" echoes only the first two of these poets obliquely, and foreshadows the symbolism of the late century and Yeats. Since Rossetti excelled in artificial, syncretic, complex, and exotic poetry, it is unfortunate that he was unable to complete more works of this kind. (p. 193)

Florence Saunders Boos, in her *The Poetry of Dante G. Rossetti: A Critical Reading and Source Study*, Mouton, 1976, 311 p.

SOURCES FOR FURTHER STUDY

Doughty, Oswald. *A Victorian Romantic: Dante Gabriel Rossetti.* London: Oxford University Press, 1949, 712 p.

> The definitive biography.

Ford, George H. "Rossetti." In his *Keats and the Victorians: A Study of His Rise to Fame, 1821-1895*, pp. 93-148. Hamden and London: Archon Books, 1962.

> Demonstrates the profound influence of Keats's works on Rossetti. Ford concludes that Rossetti "is the link between Keats and later writers, and through his example and influence, the Keatsian strain becomes predominant in later nineteenth-century poetry."

Sharp, William. *Dante Gabriel Rossetti: A Record and a Study.* London: Macmillan and Co., 1882, 432 p.

> A detailed descriptive survey of Rossetti's paintings and poetry, prefaced by a lengthy biographical chapter.

Stevenson, Lionel. "Rossetti as Poet." In his *The Pre-Raphaelite Poets*, pp. 18-77. Chapel Hill: University of North Carolina Press, 1972.

> Examines the imagery, meter, and verbal techniques of Rossetti's verse, as well as the predominant note of despondency found throughout the poet's work.

Vogel, Joseph F. *Dante Gabriel Rossetti's Versecraft.* Gainesville: University of Florida Press, 1971, 111 p.

> A detailed analysis of the meter, stanzaic structures, rhyme, and other devices in Rossetti's poetry.

Waugh, Evelyn. *Rossetti: His Life and Works.* New York: Dodd, Mead and Co., 1928, 232 p.

> A lively biography which concentrates primarily upon Rossetti's personal relationships and his work as a painter.

Philip Roth

1933-

(Full name Philip Milton Roth) American novelist, short story writer, essayist, autobiographer, and critic.

INTRODUCTION

*O*ne of the most prominent and controversial writers in contemporary literature, Roth draws heavily upon his Jewish-American upbringing and his life as a successful author to explore such concerns as the search for self-identity, conflicts between traditional and contemporary moral values, and the relationship between fiction and reality. The scatological content of some of his works and his harsh satiric portraits of Jewish life have inspired considerable critical debate. While some commentators view his work as anti-Semitic, perverse, or self-indulgent, others laud Roth's skill at rendering dialect, his exuberance and inventiveness, and his outrageous sense of humor. John N. McDaniel remarked: "No other living writer has so rigorously and actively attempted to describe the destructive element of experience in American life—the absurdities and banalities that impinge upon self-realization."

Roth was born in Newark, New Jersey. After graduating from Weequahic High School in 1950, he enrolled at Newark College of Rutgers University. Dissatisfied with what he considered the school's "provincialism," Roth transferred to Bucknell University in Pennsylvania in 1951. There he published his first story, "Philosophy," in the literary magazine *Et cetera*, which he helped to found and edit, and graduated magna cum laude and Phi Beta Kappa with a bachelor's degree in English in 1954. Receiving his master's degree in English from the University of Chicago in 1955, Roth served briefly in the United States Army but was discharged due to a back injury he sustained during basic training. Although he returned to study for his Ph.D in English at the University of Chicago, Roth withdrew to pursue his writing career in 1957. With the aid of a grant from the National Institute of Arts and Letters, the Houghton Mifflin Literary Fellowship, and a

Guggenheim fellowship, Roth was able to complete his first book, *Goodbye, Columbus, and Five Short Stories* (1959). He began teaching at the Writers' Workshop at the University of Iowa in 1960, and in 1962 he became a writer-in-residence at Princeton University. Roth resigned to become a full-time author following the financial success of his third novel, *Portnoy's Complaint* (1969).

Roth received the National Book Award in 1959 for his first work, *Goodbye, Columbus.* In the acclaimed novella, which was adapted for film by Paramount in 1969, Roth satirizes American materialistic values by focusing on the conflicting emotions of Neil Klugman, a lower-middle-class Jewish man struggling to adjust to the unfamiliar lifestyle of Brenda Patimkin, a wealthy Jewish suburbanite with whom he falls in love. Roth's first novel, *Letting Go* (1962), explores the anxieties and moral dilemmas faced by college-educated members of the generation that came of age during the 1950s. Compared by some critics to Henry James's novel *The Portrait of a Lady* in its free, unconfined style, the novel initially garnered mild notices but eventually gained status as one of Roth's best novels. Scott Donaldson commented: "*Letting Go* is a major novel and deserves to stand with the works of the master whose name Philip Roth so often and appropriately invokes. Like James, he is one of those writers on whom very little is lost." *When She Was Good* (1967), Roth's only novel to feature a female protagonist and a Protestant, midwestern setting, attracted negative reviews for its humorless portrait of an imperious middle-class housewife.

Roth is credited with propelling Jewish-American fiction into the realm of popular culture with his next novel, *Portnoy's Complaint.* Originally appearing as a series of sketches in *Esquire, Partisan Review,* and *New American Review,* the novel takes the form of a profane, guilt-ridden confession related by Alexander Portnoy to a silent psychoanalyst, Dr. Spielvogel. Decrying his Jewish upbringing, Portnoy wrestles with his Oedipal complex, obsession with Gentile women, and sexual fetishes in an attempt to free himself from the restrictions of his cultural background. Following the book's publication, scholars and Jewish-Americans labeled Roth an anti-Semitic Jew and objected to the novel's sexually explicit content and what they considered Roth's degrading treatment of Jewish life. However, *Portnoy's Complaint* also won praise for its ethnic humor, adroit dialogue, and psychological insight. It remains Roth's best-known work to date.

Following the publication of *Portnoy's Complaint,* a backlash of preponderantly negative criticism seemed to follow the appearance of Roth's novels of the 1970s. *Our Gang* (1971), a political satire of ex-President Richard Nixon and his administration, was faulted as heavy-handed and sophomoric; *The Breast* (1972), a Kafkaesque fantasy in which a professor is transformed into a six-foot mammary gland, received similar censure (though some later scholars have praised the novel's ambiguity and multiplicity); and *The Great American Novel* (1973), in which Roth lampoons the myths surrounding baseball and American culture, was regarded as less accomplished than Bernard Malamud's tribute to the same sport, *The Natural.*

Much of Roth's ensuing work is about the relationship of fiction to reality. *My Life as a Man* (1974) concerns a novelist named Peter Tarnopol who is writing about a controversial novelist named Nathan Zuckerman. Although some reviewers faulted the book as a recapitulation of Roth's previous works, Peter S. Prescott called *My Life as a Man* "[Roth's] best, . . . most complex and most ambitious novel," and Isa Kapp deemed the book "a brilliant documentary on the writing of American fiction." Zuckerman reappears in several of Roth's later novels, including *The Ghost Writer* (1979), in which the young author gains notoriety and sparks intense critical debate with his salacious novel *Carnovsky,* much as Roth did with *Portnoy's Complaint.* Two subsequent volumes, *Zuckerman Unbound* (1981) and *The Anatomy Lesson* (1983), trace Zuckerman as he encounters the joys and disadvantages of fame and then succumbs to the terrors of writer's block. These books examine such topics as the difficulties of familial and sexual relationships and the conflicts between traditional and contemporary moral values. *The Ghost Writer, Zuckerman Unbound,* and *The Anatomy Lesson* were collected along with a previously unpublished novel, *The Prague Orgy,* in *Zuckerman Bound: A Trilogy and Epilogue* (1985). In *The Prague Orgy,* Zuckerman travels to Czechoslovakia to attempt to secure the unpublished manuscripts of a deceased Yiddish writer. While continuing to develop themes and conflicts characteristic of the Zuckerman books, Roth compares the roles of literature and writers in the free world with those in the Eastern European communist states.

Roth received the National Book Critics Circle Award for his next novel, *The Counterlife* (1987). Often considered the best of the Zuckerman books, *The Counterlife* chronicles Zuckerman's travels to Israel, where his brother has joined a militant terrorist group, and then to England, where he combats English anti-Semitism. In this novel, Roth makes use of abrupt shifts in plot and point of view to offer a variety of perspectives on such subjects as death, literature, and the meaning of Judaism. Roth's next novel, *Deception* (1990), is made up entirely of snippets of pre- and post-coital conversation between a woman and a man. Combining fiction and autobiography, the novel serves in some ways as a reply to Roth's critics. The man, who is named Philip, tells the woman in one passage: "I write fiction and I'm told its autobiography. I write autobiography and I'm told it's fiction, so since I'm so dim and they're so smart, let *them* decide."

Negative criticism of Roth's works has ranged from charges of anti-Semitism to degrading portrayals of women, obscenity bordering on pornography, repetitiveness of theme, and a self-centered lack of humanity toward characters other than his protagonists. The positive response to his work, however, is equally strong, and Roth's supporters have consistently maintained that he is a deeply moral writer. They argue that his books are humorous in a fantastic sense, and that his satires, while written from a Jewish perspective, offer universal insight into the foibles of American life. The quality and variety of critical opinion that greets

each new book by Roth indicates his standing as a major contemporary novelist. Although he will not please everyone, he is, in the words of John Gardner, "on good terms with the hunchbacked muse of the outrageous."

(For further information about Roth's life and works, see *Concise Dictionary of Literary Biography, 1968-1988; Contemporary Authors*, Vols. 1-4; *Contemporary Authors New Revision Series*, Vols. 1, 22; *Contemporary Literary Criticism*, Vols. 1, 2, 3, 4, 6, 9, 15, 22, 31, 47, 66; *Dictionary of Literary Biography*, Vols. 2, 28; *Dictionary of Literary Biography Yearbook; 1982;* and *Major Twentieth Century Writers.*)

CRITICAL COMMENTARY

THEODORE SOLOTAROFF
(essay date 1970)

[An American critic who helped evaluate and direct the course of recent American literature, Solotaroff is a former editor of *New American Review* (now *American Review*), a literary magazine that has challenged the aesthetic and ethical criteria by which contemporary writing is often judged. In the following excerpt from an essay originally published in his 1970 study *The Red Hot Vacuum, and Other Pieces on the Writing of the 1960s*, Solotaroff recounts his personal encounters with Roth and appraises Roth's early works from *Goodbye, Columbus* to *Portnoy's Complaint*.]

One day in the fall of 1957, I was sitting in a course on Henry James at the University of Chicago. The semester had just begun, and there were a few new faces: one that I had been noticing belonged to a handsome, well-groomed young man who stood out in the lean and bedraggled midst of us veteran graduate students as though he had strayed into class from the business school. The text for the day was *Daisy Miller,* and toward the end of the hour, one of the other students began to run away with the discussion, expounding one of those symbolic religious interpretations of the story that were in fashion at the time everywhere but at Chicago. Eventually the instructor asked me what I thought of this reading, and in the rhetoric I had learned from my mentors among the Chicago critics, I said that it was idiotic. I was immediately seconded by the debonair young man, who, in a very precise and concrete way, began to point out how such a reading turned the purpose and technique of the story inside out. Like two strangers in a pickup basketball game

who discover they can work together, we passed the argument back and forth for a minute or two, running up the score of common sense. It was one of those fine moments of communication that don't occur every day in graduate English courses, and after class we met, shook hands, and exchanged names. His was Philip Roth. (p. 133)

During this year I read several of the stories in manuscript that were to appear two years later in *Goodbye, Columbus.* Raised as I had been, so to speak, on the short-story-as-a-work-of-art, the cool, terse epiphanies of the Joyce of *Dubliners,* the Flaubert of *Un Coeur simple,* of Katherine Mansfield and Hemingway, I didn't at first know how to respond to a story in which the narrator says:

> Though I am very fond of desserts, especially fruit, I chose not to have any. I wanted, this hot night, to avoid the conversation that revolved around my choosing fresh fruit over canned fruit, or canned fruit over fresh fruit; whichever I preferred. Aunt Gladys always had an abundance of the other jamming her refrigerator like stolen diamonds. "He wants canned peaches. I have a refrigerator full of grapes I have to get rid of. . . . " Life was a throwing off for poor Aunt Gladys, her greatest joys were taking out the garbage, emptying her pantry, and making threadbare bundles for what she still referred to as the Poor Jews in Palestine. I only hope she dies with an empty refrigerator, otherwise she'll ruin eternity for everyone else, what with her Velveeta turning green, and her navel oranges growing fuzzy jackets down below.

But my resistance quickly toppled like tenpins. It was like sitting down in a movie house and suddenly seeing there on the screen a film about the block on which I had grown up: the details of place, character, incident all intimately familiar and yet new, or at least never appreciated before for their color and interest. This story of Neil Klugman and Brenda Patimkin was so simple, direct, and evident that it couldn't be "art," and yet I knew that art did advance in just this way: a sudden sweeping aside of outmoded complexities for the sake of a fresh view of experience, often so natural a view and so common an experience that one wondered why writers hadn't been seeing and doing this all along. The informal tone of the prose, as relaxed as conversation, yet terse and fleet and right on the button; the homely images of "stolen diamonds," of the Velveeta, and the oranges, that make the passage glow. Such writing rang bells that not even the Jewish writers had touched; it wasn't Malamud, it wasn't even Saul Bellow: the "literary" fuzz of, say, Augie March had been blown away, and the actualities of the life behind it came forth in their natural grain and color, heightened by the sense of discovery.

Such writing is much more familiar today than it was ten years ago: indeed, it has become one of the staples of contemporary fiction. But at the time the only other writer who seemed to be so effortlessly and accurately in touch with his material was Salinger. For a year or so after reading Catcher in the Rye, I hadn't been

able to walk through Central Park without looking around for Holden and Phoebe Caulfield, and now here was this young semblable of mine who dragged me off for a good corned-beef sandwich or who gave me a push when my car wouldn't start, and who, somehow, was doing for the much less promising poetry of Newark, New Jersey, what the famous Salinger was doing for that of Central Park West. Moreover, if Roth's fiction had something of Salinger's wit and charm, the winning mixture of youthful idealism and cynicism, the air of immediate reality, it was also made of tougher stuff, both in the kind of life it described and in the intentions it embodied. Salinger's taste for experience, like that of his characters, was a very delicate one; Roth's appetite was much heartier, his tone more aggressive, his moral sense both broader and more decisive.

What fascinated me most about stories like **"Goodbye, Columbus," "The Conversion of the Jews,"** and **"Defender of the Faith"** was the firm, clear way they articulated the inner situation we sensed in each other but either took for granted or indicated covertly—by a reference to Isabelle Archer as a *shiksa,* or by a takeoff on the bulldozing glottals of our father's speech, as we walked away from our literature or linguistics course. In such ways we signaled our self-ironic implication in things Jewish, but Roth's stories dealt directly with the much touchier material of one's efforts to extricate himself, to achieve a mobility that would do justice to his individuality. Social mobility was the least of it. This was the burden of **"Goodbye, Columbus,"** where Neil Klugman's efforts early in the story to latch and hold on to the little wings of Brenda Patimkin's shoulderblades and let them carry him up "those lousy hundred and eight feet that make summer nights so much cooler in Short Hills than they are in Newark" soon take on the much more interesting, and representative, struggle to have her on his own terms, terms that lie well beyond money, comfort, security, status, and have to do with his sexual rights and ultimately his uncertain emotional and moral identity. At the end of the story, Neil stands in front of the Lamont Library and at first wants to hurl a rock through the glass front; but his rage at Brenda, at the things she had been given and has sacrificed him for, soon turns into his curiosity about the young man who stares back at him in the mirrored reflection and who "had turned pursuit and clutching into love, and then turned it inside out again . . . had turned winning into losing and losing—who knows—into winning. . . . "

Neil's prickly and problematic sense of himself, his resistance to the idea of being a bright Jewish boy with an eye for the main chance, for making sure, an idea that was no stranger to other desires—well, this was not simply fiction to me. Nor was the Patimkin package, where horse shows and Big Ten basketball and classy backhands still came wrapped in Jewish conformity and ethnocentricity. In story after story there was an individual trying to work free of the ties and claims of the community. There was Ozzie in **"The Conversion of the Jews,"** who would not have God hedged in by the hostility of Judaism to Christianity; there was Sergeant Marx in **"Defender of the Faith,"** who finally refused to hand over any more of his sense of fairness and responsibility to the seductive appeals of Jewish solidarity; or, on the other hand, there was Eli Peck, who refused to close the book of Jewish history to be more at ease with his landsmen in Suburbia. Or there was even poor Epstein, who managed to pry apart the iron repressions of Jewish family life to claim some final gratifications for himself. Or there was my special favorite, a very early story called **"You Can't Tell a Man by the Song He Sings,"** in which a nice Jewish boy learns from two Italians—a juvenile delinquent and an ex-radical guidance teacher—that some dignities have to be won against the rules and regulations of upward mobility.

Such themes were as evocative to me as a visit from my mother, but I knew then I couldn't write the stories that embodied them in the way that Roth had. It was not just a matter of talent but of the intricate kind of acceptance that joins one's talent to his experience so that he can communicate directly. Though Roth clearly was no less critical of his background than I was, he had not tried to abandon it, and hence had not allowed it to become simply a deadness inside him: the residual feelings, mostly those of anxiety, still intact but without their living context. That is to say, he wrote fiction as he was, while I had come to write as a kind of fantasist of literature who regarded almost all of my actual experience in the world as unworthy of art. A common mistake, particularly in the overliterary age of the late Forties and Fifties, but a decisive one. So if I envied Roth his gifts, I envied even more his honesty, his lack of fastidiousness, his refusal to write stories that labored for a form so fine that almost any naturalness would violate it. The gross affluences and energies of the Patimkins, the crudities of Albie Pelagutti and Duke Scarpa, even the whining and wheedling of Sheldon Grossbart turned him on rather than put him off. Once, I remember, I balked. There is a scene in **"Epstein"** where his wife discovers his rash that they both believe is venereal, and an ugly and not very funny description follows of their fight in the nude. "Why all the *schmutz*?" I asked him. "The story is the *schmutz*," he snapped back.

Our relationship had its other ups and downs. After he dropped out of graduate school, Roth went on teaching in the college, an impressive post to me, if not to him (he was to give it up after a year and head for New York). And since he was publishing his work and looked to be making good use of his bachelor years, he seemed, at least on the surface (which was where my envy led me to look), to have the world by the tail. On the other hand, the world in those days seemed, at least on the surface, to have me by the tail. . . . Roth was visibly well off and I was visibly not, and it made certain differences. At one point I borrowed some money from him, which made us both uncomfortable until it was paid back. One evening he and his date, my wife and I, went to hear a lecture by Saul Bellow—our literary idol—and afterward went out for a beer. His girlfriend, though, ordered a scotch, and into the discussion of what Bellow had said and could have said there intruded an awkward moment at each round of drinks. Or there was a party he came to at my place to celebrate the arrival of bock beer (our version of the rites of spring). As I've suggested, Roth and I shared our past and our opinions much more than we shared our present lives. When we met, it was almost always at his place. My apartment, over in the Negro section, with its Salvation Army decor and its harassed domesticity, seemed both to touch him and make him nervous. I remember him sitting on the edge of a couch, over which I had just nailed on an old shag rug to cover the holes, waiting like a social worker while my wife got our oldest son through his nightly asthma. Then the other guests arrived, the beer flowed, and we turned on with our favorite stimulant—Jewish jokes and caustic family anecdotes—dispensed principally by Roth, whose fantastic mimicry and wit soon had us rolling in our chairs.

That evening came back to mind a few years later when I was reading Roth's first novel, *Letting Go,* which is set mainly in Hyde Park and which deals with the ethos of the graduate-student/young-instructor situation during the Fifties: the "Age of Compassion," as Gabe Wallach, the protagonist, aptly puts it. The story mainly follows Wallach's involvement with Paul and Libby Herz, a needy young couple (money is only the beginning of it), and with Martha Reagenhart, a voluptuous and tough-minded girl who has two children to support and who is looking for some support herself. Attracted both by Libby's frailty and by Martha's strength, and unable to make much contact with the surly Herz, Wallach, an attractive bachelor in comfortable circumstances, spends much of the novel sitting on the edge of his scruples, worrying whether too much or too little is being asked of him, a dilemma he shares with Herz, whose moral self-consciousness takes over whenever the point of view shifts to his side of the story. All of this reckoning of the wages of conscience is accompanied by cool, satirical observation, more successfully of the Jewish background of Gabe and Paul than of their professional life, which Roth used mostly to even a few scores. The best writing in the book came in the scenes in a Detroit boardinghouse when Herz's effort to push Libby through an abortion gets tangled up with the schemes of the retired shyster, Levy, to "help" the pathetic Korngold extract money from his son and to move the cases of underwear that Korngold hoards in his room, waiting for the market to improve.

Like a good many other citizens of Hyde Park, my wife and I furnished a trait here, an anecdote there, but the material was more thoroughly fictionalized in our case than in some others. What Roth was mainly drawing on, I felt, was a certain depressiveness that had been in the air: the result of those long Chicago winters, the longueurs of graduate school and composition courses, the financial strains, the disillusionment with the university (this was the period in which the Hutchins experiments were being dismantled and the administration was waging a reign of respectability in all areas), and the concomitant dullness of the society-at-large, which had reached the bottom of the Eisenhower era. But mostly this depressiveness was caused by the self-inflicted burdens of private life, which in this age of conformity often seemed to serve for politics, art, and the other avenues of youthful experience and experiment. One of the principal occupations in Hyde Park seemed to be difficult marriages: almost everyone I knew was locked into one. This penchant for early marriage and child-rearing, or for only slightly less strenuous affairs, tended to fill the vacuum of commitment for sophisticated but not especially stable young couples and fostered a rather pretentious moralism of duty, sacrifice, home therapy, experiment with domestic roles—often each other's—working things out, saving each other. It was a time when the deferred gratifications of graduate school and the climb to tenure and the problems of premature adjustment seemed the warranty of "seriousness" and "responsibility": those solemn passwords of a generation that practiced a Freudian/Jamesian concern about motives, pondered E. M. Forster's "only connect," and subscribed to Lionel Trilling's "moral realism" and "tragic sense of life." In contrast to today, everyone tried to act as though he were thirty.

Some of this Roth had caught and placed at the center of *Letting Go.* As the title suggests, the novel is a study of entangling attachments, beginning with Gabe's effort to release himself from his widowed father's possessiveness and ending with his frantic effort to complete, and thereby end, his intervention in the life of the Herzes, through helping them to adopt a child. In between, a host of characters push and pull, smother and neglect each other, usually under the guise of solicitude or obligation. At one point Wallach puts it for himself, Herz, and most of the others: "I knew it was not from my students or my colleagues or my publications, but from my private life, my secret life, that I would extract whatever joy—or whatever misery—would be mine." By "private life" he means relationships and their underlying *Realpolitik* of need, dependency, and control.

It was evident that *Letting Go* represented a major effort to move forward from *Goodbye, Columbus.* The theme of communal coerciveness and individual rights that dominates most of the stories had been opened out to deal with the more subtle perversions of loyalty and duty and creaturely feeling that flow through the ties of family, marriage, friendship. A very Jamesian theme: *The Portrait of a Lady* figures almost immediately in *Letting Go,* as a reference point for its interest in benevolent power plays. Also, in bringing his fiction more up to date with the circumstances and issues of his life, Roth had tried for a more chastened, Jamesian tone. The early chapters have some of the circumspect pace and restrained wit of the Master: well-mannered passages of nuance and implication, the main characters carefully observed, the theme tucked neatly away in the movement of action, thought, and dialogue. The book sails gracefully along for about 150 pages or so. Then it begins to turn as gray and bitter as the Chicago winter and, in time, as endless.

What went wrong? As I have indicated, the Hyde Park we had known had not been an especially chipper place, and there was plenty of reason to deal with it in terms of its grim domesticity. Still, Roth had laid it on and laid it on. If Gabe and Martha have the Herzes for dinner, the mutual strains will be as heavy as a bad Ph.D oral, and afterward Gabe and Martha will fight about who paid for what. If Paul's passion for Libby revives at a party, it will cool before they can get around the corner. If some children are encountered at a playground with their grandmother, it is because their mother has just tried to flush herself down a toilet bowl at Billings Hospital. In this morbid world, sibling rivalry leads to homicide, intermarriage to being abandoned by both the Catholic and Jewish families, adoption proceedings to a nervous breakdown. Not even a stencil can get typed without fear and trembling.

All of which added up, I felt, not only to an exaggeration of the conditions but to an error of vision. I wondered if this *error* might have something to do with the surface view we had of each other's lives: his apparent fortune, my apparent misfortunes: clearly the germ, at least, of the Wallach-Herz relationship. As I was subsequently to realize, my view of him that year was full of misapprehensions: behind the scenery of ease and success he had been making his payments to adversity: a slipped disc, for one thing; a tense and complicated affair, some aspects of which were to figure in Gabe's relationship with Martha. On the other hand, behind the scenery of adversity in a life like mine, there were positive purposes and compensations that he had not taken into account, and that made the struggle of those years tolerable and possibly significant. Though Wallach is a scholar and Herz a novelist, they might as well be campus watchmen for all the interest they have in their work, in ideas, even in their careers. While this ministers to the central concerns of the novel, it deprives both of them of force and resistance, for, stripped of any aggressive claim on the world, they have little to do but hang around their women and guiltily talk about "working it out"—the true title of the novel. The only character who has any beans is Martha, which is partly owing to the fact that, having two children to support and raise, her life intentions are to some degree objective. Otherwise there are only the obsessive, devouring relationships and the malaise they breed: Libby perpetually waiting to be laid, Paul reminding her to put on her scarf, Gabe consumed by his sense of his obligations and his distrust of it, Martha demanding that payment be made for satisfactions given. From such characters, little natural dynamic can develop, and Roth can only forge on and on in his relentlessly bleak way: now analytic, now satirical, now melodramatic—giving Libby an adopted baby, Paul a religious turn, Martha a dull, dependable husband, and Gabe a wild adventure in Gary with the extortion-minded husband of the girl who bore the baby—none of it especially convincing, none of it quite able to lift up and justify the burden of the pessimism. (pp. 134-40)

When *Letting Go* came out, I was working at *Commentary*, a job that had come my way as the result of an essay that the *TLS* had asked me to write on Roth's recommendation. Since he hadn't liked the essay at first and since I was as touchy as Paul Herz proved to be about such matters as gratitude and pride, there had been a falling out. In New York, however, the relationship resumed, and with fewer of the disparities and diffidences that had made it tense and illusionary. As time went on, there were also reasons to level with each other: we were both separated, both in analysis, both in a state of flux. So we would get together, now and then, for dinner, and talk about problems and changes. One evening I dropped by his new place on East Tenth Street to borrow a book. It was bigger and much better furnished than mine, and he wanted me to know—screw the guilt—he intended to be comfortable here and to sink some new roots. But, for all that, the place looked as bare and provisional as mine: we might as well have both been living in tents, neither of us bachelors so much as husbands *manqué*. A portable typewriter was sitting on the dining-room table, and a lot of manuscript pages were spread around it.

"What's that?" I asked.

"It's a novel." He looked at it without much pleasure. "I've written it once, and now I'm writing it again."

It was strange to realize that he, too, got hung up. I had always assumed that he was like Chekhov, who said that he wrote "as easily as a bird sings."

Perhaps he noticed my silly smile. "You know

something?" he said. "There's not a single Jew in it." He went on about the strangeness of imagining, really imagining, a family that was not a Jewish family, that was what it was by virtue of its own conditioning and conditions, just as the Jews were, but which were not just those of "the others"—the Gentiles. Something like that—though he put it, as always, more concretely—acting out, with that gift of mimicry that was always on tap, the speech and the slant of some small-town citizen of middle America.

The novel, of course, turned out to be *When She Was Good,* two years, and several more revisions later. It was easy to see why the book had been a trial for Roth to write. Liberty Center is so far from his line of territory that everything had to be played by ear, so to speak. The town hardly exists as a place, as something seen in its physical actuality; it is rather the spirit of the American Protestant ethic circa 1948, whose people and mores, interests and values, emerge from the impersonation of idiom and tone: Liberty Center as it might have been presented not by Sinclair Lewis but by Ruth Draper. In order to bring this off, Roth had had to put aside his wit, color, and élan, keep his satirical tendency tightly in check, and write the novel in a language of scrupulous banality. This impersonality was far removed from the display of temperament that animated **"Goodbye, Columbus"** as the life of the bitchy heroine, Lucy Nelson, so meager and so arduous, is from that of the bitchy Brenda Patimkin.

Yet, for all the improvisation and guesswork, the surface of *When She Was Good* is solid and real, and though true to the dullness of Liberty Center's days and ways, it is beautifully constructed to take on momentum and direction and to hit its target with shattering impact, like some bland-looking object in the sky that turns out to be a guided missile. As in *Letting Go,* the theme is the wages of possessiveness and self-righteousness, but as embodied by and embedded in Lucy Nelson's raging, ball-breaking ego, it takes on a focus and power that had dissolved in the miasmic male earnestness of the previous novel. There is no false gallantry or temporizing about Lucy. Any ambivalence has been burned away, and Roth presents her and her will to power dead-to-rights. Because of this sureness of feeling, he can also present her in the round—terrible when crossed but touching in her aspirations and inexperience, her baffled need for a fathering trust, the victim as well as the avenger of her grandfather's wishy-washy Good Samaritanism, of her parasitic father's disgrace and her mother's passivity, of the family's stalled drive for respectability, and, eventually, of her husband's arrested adolescence. But from the moments early in the novel when Lucy turns in her drunken father to the police and then bars his way back into the family, the blind force of her aggression, screened by her faith in duty and responsibility and in her moral superiority, begins to charge the novel and to shape her destiny. She is unable to break off her romance with Roy Bassart until she has him safely installed in photography school and thereby ends up pregnant. She refuses the abortion she herself sought when it is offered by her father and when she learns that her mother had had one. She enters into a shotgun marriage with Roy, whom she has come to despise, with herself holding the gun. At each turn of her fate, skillfully paired with another and better alternative, it is Lucy's master emotion—her rage against her father—that directs her choice as surely as Nemesis. And some years later, when her father writes home from the jail he has landed in and thereby pulls her mother away from marriage to a man Lucy can finally respect, she turns it all against Roy in a climactic outburst of verbal castration, and then lets loose the furies of self-righteousness that drive her to madness and death. Like her grandfather's demented sister who had to be sent back to the state hospital because she followed Lucy to school and created a public nuisance, Lucy has been unable to understand "the most basic fact of human life, the fact that I am me and you are you."

In telling Lucy's story as circumspectly as he could, Roth has placed it within a context of cultural factors. Her grandfather had come to Liberty Center to escape from the brutality of the northern frontier, and the town stands in his mind, as it comes to stand in the reader's, as the image of his desire: "not to be rich, not to be famous, not to be mighty, not even to be happy, but to be civilized." Though Lucy rejects the tepid Protestantism on which Willard stands fast, she worships at the same shrine of propriety, which is the true religion of Liberty Center, and whose arbiters are the women. If men like her father and her husband founder in the complexities of society, it is the women who are supposed to straighten them out. They are the socializing agents, and the town's football stars and combat heroes, its reprobates and solid citizens, alike bow to their sway. When the high-school principal says to Roy and Lucy, "So this is the young lady I hear is keeping our old alum in line these days," he is referring to the community norm which Lucy will carry to an extreme.

Still, the cult of Momism in Liberty Center hardly added up to a pressing contemporary note, and the novel tended to be dismissed by most of the influential reviewers as slight, inauthentic, retrograde, or otherwise unworthy of Roth's talents. Coupled with the mixed reception of *Letting Go,* his reputation was slipping. Moreover, as much as I liked *When She Was Good,* it was further evidence that he was locked into this preoccupation with female power which was carrying his fiction into strange and relatively arid terrain. I knew that he had been writing plays in the last few years and had spent a lot of time watching the improvisations of the Second City Group—another part of our

Chicago days that had accompanied us to New York—and I wondered if his own theatricality would lead him in that direction. But we seldom saw each other during this time. I was editing *Book Week* during the long newspaper strike, hadn't written anything for a year, and was going through a crisis or two of my own, and if we met at a party or something, we exchanged a word or two and looked around for more cheerful company. I remember thinking that we had both come a long way since Chicago—much of it out to sea.

A few months after *When She Was Good,* Roth published a sketch in *Esquire.* It was a memoir of a Jewish boyhood, this time told to an analyst, and written with some of his former verve and forthrightness. Even so, it ventured little beyond a vein that had been pretty well worked by now: the beleaguered provider who can't even hold a bat right; the shatteringly attentive mother; the neglected, unhappy sister; the narrator, who is the star of every grade and the messiah of the household. In short, the typical second-generation Jewish family; and after all the writers who had been wrestling with it in the past decade or two—Herbert Gold, Wallace Markfield, Bruce Jay Friedman, Arnold Wesker, Mordecai Richler, Irwin Faust, Roth himself, to name only a few—Roth's latest revelations were hardly news. Nor did a psychoanalytic setting seem necessary to elicit the facts of Jack Portnoy's constipation or Sophie's use of a breadknife to make little Alex eat. After five years of reading manuscripts at *Commentary,* such stuff was coming out of my ears. Perhaps Roth was only taking a small writer's vacation from the labor that had gone into his last novel or returning to the scene of his early success for a quick score. I hoped so.

But soon after came **"Whacking Off"** in *Partisan Review:* hysterical, raw, full of what Jews call self-hatred; excessive in all respects; and so funny that I had three laughing fits before I had gone five pages. All of a sudden, from out of the blue and the past, the comedian of those Chicago sessions of nostalgia, revenge, and general purgation had landed right in the middle of his own fiction, as Alex Portnoy, the thirteen-year-old sex maniac.

> Jumping up from the dinner table, I tragically clutch my belly—diarrhea! I cry, I have been stricken with diarrhea!—and once behind the locked bathroom door, slip over my head a pair of underpants that I have stolen from my sister's dresser and carry rolled in a handkerchief in my pocket. So galvanic is the effect of cotton panties against my mouth—so galvanic is the *word* "panties"—that the trajectory of my ejaculation reaches startling new heights: leaving my joint like a rocket it makes right for the light bulb overhead, where to my wonderment and horror, it hits and hangs. Wildly in the first moment I cover my head, expecting an explosion of glass, a burst of flames—disaster, you see, is never far from

my mind. Then quietly as I can I climb the radiator and remove the sizzling gob with a wad of toilet paper. I begin a scrupulous search of the shower curtain, the tub, the tile floor, the four toothbrushes—God forbid!—and just as I am about to unlock the door, imagining I have covered my tracks, my heart lurches at the sight of what is hanging like snot to the toe of my shoe. I am the Raskolnikov of jerking off—the sticky evidence is everywhere! Is it on my cuffs too? In my *hair?* my *ear?* All this I wonder even as I come back to the kitchen table, scowling and cranky, to grumble self-righteously at my father when he opens his mouth full of red jello and says, "I don't understand what you have to lock the door about. That to me is beyond comprehension. What is this, a home or a Grand Central station?" " . . . privacy . . . a human being . . . around here *never,*" I reply, then push aside my dessert to scream "I don't feel well—*will everybody leave me alone?*"

And so on. A few minutes later Alex is back in his kingdom, doubled over his flying fist, his sister's bra stretched before him, while his parents stand outside:

"Alex, I want an answer from you. Did you eat French fries after school? Is that why you're sick like this?
"Nuhhh, nuhhh."
"Alex, are you in pain? Do you want me to call the doctor?
Are you in pain, or aren't you? I want to know exactly where it hurts. *Answer me.*"
"Yuhh, yuhhh—"
"Alex, I don't want you to flush the toilet," says my mother sternly. "I want to see what you've done in there. I don't like the sound of this at all."
"And me," says my father, touched as he always was by my accomplishments—as much awe as envy—"I haven't moved my bowels in a week." . . .

This was new, all right, at least in American fiction—and, like the discovery of fresh material in *Goodbye, Columbus,* right in front of everyone's eyes. Particularly, I suppose, guess, of the "Jewish" writers' with all that heavily funded Oedipal energy and curiosity to be worked off in adolescence—and beyond. And having used his comic sense to carry him past the shame that surrounds the subject of masturbation, and to enter it more fully than I can suggest here, Roth appeared to gain great dividends of emotional candor and wit in dealing with the other matters in **"Whacking Off."** The first sketch maintained a distance of wry description between Portnoy and his parents, but here his feelings—rage, tenderness, contempt, despair, and so on—bring everything up close and fully alive. And aided by the hard-working comedy team of Jack and Sophie Portnoy, the familiar counters of Jewish anxiety (eating hamburgers and french fries outside the home leads directly to a colostomy; polio is never more than a sore throat away; study an instrument, you never know; take shorthand in school, look what it did for

Billy Rose; don't oppose your father, he may be suffering from a brain tumor) become almost as hilarious as Alex's solo flights of passion. Against the enveloping cloud of their fear and possessiveness, his guilt, and their mutual hysteria, still unremitting twenty years later, Alex has only his sarcasm and, expressive phrase, private parts. He summons the memories of his love as well as of his hate for them, but this only opens up his sense of his vulnerability and, from that, of his maddening typicality:

Doctor Spielvogel, this is my life, my only life, and I'm living it in the middle of a Jewish joke! I am the son in the Jewish joke—*only it ain't no joke!* Please, who crippled us like this? Who made us so morbid and hysterical and weak? . . . Is this the Jewish suffering I used to hear so much about? Is this what has come down to me from the pogroms and the persecutions? Oh my secrets, my shame, my palpitations, my flushes, my sweats! . . . Bless me with manhood! Make me brave, make me strong! Make me *whole!* Enough being a nice Jewish boy, publicly pleasing my parents while privately pulling my putz! Enough!

But Portnoy had only begun to come clean. Once having fully entered his "Modern Museum of Gripes and Grievances," there was no stopping him. Or Roth. Having discovered that Portnoy's sexual feelings and his "Jewish" feelings were just around the corner from each other and that both were so rich in loot, he pressed on like a man who has found a stream full of gold—and running right into it, another one. Moreover, the psychoanalytic setting had given him now the freedom and energy of language to sluice out the material: the natural internal monologue of comedy and pain in which the id speaks to the ego and vice versa, while the superego goes on with its kibitzing. At the same time, Portnoy could be punched out of the analytic framework like a figure enclosed in cardboard and perform in his true role and vocation, which is that of a great stand-up comic. Further, those nagging concerns with close relationships, with male guilt and female maneuvering, from his two novels could now be grasped by the roots of Portnoy's experience of them and could be presented, not as standard realistic fare, but in a mode that was right up-to-date. If the background of *Portnoy's Complaint* is a classical Freudian one, the foreground is the contemporary, winging art and humor of improvisation and release, perhaps most notably that of Lenny Bruce.

In short, lots of things had come together and they had turned Roth loose. The rest of *Portnoy* was written in the same way—as series of "takes"—the next two of which were published in *New American Review,* the periodical which I was now editing. It may be no more than editorial bias speaking here, but I think these are the two richest sections of the book. "The

Jewish Blues" is a sort of "coming of age in Newark, New Jersey," beginning with the erotic phenomena of the Portnoy household and carrying through the dual issue of Alex's adolescence: maleness and rebellion. On the one hand, there are those early years of attentively following Sophie Portnoy through her guided tour of her activities and attitudes, climaxed by a memory of one afternoon when, the housework all done "with his cute little assistance," Alex, "punchy with delight" watches his shapely mother draw on her stockings, while she croons to him "Who does Mommy love more than anything in the whole wide world?" (a passage that deserves to live forever in the annals of the Oedipal Complex). On the other hand—"Thank God," breathes Portnoy—there are the visits with his father to the local bathhouse, the world of Jewish male animal nature, "a place without *goyim* and women [where] I lose touch instantaneously with that ass-licking little boy who runs home after school with his A's in his hand. . . . " On the one hand, there is the synagogue, another version of the dismal constraints and clutchiness of home; on the other, there is center field, where anything that comes your way is yours and where Alex, in his masterful imitation of Duke Snider, knows exactly how to conduct himself, standing out there "as loose and as easy, as happy as I will ever be. . . . " This is beautiful material: so exact in its details, so right in its feeling. And, finally, there is the story of his cousin Heshie, the muscular track star, who was mad about Alice Dembrowsky, the leggy drum majorette of Weequahic High, and whose disgraceful romance with this daughter of a Polish janitor finally has to be ended by his father, who informs Alice that Heshie has an incurable blood disease that prevents him from marrying and that must be kept secret from him. After his Samson-like rage is spent, Heshie submits to his father, and subsequently goes into the Army and is killed in action. But Alex adds his cause to his other manifold grounds of revolt, rises to heights of denunciation in the anti-Bar Mitzvah speech he delivers to Spielvogel ("instead of wailing for he-who has turned his back on the saga of *his people,* weep for your pathetic selves, why don't you, sucking and sucking on that sour grape of a religion"); but then is reminded by his sister of "the six million" and ends pretty much where he began.

Still circling back upon other scenes from his throbbing youth, as though the next burst of anger or grief or hysterical joking will allow him finally to touch bottom, Portnoy forges on into his past and his psyche, turning increasingly to his relations with the mysterious creatures called "shiksas" as his life moves on and the present hang-ups emerge. His occupation is that of Assistant Commissioner of Human Opportunity in the Lindsay Administration, but his preoccupations are always with that one thing his mother didn't give him back when he was four years old, and all of his sweet young Wasps, for all of their sociological interest, turn out to be only an extension of the fantasies of curiosity and self-excitement and shame that drove Alex on in the bathroom. Even "the Monkey," the glamorous fashion model and fellow sex maniac, the walking version of his adolescent dream of "Thereal McCoy," provides mostly more grist for the relentless mill of his narcissism and masochism. All of which Portnoy is perfectly aware of, he is the hippest analysand since Freud himself; but it still doesn't help him to give up the maddeningly seductive voice inside his head that goes on calling "Big Boy." And so, laughing and anguishing and analyzing away, he goes down the road to his breakdown, which sets in when he comes to Israel and finds that he is impotent.

I could go on writing about *Portnoy,* but it would be mostly amplification of the points I've made. It's a marvelously entertaining book and one that mines a narrow but central vein more deeply than it has ever been done before. You don't have to be Jewish to be vastly amused and touched and instructed by *Portnoy's Complaint,* though it helps. Also you don't have to know Philip Roth to appreciate the personal triumph that it represents, though that helps too. (pp. 141-48)

Theodore Solotaroff, "Philip Roth: A Personal View," in *Critical Essays on Philip Roth,* edited by Sanford Pinsker, G. K. Hall & Co., 1982, pp. 133-48.

IRVING HOWE

(essay date 1972)

[A longtime editor of the leftist magazine *Dissent* and a regular contributor to *The New Republic,* Howe is a highly respected literary critic and social historian who initially championed Roth following the publication of his first book, *Goodbye, Columbus.* In the influential essay excerpted below, Howe amends his earlier praise, characterizing Roth as a "minor writer" of unrealized talent. This piece, which many scholars believe has influenced negative critical reaction to most of Roth's books of the 1970s, has been variously commended for its insights and faulted for its de-emphasis of Roth's recognized talents.]

. . . the will takes pleasures in begetting its own image.

—J. V. Cunningham

When Philip Roth published his collection of stories, *Goodbye, Columbus,* in 1959, the book was generously praised and I was among the reviewers who praised it. Whatever modulations of judgment one might want now to propose, it is not hard to see why Roth should have won approval. The work of a newcomer still in his twenties, *Goodbye, Columbus* bristled with a literary self-confidence such as few writers two or three decades older than Roth could command. His stories were immediately recognizable as his own, distinctive in voice, attitude, and subject; they possessed the lucidities of definition, though I would now add, lucidities harsh and grimacing in their over-focus. None of the fiction Roth has since published approaches this first collection in literary interest; yet, by no very surprising turn of events, his reputation has steadily grown these past few years, he now stands close to the center of our culture (if that is anything for him to be pleased about), and he is accorded serious attention both by a number of literary critics and those rabbis and Jewish communal leaders who can hardly wait to repay the animus he has lavished upon them. At least for a moment or two, until the next fashion appears, we are in the presence not only of an interesting writer but also a cultural "case." (p. 69)

For good or bad, both in the stories that succeed and those that fail, *Goodbye, Columbus* rests in the grip of an imperious will prepared to wrench, twist, and claw at its materials in order to leave upon them the scar of its presence—as if the work of fiction were a package that needed constantly to be stamped with a signature of self. With expectations of being misunderstood I am tempted to add that, despite their severe and even notorious criticisms of Jewish life in America, Roth's stories are marked by a quintessentially "Jewish will," the kind that first makes its historical appearance in the autobiography of Solomon Maimon, where the intellectual aspirant sees himself as a solitary antagonist to the world of culture which, in consequence, he must conquer and reduce to acknowledgment.

The will dominating *Goodbye, Columbus* clamors to impose itself—in part through an exclusion of inconvenient perceptions—upon whatever portions of imagined life are being presented. And that is one reason these stories become a little tiresome upon rereading: one grows weary of a writer who keeps nagging and prodding and beating us over the head with the poker of his intentions. What is almost always central in Roth's stories is their "point," their hammering of idea, and once that "point" is clear, usually well before a story's end, the portrayal starts to pale, for not enough autonomous life remains and too much of the matter seems a mere reflex of the will's "begetting."

Even in regard to details of milieu and manners, for which Roth has been frequently praised, the will takes over and distorts. In his title novella, **"Goodbye, Columbus,"** there are some keen notations—the refrigerator in the basement bulging with fruit, the turgidities of the wedding—which help to characterize the newly-rich Patimkins in their suburban home. And there are moments of tenderness—a quality not abundant in Roth's work—during the romance between

Neil Klugman, the poor Newark boy, and Brenda Patimkin, the self-assured Radcliffe girl (though nothing she says or does could persuade one that she would ever have been admitted to Radcliffe). Yet if the novella is read with any care at all, it becomes clear that Roth is not precise and certainly not scrupulous enough in his use of social evidence. The Patimkins are easily placed—what could be easier for a Jewish writer than to elicit disdain for middle-class Jews?—but the elements of what is new in their experience are grossly manipulated. Their history is invoked for the passing of adverse judgment, at least part of which seems to me warranted, but their history is not allowed to emerge so as to make them understandable as human beings. Their vulgarity is put on blazing display but little or nothing that might locate or complicate that vulgarity is shown: little of the weight of their past, whether sustaining or sentimental; nothing of the Jewish mania for culture, whether honorable or foolish; nothing of that fearful self-consciousness which the events of the mid-20th century thrust upon the Patimkins of this world. Ripped out of the historical context that might help to define them, the Patimkins are vivid enough, but as lampoon or caricature in a novella that clearly aims for more than lampoon or caricature. (pp. 69-70)

Roth's stories begin, characteristically, with a spectacular array of details in the representation of milieu, speech, and manners and thereby we are led to expect a kind of fiction strong in verisimilitude. But then, at crucial points in the stories, there follow a series of substitutions, elements of incident or speech inserted not because they follow from the logic of the narrative but because they underscore the point Roth wishes to extract from the narrative. In **"The Conversion of the Jews"** a bright if obnoxious Jewish boy becomes so enraged with the sniffling pieties of his Hebrew-school teacher, Rabbi Bender, that he races out of the classroom and up to the roof, threatening to jump unless the rabbi admits that "God can do anything" and "can make a child without intercourse." The plot may seem a bit fanciful and the story, as Mr. Solotaroff justly remarks, "inflated to get in the message"—but no matter, at least our attention is being held. Then, however, comes the breaking point, when the writer's will crushes his fiction: Ozzie "made them all say they believed in Jesus Christ—first one at a time, then all together." Given the sort of tough-grained Jewish urchin Ozzie is shown to be, this declamation strains our credence; it is Roth who has taken over, shouldering aside his characters and performing on his own, just as it is Roth who ends the story with the maudlin touch of Ozzie crying out, "Mamma. You should never hit anybody about God. . . . " Scratch an Ozzie, and you find a Rabbi Bender.

A richer and more ambitious story, **"Eli the Fanatic"** suffers from the same kind of flaws. An exotic yeshivah sponsored by a Hasidic sect settles in Woodenton, a comfortable suburb. The local Jews feel hostile, tension follows, and Eli Peck, a vulnerable Woodenton Jew, undergoes a kind of moral conversion in which he identifies or hallucinates himself as a victim in kaftan. It is difficult, if one bears in mind Roth's entire work, to take at face value this solemn espousal of yeshivah Orthodoxy as the positive force in the story; I cannot believe that the yeshivah and all it represents has been brought into play for any reason other than as a stick with which to beat Woodenton. Tzuref, the yeshivah principal, is well-drawn and allowed to speak for his outlook, as Aunt Gladys in **"Goodbye, Columbus"** is not: which is one reason this story builds up a certain dramatic tension. But again Roth feels obliged to drop a heavy thumb on the scales by making his suburbanites so benighted, indeed, so merely stupid, that the story finally comes apart. Here is a Woodenton Jew speaking:

> Look, I don't even know about this Sunday school business. Sundays I drive my oldest kid all the way to Scarsdale to learn Bible stories . . . and you know what she comes up with? This Abraham in the Bible was going to kill his own *kid* for a sacrifice. She gets nightmares from it, for God's sake. You call that religion? Today a guy like that they'd lock him up.

Now, even a philistine character has certain rights, if not as a philistine then as a character in whose "reality" we are being asked to believe. To write as if this middle-class Jewish suburbanite were unfamiliar with "this Abraham" or shocked by the story of the near-sacrifice of Isaac, is simply preposterous. Roth is putting into the character's mouth, not what he could plausibly say, but what Roth thinks his "real" sentiments are. He is not revealing the character, but "exposing" him. It is a crucial failure in literary tact, one of several in the story that rouse the suspicion Roth is not behaving with good faith toward the objects of his assault.

This kind of tendentiousness mars a number of Roth's fictions, especially those in which a first-person narrator—Neil Klugman, Alex Portnoy—swarms all over the turf of his imaginary world, blotting out the possibility of multiple perspective. It is a weakness of fictions told in the first person that the limits of the narrator's perception tend to become the limits of the work itself. (pp. 71-2)

To these strictures I would offer one exception, the Roth story that, oddly, was most attacked by his rabbinical critics: **"Defender of the Faith."** This seems to me a distinguished performance, the example of what Roth might have made of his talent had he been stricter in his demands upon himself. Roth's description of the story is acute: "It is about one man who uses his own religion, and another's uncertain conscience, for selfish ends; but mostly it is about this other man, the narrator, who because of the ambiguities of being a member of a particular religion, is involved in a taxing, if mistaken, conflict of loyalties." This conflict is at once urgent for those caught up in it and serious in its larger moral implications. Nathan Marx, back from combat duty in Germany, is made First Sergeant of a training company in Missouri; he is a decent, thoughtful fellow whose sense of being Jewish, important though it is to him, he cannot articulate clearly. A few recruits in his company, led by Sheldon Grossbart, attach themselves to Marx, presumably out of common feeling toward the problem of being Jews in an alien setting, but actually because Grossbart means to exploit this sense of solidarity in behalf of private ends—he looks forward to the crucial favor of not being sent overseas to combat. As Roth comments, Grossbart is "a man whose lapses of integrity seem to him so necessary to his survival as to convince him that such lapses are actually committed in the name of integrity." At the end of the story, Sergeant Marx, incensed at the manipulation to which he has been subjected, makes certain that Grossbart is indeed shipped overseas, while he, Marx, braces himself to face the consequences of an act he admits to be "vindictive."

The power of this story derives from presenting a moral entanglement so as to draw out, yet not easily resolve, its inherent difficulties. Unattractive as Grossbart may be, his cunning use of whatever weapons come to hand in order to protect his skin seems entirely real; one would have to be thoroughly locked into self-righteousness not to be drawn a little, however shamefacedly, to Grossbart's urgency. The willingness of Marx to bend the rules in behalf of the Jewish recruits is plausible, perhaps even admirable; after all, he shares their loneliness and vulnerability. Established thereby as a figure of humaneness, Marx commits an act that seems shocking, even to himself, so that he must then try to resist "with all my will an impulse to turn back and seek pardon for my vindictiveness." If it is right to punish Grossbart, Marx also knows the punishment is cruel, a result, perhaps, of the same Jewish uneasiness that had first made him susceptible to Grossbart's designs.

The story does not allow any blunt distribution of moral sympathies, nor can the reader yield his heart to one character. Before the painfulness of the situation, Roth's usual habit of rapid dismissal must melt away. We are left with the texture of reality as, once in a while, a writer can summon it.

Neither before nor after **"Defender of the Faith"** has Roth written anything approaching it in compositional rigor and moral seriousness. It may, however, have been the presence of this story in *Goodbye, Columbus* that led reviewers, including myself, to assume that this gifted new writer was working in the tradition of Jewish self-criticism and satire—a substantial tradition extending in Yiddish from Mendele to Isaac Bashevis Singer and in English from Abraham Cahan to Malamud and Bellow. In these kinds of writing, the assault upon Jewish philistinism and the mockery of Jewish social pretension are both familiar and unrelenting. Beside Mendele, Roth seems soft; beside Cahan, imprecise. But now, from the vantage point of additional years, I think it clear that Roth, despite his concentration on Jewish settings and his acerbity of tone, has not really been involved in this tradition. For he is one of the first American-Jewish writers who finds that it yields him no sustenance, no norms or values from which to launch his attacks on middle-class complacence. (pp. 72-3)

The standard opinion of Roth's critics has been that his two novels, *Letting Go* and *When She Was Good,* and slight luster to his reputation, and there is not much use in arguing against this view. Yet it should be noticed that there are patches of genuine achievement in both books, sometimes a stumbling, gasping honesty. They are not novels that yield much pleasure or grip one despite its absence, but both are marked by tokens of struggle with the materials of American life. And there are moments that come off well—the persistence of the battered divorcee, Martha Reganhart (*Letting Go*), in raising her children decently, the precocious eeriness of little Cynthia Reganhart, the struggle of Lucy (*When She Was Good*) to raise herself above the maudlin stupor of her family. Conventional achievements all of these are, and of a kind novelists have often managed in the past—of a kind, also, they will have to manage in the future if the novel is to survive. But right now, in our present cultural situation, this is hardly the sort of achievement likely to win much attention, as Roth evidently came to see. (pp. 73-4)

The cruelest thing anyone can do with *Portnoy's Complaint* is to read it twice. An assemblage of gags strung onto the outcry of an analytic patient, the book thrives best on casual responses; it demands little more from the reader than a nightclub performer demands: a rapid exchange of laugh for punchline, a breath or two of rest, some variations on the first response, and a quick exit. Such might be the most generous way of discussing *Portnoy's Complaint* were it not for the solemn ecstasies the book has elicited, in line with Roth's own feeling that it constitutes a liberating act for himself, his generation, and maybe the whole culture.

The basic structural unit of *Portnoys' Complaint* is the skit, the stand-up comedian's shuffle and patter that come to climax with a smashing one-liner—indeed, it is worth noticing that a good many of our more "advanced" writers during the last two decades have found themselves turning to the skit as a form well-suited to the requirements of "swinging" and

their rejection of sustained coherence of form. The controlling tone of the book is a shriek of excess, the jokester's manic wail, although, because it must slide from skit to skit with some pretense of continuity, this tone declines now and again into a whine of self-exculpation or sententiousness. And the controlling sensibility of the book derives from a well-grounded tradition of feeling within immigrant Jewish life: the coarse provincial "worldliness" flourishing in corner candy-stores and garment centers, at cafeterias and pinochle games, a sort of hard, cynical mockery of ideal claims and pretensions, all that remains to people scraped raw by the struggle for success. (p. 74)

Much of what is funny in Roth's book—the Monkey's monologues, some rhetorical flourishes accompanying Alex's masturbation, Sophie Portnoy's amusement at chancing upon her son's sexual beginnings—rests on the fragile structure of the skit. All the skit requires or can manage is a single broad stroke: shrewd, gross, recognizable, playing on the audience's embarrassment yet not hurting it too much, so that finally its aggression can be passed off as good-fellowship. (We all have Jewish mamas, we're all henpecked husbands, we all pretend to greater sexual prowess than. . . .) The skit stakes everything on brashness and energy, both of which Roth has or simulates in abundance. Among writers of the past Dickens and Céline have used the skit brilliantly, but Dickens always and Céline sometimes understood that in a book of any length the skit—as well as its sole legitimate issue, the caricature—must be put to the service of situations, themes, stories allowing for complication and development. (A lovely example of this point can be seen in the skits that Peter Sellers performs in the movie version of *Lolita.*)

It is on the problem of continuity that Portnoy—or, actually, Roth himself—trips up. For once we are persuaded to see his complaints as more than the stuff of a few minutes of entertainment, once we are led to suppose that they derive from some serious idea or coherent view of existence, the book quickly falls to pieces and its much-admired energy (praised by some critics as if energy were a value regardless of the ends to which it is put) serves mainly to blur its flimsiness. Technically this means that, brief as it is, the book seems half again too long, since there can be very little surprise or development in the second half, only a recapitulation of motifs already torn to shreds in the first.

It is worth looking at a few of the book's incoherences, venial for a skit, fatal for a novel. Alex is allowed the human attribute of a history within the narrative space of the book, presumably so that he can undergo change and growth, but none of the characters set up as his foils, except perhaps the Monkey, is granted a similar privilege. Alex speaks for imposed-upon, vulnerable, twisted, yet self-liberating humanity; the other characters, reduced to a function of his need, an echo of his cry, cannot speak or speak back as autonomous voices but simply go through their paces like straight-men mechanically feeding lines to a comic. Even more than in Roth's earlier work, the result is claustrophobia of voice and vision: *he never shuts up,* this darling Alex, nor does Roth detach himself sufficiently to gain some ironic distance. The psychic afflictions of his character Roth would surely want to pass up, but who can doubt that Portnoy's cry from the heart—enough of Jewish guilt, enough of the burdens of history, enough of inhibition and repression, it is time to "let go" and soar to the horizons of pleasure—speaks in some sense for Roth?

The difficulty that follows from this claustrophobic vision is not whether Mrs. Portnoy can be judged a true rendering, even as caricature, of Jewish mothers—only chuckleheads can suppose that to be a serious question!—but whether characters like Mr. and Mrs. Portnoy have much reality or persuasiveness within the fictional boundaries set by Roth himself. Sophie Portnoy has a little, because there are moments when Alex, or Roth, can't help liking her, and because the conventional lampoon of the Jewish mother is by now so well established in our folklore it has almost become an object of realistic portraiture in its own right. As for Mr. Portnoy, a comparison suggests itself between this constipated *nudnik* whom Alex would pass off as his father and "Mr. Fumfotch" in Daniel Fuchs's novel *Homage to Blenholt.* Fuchs's character is also a henpecked husband, also worn down by the struggle for bread, but he is drawn with an ironic compassion that rises to something better than itself: to an objectivity that transcends either affection or derision. In his last novel Fuchs remarks, while writing about figures somewhat like those in Roth's work, "It was not enough to call them low company and pass on"—and if this can be said about Depression Jews in Brighton Beach, why not also about more or less affluent ones in the Jersey suburbs?

We notice, again, that Portnoy attributes his sexual troubles to the guilt-soaked Jewish tradition as it has been carried down to him by his mother. Perhaps; who knows? But if we are to accept this simplistic determinism, why does it never occur to him, our Assistant Commissioner of Human Opportunity who once supped with John Lindsay in the flesh, that by the same token the intelligence on which he preens himself must also be attributed to the tradition he finds so repugnant—so that his yowl of revulsion against "my people," that they should "stick your suffering heritage up your suffering ass," becomes, let us say, a little ungenerous, even a little dopey.

And we notice, again, that while Portnoy knows that his sexual difficulties stem from his Jewishness, the patrician New England girl with whom he has an affair also turns out to be something of a sexual failure: she will not deliver him from the coils of Jewish guilt through the magic of fellatio. But if both Jewishness and Protestantism have deeply inhibiting effects on sexual performance—and as for Catholicism, well, we know those Irish girls!—what then happens to this crucial flake of Portnoy's wisdom, which the book invites us to take with some seriousness? As for other possible beliefs, from Ethical Culture to Hare Krishna, there can surely be little reason to suppose they will deliver us from the troubles of life which, for all we know, may be lodged in the very nature of things or, at the least, in those constraints of civilization which hardly encircle Jewish loins exclusively.

There is something suspect about Portnoy's complaining. From what he tells us one might reasonably conclude that, in a far from perfect world, he is not making out so badly; the boys on his block, sexual realists that they are, would put it more pungently. Only in Israel does he have serious difficulties, and for that there are simple geographical solutions. What seems really to be bothering Portnoy is a wish to sever his sexuality from his moral sensibilities, to cut it away from his self as historical creature. It's as if he really supposed the super-ego, or *post coitum triste,* were a Jewish invention. This wish—Norman O. Brown as a *yingele*—strikes me as rather foolish, an adolescent fantasy carrying within itself an inherent negation; but it is a fantasy that has accumulated a great deal of power in contemporary culture. And it helps explain, I think, what Roth's true feelings about, or relation to, Jewishness are. *Portnoy's Complaint* is not, as enraged critics have charged, an anti-Semitic book, though it contains plenty of contempt for Jewish life. Nor does Roth write out of traditional Jewish self-hatred, for the true agent of such self-hatred is always indissolubly linked with Jewish past and present, quite as closely as those who find in Jewishness moral or transcendent sanctions. What the book speaks for is a yearning to undo the fate of birth; there is no wish to do the Jews any harm (a little nastiness is something else), nor any desire to engage with them as a fevered antagonist; Portnoy is simply crying out to be left alone, to be released from the claims of distinctiveness and the burdens of the past, so that, out of his own nothingness, he may create himself as a "human being." Who, born a Jew in the 20th century, has been so lofty in spirit never to have shared this fantasy? But who, born a Jew in the 20th century, has been so foolish in mind as to dally with it for more than a moment?

What, in any case, *is Portnoy's Complaint*—a case-history burlesqued which we are invited to laugh at, or a struggle of an afflicted man to achieve his liberation, which we are invited to cheer on? Dr. Bruno Bettelheim has written a straight-faced essay purporting to be the case notes of Alex's psychoanalyst, Dr. O. Spielvogel, who can barely restrain his impatience with Alex's effort to mask his true problems with "all the clichés of a spoiled Jewish childhood."

> A few times I [Dr. Spielvogel] indicated the wish to say something, but he only talked on the more furiously. . . . This extremely intelligent young Jew does not recognize that what he is trying to do, by reversing the Oedipal situation, is to make fun of me, as he does of everyone, thus asserting his superiority. . . . His overpowering love for his mother is turned into a negative projection, so that what becomes overpowering is the mother's love for him. . . . While consciously he experienced everything she did as destructive, behind it is an incredible wish for more, more, more. . . .

Now this is amusing, though not as amusing as the fact that it often constitutes the line of defense to which Roth's admirers fall back when the book's incoherence is revealed ("after all, it's a patient on the couch, everyone knows you can't take what he says at face value. . . . "). But to see the book in this light, as the mere comic record of a very sick man, is radically to undercut its claims for expressing radical new truths. Roth, never unwary, anticipates the problem by having Portnoy say, "Is this truth I'm delivering up, or is it just plain *kvetching?* Or is *kvetching* for people like me a *form* of truth?" Well there's *kvetching* and *kvetching.* At times it can be a form of truth, but when the gap is so enormous between manifest content and what Dr. Spielvogel *cum* Bettelheim takes to be its inner meaning, then *kvetching* becomes at best an untruth from which the truth must be violently wrenched.

It seems hard to believe that Roth would accept the view that his book consists merely of comic griping; certainly the many readers who saw it as a banner behind which to rally would not accept that view. For, in a curious way, *Portnoy's Complaint* has become a cultural document of some importance. Younger Jews, weary or bored with all the talk about their heritage, have taken the book as a signal for "letting go" of both their past and perhaps themselves, a guide to swinging in good conscience or better yet, without troubling about conscience. For some Gentile readers the book seems to have played an even more important role. After the Second World War, as a consequence of certain unpleasantnesses that occurred during the war, a wave of philo-Semitism swept through our culture. This wave lasted for all of two decades, in the course of which books by Jewish writers were often praised (in truth, overpraised) and a fuss made about Jewish intellectuals, critics, etc. Some literary people found this hard to bear, but they did. Once *Portnoy's Complaint* arrived, however, they could almost be heard breathing a sigh of relief, for it signaled an end to philo-Semitism in American culture, one no longer had to listen to all that talk about Jewish morality, Jewish endurance,

Jewish wisdom, Jewish families. Here was Philip Roth himself, a writer who even seemed to know Yiddish, confirming what had always been suspected about those immigrant Jews but had recently not been tactful to say.

The talent that went into *Portnoy's Complaint* and portions of *Goodbye, Columbus* is real enough, but it has been put to the service of a creative vision deeply marred by vulgarity. It is very hard, I will admit, to be explicit about the concept of vulgarity: people either know what one is referring to, as part of the tacit knowledge that goes to make up a coherent culture, or the effort to explain is probably doomed in advance. Nevertheless, let me try. By vulgarity in a work of literature I am not here talking about the presence of certain kinds of words or the rendering of certain kinds of actions. I have in mind, rather, the impulse to submit the rich substance of human experience, sentiment, value, and aspiration to a radically reductive leveling or simplification; the urge to assault the validity of sustained gradings and discriminations of value, so that in some extreme instances the concept of vulgarity is dismissed as up-tight or a mere mask for repressiveness; the wish to pull down the reader in common with the characters of the work, so that he will not be tempted to suppose that any inclinations he has toward the good, the beautiful, or the ideal merit anything more than a Bronx cheer; and finally, a refusal of that disinterestedness of spirit in the depiction and judgment of other people which seems to me the writer's ultimate resource.

That I have here provided an adequate definition of vulgarity in literature I do not for a moment suppose—though I don't know of a better one. It ought, however, to serve our present purposes by helping to make clear, for example, the ways in which a book like *Portnoy's Complaint,* for all its scrim of sophistication, is spiritually linked with the usual sentimental treatment of Jewish life in the work of popular and middlebrow writers. Between *Portnoy's Complaint* and *Two Cents Plain* there is finally no great difference of sensibility.

Perhaps the matter can be clarified by a comparison. Hubert Selby's novel, *Last Exit to Brooklyn,* portrays a segment of urban life—lumpen violence, gang-bangs, rape, sheer debasement—that is utterly appalling, and the language it must record is of a kind that makes Roth seem reticent; yet as I read Selby's book there is no vulgarity in it whatever, for he takes toward his barely human figures a stance of dispassionate objectivity, writing not with "warmth" or "concern" but with a disciplined wish to see things as they are. He does not wrench, he does not patronize, he does not aggrandize. Repugnant as it often is, *Last Exit to Brooklyn* seems to me a pure-spirited book; amusing as it often is, *Portnoy's Complaint* a vulgar book. (pp. 74-7)

Irving Howe, "Philip Roth Reconsidered," in *Commentary,* Vol. 54, No. 6, December, 1972, pp. 69-77.

HAROLD BLOOM

(essay date 1985)

[Bloom is a prominent American critic and literary theorist. In the following review of Roth's *Zuckerman Bound*, an omnibus volume containing the novels *The Ghost Writer, Zuckerman Unbound, The Anatomy Lesson,* and *The Prague Orgy*, Bloom praises the collection as "the novelists's finest achievement to date, eclipsing even his best single fictions, the exuberantly notorious *Portnoy's Complaint* and the undervalued and ferocious *My Life as a Man.*"]

Philip Roth's *Zuckerman Bound* binds together *The Ghost Writer, Zuckerman Unbound* and *The Anatomy Lesson,* adding to them as epilogue a wild short novel, *The Prague Orgy,* which is at once the bleakest and the funniest writing Roth has done. The totality is certainly the novelist's finest achievement to date, eclipsing even his best single fictions, the exuberantly notorious *Portnoy's Complaint* and the undervalued and ferocious *My Life as a Man. Zuckerman Bound* is a classic apologia, an aggressive defense of Roth's moral stance as an author. Its cosmos derives candidly from the Freudian interpretation of ambivalence as being primal, and the Kafkan evasion of interpretation as being unbearable. (p. 1)

Zuckerman Bound merits something reasonably close to the highest level of esthetic praise for tragicomedy, partly because as a formal totality it becomes much more than the sum of its parts. Those parts are surprisingly diverse: *The Ghost Writer* is a Jamesian parable of fictional influence, economical and shapely, beautifully modulated, while *Zuckerman Unbound* is more characteristically Rothian, being freer in form and more joyously expressionistic in its diction. *The Anatomy Lesson* is a farce bordering on fantasy, closer in mode and spirit to Nathanael West than is anything else by Roth. With *The Prague Orgy,* Roth has transcended himself, or perhaps shown himself and others that, being just past 50, he has scarcely begun to display his powers. I have read nothing else in recent American fiction that rivals Thomas Pynchon in *The Crying of Lot 49* and episodes like the story of Bryon the light bulb in the same author's *Gravity's Rainbow. The Prague Orgy* is of that disturbing eminence: obscenely outrageous and yet brilliantly reflective of a paranoid reality that has become universal.

But the Rothian difference from Nathanael West and Thomas Pynchon also should be emphasized. Roth paradoxically is still engaged in moral prophecy; he continues to be outraged by the outrageous—in societies, others and himself. There is in him nothing of West's gnostic preference for the posture of the satanic editor, Shrike, in *Miss Lonelyhearts,* or of Mr. Pynchon's cabalistic doctrine of sado-anarchism. Roth's negative exuberance is not in the service of a negative theology, but intimates instead a nostalgia for the morality once engendered by the Jewish normative tradition.

This is the harsh irony, obsessively exploited throughout *Zuckerman Bound,* of the attack made upon Zuckerman's *Carnovsky* (Roth's *Portnoy's Complaint*) by the literary critic Milton Appel (Irving Howe). Zuckerman has received a mortal wound from Appel, and Roth endeavors to commemorate the wound and the wounder, in the spirit of James Joyce permanently impaling the Irish poet, physician and general roustabout, Oliver St. John Gogarty, as the immortally egregious Malachi (Buck) Mulligan of *Ulysses.* . . . Roth, characteristically scrupulous, presents Appel as dignified, serious and sincere, and Zuckerman as dangerously lunatic in this matter, but since the results are endlessly hilarious, the revenge is sharp nevertheless.

Zuckerman Unbound makes clear, at least to me, that Roth indeed is a Jewish writer in a sense that Saul Bellow and Bernard Malamud are not, and do not care to be. Bellow and Malamud, in their fiction, strive to be North American Jewish only as Tolstoy was Russian, or Faulkner was American Southern. Roth seems prophetic in the biblical tradition. His absolute concern never ceases to be the pain of the relations between children and parents, and between husband and wife, and in him this pain invariably results from the incommensurability between a rigorously moral normative tradition whose expectations rarely can be satisfied, and the reality of the way we live now. Zuckerman's insane resentment of the moralizing Milton Appel, and of even fiercer feminist critics, is a deliberate self-parody of Roth's more-than-ironic reaction to how badly he has been read. Against both Appel and the swarms of maenads, Roth defends Zuckerman (and so himself) as a kind of Talmudic Orpheus, by defining any man as "clay with aspirations."

What wins over the reader is that both defense and definition are conveyed by the highest humor now being written. *The Anatomy Lesson* and *The Prague Orgy,* in particular, provoke a cleansing and continuous laughter, sometimes so intense that in itself it becomes astonishingly painful. One of the many esthetic gains of binding together the entire Zuckerman ordeal (it cannot be called a saga) is to let the reader experience the gradual acceleration of wit from the gentle Chekhovian wistfulness of *The Ghost Writer* on to the Gogolian sense of the ridiculous in *Zuckerman Unbound* and then to the boisterous Westian farce of *The Anatomy Lesson,* only to end in the merciless Kafkan irrealism of *The Prague Orgy*. . . .

When last we saw the afflicted Zuckerman, at the close of *The Anatomy Lesson,* he had progressed (or regressed) from painfully lying back on his play-mat, Roget's Thesaurus propped beneath his head and four women serving his many needs, to wandering the corridors of a university hospital, a patient playing at being an intern. A few years later, a physically recovered Zuckerman is in Prague, as visiting literary lion, encountering so paranoid a social reality that New York seems by contrast the Forest of Arden. Zuckerman, "the American authority on Jewish demons," quests for the unpublished Yiddish stories of the elder Sisovsky, perhaps murdered by the Nazis. The exiled younger Sisovsky's abandoned wife, Olga, guards the manuscripts in Prague. In a deliberate parody of Henry James's *Aspern Papers,* Zuckerman needs somehow to seduce the alcoholic and insatiable Olga into releasing stories supposedly worthy of Sholom Aleichem or Isaac Babel, written in "the Yiddish of Flaubert."

Being Zuckerman, he seduces no one, and secures the Yiddish manuscripts anyway, only to have them confiscated by the Czechoslovak Minister of Culture and his thugs, who proceed to expel "Zuckerman the Zionist agent" back to "the little world around the corner" in New York City. In a final scene subtler, sadder and funnier than all previous Roth, the frustrated Zuckerman endures the moralizing of the Minister of Culture, who attacks America for having forgotten that "masterpiece" by Betty MacDonald, *The Egg and I.* Associating himself with K., Kafka's hero in *The Castle,* Zuckerman is furious at his expulsion, and utters a lament for the more overt paranoia he must abandon:

> Here where there's no nonsense about purity and goodness, where the division is not that easy to discern between the heroic and the perverse, where every sort of repression foments a parody of freedom and the suffering of their historical misfortune engenders in its imaginative victims these clownish forms of human despair.

That farewell-to-Prague has as its undersong: here where Zuckerman is not an anomaly, but indeed a model of decorum and restraint compared to anyone else who is at all interesting. Perhaps there is another undertone: a farewell-to-Zuckerman on Roth's part. The author of *Zuckerman Bound* at last may have exorcised the afterglow of *Portnoy's Complaint.* (p. 42)

Harold Bloom, "His Long Ordeal by Laughter," in *The New York Times Book Review,* May 19, 1985, pp. 1, 42.

SOURCES FOR FURTHER STUDY

Baumgarten, Murray, and Gottfried, Barbara. *Understanding Philip Roth.* Columbia: University of South Carolina, 1990, 276 p.
    Overview of Roth's works intended for students and nonacademic readers.

Jones, Judith Paterson, and Nance, Guinevera A. *Philip Roth.* New York: Frederick Ungar Publishing Co., 1981, 181 p.
    Biographical and critical overview of Roth's life and first eleven books. Includes a bibliography.

McDaniel, John N. *The Fiction of Philip Roth.* Haddonfield, N. J.: Haddonfield House, 243 p.
    Examines Roth's fiction for the purpose of "clarifying Roth's place within the community of writers, Jewish and non-Jewish, now practicing their craft in America."

Milbauer, Asher Z., and Watson, Donald G., eds. *Reading Philip Roth.* Houndmills, England: MacMillan Press, 205 p.
    Collection of previously unpublished essays intended to "extend the critical understanding of Philip Roth's fiction and to clarify some fundamental misunderstandings of his intentions and meanings."

Pinsker, Sanford. *Critical Essays on Philip Roth.* Boston: G. K. Hall & Co., 1982, 278 p.
    Reprints important commentary on Roth by such critics as Leslie Fiedler, Stanley Edgar Hyman, and Alfred Kazin.

Rodgers, Bernard F., Jr. *Philip Roth.* Edited by Warren French. Boston: Twayne Publishers, 1978, 192 p.
    Questions the critical tendency to view Roth as an exclusively Jewish writer and devotes separate chapters to both prominent and lesser-studied works.

Jean-Jacques Rousseau

1712-1778

Swiss-born French essayist, autobiographer, novelist, dramatist, and poet.

INTRODUCTION

Rousseau was an eighteenth-century Swiss-born French philosopher, political theorist, and composer who is recognized as one of the greatest thinkers of the French Enlightenment. A prolific writer on many topics, he has been variously cited as intellectual father of the French Revolution, founder of the Romantic movement in literature, and engenderer of most modern pedagogical movements. The broad influence of his thought originates not only from his best-known political and philosophical treatises—*Du contrat social; ou, Principes du droit politique* (1762; *The Social Contract*), *Discours sur les sciences et les arts* (1750; *Discourse on the Sciences and the Arts*), and *Discours sur l'origine et les fondemens de l'inégalité parmi les hommes* (1755; *Discourse upon the Origin and Foundation of the Inequality among Mankind*)—but also from his eloquent novels and autobiographical writings—*La Nouvelle Héloïse* (1764), *Emile, ou de l'éducation* (1762; *Emilius and Sophia; or, A New System of Education*), and *Les Confessions de J. J. Rousseau* (1782-89; *The Confessions of J. J. Rousseau*). However, Rousseau's life and works remain controversial despite their tremendous impact on Western thought. According to François Mauriac, "it is the artist in [Rousseau] that charms and that has poisoned the world."

Rousseau was born in 1712 to Isaac, a Genevese watchmaker, and Suzanne Bernard, daughter of an upper middle-class Genevese family. His mother died a few days after his birth, and until age ten he lived with his irresponsible father, who "educated" him by reading Calvinist sermons and seventeenth-century romance novels aloud. His father subsequently abandoned him to the tutelage of an uncle who apprenticed him at age thirteen to an abusive engraver. Young Rousseau endured three miserable years of apprenticeship before fleeing Geneva in 1728. A Roman Catholic priest directed him to the town of Annecy. There Rousseau met 29-year-old Mme. de Warens, who supported herself by taking in and encouraging Catholic converts. Under her protection he was sent to a hospice in Turin, where he converted to Catholicism, thereby effectively forfeiting his Genevese citizenship. He remained for several months, working variously as an engraver and a lackey. He returned to Annecy the following spring intending to enter the priesthood, but instead he taught music to girls of the wealthiest families in the area. In 1731, after an unsuccessful search for employment in Paris, he once again returned to Mme. de Warens, who by this time had moved to her small farm, Les Charmettes, near Chambéry, where Rousseau claimed he passed the happiest years of his life. Ultimately he became her lover, although he regarded himself more as her son than as her lover, affectionately calling her "Maman." Staying with her until 1740, he studied music, read philosophy, science, and literature, and began to compose and write.

Following his departure, Rousseau became a tutor in Lyons for a year, then returned once more to Paris in late 1742, when he presented a new system of musical notation to the Académie des Sciences, but without success. With the publication of his *Dissertation sur la musique moderne* in 1743, together with the composition of an opera and a comedy, *Les muses galantes* and *Les prisonniers de guerre,* he was appointed private secretary to the French ambassador in Venice. He lost the post the following year. In 1745, while in Paris, he initiated a lifelong intimacy with Thérèse Levasseur, a chambermaid by whom he reputedly had five children, all of whom were sent to a foundling home at birth. In Paris he came to know many prominent people, including Voltaire, Friedrich von Grimm, Georges Louis Buffon, Pierre Marivaux, Bernard Fontenelle, and Denis Diderot. The latter became his confidant and asked Rousseau to write articles on music and economics for the *Encyclopédie.* Thus began Rousseau's erratic association with the Encyclopedists and philosophes. In 1749, while walking to Vincennes to visit Diderot, who was imprisoned there, Rousseau read an announcement of a prize essay contest, sponsored by the Dijon Academy, on the question: Has the revival of the arts and sciences tended to purify morals? He responded in the negative, eloquently stating that culture had ruined morality. The *Discourse on the Sciences and the Arts,* while winning him the prize and immediate fame, provoked a three-year series of acrid literary disputes. During this time Rousseau also completed all the entries pertaining to music in the *Encyclopédie.* He later compiled and published these separately as the *Dictionnaire de musique* (1768; *A Dictionary of Music*).

In 1752 Rousseau composed an Italianate operetta, *Le Devin du village* (*The Cunning Man*), which was first performed before the royal court at Fontainebleau.

Its great success contributed to the growing popularity of Italian music, thereby setting Rousseau in opposition to Jean-Phillipe Rameau and advocates of French music. When the Dijon Academy announced another essay competition in 1754, Rousseau wrote a sequel to his first *Discourse* entitled *Discourse upon the Origin and Foundation of the Inequality among Mankind.* Essentially a diatribe against despotism and private property, he sought to expose and denounce artificially instituted social inequality by describing a hypothetical state of natural man. He believed that human beings are essentially good and potentially perfect. Human faults arise from the corrupting influences of conventional society—inequality, despotism, and privately owned property—which, he claimed, progressively restrict freedom and lessen moral virtue. In order to restore humanity to its natural goodness, Rousseau called for a return to nature so far as is practicable.

In 1756, following a sojourn in Geneva, where he reembraced Calvinism and recovered his citizenship, Rousseau settled at Montmorency in the "Hermitage," a house offered to him by Mme. d'Épinay, a friend of the Encyclopedists. In the seclusion of the Hermitage, and later in that of "Montlouis," Rousseau began and completed the works that were to make him one of the most famous writers of his time. In *La Nouvelle Héloïse,* an epistolary novel, he demonstrated the triumph of a primitive family unit over the corruption of modern society. This work exhibited the author's interest in common people and championed the aggrandizement of nature—motifs later embraced by Romantic writers in France and elsewhere. In the *Lettre à d'Alembert sur les spectacles* (1758; *Letter to d'Alembert on the Theater*) Rousseau declared the theater to be useless and harmful and called for its suppression—despite his own previous theatrical productions. *Emile* explicated his scheme for "natural" education in which man would preserve his fundamentally good instincts, while *The Social Contract,* initially stating that "Man is born free and is everywhere in chains," outlined the social order that would enable human beings to be natural and free—acknowledging no other bondage save that of natural necessity.

The Parlement of Paris condemned *Emile* and *The Social Contract* in 1762, compelling Rousseau to flee to Switzerland. There, too, his works were banned, and he was banished. He defended his writings in the *Lettre à Christophe de Beaumont* (1763), an attack on the archbishop of Paris, who had condemned *Emile;* and, in response to a published defense of the Council of Geneva decree that had ordered the burning of *Emile* and *The Social Contract,* he wrote the *Lettres écrites de la montagne* (1764). Upon its publication, opposition by the Protestant clergy in Switzerland grew even stronger, and in 1766 Rousseau fled the Continent. David Hume provided refuge in Derbyshire, England, but Rousseau, whose recent adversities had affected his reasoning abilities, began to suspect him of collusion with the Parisian philosophes, whom he imagined were conspiring to ruin his reputation. Paranoid and panicked, he fled to France in 1767.

Rousseau assumed the name Renou and wandered throughout France, never remaining anywhere for long. During this period he married Thérèse in a civil ceremony and wrote his *Confessions.* In 1770 he returned to Paris and resumed his real identity unmolested. Determined to defend himself against the "conspirators," Rousseau read excerpts from his *Confessions* in the fashionable salons of Parisian society until Mme. d'Épinay requested police intervention to stop him from continuing. In 1771, when the Confederation of the Bar—noble Polish nationalists—requested his advice on institutional reform in Poland, he wrote *Considérations sur le gouvernement de Pologne et sur sa réformation projettée.* In the same year, as a means of further self-justification, he wrote *Rousseau juge Jean-Jacques: Dialogues.* (Four years later he tried to place this work on the altar of the Cathedral of Notre-Dame but was prevented by a locked gate from doing so—a rebuff that caused him to believe in despair that even God had joined the "conspiracy" against him.) Rousseau's madness lessened during the last two years of his life. He lived in seclusion with Thérèse and wrote *Les Rêveries du promeneur solitaire* (1782; *The Reveries of the Solitary Walker*), which details the beauty of nature and man's feelings for nature. On 2 July 1778 he uttered his last words: "It is true so soon as it is felt." He was buried on the Île des Peupliers at Ermenonville. During the Revolution, his remains were reinterred in the Pantheon in Paris.

Critics have long considered much of Rousseau's work extremely controversial, if not decidedly revolutionary; Rousseau's comment on his *Confessions* as "an undertaking, hitherto without precedent" is representative of early critical opinion of his canon in general. In 1790 Edmund Burke criticized Rousseau for "giving rise to new and unlooked-for strokes in politics and morals" and declared that "the writings of Rousseau lead directly to shameful evil." Yet not all English critics shared this opinion. Sir James Mackintosh credited Rousseau as one "who unshackled and emancipated the human mind." Continental critics, during and following the Revolution, maintained a similar stance, with Burke writing of them: "Him [Rousseau] they study, him they meditate; him they turn over in all the time they can spare. . . . Rousseau is their canon of holy writ; in his life he is their canon of *Polyclitus;* he is their standard figure of perfection." Indeed, Rousseau's writings were widely read and critically acclaimed throughout Europe well into the early nineteenth century. Thomas Green claimed Britons generally esteemed Rousseau as "without exception, the greatest genius and finest writer that ever lived." Nevertheless, English enthusiasm for Rousseau began to wane by 1814—the watershed year for sympathetic English criticism. By the mid-1820s Rousseau's political writings drew serious objections and were labeled "dangerous moonshine." According to Edmund Gosse: "His influence was like a snow man in the sun; it melted and dripped from every limb, from all parts of its structure." By the end of the Georgian period Rousseau was regarded with contempt, as a detestable man whose works were not to be read—except in secret. Thus Rousseau generally remained neglected in the English-speaking world, only mentioned captiously and disparagingly through the turn of the century. One exception is noteworthy, however: John Morley's classic 1873 monograph, *Rousseau.*

In the early twentieth century, English critics of Rousseau acknowledged that they suffered, in the words of Gosse, from a "stigma which [had] lain on England for a hundred years of being dry with cynical neglect of Rousseau while all the rest of the threshing-floor of Europe was wet with the dews of vivifying criticism." As the bicentenary of Rousseau's birth approached, English commentary began to mirror Continental views as scholars reassessed the import of the writer's life and ideology. Critics became increasingly sentient of Rousseau's principles, especially toward the contradictory nature of much of his thought. J. Middleton Murry attributed Rousseau's penchant for paradox to an "unremitting endeavour to express an intuitive certainty in intellectual terms. . . . He seems to surge upwards on a passionate wave of revolutionary ideas, only to sink back into the calm of conservative or quietist conclusions." By mid-century, the anchoritic qualities of his life were more appreciated than denigrated. Jacques Maritain, though generally unsympathetic toward Rousseau's views, noted that the man "gives us in his very unsociability, his sickly isolation, a lyrical image, as dazzling as it is deceptive, of the secret needs of the spirit in us." In recent years, critical attention has shifted from a "paternity" approach—study of Rousseau's "formative influence" on modern society as the father of certain ideas, movements, and events—to attempts at lucid interpretation of the actual meaning of his thought.

Rousseau—the mournful lunatic, the noble savage, the irreverent revolutionary—has fascinated generations of readers with his eloquently frank autobiographical writings, his illuminating observations on the nature and spirit of man, and his often disputatious, enigmatic sociopolitical theories. Exonerated or condemned, Rousseau and his thought continue to attract scholars and critics. In the words of R. A. Leigh, Rousseau "is not only the most original, the most profound and the most controversial of all the great eighteenth-century writers: he is also the most topical. . . . He will always remain both the prophet and the critic of modern times."

(For further information about Rousseau's life and works, see *Literature Criticism from 1400 to 1800*, Vol. 14.)

CRITICAL COMMENTARY

HAVELOCK ELLIS

(essay date 1912)

[Ellis was a pioneering sexual psychologist and a respected English man of letters. In the following excerpt from an essay first published in the *Atlantic Monthly* in 1912, he discourses upon Rousseau's wide influence and philosophic roots, claiming that Rousseau "effected a spiritual revolution which no mere man of letters has ever effected, a revolution only comparable to that effected by Christianity."]

Two centuries after his birth, Jean-Jacques Rousseau continues to exert a potent and disturbing influence; we still have among us his ardent advocates, his bitter enemies. For the most part, during the century that follows the death of any mere writer of books, he falls back into the historic background; the battles that may once have raged around him have subsided; and those persons who are still sufficiently interested to like or dislike his work combine to adjust him in the niche, large or small, which he is henceforth destined to occupy. It is so even with the greatest. Less than a century has passed since Goethe died; for some he is in the modern world 'the master of those who know'; for others he is 'a colossal sentimentalist'; but each party recognises it has something big to deal with and there is no longer any inclination to fall into violent dispute. Not so with Rousseau. This man, who filled the second half of the eighteenth century, who inspired most of the literary and even social movements of the nineteenth century, remains a living and even distracting force in the twentieth century. At the present time there is probably more written about Rousseau than about any contemporary man of letters with the possible exception of Tolstoy, and Tolstoy, we may remember, was an avowed disciple of Rousseau. We have made up our minds about Voltaire, even about Diderot, but we have not made up our minds about Rousseau. According to the point of view, and the special group of alleged facts on which attention is concentrated, Rousseau figures as the meanest of mankind, as a degenerate pervert, as an unfortunate lunatic, as a suffering and struggling man of genius, as the noble pioneer of all the great humanitarian and progressive movements in the modern world, and as the seductive and empty rhetorician who is leading society astray from the orderly paths of civilisation into the abyss of anarchy. (pp. 95-6)

Since those who revile the name of Rousseau are at one with those who adore it in magnifying the extent of his influence, it becomes easier than it would otherwise be to estimate what our modern world presumably owes to Rousseau. It may be interesting to touch on two of these things: the Revolution and Romanticism.

The whole Revolution, say its friends and its enemies alike, was Rousseau; Berthelot, the great man of science, declared it in solemn admiration a quarter of a century ago. Lasserre, the acute critic, declares it in bitter indignation today. Rousseau was not, indeed, consciously working towards the Revolution, and he would have loathed its protagonists who acted in his name, just as Jesus would have loathed the scribes and Pharisees who have masqueraded in his Church. But, as we look back, it is easy to see how Rousseau's work, and Rousseau's alone among the men of his generation pointed to revolution. They appealed to intelligence, to good sense, to fine feeling, to elevated humanitarianism; but it is not these things of which revolutions are made. Rousseau appealed to fundamental instincts, to soaring aspirations, to blind passions, to the volcanic eruptive elements in human nature, and we are at once amid the forces of revolution. No wonder that all the men of the Revolution fed themselves on Rousseau's words. Not a single revolutionary, Mallet du Pan noted in 1789, but was carried away by Rousseau's doctrines, and burning to realise them. Marat was seen in public enthusiastically reading aloud the **Social Contract,** and Charlotte Corday, who slew him, was equally the fervent disciple of Rousseau. There was one other man beside Rousseau who had a supreme part in moulding the Revolution, at all events so far as concerns its final outcome. It is interesting to hear that this man, Napoleon, declared to Lord Holland that without 'that bad man' Rousseau there would have been no Revolution. Since the Christianisation of the Roman Empire there have been four great movements of the human spirit in

Principal Works

Dissertation sur la musique moderne (essay) 1743

*Discours qui a remporté le prix à l'Academie de Dijon. En l'année 1750. Sur cette Question proposée par la même Académie: Si le rétablissement des Sciences et des Arts a contribué à épurer les moeurs (essay) 1750

[A Discourse, to which the Prize was Adjudged by the Academy of Dijon on this Question: Whether the Reestablishment of Arts and Sciences has Contributed to Purify our Morals, 1752]

Le Devin du village (operetta) 1752

[The Cunning Man, 1766]

Lettre sur la musique françoise (criticism) 1753

Discours sur l'origine et les fondemens de l'inégalité parmi les hommes (essay) 1755

[A Discourse upon the Origin and Foundation of the Inequality among Mankind, 1761]

Discours sur l'oeconomie politique (essay) 1758

†A M. D'Alembert, de l'Académie Françoise, de l'Académie Royale des Sciences de Paris, de celle de Prusse, de la Société Royale de Londres, de l'Académie Royale des Belles-Lettres de Suède, & de l'Institut de Bologne. Sur son Article Genève dans le VIIme Volume de l'Encyclopédie, et particulièrement, sur le projet d'établir un Théatre de Comédie en cette ville (essay) 1758

[A Letter from M. Rousseau to M. d'Alembert Concerning the Effects of Theatrical Entertainments on the Manners of Mankind, 1759]

Lettre de J. J. Rousseau à Monsieur de Voltaire (letter) 1759

‡Lettres de deux amans, habitans d'une petite ville au pied des Alpes. 6 vols. (novel) 1761; also published as La Nouvelle Héloïse, 1764

[Eloisa; or, a Series of Original Letters Collected and Published by J. J. Rousseau, 1761]

Du contrat social; ou, Principes du droit politique (essay) 1762

[A Treatise on the Social Compact; or the Principles of Politic Law, 1764; also published as An Inquiry into the Nature of the Social Contract; or, Principles of Political Right, 1791]

Émile, ou de l'éducation. 4 vols. (novel) 1762

[Emilius and Sophia; or, A New System of Education, 1762-63]

Letters écrites de la montagne (essays) 1764

Dictionnaire de musique (dictionary) 1768

[A Dictionary of Music, 1779]

Rousseau juge de Jean Jacques: Dialogues (autobiography) 1780

Considérations sur le gouvernement de Pologne et sur sa réformation projettée (essay) 1782

§Les Rêveries du promeneur solitaire (essays) 1782

[The Reveries of the Solitary Walker published in The Confessions of J. J. Rousseau: with the Reveries of the Solitary Walker, 1783-91; also published as The Reveries of A Solitary, 1927]

Les Confessions de J. J. Rousseau. 4 vols. (autobiography) 1782-89

[The Confessions of J. J. Rousseau: with the Reveries of the Solitary Walker. 4 vols., 1783-91]

Nouvelles lettres de J. J. Rousseau (letters) 1789

[Original Letters of J. J. Rousseau, 1799]

Oeuvres complètes. 4 vols. (essays, novels, poems, and autobiographies) 1959-64

Correspondance complète. 45 vols. (letters) 1965-86

*This work is commonly known in French as Discours sur les sciences et les arts and in English as Discourse on the Sciences and Arts.

†This work is commonly referred to in French as Lettre à d'Alembert sur les spectacles and in English as Letter to d'Alembert on the Theater.

‡This work is sometimes known as Julie; ou, La Nouvelle Héloïse.

§This work first appeared with the publication of Les Confessions in 1782.

Christendom—the Renaissance, the Reformation, the Counter-Reformation, and the Revolution. Three of these movements have been so diffused in time and space that we are scarcely justified in closely associating even one of them with the influence of a single man. But the Revolution, incalculably vast as its results have been, was narrowly circumscribed. It is comparatively easy to measure it, and when so measured its friends and its foes ascribe it—so far as any complex social-economic movement can be associated with one man— to Rousseau.

Mainly by virtue of his relation to the Revolution, Rousseau is claimed as the pioneer of Modern Democracy, alike in its direction towards Socialism and its direction towards Anarchism. For both these democratic movements—the collectivistic as well as the individualistic—rest on those natural instincts which it was Rousseau's mission to proclaim. The democracy which insists that the whole shall embody every unit, and the democracy which insists that each unit shall have its own rights against the whole, alike appeal to deep emotional reasons to which the humblest respond. 'There would have been no Republic without Rousseau,' says Lemaître. Republicanism, Socialism, Anarchism—these are the three democratic movements which have been slowly permeating and transforming the political societies of men since the Great Revolution of 1789, and we are asked to believe that the germs of all were scattered abroad by this one man, Rousseau.

The chorus of voices which acclaims or accuses Rousseau as the creator of Romanticism is even greater than that which finds in him the inventor of Revolutionary Democracy. The Revolutionary Movement and the Romantic Movement are one, we are told, and Rousseau was responsible for both. What, it may be asked, is Romanticism? There is not much agreement on this point. Lasserre, one of its ablest and most absolute opponents, tells us that it is 'a general revolution of the human soul' which may be described as 'a system of feeling and acting conformably to the supposed primitive nature of mankind,' and since we do not know what the primitive nature of mankind is, Romanticism becomes, in opposition to the classical spirit in general and the Gallic spirit in particular, 'absolute individualism in thought and feeling,' or in other words, 'a disorder of the feelings and ideas which overturns the whole economy of civilised human nature.' This definition is itself individualistic—and therefore on the theory Romantic—but it may, for the moment, serve. Fortunately, though there is no agreement as to what Romanticism is, there is less dispute as to the writers who may be termed Romantic.

It is a remarkable fact that though Rousseau so largely filled the second half of the eighteenth century he had little influence on its literature in France. He was the adored prophet, preacher, teacher, but not the inspired and inspiring artist with a new revelation of Nature peculiarly apt for literary uses. Beaumarchais, who here dominated that period, belongs to altogether another tradition. Only Bernardin de Saint-Pierre was the follower, as he was also the friend, of Rousseau, and *Paul and Virginia* opens the great literary tradition of Rousseau. The first notable names in French literature which we can at all associate with Rousseau are dubious names, more dubious perhaps than they deserve to be, but still distinctly dubious. It is highly probable that the **Confessions** moved Casanova to write his own immortal *Mémoires*. It is certain that they inspired that interesting picture of an unwholesome mind, the *Monsieur Nicolas* of Restif de la Bretonne, the 'Rousseau du ruisseau,' as he has been wittily and accurately termed. We must even recognise that Rousseau was the adored exemplar of the Marquis de Sade, who, in *Aline et Valcour,* makes Valcour, here speaking probably for his author, assert that Rousseau encouraged him to devote himself to literature and philosophy. 'It was in the conversation of this deep philosopher, of this true friend of Nature and of Man, that I acquired my dominant passion for literature and the arts.'

In Germany, earlier than elsewhere, the influence of Rousseau was profoundly felt by men of an altogether different type of character. In France, Rousseau could only be potent by stimulating a revolutionary reaction against everything which had long been regarded as the classic norm from which no deviation was possible; that was why the morbid and unsound personalities in literature, rightly finding a real point of contact with Rousseau, felt his influence first. But an altogether different tradition, if we look beyond cosmopolitan aristocratic circles, prevailed in Germany. Here the subjective emotionalism of Rousseau, his constant appeal to the ultimate standard of Nature, were so congenial to the Teutonic spirit that they acted as an immediate liberating force. Rousseau was Kant's supreme master; only one portrait, Rousseau's, hung on the walls of the philosopher's simple study; all his doctrines in the three Critiques may be regarded (Thomas Davidson has ingeniously argued) as a formal crystallisation of Rousseau's fluid eloquence. Fichte also was largely moulded by Rousseau, as were Herder and Lessing. Goethe in the final stages of his long development aimed at serenely objective Neo-classic ideals which were far indeed from Rousseau, but at the outset he was as thorough a disciple as Kant. He went on pilgrimage to the beautiful island in the Lake of Bienne once hallowed by Rousseau's presence; his Werther is manifestly the younger brother of Saint-Preux, and it may be, as some have claimed, that without Rousseau there could have been no *Faust.*

It was not until the nineteenth century that the Romantic Movement finally burst into magnificent life in France. Chateaubriand appears as the quintessence of Romanticism, a more pure embodiment of its literary quality than even Rousseau himself. Senancour, especially as he shows himself in his *Obermann,* was an equally typical and much more genuine representative of the Movement. Madame de Staël, one of the first to write about Rousseau, was penetrated by his spirit, and became the revealer to France of Romantic Germany. Alfred de Musset was a Romantic through Byron, rather than directly from Rousseau. Victor Hugo, Lamartine, George Sand, even at times Balzac, all belonged to Romanticism. Michelet, writing history by the sole light of his own personal emotions, was peculiarly a Romantic. Flaubert, in a later generation, was Romantic on one side, altogether alien from Romanticism, as were his fundamental ideals. But during the first half of the nineteenth century in France, with the possible exception of Stendhal—for even he was really affected by the movement—it is not easy to name any notable figure in literature who was outside Romanticism. Rousseau's influence had become so all-pervading that, like the universal pressure of the air, it was sometimes unperceived by those who were experiencing it. Louis Dumur has pointed out that Alfred de Musset in his *Confession d'un Enfant du Siècle,* when trying to discover the sources of Romanticism, never so much as mentions Rousseau.

The attitude of England towards Romanticism and towards Rousseau was different from either that of Germany or of France. The Germans were made conscious by Rousseau of their own unconscious impulses. The French were forced to undergo a violent conversion. But the English were Romanticists already from the outset and here the Romantic Movement could effect no revolution. All Rousseau's literary inspirations and aesthetic ideals had come, directly or indirectly, from England: Richardson's *Clarissa,* Kent's English garden, Locke's philosophy, English independence and English freedom, these were the things which had aroused the emulation or stirred the enthusiasm of Rousseau. English influence equally stimulated also the great apostle of Romanticism, and Chateaubriand composed *Atala* and *René* in Hyde Park. These splendid flowers were therefore easily acceptable in England for they clearly raised from English seeds. Rousseau's influence recognised and unrecognised, reached English Romanticism, but Rousseau was here only giving back in a more highly developed form what he had himself received from England.

If we look beyond the Romantic Movement in its narrower literary sense, we still find that the influence of Rousseau remains just as plainly visible, in Russia, for instance. It is unnecessary to say that the greatest writer of modern times in Russia, the greatest writer in the world of his day, was from his earliest years a disciple of Rousseau; Tolstoy read and re-read the twenty volumes of Rousseau's works until some of the pages became so familiar that it seemed to him he had written them himself; he wore Rousseau's portrait next his skin as the devout Russian wears the cross; it was, he himself said, worship rather than admiration which he experienced for Rousseau; even shortly before his death he wrote that the two chief formative influences of his life had been Rousseau and the Gospels.

If we turn away from the apostles and the propagandists of avowed emotional revolution, we have not yet escaped Rousseau. The austere Emerson equally has his roots in Rousseau, if he was not actually, as Davidson termed him, 'the most loyal disciple Rousseau ever had.' The Transcendentalist was here at one with the Positivist. George Eliot, equally alien in temperament, was an equally ardent admirer of the **Confessions;** Rousseau, she said, 'quickened' her mind, not by imparting any new beliefs, but by 'the mighty rushing wind of his inspiration'; he 'made man and nature a fresh world of thought and feeling to me.' It was an accurate characterisation of the kind of power by which Rousseau has so often held the souls of men and women.

In the twentieth century the same potent force is still quickening ardent and aspiring souls who strive to create new ideals. Moreover, Rousseau is still the precursor even of those who are unconscious of his influence. He had long ago anticipated our latest philosophies. William James is counted the founder of Pragmatism, but the conception of 'truth' as 'practical truth' or 'cash value' rather than 'science,' was so clearly set forth in **Emile** and the second half of the **Nouvelle Héloïse,** that Schinz has been able to argue that 'the greatest of the Pragmatists is—and will probably remain—Jean-Jacques Rousseau.' So also with the fashionable Bergsonian philosophy of the day, with its depreciation of reason and its insistence on the vital force of instinct. That also is laid down, with a less subtle elaboration but not with less emphasis, by Rousseau.

Even those for whom Rousseau is nothing but a poison have not escaped the operation of that seductive venom. Nietzsche, the most conspicuous and influential thinker of these latter days, was absolutely opposed to Rousseau. Rousseau's 'Nature,' his 'good man,' his sentiment, his weaknesses, especially his lack of aristocratic culture and his plebeianism—against all these things Nietzsche's hatred was implacable. Yet Rousseau was in his own blood. 'Nietzsche,' says Alois Riehl, 'is the antipodes of Rousseau, and yet his spiritual relation. He is the Rousseau of our time.'

In thus estimating the hold of Rousseau over the things which have been counted precious since the days in which he lived, we have the authority even of those who rebel against his influence. But there is always a fallacy involved in such attempts to fasten an unlimited responsibility upon any human figure, not excepting the greatest. Even the supreme man of genius, as Dumur truly says, is no aerolite from another sphere, no bolt from the blue. The most absolute innovator has found the terms of his fruitful ideas in ancient tradition. The most potent revolutionary owes his power to the fact that in his day certain conditions, especially economic and social conditions, combine to produce a vacuum his spirit is peculiarly fitted to fill. The name of Darwin is immortally associated with the idea of evolution, but the idea had been slowly germinating through thousands of years, sometimes in brains of as great a calibre as his own, until the moment arrived when at last fruition was possible, and the cautious, deliberate Darwin calmly completed the work of the ages. Even the great movement of Christianity, which sometimes seems to us so mighty as to be beyond the reach of reason to fathom, is seen to be necessary and inevitable when we realise the conditions under which it arose and see the figure of Jesus slowly hammered and annealed into the shape which best satisfied the deepest cravings of an epoch. Rousseau—again alike by friends and foes—has been counted, like Jesus, a prophet issuing with a new law from the desert into a decadent civilisation he was destined to dissolve and renew; he has been regarded as a great reformer of Christianity such as Luther was, the incarnation of a new wave of Christianity, adding to the renovation of its essential qualities—its abandonment to emotion, its magnification of the poor and humble, its insistence on charity—a new set of notes, a trend towards political realisation, a fresh ideal of natural beauty, a justification of passion, a refinement of voluptuous sentiment, which adjusted Christianity to the modern soul as it had never been adjusted before. Luther had de-Catholicised Christianity; Rousseau, who in his own person united the two traditions, while yet retaining the plebeian and individualistic basis which Luther established, re-Catholicised Christianity on a new plane, even though in the end he stood aloof from Christianity, and created a Church whose dogmas rested on the universal authority of instincts and emotions.

Yet, just as we can counterpart every Christian rite and dogma outside Christianity, so also it is easy to duplicate every tenet and tendency in Rousseau. Marivaux, within narrower limits and with a more restrained method, was a sympathetic and original moralist, a delicate artist, a subtle psychologist, to a degree that Rousseau never attained; in his earliest work Rousseau was frankly an imitator of Marivaux. The Abbé Prévost, again, more than any man had let the flood of early English romanticism into France, had translated *Clarissa,* and himself written novels of wild and sombre romantic passion; Rousseau knew Prévost, he was profoundly affected by his novels. Locke, in another sphere, had set forth epoch-making reflections on political government, and had written an enlightened treatise on education; the author of the **Social Contract** and **Emile** clearly reveals how much he owed to 'the wise Locke.' Before ever he began to write, Rousseau had soaked his mind in books and meditated on them in his perpetual long walks; he was brought up on romances, he had read everything he could find, English travel books especially, about savages in 'the state of Nature'; he had absorbed all that matters in the literature of the seventeenth century, though he knew comparatively little of the literature of his own century; without any guidance, by unerring instinct, he had seized on the things that fed his own mood, from Plutarch to Petrarch. Even without going outside the pale of Catholic Christianity, he could, had he known it, have found the authority for every intimate and daring impulse of his own heart.

The ideas and the emotions, therefore, which Rousseau manifested were by no means unique. The temperament he had inherited furnished the most exquisitely fertile of all conceivable soils for these seeds to flourish in. But the seeds were not new seeds and for the most part we can trace with precision the exact source from which each of them reached Rousseau. Moreover, when we come, calmly and critically, to measure and to weigh the ideas and the emotions we find in Rousseau's books, it happens, as often as not, that they fail to stand our tests. If we explore the **Social Contract,** we find that every page swarms with bold propositions for which no proof is, or can be, supplied. Rousseau had borrowed Hobbes's conception of sovereignty and Locke's conception of popular government and amalgamated them into the image of a Sovereign People which can do no wrong and governs by its own direct *fiat,* in such a way that the will of each finds its part in the will of all. No doubt it is a magnificent idea and it is still alive in the world moulding political institutions; it is responsible for the establishment of the Referendum which has had a certain vogue in new political constitutions and we are constantly endeavouring, however much in vain, to approach its realisation. But when we examine Rousseau's exposition of this idea, we find that verbal logic takes the place of inductive reasoning, that impassioned declamation is the agent of persuasion, and that the very lucidity of the statement only brings out more clearly the glaring inconsistencies and absurdities which the argument involves.

If we turn to a very different book, though not less famous and in its own way not less influential, we encounter the same experience. **La Nouvelle Héloïse,** in the effect it has had on the writing of novels, is second to none, except *Don Quixote.* Schopenhauer, himself a great literary artist, counted **La Nouvelle Héloïse** among the four great novels of the world. Shelley, who was a fine critic as well as a great poet, was enraptured by the 'sublime genius and more than human sensibility' displayed in this book, as well as by 'the divine beauty of Rousseau's imagination,' as he realised it on sailing across the famous lake which is the scene of the novel. A more modern French critic finds that 'Julie has the tongue of an apostle, she is our greatest orator after Bossuet.' That is a eulogy which may well serve to condemn any novel, but it is probably the most favourable judgment which from the modern standpoint can be bestowed upon Rousseau's novel. This novel so unlike a novel yet re-created the novel; that is admitted. Today **La Nouvelle Héloïse,** for all the fine passages we may discover in it, is far less agreeable to read than the best of those novels by Marivaux, Prévost, and the younger Crébillon which it replaced in popular esteem. Its sentimental rhetoric is now tedious; as a story it fails to enchain us; of subtle characterisation or dramatic vigour we find nothing; as a work of art it is incomparably inferior to *Clarissa Harlowe* on which it was modelled.

If we look more broadly at Rousseau's work, the results of critical examination are similar. The world's great teachers are, for the most part, impressive by the substantial unity of the message they have proclaimed; we feel a convincing harmony between that message and the personality behind it. So it is with Marcus Aurelius and so with Thoreau. It is so, also, on what may seem a lower ethical plane, with Rousseau's chief contemporaries, with Voltaire and with Diderot. It is not clearly so with Rousseau. He often seems like an exquisite instrument, giving forth a music which responds to the varying emotions of the hand that strikes it. He is the supreme individualist, and yet his doctrines furnish the foundations for socialism, even in its oppressive forms. He is the champion of the rights of passion, and yet he was the leader in a movement of revolt against licentiousness, of return to domesticity and the felicities of family life and maternal devotion to children. He was opposed to the emancipation of women, even to the education of women side by side with men; he is denounced by the advocates of women's rights who see in the philosophers whom he opposed the pioneers of their own movement, and yet he was acclaimed as the liberator of womanhood; noble women, from Madame Roland onwards, were his enthusiastic disciples, the literary promulgators of his genius are headed by two distinguished women, Madame de Staël and Madame de Charrière.

Still more discordant seems to many the clash of Rousseau's doctrines with Rousseau's life. The uncompromising champion of virtue was nearly forty years old before he learnt how to earn his own living honestly. The regenerator of love was a solitary sensuous sentimentalist. The author of **Emile,** the gospel of childhood, put away his own children—if indeed he ever really had any—as foundlings.

When we thus critically survey Rousseau's books and personality, it is difficult to avoid the conclusion that, to a large extent, Rousseau has represented a backward movement in civilisation. His influence has tended to depreciate the value of the mighty instrument of reason by which civilisation is mainly wrought; it has consecrated prejudice under the sacred names of Nature and instinct; it has opened the way to the triumph of plebeianism and the sanctification of mob-rule; it has tended, by casting off the restraints on emotion, to an unwholesome divorce between the extravagancies of feeling and the limitations of life.

It is on this note, at all events, that so many discussions of Rousseau finally rest: Rousseau was a 'degenerate' from birth, and his teaching is the disorganisation of civilised society. Yet, even if we believe that there are elements of truth in such a view, we can scarcely choose this standpoint for our final survey of Rousseau. When we bear in mind that the most aspiring efforts of the noblest souls during more than a century have been directly or indirectly inspired by this man, it becomes clear that to attaint Rousseau is to stain our own human nature, to place ourselves in the ranks of the Yahoos. For, there can be no doubt, unreasonable as it may be to regard Rousseau or any other man as the primary cause of any great social movement, it is he, more than any man, who has moulded the form of our spiritual activities and shaped our ideals. His passions have become the atmosphere in which we

move. Since the days of feverish activity which Rousseau spent in his little hermitage at Montmorency, not merely our aims in politics, but our feeling for religion, our feeling for love, our feeling for Nature, have been renovated. They would have been renovated even if Rousseau had never lived, though perhaps not so thoroughly, yet, as things are, the new forms they have assumed have been determined by this solitary dreamer. 'Religion,' said Butler in the orderly and reasonable eighteenth-century manner, 'is a useful piece of information concerning a distant region of which otherwise we should have had no explanation': the mystic enthusiasm of the Vicaire Savoyard would alone have sufficed to sweep away for ever so pedestrian a conception of religion. Before Rousseau, love was a highly refined form of social intercourse, a species of gallantry conducted with self-restraint and all the formalities of its special etiquette; any extravagance, whether in feeling, in speech, or in action, was banished. But when Saint-Preux, oppressed by his high-strung passions, came to the rock at Meillerie to pour forth in solitude the flood of his sentimental tears, all the witty refinements of eighteenth-century gallantry, for good or for evil, were finally swept away; extravagancy was free to lay down the law of love. It was Rousseau who enabled Mirabeau in his first letter to Julie Danvers (whom he had never seen) to declare: 'I, also, am a lover, have emptied the cup of sensibility to the dregs, and could give a thousand lives for what I love': it was Rousseau who laid down a new etiquette of love which every petty poet and novelist still adheres to. Finally, Rousseau renovated our feeling for Nature. The geometrically minded eighteenth century could see nothing beautiful in Nature until trimmed into symmetry by the hands of man; even for Madame de Staël the Alps were merely 'a magnificent horror.' But Rousseau, who told Bernardin de Saint-Pierre that he 'would rather be among the arrows of the Parthians than among the glances of men,' only breathed freely and thought freely in the solitude of mountains and forests and torrents, and here also he has inoculated mankind with the virus of his own passion. In all these ways (as indeed Höffding has pointed out in what is, so far as I know, the most profound statement of Rousseau's philosophic position), Rousseau stood, in opposition to our artificial and inharmonious civilisation, for the worth of life as a whole, the simple undivided rights of life, the rights of instinct, the rights of emotion. This was his assertion of Nature. This was the way in which he renovated life, and effected a spiritual revolution which no mere man of letters has ever effected, a revolution only comparable to that effected by Christianity, of which indeed it was but a modern renascence.

Yet the man who wielded, and continues to wield, this enormous power over the world cannot be called one of its great men. In intellect, one sometimes thinks, he was not conspicuously above the average; in what we conventionally call moral character, he was at the outset conspicuously below it. Ill-born and ill-bred, morbidly shy and suspicious, defective in virility, he was inapt for all the social ends of life, mentally and physically a self-torturing invalid. No man more absolutely than Rousseau has ever illustrated the truth of Hinton's profound saying that the affinities of genius are not with strength but with weakness, that the supreme man of genius is the man who opposes no obstacle to the forces of Nature of which he is the channel. Or, as St. Paul had declared long previously in a passage which seems to bear the same sense, it is the despised and rejected things of the world, even the things which are not, that God has chosen to put to nought the things that are.

It may, indeed, be pointed out to those who insist on the ludicrous, mean, and contemptible incidents in Rousseau's early life—only known to us through his own narration of them—that, as Lemaître said in a book that is, for the most part, superficial as well as unsympathetic, Rousseau's life was a process of moral evolution, a continuous purification completed by 'insanity,' or, as Rousseau himself put it, 'a purification in the furnace of adversity.' It is this process which largely gives the clue alike to his intellect and to his moral contradictions. Rousseau's abandonment to emotion was always checked by his timidity, by the perpetual searching suspicion which he applied to himself as well as to others. That is how it comes to pass that we may find in his writings the warrant for the most contradictory doctrines. It was so in the political field. In 1754 in the **Discours sur l'Inégalité,** he proclaimed that revolt of the non-possessors against the possessors of property which has since fermented so mightily in the world. But towards the end of his life, in the Constitution for Poland which he prepared at the request of the Poles, he had become in these matters a timid opportunist: 'I do not say that we must leave things as they are; but I do say that we must only touch them with extreme circumspection.' The contrast between Rousseau's apparent abandonment of his children and the fervour which in **Emile** he expended over the parental training of children has often been set forth to his discredit. But, as he himself viewed the matter, that gospel of childhood was simply the atonement for his own neglect. He displayed throughout a very passion of expiation. Born defective, beset on every side, he was yet of those who, according to the ancient metaphor of Saint Augustine, make of their dead selves the rungs of a ladder to rise to higher things. To some he seems to have been a kind of moral imbecile. But Thérèse, the mistress-wife who had been at his side during the whole of the period of his literary life and knew his weaknesses as no other could know them, said after his death: 'If he was not a saint, who ever was?' To view

Rousseau rightly, we must see him, on the one hand, as the essential instrument of genius, a reed stirred to magnificent music by all the mighty winds of the spirit, and on the other hand, as a much-suffering man, scourged more than most men by human frailties, and yet for ever struggling to aspire. In this double capacity, at once the type of genius and the type of humanity, we learn to understand something of the magic of Rousseau's influence; we learn to understand how it is that before this shrine the most unlike persons in the world—the Marquis de Sade as well as Emerson, Charlotte Corday as well as Kant—have alike bowed in reverence.

Rousseau was a creature of clay. He was also a devouring flame. But of such blended fire and clay, in the end, the most exquisite products of the divine potter's art are formed. Under that stress Rousseau's character was slowly purified to the highest issues. Under that same stress was finally woven the delicate and iridescent texture of the finest style which French speech has ever assumed. The great traditions of the literary art of France—through Montaigne, Pascal, La Bruyère—reached at last in the furnace of this man's tortured soul their ultimate perfection of sensitive and intimate beauty. This style, which is the man himself, the style of the **Confessions** and the **Rêveries,** alone serves to make these books immortal. Here in his art the consuming fire and the soft clay of Rousseau's temperament are burnt to shapes of a beauty that is miraculous and stirs the depths of the soul. What indeed can we say, in the end, of all the operation of this man's spirit on the world save that it is a miracle, with effects that immeasurably transcend their causes? The water, if not the very mud, is turned into wine, and a few small loaves and fishes suffice for the feeding of the nations. (pp. 97-112)

Havelock Ellis, "The Bicentenary of Rousseau," in his *From Rousseau to Proust,* Houghton Mifflin Company, 1935, pp. 95-112.

BERTRAND RUSSELL

(essay date 1946)

[Russell was an English philosopher and mathematician who gained recognition for his support of various social and political concerns. For his work in a number of literary genres, he was awarded the Nobel Prize in literature in 1950. In the following excerpt, he provides an analysis of Rousseau's theology and political theory.]

Jean Jacques Rousseau (1712-78), though a *philosophe* in the eighteenth-century French sense, was not what would now be called a 'philosopher'. Nevertheless he had a powerful influence on philosophy, as on literature and taste and manners and politics. Whatever may be our opinion of his merits as a thinker, we must recognize his immense importance as a social force. This importance came mainly from his appeal to the heart, and to what, in his day, was called 'sensibility'. He is the father of the romantic movement, the initiator of systems of thought which infer non-human facts from human emotions, and the inventor of the political philosophy of pseudo-democratic dictatorships as opposed to traditional absolute monarchies. Ever since his time, those who considered themselves reformers have been divided into two groups, those who followed him and those who followed Locke. Sometimes they cooperated, and many individuals saw no incompatibility. But gradually the incompatibility has become increasingly evident. At the present time, Hitler is an outcome of Rousseau; Roosevelt and Churchill, of Locke.

Rousseau's biography was related by himself in his *Confessions* in great detail, but without any slavish regard for truth. He enjoyed making himself out a great sinner, and sometimes exaggerated in this respect; but there is abundant external evidence that he was destitute of all the ordinary virtues. This did not trouble him, because he considered that he always had a warm heart, which, however, never hindered him from base actions towards his best friends. (p. 660)

There is much in Rousseau's work which, however important in other respects, does not concern the history of philosophical thought. There are only two parts of his thinking that I shall consider in any detail; these are, first, his theology, and second, his political theory.

In theology he made an innovation which has now been accepted by the great majority of Protestant theologians. Before him, every philosopher from Plato onwards, if he believed in God, offered intellectual arguments in favour of his belief. The arguments may not, to us, seem very convincing, and we may feel that they would not have seemed cogent to anyone who did not already feel sure of the truth of the conclusion. But the philosopher who advanced the arguments certainly believed them to be logically valid, and such as should cause certainty of God's existence in any unprejudiced person of sufficient philosophical capacity. Modern Protestants who urge us to believe in God, for the most part, despise the old 'proofs', and base their faith upon some aspect of human nature—emotions of awe or mystery, the sense of right and wrong, the feeling of aspiration, and so on. This way of defending religious belief was invented by Rousseau. It has become so familiar that his originality may easily not be appreciated by a modern reader, unless he will take the trouble to compare Rousseau with (say) Descartes or Leibniz.

'Ah, Madame!' Rousseau writes to an aristocratic lady, 'sometimes in the privacy of my study, with my

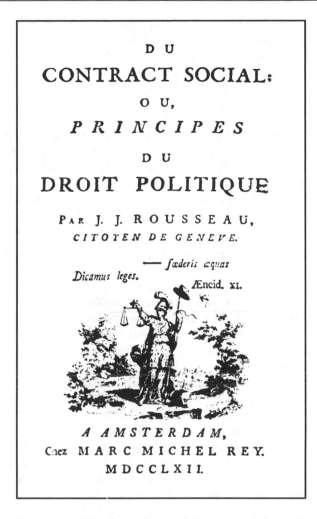

Title page of the first edition of *Du contrat social* (1762).

hands pressed tight over my eyes or in the darkness of the night, I am of opinion that there is no God. But look yonder: the rising of the sun, as it scatters the mists that cover the earth, and lays bare the wondrous glittering scene of nature, disperses at the same moment all cloud from my soul. I find my faith again, and my God, and my belief in Him. I admire and adore Him, and I prostrate myself in His presence.'

On another occasion he says: 'I believe in God as strongly as I believe any other truth, because believing and not believing are the last things in the world that depend on me.' This form of argument has the drawback of being private; the fact that Rousseau cannot help believing something affords no ground for another person to believe the same thing.

He was very emphatic in his theism. On one occasion he threatened to leave a dinner party because Saint Lambert (one of the guests), expressed a doubt as to the existence of God. *'Moi Monsieur,'* Rousseau exclaimed angrily, *'je crois en Dieu!'* Robespierre, in all things his faithful disciple, followed him in this respect also. The 'Fête de l'Etre Suprême' would have had Rousseau's whole-hearted approval.

'The Confession of Faith of a Savoyard Vicar', which is an interlude in the fourth book of *Emile*, is the most explicit and formal statement of Rousseau's creed. Although it professes to be what the voice of nature has proclaimed to a virtuous priest, who suffers disgrace for the wholly 'natural' fault of seducing an unmarried woman, the reader finds with surprise that the voice of nature, when it begins to speak, is uttering a hotch-pot of arguments derived from Aristotle, St Augustine, Descartes, and so on. It is true that they are robbed of precision and logical form; this is supposed to excuse them, and to permit the worthy Vicar to say that he cares nothing for the wisdom of the philosophers.

The later parts of *'The Confession of Faith'* are less reminiscent of previous thinkers than the earlier parts. After satisfying himself that there is a God, the Vicar goes on to consider rules of conduct. 'I do not deduce these rules,' he says, 'from the principles of a high philosophy, but I find them in the depths of my heart, written by Nature in ineffaceable characters.' From this he goes on to develop the view that conscience is in all circumstances an infallible guide to right action. 'Thanks be to Heaven,' he concludes this part of his argument, 'we are thus freed from all this terrifying apparatus of philosophy; we can be men without being learned; dispensed from wasting our life in the study of morals, we have at less cost a more assured guide in this immense labyrinth of human opinions.' Our natural feelings, he contends, lead us to serve the common interest, while our reason urges selfishness. We have therefore only to follow feeling rather than reason in order to be virtuous.

Natural religion, as the Vicar calls his doctrine, has no need of a revelation; if men had listened to what God says to the heart, there would have been only one religion in the world. If God has revealed Himself specially to certain men, this can only be known by human testimony, which is fallible. Natural religion has the advantage of being revealed directly to each individual.

There is a curious passage about hell. The Vicar does not know whether the wicked go to eternal torment, and says, somewhat loftily, that the fate of the wicked does not greatly interest him; but on the whole he inclines to the view that the pains of hell are not everlasting. However this may be, he is sure that salvation is not confined to the members of any one Church.

It was presumably the rejection of revelation and of hell that so profoundly shocked the French government and the Council of Geneva.

The rejection of reason in favour of the heart was not, to my mind, an advance. In fact, no one thought of this device so long as reason appeared to be on the side of religious belief. In Rousseau's environment, reason, as represented by Voltaire, was opposed to religion, therefore away with reason! Moreover reason was abstruse and difficult; the savage, even when he has dined, cannot understand the ontological argument, and yet the savage is the repository of all necessary wisdom. Rousseau's savage—who was not the savage known to anthropologists—was a good husband and a kind father; he was destitute of greed, and had a religion of natural kindliness. He was a convenient person, but if he could follow the good Vicar's reasons for believing in God he must have had more philosophy than his innocent naïveté would lead one to expect.

Apart from the fictitious character of Rousseau's 'natural man', there are two objections to the practice of basing beliefs as to objective fact upon the emotions of the heart. One is that there is no reason whatever to suppose that such beliefs will be true; the other is, that the resulting beliefs will be private, since the heart says different things to different people. Some savages are persuaded by the 'natural light' that it is their duty to eat people, and even Voltaire's savages, who are led by the voice of reason to hold that one should only eat Jesuits, are not wholly satisfactory. To Buddhists, the light of nature does not reveal the existence of God, but does proclaim that it is wrong to eat the flesh of animals. But even if the heart said the same thing to all men, that could afford no evidence for the existence of anything outside our own emotions. However ardently I, or all mankind, may desire something, however necessary it may be to human happiness, that is no ground for supposing this something to exist. There is no law of nature guaranteeing that mankind should be happy. Everybody can see that this is true of our life here on earth, but by a curious twist our very sufferings in this life are made into an argument for a better life hereafter. We should not employ such an argument in any other connection. If you had bought ten dozen eggs from a man, and the first dozen were all rotten, you would not infer that the remaining nine dozen must be of surpassing excellence; yet that is the kind of reasoning that 'the heart' encourages as a consolation for our sufferings here below.

For my part, I prefer the ontological argument, the cosmological argument, and the rest of the old stock-in-trade, to the sentimental illogicality that has sprung from Rousseau. The old arguments at least were honest: if valid, they proved their point; if invalid, it was open to any critic to prove them so. But the new theology of the heart dispenses with argument; it cannot be refuted, because it does not profess to prove its points. At bottom, the only reason offered for its acceptance is that it allows us to indulge in pleasant dreams. This is an unworthy reason, and if I had to choose between Thomas Aquinas and Rousseau, I should unhesitatingly choose the Saint.

Rousseau's political theory is set forth in his *Social Contract*, published in 1762. This book is very different in character from most of his writing; it contains little sentimentality and much close intellectual reasoning. Its doctrines, though they pay lip-service to democracy, tend to the justification of the totalitarian State. But Geneva and antiquity combined to make him prefer the City-State to large empires such as those of France and England. On the title-page he calls himself 'citizen of Geneva', and in his introductory sentences he says: 'As I was born a citizen of a free State, and a member of the Sovereign, I feel that, however feeble the influence of my voice may have been on public affairs, the right of voting on them makes it my duty to study them.' There are frequent laudatory references to Sparta, as it appears in Plutarch's *Life of Lycurgus.* He says that democracy is best in small States, aristocracy in middle-sized ones, and monarchy in large ones. But it is to be understood that, in his opinion, small States are preferable, in part because they make democracy more practicable. When he speaks of democracy, he means, as the Greeks meant, direct participation of every citizen; representative government he calls 'elective aristocracy'. Since the former is not possible in a large State, his praise of democracy always implies praise of the City-State. This love of the City-State is, in my opinion, not sufficiently emphasized in most accounts of Rousseau's political philosophy.

Although the book as a whole is much less rhetorical than most of Rousseau's writing, the first chapter opens with a very forceful piece of rhetoric: 'Man is born free, and everywhere he is in chains. One man thinks himself the master of others, but remains more of a slave than they are.' Liberty is the nominal goal of Rousseau's thought, but in fact it is equality that he values, and that he seeks to secure even at the expense of liberty.

His conception of the Social Contract seems, at first, analogous to Locke's, but soon shows itself more akin to that of Hobbes. In the development from the state of nature, there comes a time when individuals can no longer maintain themselves in primitive independence; it then becomes necessary to self-preservation that they should unite to form a society. But how can I pledge my liberty without harming my interests? 'The problem is to find a form of association which will defend and protect with the whole common force the person and goods of each associate, and in which each, while uniting himself with all, may still obey himself alone, and remain as free as before. This is the fundamental problem of which the Social Contract provides the solution.'

The Contract consists in 'the total alienation of each associate, together with all his rights, to the whole community; for, in the first place, as each gives himself absolutely, the conditions are the same for all; and this being so, no one has any interest in making them burdensome to others'. The alienation is to be without reserve. 'If individuals retained certain rights, as there would be no common superior to decide between them and the public, each, being on one point his own judge, would ask to be so on all; the state of nature would thus continue, and the association would necessarily become inoperative or tyrannical.'

This implies a complete abrogation of liberty and a complete rejection of the doctrine of the rights of man. It is true that, in a later chapter, there is some softening of this theory. It is there said that, although the social contract gives the body politic absolute power over all its members, nevertheless human beings have natural rights as men. 'The sovereign cannot impose upon its subjects any fetters that are useless to the community, nor can it even wish to do so.' But the sovereign is the sole judge of what is useful or useless to the community. It is clear that only a very feeble obstacle is thus opposed to collective tyranny.

It should be observed that the 'sovereign' means, in Rousseau, not the monarch or the government, but the community in its collective and legislative capacity.

The Social Contract can be stated in the following words. 'Each of us puts his person and all his power in common under the supreme direction of the general will, and, in our corporate capacity, we receive each member as an indivisible part of the whole.' This act of association creates a moral and collective body, which is called the 'State' when passive, the 'Sovereign' when active, and a 'Power' in relation to other bodies like itself.

The conception of the 'general will', which appears in the above wording of the Contract, plays a very important part in Rousseau's system. I shall have more to say about it shortly.

It is argued that the Sovereign need give no guarantees to its subjects, for, since it is formed of the individuals who compose it, it can have no interest contrary to theirs. 'The Sovereign, merely by virtue of what it is, is always what it should be.' This doctrine is misleading to the reader who does not note Rousseau's somewhat peculiar use of terms. The Sovereign is not the government, which, it is admitted, may be tyrannical; the Sovereign is a more or less metaphysical entity, not fully embodied in any of the visible organs of the State. Its impeccability, therefore, even if admitted, has not the practical consequences that it might be supposed to have.

The will of the Sovereign, which is always right, is the 'general will'. Each citizen, *quâ* citizen, shares in the general will, but he may also, as an individual, have a particular will running counter to the general will. The Social Contract involves that whoever refuses to obey the general will shall be forced to do so. 'This means nothing less than that he will be forced to be free.'

This conception of being 'forced to be free' is very

metaphysical. The general will in the time of Galileo was certainly anti-Copernican; was Galileo 'forced to be free' when the Inquisition compelled him to recant? Is even a malefactor 'forced to be free' when he is put in prison? Think of Byron's Corsair:

O'er the glad waters of the deep blue sea,
Our thoughts as boundless and our hearts as free.

Would this man be more 'free' in a dungeon? The odd thing is that Byron's noble pirates are a direct outcome of Rousseau, and yet, in the above passage, Rousseau forgets his romanticism and speaks like a sophistical policeman. Hegel, who owed much to Rousseau, adopted his misuse of the word 'freedom', and defined it as the right to obey the police, or something not very different.

Rousseau has not that profound respect for private property that characterizes Locke and his disciples. 'The State, in relation to its members, is master of all their goods.' Nor does he believe in division of powers, as preached by Locke and Montesquieu. In this respect, however, as in some others, his later detailed discussions do not wholly agree with his earlier general principles. In Book III, Chapter I, he says that the part of the Sovereign is limited to making laws, and that the executive, or government, is an intermediate body set up between the subjects and the Sovereign to secure their mutual correspondence. He goes on to say: 'If the Sovereign desires to govern, or the magistrate to give laws, or if the subjects refuse to obey, disorder takes the place of regularity, and . . . the State falls into despotism or anarchy.' In this sentence, allowing for the difference of vocabulary, he seems to agree with Montesquieu.

I come now to the doctrine of the general will, which is both important and obscure. The general will is not identical with the will of the majority, or even with the will of all the citizens. It seems to be conceived as the will belonging to the body politic as such. If we take Hobbes's view, that a civil society is a person, we must suppose it endowed with the attributes of personality, including will. But then we are faced with the difficulty of deciding what are the visible manifestations of this will, and here Rousseau leaves us in the dark. We are told that the general will is always right and always tends to the public advantage; but that it does not follow that the deliberations of the people are equally correct, for there is often a great deal of difference between the will of all and the general will. How, then, are we to know what is the general will? There is, in the same chapter, a sort of answer:

'If, when the people, being furnished with adequate information, held its deliberations, the citizens had no communication one with another, the grand total of the small differences would always give the general will, and the decision would always be good.'

The conception in Rousseau's mind seems to be this: every man's political opinion is governed by self-interest, but self-interest consists of two parts, one of which is peculiar to the individual, while the other is common to all the members of the community. If the citizens have no opportunity of striking logrolling bargains with each other, their individual interests, being divergent, will cancel out, and there will be left a resultant which will represent their common interest; this resultant is the general will. Perhaps Rousseau's conception might be illustrated by terrestrial gravitation. Every particle in the earth attracts every other particle in the universe towards itself; the air above us attracts us upward while the ground beneath us attracts us downward. But all these 'selfish' attractions cancel each other out insofar as they are divergent, and what remains is a resultant attraction towards the centre of the earth. This might be fancifully conceived as the act of the earth considered as a community, and as the expression of its general will.

To say that the general will is always right is only to say that, since it represents what is in common among the self-interests of the various citizens, it must represent the largest collective satisfaction of self-interest possible to the community. This interpretation of Rousseau's meaning seems to accord with his words better than any other that I have been able to think of.

In Rousseau's opinion, what interferes in practice with the expression of the general will is the existence of subordinate associations within the State. Each of these will have its own general will, which may conflict with that of the community as a whole. 'It may then be said that there are no longer as many votes as there are men, but only as many as there are associations.' This leads to an important consequence: 'It is therefore essential, if the general will is to be able to express itself, that there should be no partial society within the State, and that each citizen should think only his own thoughts: which was indeed the sublime and unique system established by the great Lycurgus.' In a footnote, Rousseau supports his opinion with the authority of Machiavelli.

Consider what such a system would involve in practice. The State would have to prohibit churches (except a State Church), political parties, trade-unions, and all other organizations of men with similar economic interests. The result is obviously the Corporate or Totalitarian State, in which the individual citizen is powerless. Rousseau seems to realize that it may be difficult to prohibit all associations, and adds, as an afterthought, that, if there *must* be subordinate associations, then the more there are the better, in order that they may neutralize each other.

When, in a later part of the book, he comes to consider government, he realizes that the executive is inevitably an association having an interest and a general will of its own, which may easily conflict with that of the community. He says that while the government of a large State needs to be stronger than that of a small one, there is also more need of restraining the government by means of the Sovereign. A member of the government has three wills: his personal will, the will of the government, and the general will. These three should form a *crescendo,* but usually in fact form a *diminuendo.* Again: 'Everything conspires to take away from a man who is set in authority over others the sense of justice and reason.'

Thus in spite of the infallibility of the general will, which is 'always constant, unalterable, and pure', all the old problems of eluding tyranny remain. What Rousseau has to say on these problems is either a surreptitious repetition of Montesquieu, or an insistence on the supremacy of the legislature, which, if democratic, is identical with what he calls the Sovereign. The broad general principles with which he starts, and which he presents as if they solved political problems, disappear when he condescends to detailed considerations, towards the solution of which they contribute nothing.

The condemnation of the book by contemporary reactionaries leads a modern reader to expect to find in it a much more sweeping revolutionary doctrine than it in fact contains. We may illustrate this by what is said about democracy. When Rousseau uses this word, he means, as we have already seen, the direct democracy of the ancient City-State. This, he points out, can never be completely realized, because the people cannot be always assembled and always occupied with public affairs. 'Were there a people of gods, their government would be democratic. So perfect a government is not for men.'

What we call democracy he calls elective aristocracy; this, he says, is the best of all governments, but it is not suitable to all countries. The climate must be neither very hot nor very cold; the produce must not much exceed what is necessary, for, where it does, the evil of luxury is inevitable, and it is better that this evil should be confined to a monarch and his Court than diffused throughout the population. In virtue of these limitations, a large field is left for despotic government. Nevertheless his advocacy of democracy, in spite of its limitations, was no doubt one of the things that made the French Government implacably hostile to the book; the other presumably, was the rejection of the divine right of kings, which is implied in the doctrine of the Social Contract as the origin of government.

The Social Contract became the Bible of most of the leaders in the French Revolution, but no doubt, as is the fate of Bibles, it was not carefully read and was still less understood by many of its disciples. It reintroduced the habit of metaphysical abstractions among the theorists of democracy, and by its doctrine of the general will it made possible the mystic identification of a leader with his people, which has no need of confirmation by so mundane an apparatus as the ballot-box. Much of its philosophy could be appropriated by Hegel in his defence of the Prussian autocracy. Its first-fruits in practice were the reign of Robespierre; the dictatorships of Russia and Germany (especially the latter) are in part an outcome of Rousseau's teaching. What further triumphs the future has to offer to his ghost I do not venture to predict. (pp. 666-74)

Bertrand Russell, "Rousseau," in his *A History of Western Philosophy, and Its Connection with Political and Social Circumstances from the Earliest Times to the Present Day,* Allen and Unwin Ltd. 1946, pp. 660-74.

J. B. PRIESTLEY
(essay date 1960)

[A highly prolific English man of letters, Priestley was the author of numerous popular novels that depict the world of everyday, middle-class England. His best-known critical work is *Literature and Western Man* (1960), a survey of Western literature from the invention of movable type through the mid-twentieth century. In the following excerpt, he considers Rousseau's influence upon the development of Romantic literature.]

It was inevitable that Jean-Jacques Rousseau should have quarrelled bitterly with Voltaire and the Encyclopaedists. As Lytton Strachey has pointed out: " . . . he possessed one quality which cut him off from his contemporaries, which set an immense gulf betwixt him and them: he was modern . . . he belonged to another world." We are still living in the world that owes much, for good or evil, to Rousseau; but the age that flourished just after his death in 1778, the Romantic Age, owed a great deal more to him: its most characteristic attitudes of mind either were imitated from him or were exaggerations of various attitudes of his. It is not a matter of vague influences but of direct inspiration: the Romantics, first in Germany, then in England, later in France and elsewhere, discovered in him their prophet. No doubt the Age of Reason, decaying to make room for its opposite, would sooner or later have been succeeded by an Age of Romance, even if there had been no Rousseau, but he hurried on the process of transformation; he was the catalyst. So large was Rousseau's legacy to romantic literature that, before estimating it, we had first better dispose of those elements in later eighteenth-century life that contributed to the Romantic Age without the intervention of Rousseau.

These elements belong to the natural reaction against the Age of Reason, against the over-valuation of consciousness, against what was rational, general, abstract, public, existing only in daylight, not in the dark. A one-sided attitude, if persisted in, inevitably produces its opposite, equally one-sided. Too much dependence upon reason sooner or later inspires the glorification of unreason. So the later eighteenth-century ushers in a new and widespread interest in the occult; it was a time when pseudomystical secret societies flourished all over Europe, when charlatans like Cagliostro found their way into the highest society, when alchemy and astrology, love-philtres and elixirs of youth, became fashionable and profitable again, as in the Renaissance. These new or revived tastes owned nothing directly to Rousseau but ultimately contributed something to romantic literature. (pp. 113-14)

All those critics who have tried to explain the difference between the Classical and the Romantic would have saved much time, temper and paper if they had been acquainted with the discoveries of depth psychology. For the Classical depends upon conscious mind, the Romantic upon the unconscious. So each misjudges the other: the Classical considers the Romantic unbalanced, childish, mad; the Romantic sees the Classical as drearily formal, tedious, lifeless. When either is hopelessly one-sided, it moves towards death; the Classical, deprived of zestful energy, dying of anaemia and boredom; the Romantic, losing all contact with reality, destroying itself in madness. When Rousseau was dying, after suffering for years from persecution mania, he thought himself "alone on the earth" and condemned to be alone for eternity. The fantasies of the unconscious had invaded his consciousness; he was living in a dream, or indeed a nightmare, out of which he could not wake himself. Not only his outlook and opinions but the major events of his life, the very shape of it, had been dominated by his unconscious. He lived the romanticism he was to bequeath to the age that followed him. His life and work, as Romain Rolland observes, "offer in literary history the case, perhaps unique, of a man of genius, upon whom genius descended not only unsolicited, but against his will." Will belongs to the conscious mind; the genius of Rousseau exploded from the unconscious. He describes the very moment of this explosion, on a hot summer day on the road to Vincennes, where he was going to visit Diderot, who was imprisoned there. He was thirty-seven, and had spent years wandering and idling and brooding, making little use of his quite able conscious mind, but storing energy, stoking up the boilers, so to speak, in his unconscious. Then in an instant, as he tells us, he lived in another world, he became another man. 'Great truths' descended upon him in a torrent; he saw in a flash his life's work. A prophet was born. The shy Swiss idler became an impassioned orator, an author of great force

and originality, whose influence was so strong and far-reaching that a massive genius like Tolstoy, a century later, could declare himself to be inspired by Rousseau's teaching and example. The immediate effect of his political and social discourses, and his didactic fiction and confessions, was electrical. It was as if, by-passing the wary and dubious conscious mind, unconscious called to unconscious. But then of course the time was ready: the solution had been prepared, and here was the catalyst.

There are elements in Rousseau, reaching from Kant to Marx, that must be ignored here, but sufficient is left to show how much the Romantic Age owed to Rousseau's unconscious bursting like a dam. It is not that all the romantic poets and story-tellers wished to imitate him; we are not considering here an ordinary literary influence; but what was released in him soon came, with of course many individual differences and developments, to be released in them. So the age represents first the reaction and then the triumph of the unconscious, challenging and then defeating the rational conscious mind. The medal was not refashioned but merely reversed. What had been formerly admired was now despised; what had been distrusted and feared was now exalted. Created in this way, Romantic Western Man is as unbalanced and one-sided as Rational Western Man had been. There is, however, one important difference. In the previous age, the authors were expressing the society of their time; Molière and Louis XIV . . . had more or less the same outlook; Pope the poet and John Churchill, Duke of Marlborough, knew they were living in the same world. But when we come to the Romantic Age, we are no longer concerned with the character of a whole society but only with one small, though deeply significant, part of it; so that, for example, Chateaubriand the Romantic and Napoleon have not at all the same outlook; and Byron the poet and Arthur Wellesley, Duke of Wellington, seem to be living in two very different worlds. Literature has begun to move away from the general society of its time; and this oblique movement, as we shall see, now continues down to our own day.

Everything released by the explosion of Rousseau's unconscious, creating romanticism, must necessarily be intensely private, never general and public. So the romantic writer, like Rousseau, is not at home in society. He must discover himself in solitude, far from salons and cities, musing in the forest, lost in reverie among the mountains or on the seashore. He is not trying to express what men in general are thinking and feeling, not seeking any common denominator. It is what arises from the depths of his own being—really whatever comes from the unconscious—that deserves expression, which means that, when all is well with his genius, he will in fact discover for us original and profound truths, states of mind never described before, hidden treasures of the soul, but that, when he is below his best, he will tend to be merely affected, egoistic, even touched with megalomania. Exploring himself, he will give us what is either far richer and more valuable than common-sense or considerably worse, just nonsense. This is the risk the romantic writer and his readers run. But it is worth running because the romantic writer in his moments of genius illuminates, with an effect that is magical, the reader's own depths. For that balance of thought and feeling understood by the conscious mind and the classical writer, the Romantic, who sees nothing in this balance but tedium and lifelessness, substitutes the sense of infinity, the sudden ecstasy justifying all the mere mechanics of living, the supreme magical moment.

So the Romantic, following both Rousseau's practice and precept, seeks solitude and reverie. He is a wanderer, like the remote ancestors stirring in his unconscious; to become a settled member of a society is to frustrate his genius. Though longing for the most intensely sympathetic relationship with another soul, in undying love, eternal friendship, he is for ever being misunderstood, the world of men being the wretched thing it is, and almost welcomes the persecution that for poor Rousseau became a nightmare mania. Now the young child is only struggling into full consciousness and still enjoys a profoundly satisfying relation, through the unconscious, with Nature, like the *participation mystique* of primitive men; so to the Romantics, again following Rousseau, the child is no longer a half-grown man or woman, the young of our species, but the archetypal holy innocent, whose joy and unthinking wisdom we should try to recapture if only for a moment, whose happiness irradiates a lost world. So the cult of childhood begins. A companion figure to the holy child is the unspoilt savage, the dusky Arcadian, flower-crowned in some Eden of the South Seas or the Amazonian jungle, whose very existence proves how hollow and false our boasted civilisation is. It is true that the literary members of this cult did not take leave of civilisation to share the lives of these glorious creatures—for they could hardly expect to find them on walking tours or visits to Italy—but they lived with them in imagination and various editions of their works. And again, Rousseau, whose political theory is haunted by this dream, began it.

The magical images of the unconscious are projected by the Romantic on Nature and Woman. What seemed 'a horrid wilderness' to the Age of Reason, which hurried through it in search of roast chicken and clean linen, is now welcomed as a reflection, beautiful or terrible, of the beauty or storm in the Romantic's soul. Nature, especially when remote from traffic and agriculture, responds like a devoted mistress to his every mood. Oceans and mountains, forest and heath, provide the enchanted scenery for his unending drama of the defiant lonely spirit. But somewhere across the ocean or beyond the mountains is the Woman for whom the Romantic is searching, the Woman who will lead him out of his dream of love, those erotic reveries that Rousseau describes, into a real but endlessly ecstatic relationship. The love is there, as it is in the mind of a dreamy adolescent, before the Woman. And as there arise from the unconscious certain strange symbolical images of the other sex, images that may be vague but are still illuminated by the green and gold of the depths, the Romantic turns away from ordinary sensible women who cannot help thinking about children, houses and a steady income. So there flit through the literature of this age feminine creatures who are anything but ordinary sensible women, a host of faerie beings, nymphs, water sprites, savage queens, Oriental princesses, mysterious gipsy girls, anybody in fact who is sufficiently strange and cannot be domesticated. For love here is a pursuit, a torment, an unquenchable thirst, a fleeting ecstasy, a bitter aftermath, disillusion, unending regret, anything but the foundation of an enduring and fruitful relationship between a man and a woman. The Romantic, following Rousseau, is not turning outward, to look at and enjoy women as they are, but continues to turn inward, lost in erotic dreams and reveries, entangled in the uncriticised, unchecked fantasies of the unconscious.

Unless the end, however, is to be madness—as it so often was—a sense of reality must break in, the conscious mind must make its comparisons, and then unless some sort of balance can be arrived at, the result is the famous romantic melancholy, the canker and the worm, the inexplicable sadness, the gnawing homesickness that never knew a home. It was said of one romantic poet: "He wanted better bread than could be made of wheat", and that is true of them all. So they go in search of the blue flower, the lost kingdom of childhood, the happy valley of Arcadia, the forests of fairyland, the tower where they will find at last the strange woman who will enchant them for ever, forgetting if they are foolish, remembering if they grow wiser, that these things do not exist in the outward world, as revealed to consciousness, but belong, with much else, to the hidden realm of the unconscious, to the dreamer in his dream, to the solitary drama of the soul. To ignore the romantic as an aspect of life is to be blind to the rainbow; to accept the romantic as a way of life is to try and pack a rainbow in a crate. Rousseau cannot be considered among the poets, but he was a creator of poets, just because his example helped to release the dark energy, the zest that consciousness can control but cannot produce, the magical symbols that transform verse into unforgettable poetry, all from the depths of the unconscious. The conscious mind can accept and refine, but cannot create those phrases and lines that seem pregnant with many meanings and haunt us like music. The best of the authors of the Romantic Age opened themselves to the fire and sorcery of the unconscious without abandoning themselves to it, without leaving the conscious mind helpless, its will and judgment shattered, its sense of reality lost forever. The less fortunate of them drifted rudderless into the dark, beyond communication, into madness. Rousseau, the prophet of Romance, the prototype of the romantic writer, ran the whole course. He ended by seeing the world as a conspiracy against him. Drifting into madness, he cried: "Here I am, alone on the earth, no brother, neighbour, friend, society, save myself . . ." He had turned his gaze inward too long, stared too hard into the dark depths of the unconscious. He should have looked the other way, for it is our consciousness that shows us brothers, neighbours, friends, society.

"Man is born free; and everywhere he is in chains." It is the most famous of all Rousseau's pronouncements, and it still reverberates. So far as it merely means that men in our civilisation have allowed a reasonable personal liberty to be dangerously reduced by power organisations, it was true when he wrote it, and it is true today, when we cannot even move about the world without state permission. But in its larger sense, it is untrue and perilously misleading. However man may be regarded, he is not born free. A baby is not free but severely conditioned by its helplessness. Primitive men, moving fearfully and warily in their own elaborate world of menacing spirits, taboos and tribal customs, have less freedom than we have. With the famous *Social Contract* and the arguments that Rousseau based upon it, we have nothing to do here. But what does concern us, because it is something he bequeathed to the Romantic Age and we have not done with it even yet, is his idea that freedom has nothing to do with any appreciation of necessity, any accommodation to the real world, the right balance between the conscious mind, looking outward, and the unconscious; but that, in practice if not in theory, man comes nearest to freedom by breaking that balance, by interpreting the objective world entirely in terms of the subjective inner world of dream and desire, by running away from any challenge to that inner world, escaping from, instead of facing and mastering, reality. A man who prefers erotic reveries to living in love with a real woman will certainly have more liberty, but all that it offers him is an unrewarding erotic relationship with himself. He will be freer if, like Rousseau, he deposits the children he has by his mistress in foundling hospitals, but only at the price of forfeiting parenthood and self-respect. He has more freedom as something; but not as a father, good lover or husband, decent citizen. The complete Romantic, for ever looking inward, swelling his ego into vast proportions, may tell us that he demands freedom to be completely himself—and undoubtedly there are times in an artist's life when he must have such freedom at all costs—but if he keeps running away, refusing to be bound by any obligation, then he cuts down this self by not allowing it new functions, responsibilities, relationships, diminishing instead of enriching his real life, until at last, when the final and narrowing path of escape turns into a *cul-de-sac,* he cries out in terrible despair that he is alone. Thus there is all of romanticism, exploding from the unconscious, in Rousseau: its sudden release of creative energy, its triumph as an aspect of life to be celebrated in literature, its ultimate danger, hurrying to despair and madness, when it is taken unchecked as a way of life. (pp. 116-21)

J. B. Priestley, "Rousseau and the Romantic Age," in his *Literature and Western Man,* Harper & Brothers, 1960, pp. 113-21.

SOURCES FOR FURTHER STUDY

Babbitt, Irving. *Rousseau and Romanticism.* Cleveland: World Publishing Co., 1955, 324 p.

> Seminal study of Rousseau's impact on the development and character of the Romantic movement. Babbitt contends that Rousseau provides "the most significant illustrations of it."

"Rousseau for Our Time." *Daedalus: Proceedings of the American Academy of Arts and Sciences* 107, No. 3 (Summer, 1978).

> Special issue includes studies of Rousseau's influence on utopian theory, politics, the drama, education, anthropology, and autobiography.

Dent, N. J. H. *Rousseau: An Introduction to his Psychological, Social and Political Theory.* New York: Basil Blackwell, 1988, 258 p.

> Close study of the ideas and arguments of the *Discourses, The Social Contract,* and *Emile.*

Harvey, Simon; Hobson, Marian; Kelley, David; and Taylor, Samuel S. B. *Reappraisals of Rousseau.* Totowa, N.J.: Barnes & Noble Books, 1980, 312 p.

> Selection of contemporary critical essays in English and French, concentrating on Rousseau's psychological experience, his politics, his writing, and his intellectual relationships.

Leigh, R. A., ed. *Rousseau After Two Hundred Years: Proceedings of the Cambridge Colloquium.* Cambridge: Cambridge University Press, 1982, 299 p.

> Collection of scholarly essays, including "From Orangutan to the Vampire: Towards an Anthropology of Rousseau," by Christopher Frayling and Robert Wokler, among others.

Morley, John. *Rousseau.* London: Chapman and Hall, 1873, 2 vols.

> Seminal biography, including interpretation of Rousseau's major works.

Saki

1870-1916

(Pseudonym of H[ector] H[ugh] Munro) English short story writer, novelist, journalist, and historian.

INTRODUCTION

*T*he reputation of H. H. Munro (Saki) rests primarily on his short stories, which convey whimsical humor, fascination with the odd and eerie, and worldly disillusionment with hypocrisy and banality. Written between the end of Queen Victoria's reign and the beginning of World War I, Munro's works memorialize a comfortable world of upper-class town houses, tea parties, and weekends in the country that his characters may deride but in which they never completely lose faith. The stories present characters who, through capriciousness or eccentric behavior, get into odd situations from which they usually escape by means of their quick wits; at the same time, their clever remarks and cynical views expose the arbitrariness and artificiality of their society. Munro's narratives often go beyond straightforward realism, however, when employing surprise endings or depicting strangely human animals and children embattled with adults.

Munro was born in the Far East, where his father was a colonel in the British military police. Upon the death of his mother, Munro and his two siblings were sent to live with their grandmother and aunts in Devon, England. The aunts squabbled endlessly over trivialities, involved the children in their petty jealousies, and imposed on their young charges a strict Victorian regimen that included permanently closed windows and little outside play. After some casual tutoring at home, ten-year-old Munro was sent to school. In 1887, Colonel Munro retired and returned to England to look after his nearly-grown children. Over the next few years, he completed their education by traveling with them extensively throughout the Continent. Munro subsequently spent about a year with the Burma police, returned to England, and moved to London in 1894. He worked at the British Museum and published only a short story, "Dogged," during the next six years. Munro wrote *The Rise of the Russian Empire* in 1900 and, from 1902 to 1909, was a foreign correspondent for the *Morning Post* in the Balkans and Paris. Returning to London, he wrote short stories and several novels until the outbreak of the First World War. Refusing a commission as an officer, Munro enlisted as a private and was killed in France in 1916.

In 1900 Munro collaborated with popular cartoonist Francis Carruthers Gould to produce a series of cartoons that use figures from Lewis Carroll's *Alice's Adventures in Wonderland* to satirize current political events. The cartoons by Gould and the comic sketches written under Munro's pseudonym, Saki—which was borrowed from Edward Fitzgerald's translation of Omar Khayyám's *Rubáiyát*—were an immediate success. In 1901 Munro began contributing short sketches to the *Westminster Gazette* about the adventures of a witty, acerbic young man named Reginald. These sketches, which are often set in fashionable drawing rooms, country homes, and other places where the wealthy congregate, are narrated either by Reginald himself or by an older friend called "the Other," and reveal Reginald to be a humorous observer of upper-class manners as well as a somewhat dandified self-admirer. In an attempt to repeat the success of the Alice sketches, Munro and Gould parodied Rudyard Kipling's *The Jungle Book* and *Just So Stories* in "The Political Jungle Book" and "Not So Stories" for the *Westminster Gazette* in 1902, but these political satires were not nearly as popular as the Alice series.

During his tenure as foreign correspondent, Munro published his first collection of stories, entitled *Reginald* (1904). In 1910, his second collection of short fiction was published, misleadingly titled *Reginald in Russia*—only the title story concerns Reginald. The rest of the tales continue Saki's satiric examination of upper-class country life or venture into fable-like lessons. "Gabriel-Ernest" tells the macabre story of a werewolf posing as a boy, who vanishes after devouring a child. This successful collection was followed by *The Chronicles of Clovis* (1912), which introduced two main characters, Clovis Sangrail and Bertie Van Tahn. Although both characters are akin to Reginald, Clovis is more likeable than either Reginald or Bertie; while he delights in absurd situations and in deflating the pretensions of others, he often has sympathy for those in real trouble. By contrast, the perpetually adolescent Bertie fails to see when humor at the expense of others turns into cruelty. A masterpiece in the collection, "Tobermory," is about a self-possessed talking cat that disturbs a weekend party in the country by threatening to reveal the guests' secrets that he has overheard.

In 1912, Munro published a novel, *The Unbearable Bassington,* whose hero, Comus Bassington, resembles Reginald with an undeniable mean streak. Munro continued writing stories for newspapers, and

these works were collected in *Beasts and Super-Beasts* (1914); as the title suggests, animal stories take up a large part of the collection. Munro's second novel, *When William Came: A Story of London under the Hohenzollerns* (1914), is a fantasy about life in England under German occupation led by Kaiser Wilhelm. After searching for grounds for sincere patriotism and reasons to affirm the best of English society, the novel ends ambiguously as Londoners assemble in Hyde Park for a march by Boy Scouts, who mysteriously never appear. In 1914, Munro wrote a play, *The Watched Pot.* A comedy of manners set in a drawing room, the play concerns the efforts of several young women to marry a wealthy man whose aunt resists their attempts to displace her as ruler of her nephew's household. Two collections of Munro's stories appeared posthumously, *The Toys of Peace* (1919) and *The Square Egg* (1924).

Popular and respected as a master of the short story during his own lifetime, throughout the twentieth century Munro has been ranked with the Frenchman Guy de Maupassant and the American O. Henry as a craftsman of the first order. Funny, original, sometimes bizarre, and at times creepily frightening, Munro's work has influenced writers such as P. G. Wodehouse, whose farcical stories of well-heeled, scatterbrained young men-about-town are reminiscent of the Reginald stories. The world Munro described has easily identifiable traits: the setting is the turn of the century; England is treated as the center of the civilization; life has been made comfortable for the protagonists by others; and a young man need only concern himself with his social life and the quality of the food, drink, and entertainment provided. Significantly, women in Munro's work are usually hateful guardian aunts or elderly duchesses; rarely are females depicted as young, attractive girls of sexual interest to the main characters. Munro remained a bachelor throughout his life, and this fact plus some suggestiveness in his work has led modern readers to conclude that he was homosexual.

Critics often mention the apparent cruelty and heartlessness in Munro's stories. Writing in 1940 in the *Atlantic Monthly,* Elizabeth Drew explained and justified this lack of compassion: "The cruelty is certainly there, but it has nothing perverted or pathological about it. . . . It is the genial heartlessness of the normal child, whose fantasies take no account of adult standards of human behavior, and to whom the eating of a gypsy by a hyena is no more terrible than the eating of Red Ridinghood's grandmother by a wolf. The standards of these gruesome tales are those of the fairy tale; their grimness is the grimness of Grimm." Although terrible things happen in Munro's stories, he provides a satisfying sense of justice done and human decency restored that can appeal to children and adults alike. Modern commentators have argued that there is a serious side to Munro that goes beyond mere entertainment to explore weighty moral issues. Certainly his novels were philosophical to a degree and some of his stories addressed serious concerns, however, Munro will remain most noted for his stories, which Noël Coward claimed clearly evinced "the verbal adroitness of Saki's dialogue and the brilliance of his wit."

(For further information about Saki's life and works, see *Concise Dictionary of British Literary Biography*, Vol. 5; *Contemporary Authors*, Vols. 104, 130; *Dictionary of Literary Biography*, Vol. 34: *British Novelists, 1890-1929: Traditionalists; Major Twentieth-Century Writers;* and *Twentieth-Century Literary Criticism*, Vol. 3.)

CRITICAL COMMENTARY

L. P. HARTLEY

(essay date 1927)

[Author of the acclaimed novel trilogy *Eustace and Hilda* (1944-47), Hartley was an English novelist and short story writer whose fiction is unified by the theme of the search for individuality and meaning in the post-Christian era. A literary critic as well, he contributed reviews for many years to *The Saturday Review, Time and Tide, The Spectator*, and other periodicals. In the following excerpt, he admires the savagery of Saki's wit and praises the craftsmanship of his work.]

It is not easy to write about "Saki," for he needs neither interpreter nor prophet. What he was like himself we do not know, though the introductions furnished by various distinguished authors to . . . his collected works, give us some idea. Among other things he was clearly a hero, for he joined the Army when war broke out, at the age of forty-four, as a private; and two years later, promoted to corporal, he was killed in action. How different in its setting the last two years of his life from the drawing-rooms and fashionable resorts in which his Muse loved to wander! If indeed a Muse as impatient, succinct and epigrammatic as his could be said to wander: "march" is a more accurate description of her gait; she moves with a military precision, is always on iron rations, always under orders, an Amazon among her gentler sisters.

Whatever then Munro the man, Munro the writer was a literary soldier, disciplined, not irregular, who went the nearest way to his objective and generally took it. One cannot, in thinking of him, get away from the military metaphor. His style indeed was a more delicate weapon than modern soldiers carry; it is a sister-blade to Max Beerbohm's, stouter than his perhaps, and more prone to frontal attacks, but not less piercing and leaving as clean a wound. The conduct of his narratives, brief or long, resembles a campaign; the rough, rebellious surface of life is mapped out; its defences are

carefully enveloped, then taken by surprise; finally with a grand assault its stronghold is reduced, and the whole barren region is added to the orderly empire of art. How his stories sparkle, sometimes with a distracting glitter! What traces do they not bear of spit and polish, of superfluity discarded, of symmetry achieved! Hardy, ascetic, mobile, what agonies of private drilling must they have gone through, before they were allowed to appear in public, on parade, no paragraph incomplete, no comma missing, no sentence awry!

It is true that amid the rattle of rifles and light arms we seldom detect the boom of a heavy gun. "Saki" carried few heavy guns. What weight he had (and it was considerable) was a personal quality and, like charity, it stayed at home, forming the emplacement from which his machine-guns directed their devastating fire. Without this savage fundamental seriousness his shots would have gone astray; we should have heard their impressive rattle, we should not have seen the victims fall. We may tire of his exhibitions of marksmanship; we may feel, in moments of satiety, that he is only bringing down clay pigeons; but all the same there is no disputing the deadliness of the shot or the accuracy of the aim. Exactly from what dump Munro drew his ammunition it is hard to say, but it was inexhaustible. He hated, and he believed. Perhaps it would be true to say that he hated what he believed in, and believed in what he hated. He believed that Nature was red in tooth and claw and that life was cruel, and he had some kind of respect for the qualities in men which were consonant with such a view of life. He believed in living dangerously, and he never mentions death, single or multitudinous, accidental or contrived, without a throb of delight. Here is a scrap of dialogue showing how his Comic Spirit feasted on the idea of mortality:

"Good gracious! How many lives have been lost?"
"Heaps, I should say. The second housemaid has already identified three bodies that have floated past the billiard-room window as being the young man she's engaged to. Either she's engaged to a large as-

Principal Works

sortment of the population round here, or else she's very careless at identification. Of course it may be the same body coming round again and again in a swirl; I hadn't thought of that."

We are reminded of Captain Harry Graham and "The Ruthless Rhymes." But for Munro cruelty was not so much the vehicle of humour as the source. It was not an escape from life but an intensification of it. "Gentle dullness ever loves a joke," said Pope, but he would not have so described "Saki," who was always willing to wound, and never afraid to strike. He loves the spectacle of mankind brought to misfortune and ridicule by its follies. He loves to see the unwary pedestrian slipping on the orange-peel. He tolerates, he delights in practical jokes; discomfiture and humiliation are as breath to his nostrils, balm to his soul, and he always thinks them funny. Time and again, as one of his characters is artlessly preparing to sit down, does he (metaphorically) pull away the chair and start the general laugh. He loathes meekness and weakness; irony, the refuge of sensitive minds from the world, is unknown to him; he is a satirist pure and simple.

Yet though he acquiesces in cruelty he does not spare the cruel. Comus Bassington, the hero of his most considerable book, is within the limits of his intelligence as odious a character as has ever been drawn. The passage in which, when at school, he canes the new boy who had been recommended to his protection, is a masterpiece of venom. All the more hateful characteristics of schoolboys, their herd-instinct, their desire and power to hurt, their ability to rise in their own esteem only upon the abasement of others, their fertility and resourcefulness in cruelty, all these traits are in a few

brief pages exquisitely delineated. It is a passage which any one of Munro's characters, could he have obtained it, would have rushed to place in the hands of some apprehensive mother who was sending off her boy to school. There must be numbers of people who, having read it, have decided not to let their offspring face such an ordeal. But Munro has provided Comus with an Achilles heel. In the ways of the world he is fundamentally stupid—he doesn't know which side his bread is buttered; and so, as the moralist would say, he is shipped off to Nigeria to die of fever. His mother had doted on him, as far as her realisation that, if there were five plovers' eggs he would always take three, permitted her to dote. He and her one Old Master, cherished symbol of overt respectability and latent wealth, were the apples of her eye. On the same day, almost at the same moment, she finds she has lost both; Comus is dead and the picture is declared a copy.

The Unbearable Bassington would be a better book, as Mr. Baring has pointed out, if it showed a sense of pity. It does, twice. Once when Lady Caroline hears of Comus's death; once when Elaine talks to the explorer and big-game hunter whose active life had been cut short by an accident. The passage is worth quoting, for it shows a side of Munro that he usually concealed. Generally he takes his stand with the big battalions; here he ranges himself with Cato, who preferred to find himself on the losing side. The passage is very poignant:

"You are a person to be envied," [Elaine] said to Keriway; "you have created a fairy-land, and you are living in it yourself."
"Envied?"
He shot the question out with sudden bitterness. She looked down and saw the wistful misery that had come into his face.
"Once," he said to her, "in a German paper I read a short story about a tame crippled crane that lived in the park of some small town. I forget what happened in the story, but there was one line that I shall always remember: 'It was lame, that is why it was tame.'"
He had created a fairyland but assuredly he was not living in it.

"Saki" then had a softer side, but it was the ferocious quality of his mind that gave life and impetus to his stories. This ferocity, let us hasten to add, is present in some, indeed in most, of his tales only as a rumour or a perfume, expressing itself in a thousand delicious shafts of malice, a hundred ingenious *dénouements*. Sometimes he thinks a story is funny in proportion as it is "tall"; sometimes his wit declines into facetiousness. But at its best it is admirable. True, the dialogue is artificial—people don't talk like that; but no doubt they would if they could. O! to be a Clovis, one thinks enviously, or a Reginald, who can subdue with a word the most insistent bore, encounter on equal terms the most brilliant Duchess. To have a life crammed with mirth-provoking incidents; to meet only two sorts of people; grindstones on which to sharpen the arrows of one's wit, plump defenceless bodies in which to plunge them. Though it is depressing to discover that not even Munro's silliest character, not even Merla Blathlington herself, can keep up her stupidity for long; she has to say something clever, or her creator would die of boredom. Munro will have a lasting reputation. His wit is not merely verbal, never merely a trick; it refreshes itself at a hundred sources and all his experience goes to feed it. His characters have a similarity, sometimes a sameness; his wit has an inexhaustible fertility and (a rare thing in this class of writing) it is reinforced by a sense of humour no less omnivorous. Dapper yet virile, cruel yet without personal animosity, the figure of "Saki" will be cherished by all who love first-rate craftsmanship in letters. (pp. 214, 216-17)

L. P. Hartley, "Saki," in *The Bookman,* London, Vol. LXXI, No. 424, January, 1927, pp. 214, 216-17.

ELIZABETH DREW
(essay date 1940)

[In the following essay, Drew asserts that Saki's wit is brilliant, polished, and artistically mature—though sometimes cruel.]

Hector Hugh Munro, born in India in 1870, a delicate child who was not expected to live, was brought up from the age of two in a damp, dark country house in Devonshire, surrounded by high walls and hedges. Here he and his brother and sister, placed in the care of two dragonlike aunts, were virtually prisoners, mewed in behind closed windows at night and in all bad weather, and permitted to play only on the front lawn in summer—'the kitchen garden being considered too tempting a place, with its fruit trees.' Both the aunts, Miss Munro tells us in her memoir of her brother, 'were guilty of mental cruelty.' Their methods are described in those of the aunt in **'The Lumber Room.'**

It was her habit, whenever one of the children fell from grace, to improvise something of a festival nature from which the offender would be rigorously debarred; if all the children sinned collectively they were suddenly informed of a circus in a neighbouring town, a circus of unrivalled merit and uncounted elephants, to which, but for their depravity, they would have been taken that very day.

'We often longed for revenge with an intensity I suspect we inherited from our Highland ancestry,' says Miss Munro, and Hector 'sublimated' that longing in

the finest of his sketches in the *macabre*—**'Sredni Vashtar.'** In that story we share all Conradin's feelings of exultant practical triumph over the aunt who made his life a misery, and the story itself remains as a symbol of Saki's own spiritual triumph over the Brontosauri rather than Montessori methods of his upbringing. For in his art, as in his life, there is no trace of the repressed or neurotic temperament which might have been expected.

He spent a cosmopolitan youth traveling on the continent with his father, a year in India with the Military Police, several years in Russia, the Balkans, and Paris as a newspaper correspondent, and then settled down as a free-lance journalist in London. At the outbreak of the Great War, when he was forty-four, he at once enlisted in the ranks, and he was killed in the attack on Beaumont-Hamel on November 13, 1916.

Admirers, in their natural wish to do justice to a man they loved, have pointed to passages in Saki's works in which he reveals his personality directly, and from which it is possible to construct the man of flesh and blood behind the mask of mockery he chose to wear. But such criticism does him no service. He deliberately chose a pseudonym for his writings—Sákí, the cupbearer whose 'joyous errand' was to serve the guests with wine in the *Rubáiyát* of Omar Khayyám. He never sought intimacy with his readers, or gave them his confidence. He asks nothing from them but lips that can laugh, flesh that can creep, and legs that can be pulled. Saki, in fact, agreed with the eighteenth-century essayist, Shaftesbury:—

I hold it very indecent for anyone to publish his meditations, reflections and solitary thoughts. Those are the froth and scum of writing, which should be unburdened in private and consigned to oblivion, before the writer comes before the world as good company.

Saki is the most impersonal of artists. His private emotions and enthusiasms, meditations or thoughts, have no place in the world of his art. Saki is not Hector Munro, any more than Elia is Charles Lamb. But the methods of the two writers are completely opposed. Lamb dowered Elia with all his own most lovable characteristics: his warm heart, his genius for friendship, his love of life. Hector Munro, though he was richly endowed with all these qualities, denied them to Saki. That artist, in all his short sketches and stories, is allowed but three strains in his nature: the high spirits and malicious impudence of a precocious child; the cynical wit of the light social satirist; and the Gaelic fantasy of the Highlander. We meet these three in turns: the irresponsible imp who invents unlimited extravagant practical jokes to mystify and enrage and outwit the heavy-minded adult world; the ironic mocker who speaks in the quips of Clovis and Reginald and the Duchess; and the Celt who sees the kettle refuse to boil when it has been bewitched by the Evil Eye, or hears Pan's laughter as he tramples to death the doubter of his powers.

Hilaire Belloc once wrote a poem beginning,—

Matilda told such awful lies
It made you gasp and stretch your eyes.

Matilda came to a bad end, but Saki's child and adult liars never come to bad ends. Triumphantly they discomfit the forces of dullness and of feeble counter-deception opposed to them, and prove indisputably that fiction is stronger than fact. It must be owned that there are times when we tire of these *enfants terribles* of all ages, just as we can have too much of Mr. P. G. Wodehouse's dithering dukes and prize pigs; but at his best the fiendish capacity for unveracious invention with which Saki endows his children, and the amazing mendacities with which his young men and women confute the commonplace, are the fine art of lying at its finest. My own favorites are the story spun by the ingenious niece of the house to the nervous caller, with the innocent opening, 'You may wonder why we keep that window open on an October afternoon,' or the visit of the Bishop to organize a local massacre of the Jews, invented by Clovis to animate a family in need of an 'unrest cure.' This, since it involved action as well as equivocation, perhaps belongs more truly to the stories dealing with elaborate hoaxes and practical jokes—such as the tale of Leaonard Bilsiter, who liked to hint of his acquaintance with the unseen forces of 'Siberian magic' but was somewhat horrified when it appeared that his powers had changed his hostess into a she-wolf; or that of the titled lady who was mistaken for the new governess and plays the part by teaching the children the history of the Sabine Women by the Schartz-Metterklume method of making them act it for themselves.

There is an element of cruelty in a practical joke, and many readers of Saki find themselves repelled by a certain heartlessness in many of his tales. The cruelty is certainly there, but it has nothing perverted or pathological about it. He is not one of those whose motto might be 'Our sweetest songs are those that tell of sadist thought.' It is the genial heartlessness of the normal child, whose fantasies take no account of adult standards of human behavior, and to whom the eating of a gypsy by a hyena is no more terrible that the eating of Red Ridinghood's grandmother by a wolf. The standards of these gruesome tales are those of the fairy tale; their grimness is the grimness of Grimm.

The other element in Saki's cruelty springs from a certain unsparing consistency of vision which will allow no sentiment to intrude. He speaks of one young man as 'one of those people who would be enormously improved by death,' and he never hesitates to supply that embellishment himself on suitable occasions. Stories such as **'The Easter Egg'** and **'The Hounds of Fate'** are tragedies entirely without pity, but their callousness is consistent with the hard cynical sanity which is behind even his lightest satire, and gives it its strength. His mockery is urbane but ruthless. His wit is in the tradition of Wilde and the lesser creations of E. F. Benson's *Dodo* and Anthony Hope's *Dolly Dialogues,* and in the modern world he has affinities with Noel Coward and the early Aldous Huxley. Like them, he creates an artificial world enclosed in an element outside of which it could no more exist than we could exist outside our envelope of ether. It is embalmed in the element of Wit. To talk about Saki's 'characterization' is absurd. His characters are constructed to form a front against which his light satiric artillery can most effectively be deployed. The forces against him are the common social vices of Vanity Fair: humbug and hypocrisy, greed and grab, envy and uncharitableness, sheer dullness and fatuity. Comus Bassington, listening to scraps of conversation at an At Home, comments: 'I suppose it's the Prevention of Destitution they're hammering at. What on earth would become of all these dear good people if anyone should start a crusade for the prevention of mediocrity?' The crusade would be a disaster, for it would extinguish Lucas Bassett, the young poet who had the triumphant inspiration of the couplet

Cousin Teresa takes out Caesar,
Fido, Jock and the big borzoi,

and whom we see at the end of the story docketed for a knighthood under the letter L.

'The letter L,' said the secretary, who was new to his job. 'Does that stand for Liberalism or liberality?'

'Literature,' explained the minister.

And the crusade would probably eliminate all those ardent slum workers and society socialists 'whose naturally stagnant souls take infinite pleasure in what are called "movements" '; those Wodehouse-like money-eyed aunts and impecunious and irresponsible nephews; those drones and butterflies 'to whom clear soup is a more important factor in life than a clear conscience'; and those odious children whose ghastly pranks turn us into keen supporters of the canonization of good King Herod.

But the situations and characters which, left to themselves, would develop into what Jane Austen called 'the elegant stupidity of a private party' develop instead into hilarious gayety and crackling brilliance, and it is Saki's wit and not his satirical material, or any of his other literary material, which will make him live. It is his sheer good fun and good spirits and capacity to be such persistent good company. His power to comment that 'so many people who are described as rough diamonds turn out to be only rough paste'; his power to describe the unsophisticated diner-out consulting the wine list 'with the blank embarrassment of a schoolboy suddenly called on to locate a Minor Prophet in the tangled hinterland of the Old Testament'; or his impudent morsels of dialogue.

> 'Such an exquisite rural retreat, and so restful and healing to the nerves. Real country scenery; apple blossom everywhere.'

> 'Surely only on the apple trees?'

'As a companion he was an unfailing antidote to boredom,' wrote one of his friends. It is an epitaph anyone might envy. (pp. 96-8)

Elizabeth Drew, "Saki," in *The Atlantic Monthly,* Vol. 166, No. 1, July, 1940, pp. 96-8.

GRAHAM GREENE

(essay date 1950)

[Greene is one of the most important novelists in modern English literature. In his major works, he explored the problems of spiritually and socially alienated individuals living in the corrupting societies of the twentieth century. In the following essay, he traces the source of Saki's sharp wit and generational bitterness to his unhappy childhood. Greene's remarks were first published in 1950 as an introduction to *The Best of Saki.*]

There are certain writers, as different as Dickens from Kipling, who never shake off the burden of their childhood. The abandonment to the blacking factory in Dickens's case and in Kipling's to the cruel Aunt Rosa living in the sandy suburban road were never forgotten. All later experience seems to have been related to those months or years of unhappiness. Life which turns its cruel side to most of us at an age when we have begun to learn the arts of self-protection took these two writers by surprise during the defencelessness of early childhood. How differently they reacted. Dickens learnt sympathy, Kipling cruelty—Dickens developed a style so easy and natural that it seems capable of including the whole human race in its understanding: Kipling designed a machine, the cogwheels perfectly fashioned, for exclusion. The characters sometimes seem to rattle down a conveyor-belt like matchboxes.

There are great similarities in the early life of Kipling and Saki, and Saki's reaction to misery was nearer Kipling's than Dickens's. Kipling was born in India. H. H. Munro (I would like to drop that rather meaningless mask of the pen name) in Burma. Family life for such children is always broken—the miseries recorded by Kipling and Munro must be experienced by many mute inglorious children born to the civil servant or the colonial officer in the East: the arrival of the cab at the strange relative's house, the unpacking of the boxes, the unfamiliar improvised nursery, the terrible departure of the parents, a four years' absence from affection that in child-time can be as long as a generation (at four one is a small child, at eight a boy). Kipling described the horror of that time in 'Baa Baa Black Sheep'—a story in spite of its sentimentality almost unbearable to read: Aunt Rosa's prayers, the beatings, the card with the word LIAR pinned upon the back, the growing and neglected blindness, until at last came the moment of rebellion.

> 'If you make me do that,' said Black Sheep very quietly, 'I shall burn this house down and perhaps I will kill you. I don't know whether I *can* kill you—you are so bony, but I will try.'

> No punishment followed this blasphemy, though Black Sheep held himself ready to work his way to Auntie Rosa's withered throat and grip there till he was beaten off.

In the last sentence we can hear something very much like the tones of Munro's voice as we hear them in one of his finest stories, **"Sredni Vashtar."** Neither his Aunt Augusta nor his Aunt Charlotte with whom he was left near Barnstaple after his mother's death, while his father served in Burma, had the fiendish cruelty of Aunt Rosa, but Augusta ('a woman', Munro's sister wrote, 'of ungovernable temper, of fierce likes and dislikes, imperious, a moral coward, possessing no brains worth speaking of, and a primitive disposition') was quite capable of making a child's life miserable. Munro was not himself beaten, Augusta preferred his younger brother for that exercise, but we can measure the hatred he felt for her in his story of the small boy Conradin who prayed so successfully for vengeance to his tame ferret. ' "Whoever will break it to the poor child? I couldn't for the life of me!", exclaimed a shrill voice, and while they debated the matter among themselves Conradin made himself another piece of toast.' Unhappiness wonderfully aids the memory, and the best stories of Munro are all of childhood, its humour and its anarchy as well as its cruelty and unhappiness.

For Munro reacted to those years rather differently from Kipling. He, too, developed a style like a machine in self-protection, but what sparks this machine gave off. He did not protect himself like Kipling with manliness, knowingness, imaginary adventures of soldiers and Empire Builders (though a certain nostalgia for such a life can be read into *The Unbearable Bassington*): he protected himself with epigrams as closely set as currants in an old-fashioned Dundee cake. As a young man trying to make a career with his father's help in the Burma Police, he wrote to his sister in 1893 complaining that she had made no effort to see [Oscar Wilde's play] *A Woman of No Importance.* Reginald and Clovis are children of Wilde: the epigrams, the absurdities fly unremittingly back and forth, they dazzle and delight, but we are aware of a harsher, less kindly mind behind them than Wilde's. Clovis and Reginald are not creatures of fairy tale, they belong nearer to the visible world than Ernest Maltravers. While Ernest floats airily like a Rubens cupid among the over-blue clouds, Clovis and Reginald belong to the Park, the tea-parties of Kensington, and evenings at Covent Garden—they even sometimes date, like the suffragettes. They cannot quite disguise, in spite of the glint and the sparkle, the loneliness of the Barnstaple years—they are quick to hurt first, before they can be hurt, and the witty and devastating asides cut like Aunt Augusta's cane. How often these stories are stories of practical jokes. The victims with their weird names are sufficiently foolish to awaken no sympathy—they are the middle-aged, the people with power; it is right that they should suffer temporary humiliation because the world is always on their side in the long run. Munro, like a chivalrous highwayman, only robs the rich: behind all these stories is an exacting sense of justice. In this they are to be distinguished from Kipling's stories in the same genre—**"The Village That Voted the Earth Was Flat"** and others where the joke is carried too far. With Kipling revenge rather than justice seems to be the motive (Aunt Rosa had established herself in the mind of her victim and corrupted it).

Perhaps I have gone a little too far in emphasizing the cruelty of Munro's work, for there are times when it seems to remind us only of the sunniness of the Edwardian scene, young men in boaters, the box at the Opera, long lazy afternoons in the Park, tea out of the thinnest porcelain with cucumber sandwiches, the easy irresponsible prattle.

'Never be a pioneer. It's the Early Christian that gets the fattest lion.'

'There's Marion Mulciber, who *would* think she could ride down a hill on a bicycle; on that occasion she went to a hospital, now she's gone into a Sisterhood—lost all she had you know, and gave the rest to Heaven.'

'Her frocks are built in Paris, but she wears them with a strong English accent.'

'It requires a great deal of moral courage to leave in a marked manner in the middle of the second Act when your carriage is not ordered till twelve.'

Sad to think that this sunniness and this prattle could not go on for ever, but the worst and cruellest practical joke was left to the end. Munro's witty cynical hero, Comus Bassington, died incongruously of fever in a West African village, and in the early morning of 13 November 1916, from a shallow crater near Beaumont Hamel, Munro was heard to shout 'Put out that bloody cigarette.' They were the unpredictable last words of Clovis and Reginald. (pp. 127-31)

Graham Greene, "The Burden of Childhood," in his *Collected Essays,* The Viking Press, 1969, pp. 127-31.

V. S. PRITCHETT
(essay date 1957)

[A modern master of the short story, Pritchett is one of the world's most respected and well-read literary critics. In the following excerpt, he asserts that Saki's intellectual position as an outsider enables him to provide incisive and scathing social commentary.]

"I'm living so far beyond my income," says one of the characters in Saki's *The Unbearable Bassington,* "that we may almost be said to be living apart." That is a pointer to Saki's case: it is the fate of wits to live beyond the means of their feeling. They live by dislocation and extravagance. They talk and tire in the hard light of brilliance and are left frightened and alone among the empty wine-glasses and tumbled napkins of the wrecked dinner-table. Saki was more than a wit. There was silence in him as well. In that silence one sees a freak of the travelling show of story-tellers, perhaps a gifted performing animal, and it is wild. God knows what terrors and cajoleries have gone on behind the scenes to produce this gifted lynx so contemptuously consenting to be half-human. But one sees the hankering after one last ferocious act in the cause of a nature abused. The peculiar character called Keriway who crops up unexplained in the middle of the Bassington novel tells the story of a "tame, crippled crane." "It was lame," Keriway says, "that is why it was tame."

What lamed and what tamed Saki? The hate, passion, loneliness that closed the hearts of the children of the Empire-builders? Like Thackeray, Kipling and Orwell, Saki was one of the children sent "home" from India and Burma to what seemed to them loveless care. Saki did not suffer as Kipling suffered, but we hear of an aunt whom his sister described as a woman of "ungovernable temper, of fierce likes and dislikes, imperious, a moral coward, possessing no brains worth speaking of and a primitive disposition." A Baroness Turgenev, in short. She is thought to be the detested woman in **"Sredni Vashtar,"** one of Saki's handful of masterpieces, the tale of the boy who plotted and prayed that she should be killed by a ferret. Boy and ferret were satisfied. But something less pat and fashionably morbid than a cruel aunt at Barnstaple must lie behind

Saki's peculiarity, though she may go some way to explain his understanding of children. We are made by forces much older than ourselves. Saki was a Highland Scot and of a race that was wild and gay in its tribal angers. Laughter sharpens the steel. He belonged—and this is more important—to an order more spirited, melancholy, debonair and wanton than the puddingy Anglo-Saxon world south of the Border, with its middle-class wealth, its worry and its conventions. He could not resist joining it, but he joined to annoy. *The Unbearable Bassington* is a neat piece of taxidermy, a cheerful exposure of the glass case and contents of Edwardian society, a footnote to *The Spoils of Poynton.* In a way, Saki has been tamed by this society, too. Clovis likes the cork-pop of an easy epigram, the schoolboy hilarity of the practical joke and the fizz of instant success—"The art of public life consists to a great extent of knowing exactly where to stop and going a bit further" and so on—he is the slave of the teacup and dates with every new word. His is the pathos of the bubble. But Saki has strong resources: he is moved by the inescapable nature of the weariness and emptiness of the socialite life, though unable to catch, like Firbank, the minor poetry of fashion. Francesca is too shallow to know tragedy, but she will know the misery of not being able to forget what she did to her son, all her life. She is going to be quietly more humiliated every year. And then, Saki's other resource is to let the animals in with impudent cruelty. The leopard eats the goat in the Bishop's bathroom, the cat rips a house-party to pieces, the hounds find not a fox but a hyena and it comfortably eats a child; the two trapped enemies in the Carpathian forest make up their feud and prepare to astonish their rescuers with the godly news but the rescuers are wolves. Irony and polish are meant to lull us into amused, false comfort. Saki writes like an enemy. Society has bored him to the point of murder. Our laughter is only a note or two short of a scream of fear.

Saki belongs to the early period of the sadistic revival in English comic and satirical writing—the movement suggested by Stevenson, Wilde, Beerbohm, Firbank and Evelyn Waugh—the early period when the chief target was the cult of convention. Among these he is the teaser of hostesses, the shocker of dowagers, the mocker of female crises, the man in the incredible waistcoat who throws a spanner into the teacup; but irreverence and impudence ought not to be cultivated. They should occur. Otherwise writers are on the slippery slope of the light article. Saki is on it too often. There is the puzzling, half-redeeming touch of the amateur about him, that recalls Maurice Baring's remark that he made the mistake of thinking life more important than art. But the awkwardness, the jumpiness in some of these sketches, the disproportion between discursion and incident or clever idea has something to do with the journalism of the period—Mr. Evelyn

Munro in the enlisted-man's uniform of the 22nd Batallion, Royal Fusiliers.

Waugh's suggestion—and, I would add, some connection with the decadence of club culture. The great period of that culture was in the mid-nineteenth century: by the early 1900s it had run into the taste for the thin, the urbane and the facetious; and to sententious clichés: Lady Bastable is "wont to retire in state to the morning-room"; Clovis makes a "belated appearance at the breakfast-table"; people "fare no better" and are "singularly" this or that. The cinema, if nothing else, has burned this educated shrubbery out of our comic prose. But Saki's club prose changes when he is writing descriptions of nature (in which he is a minor master) when he describes animals and children or draws his sharp new portraits. His people are chiefly the stupid from the county, the natterers of the drawing-room and the classical English bores, and though they are done in cyanide, the deed is touched by a child's sympathy for the vulnerable areas of the large mammals. He collected especially the petty foibles and practical vanities of women (unperturbed by sexual disturbance on his part), and so presented them as persons, just as he presented cats as cats and dogs as dogs.

Eleanor hated boys and she would have liked to have whipped this one long and often. It was perhaps the yearning of a woman who had no children of her own.

Or there is the scene between the pleasant Elaine who, having just become engaged to be married, decides to increase her pleasure by scoring off her aunt, and her country cousin who has also just got engaged. Saki is clear that Elaine is a thoroughly nice girl:

> "There is as much difference between a horseman and a horsy man as there is between a well-dressed man and a dressy one," said Elaine judicially, "and you may have noticed how seldom a dressy woman really knows how to dress. An old lady of my acquaintance observed the other day, some people are born with a sense of how to clothe themselves, others acquire it, others look as if their clothes had been thrust upon them."

A stale joke? Beware of Saki's claws; he goes on in the next sentence:

> She gave Lady Caroline her due quotation marks, but the sudden tactfulness with which she looked away from her cousin's frock was entirely her own idea.

Saki's male bores and male gossips are remarkable in our comic literature, for he does not take the usual English escape of presenting them as eccentrics. Bores are bores, classifiable, enjoyable like anacondas or the lung-fish. There is Henry Creech with "the prominent, penetrating eyes of a man who can do no listening in the ordinary way and whose eyes have to perform the function of listening for him." And bores have lives. When Stringham made a witty remark for the first time in his life in the House of Commons one evening, remarking indeed that, "the people of Crete unfortunately make more history than they can consume locally," his wife grasped that some clever woman had got hold of him and took poison. (p. 18)

I do not much care for Saki's supernatural stores, though I like the supernatural touch: the dog, for example, in *The Unbearable Bassington,* at the ghastly last dinner-party. His best things are always ingenious: the drama of incurring another's fate in **"The Hounds of Fate,"** the shattering absurdity of **"Louis,"** the artificial dog; and the hilarious tale of the tattooed Dutch commercial traveller who is confined to Italy because he is officially an unexportable work of art. The joke, for Saki, is in the kill. On the whole, it is the heart that is aimed at. He is always richly informed in the vanities of political life and does it in a manner that recalls Disraeli. Except for novels by Belloc, there has been none of this political writing since. Artificial writers of his kind depend, of course, on the dangerous trick-logic of contrivance. Success here is a gamble. For morality he substitutes the child's logic of instinct and idea.

The Unbearable Bassington is one of the lasting trifles. Its very surprising quality is the delicate apprehension of pleasure and misery. Saki was short of pity.

He was an egotist and had no soothing word for pain. He knew that certain kinds of pain cannot be forgotten. Self-dramatisation, self-pity, none of the usual drugs, can take that stone from the heart. He is thoughtful but will offer nothing. In this frivolous novel Saki begins to mature. His next novel, *The Coming of William,* written in 1912 and warning lazy and corrupt Society of the German menace, was good propaganda. He imagined an England annexed to Germany and it makes uncomfortable reading; for silly Society turns instantly to collaboration. There is a more serious discomfort here; a disagreeable anti-Semitism shows more plainly in this book and one detects, in this soldierly sado-masochist, a desire for the "discipline" of authoritarian punishment. He is festive and enjoyable as the wild scourge; but the danger obviously was that this performing lynx, in the demi-monde between journalism and a minor art, might have turned serious and started lecturing and reforming his trainer. In earlier and more spontaneous days, he would have eaten him. (pp. 18-19)

V. S. Pritchett, "The Performing Lynx," in *The New Statesman & Nation,* Vol. LIII, No. 1347, January 5, 1957, pp. 18-19.

JANET OVERMYER
(essay date 1964)

[In the following essay, Overmyer maintains that Saki does not employ cruel humor gratuitously or sadistically, but to express disdain for the waste of human potential.]

Hector Hugh Munro—who wrote under the apt pseudonym of Saki—has had a strange and interesting popularity. At no time during his life or after his death in battle in 1916 was he a best-selling author in the usual sense of the word. Several essays and book reviews, but no major critical studies of his work, have appeared. The only available information about his personal life is that contained in the comparatively brief biography written by his sister, Ethel M. Munro.

Yet he has attracted the attention of such literary figures as S. P. B. Mais, A. A. Milne, Christopher Morley, and Graham Greene. His popularity, if not outstanding, has been steady enough to cause two publishers to reprint his short stories while one also keeps in print his two novels and three plays. His public may be smaller than that of some authors, but it is faithful and growing. Saki would seem to be something of a specialized and acquired taste, like olives stuffed with anchovies.

That he is unique is at once obvious. Futile attempts to pin him down have at one time or another compared him to: the Restoration dramatists, John Dryden, Jonathan Swift, Alexander Pope, William Makepeace Thackeray, Robert Louis Stevenson, Rudyard Kipling, Max Beerbohm, Ronald Firbank, Charles Lamb, James Barrie, Eric Parker, Kenneth Grahame, Oscar Wilde, Aldous Huxley, Evelyn Waugh, and George Orwell. Other authors may also be added—Thomas Hardy and Roald Dahl, for instance. The very length of the list and diversity of authors indicate the difficulty of pigeon-holing Saki.

His trademark is his wit, and to this may, in part perhaps, be attributed the absence of effusive and widespread acclaim. Our Puritan heritage still insists that no one who is funny can at the same time be profound. Saki's subject matter also seems remote; he is the satirical chronicler of the leisurely Edwardian era, which was characterized by week-long house parties, proper afternoon teas, servant difficulties, and the suffragette movement—a way of life that died with the First World War. The upper classes with which Saki was familiar and of which he wrote almost exclusively are no longer, even in England, as much looked up to as pace setters as they once were. The stately homes of England that once echoed the clever conversations of titled guests now resound to the tramping of tourists.

Also, fiction today dwells on the common man, the Willy Lomans and the Walter Mittys. It concerns itself with the inactive, the trapped, the frustrated; it is not receptive to Saki's protagonists, uncommon to say the least, who strike out boldly and outrageously, if sometimes foolishly and blunderingly, attempt grandly to solve their problems, and frequently succeed.

Not only Saki's content but his style also seems to be at war with contemporary fiction. Saki is a succinct, precise story teller; no character sketches or slice-of-life incidents for him. He is not particularly concerned with characterization at all, except as it emphasizes his ideas and sharpens his satire. This slight dehumanization of his people serves his purpose well, but fiction today demands people first, story second. At first reading, Saki may seem to consist of little more than cleverness, an amusing but thin façade behind which no lasting ideas lurk. A look at Saki's short stories, which represent his best and most characteristic work, will show whether or not this is true.

The façade, if that is what it is, is well constructed; Saki is a delightfully easy author to read. His aptness of expression is perfect; his stories move rapidly and frequently end with a twist; and he is wondrously witty. His wit constantly sparks from the mouth of an outrageous protagonist named Reginald, Clovis Sangrail, or Bertie van Tahn—a frank, conceited, irreverent, and charming man about town. He comments openly on people and situations, gets himself and oth-

ers into and out of embarrassing predicaments, and continually lands on his well-shod feet. He or his counterpart, who may be feminine, spouts such epigrams as "Waldo is one of those people who would be enormously improved by death"; "They have the air of people who have bowed to destiny and are not quite sure whether the salute will be returned"; and "The cook was a good cook, as cooks go; and as cooks go she went." This persona is fond of such practical jokes as disrupting a house party by placing a false suicide note on a respectable lady's door, supposedly turning a lady into a hyena for the benefit of a dinner party, and boarding a rooster and pig in a politician's bedroom to keep his mind off politics.

Saki is also fond of the macabre, and aniticipates the current "theatre of the absurd" by blending it with wit. The result is such a story as **"Esmé,"** a tale of two ladies on horseback and their difficulties with a hyena which takes up with them, devours a gypsy child, is struck down and killed by an automobile, and buried by the driver under the impression that it was a pet dog. He makes restitution by presenting the supposed owner with a diamond brooch. Not only the situation but the dialogue maintains the delicate balance between the comic and the gruesome:

" 'Do you think the poor little thing suffered much?' came another of her futile questions.

" 'The indications were all that way,' I said; 'on the other hand, of course, it may have been crying from sheer temper. Children sometimes do.' "

But no matter how engaging, style is not, after all, its own excuse for being. It should not be laid on, like frosting, to hide unbaked content. But Saki's stylistic blend of wit and cruelty is not used to cover, but to expose. This combination is daubed on the tips of pointed barbs which are carefully aimed to puncture the weaknesses and affectations of those persons for whom Saki had an especial dislike, and who may all be included in the elastic category of fools. Saki did not suffer fools gladly; indeed, he did not suffer them at all. It might well have been his motto, emblazoned on his coat of arms, had he possessed a coat of arms.

Saki is impatient with the foibles of bores, cowards, the idle, useless rich, those lacking a sense of humor, "popular" poets, suffragettes, most women, especially aunts, politicians, and all the pompously self-righteous. He gives them such names as Ada Spelvexit, Hortensia Bavvel, Sir James Beanquest, Demosthenes Platterbaff, and Sir Wilfrid Pigeoncote. The ridiculous names and the absence of characterization in depth tend to so dehumanize them that the reader will not sympathize with them and the satire can then scathe more effectively.

Above all Saki recoils from "the mapped life,"

which is led by fools. The story of that name defines it:

> "We are able to live our unreal, stupid little lives on our particular Mappin terrace, and persuade ourselves that we really are untrammelled men and women leading a reasonable existence in a reasonable sphere. . . . We are trammelled by restrictions of income and opportunity, and above all by lack of initiative. . . . We are just so many animals stuck down on a Mappin terrace, with this difference in our disfavour, that the animals are there to be looked at, while nobody wants to look at us. As a matter of fact there would be nothing to look at. . . . It's the dreadful little everyday acts of pretended importance that give the Mappin stamp to our life."

But as Saki is capable of biting satire he is also capable of its opposite, heartfelt compassion. His tender solicitude shows as he relates the bittersweet concern for the church mice in **"The Saint and the Goblin"**; the description of the "elderly gentleman" in **"Dusk"** who "belonged unmistakably to that forlorn orchestra to whose piping no one dances"; and the heartbreaking doomed friendship of the little bird and the effigy of the Lost Soul in **"The Image of the Lost Soul."**

His compassion and cruelty come into careful balance when he writes of children. Saki loved and understood children as only a few adult writers are privileged to do, but his view of childhood is dark. He does not sketch the carefree, merry existence that adults like to think children lead. Instead, the children inhabit their own private, often grim world, one which is perfectly understandable to another child, but rarely to an adult. Children revel in the grimness since it is one way of alleviating the very cruelty of their actual existence. Children are cruel to one another because they openly and reasonably express their feelings of dislike. They are cruel to adults because the entire adult world is against them, and they are helpless to resist. They must therefore snatch their revenge whenever the opportunity arises. Saki chronicles children's cruelty with compassion; and this is not a paradox. He pities them, for they need pity; they must retaliate in kind because it is all they know.

Interwoven with Saki's attitude toward fools and children are four main themes, all of which fall under the general heading of man in relation to his environment. The themes are: supernatural beings and events, religion, hypocrisy, and death. The first two have in common their suggestion of tentative answers to man's questions about the unknown; the latter two have in common their inevitability.

From evidence in the stories, and from an actual incident in his own life when he saw a black dog which appeared only to those to whom bad news was coming and which presaged the death of his father, it is appar-

ent that Saki took the supernatural seriously. Saki's characters have dreams which predict horse race winners, see signs which foretell death, put spells on one another, turn into ghosts or animals, and are startled by animals which have supra-animal powers. At no time is a rational explanation for these occurrences offered, and no character doubts their other-worldly source.

Saki's opinion of religion connects with his opinion of hypocrisy. Men endlessly pretend to one another, for both trivial and serious reasons. They glibly utter the "polite" white lie of thanking the giver for a useless Christmas gift, as in **"Down Pens,"** and they just as readily dole out their friendship and pity openly to one of lower station only when it should be to their advantage, as in **"The Wolves of Cernogratz."**

Hypocrisy mars not only man's relation to man but man's relation to God. True Christians, actively practicing what they are supposed to believe, are almost impossible to find. Such stories as **"A Touch of Realism,"** in which two Jews are marooned on a moor in a snowstorm as part of a Christmas game, and **"The Story of St. Vespaluus,"** in which a supposed Christian near-martyr is actually a pagan, indicate that Saki distrusted genuine religious practices.

Polite tale-telling would thus seem to be necessary not only for a smooth-running society, but a smooth-running conscience. Man cannot face the truth about himself. Perhaps one reason why religion in Saki's stories is unworkable is that it will not permit man to lie to himself.

References to death recur repeatedly. It may be referred to flippantly, as in **"The Lull,"** when a young girl describes the housemaid's identification of three bodies that have floated past the window during a supposed storm as her fiancé. At times it is unavoidable doom, as in **"The Hounds of Fate,"** when a young man is killed because of his resemblance to another; and at times it is a triumph of the human spirit as in **"The Easter Egg"** when a coward gives his life to save that of a prince. Saki's preoccupation with death would seem to say that an awareness of man's final end colors his every action. No matter how high he rises, death waits. But it need not be a total defeat; it may, in fact, be a victory. There is a correlation between this belief and the Christian philosophy, although the victory in Saki's stories refers to man's triumph over himself, not over death.

From a consideration of those persons Saki attacks and those themes that most interest him can be evolved an idea of his basic philosophy. All of his writing life Saki saw through a glass darkly. He attacks mercilessly because he sees life so clearly, both as it is and as he feels it should be. He cares so deeply about mankind that he cannot bear to see people dissipate their tastes and talents on the inconsequential. He so wants to incite them to productive action in order that they may achieve the great goals of which they are capable that he becomes cruel in pointing up their defects. And he finds it necessary to cover this bitter pill of cruelty with the jelly of wit. But the pill is still visible.

The jelly has two purposes. First, coating the bitterness makes the pill easier to swallow. For Saki attacks not *him,* but *me,* and no one enjoys having his own failings blatantly trumpeted. Saki's poker-faced satire exposes the faults of its reader as well as its victim, while it seems merely to be relating an amusing incident. While the reader is laughing, the rapier is slipping, almost unfelt, between his own shoulder blades. He must watch that he does not say, "How ridiculous he is," but "How ridiculous I am."

Wit is also a protection for Saki, as it is for Reginald-Clovis-Bertie—it wounds others before they can wound him. And it keeps the insensitive at a distance so they will not discover the sincere solicitude Saki felt for his fellows. For Saki, unlike Swift, can pity as hugely as he condemns because, as is evident from his many compassionate insights, he identifies himself with foolish, struggling, inept mankind.

But even while he is urging man on he says that, ironically, there is a barrier to complete success. Just as children can never win out against adults, so man can never win out against a force more powerful than he, which may be referred to as fate. Man may transcend himself for a moment and achieve a truly glorious triumph; but then he will be slapped back. And the final defeat is that of death. Nevertheless he must keep trying. The heroes are not those who win, for no one can win, but those who persist until they gain some small success before the greater power intervenes. It is the attempt that exalts.

It is not the purpose of this [essay] to reduce Saki's work to a serious philosophical treatise. For above all his stories are fun to read, they effervesce. But like all outstanding humorists, he is funny for a more trenchant purpose than to win the passing smile. The straw man of incontemporaneity set up originally has been demolished. Those characteristics of Saki's work that would seem to make it obsolete are mainly the surface ones of subject matter and style. The underlying philosophy is not trivial: Keep trying in the face of almost certain defeat. As a credo for modern man it is not outworn. (pp. 171-75)

Janet Overmyer, "Turn Down an Empty Glass," in *The Texas Quarterly,* Vol. VII, No. 3, Autumn, 1964, pp. 171-75.

NOËL COWARD
(essay date 1967)

[Coward is one of the most popular dramatists of the twentieth century. His reputation rests primarily on sophisticated comedies of manners—including *Hay Fever, Private Lives,* and *Blithe Spirit*—that he wrote prior to the end of World War II. Coward depicted the follies, pretensions, and unconventional love affairs of vain, affluent hedonists whose glib behavior reflects the spirit of the post-World War I generation. In the following excerpt, he acknowledges Saki's artistic skill, but claims that it is inextricably tied to the Edwardian era he depicted.]

Many writers who raise youthful minds to a high pitch of enthusiasm are liable, when re-read in the cold remorseless light of middle age, to lose much of their original magic. The wit seems laboured and the language old-fashioned. Saki does not belong to this category. His stories and novels appear as delightful and, to use a much abused word, sophisticated, as they did when he first published them. They are dated only by the fact that they evoke an atmosphere and describe a society which vanished in the baleful summer of 1914. The Edwardian era, in spite of its political idiocies and a sinister sense of foreboding which, to intelligent observers, underlay the latter part of it, must have been, socially at least, very charming. It is this evanescent charm that Saki so effortlessly evoked. True, beneath the lightly satirical badinage of *When William Came* he sounds a prophetic note of warning which shows that he was by no means insensitive to the growing international tension. The idea of England being occupied by Germany, which I shamelessly borrowed for my play *Peace in Our Time* must have been fairly startling to the upper-middle-class complacency of 1912. It might have been more so if Saki had been more widely read, but alas he had only a limited public, possibly for the usual reason that he was ahead of his time. I don't feel, however, that this conclusion is really a valid one. At whatever time he had written, his talent, enchanting as it is to devotees like myself, lacks the necessary ingredients of a "best seller." It is too unsentimental and too superficially flippant. On the rare occasions, such as the end of *The Unbearable Bassington,* when he attempts tragedy, the result is unconvincing and disconcertingly abrupt. His essays in the macabre are more successful. The sinister quality of **"Sredni Vashtar"** and **"The Easter Egg"** can be remembered with an authentic shudder. High comedy was undoubtedly his greatest gift. **"The Schartz-Metterklume Method," "The Unrest-Cure"** and **"Tobermory"** and **"The Open Win-**

dow" are masterpieces. I have often wondered, if he had survived World War I, how he would have reacted to the years immediately following it, that much maligned period now glibly referred to as "the Hectic Twenties" when upstart Michael Arlens and Noël Cowards flourished like green bay trees in the frenzied atmosphere of cocktail parties, treasure hunts, Hawes and Curtis dressing gowns, long cigarette holders and enthusiastically publicised decadence. He would undoubtedly have found many targets for his sardonic wit in that gay decade but I have an instinctive feeling that it wouldn't really have been his cup of tea. His satire was based primarily on the assumption of a fixed social status quo which, although at the time he was writing may have been wobbling a bit, outwardly at least, betrayed few signs of its imminent collapse. His articulate duchesses sipping China tea on their impeccable lawns, his witty, effete young heroes Reginald, Clovis Sangrail, Comus Bassington, with their gaily irreverent persiflage and their preoccupation with oysters, caviar and personal adornment, finally disappeared in the gunsmoke of 1914. True, a few prototypes have appeared since but their elegance is more shrill and their quality less subtle. Present-day ideologies are impatient, perhaps rightly, with aestheticism. World democracy provides thin soil for the growing of green carnations, but the green carnations, long since withered, exuded in their brief day a special fragrance, which although it may have made the majority sneeze brought much pleasure to a civilised minority. In this latter group I am convinced that there will always be enough admirers of Saki to keep his memory fresh. I cannot feel that he would have wished for more. (pp. xiii-xiv)

H. H. Munro, in his introduction to *The Complete Works of Saki,* Doubleday & Company, Inc., 1976, 944 p.

JOAN AIKEN
(essay date 1978)

[An English novelist, short story writer, and author of books for children, Aiken typically combines elements from such diverse genres as fairy tales, historical fiction, and gothic romance. Her characters battle such evils as the poverty of London's slums, kidnappings, and murderous villains, yet these terrors are presented on such an extreme level that they become less real, and therefore less threatening and more comic. In the following essay, Aiken examines motifs in Saki's novel *The Unbearable Bassington,* concluding that the central theme of the work is the conflict between youth and age.]

Saki's writing is composed of four elements. Most peo-

ple, asked to name their primary association with his work, would probably think of wit and absurdity; the dry fantasy of **"Tobermory,"** the Wildean quips of the Clovis and Reginald stories. And this wit does run through all his writing; even the saddest and most sinister stories—such as **"The Hounds of Fate"** or **"The Wolves of Cernogratz"**—contain their touches of dry humour, their sharp satirical portraits. The second element in his work is, of course, his feeling for tragedy and the supernatural, his Celtic sense of doom, which, likewise, is almost always present, even under the most light-hearted foolery: nothing ever turns out quite right in a Saki story, no plan ever succeeds, or, if it does, it rebounds and the success brings worse calamity on the perpetrator than failure would have done. Munro's childhood in Burma, his fondness for Eastern literature combined with the Celtic strain to give him a powerful sense of predestination, of fatalism. Wherever his characters go, however they act, nothing is really going to affect the ultimate outcome for them; destiny is bound to overtake them. His writing is concerned with Nemesis, rather than the culpabilities and developments of human nature.

The last two, minor but continuous, elements in his work are his active delight in town life, and his deep devotion to the country. Idyllic descriptions of London parks, clubs, theatres, Mayfair drawing-rooms, are only surpassed by nostalgic evocations of Devon lanes, farmyards, moors, and woods; the short stories are fairly equally divided between town and country settings. His novel *When William Came* shifts rhythmically in scene between London and the country, as if Munro liked to give himself a breath of country air at regular intervals—in the same way that Trollope indulged himself by inserting hunting scenes into his political novels.

Only *The Unbearable Bassington* among Saki's works is almost entirely located in London; it is essentially a town book, set within the boundaries of Mayfair and Westminster, as if the writer had deliberately planned an urban satire in order to give the most telling possible emphasis to the hero's final exile.

There is one single and significant exception to this London setting, the oddly unrelated chapter in which Elaine, the girl whom Comus loses to a more calculating rival, goes riding in the country. This in itself comes as a small shock to the reader: one even asks oneself what Elaine, a town girl, was *doing* out there in the middle of some unspecified shire, where she accidentally encounters an ex-suitor, now ill and impoverished and lodging at a farm. This scene is in contrast to the main mood of the book; instead of sharp cynicism it breathes a gentle melancholy. And it bears so little relation to the plot that the reader feels the whole incident has been introduced in order to lead up to a brief anecdote about a hurt crane in a German park, and the key sentence: *'It was lame, that was why it was tame,'* a forewarning of the book's end, the despair of being reduced by circumstances to a hideously uncongenial existence. Elaine will discover this for herself, and so, even more drastically, will Comus. The line about the crane is charged with meaning. But why did Saki elaborately set up a country background in order to deliver this message? It is as if, longing for a change of scene, he suddenly and arbitrarily abandoned his own unities.

Apart from this single odd divergence, *The Unbearable Bassington* is constructed with beautiful economy and neatness. It is a sharp, tough book; the gentler side of Munro's nature, as manifested almost entirely by his attitude to animals, a few old people and the countryside, is significantly lacking; the story's tragedy is virtually unrelieved by any touch of sympathy. Even Elaine, with her 'look of grave, reflective calm' and resemblance to a Leonardo portrait, is a malicious girl, who appears to be motivated mainly by a wish to put down and outdo her cousin.

> 'As an old lady of my acquaintance observed the other day, some people are born with a sense of how to clothe themselves . . . others look as if their clothes had been thrust upon them.' [Elaine] gave Lady Caroline her due quotation marks, but the sudden tactfulness with which she looked away from her cousin's frock was entirely her own idea.

Only one minor character, Lady Veula Croot, is in the least degree sympathetic; the others are either brilliantly depicted bores—Saki shares with Jane Austen the ability to portray a bore without *being* boring—or cruel wits; the bores continuously give utterances to inanities which are instantly pounced on and held up to ridicule by the wits:

> 'The tears in their eyes and in their voices when they thanked me, would be impossible to describe.'

> 'Thank you all the same for describing it,' said Comus.

> 'I pointed out at some length a thing that few people ever stop to consider—'

Francesca went over immediately but decorously to the majority that will not stop to consider.

The wits and the bores together make up London society, and spend their time jostling round the Mayfair scene of bridge afternoons, dinners, concerts, first nights and private views.

Comus Bassington, the main figure, was said by Saki's sister, Ethel Munro, to have been based on a real character. Even if the character was taken from life, however, it is almost certain that the plot was Munro's invention; its structure shows all the workmanlike elegance manifested in his short stories. The theme is simple: Comus's mother, Francesca, a selfish, materialistic woman, is activated entirely by the wish to maintain her occupance of her desirable London house, which is due to pass to a niece upon the niece's marriage. Can she persuade Comus, Francesca wonders, to marry the niece, and so secure the house? Or, failing that, can she manoeuvre Comus into a well-paid job, so that he can support her, or, failing that, marriage to an heiress? But relations between mother and son have deteriorated to such a pitch that Francesca has only to indicate a wish for Comus to frustrate it. He blocks her aims in three swift, irreversible moves: by casual, unnecessary cruelty to the niece's schoolboy brother, by public ridicule of the family friend who might have found him a job in the diplomatic service, and by wantonly throwing away his chances with the heiress, Elaine, who is really fond of him, but, piqued by his total lack of consideration, accepts an equally egotistical but far shrewder man, Courtenay Youghal. He, Saki assures the reader, will make her even more unhappy than Comus would have.

The reader may take leave to doubt this. Comus differs from Clovis, Reginald, or Bertie van Tahn, the heroes of Saki's short stories, in that his charm has to be taken on trust. Saki frequently asserts that his hero is delightful, captivating, overflowing with wit and spirits—'In many respects he was adorable; in all respects he was certainly damned'—but we never see his charm in action; on the page, Comus is *never* adorable. He is by turns cruel, petulant, tiresome, teasing, sulky, slightly dishonest, selfish, and demanding, borrowing money from Elaine, and urging his mother to sell her greatest treasure, her cherished Dutch Old Master. Comus's rival, Courtenay, is represented as a far more civilized, if not more likeable person, and though we are informed that Courtenay is shallow and will never achieve anything, there seems no reason to suppose that Comus is any better. The latter, with his complete rejection of work, spendthrift habits 'frank and undisguised indifference to other people's interests' is, ahead of his time, the complete drop-out. But this, I think, reinforces Saki's point. We are not being asked to lament the waste of a brilliant career, or a valuable life, when Comus, sacrificed at last to his mother's callous selfishness, is shipped off to a dismal job in West Africa where he will die of fever. The book's indignation is deployed in the simple perennial battle of youth against age, youth feeling itself cut off too soon. This was a recurrent theme in Saki's work.

'If you knew how I hate death! I'm not a coward, but I do so want to live. Life is so horribly fascinating when one is young, and I've tasted so little of it yet!' cries the main character in his play *The Death-Trap*. And Kurt, in *Karl-Ludwig's Window:* 'I can't die in three minutes. O God! I can't do it. It isn't the jump I shrink from now—it's the ending of everything. It's too horrible to think of. To have no more life! Isadora and the Baron and millions of stupid people will go on living, every day will bring them something new, and I shall never have one morsel of life after these three minutes.' This is the theme of *The Unbearable Bassington.*

Although Munro was reported to have been on cordial and devoted terms with his father, one cannot help suspecting that strong unacknowledged feelings of rebellion against parental authority must have manifested themselves in this novel.

Born in Burma in 1870, Hector Munro was shipped back to England at age two, after his mother's death, with the prognosis that he would not live to grow up. This view prevailed all through his childhood; no wonder life seemed so precious to him. To understand how hopeless he must have felt as a child, one has only to read **"Sredni Vashtar."** Brought up by two wildly paranoid aunts and an ineffective grandmother, he had a fairly harrowing childhood, mitigated by strongly affectionate relations with his elder brother and sister, and love for animals and the Devon countryside in which they lived. Hector had brain-fever at nine and was taught by governesses until the age of fourteen because he was too delicate to go to school. In all, he had only three years' schooling. And yet, in spite of this extreme frailty, it seems to have been considered perfectly in order that Hector and his brother (whose bad eyesight rendered him unfit for the army) should return to Burma in their early twenties to take jobs in the Burma police force. One can hardly imagine a more unsuitable career for the boy who was too ill to go to school, who was interested in history, drawing, literature, the arts. His father, of course, came of an 'Army' family—and also belonged to the filicidal generation, stigmatized by Nicholas Mosley in his life of Julian Grenfell, who so lavishly and enthusiastically sent off their sons to be massacred in the trenches in World War I—where, in fact, Saki was to die. Child sacrifice was highly acceptable in the early decades of the twentieth century. Even so it seems astonishing that Colonel Munro—who, by all accounts, was an intelligent, affectionate parent—should have showed such a total lack of perception of his son's basic nature and needs as to ship him out to Burma. Plainly Hector suffered badly from homesickness; his letters, though characteristically amusing and descriptive, showed this:

'Owl and oaf thou art, not to see [Oscar Wilde's] *Woman of No Importance* and [Miguel Pinero's] *Second Mrs T.,* the plays of the season; what would I not give to be able to see them!' 'The most welcome noise . . . is the whistle of the steamboat, especially when it brings English mail.'

Hector's unfitness for the tropical environment was soon made manifest by seven spells of fever in thirteen months, and he had to return to convalesce in England. Thereafter he took to the kind of career that really suited him—town life, literature, and journalism in London. *Bassington* was written in 1912, after he had published three collections of short stories, *Reginald, Reginald in Russia,* and *The Chronicles of Clovis*—all dealing with elegant, clever, amusing young men, thoroughly at home in their society.

But Comus Bassington is not charming, nor likeable, nor even particularly clever. Why? Because he was drawn from the life, and the writer's fondness for the real character blinded him to its imperfections? Conceivably so. But I believe the real reason is that Comus, emerging from the author's subconscious, is the archetypal child, stamping, sulking under punishment, in rebellion against parental tyranny. Bassington is an early book about the generation gap.

The end of the story, as always in Saki's work, is hinted at, not explicitly related, and is conveyed in three brief, telling scenes: Comus lingering in the theatre after the crowds have left, knowing that he will never set foot there again; and the shrilly hypocritical farewell party given by his mother, at which none of his own friends are present, and over which a shadow is cast by the appearance of the family ghost, a small black dog said to portend a death. The dog is seen only by Comus and the sympathetic Lady Veula. This is the sole touch of supernatural that Saki, a master of the uncanny, allows himself in the book. Elsewhere in his writing he wisely confined para-normal occurrences to short stories, perhaps feeling such things out of place in more serious work. However the ghost-dog was from real experience; Saki himself saw it in Paris when his father was dying in England; it was a Munro family haunt.

We do not follow Comus to the West African swamp where he will die of fever. Instead, as if we are entering into the sulky, exiled child's own imagination—'I'll go away and I'll die and *then* you'll be sorry!' we see the effect of his death on his mother, who realizes too late that she has loved him all along, that he is the only valuable thing in her life. And—another twist of the arm by the angry child—Francesca need not leave her house, the niece has become engaged to a man in the foreign service, and will not be able to marry for years. The niece too has been sacrificed. And—yet another twist—her son's death is announced to Francesca simultaneously with the discovery that her treasured Old Master is, in fact, only a copy.

See! the angry child cries, even your precious old picture isn't really any good!

This last touch, I feel, is one of Saki's rare lapses in technique. The end would have been more truly tragic if the picture had been real, underlining Francesca's realization that she had lost something far more valuable. Saki could not resist that final teasing twist, as if he longed to expose to the ultimate degree the worthlessness of the older generation's values, and this detail, I think, demonstrates completely that he was identifying with Comus, and raging at his useless immolation on the altar of bygone idols. (pp. 5-11)

Joan Aiken, in an introduction to *The Unbearable Bassington* by Saki, 1978. Reprint by Oxford University Press, 1982, pp. 5-11.

SOURCES FOR FURTHER STUDY

Drake, Robert. "Saki's Ironic Stories." *Texas Studies in Literature and Language* V, No. 3 (Autumn 1963): 374-88.

> Attempts to demonstrate that "Saki's stories which are not humorous seem, if they have no other bond in common, to have a pervading irony." Drake adds: "This irony usually consists in the principal character's bringing about his own downfall by scorning as 'unreal' some aspect of total reality."

Gillen, Charles H. *H. H. Munro (Saki)*. Twayne's English Author Series, edited by Sylvia E. Bowman. New York: Twayne Publishers, 1969, 178 p.

> Biographical and critical study. Gillen, claiming that critics have traditionally focused on Munro as a shrewd commentator on pre-1914 Great Britain, states: "this study attempts to show the determination with which he ventured into other fields of writing and the innate ability which enabled him to win a measure of success as a versatile writer."

Langguth, A. J. *Saki: A Life of Hector Hugh Munro, with Six Short Stories Never before Collected.* New York: Simon and Schuster, 1981, 366 p.

> Biography. Langguth also reprints the stories "The Pond," "The Holy War," "The Almanack," "A Housing Problem," "A Sacrifice to Necessity," and "A Shot in the Dark."

Munro, E. M. "Biography of Saki." In *The Square Egg and Other Sketches, with Three Plays,* by H. H. Munro, pp. 3-103. New York: The Viking Press, 1929.

> Anecdotal remembrances by Munro's sister, who is assumed to have destroyed many of Munro's papers and effects that would allow a more complete biography. This essay is particularly valued for the letters by Munro that it reprints.

Porterfield, Alexander. "Saki." *The London Mercury* XII, No. 70 (August 1925): 385-94.

> Critical survey that concludes that Munro will be remembered for his short stories rather than his novels.

Stevick, Philip. "Saki's Beasts." *English Literature in Transition* 9, No. 1 (1966): 33-7.

> Freudian reading of Munro's *Beasts and Super-Beasts.*

J. D. Salinger

1919-

(Full name Jerome David Salinger) American novelist and short story writer.

INTRODUCTION

*B*est known for his controversial novel *The Catcher in the Rye* (1951), Salinger is recognized by critics and readers alike as one of the most popular and influential authors ot American fiction to emerge after World War II. Salinger's reputation derives from his mastery of symbolism, his idiomatic style, and his thoughtful, sympathetic insights into the insecurities that plague both adolescents and adults. Robert Coles reflected general critical opinion when he lauded Salinger as "an original and gifted writer, a marvelous entertainer, a man free of the slogans and clichés the rest of us fall prey to." *The Catcher in the Rye,* now regarded as a classic work of adolescent angst, drew such great attention during the 1950s that those years have been called "The Age of Holden Caulfield," in honor of the novel's sensitive, alienated sixteen-year-old protagonist. The book's vast appeal drew many readers to Salinger's subsequent short fiction, *Nine Stories* (1953), and the novella collections *Franny and Zooey* (1955) and *Raise High the Roofbeam, Carpenters, and Seymour: An Introduction* (1963). In his novellas, Salinger chronicled the Glass family, a group of seven gifted siblings led by their seer-artist and elder brother, Seymour. Salinger has chosen not to publish since 1965, and he has fallen relatively out of critical notice since the early 1960s, when his works attracted virtually a storm of attention. Nevertheless, as the consistent high sales of Salinger's books attest, he continues to speak with warmth and immediacy to succeeding generations of readers.

Salinger's upbringing was not unlike that of Holden Caulfield, the Glass children, and many of his other characters. Raised in Manhattan, he was the second of two children of a prosperous Jewish importer and a Scots-Irish mother. He was expelled from several private preparatory schools before graduating from Valley

Forge Military Academy in 1936. While attending a Columbia University writing course, he had his first piece of short fiction published in *Story,* an influential periodical founded by his instructor, Whit Burnett. Salinger's short fiction soon began appearing in *Collier's, The Saturday Evening Post, Esquire,* and, most notably, *The New Yorker.* Along with such authors as John O'Hara and John Cheever, Salinger helped to develop the sharp, ironic style that characterizes the *New Yorker* school of fiction. His many contributions to the magazine include "For Esmé—with Love and Squalor," a highly popular story in which a soldier's ingenuous friendship with a young English girl saves him from a nervous breakdown. "I'm Crazy" and "Slight Rebellion off Madison," both of which were published in periodicals during the 1940s, introduced readers to a young man named Holden Caulfield, who would eventually become the narrator of *The Catcher in the Rye.*

Self-critical, curious, and compassionate, Holden is a moral idealist whose attitude is governed by a dogmatic hatred of hypocrisy. He reveres children for their sincerity and innocence and seeks to protect them from the immorality that he believes contaminates adult society. Holden's younger brother, Allie, who died at the age of eleven and is always in Holden's thoughts, functions as a symbol of unblemished goodness. *The Catcher in the Rye* opens in a sanitarium, where Holden is recuperating from a physical and mental breakdown. Throughout the novel, Holden offers comments on the flaws and merits of American society, through which readers may evaluate Holden's own morals and values. Holden describes his expulsion from Pencey Prep, a select preparatory school, and his decision to hide out in New York City for a while before returning to his parent's home there. While in New York, he struggles between wanting to return to scenes of his youth and venturing into a mature adult lifestyle. He becomes disillusioned by a gifted jazz musician's contrived performance at a night club and is reminded of his older brother, whose career as a Hollywood screenwriter Holden regards as a waste of creative talent. In another pivotal scene, Holden decides to lose his virginity to a prostitute but sympathizes with her plight and changes his mind.

Several of Holden's attempts to connect with young adults go awry. A date with a young woman he considers a "phony" leads him to despise his own conventionality, and a meeting with Carl Luce, an older schoolmate, at a bar becomes embarrassing when Holden gets drunk and asks personal sexual questions. Critics have noted that much of the book's humor stems from Holden's misconceptions of adulthood. Although Luce is more sexually experienced than Holden, he is not as mature as Holden believes him to be. After these failed efforts at communication, Holden flees to his younger sister, Phoebe, the only person he

completely trusts. Many reviewers concur with S. N. Behrman's comment that Phoebe Caulfield is "one of the most exquisitely created and engaging children in any novel." A precocious ten-year-old, Phoebe functions as Allie's living counterpart and Holden's salvation. After discussing Holden's problems, Phoebe asks her brother if he likes anything about his life. Revealing his obsession with the past and his inability to cope with the present, Holden tells his sister of his wish to be a "catcher in the rye"—one who stands on the edge of a cliff near a rye field where thousands of children play. Holden explains: "What I have to do, I have to catch everybody if they start to go over the cliff. . . . That's all I'd do all day." Phoebe is disgusted at Holden's unrealistic yet honorable goal.

After several more bids to communicate with others, Holden arrives at Phoebe's school to leave a note and is horrified by obscenities scrawled on the building's wall. He has seen similar vulgarities on the walls of the Natural History Museum, a favorite childhood haunt. Despondent at this perversion of his idealized past, Holden finally accepts that the world will change despite his attempts to preserve it. In the novel's climactic scene, Holden watches as Phoebe rides the Central Park carousel in the rain, and his illusion of protecting children's innocence is symbolically shattered. James Bryan observed: "The richness of spirit in this novel, especially of the vision, the compassion, and the humor of the narrator reveal a psyche far healthier than that of the boy who endured the events of the narrative. Through the telling of his story, Holden has given shape to, and thus achieved control of, his troubled past." Despite such praise, *The Catcher in the Rye* has been recurrently banned by public libraries, schools, and bookstores due to its presumed profanity, sexual subject matter, and rejection of traditional American values.

Like *The Catcher in the Rye, Nine Stories* continues to provoke controversy and commentary. The volume's first story, "A Perfect Day for Bananafish," which introduces the character of Seymour Glass and recounts his suicide, has been read alternately as a satire on bourgeois values, a psychological case study, and a morality tale. Perhaps equally controversial is the book's concluding piece, "Teddy," whose title character has been seen as a juvenile version of Seymour. In this story of a boy who is apparently both a genius and a genuine holy man, Salinger gives his most overt expression to the Zen-Buddhist ideals that inform all of his fiction. This story also sets forth some puzzling ambiguities, notably whether Teddy commits suicide by jumping into an empty pool or is pushed by his envious younger sister. Although the protagonists of the remaining *Nine Stories* are not as intensely spiritual as Seymour and Teddy, the search for spiritual meaning in a superficial world is a thread that unites all the characters. From the pretentious, tender-hearted art-school instructor in "De Daumier-Smith's Blue Period" to the four-year-old Lionel Tannenbaum experiencing his first dose of adult hatred and bigotry in "Down at the Dinghy," the persons depicted in *Nine Stories* are disillusioned souls seeking some spiritual purity.

Franny and Zooey, which were originally published separately in *The New Yorker*, stand with several of the *Nine Stories* as Salinger's most acclaimed short fiction. Critics praise *Franny* for its satisfying structure and the appealing portrait of its young heroine, who suffers an emotional and spiritual breakdown while attending college. *Zooey*, the accompanying account of Zooey Glass's attempt to relieve his sister's malaise, is praised for its meticulous detail and psychological insight. *Raise High the Roofbeam, Carpenters, and Seymour: An Introduction*, sometimes faulted as formless and sentimental, are somewhat rambling anecdotes of Seymour narrated by Buddy Glass, whom Salinger has called "my alter-ego." The publication of these novellas prompted many critics to condemn the Glass family as self-centered, smug, and perfect beyond belief, while some asserted that Salinger was too absorbed in his fictitious siblings to maintain the artistic control necessary for literary art. Whatever the flaws detected, however, few deny the immediacy and charm of the Glass clan, who are so successfully drawn that numerous people over the years have reportedly claimed to have had a cocktail with or met the brother-in-law of a Glass.

Salinger's last published story under his own name, "Hapworth 16, 1924," appeared in *The New Yorker* in 1965. This piece is written in the form of a letter from summer camp by seven-year-old Seymour Glass. According to several reviewers, "Hapworth 16, 1924" ties together the Glass family saga by suggesting reasons for Seymour's later suicide. Although Salinger has published no known works since this period, critics continue to acknowledge the artistic value of much of his fiction, his influence on the style and substance of other writers, and, above all, his place of honor among young readers. In *The Catcher in the Rye* as well as his short fiction, Salinger displays what Stanley Edgar Hyman termed his "marvelous sensitivity to the young, to the language, to the fraudulence of contemporary America," all of which earn him a distinctive place in contemporary American letters.

(For further information about Salinger's life and works, see *Concise Dictionary of American Literary Biography, 1941-1968*; *Contemporary Authors*, Vols. 5-8; *Contemporary Literary Criticism*, Vols. 1, 3, 8, 12, 56; *Dictionary of Literary Biography*, Vols. 2, 102; and *Short Story Criticism*, Vol. 2.)

CRITICAL COMMENTARY

S. N. BEHRMAN

(essay date 1951)

[An American playwright, short story writer, critic, and essayist, Behrman was an important exponent of the American comedy of manners. His works often combined social, political, and philosophical commentary with sophisticated humor to expose the incongruities of human behavior. The following essay, excerpted from a highly laudatory review of *The Catcher in the Rye*, focuses on Salinger's vivid characterizations.]

Holden Caulfield, the sixteen-year-old protagonist of J. D. Salinger's first novel, *The Catcher in the Rye*, . . . refers to himself as an illiterate, but he *is* a reader. One of the tests to which he puts the books he reads is whether he feels like calling the author up. He is excited about a book by Isak Dinesen and feels like calling her up. He would like to call up Ring Lardner, but an older brother has told him Lardner is dead. He thinks *Of Human Bondage* is pretty good, but he has no impulse to put in a call to Maugham. He would like to call up Thomas Hardy, because he has a nice feeling about Eustacia Vye. (Nobody, evidently, has told him the sad news about Hardy.) Mr. Salinger himself passes his unorthodox literary test with flying colors; this reader would certainly like to call *him* up.

Mr. Salinger's brilliant, funny, meaningful novel is written in the first person. Holden Caulfield is made to tell his own story, in his own strange idiom. Holden is not a normal boy. He is hypersensitive and hyperimaginative (perhaps these are synonymous). He is double-minded. He is inexorably self-critical; at various times, he refers to himself as yellow, as a terrible liar, a madman, a moron. He is driven crazy by "phoniness," a heading under which he loosely lumps not only insincerity but snobbery, injustice, callousness to the tears in things, and a lot more. He is a prodigious worrier. . . . He is moved to pity unconscionably often. He has few defenses. For example, he is driven frantic by a scrawled obscenity some vandal has chalked on the wall of his ten-year-old sister Phoebe's

Principal Works

The Catcher in the Rye (novel) 1951

Nine Stories (short fiction collection) 1953; also published as For Esmé—with Love and Squalor, and Other Stories, 1953

Franny and Zooey (short fiction collection) 1955

Raise High the Roofbeam, Carpenters, and Seymour: An Introduction (short fiction collection) 1963

school. Grown men sometimes find the emblazoned obscenities of life too much for them, and leave this world indecorously, so the fact that a sixteen-year-old boy is overwhelmed should not be surprising. (p. 71)

The book covers Holden's last day at Pencey, a fashionable prep school, from which he has flunked out, and the following two days, which he spends in hiding in New York City. Stradlater, Holden's roommate, is handsome, gross, and a successful amorist. On Holden's last night at school, a Saturday night, he is in a frenzy of jealousy because Stradlater has dated up Jane Gallagher, with whom Holden is in love. The hero and heroine of this novel, Holden's dead brother Allie and Jane Gallagher, never appear in it, but as they are always in Holden's consciousness, together with his sister Phoebe—these three constitute his emotional frame of reference—the reader knows them better, finally, than the characters Holden encounters, who are, except for Phoebe, marginal. It is characteristic of Holden that although he is crazy about Jane, always thinking of her, always wanting to call her up, he never does call her up. He is always about to but doesn't, because he's never "in the mood." ("You really have to be in the mood for that stuff.") Perhaps he means that circumstances and his feelings are always too chaotic at the particular moment—that he wants to appear before Jane when everything is in order and he is in control of himself. Or perhaps he wishes to keep his memory of Jane inviolate and consecrated, like his memory of Allie; perhaps he is afraid of finding her innocence tarnished—not in a sexual sense, because eventually he is sure that Stradlater didn't "get to first base with her," but simply of finding her no longer what she was, possibly finding that she has become, in short, a phony. He keeps calling up a girl named Sally Hayes, whose manifest phoniness gives him "a royal pain," but he writes that off as the overhead of sex. He can never risk it with Jane.

While Stradlater is shaving before going to meet Jane, he asks Holden to write a classroom composition for him. "Anything descriptive," Stradlater says. "A room. Or a house. . . . Just as long as it's as descriptive as hell. . . . Just don't do it *too* good, is all. . . . I mean

don't stick all the commas and stuff in the right place." The implication that all there is to writing a composition is a sense of direction about commas also gives Holden "a royal pain." "I mean," he explains, "if you're good at writing compositions and somebody starts talking about commas. Stradlater was always doing that. He wanted you to think that the only reason *he* was lousy at writing compositions was because he stuck all the commas in the wrong place. . . . God, how I hate that stuff !"

While Stradlater is out with Jane, Holden, knowing his roommate's technique on the back seats of cars, takes terrific punishment from his imagination. Nevertheless, he sits down to write a composition for the absent Don Juan:

The thing was, I couldn't think of a room or a house or anything to describe the way Stradlater said he had to have. I'm not too crazy about describing rooms and houses anyway. So what I did, I wrote about my brother Allie's baseball mitt. It was a very descriptive subject. It really was. My brother Allie had this left-handed fielder's mitt. He was left-handed. The thing that was descriptive about it, though, was that he had poems written all over the fingers and the pocket and everywhere. In green ink. He wrote them on it so that he'd have something to read when he was in the field and nobody was up at bat. He's dead now. He got leukemia and died when we were up in Maine, on July 18, 1946. You'd have liked him. He was two years younger than I was, but he was about fifty times as intelligent. He was terrifically intelligent. His teachers were always writing letters to my mother, telling her what a pleasure it was having a boy like Allie in their class. . . . They really meant it. But it wasn't just that he was the most intelligent member in the family. He was also the nicest, in lots of ways. He never got mad at anybody. . . .

(pp. 71-2)

Holden copies Allie's poems from his baseball mitt. He tells you casually, "I happened to have it with me, in my suitcase." Very much later, we discover that the only person to whom Holden has ever shown this mitt is Jane. ("She was interested in that kind of stuff.") Allie is always there. Sitting in his hotel room in New York, Holden feels he is sunk, and he starts talking to Allie. He remembers that he and another boy were going on a bicycle jaunt with their BB guns, and Allie asked to come along, and Holden wouldn't let him:

So once in a while, now, when I get very depressed, I keep saying to him, "Okay. Go home and get your bike and meet me in front of Bobby's house. Hurry up." It wasn't that I didn't use to take him with me when I went somewhere. I did. But that one day, I didn't. He didn't get sore about it—he never got sore about anything—but I keep thinking about it anyway, when I get very depressed.

Holden is always regretting that you didn't know Allie. "You'd have liked him," he keeps saying: the human impulse to make a silent voice audible to others, a lost essence palpable.

By the time Stradlater returns from his date with Jane, Holden is sure that he has slept with her, and Stradlater helps him to think so, without being actually caddish. Stradlater asks for the composition; he is furious when he reads it, because it is about a baseball glove rather than a room or a house. Holden tears the composition up. He has a fight with Stradlater and gets a bloody nose. Shortly after that, he decides he can't stay another minute in Pencey and will go to New York, though his parents don't expect him until Wednesday.

Holden goes to say goodbye to Mr. Spencer, his nice old history teacher. It worries the boy that while his teacher is saying edifying valedictory things to him, he becomes acutely concerned about the winter quarters of the ducks in the Central Park lagoon. . . . This worry about the ducks stays with Holden all through his adventures in New York. On his second night, he has an irresistible impulse to go to Central Park and see what the ducks are doing. In his avidity to find them, he pokes in the grass around the lagoon, to see if they are sleeping there, and nearly falls in the water. No ducks. Beginning to shiver, he is sure he is going to die of pneumonia, and he decides to sneak into his parents' apartment to see Phoebe once more before he dies.

This Phoebe is one of the most exquisitely created and engaging children in any novel. She is herself a prolific novelist, who is not deterred from starting a new book merely because she hasn't finished the last one. They are all about an attractive girl detective named Hazle Weatherfield. Hazle's father is "a tall attractive gentleman about 20 years of age." When Holden tiptoes into Phoebe's room, she is asleep. As befits an author, Phoebe has numberless notebooks. Before Holden wakes Phoebe, he has a look at her notebooks and her schoolbooks. Phoebe's middle name is Josephine, but Holden finds "Phoebe Weatherfield Caulfield 4B-1" written on the flyleaf of her "Arithmetic Is Fun!" Phoebe keeps changing her middle name, according to caprice. In a little list of variations, Holden finds "Phoebe Weatherfield Caulfield, Esq." "Kids' notebooks kill me," Holden says. He devours Phoebe's.

Holden wakes Phoebe. The moment she opens her eyes, she wants to know whether Holden has received her letter announcing that she is going to appear in a school play, *A Christmas Pageant for Americans.* "It stinks but I'm Benedict Arnold," she tells him excitedly. "I have practically the biggest part." Then, after her theatrical excitement simmers down, she remembers that Holden wasn't expected home until Wednesday, and she learns that he has been kicked out of school. She hits him with her fist. "Daddy'll *kill* you!" she cries.

Holden lights a cigarette and tries to explain, but can't get much further than saying that the school was full of phonies and they depressed him. "You don't like *any*thing that's happening," she says. This accusation, in which Holden recognizes that there is a fundamental truth, also depresses him. He tries desperately to justify himself. He enumerates things and people he does like—his brother Allie, for instance. Phoebe replies sagely that it is easy to like people who are in Heaven. Holden, miserable, cannot marshal all his likes. There was, he remembers, a frail boy who was so bullied by some thug schoolmates that he jumped out of a window to escape them. A teacher, Mr. Antolini, picked the boy up and put his own coat around him—"He didn't even give a damn if his coat got all bloody"—and for this teacher Holden has always had a special feeling. Near Phoebe, Holden begins to feel better. (pp. 72-4)

Everybody, says Holden, accuses him of acting twelve years old. It's partly true, he admits, but not all true, because "sometimes I act a lot older than I am—I really do—but people never notice it." These perpetual insistences of Holden's—"I really am," "I really do," "It really does"—after he has explicitly said something, reveal his age, even when he is thinking much older, as when he says, "People always think something's *all* true." Although Holden thinks lots of things are funny, he hasn't much sense of humor; he has the deadpan literalness and the all-or-nothing combativeness of the passionate adolescent. Salinger's use of reiteration and redundancy in Holden's self-communion conveys this. After a passage describing his schoolmate Robert Ackley as pimply, dirty, disgusting, and nasty, and as having a terrible personality, he tells you, "I wasn't too crazy about him, to tell you the truth." . . . He is so aware of the danger of slipping into phoniness himself that he has to repeat over and over "I really mean it," "It really does." When he is not communing with himself but is in actual situations, these reiterations disappear; the dialogue and the descriptions are economical and lean.

The literalness and innocence of Holden's point of view in the face of the tremendously complicated and often depraved facts of life make for the humor of this novel: serious haggles with belligerent taxi-drivers; abortive conversational attempts with a laconic prostitute in a hurry; an "intellectual" discussion with a pompous and phony intellectual only a few years older than himself; an expedition with Sally Hayes, which is one of the funniest expeditions, surely, in the history of juvenilia. Holden's contacts with the outside world are generally extremely funny. It is his self-communings that are tragic and touching—a dark whirlpool churning fiercely below the unflagging hilarity of his surface activities. Holden's difficulties affect his nervous system but never his vision. It is the vision of an innocent. To the lifeline of this vision he clings invincibly, as he does to a phonograph record he buys for Phoebe (till it breaks) and a red hunting cap that is dear to him and that he finally gives to Phoebe, and to Allie's baseball glove. He has a hunger for stability. He loves the Museum of Natural History because the figures in the glass cases don't change; no matter how often you go, the Eskimo is still there catching fish, the deer drinking out of the water hole, the squaw weaving the same blanket. You change the circumstances of your visit—you have an overcoat on one time when you didn't before, or you may have "passed by one of those puddles in the street with gasoline rainbows in them," but the squaw and the deer and the Eskimo are stable. . . . Holden knows things won't remain the same; they are dissolving, and he cannot reconcile himself to it. He hasn't the knowledge to trace the process of dissolution or the mental clarity to define it; all he knows is that he is gasping in the avalanche of disintegration around him. And yet there is an exhilaration, an immense relief in the final scene of this novel, at the Central Park carrousel with Phoebe. ("I felt so damn happy all of a sudden, the way old Phoebe kept going around and around.") Holden will be all right. One day, he will probably find himself in the mood to call up Jane. He will even become more tolerant of phonies—it is part of the mechanics of living—as he has already had to endure the agony of saying "Glad to've met you" to people he isn't glad to have met. He may even, someday, write a novel. I would like to read it. I loved *this* one. I mean it—I really did. (pp. 75-6)

S. N. Behrman, "The Vision of the Innocent," in *The New Yorker*, Vol. XXVII, No. 26, August 11, 1951, pp. 71-6.

DAVID L. STEVENSON
(essay date 1957)

[In an overview of Salinger's fiction, Stevenson suggests that Salinger's short stories are powerful because they accurately reflect the emotional predicament of men and women in modern society.]

Because of [his] diffidence to things dedicatedly literary, Salinger is usually identified by book reviewers, and properly, as a *New Yorker* writer, implying thereby both city wit and surface brilliance in his use of prose and stylized irony of situation in his use of plot. (p. 215)

Salinger is surely one of the most skillful practioners of the *New Yorker* short story or sketch. And, invidious critics aside, his sketches show it to be, at its best, one of the truly distinctive and definable fictional types of mid-century American letters. This kind of story contains no more than two or three characters,

seen always at a moment of crisis in one of their lives. The concentration is on the crisis: the relationships which have led to it are indistinct, only suggested by the tone of the dialogue, by characters' momentary actions and gestures. The Salinger-*New Yorker* story is always a kind of closet scene between Hamlet and his mother with the rest of the play left out. It accomplishes its shock of surprise, and it evokes our emotions, by a frugal underplaying of plot and event, by its very minimizing of narrative. The reader is usually not projected into the problems of its characters because he is not given enough of the fabric of their lives to make such projection possible.

What a Salinger story *does* involve the reader in is something quite different. It is his awareness that the crisis of the sketch is a generic one of our time and place. The crisis of the usual *New Yorker* story may be fairly casual, and we have come to expect a Salinger story to be more stern in its implications because its roots are stronger and probe more deeply. But its crisis runs true to form. Salinger does not take you out of yourself into a living, substantial world of fiction. He throws you back into your own problems, or into an awareness of them in your contemporaries. His characters do not exist in a rich narrative, in a detailed setting, so that they become wholly separable, fictional beings. Rather they give us a feeling of our own sensitivity to compensate for their lack of created density.

One can best illustrate this quality of a Salinger story by comparing his *New Yorker* sketch **"Pretty Mouth and Green My Eyes"** [from *Nine Stories*] with Hemingway's "The Short Happy Life of Francis Macomber." The two stories offer the same basic character relationships: passively suffering husband, aggressively lustful wife, and casual, opportunistic lover. In Hemingway's version, however, the characters are embedded in a full, complex plot in which motive and event are made inexorably overt. The tensions of the characters are in open balance for the reader, and the husband's declared failure of nerve is what provokes his wife's ruthless retaliation in taking a lover. The Macombers exist in the round as "created" individuals in a self-contained narrative which could be translated into mandarin and remain comprehensible.

Part of the virtue of **"Pretty Mouth and Green My Eyes,"** on the other hand, is that it is not a self-contained narrative. We know of the characters only that they are apartment dwellers in New York. They exist as voices on a telephone to illustrate the desperate irony of a husband calling his wife's latest lover, after a party the three of them have attended, at the moment when the lover is in bed with the wife. The tearing crisis of the story is the husband's slow realization, as he complains in hideously maudlin, drunken terms of his wife's infidelities, that he has put his own self-respect beyond the point of salvage. Salinger's characters, here, come alive *New Yorker* fashion through the skillful veri-similitude of their conversation. . . . They are impor-tant to us in direct proportion to our recognition of them as generic sketches of our urban, childless, apart-mented men and women, alienated by the hectic nature of their lives from all quiet interflow of love and affec-tion.

One significant element in the structure of a Sal-inger story, then, and a source of his power over us, is that his characters come alive in our recognition of them. In complementary fashion, an equally significant element is the effect on us of the special kind of crisis he asks us to identify. As in **"Pretty Mouth and Green My Eyes,"** it is a crisis in a character's life that results from an erosion of personality peculiar to upper mid-dle-class, mid-century America. It is related to our sense of the heightened vulnerability of men and women to emotional disaster.

I am not prepared to argue that the Salinger spe-cies of crisis is unique, and that other ages did not feel themselves alienated from inner security and outward affection. *Hamlet* alone would suffice. I should only as-sert that in our time and place, the individual estranged from his fellows seems peculiarly understandable and therefore touching to us. (pp. 215-16)

Salinger's short stories are all variations on the theme of emotional estrangement. In **"Down at the Dinghy,"** a small boy runs away when he overhears his father referred to as a "kike." In **"Uncle Wiggily in Connecticut,"** two women, unsuccessful adventurers in love, let a Connecticut afternoon drift away on high-balls and reminiscences, while the timid child of one of them retreats farther and farther into compensatory fantasy as the two women get progressively more sod-den. In **"A Perfect Day for Bananafish,"** a young sol-dier released from an army hospital confronts his wife's complicated indifference during their first reunion. When he is forced to weigh a small child's warm, intu-itive sympathy against his wife's society prettiness, he shoots himself. The actions of the characters in all these stories could seem arbitrary, judged by the sketchiness of Salinger's narrative. In fact, however, the actions seem real and shocking because they are the kind of thing we can anticipate from the needs and stresses we share at least in part with the characters. (p. 216)

There is a further fictional device used . . . in [Salinger's] short stories. . . . It is his use of almost Chaplin-like incidents and dialogue, half-amusing, half-desperate, to keep his story always hovering in ambivalence between comedy and tragedy. Whenever a character approaches hopelessness in a Salinger sketch, he is getting there by the route of the comic. It is usually both the character's way of holding on for a moment longer (as when the husband in **"A Perfect Day for Bananafish"** goes out of his way to insult a proper dowager just before he kills himself) and, at its

sharpest, a way of dramatic irony, a way of heightening the intensity of a character's predicament (as when Holden [in *The Catcher in the Rye*] attempts to be bored with sex to get rid of a prostitute). . . .

When one is reading Salinger, one accepts his carefully placed "New Yorkerish" style and tone, and surrenders one's mind almost completely. It is only when you put the story aside and turn to other contem-porary writers and to other fictional methods and tech-niques that you begin to wonder whether the immedia-cy and vividness of Salinger might be limited in power. Nowhere in Salinger do we find ourselves plunged into the emotional coiling and recoiling provoked by pas-sages from Styron's novel, *Lie Down in Darkness*. No-where in Salinger is a character moved against the murky intensity-in-depth of a Nelson Algren Chicago scene, in *The Man with the Golden Arm*. Nowhere is a char-acter revealed by the great clots of heterogenerous de-tail yoked together in single crowded sentences, as by Saul Bellow in *The Adventures of Augie March*.

But despite the temptations of comparison there remains one's conviction that Salinger is deeply and se-riously committed in his fiction. Further, a little re-search into the Salinger canon reveals that two of his major creations, Holden Caulfield and Seymour Glass, the young husband of **"A Perfect Day for Banana-fish,"** have deep roots in Salinger's own imagination. His novel, in its way, is as much a final version of "work in progress" as are the novels of his more literary contemporaries, pulled together from fragmentary ex-cursions as short stories in *Partisan Review*, in *Hudson Re-view*, in *New World Writing*. Only with Salinger, the pro-fessional, early sketches of Holden Caulfield occur in a series of stories published in *The Saturday Evening Post*, *Collier's*, and in the *New Yorker*, in the years 1944-1946. And Seymour Glass turns out to have rich interconnec-tions in Salinger's mind with the uncle of the runaway boy of **"Down at the Dinghy,"** with the older brother of the heroine in a sketch **"Franny,"** and with the bridegroom in a novelette **"Raise High the Roofbeam, Carpenters."**

This extrinsic information helps verify one's feel-ing that there is actually more weight to his explora-tions of human alienation than his bright dialogue and his frugal use of background and event might suggest. Moreover, Salinger's non-literary status leaves him, as a serious writer, almost unique as a wholly free agent, unhampered by the commitments of his more dedicat-ed contemporaries to one or another school of critics. One might guess that this is Salinger's most precious asset. Rather than wishing quarterly significance or "greatness" on him, we can be content to take him for what he is: a beautifully deft, professional performer who gives us a chance to catch quick, half-amused, half-frightened glimpses of ourselves and our contemporaries, as he confronts us with his brilliant mirror images. (p. 217)

David L. Stevenson, "J. D. Salinger: The Mirror of Crisis," in *The Nation,* New York, Vol. 184, No. 10, March 9, 1957, pp. 215-17.

WILLIAM WIEGAND
(essay date 1958)

[In an analysis of Salinger's protagonists, Wiegand asserts that the characters are "bananafish" who are so glutted with experience, perceptions, and love that they are unable to function in society. The critic also explores the various ways that Salinger tries in his fiction to resolve this "spiritual illness."]

Salinger has, in a measure, revived the dormant art of dialect in American fiction. His ear has detected innumerable idiomatic expressions that were simply unrecorded before. And with this gift he has been able to reach a level of readers that Mark Twain, for example, was able to reach. Unlike others who have made the attempt to transcribe distinctive speech patterns, Salinger has succeeded, as few beyond Twain have, in making his characters something more than cracker-barrel philosophers or, worse, good-natured boobs.

But this achievement is somewhat self-evident. I prefer to justify Salinger on a second basis: namely, the coherence of his particular vision of the world. This is essentially the vision of his heroes—of Holden Caulfield, Seymour Glass, Teddy, Franny, Daumier Smith, and the rest. The important question in Salinger is why these intelligent, highly sensitive, affectionate beings fight curious, gruelling battles, leaderless and causeless, in a world they never made.

In simple terms, they are a family of non-conformists and Salinger documents their brotherhood by presenting several of them as brothers and sisters in **"Franny," "Raise High the Roofbeam, Carpenters,"** and **"Zooey,"** his most recent stories. However, this is not traditional non-conformity. Logically, the enemy of the non-conformist is society or some oppressive segment of society; and in the recent tradition from Sinclair Lewis's Arrowsmith and Hemingway's Frederick Henry right down to Ayn Rand's Howard Roark, the non-conformist hero is constantly threatened by external forces which seek to inhibit and to destroy him. With the Salinger hero, however, the conflict is never so cleanly drawn. . . . He is a victim not so much of society as of his own spiritual illness.

Salinger has spent much of his career seeking a cure for this illness; however, before we examine that search, we need a somewhat more precise definition of the illness. Perhaps it is best described in his second to last story **"Raise High the Roofbeam, Carpenters,"** a work which amplifies and explains the first of the *Nine Stories,* **"A Perfect Day for Bananafish."** . . . Without **"Raise High the Roofbeam, Carpenters"** the suicide which closes **"A Perfect Day for Bananafish"** appears motivated chiefly by Seymour's inability to put up with his bourgeois wife. With **"Raise High the Roofbeam, Carpenters,"** however, we see Seymour as a man not deprived of, but rather surfeited with, the joy of life. Salinger's sole excuse for Seymour's desperate social irresponsibility is this same curious surfeit of sensation.

We learn, for example, in the course of **"Raise High the Roofbeam, Carpenters,"** that Seymour does not show up for his wedding because he is too "happy," or as he puts it in his journal, he is "too keyed up . . . to be with people." The nature of this happiness is further illuminated through the use of a boyhood experience of Seymour's: at the age of twelve he threw a stone at a young girl, scarring her for life. Seymour's brother, the narrator, explains the incident this way:

> We were up at the Lake. Seymour had written to Charlotte, inviting her to come and visit us, and her mother finally let her. What happened was, she sat down in the middle of our driveway one morning to pet Boo Boo's cat, and Seymour threw a stone at her. He was twelve. That's all there was to it. He threw it at her because she looked so beautiful sitting there in the middle of the driveway with Boo Boo's cat. Everybody knew that, for God's sake—me, Charlotte, Boo Boo, Waker, Walt, the whole family.

Seymour's own understanding of his malady is a more poetic one. He writes in his journal:

> If or when I do start going to an analyst, I hope to God he has the foresight to let a dermatologist sit in on the consultation. A hand specialist. I have scars on my hands from touching certain people. Once, in the park, when Franny was still in the carriage, I put my hand on the downy pate of her head and left it there too long. Another time, at Loew's Seventy-second Street, with Zooey during a spooky movie. He was about six or seven, and he went under the seat to avoid watching a scary scene. I put my hand on his head. Certain heads, certain colors and textures of human hair leave permanent marks on me. Other things too. Charlotte once ran away from me outside the studio, and I grabbed her dress to stop her, to keep her near me. A yellow cotton dress I loved because it was too long for her. I still have a lemon-yellow mark on the palm of my right hand. Oh, God, if I'm anything by a clinical name, I'm a kind of paranoiac in reverse. I suspect people of plotting to make me happy.

The "skin disease" which Seymour sees himself

Early dust jacket for *The Catcher in the Rye*.

afflicted with in 1942 apparently becomes worse. By 1948, the date of his suicide, the "lemon-yellow marks" have attained weight and shape; he has become mortally ill.

During the course of his interlude with the little girl on the beach in **"A Perfect Day for Bananafish,"** he says to her:

> "You just keep your eyes open for any bananafish. This is a perfect day for bananafish."
>
> "I don't see any," Sybil said.
>
> "That's understandable. Their habits are very peculiar. . . . They lead a very tragic life. . . . You know what they do, Sybil?"
>
> She shook her head.
>
> "Well, they swim into a hole where there's a lot of bananas. They're very ordinary-looking fish when they swim *in*. But once they get in, they behave like pigs. Why I've known some bananafish to swim into a banana hole and eat as many as seventy-eight bananas. . . . Naturally after that they're so fat they can't get out of the hole again. Can't fit through the door."
>
> . . . "What happens to them?"
>
> . . . "Well, I hate to tell you, Sybil. They die."
>
> "Why?" asked Sybil.
>
> "Well, they get banana fever. It's a terrible disease."

In other words, Seymour, a bananafish himself, has become so glutted with sensation that he cannot

swim out into society again. It is his own banana fever, not his wife who is at fault, or his mother-in-law. If they are stupid and insensitive, **"Raise High the Roof-beam, Carpenters"** shows them also to be without malice, and hence basically as inculpable for the bananafish's condition as is the Matron of Honor, who represents the whole level-headed society in criticizing Seymour for his peccadilloes. (pp. 4-7)

In **"A Perfect Day for Bananafish,"** [Salinger's] awareness that his hero is "diseased" is still intuitive, I think. Although the "bananafish" metaphor is brilliant in itself, the insight is somewhat neutralized by Salinger's apparent blame of the wife and the mother-in-law for Seymour's suicide. The two women are, at any rate, mercilessly satirized in the telephone conversation through the mother-in-law's constant interruption of the impassioned discussion of Seymour's perilous mental health with questions like "How's your blue coat?" and "How's your ballerina?" As a result, Seymour seems . . . a victim of an external force, namely, the bourgeois matriarchy. . . . When the important bananafish symbol arrives later in the story, it is impossible to do much with it. There is no demonstrated connection between society's insensitivity and Seymour's zaniness.

The problem recurs again in the next story, **"Uncle Wiggily in Connecticut,"** but not without growing evidence that Salinger is ready to resist the easy answer that the bouregoisie and/or the war is responsible for the bananafish's condition. Here, for example, it is quite clear that it is Eloise Wengler's tormenting memories of her lost lover, Walter, that makes her unable to swim out of the cave into her proper place in Exurbia. Although "the war" is a factor in her despair since her lover is killed in it, he dies not in battle but in an "absurd" camp accident; likewise, her militantly bourgeois husband may contribute to her unhappiness, but she is allowed to repay him in kind. No mere victim of society, Eloise is a bitch, not only with her husband, but with her daughter and her maid as well. She takes the revenges of an invalid.

This story contains the first clear explanation of banana fever: it is the sense of what is missing that causes the suffering. Here, the lover's death brings the loss. Death, of course, is the most primitive way of making loss concrete; it is the villain of [Salinger's early] war stories and it is still the villain here. In **"Uncle Wiggily in Connecticut,"** however, we have Salinger's first sign of awareness that this sense of loss ought to be overcome, the first sign, in other words, that remembering too much is a bad thing. Eloise, for example, resents her daughter's habit of inventing invisible playmates, Mickey Mickeranno and Jimmy Jimmereeno, to take to bed with her at night. Unconsciously, Eloise knows that Walter, her lost lover, is as invisible as Ramona's boyfriends. She forces Ramona to move into the middle of the bed to prevent her daughter from lying with an invisible lover, as she has had to lie with one in the years since Walter's death. She knows the consequences: her bitchiness.

These "consequences" show that Salinger was not yet willing to settle completely for a story about somebody with banana fever. In the war, he learned that actions not only had social causes but also social consequences, so he must indicate that Eloise's unhappiness affects others. In this way he absolved himself from having written an isolated, clinical report about one of the hyper-sensitive. (pp. 9-10)

In **"For Esmé—with Love and Squalor"** we have an interesting development in the record of the bananafish: Salinger allows himself his first *explicit* statement of what is wrong with his heroes. Actually, he allows Dostoievski to make the statement for him; "Dear God, life is hell . . . Fathers and Teachers, I ponder, what is hell? I maintain it is the suffering of being unable to love." Although Dostoievski's lament probably does not accurately describe Sergeant X's condition, nor that of Salinger's other heroes for that matter, most of whom love too much; still the God that the Sergeant requires is clearly a God of redemption, not of justice. What the bananafish needed was to be saved; where justice lay was no longer certain. (p. 11)

The five stories published since *The Catcher in the Rye* ("De Daumier-Smith's Blue Period," "Teddy," "Franny," "Raise High the Roofbeam, Carpenters" and "Zooey") explore a solution for the bananafish, first, in terms of union with God and, finally, in terms of re-union with society.

The stories demonstrate that although the bananafish is incapacitated by the weight of his experi-

ence, he is also afflicted with a psychological conflict between the desire to participate in and the need to withdraw from society. He is a non-conformist, but a paralyzed one, unlike Arrowsmith, for example, who was moving full-tilt toward a private goal, or Huckleberry Finn, who was making his precipitate escape away from society, unwilling to be captured. The Salinger hero, on the other hand, is carried along in the currents of his own psyche, neither toward nor away from anything. He drifts in a course more or less parallel to that of society, alternately tempted and repelled, half inclined to participate, and half inclined to withdraw.

In **"De Daumier-Smith's Blue Period,"** the miracle regeneration of **"For Esmé"** recurs, this time in terms of a frankly mystical Experience. Salinger himself, only half ironically, uses the capital "e" to describe it, perhaps to indicate that it takes a momentary union with God in order to achieve a real insight into a man's relationship with his fellows.

The reconciliation to the idea of participation without illusion is pushed to fantastic new extremes in **"Teddy,"** in some ways Salinger's most unexpected story. In **"Teddy,"** reconciliation becomes Oriental resignation. The transition from the personal mysticism to the formal Eastern self-immolation which Teddy practices does not occur, however, without certain schizophrenic symptoms in both the form of the story and in its main character. It is the only one of Salinger's stories that is utterly incredible, and yet he goes to his usual pains to document its reality.

What Teddy, this ten-year-old Buddha, has achieved in Salinger's bargain with the East is, of course, invulnerability, the persistent wish of all bananafish. The knowledge that De Daumier-Smith comes to by hard Experience, Teddy is granted early through mystic revelation. He then withdraws, as all great religious figures have, to be better able to participate. In Teddy's case, he removes himself from the boorish concerns of a society represented by his father and sister in order that he may be invulnerable to the malice of his father and sister, and be able to do good in return. He writes in his diary, for example: "See if you can find daddy's army dog tags and wear them whenever possible. It won't kill you and he will like it."

The recent publication of **"Franny"** revived the dilemma of participation or withdrawal. Here, the Zen-Buddhist material is not as well integrated on a story level as in **"Teddy,"** since Franny merely wishes to believe in a way of living the validity of which Teddy has had satisfactory mystic revelation. But because the tension is more psychological in **"Franny,"** and because God is sought this side of oblivion, it is a more touching story.

In the main scene in the restaurant with her boyfriend, Franny is graphically split between the desire to withdraw and the need to participate. She has arrived to spend the weekend with Lane, already apprehensive that she will find the kind of insensitivity she has found in him many times before. She would like to be the good-time girl that Lane wants, but this time she cannot bear his egocentricity, his counterfeit participation in the world. She retreats to the stall in the Ladies' Room to weep for him and for all the others, one presumes, who, like Lane, are devoted to the Flaubertian view of society, that mean focus on personal vanity, which so offends Franny. Franny, a bananafish, sees all the beautiful possibilities instead, and she suffers for it. She tries to communicate with him again, finally withdraws once more and falls insensible to the ground. Her courage, however, has touched something in the boy at last. After her final collapse, he is kind to her, half understanding, but she ends making her final whispered appeal to God.

Pity for the bananafish ends with **"Franny."** The function of Salinger's two most recent stories, both long, didactic, and largely unsymmetrical, is to restore the stature of the bananafish. In **"Raise High the Roofbeam, Carpenters,"** he removes the shame from the disease by showing Seymour Glass as a superior man. In **"Zooey,"** he shows that reconciliation with society is possible if the bananafish, with courage, practices the act of Christian love.

"Raise High the Roofbeam, Carpenters" affirms the bananafish in spite of the fact that the reader knows that Seymour Glass is to end as Teddy did, embracing death. Its very title, first of all, is a paean for the bridegroom, a singularly appropriate symbol for all the Salinger heroes, who are young people, people uninitiated, unconsummated, unassimilated. The story thus is a celebration of experiences, rather than a dirge for them. Moreover, it celebrates for the first time, the sensitivity of the hero, marking perhaps a final surrender of the author's identification with the hero and a beginning of appreciation for him. If Seymour is a sick man, he is also a big man and that becomes an important thing here.

While the story explains the suicide of Seymour in **"Bananafish,"** it also makes that suicide seem a little irrelevant. It is Seymour's life, his unique way of looking at things that concerns Salinger here, and although he is obliged to mention the subsequent death of Seymour early in the story, he refers to it simply as "death," rather than suicide. For a change, the remark seems incidental, rather than a calculated understatement, the device Salinger consistently uses when he talks about what touches him particularly.

Concerned with Seymour's life rather than his death, Salinger is at last able to expose the bananafish here. Banana fever no longer seems the shame that it did in **"Pretty Mouth and Green My Eyes," "The Laughing Man," "For Esmé—with Love and Squa-**

lor," and in **"A Perfect Day for Bananafish"** itself where Seymour can express himself only to a little girl, and ambiguously at that. The secretly prying eyes of others he is unable to bear. Witness the curious scene on the elevator when he accuses a woman in the car of staring at his feet. This happens less than a minute before he puts a bullet through his head.

In **"Raise High The Roofbeam, Carpenters,"** the frank advocacy of Seymour enables Salinger to transcend the limits of the tight pseudo-poetic structure which hamstrings so much of modern short fiction. Because the story is partisan, it must be analytic as well as metaphoric. No longer deceived into thinking his characters are prey to simple grief or to bourgeois insensitivity, rather than to beauty, he is able to expose them at last. The loosening of form, which begins with **"For Esmé—with Love and Squalor,"** culminates with Seymour's throwing the stone at Charlotte, the affirmation of the effort for expression and communication even at the expense of exposure and pain.

Finally, it takes Zooey, in the story which bears his name, to communicate the new awareness and to act upon it. The redeeming union with the divine is the same as union with society, Zooey believes. If Buddy remains unreconstructable, Zooey, the youngest Glass son, comes to recognize that to be a deaf-mute in a high silk hat or a catcher in the rye is not the privilege of many.

Essentially, Zooey is a man of action. Appropriately enough, his profession is acting. Although he does not care much for a great deal of the world, he participates in it. He performs in television scripts which he detests; he meets people for lunch he does not like; he argues with his mother; he challenges his sister; he even dares to deface the shrine of the long-dead Seymour. In none of these things is he remotely self-immolating or contemplative, in the manner of Teddy; in none of them does he seek an "affinity." It is suggested that it is because Zooey alone among the Glasses has "forgiven" Seymour for his suicide that he is enabled to take a more involving and distinctly Western view of society. Zooey's final advice to his sister Franny, who has had aspirations to the stage, is: "The only thing you can do now, the only *religious* thing you can do, is *act.* Act for God, if you want to—be *God's* actress, if you want to. What could be prettier? You can at least try to, if you want to—there's nothing wrong in *try*ing."

Action then is the remedy here, and although remedies come and go in Salinger, it is perhaps most important because when action becomes an end in itself, it becomes possible to distinguish again between the deed and the doer. Zooey remonstrates with Franny about it: ". . . what I don't like—and what I don't think either Seymour or Buddy would like *either,* as a matter of fact—is the way you talk about all these people. I mean you just don't despise what they represent—you despise them. It's too damn personal, Franny. I mean it." Zooey's aim is to recognize that principles exist by which men live; and that without action, things are neither good nor bad. Principles vanish. The bananafish's mind is full of still photographs; action thaws these photographs; action again makes judgments possible. It forestalls the rapt contemplation of moments that have no meaning to others and which tend to isolate each individual in his own picture gallery. To transcend the particular for the sake of the general is to overcome the paralyzed moment for the sake of the principle which animates it.

Although this is a new step for Salinger, one must observe that throughout the story, he keeps Buddy's opinion in abeyance. In the speech quoted above, Zooey suggests that Buddy and Seymour agree with him about the distinction between the deed and the doer. But the shadow of Buddy and Seymour would suggest otherwise. Zooey's consent to participate is as much rebellion from as it is practice of the way of life of his older brothers. As a matter of cold fact, principles have always gotten in the way for the bananafish because principles, ideas, systems are too far away from life as the bananafish lives it. That is why every participation in the social system has turned out to be counterfeit in the end. (pp. 12-17)

William Wiegand, "J. D. Salinger: Seventy-Eight Bananas," in *Chicago Review,* Vol. 11, No. 4, Winter, 1958, pp. 3-19.

IHAB HASSAN

(essay date 1961)

[An Egyptian-born American critic, Hassan has written and edited numerous literary studies, including *Radical Innocence: The Contemporary American Novel*, from which the following commentary is excerpted. In a generally appreciative overview of Salinger's writings, Hassan discusses his characters' "rare quixotic gestures" and identifies them as central to the meaning of Salinger's fiction. Salinger's inclusion in Hassan's study is considered to have been significant in gaining Salinger credence among critics.]

The dramatic conflict which so many of Salinger's stories present obviously does not lend itself to sociological classification. It is more loving and particular, and it partakes of situations that have been traditionally available to literature. The conflict, however, suggests a certain polarity between what might be called, with all due exaggeration, the Assertive Vulgarian and the Responsive Outsider. Both types recur with sufficient frequency to warrant the distinction, and their inter-

play defines much that is most central to Salinger's fiction. The Vulgarian, who carries the burden of squalor, stands for all that is crude, venal, self-absorbed, and sequacious in our culture. He has no access to knowledge or feeling or beauty, which makes him all the more invulnerable, and his relationship to the world is largely predicated by Buber's I-It dyad. He or she can be rich or poor: . . . Sandra and Mrs. Snell in "**Down at the Dinghy,**" Joanie in "**Pretty Mouth and Green My Eyes,**" The Matron of Honor in "**Raise High the Roof Beam, Carpenters,**" Maurice, Stradlater, or any number of others in *The Catcher in the Rye.* These, in a sense, are Spiritual Tramps, as Seymour called his wife in "**A Perfect Day for Bananafish,**" though he might have better said it of her mother. The Outsider, on the other hand, carries the burden of love. The burden makes of him sometimes a victim, and sometimes a scapegoat saint. His life is like "a great inverted forest/with all foliage underground." It is a quick, generous, and responsive life, somehow preserved against hardness and corruption, and always attempting to reach out from its isolation in accordance with Buber's I-Thou dyad. Often there is something in the situation of the Outsider to isolate him, to set him off, however slightly, from the rest of mankind. He might be a child or an adolescent, might wear glasses or appear disfigured, might be Jewish, though seldom is he as crippled or exotic as the characters of Capote and McCullers often are. His ultimate defense, as Rilke, to whom Salinger refers, put it, is defenselessness. . . . Boo Boo Tannenbaum (Glass) and her son, Lionel, Seymour and other members of the Glass family, Holden and Phoebe, in the previous stories, are examples of that type.

The response of these outsiders and victims to the dull or angry world about them is not simply one of withdrawal: it often takes the form of a strange, quixotic gesture. The gesture, one feels sure, is the bright metaphor of Salinger's sensibility, the center from which meaning drives, and ultimately the reach of his commitment to past innocence and current guilt. It is a gesture at once of pure expression and of expectation, of protest and prayer, of aesthetic form and spiritual content—as Blackmur would say, it is behavior that sings. There is often something prodigal and spontaneous about it, something humorous or whimsical, something that disrupts our habits of gray acquiescence and revives our faith in the willingness of the human spirit. But above all, it gives of itself as only a *religious* gesture can. In another age, Cervantes endowed Don Quixote with the capacity to perform it, and so did Twain and Fitzgerald endow their best creations. For the gesture, after all, has an unmistakably American flourish. The quest of American adolescents, as we saw, has always been for an idea of truth. It is this very idea of truth that the quixotic gesture is constantly seeking to embody. The embodiment is style in action: the twist and tang, the stammering and improvisations, the glint and humor of Salinger's language. Hence the examples of . . . the man about to commit suicide who makes up a story about bananafish for a little girl, the lover who calls the sprained ankle of his sweetheart Uncle Wiggily, the young man who insists on giving half a chicken sandwich to a stranger, the college girl who trains herself to pray incessantly and does so in the toilet of a restaurant, and the bridegroom who is too happy to appear at his wedding. Out of context these may well sound trite or crazy; in their proper place they are nodes of dramatic significance.

But gesture is language too. The quixotic gesture, the central dramatic metaphor, to which Salinger has committed himself defines the limits of his language and the forms his fiction takes. When the gesture aspires to pure religious expression—this is one pole—language reaches into silence. To a writer of fiction, this is a holy dead end, much as the experiments of Mallarmé, say, impose a profane—that is, aesthetic—limit on the language of poetry. (One of "The Four Statements" of Zen, we recall, is: "No dependence upon words and letters.") When, on the other hand, the gesture reveals its purely satiric content—this is the other pole—language begins to lapse into sentimentality. This is the most persistent charge leveled against Salinger. Salinger's "sentimentality," however, is not obedient to the *New Yorker* doctrine of sardonic tenderness, which is really a way of grudging life emotions that the writer feigns to indulge. But if sentimentality means a response more generous than the situation seems objectively to warrant, then Salinger may choose to plead guilty. And he would be right to do so, for the spiritual facts of our situation invite us to reconceive our notions of dramatic objectivity, and the right kind of emotional excess, nowadays, can be as effective as the sharpest irony.

Between the poles of silence and sentiment, language reels and totters. Salinger's cumbersome experiments with character, tense, and point of view in his most recent stories betray his efforts to discover a language which can reconcile the worldless impulse of love to the discursive irony of squalor. In the past, while the quixotic gesture could still convey the force of his vision, reconciliation took the shape of the short story, that genre so richly exploited by the single lyric impulse seeking embodiment in dramatic form. But the quixotic motif seems no longer commensurate with the complex spiritual states by which Salinger has lately been possessed. Language must be refracted into its components—speech, letters, diaries, etc.—and the form of the short story itself must be broken and expanded into something that is neither a short story proper nor yet a novelette. In this development, the risks Salinger has taken with his art are contained in the

risks he must take with his religious view of things. (pp. 261-64)

The earliest stories of Salinger appeared, for the most part, in magazines to which we refer as slicks, though four of these were also published in the now defunct *Story*. The majority of these pieces makes an uneasy lot, and some are downright embarrassing—it is gratifying to find that Salinger has excluded them all from [*Nine Stories*]. (pp. 265-66)

The second phase of Salinger's career includes at least three stories which are among the very best he has written: **"Uncle Wiggily in Connecticut," "Down at the Dinghy,"** and **"For Esmé—with Love and Squalor."** This phase also marks the level of his most sustained achievement. The cellophane transparency and geometric outlines of the earlier pieces give way to a constant energy of perception and irritation of the moral sense. Here, in a world which has forfeited its access to the simple truth, we are put on to the primary fact of mendacity. Here, where the sources of love are frozen and responsiveness can only survive in clownish attire, we are jolted by the Zen epigraph: "We know the sound of two hands clapping. But what is the sound of one hand clapping?" (p. 267)

In **"A Perfect Day for Bananafish,"** the taste of life's corruption is so strong in the mouth of Seymour Glass, and the burden of self-alienation, even from his wife, Muriel, is so heavy, that suicide seems to him the only cleansing act possible. While Muriel is engaged in a drab and vindictive long-distance conversation with her mother, for whom the mere name of a fashionable analyst is insurance against all the ills and mysteries of the universe, Seymour entertains a little girl at their hotel beach. . . . The contrast between the monstrous and psychotic Seymour, as seen by his mother-in-law—she is genuinely worried about her daughter—in the first half of the story, and Seymour with Sybil at the beach makes the silent ironic statement of the piece. Yet even Sybil cannot prevent the world, ruthless as it is with the power of spiritual vulgarity, from collecting its toll. One feels, however, that the story needs the background of the later Glass family narratives to give Seymour's suicide its full reference.

If Seymour Glass . . . concedes the victory to the world much too easily, Walt Glass and Eloise, in **"Uncle Wiggily . . . ,"** do not. The plight of Eloise, who survived the tender and imaginative Walt to lead a conventional married life in Connecticut, is clear. The hysteria of Eloise focuses on her lonely and sensitive daughter, Ramona, who *could* be the illegitimate child of Walt, and is certainly the living reminder of the vision Eloise has compromised and the innocence she has lost. Again the contrasts between the embittered and knowing Eloise and her inane visitor, Mary Jane, between Walt, the dead lover, and Lou, the oafish husband, serve to heighten the inability of the self to reveal itself to another. All that is left to Eloise by way of recognition is the spontaneous and quixotic gesture of kissing the glasses of Ramona, whom she has bullied into conformity and disillusionment. In another story, **"The Laughing Man,"** the end of Innocence is more obviously compounded with the end to Romance, and the pressure of adult on boyhood disenchantment is rendered particularly effective by the use of a narrator who, like Lardner's narrators, serves to elicit from the situation more irony than they intend. . . . Here the story of the fabulous Laughing Man is itself the quixotic gesture which has the power to influence the youthful audience of boys, including the narrator of Salinger's story, but is powerless to save Gedsulski himself.

Wistful as these stories may appear, Salinger's ideas of innocence and romance, of the urgency of truth and readiness of imagination, take on a broad social meaning. The stories present in poignant, ironic, and roundabout ways the radical absence of communion; they define the scope of our guilt. (It is this helpless sense of *shame* that pieces like **"Just Before the War with the Eskimos"** and **"Pretty Mouth and Green My Eyes"** dramatize so fastidiously.)

The easy efficient gestures of social amenities, which usually conceal an abyss of human failure, are not even present in **"Down at the Dinghy."** Quite simply, the story is that of sensitive, four-year-old Lionel Tannenbaum who hears the housemaid, Sandra, denounce his father as a "big sloppy kike." Lionel does not fully understand the opprobrium of the term, but the tones and inflections of hate are unmistakable. He runs away to hide his shame and fear in a dinghy, from which his wise mother, née Boo Boo Glass, attempts to rescue him back to a troubled world:

> "Well, that isn't too terrible," Boo Boo said, holding him between the two vises of her arms and legs. "That isn't the *worst* that could happen." She gently bit the rim of the boy's ear. "Do you know what a kike is, baby?"

> Lionel was either unwilling or unable to speak up at once. At any rate, he waited till the hiccupping aftermath of his tears had subsided a little. Then his answer was delivered, muffled but intelligible, into the warmth of Boo Boo's neck. "It's one of those things that go up in the *air*," he said. "With *string* you hold."

The ignorance of Lionel is as consonant with the immediate requirements of the story as it is with Salinger's larger intentions. Here as elsewhere, what Salinger has undertaken to discover is that old, ironic discrepancy between illusion and reality. But in an age of mass reactions and semantic instability, the distance between illusion and reality must increase to the extent that the opportunities of self-deception are multiplied. In these circumstances, the child becomes both the dramatic analogue and corrective to our modes of awareness, both the victim and savior of our squalor. His lack of experience is at once parallel and antithetical to our blind immersion in experience and his natural sagacity is the corrective to our practiced insensibility. It is much as if Salinger meant innocence to be, in our particular situation, the redemption of our ignorance. And it is perhaps only by the grace of something like the tender playfulness which Boo Boo exhibits toward her outraged son that we can recapture the sense of reality, beyond ignorance, beyond innocence. We concede this ungrudgingly, and in conceding still ask: is this all that so gifted an author can do with the deep-down complexity of a Jew's fate in our culture?

The mode of irony, shield of Perseus against the Medusa face of our time, qualifies the elegiac motive of Salinger's stories. But even irony must exhaust its resources, and a time must come for love to show its face in the noonday light. To the unabashed lyricism of **"For Esmé—with Love and Squalor,"** one can only respond joyously. The story is a modern epithalamium, written on the occasion of Esmé's wedding. The narrator, who carries his autobiographical burden sprightly and high, recollects the time he was a sergeant stationed with the invasion forces in England. On a rainy afternoon he wanders into a church, and is struck by the angelic voice of Esmé, a girl singing in a choir. Later he meets her, escorted by a governess and a younger brother, in a tearoom. She rescues him from boredom and loneliness by her wonderful gifts of pertness and sensibility—precocity, which is the concession adults make to the understanding of children, is not the point of the story. The young lady—for she has a title—promises to write him, and in return asks him to write for her a story of squalor. Sometime afterward, we see him at the front, in the third person, suffering from an acute case of battle fatigue. The intolerable Clay, an eternal vulgarian, is his only companion. Squalor, real and tangible like the dust of death, has settled all about him—until he finds a battered package from Esmé, in which she has quixotically enclosed her dead father's watch. The narrator can finally fall asleep, for he knows that hell, which Dostoyevsky defined as the suffering of being unable to love, has been kept in abeyance for another day. The inscription a German Nazi woman had scrawled on Goebbels' *Die Zeit ohne Beispiel*, "Dear God, life is hell," is superseded by the statement of Father Zossima which the narrator appends to it. The horrendous social fact of our century and the outstanding spiritual motive of the age—genocide and love—are united in the history of a single American soldier, Staff Sergeant X. Thus the style of personal encounter in the first half of the story redeems the waste and anonymity of the second half. Thus may love overreach squalor as only love can, and the sound of two hands clapping may be heard the world around. (pp. 267-72)

The view that Salinger's most recent work predicts something of a new trend is vaguely supported by the troubled, spiritualistic bent which the latest six narratives share. The content of these stories invites some comparison with the ideals of Mahayana Buddhism and primitive Christianity, and also invites the condemnation of those who feel that "mysticism" is out of place in literature. The trend, nevertheless, is a natural outcome of Salinger's earlier interests. For it is not difficult to imagine how protestant disaffiliation may lead to holy unattachment, and how mysticism may appear, beyond childhood or adolescence, the last resort of innocence. If love is to survive in a world where personal communication has signally failed, then it can at least survive in universal compassion: love betrayed into dumbness may still speak in silence. (p. 276)

Two of the cardinal assumptions in Salinger's work find expression in the Buddhist ideas of *tanha,* or blind self-demandingness, and of *moksha,* a state of liberation achieved by the kind of impersonal compassion which "The Parable of the Mustard Seed" exemplifies. In Mahayana Buddhism particularly, a religion of the Middle Way which avoids the excesses of worldliness and asceticism, the characters of Salinger seem to find a gentle and practical ideal against which their actions may be gauged. The ideal is matter-of-fact rather than mystical, and its emphasis in the Zen Buddhist variant, to which Salinger refers most directly, is on effortless and continuous love, on the superrational insights of the Koan exercises, on the poetic concreteness of Haiku, on the virtues of silence, and on the unmediated vision of nature. For Zen is essentially a condition of being in which, without losing our identity, we are at one with the universe, and it requires, as does Haiku poetry, a certain harmony between our imaginative and spiritual responsiveness to all things. It becomes evident that these qualities of Zen define some of the interests which Salinger has constantly kept at heart, and that Zen itself, in Salinger's work, makes up to an odd way of criticizing contemporary failures. (pp. 276-77)

Art, unfortunately, sometimes falls short of the best spiritual intentions. This is evident in the two narratives which usher Salinger's "religious phase" in **"Teddy,"** the story of the strange boy who believes in Vedantic incarnation and detachment, and who vaguely foresees death, is much less satisfactory because it draws on notions that are alien to the West than because it fails to relate, within the dramatic structure of its narrative, the egoism of Teddy's parents and the ambiguous malice of his sister to the peculiar source of his own repose. There is also in **"Teddy,"** and much more in **"De Daumier-Smith's Blue Period,"** an uneasy juxtaposition of aesthetic and spiritual motives which are sometimes blurred and sometimes too simply resolved. In the latter story, the central character recollects, in manhood, the guiding revelation of his adolescence.

On the surface, the revelation takes a quasi-mystical form. De Daumier-Smith discovers that art is less important than the sacramental view of life, which can itself transform, better than the creative imagination, the objects of ugliness and misery—the enameled urinals and bedpans of an orthopedic appliance shop—into "a shimmering field of exquisite, twice-blessed enamel flowers." But as Gwynn and Blotner have argued in their pamphlet on Salinger, a sexual element enters into the story—witness the imagery—and brings to a religious situation the Oedipal complications of a young art instructor in love with a nun whose drawings—and only the drawings—he has seen. The piece serves to remind us that the power of sexuality is never directly acknowledged in Salinger's work, and that love, when it is not refined into a transcendent or artistic ideal, centers on relations from which sex is notably absent: the love of a woman for a dead sweetheart or a boy for his little sister, or the Glasses for one another. (pp. 277-78)

"It is the duty of the man of letters to supervise the culture of language, to which the rest of culture is subordinate," Allen Tate has said, "and to warn us when our language is ceasing to forward the ends proper to man. The end of social man is communion in time through love, which is beyond time." The style J. D. Salinger has created shows clearly what human ends may be considered proper, and it carries its own warnings about the ways language may come to fail man. Beneath the tingling surface, the constant play of humor and perception, the ebullience of emotions, which are all part of Salinger's generosity, there always lurks the sad reality of human failure; and it is much as if the responsiveness, both spiritual and imaginative, of Salinger's language is constantly trying not only to reveal but also to expiate the burden of these failures.

Thus whimsey and humor, when they are not simply forms of facetiousness, prove themselves to be quixotic modes of communion or understanding. Vincent Caulfield, for instance, hits it off immediately with little Mattie Gladwaller [in an early story] when he says to her: "If A has three apples, and B leaves at three o'clock, how long will it take C to row five thousand miles upstream, bounded on the north by Chile?" Seymour's funny comments on bananafish or Walt's quip about Uncle Wiggily—this is a standard Glass technique—are likewise little testaments of love. There are times, however, when Salinger's wit, itself a form of satiric awareness, seems more biting and hyperbolic— Franny describes a Bennington-Sarah Lawrence type of girl by saying that she "looked like she'd spent the whole train ride in the john, sculpting or painting or something, or as though she had a leotard under her dress." The source of humor can also be found in the intimate and disconcerting gesture which reveals actor to witness, and witness to reader, in a peculiar light— . . . Spencer picks his nose, making out "like he was only pinching it," while doling out advice to Holden Caulfield. But of the different kinds of humor Salinger uses, humor of contrast and situation, of action and characterization, of sudden perception and verbal formulation—Salinger seems to be fond of strung expressions like "the God-and-Walter Winchell section of the Stork Club"—of all these it may be said that their ultimate function is to sharpen our sense of the radical discrepancy between what is and what ought to be.

The discrepancy is apparent in the verbal nature of his style which itself attempts to convey the difficulty of communication between human beings. Adolescents as well as adults are constantly groping for the life-giving Word. Their recourse to such expressions as "Oh, I don't know," and "You know what I mean," to oaths and obscenities, to trailing, fragmentary speeches and fierce emphases on neutral syllables, to solecisms, repetitions, clichés, and asides, betrays both the urgency of their need and the compulsion to save their utterances from the fate of mere ejaculation.

Even the structure of Salinger's stories—the obsessive use of first person narration or intimate dialogue, of epistolary and diary techniques, of the confessional tone—even the structure calls our attention to the tight, lucent caul from which the captive self seldom escapes. It is not accidental that the recording consciousness of the later stories, Buddy Glass, describes himself as "the odd man out," or that so many crucial experiences seem to take place within the tiled sanctum of the Glass bathrooms. The rambling, ranting, devotional forms of these narratives equally deny the classic precepts of the short story and the well-made novelette. As Buddy puts it, the short story form eats up fat little undetached writers like him whole. This is quite in keeping with Salinger's purpose, which is to discover the form of confession and communion, the way the self can be made available to another, the point at which the irrelevant fact and transcendental idea silently meet. The purpose is not easy to achieve. Two warring impulses of the soul distend the shape of Salinger's most recent fiction: one cries in outrage at a world dominated by sham and spiritual vulgarity, the other knows, as Seymour did, that Christ ordered us to call no man a Fool. Revulsion and holiness make up the rack on which Salinger's art still twitches.

In retrospect, the artistic identity of Salinger, which also may be called his limitation, appears clear enough. Despite his striking gifts for dialogue—Salinger had once expressed the hope of becoming a playwright—the broad sense of dramatic participation is lacking in his fiction. The lack is not occasioned by the refusal of Salinger's characters to engage reality; rather is it occasioned by their insistence to engage no more of reality than they can ultimately criticize. Their access to social facts remains limited. And their very identity, their recurrent types and their intransigence

toward experience, often admits to their vision—and to ours, since no other vision qualifies theirs—such extremes of corruption and innocence as make the complex entanglements of life beyond their reach. Then, too, the cult they make of vulnerability, of amateurism in life, which is the very opposite of Hemingway's cult of professionalism, diffuses the pressure of Salinger's insight onto a rather thin surface. The quixotic gesture—Seymour searching for God by poking his finger into ashtrays—is made to carry a heavier burden of meaning than it can sustain. Love averts itself easily in whimsey or laughter. The highest candor requires us to praise things by adjectives no more complex than the word "nice."

But from the early search for innocence to the later testament of love, from the slick adequacy of his earlier style to the tense lyrical form of his later, if not latest, stories, Salinger has kept faith with the redeeming powers of outrage and compassion. His faith in these has not always allowed him to reconcile their shifting focus or to create the forms of dramatic permanence. When reconciliation is granted, when the rare, quixotic gesture, striking through, becomes the form of fiction, incarnate and ineluctable, we see Salinger at last for what he is: an American poet, his thin and intelligent face all but lost among the countless faces of the modern city, his vision, forever lonely and responsive, troubled by the dream of innocence and riddled by the presence both of love and of squalor. What saves Salinger's vision from sentimentality is the knowledge that no man can give an object more tenderness than God accords to it. His heroes, children, adolescents, or adult victims to the affluence of their own spirit, play upon our nostalgia for a mythic American past. They also manage to raise nostalgia to the condition of hope. (pp. 286-89)

Ihab Hassan, "J. D. Salinger: Rare Quixotic Gesture," in his *Radical Innocence: Studies in the Contemporary American Novel,* Princeton University Press, 1961, pp. 259-89.

MALCOLM BRADBURY
(essay date 1969)

[An English novelist, short story writer, playwright, and editor, Bradbury is also regarded as one of the United Kingdom's most respected authorities on the modernist tradition in novels. In the following essay, excerpted from his acclaimed work *What Is a Novel?*, he examines *The Catcher in the Rye* as a picaresque novel.]

At first sight, *The Catcher in the Rye* seems to be a fairly loose comic novel of adventures, some of them amusing and some not, which happen to a boy of sixteen when he slips away from his prep-school in Pennsylvania and goes off to New York on his own. Over a period of forty-eight hours, from the time he is expelled from the school to the time he rejoins his family, Holden Caulfield, who narrates his own story, is in a kind of limbo, a state of extreme freedom. He has escaped both from his responsibilities and from those who are responsible for him, and it would seem that, in the big city, almost anything could happen to him. A great deal does; once he is in the city, the novel's action moves rapidly through a great many settings and involves many different kinds of characters, people met casually from the crowd and then lost to sight again. In short, the novel is picaresque, proceeding not through old-established relationships in a stable community but by passing encounters in a constantly changing one. These adventures can be in significant sequence, which can be of a very loose kind, illustrating how very various and unexpected life is, or of a very tight kind. And I think that normally, as we reflect on a novel, we would start looking for lines of development that link the sequence together or explain *how* it develops, why these events should follow in this order. So we can ask all sorts of questions: about the world that is explored, and about the character. Does that world have any features that make it consistent? By the end of the novel, have we acquired a sense of the workings of one whole sector of society? Or is it perhaps consistent in a different way: do, for instance, most of the episodes seem in some way to illustrate how immoral or corrupt society, or this society, is? And what of the character's way of experiencing his movement through the novel? Does he or she develop, undergo a psychological or emotional change, or learn something from his experiences? (pp. 58-9)

[Is *The Catcher in the Rye*] a picaresque novel of adventures, perhaps mainly calculated to produce a comic effect? Is it a novel about the squalor of the world and how it cannot really be lived in, a novel presenting Holden as a 'rebellious saint' trying to overcome squalor with love and protect the innocent against life? Or is it a novel about a boy who sees through the sham of his society, recognises it as commercial and exploitative: in short, a classic work of protest, as other critics have suggested? Or is it perhaps a novel less reacting against the given world than a novel of quest, involving a psychological development in which Holden seeks to see how his beliefs and attitudes square with those of an adult world that he is on the verge of entering? All these amount to very different suggestions about how the novel coheres: about the primary basis of its development and structure. And to come to a view of it, we will need to look closely at the whole book and try to come to some conclusions about what Salinger is seeking to develop as he writes. There is not space enough

to do this in the kind of detail we should, in our own minds. And even if we have done it properly we could, of course, still disagree; indeed the book itself may thrive on such an ambiguity.

How, then, does the novel develop? Let us look first at the world in which the action is conducted, and how we are led through it. Clearly, we are led by a narrator who is not the novelist but is an agent implicated in the action: who is, in fact, at its very centre. The world is formed entirely around him and what happens to him. He leads us through the two main settings of the story: Pencey Prep, the exclusive boys' school in Pennsylvania where he is a boarder, and New York City, or rather those parts of it that are likely to be known to a college boy who is a resident. The social world of the book is a middle-class one, and Salinger/Holden creates it with a kind of lovingness, a realistic fascination with places and *mores,* tones of voice and styles of behaviour, that give the book a dense specificity. Holden is a very exact recorder of his situation and what is more, of his environment, which he fills out even as he reacts to it. He is always observing, watching, registering; the world is a crucial lesson in all its detail. And because he reacts to what he understands, we see more than the surface of this world; we see its inconsistencies, its oddities of behaviour, its primary obsessions. The obsessions are with wealth and getting on, with money and success, with ordering and systematising experience so that it fits those forms of success, with refusing to be interested in failure. So many of the events and settings illustrate all this, in precise ways; Holden moves from one scene to another in the narrative present, then illustrates from the narrative past, in order to build up the web, a web from which the human centre is often missing. The events through which he passes are vignettes of a fairly consistent culture, in which—at least by Holden's view—most people behave in the same kinds of way.

So the society has a general tendency, as we see it through Holden and through the novelist. But it is not a society created as a social realist would create it; Salinger isn't attempting to show us the dark underside of American society or the complex social tensions of urban life. He illustrates through manners and interludes, and as the novel builds up and we relate those vignettes, we recognise a squalid consistency in the entire order while not, I think, finding only a basically social *origin* for that consistency. In other words, it does involve a consistency in the particular society of America in the late 1940s in which Holden lives; but it also involves a consistency in the world of adult life as such. Adulthood is seen very much as a state of social acceptance—or at least is seen, as in Mr. Spencer and Mr. Antolini, as a way of thinking about life in terms of being mature and thinking about the future and having a realistic view of one's place in the world. But that is because adults tend to think like that, by a kind of adult necessity. And of course Holden is trying to be an adult, to be mature, in certain respects at least. He wants to appear sexually and socially sophisticated, and a lot of the comedy derives from his assumption of very sophisticated attitudes. But at the same time he stands somewhat outside this society. This is not because he protests in a general way about its basic relationships as such; it is not in that sense a novel of protest. It is rather because he stands at a time of life when he must neither accept nor reject it completely; where he is innocent enough to gaze in bewildered wonder at its inconsistencies; but where of course he is ironically implicated, because boys of sixteen must grow up into men.

This society is of course created by the author, who invents all its details, but it is created in relation to Holden and he is made capable of providing a judgment on it. The judgments need not be the author's; that, too, is something we must sense out. As far as Holden is concerned, it is not an invention but the given world he has to live in. So how is it evaluated? To a large extent, of course, it is evaluated through Holden's judgments, which at first often seem comically quirky but which gradually take on a consistency and depth. By choosing to evaluate it through Holden, Salinger of course is able to explore not only the society but Holden too. And in doing that he is able to make Holden's perspective, which at the beginning seems simply one of amusingly created responses, into a moral integrity. And that too is a principle of the novel's development; the events and episodes being calculated toward doing that as well as toward exploring the social world. That is to say, most of the events in the novel, however episodic they may seem at first, are calculated either to extend his knowledge of the world as it is or to reinforce or extend his particular values and preferences. This means that Holden's values don't just come out of the world as it is, the world we explore, but have certain more personal sources. Holden sees, as we have said, from an adolescent perspective; but it isn't the perspective of all adolescents, as the school scenes at Pencey show. Rather they come from Holden's way of grouping certain significant moments in his life and putting a special value on these. And these moments usually have to do either with nostalgia about childhood, or children, or about his own family: especially his sister Phoebe and his dead brother Allie. This gives him a localised moral world from which to see life. So the ethic Holden expresses is more or less present in him from the first. He normally expresses it in terms of strong immediate responses and preferences, stated through an evocative, value-laden, adolescent slang ('It made me puke'; 'She gave me a pain in the ass'). Holden is perfectly open to experience; he does, however, have strong convictions about it. And

to see all these effects working—the creation of a broad world, the creation of values and attitudes toward it, and the creation of a smaller world of the family and children out of which these attitudes come—we need to start grouping certain of the scenes of the book and getting them into perspective.

There is not space to do this in detail, but a few broad hints here can be given; rather they are tentative suggestions. In the early part of the book, the events of the day at Pencey, on the Saturday of the football game, are given in loose sequence. Holden does this and that; people come in and out; from time to time Holden remembers something in the past and introduces it in the telling. The sequence builds up to Holden's 'impulse' to leave that night and rest up in New York for a few days. But there is in fact a certain degree of consistency about what we are told. For instance, we see the school in two different lights: the light of its function in the world, to minister to the needs of society, to attempt to mould boys for their social roles; the light of its more 'real' culture of dormitories, dating, bull-sessions in which the boys compare sexual experiences. Holden is in fact separated from both cultures, which in fact link up with one another. He is not separated completely, though. He clearly needs to withdraw from the school's world of damaged innocence, but at the same time he needs to involve his affections in it, and 'miss' it. His emotions take him backwards toward nostalgia but forward to new events.

When he gets to New York, the same pattern extends and also gets complicated. On the one hand it is a confusing, anonymous and vast city, a city for growing up in; a city of adulthood where things are not what they seem and the signs of turmoil are finally those dirty words about sex that are written on the walls and cannot be erased. But it is also the city of Holden's childhood, and of other children. Holden's movements and emotions again seem casual; but he does have certain set patterns to follow deriving from both of these versions of the city. He knows college-set New York, sophisticated and mildly experienced: you meet girls under the clock at the Biltmore, you go to the theatre and the skating rink at Radio City, you go to Eddie's in the Village and listen to jazz. You ask for liquor and if the waiter thinks you are under age you drink coke. But behind that map of Manhattan lies another—the schoolchild's New York, an unsophisticated world of the lake in Central Park, the Museum of Natural History, the zoo, the carousel. Holden explores both worlds at once and tries to bring them into relation. So the episodes of this section are very mixed but again have certain patterns to them. Some involve salutary shocks about the world ahead (the episode with the whore and the elevator man); others are both instructive and salutary (the conversation with Luce or Mr. Antolini, with its ambiguous conclusion in Antolini's apparent homosexual advance); and some seem to suggest a role for Holden in relation to childhood—he can be a catcher in the rye, the adult who is the protector of childish innocence. Over these episodes, Holden obviously develops and his attitudes change. He is hunting for his own adulthood, but doesn't want to lose his childhood. He sees his childhood dropping away from him (as in the scene . . . when, after recalling the joys of going to the museum, he decides not to go in). He realises the impossibility of rubbing out all the dirty words from the world. He also realises that many of the characters who might help him to an adult world finally disappoint him. He ends up in the middle of a complex of contradictions. He thinks he will leave town and 'go out west and all'. But he doesn't, because Phoebe persuades him not to; and he ends the sequence apparently as the catcher in the rye, watching from the sides as Phoebe turns and turns on the carousel of her childhood and feeling 'so damn happy all of a sudden'. (pp. 60-4)

The scene is, in a sense, more than Holden says it is, because it not only tells his happiness but draws together various themes and depends on various contrasts—with the commercial Christmas-time we have just been seeing, for example. It recreates the pattern of the 'catcher in the rye' story: Holden as the older, protective watcher observing the happiness of childhood and its lack of concern about where it is going. Holden wears his hunting cap, a protective device he has kept donning through the story, and which has been associated with childhood: Phoebe has just been wearing it, and it has almost become for us a mildly symbolic badge of innocence. It is the novelist who creates this sense of significance, finally; particularly in the interesting verbal ambiguity of the last line, which suggests that religious feeling is what, in an oblique and unstated way, Holden has been looking for. The absence of God, the absence of veneration for things, seems here to be redeemed; we recall other moments like this one, such as the scene where Holden refuses to throw snowballs at the car and the fire hydrant because they 'looked so nice and white'. If the image serves Holden as a secure moment of happiness, it serves the reader even more. But there are also ironies in it that are surely beyond Holden's seeing. It starts to rain, and the hunting cap gives him 'a lot of protection, in a way' but doesn't stop him getting soaked. Holden has already been feeling ill, and the next thing we learn—Holden deliberately doesn't give the reasons or the details—is that this is followed by illness. 'I practically got T. B.,' Holden has earlier told us, from his post-narrative position. Holden's real power to protect childhood, moreover, is already in question; and, as in the image of the catcher on the cliff, with Holden himself threatened with toppling over backwards too, the scene suggests that his position is neither lasting nor safe. He does not belong on the innocent roundabout of the young; he is

out and exposed to the weather. His idealised image is real enough here, but also qualified—and really by the novelist, who would seem to be suggesting in the situation more than Holden actually understands or knows.

This brings us back to the question of the point of view of the book. The main action takes place some time before the time of writing; but between those two points in time something has happened to Holden, which is not stated directly by him. Holden has indeed gone 'out west and all', but not in the way he intended—he is in hospital on the west coast, apparently with something like T. B. but also under psychiatric treatment. . . . All this brings alive in the story those signs of oncoming illness we have had touched into the telling; Holden's feeling 'spooky' and his getting wet in the rain; the warnings of Mr. Antolini about 'This fall I think you're riding for'. This involves additional meanings—meanings beyond Holden's way of looking at these events at this time and place—and these have to be worked into the story by the novelist: the novelist who in some fuller sense *does* know what the story means. Salinger has created a world of very immediate experiences and actions; created a narrator who is very open to experience and does to a considerable extent interpret it for us; but there are certain touches of distance that separate novelist and his narrator Holden.

The question of whether Holden is a reliable narrator, a sane or honest one, is one possible area of separation, but perhaps not the most important. Holden's engaging admission that the story is 'crazy', 'madman stuff ', doesn't so much throw doubt on his accuracy or viewpoint as encourage us to respect his independence. But it does provide a way in which he is seeing the story in a different way from us. The real touches of distance come from tone and technique. At one level, they come from the comedy, which makes Holden sympathetically farcical. But even that is understandable in terms of his viewpoint. More important is the way Salinger creates a contradiction in Holden; between his essential openness to experience and his essential innocence. All that is important to Holden comes out of life, and so his attitudes can be presented as moments of immediate emotional response that flow out of the run of the living. But it is innocence that makes Holden open to experience; and it is also experience that is the obverse of innocence. One has to grow up, face 'reality', be mature. The childish eye cannot *remain* childish. So Holden's adventures bring him to the edge of the crucial cliff that brings the innocent out of childhood and which is—in this novel, surely—a version of the fall of man. 'I think that one of these days', he (Mr. Antolini) said, 'you're going to have to find out where you want to go. And then you've got to start going there'. Holden sees himself that simply by continuing through the line of experience one reaches a point where the vision is questioned. Hence perhaps his getting run down; hence perhaps the gap between novelist and narrator; hence the discovery that Holden is thinking of going back to school, and his experiences must start opening out again. (pp. 65-7)

The story, then, focuses on a crucial phase in Holden's life, the point at which one crosses the line from innocence to experience. The crossing involves a fall and a decline; it also involves a kind of moral schizophrenia. The innocent eye involves a love of the world, an appreciation of it, an attempt to reconcile the love and the squalor in it. But the squalor itself threatens to engulf the innocent eye. Holden comes to learn that 'you can't ever find a place that's nice and peaceful, because there isn't any'. The theme of the novel is indeed in some sense religious: how do we come to accept a world in some respects evil and corrupt, yet is our only world. The presence of the novelist in the themes and episodes raises these questions, and raises them beyond and outside Holden. He, in fact, must go on to grow up; but the innocence of vision he presents may help us to perceive the world in a different way. So we, in seeing not only Holden but the way the novelist has created Holden and his world, see the book as a much more enduring meaning than Holden does. We know, more than he does, what to think about it; we know it as a fictional work, a created whole. (p. 67)

To a considerable extent, *The Catcher in the Rye* is a book that follows life through with an empirical curiosity, and many of the things in it are surely designed to interest in that life for its own sake. At the same time, it is also concerned with making central and crucial a particular point in human experience—the point at which the child becomes adult and at which an innocent and hopeful love, a desire to protect life, becomes a profound human problem. Holden's special world does not stay intact, but it has been imagined and created up to the limit of its possibilities, and out of it a value and a meaning emerges. It is a value and meaning that comes from Salinger's control and management; and we will not really understand it unless we respond, whether consciously or unconsciously, to that control and management. It consists of a story that moves us through a social world and a moral world internal to that story, and it is up to us to look how the values by which we judge the story come out of what is given of that internal world. (pp. 67-8)

Malcolm Bradbury, "Reading a Novel," in his *What Is a Novel?* Edward Arnold (Publishers) Ltd., 1969, pp. 57-69.

SOURCES FOR FURTHER STUDY

Belcher, William F., and Lee, James W., eds. *J. D. Salinger and the Critics.* Belmont, CA: Wadsworth Publishing, 1962, 179 p.

Reprints ten critical essays on Salinger's stories and several on *The Catcher in the Rye.*

Hamilton, Ian. *In Search of J. D. Salinger.* New York: Random House, 1988, 222 p.

Controversial biography that prompted Salinger to initiate a successful lawsuit to halt its publication. Revised according to court orders, this biography focuses on the years prior to Salinger's retreat in the 1960s and draws largely from early letters by Salinger.

Laser, Marvin, and Fruman, Norman. *Studies in J. D. Salinger: Reviews, Essays, and Critiques of "The Catcher in the Rye" and Other Fiction.* New York: Odyssey Press, 1963, 272 p.

Critical anthology focusing primarily on *The Catcher in the Rye.* Among the reprinted essays are several on general subjects and the short fiction, including four interpretations by various critics of "For Esmé—with Love and Squalor."

Lundquist, James. *J. D. Salinger.* New York: Frederick Ungar Publishing, 1979, 194 p.

Critical study examining Salinger's continued popularity in spite of his long lapse in publishing. The book also contains chapters on Zen elements in *Nine Stories* and the Glass family series.

Modern Fiction Studies 12, No. 3 (Autumn 1966).

Issue devoted to Salinger. Among the seven articles included are pieces on *The Catcher in the Rye*, "For Esmé—with Love and Squalor," and "Pretty Mouth and Green My Eyes," as well as a selected checklist of criticism.

Wisconsin Studies in Contemporary Literature 4 (Winter 1963).

Whole issue on Salinger. Writers represented include Ihab Hassan, Joseph L. Blotner, and Donald M. Fiene, who contributed a primary and secondary bibliography.

George Sand

1804-1876

(Pseudonym of Amandine Aurore Lucile Dupin Dudevant) French novelist, dramatist, and essayist.

INTRODUCTION

Sand was one of France's most celebrated and controversial writers. Extremely prolific, she wrote effortlessly, as she said, "much as another person might garden." Yet despite her spontaneous method of composition, she maintained an amazing richness of style and unity of construction. Henry James said of her, "no writer has produced such great effects with an equal absence of premeditation." She produced nearly sixty novels, a lengthy autobiography, numerous essays, twenty-five plays, and approximately 20,000 letters. Relatively few of her works are studied today, however, and she is primarily remembered for her bold behavior as a young woman, wearing trousers, smoking cigars, and openly engaging in love affairs with prominent artistic figures including French novelist and dramatist Prosper Mérimée, French poet Alfred de Musset, and an infamous nine-year liaison with Polish pianist and composer Frédéric Chopin. The fascination with Sand as a personality is evidenced in the numerous biographies detailing every facet of her life, but serious critical studies of her work are lacking.

Sand's parents, who married one month before her birth, were of dissimilar backgrounds: her mother was a bird trainer's daughter while her father was an officer, only a few generations removed from royalty. Following her father's death when she was four, Sand was entrusted to her paternal grandmother's care and was raised at the family estate of Nohant in Berry, a historical region in central France. At eighteen, Sand married a local army officer, Casimir Dudevant, and soon became the mother of two children. Although the first years of marriage and motherhood were happy, Sand became increasingly restless and, in 1831, left her husband and moved to Paris, determined to pursue a literary career. With the help of Jules Sandeau, Sand wrote several articles published in the Parisian newspaper *Le*

Figaro under the pseudonym Jules Sand. Following the publication of two novels, also written in collaboration with Sandeau, she began her career in earnest, writing independently under the name of George Sand.

Sand's years in Paris developed into a series of colorful and notorious affairs, including a brief encounter with Mérimée and a six-year involvement with de Musset. Sand later fell in love with and actively pursued Chopin. Initially put-off by her unusual way of life, Chopin soon became enchanted by Sand's unique charm and intelligence. Their nine-year liaison culminated in a period of great artistic productivity for both. In addition to her romantic involvements, Sand developed lasting friendships with such French contemporaries as novelist Honoré de Balzac, critic Charles Sainte-Beuve, and painter Eugène Delacroix. One of her most significant literary friendships was with novelist Gustave Flaubert, begun later in life and well-documented in their published correspondence. Opposites in virtually every respect, they vigorously debated their conflicting literary philosophies. Following her death, Flaubert said, "One had to know her as I knew her to realize . . . the immensity of tenderness in that genius. She will remain one of the splendors of France and unmatched in her glory."

Critics usually divide Sand's literary career into four periods. The works of her first period reflect her rebellion against the bonds of marriage and deal largely with the relationships between men and women. Clearly influenced by English poet Lord Byron and French philosopher Jean-Jacques Rousseau, Sand wrote romantic novels full of passionate personal revolt and ardent feminism, attitudes which went against societal conventions and outraged her early British and American critics. These early novels, including *Indiana* (1832), *Lélia* (1833), and *Jacques* (1834), were extremely successful and established Sand as an important literary voice for her generation. Her second period, characterized by such novels as *Consuelo* (1842-43) and *Le meunier d'Angibault* (1845; *The Miller of An-*

gibault), reflects Sand's increasing concern with contemporary social and philosophical problems. These novels were strongly influenced by French philosopher and politician Pierre Leroux, and deal specifically with humanitarianism, Christian socialism, and Republicanism. Considered by many to be her least plausible works, their tone is often didactic and their plots obviously contrived. Sand next wrote pastoral novels, depicting rural scenes and peasant characters. Set in her native Berry *La mare au diable* (1846; *The Haunted Marsh*) and *François le champi* (1847-8; *Francis the Waif*) were inspired by her love of the French countryside and her sympathy with the peasants. Realistic in background detail and distinguished by their gentle idealism, they are considered by many critics to be Sand's finest novels. Although she continued writing until her death, few of the works written after her pastoral period are remembered today. The most interesting and lasting products of her later years are her autobiography, *Histoire de ma vie* (1854-55; *My Life*), and her voluminous *Correspondance, 1812-1876* (1883-95).

Considering the moral climate of her time and her open hostility to societal conventions, it was perhaps inevitable that Sand should become better known for her personal life than for her considerable literary accomplishments. From the beginning of her career, Sand's flamboyant lifestyle interfered with serious critical assessment of her works. However, although moral prejudice dominated British and American criticism of her works through the 1860s, she eventually won acceptance as an artist during her own lifetime and is now noted for her bold exploration of such issues as sexual freedom and independence for women. While Sand is not ranked among the finest French writers, the importance of her contribution to nineteenth-century French literature is acknowledged.

(For further information about Sand's life and works, see *Nineteenth-Century Literature Criticism*, Vol. 2.)

CRITICAL COMMENTARY

JOSEPH MAZZINI
(essay date 1839)

[In the following excerpt, Mazzini counters critical accusations of immorality in Sand's early novels *Indiana* and *Lélia*.]

[George Sand] has suffered—she revolted,—she has

struggled—she has sought, hoped, found; and she has told us *all*. The long series of her compositions form a grand confession. Spirits young, pure, and innocent, not worn by unhappiness, whom contact with the world has not yet endowed with the knowledge of evil, may well—perhaps, should—abstain from reading it; but let the rest, numerous as they are, boldly go

Principal Works

Indiana (novel) 1832
  [Indiana, 1881]
Valentine (novel) 1832
  [Valentine, published in The Masterpieces of George Sand, 1902]
Lélia (novel) 1833
  [Lélia, 1978]
Jacques (novel) 1834
  [Jacques, 1847]
André (novel) 1835
  [André, 1847]
Mauprat (novel) 1837
  [Mauprat, 1847]
Spiridion (novel) 1838-39; published in periodical Revue des deux mondes
  [Spiridion, 1842]
Le compagnon du tour de France (novel) 1841
  [The Companion of the Tour of France, 1847]
Consuelo (novel) 1842-43; published in periodical La Révue indépendante
  [Consuelo, 1846]
Jeanne (novel) 1844

Le meunier d'Angibault (novel) 1845
  [The Miller of Angibault, 1847]
La mare au diable (novel) 1846
  [The Haunted Marsh, 1848]
François le champi (novel) 1847-48; published in periodical Journal des débats
  [Francis the Waif, 1889]
La petite Fadette (novel) 1848-49; published in periodical Le Crédit
  [Little Fadette, 1849]
Histoire de ma vie. 20 vols. (autobiography) 1854-55
  [My Life, 1979]
Elle et Lui (novel) 1859
  [She and He, 1978]
Le marquis de Villemer (novel) 1860; published in periodical Revue des deux mondes
  [The Marquis of Villemer, 1871]
Flamarande—Les deux frères (novel) 1875; published in periodical Revue des deux mondes
Correspondance, 1812-1876. 6 vols. (letters) 1883-95

through the whole; they cannot, we say it with profound conviction, but rise the better. (p. 27)

[Her works] contain the history of her soul's life—the most complete autobiography, the most striking in its truth, and useful truth, that we know. Taken as a whole, they offer us an ascending line of progress towards good that is going on even whilst we are writing. *Indiana, Lélia, Jacques,* the *Lettres d'un Voyageur, Spiridion,* appear to us to mark the culminating points; her other productions come in, as valleys between the mountains, among the five books we have just named, and establish in some sort their continuity.

We know not in what manner *Indiana* has been read, so that an accusation of immorality against the author could be drawn from it; but we do know, that we read it before knowing this accusation, that we have re-read it before writing these lines, and that, on both occasions, we have found in it weighty precepts and a powerful lesson of morality. . . . The morality of a literary performance appears to us to consist far less in the choice of the things represented, of topics, than in the manner in which they are treated, in the final effect which the book, by whatever means, produces on the soul. Whether virtue be unsuccessful or triumphant, whether evil finds its penalty or remains unpunished, in the work, matters little, if we are taught to revere and love virtue notwithstanding its misfortunes, to abhor evil notwithstanding the seductiveness of the temporal and temporary good fortune that may attend it. Not to the eyes, but to the heart, should the author speak; to our own hearts in particular should he remit the hatred of evil and the punishment of the guilty. . . . Towards this kind of emotion it appears to us the soul must be impelled in reading *Indiana;* and the end, the inevitable consequence, is aversion for the seducer. Wherefore has it been said that *Indiana* is a *plea* against marriage? It is not even one against the husband. Certainly the inconveniences of a union between two persons whose incompatibility is beforehand written on every feature of their existence, are there strongly pointed out. But is that doing a work of immorality? Delmare, old, infirm, in character violent and domineering, is he, in the opinion of most persons, a suitable companion for a very young, beautiful, and impassioned woman, whose heart rebounds at all oppression? Unions like that, destructive of all happiness, are they not themselves a covert for great immorality, by rendering seduction a hundred times more to be feared? George Sand has made this thoroughly felt. . . . Never was there a portrait sketched with so absolute an intention of calling forth disgust, as that of Raymon; never any with so much art not to render the individuality too hateful at the risk of destroying the effect of the lesson. Raymon, with his talents and success in society—a seducer by liking, and indefatigable from the love of triumph . . .

is the very type of the dangerous seducer so often to be met in the world: his love is thoroughly that *love-passion,* a hideous compound of sensuality and vanity, that exercises so powerful a charm—fascination we might say—over the weakness of inexperience. And in *Indiana,* he is laid bare to the eye—a hundredfold beneath the husband-oppressor, cowardly, cruel, criminal as selfishness, of which he is the very highest expression. And the consequences of the seduction stand before the face of each of them, all frightful and irremediable; before the seducer, the corpse of poor Noun; before the seduced, the wreck of her illusion. For Indiana is *illusion:* she believes in goodness beyond the line of duty; she trusts blindly to the realisation of the ideal love that she bears in her own bosom, to the sincerity of the passion expressed, to the man's constancy, to a few glowing words whose source she has never studied. It is sufficient to read the letter of Indiana . . . to understand the mystery of her unhappiness; the secret of the book is contained in the ejaculation that the author puts into the mouth of Indiana herself, when Raymon reproaches her with having learnt love from romances, in the usual fashion of waiting-maids: *"What alarms and terrifies me is, that you are right,"* says Indiana. These words appear to us to contain—and we appeal to the sex as judges—a warning for all women of hearts ready to sacrifice duty to hope, more efficacious than twenty commonplaces of morality. How is it that puritanical criticism has forgotten these? How has it been forgotten that the author was writing, not an apology, but the history of Indiana—that the epithet *crime* is not spared to the flight of Indiana—that a passage of the tenth chapter reproaches her "with being too soon disheartened with her lot, and with not having given herself the pains of trying to make her husband better?" And why is there forgotten the love of Ralph—a love of the heart, respectful, and devoted, uniting in itself something of the three-fold affection of the lover, the husband, and the father, a happy contrast with Raymon's harassing, unrestrained, and daring love of the imagination—which, till then mute, dares not manifest itself but at a moment of solemnity, and when the tomb of the *husband* has long been closed? Strange that the criticism which stigmatised the book as *immoral* should have quietly got rid of Ralph by calling him "a stupid cousin." (pp. 28-30)

In a class more elevated, more open to exceptions—near [Goëthe's] Faust and [Byron's] Manfred— must be placed *Lélia.* This is not a immoral work—far from it; but for young spirits, who have not passed the double initiation of meditation and suffering, *Lélia* is a dangerous book. . . . *Lélia* is food for the strong; let the weak abstain, for there is in it that which may be the salvation of strong and tried organisations, but which may kill the tender and frail. It is a lesson whose aim is sanctified; but the details are horrible—such, perhaps, as may be necessary to act on society in a state

of gangrene. Doubtless, courage was required to trace this picture of desolation, in which hope after hope is unlinked, torn by some diabolical hand from the tree of life, and falling, like dead leaves, into the sepulchre of decay and nothingness. . . . Courage also is required to read it to the end; for we fear, at each step we take, that we are bordering on the desert of spiritual suicide: as before very general formula we feel a sensation of dizziness; and it is a formula of destruction, of negation without change, that *Lélia* undertakes to teach us. And yet hers is truly a high and sacred formula. The work of destruction that she fulfils, is that of a world worn out and corrupted, that rules over us yet, though in its agony. It is the world of *individuality,* the world that proposed to itself no other end, no other reason for its existence, than the search after prosperity. This, taken as the end of life, necessarily results in selfishness.

Lélia, whether the author intended it or not, is a symbol. The *dramatis personae* exist not as human beings; they are speaking and moving formulas; and hence it is that they strike on the brain rather than on the heart; they cause us not to weep, as *Indiana*—they make us think. Trenmor is human *reason*—reason pure, solitary, dry, deprived of impulse and sensibility. Stenio is *passion,*—not that of the heart, but empthatically that of the imagination. Pulcherie is *sensualism,*—calm, logical, and elevated even to theory. Magnus is still sensualism, but that of the instinct, fiery, unreflecting, and at enmity with superstition. Lélia is the wandering spirit on the search amid all these varieties; she is the other half of Faust, the woman-Faust. . . . What seeks she? Temporal happiness. And what seek all these personifications, all these *ideas* we would say, that are revolving round her like spectres, whom she follows each in turn? Temporal happiness: the one by the enjoyments of the flesh, or by repentance and humiliation before God; another by the exaltation of the poetic faculties; a third by the philosophic calm of stoicism; but all, whatever they may say, are only occupied with their existence. This, indeed, is the mother-principle in Faust; only as man lives more by the brain, and woman by the heart, whilst Faust seeks happiness in knowledge, Lélia seeks it through love; we feel that there rules in Faust a deep craving for power—in Lélia, a deep craving for life, for the expansion of sympathy. In Goëthe, Mephistophiles is destined to destroy power by doubt, much as he appears desirous of satisfying it by degrees. In George Sand, Trenmor destroys love, much as he appears to protect Stenio by his sympathies. Trenmor—Reason— the being who thinks, but whose heart beats not—who, instead of thinking how to *direct* the passions— instruments that God has placed at our disposal for good—fancies "that where they finish, man begins," and in whom the extinct passions have left only a mass of recollections and reflections, whose life is only the intellectual life, the *me* that contemplates and communes not—in a word, the being that muses . . .—Trenmor sways Lélia. She has a heart less ardent and less powerful than his mind; her faculties are inferior to his musings. Tormented by a lively thirst for love, but bent on there meeting with absolute and infallible happiness, when she finds it not there,—when in submitting her experience to the cool analysis of individual reason, she finds only the *finite* to satisfy a spirit full of aspirations for the infinite, she curses life and love;—she leaves herself to be tossed between scepticism and faith, and resumes her internal struggle, her desires and her impotence, with this sorrowful cry. "Happy those who can love." (pp. 32-3)

Bound as she is in the folds of a philosophy that steps not beyond the *individual,* she never rises to the conception of the *social* life of her mission in the world; between her and the crowd there is no exchange; "she has no sympathy for the human race, though she suffers the same evils, and sums up in herself all the sorrows scattered on the face of the earth." She comprehends not God in humanity; she prays not with it; she looks aside at her own weak and solitary individuality; thence it is she fears it, and feels ready to revolt from it. . . . In causing us to be born from one man, and in making us beings eminently social, God willed that our power for good should be enlarged just so much as we shall be careful to steep it in the common spring, and he has condemned to bareness all philosophy that aims at confining itself within the circle of individuality.

Lélia is the development of this principle as to woman, as Faust—more perhaps by the instinct of genius, and by a logical necessity, than from the intention of the author—is as to man. Goëthe found man marching in the path of science without any other aim than *his* pride and *his* happiness; George Sand found woman marching in the path of love without any other aim than the full budding of *her* faculties, *her* happiness; and both have inscribed at the goal of these two courses— "Impotence and nothingness." By what fatality, by what injustice—so much the greater that Goëthe stopped there, and George Sand has advanced—has the first had absolution, while the latter remains under the burden of an accusation of immorality. Why has it been made a crime for one to have proved by a *tableau*— frightful we confess—that it is an illusion to desire happiness in life and love, of what kind soever it may be, while the other has been praised for having taught that to seek happiness in knowledge and power is an illusion often criminal? Is it from weakness of perception, or from malignity, that criticism has persisted in reading and judging as a vulgar tale what evidently is not so? (p. 34)

[*Lélia* and *Indiana*] are, of the longer works of Madame Aurore Dupin, those which have called forth the most exclamations against the immorality of the author; and if we have succeeded in pointing out a more just and more favourable route for the appreciation of these works, our task is nearly completed. We only desire to provoke a fresh and more considerate examination. We ask this, upright in conscience, proud of being the first to demand it in this country, and convinced . . . that there is benefit in reconciling society with genius. . . .

Those who shall undertake the examination we ask, will certainly find some hasty passages, some crude descriptions, that we should like better to be able to suppress; they will find some phrases hazarded, in which the abuses, the absurdities, the prejudices, and the vices of society are expressed by the collective word *"society,"* some where there is used *"marriage"* in place of *"persons married."* But, looking over a few details to get at the *ensemble,* judging the spirit rather than the letter, we are sure they will find true and high morality where superficial critics have pronounced themselves scared. . . . [Never] in the pages of George Sand is vice presented in a way to seduce the young imagination, never does virtue appear but surrounded with that glory of art that impels us to prostrate ourselves before it; there is always a protest in the face of crime, aspiration after good in the face of evil. They will find that it is not the *institution* of marriage, but the corruption of that holy institution; that not husbands, but *bad* husbands are dealt with; that if she has been led to think that "the scandal and disorder of women are *very often* provoked by the brutality or infamy of men, and that a husband who wantonly neglects his duties in idle talk, merriment, and drinking, is sometimes less excusable than the wife who betrays hers in tears, in affliction, and in repentance," she is at the same time ready to revere "that grand, noble, excellent, *voluntary,* and *eternal* love," which is marriage such as Christianity made it, such as St. Paul explained it. . . . (p. 35)

And above all this, if they shall desire to reflect more conscientiously than has yet been done, they will discover that cry of deep and solemn sadness that springs from almost all the writings of Madame Aurora Dupin. . . . They will then demand, astonished, how this woman, a writer that fulfils with extraordinary powers a mission in the world of Art so substantially austere, could have been so mistaken, so little understood, so calumniated? And, thinking on the storm of misfortune that swept over her years of youth . . . , they will pardon the errors and the reaction that has signalised the first part of her course who has never betrayed the cause of truth, who has always pleaded the cause of suffering, and who has never, under trial, lost sight of the goal that alone could save her. (p. 36)

Joseph Mazzini, in an originally unsigned essay titled "George Sand," in *Monthly Chronicle,* Vol. IV, July-December, 1839, pp. 23-40.

GEORGE BRANDES

(essay date 1890?)

[In the excerpt below, Brandes examines Sand's use of characterization in her novels.]

Most undoubtedly [George Sand] was the idealist, all her life long; but it was not really the desire to delineate human beings as "they ought to be" which inspired her to write, but the desire to show what they could be if society did not hamper their spiritual growth, corrupt them, and destroy their happiness; hence, in her delineations of the representatives of "society" no leniency was shown. What George Sand originally meant to give was a picture of life as it is, of reality as she had experienced and observed it; what she gave was the feminine enthusiast's view of reality. The section she saw was a patch of earth with the brightness of heaven over it. Her clear-sightedness was the clear-sightedness of the poet. (p. 133)

[*Indiana, Valentine, Lélia,* and *Jacques* are books] which possess little literary interest for the reader to-day: the characters are vague idealisations; the plots are improbable, as in *Indiana,* or unreal, as in *Lélia* and *Jacques;* the harmonious sonority of her style does not save the author from the reproach of frequent lapses into magniloquence; in the letters and monologues she is often the poetical sermoniser. And yet there is a fire in these works of George Sand's youth which gives light and warmth to this day; they struck a note which will go on sounding for ages. They emit both a wail and a war-cry, and where they penetrate they carry with them germs of feelings and thoughts, the growth of which this age has succeeded in checking, but which in the future will unfold and spread with a luxuriant vigour of which we can only form a faint conception. (p. 137)

It was in the rôle of the psychologist and story-teller, not in that of the reformer, that she at first appeared before the public. In *Indiana,* as in *Valentine,* the fervour, the poetical impulses, the enthusiastic passions and stormy protests of youth, are the proper contents of the book; there is much psychological and little personal history. Nevertheless there was in the nature of the feeling described (feelings free from any trace of viciousness, yet at variance with the decrees of society), and still more in the reflections interspersed throughout the tale, something which actually struck at the foundations of society. (p. 141)

[In *Lélia* and *Jacques*] their authoress's Byronic "Weltschmerz" and declamatory tendency reach high-water mark. In *Lélia* she represented her ideal great, unsensual, profoundly feeling woman, and provided her with an opposite in her sister, Pulchérie, a luxurious courtesan. Taking her own character and separating the two sides of it, she formed Lélia after the Minerva-image, Pulchérie after the Venus-image in her own soul; the result being, not unnaturally, rather two symbolic personages than two human beings of flesh and blood. In *Jacques* she approached the problem of marriage from a new side. In *Indiana* she had portrayed a brutal, in *Valentine* a refined, cold husband; but now she equipped the husband with the qualities which in her eyes were the highest, and wrecked his happiness upon the rock of his own elevated character, which his insignificant young wife is not capable of understanding and continuing to love. The authoress has endeavoured to impart additional force to her own opinions by putting them into the mouth of the wronged husband. He himself excuses his wife. . . .The extravagance of Romanticism is most noticeable in the final catastrophe. Jacques can think of no better means of liberating Fernande than a suicide committed in a manner which to her will give it the appearance of an accident. This transports us at once into the region of unreality. But the unreality in this novel is, generally speaking, more apparent than actual. It is easy for modern criticism to point out the absence of any indications of locality, of real occupations, &c., &c.; the personages in George Sand's early novels have no occupation and no aim but to love. The reality of these books is a spiritual reality, the reality of feeling. . . . [We] must remember that George Sand's characters are not supposed to be average men and women. She describes unusually gifted beings. Indeed, in these early works she has done little else than delineate and explain her own emotional life. She places her own character in every variety of outward circumstance, and then, with a marvellous power of self-observation and unerring skill, draws the natural psychological conclusions. It is interesting to observe how the constant craving to find a masculine mind which is the equal of her own, leads her to a kind of self-duplication in two sexes. Ardently as she exalts love, strongly as she allows it to influence the life of the great woman and of the great man, nevertheless both of these, Jacques as well as Lélia, are inspired by a still stronger, still more ideal feeling, that of friendship for a noble member of the opposite sex, by whom they are understood. In comparison with this profound mutual understanding, Lélia's love for Sténio, Jacques' for Fernande, seem merely the weaknesses of these two great souls. Lélia has an understanding friend and equal in Trenmor, Jacques in Sylvia. Jacques would love Sylvia if she were not his half-sister, or rather if he were not compelled to suspect that she is; but there is a beauty in their mutual relationship, such as it is, to which merely erotic relations could hardly attain. (pp. 143-45)

Characters such as these illustrate the strong instinct of friendship which George Sand possessed, and which was quite in the spirit of the youthful Romanticism of the period. Her *Lettres d'un Voyageur,* which follow the first group of novels, and begin immediately after the separation from Alfred de Musset in Venice, give us an insight into her friendships. (p. 146)

In no other of her works is she so eloquent, in none of the later ones do her periods flow in such long, lyrically rhetorical waves. Nowhere better than here can we study her personal style, as distinguished from the dialogue of her novels. Sonority is its most marked feature. It rolls onward in long, full rhythms, regular in its fall and rise, melodious in joy, harmonious even in despair. The perfect balance of George Sand's nature is mirrored in the perfect balance of her sentences—never a shriek, a start, or a jar; a sweeping, broad-winged flight—never a leap, nor a blow, nor a fall. The style is deficient in melody, but abounds in rich harmonies; it lacks colour, but has all the beauty that play of line can impart. She never produces her effect by an unusual and audacious combination of words, seldom or never by a fantastic simile. And there is just as little strong or glaring colour in her pictures as there is jarring sound in her language. She is romantic in her enthusiasms, in the way in which she yields unresistingly to feelings which defy rules and regulations; but she is severely classical in the regularity of her periods, in the inherent beauty of her form, and the sobriety of her colouring. (pp. 146-47)

[Of the purely poetic tales of the second period of her literary career,] *La Marquise* is, in my estimation, undoubtedly the best; indeed, taking nothing but art into consideration, it is possibly her most perfect work. I fancy it must have been inspired by the memory of her kind-hearted, dignified grandmother. It fascinates by its combination of the spirit and customs of the eighteenth century with the timid, more spiritually enthusiastic amatory passion of the nineteenth. (p. 151)

George Sand has written nothing more graceful. The sly sarcasm in [the] conclusion, a quality which also distinguishes the equally charming and equally suggestive little tale, *Teverino,* but which is not frequently met with in her writings, is quite in the spirit of the eighteenth century; and the style has that conciseness which is, as a rule, an indispensable quality in a work destined to descend to future generations. *La Marquise* has a rightful claim to a place in every anthology of French masterpieces.

Amongst the works which George Sand now proceeds to write is a whole series in which she represents her conception of woman's nature when it is uncorrupted. The women she draws are chaste and proud and energetic, susceptible to the passion of love, but remaining on the plane above it, or retaining their purity even when they yield to it. She inclines to attribute to woman a moral superiority over man. But the natures of her heroes, too, are essentially fine, though in the ruling classes tainted by the inherited tendency to tyrannise over woman and the lower classes. . . . Women like Fiamma in *Simon,* Edmée in *Mauprat,* Consuelo in the novel of the same name . . . , are fine specimens of George Sand's typical young girl. Her rôle is to inspire, to heal, or to discipline the man. She knows not vacillation; resolution is the essence of her character; she is the priestess of patriotism, of liberty, of art, or of civilisation. (p. 153)

Side by side with the books which have the high-minded young girl as heroine, we find one or two in which the mature woman is the central figure—in which George Sand has given a more direct representation of her own character. Such are *Le Secrétaire intime,* a comparatively weak story, and *Lucrezia Floriani,* one of the most remarkable productions of her pen. Of this latter book, it may with truth be said that it is not food for every one. . . . To most readers it will seem a forbidding or revolting literary paradox; for it aims at proving the modesty, nay, the chastity of an unmarried woman (an Italian actress and play-writer) who has four children by three fathers. But it is a book in which the authoress has successfully performed the difficult task she set herself, that of giving us an understanding of a woman's nature which is so rich and so healthy that it must always love, so noble that it cannot be degraded, so much that of the artist that it cannot rest content with a single feeling, and has the power to recover from repeated disappointments. (pp. 153-54)

The contrast between *Lucrezia Floriani* and the short series of simple, beautiful peasant stories which follow it after a short interval . . . seems at first sight a very marked one. In reality, however, the gulf separating *Lucrezia* from *La Mare au Diable, François le Champi,* and *La petite Fadette* is not so wide as it appears. What attracted George Sand to the peasants of Berry, to the rustic idylls of her native province, was the very same Rousseau-like enthusiasm for nature that had lent impetus and weight to her protests against the laws of society. . . . Her French peasants are very certainly not "real" in the same sense as Balzac's in *Les Paysans;* they are not merely represented with a sympathy which is as strong as his antipathy, but are made out to be amiable, tender-hearted, and sensitively delicate in their feelings; they are to real French peasants what the shepherds of Theocritus were to the real shepherds of Greece. Nevertheless, these tales have one merit which they owe entirely to their subject-matter and which George Sand's other novels lack—they possess the charm, always rare, but doubly rare in French literature, of naïveté. All that there was of the peasant girl, of the country child, in George Sand; everything in her which was akin to the plants that grow, to the breeze that blows, knowing not whence it cometh nor whither it goeth; all that which, unconscious and dumb, was so legible in her countenance and behaviour, but was so often nullified in her works by sentimentality and phrase-mongering, revealed itself here in its childlike simplicity. (pp. 156-57)

[*La Mare au Diable*] is the gem of these village tales. In it idealism in French fiction reaches its highest level. In it George Sand gave to the world what she declared to Balzac it was her desire to write—the pastoral of the eighteenth century. (p. 157)

George Brandes, "George Sand," in his *Main Currents in Nineteenth Century Literature: The Romantic School in France, Vol. V,* translated by Diana White and Mary Morison, 1904. Reprint by Boni & Liveright, Inc., 1924, pp. 132-57.

PROSSER HALL FRYE

(essay date 1908)

[In the following excerpt, Frye praises the spontaneity and creativity of Sand's novels despite what he perceives as their "fault of saying too much."]

English literature is distinguished from French by its preference, at least in effect, for improvisation and inspiration. And it is for this reason, because these are so exactly the characteristics of her writing, that George Sand deserves the attention of the English reader. . . . Her spontaneity, ease, and fluency, her individuality, sensibility, and inventiveness are the positive virtues which most please the English sense; while the vices of their reverse—her diffuseness, confusion, and haziness, her irregularity, extravagance, and wilfulness, in fine her lack of discipline—are all defects which the English least notice or most readily excuse. She had no art in the strict sense; but she had inspiration, its virtues and vices, its qualities and defects. (p. 41)

[In] spite of the charm of her writing, almost irresistible in the wooing of the soft slow sentences, the inevitable weaknesses of the facility which stood her in place of literary method have been observed over and over, particularly where they are most noticeable, in her construction. Her lack of fundamental plan, of architectural design, has impaired a work that otherwise would have in perfection, as it now has in bulk, few peers. Sentences she could write, and chapters, exquisite in touch and feeling,—few better; but alas! for all their delicacy, fragments. When it comes to building up piece by piece a single whole, an entire fabric with the subdual of many parts to the perfect harmony of one great purpose,—there her weakness, the weakness of facility, is manifest. (p. 42)

With her quick, sensitive, and rather shallow nature she was by no means so likely to distinguish herself through the manifestation of intellect and will in literature as through the manifestation of sentiment and emotion—not so much in composition as in style. . . . [George Sand's writing] is full of colour and feeling, it is splendidly romantic; but when one comes to consider it as a whole, to look toward its end and reflect upon its tendency, one is struck by its ineptitude to its purpose. (p. 45)

For the careful and consistent reader one of the most painful experiences is prepared by the frequency with which she falls away in the latter part of her novels from the high standard of her beginnings,—and that not merely in her early work, when she was learning her trade, but in the work of after periods as well, when she had served along apprenticeship to her art. . . . And it is sadder still to find for oneself a book of such fair promise, which might have been completed faultlessly within the limit of three hundred pages, running on into a wreck of diminishing climaxes and crises and feeble after-thoughts, until it expires tardily of sheer exhaustion, without the needed apology for being so long a-dying, at more than twice its natural age,—spoiled for no other apparent reason than that the writer wrote too easily to stop when she had finished. . . . It is hardly exaggeration to advise one wishing to read George Sand's best work to read only the first halves of her novels.

And yet the difficulty were not to be so escaped. This fault of saying too much, this plethora of words occurs again and again over smaller areas than an entire book. With the inveteracy of disease it infects the whole system. The author is not willing to make the reader a suggestion, to drop him a hint, to risk herself to his perspicacity. She must needs explain—often more for her own sake than for his, it would appear—until there is left over event and motive hardly a single shadow for him to penetrate, but everything lies exposed in an even glare of revelation, like the monotonous landscape of our great western prairie, without concealment or mystery. There are no skeletons in George Sand's closet; she has got them all out into the middle of the floor. And her dialogue is as prolix as her analysis. Her characters seem possessed with her own fondness for explication, and invariably talk matters out to a finish, however trivial, so that the reader is constantly outrunning the writer with a sense at the end of disillusion and disappointment. (pp. 46-8)

Perhaps this faultiness, behind which lies always her too ready fluency, may be explained, or at least illustrated, by her manner of work. It is well known nowadays, when the personal habits of authors are more studied than their books, that she wrote at night for certain fixed hours with the regularity of a day-labourer. . . . The story goes of her that if she happened to finish the novel on which she was employed an hour or even less before her time was up for the night, she would calmly set the manuscript away, the ink still damp on the page, and placidly begin another, composing rapidly as she went until the clock released her. Whether rightly or wrongly one misses something here—the fond lingering over the old work, the patient review and minute revision, the reluctance to part with the child of the brain which makes every *finis* to the author a lover's parting and which is so characteristic of the French writers of the century. (pp. 48-9)

[However] there is something very like grandeur—the grandeur of renunciation, perhaps—in this ability of hers to put away the past when she was done with it, to leave her work to its deserts without just one more backward look, just one more correction, and to pass on confidently to the next duty without worrying over what was gone. . . . At all events it shows a self-detachment, a sobriety and moderation which is often sadly to seek in French literary workmanship of the modern school, with its long brooding, its slow coagulation, its overlaid and half-addled conception. . . . (pp. 50-1)

But for all this excess of care we might well wish that George Sand had, without going too far, shown a little more concern for what she had done, a little more for what she was about to do, were it reasonable to suppose that all her errors were due to her habits of work and could have been retrieved by revision. Much, however, of her defective construction must be charged to another cause. A certain indefiniteness of conception, a failure to decide the end from the beginning and write up to it—in short, a powerlessness to fix and realise the idea of a book, is equally a condition of her structural frailty. (p. 52)

[As a result of] the vivacity of her feelings, she was at her best when she centred her novels neither in a doctrinal *motif* nor a merely personal emotion, but in some simple episode of common life which she had noticed and been touched by. Her masterpieces are few in number—as any one's must be—but they are perfect in their kind:—*la Mare au diable, la Petite Fadette, François le champi. Les Maîtres sonneurs,* of the same attempt as the others, errs by excessive development; it overreaches and outruns itself and in spite of much good grows wearisome by its length; while *Jeanne* and the *Meunier d'Angibault,* which are sometimes classed with these, show traces of confusion due partly to the introduction of extra-literary ideas and partly to the mixture of idyllic and social elements; so that none of these latter three can be ranked as masterpieces beside the former. Her own district of Berri, which she always loved and to which she returned more and more in later life, furnished her with the setting for these flawless gems. . . . The simple, unpretentious life of the peasant amid his fields with his robust loves and hates, hopes and fears, was a discovery in comparative hu-

manity to French letters. The healthfulness and freshness of these idyls, full of the air of wood and lawn, the breath of morning and evening, is a revelation after the stale intrigue skulking away in the close and tainted atmosphere of city rooms. They justify to the English reader the existence of French fiction. It may be, as [the French critic M. Vincent de Paul] Brunetière declares, that George Sand made the French novel capable of sustaining thought; it is of infinitely greater credit to her to have shown that it was possible for the French novel to carry good, clean, wholesome sentiment. No reader of modern French fiction can return to these stories without feeling that there life, as well as literature, has been triumphantly vindicated against *naturalism,* and without feeling, too, that his heart has been purified and gladdened by contact with a simple and sincere art. (pp. 60-2)

Prosser Hall Frye, "George Sand," in his *Literary Reviews and Criticisms,* G. P. Putnam's Sons, 1908, pp. 29-62.

BENEDETTO CROCE

(essay date 1923)

[In the excerpt below from an essay that first appeared in 1923 in *Poesia e non poesia: Note sulla letteratura europea del secolo decimonono,* Croce discusses Sand's portrayal of sexual love in her novels.]

We read to-day with effort the hundred and more volumes of Georges Sand, which made our grandmothers shiver and grow pale, and the re-reading of them fails of giving pleasure, like a game that has ceased to amuse, because the trick of it has been discovered. (p. 206)

Georges Sand was undoubtedly one of the most noteworthy representative of European moral life in the twenty years prior to the revolution of 1848. She represented this practical side of life chiefly and energetically by means of a strange Utopia, which may be termed "the religion of love." . . . From the point of view of this religion, the value and meaning of life are to be found in love, just in love, understood sexually; and Eros is the god, although the rhetorical phraseology of the day preferred to formulate its thought with a certain degree of unction and spoke of "love" as "coming from God."

Love, being the highest and indeed the only act of the religious cult, does not recognize any law as superior to itself: as soon as it appears, it has the right of obtaining satisfaction, "the right of passion." And it is sovran: it does not tolerate a division of its kingdom with other affections: every other passion must serve it, receive orders from it and submit to it. It is also unique and eternal; and when it seems to vary in its objects, the fault lies with society, which embarrasses it with its foolish and tyrannical laws, or with material accidents, which trouble it, for in its essence it is constancy and fidelity. He who loves without return should respect the passion for another object in the beloved, and love ordains self-sacrifice, in order that passion may celebrate the sacred rite in full joy and freedom: in making this sacrifice, duty is performed, the heroism of the perfect lover is attained. (pp. 208-09)

When we recognize . . . the altogether sensual and pathological origin of Sand's theories, of her religion of love, and admit the accusation of immorality brought against them, we have already implicitly granted that they are without doctrinal or philosophical importance, and without any value as truth. Truth, however bitter it may be and pessimistic it may seem to be, is always moral and a source of morality. Sand was unable to extract truth from her nervous spasm, which she expressed in formulas possessing only the semblance of being theoretical. But her ideology did not even become poetry and art, when translated into the form of fiction, because art too is truth and demands sincerity towards one's self, a superior sincerity which vanquishes one-sided practical interest and penetrates to the recesses of the soul, dissipating or clearing the clouds that obscure it. Sand's was not a profound mind . . . , she was absorbed in dreaming; in weaving the web of her imaginings, as the woman she was. And being a woman, she never conceived that art should be respected, but always held it to be the natural outlet for her own sensibility and for her own intellectuality. As woman again, she brought practical sense into the things of art, domestic economy and commercial knowledge, aiming always at making above all what is called the romance, the pleasing book, and at making many of them, because many produced much fruit. She observed reality, but who does not? She even observed it with attention; but her work consisted, as she said, in "idealizing it." . . . [It] is generally admitted and recognized . . . that Georges Sand's novels are defectively composed or lack composition, but it is not observed that this was due in her case to the lack of vigorous thought, or rather of an inspiring poetic motive, owing to which she abandoned herself to chance as regards personages and events, which might be this or the opposite, and since they had little cohesion, it was not difficult for her to change or turn into its opposite this or that one of her novels, to change the fate of *Indiana* or of *Lélia,* making Indiana and Ralph marry or making Lélia die in a convent. She frequently also began her narratives, such as *Mauprat,* with force and vigour; but when we anticipate that a theme from such a beginning should attain to its full significance in the course and ending of the story, we find her losing herself in the conventional, in intrigues and in trivial adventures.

Lyricism as "setting" and the "agreeable" side of romantic love are to be found in all her works in different proportions, sometimes the one, sometimes the other preponderating. In *Lélia,* which is her greatest poetical effort, the former predominates: here everything sparkles and echoes, so that the eye becomes, as it were, dimmed, the ear seduced and deafened. The personages of *Lélia* are neither allegories nor poetical individuals: they are not allegories, because they lack definite concepts, nor poetical individuals, because they lack definiteness of character. This poem in prose, this feminine *Faust,* also fails to resolve itself into a succession of lyrics, because instead of lyrics, it abounds in emphasis and declamation. (pp. 214-17)

The characters of *Jacques* are also dreams of erotic sensuality: the hero himself, mysterious, most perfect, an idler, whose supreme need and occupation is pure love (not love that is pure), and all the more agreeable to women, since he is capable of sometimes disappearing, so that they may occupy themselves with their pleasures undisturbed. . . . (pp. 218-19)

The art is there all the more easy, because the story is developed by letters, all of them in the same florid style, letters that are not letters save by means of a gross artifice, discussing and recounting previous events and informing the reader of what is necessary for his information. This is art of a second-rate quality, like that of the first romance, *Indiana,* which gave fame to the authoress, and is the type of so many others of her novels, in which the craftsmanship predominates. There is not one poetical motive or idea in the whole of that celebrated romance: the theme . . . is treated externally and materially, complicated but not developed by means of strange events, surprises and suicides, crossings of the ocean, and the like. (p. 219)

Certainly qualities of a secondary order are very much in evidence in Sand. She is an authoress of extraordinary fluidity and abundance, although giving but slight relief to her characters, and she knows how to tell a story with vivacity. But perhaps the only places where her writing is illuminated with a touch of poetry are her descriptions of "natural scenery," universally praised, which corresponded to a true emotion in her, to a small melody that sang itself in her soul, in the midst of the din caused there by the passions artificially intensified and by ill-thought-out ideas, and in the midst of conventionalisms and expedients of the craft. Something of the florid, rhetorical and verbose is to be found in them also; but sometimes these are able to render rather successfully the feeling of waiting, of melancholy, of abandonment, of purification, of gladness, which Sand infused into the spectacles of nature. (pp. 220-21)

As is well known, Georges Sand gave herself to the cultivation of humanitarian and especially of socialistic ideals in the second period of the four into which critics are wont to divide her too copious production. (p. 222)

Consuelo belongs to [this] period, standing between the historical novel—as it was then understood, introducing great historical personages and placing them in relation to other imaginary personages and showed them as immersed in politics, intrigues and love affairs with one another—and the novel of socialistic tendencies. Consuelo is another incarnation of Lélia, an extraordinary woman, daughter of a street singer, herself a singer, but in some unknown manner endowed with the greatest possible knowledge of things in general and of the human heart, of the greatest will-power, of the greatest rectitude, of the greatest tact and practical sense, and in addition acutely intellectual and critical with a mind that meditates upon God and human destiny. In the novel, the miracles that she accomplishes follow one another: the idealization or idolization usual with Sand, unites with adventures piled upon one another, to compose a perfect novel in supplements. . . . How little capable was Sand of going deeply into anything is to be seen in the figure of Count Albert. . . . This figure is well conceived, but

Drawing of Sand by French poet Alfred de Musset.

quickly becomes superficialized and lost in narratives of strange events, terrifying apparitions and intrigues.

It is true that Sand, in the third period of her production as classified by the critics . . . , is supposed then to have composed at last her masterpieces, the idyllic novels, and to have thus bestowed upon France a kind of literature that she still lacked. I do not deny that *La mare au diable, La petite Fadette, François le champi, Les maîtres sonneurs,* and one or two like them, are very graceful books, full of gentleness and goodness, far better arranged and proportioned than the foregoing, written with greater care and with an able adaptation of peasant speech. But, to tell the truth, there does not seem to be anything poetical that comes to light in these novels, but rather the virtuosity of the expert authoress of pleasing books. A certain preparatory tone makes itself indeed felt in the best of them, *La mare au diable:* we feel there the intention of moving and delighting us with a story of innocence and tenderness. (pp. 224-26)

The accuracy of Georges Sand in portraying the life of peasants in this and others of her novels has been contested, and, as is always the case, under the guise of an unjust criticism is to be found concealed another criticism which is just, namely, annoyance at the mannered style of these edifying and consoling narratives. (p. 227)

And what shall we say finally as to the last manner, that of the fourth period of Georges Sand, when she returned to love stories no longer of the fields but of the city, returned appeased and without the fictions of rebellion and apostolate which had shaken her in the past? The recognized masterpiece of this period is *Le marquis de Villemer.* . . . It is one of those novels read with delight by young ladies, married women and gentlemen, and enjoys the favour of good society, being praised there as an *exquise.* If, however, you are simply a lover of poetry, I would counsel you to avoid it and others like it, because they would seem to you to be insipid and would perhaps arouse your indignation at their pretence of art. (pp. 228-29)

Benedetto Croce, "Georges Sand," in his *European Literature in the Nineteenth Century,* translated by Douglas Ainslie, Alfred A. Knopf, 1924, pp. 206-29.

GAMALIEL BRADFORD

(essay date 1930)

[In the following excerpt, Bradford claims idealism to be the "distinguishing feature and the fundamental characteristic of George Sand's temperament."]

Through all [her] mad adventures and strange experiences the distinguishing feature and the fundamental characteristic of George Sand's temperament was her essential idealism. . . . [Always] she retained an extraordinary, persistent power of self-delusion about persons and things. The remarkable point is that, especially in earlier years, the delusion was accompanied by the most piercing bursts and flashes of clear vision, of cynical disillusion, when for the moment all the bare ugliness of fact and truth stood out in its prevailing horror. No one could appreciate this horror or state it more clearly or violently, for the time, than she did. (pp. 206-07)

The most striking illustration of George Sand's idealism is her Autobiography, the *Histoire de Ma Vie.* Here everything is in a sense veracious. There is truth of detail, undeniable record of indisputable fact. Yet somehow, over everything, there is a sweet, sunlit glow, a pervading atmosphere of gentle tenderness, which transforms and transfigures, gives a touch of unreality, or more properly of ideality, to the most unpromising incidents and the most unattractive people. (p. 208)

The climax, the fine flower, the full embodiment of George Sand's ideal instinct and genius for friendship, appear in the correspondence between her and Flaubert, which, like those between Goethe and Schiller, or between Emerson and Carlyle, is one of the great spiritual exchanges of the world, and is perhaps the most remarkable. What is striking is the complete difference of the two correspondents. Flaubert, in theory at any rate, was the least idealistic of men, cold-blooded, keen-sighted, cynical, realistic in his mental attitude. George Sand was visionary, imaginative, a weaver of dreams. Yet by sheer breadth of character and loftiness of spiritual purpose and level, they were able to understand, to respect, to enjoy, and to love each other. And what is further notable is the way in which George Sand secures and maintains her spiritual superiority. (pp. 211-12)

If George Sand was an idealist in artistic method and attitude, she was quite as much so in artistic achievement. Not for her was the slow, laborious rendering of the sordid detail of the surface of life, but there was always the impetuous effort to transfigure reality with ideal beauty. Sometimes this was accomplished by artistic climaxes, and when these grew naturally and logically out of the movement and development of the story, they were often in a high degree impressive and effective, as with the admirable theatrical triumphs of Consuelo, which it is impossible for any sympathetic reader to resist. And again there was deference to the cheap romantic devices of the day, the hidden trapdoors, the mysterious caverns, the tricks and passwords, which make the later portion of this same *Consuelo* rather wearisome to the modern reader.

Even in the best of her novels George Sand was too much inclined to claptrap of this sort. . . . (pp. 226-27)

The same idealism of handling appears in the region of character. This was never George Sand's strong-point, and her range and variety of human types is comparatively limited. For women it may well be said that the only figure she drew with real power and success was herself. There is always a contrasted type, for purposes of conflict and comparison, the Anais of *Valentine,* the Pulchérie of *Lélia,* the Amélie of *Consuelo.* But in all the novels the same heroine appears, strong, modest, self-contained, unpretentious but dominant and dominating, Valentine, Indiana, Consuelo, the Thérèse of *Elle et Lui,* Lucrezia Floriani, above all, Lélia, and always this heroine is George Sand. It is curious to see how the same personage is manifest in the autobiography, *Histoire de Ma Vie,* and always with the leading position, the *beau rôle.* The extraordinary thing is that this figure should be so dominant and so charming, and every one of these heroines commends herself with a winning magic that is difficult to understand.

It is far otherwise with the heroes. . . . The men of George Sand fall into two distinct types. There is the spoiled, high-strung, over-sensitive child, who is chiefly embodied in Alfred de Musset, the Bénédicts, the Sténios, man as George Sand really saw him, a creature to be petted and nursed and fostered and despised. And there is the hero whom she would have liked to see, the Trenmor of *Lélia,* Albert in *Consuelo,* who combines the passions of the man with the intellect of the god. And under it all you cannot help feeling a vast instinctive contempt, a sense that the sole function of the male is to fecundate the female and then die. (pp. 227-28)

It is curious to reflect that this conception of the great feminine idealist finds its counterpart, to a large extent, in the treatment of the world's great realistic artist, Shakespeare. The men of Shakespeare certainly appear—to other men—more real than those of George Sand, but their reality is to the full as earthy as that of her men. And Shakespeare's women have the same ideal superiority, the Portias, the Violas, the Imogens, have all the celestial, sustained perfection that belongs to Lélia and Consuelo.

But undoubtedly what most idealizes these various elements in George Sand is the charm and the magic of her style. It is not in all ways a perfect style. It is too facile, too flowing, at times almost approaching the slipshod. But its very quality of improvisation gives it a divine ease and grace which all the long labor of Flaubert could never equal. There is a depth and a delicacy of rhythm, which no translation can suggest, but which is hardly surpassed in any French prose anywhere. (p. 229)

Gamaliel Bradford, "Eve and the Pen: George Sand," in his *Daughters of Eve*, Houghton Mifflin Company, 1930, pp. 201-39.

━━━━━

NANCY ROGERS
(essay date 1979)

[In the excerpt below, Rogers considers the "undeniable richness" of Sand's "erotic imagination" and comments on how it translated into her early novels *Indiana*, *Valentine*, and *Lélia*.]

[The] question of Sand's sexual contradictions is an interesting one in light of her depiction of sexual roles, especially the crossing of the boundaries of individual sexual identity, in her early novels. (p. 19)

The comparatively bold depiction of sex in George Sand's early novels is somewhat surprising in light of [the general predilection during her day] for veiled eroticism; this is doubly true since the author was a woman. . . . [Love] between man and woman as George Sand describes it is hardly the spiritually uplifting, ethereal bond which is exalted by Chateaubriand. Rather than presenting love as a soft, feminine, passive union of two souls, Sand's novels display a daring, active, violently physical sensation defined as love. (pp. 20-1)

The imagery of fire, fever, and vertigo is almost constantly associated with "love" in Sand's first novel [*Indiana*], so much so that "love" must be equated to "sex"—a violent physical reaction which renders the lover almost physically ill. The second novel, *Valentine,* presents an even stronger picture of love as physical sensation. . . . The touch of a hand, an emotionally and erotically charged game of hide and seek, or an unexpected look is enough to cause breasts to heave and blood to rise, leading to a state resembling death. . . . The intensity of this kind of physical disorganization is a central feature of the sexual encounter as Sand envisions it; the body is disturbed and disoriented to the extent that the lover loses total control of his corporeal self. . . . [The] disintegration of both the body and mind by the intensity of sexual passion is a major theme in [*Lélia*], in which the ossianic priest, Magnus, is driven mad by his desire for the statue-woman. . . . In this novel Sand examines the conflict between spiritual and physical love, the psychology of sexual frustration and frigidity, and the notion of idolatry in love, a concept which she condemns. Here, sexual satisfaction is "le but inconnu," a tormenting need which is never satisifed. Erotic images fill the pages of *Lélia*, but sexual encounters, although voluptuous, violent, and tumultuous, are never complete, at least for the heroine: the lovers are left unfulfilled, their passion a de-

structive force. Sand describes this void with an almost cruel authenticity, making *Lélia* one of the boldest of romantic novels. And yet physical passion and pleasure are praised in this ethereal, spiritual novel; the courtesan Pulchérie . . . , Lélia's sister, exists for pleasure and is the only satisfied and complete character in the work, for she understands the limits of happiness and accepts life as it is. . . . [She] is a vibrant, positive personage in the work, serving as the incarnation of physical pleasure as a genuine means of human fulfillment.

The breadth of Sand's erotic imagination is demonstrated by her investigation of the darker elements of sex, those erotic possibilities such as violence, pain, masochism, and death explored by the Marquis de Sade and the Gothic novelists. (pp. 21-2)

However, she does not imply that sex is limited to the "darker" elements: indeed, these novels exhibit a wealth of light, "innocent" features which arouse passion. The sounds, odors, and forms of nature, for example, are presented as temptations to sexual union. . . . Sand also sees other seemingly innocent elements as stimuli to sexual passion: music, for example, is described as "le langage de toute passion forte," and lovers are aroused by its message; articles of clothing, such as Indiana's scarf and Valentine's handkerchief, are capable of becoming objects of fetishism; and prayer, seemingly a spiritual activity, is a catalyst to passion as well. . . . Thus we see that the young Sand examines myriad elements of sexuality with an originality which reveals a fertile imagination and a curiosity about sex which distinguishes her from many of her fellow romantics. The author refuses to shy away from subjects considered taboo at the moment; instead she goes so far as to imply that sex is a major component of many human behavior patterns which are usually considered "pure." (pp. 23-4)

The existential questions "Who am I?" and "Who is he?" were a key element in the dilemma of romantic man as he wrestled with his inner self, alienated from his milieu. This dilemma figures prominently in Sand's method of portraiture, for characters seem to have more than one identity depending upon who is looking at them. Sand profoundly explores changing identities, the masks and disguises that people wear, and the various social roles which individuals assume. But it is one particular manifestation of the Sandian question of identity which interests us here: the merging or metamorphosis of identity, especially in the sexual act.

Sand's first three novels display a phenomenon which was initially manifested in the work *Rose et Blanche*, written . . . with Jules Sandeau. The two women of the title are an actress and a nun, respectively, whose temperaments and tastes are diametrically opposed but who serve, at least implicitly, as alter egos. Each of Sand's next three works contains a pair of young women counterparts whose fusion is of central importance to the structure of the work.

In *Indiana* the two women, Indiana and her "femme de chambre créole" Noun, are both desired by the callous Raymon de Ramière. This sexual triangle will be repeated in the next two novels, but there the ultimate merging of the two women is perhaps presented in the most dramatic manner. . . . The robust Noun and the sickly Indiana seem to represent, on the surface at least, the active and passive elements of human sexuality: Noun forcefully pursues love, . . . becomes pregnant, and in a half-wild state, commits suicide; Indiana, on the other hand, passively accepts Raymon's love, hopes that their relationship will remain spiritual, faints when kissed, and uses her will and reason to resist him until she finally gives in to her passion. . . . [It is] through Raymon that the two become physically metamorphosed; in a powerful erotic scene . . . he finally possesses Indiana through the body of Noun.

Valentine, as well, examines the relationship between two young women counterparts and a man who is attracted to both of them. In this instance the two, Valentine and Louise, are sisters and they act out both sibling and feminine rivalry in a way which would have been impossible for the Creole "soeurs de lait." Here, the brunette Louise is the active one: she has pursued love, become pregnant (like Noun), and sacrificed her material well-being for sexual passion. . . . She is also capable of intense jealousy, even of her own sister, and is so cruel to Valentine that her rebukes hasten the latter's death soon after that of Bénédict. The gentle, blond Valentine is more cautious, prudent, and modest, pulling away from love and attempting to extinguish her passion for Bénédict; she is incapable of understanding the violent jealousy and cruelty of her sister, yet accepts it as her just punishment for having committed adultery. . . . The intimate ties between Louise and Valentine are further strengthened by the convention of naming, a device which solidifies the fusion of their beings by means of a complex, convoluted interrelationship. Valentine was reared as a small child by her older sister, and the two refer to each other as if they had enjoyed a mother/daughter relationship. So, naturally, when Louise has a son, she names him Valentin after her sister/daughter. The young man is blond like his aunt and so closely resembles her in both appearance and character that his mother soon becomes jealous of their attachment. In addition, Valentine and Bénédict take charge of the education of Valentine, treating him as if he were their own son and thus usurping the mother's role. And when Valentin marries Athénais, the *fermière* to whom Bénédict had been engaged, his daughter is named Valentine; this pale blond child is not reared by her mother but by her grandmother, Louise, who has now reintegrated the roles of

sister and mother to take charge of another Valentine. Thus, the female roles of mother/sister/daughter/aunt/lover are in a constant state of flux in this novel, shifting and changing so that no one role remains distinct. One other facet of the naming convention completes the fusion of Louise and Valentine: this is the fact that Valentine's full name is Louise-Valentine, proof that each is merely one portion of a complete woman. (pp. 24-6)

The third set of sisters in Sand's first novels consists of Lélia and Pulchérie, two women who overtly represent contrasting possibilities of existence. Their psychosexual profiles are the basis of their ideologies; thus, the question of identity is a more serious problem here. The heroine Lélia, as a single entity, is viewed by others as a mass of impossible contradictions: angel/devil, fire/ice, monster/mistress, man/woman, sister/mother/lover. She never becomes a fully integrated being for either Magnus or Sténio, both of whom fail to possess her. The Rose/Blanche, actress/nun syndrome is dramatically manifested here by the sensual courtesan Pulchérie and the spiritual poetess Lélia. The two meet at an orgiastic feast after years of separation, and the central portion of *Lélia* relates their reunion, culminating in a merging of their identities as Sténio possesses Pulchérie's body, convinced that she is Lélia. (pp. 26-7)

It is evident that George Sand is attempting to analyze and define female sexuality through these pairs of sister heroines. Each pair represents a shifting, unstable psychosexual nature, a kind of sexual schizophrenia which must be resolved. The author accomplishes the reunion of the many facets of female eroticism through a kind of metamorphosis of two identities, roughly representing the binary oppositions of body and soul, senses and emotions, active and passive, male and female. Such union is achieved in erotic scenes which, although varied in each novel, involve violent sexual fusion. The central triangle in each case is the same: a male figure is attracted to and caught between two different, almost opposite, females. The androgynous fission which has occurred to produce these two types can only be resolved through this figure of a third, the "other," the desiring male; metamorphosis occurs with him as the mediator, either in his mind, as in *Valentine,* or through his body, as in *Indiana* and *Lélia.* The repetition of this pattern in the three novels indicates an underlying subconscious network through which Sand explores the ambiguities and contradictions of sexual identity. She thus applies the existential question "Who am I?" to two (or more) facets of the same personality.

Whether the young author uses her novels as a means of defining her own psychosexual orientation is difficult, if not impossible, to state definitively. . . . The erotic nature of her first novels seems to indicate that Sand was never able to integrate her diverging sexual tendencies, thus justifying, to a certain extent, the critics' perplexity.

What is more important for her art, however, is the undeniable richness of her erotic imagination; of the romantic novelists, only Balzac rivals her in this aspect of creativity. Her perhaps intuitive perception of sexual schizophrenia and the consequent hunger for fusion is all the more striking when one considers the comparative temerity of the romantic novel in general. Sand has been called the first modern, liberated woman; her gloriously pre-Freudian explorations of female psychosexuality support that claim. (pp. 34-5)

Nancy Rogers, "Psychosexual Identity and the Erotic Imagination in the Early Novels of George Sand," in *Studies in the Literary Imagination,* Vol. XII, No. 2, Fall, 1979, pp. 19-35.

V. S. PRITCHETT

(essay date 1979)

[Pritchett, a modern British writer, is respected for his mastery of the short story and for what critics describe as his judicious, reliable, and insightful literary criticism. Here, he explores the autobiographical nature of Sand's work.]

[George Sand] is shamelessly autobiographical. The love affair of the week, month or year, along with mysticism, socialism and The People was transposed into the novel that promptly followed; she spoke of herself as "the consumer" of men and women too, and the men often turned out to be projections of herself. The passions of her characters, their powerful jealousies, their alternations of exaltation and gloom, were her own. She was half Literature.

Her finer powers emerged when her fame as a novelist declined, above all in her *Histoire de ma vie,* in her lively travel writing and her letters. In her letters there is no need of Gothic castles or dreadful ravines: her mundane experience was extraordinary enough in itself. As a traveller she had eyes, ears and verve. The short pastoral novels *La mare au diable* (*The Haunted Pool*) or *François le Champi* (*The Country Waif*) are serene masterpieces drawn from her childhood and her love of nature, which awakened her senses as they awakened Colette's. She was close to the peasants of Nohant. The self is in these tales, but it is recollected or transposed in tranquility—in her own early life she had known what it was to be a waif, albeit a very fortunate one. These works have never lost their quiet, simple, truth-telling power. . . . (p. 117)

[George Sand's] inner class conflict enriched both

[her] exuberant imagination and those sympathies with the poor which took her into radical politics; strangely like Tolstoy—but without his guilt or torment—she turned to presenting the peasantry not as quaint folk or a gospel, but as sentient, expressive beings. . . . She had the humility and concern to discard dramatic earnestness without losing her psychological acumen or her art as a story teller who keeps her people in focus as the tradition of Pastoral does: very often her best work is a gloss on traditional forms.

In the feminist foreground of the present revival [of interest in George Sand] is *Lélia,* the confessional novel which she wrote at the age of twenty-nine. . . . Lélia is intended to be a Romantic heroine, a doomed but indomitable soul, one pursuing a mystical quest for spiritual love. She is beautiful, intellectual, independent, yet tormented by a sensuality that is nevertheless incapable of sexual happiness. She cannot be a nun like Santa Teresa nor can she be a courtesan or married woman. (pp. 117-18)

It is important to remember . . . that George Sand's prose feeds on a sensibility to music which dated from her childhood; she was alert to all sounds in nature and to all delicacies and sonorities of voice and instrument. (Her novels might be described as irresistible overtures to improbable operas which are—as they proceed—disordered by her didactic compulsion.) *Lélia,* I think, rises above this, because it is so personal and arbitrary in its succession of sounds and voices, and we are bounced into accepting the hyperbole as we would be if it were sung, though we may be secretly bored by the prolonging of the moans.

In *Lélia,* we listen to five voices: there is the voice of Sténio, the young poet lover whom Lélia freezes with Platonic love; she is an exalted *allumeuse;* there is Trenmor, the elderly penitent gambler and stoic—her analysis of the gambler's temperament is the best thing in the book: George Sand was at heart a gambler—there is Magnus, the fanatic priest who is made mad by the suppression of his sexual desires and who sees Lélia as a she-devil; there is Pulchérie, Lélia's sister, a genial courtesan living for sexual pleasure; and Lélia herself, defeated by her sexual coldness, horrified by the marriage bed, the mocker of a stagnant society, religion and the flesh. She is sick with self-love and her desires approach the incestuous: she seeks weak men who cannot master her, to whom she can be either a dominating mother, sister or nurse.

In chorus these voices sing out the arguments for and against spiritual love. As in opera, the plot is preposterous and scenes are extravagant and end without warning. (pp. 120-21)

Lélia is one of those self-dramatizations that break off as mood follows mood. She asks what God intended for men and women: whether he intended them to meet briefly and leave each other at once, for otherwise the sexes would destroy each other; whether the hypocrisy of a bourgeois society is the enemy; whether intellectual vision must be abnormal; whether poetry and religion corrupt. All the voices are George Sand herself—and very aware, as she frankly said, that she belonged to a generation which, for the moment, was consciously out to shock. . . .

One can see how much of the book comes out of Hoffmann and even more precisely from Balzac's equally chaotic and melodramatic *La Peau de chagrin.* . . . Both writers feel the expanding energies of the new century; both have the confident impulse toward the Absolute and to Omniscience; but hers is the kind of imagination and intellect that breaks off before suggesting a whole. Balzac and Sand were both absorbed by an imaginative greed; they worked themselves to the bone, partly because they were like that, partly because they created debts and openly sought a vast public. Their rhetoric was a nostalgia for the lost Napoleonic glory.

How thoroughly she toiled in her social-problem novels! The tedious *Compagnon du Tour de France* is a garrulous study of the early trade unions, a politically pious book, enlivened by her strong visual sense. In the far more sympathetic *Mauprat* she goes to the heart of her life-long debt to Rousseau. . . . (p. 123)

George Sand herself did not think we should be punished for our sins or our grave faults of character, but that we were called upon to learn from them: they were—*grace à* Rousseau—opportunities for interesting self-education and reform. She is not a doctrinaire like Gorki in his communist phase. Her advantage as a woman is that she is a psychologist who gives hostilities their emotional due: they are indications of the individual's right to his temperament. She may have been a domineering, ruthless woman and very cunning and double-minded with it, but there is scarcely a book that is not redeemed by her perceptions, small though they may be.

She understands the rich very well—'There are hours of impunity in château life'—and she thinks of the poor as individuals but flinches from them as a case. Two words recur continually in her works: 'delirium,' which may be ecstatic, bad, or, more interestingly, a psychological outlet; and 'boredom'—energy and desire had been exhausted. One can see that she is woman but not Woman. The little fable of *François de Champi* shows that she used every minute of her life; for not only was she in a fortunate sense a waif, as I have said, but an enlightened waif; and we note that when François grows up he marries the widow who has been a mother to him. Most of George Sand's men were waifs in one way or another; the Higher Incest was to be their salvation. Women were the real power figures, whereas men were consumable. She liked to pilfer their brains. (p. 124)

V. S. Pritchett, "George Sand," in his *The Mythmakers: Literary Essays,* Random House, 1979, pp. 115-27.

SOURCES FOR FURTHER STUDY

Blount, Paul G. *George Sand and the Victorian World.* Athens: The University of Georgia Press, 1979, 190 p.

> Traces the evolution of Victorian attitudes towards Sand's work and provides valuable references to important early reviews and essays.

Cate, Curtis. *George Sand: A Biography.* Boston: Houghton Mifflin Co., 1975, 812 p.

> The first major biography of Sand since André Maurois's *Lélia: The Life of George Sand.*

Crecelius, Kathryn J. *Family Romances: George Sand's Early Novels.* Bloomington: Indiana University Press, 1987, 183 p.

> Provides criticism and interpretation on Sand's early works.

Maurois, André. *Lélia: The Life of George Sand.* Translated by Gerard Hopkins. New York: Harper & Brothers, 1953, 482 p.

> An authoritative biography.

Naginski, Isabelle Hoog. *George Sand: Writing for Her Life.* New Brunswick, N.J.: Rutgers University Press, 1991, 281 p.

> Analysis of the early novels of George Sand.

Rea, Annabelle. "Maternity and Marriage: Sand's Use of Fairy Tale and Myth." *Studies in the Literary Imagination* XII, No. 2 (Fall 1979): 37-47.

> Analyzes elements from fairy tales, myths, legends, and archetypal patterns found in Sand's novels.

Carl Sandburg

1878-1967

(Full name Carl August Sandburg; also wrote under pseudonyms Charles A. Sandburg, Militant, and Jack Phillips.) American poet, biographer, autobiographer, novelist, journalist, songwriter, editor, and author of children's books.

INTRODUCTION

*O*ne of America's most celebrated poets during his lifetime, Sandburg developed a unique and controversial form of free verse that captured the rhythms and color of Midwestern American vernacular. While some critics have dismissed Sandburg for his sentimental depictions of urban and agrarian landscapes and for his simple style, others have lauded his rhapsodic and lyrical technique and his effective patterns of parallelism and repetition. In *Chicago Poems* (1916), his first major collection and one of his most respected works, Sandburg employs images and topics not commonly considered poetical to paint realistic portraits of common people in such environments as the railroad yard, the marketplace, and the factory. Louis D. Rubin affirmed Sandburg's unique approach: "Sandburg's particular talent is that he opens up areas of our experience which are not ordinarily considered objects of aesthetic contemplation, through language that enables him, and us, to recognize such experience in new ways."

Sandburg was one of seven children born to hardworking, conservative Swedish immigrants in Galesburg, Illinois. Although Sandburg's parents were fluent in both English and Swedish, they did not encourage their children's education. Sandburg developed an interest in reading and writing but was forced to leave school at age thirteen to help supplement the family income. Before borrowing his father's railroad pass at age eighteen to visit Chicago for the first time, Sandburg drove a milk wagon, worked in a barber shop, and was an apprentice tinsmith. He would later utilize the images and vernacular he was exposed to during such experiences to create verse reflective of the working class.

After spending three and a half months traveling through Iowa, Missouri, Kansas, and Colorado on the railroad, Sandburg volunteered for service in the Spanish-American War in 1898, and served in Puerto Rico. As a veteran he was offered free tuition for a year at Lombard College in Galesburg. He studied there for four years, but left in 1902 before graduating. It was at Lombard that Sandburg began to develop his talents for writing, encouraged by the scholar Philip Green Wright. On a small hand press in the basement of his home, Wright set the type for Sandburg's first publications: *In Reckless Ecstasy* (1904), *Incidentals* (1907), *The Plaint of a Rose* (1908), and *Joseffy* (1910). These four slim volumes contain Sandburg's juvenilia and are stylistically conventional. In retrospect Sandburg declared them "many odd pieces . . . not worth later reprint."

Sandburg gained recognition when Harriet Monroe, editor of the progressive literary periodical *Poetry: A Magazine of Verse,* published six of Sandburg's poems in 1914. During this time Sandburg cultivated literary friendships with, among others, Edgar Lee Masters, Vachel Lindsay, Amy Lowell, and Sherwood Anderson, and gained the attention of Henry Holt and Company, the firm that was to publish his first major volume of poetry, *Chicago Poems.* This collection, with its humanistic renderings of urban life, place descriptions, and casual assemblage of character sketches, provides a stark but idealistic view of the working class. While "Chicago," one of Sandburg's most celebrated poems, depicts the faults of the midwestern metropolis, it also praises what Sandburg considered the joy and vitality integral to life there. "Chicago," along with the poem "Skyscraper," which proclaims that buildings have souls, initiated what was to be called the "Chicago Myth," or the belief that Chicago was somehow tougher than other cities but also more genuine and robust. *Chicago Poems* is generally regarded as one of Sandburg's finest poetic achievements, but initial reaction to the volume was mixed, with many reviewers finding the subject matter startling and the prosaic poetry oddly structured.

While *Chicago Poems* depicts the urban experience, Sandburg's next volume, *Cornhuskers* (1918), explores the realities of agrarian life. In such poems as "Prairie" and "Laughing Corn," Sandburg expresses his fondness for family life and nature. Also included in this collection are a number of war poems with images of soldiers who died in conflicts previous to World War I. *Smoke and Steel,* published in 1920, addresses complex postwar issues such as industrialization and urbanization and was less optimistic and idealistic than Sandburg's earlier works. With *Slabs of the Sunburnt West* (1922), Sandburg began using a technique in which a series of images are presented in parallel forms as well as in rough, colloquial language. In 1928 Sandburg published his fifth significant volume of poetry, *Good Morning, America.* This collection begins with

his thirty-eight "Tentative (First Model) Definitions of Poetry," but because Sandburg never developed a consistent critical theory of poetry, these definitions are generally considered unenlightening. In this volume Sandburg delves into mythology, history, and universal humanism through extended use of proverbs and folk idioms. His concentration on historical fact foreshadowed the content of Sandburg's epic prose-poem, *The People, Yes* (1936). In this work, which he crafted over a period of eight years, Sandburg fused American colloquialisms with descriptions of historical and contemporary events to create a collection of verbal portraits of the American people. Because Sandburg chose to allow his subjects to speak for themselves, many critics accused him of foregoing the role of poet for folklorist. While considered an important historical and cultural reflection of the American people, *The People, Yes* is not widely regarded as poetry in the traditional sense.

Sandburg won the Pulitzer Prize in 1951 for *Complete Poems* (1950), a cumulation of his six previous volumes of poetry. While numerous critics commented briefly on the occasion of its publication, few took the opportunity to evaluate the whole of Sandburg's poetic career. William Carlos Williams represents the general critical response to this volume: "Carl Sandburg petered out as a poet ten years ago. I imagine he wanted it that way. His poems themselves said what they had to say, piling it up, then just went out like a light. He had no answers, he didn't seek any." However, while many critics spoke nostalgically about the "Chicago Poet" of 1916, they failed to acknowledge or comment upon the seventy-two poems published for the first time in *Complete Poems.* Recent commentators use such poems as "The Fireborn Are at Home in Fire" and "Mr. Longfellow and His Boy" to demonstrate Sandburg's continuing stylistic and thematic development, which was also evident in his last volume, *Honey and Salt* (1963). Despite the fact that some commentators noted a quiet and reflective mastery of the poetic craft in the title poem, "Foxgloves," and "Timesweep," *Honey and Salt* generated little critical attention.

In addition to his poetry, Sandburg also produced a multivolume biography of Abraham Lincoln in which he related incidents from Lincoln's life in the manner of a story rather than as a series of historical facts. Although some critics expressed their uneasiness with Sandburg's artistic license, most praised his vivid, "folksy" presentation and the enormous amount of factual detail he included in the biography. In *Abraham Lincoln: The Prairie Years* (1926), which consists of two volumes, Sandburg explored Lincoln's youth and his adult life before he became President. The four-volume *Abraham Lincoln: The War Years* (1939) opens with Lincoln departing Springfield, Illinois, to serve as President and concludes with the return of Lincoln's body to Springfield for burial. The latter volumes offer a panoramic view of the Civil War and feature a large cast of well-developed historical figures, including government officials, soldiers, and common citizens. Sandburg achieved a sense of drama and intrigue by developing events in sequential order from the viewpoints of those involved and by meticulously recreating historical events. Sandburg was awarded the Pulitzer Prize in history for *Abraham Lincoln: The War Years.* While Sandburg won fame primarily as a poet and as a biographer of Lincoln, he was also recognized for several other literary activities. He wrote several volumes of tales for children, known collectively as the "Rootebaga Stories" and a historical novel set in America, *Remembrance Rock,* which spans the arrival of the Pilgrims to the onset of World War II.

Sandburg was an eminent figure of the "Chicago Renaissance" and the era encompassing World War I and the Great Depression, but his reputation waned in mid-century when his folksy and regional approach was overshadowed by the allusive and cerebral verse

of such poets as Ezra Pound and T. S. Eliot. While Sandburg continued to depict ordinary people in their everyday settings, other poets were gaining critical acclaim for internalizing and codifying experiences. Nonetheless, some recent commentators purport that this disfavor was a result of the whims of various critical movements, and not based on the strength or significance of Sandburg's poetic contribution. Dan G. Hoffman asserts: "[Sandburg] was a realistic voice which caught the cacaphonous choruses of 'the mob—the crowd—the mass' and made a new poetry in a new form, from the jangling noises about our ears."

(For further information about Sandburg's life and works, see *Concise Dictionary of Literary Biography, 1865-1917; Contemporary Authors,* Vols. 7-8, 25-28; *Contemporary Authors New Revision Series,* Vol. 35; *Contemporary Literary Criticism,* Vols. 1, 4, 10, 15, 35; *Dictionary of Literary Biography,* Vols. 17, 54; *Major 20th-Century Writers; Poetry Criticism,* Vol. 2; and *Something About the Author,* Vol. 8.)

CRITICAL COMMENTARY

LOUIS UNTERMEYER

(essay date 1918)

[Untermeyer was an American anthologist of poetry and short fiction. In the following excerpt, he studies Sandburg's first two major volumes of poetry, *Chicago Poems* and *Cornhuskers*.]

When Carl Sandburg's *Chicago Poems* appeared two years ago, most of the official votaries and vestrymen in the temple of the Muse raised their hands in pious horror at this open violation of their carefully enshrined sanctities. In the name of their belovéd Past, they prepared a bill of particulars that bristled with charges as contradictory as they were varied. They were all united however on one point—Sandburg's brutality. In this they were correct. (p. 263)

As in *Chicago Poems,* the first poem of his new volume—*Cornhuskers*—brims with an uplifted coarseness, an almost animal exultation that is none the less an exaltation.

I was born on the prairie, and the milk of its
  wheat, the red of its clover, the eyes of its
  women, gave me a song and a slogan.
Here the water went down, the icebergs slid with
  gravel, the gaps and the valleys hissed, and the
  black loam came.

(pp. 263-64)

These are the opening lines of **"Prairie,"** a wider and more confident rhythm than Sandburg has yet attempted. The gain in power is evident at once and grows with each section of this new collection. The tone in *Cornhuskers* has more depth and dignity; the note is not louder, but it is larger. In *Chicago Poems* there were times when the poet was so determined to worship ruggedness that one could hear his adjectives strain to achieve a physical strength of their own. One occasionally was put in mind of the professional strong man in front of a mirror, of virility basking in the spotlight, of an epithet exhibiting its muscle. Here the accent is less vociferous, more vitalizing; it is a summoning of strong things rather than the mere stereotypes of strength. Observe the unusual athletic beauty of **"Leather Leggings," "Always the Mob," "The Four Brothers,"** and [**"Prayers of Steel"**]. . . .

These and a dozen others seem a direct answer to Whitman's hope of a democratic poetry that would express itself in a democratic and even a distinctively American speech. He maintained that before America could have a powerful poetry our poets would have to learn the use of hard and powerful words; the greatest artists, he insisted, were simple and direct, never merely "polite or obscure." "Words are magic . . . limber, lasting, fierce words," he wrote in an unfinished sketch for a projected lecture. "Do you suppose the liberties

---

Principal Works

*In Reckless Ecstasy (poetry) 1904

*Incidentals (poetry) 1907

*The Plaint of a Rose (poetry) 1908

*Joseffy (poetry) 1910

Chicago Poems (poetry) 1916

Cornhuskers (poetry) 1918

The Chicago Race Riots (journalism) 1919

Smoke and Steel (poetry) 1920

Rootabaga Stories (fables) 1922

Slabs of the Sunburnt West (poetry) 1922

Rootabaga Pigeons (fables) 1923

Abraham Lincoln: The Prairie Years (biography) 1926

Carl Sandburg (autobiography) 1926

Selected Poems (poetry) 1926

Good Morning, America (poetry) 1928

Mary Lincoln: Wife and Widow (biography) 1932

The People, Yes (poetry) 1936

Abraham Lincoln: The War Years (biography) 1939

Home Front Memo (journalism/radio broadcasts) 1943

Remembrance Rock (novel) 1948

Complete Poems (poetry) 1950

Always the Young Strangers (autobiography) 1955

Honey and Salt (poetry) 1963

The Letters of Carl Sandburg (letters) 1968

*These volumes were published under the name Charles A. Sandburg.

---

shows a cosmic use of penetrating patois; it is Sweden-borg in terms of State Street. This mysticism shines out of **"Caboose Thoughts, Wilderness, Southern Pacific, Old Timers."** And it is always a more extended and musical spirituality than the earlier volume; the new collection may not be more dynamic, but it is more lyric.

The struggles, the social criticism, the concentrated anger, and the protests are here as prominently as in *Chicago Poems,* but they assert themselves with less effort. The war has temporarily harmonized them; they are still rebellious, but somehow resigned. The chants of revolt are seldom out of tune with Sandburg's purely pictorial pieces. Both are the product of a strength that derives its inspiration from the earth; they are made of tough timber; they have "strong roots in the clay and worms." (p. 264)

Louis Untermeyer, "Strong Timber," in *The Dial,* Chicago, Vol. LXV, October 5, 1918, pp. 263-64.

AMY LOWELL
(essay date 1920)

[Lowell, an American poet and critic, was a proponent of Imagism in American verse. In the following excerpt, she examines manifestations of Sandburg's socialistic political ideology in his poetry.]

Two men speak in Mr. Sandburg, a poet and a propagandist. His future will depend upon which finally dominates the other. Since a poet must speak by means of suggestion and a propagandist succeeds by virtue of clear presentation, in so far as a propagandist is a poet, just in that ratio is he a failure where his propaganda is concerned. On the other hand, the poet who leaves the proper sphere of his art to preach, even by analogy, must examine the mote in his verse very carefully lest, perchance, it turn out a beam.

In my study of Mr. Sandburg in *Tendencies in Modern American Poetry* I pointed out this danger of his practice. Then I had only one book to go upon, now I have three, [the latest being *Smoke and Steel*], and the danger seems to me to be looming larger with terrific speed. It may be that Mr. Sandburg has determined to stuff all his theories into one book and let it go at that. In which case there cannot be too much objection, but I fear—oh, I fear.

Mr. Sandburg loves people, perhaps I should say the "people." But I believe it is more than that. I think he has a real love for human beings. But evidently, from his books, his experience with people is limited to a few types, and it is a pity that these types should

---

and the brawn of These States have to do only with delicate lady-words? with gloved gentlemen-words?" Later he said, "American writers will show far more freedom in the use of names. Ten thousand common and idiomatic words are growing, or are today already grown, out of which vast numbers could be used by American writers—words that would be welcomed by the nation, being of the national blood."

No contemporary is so responsive to these limber and idiomatic phrases as Sandburg. His language lives almost as fervidly as the life from which it is taken. And yet his intensity is not always raucous; it would be a great mistake to believe that Sandburg excels only in verse that is heavy-fisted and stentorian. . . .

This creative use of proper names and slang (which would so have delighted Whitman), this interlarding of cheapness and nobility is Sandburg's most characteristic idiom as well as his greatest gift. And it is this mingling that enriches his heritage of mingled blood; the rude practical voice of the American speaks through a strain of ruder Swedish symbolism. Beneath the slang, one is aware of the mystic; *Cornhuskers*

so often be the kind of persons whom only the morbidly sensitive, unhealthily developed, modern mind has ever thought it necessary to single out for prominence—prominence of an engulfing sort, that is. If we admit that the degraded are degraded there is not much danger of losing our perspective; if we hug them to our hearts and turn a cold shoulder to the sober and successful of the world, then we are running fast toward chaos. . . .

In *Cornhuskers* Mr. Sandburg seemed content to let the back alley folk stay in the back alleys. He spoke to us of other things, of the great, wide prairies, for instance, and, in so speaking, achieved a masterpiece. He gave his lyrical gift far more space than he usually allows, and the result was some of the finest poems of the modern movement. For Mr. Sandburg has a remarkable originality. His outlook is his own, his speech meets it, together the two make rarely beautiful poetry, when Mr. Sandburg permits. Then conscience pricks him, the "people" rise and confront him, gibbering like ghouls, he experiences an uneasy sense of betrayal and writes "Galoots" for example. I think these things hurt Mr. Sandburg as much as the things they represent hurt him. If they did not hurt him they would not have become an obsession. Much morbid verse has been written by tortured lovers, and we shall never understand these particular poems of Mr. Sandburg's until we realize that he too is a tortured lover, a lover of humanity in travail. It is seldom that the kind of exaggerated misery which Mr. Sandburg feels produces good poetry, and these poems are seldom successful.

I do not wish to imply that all the poems in [*Smoke and Steel*] are the results of the mood in question. That would be far from the case, but the proportion of such poems is too great for the thorough satisfaction of a reader who is a profound admirer of Mr. Sandburg at his best—and, shall I add, his most lyrical. The book is divided into eight sections, of which only two, "Mist Forms" and "Haze" are frankly lyrical, while another two, "People Who Must" and "Circle of Doors," are as frankly the other thing, which, for want of a better name, we may call "the obsession." But this obsession creeps into many poems in the sections, "Playthings of the Wind" and "Passports"; even when "it," specifically, is not present, some crude and irrelevant turn of speech, the outgrowth of it, will crop up and ruin an otherwise noble thing. Colloquialisms, downright slang, have their place in poetry as in all literature. My contention here is not that Mr. Sandburg does not often use them with happy effect, but that quite as often he drags them in where (to my ear, at least) they should emphatically not be. A line like "We'll get you, you sbxyzch!" may be perfect realism, but it hurts the reader, as does "stenogs" and "thingamajig." The last appears in a poem in which it is at least in place if we admit the poem itself, **"Manual**

System,"** to a place anywhere; but "stenogs" is smashed into a serious poem called **"Trinity Peace,"** which is built around a highly poetic thought. "Stenographers" would not have been out of order, because it is a mere description of a calling, and in one stanza Mr. Sandburg is enumerating people by their callings; to shorten the word into "stenogs" brings in an element of cheapness, which in this instance has no dramatic value, and so rivets the attention as to break the force of the poem. One can skip such sheer propaganda as **"Alley Rats," "The Mayor of Gary"** and **"The Liars,"** if one wants to, but it is hard to have something otherwise beautiful spoiled by a line or a word, which is hopelessly out of key. It dislocates the mood of appreciation, and is, I believe, the chief cause why the general reader does not yet entirely recognize how fine and true a poet Mr. Sandburg is.

Having registered my protest, which is the disagreeable part of the critic's work, let me immediately admit that one of Mr. Sandburg's excellencies is that he sets down the life about him, that very life of the people of which I have been speaking. When he sees it as a poet, he makes it poetically adequate; it is only when he sees it obliquely as a biased sentimentalist that he injures it and himself. He has an inclusive vision, something which gathers up the essences of life and work and relates them to the pulsing fabric which is the whole energy of human existence. His **"Prairie"** was not only a slice of Mother Earth, it was Mother Earth cherishing her children. So, in **"Smoke and Steel,"** we have not a mere metal being manufactured, not mere men toiling at their work—we have man's impulse to spend himself in creation and the far ramifications of what that creation means. . . .

"Smoke and Steel" is worthy to stand beside **"Prairie."** There is an epic sweep to this side of Mr. Sandburg's work. Somehow it brings the reader into closer contact with his country, reading these poems gives me more of a patriotic emotion than ever "The Star-Spangled Banner" has been able to do. This is America, and Mr. Sandburg loves her so much that suddenly we realize how much we love her, too. What has become dulled by habit quickens under his really magical touch. Freight cars mean all the prosperity of the country; in the first stanza of **"Work Gangs"** they become a great chorus of men's hearts building a land to live in, to grow and make homes and happiness in. Because he can do this Mr. Sandburg has a glorious responsibility set on his shoulders.

The seeing eye—Mr. Sandburg has it to a superlative degree, and, wedded to it, an imaginative utterance which owes nothing whatever to literature or tradition. It is a fascinating and baffling study this of examining how Mr. Sandburg does it. The technique of this magic is so unusual that no old knowledge applies. It is, more than anything else, the sharp, surprising rightness of his descriptions which gives Mr. Sandburg his high position in the poetry of today. . . .

Some people have had difficulty in understanding Mr. Sandburg's rhythms, these long, slow cadences, like the breath of air over an open moor. Indeed they are the very gift of the prairies, for where else do we find them? Not in Whitman, not in the Frenchmen, not among his contemporaries. Mr. Sandburg's ear seldom fails, I can recall but one instance of a false notation. In **"How Yesterday Looked,"** occurs this stanza:

Ask me how the sunset looked on
  between the wind going
Down and the moon coming up and
  I would struggle
To tell the how of it.

This may be a typographical error, for the beat of the cadence requires the first line to end after "looked on," the second line after "coming up," and the rest of the stanza to be contained in the third line. But, even here, the error occurs merely in the break of the lines and not in the cadence per se.

There is one thing we can say with Mr. Sandburg's three books in front of us. Either this is a very remarkable poet or he is nothing, for which the minors he clearly has no place. He has greatly dared, and I personally believe that posterity, with its pruning hand, will mount him high on the ladder of poetic achievement.

Amy Lowell, "Poetry and Propaganda," in *The New York Times Book Review,* October 24, 1920, p. 7.

STEPHEN VINCENT BENÉT

(essay date 1936)

[Benét was an American poet and fiction writer. In the excerpt below, he praises Sandburg's *The People, Yes* for its celebration and documentation of American life and vernacular.]

Carl Sandburg occupies a unique position in the contemporary American scene. When he first came before the public, with *Chicago Poems,* he was labeled by the people who love to label things—largely on such poems as **"Chicago"** and **"To a Contemporary Bunk-Shooter"**—as a brutal realist and a smasher of idols. Yet that same book showed a poet who could work with great sensitiveness and grace, and bring to his work not only an interest in live words and live people but a sort of folk fairytale quality that was as far east of automatic realism as it was west of sentimentality. He has always been an American but his Americanism has never been a horse-and-buggy hired for the occa-

sion—he talks United States because that is his language and he talks it with a sure tongue. . . .

[In] *The People, Yes,* he brings us the longest and most sustained piece of work he has yet done in verse. It is a book that will irritate some; and some will find it meaningless. . . . It deals with people; it deals with these times. But Carl Sandburg has his own way of going about things. He will go back to the Tower of Babel if he feels like it; he will go forward to the wreck of the skyscrapers. . . .

And there is something to be said about the man who was feeding a hatful of doughnuts to a horse, explaining to the curious, "I want to see how many he'll eat before he asks for a cup of coffee." There is something to be said about doctors and restaurant cashiers, about airplane stunters and mine strikers and city editors, about the railroad engineer on the Pennsy, directing in his will that they should burn his body as a piece of rolling stock beyond rehabilitation and repair and scatter the ashes from the cab on the Beverley curve, and about the bottom of the sea which accommodates the mountain ranges. *The People, Yes* is not a dogmatic book and it turns corners and goes around alleys. It is full of proverbs, questions, memoranda, folklore, faces and wonderings. It is a fresco and a field of grass and a man listening quietly to all the commonplace, extraordinary things that people say. Yet it has its own coherence and its own confidence.

It is hard to get all the people into any one book. You forget two martins on the shore of Lake Michigan, you forget the hobo who said, "Give me something to eat. I'm so thirsty I don't know where I'm going to sleep tonight." And then you have to turn around and start over again. Otherwise, you begin to talk about case histories, proletarians, the lower classes, the typical American farmer, the rabble, the intelligent voters. . . . But Carl Sandburg doesn't do that. He knows all that has been said against the people—and said in this country, past and present.

It is unfair to pick bits out of a poem that owes its power to its mass and its cumulative effect, to its rambling diversions, even to its occasional long-windedness and hold them up like dress samples in front of the reader. But Sandburg's attitude is an important one and I have to quote to show how that attitude expresses itself. Though quotations, no matter how selected, will not give the full flavor of this book. For it is the people themselves who are celebrated here—more completely perhaps than by any American poet since Whitman and with as essential a love. The people "so often sleepy, weary, enigmatic," the people so often saying "aw nuts, aw go peddle yer papers," saying, "Men will yez fight or will yez run?" and "The coat and pants do the work but the vest gets the gravy," are yet the rock and the spring and the good ground.

The people will live on.
The learning and blundering people will live on,
They will be tricked and sold and again sold
And go back to the nourishing earth for root-
　holds. . . .
. . . This reaching is alive.
The panderers and liars have violated and smutted
　it.
Yet this reaching is alive yet for lights and keep-
　sakes.

And, if Sandburg writes with honesty, he also writes, and with a biting anger, of the rare and suave folk who pay themselves a fat swag of higher salaries while they out wages, of the pay day, patriots that Lincoln called "respectable scoundrels," of all those who deny, debauch, oppress, mock, enslave the people, of all those who say, "Your people, sir, is a great beast," covertly or openly, in past times or now. (p. 1)

This voice does not come from Moscow or Union Square. It comes out of Western America, soil of that soil and wheat of that wheat, and it is the voice of somebody who knows the faces, the folkwords and the tall tales of the people. It is as honest as it is questioning and it speaks its deep convictions in a tongue we know. And there is warning in it as well as hope. Sometimes it goes runabout; not all of it is poetry. But it is the memoranda of the people. And every line of it says "The People—Yes." (p. 2)

Stephen Vincent Benét, "Carl Sandburg—Poet of the Prairie People," in *New York Herald Tribune Books,* August 23, 1936, pp. 1-2.

ROBERT SHERWOOD

(essay date 1939)

[Sherwood was an American playwright. In the following excerpt, he provides an overview of Sandburg's biographical works on Abraham Lincoln.]

Twenty years ago Carl Sandburg of Illinois started to write the fullest, richest, most understanding of all the Lincoln biographies. His work is now complete. *The War Years* follows *The Prairie Years* into the treasure house which belongs, like Lincoln himself, to the whole human family. It has been a monumental undertaking; it is grandly realized.

The War Years begins where *The Prairie Years* ended, with Lincoln's departure from Springfield—an unknown, threatened, doubted man. It ends with the return of his body to the soil on which it grew. Mr. Sandburg's finest passages are those describing his final journey, and all the immediate aftermaths of the assassination, the shocking effect on men everywhere. Even

the wild tribesmen in the Caucasus were asking a traveler, Leo Tolstoy, to tell them of this Western man who was "so great that he even forgave the crimes of his greatest enemies." And Tolstoy told them, "Lincoln was a humanitarian as broad as the world."

The War Years is compounded of such quotations. We are enabled to look at Lincoln through thousands of contemporary eyes, including those of Tolstoy, and Jefferson Davis, and John Bright, M.P., and Hendrik Ibsen, and Nathaniel Hawthorne, and a South Carolina lady named Mary Chestnut. Mr. Sandburg gives us his own estimates of many other figures, big and little, of the period, but not of Abraham Lincoln. He indulges in no speculation as to what was going on within the heart and soul and mind of this peculiar man. If there is anything lacking in *The War Years* it is the presence of two men of the prairie years, Joshua Speed and William H. Herndon, who saw more deeply into Lincoln than did any others who ever knew him. When Lincoln stepped into the White House he stepped into a great isolation which no one—not even his old friends, Browning and Lamon, nor his secretaries, Nicolay and Hay—seems to have penetrated. In the analyses of his character provided by those who observed him at closest range the word "unfathomable" recurs again and again.

In *The Prairie Years,* with fewer documents and many more myths at his disposal, Mr. Sandburg gave greater play to his own lyrical imagination. Any one can indulge in guesswork about the raw young giant who emerged from the mists of Kentucky, and Indiana, and Sangamon County, Illinois, and Mr. Sandburg's guesses were far better than most. But in *The War Years* he sticks to the documentary evidence, gathered from a fabulous number of sources. He indulges in one superb lyrical outburst at the conclusion of the chapter in which is described the dedication of the cemetery at Gettysburg; and, in the last volume, after John Wilkes Booth has fired the one bullet in his brass derringer pistol, Mr. Sandburg writes with the poetic passion and the somber eloquence of the great masters of tragedy.

Mr. Sandburg's method is unlike that of any biographer since Homer. He starts *The War Years* with the usual appreciative Foreword surveying his source material—and this Foreword provides an excellent survey of Lincolniana—but he reveals the odd nature of his essential research when he says, "Taking my guitar and a program of songs and readings and traveling from coast to coast a dozen times in the last twenty years, in a wide variety of audiences I have met sons and daughters of many of the leading players in the terrific drama of the Eighteen Sixties." From these sons and daughters he obtained old letters and pictures and clippings, and reminiscences and rumors which led him to upper shelves in remote libraries. Thus, his "program of songs" (like Homer's) brought him into the very spirit of the people, the same people of whom—and by whom, and for whom—was Abraham Lincoln. Quite properly, Mr. Sandburg's great work is not the story of the one man's life. It is a folk biography. The hopes and apprehensions of millions, their loves and hates, their exultation and despair, were reflected truthfully in the deep waters of Lincoln's being, and so they are reflected truthfully in these volumes. (p. 1)

Any review of *The War Years* at this time can be no more than a smattering report of quickly remembered fragments. It is so great a work that it will require great reading and great reflection before any true appreciation of its permanent value can be formed. It will beget many other books. But, in the meantime, the people of this nation and this human race may well salute and thank Carl Sandburg for the magnitude of his contribution to our common heritage. (p. 14)

Robert E. Sherwood, "The Lincoln of Carl Sandburg," in *The New York Times Book Review*, December 3, 1939, pp. 1, 14.

DAN G. HOFFMAN
(essay date 1950)

[An American poet, educator, and critic, Hoffman is the author of a number of critical works, including *English Literary Criticism: Romantic and Victorian* (1963). In the following excerpt, he examines Sandburg's attempts to represent communal emotion in his works.]

"The hardest part of being a pioneer is remaining a contemporary," Morton D. Zabel wrote of Sandburg in 1936. It has been Sandburg's misfortune to see his own reputation decline during the dozen years since his most successful poetry was published. Rising to fame in the excitement of the "Little Renaissance," he continued during the '20's and '30's to be popular among readers who take their poetry seriously. When the lyricism of Aiken, Cummings and Millay set the boom decade to music, Carl Sandburg described deserted city brickyards where "Fluxions of yellow and dusk on the waters / Make a wide dreaming pansy of an old pond in the night." When the depression gave poetry of social protest its short-lived hour, Sandburg found his fame greater than it had ever been. He had been protesting for twenty years; the old lines in "Hog butcher for the world" sounded still fresh, while those of Masters and Lindsay, his fellow-rebels of the "Little Renaissance," seemed naive and quaintly dated. From the beginning an accurate observer of the urban scene, Sandburg had made city life the surface as well as the subject of his poetry. His was a realistic voice which caught the cacaphonous choruses of "the mob—the crowd—the mass" and made a new poetry, in a new form, from the jangling noises about our ears.

Sandburg has a following still, but it no longer numbers many of modern poetry's serious readers. The loose, proselike surface, the flat, colloquial diction, and the apparent lack of organization and of intensity in his verse have alienated those who see Eliot, Pound, and Wallace Stevens as the chief poetic spokesmen of the contemporary dilemma. "The age demanded an image / Of its accelerated grimace," Pound told us when the age had scarcely begun; within a few short years Sandburg's image for the age seemed singularly inappropriate. He had made an abstraction of "the people," and his poetry was to represent communal, rather than individual, emotion. This program of literary populism denied the poet access to the dark night of the soul, which must ever be an individual experience. It also limited the range of his language, as well as of his emotions, to the popular, the communal, and only too often, the common. Yet these limitations are exactly the sources of Sandburg's strength. In denying himself the experiences of the more introspective artist and the private diction of the individualistic poet, he became a pioneer in ways of feeling and speaking which most other poets neglect.

Nonetheless, Sandburg is now very much out of favor among the *avant garde,* both as poet and as social thinker. His name is rarely seen in the advanced quarterlies; when it does come up, it is attended by little praise. When *Poetry* recently published its thirty-fifth anniversary issue, the presence of Sandburg among the contributors seemed anachronistic. Indeed, it was almost a matter for wonder, as though a man were to address a memorial service held in his own honor.

Before taking for granted the justice of Sandburg's present eclipse it may be worth while to look into the reasons for his decline. Is the descent of his reputation caused solely by the New Critics' preference for intensity, form, and intellectualized content? Or is it possible that Sandburg has been neglected because most readers have neglected to learn how to read him? Why is it that, while everyone concedes him to be a pioneer in communal expression, so few have followed his lead with any success? Is this because his followers have imitated his faults without understanding his virtues? Or is it because the program to which he has dedicated his career as a poet is an unpromising, even an impossible, basis for art? (pp. 265-66)

Since his favorable critics have been at . . . a loss to understand the form of his verse, it is no surprise that his significant followers are few, though his imitators many. His casual stanzas are so difficult to reconcile with the discipline expected in traditional poetry that the critics are puzzled, and the poet attracts a kind of adulation-by-imitation from those who think that his is an easier way to spread poetry on a page. This opinion is widely held, and has contributed to the decline of Sandburg's prestige.

However, there is more form in Sandburg's verse than meets the eye. I believe a careful reading of *The People, Yes* will show a definite and ingenious organization of the very lists of proverbs and catalogues of popular phrases which seemed to Mr. Zabel to reveal "no apparent principle of contrast or structure." These lists do not, as Professor [Willard] Thorp suggested, "merely assemble the collective wisdom of the people." There is more to Sandburg's art than that; otherwise [critics] would find the files of *The World Almanac* just as satisfying as Sandburg's poems.

The most distinguished portions of *The People, Yes* are those in which the poet succeeds, or nearly succeeds, in imposing form upon his almost intractible materials. Where his scheme can be recognized, those parts of the book assume a power they did not have before that recognition. One such portion includes Sections 36 through 47, which brings to a focus several of Sandburg's major themes. A brief analysis of Sandburg's method here will clarify his intentions for us, and help make evident the direction in which his writings have pioneered. And since his faults are interfused with his virtues, we can also see the limitations of his achievement, and the dangers inherent in making that achievement an example.

In this portion of *The People, Yes,* Sandburg's theme is recovery: recovery from the economic paralysis of the depression, and more immediately, recovery of human dignity from the ravages of want, hopelessness, and fear. The assertion,

"I am zero, naught, cipher,"
meditated the symbol preceding the numbers

introduces six verse paragraphs which argue that money brings status, pride, and selfishness. Then,

Said the scorpions of hate: "The poor hate the rich. The rich hate the poor. The south hates the north. The west hates the east. The workers hate their bosses. The bosses hate their workers. . . . We are a house divided against itself. We are millions of hands raised against each other. We are united in but one aim—getting the dollar. And when we get the dollar we employ it to get more dollars."

The capitalistic economy makes men inhuman. In the next section they wrangle over "what is mine" and "what is yours" and "who says so?" Yet along with the arguing and hating there is joking and laughter, though the humor may be wry indeed.

Sandburg describes the farmers who had overproduced their crops and cattle until they were themselves near starvation. Theirs is the smoldering hatred that verges on violence:

"I want to shoot somebody but I don't know who.
"We'll do something. You wait and see.
"We don't have to stand for this skin game if we're free Americans."

Speaking through the many voices he has chosen to speak for him or to echo in his own words, Sandburg is moved to anger by the greatest of all injustices: the disavowal of human dignity, the crushing of men and of Man by the economic machine.

Have you seen men handed refusals
till they began to laugh
at the notion of ever landing a job again— . . .
                                                          (pp. 267–69)

The theme of Section 40 is, "We live only once"; we are all played for suckers by one another, but fate in the end makes suckers out of all the players. Meanwhile,

programs, inventions,
plans, promises,
hints, insinuations pour
from the professional schemers
into the ears of the people.

But as we learn in Number 41, the people are unpredictable. You can't regulate them. Section 42 presents twenty-seven proverbs and jests which illustrate their diversity and their humor. In 43 people are compared to eggs.

What sort of an egg are you? . . .
Under the microscope Agassiz studied one egg:
    chaos, flux, constellations, rainbows:
    "It is a universe in miniature."

Similarly, one man is a paradigm of humanity. There follow twenty-six samples of the jokes and quips of the people. These, like the egg, are microcosms which suggest more than they seem to contain. In Section 45 these jests accumulate with growing intensity:

They have yarns
Of a skyscraper so tall they had to put hinges
On the top two stories so to let the moon go by,
Of one corncrop in Missouri when the roots
Went so deep and drew off so much water
The Mississippi riverbed that year was dry. . . .
Of the man who drove a swarm of bees across the
    Rocky Mountains and the Desert "and didn't lose
    a bee," . . .
Of the boy who climbed a cornstalk growing so fast
    he would have starved to death if they hadn't shot
    biscuits up to him, . . .
Of mosquitoes: one can kill a dog, two of them a
    man . . .
Of Paul Bunyan's big blue ox, Babe, measuring be-
    tween the eyes forty-two ax-handles and a plug
    of Star tobacco exactly.

From Sandburg's long list of yarns I have abstracted those which point toward the climax of this portion a few pages later. The six motifs quoted above are all taken from the body of comic anecdotes which used to be told by lumberjacks about their hero, Paul Bunyan. Sandburg has long been familiar with this folklore . . . In their present context these fragments of the Bunyan yarns are piled helterskelter one upon another; the list includes other folktale motifs, too, from cowboys, engineers, farmers, sailors, sheepherders, and Negro section gangs. A common bond of humor links them in their diversity. These are the incongruities the people laugh at. Sandburg brings the old yarns up to date, too, with jokes about the high-pressure salesman who sold a cop the idea of jumping off the Brooklyn Bridge; the oil man in heaven who succumbs to his own suggestion that there are gushers in hell; and four "fantasies heard at filling stations in the midwest." They are simply old tall tales mechanized. . . . (pp. 269-70)

In these twelve poems (36-47), the scraps of comic folklore have consistently grown in length and continuity from short proverbs and one-line jests to one-paragraph anecdotes, and now, in Number 47, at last to a full poem on a single subject. The increasing length is accompanied by an acceleration of intensity. "Who made Paul Bunyan" is the climax of this development, and the rhapsodic flow of its first paragraph is among the high points of Mr. Sandburg's book and of the Paul Bunyan tales in any form.

Why should Paul Bunyan emerge as the climactic image of the age in this portion of *The People, Yes?* We remember that eleven poems ago the chain of comic links that led to Paul was fastened to the dull weight of despair. The progression from "I am zero" . . . to the ecstatic affirmation of "The people, the bookless people" is a record of the resilience of the human spirit. For Sandburg the Bunyan stories are a major triumph of the collective imagination. They fulfill in this poem the selfsame function that they played in the lives and the art of the hundreds of anonymous raconteurs who told them in the woods, when logging was a folk life which inherited directly the comic traditions of the old frontier. . . . (pp. 271-72)

Whether Sandburg learned them from oral sources or read them watered-down in books, his retelling of these motifs here lacks any distinctive flavor. Only the introductory paragraph has a truly individual tone. The flatness of his diction and the choice of anecdotes combines to defeat the poet's purpose. What was intended as a culmination of his efforts turns out an anticlimax which reveals two endemic weaknesses of Sandburg's art. One is his poetic language, the other his social thinking. A philosophy which appears so full of hope that liberal democracy will in the end prevail contains denials of those very hopes within its own statements of affirmation.

It is Sandburg's personal triumph to have fashioned from the intransigent materials of these dozen poems a form which has the power to invoke our sym-

Carl Sandburg, Librarian of Congress L. Quincy Mumford, and poet Robert Frost in Washington, D.C., 1960.

pathies for the "bottom people," and which invites us to rejoice with them in the imaginative conquests of their hero, Paul Bunyan. But we must also ask whether it was really of moment in 1936 to assume the guise of old Paul Bunyan, so big his footsteps made earthquakes, so strong he turned off waterspouts. The natural elements were not our important enemies then. Neither does it seem especially relevant to thump the expansionist tub with hosannas of a three-mile table and an ox of fantastic size. Is not this a retreat into the vanished past? The Paul Bunyan tales are not even told any longer among the lumberjacks; how is the poet justified in resurrecting them as a symbol of the contemporary popular imagination?

Sandburg is not using Paul Bunyan narrowly to represent the loggers' hero. Accurately, he saw that these tales of Paul do convey the sense of certain aspects of our national character, and these aspects are not yet extinct simply because bulldozers have displaced ox-teams in the lumbercamps. The concepts of character which such folklore preserves from our past and presents to our future are the tenets of individualism which the pioneers needed to practice in order to survive. Paul Bunyan is the last of a long line of pioneer demigods; his ancestors are Mike Fink and Davy Crockett. Riverboating and hunting died out years ago, but logging continued well into the twentieth century as a way of life which preserved the pioneer's struggles against the hostile wilderness. Hence the yarns of the older heroes were retold about Bunyan, and so survived the passing of the old frontier.

The grip of such comic figures upon the popular imagination continues despite the changing times. The virtues of the pioneers, which the Bunyan tales and other legends keep still fresh in the public mind, derive from their heroic struggle to establish human life where for ages thunderstorms had reigned unchallenged. We admire their indomitable energy; the skills and ingenuity with which they fashioned homes in a hostile wilderness; the persistence with which they seized, held, and populated the resisting earth; and their individualism, forged in the heat of unending adversity, danger, and toil. "The people will live on," Sandburg writes; "You can't laugh off their capacity to take it."

But when civilization overtakes the rugged settlement, how useful are these same virtues? The pioneer ethic of individualism was seldom fitted to deal with interpersonal relationships on other levels than self-assertive violence. The tradition of lawlessness was so cherished on the frontier that such a man as Judge Roy Bean could be celebrated in oral tradition as a hero. Bean was that member of the bench who declared, "I am the law west of the Pecos," held court in a barroom, and said, "The jury will not deliberate; and if it brings a verdict short of hangin' it'll be declared in contempt." Paul Bunyan, too, represents Activity and Will, free from Responsibility, Conscience, or Cooperation. In many ways this frontier individualism is the very antithesis of life in a democratic civilization. While these pioneer virtues may still be admired among "the people," primitive individualism of this sort survives most vigorously in the ethic of old-style business executives, who, in the assertion of their rights of ownership, leave no ground for intelligent analysis in the solution of economic problems.

The depression was the greatest of such problems. Apparently Sandburg proposes to solve its attendant problems of poverty, hopelessness, and fear by exhorting "the people" to remember Paul Bunyan and the virtues of the pioneers. This is really cold comfort for those bottom people who find themselves at the bottom exactly because there is no longer room in America for men to emulate Paul Bunyan. Sandburg's offering is more a testament of his faith in the will of the people to survive than it is even a hint toward any constructive program. He does not suggest the application of rational intelligence in the continual effort to find an equitable balance between the rights and desires of the individual and the institutions with which he lives. In Sandburg's panoramic representation of American life, as Zabel suggests, "he is pulled by so many claims on sympathy and forbearance that nothing survives the prodigious outlay of tolerance and compassion." Like many another native radical he has faith and good intentions, but has not penetrated to the core of those appearances which he records so faithfully. It is hard, too, to reconcile his celebration of rugged individualism with his well-known interest in the Socialist movement.

In resurrecting the dying folklore of a vanished way of life Sandburg resembles his only important literary forbear. Whitman, writing at the moment when industrialization was changing the landscape of the cities and the tempo of the people's lives, saw not the factory and lathe but the teamster, trapper, and Indian squaw. Both poets attempted to create an imaginary portrait of America. Both portrayed the expansive youth of the nation, but missed the maturer visage in which that youthfulness is interfused with other elements. In the modern struggle for survival, energy and resilience and determination—and even a sense of humor—are no longer enough. While these qualities may have helped avert the explosion of baffled anger into senseless violence in the 1930's, they alone did not restore our economy or regenerate our character. To maintain that they did so, or could do so, is a sentimental fiction, romantic but untrue.

A literature employing national myths may well be romantic, but if the romance is a fiction inadequate to the truth, then neither the myths nor the literature they inspire will be living things. Sandburg has performed a remarkable achievement in delineating our comic heritage, and suggesting its possibilities for poetry. But in his emphasis on the resilience and the energy of the people he overlooks many other strands in American culture which should be represented in the epic panorama he has attempted to write. The omission of these strands seriously weakens the validity of his achievement.

The aesthetic of literary populism holds that the people themselves will give language its most interesting forms and thought its most significant development. Such a belief in common speech and popular democracy as the basis for art limits the artist to one or another form of realism. He literally attempts to transcribe from nature, since the diction, structure, and content that he seeks are already expressed in the free intercourse of the common people. Sandburg seems to follow such a program in his verse, which has always reflected his early training in journalism and his highly skilled reportorial eye.

Sandburg has an unusually accurate reportorial ear, too. There is an authenticity about his slang, his yarns, his folklore, that marks him as an accurate historian of the popular imagination. He has chosen to give us his record of that imagination in the words and inflections of the many men who created its original documents. It is often said that his language is unpoetic; yet who more than Sandburg writes in the spirit of the *Lyrical Ballads?* The language that men actually use, heightened under tension by the faculty of the imagination, is the idiom which he sought in the streets, factories, and farms—the only places where that language may actually be found.

However, he suffers from the same faults which afflicted Wordsworth, and to the degree that Sandburg follows Wordsworth's program further, so he is penalized the more. It is by now clearly evident that the most promising language for poetry is that of the uncommon, rather than the common, man. The variety of common speech which Wordsworth and Coleridge sought was itself uncommon, the supercharging under emotional stress of a limited vocabulary. The result was common words in unusual juxtapositions which suggested thoughts that no amount of aristocratic diction could inspire, unless a similar intensity had produced a similar effect.

The attempt to simplify the diction of poetry is characteristic of the major poets of our time. Eliot, Yeats, and Frost, each in his own fashion, have sought to reinvigorate poetic language by overthrowing the sweet and stuffy vocabularies of the Victorians. Sandburg, too, went to the limit of his premises in his attempt to make the language of poetry come alive. But standing on Chicago street corners to set down verbatim the wry jokes from Skid Row rewarded him more often with urbanality than with the words of power we may presume he sought. Again and again the excitement of Sandburg's concepts dissipates in their conception; the language does not project the intensity of the idea.

From the looseness of his diction it is evident that Sandburg has an unusual notion of the poet's role in producing poetry. Unlike Whitman, from whom his style is usually thought to be derived, Sandburg does not attempt to achieve in the very texture of his language organic forms arising from the tensions of the ideas his images suggest. Whitman's most successful idiom was fresh because he had assimilated many new influences into the language of his poems. The rhythms of the sea, the solemnity of the King James Bible, the incremental repetitions of Biblical verse and nineteenth-century oratory, and the "barbaric yawp" of the backwoods boaster were combined to fashion a new poetic diction. This combination was an act of discipline as well as of the inexplicable processes of creation; it was an operation of intelligence and will, which in time produced an idiom that was the natural expression of the poet's sensibility.

The laxity of Sandburg's style shows that he has not subjected himself to a discipline as forceful as Whitman's. Instead, he strongly relies upon his raw material to suggest or supply the finished forms of his verse. Though he resembles other poets in his colloquial diction and his disregard of traditional forms, it is precisely in these departments that he is most at odds with the main trends in contemporary verse. We may say that "Easter, 1916," "Burnt Norton," "The Death of the Hired Man," and **"Who made Paul Bunyan"** all show a trend away from rhetoric; but Yeats, Eliot, and Frost also show a command of rhythm in the line, tension in the stanza, and compression in language that Sandburg almost never achieves. The ultimate distinction between poetic and prosaic diction is one of intensity. It is here that Sandburg fails. While his craftsmanship is considerable in many other respects, his efforts are denied a power which might be theirs but for his almost complacent reliance upon popular joke and proverb to furnish him finished language to be juggled into poems.

It may well be that what Carl Sandburg attempts to do is not a promising possibility for art. He has tried to record the emotions of a society instead of an individual. His greatest weakness is not even the sagging diction of his stanzas, but the simple fact that "the people" is and remains a faceless abstraction, just as in the people's folklore Paul Bunyan is an abstraction, rather than a personification, of size, strength, cunning, and prowess. In limiting the range of his own sensibilities to experiences which are widely shared the poet of communal emotions cuts himself off from his own deepest resources. He is also likely to underestimate—and even patronize—"the people." No writer has ever portrayed or manipulated communal emotions with the power and assurance of Shakespeare, that relentless prober of the individual soul. Except in patches, Sandburg's work is undramatic, unconcerned with the portrayal or development of character. His "people" are a hive of bees who hum snatches of human speech.

Perhaps Sandburg's major purpose was doomed from the start. In a culture as pre-eminently noncollective as ours, the poet who presents collective emotions divorced from the individual consciousness may have set himself an impossible task. He has explored a peninsula of poetry isolated from the heartland of contemporary writing. MacLeish and Stephen V. Benet have skirted his shores. John Dos Passos made poetic prose in the wake of his prosaic poems; *U.S.A.* is perhaps the only book whose plan at all resembles that of *The People, Yes.* But Carl Sandburg is a lonely figure in modern literature, a pioneer whom few have followed.

And yet *The People, Yes* has an impact, an individual stamp. It demands recognition and refuses to be forgotten. Different as it is from all other poetry produced in our time, unsuccessful as it is when judged by the standards which all other poetry demands, it billows with an imagination widely informed and widely curious which gives it a life within itself. Though its over-all structure fails to sustain it as a single poem, its parts seem more important than the whole. They are the authentic records of a single imagination the popular imagination deeply stirred. Perhaps Carl Sandburg's brighter day is yet to come, when younger writers will find in his virtues a touchstone to the development of their own. Some of them may temper his wide-ranging consciousness with their own introspection, with an intensity and a formal discipline he has failed to achieve. But surely he has much to teach them of the imaginative possession of the American past, as well as of the sensitive observation of the American scene today. (pp. 272-78)

Dan G. Hoffman, "Sandburg and 'The People': His Literary Populism Reappraised," in *The Antioch Review*, Vol. X, No. 2, June, 1950, pp. 265-78.

GAY WILSON ALLEN

(essay date 1960)

[In the following excerpt, Allen examines Sandburg's literary reputation.]

In 1950, at the age of seventy-two, Carl Sandburg published a collected edition of his poetry called *Complete Poems.* It was a heavy volume, running to nearly seven hundred large pages and spanning a generation of poetic output, from "Chicago," first published in Harriet

Monroe's *Poetry* in March, 1914, to the great elegy on Franklin Roosevelt, **"When Death Came April Twelve 1945."** In his "Notes for a Preface" Sandburg wrote, "It could be, in the grace of God, I shall live to be eighty-nine, as did Hokusai, and speaking my farewell to earthly scenes, I might paraphrase: 'If God had let me live five years longer I should have been a writer.'"

Sandburg's most severe critics would probably grant that he is a "writer," even a gifted one, but whether he deserves to be called "poet" is still disputed. (p. 315)

The "puzzlement" experienced by critics thirty years ago becomes even more persistent now after Sandburg has completed his fourscore of years. To some extent this is the natural consequence of the shift in sensibility of both poets and critics during the past three decades, but it is also in part the result of the literary role that Sandburg chose for himself at the beginning of his career, as the reception of his *Complete Poems* demonstrated. It was widely and prominently reviewed, but reviewers betrayed by their words that they had not read the book; indeed, had hardly read Sandburg since the 1920's or 1930's, for the man they wrote about was the theatrical, self-conscious "Chicago poet" and the optimistic affirmer of *The People, Yes.* There was one exception; Louis D. Rubin, Jr., began his perceptive critique in the *Hopkins Review:*

> It seems to me that the critics who most dislike the poetry of Carl Sandburg do so for precisely the wrong reasons, and that those who praise Sandburg's work do so for equally mistaken reasons. What is bad in Sandburg is not his poetics, but his sentimentality. And when he is good, it is not because he sings of the common people, but because he has an extraordinarily fine gift of language and feeling for lyric imagery.

This is an admirably clear statement of the problem. And readers will either learn to distinguish the poetry from the propaganda and sentimentality or Sandburg's name will fade from the history of twentieth-century poetry. In old age he is still one of the most vivid personalities on the American scene, but his reputation has suffered in almost direct ratio to the rise of Eliot's and Pound's, both members of his own generation; and this is unfortunate, for he has written some poetry that deserves to live.

Sandburg's early role as the poet of Chicago and the sunburnt Midwest helped him gain quick recognition. What might now be called the "Midwest myth" was then in formation, and he found it both convenient and congenial. In part this myth was the final phase of American romantic nationalism. Emerson, in his historymaking "American Scholar" address, called for literary independence from Europe; in the twentieth century a group of Midwestern writers adapted this threadbare doctrine to mean liberation from the cultural dominance of the Eastern United States. There were, of course, new experiences and environments in the region demanding newer literary techniques and a retesting of values and standards, and in the novel especially these needs were met with Realism and Naturalism which yielded stimulating and beneficial results. (pp. 316-17)

Here is the myth: other cities are "soft"; Chicago is brutal, wicked, and ugly, but to be young, strong, and proud is more important. In the first place, Chicago was not unique in its brutality or virility. For social and moral degradation, New York, Boston, or San Francisco could equal it, . . . and for business enterprise and physical expansion, Cleveland, Dallas, Seattle, and a dozen other cities were as dynamic. However, for the first three decades of the twentieth century the Midwest did produce more writers (notably, Anderson, Hart Crane, Dreiser, Fitzgerald, Hemingway, Masters, Lindsay, Frank Norris) than any other region of the United States, thus supporting the notion that the East was effete and that cultural vitality was shifting to midcontinent.

A more unfortunate influence on Sandburg's poetry than his acceptance of the Midwest myth was his own private myth, in which only the poor and oppressed have souls, integrity, the right to happiness, and the capability of enjoying life. There are only two classes in Sandburg's *Chicago Poems,* day laborers and "millionaires." He is contemptuous of the millionaire's "perfumed grief " when his daughter dies, but "I shall cry over the dead child of a stockyards hunky." Certainly a poet has a right to his sympathies, perhaps even a few prejudices—in which no poet could rival Pound. What is objectionable in Sandburg's attitudes and choice of subject in his early poems is his use of stereotypes and clichés. In **"The Walking Man of Rodin"** he finds "a regular high poem of legs" and praises the sculptor for leaving "off the head." This is one of Sandburg's worst stereotypes, leaving off the head, "The skull found always crumbling neighbor of the ankles." Consequently, in the 1930's, when proletarian sympathies were valued more than artistry or universal truth, Sandburg's reputation as a poet reached its highest point. . . . In the 1950's, when social protest was less popular or even suspect, most serious critics simply ignored Sandburg. Perhaps, however, this is the most propitious time for a re-evaluation, for discovering exactly what as a poet he is or is not.

Sandburg is not, whatever else he may be, a thinker like Robinson or Eliot; not even a cracker-barrel philosopher like Frost. So far as he has a philosophy it is pluralistic, empirical, positivistic. He loves "facts," and has made a career of collecting them to be used in journalism, speeches, biography, a novel, and poetry. Yet he is in no sense a pedant; his facts (when

they are facts and not prejudiced supposition) are alive and pertinent, and he is usually willing to let them speak for themselves. "What is instinct?" he asks in "Notes for a Preface" (and the title itself is characteristic). "What is thought? Where is the absolute line between the two. Nobody knows—as yet." He is still, he says, a "seeker." He might be called a pragmatic humanist. Certainly he is not a Naturalist, who believes that human nature is simply animal nature; or a supernaturalist, who has an equally low opinion of mankind. Among his new poems is a satire on a contemporary poet, probably Eliot, who believes that "The human race is its own Enemy Number One." There is no place for "original sin" in Sandburg's theology.

From first to last, Sandburg writes of man in the physical world, and he still regards the enemies of humanity as either social or political. Man's salvation, he thinks, is his instinctive yearning for a better world; in the practical sense: idealism, the "dream." At the end of World War II he wrote **"The Long Shadow of Lincoln: A Litany,"** in which, remembering the "liberation" of Europe and the battles of the South Pacific, he advised his countrymen to

Be sad, be kind, be cool,
remembering, under God, a dreamdust
hallowed in the ruts and gullies,
solemn bones under the smooth blue sea,
faces warblown in a falling rain.

In this role as the conscience of his nation he has written some of his best poems, neither blatantly patriotic nor mawkishly sentimental. He plays this role, in fact, more gracefully than Whitman, whose best poems are usually his least self-consciously nationalistic. (pp. 317-19)

Whitman is the older poet with whom Sandburg is most often compared, and there are superficial resemblances, in their humble origins, their anti-intellectual poses, their seeing beauty and nobility in common objects and simple people. It is true, too, that Sandburg greatly admires Whitman, and once wrote a preface for an edition of *Leaves of Grass.* Yet despite these affinities, the two poets are different in temperament, in sources of power, and especially in prosody.

Because most of Sandburg's poems are in "free verse" it has often been assumed that he has continued Whitman's verse techniques. Some of his long lines do resemble Whitman's, and achieve the same space empathy, which is one of their chief aesthetic functions. But the big difference is that Whitman composed by line units, making great use of parallelism (a "rhythm of thought"), with almost no enjambment. Sometimes he used true metrical patterns, but freely, organically. Yet regardless of metrics or their absence, his basic unit was the verse, or line—usually a complete prediction. . . . This is not Sandburg's structure, or his music. Of course he was influenced by Whitman's freedom, but his versification is usually nearer the experiments of Arno Holz in Germany and the French poets of the late nineteenth century, such as Jules Laforgue, Gustave Kahn, and Francis Vielé-Griffin, who gave currency to the term "vers libre." (p. 319)

In his first volume of poems, *In Reckless Ecstasy*, privately published (1904) and wisely never reprinted, he still used conventional rhyme and meter. . . . At some period between 1904 and 1912 Sandburg adopted the newer phrasal prosody, in which neither number of syllables or counting of accents determined the pattern. The line might be a complete statement . . . or it might be a single word:

> Bareheaded,
> Shoveling,
> Wrecking,
> Planning, etc.

Here the arrangement is mainly typographical to emphasize thought, word, and even rhythm (a kind of grammatical rhyme). But in other poems the line division is by clause or sentence, in prose rhythms, often even without any striking or "poetic" imagery. One of many examples is **"Happiness"**:

> I asked professors who teach the meaning of life to tell me what is happiness.
>
> And I went to famous executives who boss the work of thousands of men.
>
> They all shook their heads and gave me a smile as though I was trying to fool with them.
>
> And then one Sunday afternoon I wandered out along the Desplaines river
>
> And I saw a crowd of Hungarians under the trees with their women and children and a keg of beer and an accordion.

This is essentially prose, but the terse, simple language does heighten the implied definition. It is a poem by Sandburg's own theory, which we should examine before further analysis.

He began, as the title of his first book plainly reveals, with the typical romantic concept that poetry is simply words arranged to evoke emotion. In his preface he agreed with Marie Corelli (from whom he derived his title) in her praise of "reckless ecstasies of language." In his own words, "There are depths of life that logic cannot sound. It takes feeling." (pp. 320-21)

Beginning with the *Chicago Poems* and continuing through to his latest compositions, Sandburg has always created a new form—or at least format—for each poem, not counting the unconscious repetition of trivial mannerisms. He is, in fact, one of the most *formal* of all free-verse poets, with a greater sense of form than

many poets who use rhyme and meter. His control of emotion and thought fluctuates, but his architectural instinct and judgment seldom desert him.

The famous **"Chicago"** poem has a clear, logical structure. The introduction contains five short lines of brutal labels for the city—technically, synecdoches: "Hog Butcher . . ., / Tool Maker, Stacker of Wheat,. . . ." Then comes the logical development in seven long lines, which are banded and subdivided by parallelism, so perfectly balanced that they create a rhythmical pattern of their own: "They tell me . . .," "Yes, it is true . . .," but. . . . The poet flings back his answer with new similes, rising to another set of single-word attributes, displayed on the page as separate lines to balance the epithets of the opening lines of the poem: "Bareheaded, / Shouting, / Wrecking, / Planning," and,—with rising tempo,—"Building, breaking, rebuilding, . . ." (Both sense and rhythm are strengthened by placing "breaking" between "Building" and "rebuilding.") Then, more calmly, "Under the smoke . . .," "Under the terrible burden . . .," balanced by "Laughing . . . / Bragging . . .," repeated with variations in the final line, which also completes the circle, returns to the epithets of the introduction, and makes a final logical application of them.

The very next poem in this early collection, **"Sketch,"** has a decidedly different form and structure. Here syntactical and rhetorical patterns have very little to do with the line divisions, which are based on images. In his sketch the poet paints with words, but using words gives him the advantage of movement; his images are dynamic, and this enables one image to charge the contiguous image with its power.

> The shadows of the ships
> Rock on the crest
> In the low blue lustre
> Of the tardy and the soft inrolling tide.
>
> A long brown bar at the dip of the sky
> Puts an arm of sand in the span of salt.
> The lucid and endless wrinkles
> Draw in, lapse and withdraw.
> Wavelets crumble and white spent bubbles
> Wash on the floor of the beach.
>
> Rocking on the crest
> In the low blue lustre
> Are the shadows of the ships.

The ships themselves are not seen, but their presence is felt in the undulating shadows and the rhythms of the waves,

> A long brown bar at the dip of the sky
> Puts an arm of sand in the span of salt.

(pp. 326-27)

The emphasis on blue, brown, and white in the shimmering light gives the poem the form and color of a French impressionistic painting. The picture is complete without the last three lines, but the reiteration of the words and the composite images of the opening stanza (for the lines are spaced and function as a stanza) are typical of Sandburg's structure and demonstrate his sense of form. (pp. 327-28)

No schematic prosody or basic structural pattern can be educed from the study of Sandburg's *Complete Poems.* But he nevertheless has an intuitive sense of equivalence (balance and counterbalance); he likes a closed circuit in sound and sense. In his most ambitious effort to write a whole book on one theme (however general), *The People, Yes,* he made a compendium of folklore, vernacular observations, graphic descriptions of episodes and incidents in American life, and interspersed these with his epigrammatic comments. In appearance it is the most formless book he ever published; yet even in this loose composition his sense of form is apparent on every page. Section 87, for instance, begins in this way:

> The people learn, unlearn, learn,
> a builder, a wrecker, a builder again,
> a juggler of shifting puppets.
>> In so few eyeblinks
>> In transition lightning streaks,
> the people project midgets into giants,
> the people shrink titans into dwarfs.
>
>> Faiths blow on the winds
>> and become shibboleths
>> and deep growths
>> with man ready to die
> for a living word on the tongue,
> for a light alive in the bones,
> for dreams fluttering in the wrists.

The end of this section, however, raises a serious question about Sandburg's diction:

> This free man is a rare bird and when you meet
>> him take a good look at him and try
>> to figure him out because
> Some day when the United States of the Earth
>> gets going and runs smooth and pretty there
>> will be more of him than we have now.

These mixtures of slang and colloquialism ("rare bird," "figure him out," "gets going," "runs . . . pretty," etc.) were deliberately chosen to represent the speech and thinking of common people, but the objections that Coleridge raised to Wordsworth's similar theory of diction are still pertinent. Perhaps it might be argued that such usages in *The People, Yes* serve an aesthetic purpose that Sandburg probably did not consider: they serve to change pace and highlight by contrast the more dignified language that usually follows (as it does in the beginning of section 88). It is doubtful, however, that such contrasts sufficiently compensate for the loss of concentration, the diffusion of emotion,

the general arousing of prosaic connotations. Yet it cannot be denied that Sandburg is light on his feet and constantly shifts his weight and stance. And it is on the most elevated plane that the book ends, with the identification of "the people" and cosmic laws:

> The people is a polychrome,
> a spectrum and a prism
> held in a moving monolith. . . .

The People, Yes was written during the great economic depression, and when it appeared in 1936 many critics hailed it as a sociological document and political philosophy. Reading it today we can see that it was neither, and a poem should not be—better, cannot be. It is rather a psalm—or a series of psalms—written out of Sandburg's religion of humanity. This religion is less openly confessed today than it was a generation ago, and the change in religious fashions has affected Sandburg's poetic reputation. It is easy for a high church critic to rationalize his aesthetic objections to a poet who has not yet discovered original sin. (pp. 328-30)

At the age of sixty-seven . . . Sandburg was still learning; but he need not pray, after he reaches eighty-nine, for God to spare him five more years so that he may become a writer. God made him a writer, and by his own efforts he has become a poet. How long he will be read only the future can decide, but certainly he is worthy of respect and deserves to be read—the kind of immortality dearest to every poet. (p. 331)

Gay Wilson Allen, "Carl Sandburg: Fire and Smoke," in *South Atlantic Quarterly,* Vol. 59, 1960, pp. 315-31.

ARCHIBALD MACLEISH
(essay date 1967)

[MacLeish was a Pulitzer Prize-winning American poet and dramatist. The following excerpt is taken from an address delivered on the steps of the Lincoln Memorial, September 17, 1967, as part of the Carl Sandburg Memorial Ceremony.]

Sandburg had a *subject*—and the subject was belief in man. You find it everywhere. You find it announced in the title of the book in which his Chicago poem appears: *The People, Yes.* You find it in one form or another throughout the hundred odd poems and proses of which that extraordinary book is composed. You find it in other poems. And in other books. Most important of all, you find it in the echo which all these poems and these books leave in the ear—your ear and the ears of others: the echo which has made the body of Sandburg's work a touchstone for two generations of readers—almost, by this time, for three.

A touchstone of what? A touchstone of America. If ever a man wrote for a particular people, however he may have reached in his heart for all people, it was Sandburg. . . . And if ever a man was heard by those he wrote for it was Carl. Europeans, even the nearest in that direction, the English, do not truly understand him but Americans do. There is a raciness in the writing, in the old, strict sense of the word raciness: a tang, a liveliness, a pungency, which is native and natural to the American ear. And underneath the raciness, like the smell of earth under the vividness of rain, there is a seriousness which is native too—the kind of human, even mortal, seriousness you hear in Lincoln.

An American touchstone. But is there not a contradiction here? *Can* a body of work bound together by credulity constitute a touchstone for Americans? For Americans *now?* Once, perhaps, in the generation of Jefferson, or once again in the generation of Lincoln—but *now?* There is a notion around in great parts of the world—in Asia and in certain countries of Europe—that America has changed in recent years: that the last thing one can expect from America or from Americans today is credulity. It is asserted that the American people have now, as the saying goes, grown up. That they have put aside childish things, beliefs which can't be proved. That they have come to see what the world is, to put their trust in the certainties of power. That they have become, in brief, what is favorably known as "realistic": about themselves, about humanity, about the destiny of man.

Listening to contemporary speeches, reading the papers, one can see where these opinions of America may have come from. But are they true? Are they really true? Can we believe, in *this* place, thinking of *this* man, that they are true? Sandburg was an American. He was an American also of our time, of our generation. He died fifty-seven days ago. He was seen and known and talked to by many in this meeting. His struggles were the struggles of the generation to which most of us belong—the struggles of the great depression and the many wars and the gathering racial crisis and all the rest. He was a man of our time who lived in our time, laughed at the jokes our time has laughed at, shed its tears. And yet *Sandburg was a credulous man*—a man credulous about humanity—a man who believed more than he could prove about humanity. And Sandburg, though he listened to those who thought themselves realists, though he was attentive to the hard-headed, was not convinced by them. In *The People, Yes* it is said:

The strong win against the weak.
The strong lose against the stronger.
And across the bitter years and the howling winters
the deathless dream will be the stronger . . .
Shall man always go on dog-eat-dog?
Who says so?
The stronger?

And who is the stronger? . . .

What Sandburg knew and said was what America knew from the beginning and said from the beginning and has not yet, no matter what is believed of her, forgotten how to say: that those who are credulous about the destiny of man, who believe more than they can prove of the future of the human race, will *make* that future, *shape* that destiny. This was his great achievement that he found a new way in an incredulous and disbelieving and often cynical time to say what Americans have always known. And beyond that there was another and even greater achievement: that the people listened. They are listening still. (pp. 42-4)

Archibald MacLeish, "A Memorial Tribute to Carl Sandburg," in *The Massachusetts Review,* Vol. IX, No. 1, Winter, 1968, pp. 41-4.

DANIEL HOFFMAN
(essay date 1978)

[In the following excerpt, Hoffman discusses Sandburg's contribution to modern American literature.]

Nobody in America could have written [the lines of *The People, Yes*] but Carl Sandburg. They have the thumbprint of his personality, his ear for a good yarn, his sense of the revealing detail, his empathy with folk wisdom, his unique ability to transform the raw materials of common speech into a lyricism with a swing and rhythm recognizably his own. Other poets may from time to time touch on his materials, but their touch is inevitably different from Sandburg's. (p. 392)

The People, Yes [displays] Sandburg's zest for language—the language, as he called it, of "the people," the seemingly endless scroll on which he recorded their talk, their sayings, their self-contradictory wisdom, their resilience, the barbed solace of their wit. . . . "Fine words butter no parsnips," he says—perhaps he quotes a woman trying to feed a family of seven on a railroad blacksmith's pay, what his Swedish mother might have said. "Moonlight dries no mittens." But let us not too quickly conclude that Sandburg, because he values parsnips and dry mittens, therefore despises moonlight, or what moonlight—traditionally anciently, the emblem of imagination—can mean to "the people," the very sort of people whose apothegms he so delighted in making into lines of poetry. (p. 393)

[Sandburg's *Rootabaga Stories*] are a minor classic, a successful attempt to make for American children fairy tales without the supernatural, to give children stories conceived in pure delight. Sandburg, who wrote them for his own daughters, made up several dozen tales that are cadenzas upon the child's pleasure in names, in the sounds of words, in the setting loose of fantasy in a village as wide as the sight in a child's eye. Some of these tales have, or may be interpreted to have, something in them akin to a moral, but none is much burdened thereby. A pedant might extrude a lesson about the badness of being a braggart from the story of **"How Bozo the Button Buster Busted All His Buttons when a Mouse Came,"** or make a preachment about uncontrolled ambition from the tale of **"Slipfoot and How He Nearly Always Never Gets What He Goes After,"** but most readers of whatever age will prefer to take Sandburg's fables for the pleasure that is in them and let other values—I don't say higher values—follow as they may. I choose these examples from the second of Sandburg's Rootabaga volumes, for in it he did not so often lapse into the sentimentality which mars the whimsy of the first.

Rootabaga Stories are reminiscent in their plot structures of George Macdonald's fairy tales, sometimes of Kipling's *Just So Stories,* but everywhere in Sandburg the roots of his tales in literary and older folklore traditions have been pulled up and replanted in native soil. Their formulaic plots, their repetitions and increments, the way things happen in threes may suggest old Irish fairy stories or the *Hausmärchen* of the Brothers Grimm. *Rootabaga Stories* offer a child enjoyment of patterns of language and of action as old as mankind, set, not in a peasant's cottage in a frightening forest in a foreign country, nor in a king's castle behind a moat menaced by wicked enchanters or witches, but in a village of easy-going and likeable characters as friendly and engaging as Hatrack the Horse or the Potato-Faced Blind Man. The tales they tell are not like Jack the Giant Killer, or Cinderella. There are no boy-eating ogres, no cruel stepmothers in Rootabaga Country. There, children do not need the solace of imagined triumphs over their surrogate parents, as in those European folk-tale dreams. No, Sandburg's fables offer the child a sunny, cheerful world of pure pleasure, with few shadows and no menacing monsters. In the spirit of oldtime American self-reliance, Rootabaga people come to mischance only through their own flaws: Slipfoot's greed, the Button Buster's pride, the folly of the wheelbarrowmen and plasterers who keep building a tower to the moon to stop the moon moving. But no one is ever killed, or eaten, or even hurt in this country, where imagination triumphs doing the work done by magic in tales from other lands and times. (pp. 395-96)

[**"Chicago"**], perhaps overly famous, has become a sort of albatross to Sandburg's reputation. He was capable of many other notes than "Stormy, husky, brawling," but they may be drowned out in the memories of everyone who has read **"Chicago."** One such note is joyousness in the most ordinary life, in sights other poets had not noticed, sounds made by people other poets hadn't listened to. . . . (pp. 396-97)

[**"The Shovel Man"** and **"Fish Crier"**] are but two from Sandburg's scores of poems that describe and celebrate the infinite variety of American life. The first fact one confronts in reading Sandburg is his inclusiveness, his liberality. Although many of his poems are brief—I believe the best ones to be so—the sensibility of the poet embodies what Whitman once called "acceptation." Sandburg excludes nothing, or at any rate very little, of his own experience from his poetry. If what he sees on a crowded city street on a wintry day includes a fish peddlar, his poem will tell us this, and will tell us what feelings the sight of that peddlar evokes in him.

Sandburg touches many emotions as well as observing facts and faces. Alongside his celebrations of the various fulfilments of human life are his moments of poignance, of longing, as in **"Gone."** . . .(pp. 397-98)

So much has been said about Sandburg's vitality and his celebration of life that his ability to see sharply the darker side of life—its doubts, its defeats, its despairs—is often overlooked. Yet these too are among the emotions his poems keenly define. . . . (p. 398)

It is often said that Whiman is Sandburg's model, even that Sandburg is Whitman's successor. Surely he learned from Whitman the possibilities of a long prose-rhythmed strophe. And just as surely he learned even more from the Bible, where Whitman learned it, of the uses of incremental repetition. But anyone leafing through Sandburg's *Collected Poems* may be surprised at how often he used short lines, a different swing altogether from Whitman's lyrical legato. True, Whitman preceded him in glorifying the details of the common life; but I agree with Professor Gay Wilson Allen that Sandburg's divergences from Whitman are greater than his resemblances. Chief of these divergences is in these poets' attitude toward death. Sandburg has little of Whitman's welcoming of death as the unifier and completion of life; for Sandburg death is merely life's end, not its fulfilment. Death is central to Whitman's work, the deep dark river that flows through all of his lines, while Sandburg is a poet of living. His vision of life does not include tragedy.

Impatient of theory, Sandburg in the preface to his *Collected Poems* tells us that "the more rhyme there is in poetry the more danger of its tricking the writer into something other than the urge [he had] in the beginning." As Mark Van Doren justly said of him, "He feels free only when he thinks he has escaped from form. He seems to have known nothing about the freedom that flows from mastery of form." Yet at his best Sandburg contrived his own form—without apparently being aware of it as form at all. He regarded his free verse as entirely free. The question his readers ultimately have to face, because the experience of reading more than a few anthology pieces by any poet raises it, is whether the structures as well as the language Carl Sandburg devised to take the place of those he spurned have the look and the feel of necessity. As the pioneers of the prairies knew, it takes more than sod to build sod houses. There must be a rudimentary architecture to hold up the roof, keep the doors and windows hung squarely on their sills, let the smoke go up the chimney. This principle is equally true of those other indigenous structures, the skyscrapers, which Sandburg was among the first to praise in his poems. (pp. 401-02)

Sandburg is concerned with the effects and materials of his poetry but not with creating those effects from new modes of perception. He would . . . "achieve a synthesis of hyacinths and biscuits,"—or of moonlight and mittens—simply by juxtaposing the one with the other. And yet we know that his practice is a little more uncasual than his protestations. His best poems, and the best passages in his longer, uneven poems, are shaped with a kind of caring of his own.

The case against Sandburg was made by William Carlos Williams, reviewing the *Collected Poems* in *Poetry*.

[Although] many of his strictures are true, I think he undervalues Sandburg, undervalues him for not doing what he himself was doing: searching for a language, making it new, instead of finding a language ready-made as in *The People, Yes*. In the first section of this long poem Sandburg offers us a myth which the rest of the work will embody. The myth is that of the Tower of Babel. It's not that Sandburg was a naïf who didn't know what he was doing, or what he wasn't doing. His effects are very different from those of Williams, for instance, but it doesn't follow that they were not deliberate. Sandburg sets out to capture Babel, the very diction of the tongue-wagging, loquacious, self-defining entity he imagined as "the people." He did not, like Williams, or like Whitman before him, construct a central identity, a "single separate person" who is at the same time a corporate sensibility. No, his crowd of many voices . . . offer their contradictory proverbs, their yarns, their japes, and their quizzical observations. Sandburg puts in a number of characters too, quickly sketched as they drive bargains, get gypped, laugh at themselves, or shoot themselves in despair. The effect is not one of plan or structure, not one of experience understood through intellectual or analytical processes; nor is it an effect in which there is the felt coherence of an artistic unity. It's a sprawl, a packed jumble of human activity, of talk in a sometimes tedious but often interesting chaos. It is a celebration of human survival, of the vitality of the people whose language it uses. *The People, Yes* is Sandburg's lengthy charm against adversity. It survives its own randomness. More successfully than other poems written during the 1930's it depicts the character of the people who, by their grit and their guts, came through the Great Depression. It does in its lyrical, kaleidoscopic way what *The Grapes of Wrath* attempts in epic narrative.

But Dr. Williams' objections cannot be completely obviated. Here, as everywhere, he would say, Sandburg accepted that which is, while it is demanded of a great poet that he impose upon reality his own imaginative vision. Such is the unification of experience we find in Whitman, in Emily Dickinson; such is what Williams, Pound, Eliot, Stevens, and Frost each in his own way strove for.

I find something like this in Sandburg too, though not as powerfully crafted as in these other poets. What I find as the unification of his vision is in fact inherent in the very amplitude, vitality, and inclusiveness with which Sandburg's work spreads itself before us. We must accept the seeming artlessness of his diction, the sprawl of his forms, and the fact that the tensile strength of his individual lines is seldom taut, as we expect great verse to be. Yet his ear, his tone, his lilt, his voice are unmistakable. Out of what Williams termed his weaknesses Sandburg made an individual style. His work is based on the faith that poetry is a quality of life itself. It is easy to over-simplify Sandburg's view of "the people"; sometimes he oversimplified it himself. And it is easy to dismiss his conviction that in the demotic diction of American life there is a vein of real poetry; he himself often quarried more dross than the genuine article. But Sandburg's conviction that the real thing was there, that he could find and shape it into poetry, is not a mere submission to whatever is. It is this conviction that I take to be Sandburg's democratic ideal, his insistence that the lives and lingo of blue-collar people could bring him not only the subjects of art but the materials of art, and that from these he could make poetry.

Much of his work is flawed, but in at least two periods of his long career he achieved a democratic art that lasts. Sandburg's best poems still speak of lives of people in small towns, in city ghettoes, and of the energy and broken patterns of industrial life with the force, the clarity, and the pleasure that first was found in them. And the poetic vision in *The People, Yes* is felt, not in the invention of a new language or a novel presentation for poetry, but in the poet's faith that "the bookless people" could, in their adversity, provide a thesaurus of idioms commensurate with their strength to endure and their will to survive.

Like the men who broke the plains in Illinois, Carl Sandburg was a pioneer. His vision of life was neither tragic nor cheery, but inclusive of defeat, of doubt, of despair even; these conditions he found life to transcend by its own resilience. He was deeply in the American grain in his pragmatism, his hopefulness. He once said, "The past is a bucket of ashes." He wrote of the present he knew. Now that that present and his work have become parts of our past, we can look back at Sandburg's best poems with gratitude for their capturing a portion of the reality of his time. We can thank Sandburg, too, for enlarging the possibilities of subject and language for other poets who came in our century. (pp. 404–06)

Daniel Hoffman, " 'Moonlight Dries No Mittens': Carl Sandburg Reconsidered," in *The Georgia Review,* Vol. XXXII, No. 2, Summer, 1978, pp. 390-407.

SOURCES FOR FURTHER STUDY

Basler, Roy P. "Your Friend the Poet—Carl Sandburg." *Midway* 10, No. 2 (Autumn 1969): 3-15.

Overview of critical response to Sandburg's prose and poetry.

Brenner, Rica. "Carl Sandburg." In her *Ten Modern Poets,* pp. 117-48. New York: Harcourt, Brace and Company, 1930.

Biographical study focusing on Sandburg's poetic development.

Crowder, Richard. *Carl Sandburg.* New York: Twayne Publishers Inc., 1964, 176 p.

Comprehensive biographical and critical study.

Detzer, Karl. *Carl Sandburg: A Study in Personality and Background.* New York: Harcourt, Brace and Company, 1941, 210 p.

Discusses Sandburg's personal life, his working methods, and his interest in Abraham Lincoln.

Monroe, Harriet. "Comment." *Poetry: A Magazine of Verse* XXIV, No. 6 (September 1924): 320-26.

Discusses Sandburg's talent for rhythm, dialogue, and description as displayed in *Chicago Poems, Cornhuskers,* and *Smoke and Steel.*

Van Doren, Mark. *Carl Sandburg: Bibliography of Sandburg Material in the Collections of the Library of Congress.* Washington D. C.: Library of Congress, 1969, 83 p.

Critical bibliography.

William Saroyan

1908-1981

(Also wrote under pseudonyms Archie Crashcup and Sirak Goryan) American dramatist, short story writer, novelist, autobiographer, scriptwriter, essayist, and songwriter.

INTRODUCTION

Saroyan is probably best known for his plays *The Time of Your Life* (1939), for which he won the Pulitzer Prize in 1940, and *My Heart's in the Highlands* (1939). The son of Armenian immigrants, Saroyan wrote about the lighter side of the immigrant experience in America, with special emphasis on humor and family life, which are central to Armenian culture. Most of his works are set in the United States and reveal his appreciation of the American dream and his awareness of the strengths and weaknesses of American society.

The son of a Presbyterian minister, Saroyan began selling newspapers at the age of eight and worked at various jobs while still in school. He began writing at the age of thirteen. His work first became widely known in 1934, when *Story* magazine published "The Daring Young Man on the Flying Trapeze." By the late 1930s Saroyan had a national reputation as a writer of short fiction and turned his attention to playwriting. Although he was awarded the Pulitzer Prize in drama in 1940 for *The Time of Your Life*, he refused it because he did not believe in critical or commercial sanctions for art. By the time he reached middle age, Saroyan's early success had faded. Many critics cite Saroyan's refusal to adapt his writing to changes in American life as a significant factor in the decline of his literary reputation. During the Depression, Saroyan's fiction, with its nostalgia for an earlier, better time, was welcomed with relief by an American public who sought escape from the bleak reality of their lives. With the advent of World War II, however, the changing values and tastes of more cynical readers made Saroyan's stories of the goodness of human beings seem simplistic and superficial. Biographers also attribute Saroyan's change in fortune to his excessive drinking and gambling. In his memoirs Saroyan wrote: "Three years in the Army and a stupid marriage had all but knocked me out of the picture and, if the truth is told, out of life itself." In recent years, there has been renewed appreciation of Saroyan's early plays and stories.

Saroyan's early, romantic themes included man's innate goodness, men's dreams as they are changed by the passage of time, and personal isolation as the ultimate tragedy. Death, for him, is as natural as life; in fact, its closeness should lead to an intensified view of the preciousness of life. His outlook has been called that of a facile optimist. Later in his career, however, he grappled with darker themes in such works as *Hello Out There* (1941) and *The Cave Dwellers* (1957).

Because Saroyan was defiantly unliterary, it is difficult to trace his literary influences. He bears some similarity to Sherwood Anderson, as Howard Floan notes, in his indifference to plot, his overplaying of sincerity and spontaneity, his homely philosophy, his preference for outcasts, his contempt for formal education, and his distrust of creeds combined with a nearly mystical reverence for life. His early work seemed to imitate Ernest Hemingway's in its clipped dialogue and sparse descriptions; yet Saroyan has acknowledged only the influence of Bernard Shaw, and has hoped to have a similar effect on the public. His own estimation of himself runs thus: "I am so innately great that by comparison others who believe they are great or act as if they are great seem to me to be only pathetic, although occasionally charming." His stories (which he sometimes wrote at the rate of one per day) have always received kinder attention than have his plays or novels. According to Elizabeth Bowen, "probably since O. Henry nobody has done more than William Saroyan to endear and stabilize the short story." Between 1934 and 1940 he wrote more than 500 stories, and, says Floan, "he learned to get into his story immediately; to fit character, setting, and mood to the action; to express with colloquial vigor what his people were capable of saying, and to imply much about what they were able to feel." Many of Saroyan's stories are based on himself and his family. He claimed, for example, that nothing in *My Name is Aram* (1940) is entirely fiction. All humanity, he believes, is contained in the "proud and angry Saroyans."

His plays are fantastical and surrealistic, employing incidents rather than strong plots. Floan believes that it is a sense of pageantry which holds most of his plays together. This form "was such a fundamental departure from the main conventions of the modern drama—from the theater of ideas that has come down to us from Ibsen and Shaw—that, when Saroyan's two most remarkable plays appeared, *My Heart's in the Highlands* and *The Time of Your Life*, critics had difficulty classifying them."

Saroyan's work has been widely reviewed, but has rarely received serious critical analysis. In structure and in philosophy, his writing is simple, an attribute for which he has been both praised and scorned. Many critics contend that Saroyan did not grow as an artist after the 1940s, that his subject matter and outlook were stuck in the Depression/World-War-II era, and that he did not challenge himself to vary from his proven formulae. Especially in the later years, critics were almost unanimous in calling Saroyan's work overly sentimental. Although many have claimed that his loosely structured, anecdotal stories and memoirs overflow with sentiment and description and lack structure and form, Saroyan's works are still widely read. His special talent lay in his ability to create poetic, humorous characters and situations, and, as one critic said, "to write from joy, which is . . . sparse as a tradition in our literature."

(For further information about Saroyan's life and works, see *Contemporary Authors*, Vols. 5-8, 103 [obituary]; *Contemporary Authors New Revision Series*, Vol. 30; *Contemporary Literary Criticism*, Vols. 1, 8, 10, 29, 34, 56; *Dictionary of Literary Biography*, Vols. 7, 9, 86; *Dictionary of Literary Biography Yearbook: 1981*; and *Major Twentieth-Century Writers*.)

CRITICAL COMMENTARY

JOHN GASSNER

(essay date 1954)

[Gassner was a Hungarian-born American critic, editor, and translator. In the excerpt below, he discusses the popularity of *The Time of Your Life*, claiming that Saroyan "epitomized both [American playwriting's] virtues and defects in the plays which gave him a reputation on Broadway." Portions of this excerpt were originally published in *One Act Play Magazine* in February 1940.]

When William Saroyan's celebrated fugue on the futilities and joys of living [*The Time of Your Life*] opened in the fall of 1939, the troubled anticipations of its pro-

Principal Works

The Daring Young Man on the Flying Trapeze, and Other Stories (short stories) 1934

Inhale and Exhale (short stories) 1936

Little Children (short stories) 1937

Love, Here Is My Hat, and Other Short Romances (short stories) 1938

The Trouble with Tigers (short stories) 1938

My Heart's in the Highlands (play) 1939

The Time of Your Life (play) 1939

My Name Is Aram (short stories) 1940

Harlem As Seen by Hirschfield (play) 1941

Hello Out There (play) 1941

Jim Dandy (play) 1941; reprinted as Jim Dandy: Fat Man in a Famine, 1947

The Human Comedy (novel) 1943

A Decent Birth, a Happy Funeral (play) 1949

The Assyrian, and Other Stories (short stories) 1950

Rock Wagram (novel) 1951

The Bicycle Rider in Beverly Hills (autobiography) 1952

The Laughing Matter (novel) 1953

The Cave Dwellers (play) 1957

Here Comes, There Goes, You Know Who (autobiography) 1962

Boys and Girls Together (novel) 1963

Not Dying (autobiography) 1963

One Day in the Afternoon of the World (novel) 1964

---

ducers were quickly dispelled. By rights the play should have failed, according to Broadway showmen, since it departed from the rules of playwriting. According to ordinary Broadway playwrights, too, failure awaited the seemingly scrambled improvisations with which a short-story writer violated both practical and academic precepts. The difficulties the . . . production encountered in Boston suggested a dire fate. Directors were changed midstream and the original setting, an abstract one, was scrapped in favor of a realistic one. And even after the play, instead of being abandoned in Harvard's backyard, reached Broadway, puzzled logicians wondered how illogic and inattention to dramatic action-plot could win plaudits from usually harsh critics. Saroyan, who had proclaimed himself the wild man of the theatre and—with touching candor—also a genius, was now admitted to respectable company (he had a Broadway "hit") while his claims to transcendent merit were wholeheartedly accepted by all but a small minority of the theatre's devotees. In time, the New York Drama Critics Circle and The Pulitzer Prize Committee, long at odds, . . . put their seal of approval on

The Time of Your Life, voting it the "best play" of the first war-time season.

Actually, the mystery of Saroyan's success was no mystery at all. It was the result of an instinctively arrived at accommodation between two schools of theatre that had been at war with each other during the depression-harassed thirties—the school that made social awareness the primary test of playwriting and the school that would have preferred playwrights to sublimate the times into poetry, fantasy, and abstraction.

Saroyan, himself a depression period writer ever since he wrote about starvation in **"The Daring Young Man on the Flying Trapeze,"** obliged in the play in a variety of ways. He not only drew a picture of poverty and unemployment with characterizations of an actor and a Negro musician, but painted a backdrop of "social significance" by supplementing the foreground action with a waterfront strike which provided conversation for a class-conscious dockworker and a voluble policeman. . . . Saroyan ranged himself on the side of the common people, too, by sympathizing with a hapless young harlot. . . . He consigned her persecutor, the Vice Squad detective Blick, to scorn and ultimate assassination by "Kit Carson," an ex-frontiersman with delusions of grandeur—a symbol, no doubt, of the gallant West and the good old American spirit of freedom. Saroyan also had uncomplimentary words for wealth based on economic exploitation, and gave Joe, his wealthy hero who plays the roles of observer, intercessor, and philosopher in the play, an acute case of social conscience. (pp. 297-98)

There was little doubt that this mélange was frequently refreshing and evocative on the busily occupied stage. And the very fact that Saroyan put virtually everybody except the villainous Vice Squad officer, himself a psychological mess, into the same boat helped to "sublimate" the social content of the play. Here, in other words, there was no evidence of the sharp cleavage between capital and labor favored by the doctrinaire political left. The moral to be drawn from Saroyan's picture, and the moral the author himself explicitly drew, was that life being as full of frustration as it is, we should make the most of our time—"in the time of your life" *live.* Not content, however, with this counsel, hardly novel and surely not so challenging as to suggest any passionate involvement in the conflicts posed by the depression and by the rise of Hitler, Saroyan proved the possibility of "living" by extracting as much courage and spirit from his honky-tonk habitués as anyone could wish. Both the common and the uncommon people of the play were, in one respect or another, marvelously vital, imaginative, or sensitive. . . . And for very good measure, Saroyan spun a world in which everything was possible: Thus, Kitty the magdalen is redeemed and married, with help from Joe, to Joe's handsome and simple-hearted protégé, and villainy is destroyed when "Kit Carson," using his antique frontier-weapon, stalks the Vice Squad insect and shoots him dead for insulting a lady—to wit, Kitty Duval. No consequences to "Kit Carson" are expected from this act of private reprisal, so much simpler in dramatic fancy than resistance to Hitler's battalions of evil outside the theatre. And since even Saroyan did not allege that the war of good and evil was at an end, he made Joe bequeath his own, unused, gun to "Kit Carson" for further exploits when and if called for. (pp. 298-99)

Curiously enough Saroyan's extravagance, which, coldly considered, is infantile, proved to be quite entrancing; and not merely because all of us indulge in wishful thinking or because, as the cliché goes (and cliché and Saroyan were bizarrely related), there is a child in the heart of each of us, but because Saroyan's bravura carried the day. His bravura had been tender and casual in his first play *My Heart's in the Highlands,* produced earlier in the same year, and it had made that long one-acter a unified fancy. *The Time of Your Life* was disunified and sprawling; it was less completely self-contained than its predecessor. But here, too, Saroyan did not withhold his hand from dispensing the bounty of an Americanized, plebeianized fairyland, and he poured a good deal of robust humor and even some tonic of irony into his largesse.

Saroyan, in short, was able to live in two worlds—those of social reality and fantasy—at the same time. The play, coming as it did at the beginning of World War II which ended a decade during which those worlds had stood miles apart in the consciousness of writers, was a fitting valedictory to the militant social theatre movement of the thirties soon to be memorialized in Harold Clurman's book about the Group Theatre under the title of *The Fervent Years.* (p. 299)

[The] Group Theatre, the most talented company to follow social consciousness as an article of faith in the thirties, . . . gave up the ghost in 1941. Henceforth, this prodigy and victim of history belonged to history—as a memory of the best ensemble acting Broadway had ever known and as an "influence" through its directors and actors—especially through Elia Kazan, Harold Clurman, and Lee Cobb, who became variously associated with the emergence of the new decade's foremost playwrights Tennessee Williams and Arthur Miller. As for Saroyan himself, the decline of his fortunes in the theatre actually became more rapid and marked than that of many less gifted and robust playwrights. Only two other full-length plays by him, *Love's Old Sweet Song* and *The Beautiful People,* and his one-act play *Hello, Out There,* all produced within the next two or three years, won any plaudits.

It would be wrong to attribute his misfortunes as a playwright to the very qualities that first drew attention to him. His breezy style and carefree inventiveness would have continued to sustain him on Broadway,

which is anything but unappreciative of gusto and unconventional playwriting. Nor can it be maintained that he was always so unconventional that he taxed the tolerance of American playgoers. It is true that for a short time in a few plays, such as *Sweeney in the Trees* and especially *Jim Dandy,* he played the extreme *surréaliste* like a hod-carrier carrying a needle. But *Jim Dandy* was widely circulated during the war on the circuit of the National Theatre Conference, the Rockefeller-supported confederation of our most active university and community theatres. And, actually, the plays with which he won his reputation as the most promising new playwright at the close of the thirties were less extreme than press reviews had suggested.

Both *My Heart's in the Highlands* and *The Time of Your Life* made only moderate demands for a suspension of disbelief on our part. Their dialogue was colloquial and clear, and their characters were recognizably human, if eccentric. Their "philosophy," when they had one, was individualistic and genial in a manner traditional in the United States. Saroyan's brassy affirmativeness was that of an American street-Arab, his irreverence that of traditional American humorists. His fancies were moderate, consisting as they did largely of propositions favored in American "low-brow" and "middle-brow" circles—namely, that the common man is the salt of the earth, that somehow things usually turn out well for him, and that he has a high-hearted capacity for endurance. . . . [The] fact that Saroyan presented his faith with whimsy and compassion and that he added a spray of rue to his bouquet for "the beautiful people" endeared him to critics.

The structure of *My Heart's in the Highlands* and *The Time of Your Life,* as well as of several later plays, was actually as realistic as his dialogue; only their premises seemed somewhat extreme and askew. He made no literary allusions. He fiddled no harmonics on the strings of bohemian alienation or left-bank sophistication. By comparison with Apollinaire's *Les Mammelles de Tiresias,* Cocteau's *Orphée,* E. E. Cummings' *Him,* and any number of *surréaliste* and expressionist plays, his work was actually that of a conformist.

The Time of Your Life is a genre picture with a wealth of chiaroscuro, enlivened by the characters who reach out differently for their desires and dreams, and are roused out of various degrees of egocentricity by a conventional enough crisis when the Vice Squad detective tries to intimidate the saloon's inhabitants and jail the gentle harlot "Kitty Duval."

Packed into a "honky-tonk," a saloon that supplies entertainment as well as hard liquor, are a number of people. They are, superficially considered, hopelessly miscellaneous. But they have one thing in common—their burden of aspiration or of frustration or of both. The young marble-game addict, the melancholy comedian, the Negro who collapses of hunger and

plays divinely when he is revived, the overzealous comedian, the naïvely persistent young man at the telephone, the prostitute who veils her past in dreams, the
sensation-seeking wealthy woman married to a comically straitlaced husband, the policeman who detests
his job, the frontiersman who blusters and lies himself
into a glorious past—who are these and others but
waifs of the world, impressing upon us the fact that we
are all waifs of one kind or another!

The interplay of these characters, the mere fact,
indeed, that they constitute a world, provides cohesion
to the play on a level of simple intelligibility. And more
cohesion is provided by the central character, Joe. Everything, every event or presence in the play, impinges
upon him. He is many things in one, this man who acquired money and sickened of it, who is alone and in-
scrutably so.

Out of his loneliness and sensitivity he has developed a pity for all mankind and a sense of justice. And
having money and time at his disposal, he has made
himself a paraclete or comforter of his fellow creatures,
giving understanding where it is needed and material
help where it is imperative. One cannot attribute supernatural or social leadership to this figure. But as a
very human person, he is the catalytic agent of a large
portion of the play. He has a mystic prototype in the
Paraclete of Evreinov's *The Chief Thing*, and a realistically characterized one in the interfering Luka of Gorky's
Night's Lodging or *Lower Depths*. Saroyan's honky-tonk, itself, is an Americanized "Night's Lodging."

In its rambling way, *The Time of Your Life* even
affords a theme. It is the need to make the most of life,
which requires endurance, compassion, and opposition
to the enemies of life represented by the vice-hunter
and bully Blick. All mankind is pitiful, indeed, in Saroyan's stage world; even the sadistic Blick—who bullies the prostitute and maltreats the Negro who comes
to her defense—is a pitiful specimen. And at the same
time Saroyan suggests obliquely that there is a degree
of evil that can be overcome only by the application of
force. Joe wants to give his gun to "a good man who can
use it," and he gives it at the end—to Kit Carson. Compassion and perception, and laughter and pity are fused
in Saroyan's play. Nothing is basically vague here, although everything is fugitive. If the work does not
come to a single point (and there is no reason why
every play must, provided it is richly alive), all its separate points are vividly realized. Only a certain sweet
tenderness dissolves them, particularly in a bedroom
scene between a simple-minded boy and a brokenhearted young harlot.

We cannot, therefore, say that Saroyan won his
early place in our theatre with a really radical departure
from American playwriting. On the contrary, he epitomized both its virtues and defects in the plays which
gave him a reputation on Broadway. Nor did he lose his

place in our professional theatre because he offered a
new dramatic form which was cravenly or obtusely rejected.

Saroyan's vogue in the theatre, which he has been
unable to recover to date, though not for want of trying, was a casualty of sheer wilfulness on his part. Like
so many of us in America, he quite appealingly wanted
to remain young forever, and therefore performed can-
ters that did not become his subject matter. He was
wont to start themes that required serious application
on his part with a view to developing them, but he was
too self-indulgent to do more than doodle around the
edges. Self-indulgence, however, is the privilege of the
young, and not of writers of whom maturity is expected after promise has been granted. Many American
playwrights failed to mature, and we may well wonder
what it was in our theatre that encouraged an arrested
adolescence. Perhaps the indulgent education to be had
in our schools gave the playwrights an insufficient
sense of discipline. Perhaps the belief that success can
be had with little effort made them too balky when
hard thought was required. Saroyan certainly made too
little effort to *think* things through and *work* things out.
If the Group Theatre was a casualty of "history," Saroyan, like other writers, was a casualty of our culture.
Indeed, he nearly made a cult out of the flouting of responsibility and discipline. Buoyancy and sentiment
proved to be inadequate substitutes for meaning even
in his often vital kind of playwriting. (pp. 299-302)

John Gassner, "Saroyan: 'The Time of Your Life'," in his *The
Theatre in Our Times: A Survey of the Men, Materials and Movements
in the Modern Theatre*, Crown Publishers, Inc., 1954, pp. 297-
302.

WILLIAM J. FISHER
(essay date 1955)

[In the excerpt below, Fisher surveys Saroyan's career, calling him "the representative American of the
mid-twentieth-century, a man baffled at the failure of
the Dream but unwilling to give it up; incapable of
facing his dilemma frankly or of articulating it meaningfully."]

The story of William Saroyan's amazing success and
rapid decline is, in microcosm, a history of American
optimism. Saroyan rose in mid-Depression as a bard of
the beautiful life, a restorer of faith in man's boundless
capacities; he has declined as a troubled pseudo-
philosopher, forced to acknowledge man's limitations,
yet uncomfortable in the climate of Evil. Indeed, he has
come to dwell on Evil in order to deny its reality, reas-
serting, blatantly and defensively now, the American

Dream of Unlimited Possibilities and Inevitable Progress. As a self-styled prophet of a native resurgence—believing in the virtue of self-reliant individualism, in the innate goodness of man and the rightness of his impulses—he has followed the tradition of American transcendentalism. (One critic has quite seriously called Saroyan the creator of "the new transcendentalism.") But it need hardly be said that Saroyan is no Emerson, either by temperament or by talent. The extent to which his later work has failed reflects, in one sense, the inadequacy of his equipment for the task he set himself. Yet it is also true that Saroyan is the representative American of the mid-twentieth-century, a man baffled at the failure of the Dream but unwilling to give it up; incapable of facing his dilemma frankly or of articulating it meaningfully.

When Saroyan's stories began appearing in the early 1930's, the literature of the day was somber with gloom or protest. And though Saroyan's fiction was also born of the Depression, often telling of desperate men, of writers dying in poverty, it nevertheless managed a dreamy affirmation. Politically and economically blind, Saroyan declared himself bent on a one-man crusade in behalf of the "lost imagination in America." In an era of group-consciousness, he was "trying to restore man to his natural dignity and gentleness." "I want to restore man to himself," he said. "I want to send him from the mob to his own body and mind. I want to lift him from the nightmare of history to the calm dream of his own soul."

This concept of restored individuality governed Saroyan's principal attitudes, his impulsive iconoclasm as well as his lyrical optimism. While Saroyan joined the protestants in damning the traditional villains—war, money, the success cult, standardization—he was really attacking the depersonalization which such forces had effected. He was just as much opposed to regimentation in protest literature as in everyday life. ("Everybody in America is organized except E. E. Cummings," he complained.) Writing about foreigners and exiles, the meek and isolated, "the despised and rejected," he celebrated the "kingdom within" each man. The artists in his stories preserved a crucial part of themselves; there was spiritual survival and triumph, let economics fall where it might. And in the glowing stories about men close to the earth of their vineyards, about glad children and fertile, generous women, Saroyan was affirming what he called the "poetry of life" and exalted with capital-letter stress: Love, Humor, Art, Imagination, Hope, Integrity.

In effect, Saroyan was restoring the perspective without which the writers of the thirties had often (for obvious reasons) reduced the individual potential to a materialism of physical survival. When a character in one of his plays insisted that food, lodging, and clothes were the only realities, another responded, "What you

say is true. The things you've named are all precious—if you haven't got them. But if you have, or if you can get them, they aren't." However limiting Saroyan's simplifications might prove, they none the less contained important truths which had been lost sight of amidst the earnestness of agitation-propaganda. If Saroyan is given any place in future literary histories, he should be credited with helping to relax ideologically calcified attitudes. (pp. 336-37)

Saroyan [became], for the moment, an important force in the American theatre—a symbol and an inspiration to playwrights, actors, and audiences. He had come to stand not only for personal freedom after the years of economic and emotional austerity, but also for freedom in style and form.

Whereas Saroyan's stories were often reminiscent of Mark Twain, Sherwood Anderson, or John Steinbeck, there was no recognizable literary tradition behind his playwriting. Rather, it was the showmanship and theatricality of the popular entertainers, made euphonious and articulate, that went into these early plays. . . . He had developed a decided preference for vaudeville over Ibsen, Oscar Wilde, and the other "serious dramatists" because it was "easygoing, natural, and American."

Thus, his best works for the stage gave the impression of a jamboree which was springing to life spontaneously, right before one's eyes. The inhibitions of both stage people and audience were lifted by a mood of gentle intoxication (sometimes alcoholic, sometimes not). The impulse to play and sing and dance was given free rein without concern for plot or didactic point. (pp. 337-38)

Saroyan's element, indeed, was the flexible time of childhood; he was at his best when writing about dreams fulfilled and faith justified. He was a teller of joyful tales and tales of high sentiment, making a revel of life and lyricizing death, hardship, and villainy.

But not long after the peak of his success at the beginning of the forties, Saroyan's writing began to change. Concerned about the onesidedness of his outlook, he set out to *justify* his unadulterated hopefulness. Instead of the airy, uncontested supremacy of beauty and happiness, there were now, as Saroyan began to see things, misery and ugliness to contend with, imperfection to account for. At the same time that he took cognizance of the dark side of life, he began trying to *prove* all for the best in the best of all possible worlds, with the result that his novels and plays became strange battlegrounds where belief struggled with skepticism. To retain his perfectionist version of man's life on earth, yet to get rid of the unpleasant realities he had come to acknowledge—this was Saroyan's new burden. (p. 338)

Among the earliest works to demonstrate that Saroyan was no longer able to dismiss "evil" casually or to proclaim "belief" summarily was his first novel, *The Human Comedy* (which Saroyan wrote originally as a motion picture in 1943). The protagonist was Saroyan's favorite character type—a young dreamer with untainted senses, a rich imagination, and warm sympathies. Instead of following the old blithe Saroyanesque line, however, the book became a study in doubt and faith, tracing prophetically the pattern of Saroyan's own career. The young hero . . . is nearing the age of disenchantment and is especially vulnerable because he has been nourished on inflated ideals and has never been allowed to know adversity. His trust in the benevolence of the universe is consequently threatened when his personal idol, an older brother, goes off to war and faces death.

The outcome is abrupt and arbitrary, as Saroyan contrived to dissolve the conflict with a happy ending. The brother is killed in the war, and the boy is about to plunge into despair when, before mourning can get under way, a wounded buddy of the dead soldier—fortuitously an orphan without ties—appears on the scene and quite literally takes the brother's place in the household as if nothing had happened. Saroyan explained this miracle by inflating his idea of brotherliness into a concept of universal oneness which permits live men to be substituted for dead ones. Since "none of us is separate from any other," according to the logic of the novel, and since "each man is the whole world, to make over as he will," the stranger is able to become at once the son, brother, and lover that his friend had been. It is as simple as this because Saroyan is running the show. Death and disaster are ruled out of order, and the boy's illusions are protected.

But Saroyan was paying a high price for the preservation of unlimited possibilities. This novel had lost all but a modicum of the Saroyanesque buoyancy. In the course of thwarting misfortune, the author had to let the boy abandon his pranks and dramas to face the prospect of sorrow. Meanwhile, there was a moral point that had to be reinforced by sermons on virtue. Large doses of speculative talk adulterated the dreamy atmosphere. Always inclined toward sentimentality, Saroyan now landed with both feet deep in mush. By dwelling on the love and goodness he had previously taken with a skip and a holler, Saroyan was suffocating spontaneity. (pp. 338-39)

The fact that [the] concept of the mutual exclusiveness of good and bad, right and wrong, beautiful and ugly has become an underlying assumption in Saroyan's struggle against disbelief is evidence of his "Americanism." (p. 339)

[*The Adventures of William Saroyan* and a novel (*The Adventures of Wesley Jackson*)] were weighted down with aimless vitriol about the indignities of war and in attempting to write seriously about statesmanship, propaganda, and international affairs, Saroyan exposed to full view his lack of intellectual discipline and integrative capacity.

Saroyan has perennially boasted an aesthetics of no-effort, denouncing "intellectualism" and contending that a man should write as a hen lays eggs—instinctively, without thought or planning. Confusing laziness with casualness and spontaneity, he has continued to oversimplify. Part of Saroyan's charm had been the way he had often, in his enthusiasm about everyday things and people, blurred but intensified the lines of his picture with superlatives: "The loveliest looking mess the girl had ever seen"; "nature at its proudest, dryest, loneliest, and loveliest"; "the crazy, absurd, magnificent agreement." But when, in his later work, he applied this indiscriminate approach to questions of morality and metaphysics, the effect became one of pretentiousness. With sweeping generalizations, he now implied that he was solving man's weightiest problems, yet without evidence of any careful or systematic consideration. . . . The allegorical scheme he concocted for *Jim Dandy* was more ambitious than Thornton Wilder's in *The Skin of Our Teeth.* The assumption of Saroyan's play, as of Wilder's, was that "everybody in it had survived pestilence, famine, ignorance, injustice, inhumanity, torture, crime, and madness." But instead of a cohesive drama about man's survival through history by the skin of his teeth, Saroyan wrote an incoherent hodge-podge in which everything turns out just jim dandy, as if there has never been a serious threat at all. (pp. 339-40)

Saroyan's efforts to provide clarification have often had [a] tendency to eliminate *all* distinctions, reducing meaning to some amorphous unit—if not to a cipher. In his yearning for a harmony, for an eradication of conflicts and contradictions, Saroyan is the heir of a tradition which, among Americans of a more reflective or mystical temperament, has included Jefferson's ideal of human perfectibility, Emerson's Oversoul, Whitman's multitudinous Self, Henry Adams' Lady of Chartres, and Waldo Franks's "Sense of the Whole."

In 1949, there appeared a volume of three full-length plays by William Saroyan, his major works for the theatre since the war. None of these plays—*Don't Go Away Mad; Sam Ego's House; A Decent Birth, A Happy Funeral*—has been given a Broadway production. Indeed so vaguely speculative are they that their author found it necessary to explain them in lengthy prefaces summarizing the plots and offering suggestions for deciphering the allegories. The pseudo-philosophical elements of Saroyan's writing had come more than ever to overshadow the vivid and the colorful.

Moreover, the preoccupation with death virtually excludes every other consideration, especially in *A De-*

cent Birth, A Happy Funeral and in *Don't Go Away Mad.* The action of the latter is set in a city hospital ward for cancer victims, and the characters are all "incurables," tortured by pain and by thoughts of their impending doom. While they clutch at prospects of the slightest delay, they brood over the crises and deaths of fellow inmates and talk endlessly about death, life, time, and the details of their physiological decadence. Yet even here, in these plays about death, Saroyan has conjured up endings of joy. . . . (p. 340)

To negate death has thus become for Saroyan the crucial test of man's free will and unlimited powers. Sometimes, instead of whisking it away by plot manipulations, he had tried to exorcise death by comic ritual, to be as airy about morbidity as he had been about little boys turning somersaults. (Many social analysts have noted the uneasy effort in America to euphemize death, glamorize it, sentimentalize it, and generally make it keep its distance.) He changed the title of his most dismal play from "The Incurables" to *Don't Go Away Mad.* He tried to lighten an act-long funeral ceremony by having burlesque comedians conduct the service while they played with yo-yos and rubber balls and blew tin horns. And some years ago he hailed George Bernard Shaw as the first man "to make a complete monkey out of death and of the theory [sic!] of dying in general." But one of Saroyan's own characters declares that "Death begins with helplessness, and it's impossible to joke about." Perhaps Saroyan has begun to suspect that for him, "Death is a lousy idea from which there is no escape."

The latest novel by Saroyan is called *The Laughing Matter* (1953). Set in the California vineyards and dealing with a family of Armenian heritage, the book has on its opening pages an atmosphere of love and warmth which recalls the earliest and best Saroyan. When the boy and girl of the family are the book's concern, their enjoyment of life and their sensitivity to the world around them—the way they savor figs and grapes, drink in the warmth of the sun, wonder about the universe—are a delight. But before long, Saroyan is trying to handle adult problems and the tale bogs down. . . . The boy, confronted by the tragic situation which is rocking the security of his beautiful family, cries to the skies, "What was the matter? What was it, always? Why couldn't anything be the way it *ought* to be? Why was everything always strange, mysterious, dangerous, delicate, likely to break to pieces suddenly?" For although his father has taught him the Armenian words, "It is right," and although everybody chants them over and over (one wise member of the family insists, meaning it, "Whatever you do is right. If you hate, it is. If you kill, it is."), nevertheless, everything goes wrong and there is death and disaster, and there is futility in the face of imperfection. And after it all, at the end of the book, still crying like an echo

in the wilderness, is the repeated refrain, "It is right!" (pp. 340, 385)

William J. Fisher, "What Ever Happened to Saroyan?" in *College English,* Vol. 16, No. 6, March, 1955, pp. 336-40, 385.

MARY McCARTHY
(essay date 1956)

[McCarthy was a prominent American novelist, literary critic, essayist, and autobiographer. In the following excerpt, originally published in a slightly different form in 1940, she discusses Saroyan's perspective on America.]

William Saroyan has been in the writing business for eight years. He still retains his innocence. . . . To keep it, he has, of course, had to follow a strict regimen—no late hours, no worries, and only a limited responsibility. That is, he has had to fight off Ideas, Movements, Sex, and Commercialism. Some of the benefits have been remarkable. He has stayed out of the literary rackets—the Hollywood racket, the New York cocktail-party racket, and the Stalinist racket, which became practically indistinguishable from both the others. What is more important, the well of inspiration, located somewhere in his early adolescence, has never run dry. He is still able to look at the world with the eyes of a sensitive newsboy, and to see it eternally brand-new and touched with wonder. The price is that the boundaries of this world are the boundaries of the newsboy's field of vision.

Saroyan is genuine, Saroyan is not mechanical, Saroyan is the real thing; he tells you this over and over again in the prefaces to his two plays, [*My Heart's in the Highlands* and *The Time of Your Life*]. It is true. If you compare him with his contemporaries, Odets and Steinbeck, the purity of his work is blinding. Puerile and arrogant and sentimental as he may be, he is never cheap. Both Odets and Steinbeck are offering the public a counterfeit literature: Odets is giving an imitation of a lacerated Bronx boy named Odets who once wrote a play; Steinbeck is giving an imitation of a serious novelist. Saroyan as a public figure does an impersonation of Saroyan, but as a writer he plays straight. Moreover, both Odets and Steinbeck suffer from a kind of auto-intoxication; they are continually plagiarizing themselves; and their frequent ascents into "fine writing" are punctuated with pauses for applause that are nearly audible. Now Saroyan, as I say, has created a public character for himself, and the chief attribute of this character is exhibitionism, but he has incorporated this character boldly into his work and let him play his role there. Vanity has become objectified and externalized; it has no need to ooze surreptitiously into the prose. Saroyan's writing remains fresh and crisp and never has the look of having been pawed over by the author. Furthermore, though Saroyan's work is all of a piece, and the same themes and symbols recur, you will rarely find a constellation of symbols repeating itself, you will rarely get the same effect warmed up for a second serving.

It may be that Saroyan's world of ice-cream cones and toys, of bicycles and bugles, and somersaults and shotguns, of hunger and of banquets that appear out of the air, of headlines that tell of distant disasters, of goodhearted grocers and lovable frauds, of drunk fairy princes and pinball games that pay, is naturally more at home in the theatre than in fiction. Or it may be that, his scope being necessarily as narrow as it is, he has exhausted the permutations of the short story and requires the challenge of a new medium. At any rate, he has written [*My Heart's in the Highlands* and *The Time of Your Life;* the former] caused a furore and the other is a hit. (pp. 46-7)

[*The Time of Your Life*] is almost pure vaudeville,

a play that is closer to *Hellzapoppin* than to anything else in the theatre.

The action of this play takes place in a San Francisco waterfront saloon in the year 1939. . . . [There] is a group of relatively simple people. . . . [These] characters seem to be trailing clouds of glory; they are beautiful and terrible just because they *are* people, Saroyan thinks. Each of them wants to do his own job, to do it tenderly, reverently, and joyfully, and to live at peace with his neighbors. Unfortunately, there are Frustrators at work, monstrous abstractions like Morality, and Labor and Capital, whose object is to flatten out these assertive individualists. The chief of these Frustrators is a Vice-Squad man named Blick, who stands for Morality, but Finance Capital is in the room in the shape of a gentleman slummer, and the voice of Labor can be heard outside in the waterfront strike. But if this universe has its devil in Blick, it has its God in Joe, . . . a charming, indolent alcoholic, whose mysterious wealth is the life-blood of the joint. Buying champagne, buying newspapers, ordering drinks for the house, giving handouts to the Salvation Army, to the boy out of a job, to the unfortunate prostitute, he keeps the people of the play going, but, being detached

Saroyan and his son, Aram, 1957.

from the life of action, he is powerless to save them from Blick. This is left for one of their own numbers, the old trapper (God the Son), who shoots the interfering moralist as calmly as if he did it every day, and regretfully throws his beautiful pearl-handled revolver into San Francisco Bay. When Joe sees that everything is straightened out, and that the two main characters are ready to start life on their own, he goes home, and the understanding is that he will not be back tomorrow.

There is no point in commenting on this intellectual structure, for it is not an intellectual structure at all, but a kind of finger-exercise in philosophy. Whenever it makes itself explicit, its juvenility is embarrassing; when it is allowed to lie somewhere behind the lines, it gives the play a certain strangeness, another dimension that is sensed but not seen. The real living elements of the play, however, owe nothing to philosophy. . . . Saroyan is still drawing on the street-life of his adolescence; it is inevitable, therefore, that his plays should belong to the theatre of that street-life, that is, to vaudeville. *The Time of Your Life* is full of vaudeville; indeed, almost every incident and character in it can be translated back into one of the old time acts. Kit Carson, the trapper, is W. C. Fields; the pinball machine that plays "America" and waves a flag when the jackpot is hit is out of Joe Cook; the toys Joe buys are a visual reminder of the juggling turn, and his money, deriving from nowhere and ostentatiously displayed, makes you think of the magic act; the young man who keeps telephoning his girl is the comic monologist; Harry the hoofer is Jimmy Durante; the boy out of a job is the stooge; and Joe (or God) . . . has that slim, weary, sardonic, city-slicker look that was the very essence of the vaudeville artist. Even the serious part of the play, the soulsearing drama involving Kitty, the beautiful prostitute, and the boy who wants to marry her, and Blick, takes you back to those short problem melodramas starring a passée actress that were occasionally interspersed with the regular acts. And *The Time of Your Life,* like an evening of vaudeville, is good when it engages the fancy and bad when it engages the feelings. (pp. 48-50)

Saroyan is in love with America, and very insistent about it. Just as a girl in his plays will be an ordinary girl and at the same time "the most beautiful girl in the world," because Saroyan is young and feeling good when he looks at her, so America is an ordinary place and at the same time "the most wonderful country in the world." This excessive, rather bumptious patriotism has created a certain amount of alarm; it has been suspected that Saroyan has joined the propagandists of the second crusade for democracy. The alarm is, I think, unjustified. Actually, the second statement is no more realistic than the first; it is not the literal fact but the state of mind that the reader is asked to believe in. And there is a kind of pathos about both statements

that arises from the discrepancy that must exist between the thing described and the description of it. How far, in the second case, the pathos is intentional it is impossible to tell, but the contrasts in Saroyan's work show that he is at least partly aware of it.

In each of these plays there is a character that, more than the "gentle people" he talks so much about, represents the America he loves. This national type, exemplified by . . . the trapper in *The Time of Your Life,* is an elderly boaster who is both a fraud and not a fraud, an impostor and a kind of saint. . . . Kit Carson moves along through the plot telling one tall tale after another. At the end, after he has shot Blick offstage, he comes into the saloon and begins a narrative that sounds exactly like all the others: "Shot a man once. In San Francisco. In 1939, I think it was. In October. Fellow named Blick or Glick or something like that." This statement is a bombshell. It gives veracity to all the improbable stories that have preceded it, and at the same time the improbable stories cast a doubt on the veracity of this statement, which the audience nevertheless knows to be true. A boast becomes a form of modesty, and the braggart is maiden-shy.

This kind of character undoubtedly belongs to the tradition of American life and especially to the tradition of the West. It is Paul Bunyan and it is also the barker. But the tradition is dead now; it died when the frontier closed on the West Coast at some point in Saroyan's childhood. The type, if it exists at all outside of W. C. Fields, is now superannuated, for such anomalous human beings could only thrive under nomadic conditions of life. Today the barker has become an invisible radio announcer, and the genial, fraudulent, patent-medicine man has turned into a business house, with a public relations counsel. The America Saroyan loves is the old America, and the plays he weaves around it are not so much daring innovations as legends. (pp. 50-2)

Mary McCarthy, "Saroyan, an Innocent on Broadway," in her *Sights and Spectacles: 1937-1956.* Farrar, Straus and Cudahy, 1956, pp. 46-52.

THELMA J. SHINN

(essay date 1972)

[In the following excerpt, Shinn contends that Saroyan's plays present both a romantic and existentialist view of life.]

Saroyan's philosophy is not a resolution of but a recognition and acceptance of the contradictions of life. He tells us that life is both funny and sad, both violent and tender, and that generally the contradictions are present in the same scene, the same person, at the same time. Consequently, critics could not define Saroyan's plays—to give one interpretation would conceal the other interpretations simultaneously maintained by the symbolism. This led many critics to reject Saroyan's works because they felt that the plays, in appealing to the irrational and to the emotional in the audience rather than to the intellectual and rational, could be dismissed as mere Romanticism. The more perceptive critics, however, suspected that there was more to Saroyan than sentimentality. (p. 185)

The nonplot symbolic dramas of Pinter, of Beckett, of Ionesco with their usually unrelieved pessimism are remarkably similar to the "romantic fantasies" of Saroyan. Saroyan displays the same disregard for spelling out meanings to the audience, the same freedom with scenery and plot, the same concentration on the individual. Much of modern drama is considered existential because the individual is trying to find for himself some meaning in this absurd universe—and the meaning, if any, appears to be within himself. In this sense, at least, the existential theme is precisely what most concerns Saroyan.

Saroyan's departure from modern theater, as well as from the theater of the 30's and 40's, is his remarkable—his critics say unrealistic—ability to find a note of affirmation, to testify finally to the rejected ideal of human dignity. (pp. 185-86)

The multiplicity of [critical interpretations of *My Heart's in the Highlands*] reflects the symbolic import of the play, a symbolism . . . exclusively American. Saroyan explores the themes of economic inequality, the plight of the artist, individual integrity, the search for beauty and the growth of awareness in a seemingly haphazard way in the simple international American stock of a small neighborhood. The Scotch bugler, the Armenian-speaking grandmother, the Polish grocer are all beautifully American. The setting is representative rather than realistic; the simple dialogue is intuitive rather than logical.

The economic inequality is implicit in the poverty of the family. . . . Saroyan's interest lies not so much in the inequality indiscriminately arising from the indifference of the external world as it does in the individual's ability to turn even this into a vehicle for the expression of human dignity. . . . Saroyan's play emphasizes the brotherhood of man and the dignity of the individual, the human relationships rather than the social "realities."

The plight of the artist theme is also treated in a universal manner by Saroyan. Though Johnny's father represents the artist, he is not alone. Saroyan recognizes the artist—the sensitive awareness to living—in each of the characters. . . . Saroyan identifies the artist as the man sensitive to the beauty which can be found in the world. His plight is in the rejection by the world of his attempts to express this beauty, and that rejection is equally wrong—or at least equally possible—whether the man is a first-rate or a tenth-rate poet. (pp. 186-87)

This search for beauty within the individual which Saroyan recognizes comes close to being the element of the divine in humanity. MacGregor, who achieves recognizable expression of beauty in his music, has his "heart in the highlands," and goes there at the end of the play. The townspeople implicitly recognize the divine origin of this gift when they bring the food as sacrifices to it. The father has created his successful poem in the person of Johnny and in himself—thus they are in this sense identical and thus MacGregor wants to come to their home to die because that is the closest he can come to the divine perception in this world.

It is Johnny's father who gains the most complete awareness of the value of the individual and of the search for beauty in this play. . . . Johnny himself, as he ends the play with "I'm not mentioning any names, Pa, but something's wrong somewhere," has only grasped half the truth—the easiest half according to Saroyan. His recognition of the injustice of a world that prevents good people from dwelling together peacefully in the goodness of the universe is the stopping point of most modern views of the world. Saroyan goes on to assert that man's search for beauty can carry him beyond the ugliness of the world to the divine within himself and within his fellow men. If this attitude must be romantic and sentimental, then Saroyan is both—and so is Emerson, Thoreau, Hart Crane, any artist who believes that man can transcend the injustice of the external world by looking within himself and that man can find a beauty within himself that is within each man. Saroyan tries to reach this inner beauty, and if he does not appeal to it with logical arguments, it may be because beauty is beyond logic. If he couches his appeal in what seems sentimental and romantic, it is because inner beauty is the source of whatever sentiment and romance man can know. Even this first play shows that Saroyan is not simply saying that life is beautiful and all men love each other. He says rather that in each man with any sensitivity there is a desire for beauty and that this desire should be followed and nurtured if there is to be any positive reality of beauty in this absurd world.

Saroyan's greatest success, *The Time of Your Life*, carries the same message as *My Heart's in the Highlands*, or messages rather, since the simple statement above can scarcely represent the levels of meaning presented in Saroyan's symbolic dramas. . . . The central set is a run-down bar where the central character sits drinking champagne and watching people. Every person (with the exception of Blick, the depersonalized symbol of the authority of the external world reminiscent of Kafka's bureaucrats) is seeking for beauty. However, it is not at all easy to dismiss this as romanticism either, even the most "apparently" romantic situation of the prostitute with the heart of gold who gets a new life through the sincere love of a man. The ingredients are romantic—because they deal with that desire for beauty within the individual which is the source of all romance—but Saroyan's treatment of the material reveals more perception than is usually attributed to him. The prostitute remembers the beauty of her childhood—when her childhood wasn't beautiful. . . . Here Saroyan's admiration for family ties is apparent, but most apparent is that the word "home" epitomized for Kitty her search for beauty. Her perception of the indefinable beauty of her family and her childhood—despite the trouble and the sadness—was her artistic achievement, her communication of beauty where it is not immediately discernible. . . . [This] attempt is infinitely better than the alternative, than the prostitution of the individual by the depersonalized destructiveness of the external world.

Saroyan's ending to this play, however, if not condemned as sentimentality, will have to be recognized as pure wish-fulfillment. (pp. 187-89)

[In *Hello Out There, Across the Board on Tomorrow Morning,* and *Death Along the Wabash,* all pessimistic plays,] Saroyan openly admits that his romantic individualists in their search for beauty do not always succeed—and this is perhaps why he said later that he repudiated *Hello Out There*—but the value of their attempts contrasted with the rest of the world still places them far above the other characters. The most romantic of these three is *Hello Out There,* where the young man says to the girl that with her he could be good—but in the light of Saroyan's other plays this can be raised above its typically sentimental interpretation. The young man's recognition of beauty in the girl makes her a symbol of his unique expression of beauty, of his poem or song, and therefore of the true goal of his restless search for beauty. (p. 190)

But we should avoid placing only one interpretation on Saroyan's symbols; the girl must also be seen in relation to Mr. Kosak of *My Heart's in the Highlands.* She is the one person who has listened to the young man, who has in a sense read his poetry and therefore given value to it. Thus at the end she blends with him through their shared perception of beauty and her last line is the same as his first line—"Hell—out there!"—which is both an attempt to communicate with the world and an acceptance of the alienation of the individual.

Across the Board on Tomorrow Morning, is even more symbolic than *Hello Out There,* leaving realistic presentation far behind. . . . The most obvious theme is the conflict and identification of illusion and reality.

Saroyan maintains in this play a precarious balance between the external and internal world, and the success of the play is that he doesn't reject either as illusory: in the delightfully drunken perception of Fritz the cab driver, "Illusion or reality, no illusion or no reality, one more drink before I go."

However, in attesting to the illusoriness of the external world at all, Saroyan is taking his stand for the internal world as before. Whether Kitty's dream of home is an illusion, whether each man's search for beauty is illusory, it is an illusion which many—Saroyan included—honor by such titles as divinity, as art, as inspiration. Simultaneously, for Saroyan at least, whether the external world is irrelevant and is going to disappear tomorrow morning or not, it is within the context of that world—with all its "delicate balance of despair and delight"—that inner reality must be expressed. . . . (pp. 190-91)

The final lines of the play, in which Fritz places a bet on Tomorrow Morning, show that Saroyan had passed beyond the wish-fulfillment he allowed himself in *The Time of Your Life.* . . . Fritz's bet symbolizes Saroyan's willingness to gamble on the desire for beauty in mankind despite his realization that the odds are against him and that he has lost before.

Death Along the Wabash is the most pessimistic of Saroyan's plays. *Hello Out There* recognized the world's rejection of the artist's perception of beauty, but held out the hope that the search for beauty would still be carried on by the individual. In *Across the Board on Tomorrow Morning,* despite the lighter tone, the conclusion . . . is even more pessimistic. This is only relieved by Fritz's willingness to continue betting on the losing horse anyway.

In *Death Along the Wabash,* no one is left to search for beauty anymore, and the world refuses to gamble on the individual. Instead, it destroys him, ostensibly because it is helping him to reach his goal—which is only attainable in heaven, or at least out of this world. The Hobo as the representative of the world is right when he says that he has destroyed the idealistic, Negro, escaped convict Joe in self-defense: a complete perception of the beauty possible within oneself does destroy the external irrelevancies for that individual, and in this sense Joe was threatening the Hobo's existence. (pp. 191-92)

This play, so reminiscent of Pinter, surpasses both the obvious theme of murder for materialistic satisfaction and the topical theme of racial discrimination—of the Hobo representing society's specific persecution of the Negro. It is the somewhat superficial concentration on the racial theme which weakens all three of [these plays]. . . . Saroyan transcends this in *Death Along the Wabash* because he is not so much trying to write as a black man as to portray the individual persecuted by the world, the individual searching for beauty who has been his main concern in the other plays. Consequently, portraying a hero that is black rather than a black hero enables Saroyan to point out parallels between discrimination against minority groups and discrimination against the individual. Except for the blatant exposition in Joe's first speech, the play is powerfully written. The speeches are generally longer and weightier than those usually found in Saroyan's plays, and the conclusion of unrelieved pessimism is hardly recognizable as the work of this affirmative playwright. . . . [The Hobo, a] powerful portrait of that portion of mankind which recognizes the external world as the only reality . . . and thus destroys the inner reality in others and in themselves, is especially significant because the Hobo's arguments appeal strongly to logic, to the rational perception of the world. Those critics who argued that Saroyan was not logical should read this play—they might note an undercurrent of resentment here of the artist who was criticized for appealing to the heart. This play gives modern society what it claims to want—a realistic pessimism and the destruction of the idealistic and romantic in mankind.

In fact, the pessimism of this play strikes deeply because Saroyan's multi-level symbolism enables him to reflect parallels between many forms of persecution and discrimination and at the same time to show the close relationship between the persecutor and his victim. Saroyan not only realizes that, as in this play, the sensitive individual, the artist, the economically oppressed, the black man or Armenian in search of something beyond what society has allotted him, will more likely than not be destroyed by the world before he can reach his goal; but even more painful is Saroyan's recognition that this destruction is likely to be at the hands of the individual's own father—from another man who could have chosen to search for beauty or fight for freedom but who sold out to the world instead for materialistic reasons.

This is not a new discovery Saroyan made just before writing Death Along the Wabash. The world had always opposed his individuals; it is only that he has preferred to place his bet on beauty, on humanity, on tomorrow morning despite the odds. He reaffirms the value of the individual in . . . The Cave Dwellers, and if one reviewer derides it for imitating Beckett by calling it "an affirmative 'Waiting for Godot'" it should be remembered that Saroyan was writing plotless symbolic drama many years before Waiting for Godot appeared in 1953. It is true that several of Saroyan's general situations reflect other plays—Wilder's Skin of Our Teeth is strongly recalled in High Time Along the Wabash and Hart and Kaufman's You Can't Take It With You provides the source for much of the merriment in The Beautiful People. Despite these recognizable influences, Saroy-

an's plays . . . are still very original and carry different messages from their models. This is equally true of The Cave Dwellers, where the characters resemble nothing so much as characters in other Saroyan plays. (pp. 192-93)

The Cave Dwellers, however, lacks the power of Saroyan's earlier works except in isolated moments. The ingredients are there, the intention is there, but somehow the use of romanticism has become an immersion in romanticism. Saroyan is pushing too hard: as Walter Kerr observed, "The sentence beginning 'Love is . . . ' occurs more times in eleven scenes than I could count, try though I did." Critics have frequently argued that Saroyan tends to state his message rather than present it dramatically, and statements do detract from the effect of this play, anyway. In fact, Saroyan protests too much this time, perhaps because he had become increasingly more aware of the loneliness of his affirmative position and the difficulties of maintaining it in the face of current conditions. . . . [We] might validly wonder whom he is trying to convince in the Cave Dwellers, the audience or himself?

However, allowing for the intrusion of sentimentality and didacticism in The Cave Dwellers, on the whole Saroyan has succeeded remarkably well in using romantic material symbolically. To one who automatically identifies any affirmation with romanticism, he is a romantic. But to recognize the world for what it is, to admit the apparent hopelessness of an affirmation of the individual, yet still to be willing to gamble on human dignity because of the value of the attempt itself sounds more like courage than romanticism. (p. 194)

Thelma J. Shinn, "William Saroyan: Romantic Existentialist," in Modern Drama, Vol. XV, No. 2, September, 1972, pp. 185-94.

MARGARET BEDROSIAN
(essay date 1982)

[In the following excerpt, Bedrosian examines Saroyan's optimism and his depiction of ethnicity in The Assyrian, Rock Wagram, and The Laughing Matter.]

What we discover in the work of this most famous and prolific of Armenian-American writers [Saroyan] is a lifelong tension between the forces of good-humored acceptance and the more insistent voice of his own experience as the orphaned son of an Armenian immigrant. . . . Saroyan's relationship to his ethnic group [is] an affinity based less on the shared values of communal life than the common experience of "wounded homelessness," of belonging to a dying race, of having been abandoned by one's father into a world devoid of security and rest.

This was an attitude he had portrayed movingly in his 1934 short story, **"Seventy Thousand Assyrians."** Here Saroyan depicts the Assyrians as the one ethnic group whose claim to world attention fell even below that of the Armenians. . . . The moral of this bittersweet tale is that the fragility of his national ties has freed the humble Assyrian barber to join the race of man, "the part that massacre does not destroy." (pp. 13-14)

Saroyan's laughter *is* sad, because the "tougher truth" of his family's and ethnic group's struggles stands at the back of his celebrations of earthy Armenian homelife, where flat bread and sun ripened grapes may nurture individual quests into a chancy world, but can't lighten the journey. Throughout, the thrust of Saroyan's life and art came from a radical existentialism, isolated from communal solace. It was an orphan's creed, sinewy and street-wise, marbled with a rigidity that rejects self-pity and forgives slowly.

The sharp edges of this worldview emerge most painfully in three works of fiction Saroyan wrote in mid-career in the early 1950s: a novella entitled *The Assyrian,* and two novels, *Rock Wagram* and *The Laughing Matter.* Expressed with increasing intensity through these works is the sense that the melancholy that plagues the "dying race"—whether Armenian or otherwise—has seeped into the protagonist's soul, where it can only find a healthy outlet in swift motion—flying, gambling, racing. When at rest, the main character finds himself in spiritual limbo, unable to adopt the ethos of his ancestors and equally incapable of creating a viable personal code. Thus in the middle of his writing career Saroyan returned to the theme of his earliest short story, **"The Daring Young Man on the Flying Trapeze,"** . . . in which the young man's refusal to be saved from starvation by the Salvation Army coupled with his steady motion to the end forms his chief claim to heroism. But, whereas the daring young man was only responsible for his own life, the middle-aged protagonists of the later period face crises of family life, where the models of their ethnic past remind them of their domestic shortcomings. With each successive work, we find the ethnic group serving a dual function, not only mirroring the central character's spiritual uprootedness, but exhorting him to pursue family ideals beyond his grasp.

In *The Assyrian,* the novella that begins the 1950 collection of stories with that name, Paul Scott reexamines the profiles of his life as he prepares to meet his approaching death. What little we know of his life falls into the typical Saroyan pattern: Scott is a zestful gambler, deriving from the swift throw of the dice a keen sense of personal freedom, the satisfaction of

beating the odds against defeat, of riding through inner turmoil on a tide of luck only confident timing and daring can compel. He has come to Lisbon, Portugal on another gamble, climaxing a lifelong search for an elusive connectedness and transcendence. In the process of following his brief meditation on his past amidst the backdrop of this gracious city, where civility soothes his restlessness, the reader finds the key to Scott's character in the constant push against constraint, social and otherwise. . . . But the cost of compulsively defying boundaries can be disease. Early in the story, Scott traces the root of his malaise to "bitterness about himself ": "He knew he didn't care about anybody else in the world, not even [his daughter] if the truth were told, he cared only about himself, and always had." . . .

The anger and shame of Scott's self-recognition will recur in the later works, accompanied by the central character's ambivalent tie to his ethnic heritage, wherein the members of a small, dying race urge family bonding. In *The Assyrian,* Paul Scott has responded to his call, having early on sided with "the tired side," "the impatient and wise side," hidden in him like a life spring until he reaches puberty. (p. 15)

Published a year after *The Assyrian,* in 1951, *Rock Wagram* picks up many of the same concerns as the earlier work, but locates them in a more specific ethnic context. As Nona Balakian briefly notes of this novel, *Rock Wagram* "is one of Saroyan's darker works, reflecting his own uneasy passage from the Old World of his beginnings to the competitive world of Hollywood and New York." Rock's "uneasy passage" is most noticeably reflected in his name change from Arak (literally meaning "swift" in Armenian) Vagramian to accommodate his acting career. The shift in social identity has deprived this second-generation Armenian of the old security of Fresno family and friends, and has placed him in a milieu where he is cautioned against assuming easy friendships.

In the tradition of the Saroyan picaresque (and American heroes in general), Rock is perpetually on the road, charting the American landscape, seeking contentment in hurtling through "a dream of cities, money, love, danger, oceans, ships, railroads, and highways." But whereas in the earlier work Paul Scott pursued his independence of family matters, Rock constantly defines himself in terms of the domestic ideal: "A man is a family thing. His meaning is a family meaning." . . . Yet falling into the overriding pattern, when it comes to embodying this ideal, Rock fails. (p. 17)

As the novel progresses, we find that Rock's inability to forge a family stems from a deeper stratum of his experience, primarily his uneasy relationship with his now deceased father. This facet of the story reminds us of the central lack in Saroyan's childhood: a flesh-and-blood father. As Armenians, both Rock and

Saroyan inherited an ethos in which family bonding was of primary concern and the role of the father critical in maintaining social cohesion. (p. 18)

Rock's determination to not repeat his father's failure continues to the end. Unlike Paul Scott who travels east to die, Rock Wagram concludes his self-exploration on a more positive note: "I don't like to work for money, but I'm going to try to do it. I'm a father, and I haven't any choice any more, that's all." . . . Yet despite this promise, the ending returns to the larger Saroyan pattern, for Rock finds himself alone, on the road, clutching the token of love (a fake coin Ann Ford has given him stamped with the ironically misspelled, "I lovea you"), rather than touching the warm reality of human intimacy.

The Laughing Matter, the darkly ironic novel that completes this sequence, intensifies and makes more explicit the tensions of the previous two works, especially with regard to the passions that split the ethnic husband from his wife. Set amidst the autumn vineyards of Fresno which Saroyan knew well, the story broods on the extent to which an unforgiving pride can ruin a family. Hearing from his wife that she is pregnant with a child not his own, Evan Nazarenus reacts with an icy rage whose every breath punishes. But as with the earlier stories, the reader can't fully understand Evan's anger without connecting it to a moribund heritage which has saddled him with a burden of "pride and loneliness." (p. 19)

Evan's questions restate the concerns of the previous protagonists even more specifically. Early loss of parental bonding and the dissolution of family ties due to cultural assimilation have left him without an emotional anchor. As a result, Evan's inability to reach out and embrace the unborn child denotes his own poverty of self, a self he's never learned to love. He thus answers his wife's plea that he accept the illegitimate child with: "I would love the stranger. I would love without pity . . . but where is there in my own stranger's heart the means and nature of such love? Where is it, Swan?" . . .

As in *Rock Wagram,* members of the ethnic group both defend and admonish the central character. Here, after Swan commits suicide, Dr. Altoun suggests that the instability of the marriage stemmed from her being non-ethnic: "With one of *us,* it would take a great deal to end a marriage." . . . (p. 20)

Though Evan's "call" is in the conditional—"I'll love you *if* you have an abortion"—passages of great descriptive simplicity present Saroyan's ideal of family life with allegorical dignity. In these vignettes, the narrative assumes a soothing symmetry that symbolizes the perfection neither Evan nor any real family can ever achieve. . . . But since such moments stand for an ideal Evan can't sustain, they give way to the opposite extreme in melodrama. (pp. 20-1)

Coming to the end of this short series of fiction, one suspects that Saroyan's personality was much more complex than his oft-expressed pseudo-philosophy of love and brotherhood would lead us to believe. In recent excerpts from a biography Aram Saroyan has written of his father, we find that loneliness and sparks of viciousness stalked Saroyan's life in fact as well as fiction. . . . What emerges from these memories is the portrait of a man who could not get close to others. . . . In short, Aram Saroyan spots the same irony in his father's life that lies at the heart of his writing: that "one of the most loveable father figures of American letters'," . . . the poet of the family, was himself totally inadequate to the demands of family life.

With regard to Saroyan's writing, the biographical perspective supports the notion that many of his excesses—his gushy sentimentality, facile worldview, smug self-confidence, and sloppy writing—were often masks for an underlying ambivalence, even a cynicism, about the value of anchoring art and relationships in disciplined thought and behavior. Genuine sentiment needs no exaggeration, but does depend on a fine emotional tuning sensitive to others. Accordingly, some critics have charged that the novel is Saroyan's least successful genre, for he had little interest in character for its own sake.

Nevertheless, we know from his portrayals of Armenians elsewhere, notably stories and vignettes of his own family in Fresno, that Saroyan could depict his people with all the color and spirit they demand, with admirable faithfulness to individual personality. But, as noted, in this fictional sequence he keeps describing the ethnic group as "dying," possibly a vague recognition of Armenia's long history of persecution; the dwindling numbers of Armenia's surrogates, the Assyrians; or the corrosive effects of assimilation into this culture. Yet beyond this minimally valid tag, there isn't much that is particularly Armenian or Assyrian or halfway "ethnic" about the characters in any of these stories, if by those terms we mean a detailed and accurate delineation of a specific people. They are merely props for the central character's introspective battles, bearing foreign-sounding names, sometimes suspicious of outsiders or quaint in speech, patient with whatever fate brings, but leaving us hard-pressed to identify them as Armenian, Assyrian, or whatnot. (pp. 21-22)

And finally, to refute another critical defense brought to Saroyan's aid, his disregard of character does not always denote an allegorical intent, just as his frequent refusal to deal with evil does not neatly transform him into an affirmative writer. Indeed, it seems more accurate to say that his preoccupation with anger and denial simply blocked interest in persons and social forces removed from his struggles. The profile of Saroyan's career thus resembles the motions of the trapeze artist in whom he first projected his symbolic self, hurtling between the poles of a flabby acceptance of the "All" and a self-punishing denial of intimacy, occasionally achieving a fragile balance in works such as *My Heart's in the Highlands,* where trust and faith lighten the impoverished lives of an ethnic family. Throughout this dialectic, Saroyan's descriptions of family and ethnicity mirrored his fluctuating and am-

bivalent loyalties. For though Saroyan identified with the orphaned independence of the Armenian people, he also knew that the axiom that had insured their survival was the truth he found toughest to embody: "Fool with the family and you've finished everything." (p. 23)

Margaret Bedrosian, "William Saroyan and the Family Matter," in *MELUS,* Vol. 9, No. 4, Winter II, 1982, pp. 13-24.

SOURCES FOR FURTHER STUDY

Calonne, David Stephen. *William Saroyan: My Real Work is Being.* Chapel Hill: University of North Carolina Press, 1983, 185 p.

> Critical biography.

Floan, Howard R. *William Saroyan.* New York: Twayne Publishers, 1966, 176 p.

> Concise biography.

Foster, Edward Halsey. *William Saroyan: A Study of the Short Fiction.* Boston: Twayne Publishers, 1991.

> Overview of Saroyan's short stories.

Hamalian, Leo, ed. *William Saroyan: The Man and the Writer Remembered.* Rutherford, N.J.: Fairleigh Dickinson University Press, 1987, 259 p.

> Memorial collection of biographical and critical essays.

Lee, Lawrence, and Gifford, Barry. *Saroyan: A Biography.* New York: Harper and Row, 1984, 338 p.

> Biography.

Saroyan, Aram. *William Saroyan.* San Diego: Harcourt Brace Jovanovich, 1983, 168 p.

> Biography written by Saroyan's son.

Jean-Paul Sartre

1905-1980

(Full name Jean-Paul Charles Aymard Sartre) French philosopher, dramatist, novelist, essayist, biographer, short story writer, journalist, editor, scriptwriter, and autobiographer.

INTRODUCTION

Sartre is regarded as among the most influential contributors to world literature in the twentieth century and, along with Martin Heidegger and Albert Camus, one of the leading proponents of the philosophical concept of existentialism. Sartre's interpretation of existentialism emphasizes that existence precedes essence and that human beings are alone in a godless, meaningless universe. He believed that individuals are thus absolutely free but also morally responsible for their actions. Sartre acknowledged the inherent absurdity of life and the despair that results from this realization but maintained that such malaise could be transcended through social and political commitment. In his prolific and diverse literary output, Sartre examined virtually every aspect of human endeavor from the position of a search for total freedom. Arthur C. Danto commented: "Sartre totalized the [twentieth] century . . . in the sense that he was responsive with theories to each of the great events he lived through."

Sartre's earliest influence was his grandfather, Charles Schweitzer, with whom he and his mother lived after his father's early death. As Sartre recalls in his childhood memoir, *Les mots* (1964; *The Words*), Schweitzer, a professor of German, instilled in him a passion for literature. Yet Schweitzer also preached the serious values of the bourgeoisie and denigrated a career in letters as precarious and unsuitable for stable middle-class people. In reaction Sartre proposed to make writing *serious*, to adopt it as the center of his life and values. He also chose it as a kind of self-justification in a world where children were not taken seriously. "By writing I was existing. I was escaping from the grown-ups," he wrote in *The Words*. An only child who was doted on by the adults in the Schweitzer home, Sartre perceived hypocrisy in his middle-class environment as manifested in his family's penchant for self-indulgence and role-playing. As a result, he held anti-bourgeois sentiments throughout his life. After completing his early education at a Parisian lycée, Sartre attended the École Normale Supérieure. There he studied philosophy and met fellow philosophy student Simone de Beauvoir, with whom he maintained a lifelong personal and intellectual relationship. Sartre spent much of the 1930s teaching philosophy and studying the works of German philosophers Edmund Husserl and Martin Heidegger. Sartre's early philosophical volumes—*L'imagination* (1936; *Imagination: A Psychological Critique*), *Esquisse d'une théorie des émotions* (1939; *The Emotions: Outline of a Theory*), and *L'imaginaire: Psychologie phénoménologique de l'imagination* (1940; *The Psychology of Imagination*)—reflect the influence of Husserl's phenomenology and focus on the workings and structure of consciousness. During this era, Sartre also wrote his first novel, *La nausée* (1938; *Nausea*), a work that depicts man's reaction to the absurdity of existence, and the short story collection *Le mur* (1939; *The Wall, and Other Stories*), an exploration of human relationships, sexuality, insanity, and the meaning of action. By the end of the decade, he had firmly established his reputation as a promising young writer.

Sartre continued to write prolifically during World War II, producing the dramas *Les mouches* (1942; *The Flies*), a retelling of the Greek story of the murder of Clytemnestra by her children, and *Huis clos* (1944; *No Exit*), a disturbing vision of hell. At this time, Sartre also wrote the philosophical work *L'être et le néant: Essai d'ontologie phénoménologique* (1943; *Being and Nothingness: An Essay on Phenomenological Ontology*), which examines man as both an object in the world and as an ordering consciousness. After the publication of this last work, considered by many scholars the most important of the first half of his career, Sartre became recognized as a major philosopher and preeminent spokesman for his generation.

While serving with the French Army during the war years, Sartre had been taken prisoner by the Germans and held captive for nine months. His experiences among fellow inmates affected him strongly. His subsequent literary and philosophical works demonstrated an increased awareness of history and politics, as well as an increased commitment to social and political action. Throughout the 1950s and 1960s, Sartre devoted much attention to world affairs, participating in political demonstrations and espousing Marxist solutions to social problems in articles later collected, along with philosophical and literary essays, in the ten-volume *Situations* (1947-1976). In *Critique de la raison dialectique, Volume I: Théorie des ensembles pratiques* (1960; *Critique of Dialectical Reason: Theory of Practical Ensembles*), considered by critics his second major philosophical work, Sartre attempts to fuse Marxism and existentialism to provide a new approach to historical analysis. Condemning capitalism and Western democratic institutions, Sartre calls for a synthesis of personal freedom and moral duty within a neo-Marxian context in order to create the foundation for social revolution. In 1964, Sartre was awarded, but refused to accept, the Nobel Prize in literature. As the result of declining health, Sartre wrote less prolifically in his last years. He died of a lung ailment in 1980.

Several of Sartre's philosophical themes are adapted from the works of Heidegger. Among Heidegger's theories influential in the development of Sartre's ideas are the importance of history as a requisite for philosophical analysis, the belief that individuals are continuously inventing their identities, and the contention that inquiry into the human condition should derive from an examination of the results of social change throughout history. Sartre and Camus, who were among the leading French intellectuals during the World War II era, also shared many similar ideas. Both writers were interested in exploring the significance of human endeavor in the twentieth century, and each recognized the need to acknowledge and overcome the absurdity of the world through commitment and action. Their fundamental philosophical differences lay in their interpretations of "the absurd"; Camus saw absurdity as the disparity between an individual's rational expectations and the irrationality of the universe, whereas Sartre viewed absurdity in terms of contingency, or the superfluous nature of existence.

Being and Nothingness: An Essay on Phenomenological Ontology is considered by many scholars to be Sartre's masterpiece. Combining technical philosophical terminology with specific, fictionalized scenarios, Sartre systematically examines what he terms "being-in-itself," or the world of things, and "being-for-itself," or the world of human consciousness. Sartre also explores such issues as how individuals view reality, how they perceive themselves and others, and how they interact, stressing humanity's complete freedom and resultant responsibility to overcome the role prescribed by society. Failure to act on this responsibility, Sartre contends, results in "bad faith" and represents an inauthentic existence. Lionel Abel remarked: "*Being and Nothingness* is probably the most complete effort that has been made in modern times to deal in a philosophically precise manner with questions which by their very nature had seemed to condemn the theorist to inexactitude."

Sartre's plays are generally recognized as successful statements of his philosophical themes of freedom, responsibility, and action. His first drama, *The Flies,* produced during the German occupation of France, subtly denounces nazism through a reenactment of Greek legend. Sartre's next play, *No Exit,* presents three characters who have been condemned to hell. This existence is symbolized by a small room from which there is no escape—the result of having lived in bad faith. The protagonists eventually realize that "hell is other people" and that the ultimate torture is to ponder one's faults for eternity through the eyes of others. *Morts sans sépulture* (1946; *The Victors*) centers on a crisis of consciousness among French Resistance fighters who have been captured and tortured by the Vichy militia. *Les mains sales* (1948; *Dirty Hands*) focuses on the struggle of Hugo, a bourgeois idealist, to prove his worth to his comrades in the Communist party. Ordered to assassinate Hoederer, a Communist leader whom he admires for his political views, Hugo wavers but finally kills him for reasons unrelated to politics. When given a chance to renounce his action after Hoederer is declared a hero, Hugo refuses, thereby affirming his good faith. *Le diable et le bon dieu* (1951; *The Devil and the Good Lord*), set in Reformation Germany, revolves around a man who first pursues absolute evil and then absolute good, only to discover the falseness of both paths. This play is generally viewed as Sartre's strongest affirmation of atheism. In *Les séquestrés d'Altona* (1959; *The Condemned of Altona*), a German boy goes insane after contemplating his father's role in the Nazi Holocaust. The boy locks himself in a room in an attempt to expiate guilt and sustain his delusion that Germany won World War II. This play also indirectly addresses the French Army's crimes during the Algerian war.

Sartre's novels are also considered reflective of his philosophical themes. His first novel *Nausea* is widely considered a classic of existentialist literature and the precursor of the *nouveau roman,* or New Novel. Taking the form of a journal kept by Antoine Roquentin, a historian working on a biography, *Nausea* relates the protagonist's growing realization of the gratuitousness and senselessness of physical objects and of his own existence, which manifests itself as a feeling of nausea and a resolve to invest meaning in his life by writing a novel that would alert the bourgeoisie to the absurdity of their existence. Sartre implies in *Nausea* that the only authentic mode of being is the aesthetic.

During World War II, Sartre developed the idea for a tetralogy of novels entitled *Les chemins de la liberté* (1947-51; *The Roads of Freedom*). In this series, which he never completed, Sartre intended to dramatize the conflict between individual liberty and social obligation among French intellectuals and artists in crisis situations. The first novel of *The Roads of Freedom, L'age de raison* (1945; *The Age of Reason*), centers on

philosophy student Mathieu Delarue's uncertainty over whether to devote himself to his pregnant mistress or to his political party. The second volume, *Le sursis* (1945; *The Reprieve*), which employs simultaneous narratives influenced by the novels of John Dos Passos, explores the ramifications of the appeasement pact that Great Britain and France signed with Nazi Germany in 1938. In the third book, *La mort dans l'âme* (1949; *Troubled Sleep*), Delarue ends his indecisiveness by attempting to defend a village under attack from the Germans. Although he is killed, Delarue expresses his ultimate freedom through his bravery.

In addition to philosophy, drama, and fiction, Sartre also wrote biographies of French writers Charles Baudelaire, Jean Genet, and Gustave Flaubert. These books—*Baudelaire* (1947), *Saint Genet, comédien et martyr* (1952; *Saint Genet, Actor and Martyr*), and *L'idiot de la famille: Gustave Flaubert de 1821 à 1857* (1971-1972; *The Family Idiot: Gustave Flaubert, 1821-1857*)—examine their subjects through the social conditions under which they wrote and the changes they underwent as a result of historical events. This method is delineated in part in the essay "Qu'est-ce que la littérature?" (1948; "What Is Literature?"). In this work, Sartre denies the necessity of critical analysis of a writer's style, which he believes is important only as a means for stating a theme. Instead, he promotes "engaged" writing, that which raises social consciousness.

Opinion on Sartre's overall achievement varies. The novelist Colin Wilson wrote in *Anti-Sartre* that "both his metaphysics and his political philosophy are invalidated by a number of serious mistakes" and suggested that his influence as a philosopher predeceased him by at least ten years. Contrary views were expressed, in *Jean-Paul Sartre: His Philosophy,* by René LaFarge, who called Sartre "a splendid example of an exceptional talent and a generous will put to the service of man," and, in *Sartre and Marxist Existentialism,* by Thomas R. Flynn, who declared that he was "the very model of the *philosophe engagé,* the conscience of his age."

(For further information about Sartre's life and works, see *Contemporary Authors,* Vols. 9-12, 97-100 [obituary]; *Contemporary Authors New Revision Series,* Vol. 21; *Contemporary Literary Criticism,* Vols. 1, 4, 7, 9, 13, 18, 24, 44, 50, 52; *Dictionary of Literary Biography,* Vol. 72: *French Novelists, 1930-1960;* and *Major 20th-Century Writers.*)

CRITICAL COMMENTARY

BENJAMIN SUHL

(essay date 1970)

[In the following excerpt, Suhl examines the relationship between philosophy, literary criticism, and literature in Sartre's system of thought.]

A philosopher described Sartre's philosophy as one "rooted in experience and directed towards the analysis of experience," of experiences which are "paradigm cases" for him. But there are, beyond these, individual phenomena which are irreducible to philosophy as a coherent body of thought. Sartre therefore relies on literature to complement philosophy and on literary criticism to mediate between literature and philosophy.

Sartre found or founded in literature vertigo and anguish as the experience of man's freedom; man's gaze as the revelation of the other, interiorized in shame when dominated, in pride when dominating; the privileged moments of a choice of being or of a profound change in direction as "paradigm cases" of the project and *praxis,* either authentic in a spirit of contestation or in bad faith in the "spirit of seriousness." Literature is also the medium in which description of the act of living discloses knowledge. Sometimes a literary "becoming" has the weight of a comprehensive philosophical or theological demonstration. [In *Nausea,*] Roquentin feels that life acquires a greater density of being when he hears the voice of commitment. In short, in literature an imaginary prereflective and reflective experience precedes philosophy, just as existence precedes essence. And since Sartre—by his reliance on literature—has been able to produce a systematic existentialist philosophy, this constitutes, in turn, a validation of literature. (p. 267)

Sartre's evolution shows a remarkable degree of consistency; it is the story of an unfolding, not of changes in direction. His career as a literary critic follows by a few years the publication of his phenomenological monographs. In the latter, he expelled interiority from consciousness and established the distinction between perception and imagination. He was one of the early enthusiastic readers of Dos Passos because that author dispensed with inner life, and, in turn, his discovery of Faulkner's "disloyal" temporality foreshadowed the development of his own ontological temporality in *Being and Nothingness.* In his other early reviews Sartre treats of Giraudoux's latent Aristotelianism, Ponge's psychoanalysis of things, Mauriac's *a priori*

essentialism, Camus's concept of absurdity from the point of view of reason, and the problem of language as that of the recuperation of being. In the style of a work, its structure, its temporality, its semantic field, its tone or its rhythm, Sartre seeks to detect the metaphysics of an author and judges it according to his own. For from the outset Sartre used literary criticism as a mediation between his philosophy and literature.

He expanded his thought in his phenomenological ontology, which permitted him to define man's project as a variant of value and aesthetic beauty as value. Commitment, arising from contingency and facticity, brought him to the need and the promise of a normative ethics. So far, modifying Freud through his existentialist psychoanalysis, Sartre had described the inauthenticity of the spirit of seriousness and asked only that one recognize one's contingency.

With the first issue of *Les Temps Modernes* Sartre, aroused by the war and the Resistance movement, manifested his involvement with social issues. Its "Présentation" announced as its aim the foundation of a synthetic anthropology. Later issues featured *What is Literature?* with its definition of aesthetic pleasure and of committed literature, and a series of articles on literary criticism in character with his existentialist ontology and his new concern for history.

With the *Baudelaire* and the *Saint Genet* Sartre created what is actually a new genre: existentialist biography. Following the elaboration of an existentialist anthropology in the [*Critique of Dialectical Reason (Critique de la raison dialectique)*], Sartre could expand and perfect his biographical criticism in the Flaubert articles. It remained the history of an author's consciousness, but it now gave greater weight to his family and social conditioning as a child. Sartre fully developed his regressive-progressive and analytico-synthetic method of research: a man's life is the endeavor to unify his world in a totalizing *praxis* in which he develops his initial project. (pp. 268-69)

The role of literary criticism as a dynamic correlation between literature and philosophy is in many respects originally and peculiarly Sartrian. Sartre did not, in spite of his *tabula rasa* point of departure in philosophy, discard any of the criteria of literary criticism to be derived from the humanistic disciplines, but he centered them on his own philosophical system. In this critical reflection on an author's work as the expression of his total existence, Sartre penetrates to the underly-

Principal Works

L'imagination (philosophy) 1936

[Imagination: A Psychological Critique, 1962]

La nausée (novel) 1938

[Nausea, 1949; also published as The Diary of Antoine Requentin, 1949]

Esquisse d'une théorie des émotions (philosophy) 1939

[The Emotions: Outline of a Theory, 1948; also published as Sketch for a Theory of the Emotions, 1962]

Le mur (short stories) 1939

[The Wall, and Other Stories, 1948; also published as Intimacy, and Other Stories, 1956]

L'imaginaire: Psychologie phénoménologique de l'imagination (philosophy) 1940

[The Psychology of Imagination, 1948]

Les mouches (drama) 1942

[The Flies, 1947]

L'être et le néant: Essai d'ontologie phénoménologique (philosophy) 1943

[Being and Nothingness: An Essay on Phenomenological Ontology, 1956]

Huis clos (drama) 1944

[The Vicious Circle, 1946; also produced as No Exit, 1946]

*Les chemins de la liberté. 3 vols. (novels) 1945-49

[The Roads of Freedom, 1947-51]

L'existentialisme est un humanisme (philosophy) 1946

[Existentialism, 1947; also published as Existentialism and Humanism, 1948]

Morts sans sépulture (drama) 1946

[Men without Shadows, 1947; also produced as The Victors, 1948]

Baudelaire (biography and criticism) 1947

[Baudelaire, 1949]

Les jeux sont faits (screenplay) 1947

[The Chips are Down, 1948]

†Situations. 10 vols. (essays) 1947-76

Les mains sales (drama) 1948

[Crime Passionnel, 1948; also published as Dirty Hands, 1949]

Le diable et le bon dieu (drama) 1951

[Lucifer and the Lord, (publication date) 1953; also published as The Devil and the Good Lord, and Two Other Plays, 1960]

Saint Genet, comédien et martyr (biography and criticism) 1952

[Saint Genet: Actor and Martyr, 1963]

Les séquestrés d'Altona (drama) 1959

[Loser Wins, 1960; also published as The Condemned of Altona, 1961]

Les mots (autobiography) 1963

[The Words, 1964]

L'idiot de la famille: Gustave Flaubert de 1821 à 1857 (biography and criticism) 1971-72

[The Family Idiot: Gustave Flaubert, 1821-1857, 1981-89]

Le scenario Freud (essays) 1984

[The Freud Scenario, 1985]

The War Diaries of Jean-Paul Sartre (diaries) 1985

*The three volumes of this sequence are: Volume 1: L'age de raison (1945; The Age of Reason, 1947); Volume 2: Le sursis (1945; The Reprieve, 1947); and Volume 3: La mort dans l'âme (1949; Iron in the Soul, 1950; also published as Troubled Sleep, 1951).

†The first volume of this series is Critique de la raison dialectique, Volume I: Théorie des ensembles pratiques (1960; Critique of Dialectical Reason: Theory of Practical Ensembles, 1976). Volume II contains the essay "Qu'est-ce que la littérature?" (1948; What is Literature?, 1949; also published as Literature and Existentialism, 1962).

---

ing metaphysics. Sartre can be a rewarding reader, ready to recognize and adopt valid discoveries in a literary work or to criticize them from the point of view of his existentialist criteria. . . . Sartre's literary criticism is a guide, a method of research, but not an *a priori* system to be imposed on original thought. To him, literary criticism is in a permanent evolution, moving back and forth from philosophy to the lived world of the author, so as to renew, to complement, to enlarge, to deepen and to explicate one by the other.

Sartre's philosophy and literary criticism exist as the antidote to most Anglo-American philosophy, preoccupied, in the words of one critic, "with the analysis of language and with problems in the theory of knowl-

edge," philosophers to whom "philosophy [is] a dialogue between philosophers, unbroken by reference to anything outside philosophy." One might perhaps say that nonexistentialist philosophy as a whole is more dominated by the tradition of its own past than is literature, thanks to its "belletristic" freedom. Taking reflection on experience as its point of departure, Sartrian literary criticism is a free and unending dialogue between the two disciplines in which he seeks a unification of many branches of knowledge, and to which he brings the criteria developed in his philosophy.

Success in one's critical endeavor is reached, by his own standards, when one has the intuition of having attained irreducibility and thus advanced to an understanding of a work and an author that explicates the greatest number of phenomena. This is exactly what Sartre has achieved: he has "reduced" traditional categories in many fields while integrating them into his concept of the original choice of being. (pp. 269-71)

Sartre's first impetus to write came from a passion to understand what he was to others. In the process he often had to think against himself, and, in tried and true phenomenological fashion, he came, as has no one before him, to understand those of whom he himself was conscious: the others. In either case, in the words of a perceptive reader of Sartre, "we can no longer formulate a general truth about ourselves which shall encompass us like a house." The most we can do is to emulate Sartre's lack of illusions, his lucidity, his wager of commitment, and his example of someone who "by inventing his own issue, invents himself." (p. 272)

Benjamin Suhl, in his *Jean-Paul Sartre: The Philosopher as a Literary Critic,* Columbia University Press, 1970, 311 p.

JUDITH ZIVANOVIC

(essay date 1971)

[In the following excerpt, Zivanovic examines the evolution of Sartre's concept of freedom as revealed in his dramas.]

A valuable prescription for those who would understand Sartre's notion of freedom should be: Don't confine your reading to *Being and Nothingness* and *Critique of Dialectical Reason.* Although Sartre deals with a wide range of subjects in the former, earlier work, he largely emphasizes individual freedom and aloneness. In the latter work, he encourages concerted social action. This seeming paradox requires a survey of the Sartre *oeuvre* to decipher, for only in this way can one fully appreciate the progression of Sartre's thought on the crucial matter of freedom. (p. 144)

The primary components of Sartre's thought may be said to form a triumvirate: Freedom-Responsibility-Action. In *Being and Nothingness,* Sartre insists that the major consequence of the fact that God does not exist, a consequence which man must recognize and accept, is that man is completely free. It is he who represents, through his freedom to act, the only destiny of mankind, and, through the acceptance of his freedom-responsibility, the legislator of all values.

Initially, the emphasis on freedom had a strongly personal nature—with *Being and Nothingness* and Sartre's first play, *The Flies,* many readers determined that for Sartre the individual must assume his own freedom as ultimately and exclusively important. His

second drama, *No Exit,* was viewed as a vivid revelation that men cannot engage in cooperative endeavors due to inevitable conflict. At this stage of his writing, however, Sartre produced his essay, *Existentialism is a Humanism.* Many critics prefer to forget this brief work and fervently wish that Sartre had done the same. Still Sartre refuses to reject any of his works; thus, we must accept the fact that he does not now reject nor did he reject in 1946 the premise of this essay—each man, desiring freedom above all, necessarily wants and strives for the freedom of the Other as well. . . . Sartre had not sufficiently elaborated in his first work the extent of the limitation to project and freedom afforded by the Other. Again, he did not sufficiently elaborate in *Existentialism Is a Humanism* how the former difficulty could be superseded in favor of a striving toward freedom for both self and the Other. Was it possible, in fact, that the critics were justified, that there was no solution to this dilemma?

Here a study of the drama provides a much needed and indispensable supplement to Sartre's philosophical works. The careful reader of Sartre's *oeuvre* cannot help but be struck by the fact that Sartre wrote a play subsequent to each progression of thought concerning his system. Yet, with the drama, he seems to be released from a good deal of the abstraction peculiar to his philosophical work. Proceeding as it does from within the inner sphere of his imagination, the drama not only quotes the key ideas of its father philosophical or critical work but expands upon the ideas, and, in fact, often foreshadows ideas to come. Such is the case with regard to the dilemma of freedom in the context of human projects.

Looking at Sartre's first drama, *The Flies,* written after Sartre's first great philosophical work and during the occupation, the reader finds an emphasis on the recognition of individual freedom on the part of one man, Orestes. . . . The play demonstrates quite clearly that the Other, in this case, the people of Argos, are necessary in order to give meaning to the act which Orestes performs; clearly, Orestes performs the act to free the people and to show them their freedom; however, the reader cannot escape the point that Orestes initially desires the act and the communion with the Argives as a means of personal commitment and to give his own life meaning. Thus, the individual in search of his own freedom and identity through commitment is primary and the devotion of the effort for the Other, while very important, is secondary to this factor.

Sartre's second play, *No Exit,* focuses on the conflict basic to human relations. Unfortunately, with one line of this play, Sartre has allowed himself to be "hung on his own catchphrase." "Hell is other people" is a line so vivid and memorable that it permits critics to handily make of the play itself an object which teaches, "Hell is [always] other people." There is, however, much more to this play than meets the eye of the person who prefers to be captivated by this catchphrase. (pp. 145-46)

[It] is the misinterpretation of Sartre's view of human interaction emanating from this play which tends to color the view of this phenomenon in the whole of his drama and perhaps the whole of his thought. Critics tend to view Sartre's play as a reflection of life as it is; they assume the fact that the characters are dead and in "hell" is only symbolic. This is partially true, but the *fact* of death is too important to Sartre to attribute only incidental meaning to that state in his three characters. The result of death is that man ceases to be a subject and becomes an immutable object over which the living are the guardians. . . . This condition is also comparable to the state of persons in bad faith—a condition of lying to oneself in order to escape responsible freedom. Thus, "dead" characters offer Sartre twofold advantages. First, he can show the immutable total antithesis of authentic existence. He can hold the condition of bad faith suspended in time. The characters can be shown as condemned, since they are dead, to repeat all of the errors which become an object lesson for the audience. Secondly, the fact that the characters are dead permits Sartre to represent the failings of those individuals who are their counterpart in life, those who are dead on earth before they are buried because they fail to choose and act. At the same time, this fact confirms that another course is possible, that life is for the living if they exist authentically. If they do not, then they are as surely dead, objectified, and meaningless as the inhabitants of that hellish Second Empire drawing room.

From this interpretation, it is easy to see the actual significance of the line, "Hell is other people." Each character has died in bad faith and can no longer change. In one way or another, he is totally dependent upon the others for even his meagre and meaningless existence. (p. 146)

The play is never meant to indicate that conflict *per se* is an evil. Obviously, when two conscious beings, two freedoms, come together, there is the potential of conflicting freedoms. . . . [Sartre] has not indicated that this basic conflict with the Other is a negative thing, but rather that for those who would live authentically, those who reject bad faith and embrace freedom, it is through such encounters with the Other that freedom is expressed and values are created. Indeed, outside of its relation to the Other and the world, freedom does not exist. Franz Gerlach of Sartre's play, *The Condemned of Altona*, vividly affirms this concept. He refuses to confront the Other and the world and to strive to give meaning to the world around himself. Even without his locked room, he would be imprisoned, for without placing himself in choice situations with the Other, his freedom is nothing. In the same

sense, Garcin, Estelle, and Inez were "dead" long before they reached their "hell" [in *No Exit*]; they had created a hell on earth through their bad faith, through their failure to act in a manner which gave meaning to freedom. Thus, it is through action in relation to the Other and the world that each man gives meaning to his freedom and to his life. This is, of course, the way which requires bearing the burden of freedom-responsibility; it is not the way of a Garcin or an Estelle.

While conflict is shown in *No Exit* as a primary factor of existence, unresolved conflict of projects is demonstrated as inherent only in relationships fostered of bad faith. It must never be overlooked that only the characters of *No Exit* of all the plays written by Sartre, are unable to change; only they are irremediably as others see them. . . . [Even so,] the small suggestion is there that a course is possible which feasibly resolves the conflict of projects, a course which requires working together with mutual respect for the Other's freedom and his project.

It would appear that little hope in this direction would be forthcoming from the oppressive atmosphere of *The Dead without Burial*. . . . [Still], Canoris, one of the prisoners, has several speeches which mark his character as the transition between the early Sartre absorbed in the notion of personal freedom as exemplified by Orestes and the later Sartre concerned with unified human effort. . . . Canoris insists that the prisoners must determine to subordinate their own desires and their attempts to justify their own existence in favor of lives useful to others.

This viewpoint, of course, is the driving force behind the character of Hoederer [in *Dirty Hands*], whose numerous speeches concerning his dedication to mankind mark him as engaged in a truly authentic existence. Hoederer [is] surely Sartre's most authentic man. . . . Goetz [in *The Devil and the Good Lord*] comes to realize that the only authentic existence lies in giving up his own vain attempts at perfection and self-justification and his former beliefs in God, Good, and Evil in an all-out effort to achieve the liberation of man. He will become the man Hoederer and the prisoners of *The Dead without Burial* were prevented by death from becoming. He will be the man that Orestes had never considered becoming. (pp. 147-49)

Sartre began to focus more diligently on limitations to freedom of which he was becoming increasingly aware. . . .

The plays begin to show that poverty and social class structure particularly are responsible for much that is oppressive and limiting in the world. (p. 150)

The new emphasis in Sartre's work is reflected in his focus on the concept of "need." . . . Sartre says of this new emphasis since his early writing, "Over against a dying child *Nausée* cannot act as a counterweight." Sartre, then, has come to believe that man is more limited in his freedom than Sartre himself originally anticipated. While each man is free within his own situation, some circumstances, such as poverty or war, make the situation so oppressive that genuine liberation is impossible *without constant revolution* to maintain freedom. This revolution must proceed from unified effort within which individual talent is utilized and the individual freely "relinquishes" a degree of his freedom in the sense that he is willing to engage in concerted effort with other men. (pp. 150-51)

This more recent recognition by Sartre of those factors in life which tend to limit freedom must not be construed, however, as a significant deviation from Sartre's original premise that man is free within his own situation. . . . For Goetz and the peasants, poverty and the division among classes which *limits* their freedom *does not eliminate* their freedom nor does it offer an excuse for inaction. It is merely the playing court in which they will engage in a contest whose rules they now know. (p. 151)

This progressive awareness, which the reader of Sartre's drama may witness groping for and gradually reaching the light, seems more abrupt when the perusal of the works is limited to Sartre's statements of philosophy. Still, what appears to the reader of *Being and Nothingness* as an inconsistency in *Existentialism Is a Humanism* and a complete break in *Critique* should appear to the reader of the entire works of Sartre as rather a constant movement and development of thought. The conflict between peoples and the necessity for individual resistance is developed in *Being* and exemplified in the action of *The Flies* and *No Exit*. The need for a shift from concerns with individual freedom to a striving for universal freedom is suggested in *Existentialism Is a Humanism* but not explained. Gradually, the explanation is accomplished in *The Dead without Burial, Dirty Hands,* and reaches its culmination in *The Devil and the Good Lord,* the logical predecessor to *Critique.* With the play, *The Condemned of Altona,* which expresses the notion of "need," the entire effort is toward an awareness of twentieth-century problems which must be corrected at all costs in order to facilitate the true liberation of man.

There is, then, nothing violently new, no break with previous thought, in this present notion of unified striving for mankind's liberation. As Sartre describes his shifts of emphasis, it is change "within a permanency." In the present order of things, Sartre endeavors to encourage an examination of a situation in order that man may recognize which elements are of his own choosing and which are simply conditions of his existence. Once he has done this, he can choose the method of procedure and make his own history. There is no fate, no bad luck, no excuse; simply man, his choices, and the situation in which he finds himself. . . . Goetz

passes through stages of awareness which Hoederer has evidently already achieved; each realizes the limitations of the possibilities of action open to him, accepts those limitations, and determines to act to the utmost within the context of these limitations. It is this recognition and this determination plus movement to action which affords these two men the opportunity to become real, existing human beings; which gives them and the world around them a true identity, a reality.

The individual freedom so crucial to Sartre's early thought is still important (all acts are necessarily initiated from the individual's awareness and abilities), but another aspect becomes equally crucial, respect for the freedom of all. Another principle likewise comes into play—no man is indispensable. (pp. 152-53)

That which Sartre requires of today's authentic man is . . . more heroic than the requirement for any Orestes. The unified action will not serve to defend each man against the anguish of life . . . ; quite the contrary. Each authentic man of today, each man who would lead in the revolution, must be willing to take a heavier burden than that of Orestes. He remains alone in his choices as the characters Hoederer and Goetz demonstrate. . . .

[Success] is possible, if highly difficult of accomplishment, when each man recognizes that difficulty is inherent in human relationships but that this difficulty must be overcome. It *must* be overcome because the principle of freedom should receive greater emphasis than each man's self-concern. It *can* be overcome because man makes himself through his free choices, thus he can create his relationship with the Other in whichever method he chooses, just as he creates his own individuality. Goetz and Hoederer forsee a chance, remote though it may be, and they determine to try it as the only authentic course. They are responsible for the weighty decisions and for the acts which they perform and their aloneness presses down upon them—the Sartrean free man is still responsible and very much alone. Now, however, his efforts are to obtain *and* cultivate his freedom *and* the freedom of the Other. (p. 154)

Judith Zivanovic, "Sartre's Drama: Key to Understanding His Concept of Freedom," in *Modern Drama*, Vol. XIV, No. 2, September, 1971, pp. 144-54.

DOUGLAS KIRSNER
(essay date 1985)

[In the following excerpt, Kirsner examines the relationship between Sartre's life and works and the psychological milieu of the modern era.]

Sartre was always interested in the relation between an individual and his or her time. The early Sartre seemed to focus on the manner in which we deny the freedom which constitutes us, while the later Sartre emphasises the limits to this freedom, which result from our familial and social contexts. In fact, Sartre devoted more pages to understanding the individual in context than to any other matter. How much can we know about a person who is free and yet situated? Sartre's study of Genet [*Saint Genet*] shows what Genet made of what was made of him. His study of Flaubert [*The Family Idiot*] asks both what Flaubert can tell us about his time and what the time can tell us about Flaubert:

> For a man is never an individual; it would be more fitting to call him a *universal singular*. Summed up and for this reason universalized by his epoch, he in turn resumes it by reproducing himself in it as a singularity. Universal by the singular universality of human history, singular by the universalizing singularity in his projects, he requires simultaneous examination from both ends.

In this article I want to look at Sartre in the same way in which Sartre treated Genet and Flaubert. Sartre himself wanted to be "as transparent to posterity . . . as Flaubert is to [him]." I want to investigate empathically Sartre's "lived experience," as the way his culture lived him as well as the way he lived his culture, in order to achieve the same end as Sartre achieved with Flaubert. How did Sartre live our contemporary culture? How did he reflect and express central problems of our time as a "universal singular"? Sartre's own view of our age is depicted in *The Critique of Dialectical Reason*. It is a pessimistic work which focusses on our radical alienation from ourselves and our world. The groups into which we are born terrorize us and dominate the very categories with which we think. Our Western world of late capitalism is ruled by a counter-finality in which loser wins. Advanced technological rationality may be seen to enshrine the final outcome of the fetishism of commodities—human beings are constituted as objects of administration. We blindly produce a world that controls us. Where technology has become the prevailing ideology, human relations often become relations between things. Freedom and choice are fundamentally illusions for there is no ground on which freedom and choice can become realized. In *Search for a Method* Sartre shows how we can use a method of cross-reference to explain the relation of the individual to society and, in *The Family Idiot,* Sartre goes further in developing a way of characterizing our time. He understands Flaubert's neurosis as

> a neurosis *required* by what I call the objective spirit . . . In the first two volumes I seem to be showing Flaubert as inventing the idea of art for art's sake because of his personal conflicts in reality, he invented it because the history of the objective

spirit led someone who wanted to write in the period 1835 to 1840 to take the neurotic position of post-romanticism, that is to say, the position of art for art's sake.

The "objective neurosis" of Flaubert's time then provided the setting and the impetus for Flaubert's subjectively conditioned creativity. Sartre's work is specific—he understands Flaubert through documents and texts and also as reflecting and expressing his own time. Sartre uses the method of empathy, which he could not use in writing about himself, in understanding the writer's lived experience.

How are we to define the "objective spirit" of our age in an effort to understand Sartre in his time and ours? I will attempt to cross-reference Sartre's own statements and writings with a view of our time in which the psychological is firmly rooted in the sociological. Sartre has often criticized psychoanalysis for its stereotyped use of categories as labels, as though psychoanalytic categories were final explanations. Sartre's work is antipsychological insofar as psychology is seen as stripping responsibility from us and placing it somewhere else in the past, i.e. insofar as it is reductionist. Yet Sartre himself uses psychological categories in a nonreductionist way in his works on Genet and Flaubert: it is difficult to discuss the singularity of an individual which includes experience of childhood without it. Sartre's ambivalence about psychoanalysis does not prevent his using a similar approach in his later works, although it is neither stereotyped nor reductionist. I will approach Sartre himself as a universal singular of our time in terms of the relationship between the objective or collective neurosis and the subjective neurosis that Sartre discusses in Flaubert. (pp. 206-08)

According to Harry Guntrip, a leading analytic thinker of the British school of object-relations, many people today suffer from schizoid problems which concern identity, "people who have deep-seated doubts about the reality and validity of their very 'Self,' who are ultimately found to be suffering various degrees of depersonalisation, unreality, the dread feeling of 'not belonging,' of being fundamentally isolated and out of touch with their world." They do not feel other people at all as being capable of being related to as they are trapped inside their own fantasy world. These people "feel cut off, apart, different, unable to become involved with real relationships."

> The schizoid sense of futility, disillusionment and underlying anxiety (is apparent) in existentialism. These thinkers, from Kierkegaard to Heidegger and Sartre, find human existence to be rooted in anxiety and insecurity, a fundamental dread that ultimately we have no certainties and the only thing we can affirm is "nothingness," "unreality," a final sense of triviality and meaninglessness. This surely is schizoid despair and loss of contact with the verities of

Sartre in 1964 with his longtime companion Simone de Beauvoir.

emotional reality, rationalised into a philosophy. Yet existentialist thinkers, unlike the logical positivists, are calling us to face and deal with these real problems of the human situation. It is a sign of our age.

I want to argue that Sartre's problematic fits this view. The most important issues in Sartre's life and work express and reflect these issues and tell us much about Sartre and our age. Often the creative writer distills much of the mood of an era, and is especially sensitive about the flavor and problems of human relations. This is not to say that Sartre's views are to be dismissed as "metaphysical pathology" (as Garaudy once called *Being and Nothingness.*) On the contrary we must read them as enlightening us about ourselves and our experience today. For the world Sartre describes is no alien one and his work has been very popular and influential. As many theories in the history of ideas express an age and are thus historically situated, so Sartre's ideas need to be historicized. This does not detract from the very real insights he made but rather tells us about the way he lived out history.

Herbert Marcuse has argued that Sartre's ontological categories are in fact the historical categories of late capitalism. While this may be true, it does not go far enough. As Sartre says, we are not lumps of clay; and what is important is not what people make of us, "but what we ourselves make of what they have made of us." We are obviously conditioned by our historical context but are also "transhistorical" beings, that is, the fact that we are born small and dependent in need of suckling is true of all cultures and of all times. We live our historical conditioning in individual ways which emanate from our own childhood relations, as Sartre reminds us in *Search for a Method. . . .* If Sartre's life and work are taken as a whole, a thread emerges which also links his world with our time—Sartre's schizoid and narcissistic world can be viewed as an instance of our neurosis. Let us look at this world in more detail. Sartre's worldview is essentially pessimistic. The world is an unfriendly viscosity bereft of meaning. Confronted with a godless world, human beings who are themselves defined as absence have an abiding sense of futility. We are not defined by what we are and will, but by what we do. There is no inner core of being. Our actions are not even within our control—loser so often wins.

Sartre's world is radically split. The "for-itself" will never be united with the "in-itself". We are "the desire to be God" but in this we are a "useless passion." Human relations are intrinsically "locked in conflict" and sadomasochistic pleasures are poor substitutes for love and friendship—all relationships are between exploiters and exploited. As the individual is an empty nonentity, life becomes a grim and constant struggle to preserve a minimal personal integrity against hostile others or else a self-deceiving loss of identity in another person, ideology or organization. We long to escape the freedom to which we are condemned. But in this we are doomed to frustration and despair.

In the world Sartre describes there is a fundamental failure of basic trust in both self and environment to provide the basis or the development of what Laing terms "primary ontological security." We are abandoned by a God who does not care and life becomes a losing battle with despair. Condemned to a freedom we do not want, we are basically deprived of the fullness of being. The good Lord does not exist but acts as a silent partner in Sartrean ontology. In fact the dialogue with the silent bespeaks a manichaeism without God— deprived of God, the world is evil and liberation is not possible.

Except perhaps in the battle of Sisyphus. For joy consists in our consciousness of not being overwhelmed and controlled by the circumstances to which we are condemned. The ability to say "no" which constituted a final refusal was, for Sartre, the ultimate foundation of choice. There was never the Promethean vision of an open future. The ability to turn the tables on one's torturers means an *incontrovertible conviction of meaning.* But even here as in *The Wall* we cannot be certain of the consequences of our not giving in to the demands of our masters. Sartre's optimism is that we "do not suffer from nothing" and Sisyphean freedom is a last-ditch stand against an otherwise invasive world. Certainly it is the freedom in chains that Sartre proclaims and sometimes rails against, but defiance can be seen as appropriate for a world where this is the only real freedom left; the very emphasis on our ontological freedom is an index of how far social freedom has ceased to exist.

Even where there are dreams of freedom, there is no exit anywhere. The theme of sequestration provides a vital underlying theme in Sartre's work. Many scenes in Sartre's literary works are set in rooms almost hermetically sealed off from the outer world. The room of the madman Pierre in *La Chambre,* the second empire drawing room of *Huis Clos,* the room in *Morts sans sépulture* where the resistance fighters await torture and death, Hoederer's room in *Les Mains sales* and that of Franz in *Les Séquestrés d'Altona,* provide some examples.

These symbolize the human situation as one of imprisonment. We are enveloped by forces beyond our control and condemned to possessing a freedom we cannot use authentically. Our inner void which demands fulfillment can never be filled. Our relations with others are intrinsically frustrating and, as if this were not enough, death destroys all the significance we thought we could attain. For Sartre, "Life does not only take place in a prison, it is itself a prison."

Sartre's interest in sequestration finds its origin in his own childhood experience of being an only child without peers who was shut up in a house where his only friends were his grandfather's books. Sartre's mother was treated as a child in the household which was ruled by Sartre's domineering grandfather. Sartre had no respect for her and came to regard her as an older sister in need of his protection. He was treated as a doll, a cute exhibition piece, an object—even a little prince. But never was he treated as a worthwhile person in his own right with real and valued feelings of his own. The young Sartre's internal reality was systematically invalidated: his being became his being-for-others. Sartre felt himself to be in the hands of adults. Feeling empty, he was an impostor playing the part he understood was expected of him by adults. The world of reason, books and ideas was substituted for the emotionally real, meaningful and confirming experience he lacked. As he experienced only his false self, he felt as malleable as clay, like a jelly fish inside, and was disgusted with what he saw as the "trivial unreality" as the world. Sartre sees childhood as a "solitary" reality in which what and how the child internalizes is beyond his control. It is scarcely surprising that his work denigrates the reality of feeling in favor of an intellectual rationality which sees the human being as a void, a lack, a nothingness.

Sartre always saw himself as marginal—as never really being in anything. He missed the games with other children in early childhood, and later only watched others' games. The proletariat was only on his horizon at the Ecole Normale and it was really only the war that brought him a sense of solidarity and membership in society. But even then, Sartre felt envious of those who did the actual fighting; as a writer he was still on the sidelines. After the war he continued to feel marginal, since he wasn't a worker but a "useless mouth" so far as the communist party was concerned. Sartre's portrait of the party man Brunet [in *The Roads of Freedom*], certainly depicts a man deceiving himself, yet the opposite position, that of Mathieu, is also untenable. Sartre says in the interviews following *La Cérémonie des adieux:* "Mathieu, Antoine Roquentin had lives other than mine, but neighbouring lives, expressing what, in my own eyes, was most profound in my own life."

Brunet's solidity was given by his identification with the party. Mathieu, the indecisive, intellectualized, evasive, bourgeois, impotent, self-searching philosophy teacher is counterposed to the solid, powerful, resolute, real proletarian man of action, Brunet. Duped by nature we are, like Mathieu, nothing at all, or else we impersonate what we are, like Brunet. Brunet, who seems like a whole man, is really a caricature, for his raison d'être is based on self-deception, on the delusional identification of being a soldier of the Party. Thus, Mathieu is ambivalent towards Brunet. He would love nothing more than to be able to make the leap of bad faith to become like Brunet. Yet he cannot act without sufficient reason—conviction must follow reason and not vice versa.

For Mathieu there is a complete split between reason and feeling. A life based on reason alone is as much a lie as one based exclusively on feeling. Demanding absolute certainty in his actions, Mathieu sees himself as an embodied refusal whose identity would be at stake in a world in which he would have to say "Yes." He defines himself *against*—like Sisyphus he knows what he is by what he is not. His nothingness forms the boundary between himself and others and prevents his merging with them. Brunet, on the other hand, does not experience his nothingness as he has merged with the Party. But Brunet's strength and identity are based on a collusively accepted myth.

Mathieu can either renounce his freedom by joining the Party or he can maintain his precarious identity by keeping his distance from the menacing world that threatens to engulf him. Mathieu has a constant grip on himself; feelings will never rule him. He will not let himself go for fear of losing himself. Feeling that there is nothing inside him is preferable to losing his boundaries altogether. To keep away from his feelings he represses them. His attachment to reason is rationalization. Mathieu and Brunet can be seen as two parts of the same person, a split personality that can never come together. The vitality is in Brunet, yet Mathieu can never reason himself into embracing it. Intellect and emotion are radically split.

Feeling himself to be a shell, Mathieu never explores any core feelings, only his defenses against them. His lack of commitment is not a happy one since there is nothing he desires more, yet at the same time fears more. He can do neither with nor without relationships. If he forgets himself for a moment, flies and cockroaches appear. If he commits himself to an action, he loses control of its consequences. Yet by not doing anything, he is pushed around by personal or impersonal forces.

Mathieu has only a pseudoindependence, invoking the outer world to give his life meaning. This characterizes the schizoid dilemma in which the self feels so empty that it relies suicidally on relationships with precisely those others who might swallow it up. Mathieu reaches a schizoid compromise in which he is "half-in and half-out" of relationship. He is sympathetic to the Party but will not join, has a lover but will not commit himself, attacks bourgeois living but remains bourgeois. His compromise means diminished desires but also diminished rewards. Feeling is erased in his general state of continuous withdrawnness. He is never really unhappy, but his life is full of chronic frustration. He is cut adrift in his own futile world, floating aimlessly, ruminating, waiting. In the aloofness and fastidiousness he so enjoys, Mathieu can remain cold, detached, even icy. Mathieu has committed a form of psychic suicide; devoid of feeling, how can he feel any point to life? Living becomes an intellectual exercise. In a life full only of missed opportunities Mathieu waits for the lightning flash which could fuse reason and emotion in a self-certain conviction; this is precisely what his radically split ego cannot achieve. Mathieu sees himself as a rotter, a washout who needs to be thoroughly cleansed. Purification comes only in his putative suicide in which he takes revenge on his past failures through firing on the approaching Germans. Mathieu knows this absurd and futile act will put the German timetable back only fifteen minutes and has warned a comrade against doing just that. Killing his first German is his first definite action—it is his own German. Commitment is for Mathieu linked with self-destruction. But Mathieu's first definite live action means that he has not only projected his bad parts on to the Germans, but also that he has put his vitality into them. This is suicidal as there is nothing left in him emotionally after his act. This demonstrates the final loss of self on the one hand subjectively and on the other a magical feeling of omnipotence which in fact is the likelihood of actual self-annihilation. Commitment for Mathieu is life and death at the same time. Doing what he most wants means self-annihilation. Moreover, Mathieu projectively identified parts of himself with the Germans as he had with the Party. The other often serves as a repository for menacing projections in the Sartrean world.

For Sartre action means losing oneself in it. There is no autonomous self behind an action or role. The waiter sees himself and is seen primarily as a Waiter. His role defines him—he cannot be in *his* actions without being his actions. The self as shell remains by not being engulfed, for neither symbiosis nor aloneness is a viable alternative. Symbiosis means a total dependence on a constricting and frustrating mother who will contract to supply all needs only at the price of the child's soul. It involves the ultimate in projective identification—everything is in the other with whom one is psychologically merged. Aloneness is being cast out helpless without relationship into the unfriendly and untrustworthy menacing wilderness. This represents the paranoid position described by the psychoanalyst Melanie Klein in which all the badness is outside and normal introjections have failed. Real relationships as opposed simply to projections of oneself on to others, are not possible. Sartre presents an ego in a primitive stage of infantile dependence, in a state of projective identification with the parent.

Sartre's analysis of "being-for-others" in *Being and Nothingness* confirms this. All human relationships are of a mutually devouring kind—one's being is swallowed up by or absorbed by another and vice versa. (pp. 211-17)

All relationships involve either sadism or masochism; one attempts to "appropriate" the "freedom" of the Other or surrenders one's own to him. But "the Other is on principle inapprehensible; he flees me when I seek him and possesses me when I flee him." Thus a satisfying sado-masochistic equilibrium is impossible; relationships are doomed to frustration. One wishes to "absorb" and "assimilate" the Other to achieve recognition, one is in perpetual danger and has no security. Again we find the paranoid position described by Melanie Klein where relationship is equivalent to persecution.

Apart from indifference—which is no relationship at all or withdrawal from relationship—hate is the only alternative relation to love. For Sartre hate involves my wishing the Other dead so that I will not be an object for him. (pp. 217-18)

According to Sartre the self, as a nothingness, is so empty, so inherently deprived of satisfactory fulfilment that he feels he needs to be certain of the Other—which he cannot be by the nature of the Other's separateness and subjectivity. This leads to a sadistic drive to incorporate or absorb the Other with the concomitant fear of destroying the very person he desires. One wants to have the Other as subject or person, not as an object or instrument. But one cannot have one's cake and eat it. One seeks to control and secure the freedom of the Other, but it is precisely the unconstrained freedom of the Other, upon which the self cannot depend, that is required for secure recognition.

Sartre's conceptions of being-for-others in the outer world are generated by the emotions of the inner world. The relationships that Sartre describes reflect the internal bad objects of a barely developed inner world. The Other upon whom the self cannot rely is the breast that may be snatched away at any time. As Guntrip remarks, "The schizoid is very sensitive and quickly feels unwanted, because he is always feeling deserted in his inner world." (p. 218)

Huis Clos is a dramatization of Sartre's analysis of being-for-others in *Being and Nothingness*. The three occupants constantly thwart and frustrate each other in the hermetically closed *"Second Empire"* drawing-room which is their Hell. Garcin concludes that "Hell is other people" since each person acts as torturer of the other two. However at one stage the door to their prison opens to Garcin's insistent knocking, but no one, including Garcin, leaves. They are *"inséparables."* Garcin claims that his reason for not leaving and for his not pushing Inez, who hates him, out of the room is his need for her "confirmation." However, if Hell really is other people, why does no one leave?

Huis Clos may be regarded as an image of the inner bad object world which is a "closed system" that is a "static internal situation." This closed system is what Sartre's concern with sequestration, with imprisonment, is basically about. This inner world of bad objects revealed by Melanie Klein is understood by Fairbairn to constitute "the most formidable resistance in psychoanalytical treatment." This inner world is often dreamed of as a torture house, a prison, or a concentration camp in which the self is a prisoner. This system is "run on hate," and the self is the victim of a large amount of persecution. Of course the prison in which the person finds himself has been erected by himself. But it is a prison which is very difficult to breach, and this indicates just how strongly the person holds on to his persecutory system of internal object-relations. Many people do not want to leave their prisons—it is felt to be far more dangerous outside.

The persecutory internal object-relationship is that of the internalized bad parents whom it is impossible to do without, since the person would then be all alone without any relationship at all. It is better to be hated than ignored—far better to be something than nothing. The closed system is part of a struggle to keep going, to have some degree of independence. Further, the internal closed system of persecution "confers a sense of power, if only over the self." Identification

with powerful objects, even where these are self-destructive, gives some security. Guntrip writes:

> The entire world of internal bad objects is a colossal defence against loss of the ego by depersonalisation. The one issue that is much worse than the choice between good and bad objects is the choice between any sort of objects and no objects at all. Persecution is preferable to depersonalisation.

This is why the inmates in *Huis Clos* dare not leave their prison. Garcin, for example, has a hate relationship with Inez, which is preferable to being alone in absolute isolation. Further, since Estelle is of no account to Garcin, it is imperative that Inez stay to provide a meaningful, if hostile, relationship. The worst ultimate terror is to be a "psyche in a vacuum." The irresolvable relationships of *Huis Clos* are staunch defenses against personal annihilation. Hell is not other people—it is being utterly alone. (pp. 219-20)

Sartre wanted to rescue subjectivity in a dehumanized world, and to find the possibility of good reciprocal relationships in a better society, yet the deeper he probed the less real these possibilities seemed. The early Sartrean self can at least refuse to be controlled, yet we find a still bleaker view developing as Sartre senses the increasing power of the social world to control even the perception of the alternatives available to us. For Sartre the world is a vast prison in which the prisoners wittingly or unwittingly collaborate in the perpetuation of their servitude.

In his personal and philosophical refusal of surrender, Sartre wants consciously directed activity to dominate the body and nature. Sartre is echoing the view of the body and the world that has enshrined the project of Western civilisation for many centuries. This is the logic of domination which views the world as there to be subdued and controlled and uses an instrumental, managerial form of rationality that regards oneself, others and the environment as objects to be quantified and manipulated. Near nuclear catastrophe and ecological disaster are part of the runaway madness of a system that uses a logic whose "paradoxical" consequence is thoughtless technologization and "development." Why should we accuse Sartrean philosophy of being schizoid when the logic of the world at large pushes us so far in that direction?

Sartre is truly a "universal singular" of our time in that he describes in his work, and represents in his approaches and perspectives, some of the foremost problems of our era. Sartre's refusal of surrender to the body, the Other, and nature is itself an instance of the logic which has led to our collective insanity today. It represents the total abandonment of basic trust in ourselves and our world to provide for our vital needs. Yet has Sartre gone too far?

The world Sartre portrays is one in which our

worst fears are seen to be finally true, but this situation need not be understood as ontologically inherent in history. Whatever else he has contributed, Sartre has expressed the vagaries and paradoxes of life in the modern world. (pp. 224-25)

Douglas Kirsner, "Sartre and the Collective Neurosis of Our Time," in *Yale French Studies,* No. 68, 1985, pp. 206-25.

ARTHUR C. DANTO
(essay date 1986)

[In the following excerpt, Danto explores the meaning of the terms "totality" and "totalization" in Sartre's early and late works.]

The terms "totality" and "totalization" occur with increasing frequency in the late philosophical writings of Sartre, and though the concepts to which they correspond were present at the beginning, they refer, in his earlier thought, primarily to the structure of the single life, whereas in the later writings they refer to social and political structures, as well as to the way or ways the individual life and the enveloping structures relate to one another. In those last, swollen, difficult works, desperately in need of editorial modulation, the problem with which Sartre struggled as a thinker almost perfectly coincided with his struggle as a person, to reconcile both his extreme independence with the social commitments in which he increasingly believed, and the unqualified metaphysical freedom of the person with his visions of societies in which the individual was fully and fulfillingly integrated. Ideologically speaking, the effort was to reconcile Existentialism, which he never forsook, with Marxism, which he could not resist. Perhaps no more revealing approach to either his life or his philosophy could be found than in tracing the adventures of totalization as the leading idea in both. In terms of one of his most audacious theses, one might say that totalization was his original project, with his life and his philosophy parallel examples of what it meant.

In *L'Être et la néant* he had written (my translation):

> Man is a totality and not a collection. Consequently he expresses himself as a whole in even his most insignificant and most superficial behaviour. In other words there is not a taste, a mannerism, or a human act that is not revealing.

It would be inevitable—it would be a matter of totalistic necessity—that Sartre would be concerned with biography in a philosophical way: that biography would

be an enfleshment of his metaphysics. In *L'Être et le néant* he announces two biographies—one of Flaubert and one of Dostoevsky—but biographical preoccupations possessed him already in his philosophical novel, *La Nausée,* whose hero, after all, is the biographer Roquentin. The difficulties Roquentin encounters in getting at the life of his subject moved Sartre, in his philosophical writings, to elaborate them as matters of ontology, and, in the other direction, moved the hero of the novel to undertake a novel which, just because a work of art, must exemplify the totalistic structure he fails to find in life. *La Nausée* itself has the form of a diary, a series of notations and memoranda—a collection—which, when read as a narrative, is fused into a totality. Since in any case "everything is revealing", since "there are no accidents in life", the concern with totalization must itself be totalized as an expression of the totality that is Sartre. Whatever else he may do, he expresses the full totality of his being, and his biographies—of Baudelaire, of Genet, and of course of Flaubert—have often been perceived as disguised essays in autobiography. It is not surprising—it is no accident, as totalizing thinkers like to say—that his one absolute masterpiece is his autobiography, in which he could confront directly, and with narcissistic enthusiasm, the personage he knew himself to be. But even in the most remote and abstract of his texts, we are never very far from autobiography. And the texts come most forcefully to life when we recognize that it is his own life he is describing.

Sartre characterizes a totality as follows in the first volume of the *Critique de la raison dialectique:* . . .

> A being which, radically distinct from the sum of its parts, is to be found, under one form or another, in each of those parts, and which enters into a relationship with itself, either with respect to one or several of its parts, or with respect to [*par rapport à*] relations which all or several of its parts sustain among themselves. . . .

Sartre uses works of art as his best examples of totalities, and insists that a totality is something made, or constructed, and hence has the status of what he terms *l'imaginaire*—the product of an act of imagination. Thus, by reading in a certain way, we confer totality on what is but a set of jottings, as in *La Nausée.* But totalization is a synthesizing activity found throughout the sphere of human practice, and dialectical reason itself is "nothing other than the movement of totalization as such". Totalization consists in an ensemble, or set, "making itself manifest to itself through the mediation of its parts". Imagination and the imaginary were among the first of Sartre's philosophical concerns. They reappear, under the rubric of totalization and totality, twenty-five years later, in the *Critique,* and seeing them together is itself an act of totalization if Sartre's evolving system is a totality.

La raison dialectique is sharply counterposed to *la raison analytique,* and Sartre over and over again throughout the *Critique* is at pains to point to things revealed to dialectical reason to which analytical reason is blind. Indeed, analytical reason is misapplied to human reality since its primary field is the *Ensoi*—the world as mere object as opposed to practice (Heidegger's distinction between *Vorhandene* and *Zuhandene* peers out from behind Sartre's terms)—or the world as mere body as opposed to consciousness or the *Pour-soi.* The *En-soi* is inert and "rongée par une infinie divisibilité". Dialectical reason, or totalization, exemplifies human reality construed as practice. Infinite divisibility was tendered by Descartes in the Synopsis to the *Meditations* as the criterion of the bodily, with indivisibility as the correlative distinguishing property of the soul or mind. Totalization is then meant, in Sartre's system, to express the kind of unity the mind has. It is a constructed or imagined unity, as with a work of art. It is not that a life need be a work of art, as in Goethe's famous imperative, but only that lives on the one hand and works of art on the other are examples of (forgive me) totalizing totalities.

Critique de la raison dialectique is addressed to social and historical unities—the second, posthumously published volume is specifically concerned with the totalization of conflict—but it is also concerned with the structure of thought or reason appropriate to these matters, so that the book moves on two levels at once. One must be reminded of the way in which Descartes, in the *Second Meditation,* demonstrates that whatever we may have learned about physical bodies, in thinking out the criteria of identity and change for the celebrated piece of wax, we have learned even more about ourselves, in reflecting on the way we have just been thinking. We are always led back to the self. It is this that perhaps vindicates the bold use of "critique" in the title—one does not lightly invite comparison with Kant—since the *Critique of Pure Reason* reflects back on to the act of reading it, almost as though the text serves as a *repoussoir* for what the mind goes through in coming to terms with it, and we learn about ourselves not just as its subject but as its readers. Sartre's *Critique* is intended, then, to exemplify what it also addresses, and we are to catch dialectical reason in the act, as we read about it. Admittedly, this is to give Sartre a certain credit not altogether licensed by the text, sprawling and arid but punctuated with brilliancies, as one might expect of a mind like his, prodded and sustained by the desperate administration of amphetamines during its composition (if that is the word). It is easier, in a way, to totalize it into the larger enterprise of Sartre's philosophy than to totalize it as such. Thus the central idea of totality and of totalization connects with the early notions of original choice and of existential psychoanalysis, both of which refer us to the single life . . . and thence to the topic of philosophical biography.

In *Les Mots,* Sartre addressed the question of what could have accounted for his having become precisely the individual he was. This, in its most general form, was the animating question of his philosophy, and certainly of the *Critique.* In "Questions de méthode"—which prefaces the *Critique* exactly as the *Discours de la méthode* (that paradigm of *la raison analytique*) prefaced Descartes's treatises on geometry, optics and meteors—Sartre lays out the problem that Existentialism raises for Marxism:

> Valéry was a petit-bourgeois intellectual. Of that there is no doubt. But not every petit-bourgeois intellectual is Valéry. The heuristic insufficiency of contemporary Marxism is contained in these two sentences. Existentialism . . . means, without being unfaithful to the principles of Marxism [*aux thèses marxistes*], to find the mediations which permit the concrete singular to be engendered—the life, the real and dated conflict, the person—from the general contradictions of productive forces and the relations to production.

It was thus that the immense study of Flaubert was meant to be a philosophical demonstration, an existentialist-marxist biography, and the crowning achievement of his life, seen as a whole. *L'être et le néant* is about *individual consciousness,* the *Pour-soi* being almost a metaphor for the *légèreté* Sartre rued in his own personality. The *Critique* is about consciousness as social, the individual as penetrated by the social whole of which he is a part. The three-volume life of Flaubert [*L'Idiot de la famille*], with the projected study of *Madame Bovary,* was to bring all this together in a *Gesamtwerk:* the social made concrete in the individual artist, the artist totalizing the structures that made him thinkable. Philosophy and biography at once, it was to be a triumph of the progressive-regressive method bravely announced in the *Critique.* (p. 753)

Sartre totalized the century, I suppose, in the sense that he was responsive with theories to each of the great events he lived through. And for a few years he did more—he represented history, he *was* history during the *années sartre,* just after 1945, when the world saw the meaning of the war, of occupation, of a Europe liberated, of a night lifted, in his work and his life. This utter identification may have spelled the *has-been-ness* to come, when the theories seemed to grate against the consciousness of the French, to be arbitrary and out of contact with reality to the point that his countrymen seemed glad to walk him to his grave and forget him. (p. 754)

Arthur C. Danto, "A Prodigious Dream of Totality," in *The Times Literary Supplement,* No. 4345, July 11, 1986, pp. 753-54.

JAY PARINI

(essay date 1988)

[In the following excerpt, Parini discusses several of Sartre's early and late works, concentrating on the novel *Nausea*, which he labels "the best thing Sartre ever did."]

This inventive, highly speculative novel [*Nausea*] is, I think, the best thing Sartre ever did. It sounds like cruel and unusual criticism to say that a writer's first book was his best, but it seems true. *Nausea,* as Iris Murdoch points out in her terse but brilliant study of Sartre's career as a writer and philosopher, "contains all his main interests except the political ones." In it, Sartre meditates on the nature of memory and of thought itself. Its hero, Antoine Roquentin, "discovers" that life is contingent, that we relate to the world not intuitively but discursively. I doubt that it's an either-or situation, but Sartre doesn't. His hero, in the process of learning how to read the world and his relation to it, becomes the embodiment of philosophical man, though Roquentin is hardly a man: he is a vehicle for Sartre's speculation. As such, he is fascinating. The novel is not a novel, per se; it is a prose-poem. Like Virginia Woolf or Joyce, Sartre often conjures moments of pure aesthetic reflection. The book is noticeably apolitical, though Roquentin's disgust with bourgeois society amounts to something like the beginning of a political position. What's good about *Nausea* is the way Sartre has reduced the human condition to its essentials, revealing a bare, abstract pattern that produces, as the title suggests, a kind of nausea.

For a man who would later become hyper-political, Sartre began with the usual Modernist detachment from overt politics, a carryover from the aestheticism of the Belle Epoque. He took no interest in the Spanish Civil War, for instance. His personal life, relations with women, his writing and teaching, absorbed him utterly. Even World War II seems to have had little effect on him. Though he formed a discussion group called "Socialism and Freedom" during the Occupation, they did little but meet periodically for a chat. Sartre never wrote an explicit word about Nazi atrocities, nor did he contribute much to the Resistance.

He began, nonetheless, to think that philosophy and literature should impinge on life. What he did was to mix his own blend of phenomenology from the previous work of Husserl and Heidegger, adding his own concern for "freedom" as it relates to individual action. He called this mixture a "philosophy of existence," and when the media labeled the new thinking "Existential-

ism," Sartre gladly accepted the term, realizing it was catchy. And why not? The central concerns of the new philosophy are contained in his massive text of 1943, *Being and Nothingness.* That somewhat impenetrable tome takes up and develops the themes presented in *Nausea,* the main one being the nature of consciousness.

Here, Sartre is a philosopher in the tradition of Descartes. His concern with "freedom" is inextricably involved with his concern for picturing consciousness. He insists, like Descartes, on the supremacy of the *cogito,* but his interests (unlike most other serious philosophers of consciousness) are psychological rather than linguistic. For him (as for Roquentin), consciousness becomes the flux between moments of perception, of being, wherein objects exist "in-them-selves" against a background of negation, of nothingness, the empty spaces between the stars. To perceive the "thinginess" of things is the beginning of Sartrean wisdom. But what about the Self? Here value comes into play (*la valeur*): that mystical entity which is noncontingent but real nonetheless. "The supreme value towards which consciousness, by its very nature, is constantly transcending itself is the absolute being of the self, with its qualities of identity, purity, permanence," writes Sartre.

Humankind seems endlessly shifting between Being and Nothing, between value and non-value, between Being-in-Itself (*être-en-soi*) and Being-for-Itself (*être-pour-soi*). This latter contrast, the in-itself versus the for-itself, has become famous. We seek, according to Sartre, the former, the (valued) thinginess of reality, the in-itself. The for-itself is an "outside" state, the sense of consciousness playing over the world of things, a state of pure consciousness. Only God, says Sartre, ever attains both senses of reality, the condition of being *en-soi-pour-soi;* the human condition denies it. This is ultimately a depressing philosophy, wherein human nature defines itself as a lack of completeness. Sartrean man is, as he notes toward the end of *Being and Nothingness,* a reverse Christ, aspiring to lose his humanness, to become God. But since God doesn't exist (because His existence defies logic), man is perpetually foiled: *"L'homme est une passion inutile."*

What's interesting, and noble, is that Sartre refuses to sink into a self-satisfied, rational despair. He declares an end to "the reign of value" in the old sense. The discovery that all human activity is a vain attempt to transmogrify man into God is the pre-condition of freedom. In *Being and Nothingness,* Sartre does not develop the implications of this newfound freedom, though, as Denis Hollier notes, in this work Sartre "encountered the imperative of an ethics." That ethics will unfold in *Existentialism Is a Humanism,* the great essay of 1946, where the Existentialist creed is codified (if not ossified). It becomes an underlying theme in the four novels gathered under the title, *The Roads of Freedom*— all written during the war and shortly after.

Oddly enough, the war years were amazingly conducive to productivity for Sartre, who wrote much of his best creative work then, excluding *Nausea*. The novels have been mentioned: not one of them has the centripetal energy of *Nausea*, but the sum of the four is considerable. As in *Nausea*, all human communication seems difficult, even impossible. The superabundance of *things* produces nausea in *Nausea*; in *Roads of Freedom* it is the horror of the flesh that produces loathing. Murdoch says: "The flesh symbolises the absolute loss of freedom, and references to its inertness, flabbiness, stickiness, heaviness form a continual accompaniment to the narrative."

It was also during the war years that Sartre wrote his two finest plays, *The Flies* (1943) and *No Exit* (1944), the former a Sartrean riff on the Electra-Orestes theme, the latter an "existential" portrait of hell, defined here as "other people." These are remarkable works, very much in accord with the Modernist theater in France. Jean Giraudoux, Cocteau, and Jean Anouilh had all refashioned Greek myths for the contemporary theater, so Sartre's *The Flies* was, if anything, *á la mode*. In his version of the myth, Orestes returns to Argos and finds it wallowing in regret, choked; the citizens "held their tongues . . . said nothing," as Jupiter says, trying to convey the cowardice of the town in the face of its king's death. The men of Argos, in a moment of recognition, plead: "Forgive us for living while you are dead." The parallel with the Occupation is implicit, with Sartre arguing that free men should assume responsibility for their actions, no matter what the consequences. (pp. 364-66)

Sartre became increasingly political—fanatically so—in the post-war years, supporting a wide range of left-wing causes and revolutionary committees. He played cat-and-mouse with the Communist Party, writing an anti-Communist play *(Dirty Hands)* in 1948 that, later, he would renounce. Wanting desperately to believe that the Soviets had, in fact, managed to create a genuine Marxist society, Sartre bent over backwards in the early fifties to support them; but this became impossible after the invasion of Hungary in 1956, and he withdrew his endorsement. In his later years, he supported a group of student Maoists called the Proletarian Left, becoming their figurehead for a while as "editor" of their crudely printed handouts. In fact, Sartre was in the late sixties a kind of hero to the student left throughout the world.

The need to rationalize his commitment to political activity led to his last major philosophical effort, *The Critique of Dialectical Reason* (1960), a projected two-volume effort of which only the first was ever published. The work was written—thirty to forty pages a day—in what Cohen-Solal describes as "a wild rush of words and juxtaposed ideas, pouring forth during crises of hyperexcitement, under the effect of contradictory drugs. . . . Everything in excess." The work meditates on the meeting between Marxism and Existentialism: an attempt to get Marxists to recognize, as Murdoch says, that "the *aventure singuliére* of human existence must be returned to the centre of the picture." Sartre was looking for ways in which individuals relate to their historical surroundings via a continuous mediation between the general and the particular; he was trying to understand the nature and place of free choice in this overall scheme.

Methods of "mediation" were sought in the human sciences—psychology, anthropology, and sociology—though Sartre keeps returning to his philosophical base, which is always the phenomenology of consciousness. Sartre came to see history as driven, as he says, "not by scientific laws or by an abstract inhuman super-purpose, but by human willed purposes, so that its explanation and being lie in a study of conscious human activity." Historical inevitability, the baseline of Orthodox Marxism, went out the window. In general, Sartre was trying to connect Marxism with the old Hegelian subject-object phenomenology of mind, and to reinstate the theme of human purpose in history. He was also trying to formulate a critique of Western culture in the guise of philosophy, though he never really accomplished this goal. Instead of making a sustained analysis of existing institutions with concrete proposals for change, he indulged in random indictments, his rhetoric swelling at times to something approaching the apocalyptic.

The failure of coherence which mars *The Critique* is even more troublesome in his last great work, *The Family Idiot*, a biographical study of Flaubert. This work obsessed Sartre in his later years, and it was finally published (in French) in 1971 (volumes I and II) and 1972 (volume III). Like his previous "biographies" of Baudelaire (1946) and Genet (1956), Sartre takes huge liberties with the genre, mixing in autobiography, philosophical rumination, and criticism. He pays scant allegiance to the facts, using them as a launching pad for speculation. The unique *mythos* of each life provides instances galore of existential choices, though one suspects that Sartre distorts the lives to fit them to his philosophical schema. He should have followed the example of his earliest hero, Roquentin, who abandons his biography of de Rollebon when he sees that no amount of factual knowledge can make another person's life any more "real." In *Nausea*, this is all part of Roquentin's mounting awareness that one cannot form an absolute notion of one's past. It is also part of Sartre's typically Modernist lack of faith in epistemological certainty. One wonders what drove him to attempt in his last major work what he had previously decided was impossible. (pp. 368-69)

Jay Parini, "Sartre's Life of Writing," in *The Hudson Review*, Vol. XLI, No. 2, Summer, 1988, pp. 363-69.

SOURCES FOR FURTHER STUDY

Desan, Wilfrid. *The Marxism of Jean-Paul Sartre.* New York: Doubleday & Co., 1965, 320 p.

    Analysis of Sartre's *Critique of Dialectical Reason.*

Greene, Norman N. *Jean-Paul Sartre: The Existentialist Ethic.* Ann Arbor, Mich.: University of Michigan Press, 1960, 213 p.

    Explication of such key concepts as freedom, being and nothingness, and God in Sartre's philosophy.

Jameson, Fredric. *Sartre: The Origins of a Style.* New Haven, Conn.: Yale University Press, 1961, 228 p.

    Exploration of Sartre's prose style.

Kern, Edith, ed. *Sartre: A Collection of Critical Essays.* Englewood Cliffs, N.J.: Prentice-Hall, 1962, 179 p.

    Studies of Sartre's fiction, drama, literary criticism, philosophy, and politics by Henri Peyre, Robert Champigny, Fredric Jameson, and other noted Sartre scholars.

Murdoch, Iris. *Sartre: Romantic Rationalist.* Studies in Modern European Literature and Thought, edited by Erich Heller. New Haven, Conn.: Yale University Press, 1953, 114 p.

    Study of Sartre's philosophical and literary works. Murdoch states: "To understand Jean-Paul Sartre is to understand something important about the present time."

Suhl, Benjamin. *Jean-Paul Sartre: The Philosopher as a Literary Critic.* New York: Columbia University Press, 1970, 311 p.

    Examines the "ascension and growth" of Sartre's literary criticism "from the vantage point of his philosophy."

Sir Walter Scott

1771-1832

(Also wrote under pseudonym Jedediah Cleishbotham)
Scottish novelist, poet, short story writer, biographer,
historian, critic, and editor.

INTRODUCTION

Scott exerted a profound influence on early nineteenth-century European literature. During his lifetime he was immensely popular, and modern
scholars consider him both the inventor of the historical novel and the first best-selling novelist. As the
anonymous and enormously prolific "Author of *Waverley,*" Scott not only elevated the novel to a status equal
to that of poetry but also influenced the way history has
been written and understood by subsequent generations of historians and novelists. Despite the unprecedented success of his novels and poetry, Scott's literary reputation and popularity underwent one of the
most pronounced reversals in the history of English literature following his death. Today his poetry is largely
ignored, and his novels attract the interest primarily of
scholars and literary historians.

Scott was born in Edinburgh to middle-class parents, the fourth surviving child of Walter Scott and
Anne Rutherford. At the age of two, he suffered an attack of polio that rendered him lame for the rest of his
life. Biographers note, however, that in spite of his illness, Scott led an active outdoor life during his childhood and developed an appreciation for the picturesque scenery that later figured so prominently in his
writings. As a child Scott was also fascinated with Scottish history and literature and retained detailed information he learned about his country's past. According to
the critic Ian Jack, "It was Scott's good fortune as a
boy to be surrounded by a sort of Greek chorus of
Scots antiquaries" from whom he absorbed both
knowledge and enthusiasm. Scott enrolled in Edinburgh High School in 1778 and five years later entered
the University of Edinburgh, studying history and law.
In 1786, he was apprenticed to his father's legal firm
and was called to the bar in 1792. While serving his apprenticeship, Scott traveled extensively in the Scottish

Border country and Highlands, where he delighted in the natural settings and rural inhabitants. In 1800 he was able to combine his love for Scottish lore and literature with his ongoing excursions into the countryside as he started collecting and editing ballads for his *Minstrelsy of the Scottish Border* (1802-03). The *Minstrelsy* contained numerous Scottish ballads that had never before appeared in print, as well as imitation ballads written by Scott and others. Although it produced only modest sales, the collection enjoyed critical favor. More importantly, with the *Minstrelsy,* as John Lauber has pointed out, Scott "discovered his proper subject, Scottish history and tradition."

The positive reception of the *Minstrelsy* and the encouragement of his friends prompted Scott to attempt an original work based on Scottish themes. His efforts resulted in *The Lay of the Last Minstrel* (1805), a narrative poem set in medieval times that, in Scott's words, was "intended to illustrate the customs and manners which anciently prevailed on the Borders of England and Scotland." The success of the *Lay* when it appeared was immediate and substantial. Determined to earn a living through his writings, Scott gave up the law as a full-time profession and beginning in 1808 with *Marmion* published a series of highly popular and remunerative poems with Scottish backgrounds and themes, including what is perhaps his best-known long poem, *The Lady of the Lake* (1810). By the time *Rokeby* appeared in 1813, however, readers were beginning to lose interest in his poetry. In addition, the triumph of the first two cantos of Lord Byron's *Childe Harold* in 1812 had convinced Scott that he could not compete with the younger poet. Anxious to retain his audience and large income, Scott decided to revise and complete a fragment of a novel that he had begun ten years before.

Entitled *Waverley; or, 'Tis Sixty Years Since,* Scott's tale of an Englishman who travels to the Scottish Highlands and becomes caught up in the Jacobite rebellion of 1745 proved a popular sensation when published in 1814. *Waverley* quickly became the most successful work of its kind ever to appear, and the novel brought huge profits to Scott and his publishers. Buoyed by his first venture as a novelist, he began writing at a rapid pace, and over the next seventeen years produced more than two dozen novels and tales in a series that has since become known as the *Waverley Novels.* He was able to maintain his prolific output not only because he never plotted his works ahead of time and seldom revised his manuscripts, but also because he maintained strenuous work habits even when gravely ill. In the *Waverley Novels,* most of which describe the lives of ordinary individuals who become involved in great historical events, Scott presented in lavish detail the speech, manners, and customs of past ages. In studying these works, critics have often divided them into three groups: the so-called "Scotch Novels," or those dealing with Scottish culture and history, including *Old Mortality* (1816) and *The Heart of Midlothian* (1818); those concerned with medieval history in England and Europe, including *Ivanhoe* (1820) and *Quentin Durward* (1823); and those focused on the Tudor-Stuart era in England, including *Kenilworth* (1821) and *Woodstock* (1826). Although the sales of the *Waverley Novels* varied, they were generally a consistent success with the public, who eagerly awaited each new work. Because writing novels was perceived with less respect than writing poetry, Scott published *Waverley* anonymously. When the success of *Waverley* increased the public's appreciation for novelists, he nevertheless chose to retain his anonymity for many years, a practice his biographers have traced both to his love of secrecy and to his perception that the mystery surrounding the novels contributed to their sales. Many of the novels were published as "by the Author of *Waverley,*" and he was often referred to simply as the "Great Unknown." Despite his policy of anonymous publication, numerous readers and critics knew of his authorship; he became the most popular writer in contemporary English literature and a highly respected and admired figure throughout Europe. In 1818 he accepted a baronetcy, becoming Sir Walter Scott.

Scott's expenditures increased as quickly as his income, and many critics and biographers have tied his enormous output directly to a desire for material gain. Scott had purchased a farm in 1811 and, after renaming the property Abbotsford, began devoting huge sums of money to building, planting, and collecting relics from Scotland's past. Thus, though his income was large, his financial situation was often precarious. In 1826, disaster struck when a publishing house in which he was a silent partner failed. His debt amounted to over one hundred thousand pounds. Instead of choosing to declare bankruptcy, Scott arranged to work off the debt through his writings. The remainder of his life was devoted to the increasingly difficult task of producing saleable works in a variety of genres. Beginning in 1830 he suffered a series of strokes as he labored to pay his creditors. A trip to the Mediterranean in 1831 to regain his health proved unsuccessful, and after suffering further strokes and paralysis he died at Abbotsford in 1832.

The novelty of Scott's writing style and subject matter captivated his early audience; in fact, his writings created a vogue for Scottish culture and even led to an increase in tourism in Scotland. Many contemporary critics, however, have agreed that Scott's poetry and novels reveal glaring deficiencies, including careless construction, prolixity, and bad grammar. Yet most early reviewers acknowledged the superiority of his novels, arguing that their originality, vivid portrayal of history, and lively characters outweighed their faults.

Scott's ability to bring Scottish and English history to life—to capture the language, costumes, and settings of the past—as well as his understanding of the effects of social change upon the lives of ordinary people, were entirely new contributions to English fiction.

Scott was viewed by many early Victorians as an heroic figure whose exemplary life and courageous struggle to pay his debts were reflected in the morally irreproachable qualities of his works. Yet certain critics, prominent among them Thomas Carlyle, felt that Scott's life should not be confused with his works, which were shallow, lacking in true passion, and written largely for material gain. As the nineteenth century progressed, the increasingly sophisticated design and self-conscious art of the novel as practiced by such writers as George Eliot and Henry James caused numerous commentators to deride the disorganized plots and intellectual superficiality of Scott's fiction. Although his admirers countered by praising his enduring appeal as a storyteller and the entertainment value of the *Waverley Novels*, by the turn of the century many critics maintained that Scott could no longer be considered a major English novelist. His readership as well as his critical stock had been declining since mid century, and while the second half of the twentieth century would show mounting scholarly interest in his works, Scott, a writer who in his own day had been compared with William Shakespeare, would eventually be described by W. E. K. Anderson as the "Great Unread."

Twentieth-century critics have emphasized Scott's important role in English literary history as well as his considerable impact on nineteenth-century European literature. Literary historians have traced his influence on the masterpieces of novelists as diverse as Charles Dickens, Gustave Flaubert, Honoré de Balzac, and William Makepeace Thackeray. Scholars have also explored Scott's significant contribution—through his invention and development of the historical novel—to the history of ideas, specifically with respect to the modern concept of historical perspective. Modern studies of the *Waverley Novels* have consistently stressed the superiority of the "Scotch Novels" over the rest, and critics have given particular attention to *The Heart of Mid-Lothian,* often considered his finest novel. Scott's works have attracted increasing scholarly notice since the general proliferation of English literary scholarship that began in the 1950s, and recent commentators have explored such specific aspects of his novels as his passive heroes and his portrayal of the Middle Ages. Although his works are now largely the concern of literary specialists, Scott nevertheless remains a crucial figure in the development of the English novel and a seminal influence on nineteenth-century European literature.

(For further information about Scott's life and works, see *Dictionary of Literary Biography,* Vols. 93, 107 and *Nineteenth-Century Literature Criticism,* Vol. 15.)

CRITICAL COMMENTARY

VIRGINIA WOOLF

(essay date 1924)

[A British novelist, essayist, and short story writer, Woolf is one of the most prominent figures of twentieth-century English literature. In the following excerpt, she provides an appreciative overview of the *Waverley Novels*, balancing their entertaining qualities, idiosyncratic attractions, and memorable characters against their artistic shortcomings. Woolf's remarks were written in 1924.]

There are some writers who have entirely ceased to influence others, whose fame is for that reason both serene and cloudless, who are enjoyed or neglected rather than criticized and read. Among them is Scott. The most impressionable beginner, whose pen oscillates if exposed within a mile of the influence of Stendhal, Flaubert, Henry James, or Chekhov, can read the *Waverley Novels* one after another without altering an adjective. Yet there are no books perhaps upon which at this moment more thousands of readers are brooding and feasting in a rapture of uncritical and silent satisfaction. And if this is the mood in which the *Waverley Novels* are read, the inference is perhaps that there is something vicious about such a pleasure; it cannot be defended; it must be enjoyed in secret. Let us run through *The Antiquary* again and make a note or two as we go. The first charge that is levelled against Scott is that his style is execrable. Every page of the novel, it is true, is watered down with long languid Latin words—peruse, manifest, evince. Old metaphors out of the property box come flapping their dusty wings across the sky. The sea in the heat of a crisis is 'the devouring element'. A gull on the same occasion is a 'winged denizen of the crag'. Taken from their context it is impossible to deny that such expressions sound

Principal Works

Minstrelsy of the Scottish Border. 3 vols. [editor and contributor] (poetry) 1802-03

The Lay of the Last Minstrel (poetry) 1805

Marmion: A Tale of Flodden Field (poetry) 1808

The Lady of the Lake (poetry) 1810

The Vision of Don Roderick (poetry) 1811

The Bridal of Triermain; or, The Vale of St. John (poetry) 1813

Rokeby (poetry) 1813

Waverley; or, 'Tis Sixty Years Since (novel) 1814

The Field of Waterloo (poetry) 1815

Guy Mannering; or, The Astrologer (novel) 1815

The Lord of the Isles (poetry) 1815

The Antiquary (novel) 1816

The Black Dwarf [as Jedediah Cleishbotham] (novel) 1816; published in Tales of My Landlord, first series

Old Mortality [as Jedediah Cleishbotham] (novel) 1816; published in Tales of My Landlord, first series

Tales of My Landlord, first series [as Jedediah Cleishbotham] (novels) 1816

The Heart of Mid-Lothian [as Jedediah Cleishbotham] (novel) 1818; published in Tales of My Landlord, second series

Rob Roy (novel) 1818

Tales of My Landlord, second series [as Jedediah Cleishbotham] (novel) 1818

The Bride of Lammermoor [as Jedediah Cleishbotham] (novel) 1819; published in Tales of My Landlord, third series

A Legend of Montrose [as Jedediah Cleishbotham] (novel) 1819; published in Tales of My Landlord, third series

Tales of My Landlord, third series [as Jedediah Cleishbotham] (novels) 1819

The Abbot (novel) 1820

Ivanhoe (novel) 1820

The Monastery (novel) 1820

The Poetical Works of Walter Scott. 12 vols. (poetry) 1820

Kenilworth (novel) 1821

The Fortunes of Nigel (novel) 1822

Peveril of the Peak (novel) 1822

The Pirate (novel) 1822

Quentin Durward (novel) 1823

Redgauntlet: A Tale of the Eighteenth Century (novel) 1824

St. Ronan's Well (novel) 1824

*Tales of the Crusaders (novels) 1825

Woodstock; or, The Cavalier: A Tale of the Year Sixteen Hundred and Fifty-One (novel) 1826

† Chronicles of the Canongate, first series (short stories) 1827

Chronicles of the Canongate, second series (novel) 1828

St. Valentine's Day; or, The Fair Maid of Perth (novel) 1828; published in Chronicles of the Canongate, second series

Anne of Geierstein; or, The Maiden of the Mist (novel) 1829

Waverley Novels. 48 vols. (novels) 1830-34

Castle Dangerous [as Jedediah Cleishbotham] (novel) 1832; published in Tales of My Landlord, fourth series

Count Robert of Paris [as Jedediah Cleishbotham] (novel) 1832; published in Tales of My Landlord, fourth series

Tales of My Landlord, fourth series [as Jedediah Cleishbotham] (novels) 1832

The Poetical Works of Sir Walter Scott. 12 vols. (poetry) 1833-34

The Journal of Sir Walter Scott (journal) 1890

The Letters of Sir Walter Scott. 12 vols. (letters) 1932-37

*This work contains the novels The Betrothed and The Talisman.

†This work contains the short stories "The Highland Widow," "The Surgeon's Daughter," and "The Two Drovers."

---

wrong, though a good case might be made against the snobbery which insists upon preserving class distinctions even among words. But read currently in their places, it is difficult either to notice or to condemn them. As Scott uses them they fulfil their purpose and merge perfectly in their surroundings. Great novelists who are going to fill seventy volumes write after all in pages, not in sentences, and have at their command, and know when to use, a dozen different styles of varying intensities. The genteel pen is a very useful pen in its place. These slips and slovenlinesses serve as relaxations; they give the reader breathing space and air the book. Let us compare Scott the slovenly with Steven-

son the precise. 'It was as he said: there was not a breath stirring; a windless stricture of frost had bound the air; and as we went forth in the shine of the candles, the blackness was like a roof over our heads.' One may search the *Waverley Novels* in vain for such close writing as this. But if we get from Stevenson a much closer idea of a single object, we get from Scott an incomparably larger impression of the whole. The storm in *The Antiquary,* made up as it is of stage hangings and cardboard screens, of 'denizens of the crags' and 'clouds like disasters round a sinking empire', nevertheless roars and splashes and almost devours the group huddled on the crag; while the storm in *Kidnapped,* for all its exact detail and its neat dapper adjectives, is incapable of wetting the sole of a lady's slipper.

The much more serious charge against Scott is that he used the wrong pen, the genteel pen, not merely to fill in the background and dash off a cloud piece, but to describe the intricacies and passions of the human heart. But what language to use of the Lovels and Isabellas, the Darsies, Ediths, and Mortons! As well talk of the hearts of seagulls and the passions and intricacies of walking-sticks and umbrellas; for indeed these ladies and gentlemen are scarcely to be distinguished from the winged denizens of the crag. They are equally futile; equally impotent; they squeak; they flutter; and a strong smell of camphor exudes from their poor dried breasts when, with a dismal croaking and cawing, they emit the astonishing language of their love-making.

'Without my father's consent, I will never entertain the addresses of anyone; and how totally impossible it is that he should countenance the partiality with which you honour me, you are yourself fully aware,' says the young lady. 'Do not add to the severity of repelling my sentiments the rigour of obliging me to disavow them,' replies the young gentleman; and he may be illegitimate, and he may be the son of a peer, or he may be both one and the other, but it would take a far stronger inducement than that to make us care a straw what happens to Lovel and his Isabella.

But then, perhaps, we are not meant to care a straw. When Scott has pacified his conscience as a magistrate by alluding to the sentiments of the upper classes in tones of respect and esteem, when he has vindicated his character as a moralist by awakening 'the better feelings and sympathies of his readers by strains of generous sentiment and tales of fictitious woe', he was quit both of art and of morals, and could scribble endlessly for his own amusement. Never was a change more emphatic; never one more wholly to the good. One is tempted, indeed, to suppose that he did it, half-consciously, on purpose—he showed up the languor of the fine gentlemen who bored him by the immense vivacity of the common people whom he loved. Images, anecdotes, illustrations drawn from sea, sky, and earth, race and bubble from their lips. They shoot every thought as it flies, and bring it tumbling to the ground in metaphor. Sometimes it is a phrase—'at the back of a dyke, in a wreath o' snaw, or in the wame o' a wave'; sometimes a proverb—'he'll no can haud down his head to sneeze, for fear o' seeing his shoon'; always the dialogue is sharpened and pointed by the use of that Scottish dialect which is at once so homely and so pungent, so colloquial and so passionate, so shrewd and so melancholy into the bargain. And the result is strange. For since the sovereigns who should preside have abdicated, since we are afloat on a broad and breezy sea without a pilot, the *Waverley Novels* are as unmoral as Shakespeare's plays. Nor, for some readers, is it the

least part of their astonishing freshness, their perennial vitality, that you may read them over and over again, and never know for certain what Scott himself was or what Scott himself thought.

We know, however, what his characters are, and we know it almost as we know what our friends are by hearing their voices and watching their faces simultaneously. However often one may have read *The Antiquary*, Jonathan Oldbuck is slightly different every time. We notice different things; our observation of face and voice differs; and thus Scott's characters, like Shakespeare's and Jane Austen's, have the seed of life in them. They change as we change. But though this gift is an essential element in what we call immortality, it does not by any means prove that the character lives as profoundly, as fully, as Falstaff lives or Hamlet. Scott's characters, indeed, suffer from a serious disability; it is only when they speak that they are alive; they never think; as for prying into their minds himself, or drawing inferences from their behaviour, Scott never attempted it. 'Miss Wardour, as if she felt that she had said too much, turned and got into the carriage'—he will penetrate no further into the privacy of Miss Wardour than that; and it is not far. But this matters the less because the characters he cared for were by temperament chatterboxes; Edie Ochiltree, Oldbuck, Mrs. Mucklebackit talk incessantly. They reveal their characters in talk. If they stop talking it is to act. By their talk and by their acts—that is how we know them.

But how far then can we know people, the hostile critic may ask, if we only know that they say this and do that, if they never talk about themselves, and if their creator lets them go their ways, provided they forward his plot, in complete independence of his supervision or interference? Are they not all of them, Ochiltrees, Antiquaries, Dandy Dinmonts, and the rest, merely bundles of humours, and innocent childish humours at that, who serve to beguile our dull hours and charm our sick ones, and are packed off to the nursery when the working day returns and our normal faculties crave something tough to set their teeth into? Compare the *Waverley Novels* with the novels of Tolstoy, of Stendahl, of Proust! These comparisons of course lead to questions that lie at the root of fiction, but without discussing them, they reveal unmistakably what Scott is not. He is not among the great observers of the intricacies of the heart. He is not going to break seals or loose fountains. But he has the power of the artist who can create a scene and leave us to analyse it for ourselves. When we read the scene in the cottage where Steenie Mucklebackit lies dead, the different emotions—the father's grief, the mother's irritability, the minister's consolations—all rise spontaneously, as if Scott had merely to record, and we have merely to observe. What we lose in intricacy we gain perhaps in spontaneity and the stimulus given to our own creative powers. It is true that Scott creates carelessly, as if the parts came together without his willing it; it is true also that his scene breaks into ruin without his caring.

For who taps at the door and destroys that memorable scene? The cadaverous Earl of Glenallan; the unhappy nobleman who had married his sister in the belief that she was his cousin; and had stalked the world in sables ever after. Falsity breaks in; the peerage breaks in; all the trappings of the undertaker and heralds' office press upon us their unwholesome claims. The emotions then in which Scott excels are not those of human beings pitted against other human beings, but of man pitted against Nature, of man in relation to fate. His romance is the romance of hunted men hiding in woods at night; of brigs standing out to sea; of waves breaking in the moonlight; of solitary sands and distant horsemen; of violence and suspense. And he is perhaps the last novelist to practice the great, the Shakespearean art, of making people reveal themselves in speech. (pp. 139-43)

Virginia Woolf, " 'The Antiquary'," in her *Collected Essays, Vol. I,* Harcourt Brace Jovanovich, Inc., 1967, pp. 139-43.

DAVID DAICHES
(essay date 1951)

[Daiches is a prominent English scholar and critic who has written extensively on English and American literature. In the following excerpt, he offers an extended assessment of what he considers to be Scott's best works, the "Scotch Novels." This essay was first published in *Nineteenth-Century Fiction* in September 1951.]

The novels on which Scott's reputation as a novelist must stand or fall are his 'Scotch novels'—those that deal with Scottish history and manners—and not even all of those. *Waverley, Guy Mannering, The Antiquary, Old Mortality, The Heart of Midlothian, Rob Roy, The Bride of Lammermoor, A Legend of Montrose* and *Redgauntlet*—all, except *Redgauntlet,* earlier novels—constitute Scott's list of masterpieces. There are others of the *Waverley Novels* of which no novelist need be ashamed, many with excellent incidental scenes and memorable character studies, but this group of Scottish novels all possess Scott's characteristic virtues, and they represent his particular kind of fiction at its very best.

The fact that these novels are all concerned with Scottish history and manners is intimately bound up with the reasons for their being his best novels. For Scott's attitude to life was derived from his response to the fate of his own country: it was the complex of feelings with which he contemplated the phase of Scottish history immediately preceding his own time that provided the point of view which gave life—often a predominantly tragic life—to these novels. Underlying most of these novels is a tragic sense of the inevitability of a drab but necessary progress, a sense of the impotence of the traditional kind of heroism, a passionately regretful awareness of the fact that the Good Old Cause was lost forever and the glory of Scotland must give way to her interest.

Scott's attitude to Scotland, as Edwin Muir pointed out some years ago in a thoughtful and provocative study, was a mixture of regret for the old days when Scotland was an independent but turbulent and distracted country, and of satisfaction at the peace, prosperity and progress which he felt had been assured by the Union with England in 1707 and the successful establishment of the Hanoverian dynasty on the British throne. His problem, in one form or another, was the problem of every Scottish writer after Scotland ceased to have an independent culture of her own: how to reconcile his country's traditions with what appeared to be its interest. Scott was always strongly moved by everything that reminded him of Scotland's past, of the days of the country's independence and the relatively recent days when the Jacobites were appealing to that very emotion to gain support for their cause. He grew up as the Jacobite tradition was finally ebbing away, amid the first generation of Scotsmen committed once and for all to the association with England and the Hanoverian dynasty. He felt strongly that that association was inevitable and right and advantageous—he exerted himself greatly to make George IV popular in Scotland—yet there were strong emotions on the other side too, and it was these emotions that made him Tory in politics and that provided the greater blessing of leading him to literature and history. (pp. 90-2)

This conflict within Scott gave life and passion to his Scottish novels, for it led him to construct plots and invent characters which, far from being devices in an adventure story or means to make history look picturesque, illustrated what to him was the central paradox of modern life. And that paradox admitted of the widest application, for it was an aspect of all commercial and industrial civilizations. Civilization must be paid for by the cessation of the old kind of individual heroic action. Scott welcomed civilization, but he also sighed after the old kind of individual heroic action. Scott's theme is a modification of that of Cervantes, and specifically, *Redgauntlet* is Scott's *Don Quixote.* (p. 92)

The Jacobite movement for Scott was not simply a picturesque historical event; it was the last attempt to restore to Scotland something of the old heroic way of life. This is not the place for a discussion of the real historical meaning of Jacobitism—I am concerned at present only with how Scott saw it and how he used it in his novels. He used it, and its aftermath, to symbolize at once the attractiveness and the futility of the old Scotland. *That* Scotland was doomed after the Union of Parliaments of 1707 and doubly doomed after the Battle of Culloden in 1746; the aftermath of 1707 is shown in *The Heart of Midlothian* and of 1746 in *Redgauntlet*. In both novels, explicitly in the latter and murmuring in an undertone in the former, there is indicated the tragic theme (for it *is* tragic) that the grand old causes are all lost causes, and the old heroic action is no longer even fatal—it is merely useless and silly. One thinks of the conclusion of Bishop Hurd's *Letters on Chivalry and Romance:* 'What we have gotten by this revolution, you will say, is a great deal of good sense. What we have lost is a world of fine fabling.' But to Scott it was more than a world of fine fabling that was lost; it was a world of heroic ideals, which he could not help believing should still be worth something. He knew, however, even before it was brought home to him by Constable's failure and his consequent own bankruptcy, that in the reign of George IV it was not worth much—certainly not as much as novels about it.

Scott has often been presented as a lover of the past, but that is a partial portrait. He was a lover of the past combined with a believer in the present, and the mating of these incompatible characters produced that tension which accounted for his greatest novels. (pp. 93-4)

It is this ambivalence in Scott's approach to the history of his country—combined, of course, with certain remarkable talents which I shall discuss later—that accounts for the unique quality of his Scottish novels. He was able to take an *odi et amo* attitude to some of the most exciting crises of Scottish history. If Scott's desire to set himself up as an old-time landed gentleman in a large country estate was romantic, the activities by which he financed—or endeavoured to finance—his schemes were the reverse, and there is nothing romantic in James Glen's account of Scott's financial transactions prefixed to the centenary edition of his letters. He filled Abbotsford with historical relics, but they were relics, and they gave Abbotsford something of the appearance of a museum. He thus tried to resolve the conflict in his way of life by making modern finance pay for a house filled with antiquities. This resolution could not, however, eliminate the basic ambivalence in his approach to recent Scottish history: that remained, to enrich his fiction.

This double attitude on Scott's part prevented him from taking sides in his historical fiction, and Sir Herbert Grierson has complained, though mildly, of this refusal to commit himself. 'Of the historical events which he chooses for the setting of his story,' writes Sir Herbert, 'his judgment is always that of the good sense and moderated feeling of his own age. He will not take sides out and out with either Jacobite or Hanoverian, Puritan or Cavalier; nor does he attempt to transcend either the prejudices or the conventional judgment of his contemporaries, he makes no effort to attain to a fresh and deeper reading of the events.' Sir Herbert partly answers his own criticism later on, when he concedes that Shakespeare likewise concealed his own views and did not stand clearly for this or that cause. But there are two questions at issue here. One is whether Scott's seeing both sides of an historical situation is an advantage or a disadvantage to him as a novelist; the other is whether, as Sir Herbert charges, he accepts the prejudices or the conventional judgment of his contemporaries and 'makes no effort to attain to a fresh and deeper reading of the events'. I should maintain that his seeing both sides is a great advantage, and, as to the second point, that, in terms of his art, Scott *does* attain to a fresh and deeper reading of the events. I say in terms of his art, because I of course agree that there is no overt philosophizing about the meaning of history in Scott's novels. But the stories as told by Scott not only 'attain to a fresh and deeper reading of the events', but also, I submit, do so in such a way as to illuminate aspects of life in general. As this is the crux of the matter, it requires demonstration in some detail.

Let us consider first *Waverley,* Scott's initial essay in prose fiction, and a much better novel, I venture to believe, than most critics generally concede it to be. . . . [The] plot is built around an Englishman's journey into Scotland and his becoming temporarily involved in the Jacobite Rebellion on the Jacobite side. How does he become so involved and how are the claims of the Jacobite cause presented? First he becomes angry with his own side as a result of a series of accidents and misunderstandings (undelivered letters and so on) for which neither side is to blame. In this mood, he is willing to consider the possibility of identifying himself with the other side—the Jacobite side—and does so all the more readily because he is involved in friendly relations with many of its representatives. He admires the heroism and the clan spirit of the Highlanders, and their primitive vigour (as compared with the more disciplined and conventional behaviour of the Hanoverian troops with whom he formerly served) strikes his imagination. He becomes temporarily a Jacobite, then, not so much because he has been persuaded of the justice of the cause, or because he believes that a Jacobite victory would really improve the state of Britain, but because his emotions have become involved. It has become a personal, not a national, matter.

It should be noted further that Waverley goes into the Highlands in the first place simply in order to satisfy a romantic curiosity about the nature of the Highlanders, and it is only after arriving there that he succumbs to the attractions of clan life. Not that his reason ever fully succumbs: though he comes to realize the grievances of the Highland Jacobites, he has no illusions about their disinterestedness or their political sagacity, and even when he does surrender emotionally he remains critical of many aspects of their behaviour. Thus it is emotion against reason, the past against the present, the claims of a dying heroic world against the colder but ultimately more convincing claims of modern urban civilization.

The essence of the novel is the way in which these conflicting claims impinge on Waverley. It is worth noting that Waverley, though he began his progress as a soldier in the army of King George, did not set out completely free of any feeling for the other side. Though his father had deserted the traditions of his family and gone over completely to the Government, his uncle, who brought him up, was an old Jacobite, and his tutor, too, though an impossible pedant who had little influence on Waverley, supported the old régime in both Church and State. Waverley thus belonged to the first generation of his family to begin his career under the auspices of the new world— specifically, to become a soldier of King George as a young man. That new world was not yet as firmly established in Scotland as it came to be during Scott's own youth: there was still a possibility of successful rebellion in Waverley's day, but none in Scott's. It was too late for Scott to become a Jacobite, even temporarily, except in his imagination, so he let Waverley do it for him. The claims of the two sides are a little more evenly balanced for Waverley than for Scott, yet even in the earlier period the issue is never really in doubt, and Waverley's part in the Jacobite rebellion must be small, and must be explained away and forgiven by the Government in the end. Above all, it must be a part entered into by his emotions on personal grounds rather than by his reason on grounds of national interest.

I have said that the essence of *Waverley* is the way in which the conflicting claims of the two worlds impinge on the titular hero. The most significant action there cannot concern the hero, but involves the world in which he finds himself. It is important, of course, that the hero should be presented as someone sensitive to the environment in which he finds himself; otherwise his function as the responsive observer could not be sustained. To ensure that his hero is seen by the reader as having the proper sensitivity, Scott gives us at the opening of the book several chapters describing in detail Waverley's education and the development of his state of mind. Waverley's education, as described in Chapter Three, is precisely that of Scott himself. By his undisciplined reading of old chronicles, Italian and Spanish romances, Elizabethan poetry and drama, and 'the earlier literature of the northern nations', young Waverley was fitted to sympathize with the romantic appeal of the Jacobite cause and its Highland support-

ers. This, as we know from Lockhart and from Scott's own account, was Scott's own literary equipment, and it qualified Waverley to act for him in his relations with the Scottish Jacobites. (pp. 95-8)

The subtitle of *Waverley* is ' 'Tis Sixty Years Since', and the phrase is repeated many times throughout the book. It deals, that is to say, with a period which, while distant enough to have a historical interest, was not altogether out of the ken of Scott's own generation. In the preface to the first edition of *The Antiquary,* his third novel, Scott wrote: 'The present work completes a series of fictitious narratives, intended to illustrate the manners of Scotland at three different periods. *Waverley* embraced the age of our fathers, *Guy Mannering* that of our youth, and the *Antiquary* refers to the last years of the eighteenth century.' (Scott, it will be remembered, was born in 1771.) As Scott comes closer to his own day, the possibilities for heroic action recede and the theme of the lost heir is introduced as a sort of substitute. It was with recent Scottish history that Scott was most concerned, for the conflict within himself was the result of relatively recent history. The Jacobite Rebellion of 1745 was the watershed, as it were, dividing once and for all the old from the new, and Scott therefore began his novels with a study of the relation between the two worlds at that critical time. It was not that the old Scotland had wholly disappeared, but that it was slowly yet inevitably disappearing that upset Scott. Its disappearance is progressively more inevitable in each of the next two novels after *Waverley.*

Guy Mannering is not in the obvious sense a historical novel at all. It is a study of aspects of the Scottish situation in the days of the author's youth, where the plot is simply an excuse for bringing certain characters into relation with each other. Once again we have an Englishman—Colonel Mannering, who, like Edward Waverley, shares many of his creator's characteristics—coming into Scotland and surrendering to the charm of the country. Scott has to get him mixed up in the affairs of the Bertrams in order to keep him where he wants him. Round Guy Mannering move gypsies, smugglers, lairds, dominies, lawyers and farmers, and it is to be noted that none of these characters, from Meg Merrilies to Dandie Dinmont, belongs to the new world: they are all essentially either relics of an earlier age, like the gypsies, or the kind of person who does not substantially change with the times, like that admirable farmer Dandie. These people are made to move around the Bertram family, or at least are brought into the story through some direct or indirect association with that family, and the family is decayed and impoverished. The lost heir is found and restored, and, largely through the benevolent offices of an English colonel, a Scottish landed gentleman is settled again on his ancestral acres. That is how things happen in the days of Scott's youth: no clash of arms or open conflict of two worlds, but the prophecies of gypsies, the intrigues of smugglers, the hearty activities of farmers, all set against the decay of an ancient family and all put to right in the end with the help of a gypsy, an English officer, and a Scottish lawyer. If the heroic element is less than in *Waverley,* the element of common life is greater, and the two virtues of honesty (in Dinmont) and urbanity (in Counsellor Pleydell) eventually emerge as those most worth while.

Counsellor Pleydell is a particularly interesting character because he represents that combination of good sense and humanity which Scott so often thought of as mediating between extremes and enabling the new world to preserve, in a very different context, something of the high generosity of the old. Pleydell is a lawyer, essentially middle class and respectable, but he is drawn with such sympathy that he threatens to remove most of the interest from the rather artificial main plot and share with Dandie Dinmont the reader's chief attention. If the gypsy Meg Merrilies provides something of the old-world romantic note—and she does so with great vigour and effectiveness—the lawyer and the farmer between them represent the ordinary man providing comfort for the future. The bluff courage and honesty of the farmer and the kindly intelligence of the lawyer dominate the story at the end. (pp. 101-03)

The scene of *The Antiquary* is the Scotland of Scott's own day. The external plot, which is once again that of the lost heir, is, as usual, not to be taken seriously: its function is to bring the faintly drawn Englishman Lovel into Scotland and so set the appropriate characters into motion. In three successive novels Scott begins by bringing an Englishman into Scotland, by sending forth an observer to note the state of the country at the time represented by the novel's action. Lovel, of course, is no more the hero of *The Antiquary* than Christopher Sly is the hero of *The Taming of the Shrew,* and his turning out at the end to be the lost heir of Glenallan is the merest routine drawing down of the curtain. The life of the novel—and it has abundant life—centres in the Scottish characters whom the plot enables Scott to bring together, and in their reactions to each other. (pp. 105-06)

The characteristic tension of Scott's novels is scarcely perceptible in *The Antiquary,* though I think it can be discerned by those who look carefully for it. In *Old Mortality* it is present continuously and is in a sense the theme of the story. In this novel Scott goes back to the latter part of the seventeenth century to deal with the conflict between the desperate and embittered Covenanters and the royal armies intent on stamping out a religious disaffection which was bound up with political disagreements. Though this was an aspect of Scottish history which, in its most acute phases at least, was settled by the Revolution of 1689, it represented a type of conflict which is characteristic

of much Scottish history and which Scott saw as a struggle between an exaggerated royalism and a fanatical religion. It should be said at the outset that as a historical novel in the most literal sense of the word—as an accurate picture of the state of affairs at the time—this is clearly Scott's best work. Generations of subsequent research have only confirmed the essential justice and fairness of Scott's picture of both sides. The only scholar ever seriously to challenge Scott on this was the contemporary divine, Thomas McCrie, who made an attack on the accuracy of Scott's portrait of the Covenanters, but posterity has thoroughly vindicated Scott and shown McCrie's attack to have been the result of plain prejudice.

But we do not read *Old Mortality* for its history, though we could do worse. We read it, as Scott wrote it, as a study of the kinds of mentality which faced each other in this conflict, a study of how a few extremists on each side managed, as they so often do, to split the country into warring camps with increasing bitterness on the one side and increasing cruelty on the other. (pp. 107-08)

If Scotland had not torn itself in two before the issues presented in the eighteenth century were ever thought of, the fate of the country might have been different, and Scott's study of the last of the Scottish civil wars before the Jacobite Rebellions is thus linked with his major preoccupation—the destiny of modern Scotland. If moderate men on both sides could have won, the future would have been very different. But, though there were moderate men on both sides and Scott delighted to draw them, their advice in the moments of crisis was never taken. There is no more moving passage in the novel than the description of Morton's vain attempt to make his fanatical colleagues behave sensibly before the Battle of Bothwell Brig. There is a passion behind the telling of much of this story that is very different from the predominantly sunny mood of *The Antiquary.* The extremists prevail, the Covenanting army is destroyed, and a victorious Government takes a cruel revenge on embittered and resolute opponents. This is one novel of Scott's where the moderate men do not remain at the end to point the way to the future. (p. 109)

Harry Morton, the observer, the man who sees something good on both sides and is roped into the Covenanting side by a series of accidents, represents the humane, intelligent liberal in a world of extremists. *Old Mortality* is a study of a society which had no place for such a character: it is essentially a tragedy, and one with a very modern ring.

If *Old Mortality* is, from one point of view, Scott's study of the earlier errors which made the later cleavage between Scotland and her past inevitable (for it is true to say that after the Covenanting wars the English saw no way but a union of the two countries to ensure the perpetual agreement of the Scots to the king chosen by England and to prevent the succession question from being a constant bugbear), *Rob Roy* is a return to his earlier theme, a study of eighteenth-century Highland grievances and their relation to Scotland's destiny. It is, in a sense, a rewriting of *Waverley* and the main theme is less badly presented. The compromise character here is the ever-delightful Bailie Nicol Jarvie, the Glasgow merchant who is nevertheless related to Rob Roy himself and, for all his love of peace and his commercial interests, can on occasion cross the Highland line into his cousin's country and become involved in scenes of violence in which, for a douce citizen of Glasgow, he acquits himself very honourably.

Rob Roy represents the old heroic Scotland, while the worthy Bailie represents the new. The Union of 1707 may have been a sad thing for those who prized Scotland's independence, but to the Bailie and his like it opened up new fields for foreign trade, and brought increased wealth. . . . Rob Roy is courageous and sympathetic, and Helen Macgregor, his wife, is noble to the verge of melodrama, but they represent a confused and divided Highlands and are, after all, nothing but glorified freebooters. Scott, in the person of Francis Osbaldistone, pities their wrongs and feels for their present state, but he knows that they and what they stand for are doomed—indeed, they admit it themselves—and throws in his lot with the prudent Bailie. (pp. 110-11)

There are two pivots to this novel; one is the relations between Francis Osbaldistone and his friends with Rob Roy and *his* friends, and the other is Francis's relations with his uncle and cousins. It is, I believe, a mistake to regard the family complications in *Rob Roy* as mere machinery designed to provide a reason for young Osbaldistone's journey into Scotland: they loom much too largely in the novel for that. They represent, in fact, a statement of the theme on which the Rob Roy scenes are a variation—the impossibility of the old life in the new world. Francis's uncle is an old-fashioned Tory Jacobite squire, completely gone to seed, and his sons are either fools or villains. This is what has become of the knights of old—they are either freebooters like Rob Roy, shabby remnants of landed gentry like Sir Hildebrand, or complete villains like Rashleigh. Francis's father had escaped from this environment to embrace the new world wholeheartedly and become a prosperous London merchant. He is at one extreme, Bailie Nicol Jarvie is the middle figure, and Rob Roy is at the other extreme. But the pattern is more complicated than this, for the novel contains many variations on each type of character, so much so, in fact, that it is an illuminating and accurate picture of Scottish types in the early eighteenth century. And through it all runs the sense of the necessity of sacrificing heroism to prudence, even though heroism is so much more attractive. (pp. 112-13)

Of *The Heart of Midlothian,* which most critics consider the best of Scott's works, I shall say nothing, since I have analysed it in accordance with the view of Scott here developed in the introduction to my edition of the novel.

The Bride of Lammermoor, which followed *The Heart of Midlothian,* presents the conflict between the old and the new in naked, almost melodramatic terms: the decayed representative of an ancient family comes face to face with the modern purchaser of his estates. The book is stark tragedy, for the attempted compromise—the marriage between the old family and the new—is too much for circumstances, and the final death of hero and heroine emphasizes that no such direct solution of the problem is possible. (pp. 113-14)

A Legend of Montrose—the companion piece of *The Bride of Lammermoor* in the third series of *Tales of My Landlord*—is a slighter novel than those I have been discussing: it lives through one character only, Captain Dugald Dalgetty, the only military figure in English literature beside whom Fluellen looks rather thin. But this one character is sufficient to illuminate the whole story, since, in a tale concerning the Civil War of the 1640s, he represents the most complete compromise figure—the mercenary soldier, trained in the religious wars of the Continent, willing to fight on and be loyal to any side which pays him adequately and regularly. This is another novel of a divided Scotland—divided on an issue foreshadowing that which divides the two camps in *Old Mortality.* Here again we have Highland heroism presented as something magnificent but impossible, and the main burden of the novel falls on Dugald Dalgetty, mercenary and pedant (a most instructive combination to those interested in Scott's mind), the man of the future who, ridiculous and vulgar though he may be, has a firm code of honour of his own and performs his hired service scrupulously and courageously.

After *The Bride of Lammermoor* and *A Legend of Montrose* Scott turned to other fields than relatively recent Scottish history, and in *Ivanhoe* he wrote a straight novel of the age of chivalry without any attempt to relate it to what had hitherto been the principal theme of his prose fiction—the relations between the old heroic Scotland and the new Anglicized, commercial Britain. . . . But he returned later to the theme which was always in his mind, and in *Redgauntlet* produced if not certainly the best, then the most illuminating of his novels.

Redgauntlet is the story of a young Edinburgh man who becomes involved against his will in a belated Jacobite conspiracy some twenty years after the defeat of Prince Charlie at Culloden. The moving spirit of the conspiracy turns out to be the young man's own uncle (for, like so many of Scott's heroes, young Darsie Latimer is brought up in ignorance of his true parentage), who kidnaps him in order that, as the long-lost heir to the house of Redgauntlet, he may return to the ways of his ancestors and fight for the Pretender as his father had done before him. Darsie, of course, has no liking for this rôle so suddenly thrust upon him, and is saved from having to undertake it by the complete collapse of the conspiracy. That is the barest outline of the plot, which is enriched, as so often in Scott, with a galaxy of characters each of whom takes his place in the complex pattern of late eighteenth-century Scottish life which the novel creates.

As with most of the Scottish novels, the story moves between two extremes. On the one hand, there is the conscientious lawyer Saunders Fairford, his son Alan, who is Darsie's bosom friend and with whom Darsie has been living for some time before the story opens, and other characters representing respectable and professional Edinburgh. Saunders Fairford is Scott's portrait of his own father, and the figure is typical of all that is conventional, hard-working, middle class, unromantic. At the other extreme is Darsie's uncle, a stern fanatical figure reminiscent of Balfour of Burley. Between the two worlds—that of respectable citizens who are completely reconciled to the new Scotland and that of fanatical Jacobites engaged in the vain task of trying to recreate the old—Scott places his usual assortment of mediating figures, from the blind fiddler, Wandering Willie, to that typical compromise character, the half-Jacobite Provost Crosbie. This is the Scotland in which Scott himself grew up and in which he recognized all the signs of the final death of the old order. For most of the characters Jacobitism is now possible only as a sentiment, not as a plan of action. But to Redgauntlet, who has dedicated his life to the restoration of the Stuarts, it is a plan of action, and the tragedy—for the novel is essentially a tragedy—lies in the manner of his disillusion. (pp. 114-16)

It is important for a proper understanding of Redgauntlet's character to note that his zeal is not only for the restoration of the Stuarts; it is, in some vague way, for the restoration of an independent Scotland, and his dominant emotion is Scottish nationalism rather than royalism. Scott made him a symbol of all that the old, independent Scotland stood for, and that is why his fate was of so much concern to his creator. . . . Scott, who burst into tears when he heard of old Scottish customs being abolished and who protested in horror when, at the uncovering of the long-hidden crown jewels of Scotland, one of the commissioners made as though to place the old Scottish crown on the head of one of the girls who were present—the Scott who, in his heart, had never really reconciled himself to the Union of 1707 (though he never dared say so, not even

in his novels), was portraying in the character of Redgauntlet something of himself, something, perhaps, of what in spite of everything he wished to be. But as Darsie Latimer—who is clearly a self-portrait, though a partial one—he only touched the fringe of that tragedy, without becoming involved in it. (p. 118)

Basing Scott's claim on these Scottish novels, what then was his achievement and what is his place among British novelists? It might be said, in the first place, that Scott put his knowledge of history at the service of his understanding of certain basic paradoxes in human society and produced a series of novels which both illuminates a particular period and throws light on human character in general. His imagination, his abundant sense of life, his ear for vivid dialogue, his feeling for the striking incident, and that central, healthy sense of the humour of character, added, of course, essential qualities to his fiction. But it was his tendency to look at history through character and at character through the history that had worked on it that provided the foundation of his art. Scott's might be called a 'normal' sensibility, if such a thing exists. He has no interest in aberrations, exceptions or perversions, or in the minutiae of self-analysis—not unless they have played a substantial part in human history. Fanaticism, superstition, pedantry—these and qualities such as these are always with us, and Scott handles them again and again. But he handles them always from the point of view of the ordinary sensitive man looking on, not from their *own* point of view. We see Balfour of Burley through Morton's eyes, and Redgauntlet through Darsie Latimer's. We feel for them, understand them even, but never live with them. That is what I mean when I talk of Scott's *central* vision: his characters and situations are always observed by some one standing in a middle-of-the-road position. That position is the position of the humane, tolerant, informed and essentially happy man. It is fundamentally the position of a sane man. Scott was never the obsessed artist, but the happy writer.

Scott's abundant experience of law courts, both in Edinburgh and in his own sheriffdom, gave him a fund of knowledge of ordinary human psychology, and he had besides both historical knowledge and imagination. His eccentrics are never as fundamentally odd as Dicken's eccentrics: they are essentially ordinary people, people he had known in one form or another. Most important of all, Scott *enjoyed* people, in the way that Shakespeare must have done. They live and move in his novels with a Falstaffian gusto. There is indeed something of Shakespeare in Scott—not the Shakespeare of *Hamlet* or *Othello*, but the Shakespeare of *Henry IV* or *Twelfth Night*, and perhaps also of *Macbeth*. His gift for dialogue was tremendous, and his use of Scottish dialect to give it authenticity and conviction is unequalled by any other Scottish novelist except very occasionally John Galt, Stevenson in *Weir of Hermiston*, and perhaps Lewis Grassic Gibbon in our own century. In spite of all the tragic undertones in so many of his novels, most of them are redeemed into affirmations of life through the sheer vitality of the characters as they talk to each other. Scott's gallery of memorable characters—characters who live in the mind with their own individual idiom—cannot be beaten by any other British novelist, even if we restrict the selection to some eight of Scott's novels and ignore all the rest. But they are not merely characters in a pageant: they play their parts in an interpretation of modern life. I say of 'modern life' to emphasize the paradox: Scott, the historical novelist, was at his best when he wrote either about his own time or about the recent past which had produced those aspects of his own time about which he was chiefly concerned.

Of course Scott was often careless. He wrote fast, and employed broad brush strokes. Sometimes we feel that he wholly lacked an artistic conscience, for he could do the most preposterous things to fill up space or tie up a plot. His method of drawing up the curtain is often clumsy, but once the curtain is up, the life that is revealed is (in his best novels) abundant and true. Scott can be pompous in his own way when his inspiration flags, but he never fools himself into mistaking his pomposity for anything else. Above all, though he is concerned about life he is never worried about it. We read his best novels, therefore, with a feeling of immense ease and satisfaction. We may be moved or amused or excited, but we are never worried by them. His best novels are always anchored in earth, and when we think of Helen Macgregor standing dramatically on the top of a cliff we cannot help thinking at the same time of the worthy Bailie, garrulous and kindly and self-important; Counsellor Pleydell is the perfect antidote to Meg Merrilies, and even Redgauntlet must give way before Wandering Willie and Provost Crosbie. The ordinary folk win in the end, and—paradox again—the Wizard of the North finally emerges as a novelist of manners. (pp. 119-21)

David Daiches, "Scott's Achievement as a Novelist," in his *Literary Essays,* 1956. Reprint by Philosophical Library Publishers, 1957, pp. 88-121.

THOMAS CRAWFORD

(essay date 1982)

[In the following excerpt, Crawford provides a modern assessment of Scott's poetry, focusing on the ballad epics *The Lay of the Last Minstrel, Marmion,* and *The Lord of the Isles.* The critic discusses Scott's structural principles, narrative techniques, descriptive methods, and treatment of landscape.]

When the young Scott attempted wholly original poetry in the ballad measure, he at first wrote nothing so good as his interpolations into traditional ballads, few though these were. Years later, in *The Antiquary,* he went back to the method and the mood of the interpolated stanzas of "Kinmont Willie." Using the traditional "Red Harlaw" as his starting point, he gave his own ballad on that topic to one of his impressive spey-wives, Elspeth of Craigburnfoot. Elspeth's ballad succeeds because it is in character, and deliberately fragmentary. The too explicit **"Eve of St. John"** and **"Glenfinlas"** have been replaced by a mysterious, irrational sequence; and Scott's poetry has gained enormously by his adoption of a *persona.*

Elspeth's ballad is one of a remarkable series of varied lyrics scattered through the novels and longer poems, which are at one and the same time the apotheosis of *pastiche* and the concentrated expression of Scott's own personality. Comparing Scott's lyrics with Burns's, Grierson claims that Scott is more impersonal than Burns: "Even Burns in his recast of folk-songs frequently charges them with more of his personal feelings. . . . Scott's revivals of older strains, aristocratic as often as folksong, are in a purer style." But Grierson ignores the fact that Burns's best lyrics are often dramatic lyrics, implying a *persona* ("My luve she's but a lassie yet," "Tam Glen," "Thou hast left me ever, Jamie"), while Scott's are impregnated with the spirit of the works in which they appear, which in its turn is Scott's own. Take Lucy Ashton's song from Ch. III of *The Bride of Lammermoor:*

> Look not thou on beauty's charming,
> Sit thou still when kings are arming,
> Taste not when the wine-cup glistens,
> Speak not when the people listens,
>
> Stop thine ear against the singer,
> From the red gold keep thy finger,
> Vacant heart, and hand, and eye,
> Easy live and quiet die.

In its context it is related to the defect in Lucy's character that is part cause of the novel's catastrophe, and is thus the emanation of Lucy, not Scott. At the same time it is connected with preoccupations of the author's own, with the wistful contemplation of temptations. Beauty charmed Scott only in a "respectable" and gentlemanly manner, not in Burns's or Byron's fashion: he would have dearly liked to be a soldier, but his lameness prevented him from serving fully when the kings of Europe were arming. In days when the people required leadership, all he could give them—magnificent though it was—was a picture of their past; the red gold and the wine cup attracted him greatly;

William Hazlitt on Scott the historical novelist:

Sir Walter Scott is undoubtedly the most popular writer of the age—the "lord of the ascendant" for the time being. He is just half what the human intellect is capable of being: if you take the universe, and divide it into two parts, he knows all that it *has been*; all that it *is to be* is nothing to him. His is a mind "reflecting ages past"—he scorns "the present ignorant time." He is "laudator temporis acti"—a "prophesier of things past." The old world is to him a crowded map; the new one a dull, hateful blank. He dotes on all well-authenticated superstitions; he shudders at the shadow of innovation. His retentiveness of memory, his accumulated weight of prejudice or romantic association, have overlaid his other faculties. The cells of his memory are vast, various, full even to bursting with life and motion; his speculative understanding is rather flaccid, and little exercised in projects for the amelioration of his species. His mind receives and treasures up every thing brought to it by tradition or custom—it does not *project* itself beyond this into the world unknown, but mechanically shrinks back as from the edge of a prejudice. The land of abstract reason is to his apprehension like *Van Diemen's Land*, barren, miserable, distant, a place of exile, the dreary abode of savages, convicts, and adventurers. Sir Walter would make a bad hand of a description of the *millennium*, unless he could lay the scene in Scotland five hundred years ago, and then he would want facts and worm-eaten parchments to support his style. Our historical novelist firmly thinks that nothing *is* but what *has been*; that the moral world stands still, as the material one was supposed to do of old; and that we can never get beyond the point where we are without utter destruction, though every thing changes, and will change, from what it was three hundred years ago to what it is now—from what it is now to all that the bigoted admirer of the "good old times" most dreads and hates.

William Hazlitt, in an unsigned essay in *The New Monthly Magazine*, April, 1824.

---

often it must have seemed to him that there was an emptiness at the centre of his being—"vacant heart," if not hand or eye; and Abbotsford, for all the bustle of its social life, for all the hunting and fishing and entertaining, was surely in essence a retreat: the direct opposite of political and military life, and a substitute for strenuous action in the real world. Thus I do not think it is fanciful to trace the elements of this beautiful dramatic lyric to Scott's own experience, and to suggest that its mainspring is the author's ironical self-criticism.

Unlike Burns, Scott did not generally have a tune in mind when writing a lyric—but, despite the assertion that he had no ear for music, he could sometimes almost rival Burns in this strain, as in **"Bonny Dundee"** and **"Donald Caird"**; and his handling of vernacular Scots in this last song has all the vitality of the Scots dialogue in the novels. The most characteristic moods in Scott's lyrics are robust action, elegiac sadness, extreme, even stark poignancy, and the monolithic sublime. For robust action we need go no further than Flora MacIvor's song, **"There is mist on the mountain"** from Ch. XXII of *Waverley;* for stark poignancy, Madge Wildfire's **"Proud Maisie"** in Ch. XL of *The Heart of Midlothian;* for elegiac sadness united to a magical strain of high poetry, **"Rosabelle"** in *The Lay of the Last Minstrel*, Canto VI; and for the monolithic sublime, Rebecca's hymn in Ch. XXXIX of *Ivanhoe*, which contains within itself all the grandeur of the Hebrew strain in Scottish Presbyterianism. There are literally scores of fine stanzas and lines scattered throughout Scott's numerous lyrics, and a handful of songs as perfect as any ever written in Scotland. . . . One can only marvel that the popular handbooks on English romantic poetry and the "romantic imagination" ignore such poems; often, there is not even a single entry for Scott in the index.

Scott's longer poems grew out of his ballad imitations; thus, *The Lay of the Last Minstrel* was originally conceived as a ballad but grew into a longer work under the influence of medieval English romances. He began it in the *Christabel* measure, but soon varied it either with straight octosyllabics, his favourite form, or with one derived from late medieval romances. This latter occurs much oftener in *Marmion,* where octosyllabic couplets are repeated two, three, or even more times, then interrupted by a six-syllabled line, followed by another group of eights, then a second six, rhyming with the first. The effect of the three-stressed line has been well compared to the breaking and falling of a wave.

By the time he wrote *The Lady of the Lake* and the later poems, Scott's lines of eight had developed a "massed and cumulative force" of their own, just like that of the old pentameter; as the line pattern became less broken, his poems exhibited a facile monotony that had been inherent in them from the beginning.

If Scott's versification builds up to parallel climaxes, so, too, does his syntax—a characteristic which Donald Davie has described, in a phrase borrowed from the linguist Roman Jakobson, as "the poetry of grammar." Scott's poetical rhetoric repeats identical constructions in order to produce syntactic augmentation, a "principle of organization" which he uses along with the other repetitive orderings of rhyme and metre. As Davie says:

it is when the traditional principles of order are reinforced by grammatical patterning and parallels that we recognize a poetry thoroughly achieved, structured through and through; and elegant variation, the saying of one thing many ways, brings with it for Scott this additional source of order.

But the "many ways" change what is being said, and give us a poetry that is quite alien to modern English modes, where the short or medium-length lyric is the norm, concentration a virtue, and expansiveness a positive defect. The type of order which is created by all Scott's metrical and syntactic accumulation, by all the elegant variations, may perhaps be regarded as his personal adaptation of that "Celtic ornamentation of a surface" which has often been considered one of the abiding features of Scottish literature. And it exists alongside another principle of order—that of narrative structure, of the tale itself.

In *Marmion* and the later poems, we react in the first place as we do to any other narrative—to the total shape, which in its turn is concerned with the creation and resolution of suspense, with the spectacle of persons and things, with recognitions and reversals, with the contrast and interplay of the expected and the unexpected. Scott's ballad epics consist primarily of situations: rhythms, rhymes, images and "the poetry of grammar" are therefore means to an end. And, as so often in the *Waverley Novels* also, the most striking elements within these situations are description and dialogue. Any of the longer poems provides a typical example; the situations are both visually and dramatically conceived, just as in the most successful modern popular modes—the film, the TV play, and the comic strip—and, what is more important, just as in the best popular ballads in the *Minstrelsy*. Thus the union of sight and sound, of drama and picture, is part of the ballad's contribution to the *Lays,* as it is later part of the ballad's contribution to the novels. Not only are dialogue and narrative linked so that the one interpenetrates the other, as in the scene of Marmion's death, but both dialogue and description are often subordinated to the characters and indeed to their social typology.

Scott's situations are so intensely seen and heard that it seems almost certain they must have existed in the first instance as mental pictures and speech heard with the mind's ear. The creative process with Scott would thus seem to have comprised, firstly, the visualisation of a series of scenes, then secondly, their *translation* into his chosen medium of verse or prose. In the *Lays,* the subsidiary units of the medium itself were often not so much words and images that Scott had impregnated with his own personality after the fashion of a modern lyric poet, as standard currency, like Homeric diction or the stock phrases of ballads and popular poetry. His expressions are often lifted bodily from other poets, or from the *clichés* of everyday life:

> But Isabel, who long had seen
> Her pallid cheek and pensive mien,

> And well herself the cause might know,
> Though innocent, of Edith's woe,
> Joy'd, generous, that revolving time
> Gave means to expiate the crime.

Scott's originality consists partly in his disposition of the larger situations rather than in his language as such. Nevertheless when he is working at full stretch, his "translations" can be intensely and beautifully vivid, as in Canto II of *Marmion,* where two abbesses and a blind and aged abbot sit in judgment on the guilty nun, Constance Beverley, in surroundings of Gothic gloom and horror, or—in *The Lay of the Last Minstrel*—William of Deloraine's wild ride form Branksome to Melrose.

Early critics of Scott's poetry spoke much of his descriptive powers, and one of the most acute of these, Adolphus, pointed out that his descriptions were often conceived in terms of a framed and painted picture rather than as direct renderings of reality. Adolphus also noted Scott's "marked attention . . . to what is called in painting Chiaroscuro"; there are, he said, very few of his "poetical descriptions . . . which do not owe part of their beauty to the distribution of light and shade," and he is always concerned "to point out some remarkable appearance of illumination or obscurity" [see Additional Bibliography]. To this might be added his fondness for moving pictures or pageants, especially processions, and his addiction to the poetical equivalent of "glorious technicolor," like the description of Lord Ronald's fleet at the beginning of *The Lord of the Isles.* The pageantry and cinematic quality reach their highest expression in the battle scenes at the end of *Marmion* and *The Lord of the Isles.* In *The Lord of the Isles,* Bruce slays a murderer with a brand snatched from the fire:

> The spatter'd brain and bubbling blood
> Hiss'd on the half-extinguish'd wood,
> The miscreant gasp'd and fell!

After Bruce's fight to liberate his ancestral castle from the English,

> . . . on the board his sword he toss'd,
> Yet steaming hot; with Southern gore
> From hilt to point 'twas crimson'd o'er.

In passages like these, or in the incident at Bannockburn where the Lord of Colonsay manages to slay d'Argentine, the knight who has given him his own death-wound, Scott's intensely visual and literal imagination was able to fashion out of his almost juvenile fascination with the horrors of war an anti-poetry of action that is far superior to the more conventional heroics for which he is famous.

In discussing Scott's descriptive verse, Adolphus notes that he never separates nature from human society, and that

There is, indeed, throughout the poetry of this author, even when he leads us to the remotest wildernesses, and the most desolate monuments of antiquity, a constant reference to the feelings of man in his social condition; others, as they draw closer to inanimate things, recede from human kind; to this writer even rocks and deserts bear record of active and impassioned life, nay sometimes appear themselves inspired with its sensations; the old forgotten chieftain groans in the lonely cavern, and with "tears of rage impels the rill"; the maid's pale ghost "from rose and hawthorn shakes the tear," and the "phantom knight" shrieks along the field of his battles.

Such an attitude to nature is not so much "Augustan" as "pre-Romantic," for the persons whom Scott finds inseparable from his lonely places—the chieftain, the maid of balladry, and the phantom knight—are not those that would most readily occur to Pope or Johnson. There is, however, one aspect of Scott's treatment of landscape which is undoubtedly new—the poetical fusion of landscape with the sentiment of nationality. In previous Scottish poetry there is much evocation of a characteristically northern landscape, but without the specific and obvious infusion of national as distinct from local feeling. One thinks of the introductions to the various books of Gavin Douglas's *Aeneid,* of Thomson's *Winter,* of Burns's occasional sketches of the Ayrshire pastoral landscape. But it was reserved for Scott to strike such a note as the depiction of James V's incursion into the Trossachs in Canto I of *The Lady of the Lake,* or of Loch Coriskin and the Coolins in *The Lord of the Isles,* or of the border and lowland scenery of past and present in *The Lay of the Last Minstrel* and *Marmion.* The union of nationality with the perception of landscape becomes embarrassingly explicit in the rhetorical apostrophe which follows the often quoted:

> Breathes there the man, with soul so dead,
> Who never to himself hath said,
> This is my own, my native land!

The succeeding stanza begins:

> O Caledonia! stern and wild,
> Meet nurse for a poetic child!
> Land of brown heath and shaggy wood,
> Land of the mountain and the flood,
> Land of my sires! what mortal hand
> Can e'er untie the filial band,
> That knits me to thy rugged strand!

These hackneyed and oratorical lines exhibit a response to landscape that seems typically Scott's and which he renders with greater subtlety in many other passages—as, for example, this one, also from *The Lay of the Last Minstrel*—

> From the sound of Teviot's tide,
> Chafing with the mountain's side,

> From the groan of the wind-swung oak,
> From the sullen echo of the rock,
> From the voice of the coming storm,
> The Ladye knew it well!
> It was the Spirit of the Flood that spoke,
> And he call'd on the Spirit of the Fell.

(pp. 34-42)

[The] strain of melancholy so noticeable in Scott's . . . ballad imitations is developed in the *Lays* to the point where it becomes mourning for Scotland's vanished independence. When the "last minstrel" is asked by the company at Branksome:

> Why he, who touch'd the harp so well,
> Should thus, with ill-rewarded toil,
> Wander a poor and thankless soil,
> When the more generous Southern Land
> Would well requite his skilful hand,

his reply is the "Breathes there the man, with soul so dead" passage already quoted, which soon, however, modulates into the nostalgic

> Still, as I view each well-known scene,
> Think what is now, and what hath been,
> Seems as, to me, of all bereft,
> Sole friends thy woods and streams were left;
> And thus I love them better still,
> Even in extremity of ill.

Thus the romantic-nationalistic attitude to landscape is to some extent a compensation for the desolate state of Scotland in the present. A similar mood occurs in *Marmion,* when a Highland tune puts Scott in mind of Scottish emigrants to Canada and America, chanting

> the lament of men
> Who languish'd for their native glen . . .
> Where heart-sick exiles, in the strain,
> Recall'd fair Scotland's hills again!

This is as close as Scott ever comes to what David Craig calls doing justice "to both the inevitability" of contemporary developments "and the losses involved"; the trouble is that he does not come close enough, and that his awareness is projected back into the past.

In the introduction to Canto V of *Marmion,* Scott shows himself quite conscious of his escapist role. After a glance at the danger to Kingship from the democratic and anti-royalist movements of his time, he goes on:

> Truce to these thoughts!—for, as they rise,
> How gladly I avert mine eyes,
> Bodings, or true or false, to change,
> For Fiction's fair romantic range,
> Or for Tradition's dubious light,
> That hovers 'twixt the day and night:
> Dazzling alternately and dim,
> Her wavering lamp I'd rather trim,
> Knights, squires and lovely dames to see,
> Creation of my fantasy. . . .

But what he finally beholds in "Fiction's fair romantic range" is the national disaster of Flodden, and in the Spenserians which preface *The Lord of the Isles* he sees himself as

> a lonely gleaner I,
> Through fields time-wasted, on sad inquest bound,
> Where happier bards of yore have richer harvest found.

Scott's conscious motive, in these Scottish Lays, seems identical with his intention in *The Minstrelsy of the Scottish Border:*

> By such efforts, feeble as they are, I may contribute somewhat to the history of my native country; the peculiar features of whose manners and character are daily melting and dissolving into those of her sister and ally. And, trivial as may appear such an offering, to the manes of a kingdom, once proud and independent, I hang it upon her altar with a mixture of feelings, which I shall not attempt to describe.

After this, Scott quotes some lines from an anonymous poem, *Albania,* published in 1742, which end:

> Hail! dearest half of Albion, sea-wall'd!
> Hail! state unconquer'd by the fire of war,
> Red war, that twenty ages round thee blaz'd!
> To thee, for whom my purest raptures flow,
> Kneeling with filial homage, I devote
> My life, my strength, my first and latest song.

In the General Preface to the *Waverley Novels,* however, he tells us that the purpose of his own "latest song"—the prose romances—was to serve Scotland by interpreting her to the English. In this he was following Maria Edgeworth, who

> may be truly said to have done more towards completing the Union than perhaps all the legislative enactments by which it has been followed up.

> Without being so presumptuous as to hope to emulate the rich humour, pathetic tenderness, and admirable tact which pervade the works of my accomplished friend, I felt that something might be attempted for my own country, of the same kind with that which Miss Edgeworth so fortunately achieved for Ireland—something which might introduce her natives to those of the sister kingdom in a more favourable light than they had been placed hitherto, and tend to procure sympathy for their virtues and indulgence for their foibles.

Comparison of these extracts suggests a certain deterioration in Scott's attitude to his native country between the *Minstrelsy* and the *Waverley Novels:* the pessimistic antiquarian had turned into a loyal subject displaying his ancestors and their quaint dependants to the Conqueror. (pp. 46-9)

Thomas Crawford, in his *Scott,* revised edition, Scottish Academic Press, 1982, 132 p.

SOURCES FOR FURTHER STUDY

Devlin, D. D. *The Author of "Waverley": A Critical Study of Walter Scott.* London: Macmillan, 1971, 142 p.

> A detailed study of five Scott novels: *Waverley, A Legend of Montrose, Rob Roy, The Bride of Lammermoor,* and *Redgauntlet.* Devlin focuses on Scott's portrayal of the past and on the structural functions of his comic characters.

Hart, Francis R. *Scott's Novels: The Plotting of Historic Survival.* Charlottesville: University Press of Virginia, 1966, 371 p.

> A detailed study of the *Waverley Novels.* Hart divides his overview of the novels into four sections: "The Quixotic Tragicomedy of Jacobitism," "Opposing Fanaticisms and the Search for Humanity," "The Historical Picturesque and the Survivals of Chivalry," and "The Falls and Survivals of Ancient Houses."

Jack, Ian. *Walter Scott.* 1958. Reprint. Writers and Their Work, no. 103. London: Longman Group, 1971, 38 p.

> A general introduction to Scott and his writings.

Johnson, Edgar. *Sir Walter Scott: The Great Unknown.* 2 vols. New York: Macmillan, 1970.

> The definitive modern biography.

Lauber, John. *Sir Walter Scott.* New York: Twayne Publishers, 1966, 166 p.

> A concise introduction to Scott and his works.

Wilson, A. N. *The Laird of Abbotsford: A View of Sir Walter Scott.* Oxford: Oxford University Press, 1980, 197 p.

> A laudatory study of Scott and his works, with chapters on his poetry and various aspects of the novels, including the author's religion, medievalism, and heroines.

Robert W. Service

1874?-1958

(Full name Robert William Service) Scottish-born Canadian poet, novelist, and autobiographer.

INTRODUCTION

During the early twentieth century, Service was one of North America's most popular poets, and his work is still widely read. He is best known for his playfully rhythmic verses that celebrate life and adventure in the Yukon, particularly "The Shooting of Dan McGrew" and "The Cremation of Sam McGee." Because of the marked influence of Rudyard Kipling's work on his verse, Service has often been called "the Canadian Kipling."

Born in England and educated in Glasgow, Scotland, Service moved to Canada when he was twenty years old. He traveled extensively in British Columbia and worked at a variety of jobs until he was hired by a Vancouver bank in 1902. Two years later, Service was assigned to a Yukon branch, where he remained for eight years and gathered material for his ballads. His first volume of verse, *Songs of a Sourdough* (also published as *The Spell of the Yukon*), was published in 1907 and was an instant success. The royalties from this book enabled Service to publish more verse and his first novel, *The Trail of Ninety-Eight: A Northland Romance* (1910). Service worked as a war correspondent for a Toronto newspaper during the Balkan War of 1912-13; he later covered events in France during World War I and also worked as an ambulance driver. After the war, Service remained in France, where he wrote most of his remaining verse and novels. In 1940, when the Nazis invaded France, Service was forced to leave and return to Canada. While in North America he spent time in Hollywood, where he wrote his two-volume autobiography. After World War II, Service returned to France and lived in retirement on the French Riviera until his death in 1958.

A poet who deliberately omitted the word "poem" from his book titles, Service was quoted as saying, "Verse, not poetry, is what I was after—something the man in the street would take notice of and the sweet old lady would paste in her album; something the schoolboy would spout and the fellow in the pub would quote." *Songs of a Sourdough* achieved this type of popularity, selling more than two million copies by 1940. The most famous poems in *Sourdough* are "The Shooting of Dan McGrew" and "The Cremation of Sam McGee," which mythologize the adventure and masculine vigor of life during the Klondike Gold Rush at the turn of the century. In these poetic ballads, which are designed as dramatic monologues, Service incorporated popular Yukon slang of the day with a memorable cadence and rhyme scheme. After the publication of *Sourdough* and another volume of verse, *Ballads of a Cheechako* (1909), Service wrote his first novel, *The Trail of Ninety-Eight,* which was also extremely successful. Service intended it to be, in his words, "the only fictional record of the gold rush." He modeled the novel's main character, Athol Meldrum, after himself. Meldrum is a drifter and romantic dreamer who has considerable moral fiber and courage, but, unlike Service, is destined to fail rather than succeed. *The Trail of Ninety-Eight* was later produced as a movie, as were several of Service's other novels.

In addition to the poetry and prose inspired by the Yukon, Service wrote books based on his experiences in the bohemian circles of Europe before World War I. The most popular work he wrote about this period is *The Pretender: A Story of the Latin Quarter,* which was published in 1914. This novel is a high-spirited, if slightly cynical account of avant-garde life in Paris. During the war years in France, Service's employment as a reporter and ambulance driver provided him with inspiration for one of his best-known books of verse, *Rhymes*

of a Red Cross Man (1916). It was this volume that enabled Service to gain a degree of distinction as a poet in his own right, and not merely as a devotee of Kipling, as critics had hitherto alleged. Many critics praised *Rhymes of a Red Cross Man* for displaying a genuine empathy with the common soldier's circumstances and for evoking deep feelings of patriotism in the reader. The volumes of verse Service wrote after the Second World War are more autobiographical and opinionated than any of his previous collections. *Songs of a Sun-Lover,* published in 1949, was Service's first postwar book of verse. In it he demonstrated his distinctive brand of rhyme-making, but also presented his opinions on such serious issues as poetry, politics, human nature, and religion. The bulk of Service's later verse was published under the title *More Collected Verse* in 1955. But it is his earlier ballads that are responsible for his continuing fame.

Because his poetry is deliberately anti-intellectual, Service has been alternately attacked or ignored by literary critics. Several recent scholarly articles on his work, however, have argued that the literary standards by which it has been judged are inapplicable, because Service's verse falls into an oral, folkloric tradition, and its formal aspects are of secondary importance. Written to appeal to the unsophisticated and the traditionalist, Service's verse is widely anthologized and continues to find a large and receptive audience.

(For further information about Service's life and works, see *Contemporary Authors,* Vol. 115; *Dictionary of Literary Biography,* Vol. 92: *Canadian Writers, 1890-1920; Something about the Author,* Vol. 20; and *Twentieth-Century Literary Criticism,* Vol. 15.)

CRITICAL COMMENTARY

W. A. WHATLEY
(essay date 1921)

[In the following excerpt, Whatley discusses the two major divisions of Service's work: the poems written before World War I, which focus on life in the Yukon, and those written during the war, which deal with the soldier's experience. Whatley also examines the influence of Rudyard Kipling on Service's poetry.]

The work of Robert W. Service falls naturally into two divisions. The first of these consists of his entire poetic output prior to the Great War. The major theme of the verse of this period is the interpretation of the life of the Great North, with its pendulum-sweep from the

heroic to the mean, and its direct contact with the primary forces of Nature; it is to this verse that Service owes his title of "the Kipling of the Northwest." The second division of Service's work is made up of poems written during the war and dealing with soldier life at first hand, being the direct result of the author's experiences in trench, camp, and hospital while in active service with the Red Cross at the Front.

In the pre-war verse of Service, the influence of Kipling is unmistakably and universally manifest. The poems of this period are, in the main, poems of adventure which are modeled, either consciously or unconsciously, upon the lines of the Kipling poem of the

"Rhyme of the Three Sealers" type. In the *Ballads of a Cheechako*, the *Rhymes of a Rolling Stone*, and *The Spell of the Yukon*, the Kipling attitude toward the life of the wild and the primitive is the prevailing *motif*. Service, as well as Kipling, looks upon the North as the last stronghold of the hostile forces of Nature, into which man penetrates only as a rash and audacious intruder, but in which he has no legitimate place or standing.

This identity of feeling and spirit which characterizes the work of Kipling and Service is evident upon the most cursory examination of representative poems. (p. 300)

The Arctic scenes of both poets are drawn in the same light, are shaded with the same colors; the reactions of both to the inspiration of the North are in the same spirit.

In addition to this parallelism, there are other and more technical evidences of the influence of Kipling in Service's earlier work. His metrical forms and rhyme-schemes show a marked similarity to those of Kipling. . . . The ballad form is a prime favorite with Service; and in this, as in more minute features of his verse, the Kipling influence is evident.

Only in the matter of diction is there any appreciable difference to be noted; and the distinction here lies in something which is difficult to define, but which

permeates the style of Service and serves to differentiate it subtly from that of Kipling. The style of both poets is spontaneous and virile; but there is an innate *American* quality in the diction of the one which distinguishes it from that of the other. It would be difficult, or rather impossible, to point out the exact nature of this difference without having recourse to minute and exhaustive analysis; the difference lies more in the nice shadings of habitual and local usages of language than in anything else, and its presence is more easily felt than pointed out. Service acquired his knowledge of the North through intimate and hard experience, and the language in which he celebrates its splendors and terrors is the *bona fide* speech of the North. Kipling's acquaintance with the North is at second hand, or at the best was made from the deck of a steamer. The difference in the degree of familiarity has left its trace upon the diction of both poets, if not upon the spirit of their works.

There is a tendency on the part of the general reader to class Service as a simple American echo of Kipling; and in so far as his early poetry is concerned, it is to be frankly acknowledged that Service is deeply in Kipling's debt. But Service is really more than a mere imitator—rather, he is an enthusiastic follower. He is a kindred spirit, an American continuation of the Kipling tradition—if such a thing as a Kipling tradition may be said to have come into existence so soon. (pp. 301-02)

As a war poet, Service has definitely assumed the position which Kipling, in view of his past achievements, might have been expected to occupy. One of the many surprises which were brought in by the year 1914 and its immediate successors was the complete and dismal failure of the greatest living English poet to live up to the spirit of the occasion. . . . [It] was left to Service, hitherto a simple follower of the elder poet, to sing the saga of the trenches, the hospital, and the camp.

The war-verse of Service is sincere and vital; it does not leave the impression, as is the case with the large majority of Kipling's poems, of having been written for a purpose. It is not tainted with the evidence of propaganda. It is a spontaneous interpretation of the spirit of the war through the lips of one who experienced it, throughout the various phases of its four years of conflict and toil, at first hand. It is instinct with the life of the "carry-on" spirit, the determination to make the best of conditions which were well-nigh unbearable, to see the stupendous task through to a definite and satisfactory ending.

The influence of Kipling is not so universally noticeable in this verse as in that of the pre-war period; the vividness of his experience of the Great Adventure seems to have inspired Service to break away into more individual and original lines. A number of these poems, nevertheless, show the old influence as plainly as do their predecessors; such productions, for instance, as **"Going Home,"** which is as evident an adaptation of "Danny Deever" as is **"The Song of the Mouth-Organ"** of another famous Kipling poem. **"The Red Retreat," "A Song of Winter Weather,"** and **"Funk"** are reactions to trench life and campaign incident which show the influence of the *South African Ballads*, in structure, diction, and spirit; while **"Jean Desprez"** is equally traceable to such Kipling influences as "The Ballad of East and West" and "The Ballad of the King's Mercy." **"The Man From Athabaska"** marks the transition from the poetry of the North to that of the war, and is not lacking in evidences of the influence of Kipling, being somewhat reminiscent of the latter's "M.I."

In a second class of war poems, the Kipling influence is less evident. These have a more intimate, personal ring; and in this they show a marked departure from the Kipling model. In truth, Kipling is surprisingly neglectful of the individual for a poet of his magnificent range. He is interested in the interpretation of the type, and either fails to attempt or is incapable of the expression of individual reactions. Service, on the other hand, has a deeper personal sympathy; and where Kipling depicts the soldier class as an entity, *en masse*, Service develops the reaction of the individual soldier himself. (pp. 302-04)

There is a final group of poems among the *Rhymes of a Red Cross Man* which show no appreciable Kipling influence. These are purely personal reactions of the poet himself to the war, and the influences to be traced between their lines are anything but Kiplingesque. If anything, they are more reminiscent of the work of Rupert Brooke than of that of any other recent poet. Of these, **"Tricolour"** and **"The Lark"** are perhaps the best, although **"The Fool"** is almost equally good. (p. 306)

Thus Service, while he may be the inferior of Kipling in original gift of poetic genius and in versatility, is at least not justly condemned as an imitator and nothing more. That he is indebted to Kipling in no small degree, no one can deny; but it is equally undeniable that his work possesses merit of its own, which is not attributable to any exterior influence, and is only to be credited to the possession of native poetic genius. (pp. 307-08)

W. A. Whatley, "Kipling Influence in the Verse of Robert W. Service," in *The Texas Review*, Vol. VI, No. 4, July, 1921, pp. 299-308.

MARTIN BUCCO
(essay date 1965)

[In the following excerpt, Bucco examines the folkloric qualities of Service's poetry.]

To millions of people Dan McGrew and Sam McGee are as familiar as Prince Hamlet and Gunga Din. At schools, colleges, camps, bars, clubs, conventions, smokers, and parties, the "manly" metrics of Robert W. Service are parodied and recited—perhaps more than any other North American verse. Yet fictive characters who flourish in the popular imagination do not always attract critical attention to themselves, to their contexts, or to their creators. Literary analysts who focus on complexity, nuance, and stylistic innovation dismiss Service's achievement as naive, banal, and facile. As "folk poetry," however, the early efforts of "The Bard of the Yukon" merit study. Since the folklorist customarily deals with non-aesthetic facts, he values Service's contribution for what it is, rather than for what it is not. (p. 16)

Although in British Columbia he became a bank clerk instead of a prospector, Service's sedentary occupation perpetuated his romantic outlook. He saturated himself in oral and written tales of northwestern North America. . . . The stories about exploration and danger that Service appropriated from folklore, myth, and ritual are ideal narrative material, and his own background helped integrate cultural patterns from diverse traditions. The quality of collective authorship which marks his early ballads stems from his capacity for defining in bold emotion, vivid images, dynamic meter, and fierce rhyme an unsophisticated people's feelings, attitudes, beliefs, sorrows, and aspirations. . . . His curiosity about the dwindling group of isolated muckers—Stampeders in the Gold Rush of 1898—their native intelligence, memory, and imagination, along with his own affinity for the foibles and folly of low society, down-and-outers, riffraff, and people uncontaminated by learned tradition, was highly suitable for a rich folk literature. Unlike the "folksy" Edgar A. Guest, Service saw vice as dramatically more vital than virtue. Therefore, in telling the inside story of the Yukon, he created a "Red Light Atmosphere" and tried through hard Anglo-Saxon and picturesque slang to blend realism and romanticism. Service longed to recreate a past that "otherwise would be lost forever."

The durable *Spell of the Yukon and Other Verses* . . . along with *Ballads of a Cheechako* . . . and the isolated Northland poems in his later volumes contain two strong mythic themes: Wonder and Initiation. The state of wonder or mystification results from Man's confrontation with environmental austerities and associations; the initiatory rites (*rites de passage*) involve quests and tasks. More often than not, these two "archetypal patterns"—treated tragically, comically, or tragicomically—blend in particular poems.

Some spectacular images of nature that cram Service's pages—legendary cliches that inflate the mind—are northern lights, groaning ice, burning sunsets, great stars, profound crevasses, blinding snow, bludgeoning silence, ice-locked land, rivers of blood, glacier-glutted streams, fanged mountains, fantastic sky colors, giant canyons, roaring avalanches, and the nail-driving wind. The barbaric land is alive with pine, spruce, tundra, and moss. Real and imaginary wolves, moose, deer, bears, foxes, panthers, and men prowl this land—at times an Earthly Paradise, at times a Howling Wilderness. Ostensibly, most men there seek gold. They dream, prospect, camp, hunt, fish, find, fail, drink, gamble, fornicate, lose, understand. The talk mainly is of claims, caches, grub-stakes, pay-streaks, pokes, kilters, picks, pans, bed-rock holes, sluicing-boxes. When not in log or stone settlements, the men sleep in tents and thrive on tinned tomatoes, embalmed beef, sourdough bread, rusty beans, and moldy bacon. Culture comes in the form of the Bible and the mouth organ. The initiate is either the narrator, another person, or a few men. Always preferring the ordeals of raw nature to the comforts of urban confinement, the seekers set forth on a quest involving challenge, struggle, hardship; the end—in simplest terms—is death or survival, failure or success. Those who succeed (and some who die) are real men, code heroes, a quasi-religious Brotherhood of the North.

At bottom, all religion rests on the memory of environmental mystery and holiness. Viewing the North land ambivalently—loving its freshness and freedom, hating its famine and scurvy—the successful old prospector of **"The Spell of the Yukon"** yet is awed by it all. . . . Weary of champagne, the old prospector remembers the early struggle, and his recollection of the heroic land strengthens him. In terms of mythology, his desire to return to the Other World signifies a need to regain a lost power; in terms of psychology or religion, a rebirth. Similarly, the speaker in **"The Prospector"** who revisits the ghost-ridden Bonanza concludes that his sacred dream made the search for gold good. Reality was in the quest, not in the lucre. As such, one could readily substitute a Holy Mission, the Holy Grail, or God.

Conspicuous in many of Service's hyperbolic figures of speech is the wide-spread custom of viewing the land as an Earth Mother. Service's most complete contribution to this folk motif is the personification of a forbidding yet just Mother Earth in **"The Law of the Yukon."** Here she is a celibate queen crushing the weak who come to rape, but embracing the strong who come to serve. Dreaming of her future blessed condition, of her good reputation, of motherhood, of fame, of bestowing riches "in the eager lap of the world," Queen Yukon clearly represents a frontier people's aspirations and enterprise. (pp. 17-19)

Besides portraying ancient and traditional frontier religious fervor, the agnostic Service also gives expression to pantheistic tendencies found in the folk. **"The Three Voices,"** for example, depicts the sea, wind, and stars imparting sentimentalities about bravery, freedom, and God. The stars singing of "the God in man" sounds like nineteenth-century romantic transcendentalism, and both the Adamic Emerson and Thoreau would agree that "a star or soul is part of the whole."

The universal belief in a god of place (*deus loci*) who confers benefits—material and spiritual—to pilgrims at his shrine makes the rich and awesome North an ideal place for dislocating "standard" values, for finding the self, and for establishing a new relationship between that self and the universe. The speaker in **"The Heart of Sourdough,"** his kit packed, is leaving, "ere another day is done," to seek things elemental and timeless. Though the mighty land will best the puny man, the wild romantic fight for survival is a blessing—one feels fully *alive*! The "Envoy" to *The Spell of the Yukon* insists that "even to win is to fail." The catalog of natural wonders in **"The Call of the Wild"** . . . beckons a man from the cradle of convention to the knowledge of self. (pp. 19-20)

Sometimes the journey is neither for God nor Self, but simply for the sake of duty or humanity. **"Clancy of the Mounted Police,"** for example, eulogizes the duteous Scarlet Riders. Talking as tall as Paul Bunyan or Mike Fink, Constable Clancy boasts that he can "cinch like a bronco the Northland, and cling to the prongs of the Pole." Into the Great White Silence moves the red-headed Mountie to rescue a starving madman on the banks of the Nordenscold. "Suffering, straining, striving, stumbling, struggling on," Clancy gets his man—and frostbite gets the heroic Constable's toes. Another frosted man—the teller of **"My Friends"**—ironically describes how two guilt-ridden criminals—a murderer and a thief—nurse him, haul him a hundred stormy miles to the nearest Mounted Police post, and then are arrested, men "wicked beyond belief."

Almost unprincipled beyond credulity is "the lady that's known as Lou" in one of Service's most famous ballads—**"The Shooting of Dan McGrew."** According to the balladeer's testimony, the editor of the *White Horse Star* urged him to give as his "piece" at the next church concert "something about our own bit of earth." Tired of reciting "Casey at the Bat," "The Face on the Barroom Floor," or "Gunga Din," Service determined to tell a story by musical suggestion. Strolling through town on a rowdy Saturday night, Service invented the opening line: 'A bunch of the boys were whooping it up in the Malamute saloon . . ." His plot he discovered later that evening when the bank guard, thinking a thief had broken in, fired a shot at Service—but missed. Before five the next morning the tale of the celebrated shooting was on paper. Notwithstanding Service's judgment that the ballad was indecorous for recitation at the church concert, the setting, conflict, and action are felicitous as folklore. Hence, even the famous Sourdough, Klondike Mike, came to believe the rumor that he had witnessed the love triangle, the drinking, piano-playing, gambling, swearing, gun-fighting, and double expiration in the frontier barrel house. Oddly enough, the demise of Dan McGrew is no more pivotal in the tale than that of the Stranger—as much a folk type as the Gambler and the Prostitute. Indeed, what might account, in part, for the ballad's wide appeal is its mystifying lack of organic centrality. Certainly, the first-person peripheral narrator sympathizes with the besotted Stranger more than he does with the undercharacterized McGrew. Further, the psychological conflict between the Stranger and Lady Lou is as desperate as the shooting between the Stranger and McGrew; and, finally, the common folk theme of true love and revenge rides tandem with that of forsaken love and greed. Contrast, repetition, heavy-handed rhythm, and climactic order carry conventional associations until the tag end. Fortunately, Lou's greed is as plausible (on second thought) as the narrator's black humor.

Besides the doomed gunfighters, Service versifies such fated humans as Dago Kid, Sailor Swede, Ole Olson, and Hard-Luck Harry, along with a host of nameless figures. In the vernacular of folk memory, Ole Olson of **"The Ballad of the Northern Lights"** spins his yarn to a stranger: the Big Stampede and the Trail of '98, when the Klondike was the center of the world and local legend ran wild. Broke after rioting in the "siren town," each of the "Unholy Trinity" dream of a dead relative who promises the Golden Land. The folkloristic vision of fate spur their greedy kin to seek the lone moose trail along the Arctic rim. In time, the fevered men are driven mad by the fantastic Northern Lights—in Eskimo lore the capering spirits of the dead. After Dago Kid shoots himself and Sailor Swede freezes, Ole Olson staggers to the crater of a low, round mountain by the Polar rim and stakes "the source and spring of the mystic Northern Lights." For ten dollars, Ole now offers to the stranger at the bar a quarter share in the crater full of radium (worth a million dollars a pound). In this tall tale about hidden treasure, a variation on the old story about selling the Brooklyn Bridge

to bumpkins, Ole settles for the loan of a dollar. (pp. 20-1)

Of Service's tall tales, none surpasses **"The Cremation of Sam McGee"**—a comic version of the wide-ranging folktale of the return from the dead. Sam McGee's fiery resuscitation rates him high in the hierarchy of Northern folk heroes—higher, to be sure, than the anonymous Southwest buffalo hunter who crawled into a buffalo robe during a storm and endured emprisonment until the frozen skin was thawed out by fire. Service avers that he first heard the cremation yarn at a party in White Horse, where a miner from Dawson preambled it with the declaration that he would "tell a story that Jack London never got." Excited, Service (he states early in his autobiography that pictures of burning saints in Fox's *Book of Martyrs* gave him a "gruesome delight") afterwards left the party for a moonlit trail and began composing the key to his success: *"There are strange things done in the midnight sun . . ."* He claims that he finished the fourteen stanzas in six hours and spontaneously wrote it down the next day. As well as breaking the law of nature, Service's Southern prospector also disrupts the code of honor of the Brotherhood of the North—a type of inverse brag; instead of "grinning" about the Polar cold or "laughing it off," he whines. A true code hero bent on keeping his promise to cremate the frozen body, McGee's trail companion voices the ballad's grotesque humor and irony, first when he declares that the derelict *Alice May* will serve as "my cre-ma-tor-eum" and later when he explains that he "stuffed" his friend in the glowing coal, but had to hike away from the "sizzle." In short, Sam's is no Beowulfian cremation. The final sight of the grinning McGee and the sound of his peppery appeal is legion:

> "Please close that door.
> It's fine in here, but I greatly fear you'll
> let in cold
>   and storm—
> Since I left Plumtree, down in Tennessee,
> it's the first
>   time I've been warm."

(pp. 22-3)

In several of Service's poems, conspicuous supernatural and superstitious folk elements occur. **"The Ballad of the Black Fox Skin,"** for example, features shapeshifting, a motif common to thousands of far-flung anecdotes. In many North American Indian tales, transformation or metamorphosis facilitates homicide. The black fox pelt, according to "squaw tales," comes from the unkillable devil-fox, a well-known folk creature. Scuffling over the pelt of the murdered "man-with-no-name," Windy Ike hurls his mistress-accomplice, Claw-fingered Kitty, over a bluff and into the icy river; the note found beside the hole through which Ike himself later perishes reads:

> "Here met his fate by evil luck a man who lived in
> sin,

And to the one who loves me least I leave this black fox skin."

No one ever retrieves the pelt, but the narrator certifies that "one man said he saw the tread of *hoofs* deep in the ground."

Here and elsewhere Service, like the quizzically folk-conscious Hawthorne, employs the literary device of alternative possibility. **"The Ballad of One-Eyed Mike,"** another example, pictures the hypnotic dream of the persecuted crystal-eyed speaker. The river before him shrinks to a backdrop for wobbly flakes, wriggling snakes, and goblin eyes, reminding one of Coleridge's "The Rime of the Ancient Mariner." Then Mike's dead enemy, seeking atonement, looms as an "inky blot"; folkloristic terms for this phenomenon are floater, fireball, will-o'-the-wisp, or *ignis fatuus.* Even after his haunting dream, the appearance-reality dilemma remains, for Mike discerns "something" bobbing in the black water before it heads down-stream. Not only hallucination, but folkish premonition—parapsychology today—informs "Lost." Bathetically freezing to death in a blizzard, the "erring" son envisions his old parents and the old home trail; simultaneously, his mother presages his peril, hears his cry, and then sees her boy's frozen face pressed to the window pane. Old Father explains that what Mother heard was a wounded bird, and what Mother saw was snow falling from the maple tree. (pp. 24-5)

Undoubtedly, Service's humorous or pathetic grotesquerie derives, in part, from new ways of living in the raw subartic wilderness and from the sense that the single man—no matter how communal or community-minded—is, after all, discrete. These aspects of frontier individualism impart to Service's Yukonistic *mores* the kind of unity and coherence discoverable in the local color tradition of New England's Harriet Beecher Stowe, California's Bret Harte, and Indiana's Edward Eggleston. However singular, Service's characters do share, among other things, common interests, lingo, legends, rituals, tales, beliefs, and skills. As a folk poet, Service cherished the protrusive differences between the Sourdoughs and the Outsiders. Likewise, earlier writers relied on such sub-literary ingredients as purple passages, exaggerated metaphors, and exuberant contrasts to express the folkways of stampedes to gold-ored California, Colorado, Nevada, and South Dakota.

Service's representative subjectivism frequently colors sense data, but he honestly reports that adventuring, westering, and prospecting more often bring gall and wormwood than milk and honey. His treatment of frontiering through archetypal folk patterns rather than through naturalistic social documentation does not veil his majestically unresponsive, supremely indifferent, and glaringly ruthless deterministic universe. But because the optimistic romanticism of the buoyant Adamic journey (a combination in Service of learned and unlearned traditions) overrides any pessimistic naturalism, he is fundamentally American. The European or Eastern American who seeks personal Manifest Destiny, whether he succeeds or fails, is better off for having discarded the stable and effete ways for the dynamic and manly. Folkloristically sympathetic with such economic failure as he depicts in **"The Wage Slave,"** Service, however, reveals no contemporary concern for promoting security, equality, and prosperity for all men.

For many, Service's inspired myth of Northern glory replaced the tired myth of Outside shame. In short, indisputable Natural Law imposed order upon the interplay of mutualism and rivalry in the struggle for existence; the moral sentiment and the code of the Brotherhood of the North relied heavily on feelings of sublimity and inflated notions of poetic justice. Because the stampeders could not naturally forget their pasts—a source of dramatic contrast and psychological conflict—they gained not only experience of the New World, but also wisdom of the Old Self. For, as in seeking gold, the value in searching for some part of the Self is in the quest. In trying to define self, past, and place, Service also defined a folk, introducing them to one another, to Outsiders, and to their heirs. Like the mythic prospectors of the Glory Trail, today's Northlander—learned or unlearned—bears the burden of his past, but instead of willing vainly to "get shut of it," the modern Sourdough knows that his health, vanity, and pride need a vivid sense of tradition—Inside and Out—and that the folk poetry of Robert Service is a signal part of that tradition. . . . (pp. 25-6)

Martin Bucco, "Folk Poetry of Robert W. Service," in *Alaska Review,* Vol. II, No. 1, Fall, 1965, pp. 16-26.

EDWARD HIRSCH
(essay date 1976)

[In the following excerpt, Hirsch presents a structural analysis of Service's Yukon ballads, explaining their success as dramatic monologues.]

From the time that he published his first book of poetry in 1907, Robert W. Service's long rhyming narratives, written about the romance and hardship of the gold miner's life in the Canadian wilderness, have been extraordinarily popular. Their success was nearly instantaneous and by now many of his poetic characters have firmly lodged themselves into the popular imagination. (p. 125)

Despite their enormous popularity, Service's

poems have been essentially neglected by literary scholars and critics intent on the products of elite culture. One aspect of the problem is that most scholars have confronted the poems with literary rather than sociological questions. Another is that there is some confusion concerning Service's actual intent and literary position. For though the ballads may initially appear to have been written as elite poetry, they have been most often read and transmitted as oral monologues by the people who have in fact loved them. Part of the disparity between their popularity and their literary reputation may lie in this distinction: that whereas Service's poems have been judged against other more essentially literary artifacts (and thus deemed unsuccessful), by the aesthetics of monologue composition and performance they are actually quite successful. It is important to add that Service's poems, and parodies of those poems, form an essential part of almost every monologuist's repetory. But as the few literary critics who have dealt with Service have noted, even to literary audiences the natural oral and dramatic dualities of Service's verse almost demand, certainly invite, and perhaps even create their own performing context. (pp. 125-26)

Service himself has stated that he wanted verse instead of poetry—"something the schoolboy would spout and the fellow in the pub would quote." Insofar as that was his goal, he had indeed been successful. Therefore, by defining Service's ballads as poems which are particularly conducive to monologue performance, we at least partially account for the difference of opinion concerning Service's achievement. Moreover by viewing Service's ballads not only as poems but as texts for monologue performance, we can also account for Service's emergence as both a folk and a popular poet, two distinctions which do not always correspond. In so far as they are performed as monologues, Service's poems belong to a long tradition of oral literature (though with important differences) and hence are able to speak to specific small groups in immediate ways, even as ballads, stories, and songs do. Yet as written literature, they also have a greater circulation and are able to reach, in nearly exact form, a far wider literate audience. There can be little doubt that Service's poems have become far more widely known because they have fulfilled this dual role.

Our initial position is now clear: since Service's ballads were largely intended for public recitation and have been essentially accepted and transmitted as monologues, it is in that light which they should be studied. It is interesting to note that the very things which make Service's poems unacceptable to literary scholars also make them acceptable as monologues intended for performance. For example, Service's verse, like nursery rhymes and other forms of popular poetry, conforms closely to an ideal metrical rule . . . , thus

specifically defying Ezra Pound's 1912 Imagist dictum that poetry should be composed in the sequence of the musical phrase, not to the beat of the metronome. Although this metrical regularity may be distasteful to a literati trained on stylistic nuances and metrical subtleties, Service's "clanging rhythms" serve several functions for the performer. First, they serve as a mnemonic device. Second, they allow the performer to concentrate—and to concentrate on—the drama of a story. The metrical strength not only helps to attract and to keep an audience's attention, but it also draws on the underlying metrical regularity which serves to modulate the tone and quickness of the speaking voice, hence avoiding monotony. The dramatic element of the performer's voice is in many ways necessary for the full success of Service's poems. And yet there must be something in the structure and content of the poems themselves that warrants their repeated performance. It seems likely, perhaps even requisite if they are to remain popular, that in some manner the poems articulate the needs and conflicts of the community to which they speak. (pp. 126-27)

[Since] the poems are still primarily transmitted through the written medium, and since the monologue performers are to a large extent bound by the substance of the printed text, an analysis of the material as written seems to be preliminary to other investigations. (p. 127)

By employing a structural approach we hope to reveal what is most essential to the meaning and character of the poems. Furthermore, we hope to show that the structure of the form (i.e. the metrical schema) corresponds to the structure of the content (i.e., the story the ballads tell) and that these unique analogues illuminate what is most important in the poems. Throughout this paper we will also be saying things about the nature and aesthetics of monologue performance.

We have chosen for the text of our analysis Service's Yukon ballads. . . . These ballads form a self-contained unit both in terms of the subject matter and metrical forms, and are the poems of Robert Service which are most often used, in fact almost exclusively used, by monologue performers. Though there is a great deal of diversity within the poems, it will be argued that there is at least an implicit unity in the substantive body of the material.

We begin our discussion with a lyric poem entitled **"Prelude"** which Service used as a preface to *Bar-Room Ballads,* not because it belongs to what we have depicted as the Yukon ballads, but because it illuminates several important aspects of Service's method and style. Most important of all, the poem essentially dramatizes the dichotomy between high-brow and low-brow, the Opera and the tavern, "the graceless hobo" and "the Land of Letters." The poem proceeds by a series of careful binary oppositions. . . . The rhyme scheme, a feminine-masculine alteration (abab-cdcd), emphasizes this set of binary oppositions by always rhyming one of the high-brow—low-brow juxtapositions as opposed to any two like assertions or negations. Thus "unable" and "table" are rhymed, or "pity" and "ditty"; later such rhymes occur as "fetters" and "Letters" and "booze" and "Muse." The tone is both comic and serious, defensive and aggressive. Service achieves this remarkable effect by paralleling a serious word or emotion (pity) with a comic or low-brow one (ditty). In spite of the humor, however, notice that the negations are preliminary and are always rhetorically countermanded by one of the assertions. The poem ends on an aggressive, defiant note.

> A bar-room bard . . . so if a coin you're flinging,
> Pay me a pot, and let me dream and booze;
> To stars of scorn my dour defiance ringing,
> With battered banjo and a strumpet Muse.

Other oppositions, sometimes implicit, are developed as the down-and-out versus the wealthy, the graceless versus the elegant, the raucous versus the elite and self-contained, the drunken versus the sober.

"Prelude," like all of Service's poems, establishes a true democracy of language and consciously poses a colloquial diction which speaks to the masses against a sophisticated and elegant diction which speaks to the few. In Nietzschean terms the Dionysian is set against the Apollonian; in Marxist terms the working or lower class is implicitly set against the aristocratic or upper class. This is particularly crucial not only because it illuminates important aspects of Service's attitudes (which are defensive and aggressive, self-conscious and defiant) toward his high culture poetic contemporaries, but because of the values which it extolls and the community to which his verse naturally addresses itself. As they unfold, Service's poems indicate an awareness that he will be judged and misjudged by his more refined poetic peers. It can also be argued that Service's self-defined relation to those peers has analogues in the rugged Yukon miners' ambiguous relations to their safer, middle-class contemporaries who live in more domesticated territories, and thus corresponds to the binary oppositions which will be established in the Yukon ballads. It can also be stated that the verse articulate the values and conflicts of the Yukon miners and, probably to a lesser degree, of the monologue performers and their audiences who have nothing to do with the Yukon. The final judgement about the expressive value of an art form of Service's kind must still be based on the range of its popularity. And Service's ballads are certainly popular. What we have designated as Service's Yukon ballads depict a language of oppositions which is structured within the overall language and on which any of the single ballads may draw. These oppositions may be seen in a general schematic framework which has elements from all of the ballads, but of which elements *all* are almost never contained in any given ballad. (pp. 128-30)

The primary and omnipresent conflict of Service's Yukon ballads is the opposition between life in the Yukon and life in other places. While life in the Yukon is explicitly dramatized and individuated, life in other places is usually assumed implicitly, or conceptualized in only the most general and stereotypic terms. This pattern also corresponds to Service's dramatization of the low-brow/high-brow poetic conflict where the low-brow is assertively and dramatically revealed while the high-brow is presented only in the most general terms. Nonetheless (these ballads are, after all, ostensibly about the Yukon), if only from the most obvious juxtaposition of elements, it is possible to establish Service's defining characteristics of life outside the Yukon.

In Lévi-Strauss' terms, which are indeed relevant, Service's poems dramatize the ongoing conflict between nature and culture, the terribly raw (Dionysian man) and the elaborately cooked (Apollonian man). The terribly raw, or life in the Yukon, is associated with the hard, physical life, which in turn means life in constant confrontation with death, a natural preoccupation of the gold miners. Implicit in this is the opposition of an easy life, which is also the secure but tedious life in other places. This middle-class safety, or civilization,

Robert Service in uniform, 1916.

which we shall term death-in-life since it guarantees a secure physical life but implies a kind of spiritual death or mediocrity, defines an existence without promise (gold) or sacrifice (inherent in conditions of life in the wilderness). Its traditional virtues are warmth (both in a literal and a metaphorical sense), the security of a family, the stability of a job and a regular income. Life in the Yukon, however, which we shall term life-in-death since the barren, frozen, impoverished and dark conditions of the Yukon imitate a certain kind of physical death at the same time that they promise a high spiritual or romantic life, is of exactly the opposite order. Service's poems rationalize (often they are openly nostalgic for) the renunciation of all that life in the Yukon is not—safe, secure, and boring—while simultaneously exhibiting a longing for that familiar existence. Life in the Yukon might feasibly be equated with a physical and beastly Hell, but with the promise of Heaven (i.e., gold or extreme wealth). Dependent upon the miner's mood, be it hope or despair, the home life will take on the opposing qualities; thus it will be pictured as either Heaven or Hell, whereas when the average gold miner left it was only earth. This may, in fact, reverse (at least temporarily) what we have described as the death-in-life of middle-class life. To extend the Heaven/Hell metaphor, it is also possible to see Heaven, or the promise of gold, as the hopeful future, as opposed to Hell which is the barren present. It is only the fantastic promise of wealth that can be used to justify the risk and extreme poverty of the present. Service has localized the metaphor of Hell by making it frighteningly cold as opposed to frighteningly hot as it is usually portrayed. Finally, without the promise of gold it would be impossible to rationalize the renunciation of a secure life outside of the Yukon. Service's ballads inevitably draw on the ambiguities of that renunciation, and on the central emotional conflicts of the gold miner's existence.

One aspect of the conflict is the role that the saloon often plays in the implicit struggle between life styles. Having characteristics of both styles of life, the bar-room is something of a mediator between the two styles. Thus it can be defined as neutral territory, a social arena, a place where the conflicts can be localized. Similarly, it is both domestic and wild, a place of rest and leisure, a locale where ballads are both performed and dramatized. (pp. 130-32)

The way in which the bar-room acts as both a secondary world (a place where the art form is performed), and a primary world (a place where the dramatization takes place), and thus represents aspects of life in the Yukon and life outside the Yukon, can best be illustrated by the following chart:

Yukon	Bar-Room	Middle-Class Life
open spaces	closed space, but surrounded by the wilderness	closed space, house
extreme cold	warm, but surrounded by the cold	well-protected warmth
extremely dark	light, but surrounded by the darkness	well-lit
individual miners— alone	individual miners with other miners—social	individual miners with others— family
no women	barmaids, prostitutes, kept women, etc.	wives, daughters, mothers
sober	drunk	sober
no love	sex, cards, drink	familial love
North	North, but first stop into and out of the Yukon	South

(p. 132)

Perhaps the most perfect example of a poem in which the barroom is a dramatic as opposed to a performing center (as in most of the Bar-Room Ballads) that mediates the essential conflict is in **"The Shooting of Dan McGrew."** This ballad primarily dramatizes love or sexual conflict. McGrew's reality (alone) and his dream of reality (a wife, a home) are mediated by the presence of the lover who betrayed him. His despair is founded on the clear juxtaposition of what he has and what he wants, and by the fact that he has lost his mediator, the lady Lou. The bar-room is the place where he expresses his feelings (by playing the piano) and indicates his poverty (by looking as if he's been in Hell). The ballad also opposes his physical wealth with his physical longing; the bar, for example, is characterized as a social arena where no one cares for each other (though they are together) and is in itself juxtaposed against a real home, even as a faithful Lou (as opposed to Lou as she really is, unfaithful), is juxtaposed against a real wife. The gunfight between Dan McGrew and the nameless miner takes place in the bar, which is the localizer of the conflict. Thus the bar serves as a kind of stage *for* the dramatization as well as an essential element *in* the dramatization. It is both backgrounded and foregrounded, the thematic center of the story of true love and revenge, forsaken love and greed. Thus the saloon is both a secondary and a primary world.

This is not to say that the bar-room is always a mediator for the oppositions of death-in-life and life-in-death. Sometimes the conflicts are set in direct dynamic tension with only the Yukon as the locale, as in **"The Cremation of Sam McGee"** where the mediation takes place in offsetting journeys. The absence of the bar, in fact, tends to heighten the juxtapositions of reality in the Yukon (Hell) and nostalgia for life outside the Yukon (which becomes Heaven). We can thus argue that the mediators change, but the overall binary oppositions remain static. Once again, the conflicts of any given poem draw from and rely upon this communal set of oppositions as established in the chart, although the chart is not identical to the conflicts in any given poem.

It is now time to proceed with a detailed analysis of a single text, **"The Cremation of Sam McGee"** both in terms of content and the metrical form used. (pp. 133-34)

We have chosen **"The Cremation of Sam McGee"** for our ballad *par excellence* because it is one of the most popularly performed monologues, it is metrically representative of all of the Yukon ballads, and at the same time it is somewhat difficult to conceptualize against the backdrop of our chart of binary oppositions, particularly since there is no bar-room to localize the conflict. The poem is ostensibly not about the conflict between middle-class life and life in the Yukon at all, and yet it will be illustrated that in terms of the underlying structure, on both the literal and symbolic levels, the poem is 'about' the juxtaposition of the life-in-death and death-in-life tension.

The metrical form of **"The Cremation of Sam McGee"** is basically an alternating anapestic and iambic heptameter, the pattern of which is consistently varied by substituting an iamb for an anapest in the last foot of each line. This creates the kind of rhythm which Mike Harding finds inherently necessary for good monologues. Once again, the language is colloquial and straightforward, immediately comprehensible. Since the form is highly conventional, both in terms of rhyme and meter, the reader can concentrate on the narrative elements of the story. (p. 135)

The first stanza and the last (the introduction and the denouement) create a frame within which the poem establishes its oppositions. The story is considered strange because it is supernatural, a tale of death and ressurection meant to astonish and perhaps frighten. However, as will be illustrated, under the exotic surface the poem expresses the normative values, feelings, and tensions of Service and the Yukon miners whom he portrays. The story also appears strange, at least to the narrator, because Sam McGee is unlike the other miners insofar as he is weak and cowardly and exceptionally obsessed by the cold. For that very reason he is an exceptional example of the ambiguous feelings which any gold miner in the Yukon would have to have. Structurally, the poem reveals and works out through "build up, attack, and pay off " many of the most crucial literal and symbolic binary oppositions of our chart.

After the introductory stanza, which might be viewed as a frame for the poem, the ballad begins in earnest with a series of implicit oppositions. As the first stanza progresses, the reader discovers, or might discover, that he is getting not a dramatization but a setting of oppositions already defined in our binary set. The actual dramatization, or the literal present, does not in fact focus until the third stanza. (p. 137)

What appears to be the first journey of the poem, but which, as we have seen, is in fact the second (implicit in Sam McGee's presence in the Yukon) takes place in stanza three. The next stanza fully articulates the Yukon-as-death theme (which will be played to its ultimate logical conclusion) by establishing and extending the symbolic metaphor of cold. (p. 138)

Thus we have the continuation of the journey in the Yukon . . . and Sam McGee's death. The narrator is forced to continue the journey . . . , and symbolic return both to the South and to the security of the womb. It is important that at this point in the poem (stanza eight) Sam McGee is dead, and his body is icy cold, but his journey back, which concludes with cremation and thus a final or second death, essentially culminates in resurrection. This is the second birth ("Now Sam McGee was from Tennessee") and we have come full cycle back to the South ("Since I left Plumtree, down in Tennessee, it's the first time I've been warm."). This of course makes for a neat closure, accentuated by the repetition of the first stanza of the poem at the end. (pp. 138-39)

In so returning, the theme of death in the Yukon (and how in this case it overwhelms spiritual life so as to make that life meaningless) is pushed to its logical extreme. As life in the Yukon becomes more and more closely identified with Hell, life in Tennessee becomes more closely identified with Heaven. . . . It is only because of Sam McGee's exceptional cowardice and fear of the cold that Tennessee becomes fully and literally associated with Heaven, and the cycle is thus completed, the theme pushed to its logical conclusion. This conclusion contains a reversal or violation of our established categories. It is in death, after all, that Sam McGee finds a second life. But what is perhaps most interesting of all is that Sam McGee's case is only exceptional in terms of its intensity, not in terms of its impulse. In fact, the essential oppositions categorized— warmth and cold, security and insecurity, or danger contemporaneous with promise—are common to all of the ballads. Because of the absolute intensity of Sam McGee's feelings, the terms are pushed to their logical extremes. At this point the tale becomes strange and supernatural, but the oppositions nonetheless remain normative. Thus, one of Service's most extraordinary ballads fits into our schema of binary oppositions. (pp. 139-40)

Edward Hirsch, "A Structural Analysis of Robert Service's Yukon Ballads," in *Southern Folklore Quarterly*, Vol. XL, Nos. 1 & 2, March-June, 1976, pp. 125-40.

CARL F. KLINCK

(essay date 1976)

[In the following excerpt, Klinck discusses Service's later verse.]

Two poems, **"Dan McGrew"** and **"Sam McGee,"** had brought Robert Service fame and fortune. They had given him the freedom to pursue a career of rhyming which lasted fifty years and yielded more than two thousand pages of printed verse. Late in his life he estimated wryly that he had written thirty thousand couplets, and employed more than ten thousand rhymes. (p. 171)

[Service's *Collected Verse* and *The Complete Poems*] were succeeded by *Collected Poems*, copyrighted by the author in 1940. *The Bar-Room Ballads* . . . were made Book Six in this new collection, but the inconsequential *Twenty Bath-Tub Ballads* . . . were omitted. These facts indicate a hiatus in his writing of verse, certainly in his publication of verse, between *Ballads of a Bohemian* . . . and 1940—that is, through the "thriller" twenties, the possibly lazy thirties, and the war-time forties. It is difficult, however, to determine how many verses written during the hiatus went into the first volumes of Service's post-war series of poetic books which began with *Songs of a Sun-Lover*, published in 1949. Not much, therefore, can be said to identify any poetic production of the Nice and second Hollywood periods, which ended in 1946. In that year, with the removal of Service's household to Monte Carlo, the remarkable Monaco period began.

This Monaco verse has considerable biographical and critical value, for it rounds out, on Service's own terms, the story of his life and thought. Most of it was published in separate volumes before the large collected editions were made. In the various titles, the sacred word "poem" is conspicuously avoided: [*Songs of a Sun-Lover, Rhymes of a Roughneck, Lyrics of a Low-brow, Rhymes of a Rebel, Songs For My Supper, Carols*

of an Old Codger, Rhymes For My Rags, and *Cosmic Carols*]. . . . (pp. 171-72)

All of these later publications show that Service was surveying his past in terms of the present in which he found himself. *Songs of a Sun-Lover* . . . seems to be related in a special way to the prose works of the 1940s, when he was turning his attention from Paris to the south of France, and, with the fresh experiences of war-time residence in North America, writing his biographies, *Ploughman of the Moon* . . . and *Harper of Heaven.* . . . Some of the songs in *A Sun-Lover* may have been "harped" in the early 1940s. Certainly this book is dedicated to Provence: "O Land of Song! O golden clime!" In a lyric for his seventy-fifth birthday on the 16th of January, 1949, he was in a mood to "whoop it up" and let the world know that he was still alive. Coming to terms with his destiny was going to be necessary, but chiefly as part of an on-going career in song.

Songs of a Sun-Lover gave him an opportunity to reappear as the same old poet with an even stronger assertion of his aims. His *apologia* for his early and his forthcoming verse runs through this first of the Monaco books; it is most clearly stated in **"A Verseman's Apology"**,

Alas! I am only a rhymer,
I don't know the meaning of Art;
But I learned in my little school primer
To love Eugene Field and Bret Harte.
I hailed Hoosier Ryley with pleasure,
To John Hay I took off my hat;
These fellows were right to my measure,
.......................And I've never gone higher than that.
For God-sake don't call me a poet,
..............................For I've never been guilty of that.
And I fancy my grave-digger griping
As he gives my last lodging a pat:
"That guy wrote McGrew;
'Twas the best he could do" . . .
So I'll go to my Maker with that.

In an intermediate stanza he declared that

The Classics! Well, most of them bore me
The Moderns I don't understand. . . .

(pp. 174-75)

There was some over-statement in this; he knew, for example, what a Pullman porter at Montreal meant when that polished servant of travellers declared that he owned all of Service's books of verse, but his taste was "Eliot and Auden". In **"Book-Lover"** Service gave an impressive list of great authors on his library shelves which he now no longer read. In **"My Library"** he confessed with shame that he was too old to read his thousand books, but that he "wallowed" in "the Daily Press." It was part of his programme for living and writing in the world of the present day with plenty of time for communion with nature. In this way he hoped to stay in touch with "simple folk." . . . (p. 175)

A few Yukon ballads, included in *Sun-Lover*, showed that this was indeed the McGrew and McGee storyteller that readers remembered. The comedy was in Service's coarsest vein, and he added to his Northern characterizations the first of a series of effective ballads about Montreal Maree, a dance hall girl "as pretty as a pansy, wi' a heart o' Hunker gold." The tuneful lyric about **"Marie Vaux of the Painted Lips"** is a welcome addition to this book: under the title of **"The Last Supper"** it had first appeared in *The Trail of Ninety-Eight* as the work of the "Pote", Ollie Gaboodler. Service was now claiming it as his own. There is further sympathy for fallen women in **"Babette"**, **"No Lilies for Lisette"**, and **"White Christmas"**; these evidently belong to the Bohemian period. There are also compassionate portrayals of the various unhappy fates of an actor, a millionaire, a little Jewish orphan, an opera singer, a tippler, a murderer, a motorcycle racer and his girl, a boxer, and the deserted sweetheart of a soldier boy. Service's portrait gallery, already packed with distinctively drawn likenesses of a host of characters, would have many more additions before he laid down his pen.

In *Sun-Lover* Service displayed a growing tendency to make explicit attacks upon war, political injustices, and oppression of the poor. The realism with which he now went to the heart of a matter was sharper than the realism of setting in the thrillers, or the realism of human activity in the earlier vignettes. But his ideas were still incorporated in the doings of men and women, often through the device of using these characters as the ostensible speakers of the lines of a poem. His favourite technique involved a brief, effective presentation of a situation followed by an expression of the consequences thereof in a rhetorical or ironic ending. He was tireless in his search for the unique word or phrase. (pp. 176-77)

In **"God's Battle-Ground"** he laid the foundations of his opinions about divinity. . . .

God is not diminished by offering to man the freedom to act in gentle kindliness or in evil ways. God being "What is," the struggle is also God's: the struggle is human and divine. Thus, for Service, life was God's experiment, and it called for active realism, not for "abstract terms," which appeared to set God at a distance from daily life. (p. 178)

There is a sense in which, for him, life and all his writings were religious, for he was dedicated to finding and reporting little dramas of human experience; vignettes were revelations of mingled success and failure on an individual scale. A report of life as lived was a form of identification with the universe. . . . The poet is a "maker": it is his business to construct an accurate verbal transcription of what he can see and know. It is his mood that counts. "Goodness is Godness," and Goodness is kindliness, compassion, love, peace, tolerance, and opposition to tyranny and oppression. "To

fight that Mankind may be free . . . ," he said, "There is our Immortality." It seemed a high calling from which a versifier of the "common" lot was not excluded.

It will not be possible to trace restatements of these themes through all the Monaco books, although the next one, *Rhymes of a Roughneck* . . . , shows an interesting development beyond the conclusion of **"Prayer."** Praying was not in Service's line. . . . Yet "when the *Cross* I see / I make the sign." Some of the later books have sections entitled "Rhymes for Reverence." Perhaps one should not be startled when one turns to the last page of *Roughneck* where a [Roman cross] appears under the title **"Rhyme For My Tomb"**. (pp. 179-80)

The *Roughneck* book may be regarded as a supplement to *Sun-Lover*, for the Rhymes are grouped under headings appropriate to both books: "Low-brow Lyrics," "Garden Glees," "Library Lays," "Poems of Compassion," "Ribald Rhymes," "Vignettes in Verse," and "Mortuary Muse." A fair choice from the numerous offerings in each of the categories respectively would include **"McCluskey's Nell"** (a Montreal Maree ballad); **"My Pal"** ("Brave bird, be lyric to the last. . . . And so will I, / And so will I"); **"Amateur poet"** ("To make my rhyme come right, / And find at last the phrase unique / Flash fulgent in my sight"); **"The Under-Dogs"** ("What have we done, Oh Lord, that we / Are evil starred?"); **"Include Me Out"** ("I grabbed the new *Who's Who* to see / My name—but it was not . . . / The book I held was *Who WAS Who* / Oh was I glad—and how!"); **"Humility"** ("Yet if in sheer humility / I yield this yokel place, / Will he not think it mockery / And spit into my face"); and **"The Hand"** ("How merciful a Mind / My life has planned!").

In such verses there are few significant differences from those in *Songs of a Sun-Lover*. Yet one may sense Service's growing tendency to stress the lamentable in human existence and to moralize about it; at the same time there is no retreat from the policy of illustrating nearly everything by means of vignettes and suggestive images. The pronoun "I" (so often used) belongs to his *persona*, his fictional participant, but the author's heart is in that "I" more sympathetically than ever before. He cannot resist being part of all that he had met. Also, he gives evidence of renewed and stronger literary interests: he had been recalling and rereading his favourite authors. In **"God's Skallywags"** he asserts that he would set Villon, Baudelaire, Byron, Poe, Wilde, Francis Thompson, and Burns high above the "merely holy" writers. He praises Maeterlinck as "a forgotten master," communes with the spirit of Thomas hardy as one of the "Great Rejected Poets," and gives "his vote" to Cervantes rather than to Shakespeare.

One of the novel features of *Rhymes of a Roughneck* is the appearance of travel verses. The first instalment of a series which would range through several books from ribaldry to indignation was saucily entitled "Dago Ditties." As a **"Tourist"** he preferred "to Mike Angelo / The slim stems of a lady tourist"; and as a **"Florentine Pilgrim"** he thought "better than a dozen Dantes" was "something cute in female scanties." What he wrote about **"The Pigeons of St. Marks"** can be left to the imagination. Yet there was reverence for genius and art. The Leaning Tower of Pisa reminded him that Galileo had stood there; and the Apollo Belvedere was "A bit o'frozen music." (pp. 180-81)

[*Songs For My Supper*] was the fifth of the Monaco books and stood at the end of the collection entitled *More Collected Verse,* published in 1955 while Service was still alive and writing. (p. 186)

There are several . . . unusual features in this book of *Songs.* Service here drops his Rolls Royce contentment and puts on the mask of a bard, eighty years of age, who must work for his bread because no one will buy his books. In fact he was very rich, but this device served to identify himself with the poor, the unemployed, the underprivileged, the prisoners of toil, the unwilling soldiers, and the doomed felons. He had experienced in early life all but the last two of these misfortunes. The theme is, once more, resentment on behalf of those whom systems of various kinds have caged. Service was an exponent of liberty, not of equality, not of fraternity, and not of communism. He was an individualist to the end.

In "Domestic Ditties" he accepts his place as Grandpa, more or less shelved by his family, while he relives in memory some childhood scenes. "Rhymes for Irony" is his general term for paradoxes and surprise endings concerned with miscellaneous subjects ranging here from the sex obsessions of cats and the slovenliness of Beethoven to his own anger at the *Morning Star* for printing a fleshy picture of himself as a "tycoon." In "Lyrics of the Lost" and "Lyrics for Reverence," he took up the themes and methods in which he excelled, and demonstrated ever-fresh descriptions of characters

and their human problems. He scrupulously avoided repetition of settings and statements.

Very much the same applies to *Carols of an Old Codger* . . . , *Rhymes For My Rags* . . . , and the undated *Cosmic Carols,* published when he was over eighty years of age and republished in *Later Collected Verse* after his death. In these books he maintains the pose of a poor old man whose books are not selling because his rhymes and rhythms are outmoded. There is still a substantial number of vignettes, notably two saucy Yukon ballads. . . . (pp. 186-87)

As evidence of continuing good humour, he was still indulging in "Lyrics for Levity" and "Derisive Ditties," which were exercises in irony spreading over into "Rhymes for Resignation" about Clemenceau, Mistinguette, Ernie Pyle, Einstein, Tom Paine, Dylan [Thomas], Monticelli, and Benjamin Franklin.

Inevitably, however, he felt impelled to write postscripts on life and rhyme. He had often described his attitude toward religion as agnosticism, or simply "reverence," in the absence of certainty. (pp. 189-90)

The "riddle of Reality," which was basic to his thinking about life and religion, had also been the key to his literary practice when he wrote vignettes, which were characterized by the dramatic interplay of favourable and unfavourable forces in human lives. He was not inclined to label much that he described as wholly good or wholly evil. The riddle of life and of lives demanded ironic treatment. This attitude is confirmed in a stanza introducing the valuable "unpublished" selections in *Later Collected Verse:*

I don't believe in all I write,
  But seek to give a point of view;
Am I unreasonable? Quite!
  I'm ready to agree with you . . .
Times, though opponents we deride,
  Let's try to see the other side.

(pp. 190-91)

Carl F. Klinck, in his *Robert Service: A Biography,* Dodd, Mead & Company, 1976, 199 p.

SOURCES FOR FURTHER STUDY

Atherton, Stanley S. "The Klondike Muse." *Canadian Literature* No. 47 (Winter 1971): 67-72.

> Discusses Service's attempts to create in his works a mythology about the Yukon. In Atherton's estimation, Service only partially succeeded at this goal because of his eclectic selection of Northern physical and climatic characteristics.

Bynner, Witter. "Poetry from the Trenches." *The Dial* LXI, No. 731 (14 December 1916): 531-32.

> Review of *Rhymes of a Red Cross Man*, noting both Service's indebtedness to Kipling and his ability to accurately depict life on the battlefield.

McCarthy, Clare. "The Poetry of Robert Service." *Contemporary Review* 234, No. 1360 (May 1979): 276-77.

Praises the *Collected Poems of Robert Service* and notes the range of expression reflected in Service's poetry.

Phelps, Arthur L. "Robert W. Service." In his *Canadian Writers,* pp. 28-35. Toronto: McClelland and Stewart, 1951.

Contends that Service's anti-intellectual stance and robust verbal technique were instrumental in creating a voice for the Canadian North and in contributing to the popularity of his verse.

Review of *The Spell of the Yukon and Other Verses,* by Robert W. Service. *The Sewanee Review* XVII, No. 3 (July 1909): 381-82.

Discusses Service's poetic style, remarking that his poetry deals too rawly with the harsh realities of life in the Yukon, though it shows considerable skill and vigor.

Untermeyer, Louis. "Our Living Laureates." *The Bookman,* New York LIV, No. 5 (January 1922): 481-84.

Sarcastically names Service and Edgar A. Guest poet laureates of North America, and offers tongue-in-cheek praise for *Ballads of a Bohemian.*

Anne Sexton

1928-1974

(Born Anne Gray Harvey) American poet, short story writer, dramatist, and author of children's books.

INTRODUCTION

Sexton was among the best-known of the often controversial Confessional poets, a group composed primarily of New England writers who rose to prominence during the 1950s and early 1960s. Like such fellow Confessionalists as Robert Lowell and Sylvia Plath, she wrote highly introspective verse that revealed intimate details of her emotional troubles, including the severe depression from which she suffered for most of her adult life and which led to her suicide. Characterized by vivid imagery and daring metaphors, Sexton's early work deals intensively with her psychic traumas and her attempts to overcome mental illness. While she began her career as a highly methodical poet who wrote within formal metrical and rhyme schemes and reworked her manuscripts through several drafts, Sexton composed her later poems in various experimental forms, often with little or no revision. In addition to focusing upon her emotional life, Sexton's later work includes frequent allusions to mythology, fairy tales, and Christian motifs, and explores such topics as romantic love, motherhood, and relationships between the sexes.

Sexton spent most of her life in the affluent, upper-middle-class suburbs of Boston. She married at age nineteen and attempted to settle into the role of housewife and mother. During her early twenties, however, Sexton began to experience bouts of depression that eventually led to hospitalization. After the birth of her second daughter in 1955, Sexton attempted suicide and was placed under the care of Dr. Martin Orne who encouraged her to write poems as a form of therapy. After her release, Sexton joined John Holmes's writing course at the Boston Center for Adult Education and later won a scholarship to the Antioch Writer's Conference where she studied under W. D. Snodgrass, whose confessional poem "Heart's Needle" she deeply admired and attempted to emulate. At Snodgrass's suggestion, Sexton also enrolled in Robert Lowell's graduate writing seminar at Boston University where she became friends with Sylvia Plath and George Starbuck, among others. Under the auspices of Snodgrass and Lowell, Sexton began writing extremely personal verse concerning her experiences as a mental patient. When she composed enough poems to consider compiling a book, however, Holmes discouraged her from publishing, expressing in a letter to Sexton his fear "that what looks like a brilliant beginning might turn out to be so self-centered and so narrowed a diary that it would be clinical only." Sexton responded to this evaluation by writing "For John Who Begs Me Not to Inquire Further," a poem that expresses the psychological motives underlying Confessionalism. She included this piece in her first collection, *To Bedlam and Part Way Back* (1960), which, along with ensuing volumes, rapidly gained her a reputation as an important new poet. During the 1960s, Sexton gave spirited public readings accompanied by the musical group Her Kind. She also wrote several highly regarded children's books with Maxine Kumin, her close friend and fellow poet. Yet despite her literary success, Sexton continually battled depression and psychosis. She repeatedly attempted suicide and was committed twice more to mental institutions by her family. In 1974, she ended her life by carbon monoxide poisoning.

Sexton's early belief that complete honesty and self-revelation were essential to her creative work is strongly reflected in *To Bedlam and Part Way Back.* "You, Dr. Martin," for instance, candidly portrays her desolate existence in a psychiatric ward. In "The Double Image," one of her most acclaimed works, Sexton describes the conflict between her desire to be a loving and devoted mother and daughter and her withdrawal into psychosis. "Elizabeth Gone" and "Some Foreign Letters" concern the death of her beloved Great-Aunt Anna, a figure who reappears in numerous works by Sexton, including "The Nana-Hex" and *Mercy Street.* Other poems, while thematically and tonally impersonal, focus on the emotional states of fictional narrators. More than any of her later writings, the poems in *To Bedlam and Part Way Back* conform to traditional structural patterns. In her second collection, *All My Pretty Ones* (1962), Sexton began to experiment with a less formal, more intuitive and spontaneous approach to composition. In many of these poems, particularly the title piece, Sexton confronts her ambivalent feelings toward her parents and expresses grief over their deaths. Sexton's penchant for vivid imagery is evident in "Letter Written on a Ferry While Crossing Long Island Sound," in which a surrealistic vision of floating nuns represents the narrator's yearning for a heavenly blessing and "In the Deep Museum," a vision of Christ's martyrdom in which He is eaten alive by rats.

Sexton received the Pulitzer Prize in poetry for her third collection, *Live or Die* (1966), which many critics consider her finest volume. While her earlier poems are mostly cathartic outpourings of emotion, Sexton's pieces in *Live or Die* evince a more controlled, analytical approach to the Confessional style as she contemplates possible causes for her psychological anguish. In "Those Times . . . " and "Imitations of Drowning," for example, she related some of the traumatic incidents from her childhood. The major theme of this collection involves the choice that Sexton must make between life, with its attendant joys and miseries, and death, through suicide. The final poem in the collection, "Live," affirms her decision to continue living.

Most commentators regard *Love Poems* (1969) and *Transformations* (1971) as the last accomplished collections of Sexton's career. While the pieces in *Love Poems* chronicle an extramarital love affair, *Transformations* develops a sardonic pastiche of the fairy tales of the Brothers Grimm. In the latter volume, Sexton abandons Confessionalism and adopts the persona of a middle-aged witch who perverts the legends of such archetypal heroines as Rapunzel and Cinderella. Her version of Rapunzel, for instance, involves a love triangle between Rapunzel, the witch who holds her captive, and the prince who rescues her. In "Cinderella," Sexton cynically compares the well-known fairy tale to equally unlikely stories in which the desires of the downtrodden are miraculously gratified.

In *The Book of Folly* (1972), Sexton returned to the Confessional mode, reiterating themes of trauma, anguish, and alienation. Her occasional interest in religious symbolism resurfaces in "The Jesus Papers," a nine-poem sequence depicting the life of Christ through images of birth, death, and sacrifice. The predominate theme in her final collections, *The Death Notebooks* (1974) and *The Awful Rowing Toward God* (1975), is the desire for salvation through a transcendent mystical experience. "The Death Baby," a sequence from *The Death Notebooks,* makes use of the image of the title figure to express a complex range of associations, including Sexton's hunger for spiritual fulfillment. The infant also represents her obsession with mortality, a force that impels her toward self-destruction but which paradoxically provides the chief inspiration for creative endeavors that give meaning to her life. In the poems that conclude *The Awful Rowing Toward God,* Sexton envisions a journey by boat to confront her Creator; the last poem in the sequence, "The Rowing Endeth," describes the climax of her spiritual quest, as God challenges her to a poker game and draws the winning hand. Several additional volumes of Sexton's writings have been issued posthumously, some edited by her daughter, Linda Gray Sexton. *45 Mercy Street* (1976) contains "The Divorce Papers," written shortly before Sexton's death, in which she describes her divorce and the failed romances that followed. The title sequence in *Words for Dr. Y* (1978), a collection of poems and short stories, recounts in verse a series of sessions with her psychotherapist.

When Sexton's poems first appeared, a critical debate ensued that continues to dominate evaluations of her work. While several commentators echoed John Holmes's condemnation of them as solipsistic, others perceived in them an honesty and technical control that effectively transcend her narrow subject matter. Comparing her style to that of other Confessionalists, J. D. McClatchy observed: "More than the others, Sexton resisted the temptations to dodge or distort, and the continuity and strength of her achievement remain the primary witness to the ability of confessional art to render a life into poems with all the intimacy and complexity of feeling and response with which that life has been endured." Although generally regarding her work as uneven, critics have increasingly lauded her stylistic innovations and unflinching examination of formerly taboo subjects, including female sexuality and mental illness, as abiding aspects of her art. According to Max-

ine Kumin, Sexton "delineated the problematic position of women—the neurotic reality of the time—though she was not able to cope in her own life with the personal trouble it created. If it is true that she attracted the worshipful attention of a cult group pruriently interested in her suicidal impulses, her psychotic breakdowns, her frequent hospitalizations, it must equally be acknowledged that her very frankness succored many who clung to her poems as to the Holy Grail. Time will sort out the dross among these poems and burnish the gold. Anne Sexton has earned her place in the canon."

(For further information about Sexton's life and works, see *Contemporary Authors*, Vols. 1-4, 53-56 [obituary]; *Contemporary Authors New Revision Series*, Vol. 3; *Contemporary Authors Bibliographical Series*, Vol. 2; *Contemporary Literary Criticism*, Vols. 2, 4, 6, 8, 10, 15, 53; *Dictionary of Literary Biography*, Vol. 5: *American Poets Since World War II; Concise Dictionary of Literary Biography, 1941-1968; Poetry Criticism*, Vol. 2; and *Something about the Author*, Vol. 10.)

CRITICAL COMMENTARY

JAMES DICKEY

(essay date 1961)

[Dickey is an American novelist and critic. In the following excerpt from his review of *To Bedlam and Part Way Back*, he voices his disapproval of Sexton's personal themes.]

[The poems of *To Bedlam and Part Way Back*] so obviously come out of deep, painful sections of the author's life that one's literary opinions scarcely seem to matter; one feels tempted to drop them furtively into the nearest ashcan, rather than be caught with them in the presence of so much naked suffering. The experiences she recounts are among the most harrowing that human beings can undergo: those of madness and near-madness, of the pathetic, well-meaning, necessarily tentative and perilous attempts at cure, and of the patient's slow coming back into the human associations and responsibilities which the old, previous self still demands. In addition to being an extremely painful subject, this is perhaps a major one for poetry, with a sickeningly frightening appropriateness to our time. But I am afraid that in my opinion the poems fail to do their subject the kind of justice which I should like to see done. Perhaps no poems could. Yet I am sure that Mrs. Sexton herself could come closer than she does

here, did she not make entirely unnecessary concessions to the conventions of her literary generation and the one just before it. One can gather much of her tone and procedure from quotations like "You, Doctor Martin, walk / from breakfast to madness," and "All day we watched the gulls / striking the top of the sky / and riding the blown roller coaster." "Riding the blown roller coaster" is a kind of writing I dislike to such an extent that I feel, perhaps irrationally, that everyone else including Mrs. Sexton ought to dislike it, too, for its easy, A-student, superficially-exact "differentness" and its straining to make contrivance and artificiality appear natural. One would hope that a writer of Mrs. Sexton's seriousness, and with her terrible story to tell, would avoid this kind of thing at any price. Yet a large part of her book is composed of such figures. In the end, one comes to the conclusion that if there were some way to relieve these poems of the obvious effort of trying to be poems, something very good would emerge. I think they would make far better short stories, and probably in Mrs. Sexton's hands, too, than they do poems. As they are, they lack concentration, and above all the profound, individual linguistic suggestibility and accuracy that poems must have to be good. As D. H. Lawrence once remarked in another connection, they don't "say the real say". But Mrs. Sexton's candor,

---

Principal Works

To Bedlam and Part Way Back (poetry) 1960

All My Pretty Ones (poetry) 1962

*Selected Poems (poetry) 1964

Live or Die (poetry) 1966

Love Poems (poetry) 1969

Transformations (poetry) 1971

The Book of Folly (poetry) 1972

The Death Notebooks (poetry) 1974

The Awful Rowing Toward God (poetry) 1975

45 Mercy Street (poetry) 1976

Anne Sexton: A Self-Portrait in Letters (letters) 1978

Words for Dr. Y (poetry) 1978

The Complete Poems (poetry) 1981

*Contains poems from To Bedlam and Part Way Back
and All My Pretty Ones.

---

her courage, and her story are worth anyone's three dollars. (pp. 318-19)

James Dickey, in a review of "To Bedlam and Part Way Back," in *Poetry,* Vol. XCVII, No. 5, February, 1961, pp. 318-19.

J. D. MCCLATCHY

(essay date 1975)

[The poetry editor for the *Yale Review,* McClatchy is the author of the verse collections *Scenes from Another Life* (1981) and *Stars Principal* (1986). In the following excerpt, he charts the evolution of Sexton's poetic voice.]

[Anne Sexton] has described herself as "a primitive," yet is master of intricate formal techniques. Her voice has steadily evolved and varied and, at times, sought to escape speaking of the self, but her strongest poems consistently return to her narrow thematic range and the open voice of familiar feelings. . . . For the source of her first fame is still the focus of her work: she is the most persistent and daring of the confessionalists. Her peers have their covers: Lowell's allusiveness, Snodgrass's lyricism, Berryman's dazzle, Plath's expressionism. More than the others, Sexton has resisted the temptations to dodge or distort, and the continuity and strength of her achievement remain the primary witness to the ability of confessional art to render a life into poems with all the intimacy and complexity of

feeling and response with which that life has been endured.

Endurance has always been her concern: why must we? how can we? why we must, how we do: "to endure, / somehow to endure." It is a theme which re-enacts not only the continuing source of her poetry but its original impulse as well. (pp. 1-2)

Sexton's business with words—the ordering of statement and instinct—is the adjustment of their demands to her experience: in her figure, to made a tree out of used furniture. Though her attitudes towards form have evolved, from the beginning there has been an uneasy ambivalence: the poet insisting on control, the person pleading "Take out rules and leave the instant," as she says in one interview. Her solution has been to use the metaphor of deceit, but to reverse it into a very personally inflected version of form. . . . Though her early work occasionally forces itself with inversions and stolid High Style, her concern for the precisions of voice and pace reveal her care in indulging a lyric impulse only to heighten the dramatic. . . . For the poet, form functions to articulate the details and thrust of her actual experience, while for the reader it guides his dramatic involvement in the recreation: both convictions converging on authenticity, on realization. And so the voice is kept conversational, understated by plain-speech slang or homely detail—its imagery drawn from the same sources it counterpoints, its force centered in the pressure of events it contours, the states of mind it maps. This is clearly the case with the poems of madness in the first section of *To Bedlam and Part Way Back.* (pp. 4-5)

[The confessions in *All My Pretty Ones*] converge towards the present, and the chronicle begins to include more immediate and intimate events. Previously worked aspects of and approaches to her experience are here retried: **"The Operation"** clearly derives from **"The Double Image," "The House"** expands **"Some Foreign Letters."** The greater assurance of her verse likewise allows Sexton to experiment successfully with open forms and new voices. (pp. 13-14)

The oneiric organization of **"The House"** looks forward to the important changes that her next, and decisive, book *Live or Die* (1966) announces. With its longer poems in open forms which more subtly accommodate a greater range of experience, and with a voice pitched higher to intensify that experience, *Live or Die* represents not a departure from her earlier strengths but the breakthrough into her distinctive style. Perhaps the most immediate aspect of that style is its use of imagery. . . . This is the sort of imagery that will be exploited even more extremely in later books where "like" becomes the most frequently encountered word. It is a technique that risks arbitrary excesses and embarrassing crudities, that at its best can seem but a slangy American equivalent of Apollinaire's surrealism. . . . Sexton's use of images is primarily psychotropic—used less for literary effect than as a means to pry deeper into her psychic history, to float her findings and model her experience. . . . Sexton's commitment to honest realization is thus only carried to a deeper level, the final source of memory. And if Rimbaud was right to demand of such associative poetry a *"dérèglement de tous les sens,"* it can be seen as Sexton's necessary road of excess through her experiences of madness and the disorientation of her past so that her metaphors are a method not to display similarities but to discover identities. (pp. 17-18)

The survival achieved, the rebirth delivered, is then praised in *Love Poems* (1969), in many ways her weakest collection since most of it is sustained by language alone. Its self-celebration tends either to avoid or invent the experience behind it, or revolves on minimal events. . . . Secure in her use of free verse, Sexton crafts these poems with equivalents: litanies of images which are more often additional than accumulative. (p. 22)

The masks she wears in *Love Poems* do not hide Sexton's confessional impulse, they avoid it. Her motive may well have been to search out new voices. Certainly this is the case with her next work, *Transformations* (1971). . . . Like *Love Poems,* it seems content to present women in their roles, from princess to witch, with the poet merely presiding as "Dame Sexton." . . . [Her] "transformations" [of various tales] exaggerate and so distort the originals to create contemporary camp. And indeed the tales are blown up like pop-art posters by means of an irreverently zippy style, slangy allusions, and a strongly Freudian slant to her stories. But what draws *Transformations* into this discussion is Sexton's inability to keep her characteristic concerns from seeping into what would otherwise seem her most distanced work. (pp. 22-3)

[The] psychoanalytical uses of the word "transformations" bear on Sexton's work. It can refer both to the variations of the same thematic material represented in a patient's dreams or experience, and to the process by which unconscious material is brought to consciousness. So too Sexton's poems are variations on themes familiar from her earlier work. . ., transformed into fantasies or dreams discovered in the Grimm tales which are anyone's first "literature" and become bound up with the child's psyche. (p. 24)

[The] most significant and successful poem in *The Death Notebooks* is "Hurry Up Please It's Time," a sort of long, hallucinatory diary-entry: "Today is November 14th, 1972. / I live in Weston, Mass., Middlesex County, / U.S.A., and it rains steadily / in the pond like white puppy eyes." The style is pure pastiche, mixing dialect and dialogue, nursery rhymes and New Testament, references ranging from Goethe to Thurber, attitudes veering between arrogance and abasement. At

times she is "Anne," at times "Ms. Dog"—becoming her own mock-God. She can sneer at herself ("Middle-class lady, / you make me smile"), or shiver at what "my heart, that witness" remembers. The recaptured spots of time—say, a quiet summer interlude with her husband and friends—are run into projected blotches spread towards the death to come. And though its expansive free-form dilutes all but its cumulative force, the poem is an advance on the way **"The Death of the Fathers"** had whispered its confessions. It may even prefigure the manner which confessional poetry generally may later assume. But whatever it may predict, it remains as evidence of Sexton's steady boldness, her readiness to risk new experiments in verse to record renewed perceptions of her experience in life. . . . Her courage in coming true has not only made Sexton one of the most distinctive voices in this generation's poetry, but has revealed in its art and its honesty a life in which we can discover our own. (p. 33)

J. D. McClatchy, "Anne Sexton: Somehow to Endure," in *The Centennial Review,* Vol. XIX, No. 2, Spring, 1975, pp. 1-36.

MAXINE KUMIN
(essay date 1981)

[Kumin is an accomplished poet and novelist whose works probe the human relationship to nature and celebrate the redemptive qualities of the natural world. While her verse has often been compared to that of Sexton, who was a close friend and collaborator, Kumin focuses predominately on life-affirming experiences rather than personal anguish. In the following excerpt from her introduction to Sexton's *The Complete Poems,* she assesses Sexton's contribution to contemporary poetry.]

It seems presumptuous, only seven years after her death, to talk about Anne Sexton's place in the history of poetry. We must first acknowledge the appearance in the twentieth century of women writing poetry that confronts the issues of gender, social role, and female life and lives viewed subjectively from the female perspective. The earlier world view of the poet as "the masculine chief of state in charge of dispensing universal spiritual truths" (Diane Middlebrook, *The World Into Words*) has eroded since World War II, as have earlier notions about the existence of universal truths themselves. Freed by that cataclysm from their clichéd roles as goddesses of hearth and bedroom, women began to write openly out of their own experiences. Before there was a Women's Movement, the underground river was already flowing, carrying such diverse cargoes as the poems of Bogan, Levertov, Rukeyser, Swenson, Plath, Rich, and Sexton.

The stuff of Anne's life, mercilessly dissected, is here in the poems. Of all the confessional poets, none has had quite Sexton's "courage to make a clean breast of it." Nor has any displayed quite her brilliance, her verve, her headlong metaphoric leaps. As with any body of work, some of the later poems display only ragged, intermittent control, as compared to **"The Double Image," "The Operation,"** and **"Some Foreign Letters,"** to choose three arbitrary examples. The later work takes more chances, crosses more boundaries between the rational and the surreal; and time after time it evokes in the reader that sought-after shiver of recognition.

Women poets in particular owe a debt to Anne Sexton, who broke new ground, shattered taboos, and endured a barrage of attacks along the way because of the flamboyance of her subject matter, which, twenty years later, seems far less daring. She wrote openly about menstruation, abortion, masturbation, incest, adultery, and drug addiction at a time when the proprieties embraced none of these as proper topics for poetry. Today, the remonstrances seem almost quaint. Anne delineated the problematic position of women— the neurotic reality of the time—though she was not able to cope in her own life with the personal trouble it created. If it is true that she attracted the worshipful attention of a cult group pruriently interested in her suicidal impulses, her psychotic breakdowns, her frequent hospitalizations, it must equally be acknowledged that her very frankness succored many who clung to her poems as to the Holy Grail. Time will sort out the dross among these poems and burnish the gold. Anne Sexton has earned her place in the canon. (pp. xxxiii-xxxiv)

Maxine Kumin, "How It Was: Maxine Kumin on Anne Sexton," in *The Complete Poems* by Anne Sexton, Houghton Mifflin Company, 1981, pp. xix-xxxiv.

GREG JOHNSON
(essay date 1984)

[In the essay excerpted below, Johnson asserts that Sexton's poetry, as a record of her own struggle toward wholeness, possesses a special relevance in an increasingly chaotic, disjointed society.]

At the heart of Anne Sexton's poetry is a search for identity, and her well-known infatuation with death— the cause of her rather notorious fame, and the apparent reason her work is often dismissed as beneath seri-

ous consideration—has little to do with this search; in her best work, in fact, it is most often an annoying irrelevancy, however potent it seems in its occasional command of the poet's psyche. Quite simply, Sexton's poetry is a poetry of life, and if her work is "confessional" at times, or even most of the time, this does not mean that the poet's confessions (the word itself is misleading) necessarily describe experiences ridden with guilt or pain. This is where Sexton's poetry diverges so dramatically from that of Sylvia Plath, of whom she is frequently seen as a kind of epigonic follower. Plath mythologizes death with great power and succinctness, and places herself at the center of a myth whose message is "blackness—blackness and silence"; her vision is brutally nihilistic, and she embraces it willingly. Plath's struggle is that of the mythmaker—primarily artistic rather than personal, since the personal self is mercilessly pared away in her poetry (as are all other selves) in deference to the controlling myth. Anne Sexton, on the other hand, speaks longingly and lovingly of a world of health, of childlike wholeness—a world toward which she struggles valiantly and against insuperable odds. To understand her poetry as a record of this struggle, and as a testament to its value and importance, is to appreciate its special relevance to the contemporary world, a world of increasing disjunction between personal and social selves and one whose chaotic, literally "maddening" effect on the individual mind Anne Sexton manages to convey with that blend of craft and vulnerability that is her special magic.

Unlike Plath, and certainly unlike Robert Lowell—with whom her name is also frequently and pointlessly linked—Sexton is a Primitive, an extraordinarily intense artist who confronts her experience with unsettling directness, largely innocent of "tradition" and privately developing an idiom exactly suited to that experience. As Louis Simpson remarked after the publication of her first book, "This then is a phenomenon . . . to remind us, when we have forgotten in the weariness of literature, that poetry can happen." The reader's sense of the direct and seemingly spontaneous quality of Sexton's earliest volumes—*To Bedlam and Part Way Back* (1960), *All My Pretty Ones* (1962) and *Live or Die* (1966)—can partially be explained by noting that she first began writing poetry, at the age of twenty-eight, as a form of personal therapy, a way of formalizing past traumas and of coping with an increasing sense of disorientation in her conventional role of suburban wife and mother. Her emotional instability, including her suicidal impulses, contributed to the immediacy, rawness and power of much of the poetry. This kind of therapy no doubt helped the poet in her personal life, but what is heroic in Sexton's case, and particularly relevant to her readers, is the earnestness and scrupulosity with which she mastered her craft, developed her highly original voice, and set about the task of communicating her experience to others. That Anne Sexton herself later succumbed to the "weariness of literature"—her later work, on the whole, is distinctly inferior to her early poetry, and verges at times on self-parody—and finally to her own destructive impulses, does not diminish the value and irresistible power of her finest achievements, which speak to us in a voice by turns inspired and beleaguered, joyful and aggrieved, lost in the confusions of self but found, ultimately, in her masterful articulation of her experience as a whole, a complex experience which serves as a painfully truthful mirror of the age.

Sexton's first two volumes have much in common, both in their multi-faceted handling of the identity theme and in their adherence to rather strict poetic forms. In both there is a constructive relationship between the deeply painful, inchoate materials—experiences in a mental institution, the loss of the poet's parents, and unceasing struggle to define her own selfhood—and the restraining, masterful form of the poems themselves. There is little sense that the poet is arbitrarily forcing her experiences into rigid, inappropriate shapes, primarily because she convinces us that she has pierced to the core of those experiences to discover shapes inherent in them; the formal, measured quality of the verse not only indicates the poet's necessary caution in dealing with her turbulent materials, but also establishes a crucial distance from which she may safely view her continuing struggle and present it to her readers in palatable form. Yet the controlled, meditative voice of these early poems is frequently mingled with an openly vulnerable, "confessional" voice, one which conveys genuine, childlike experiences of pain and terror. The poems are neither songs of innocence nor experience, but continually oscillate between conflicting states of mind, admitting continued disorientation while simultaneously creating an impressive poetic order.

An important difference between the first two books should be recognized, however *To Bedlam and Part Way Back* comprises an ordering of a specific, urgent experience—the descent into madness and a partial return—while *All My Pretty Ones* broadens from this painful but rich experience to consider more general themes of loss (especially the loss of parents) and upon an explicit need to define the poet's self in terms of the world. Although Sexton's books describe an ongoing personal development and flow naturally one into the other, each of the early volumes has a distinct identity and merits separate discussion. As Geoffrey Hartman has noted, *To Bedlam and Part Way Back* is not merely a collection of poems but "truly a *book*," and there is ample evidence that Sexton organized the volume with meticulous care. The shorter lyrics in Part One deal with a cluster of obsessive themes, all related to the poet's search for identity, while the pair of long,

meditative poems in Part Two achieve a tentative but emotionally satisfying resolution. (pp. 2-3)

By far the majority of poems in *To Bedlam and Part Way Back* explore the poet's identity in terms of other women. There are poems about being buried alive ("The Moss of His Skin"), paralysis within a marriage and its "pantomime of love" ("The Farmer's Wife"), the literal paralysis of the goddess Diana, changed forever to a laurel tree and noting in despair that "blood moves still in my bark bound veins" ("Where I Live in This Honorable House of the Laurel Tree"). In one of the most moving of these poems, "Unknown Girl in the Maternity Ward," Sexton dramatizes the relationship between a mother and her daughter with a typical mingling of tenderness and a hopeless sense of estrangement. The mother can only consider her child a "fragile visitor," her "funny kin," and the reason is the mother's lack of her own selfhood, since she is, after all, "unknown". (p. 4)

In seeking to define her own identity through poetic fictions about other women, and about relationships between women, Sexton merely sees her own identity as inferior and finds that genuine relationship is unavailable. Later volumes will explore the causes behind her failure to "connect" meaningfully with others, but in *To Bedlam and Part Way Back,* her failure leads directly into madness. Although she pictured herself, wryly, as "a secret beatnik hiding in the suburbs in a square house on a dull street," any pride she might have taken in her role as poet seems cancelled by this image of herself as a misfit, someone who did not live in that "good world" she envied her great aunt and could not create for herself. One senses that Anne Sexton felt herself forced into poetry, that her inability to find satisfaction in a conventional role made the pose of a "secret beatnik," a rebel—in the sense that both poetry and madness are forms of rebellion—her only means of survival. Unlike Emily Dickinson, who felt that "Much Madness is divinest Sense" and whose extreme self-sufficiency (however "mad" it might have appeared to her Amherst contemporaries) was the sign of a fully realized identity, Sexton desperately needed the approval of others: "I want everyone to hold up large signs saying YOU'RE A GOOD GIRL." Her belief that she had failed to be "good," and that she had no way of finding a "good world," led to a madness that was not divinest sense but hellish chaos, a threatened disintegration of selfhood.

This linking of madness with evil, with the inability to be "good," recurs in Sexton's poems dealing with her experiences in mental institutions. She continues to lament her sense of loss and disorientation: "They lock me in this chair at eight a.m. / and there are no signs to tell the way" ("Music Swims Back to Me"). In the first stanza of this poem she pictures herself as an orphan seeking the way home. . . . These lines, like

Ophelia's mad speeches, blend irreality and the absence of sequential thought with a terrifying, sane intuition; immersed in a surreal, abandoned world, the speaker nonetheless understands her need to escape, to find "sign posts" back toward health.

Does Sexton imagine any way out of this impasse, any way to escape the debilitating terrors of a consciousness plagued by a conviction of its own evil? One possibility is to replace self-loathing with an open acceptance of evil—even admitting the likelihood that she is "not a woman." What is remarkable, however, is not this admission itself but the lively, almost gleeful tone in which it is uttered:

> I have gone out, a possessed witch,
> haunting the black air, braver at night;
> dreaming of evil, I have done my hitch
> over the plain houses, light by light:
> lonely thing, twelve-fingered, out of mind.
> A woman like that is not a woman, quite.
> I have been her kind.

("Her Kind")

"A woman like that is misunderstood," Sexton adds wryly, but the poem is a serious attempt to understand such a woman—her sense of estrangement, her impulse toward death—by internalizing evil and giving it a voice: a chortling, self-satisfied, altogether amiable voice which suggests that "evil" is perhaps the wrong word after all. Sexton's witch, waving her "nude arms at villages going by," becomes something of value to the community, performing the function Kurt Vonnegut has called the "domestication of terror." Unlike Plath's madwoman in "Lady Lazarus"—a woman at the service of a private, unyielding anger, a red-haired demon whose revenge is to "eat men like air"— Sexton's witch is essentially harmless. Although she remains vulnerable—"A woman like that is not afraid to die"—she rejects anger in favor of humor, flamboyance, self-mockery. She is a kind of perverse entertainer, and if she seems cast in the role of a martyr, embracing madness in order to domesticate it for the rest of the community—making it seem less threatening, perhaps even enjoyable—it is nevertheless a martyrdom which this aspect of Sexton accepts with a peculiar zest.

Poems like **"Her Kind"** and **"Music Swims Back to Me"** help create the famous, fatally glamorous mask of Anne Sexton—part lovable witch, part helpless madwoman—for which she became famous, and which is often discussed as if it were the only self present in Sexton's poetry. Denise Levertov, in her well-intentioned, somewhat patronizing remarks on Sexton's suicide, suggested that Sexton was "too intensely troubled to be fully aware of her influence or to take on its responsibility. Therefore it seems to me that we who are alive must make clear, as she could not, the distinction between creativity and self-destruction." But Sexton did take on a personal responsibility for the

interest her work aroused—she sent cheerful, supportive letters, for instance, to the countless victims of mental illness who wrote to her—and much of her poetry, from the first volume onward, expresses anguish over her destructive impulses, with an awareness that they are threatening to her poetry as well as to her personal well-being.

Part Two of *To Bedlam and Part Way Back* contains only three poems, but they are long, reflective works which attempt to take stock of the poet's progress, to state a rationale for her kind of poetry, and especially to acknowledge lifelong conflicts that have prevented a healthy development of self. These goals are directly addressed in the volume's longest and finest poem, **"The Double Image."** Here the poet gathers all her themes into a single autobiographical narration, seeking that "certain sense of order" through a careful, measured recounting of her seemingly chaotic and random experiences. Like many of Sexton's more somber, reflective poems, **"The Double Image"** is addressed to her daughter, establishing the crucial dynamic between the poet's desire for an affectionate, healthly relationship with the child, and her yearning toward the madness that threatens to separate them. The poem's tender, carefully modulated voice is firmly aligned on the side of health, but the poet remains aware of her continued vulnerability. She sees her madness as an unknown, demonic force, an "ugly angel" whose voice enchants the poet—much like the "disquieting muses" in Plath's analogous narrative. After giving way to madness and losing her child, Sexton has returned as a "partly mended thing," still unable to assume a healthy identity. . . . The poem's title refers to Sexton's mother and daughter, seen as potent forces pulling her simultaneously in two directions. Sexton's mother (certainly a cold, uncaring figure in this poem) represents "the stony head of death," while the final lines speak of the daughter's inestimable value for the poet's present self, not only as a symbol of the life-force but as a hopeful foreshadowing of her own developing selfhood. . . . (pp. 4-6)

In Sexton's second volume, *All My Pretty Ones* (1962), she broadens her scope from consideration of the specific, urgent experience of madness to consider more universally comprehensible forms of loss. Sexton's parents died in 1959, and though she insisted at the time that she would not write poems about them, she later changed her mind. The first part of this volume contains **"The Truth the Dead Know," "All My Pretty Ones"** and **"Lament,"** poems dealing with her parents' deaths and among the finest she ever wrote. Not surprisingly, the ostensible theme of bereavement is mingled with an examination of the poet's continuing struggle toward identity. In that strange, bitter elegy, **"The Truth the Dead Know,"** Sexton seems to eschew the common rituals of mourning: "Gone, I say and walk from church, / refusing the stiff procession to the grave"; she prefers, instead, to "cultivate myself" and to avoid such a powerful intimation of mortality as the death of both parents within a few months. The poem ends, however, by emphasizing not her own refusals but those of the dead, and into her voice creeps something like envy. . . . (p. 7)

A far gentler, more nostalgic poem like **"Young"** recalls the poet's innocence as a "lonely kid" whose relationship to her mother was not yet perceived as a "funnel"; and in **"Old Dwarf Heart"** she creates a separate, mythical self—again resembling Plath's disquieting muses—who insists upon "the decay we're made of": "When I lie down to love, old dwarf heart shakes her head." Sexton can never escape this destructive self ("Where I go, she goes"), which is perceived as having originated in a vicious Oedipal "tangle," but the loss of her parents does give her a kind of grim new beginning, and the rest of the volume explores various avenues of escape.

In her attempt to counter the truth the dead know with a gentler, more humanizing truth, Sexton seeks out two major sources of comfort: religious belief and domestic love. Her early cluster of religious poems, forming Part Two of *All My Pretty Ones*, initiates a theme that will recur throughout her work—especially

Sexton with her husband Kayo and daughters, Joy (left) and Linda, in 1957.

in her posthumous volume, *The Awful Rowing Toward God* (1975)—but she seemed to find little solace in her religious ponderings; at times, in fact, they only increase her sense of guilt. In **"With Mercy for the Greedy,"** addressed to a Catholic friend who tried to convert the poet, Sexton says with childlike sincerity: "I detest my sins and I try to believe / in the Cross. I touch its tender hips, its dark jawed face, / its solid neck, its brown sleep." Unlike Emily Dickinson, who saw herself locked in a battle of wills with God the Father, a Puritan Nobodaddy who threatened her own sense of self, Sexton was drawn toward the image of a gentle, redemptive Christ, a God who was palpably human. But she concludes, ruefully, "Need is not quite belief," and explains, with typical Sexton wryness, "I was born doing reference work in sin . . . " In Part Three, which consists of a single poem, **"The Fortress,"** Sexton insists that the love between herself and her daughter has greater redemptive power than any religious belief. The poet has a sense of her own value, however fleeting, in her protectiveness toward her daughter: "What ark / can I fill for you when the world goes wild?" Although she knows that "Life is not in my hands" and cannot promise that her daughter will find happiness, the poem emphasizes their tender domestic alliance, the "fortress" their togetherness forms against the "bombs" of experience.

In one of the volume's most impressive poems, **"Letter Written on a Ferry While Crossing Long Island Sound,"** Sexton makes an ordinary boat ride into the occasion of an optimistic, even transcendent spiritual vision. (p. 8)

With two accomplished volumes behind her, with a blossoming career and innumerable devoted readers, she summoned the courage to bluntly question the value of living—to decide whether, in fact, the pain of life does not outweigh its rewards. In **"The Black Art"** she insisted: "A woman who writes feels too much, / those trances and portents!" Her decision to explore fully those excessive feelings, to relate her mysterious "trances and portents" to her central concerns of identity, poetry and survival, helped her toward *Live or Die* (1966), winner of a Pulitzer Prize and the finest achievement of her career. The volume's title represents an ultimatum; the poems themselves, arranged in chronological order and reading, as Sexton herself noted, like a "fever chart," show the poet moving toward a stark confrontation with her suicidal impulses and with her "portent" that life as a whole—not only for her, but perhaps for everyone—is simply not worthwhile. And yet, as one astute reviewer, Thomas P. McDonnell, noted at the time *Live or Die* was first published, Sexton gives us more than "impulses": "(this) is not a poetry of spasmodic revelation or of occasional incident transformed from similitude to artifact: in its continuing wholeness one perceives the suggestion of a journey." It was a journey, as *Live or Die* makes clear, upon whose outcome rested her life itself, and one she approaches with great courage and her developed artistic powers.

Carl Jung, discussing the obstacles to personal growth, notes that venturing into "obscurity and darkness" is absolutely essential in the quest for a new stage of development, a higher individuation of self. For Anne Sexton, there were two kinds of "darkness"—her madness, which represented personal defeat; and that agonizing uncertainty about her life and her identity which could only be eased through poetry and whose resolution—even if temporary—could represent significant progress toward mental stability and a secure sense of self. In *Live or Die,* Sexton has greatly matured as woman and as poet: she does not glorify madness, setting herself apart from the rest of humanity, but rather perceives it as an ignoble escape and, most of all, as a colossal waste of time. The most fearsome "obscurity and darkness," Jung suggests, lies in a sane, ego-centered approach toward personal problems, not in a surrender to the chaotic promptings of the id. In her third volume Sexton recognizes this truth, and the recognition helps produce some of her finest poetry. (pp. 9-10)

In **"Wanting to Die,"** Sexton notes that her own body, her essential physical self, is only a "bad prison" that should be emptied of breath, of life. Through poetry she sought liberation from this cruel and unnecessary prison, a liberation that could come only through a compassionate acceptance of her own flawed but redeemable self. Thus her emphasis in *Live or Die* is not upon "confession," with its implication of guilt, but upon compassion for herself and for all those who have influenced her personal existence. Seeking out the origin of her illness in childhood traumas and inadequate relationships with her parents, she is not interested in assigning blame but in bringing to light the dismal facts themselves; there is a new, strong impulse to face past realities and to assess their impact on the present. If this produced only a partial liberation, at least it represented an *earned* freedom that could directly affect the poet's life—acting as a form of therapy—and intensify the honesty of her art as well. (p. 11)

After *Live or Die,* Sexton's personal evolution began to seem increasingly frenetic and directionless. In her later volumes she assumes various effective guises—the witty lover of *Love Poems* (1969), the ribald folklorist of *Transformations* (1971), the religious seeker of *The Awful Rowing Toward God* (1975)—but never again does she achieve the immediacy and fullness of *Live or Die,* a book that shows her largest, most personal issue examined with her utmost energy and clarity. In a sense, her later books are elaborate footnotes to that volume, developing ancillary themes and exploring areas of existence which become important

once Sexton has made her crucial decision to live. And, as many critics have noted, she began to abandon the careful craftsmanship so evident in the early volumes, producing a large number of poems but letting their quality suffer a noticeable decline. Increasingly uncertain about the direction of her career, Sexton began to rely on the familiar, melodramatic voice of her earlier work, frequently repeating herself and no longer seeming able, or willing, to hone that voice through a rigorous attention to form, or to deepen its implications through fresh or surprising insights. As an artist, in short, she seems to stop growing. As a result, the American literary myth that a writer is only as good as her last book has been extremely damaging to Sexton, as expressed in the form of harsh or dismissive reviews of her last volumes. The recently issued collected edition of her work, however, should force readers to take another look, and especially to rediscover the value of Sexton's important earlier work.

In a letter written a few weeks before her death, Sexton remarks upon the famous closing poem of *Live or Die:*

> I do not know how I feel about such an old poem as **"Live"** in *Live or Die.* The poems stand for the moment they are written and make no promises to the future events and consciousness and raising of the unconscious as happens as one goes forward and does not look backward for an answer in an old poem.

A typically breathless, headlong statement, one which contains—with the advantage of hindsight, we can see it easily—a veiled warning, as well as a surprisingly harsh contempt of "old poems" representing experiences that are past, dead, no longer available to the poet (and, it would seem, no longer interesting to her). On the surface, it also suggests an unwillingness to *learn* from experience, to assimilate past insights into the vulnerable present consciousness as talismanic reminders, if not as forms of positive moral instruction. But actually the statement is consistent with Sexton's poetry as a whole, and merely states once again the darker side of her belief: one cannot go backward, and the poet can "make no promises" that artistic resolutions can remain valid beyond the experience of a particular poem. "Experiment escorts us last," as Emily Dickinson wrote, and Sexton shared this frightening awareness of the uncertain, friable nature of personal evolution, of the pitfalls lying in wait at every turn of experience. What remains for us, after her death, is to admire her spirit in facing that experience, to rejoice in her momentary triumphs and to recognize, in the poems themselves, her ultimate survival. (pp. 12-13)

Greg Johnson, "The Achievement of Anne Sexton," in *The Hollins Critic,* Vol. XXI, No. 3, June, 1984, pp. 1-13.

DIANE MIDDLEBROOK

(essay date 1985)

[An American poet and educator, Middlebrook is the author of *Anne Sexton: A Biography* (1991). In the following excerpt, she traces the development of Sexton's career.]

When Anne Sexton's posthumous *Complete Poems* came out four years ago, poet Katha Pollitt summarized the negative judgment many critics arrived at in their reviews: "the sheer quantity of inferior work does tend to dull one's response to the gems. One puts down this enormous book with the nagging feeling that all along a slim volume of verse was trapped inside it." Contemporary poets tend to be assessed by the carat: prized for glitter, durability and for scale that permits resetting in an anthology. As Pollitt says, "the gems are there" in Sexton, too.

Yet the appearance of a complete poems also presents an opportunity to pose questions about a writer whose entire body of work is the necessary critical context. How are the gems related to surrounding poems? Is the un-gemlike work inferior as art, or does it represent different artistic goals? Sexton's method of writing, which she referred to as "milking the unconscious," often produced a loosely-structured poetry dense with simile, freaked with improbable associations. In a poem addressed to James Wright, Sexton herself acknowledged she knew the effect offended certain tastes: "There is too much food and no one left over / to eat up all the weird abundance" (**"The Black Art"**). Weird: uncanny, magical, unconventional. While some of Sexton's most admired poems work, like little machines, on well-oiled armatures of rhythm or rhyme (such as **"All My Pretty Ones," "The Starry Night," "Wanting to Die"**), others equally powerful depend on manic or despairing or ecstatic cascades of association (**"The Furies," "O Ye Tongues"**) that flow like an open spigot. The gems, or closed forms, tend to be early; the looser style, later. In this collection, the reader can watch Sexton evolve her second style as a way of exploring a changing relation to her subject matter.

Sexton's *Complete Poems* is a compilation of the eight books she saw into print, plus an edited collection of work left in manuscript at the time of her death. . . . The early poetry (*To Bedlam and Part Way Back,* 1960; *All My Pretty Ones,* 1962) holds up very well. But as this volume shows, Anne Sexton made bolder exploration of her lifelong subject—her experiences of madness—in later work, beginning with the

volume *Live or Die* (1966). Mining the realm of the unconscious as she had been taught by both psychotherapy and contemporary writing, after 1962 Sexton became increasingly preoccupied with the psychological and social consequences of inhabiting a female body.

Because Sexton's writing seems so personal she is often labeled a "confessional" poet and grouped (to her disadvantage) with poets such as Lowell, Berryman, Roethke, and Plath. But Sexton resisted the label "confessional"; she preferred to be regarded as a "storyteller." To emphasize that she considered the speaking "I" in her poetry as a literary rather than a real identity, Sexton invariably opened her public performances by reading the early poem **"Her Kind."** These are the first and last stanzas:

> I have gone out, a possessed witch,
> haunting the black air, braver at night;
> dreaming evil, I have done my hitch
> over the plain houses, light by light:
> lonely thing, twelve-fingered, out of mind.
> A woman like that is not a woman, quite.
> I have been her kind.
>
>   . . .
>
> I have ridden in your cart, driver,
> waved my nude arms at villages going by,
> learning the last bright routes, survivor
> where your flames still bite my thigh
> and my ribs crack where your wheels wind.
> A woman like that is not ashamed to die.
> I have been her kind.

No matter what poetry she had on an evening's agenda, Sexton offered this persona as a point of entry to her art. "I" in the poem is a disturbing, marginal female whose power is associated with disfigurement, sexuality, and magic. But at the end of each stanza, "I" is displaced from sufferer onto storyteller. With the lines "A woman like that . . . I have been her kind" Sexton conveys the terms on which she wishes to be understood: not victim, but witness and witch. (pp. 293-94)

Sexton's *Complete Poems* yields most when read as if it contained a narrative: an account of a woman cursed with a desire to die. Why is she different from other women? Where did the curse come from? A story line with a beginning, middle, and end takes shape in *Complete Poems* as Sexton systematically exhausts a set of culturally acceptable explanations for the condition of her kind. These are, first, a psychiatric explanation; later, a sociological explanation; and finally a spiritual explanation.

The story begins with the discovery of the poet in the sick person. The narrator of Sexton's first book is a woman "part way back" from Bedlam—that is, not yet restored to the family home as wife and mother—contemplating what took her to the mental hospital: the preference for suicide over motherhood as she had learned that role from her own mother (**"The Double Image"**). Bedlam has been a school which taught a valuable lesson: the power of signs.

> I tapped my own head;
> it was glass, an inverted bowl.
>
> . . .
>
> if you turn away
> because there is no lesson here
> I will hold my awkward bowl,
> with all its cracked stars shining
> like a complicated lie.

("For John, Who Begs Me
Not to Enquire Further")

From now on, she will be a poet of the tapped head: the mad housewife.

Condensed into the metaphor of the broken kitchen bowl are most of the meanings Sexton associates with her own liberation into poetry. Before she tapped meanings from her head, the bowl—her womanly identity—revealed but enclosed her (like Plath's bell jar); only through costly breakage did the identity begin to shine with complex significance. Breakage ruined the bowl for kitchen use but endowed it with a more precious moral utility. Further, the act of offering her own breakage as a gift shifted her relation both to her suffering and to the beholder. In the metaphor of the bowl whose cracks become stars, Sexton avows belief that her experience has been redeemed by its transformation into the social medium of language. "Star" in her personal mythology will from now on designate that place—the poetic symbol—where the language of private suffering grows radiant and magically ambiguous.

Sexton began writing poetry as a form of therapy, at her doctor's suggestion. In her first two books, she uses a good many references to this therapy and occasionally speaks of herself almost objectively as a case history. These are her most admired books. They are also her most "confessional" books in that they establish that her maladjustment as a woman is to be her subject as a poet.

By 1962, Sexton's poetry had won a respectful audience. But as a psychiatric patient she had experienced many setbacks and relapses. She had changed as an artist; as a sick woman, she did not change: repetition of destructive patterns was one of the symptoms of her illness. To survive as a poet meant to attain another, a less reportorial relation to the subject of her pathology. Beginning with poems written for her third volume, *Live or Die*, Sexton gradually abandoned the polarity sick / well which gives underlying structure to the poems of *Bedlam* and *Pretty Ones*. In the poetry of *Live or Die* Sexton begins to explore the suspicion that what she suffers from is femaleness itself, and is probably incurable. "—I'm no more a woman / than Christ

was a man," she says in a dream (**"Consorting with Angels,"** *Live or Die*). Behind this claim are questions that eventually dominate her last, religious poems: what kinds of social significance has *her* suffering? Is it too specifically female to contain spiritual meaning? Can a woman speak for Man? More and more for Sexton the problematic will not lie between being insane and being healthy, but within being female. To be female is to be defective. (pp. 295-96)

In my reading of Sexton's *Complete Poems, Love Poems* (1969) and *Transformations* (1971) form a dyad. *Love Poems* exposes the dilemma of the female poet trying to write within the conventions of the literary genre of love poetry: *Transformations* explains this dilemma by situating sexual love in its social context: the marriage contract that stabilizes the social order. Both have an unsettling, masochistic tone. The speaker of *Love Poems* experiences her body as a hoard of attributes, desirable only in dismemberment. "Love" is the anxious energy she feels as her body parts come to life under the prospective or actual gaze of a man. . . . (p. 300)

Transformations also presents women as some of their parts; but since Sexton adopts here the plots of fairy tales from Grimm, by which children are instructed in the repression and displacement of libido, the consciousness is perhaps more acceptable than it feels in the radically masochistic *Love Poems*. The tale-teller of *Transformations* is "a middle-aged witch, me"—the woman who has done her hitch over the plain houses but is not a woman quite. She designates as the chosen auditor of these stories a boy of sixteen ("He is sixteen and he wants some answers. / He is each of us") who has found a gold key and is about to learn the use of it.

> Its secrets whimper
> like a dog in heat.
> He turns the key.
> Presto!
> It opens this book of odd tales.

These narratives are adapted directly from Grimm; what Sexton underscores in retelling is the phallic key. The wisecracking witch supplies prologues which emphasize roles and strategies within the system of exchange where sexuality is the coin circulated among the generations to replenish the family and define differences between masculine and feminine identities. . . . Sexton said *Transformations* was "as much about me" as any of her first-person lyrics, and it is. Yet in neither *Love Poems* or *Transformations* is the pathological conceived as merely personal. If Sexton's *Complete Poems* can be read as a woman's story of her wish to die, these explore the death wish as a response to the emptiness of sexuality experienced as a commodity— its repetitiousness, its fetishes.

In the last three books Sexton saw through publication, another appetite emerges: the hunger for redemption. Sexton reformulates, this time in religious terms, her oldest questions about the origins and meaning of her wish to die. The dyad of mother and daughter, and the oedipal triangle, scrutinized psychiatrically in earlier work, return to these volumes as potential sources of grace. In one of Sexton's most imaginative inventions, regression becomes a metaphor for spiritual quest.

The Book of Folly reintroduces the theme of mother's power of cursing or curing a sick daughter. Sexton had, in effect, two mothering figures in early childhood, and both have roles to play in Sexton's late poems. Great-aunt Anna Dingley, the loving "Nana" of Sexton's early childhood, went insane and was institutionalized shortly after Anne told her about kissing a boyfriend at age thirteen. Sexton thus associated her own sexual development with her spinster aunt's decline, and recreated the episode in numerous poems (see, especially, **"Some Foreign Letters," "Rapunzel," "The Nana-Hex"**) as well as in her play *Mercy Street,* in which the maiden aunt witnesses an incestuous episode with the father. In *Folly,* Sexton's yearning to recover the "good mother" lost first to insanity and then to death takes the form of desire for regression to the period before the heterosexual kiss divided them. (pp. 301-03)

Sexton's real mother, Mary Gray Staples Harvey, occupies another kind of ambivalent symbolism. In the late poems, Sexton locates the possibility of her redemption from insanity—the evil of being female—in the memory of her first connection to Mother Mary through the mouth. . . . Mouthing mother, her original hunger was appeased; yet appeasement was only possible in the infant stage when the female body of the mother was innocent—that is, was a source of comfort, not an object of identification. Redemption from the condition of femaleness resides, by this logic, only in the infant stage before separation has done its work and before the infant knows her name and pronoun.

In this world both symbolic and real, it is no more innocuous to be male, of course. The three ambitious sequences that end *Folly*—**"The Death of the Fathers," "Angels of the Love Affair," "The Jesus Papers"**—can be read as progressive confrontations with father figures, motivated by Sexton's defect-haunted sense of herself as a woman. If to mother a daughter is to press her into female roles, so to father a daughter is to expose her to male desire. **"The Death of the Fathers"** revisits old subject matter—young Anne Harvey's tender fascination with her father Ralph Churchill Harvey—treated in the elegiac lyrics of the earlier volumes, most poignantly in **"All My Pretty Ones," "Young," "And One for My Dame."** But by the time of writing *Folly,* Sexton has reduced the dead father to

a mere symbolic shadow of himself. In *Folly's* **"Death of the Fathers,"** he stands for the unattainable object of desire, the lover who might give her both safety and sex. But above all, he is the man she can't have: first because he's her father; again because he's a drunkard; then because he's dead; and now, when Sexton is 42, because his authenticity has been challenged by a usurper, a man claiming to have been her mother's lover. By 1971, of course, Sexton's memory of Ralph Churchill Harvey has been much mediated by years of psychotherapy. But in any case by age 42 a woman's relationship to her father, even a relationship disfigured by memories or fantasies of incest, takes its place in a social realm larger than family life.

In *The Book of Folly* this realm is theological. Sexton's most inventive explanation of femaleness in the scheme of things occurs in **"The Jesus Papers,"** the sequence of nine poems that ends *Folly.* Food metaphors dominate this sequence; most particularly, the metaphor of breast milk as a principle of generosity, a form of salvation issuing specifically from the female body. Flowing from the madonna's breast, **("Jesus Suckles")** it offers the infant his first knowledge of human connection—and its cognate, knowledge of separation. The experience of separation or the creation of the selfish ego becomes in these poems *the* principal human experience needing spiritual cure. Thus the infant Jesus, separating from the breast, fantasizes himself as a truck, an image that recalls Sexton's guilty happiness at discovering her poetic gift as won at her mother's expense. ("I did not know that my life, in the end, / would run over my mother's like a truck"—**"Those Times . . . "**). (pp. 303-04)

In Sexton's version of Christian theology, Christ's death, like her own deathwish, is meaningful to others as a source of symbolisms. For God does not dispense meaning. He dispenses in infancy the hunger for meaning, and he endows the earth with meaning-makers. In Sexton as in Christ the sufferer and the symbol-maker meet: she is the hungry woman we eat as we read her words.

These, in any case, are the symbolisms carried over into Sexton's last two books: *The Death Notebooks* and *The Awful Rowing Toward God.* (p. 306)

Sexton's firmest poems in the volume *The Death Notebooks* are built on the symbolisms radiating from this infant indentity condensing hunger / sacrifice / poetry. In both the **"Death Baby"** sequence and, further on, in the **"Furies"** sequence, the successes arise from the startling originality and intelligence with which Sexton draws on regression as a source of imagery. **"The Furies"** appears occasionally to owe something to Theodore Roethke's sequence "The Lost Son," and the final sequence, **"O Ye Tongues,"** is modeled after Christopher Smart's "Jubilate Agno." In both cases the models are structural, and have served to free

Sexton's characteristic strength: access to the matrix of symbolism, the infant psyche from which she retrieved her subject matter throughout life. (pp. 307-08)

The pair of poems that begin and end [*The Awful Rowing Toward God*] (**"Rowing"** and **"The Rowing Endeth"**) give it a solid structure. Sexton writes in **"Rowing"** that she had passed her life ignorant of God as a destination: "I grew, I grew, / and God was there like an island I had not rowed to." While writing the poems of *Awful Rowing,* Sexton was preparing to separate from her husband; projected changes in her way of life seem to lie behind Sexton's metaphor of the island as a spiritual destination with the characteristics of a new household. It "will not be perfect, / it will have the flaws of life, / the absurdities of the dinner table, / but there will be a door / and I will open it." Unlike the childhood home, unlike the "cruel houses" of married life (including the mental hospitals she has lived in), this island, she believes, houses the paternal presence who might embrace and rescue her at last.

But when she arrives, in **"The Rowing Endeth,"** "at the dock of the island called God," she does not find the expected door. No shelter; no embrace. Instead, she and God "squat on the rocks by the sea / and play—can it be true— / a game of poker." The hand she's dealt Sexton calls a royal straight flush. Instead it seems to be a run of 9-10-J-Q-K, a suit—or family—of five headed by a King and Queen; presumably, the ace is missing from this straight run, because the winning hand is God's five aces. ("A wild card had been announced / but I had not heard it / being in such a state of awe / when He took out the cards and dealt.") God, like the salesman-father named Ace in Sexton's play *Mercy Street,* is fond of a joke, and the poem ends as loser Anne joins the winner in his "untamable, eternal, gut-driven *ha-ha.*"

God's aggressive masculine presence in the poem aligns him with other father figures in Sexton's poetry, including the doctors: those she is doomed to love from a position of compliance, but from whom she will never receive healing care. God's "wild card" signifies the privilege of Him over Her everywhere—the inscrutable possession of dominance. But the poker game with God also seems to stand for a final confrontation of her delusions as delusions. There is no "door" to pass through which will retrospectively transform her history, and no magic embrace, equivalent to God's wild card, which can "get rid of the rat inside of me."

Between the first and last poems of this volume, however, Sexton writes on a variety of themes that may be regarded as "rowing" exercises, or strategies of approach to the redemptive island. In these poems her body acquires a new set of meanings, as a site for the study of the existence of evil. . . . Sexton's *Complete Poems* ends not with a "last word" but with 141 pages of unpublished work in various stages of finish. An epi-

graph for the book might well have been, "The story ends with me still rowing" (**"Rowing"**). The mysterious curse of her mental illness, and the death wish at its core, could be lifted neither by medical nor by other means; but in becoming its storyteller Sexton achieved an emancipating relation to it. "This is madness / but a kind of hunger . . . Turn, my hungers!" In the leap from madness to metaphor Sexton fled solitary confinement again and again. Arriving at the end of Sexton's *Complete Poems* brings me to the question of merit. Sexton was in many ways an interesting writer; but was she an inferior poet?—Inferior, say, to her mentor W. D. Snodgrass, her teacher Robert Lowell, her friends James Wright and Sylvia Plath, her Boston peers Adrienne Rich and Denise Levertov?

As I have been suggesting, I find Sexton a startlingly original and valuable artist. But Sexton differs from members of this group in two important ways that make it difficult to rank her among these other writers. First, she was not an intellectual. Sexton had only a high school education; she got her training as a poet in workshops. Though she had a quick mind and read widely, her thinking was intuitive rather than systematic. She did not identify herself with a literary tradition, she did not measure herself in terms of precursors, she did not acquire a critical language by which to classify and discriminate. Hers is not a poetry of ideas—aesthetic, political, philosophical, or historical.

Second, she stopped writing the kind of short lyric that remains coin of the realm in American poetry: the lyric of perfect economy composed according to an exacting formal standard, whether in meter or free verse. Critics still praise Sexton's early work for its control of the materials of disorder by means of formal effects she dismissed as "tricks." Manuscripts of early poems reveal that Sexton often began by setting herself a design problem: a stanza template with rhyme positions designated "a, b, c," etc.; then she would write a poem into the mould. She continued this practice, with good results, through 1962: her workshop years. (pp. 309-10, 312-13)

Sexton's later style developed out of the demands of her subject matter: accounting for madness. The exploratory, associational method she devised gave priority to the implacable structure of unconscious processes. This method is most successful in such poems as **"O Ye Tongues," "The Jesus Papers," "The Furies," "The Death of the Fathers," "The Death Baby,"** *Transformations*—works where the traces of a narrative adumbrate a boundary of reference within which to rationalize the flow of association. For much of Sexton's *Complete Poems,* the horizon or story line is, of course, autobiographical, focused on Sexton's attraction to death. Sexton's *Complete Poems* might be described as a psycho-narrative in verse, to which each poem is a contribution.

Moreover, the type of poem Sexton evolved was probably an inevitable creation in mid-century American poetry. It articulates the dilemma of a female recipient of certain ideas about women's place in the social order; it invests this dilemma in a single persona, a performing voice. The contemporary writings of Sylvia Plath and Adrienne Rich offer perhaps the closest analogues to Sexton's work, since their own dilemmas were equally privileged and middle class. As young *women*, all three had embraced prevailing ideologies about women's roles. All three of them seem to have been excessively susceptible to highly conventional expectations, tormented by questions about whether they were "good" daughters, students, mothers, wives. As young *artists* they had to gain recognition in a prestige system condescending to women, and the conflicts they experienced between the roles of woman and artist fueled their development. In fact, the gender specificity of much of their poetry helps us see how specifically "masculine" were the concerns of peers such as Lowell, Snodgrass, Berryman, Wright, Roethke, Ginsberg—who struggled to attain spiritual authority in the postwar consumer society littered with unusable masculine stereotypes.

But for Plath and Rich, the male-identified literary tradition eventually suggested models for transcendence uncongenial to Sexton. Both Plath and Rich essentially revised, for women's use, the poetics of romanticism which centers the poem in a visionary ego. Plath adopted the voice of a maenad; Rich evolved a powerfully personal voice of informed social criticism.

Sexton's voice remained unembarrassedly domestic. She tested notions about self and God against feelings schooled in repression, and her poems do not transcend, they explore this repression. Sexton's art celebrates word-magic, buffoonery, regression, "milking the unconscious," as inexhaustible sources of resistance to the deadly authority of the stereotypes constraining adult women's lives. Sexton's artistry was to achieve a mode of expression for this particular female consciousness, expression at once intimate and theatrical. Her audiences, mostly women, responded to that voice as the manifestation of a condition they had previously felt to be wholly personal and interior. Suddenly, poetry had expanded to acknowledge a whole new citizenry; the middle-class American woman beginning to seek liberation from confinement in domestic roles. As American poetry slowly incorporates a feminist consciousness, Sexton's work seems uncannily ahead of its time. It seems bound to endure at least as long as the social and psychological dilemmas that inspired her. (pp. 313-14)

Diane Middlebrook, "Poets of Weird Abundance," in *Parnassus: Poetry in Review*, Vols. 12-13, Nos. 1-2, 1985, pp. 293-315.

DIANA HUME GEORGE
(essay date 1987)

[In the following excerpt from her critical study *Oedipus Anne: The Poetry of Anne Sexton*, George discusses Sexton's themes and subject matter.]

Anne Sexton's poetry tells stories that are immensely significant to mid-twentieth-century artistic and psychic life. Sexton understood her culture's malaise through her own, and her skill enabled her to deploy metaphorical structures at once synthetic and analytic. In other words, she assimilated the superficially opposing but deeply similar ways of thinking represented by poetry and psychoanalysis. Sexton explored the myths by and through which our culture lives and dies: the archetypal relationships among mothers and daughters, fathers and daughters, mothers and sons, gods and humans, men and women. She perceived, and consistently patterned in the images of her art, the paradoxes deeply rooted in human behavior and motivation. Her poetry presents multiplicity and simplicity, duality and unity, the sacred and the profane, in ways that insist on their similarities—even, at times, their identity. In less abstract terms, Sexton made explicit the intimacy of forces persistently treated as opposites by the society she lived in.

I appreciate the intention of statements made since her death that caution readers against becoming enamored of Sexton's illness and that encourage concentration on the celebratory aspects of her poetry. But another cautionary note is perhaps in order: that readers not ignore the expression of poetic and personal anguish for which the celebration is counterpart and foil. "The soul is, I think, a human being who speaks with the pressure of death at his head," Sexton wrote in a 1963 letter. Her poems articulate some of the deepest dilemmas of her contemporaries about their—our—most basic fears and wishes. Although Sexton's canon reaches for the unities of human experience, she did not abandon duality, even dichotomy. Poets must transcend us in some ways to be counted great of mind, but they must also be *of* us. Her poems vibrate in that energetic, passionate area between everlasting certainty and everlasting doubt. When she perceived the sameness of everything, it was against the background of the difference; when she perceived the difference, it was in reference to the sameness—just as metaphor, the imaging of connectedness, always implies a prior discontinuity.

Sexton flashed a sparkling, multiple light on human faces from the beginning of her writing career until the month of her death. For seventeen years she spoke in a direct, intimate way of people she loved. Her concentration on human relationships produced sharp, masterful portraits of people who were worth keeping alive, or worth resurrecting. That they were often "all her pretty ones" creates part of her poetry's poignancy. Her personal relationship to many of those who people the world of her poems amplifies the resounding creation of whole, complicated characters whose compelling presence is perhaps more deeply artful for having been lived. If many of Sexton's people had not so lived, her skill and art would have been solely responsible for breathing the life into them. As it was, she most often worked from the life and perhaps must share her credit with those who died before her and those who have outlived her: her mother, her father, her daughters, her husband, her lovers, her aunt, her grandfather, and her remarkable friends. I am glad there was or is an Eleanor Boylan, whatever name she bears.

When Sexton tells her dead father that she will bend down her strange face to his and forgive him, she is speaking of what we all need to do: to bend down our faces to our fathers, living or dead, and forgive them. When she calls her mother her mocking mirror, her overthrown love, her first image, she speaks for all of us of woman born and first nurtured against "her plump and fruity skin." When she becomes the child of "elbows, knees, dreams, goodnight," she is the child in all of us, recapturing those moments when "love grew rings around me." When she says to her daughter, "Everything in your body that is new is telling the truth," she may be transcribing what she said to her daughter; she is also expressing for the collective mothers of her readership what we all want to be saying to our daughters, what we sometimes have not the courage or attentiveness to say. The mother of "life is not in my hands" tells a terrible truth, but she is also the mother of "Darling, stand still at your door, sure of yourself, a white stone, a good stone. . . ." This is a mother who tells the truth, one who gives you "the images I know."

In her lively, lonely telling of her truth, in her giving of the images she knew, Sexton looked for "uncomplicated hymns / but love has none." So the daughter who has loved and watched her mother closely enough to see "that blaze within the pilgrim woman" will also confess that this most important death does not equip her with grief. The friend who watches Eleanor Boylan talking with God, "as close as the ceiling," will warn her to speak quickly, "before death uses you up." The great aunt who climbed Mount San Salvatore, that "yankee girl, the iron interior of her sweet body," will one day career into the streets and stop passersby "to mumble your guilty love while your ears die."

In **"Her Kind"** and **"The Black Art,"** Sexton characterizes the poet as one who feels too much,

thinks too much, and lives in an atmosphere of "weird abundance." In a 1966 letter she writes about the abundance that "runs wild with love as cancer." Sexton did, in some respects, connect the sources of poetic inspiration with death. Certainly the connections between extremist art and suicide as a form of poetic destiny have been destructively romanticized. My intention in raising the point is not to confirm it but to suggest something that it indicates. The limited extent to which Sexton connected art and self-destruction may have been symptomatic of her illness. I think she would have agreed: "Suicide is the opposite of the poem." That she *might* have felt called upon to fulfill a poetic as well as personal destiny by suicide—and I do not necessarily think she did—is better viewed as symptomatic of the cultural conditions she so clearly perceived and lived with.

Poets are among the few whom our culture still invests with a ritual function. We ask them to speak the unspeakable for us, and when they do, we are capable of effecting a violently negative transference. Critical response to Sexton's poetry seems to me to bear this out. Particularly if the poet has exposed our pain, seen into our darkest selves, we need to purge ourselves of the violating member, to punish the one who has broken boundaries and violated taboos. That Christianity depends for salvation on a sacrificial lamb whose death permits us to abrogate responsibility for the human failings we call "sin" speaks of our need to transfer guilt. Sexton's identifications with the crucified Christ sometimes have the ring of a self-aggrandizing and self-appointed martyrdom. But to whatever extent she may have been martyred, it was at the invitation, if not the insistence, of an exceptionally hungry audience.

Yet we are angry with Anne Sexton for killing herself, partly because she is the same poet who wrote with such commitment and intensity of the delight of being alive. If Sylvia Plath was always removed from her readership by the consistency of her "dead hands, dead stringencies," if she was always somehow beyond the merely human, always "the arrow, the dew that flies / Suicidal, at one with the drive," Sexton was not always so. Before and after she was sometimes that, she was also the mother of **"Little Girl,"** the lover of **"Us,"** the daughter of **"Oysters,"** the child of **"Young."** She spoke to us of celebration of the sun, that "excitable gift," of all the wicked, pure, lovely fun of being alive. Perhaps we could not tolerate knowing that this was the same woman who saw "rats in the toilet." If she was more clearly one of us, then her defection was more serious. It endangered us more deeply. She was an anomaly, a fish with wings.

Many of the qualities of Sexton's poetry so often seen as inconsistent I see as part of the vitalizing struggle to make of her art a salvation both spiritual and bodily. Much like the early Blake, Anne Sexton moved between contraries with equal force, equal conviction, and equal doubt. One can experience disappointment or frustration in the presence of such vacillation and label it a failure of nerve or will or imagination—or one can experience it, as I do, as one's own truth. To make it more concrete: if you think linearly about the building of a body of truth, then you must think only in terms of progress and regress. Anne Sexton comes to happy resolutions repeatedly in her work, from poem to poem, volume to volume. *Live or Die* is structured in just such a pleasing, simple shape: after a struggle with destruction, it ends with the affirmation of life. Yet in subsequent volumes she backslides continuously, seeming to erase her previous truths, to compromise them, or to give them up. In the early *All My Pretty Ones,* Sexton first forgives her father. In later works she sometimes appears to renege on that forgiveness and to exhume the old ghost she had, we thought, laid to rest. In a literary and moral tradition presided over by *Paradise Lost* followed by *Paradise Regained,* and a theological one structured by the external resurrection of a crucified god, the linear progression of truth is denied by the return of the ghost from eternal rest.

The wish that art may carve into permanent perfection either our hope or our despair is understandable but too limiting. There is ample room in my own notion of poetry for the repeated reflections of that imperfectability that separates humans from the gods they create. The repetition of a set of emotional and mental acts is central to Anne Sexton's poetry and represents a striving after personal and poetic catharsis that is never quite achieved, even when it is claimed. Her poetry enacts the repetition compulsion that may justly be called thanatopic from one perspective. From another, the movement that seems repetitive represents an intricate tension between contraries that is at the core of all creative process. (pp. xi-xiv)

Diana Hume George, in her *Oedipus Anne: The Poetry of Anne Sexton,* University of Illinois Press, 1987, 210 p.

SOURCES FOR FURTHER STUDY

Colburn, Steven E., ed. *Anne Sexton: Telling the Tale.* Ann Arbor: University of Michigan Press, 1988, 470 p.
    Essay collection. Includes contributions by Robert Lowell, Denise Levertov, and James Dickey.

George, Diana Hume. *Oedipus Anne: The Poetry of Anne Sexton.* Urbana: University of Illinois Press, 1987, 210 p.
    Critical analysis that concentrates on the psychological aspects of Sexton's poetry.

Hall, Caroline King Barnard. *Anne Sexton.* Boston: Twayne, 1989, 192 p.
    Outlines Sexton's life and works.

McClatchy, J. D., ed. *Anne Sexton: The Artist and Her Critics.* Bloomington: Indiana University Press, 1978, 297 p.
Presents interviews with Sexton as well as reviews and essays concerning her work that "direct our attention away from the woman and back toward her art."

Middlebrook, Diane Wood. *Anne Sexton: A Biography.* Boston: Houghton Mifflin, 1991, 488 p.
    Extensive, highly controversial biography of Sexton that makes use of audio tapes of Sexton's therapy sessions with her psychiatrist, Dr. Martin Orne.

Wagner-Martin, Linda. *Critical Essays on Anne Sexton.* Boston: G. K. Hall, 1989, 254 p.
    Collection of reviews, essays, and reminiscences concerning Sexton and her work.

William Shakespeare

1564-1616

English dramatist and poet.

INTRODUCTION

Considered by critics, scholars, and the theater-going public the most important dramatist in the history of English literature, Shakespeare occupies a unique position in the pantheon of great world authors. The acknowledged Shakespearean canon of some thirty-seven plays, written in the late sixteenth and early seventeenth centuries, continues to sustain critical attention and elicit popular approval on a scale unrivaled by that accorded other writers of the period—or, for that matter, of any other time. While best known as a dramatist, Shakespeare was also a distinguished poet; his 1609 sonnet series is considered a literary masterpiece. Shakespeare's dramas and poems were composed during the English Renaissance (c. 1500-1642), a period characterized by a remarkable flowering of brilliant literature. Together with such writers as Christopher Marlowe, Sir Philip Sidney, Edmund Spenser, and others, Shakespeare drew upon elements of classical literature in the creation of distinctly English forms of poetry and drama. His work was hardly limited to strict classical idioms, however; he successfully utilized a much broader range of literary sources than any of his contemporaries. His history plays, for example, borrow heavily from contemporary English histories, and his comedies often incorporate aspects of English folklore. Moreover, Shakespeare's extraordinary linguistic abilities—his gift for complex poetic imagery, mixed metaphor, and brilliant puns—combined with a penetrating insight into human nature, are widely recognized as the makings of a unique literary genius. Shakespeare's dramatic imagination and unparalleled ability to capture and express universal concerns led his contemporary Ben Jonson to declare that Shakespeare "was not of an age, but for all time."

Shakespeare was probably born on 23 April 1564, though the precise date of his birth is uncertain.

His father, John Shakespeare, belonged to the merchant class; with increasing prosperity, he acquired a series of municipal offices in Stratford-upon-Avon. His wife, Mary Arden, came from a yeoman family of slightly higher social standing and was a minor heiress to some land in Warwickshire. It is thought that Shakespeare attended the local grammar school, the King's New School, where the main course of instruction was in Latin. There, students were taught rhetoric, logic, and ethics and studied works by classical authors Terence, Plautus, Cicero, Vergil, Plutarch, Horace, and Ovid. This, it is believed, was the extent of Shakespeare's education; there is no evidence that he attended university. Instead, in 1582, at the age of eighteen, he married Ann Hathaway of Stratford. Their first child, Susanna, was born six months later, followed by twins, Hamnet and Judith, in 1585. Shakespeare's life from this date until 1592, when he became known as a dramatist, is not well documented. Scholars surmise that in these so-called "dark years" he probably became acquainted with professional acting companies touring the provinces and made his way to London, where his first plays, the three parts of the Henry VI history cycle, were presented in 1589-91. The first reference to Shakespeare in the London literary world dates from 1592, when dramatist Robert Greene alluded to him as "an upstart crow" in his *Greenes, groats-worth of witte, bought with a million of Repentance* (1592). Shakespeare's literary reputation was apparently little affected by Greene's barb, and in the next few years it grew tremendously. While experimenting with classical dramatic forms in the early tragedy *Titus Andronicus* (1593-94) and elsewhere, Shakespeare issued a pair of narrative poems directly modeled after Ovid's *Metamorphoses*: *Venus and Adonis* (1593) and *The Rape of Lucrece* (1594). These works, which acknowledged the current fashion for poems on mythological themes, were immensely successful, establishing "honey-tongued Shakespeare"—as his contemporary Francis Meres called him—as a poet of the first rank. Shakespeare further established himself as a professional actor and playwright when he joined the Lord Chamberlain's Men, an acting company formed in 1594 under the patronage of Henry Carey, Lord Hunsdon. The members of this company included the renowned tragedian Richard Burbage; the famous "clown" Will Kempe, who was one of the most popular actors of his time; and John Heminge, who served as business manager for the company. In 1594 they began performing at the Theatre and the Cross Keys Inn, moving to the Swan Theatre on Bankside in 1596 when municipal authorities banned the public presentation of plays within the limits of the City of London. In 1599 Shakespeare and other members of the company financed the building of the Globe Theatre, the most famous of all Elizabethan playhouses. As a result, they became "sharers," not only in the actors' portion of the profits, but in the theater owners' as well. Ensuing economic independence was an important element in the unusual stability of their association. They became the foremost London company, performing at Court on thirty-two occasions between 1594 and 1603, whereas their chief rivals, the Lord Admiral's Men, made only twenty appearances at Court during these years. The success of the Lord Chamberlain's Men is largely attributable to the fact that after joining the group in 1594, Shakespeare wrote for no other company.

In 1603, shortly after his accession to the throne, James I granted the Lord Chamberlain's Men a royal patent, and the company's name was altered to reflect the King's direct patronage. Records indicate that the King's Men remained the most favored acting company in the Jacobean era, averaging a dozen performances at Court each year during the period. In addition to public performances at the Globe Theatre in the spring and autumn, the King's Men played at the private Blackfriars Theatre in winter and offered evening performances there. Many of Shakespeare's late plays were first staged at Blackfriars, where the intimate setting facilitated Shakespeare's use of increasingly sophisticated stage techniques. Surviving records of the playwright's business transactions indicate that he benefited financially from his long career in the theater: he invested in real estate, purchasing properties in both Stratford and London, and by 1596 had attained sufficient status to be granted a coat of arms and the accompanying right to call himself a gentleman. By 1610, with his fortune made and his reputation as the leading English dramatist unchallenged, Shakespeare appears to have largely retired to Stratford, although business interests kept him in London from time to time. Shakespeare completed his will on 25 March 1616 and died on April 23. He was buried in the chancel of Trinity Church in Stratford, with this epitaph: "Good frend for Jesus sake forbeare, / to digg the dust encloased heare: / Bleste be the man that spares thes stones, / and curst be he that moves my bones."

The publication history of Shakespeare's plays is extremely complex and the subject of much scholarly debate. The earliest collected edition of his dramas, known as the First Folio, was compiled by his fellow-actors John Heminge and Henry Condell and published posthumously in 1623. The First Folio, which classifies the dramas into distinct genres of comedy, history, and tragedy, contains thirty-six of the thirty-seven plays now regarded as indisputably Shakespearean. (*Pericles* [1609] is not included, and the authorship of *The Two Noble Kinsmen* [1613] remains uncertain.) Of the works included, thirteen had not been published before. The remainder were first printed in unauthorized "quarto" editions apparently based on prompt-book copies of the plays or on reconstructions by some of the actors in the original performances. Although the First Folio is considered authoritative for a number of plays, recent textual scholarship tends to call for broad consideration of *all* versions of a Shakespearean drama, since the quartos sometimes clarify passages that are confused or garbled in the Folio. The quartos also occasionally include valuable stage directions employed in early presentations.

Shakespeare's approach to drama was markedly eclectic. He appropriated stylistic elements from Roman classicism—specifically comedy as defined by Plautus and Terence and tragedy by Seneca—medieval morality plays, French popular farce, and modern Italian drama such as the improvised comedic forms of the commedia dell'arte. Shakespeare's use of these sources was not purely imitative, however; he experimented with traditional forms in an original way. Of the three genres, the comedies reveal the closest affinity to the themes of Italian Renaissance literature. Scholars typically separate these plays into various general categories. The "early" comedies, as the name implies, are among the first works Shakespeare wrote. The plays in this group, such as *The Comedy of Errors* (1592-94), *The Taming of the Shrew* (1593-94), and *Love's Labour's Lost* (1594-95), generally adhere closely to established comedic forms. The "romantic" comedies from the period 1596-1602, including *A Midsummer Night's Dream* (1595-96), *The Merchant of Venice* (1596-97), *As You Like It* (1599), and *Twelfth Night* (1601-02), display a consistency in style and subject matter and especially focus on themes of courtship and marriage. While most of these works are also indebted to Italian predecessors—*As You Like It,* derived from English sources, is the notable exception—Shakespeare introduced his own comedic inventions, and as a group, the "romantic" comedies comprise his most popular and critically esteemed comedies. These plays commonly feature imaginary "realms," such as Belmont or the Forest of Arden, that provide a counterpoint to, or escape from, the restrictions of society. In the relative freedom of such places, conflicts are resolved, permitting a happy ending that typically involves marriage and a return to a reinvigorated society. Shakespeare thus invested the romantic comedies with narrative complexity and compelling moral ambiguity. Shakespeare's "dark" comedies, including *Troilus and Cressida* (1601-02), *All's Well That Ends Well* (1602-03), and *Measure for Measure* (1604), are characterized by marked seriousness in theme, somberness in tone, and strange, shifting narrative perspectives. Some critics argue that a separate "romance" genre should be assigned to such tragi-comic later works as *The Tempest* (1611), but others completely reject this idea. This group, which also includes *Cymbeline* (1609-10) and *The Winter's Tale* (1610-11), is characterized by an emphasis on themes of separation and loss. These plays typically include a wandering journey that ultimately results in a reunion amid a spirit of forgiveness and reconciliation.

Departing from the inspired eclecticism of the comedies, the history plays reflect Shakespeare's reliance on two principal sources, Edward Hall's *The Union of the Two Noble and Illustre Families of Lancastre and York* (1548) and Raphael Holinshed's *Chronicles of England, Scotlande, and Irlande* (1587). Both works advance the belief that divine providence led England toward unified government under Tudor rule, and some critics suggest that Shakespeare's history plays were written to further legitimize this so-called "Tudor myth." Eight of the ten history plays collectively trace the English monarchy from the fourteenth century Plantagenets to the emergence of the Tudors in the sixteenth century. They are commonly grouped in two "tetralogies": the first contains the three parts of *Henry VI* and *Richard III* (1592-93); the second, depicting chronologically earlier events but written later in Shakespeare's career, includes *Richard II* (1595), the two parts of *Henry IV* (1596-98), and *Henry V* (1599). This last work presents the king as the triumphant leader of his people in a glorious battle against the French. Some commentators claim that rather than defending Tudor authority, the history plays subtly expose the political defects of divine right monarchy. In illustration of this point, such scholars note that on the night before the Earl of Essex's ill-fated uprising against Elizabeth I in 1601, some of Essex's followers arranged a performance of *Richard II* in the hope that Shakespeare's depiction of the deposing of an unfit monarch would generate support for their cause. The history plays are considered successful works from a dramatic point of view. Shakespeare fully realized his capacity for investing plot with extraordinary dramatic tension and demonstrated his flair for original characterization through the use of subtle, ironic language. Such figures as Richard II, Richard III, and Henry V are fully developed personages whose depiction, critics agree, transcends mere historical reportage. In addition, Falstaff in *1* and *2 Henry IV* is acclaimed as one of Shakespeare's most imaginative comic characterizations.

Shakespeare's tragedies, like his comedies, are commonly divided into separate though related categories, the "Roman" tragedies and the "great" tragedies. As their nomenclature suggests, the Roman plays drew their inspiration from histories of classical antiquity, chiefly from a translation of Plutarch's *Parallel Lives* by Sir Thomas North, published as *The Lives of the Noble Grecians and Romanes* in 1579. The major tragedies of this type, *Julius Caesar* (1599) and *Antony and Cleopatra* (1606-07), explore the themes of political intrigue and personal revenge and are distinguished by their clear, poetic discourse and ironic representation of historical incidents. The four great tragedies are similar thematically to the Roman plays insofar as their principal subject is the fall of high public figures. However, the sources for their documentation were usually medieval rather than classical. *Hamlet* (1600-01), regarded by many critics as Shakespeare's finest work, is based on the story of Hamlet, Prince of Denmark, which first appeared in the *Historia Danica,* a Latin text by the twelfth-century historian Saxo Grammaticus. *King Lear* (1605) improvises on the legend of a British king and his disastrous decision to divide his kingdom equally among his daughters. *Macbeth* (1606), which explores the issue of regicide, is derived from the history of an ancient Scottish king, Duncan. *Othello* (1604), a story of domestic intrigue set in the Venetian Republic, is taken from a Renaissance source, Giovanni Battista Giraldi Cinthio's *Hecatommithi* (1565). Special mention should be made of *Romeo and Juliet* (1595-96). Although frequently judged by critics to be of a lesser rank than the great tragedies, it remains one of the most frequently performed of Shakespeare's dramas. This tale of love thwarted by the pointless feuding of the lovers' families reworks a well-known story of medieval Italian origin.

The four great tragedies display the greatest intensity of tragic pathos of all Shakespeare's dramas. In these works Shakespeare characteristically presents the fall of the heroes in terms that suggest a concomitant collapse of all human values or, more, a disordering of the universe itself. As Othello states after he has killed Desdemona, "Methinks it should be now a huge eclipse / Of sun and moon". Similarly, after King Lear's daughters rebel against him, he wanders in a thunderstorm of near-cataclysmic proportions. Scholars have suggested that such vividly portrayed upheavals reflect a generalized anxiety among Shakespeare's contemporaries that underlying social, political, and religious tensions would upset the hierarchical order of the Elizabethan world.

The *Sonnets* are also considered a central work in the Shakespeare canon. Like the dramas, the sonnets are patterned after a literary model widely imitated in Shakespeare's age: the sonnets of Petrarch. Shakespeare's sonnets are arranged in a narrative order. They consist of a series of metaphorical dialogues between the poet and two distinct personalities: Sonnets 18 to 126 are addressed to a fair young man, or "Friend," and are concerned with the themes of beauty, friendship, and immortality; Sonnets 127 to 154 are addressed to a "Dark Lady" who is described as sensual, coarse and promiscuous. The intensity of feeling revealed in the poems, as well as the vividness of the personalities described by the poet, have led many critics to believe that the *Sonnets* are primarily autobiographical. But this conclusion is not universally accepted. Many critics point out that the sequence of the sonnets appears to have been altered in the course of publication, irrevocably dimming the original meaning of the text. Although the circumstances surrounding the composition of the *Sonnets* continues to be disputed, their brilliant versification and subtle analysis of human emotion are together regarded as the work of a unique poetic genius. Consequently, scholars often place the *Sonnets* on an equal level with Shakespeare's dramas. Thus, considered as a complete entity, the Shakespeare canon has over the centuries obtained an unparalleled critical significance and has exerted an unprecedented influence on the development of world literature.

(For further information about Shakespeare's life and works, see *Dictionary of Literary Biography,* Vol. 62: *Elizabethan Dramatists; Shakespearean Criticism,* Vols. 1-18; and *Shakespeare for Students.*)

CRITICAL COMMENTARY

A. C. BRADLEY

(essay date 1905)

[Bradley was a major Shakespearean critic whose work culminated the method of character analysis initiated in the Romantic era. His *Shakespearean Tragedy* (1904; revised edition, 1905), an examination of *Hamlet, Othello, King Lear,* and *Macbeth,* is widely regarded as an indispensable contribution to critical understanding of the tragic genre in Shakespeare's canon. In the following excerpt from this work, Bradley outlines the characteristic features of Shakespearean tragedy.]

A Shakespearean tragedy . . . may be called a story of exceptional calamity leading to the death of a man in high estate. But it is clearly much more than this, and we have . . . to regard it from another side. No amount of calamity which merely befell a man, descending from the clouds like lightning, or stealing from the darkness like pestilence, could alone provide the substance of its story. Job was the greatest of all the children of the east, and his afflictions were well-nigh more

*Principal Works

1 Henry VI (drama) 1589-90

2 Henry VI (drama) 1590-91

3 Henry VI (drama) 1590-91

Richard III (drama) 1592-93

The Comedy of Errors (drama) 1592-94

Venus and Adonis (poetry) 1593

The Taming of the Shrew (drama) 1593-94

Titus Andronicus (drama) 1593-94

The Rape of Lucrece (poetry) 1594

The Two Gentlemen of Verona (drama) 1594

King John (drama) 1594-95

Love's Labour's Lost (drama) 1594-95

Richard II (drama) 1595

A Midsummer Night's Dream (drama) 1595-96

Romeo and Juliet (drama) 1595-96

1 Henry IV (drama) 1596-97

The Merchant of Venice (drama) 1596-97

The Merry Wives of Windsor (drama) 1597

2 Henry IV (drama) 1598

Much Ado about Nothing (drama) 1598-99

As You Like It (drama) 1599

Henry V (drama) 1599

Julius Caesar (drama) 1599

Hamlet (drama) 1600-01

The Phoenix and Turtle (poetry) 1601

Troilus and Cressida (drama) 1601-02

Twelfth Night (drama) 1601-02

All's Well That Ends Well (drama) 1602-03

Measure for Measure (drama) 1604

Othello (drama) 1604

King Lear (drama) 1605

Macbeth (drama) 1606

Antony and Cleopatra (drama) 1606-07

Coriolanus (drama) 1607-08

Pericles (drama) 1607-08

Timon of Athens (drama) 1607-08

Sonnets (poetry) 1609

Cymbeline (drama) 1609-10

The Winter's Tale (drama) 1610-11

The Tempest (drama) 1611

Henry VIII (drama) 1612-13

The Two Noble Kinsmen [with John Fletcher] (drama) 1613

†Mr. William Shakespeares Comedies, Histories, & Tragedies (drama) 1623

†Mr. William Shakespeares Comedies, Histories, and Tragedies (drama) 1632

†Mr. William Shakespear's Comedies, Histories, and Tragedies (drama) 1663

†Mr. William Shakespear's Comedies, Histories, and Tragedies (drama) 1685

Arden Shakespeare Series (drama and poetry) 1954-82

The Riverside Shakespeare (drama and poetry) 1974

The New Cambridge Shakespeare (drama and poetry) 1983-

*Dramas are ordered by date of first performance and poetic works are arranged by date of publication. This chronology conforms to that determined by G. Blakemore Evans in The Riverside Shakespeare (1974).

†These volumes are commonly termed The First Folio, The Second Folio, The Third Folio, and The Fourth Folio. A number of Shakespeare's plays included in them were first printed in unauthorized quarto editions.

---

than he could bear; but even if we imagined them wearing him to death, that would not make his story tragic. Nor yet would it become so, in the Shakespearean sense, if the fire, and the great wind from the wilderness, and the torments of his flesh were conceived as sent by a supernatural power, whether just or malignant. The calamities of tragedy do not simply happen, nor are they sent; they proceed mainly from actions, and those the actions of men.

We see a number of human beings placed in certain circumstances; and we see, arising from the co-operation of their characters in these circumstances, certain actions. These actions beget others, and these others beget others again, until this series of interconnected deeds leads by an apparently inevitable sequence to a catastrophe. The effect of such a series on imagination is to make us regard the sufferings which accompany it, and the catastrophe in which it ends, not only or chiefly as something which happens to the persons concerned, but equally as something which is caused by them. This at least may be said of the principal persons, and, among them, of the hero, who always contributes in some measure to the disaster in which he perishes.

This second aspect of tragedy evidently differs greatly from the first. Men, from this point of view, appear to us primarily as agents, 'themselves the authors of their proper woe'; and our fear and pity, though they will not cease or diminish, will be modified accordingly. We are now to consider this second aspect, remembering that it too is only one aspect, and additional to the first, not a substitute for it.

The 'story' or 'action' of a Shakespearean tragedy does not consist, of course, solely of human actions or deeds; but the deeds are the predominant factor. And these deeds are, for the most part, actions in the full sense of the word; not things done "tween asleep and wake,' but acts or omissions thoroughly expressive of the doer,—characteristic deeds. The centre of the tragedy, therefore, may be said with equal truth to lie in action issuing from character, or in character issuing in action.

Shakespeare's main interest lay here. To say that it lay in *mere* character, or was a psychological interest, would be a great mistake, for he was dramatic to the tips of his fingers. It is possible to find places where he has given a certain indulgence to his love of poetry, and even to his turn for general reflections; but it would be very difficult, and in his later tragedies perhaps impossible, to detect passages where he has allowed such freedom to the interest in character apart from action. But for the opposite extreme, for the abstraction of mere 'plot' (which is a very different thing from the tragic 'action'), for the kind of interest which predominates in a novel like *The Woman in White,* it is clear that he cared even less. I do not mean that this interest is absent from his dramas; but it is subordinate to others, and is so interwoven with them that we are rarely conscious of it apart, and rarely feel in any great strength the half-intellectual, half-nervous excitement of following an ingenious complication. What we do feel strongly, as a tragedy advances to its close, is that the calamities and catastrophe follow inevitably from the deeds of men, and that the main source of these deeds is character. The dictum that, with Shakespeare, 'character is destiny' is no doubt an exaggeration, and one that may mislead (for many of his tragic personages, if they had not met with peculiar circumstances, would have escaped a tragic end, and might even have lived fairly untroubled lives); but it is the exaggeration of a vital truth.

This truth, with some of its qualifications, will appear more clearly if we now go on to ask what elements are to be found in the 'story' or 'action,' occasionally or frequently, beside the characteristic deeds, and the sufferings and circumstances, of the persons. I will refer to three of these additional factors.

(*a*) Shakespeare, occasionally and for reasons which need not be discussed here, represents abnormal conditions of mind; insanity, for example, somnambulism, hallucinations. And deeds issuing from these are certainly not what we called deeds in the fullest sense, deeds expressive of character. No; but these abnormal conditions are never introduced as the origin of deeds of any dramatic moment. Lady Macbeth's sleepwalking has no influence whatever on the events that follow it. Macbeth did not murder Duncan because he saw a dagger in the air: he saw the dagger because he was about to murder Duncan. Lear's insanity is not the cause of a tragic conflict any more than Ophelia's; it is, like Ophelia's, the result of a conflict; and in both cases the effect is mainly pathetic. If Lear were really mad when he divided his kingdom, if Hamlet were really mad at any time in the story, they would cease to be tragic characters.

(*b*) Shakespeare also introduces the supernatural into some of his tragedies; he introduces ghosts, and witches who have supernatural knowledge. This supernatural element certainly cannot in most cases, if in any, be explained away as an illusion in the mind of one of the characters. And further, it does contribute to the action, and is in more than one instance an indispensable part of it: so that to describe human character, with circumstances, as always the *sole* motive force in this action would be a serious error. But the supernatural is always placed in the closest relation with character. It gives a confirmation and a distinct form to inward movements already present and exerting an influence; to the sense of failure in Brutus, to the stifled workings of conscience in Richard, to the half-formed thought or the horrified memory of guilt in Macbeth, to suspicion in Hamlet. Moreover, its influence is never of a compulsive kind. It forms no more than an element, however important, in the problem which the hero has to face; and we are never allowed to feel that it has removed his capacity or responsibility for dealing with this problem. So far indeed are we from feeling this, that many readers run to the opposite extreme, and openly or privately regard the supernatural as having nothing to do with the real interest of the play.

(*c*) Shakespeare, lastly, in most of his tragedies allows to 'chance' or 'accident' an appreciable influence at some point in the action. Chance or accident here will be found, I think, to mean any occurrence (not supernatural, of course) which enters the dramatic sequence neither from the agency of a character, nor from the obvious surrounding circumstances. It may be called an accident, in this sense, that Romeo never got the Friar's message about the potion, and that Juliet did not awake from her long sleep a minute sooner; an accident that Edgar arrived at the prison just too late to save Cordelia's life; an accident that Desdemona dropped her handkerchief at the most fatal of moments; an accident that the pirate ship attacked Hamlet's ship, so that he was able to return forthwith to Denmark. Now this operation of accident is a fact, and a prominent fact, of human life. To exclude it *wholly* from tragedy, therefore, would be, we may say, to fail in truth. And, besides, it is not merely a fact. That men may start a course of events but can neither calculate nor control it, is a *tragic* fact. The dramatist may use accident so as to make us feel this; and there are also other dramatic uses to which it may be put. Shakespeare accordingly admits it. On the other hand, any *large* admission of chance into the tragic sequence would certainly weaken, and might destroy, the sense of the causal connection of character, deed, and catastrophe. And Shakespeare really uses it very sparingly. We seldom find ourselves exclaiming, 'What an unlucky accident!' I believe most readers would have to search painfully for instances. It is, further, frequently easy to see the dramatic intention of an accident; and some things which look like accidents have really a connection with character, and are therefore not in the full sense accidents. Finally, I believe it will be found that almost all the prominent accidents occur when the action is well advanced and the impression of the causal sequence is too firmly fixed to be impaired.

Thus it appears that these three elements in the 'action' are subordinate, while the dominant factor consists in deeds which issue from character. So that, by way of summary, we may now alter our first statement, 'A tragedy is a story of exceptional calamity leading to the death of a man in high estate,' and we may say instead (what in its turn is one-sided, though less so), that the story is one of human actions producing exceptional calamity and ending in the death of such a man.

Before we leave the 'action,' however, there is an-

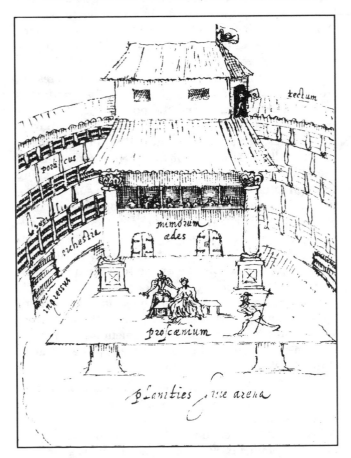

Drawing of the Swan Theatre (c.1596), attributed to Johannes de Witt. This sketch, made during Shakespeare's lifetime, is the only depiction of the interior of an Elizabethan playhouse known to survive.

other question that may usefully be asked. Can we define this 'action' further by describing it as a conflict?

The frequent use of this idea in discussions on tragedy is ultimately due, I suppose, to the influence of Hegel's theory on the subject, certainly the most important theory since Aristotle's. But Hegel's view of the tragic conflict is not only unfamiliar to English readers and difficult to expound shortly, but it had its origin in reflections on Greek tragedy and, as Hegel was well aware, applies only imperfectly to the works of Shakespeare. I shall, therefore, confine myself to the idea of conflict in its more general form. In this form it is obviously applicable to Shakespeare tragedy; but it is vague, and I will try to make it more precise by putting the question, Who are the combatants in this conflict?

Not seldom the conflict may quite naturally be conceived as lying between two persons, of whom the hero is one; or, more fully, as lying between two parties or groups, in one of which the hero is the leading figure. Or if we prefer to speak (as we may quite well do if we know what we are about) of the passions, tendencies, ideas, principles, forces, which animate these persons or groups, we may say that two of such passions or ideas, regarded as animating two persons or groups, are the combatants. The love of Romeo and Juliet is in conflict with the hatred of their houses, represented by various other characters. The cause of Brutus and Cassius struggles with that of Julius, Octavius and Antony. In *Richard II.* the King stands on one side, Bolingbroke and his party on the other. In *Macbeth* the hero and heroine are opposed to the representatives of Duncan. In all these cases the great majority of the *dramatis personae* fall without difficulty into antagonistic groups, and the conflict between these groups ends with the defeat of the hero.

Yet one cannot help feeling that in at least one of these cases, *Macbeth*, there is something a little external in this way of looking at the action. And when we come to some other plays this feeling increases. No doubt most of the characters in *Hamlet, King Lear, Othello,* or *Antony and Cleopatra* can be arranged in opposed groups; and no doubt there is a conflict; and yet it seems misleading to describe this conflict as one *between these groups.* It cannot be simply this. For though Hamlet and the King are mortal foes, yet that which engrosses our interest and dwells in our memory at least as much as the conflict between them, is the conflict *within* one of them. And so it is, though not in the same degree, with *Antony and Cleopatra* and even with *Othello;* and, in fact, in a certain measure, it is so with nearly all the tragedies. There is an outward conflict of persons and groups, there is also a conflict of forces in the hero's soul; and even in *Julius Caesar* and *Macbeth* the interest of the former can hardly be said to exceed that of the latter.

The truth is, that the type of tragedy in which the

hero opposes to a hostile force an undivided soul, is not the Shakespearean type. The souls of those who contend with the hero may be thus undivided; they generally are; but, as a rule, the hero, though he pursues his fated way, is, at least at some point in the action, and sometimes at many, torn by an inward struggle; and it is frequently at such points that Shakespeare shows his most extraordinary power. If further we compare the earlier tragedies with the later, we find that it is in the latter, the maturest works, that this inward struggle is most emphasised. In the last of them, *Coriolanus,* its interest completely eclipses towards the close of the play that of the outward conflict. *Romeo and Juliet, Richard III., Richard II.,* where the hero contends with an outward force, but comparatively little with himself, are all early plays.

If we are to include the outer and the inner struggle in a conception more definite than that of conflict in general, we must employ some such phrase as 'spiritual force.' This will mean whatever forces act in the human spirit, whether good or evil, whether personal passion or impersonal principle; doubts, desires, scruples, ideas—whatever can animate, shake, possess, and drive a man's soul. In a Shakespearean tragedy some such forces are shown in conflict. They are shown acting in men and generating strife between them. They are also shown, less universally, but quite as characteristically, generating disturbance and even conflict in the soul of the hero. Treasonous ambition in Macbeth collides with loyalty and patriotism in Macduff and Malcolm: here is the outward conflict. But these powers or principles equally collide in the soul of Macbeth himself: here is the inner. And neither by itself could make the tragedy. (pp. 11-19)

A. C. Bradley, in his *Shakespearean Tragedy: Lectures on Hamlet, Othello, King Lear, Macbeth,* second edition, Macmillan and Co., Limited, 1905, 498 p.

C. L. BARBER

(essay date 1959)

[An American scholar, Barber was one of the most important contemporary critics of Shakespearean comedy. His influential study *Shakespeare's Festive Comedy* (1959) examines the parallels between Elizabethan holiday celebrations and Shakespeare's comedies. In the following excerpt from this work, Barber explains how "the social form of Elizabethan holidays contributed to the dramatic form" of Shakespeare's early comedies.]

• • • • •

Messenger. Your honour's players, hearing your amendment,
Are come to play a pleasant comedy . . .
Beggar. . . . Is not a comonty a Christmas gambold or a tumbling trick?
Lady. No, my good lord; it is more pleasing stuff.
Beggar. What, household stuff ?
Lady. It is a kind of history.
Beggar. Well, we'll see it. Come, madam wife, sit by my side and let the world slip. We shall ne'er be younger.

—Induction to *The Taming of the Shrew*

• • • • •

Much comedy is festive—all comedy, if the word festive is pressed far enough. But much of Shakespeare's comedy is festive in a quite special way which distinguishes it from the art of most of his contemporaries and successors. The part of his work which I shall be dealing with . . . , the merry comedy written up to the period of *Hamlet* and the problem plays, is of course enormously rich and wide in range; each new play, each new scene, does something fresh, explores new possibilities. But the whole body of this happy comic art is distinguished by the use it makes of forms for experience which can be termed saturnalian. Once Shakespeare finds his own distinctive style, he is more Aristophanic than any other great English comic dramatist, despite the fact that the accepted educated models and theories when he started to write were Terentian and Plautine. The Old Comedy cast of his work results from his participation in native saturnalian traditions of the popular theater and the popular holidays. Not that he "wanted art"—including Terentian art. But he used the resources of a sophisticated theater to express, in his idyllic comedies and in his clowns' ironic misrule, the experience of moving to humorous understanding through saturnalian release. "Festive" is usually an adjective for an atmosphere, and the word describes the atmosphere of Shakespeare's comedy from *Love's Labour's Lost* and *A Midsummer Night's Dream* through *Henry IV* and *Twelfth Night.* But in exploring this work, "festive" can also be a term for structure. I shall be trying to describe structure to get at the way this comedy organizes experience. The saturnalian pattern appears in many variations, all of which involve inversion, statement and counterstatement, and a basic movement which can be summarized in the formula, through release to clarification.

So much of the action in this comedy is random when looked at as intrigue, so many of the persons are neutral when regarded as character, so much of the wit is inapplicable when assessed as satire, that critics too often have fallen back on mere exclamations about poetry and mood. The criticism of the nineteenth century and after was particularly helpless, concerned as it was chiefly with character and story and moral quality. Recent criticism, concerned in a variety of ways with structure, has had much more to say. No figure in the carpet is the carpet. There is in the pointing out of patterns something that is opposed to life and art, an ungraciousness which artists in particular feel and resent. Readers feel it too, even critics: for every new moment, every new line or touch, is a triumph of opportunism, something snatched in from life beyond expectation and made design beyond design. And yet the fact remains that it is as we see the design that we see design outdone and brought alive.

> O body swayed to music, O brightening glance,
> How can we know the dancer from the dance?

To get at the form and meaning of the plays, which is my first and last interest, I have been led into an exploration of the way the social form of Elizabethan holidays contributed to the dramatic form of festive comedy. To relate this drama to holiday has proved to be the most effective way to describe its character. And this historical interplay between social and artistic form has an interest of its own: we can see here, with more clarity of outline and detail than is usually possible, how art develops underlying configurations in the social life of a culture. The saturnalian pattern came to Shakespeare from many sources, both in social and artistic tradition. It appeared in the theatrical institution of clowning: the clown or Vice, when Shakespeare started to write, was a recognized anarchist who made aberration obvious by carrying release to absurd extremes. The cult of fools and folly, half social and half literary, embodied a similar polarization of experience. One could formulate the saturnalian pattern effectively by referring first to these traditions: Shakespeare's first completely masterful comic scenes were written for the clowns. But the festival occasion provides the clearest paradigm. It can illuminate not only those comedies where Shakespeare drew largely and directly on holiday motifs, like *Love's Labour's Lost, A Midsummer Night's Dream,* and *Twelfth Night,* but also plays where there is relatively little direct use of holiday, notably *As You Like It* and *Henry IV.*

We can get hold of the spirit of Elizabethan holidays because they had form. "Merry England" was merry chiefly by virtue of its community observances of periodic sports and feast days. Mirth took form in morris-dances, sword-dances, wassailings, mock ceremonies of summer kings and queens and of lords of misrule, mummings, disguisings, masques—and a bewildering variety of sports, games, shows, and pageants improvised on traditional models. Such pastimes were a regular part of the celebration of a marriage, of the village wassail or wake, of Candlemas, Shrove Tuesday, Hocktide, May Day, Whitsuntide, Midsummer Eve, Harvest-home, Halloween, and the twelve days of the Christmas season ending with Twelfth Night. Custom prescribed, more or less definitely, some ways of making merry at each occasion. The seasonal feasts were not, as now, rare curiosities to be observed by folklorists in remote villages, but landmarks framing the cycle of the year, observed with varying degrees of sophistication by most elements in the society. Shakespeare's casual references to the holidays always assume that his audience is entirely familiar with them:

> As fit as ten groats is for the hand of an attorney . . .
> as a pancake for Shrove Tuesday, a morris for May
> Day, as the nail to his hole . . .
>   (*All's Well That Ends Well* II. ii. 22)

A great many detailed connections between the holidays and the comedies will claim our attention later, but what is most important is the correspondence between the whole festive occasion and the whole comedy. The underlying movement of attitude and awareness is not adequately expressed by any one thing in the day or the play, but is the day, is the play. Here one cannot say how far analogies between social rituals and dramatic forms show an influence, and how far they reflect the fact that the holiday occasion and the comedy are parallel manifestations of the same pattern of culture, of a way that men can cope with their life.

THROUGH RELEASE TO CLARIFICATION

Release, in the idyllic comedies, is expressed by making the whole experience of the play like that of a revel.

> Come, woo me, woo me! for now I am in a holiday
> humour, and like enough to consent.
>   (*As You Like It* IV. i. 68-69)

Such holiday humor is often abetted by directly staging pastimes, dances, songs, masques, plays extempore, etc. But the fundamental method is to shape the loose narrative so that "events" put its persons in the position of festive celebrants: if they do not seek holiday it happens to them. A tyrant duke forces Rosalind into disguise; but her mock wooing with Orlando amounts to a Disguising, with carnival freedom from the decorum of her identity and her sex. The misrule of Sir Toby is represented as personal idiosyncrasy, but it follows the pattern of the Twelfth Night occasion; the flyting match of Benedict and Beatrice, while appropriate to their special characters, suggests the customs of Easter Smacks and Hocktide abuse between the sexes. Much of the poetry and wit, however it may be occasioned by events, works in the economy of the whole play to promote the effect of a merry occasion where Nature reigns.

F. M. Cornford, in *The Origins of Attic Comedy,* suggested that invocation and abuse were the basic gestures of a nature worship behind Aristophanes' union of poetry and railing. The two gestures were still practiced in the "folly" of Elizabethan Maygame, harvest-home, or winter revel: invocation, for example, in the manifold spring garlanding customs, "gathering for

Robin Hood"; abuse, in the customary license to flout and fleer at what on other days commanded respect. The same double way of achieving release appears in Shakespeare's festive plays. There the poetry about the pleasures of nature and the naturalness of pleasure serves to evoke beneficent natural impulses; and much of the wit, mocking the good housewife Fortune from her wheel, acts to free the spirit as does the ritual abuse of hostile spirits. A saturnalian attitude, assumed by a clear-cut gesture toward liberty, brings mirth, an accession of wanton vitality. In the terms of Freud's analysis of wit, the energy normally occupied in maintaining inhibition is freed for celebration. The holidays in actual observance were built around the enjoyment of the vital pleasure of moments when nature and society are hospitable to life. In the summer, there was love in out-of-door idleness; in the winter, within-door warmth and food and drink. But the celebrants also got something for nothing from festive liberty—the vitality normally locked up in awe and respect. E. K. Chambers found among the visitation articles of Archbishop Grindal for the year 1576 instructions that the bishops determine

> whether the ministers and churchwardens have suffered any lord of misrule or summer lords and ladies, or any disguised persons, or others, in Christmas or at May games, or any morrisdancers, or at any other times, to come unreverently into the church or churchyard, and there to dance, or play any unseemly parts, with scoffs, jests, wanton gestures, or ribald talk. . . .

Shakespeare's gay comedy is like Aristophanes' because its expression of life is shaped by the form of feeling of such saturnalian occasions as these. The traditional Christian culture within which such holidays were celebrated in the Renaissance of course gave a very different emphasis and perspective to Shakespeare's art. But Dicaeopolis, worsting pompous Lamachus in *The Acharnians* by invoking the tangible benefits of Bacchus and Aphrodite, acts the same festive part as Sir Toby baffling Malvolio's visitation by an appeal to cakes and ale.

The *clarification* achieved by the festive comedies is concomitant to the release they dramatize: a heightened awareness of the relation between man and "nature"—the nature celebrated on holiday. The process of translating festive experience into drama involved extending the sort of awareness traditionally associated with holiday, and also becoming conscious of holiday itself in a new way. The plays present a mockery of what is unnatural which gives scope and point to the sort of scoffs and jests shouted by dancers in the churchyard or in "the quaint mazes in the wanton green." And they include another, complementary mockery of what is merely natural, a humor which puts holiday in perspective with life as a whole.

The butts in the festive plays consistently exhibit their unnaturalness by being kill-joys. On an occasion "full of warm blood, of mirth," they are too preoccupied with perverse satisfactions like pride or greed to "let the world slip" and join the dance. Satirical comedy tends to deal with relations between social classes and aberrations in movements between them. Saturnalian comedy is satiric only incidentally; its clarification comes with movement between poles of restraint and release in everybody's experience. Figures like Malvolio and Shylock embody the sort of kill-joy qualities which the "disguised persons" would find in any of Grindal's curates who would not suffer them to enter the churchyard. Craven or inadequate people appear, by virtue of the festive orientation, as would-be revellers, comically inadequate to hear the chimes at midnight. Pleasure thus becomes the touchstone for judgment of what bars it or is incapable of it. And though in Shakespeare the judgment is usually responsible—valid we feel for everyday as well as holiday—it is the whirligig of impulse that tries the characters. Behind the laughter at the butts there is always a sense of solidarity about pleasure, a communion embracing the merrymakers in the play and the audience, who have gone on holiday in going to a comedy.

While perverse hostility to pleasure is a subject for aggressive festive abuse, highflown idealism is mocked too, by a benevolent ridicule which sees it as a not unnatural attempt to be more than natural. It is unfortunate that Shakespeare's gay plays have come to be known as "the romantic comedies," for they almost always establish a humorous perspective about the vein of hyperbole they borrow from Renaissance romances. Wishful absolutes about love's finality, cultivated without reserve in conventional Arcadia, are made fun of by suggesting that love is not a matter of life and death, but of springtime, the only pretty ring time. The lover's conviction that he will love "for ever and a day" is seen as an illusion born of heady feeling, a symptom of the festive moment:

> Say 'a day' without the 'ever.' No, no, Orlando! Men are April when they woo, December when they wed. Maids are May when they are maids, but the sky changes when they are wives.
>
> (*As You Like It* IV. i. 146-150)

This sort of clarification about love, a recognition of the seasons', of nature's part in man, need not qualify the intensity of feeling in the festive comedies: Rosalind when she says these lines is riding the full tide of her passionate gaiety. Where the conventional romances tried to express intensity by elaborating hyperbole according to a pretty, pseudo-theological system, the comedies express the power of love as a compelling rhythm in man and nature. So the term "romantic comedies" is misleading. Shakespeare, to be sure, does not always transform his romantic plot materials. In the

Claudio-Hero business in *Much Ado,* for example, the borrowed plot involved negative behavior on the basis of romantic absolutes which was not changed to carry festive feeling. Normally, however, as in *Twelfth Night,* he radically alters the emphasis when he employs romantic materials. Events which in his source control the mood, and are drawn out to exhibit extremity of devotion, producing now pathos, now anxiety, now sentiment, are felt on his stage, in the rhythm of stage time, as incidents controlled by a prevailing mood of revel. What was sentimental extremity becomes impulsive extravagance. And judgment, not committed to systematic wishful distortion, can observe with Touchstone how

> We that are true lovers run into strange capers; but as all is mortal in nature, so is all nature in love mortal in folly.
>
> (*As You Like It* II. iv. 53-56)

To turn on passionate experience and identify it with the holiday moment, as Rosalind does in insisting that the sky will change, puts the moment in perspective with life as a whole. Holiday, for the Elizabethan sensibility, implied a contrast with "everyday," when "brightness falls from the air." Occasions like May day and the Winter Revels, with their cult of natural vitality, were maintained within a civilization whose daily view of life focused on the mortality implicit in vitality. The tolerant disillusion of Anglican or Catholic culture allowed nature to have its day. But the release of that one day was understood to be a temporary license, a "misrule" which implied rule, so that the acceptance of nature was qualified. Holiday affirmations in praise of folly were limited by the underlying assumption that the natural in man is only one part of him, the part that will fade.

"How that a life was but a flower" (*As You Like It* V. iii. 29) was a two-sided theme: it was usually a gesture preceding "And therefore take the present time"; but it could also lead to the recognition that

> so, from hour to hour, we ripe and ripe,
> And then, from hour to hour, we rot and rot.
>
> (*As You Like It* II. vii. 26-27)

The second emphasis was implicit in the first; which attitude toward nature predominated depended, not on alternative "philosophies," but on where you were within a rhythm. And because the rhythm is recognized in the comedies, sentimental falsification is not necessary in expressing the ripening moment. It is indeed the present mirth and laughter of the festive plays—the immediate experience they give of nature's beneficence—which reconciles feeling, without recourse to sentimentality or cynicism, to the clarification conveyed about nature's limitations.

SHAKESPEARE'S ROUTE TO FESTIVE COMEDY

In drawing parallels between holiday and Shake-speare's comedy, it has been hard to avoid talking as though Shakespeare were a primitive who began with nothing but festival custom and invented a comedy to express it. Actually, of course, he started work with theatrical and literary resources already highly developed. This tradition was complex, and included folk themes and conventions along with the practice of classically trained innovators like Lyly, Kyd, and Marlowe. Shakespeare, though perfectly aware of unsophisticated forms like the morality and the jig, from the outset wrote plays which presented a narrative in three dimensions. In comedy, he began with cultivated models—Plautus for *The Comedy of Errors* and literary romance for *Two Gentlemen of Verona;* he worked out a consistently festive pattern for his comedy only after these preliminary experiments.

In his third early comedy, *Love's Labour's Lost,* instead of dramatizing a borrowed plot, he built his slight story around an elegant aristocratic entertainment. In doing so he worked out the holiday sequence of release and clarification which comes into its own in *A Midsummer Night's Dream.* This more serious play, his first comic masterpiece, has a crucial place in his development. To make a dramatic epithalamium, he expressed with full imaginative resonance the experience of the traditional summer holidays. He thus found his way back to a native festival tradition remarkably similar to that behind Aristophanes at the start of the literary tradition of comedy. And in expressing the native holiday, he was in a position to use all the resources of a sophisticated dramatic art. So perfect an expression and understanding of folk cult was only possible in the moment when it was still in the blood but no longer in the brain.

Shakespeare never made another play from pastimes in the same direct fashion. But the pattern for feeling and awareness which he derived from the holiday occasion in *A Midsummer Night's Dream* becomes the dominant mode of organization in subsequent comedies until the period of the problem plays. The relation between his festive comedy and naive folk games is amusingly reflected in the passage from *The Taming of The Shrew* which I have used as an epigraph. When the bemused tinker Sly is asked with mock ceremony whether he will hear a comedy to "frame your mind to mirth and merriment," his response reflects his ignorant notion that a comedy is some sort of holiday game—"a Christmas gambold or a tumbling trick." He is corrected with: "it is more pleasing stuff . . . a kind of history." Shakespeare is neither primitive nor primitivist; he enjoys making game of the inadequacy of Sly's folk notions of entertainment. But folk attitudes and motifs are still present, as a matter of course, in the dramatist's cultivated work, so that even Sly is not entirely off the mark about comedy. Though it is a kind of history, it is the kind that frames the mind to mirth.

So it functions like a Christmas gambol. It often includes gambols, and even, in the case of *As You Like It,* a tumbling trick. Though Sly has never seen a comedy, his holiday mottoes show that he knows in what spirit to take it: "let the world slip"; "we shall ne'er be younger." Prince Hal, in his festive youth, "daff 'd the world aside / And bid it pass" (*I Henry IV* V. i. 96). Feste sings that "Youth's a stuff will not endure" (*Twelfth Night, or What You Will* II. iii. 53).

The part of Shakespeare's earliest work where his mature patterns of comedy first appear clearly is, as I have suggested, the clowning. Although he did not find an entirely satisfactory comic form for the whole play until *A Midsummer Night's Dream,* the clown's part is satisfactory from the outset. Here the theatrical conventions with which he started writing already provided a congenial saturnalian organization of experience, and Shakespeare at once began working out its larger implications. It was of course a practice, going back beyond *The Second Shepherds' Play,* for the clowns to present a burlesque version of actions performed seriously by their betters. Wagner's conjuring in *Dr. Faustus* is an obvious example. In the drama just before Shakespeare began writing, there are a great many parallels of this sort between the low comedy and the main action. One suspects that they often resulted from the initiative of the clown performer; he was, as Sidney said, thrust in "by head and shoulders to play a part in majestical matters"—and the handiest part to play was a low take-off of what the high people were doing. Though Sidney objected that the performances had "neither decency nor discretion," such burlesque, when properly controlled, had an artistic logic which Shakespeare was quick to develop.

At the simplest level, the clowns were foils, as one of the aristocrats remarks about the clown's show in *Love's Labour's Lost* :

> 'tis some policy
> To have one show worse than the King's
> and his company.
> (*Love's Labour's Lost* V. ii. 513-514)

But burlesque could also have a positive effect, as a vehicle for expressing aberrant impulse and thought. When the aberration was made relevant to the main action, clowning could provide both release for impulses which run counter to decency and decorum, and the clarification about limits which comes from going beyond the limit. Shakespeare used this movement from release to clarification with masterful control in clown episodes as early as *2 Henry VI.* The scenes of the Jack Cade rebellion in that history are an astonishingly consistent expression of anarchy by clowning: the popular rising is presented throughout as a saturnalia, ignorantly undertaken in earnest; Cade's motto is: "then are we in order when we are most out of order" (IV. iii. 199). In the early plays, the clown is usually represented as

oblivious of what his burlesque implies. When he becomes the court fool, however, he can use his folly as a stalking horse, and his wit can express directly the function of his role as a dramatized commentary on the rest of the action.

In creating Falstaff, Shakespeare fused the clown's part with that of a festive celebrant, a Lord of Misrule, and worked out the saturnalian implications of both traditions more drastically and more complexly than anywhere else. If in the idyllic plays the humorous perspective can be described as looking past the reigning festive moment to the work-a-day world beyond, in *I Henry IV,* the relation of comic and serious action can be described by saying that holiday is balanced against everyday and the doomsday of battle. The comedy expresses impulses and awareness inhibited by the urgency and decorum of political life, so that the comic and serious strains are contrapuntal, each conveying the ironies limiting the other. Then in *2 Henry IV* Shakespeare confronts the anarchic potentialities of misrule when it seeks to become not a holiday extravagance but an everyday racket. (pp. 3-14)

. . .The sort of interpretation I have proposed . . . does not center on the way the comedies imitate characteristics of actual men and manners; but this neglect of the social observation in the plays does not imply that the way they handle social materials is unimportant. Comedy is not, obviously enough, the

Act V, Scene iii of the 1968 Franco Zeffirelli film adaptation of *Romeo and Juliet,* with Olivia Hussey as Juliet and Leonard Whiting as Romeo. Juliet: "O happy dagger, This is thy sheath; there rust, and let me die."

Major Media Adaptations: Motion Pictures and Television

A Midsummer Night's Dream, 1935. Warner (Max Reinhardt). Directors: Max Reinhardt and William Dieterle. Cast: Ian Hunter, Verree Teasdale, Victor Jory, Anita Louise, Dick Powell, Ross Alexander, Olivia de Havilland, Jean Muir, Mickey Rooney, James Cagney.

As You Like It, 1936. Twentieth-Century Fox. Director: Paul Czinner. Cast: Laurence Olivier, Elisabeth Bergner, Henry Ainley, Sophie Stewart, Mackenzie Ward, Leon Quartermaine.

Henry V, 1944. Two Cities Films (Laurence Olivier). Director: Laurence Olivier. Cast: Laurence Olivier, Leslie Banks, Renee Asherton, Esmond Knight, Leo Genn, Felix Aylmer, Harcourt Williams, Max Adrian.

Hamlet, 1948. Two Cities Films (Laurence Olivier). Director: Laurence Olivier. Cast: Laurence Olivier, Eileen Herlie, Basil Sydney, Jean Simmons, Felix Aylmer, Norman Wooland, Terence Morgan.

Macbeth, 1948. Mercury Productions (Orson Welles). Director: Orson Welles. Cast: Orson Welles, Jeanette Nolan, Dan O'Herlihy, Roddy McDowell, Edgar Barrier, Erskine Sanford.

Othello, 1952. Mercury Productions (Orson Welles). Director: Orson Welles. Cast: Orson Welles, Michael MacLiammoir, Suzanne Cloutier, Fay Compton, Robert Coote, Michael Lawrence.

Richard III, 1956. Laurence Olivier/London Films. Director: Laurence Olivier. Cast: Laurence Olivier, Ralph Richardson, John Gielgud, Claire Bloom, Cedric Hardwicke, Alec Clunes, Pamela Brown, Mary Kerridge, Norman Wooland, Helen Hayes.

Throne of Blood, 1957. Brandon Films. [Adaptation of *Macbeth;* in Japanese, with English subtitles] Director: Akira Kurosawa. Cast: Toshiro Mifune, Isuzu Yamada, Takashi Shimura, Minoru Chiaki, Akira Kubo, Takmaru Sasaki, Yoichi Tachikawa, Cheiko Naniwa.

West Side Story, 1961. Mirish/Seven Arts/Beta (Robert Wise). [Musical adaptation of *Romeo and Juliet*] Directors: Robert Wise and Jerome Robbins. Cast: Natalie Wood, Richard Beymer, Russ Tamblyn, Rita Moreno, George Chakiris.

The Bad Sleep Well, 1963. Toho. [Adaptation of *Hamlet;* in Japanese, with English subtitles] Director: Akira Kurosawa. Cast: Toshiro Mifune, Tokashi Kato, Mosayuki Mori, Tokashi Shimura, Akira Nishimura, Kamatari Fujiwara.

Othello, 1965. B.H.E. Productions (Anthony Havelock-Allan and John Brabourne). Directors: Stuart Burge and John Dexter. Cast: Laurence Olivier, Frank Finlay, Maggie Smith, Joyce Redman, Robert Lang, Derek Jacobi.

The Taming of the Shrew, 1967. Royal Films. Director: Franco Zeffirelli. Cast: Richard Burton, Elizabeth Taylor, Cyril Cusak, Michael Hordern, Alfred Lynch, Michael York, Alan Webb.

Romeo and Juliet, 1968. B.H.E. Productions/Verona Productions/Dino DeLaurentiis Cinematografica (Anthony Havelock-Allan and John Brabourne). Director: Franco Zeffirelli. Cast: Leonard Whiting, Olivia Hussey, Michael York, John McEnery, Pat Heywood, Milo O'Shea.

King Lear, 1970. Filmways/Royal Shakespeare Company (Michael Birkett). Director: Peter Brook. Cast: Paul Scofield, Irene Worth, Susan Engel, Annelise Gabold, Jack MacGowan, Alan Webb, Robert Lloyd, Ian Hogg, Tom Fleming.

The BBC Shakespeare, 1979-85. BBC [All plays].

Ran, 1985. Herald Ace/Greenwich Films. [Adaptation of *King Lear;* in Japanese, with English subtitles] Director: Akira Kurosawa. Cast: Tatsuya Nakadai, Akira Terao, Jinpachi Nesu, Daisuke Oka, Meiko Harada, Hisashi Igawa.

Hamlet, 1990. Warner. Director: Franco Zeffirelli. Cast: Mel Gibson, Glenn Close, Alan Bates, Ian Holm, Helena Bonham-Carter, Paul Scofield.

same thing as ritual; if it were, it would not perform its function. To express the underlying rhythm his comedy had in common with holiday, Shakespeare did not simply stage mummings; he found in the social life of his time the stuff for "a kind of history." We can see in the Saint George plays how cryptic and arbitrary action derived from ritual becomes when it is merely a fossil remnant. In a self-conscious culture, the heritage of cult is kept alive by art which makes it relevant as a mode of perception and expression. The artist gives the ritual pattern aesthetic actuality by discovering expressions of it in the fragmentary and incomplete gestures of daily life. He fulfills these gestures by making them moments in the complete action which is the art form. The form finds meaning in life.

This process of translation from social into artistic form has great historical as well as literary interest. Shakespeare's theater was taking over on a professional and everyday basis functions which until his time had largely been performed by amateurs on holiday. And he wrote at a moment when the educated part of society was modifying a ceremonial, ritualistic conception of human life to create a historical, psychological conception. His drama, indeed, was an important agency in this transformation: it provided a "theater" where the failures of ceremony could be looked at in a place apart and understood as history; it provided new ways of representing relations between language and action so as to express personality. In making drama out of rituals of state, Shakespeare makes clear their meaning as social and psychological conflict, as history. So too with the rituals of pleasure, of misrule, as against rule: his comedy presents holiday magic as imagination, games as expressive gestures. At high moments it brings into focus, as part of the play, the significance of the saturnalian form itself as a paradoxical human need, problem and resource. (pp. 14-15)

C. L. Barber, in his *Shakespeare's Festive Comedy: A Study of Dramatic Form and Its Relation to Social Custom,* Princeton University Press, 1959, 261 p.

L. C. KNIGHTS

(essay date 1959)

[A renowned English Shakespearean scholar, Knights disparaged the traditional critical emphasis on character as limiting the reader's response to Shakespeare's plays. In the following excerpt from *Some Shakespearean Themes* (1959), he considers Shakespeare's "exploration of the public world and its tragic consequences" in the history plays.]

With the possible exception of *Romeo and Juliet* all the more significant of Shakespeare's early plays deal with public themes: their protagonists are, ostensibly, figures from history, in actuality representative figures from the world of great affairs. It is in this area of human experience that Shakespeare made some of his keenest observations, and the interest that determined the choice of subject for—probably—his earliest plays remained active throughout his career. When we look at the whole sequence of the political plays (for this, rather than 'History plays, English and Roman', seems the best description of them) we see a steady deepening of the vision and an increasingly close relationship with work that is not formally historical or political. The connexions are close and intricate. In the public world the conflicts are no simpler, the contradictions no less deeply rooted, than in more intimate relationships or within the individual himself. Indeed the distinguishing mark of Shakespeare's handling of political actions is the clarity with which he sees them, not in terms of 'politics' (that word which, perhaps as much as any, is responsible for simplification and distortion in our thinking) but in terms of their causes in human fears and desires and of particular human consequences. His interest in politics was of a kind that led, inevitably, beyond them, and the insights that made possible *Coriolanus* were developed outside the bounds of a merely political concern. This, however, is to anticipate. All I wish to remark here is that the public world of the early plays is not, so to speak, felt from within, but it is a world that is keenly *observed*. For our present purposes

both the negative and the positive implications of this are important.

In the first four plays on English history—the three parts of *Henry VI* and *Richard III*—the conventional and formal mode (history moralized on the Tudor pattern) is increasingly qualified by reality breaking in. To say this does not of course mean that there is a simple progress from 'convention' to naturalism; it means that within the formal pattern Shakespeare can make us see and feel the human actuality. A small but significant example is the scene in *Richard III* (III, vii) in which Gloucester, suitably discovered at his devotions between a couple of bishops, pretends reluctance to take the crown, offered to him as the result of a carefully rigged meeting at the Guildhall. The comedy of the scene is simple enough, but it is entirely serious, and it lies in the contrast of what may be called the newspaper-headline view of events and what we know is the truth of the matter. Or again, in *2 Henry VI,* there is the well-known scene of Cade's oration to his men.

> CADE. Be brave then; for your captain is brave, and vows reformation. There shall be in England seven halfpenny loaves sold for a penny; the three-hooped pot shall have ten hoops; and I will make it felony to drink small beer. All the realm shall be in common, and in Cheapside shall my palfrey go to grass. And when I am king, as king I will be,—
>
> ALL. God save your majesty!
>
> CADE. I thank you good people: there shall be no money; all shall eat and drink on my score; and I will apparel them all in one livery, that they may agree like brothers, and worship me their lord.
>
> (IV. ii)

The point is not simply that Cade is a 'character', whereas Iden, say, is a type figure. That Shakespeare did not so cast him, as a mere representative of 'commotion' (III. i. 358), was not entirely because Cade offered an opportunity for a bit of incidental comedy; we may fairly assume it was because he could not suppress his interest in the actuality of the demagogue, in the private motives and muddles that at any time may make their impact—transient or more lasting—on the public world. Much of *King Henry VI* is, as it were, action seen at a distance—as children see history, or as most of us tend to see world affairs. When Shakespeare alters the focus (and this is a dramatic device that he was to use repeatedly later), we have a close-up view of what we had taken to be a pageant: history and politics begin to appear differently. And it is in the development of a particular manner of speech that the pressure of life makes itself felt.

This new kind of interest, demanding a new use of words, centres on the figure of Richard of Gloucester, who in the Third Part of *Henry VI* announces his intention of setting the murderous Machiavel to school. *Richard III* is still to some extent a political morality play in which events—like some of the speeches—are rather stiffly formalized and patterned. But Richard himself isn't simply a morality figure—Cunning Craft or Policy. The way he speaks—the way Shakespeare makes him speak—relates him directly to a world that is seen and felt close at hand. In *Henry VI* Shakespeare uses more than one style, but the following, from the Second Part (II. vi), is not uncharacteristic of that play: the speaker is the mortally wounded Clifford.

> The common people swarm like summer flies;
> And whither fly the gnats but to the sun?
> And who shines now but Henry's enemies?
> O Phoebus, hadst thou never given consent
> That Phaëthon should check thy fiery steeds,
> Thy burning car never had scorched the earth!
> And, Henry, hadst thou sway'd as kings should do,
> Or as thy father and his father did,
> Giving no ground unto the house of York,
> They never then had sprung like summer flies;
> I and ten thousand in this luckless realm
> Had left no mourning widows for our death;
> And thou this day hadst kept thy chair in peace.
> For what does cherish weeds but gentle air?
> And what makes robbers bold but too much lenity?
> Bootless are plaints, and cureless are my wounds;
> No way to fly, nor strength to hold out flight:
> The foe is merciless, and will not pity;
> For at their hands I have deserved no pity.

We have only to put beside this a passage from the opening soliloquy of *Richard III* to see how rapidly Shakespeare's resources are developing, and in what direction.

> Grim-visag'd War hath smooth'd his wrinkled
>   front;
> And now, instead of mounting barbed steeds,
> To fright the souls of fearful adversaries,
> He capers nimbly in a lady's chamber,
> To the lascivious pleasing of a lute.
> But I, that am not shap'd for sportive tricks,
> Nor made to court an amorous looking-glass;
> I, that am rudely stamp'd and want love's majesty,
> To strut before a wanton ambling nymph;
> I, that am curtail'd of this fair proportion,
> Cheated of feature by dissembling Nature,
> Deform'd, unfinish'd, sent before my time
> Into this breathing world, scarce half made up,
> And that so lamely and unfashionably,
> That dogs bark at me as I halt by them;
> Why, I, in this weak piping time of peace,
> Have no delight to pass away the time,
> Unless to spy my shadow in the sun,
> And descant on mine own deformity.
> And therefore, since I cannot prove a lover,
> To entertain these fair well-spoken days,
> I am determined to prove a villain . . .

Of this speech Mr Traversi says, 'Although a certain stilted quality survives in the movement of the verse . . . the general effect is remarkably concise and pointed. Richard's state of mind is conveyed primarily through a series of sharp visual touches directly expressed—the vision of himself as "strutting" ludicrously before a "wanton, ambling nymph", as being "barked at" by the dogs as he passes before them, as "spying" his misshapen shadow in the sun. . . . In this way, by making envy the vehicle for a criticism felt, by its very directness, not to be altogether unjustified, the speaker is humanized, transformed from the abstract incarnation of a traditional vice exploited for melodramatic effect into something like a person'. It would be difficult to improve on this account of a realistic manner that, in this play, we associate especially with Richard. There are his characteristically terse asides ('But yet I run before my horse to market'), and even the formal oration to his army before Bosworth has a colloquial vividness.

> Remember whom you are to cope withal;
> A sort of vagabonds, rascals, and runaways,
> A scum of Bretons, and base lackey peasants, . . .
> And who doth lead them but a paltry fellow,
> Long kept in Bretagne at our mother's cost?
> A milk-sop, one that never in his life
> Felt so much cold as over shoes in snow!
> Let's whip these stragglers o'er the seas again . . .
> If we conquer'd, let men conquer us,
> And not these bastard Bretons, whom our fathers
> Have in their own land beaten, bobb'd and thump'd.
> (V. iii. 316-35)

In the presentation of Richard, then, there is a new psychological interest. (It is significant that Shakespeare drew on More's vivid and dramatic presentation in his *Life of Richard III*.) But it is as the Machiavel—not the merely theatrical Machiavel, but the a-moral political 'realist'—that Shakespeare is primarily interested in him. Or perhaps we should say that the interest in the Machiavel, the public figure, is inseparable from the psychological interest in the man with a grudge against the world.

> I have no brother, I am like no brother;
> And this word 'love', which greybeards call divine,
> Be resident in men like one another
> And not in me: I am myself alone.

As Mr Danby has pointed out, this speech of Richard's, when he has killed Henry VI, looks forward to some of Shakespeare's profounder searchings of the human situation. Meanwhile we may simply notice that in the presentation of Richard Shakespeare is developing an idiom and manner in which the political world can be seen directly, can be brought closer to what the audience directly knows, or can be brought to see, of men and affairs.

This manner is brilliantly developed in *King John.*

A scene from the 1961 United Artists production of *West Side Story*, a musical adaptation of
Romeo and Juliet.

There is a new activity in the descriptive passages, as in the well-known account of the spread of anxious rumour (IV. ii. 185-202) or in the Bastard's defiance of the Dauphin's troops.

> That hand which had the strength, even at your
>   door,
> To cudgel you and make you take the hatch,
> To dive like buckets in concealed wells,
> To crouch in litter of your stable planks,
> To lie like pawns lock'd up in chests and trunks,
> To hug with swine, to seek sweet safety out
> In vaults and prisons, and to thrill and shake
> Even at the crying of your nation's crow,
> Thinking his voice an armed Englishman;
> Shall that victorious hand be feebled here,
> That in your chambers gave you chastisement?
>   (V. ii. 137-47)

As is plain from these lines, it is a manner particularly suited for the purposes of mockery or satire, and it is the Bastard's especial rôle to act as a solvent of all that is high-flown and exaggerated, whether it is literary affectation (II. i. 504-9) or social pretension:

> Now your traveller,
> He and his toothpick at my worship's mess,
> And when my knightly stomach is sufficed,
> Why then I suck my teeth and catechize

> My picked man of countries: 'My dear sir,'
> Thus, leaning on mine elbow, I begin,
> 'I shall beseech you'—that is question now;
> And then comes answer like an Absey
>   book:
> 'O sir,' says answer, 'at your best command;
> At your employment; at your service, sir:'
> 'No, sir,' says question, 'I, sweet sir, at
>   yours:'
> And so, ere answer knows what question
>   would,
> Saving in dialogue of compliment,
> And talking of the Alps and Apennines,
> The Pyrenean and the river Po,
> It draws toward supper in conclusion so.
> But this is worshipful society. . . .
>   (I. i. 189-205)

This last passage has a particular significance: by a variety of devices, including exaggerated gesture ('Thus, leaning on mine elbow, I begin . . .') and sardonic alliteration ('The Pyrenean and the river Po'), 'worshipful society' is shown from the standpoint of an outsider, but (there is neither fuss nor bitterness in the satire) one who clearly *belongs* elsewhere. As I have said in another connexion, his idiom, references and manner relate him directly to the local world, where 'St George, that swinged the dragon . . . sits on his horse back at mine hostess' door', a world where observation is direct and comment forthright.

The world into which the Bastard is introduced is the world of statecraft—the Renaissance world, where 'policy', by the end of the sixteenth century, had acquired its sinister implication. The precepts of Machiavelli's *The Prince* had of course been followed, if not formulated, before the sixteenth century; but it was not without reason that the Elizabethans saw in 'the Machiavel' a portent. In economic affairs, in national politics and international relations, perhaps more than ever before, men were becoming aware of what could be achieved by the will directed to 'rational'—that is, clearly defined—ends. In other words, there was an increasing preoccupation with the problem of power, especially of power divorced from conscience. In *Richard III* the question had been debated by the two murderers of Clarence.

> FIRST MURDERER. Where's thy conscience now?
> SECOND MURDERER. O, in the Duke of Gloucester's purse.
> FIRST MURDERER. When he opens his purse to give us our reward, thy conscience flies out.
> SECOND MURDERER. 'Tis no matter, let it go: there's few or none will entertain it.
> FIRST MURDERER. What if it come to thee again?
> SECOND MURDERER. I'll not meddle with it: it makes a man a coward . . . 'Tis a blushing shamefast spirit, that mutinies in a man's bosom; it fills a man full of obstacles . . . it is turn'd out of towns and cities for a dangerous thing; and every man that means to live well endeavours to trust to himself and to live without it.
>
> (I. iv. 125-42)

And lest this should be thought irrelevant to the main theme Richard himself was made to reveal that the basic assumption of power politics is the same as the Second Murderer's.

> Conscience is but a word that cowards use,
> Devis'd at first to keep the strong in awe;
> Our strong arms be our conscience, swords our law!
>
> (V. iii. 310-12)

The rulers in *King John* are not quite so explicit. When the contending parties meet before Angiers both the King of France and the Duke of Austria profess lofty and disinterested motives; and even John, whose 'strong possession' of the crown is much more than his 'right' (I. i. 40), can adopt at times a lofty religious tone. The upshot of the meeting of the kings is a marriage alliance determined purely by 'policy', and it is this that gives the Bastard his opportunity to comment directly on the political action.

> Mad world! mad kings! mad composition!
> John, to stop Arthur's title in the whole,
> Hath willingly departed with a part:
> And France, whose armour conscience buckled on,

> Whom zeal and charity brought to the field
> As God's own soldier, rounded in the ear
> With that same purpose-changer, that sly devil,
> That broker, that still breaks the pate of faith,
> That daily break-vow, he that wins of all,
> Of kings, of beggars, old men, young men, maids,
> Who, having no external thing to lose
> But the word 'maid', cheats the poor maid of that,
> That smooth-faced gentleman, tickling Commodity,
> Commodity, the bias of the world,
> The world, who of itself is peised well,
> Made to run even upon even ground,
> Till this advantage, this vile-drawing bias,
> This sway of motion, this Commodity,
> Makes it take head from all indifferency,
> From all direction, purpose, course, intent:
> And this same bias, this Commodity,
> This bawd, this broker, this all-changing word,
> Clapp'd on the outward eye of fickle France,
> Hath drawn him from his own determined aid,
> From a resolved and honourable war,
> To a most base and vile-concluded peace.
> And why rail I on this Commodity?
> But for because he hath not woo'd me yet . . .
> Since kings break faith upon commodity,
> Gain be my lord, for I will worship thee.
>
> (II. i. 561-88)

The Bastard's profession of self-interest—judging by his subsequent conduct—is not to be taken at its face value, but there is no doubt that his speech as a whole, with its racy colloquial turns and shrewd realism, is the pivot on which the play turns. Indeed, so far as any one speech can, it sums up Shakespeare's view of the public world at this stage of his career.

King John, it is true, is not an entirely satisfactory play. At the end the English lords, who have revolted because of what they consider John's crime against Arthur, on learning that the Dauphin intends to double-cross them return to their allegiance—'even to our ocean, to our great King John', who has been shown as anything but great; and the action is rounded off with a simple patriotic appeal—

> This England never did, nor never shall,
> Lie at the proud foot of a conqueror,
> But when it first did help to wound itself.
> . . . Nought shall make us rue,
> If England to itself do rest but true.

But the play as a whole is anything but a simple patriotic play; nor is it merely a play about past history; it is a play about international politics, which are seen with complete realism through the eyes of the Bastard. In the plays that follow, Shakespeare was to find subtler means of expressing and enforcing judgment on the presented action; and he was never again to sum up with the simple obviousness of the speech on Commodity. But the Bastard represents something fundamental in Shakespeare's outlook on the world; he represents the habit of looking at things directly, of cutting through pretence and getting behind the words that disguise reality. In the greater plays on social and political themes, Shakespeare takes a situation, an attitude, an idea, and asks, *What does this mean,* in terms of specific human causes and consequences?

In the First Part of *King Henry IV* the question that Shakespeare is asking is, What does it mean to use force for political ends, to seek and keep power? The facts of the situation—I mean the dramatic facts, not any that may be brought in from historical knowledge extraneous to the play—are clear. Henry Bolingbroke is a usurping king, who is now meeting the consequences of usurpation in precisely the way that was foretold in *Richard II.* But we are concerned not only with a succession of 'facts' but with interpretation and judgment—and judgment has to do with the way in which, at particular places within a developing context, we give or refuse imaginative assent to the varied attitudes or life-directions, revealed through the spoken word, whose struggle and interaction constitute the drama. It is certain that the rebels, the Northumberland faction, do not enlist our sympathy. Indeed they are often presented satirically, as in the comedy of their first meeting, where Worcester and Hotspur take turns in deflating each other's rhetoric:

> WORCESTER. . . . And now I will unclasp a secret book,
> And to your quick-conceiving discontents
> I'll read you matter deep and dangerous,
> As full of peril and adventurous spirit
> As to o'er-walk a current roaring loud
> On the unsteadfast footing of a spear.
> HOTSPUR. If he fall in, good night! or sink or swim . . .
>
> (I. iii. 188-94)

In spite of the moral indignation they can direct against Bolingbroke, there is really no pretence that they are setting out to right a wrong. They simply stand for factional interests whose determined pursuit is bound to lead to further bloodshed and disorder—to 'pellmell havoc and confusion' (V. i. 82). Worcester, as spokesman of the faction, may complain to Henry of 'unkind usage . . . violation of all faith and troth' (V. i. 69-70), but it is Worcester who lets us know that the public and diplomatic colouring is no more than that—

> For well you know we of the offering side
> Must keep aloof from strict arbitrement,
> And stop all sight-holes, every loop from whence
> The eye of reason may pry in upon us;
>
> (IV. i. 69-72)

and it is he who conceals the king's 'liberal and kind offer' of peace before Shrewsbury:

> It is not possible, it cannot be,
> The king should keep his word in loving us;

> He will suspect us still, and find a time
> To punish this offence in other faults:
> Suspicion all our lives shall be stuck full of eyes;
> For treason is but trusted like the fox . . .
>
> (V. ii. 4-9)

Yet the rebels' view of how the king came to his throne—and they revert to it often enough—is not far from what Henry himself admits. Hotspur speaks of 'murderous subornation' (I. iii. 163), of a hypocritical pretence of righting wrongs, whereas Henry speaks of 'necessity',

> . . . necessity so bow'd the state,
> That I and greatness were compell'd to kiss,
>
> (Part II, III. i. 73-4)

but even he admits to his son that he used considerable astuteness to 'pluck allegiance from men's hearts' (III. ii. 39 ff.), and, as he says on his death-bed,

> God knows, my son,
> By what by-paths and indirect crook'd ways
> I met this crown.
>
> (Part II, IV. v. 183-5)

The 'necessity' to which he submitted has its own laws, and although there is the accent of sincerity whenever Henry reflects on the condition of England—'my poor kingdom, sick with civil blows!' (Part II, IV. v. 133)—or urges the need for peace, he is caught in a chain of consequences from which he cannot escape,

> For all my reign hath been but as a scene
> Acting that argument . . .
>
> (Part II, IV. v. 197-8)

What we have in *1 Henry IV* therefore is a realistic portrayal of the ways of the world and an insistent questioning of the values by which its great men live—with a consequent ironic contrast between public profession and the actuality. The questioning centres on the nature of 'honour'. Shakespeare does not say that honour is unreal, a mere abstract word with which men hide reality from themselves: he simply points out—that is, the play has the effect of pointing out—that whether honour means much or little depends on the person using it. Hotspur is of course the chief exponent of Honour in the conventional sense, and the forced rhetoric with which he presents his ideal is comment enough.

> By heaven, methinks it were an easy leap,
> To pluck bright honour from the pale-faced moon,
> Or dive into the bottom of the deep,
> Where fathom-line could never touch the ground,
> And pluck up drowned honour by the locks;
> So he that doth redeem her thence might wear
> Without corrival all her dignities.
>
> (I. iii. 201-7)

But Hotspur, fundamentally immature as he is in his

aggressive self-assertion (as also, incidentally, in his relations with his wife), is not only taken seriously by the other characters, as such people have to be, he is accorded respect. For Henry he is 'a son who is the theme of honour's tongue' (I. i. 81); and although Prince Hal can produce an amusing skit on the swashbuckling hero—'he that kills me some six or seven dozen of Scots at a breakfast, washes his hands, and says to his wife "Fie upon this quiet life! I want work." ' (II. iv. 102-5)—Hal too accepts the conventions:

> Percy is but my factor, good my lord,
> To engross up glorious deeds on my behalf;
> And I will call him to so strict account,
> That he shall render every glory up . . .
>
> (III. ii. 147-50)

Honour, then, is simply military glory—a prerogative of the nobleman who can afford to forget the humbler realities of warfare.

But the play as a whole does not allow us to forget them. The element of unreality in the world of the military and political leaders—their failure to take enough into account—is made plain in various ways. There is the persistent imagery of physical violence which throughout the play reminds us that warfare is not simply a form of sport,—

> And as the soldiers bore dead bodies by,
> He call'd them untaught knaves, unmannerly,
> To bring a slovenly unhandsome corse
> Betwixt the wind and his nobility.
>
> (I. iii. 42-5)

There is deliberate juxtaposition, with an effect of implicit critical comment, as when Vernon's description of the Prince of Wales and his comrades in arms

> —Glittering in golden coats, like images;
> As full of spirit as the month of May—
>
> (IV. i. 100-1)

is followed, first, by Hotspur's invocation of Mars 'up to the ears in blood' (IV. i. 112-17), and then, almost without a pause, by Falstaff 's account of the military operations whereby a hundred and fifty scarecrows are led to take their part in the same 'glorious day' (III. ii. 133).

> I have misused the king's press damnably. I have got, in exchange of a hundred and fifty soldiers, three hundred and odd pounds. I press me none but good house-holders, yeomen's sons; inquire me out contracted bachelors . . . I pressed me none but such toasts-and-butter, with hearts in their bellies no bigger than pins'-heads, and they have bought out their services; and now my whole charge consists of ancients, corporals, lieutenants, gentlemen of companies, slaves as ragged as Lazarus in the painted cloth, where the glutton's dogs licked his sores; and such indeed as were never soldiers . . . and such have I, to fill up the rooms of them that have bought

out their services, that you would think that I had a hundred and fifty tattered prodigals lately come from swine-keeping, from eating draff and husks.

> (IV. ii. 12-36)

In short, within the space of some eighty lines, we have successive glimpses of the chivalric, the barbaric ('all hot and bleeding'), and the completely unheroic aspects of war: Shakespeare does not say that one is 'truer' than another, but Falstaff 's 'pitiful rascals'—'good enough to toss; food for powder' (IV. ii. 66)—are, after all, part of the setting in which the nobles expect to purchase honour.

It is of course from Falstaff, whose obvious comic function combines with a more serious rôle, that the main explicit criticism comes. He may be in part the personification of Misrule from whom it is the Prince's business to escape, but clearly he cannot be reduced to a morality abstraction. It is impossible to think of him, as Hal tends to do, simply as 'blown Jack' or 'guts'—his mind moves more quickly than that of anyone else in the play—but over against Hotspur's abstraction, 'honour', he does represent the life of the body, intent on its own preservation and the satisfaction of its instincts, and his philosophy is summed up in the famous soliloquy before Shrewsbury.

> Well, 'tis no matter; honour pricks me on. Yea, but how if honour prick me off when I come on? how then? Can honour set to a leg? no: or an arm? no: or take away the grief of a wound? no. Honour hath no skill in surgery, then? no. What is honour? a word. What is in that word honour? what is that honour? air. A trim reckoning! Who hath it? he that died o' Wednesday, Doth he feel it? no. Doth he hear it? no. 'Tis insensible, then? yea, to the dead. But will it not live with the living? no. Why? detraction will not suffer it. Therefore I'll none of it. Honour is a mere scutcheon; and so ends my catechism.
>
> (V. i. 129-41)

Shakespeare's philosophy, to be sure, is not Falstaff 's. Falstaff too is presented critically, as 'riot and dishonour', and even in Part I there is enough to prevent us from taking him (as we take the Bastard) for an entirely reliable commentator. Nevertheless there is a sense in which Falstaff is, as Middleton Murry calls him, 'a triumphant particular crystallization of the general element', and through him—to change the metaphor—the pervasive ironic vision comes to its sharpest focus. It is largely because Falstaff is in the play that we are able to see how flawed and unsatisfactory is the public world.

In *Henry V,* in *Julius Caesar* and, later, in *Coriolanus,* Shakespeare was to continue his exploration of the public world and its tragic contradictions, and of the rôle of the Governor. But between *1 Henry IV* and *Henry V* Shakespeare wrote *2 Henry IV*; and the Second Part of **King Henry IV** is a different kind of play from the first Part. There is certainly continuity, but there is also a new direction of interest and the action is contrived for new purposes: there is a greater involvement of the dramatist in his fable. [Yet] it seems important to emphasize once more the realism—the detached observation and irony—that has been briefly illustrated in this chapter. This shrewd understanding of men in their political and public aspects and relations (not 'disillusioned', because that implies an attitude to the self quite foreign to Shakespeare, but certainly without illusions) was an essential condition of Shakespeare's exploration of experiences that come to each man simply as individual man in his more directly personal life and relationships. It meant that the inwardness was to be something utterly different from the results of an engrossed introspection. (pp. 28-44)

L. C. Knights, in his *Some Shakespearean Themes,* 1959. Reprint by Stanford University Press, 1960, 183 p.

WOLFGANG H. CLEMEN
(lecture date 1964)

[A German Shakespearean scholar, Clemen was among the first critics to consider Shakespeare's imagery an integral part of the development of his dramatic art. In the following excerpt from a lecture delivered in honor of the 400th anniversary of Shakespeare's birth, he evaluates the characteristic elements of Shakespearean drama.]

What is the unique form, the individual quality of Shakespearian drama? Critics have often tried to answer this question by defining it as 'great drama' in an absolute sense—as a synthesis of everything which they consider to be dramatic. But if we look closer we can see that Shakespeare is exceptional and unique in the history of European drama. For this reason all the attempts which have been made to derive the basic rules and norms of drama from his work have proved to be so difficult and usually so fruitless.

In this essay I should like to define the individual and unique quality of Shakespearian drama by selecting, from the numerous possible points of view, what is perhaps most prominent in our minds. We shall commence by asking ourselves what it is that primarily occurs to us when we think of Shakespeare's plays. First of all there is a vast crowd of human figures: kings and great barons, fools and tradesmen, princesses and peasant girls, eccentrics and outcasts of society, soldiers, actors, witches and magicians, mythological figures and fairies, cardinals and pagan deities; a whole *theatrum mundi,* in fact, which appears to play in the remote past and in the immediate present as well. If we now go on to ask ourselves in what visual context this world of figures impresses itself upon us, then we see again the most varied and contrasting scenes: ceremonies of state alongside tavern drinking-bouts and rough brawls, tender love-scenes alongside court festivities, marching armies and solemn coronations, masquerades and village fêtes, assassination and pensive soliloquies, merry dances and dumb shows, songs and the melancholy music of the lute. There is similar variety in the language, for we hear stylized speeches as well as rapid prose dialogue, rich and formal Elizabethan verse alongside coarse jokes, witty repartee of high comedy and the slang of everyday speech, melodramatic rhetoric in the scenes of grand passion, and simple, terse utterances in moments of distress.

These are merely casual impressions and associations, such as may occur to all of us. Here they are only intended to indicate a starting-point from which we easily reach the first two distinctive marks which may help us to characterize the individual quality of Shakespeare's work. For Shakespeare's drama appears to be a free and open form of drama, continually changing and not subject to prescribed rules, and also a form of drama in which the most varied and mutually opposed elements combine to form a new unity.

The first of these two characteristics provides the conditions necessary for the second. So I shall begin with this first characteristic: a free form of drama. This means both that Shakespeare does not feel himself limited by any rules, any three unities or superimposed sense of decorum, and also that exceptional possibilities are provided for bold inventiveness and experiment, possibilities of which Shakespeare takes equally exceptional advantage.

This free, unrestricted form gives rise to the receptiveness of his drama for many features and suggestions from the non-dramatic literature of the time. For not only dancing and music, but also lyric and epic elements exercise their influence and are readily adopted by the poet. This is an inclusive, not an exclusive form of drama, for it has an extraordinary power of assimilation, and is consequently able to include many things which according to later standards would have been left outside the drama. Thus Shakespeare's work becomes a melting-pot for many elements of form and expression which we find in Elizabethan prose and poetry, but which Shakespeare subordinates critically and consciously to his dramatic intentions.

This receptivity for new and different material was due to the fact that the form of Shakespeare's drama was not strictly fixed or laid down. When he began to write he found that there was no predominant dramatic tradition, but on the contrary a great diversity of types of drama of various origins. There was on the one hand the neo-classical rhetorical drama in the Senecan tradition, and on the other the crude popular play.

There were Lyly's courtly comedies with their refined wit and polished dialogue, there were pastoral plays, masques employing allegory and pantomime, and Marlowe's powerful tragedies; the mystery-plays and moralities were still being performed, and Shakespeare may well have seen them in his youth in one of the neighbouring towns.

Probably no other period in the history of the European theatre has offered at one time such a great variety of different dramatic styles and possibilities; and these were not clearly separated, but capable of being combined and fused with one another in many different ways. Both the interest in drama and the participation in its creation and production were common to all classes of society; drama came into existence in the most diverse places and from a multiplicity of causes.

This varied abundance proved to be exactly the right soil, in which Shakespeare's dramatic art was able to take root and flourish. The very fact that no single clear and authoritative conception of drama could come into existence was a necessary condition for the development of the free and open form of which I have spoken. Shakespeare was not obliged to commit himself to a fixed type, and he never did; on the contrary, he continually changed his manner, from one play to the next. This lack of commitment to a particular form has given us the most flexible and adaptable type of drama in the history of the European theatre.

Let us consider for a moment the extraordinary differences between plays which follow one another. *Richard II,* with its lyrical and reflective richness and its comparative lack of sensational stage action, follows the utterly different history of *Richard III.* And what an astonishing difference there is between *The Merchant of Venice* and *A Midsummer Night's Dream,* though both are called comedies! In *The Merchant of Venice* we have what is virtually a serious play with a happy ending, and even the beginning of a tragedy of character, if we look at the figure of Shylock.

How different is *A Midsummer Night's Dream* with its inter-weaving of the world of the fairies, the mechanicals' sub-plot, and the entanglements of the Athenian lovers! Here none of the characters are at all 'true to life', with the exception of Bottom. But in spite of this *A Midsummer Night's Dream* is one of the greatest plays in the whole of literature, and if we examine its dramatic form we see that it represents a bold advance along new paths.

A comparison of the tragedies also reveals more differences than points in common, and any attempt to ascertain a kind of basic structure of Shakespearian tragedy would be fruitless unless we were to be content with a few external similarities. Following upon the tragedy of *Othello,* with the closely woven, uninterrupted progress of its plot and the clear logic of its ar-

chitecture, comes *King Lear,* which rests upon an utterly different principle of composition, in which expansion and breadth dominate, so that the plot often comes to a halt to permit a fuller portrayal of a character's state of mind.

Shakespeare had shown in *Othello* how much he was a man of the theatre and in full command of all the possibilities of the stage, but in *King Lear* it is apparent that he has attempted something quite different. For here we are faced with the great design of a new dramatic form, which in some respect even transcends the conventional framework of the theatre.

And is there anything in the whole field of satiric drama which can be compared with *Troilus and Cressida*—the strangest, boldest, most provoking and therefore the most difficult comedy Shakespeare ever wrote? This is another unique case, it is nothing less than the invention of a new dramatic form!

And finally Shakespeare's last works: the romances *Cymbeline, The Winter's Tale,* and *The Tempest.* Here, as in *King Lear,* Shakespeare has turned to a new manner of dramatic composition which seems at first to ignore the obvious dramatic effect, but which then grips the spectator in a new way. These three plays are three different solutions which emerged in the course of the search for a new dramatic form.

We are perhaps not yet sufficiently aware of Shakespeare's remarkable inventiveness, to which his development of new dramatic forms, methods of composition and combinations all bear witness. In the course of many years we have become so familiar with all these plays, most of which we have seen on the stage, that we are no longer surprised at the great differences which exist between them. We are accustomed to thinking of Shakespeare in terms of abundance and variety. So why should this not also be evident in the development of the most varied types of drama?

But a glance at Calderon, Racine, Lessing, Schiller or Ibsen can show us that such a diversity is by no means self-evident, and that in fact no other dramatist has ever been endowed with a comparable versatility in the construction and development of new dramatic forms.

Freedom from rules, the absence of overpowerful literary models, receptiveness for every impulse from outside, and the lack of a fixed dramatic form,—these were the conditions which made possible the development of an inventive creativeness able to prove, again and again, that our conventional views of what drama is are much too narrow.

But in Shakespeare's case creative invention does not mean the ability to create something new and original out of nothing, but rather the adaptation and transformation of material already present, and above all it means the combination of diverse elements to form a

Act V, Scene i of the 1948 J. Arthur Rank film production of *Hamlet,* with Laurence Olivier as Hamlet and Norman Wooland as Horatio. "Alas, poor Yorick! I knew him, Horatio, a fellow of infinite jest, of most excellent fancy."

new whole. In the course of time the diligence of schol-   ars has enabled us to pursue back to some definite source a great many motifs and even forms and figures of speech, proverbs and maxims. It is well known that Shakespeare did not, as a rule, invent the plots of his plays, but borrowed most of his subject-matter from others. Much less well known is the degree to which single details in his plays, including some of the best-known lines, are taken from some source. We believe we are hearing Hamlet's own voice and mood when he says 'There's nothing good or bad but thinking makes it so' or 'The readiness is all' or when he dwells upon the nature of man in his speech: 'What a piece of work is man!' However, each of these sayings derives from a source in medieval or Renaissance literature. And so Shakespeare's contemporary, the dramatist Greene, was not so wrong when, in his embitterment at the success of his new rival, he accused him of being 'an upstart Crow, beautified with our feathers'. It is true that, living in an age in which our concept of originality was still unknown, Shakespeare must be considered a great plagiarist. But he was not only a plagiarist, he was an 'amalgamator' as well, by which we mean that he was an adaptor of genius, and understood the art of employing everything that fell into his hands for his dramatic purposes, often by means of very slight alterations and transpositions.

This unhampered and masterly skill in borrowing from the most diverse fields, however, could only bear fruit in a form of drama which was itself unrestricted and prepared to take its basic elements from any available source.

This gift of assimilation is most evident when Shakespeare combines opposite and diverse material in order to form a new unity. For this constitutes the second feature which is especially characteristic of Shakespearian drama. It is true that the pre-Elizabethan and early Elizabethan theatre had already known the clash of contrasting features. But not until Shakespeare does this combination of diverse elements attain a level of significance and mutual relevance. Only in his plays does it result in a greater unity which can contain and resolve opposites. Let us return to *A Midsummer Night's Dream.* The world of the fairies, the night full of dreams and enchantments for the Athenian lovers, and the theatrical activities of the mechanicals—all these seem at first to have very little to do with each other. But quite apart from the various encounters in the course of the action they are interwoven with each other by means of many cross-references and subtle contrasts, and as a result we receive the impression of a thoroughly homogeneous and unified play, although it is constructed out of such different elements.

Shakespeare developed the use of contrast as an artistic device to a greater degree than other dramatists. The effect and significance of something is heightened again and again by the juxtaposition of its opposite. This use of contrast can take place on many levels: in

the language, in the interplay of character, in the combination of individual motifs and in the juxtaposition of scenes and moods. Sometimes the whole plot of a play is contrasted to a parallel sub-plot; Shakespeare found examples of this in the sub-plots of pre-Shakespearian comedy, but he developed the technique further to enable the plots to reflect and complement each other, and for one to enrich the meaning of the other. The most famous example is to be found in *Henry IV,* where the Falstaff plot is enacted in the prose scenes on a lower floor of the play, as it were, in Mistress Quickley's inn and elsewhere. However, it is much more than a contrast of language or atmosphere. For the action of the main plot is not only parodied and reflected here, but also anticipated, echoed and commented upon with incomparable skill, so that although the two plots touch each other only at a few points, they necessarily belong to each other like the two complementary halves of a single whole.

The contrast between the world of Falstaff and the world of the king is among other things a contrast of comedy and tragedy. For most of us Shakespeare's artistry in the uniting of opposites is to be seen most clearly in this combination of the serious and the light. And can we think of any other play in the literature of the world in which the blend of comedy and tragedy has been achieved more successfully? Again we may say that here, too, the unrestricted form of Shakespeare's drama was a necessary condition, for the poet never kept to the strict boundaries of tragedy and comedy.

As Dr Johnson observed,

> Shakespeare's plays are not in the rigorous and critical sense either tragedies or comedies, but compositions of a distinct kind; exhibiting the real state of sublunary nature, which partakes of good and evil, joy and sorrow, mingled with endless variety of proportion and innumerable modes of combination; and expressing the course of the world, in which the loss of one is the gain of another; in which, at the same time, the reveller is hasting to his wine, and the mourner burying his friend; in which the malignity of one is sometimes defeated by the frolick of another; and many mischiefs and many benefits are done and hindered without design.

In these apt sentences Dr Johnson has indicated that the linking of the serious and the comic, which can be found in such rich variation in Shakespeare's work, is by no means to be regarded only as an effective dramatic device, but reflects a view of the world which keeps the two poles of human existence constantly in view, and regards them as complementary. These two spheres are often combined in one and the same person, and even in the same moment. We feel that the Fool in *King Lear* is not only a jester, but a tragic figure who shares in the suffering, whose jokes incorporate the

Samuel Johnson on the merits and defects of *Romeo and Juliet*:

[*Romeo and Juliet*] is one of the most pleasing of our author's performances. The scenes are busy and various, the incidents numerous and important, the catastrophe irresistibly affecting, and the process of the action carried on with such probability, at least with such congruity to popular opinions, as tragedy requires.

Here is one of the few attempts of Shakespeare to exhibit the conversation of gentlemen, to represent the airy sprightliness of juvenile elegance. Mr. Dryden mentions a tradition, which might easily reach his time, of a declaration made by Shakespeare, that "he was obliged to kill Mercutio in the third act, lest he should have been killed by him." Yet he thinks him "no such formidable person, but that he might have lived through the play, and died in his bed," without danger to a poet. Dryden well knew, had he been in quest of truth, that, in a pointed sentence, more regard is commonly had to the words than thought, and that it is very seldom to be rigorously understood. Mercu-

tio's wit, gaiety and courage, will always procure him friends that wish him a longer life but his death is not precipitated, he has lived out the time allotted him in the construction of the play; nor do I doubt the ability of Shakespeare to have continued his existence, though some of his sallies are perhaps out of the reach of Dryden; whose genius was not very fertile of merriment, nor ductile to humour, but acute, argumentative, comprehensive, and sublime.

The Nurse is one of the characters in which the authour delighted: he has, with great subtilty of distinction, drawn her at once loquacious and secret, obsequious and insolent, trusty and dishonest.

His comick scenes are happily wrought, but his pathetick strains are always polluted with some unexpected depravations. His persons, however distressed, "have a conceit left them in their misery, a miserable conceit."

Samuel Johnson, in an endnote to his 1765 edition of *Romeo and Juliet*.

---

sphere of the absurd into the tragedy, and who makes us aware of the close relationship between the grotesque and the tragic. The gravediggers' scene in *Hamlet* and the porter's scene in *Macbeth* are interludes of light relief in a superficial sense only. In fact their grim humour serves to make us even more aware of the sombre mood of death surrounding them. And even Falstaff is far from being only a comic figure, for the effect of his words and actions is to appeal to our sense of tragedy as well as to our sense of comedy. And the same holds true of the comedies. Portia in *The Merchant of Venice*, Rosalind in *As You Like It*, Viola in *Twelfth Night*, and even Beatrice in *Much Ado About Nohing*—they are not typical figures of comedy, but women whose audacity and gaiety never allow them to forget the seriousness which underlies these qualities, and for all of them merriment and melancholy are seldom far apart.

Laughter through tears, despair masquerading behind a witty remark, cheerfulness overshadowed by melancholy—these are blends of mood, to which nobody has given better dramatic expression than Shakespeare.

This capacity to correlate opposites can be demonstrated in a great many other ways. In his essay on Shakespeare written in 1773 the German writer Herder said that Shakespeare had 'created a miraculous unity out of the most heterogeneous materials by virtue of his creative spirit'. He will have had in mind above all the way in which incongruous motifs and characters are fused to form a unity which convinces us by its imaginative power and truth to life. In this way Shakespeare's drama continually contrives to make the im-

probable seem probable and convincing. In *The Merchant of Venice*, for example, we have the old fairy-tale motif of the choice between caskets of gold, silver, and lead establishing the right suitor for Portia, and in addition to this the motif of the bond that carries a forfeit of a pound of flesh. Both these motifs are highly improbable and quite unrealistic, but the course of events in this comedy is completely dependent upon them. And the basic content of the play, its truth to life, its inner unity and immediate effectiveness are not lessened by this in the least. This is also true of the many similarly absurd or incongruous motifs which can be found, for instance, in *Cymbeline, The Winter's Tale, All's Well That Ends Well*, in *Measure for Measure* or in *The Comedy of Errors*. And it holds true for many cases of motivation and for many details of the subject matter in the tragedies as well. But we can go further than this and say that it also holds true for the artistic devices which Shakespeare employs. In the depiction of character we find primitive conventions of self-dramatization alongside the most subtle psychology, some of the plays contain long narrative episodes, and sometimes there are scenes which appear to be totally undramatic. Unrealistic conventions can be found side by side with naturalistic methods of depiction. So critics have always been able to find much that is contradictory and to discover all kinds of inconsistencies in Shakespeare's work. They have been right, but at the same time they have been wrong. For the real test in Shakespeare's case can never be the rational analysis after the event; it must be the degree to which the illusion of the theatrical performance is capable of convincing, and sometimes of overpowering, the spectator.

So we can perhaps say that there are two different forces, two basic tendencies, active in Shakespeare's work simultaneously. On the one hand there is the expansive force, which is always exploring new paths and forming new combinations, and which seems intent on breaking out of the limitations of the theatre, and on the other hand there is the binding-force, which moulds all these parts into a complete unity and correlates all the different aspects of the play. At the height of his art Shakespeare is even able to give each play an organic harmony of its own. For each of his greater plays has its individual atmosphere and mood, its characteristic imagery and dramatic technique, and above all an individual poetic idiom which pervades the whole work. And it is Shakespeare's mastery of language that enables him to achieve this inner cohesion.

This brings me to the third characteristic feature of his work. Shakespeare combined a practical sense of the theatre with poetic genius, and in the same way his work reveals the unity of a supreme stage artistry and a matchless artistry of language. In this unity each half permeates and enriches the other. The language is an end in itself only in the early plays, if at all, and in Shakespeare's hands it soon develops into the direct vehicle of dramatic representation; it becomes the medium for what has to be shown, both through the action on the stage and through the behaviour of the actors. Shakespeare's spoken text actually contains both the actor's tone of voice, movements and gestures. In fact the poet must have borne the actor in mind speaking and moving with every line he wrote. Hamlet's advice in his speech to the players—to suit the action to the word, the word to the action—was followed by Shakespeare himself in the composition of every play. The result is the uniquely fortunate case of poetic language which is of great complexity and expressiveness, but which always gives us the impression that we are listening to the speaking voice of the actor. This is another combination which has never again been achieved so successfully.

Shakespeare has to rely on the language alone to evoke all those things like the scene of action, landscape, local colour, atmosphere, and time of day, which the drama of later centuries could include in the stage directions and put into effect with the technical devices of the modern stage, such as scenery and lighting. Shakespeare has none of the technical resources of later periods at his command, but he makes a virtue of necessity, and conjures up all these things for us by the evocative power of his language. In doing so he compels our own imagination to help in this process. A great deal of action takes place on the stage in every Shakespeare play, but still more is suggested by the language, and takes place before the mind's eye, so that the spectator is called upon to take part in the creative process and to contribute himself towards the total effect of the performance of a play.

Shakespeare refers several times to the fact that his stagecraft is dependent upon the imaginative co-operation of his spectators, for example in the Prologue to *Henry V,* where the Chorus says to the audience: 'Let us . . . /On your imaginary forces work/ . . . ./ Piece out our imperfections with your thoughts!' Thus the poetic language appeals to our 'imaginary forces'. In doing this it achieves two aims. In the first place all those aspects which can only vaguely be described by terms such as local colour and atmosphere can transcend the limitations of physical reality, they can take over important functions and assume a wider, indeed a symbolic significance.

And secondly they can be adapted to the individual idiom of a particular character, and thus be integrated into his experience. As a result the statement which helps to conjure up an atmosphere for us can at the same time reveal character. Let us take one of many possible examples: Othello has just landed in Cyprus, and embraces Desdemona with the words:

> O my soul's joy!
> If after every tempest come such calms,
> May the winds blow till they have waken'd
>   death,
> And let the labouring bark climb hills of
>   seas
> Olympus-high, and duck again as low
> As hell's from heaven.
>
> (II, i, 182)

In these words Othello gives us an idea of the wide rough sea across which he has just sailed; his lines contribute to the sea-atmosphere in the play. But in these lines he also gives expression to his own dynamic character, and, although not conscious of it himself, he anticipates the way he is to go, from Heaven down to Hell. In this manner the evocative power of Shakespeare's poetic language replaces the illusion of reality otherwise provided by stage scenery and other devices. This means that the scene of action in the drama is now wider instead of narrower. For now, free of the material limitations imposed by any stage apparatus, however perfect it may be, the play can take place upon a stage which represents the whole world. This stage can present what is close at hand and what is far away at the same time, and can even disregard the limits of this world in order to provide a setting of cosmic dimensions. In Shakespeare's plays we often have the impression that more is at stake than merely a series of events involving several people; other forces seem to be involved, and beyond the world of human beings there is the world of nature, of the elements and cosmic powers, which appear to be taking part in the action. When Lear invokes the elements—the storm, the thunder and lightning—in the great scene on the heath, he is giving expression to the hurricane in his own soul, but at the same time he is calling upon the forces of nature to intervene in the course of events, as indeed they do in many different ways in this play.

Alongside this evocative power of the poetic language we may set its ability to anticipate what is coming, to make us conscious of earlier and later developments, and to enrich the single present moment with an awareness which includes the past and the future as well. And in this way the poetic language becomes an instrument with which the listener may be influenced secretly. It makes him aware of much more than the concern of the moment. It arouses expectations and tensions, reminds the hearer of what he has already been told, and makes him conscious of the way in which time slowly trickles away or hurries quickly on. And all these various effects are the specifically dramatic results of the working of the poetic language.

No other poet has ever exploited the dramatic possibilities of poetic language in such divergent ways as Shakespeare has. The idiom of verse drama, as he uses it, proves to be a flexible instrument, capable of fulfilling many different purposes and of conveying several meanings at one and the same time. And this is what I should like to define as the fourth basic feature of Shakespeare's drama: the presence of several different levels of significance and of effect. So Shakespeare's drama can be considered multi-levelled in two different ways; for it not only contains on the plane of action one or two sub-plots which vary and comment upon the theme of the main plot, but it also combines several layers of meaning. Under the surface of the external action it is possible to trace a complex network of images and concepts. These express and vary the themes of the play in a manner comparable to musical counterpoint. Similarly reminiscent of music is the way in which the *Leitmotiv* technique is applied in order to appeal to our subconscious. From the point of view of the twentieth century, it seems that here a great genius has anticipated much more recent processes of poetic composition, such as have only been examined more closely by literary criticism in the course of the last thirty years. For on this deeper level of significance we can now find the same subtle parallels and double meanings, the same indirect echoes and references, and the same forms of irony and paradox that are characteristic of modern poetry. It is true that critics have sometimes exaggerated Shakespeare's use of these techniques. But even if we make sufficient allowance for the various exaggerations of this branch of modern criticism, we must still continue to be astonished at the abundance of inner relationships, hidden allusions, and additional meanings in Shakespeare's texts.

It is difficult for us to estimate now how many of all these double meanings and ambiguities were understood by Shakespeare's own audience. However, it is very probable that the Elizabethans had a better memory for words, a more acute sense of language, and a more lively verbal imagination than we have to-day. Puns and ambiguous figures of speech were not confined to literature, but were among the colloquial habits of speech of educated people. And could we account for the large number of allusions and references to the stylistic models of the day, unless they were noticed, at least by the well-informed? This observation leads me to a further important point which I wish to suggest as the fifth characteristic feature of Shakespeare's dramatic work. These plays were written for an extremely mixed audience in which all classes of society and degrees of education were represented, and they were capable of meeting the varied expectations and demands of this mixed audience. So the various levels of significance in the plays correspond to the different levels present in the audience. Perhaps it is characteristic of all great art that it should be able to appeal to the uneducated spectator and to the cultivated sensitive person as well, and to satisfy both. But Shakespeare's range of appeal is so great that he achieves a synthesis of crude and refined effects, of simple and subtle devices. This particular balance was never regained by later dramatists, for either they were coarser and more limited, without Shakespeare's breadth and subtlety, or they were altogether more literary, and wrote without Shakespeare's uninhibited vitality for a primarily middle-class audience. 'Good plays must be straightforward in appeal' ('Gute Dramen müssen drastisch sein') stipulated Friedrich Schlegel two hundred years after Shakespeare. Shakespeare followed this principle in all of his plays, for there are certainly enough bloody murders and other sensational, heart-rending episodes and gripping scenes to delight the heart of the most unsophisticated theatregoer, from his own time till the present.

And is it not typical that Shakespeare's plays should have such a strong effect on young people! The main reason for this is the magnificent simplicity and vividness of action and situation, which possess such expressive power in themselves that we can grasp their meaning even without a specific comprehension or intellectual analysis of the text. These moments of great theatrical power are what remain in our minds when we think of performances we have seen. Brutus and Antony speaking over Caesar's body, Hamlet and the ghost on the platform, Hamlet meditating over Yorick's skull, Lear with his three daughters and the map of his kingdom, Lear with Cordelia dead in his arms, Lady Macbeth walking in her sleep with a lighted candle, Othello at Desdemona's deathbed, Timon with his guests at the last banquet. Or in the histories: the abdication scene in *Richard II,* where the golden crown is held between the hands of the two rival kings, or the scene in *Henry IV* in which the prince puts on the crown and takes it away from the bed of his dying father. All of these tableaux, interpreted in each case by the text, compress the essence of a figure, and sometimes of a whole play, into a single visual image. These symbolic moments on the stage are often more eloquent than many speeches because of their simplicity, for they can make the meaning vivid to every spectator. So young and old, novices and experts, can all be moved by Shakespeare's work. And similarly we can observe the way in which it affects our own faculties of perception on many different levels. These plays appeal to the eye as well as to the ear, to our emotions as well as to our moral judgment, and occupy our intellect in addition to our imagination. They may be compared to the richest orchestral scores which have ever been written.

But they are of course not only obvious and *drastisch* (straightforward); they do not consist solely of colourful events, for each play forms a finely woven texture of skilfully graduated and varied effects, which range from the melodious cadence of a line to the moments of great theatrical power about which we have just spoken.

The interweaving of the most diverse kinds of figures, effects, and dramatic devices—devices which are often simple and often refined, sometimes artificial and sometimes direct, often improbable but always convincing—this fact has at all times been considered an almost incomprehensible miracle. Shakespeare has always defied theories about what is possible and permissible in the theatre, and anyone who has tried to establish the derivation of his art from certain basic principles and rules has soon got into difficulties. For his plays not only overpower us with the dramatic illusion, they also give us the impression of being incomparably true to life, which makes us feel even today that he is 'holding a mirror up to nature'. In the classical period of German literature in the late eighteenth century an attempt was made to define Shakespeare's instinctive feeling for what was both dramatically effective and true to life, in terms of a phenomenon of Nature, as the Spirit of the World expressing itself in poetry, and as a form of completely irrational and subconscious creativity. Today we are more inclined to recognize a conscious artistic intention in this interweaving of different effects—a highly refined art of composition which orders all its resources with perfect harmony.

But it certainly is an art which conceals its own rules and resources to such an extent that it gives the impression of being without art, and seems utterly and totally natural. In *The Winter's Tale* Shakespeare touches upon this secret of art transformed into nature, when he makes Polixenes speak to Perdita about gardening:

POLIXENES. You see sweet maid, we marry
A gentler scion to the wildest stock,
And make conceive a bark of baser kind
By bud of nobler race. This is an art
Which does mend nature—change it rather;
　　but
The art itself is nature.

PERDITA. So it is.

(IV, iv, 92)

These last words of Polixenes certainly hold true for the whole of Shakespeare's drama.

Nevertheless we would like to ask in closing whether this true reflection of life which we have mentioned cannot be seen in relation to certain basic qualities in the construction of the plays and characters. And this now leads us to the sixth and last of our characteristic features: this is a drama of inner balance, and consequently displays the greatest possible objectivity of characterization.

Inner balance: this means, that every play contains both light and shade, both good and evil, even if these two halves are not always of exactly equal weight. None of these plays makes the attempt to lead us in one direction only, in none of them does one kind of human character dominate the stage alone, and there is no play that stays, as it were, in one key. Everywhere we find that one attitude is corrected by the other, the opposites serve to counterbalance and clarify each other. Should an extreme or exaggerated attitude assume dominance, then a moderating influence is bound to appear too, and we shall hear the commentary of a neutral observer or perhaps a parody, by means of which the balance is restored, and we are made doubly aware of the exaggeration. At Lear's side we find Kent, who makes the king's blindness and lack of moderation clear to us in the very first scene, just as Cordelia takes her place alongside Goneril and Regan, and Edgar alongside Edmund. Romeo's emotional enthusiasm is accompanied in the first part of the play by Mercutio's wit and mockery, and in *Henry IV* Hotspur's impetuousness is contrasted with the dispassionate judgment of Prince Hal. Even Hamlet has the neutral voice of Horatio at his side. We could pursue this technique of constant juxtaposition and contrast on many different levels. Besides intensifying the delineation of character it helps to produce what we have called the inner balance of the plays. But it has its roots in a concept of the totality of life which has here found an adequate form of artistic expression.

We are aware of the absence of any philosophical or religious bias in Shakespeare's plays, as opposed to the French, German, and Spanish drama of his age, and this enhances both the correspondence to real life and the equilibrium in his work. A royal decree of 1559 had forbidden the treatment of religious matters on the stage. Whereas the theatre on the Continent became a platform for theological disputes, Elizabethan drama was on the whole able to steer clear of such polemics, which usually resulted in artistic sterility. The emphasis lay on the depiction of human relationships, and a secular type of drama developed, in which the religious element is only peripheral.

Shakespearian drama cannot be identified with any dogmatic beliefs, and even less with any kind of philosophical or ideological propaganda. For although Shakespeare's depiction of character often appears to be based on Christian principles, these nearly always remain unspoken, and very rarely attain the level of clear expression.

But what Shakespeare himself really believed we do not know. And the fact that we do not know is part of the unique quality of his work, and this brings us to touch upon the personality of its creator. For the exceptional objectivity of the dramatic writing, which has always roused the admiration of critics and readers, has its roots in the fact that Shakespeare himself always remains in the background. Each of his creations has become a completely independent figure and exists in his own right. Villain and hero alike are treated with the same understanding and emerge as credible and living persons. Shakespeare does not take sides. So the world full of people which he has given us cannot be reduced to a few basic types, for the individual human beings which it displays in such astonishing abundance remain in our minds as fully rounded personalities, including in some cases even those who appear only in one single scene. For it is impossible to say that Shakespeare devoted less creative sympathy to Caliban than to Prospero, or that the treatment of Polonius reveals less loving care than the treatment of Laertes. It was this completeness of vision which Dryden must have had in mind when he described Shakespeare as 'the man who of all modern and perhaps ancient poets had the largest and most comprehensive soul'.

But what was Shakespeare's own position? We cannot tell. And if we could tell, it would mean that the incomparable objectivity of this dramatic world would be less perfect than it is. The anonymity which surrounds Shakespeare's person in the eyes of posterity is hardly a matter of chance. It is merely another way of expressing the permanent and imperishable vitality of a dramatic work which completely overshadows the personality of its author. And as a person he is indeed not so important, for he lives on in all the characters he created. (pp. 198-213)

Wolfgang Clemen, in his *Shakespeare's Dramatic Art: Collected Essays*, Methuen, 1972, 236 p.

PHILIP EDWARDS
(essay date 1968)

[In the following excerpt, Edwards discusses the thematic significance of the irregular sequence of the Dark Lady sonnets.]

Shakespeare's sonnets to the Dark Woman are a triumph of art built on a persistent demonstration of the weakness of art. What we get from these later sonnets, however, depends on the order in which we read them. A convincing order for the sequence (numbers 127-54) is extremely difficult to establish. Many critics who thought that they could make a pattern out of the sonnets to the young man have given up the task for the dark woman. [Edward Dowden wrote in *Shakespere's Sonnets* (1883)]: 'I do not here attempt to trace a continuous sequence in the Sonnets addressed to the dark-haired woman . . . ; I doubt whether such continuous sequence is to be found in them.' Most readers, in the end, are content to greet the acknowledged great poems as they come: **'My mistress' eyes are nothing like the sun' (130); 'Th' expense of spirit in a waste of shame' (129); 'Two loves I have of comfort and despair' (144); 'Poor soul the centre of my sinful earth' (146).** They can claim with reason that the poetry is not suffering in their eyes through the absence of a settled order.

But the belief that there *is* a correct order is hard to subdue. Brents Stirling has made a new attempt, based upon a theory of the way in which the printer might have disarranged the sheets of an ordered collection. In his view, the sequence ends with the great sonnets on lust and on mortification (**'Sonnet 129'** and **'Sonnet 146'**), and three sonnets are independent (**'Sonnet 128,' 'Sonnet 138,' 'Sonnet 145'**). I shall show why I disagree with such an ending, and why I find the three 'independent' sonnets necessary to the sequence, but first we have to ask what kind of an order we are looking for. We may mean the order in which they were written, an unplanned 'biographical' order. We should then have to ask whether we suppose the sonnets to have been written for and sent to a woman as a liaison progressed or whether we suppose them to be a deliberate record of an affair. The former seems very unlikely. As [William] Auden has reminded us, it is most improbable that the sonnets of the later sequence were ever sent to the woman herself. If you send sonnets to a woman in which you talk of 'the very refuse of thy deeds', and describe her as 'black as hell, as dark as night' and as 'the bay where all men ride' [**'Sonnet 150,' 'Sonnet 147,' 'Sonnet 137'**], then sooner or later she either refuses to receive the sonnets or refuses to receive the poet. The sonnets themselves show that the intended audience must have been close friends who play a game of overhearing a poet talking to his mistress; it is *they* who are meant to appreciate the pervading irony which the ostensible recipient is supposed not to discern.

Even if we regard the poems as a self-conscious record of a liaison rather than as 'spontaneous' occasional poems sent to a woman, we are still faced with a big difficulty implicit in the search for an autobiographical order. It is unlikely that autobiography will yield order; it is unlikely that a 'real-life' sequence will have the tidiness of a self-explanatory order, with a beginning, middle and end. If we are looking for a history or a diary we may expect it to look as confused as the sonnets now look, left in the order in which they were first printed.

If we turn now to look for a planned sequence, belonging only partly (if at all) to the events of Shakespeare's life, we are at once baulked, as we begin to shuffle the 1609 order, by the interference of our own expectations—the kind of interference which made critics wish to close Sidney's *Astrophil and Stella* with 'leave me O love which reachest but to dust.' Unless the closest chronological continuity can be established (and it cannot), we can only impose what we wish to find. In a set of sonnets like that which we have before us, we cannot, by re-arranging them, do more than give a personal guess at the pattern of love's progress which we think Shakespeare intended to set out.

All the same, it is my opinion that the Dark Woman sonnets were put forward by Shakespeare as a coherent sequence, a sequence which is as much imaginative as historical, as much thought out as lived out. Although I find it inconceivable that the sonnets were not born out of the deepest personal experience, what Shakespeare gave—to his friends if not to the world—seems to me a very long way from a personal diary. How much revising, re-arranging, new writing was needed in the progress from personal experience no one will ever know, but perhaps Yeats is the poet to think of in analogy.

Where is the sequence to be found? I suggest it is in the order in which the sonnets were first printed in 1609: the order in which they are still printed because no one can find a better. In *The Shakespearean Moment* (1954), Patrick Cruttwell said, 'These sonnets which deal with the lady . . . contain most of the greatness and most of the maturity of the whole sequence; they can be taken as a single poem, in the way in which (for instance) Donne's nineteen *Holy Sonnets* are a single poem'. It is possible to go further than this comparison takes us and argue that the sonnets are a single poem only if they are read in the 1609 order. (pp. 17-19)

The first face of love is described in the long sequence of poems to the young man, the second in the appended sequence to the dark woman. The first love is non-physical, a mingling of the two selves or souls into one soul; the second love is a mingling of the bodies of man and woman—will with will—without the marriage of the minds. On the one hand is love without physical intercourse; on the other is lust without spiritual intercourse. Shakespeare makes it clear that love and lust (each directed towards a different person) are intertwined in the lover. The story of the dark woman takes place *within* the narrative of the love for the youth; the fact of lust is included in the history of love. That the two experiences are meant to be seen as simultaneous can be inferred from the rather forced insertion, at the centre of each sequence, of the 'triangle' sonnets (**'Sonnet 40,' 'Sonnet 41,' 'Sonnet 42'**; and **'Sonnet 133' and 'Sonnet 134'**), in which the poet tells us of the sexual relations between the woman and the youth. In these sonnets it is clear that the poet is 'in love' with both the youth and the woman at the same time. They describe how the woman has deserted his bed for the young man's, they voice his feeling of being betrayed by both of them, and they attempt (more or less ironically) various kinds of consolation. The most profound explanation of the predicament is in **'Sonnet 144'**. . . . At one level, the poem expresses by means of puns the fear that the mistress and the beloved youth are committing fornication and that the youth will be infected with venereal disease. There is also the fear that the young man's lust will corrupt him spiritually as well as physically. If the youth *is* corrupted, then the salvation offered to the poet in loving him disappears. At another level, the complicated story of what is happening to three people can be seen as an image of what is happening to one human soul. The poet shows himself as a man swinging between salvation and damnation as he obeys the desires of his body and of his body and of his spirit. Ultimately, the living-together which the poet describes is the living-together in his own heart of the purity of love and the impurity of lust. The final fear is that his own lust will contaminate and disfigure his capacity to love, and win him soon to hell.

If the two faces of love are to be shown as present at the same time, it has also to be made clear that in essence they are distinct and separate; each kind of affection has its own sequence. It seems right that the lust-sequence should come last. Slowly, after 'all that pain', the sequence of sonnets to the fair youth reaches an equilibrium in the mutual forgiveness of faults when true minds are married (**'Sonnet 116' and 'Sonnet 120'** especially). The appending of the second sequence shows how impermanent this equilibrium is, how it is always threatened by the grosser sexual needs. The victory in the first sequence is subdued enough but even so Shakespeare questions it. By adding the Dark

Woman sonnets he shows a distrust of the resounding final chord which we shall find again and again in the plays.

The characteristic of the Dark Woman sonnets is that the suggestion of a 'real' relationship is created, running beneath poems which, sometimes ostentatiously, show their failure to crystallize and comprehend this relationship. It is the impression of failure which provides the evidence of the 'real' relationship. It is like defining God by negatives, showing the inability of language to describe Him. We may often enough indulge our fancy about the real relationship which lay behind some love poem and imagine that in life things were not quite as the poet has put it. But love poems do not usually make the effort to hint at a discrepancy; the sense of life is what most of them try to give. I suggest that the most profitable way to read the Dark Woman sonnets is to think of Shakespeare watching his creature-poet at work. The sonnets, strung along a thin line of narrative about wooing, conquest and disgust, are a poet's ordering of his own life, his answering 'the daily necessity of getting the world right'; and Shakespeare is observing his grim failure. As the affair intensifies from courtship to consummation to bitterness, Shakespeare's ironic detachment from his creature becomes less and less, but a distance is maintained throughout.

Each of the first four sonnets is a posture; each introduces a particular kind of artistic ordering which is to be followed up later. **'Sonnet 127,' 'In the old age black was not counted fair'**, proves that the dark woman is beautiful and is the first of a number of courtship poems in which the sonneteer, delighting in his own poetic wit, denies the distinction between ugliness and beauty, and hence, by traditional symbolism, denies the distinction between evil and good. The second poem, **'How oft when thou, my music, music play'st'** ['Sonnet 128'], is one of those classed as 'independent' by Professor Stirling. It seems to me the very necessary introduction of the purely conventional wooing-poem. The humble lover watches his mistress at her music, envies the keys which touch her hand and pleads for the gratification of a kiss. To explode this world of sighing poetry-love, there follows the great sonnet on lust (**'Sonnet 129'**). . . . Magnificent though this sonnet is, taken by itself, it gains a special force from its position. The early sonnets in this sequence, before the reversal in **'Sonnet 137'**, provide a study in self-deception, and the evidence for this is **'Sonnet 129.'** Here the poet has a momentary vision of himself as a madman, here he sees his courtship as the longings of lust for its reward of self-loathing. Every wooing-poem which follows this is coloured by it; the poet who has had this vision of what he is doing in seeking the favours of the dark woman goes on writing poems which 'convince' him that he is in no danger, poems in which he is able to smother his moral sense in his delight in his own poetic skill. Far from being an ending to the sequence, the sonnet on lust finds its proper place near the beginning. It poses the question to which the sequence as a whole finds that there is no answer; why does a man willingly poison himself?

In the fourth sonnet, **'My mistress' eyes are nothing like the sun'** ['Sonnet 130'], the poet explores the possibilities of the common antipetrarchan convention. . . . At first, this sonnet seems to be a direct attempt to cut through the nonsense of **'Sonnet 128'** and to come to a 'real' relationship. Rejecting idiotic comparisons, it seems a sane and human acceptance of a woman for what she is. The poet's love seems truer and warmer in its independence of poetic flattery. For the reader to see the poem only in this way, however, is to slip into the very trap which Shakespeare wants to show his poet falling into. Who is the woman who is contemplated so humanly, so warmly, so confidently? The Dark Woman, who is shortly to be shown as an agent of damnation. When we read this poem in its proper context, we can see that the final couplet conveys a double impression. First we congratulate the poet on the honesty of his love which needs no lying comparisons to assist it. Then we reflect on the continuous play in these sonnets between fairness-beauty-virtue and darkness-ugliness-vice, and we wonder whether a sophistical confusion between these two poles is not at work here too. Because all women, however beautiful, are 'belied' by being compared with goddesses, are all women equally beautiful and equally worthy of love? The poet has a right to love whom he will, and to accept a plain woman is no crime, but in so far as the ground of his acceptance is the equality of women as non-goddesses, he shows himself insensitive to the distinction (symbol of a moral distinction) between ugliness and beauty. Shakespeare does not say outright that the woman is ugly; students are taught that 'reeks' does not imply halitosis or garlic. But no one can read the poem without a sense of considerable unattractiveness in the dun breasts, black hair, pallid cheeks and breath which, if it is not sour, is not exactly sweet. The sonnet may be seen as a parody of the usual anti-petrarchan sonnet in which the poet rejects ornamental comparisons because true beauty needs no such aids. While showing that a woman gains nothing from false flattery the poet implies that physical demerits (the emblems of spiritual demerits) are of no account with him. With the gallantry of his wit, he once more confounds all distinction between women. To understand what the lover really achieves in this sonnet, we can turn to any of the later poems, **'Sonnet 150'** for example:

To make me give the lie to my true sight
And swear that brightness doth not grace the day.

The ugliness of the woman is made obvious in the

subtle poem which follows **('Sonnet 131')**. The poet jokes that in spite of her unpromising face, his mistress must be a conventional beauty because she tyrannizes over his heart like the heroine of any ordinary sonnet-sequence. He again denies distinction ('Thy black is fairest in my judgement's place') and tells us outright, for the first time, of the woman's viciousness:

In nothing art thou black save in thy deeds,
And thence this slander, as I think, proceeds.

What a great joke it is for him to be in love (if that's the word) with an ugly woman of dubious character and to be able to prove her as fair as the fairest—and, by means of the proof, insult her.

'Sonnet 132' carries the jesting on and deepens the sense of ugliness. Conventional comparisons, rejected in **'Sonnet 130,'** are trotted out with an accent which cleverly degrades the woman as they seem to praise her.

And truly not the morning sun of heaven
Better becomes the grey cheeks of the east,
Nor that full star that ushers in the even
Doth half that glory to the sober west
As those two mourning eyes become thy face.

The denial in this poem is emphatic, 'Then will I swear beauty herself is black', and the denial is promised as a consequence of her granting him 'pity'. The denial of value is a price he is willing to pay for the satisfaction of his lust.

The 'triangle' sonnets, which follow, are important in reminding us at this stage of the existence of the other kind of love and of the contamination of the higher by the lower kind. The two poems make the woman's 'black deeds' more real as they describe her promiscuity and draw her as a demon whose loathsome magnetism enslaves her victims. The extraordinary 'will' sonnets, **'Sonnet 135'** and **'Sonnet 136,'** show what wit can do to turn what is dreadful into amusement; the lover's plea for pity is advanced in a crudely physical way. His arguments for being admitted to her favours are at the level of mutual sexual satisfaction; he equates his whole being with his carnal desire and his virility:

Make but my name thy love, and love that still
And then thou lovest me, for my name is Will.
                                              ['Sonnet 136']

He is still laughing at the joke as he unites with the woman he knows the worst of in a congress whose emotional and spiritual consequences he has already foreseen in **'Sonnet 129.'** The climax of the sequence—the 'kiss' sonnet of discreeter series—is **'Sonnet 137.'** At the moment of fruition, there is immediate and overpowering revulsion. . . . The question, why does a man betray himself and swallow the bait?, continues for the rest of the sequence, but in the end there is no answer to give beyond the simple statement that it has happened.

The sequence continues with a series of sonnets written in bed. The rapid alterations of mood, the contradictions in viewpoint, may seem bewildering, but they are by no means an indication that the order is haphazard. The mood as a whole is of restless conflict in the single attempt to write the poem that makes the unbearable look bearable. **'Sonnet 138' ('When my love swears that she is made of truth / I do believe her though I know she lies')** tries to follow the pattern of conciliation used in the sequence to the young man—not to insult and despise but to recognize and accept one's own imperfections as well as those of one's partner. But the resolution has a very hollow sound; they will lie to each other and each will pretend to believe the other, for 'love's best habit is in seeming trust'. On this thin surface they will try to build, but all that they have with which to build is sexual pleasure:

Therefore I lie with her and she with me,
And in our faults by lies we flattered be.

In **'Sonnet 139,'** he shows himself afraid of his own facility for consoling himself by writing down specious excuses for the woman. The mood is very similar to the mood of **'Sonnet 35'** in which the poet begins to pur out tired exculpatory analogies on his friend's behalf, and then pulls himself up in disgust at his own lack of moral courage. [In **'Sonnet 141'** and **'Sonnet 142']** the word 'sin' enters for the first time, and the poet sees his suffering as condign punishment. Orthodox moral judgement of himself and his mistress as adulterers brings a new perspective into the sequence.

'Sonnet 143,' **'Sonnet 144,'** **'Sonnet 145,'** and **'Sonnet 146'** seem to me to be of central importance. Two of them are very weak, the other two are very powerful. Indeed, in 145 (**'Those lips that Love's own hand did make'**) we have one of the worst of all the sonnets, and in 146 (**'Poor soul the centre of my sinful earth'**) one of the best. But when he is writing badly, Shakespeare does so intentionally, not for the first or the only time (we may think of the sonnets given to the young nobles in *Love's Labour's Lost*). In each of these sonnets, Shakespeare—or rather his poet—tries to make the peculiarly unhappy fact of his predicament conform to a different poetic 'idea'; he tries out different objectifications of the intolerable position he finds himself in—and none of them 'works'. **'Sonnet 143,'** a study in whimsical self-derision, turns the lover into a neglected baby crying for the mother who is chasing a hen. If this ludicrous image for deserted lover and predatory female lowers the poet, the poem yet provides in the rounded movement of its own logic the promise of consolation:

But if thou catch thy hope, turn back to me
And play the mother's part, kiss me, be kind.

The next sonnet in the group is **'Two loves I have of comfort and despair** ['**Sonnet 144'**], which we have already discussed. Like the lust-sonnet, it gains extra depth from its position, rudely cancelling out the propositions of a weak preceding sonnet. It is followed in its turn by a remarkable song (**'Sonnet 145'**). A characteristic and understandable note on this appears in the Harbage and Bush 'Pelican' edition of the Sonnets: 'The authenticity of this sonnet, in tetrameters and rudimentary diction, has been questioned, with considerable show of reason; in any case, it is not in context with the adjacent sonnets.' The Ingram and Redpath edition says:

> These trivial octosyllabics scarcely deserve reprinting. Some editors have considered the poem spurious on account of its feeble childishness. It would seem arbitrary, however, to rule out the possibility that one of Shakespeare's trivia should have found its way into a collection not approved by him. . . .

It can surely be argued that this absurd song *does* fit the place it is given. The idea of the woman's hate, as opposed to coldness or indifference, was first introduced in **'Sonnet 142'** and is continued here and in later sonnets. The metaphor of heaven and hell makes a direct link with the preceding 'two loves' sonnet and with the mortification-sonnet which follows next. I suggest that this despised poem should be taken as a satirical picture of a poet smoothing out life's problems, whistling to keep his spirits up. All's well that ends well; the fiend flies out of the window. The feebleness of the poem is an exaggerated comment on the weakness of poetry as a means of arranging one's life or even portraying it. Yet, exaggerated as it is, it does make a comment on poetry as a whole. It uses a magic which is quite patently ineffectual, but it draws our attention to poetry as a kind of magic which may or may not work. The poem which follows [**'Sonnet 146'**] is a particularly powerful poem. Although, as with two earlier poems I have mentioned, it gains extra force from exploding a namby-pamby predecessor, I believe we must also say that it is coloured by its predecessor. The mortification-sonnet is akin to the song in being a poet's attempt to relieve the pressures on his life through the perspective of art. . . . That mortification of the pride of the flesh and a life turned towards God can be an answer to the attack of the female devil ('there's no more dying then') is ruled out by the next sonnet—

> My love is as a fever longing *still*
> For that which longer nurseth the disease.
>
> ['**Sonnet 147'**]

('still' is at least as likely to have here its modern meaning as the older meaning of 'always'.) Death is not dead: 'I desperate now approve / Desire is death.' **'Sonnet 146'** does not put the claims of religion any the less nobly because it does not serve the poet as more than

a transient insight into what might be. It may seem a greater poem because of its hint of tragedy in that a man should know what this poem knows and yet be unable to avail himself of what the poem offers. And I certainly do not think that its value is lessened if we see it as one of a series of poems in a *dramatic* sequence in which the hero, a poet, restlessly turns to different poetic images of his own troubles.

The wild music of the few remaining sonnets puts them among the greatest writing of Shakespeare. There is never a last word. The poet accepts his incurable condition as a madness in **'Sonnet 147,'** but then he goes on to degrade himself in anger (**'Sonnet 149'** and **'Sonnet 150'),** blaming *her* for entangling him:

> If thy unworthiness raised love in me,
> More worthy I to be belov'd of thee.
>
> [**Sonnet 150**]

The obscene **'Sonnet 151'** tries vainly to find refuge in the idea that there being nothing nobler in man than his sexual desire, he might find contentment in simply being the woman's drudge. **'Sonnet 152'** ends with yet another repetition of the inexplicable:

> And, to enlighten thee, gave eyes to blindness,
> Or made them swear against the thing they see;
> For I have sworn thee fair; more perjured eye,
> To swear against the truth so foul a lie.

After this, the sequence evaporates in two perfunctory sonnets on the theme of Cupid's brand heating a well.

> Past reason hunted, and no sooner had,
> Past reason hated as a swallowed bait
> On purpose laid to make the taker mad.
>
> [**'Sonnet 129'**]

The story of the poet and the dark woman is not some isolated adventure. Shakespeare is writing about sexual desire, and he portrays it as a degradation that a man cannot withstand. What is perhaps not improperly called the fear of desire is partly submerged in Shakespeare's earlier plays but it reappears at the turn of the century and in almost every play from *Measure for Measure* onwards there is an acknowledgement of the supposed disjunction between the marriage of minds and the union of bodies. In the last plays there is much that is perplexing on this subject. What we have read in the Sonnets helps to explain the chiaroscuro of Marina in the brothel, Polixenes' vision of childhood innocence and the anxiety of Prospero's spirits to keep Venus out of the wedding masque. Auden was right to conclude his essay on the sonnets with the address to all-enslaving Venus from Shakespeare's last offering, *The Two Noble Kinsmen.*

At the moment what concerns us is not Shakespeare's 'attitude to sex' but his attitude towards art. The drama of the Dark Woman sequence is not alone the drama of the curse of the granted wish, but the drama of the poet groping to materialize his emotions in verse. Shakespeare sets poetry the task of describing a certain kind of hopelessness and he shows poetry pulling like a tidal current away from hopelessness towards resolution of one kind or another. Although individual poems, however brilliant, may be 'failures' in that they are shown to be separated from the life they pretend to record, the cumulative effect of the sequence is success of the highest order, not failure. By accretion and implication, the condition is described. It will be found in some of the earlier comedies that a triumph of art can lie in a partial repudiation of art. Winning a victory by allowing a series of defeats resembles what Eliot was doing in *Four Quartets,* for there too the poetry moves round and about, trying every sort of key and tempo, cancelling out its rhetoric, defying heroics, trying to find the poetry for

A condition of complete simplicity
(Costing not less than everything).

Another poet than Shakespeare might have made

the lust-sonnet and the mortification-sonnet the culmination of his sequence; at the end of the affair the poet-lover is made to recognize the madness of desire and to turn his back on all earthly things. In his very ingenious and persuasive study, Brents Stirling writes that his hypothesis 'accounts for seemingly random displacement—the appearance of a grim sonnet on lust (**'Sonnet 129'**) between the dainty, affected **'Sonnet 128'** and **'Sonnet 130',** and the sequential absurdity of a pretty sonnet like **'Sonnet 145'** followed by the *de profundis* note of [**'Sonnet 146'**].' I have tried to show that **'Sonnet 129'** and **'Sonnet 146'** have a quite special importance in irrupting into the narrative just where they do in 1609, and in not coming at the end. Shakespeare is dealing with great complexities of the mind and the heart, on to which is added the driving need of the poet to use his art, with all *its* complexities, to make sense of his condition. The course of knowledge will not be a symmetrical graph. (pp. 19-31)

Philip Edwards, "The Sonnets to the Dark Woman," in his *Shakespeare and the Confines of Art,* Methuen & Co. Ltd., 1968, 17-32.

SOURCES FOR FURTHER STUDY

Burton, S. H. *Shakespeare's Life and Stage.* Edinburgh: Chambers, 1989, 230 p.

   General introduction to Shakespeare's life and theater.

Eastman, Arthur M. *A Short History of Shakespearean Criticism.* New York: Random House, 1968, 418 p.

   Traces the major trends and concerns of Shakespearean studies from the seventeenth century to the modern age.

Holland, Norman N., Homan, Sidney, and Paris, Bernard J., eds. *Shakespeare's Personality.* Berkeley: University of California Press, 1989, 284 p.

   Important recent compilation of critical essays covering a diversity of topics relating to the dramatist.

Muir, Kenneth, and Schoenbaum, S., eds. *A New Companion to Shakespeare Studies.* London: Cambridge University Press, 1971, 297 p.

   Outstanding selection of critical and historical essays on Shakespeare addressing all aspects of the subject.

Schoenbaum, S. *Shakespeare: The Globe & the World.* New York: Oxford University Press, 1979, 208 p.

   Lavishly illustrated survey of Shakespeare's life and career.

Wilson, J. Dover. *The Essential Shakespeare.* Cambridge: Cambridge University Press, 1932, 148 p.

   Standard introduction to Shakespeare's life and writings.

Bernard Shaw

1856-1950

(Full name George Bernard Shaw; also wrote under pseudonym Corno di Bassetto) Irish dramatist, essayist, critic, novelist, short story writer, and poet.

INTRODUCTION

Shaw is generally considered the greatest dramatist to write in the English language since Shakespeare. Following the example of Henrik Ibsen, he succeeded in revolutionizing the English stage, disposing of the romantic conventions and devices of the "well-made" play, and instituting a theater of ideas grounded in realism. During his lifetime, he was equally famous as an iconoclastic and outspoken public figure. Essentially a shy man, Shaw created the public persona of G. B. S.: showman, satirist, pundit, and intellectual jester, who challenged established political and social beliefs.

Shaw was born into genteel poverty in Dublin. His father was an alcoholic. His mother, a woman of some refinement and culture, introduced her son to music and art at an early age. In 1876 Shaw moved to London and was supported by his mother for nine years while he tended to his self-education. During this period, he wrote five unsuccessful novels and, through intensive reading, acquired a strong background in economics and politics. Shaw established himself as a persuasive orator during the 1880s, rising to prominence in the socialist Fabian Society. He also became well known as a literary critic, an art critic, a music critic, and, in 1895, the drama critic for the *Saturday Review*. G. B. S., as he now signed his work, began to be widely recognized for reviews that were witty, biting, and often brilliant.

Shaw had the unusual distinction of being a playwright whose works were successful in book form before appearing on the stage. His early plays aroused the interest of a small, enthusiastic audience, although several were rejected for performance because they were believed to be unactable or risqué. Nevertheless, six of his early dramas were collected in *Plays: Pleasant and Unpleasant* (1898) and were accompanied by lengthy explanatory prefaces that many critics consider as significant as the plays themselves. The critical and popular success of this endeavor, along with his marriage in 1898 to Charlotte Payne-Townshend, a rich Fabian, proved to be turning points in Shaw's life. From that time on, Shaw was closely associated with the intellectual revival of the English theater, two of his greatest critical successes being *Man and Superman* (1905), based on the Don Juan legend, and *St. Joan* (1923), the history of Joan of Arc. The comedy *Pygmalion* (1913), highlighting the absurdities of class distinction, was his most outstanding commercial success. Constantly revived, *Pygmalion* was adapted into the popular, long-running musical, *My Fair Lady.* During seventy-five years of literary activity that ended with his death in 1950, Shaw produced a tremendous body of work, never hesitating to publicly express his views on such subjects as feminism, war, religion, imperialism, individualism, and socialism with frankness and wit. He was awarded the Nobel Prize for literature in 1925.

Man and Superman is often held to represent a central and pivotal point in Shaw's career because it contains the fullest explication of Shaw's own ideas and beliefs to that time. *Man and Superman* is also the work in which Shaw began to explore his theories of the Life Force and Creative Evolution, ideas that were central to his personal and artistic philosophy and that he examined more fully in later works, particularly in the drama *Back to Methuselah.* Shaw conceived of the Life Force as an impersonal god of sorts, a natural force governing human affairs. Critics find that Shaw borrowed liberally from elements of many different philosophical, sociological, and scientific concepts in constructing his theory of the Life Force, most notably drawing on Friedrich Nietzsche's idea of the "Übermensch," the "overman" or "superman," the highest type to which humanity should strive; Henri Bergson's concept of *élan vital,* the creative tendency or impulse of nature toward continual adaptation and improvement; and Darwinian hypotheses of natural selection. Creative Evolution is simply the purpose and the result of the Life Force in action: the continual improvement of the race through eugenic breeding.

In book form *Man and Superman* consists of three parts: the "Epistle Dedicatory to Arthur Bingham Walkley," in which Shaw credits his friend with having inspired the play; the play's four acts; and, as an appendix, " 'The Revolutionist's Handbook and Pocket Companion,' by John Tanner, M.I.R.C. (Member of the Idle Rich Class)," a revolutionary tract and collection of aphorisms purported to be the work of a central character. Thus performances of *Man and Superman* necessarily omit large amounts of related material that Shaw originally presented with the published play. Furthermore, theater-going audiences rarely see the third act "hell scene" or dream sequence, as its inclusion results in a performance of impracticable length. Shaw

invested this third act with the bulk of the "philosophy" of the subtitle; without Act Three *Man and Superman* is generally considered a sparkling, witty, and farcical comedy of manners.

According to Homer Woodbridge, Shaw's subtitle for *Man and Superman*—"A Comedy and a Philosophy"—indicates his recognition of the dual nature of the play: a sparkling comedy, featuring skilled comic characterizations, intercut with a lengthy philosophic and religious discussion. The play's first, second, and fourth acts comprise the comedy, characterized by Shaw as "a trumpery story of modern London life, a life in which . . . the ordinary man's main business is to get means to keep up the position and habits of a gentleman, and the ordinary woman's business is to get married." Although *Man and Superman* is invested with more doctrine than any previous work of Shaw's, most of the discussion of ideas is relegated to the third act, which Shaw himself termed "wholly extraneous." The remainder of the play has proven to be an enormously successful, entertaining, and popular comedy. Shaw drew most of his characters from various treatments of the Don Juan legend, yet modified each with uniquely Shavian touches. Perhaps the most renowned of Shaw's changes was his reversal of traditionally sex-defined roles, so that in his play the woman is the ruthless pursuer of the hapless man. This inversion of the love chase is a stock comic device, occurring not only in Shakespeare but in much nineteenth-century comedy as well. Shaw, however, presented this inversion as an archetypal pattern. In assuming the universality of woman as aggressor, Shaw, according to such critics as G. K. Chesterton and Charles A. Berst, weakened the play's basic structure, since a large part of the action is predicated upon Shaw's assumption of this pattern as universal. The central figure of Ann Whitefield, Shaw claimed, was inspired by a viewing of the medieval morality play *Everyman:* "Every woman is not Ann, but Ann is Everywoman." Ann, like all women (according to Shaw) motivated primarily by the Life Force, instinctively knows that John Tanner will sire superior children and is therefore completely unscrupulous in pursuing and capturing him. The comic action derives from the obliviousness of the other characters—in particular Tanner himself—to Ann's intentions, and Tanner's horrified cross-continental flight when he realizes he is Ann's intended "victim."

A large part of the critical discussion surrounding *Man and Superman* focuses on the relationship between the hell scene in the third act and the rest of the play. In Act Three, the principal characters reappear as their actual or spiritual forebears from the Don Juan legend: John Tanner as Don Juan Tenorio, Ann Whitefield as Doña Ana de Ulloa; Roebuck Ramsden as Ana's father the Commendatore, slain by Don Juan in a duel over Ana's honor, and as the Devil, Mendoza, the brigand who briefly kidnaps Tanner during his flight from Ann. In an extension of the sex-role-reversal that Shaw established by presuming woman as the aggressor in human relationships, Shaw presented his Don Juan as the victim, and not the victimizer, of women, a man whose reputation as a philanderer was unfairly put upon him by the imploring women whom he fled. Louis Kronenberger has written of the hell scene that "nowhere in English during the twentieth century has there been a more dazzlingly sustained discussion of ideas in dialogue form," although he questions whether the scene, consisting as it does of lengthy discourse and little action, ought technically even to be considered a part of the play. In analyzing the relationship between the play's two parts, Bernard F. Dukore has noted that "parallel snatches of dialogue" occur in both parts, and that the themes of "illusion and reality, the central images of the hell scene," are also the themes that most involve the actors and actions of Acts One, Two, and Four. Dukore also remarks upon some similarities between the predilections of the characters in the framing play and their alternate *personae* in the hell scene: for example, "Member of the Idle Rich Class" Tanner deplores his social milieu much as Don Juan Tenorio condemns the idleness of dwellers in hell. Both Ann and Ana profess to be conventional and dutiful, when in fact both are duplicitous and hypocritical. Dukore further notes that although "the philosophy [of the Life Force] underlies the action of the frame play, it is implicit only. The hell scene . . . makes the philosophy explicit. The Life Force is *mentioned* in the frame play; in the inner play, it is *explained.*"

Many other critics have commented on the fact that the hell scene serves as explication of the Life Force theory, while the social comedy portion of the play demonstrates an instance of the Life Force at work. The exchange of ideas between the characters in the dream scene in some ways reinforces the relationships that already existed between them in the framing play. Ana, for example, is shown to be as dishonest and manipulative as Ann. Since the scene is Tanner's (and possibly also Mendoza's) dream, however, Tanner's forebear Tenorio comes off much more impressively than does Tanner in the rest of the play. In Acts One, Two, and Four, Tanner's heartfelt and impassioned speeches fall flat, fail to impress, or are summarily dismissed; in the hell scene, Don Juan Tenorio brilliantly outwits even the Devil. The equivocal ending of the dream scene—with Ana de Ulloa disappearing in search of "a father for the Superman!"—does not make clear if in fact she has fixed upon Don Juan as the intended father of her child, or if Tenorio, unlike Tanner, escapes this fate. It is often pointed out, however, that the dream scene in hell ends when Ann Whitefield triumphantly descends upon and "captures" Tanner. This is often taken by critics to mean that in

hell, as on earth, the Life Force has won out and in both places Ana/Ann has successfully brought down her prey, to the eventual betterment of the race. The hell scene can be, and in fact often has been, performed successfully as a separate, one-act play. When the two parts of *Man and Superman* are performed together, however, most critics concur with Dukore that "the sum is greater than the mere addition of two parts."

Shaw's idea of the dramatic hero was one "whose passions are those which have produced the philosophy, the poetry, the art, and the stagecraft of the world, and not merely [the type] who have produced its weddings, coroners' inquests, and executions." Thus, Shaw's dramas invariably present characters who undergo a synthesis of outlook following a clash between other characters or with the moral and religious conventions of their time. The heroes are often reflections of Shaw himself: vivacious, sophisticated, and lucid. A frequent and central criticism directed at Shaw as a dramatist is that his characters are intellectual rather than human creations. From the time of Shaw's earliest plays, critics have claimed that he peopled his stage with cleverly disguised strawmen, only to have his favored protagonists knock them down with Shavian declamations by the final curtain. Many commentators, however, commonly consider *Man and Superman* the play in which Shaw "gave the devil his due": although clearly espousing a particular doctrine, Shaw did allow such characters as Doño Ana, and the Devil himself, in the hell scene, to muster convincing and persuasive arguments against the ideal life of the intellect propounded by the Shavian figure of Tanner/Tenorio. Even in the play's first act, the character of Roebuck Ramsden, intended as an archetype of outdated liberalism and superseded "advanced ideas," is granted an unexpectedly sympathetic stance when the assembled characters believe they are dealing with an unmarried pregnant woman. Even though the "trumpery story of modern London life" ends with Tanner defeated (that is, engaged to marry Ann), his counterpart in the hell scene, Don Juan, triumphs, expounding brilliantly on the Life Force, which he eventually summarizes in terms that critics note can be regarded as descriptive of nature or of God: "I tell you, as long as I can conceive something better than myself I cannot be easy unless I am striving to bring it into existence or clearing the way for it. This is the law of my life. This is the working within me of Life's incessant aspiration to higher organization, wider, deeper, intenser self-consciousness and clearer self-understanding." Further, some critics, such as A. M. Gibbs, hold that in "losing" to Ann and succumbing to the Life Force, Tanner in fact wins both that which will make him happiest and accomplish the greatest general good.

As Samuel Hynes has noted, Shaw was driven by *weltverbesserungswahn*—a rage to better the world.

His vivid characters and clever dialogue only disguise his moral purpose, called Puritan by some: to expose the dilemmas, absurdities and injustices of society. Shaw turned away from the nineteenth-century concept of the English theater as a source of light entertainment, and made acceptable the drama of ideas. In this he altered the course of twentieth-century drama.

(For further information about Shaw's life and works, see *Contemporary Authors*, Vol. 104; *Dictionary of Literary Biography*, Vol. 10: *Modern British Dramatists, 1910-1945;* and *Twentieth-Century Literary Criticism*, Vols. 3, 9, 21.)

CRITICAL COMMENTARY

BERTOLT BRECHT

(essay date 1926)

[In the following essay, originally published in *Berliner Borsen-Courier* in 1926, Brecht discusses Shaw's artistic aims and techniques.]

It should be clear by now that Shaw is a terrorist. The Shavian terror is an unusual one, and he employs an unusual weapon—that of humor. This unusual man seems to be of the opinion that there is nothing fearful in the world except the calm and incorruptible eye of the common man. But this eye must be feared, always and unconditionally. This theory endows him with a remarkable natural superiority; and by his unfaltering practice in accordance with it, he has made it impossible for anyone who ever comes into contact with him— be it in person, through his books, or through his theater—to assume that he ever committed a deed or uttered a sentence without fearful respect for this incorruptible eye. In fact, young people, whose main qualification is often their love of mettle, are often held to a minimum of aggressiveness by their premonition that any attack on Shaw's habits, even if it were his insistence on wearing peculiar underwear, would inevitably result in a terrible defeat of their own thoughtlessly selected apparel. If one adds to this his exploding of the thoughtless, habitual assumption that anything that might possibly be considered venerable should be treated in a subdued manner instead of energetically and joyously; if one adds to this his successful proof that in the face of truly significant ideas a relaxed (even snotty) attitude is the only proper one, since it alone facilitates true concentration, it becomes evident what measure of personal freedom he has achieved.

The Shavian terror consists of Shaw's insistence on the prerogative of every man to act decently, logically, and with a sense of humor, and on the obligation to act in this manner even in the face of opposition. He knows very well how much courage it takes to laugh about the ridiculous and how much seriousness it takes to discover the amusing. And, like all purposeful people, he knows, on the other hand, that the most time-consuming and distracting pursuit is a certain kind of seriousness which pervades literature but does not exist anywhere else. (Like us, the young generation, he considers it naive to write for the theater, and he does not show the slightest inclination to pretend that he is not aware of this: he makes far-reaching use of his naivete. He furnishes the theater with as much fun as it can take. And it can take a lot. What draws people to the theater is, strictly speaking, so much nonsense, which constitutes a tremendous buoyancy for those problems which really interest the progressive dramatic writer and which are the real value of his pieces. It follows that his problems must be so pertinent that he can be as buoyant about them as he wishes to be, for the buoyancy is what people want.)

I seem to remember that Shaw recently expressed his opinion about the future of the drama. He says that in the future people will no longer go to the theater in order to understand. He probably means that mere reproduction of reality curiously fails to give the impression of verisimilitude. The younger generation will not contradict Shaw on this point. But I feel that Shaw's own dramatic works were able to overshadow those of his contemporaries exactly because they unflinchingly appealed to the intellect. His world is composed of opinions. The fate of his characters is identical with their opinions. Shaw, in order to have a play, invents some complications which provide his characters with opportunities to vent their opinions extensively and to have them clash with ours. (These complications can never be old and familiar enough to suit Shaw; here he really has no ambition whatever: a thoroughly ordinary usurer is worth his weight in gold; he stumbles on a patriotic girl in history, and the only important thing is that his audience be equally familiar with the story of this girl, that the sad end of the usurer be well known and gleefully anticipated, so that he can upset all the more completely our old-fashioned concepts of these

Principal Works

Cashel Byron's Profession (novel) 1886

An Unsocial Socialist (novel) 1887

The Quintessence of Ibsenism (criticism) 1891

Widowers' Houses (drama) 1892

Arms and the Man (drama) 1894

Candida (drama) 1897

The Devil's Disciple (drama) 1897

The Perfect Wagnerite (essay) 1898

Plays: Pleasant and Unpleasant [first publication] (dramas) 1898

You Never Can Tell (drama) 1899

Captain Brassbound's Conversion (drama) 1900

Love among the Artists (novel) 1900

Socialism for Millionaires (essay) 1901

Three Plays for Puritans [first publication] (dramas) 1901

Mrs. Warren's Profession (drama) 1902

*The Admirable Bashville; or, Constancy Unrewarded (drama) 1903

How He Lied to Her Husband (drama) 1904

John Bull's Other Island (drama) 1904

The Irrational Knot (novel) 1905

Major Barbara (drama) 1905

Man and Superman: A Comedy and a Philosophy (drama) 1905

On Going to Church (essay) 1905

The Philanderer (drama) 1905

Caesar and Cleopatra (drama) 1906

The Doctor's Dilemma (drama) 1906

Dramatic Opinions and Essays (essays) 1906

Getting Married (drama) 1908

The Shewing-Up of Blanco Posnet (drama) 1909

Misalliance (drama) 1910

Fanny's First Play (drama) 1911

Androcles and the Lion (drama) 1912

Pygmalion (drama) 1913

Heartbreak House (drama) 1920

Back to Methuselah (drama) 1922

Saint Joan (drama) 1923

The Intelligent Woman's Guide to Socialism (essay) 1928

The Apple Cart (drama) 1929

Immaturity (novel) 1930

The Adventures of the Black Girl in Her Search for God (short story) 1932

Music in London, 1890-94 (criticism) 1932

Too True to Be Good (drama) 1932

The Simpleton of the Unexpected Isles (drama) 1935

London Music in 1888-89 (criticism) 1937

Geneva (drama) 1938

Bernard Shaw's Rhyming Picture Guide to Ayot St. Lawrence (poetry) 1950

*This drama is an adaptation of the novel Cashel Byron's Profession.

---

types and—above all—our notions of the way these types think.)

Probably all of his characters, in all their traits, are the result of Shaw's delight in upsetting our habitual prejudices. He knows that we have the terrible habit of forcing all the attributes of a certain kind of people into one preconceived, stereotyped concept. In our imagination the usurer is cowardly, sneaky, and brutal. We would not think of permitting him to be even a little courageous, sentimental, or soft hearted. Shaw does.

Concerning heroes, Shaw's degenerate successors have awkwardly amplified his refreshing conviction—that heroes are not exemplary scholars and that heroism is a very inscrutable, but very real conglomeration of contradictory traits—to mean that neither heroism nor heroes exist. But even this does not bother Shaw. It seems he considers it healthier to live among common people than among heroes.

In the composition of his works Shaw proceeds with utmost frankness. He does not mind writing under the continuous scrutiny of the public. In order to make his judgments more emphatic, he facilitates this scrutiny: he unremittingly stresses his own peculiarities, his very individualistic taste, even his own (little) weaknesses. Thus he cannot fail to reap gratitude. Even where his opinions clash with those of the younger generation, he is listened to with glee: he is—and what more can be said about a man—a good fellow. Besides, his time preserves opinions better than emotions and moods. It seems that of all the things produced in this epoch opinions are the most durable.

It is characteristically difficult to find out the opinions of other European authors. But I assume that concerning literature they hold approximately the same view, to wit, that writing is a melancholy business. Shaw, whose opinions about everything are widely known throughout the world, clearly sets himself deliberately apart from this view of his colleagues. . . . Shaw likes to write. On his head there is no room for the crown of a martyr. His literary preoccupation does not separate him from life. On the contrary. I do not know whether it is an indication of talent, but the effect of his unmistakeable serenity and his contagious good humor is extraordinary. Shaw actually succeeds in giving the impression that his mental and bodily health increases with every sentence he writes. Reading him is perhaps not exhilarating in a dionysean manner, but it is undeniable that it is amazingly conducive to good health. And his only enemies—if we must mention them at all—are obviously exclusively people to whom health is much less of a concern.

I cannot remember a single one of Shaw's "characteristic" ideas, although I know, of course, that he has many; but I remember many things which he discovers to be characteristic of other people. In his own estimate, at any rate, his temper is more important than his individual opinions. And that speaks well for a man like him.

I feel that a theory of evolution is central for him, one which, in his opinion, differs considerably and significantly from another theory of evolution of definitely lower calibre. At any rate, his faith that man is capable of infinite improvement plays an important role in his works. It will be clearly recognized as a sincere ovation for Shaw when I admit without blushing that I unconditionally subscribe to Shaw's view although I am not thoroughly acquainted with either of the two theories mentioned above. The reason? A man with such keen intellect and courageous eloquence simply deserves my complete confidence. This is all the more true as I have considered—always and in any situation—the forcefulness of an expression more important than its immediate applicability and a man of stature more important than the sphere of his activity. (pp. 184-87)

Bertolt Brecht, "Ovation for Shaw," translated by Gerhard H. W. Zuther, in *Modern Drama*, Vol. 2, No. 2, September, 1959, pp. 184-87.

DESMOND MACCARTHY

(essay date 1946)

[MacCarthy was one of the foremost English literary and dramatic critics of the twentieth century. In the following excerpt from a 1946 radio broadcast, he contends that *Man and Superman*, in its published three-part form, contains "a central exposition of Shaw's philosophy."]

Man and Superman is one of the peaks in Bernard Shaw's dramatic work. (p. 32)

The play is a serio-comic love-chase of a man by a woman. But taken together with the preface, with the long dream interlude in Act III called "Don Juan in Hell," and with its appendix, "The Revolutionist's Handbook" (attributed to John Tanner), it remains a central exposition of Shaw's philosophy. This was the first time that his Evolutionary Religion, his conception of the Life Force as a Will striving through the minds and instincts of men to become conscious of itself, was set forth.

Yet in the play itself, with the exception of the dream interlude, there is nothing of this; and the theory which interprets sex attraction between men and women as one of the means the Life Force takes towards its end is a deduction from the play rather than a part of it. So also is the "practical" moral that selective breeding is more important than political reforms. What does, however, pervade the dialogue and action is Shaw's conception of sex and love. In *Man and Superman*, as he says in the preface, he set out to write a play in which sex attraction should be the main subject. This, he proclaimed, no dramatist had done before. The world's famous love-tragedies and love-comedies had only dramatised conflicts, either triumphant or unhappy, between lovers and marriage laws, or love and circumstance or love and moral obligations. No dramatist, he asserted, had attempted to reveal the underlying nature of a passionate mutual attraction between a particular man and a particular woman. That startling statement had some truth in it, though all it really meant was that no dramatist had yet interpreted on the stage "love" as the great German pessimist, Schopenhauer, had also interpreted it, namely as the Will of the Race expressing itself through the desires of the individual and often contrary to his or her happiness. Shaw also added that in love woman was really always the pursuer, and he pointed out that Shakespeare had unconsciously realised this in some of his plays. This theory, however, though it gains plausibility from the fact that women take love-likings as often as men, and in their own ways seek as often to win the object of their affections, cannot be accepted as sound. Still, if the case of Ann and Tanner is taken as a particular story, and not as illustrating a universal truth, this theory need not lessen our appreciation. The play is one of Shaw's most brilliant pieces of creative work.

Ann according to his philosophy is "Everywoman," though every woman is not Ann. As an individual she is excellently drawn. Instinct leads her to mark down Tanner as the father of her future children, but Tanner knows that for him marriage means loss of liberty, peace of mind, and what is far more serious, as likely as not the ruin of his revolutionary efforts. Jack Tanner, with his explosions of nervous energy, his wit, and vehement eloquence, is as vividly created as Ann.

The contrast to him is the poetical, chivalrous, romantical Octavius, the idealiser of women who is in love with Ann. "Ricky Ticky Tavy," as she half tenderly, half contemptuously calls him, instead of flying from her like his friend Jack Tanner, woos her humbly, but her deeper instincts—and through these, according to Shaw, the Life Force works—leads her to refuse him as a husband; the poetic temperament is barren—the Life Force passes it by.

But Tanner yields at last, because, as his previous incarnation Don Juan explains in the dream episode, he cannot help it. The Life Force which wills that the offspring of two particular people shall be born, is stronger even than his impulse to serve mankind in ways to which he had intended to dedicate himself. Tanner "loves" Ann in the sense of feeling this irresistible urge; at the same time he despises her. She is a bully and a liar and by "unscrupulously using her personal fascinations to make men give her what she wants," she is also "something for which there is no polite name." He knows that she will think his aspirations and efforts to reform society absurd and thwart him in so far as she dares in the interests of the family. Above all, Ann is a hypocrite, but from an ultimate point of view that was unimportant. Both Ann and Tanner, in submitting to their attraction for each other, become servants of the will of the world. They are instruments towards creating the superior race of the future—ultimately the Superman.

Now at the time Shaw wrote this play he was evidently in a state of impatient despair in regard to what political reform could achieve. In the preface he says: "There is no public enthusiast alive of twenty years' practical democratic experience who believes in the political adequacy of the electorate or the body it elects. The overthrow of the aristocrat has created the necessity of the Superman." Thus both are right to sacrifice; she, perhaps her life in child-bearing, he his happiness, aims and generous ambitions; for such things cannot compare in importance with bringing into the world a child born of their mutual attraction.

It follows, of course, that the institution of marriage which compels two people who have nothing in common save mutual sex-attraction to spend their lives together, is stupid, and that from the conception that the child is the sole end of marriage, it is absurd to make it binding. Moreover, the fact that marriage is binding makes men and women who know that they will have to spend the rest of their lives together, choose their mates for irrelevant reasons—affection, respect or self-interest. That is the moral of this serio-comedy, which keeps many people laughing who would not laugh perhaps if they really understood its drift. It is rather odd that the dramatist never again returned to the theme that in selective breeding or "eugenics," as that process is called, lay all hope of the future of mankind.

In the other characters, also, Shaw's skill in drawing types and making them speak out of themselves with arresting point is at its best. What an eye he has always had for types which were instantly recognisable and yet new to the stage or to fiction. Note here the appearance for the first time of the modern mechanician, 'Entry Straker, Tanner's chauffeur, and note too, how admirably the old-fashioned, free-thinking radical, Roebuck Ramsden, is presented, the man who can't believe that he is not still in the forefront of advanced thought, and yet is to Tanner the most ludicrous old stick-in-the-mud. The last moment of the first act, when Violet, that expertly drawn, empty-headed, possessive type of attractive girl, suddenly reveals that, instead of being the daring flaunter of conventions Tanner had hoped, she has all the time really been *married* to the man whose child she is about to bear, is one of the most amusing thunder-claps in modern comedy.

The scene at the end between Ann and Tanner, in which Ann at last gets her way, is also admirable. (pp. 32-5)

The dream-interlude, "Don Juan in Hell," is a marvellous example of Shaw's power of making the eloquence of ideas as riveting as action on the stage. Note, by the way, his contrast between Heaven and Hell.

The point which I wish to insist upon here is not that Shaw is not right in considering his Heaven superior to his Hell—it obviously is; but that his Heaven is not the contemplation of what is perfect, but of something that is struggling to become so. It is a condition in which there is still peril, where you "face things as they are"; in short, a "community of saints" which is really a community of reformers. Shaw describes them as filled with "a passion of the divine will"; but this passion is a desire to make the world better, and not a contemplation of perfection: in so far as it is a contemplative ecstasy at all, it is only rapture at the idea that perfection is possible.

What chills us, then, in his Heaven is the misgiving that the phrase "masters of reality" (so the heavenly inhabitants are described) is a euphemism for a society of people all devoted to making each other and everybody else more virtuous. Now we can imagine something better than that; and Shaw's Hell, if he had not been so unfair to it, where they value love, music and beauty for their own sakes, offers hints at any rate. (pp. 35-6)

Desmond MacCarthy, in his *Shaw,* MacGibbon & Kee, 1951, 217 p.

EDMUND WILSON

(essay date 1948)

[Wilson was an American novelist and critic. In the following excerpt from an essay written in 1936 and revised in 1948, he examines the principal themes of Shaw's dramas.]

Einstein has said that Shaw's plays remind him of Mozart's music: every word has its place in the development. And if we allow for some nineteenth-century prolixity, we can see in Shaw's dramatic work a logic and grace, a formal precision, like that of the eighteenth-century composers.

Take *The Apple Cart,* for example. The fact that Shaw is here working exclusively with economic and political materials has caused its art to be insufficiently appreciated. If it had been a sentimental comedy by Molnar, the critics would have applauded its deftness; yet Shaw is a finer artist than any of the Molnars or Schnitzlers. The first act of *The Apple Cart* is an exercise in the scoring for small orchestra at which Shaw is particularly skillful. After what he has himself called the overture before the curtain of the conversation between the two secretaries, in which the music of King Magnus is foreshadowed, the urbane and intelligent King and the 'bull-roarer Boanerges' play a duet against one another. Then the King plays a single instrument against the whole nine of the cabinet. The themes emerge: the King's disinterestedness and the labor government's sordid self-interest. The development is lively: the music is tossed from one instrument to another, with, to use the old cliché, a combination of inevitableness and surprise. Finally, the King's theme gets a full and splendid statement in the long speech in which he declares his principles: 'I stand for the great abstractions: for conscience and virtue; for the eternal against the expedient; for the evolutionary appetite against the day's gluttony,' etc. This silver voice of the King lifts the movement to a poignant climax; and now a dramatic reversal carries the climax further and rounds out and balances the harmony. Unexpectedly, one of the brasses of the ministry takes up the theme of the King and repeats it more passionately and loudly. . . . [She] launches into an extraordinary tirade in which the idea of political disinterestedness is taken out of the realm of elegant abstraction in which it has hitherto remained with the King and reiterated in terms of engineering: 'every little sewing machine in the Hebrides, every dentist's drill in Shetland, every carpet sweeper in Margate,' etc. This ends on crashing chords, but immediately the music of the cabinet snarlingly reasserts itself. The act ends on the light note of the secretaries.

This music is a music of ideas—or rather, perhaps, it is a music of moralities. . . . Shaw, like Plato, repudiates as a dangerous form of drunkenness the indulgence in literature for its own sake; but, like Plato, he then proceeds, not simply to expound a useful morality, but himself to indulge in an art in which moralities are used as the motifs. It is partly on this account, certainly, that Bernard Shaw has been underrated as an artist. Whether people admire or dislike him, whether they find his plays didactically boring or morally stimulating, they fail to take account of the fact that it is the enchantment of a highly accomplished art which has brought them to and kept them in the playhouse. . . . [Far] from being relentlessly didactic, Shaw's mind has reflected in all its complexity the intellectual life of his time; and his great achievement is to have reflected it with remarkable fidelity. He has *not* imposed a cogent system, but he has worked out a vivid picture. It is, to be sure, not a passive picture, like that of Santayana or Proust: it is a picture in which action plays a prominent part. But it does not play a consistent part: the dynamic principle in Shaw is made to animate a variety of forces. (pp. 182-84)

The principal pattern which recurs in Bernard Shaw—aside from the duel between male and female, which seems to me of much less importance—is the polar opposition between the type of the saint and the type of the successful practical man. (p. 185)

Certainly it is this theme . . . which has inspired those scenes of Shaw's plays which are most moving and most real on the stage—which are able to shock us for the moment, as even the 'Life Force' passages hardly do, out of the amiable and objective attention which has been induced by the bright play of the intelligence. It is the moment when Major Barbara, brought at last to the realization of the power of the capitalist's money and of her own weakness when she hasn't it to back her, is left alone on the stage with the unregenerate bums whose souls she has been trying to save; the moment when Androcles is sent into the arena with the lion; the moment in the emptied courtroom when Joan has been taken out to be burned and the Bishop and the Earl of Warwick are trying each to pin the responsibility on the other. It is the scene in *Heartbreak House* between Captain Shotover and Hector, when they give voice to their common antagonism toward the forces that seem to have them at their mercy. . . . It is the scene in *Back to Methuselah* when the Elderly Gentleman declares to the Oracle: 'They have gone back [the political delegation with whom he has come] to lie about your answer. I cannot go with them. I cannot live among people to whom nothing is real!'—and when she shows him her face and strikes him dead.

But now let us note—for the light they throw on Bernard Shaw in his various phases—the upshots of these several situations. In *Major Barbara,* the Christian saint, the man of learning, and the industrial superman form an alliance from which much is to be hoped. In *Androcles and the Lion,* written . . . in Shaw's amusing but least earnest middle period, just before the war, Androcles and the lion form an alliance, too, of which something is also to be hoped, but go out arm in arm after a harlequinade on the level of a Christmas pantomime. In *Heartbreak House,* which was begun in 1913 and not finished till 1916, the declaration of war by the unworldlings takes place in the midst of confusion and does not lead to any action on their part.

In *Back to Methuselah,* of the postwar period, the Elderly Gentleman is blasted by the Oracle in a strange scene the implications of which we must stop to examine a moment. The fate of the Elderly Gentleman is evidently intended by Shaw to have some sort of application to himself: though a member of a backward community in which people have not yet achieved the Methuselah-span of life, he differs from his fellows at least in this: that he finds he cannot bear any longer to live among people to whom nothing is real. So the Oracle shrivels him up with her glance.

But what is this supposed to mean? What *is* this higher wisdom which the Elderly Gentleman cannot contemplate and live? So far as the reader is concerned, the revelation of the Oracle is a blank. The old system of Bernard Shaw, which was plausible enough to pass before the war, has just taken a terrible blow, and its grotesque and gruesome efforts to pull itself together and function give the effect of an umbrella, wrecked in a storm, which, when the owner tries to open it up, shows several long ribs of steel sticking out. The Life Force of the man and woman in *Man and Superman* no longer leads either to human procreation or to social-revolutionary activity. The Life Force has been finally detached from socialism altogether. In the *Intelligent Woman's Guide,* Shaw will reject the Marxist dialectic as a false religion of social salvation; but the Life Force is also a religious idea, which we have always supposed in the past to be directed toward social betterment, and now, in *Back to Methuselah,* we find that it has misfired with socialism. Socialism has come and gone; the planet has been laid waste by wars; the ordinary people have all perished, and there is nobody left on earth but a race of selected supermen. And now the race of superior human beings, which was invoked in *Man and Superman* as the prime indispensable condition for any kind of progress whatever but which was regarded by Shaw at that time as producible through eugenic breeding, has taken here a most unearthly turn. It has always been through the superman idea that Shaw has found it possible to escape from the implications of his socialism; and he now no longer even imagines that the superior being can be created by human idealism through human science. The superior beings of *Back to Methuselah* are people who live forever; but they have achieved this superiority through an unconscious act of the will. When they achieved it, what the Life Force turns out to have had in store for them is the mastery of abstruse branches of knowledge and the extra-uterine development of embryos. Beyond this, there is still to be attained the liberation of the spirit from the flesh, existence as a 'whirlpool in pure force.' (pp. 186-88)

Humanity, in *Back to Methuselah,* has dropped

out for the moment altogether. The long-livers of the period of progress contemporary with the Elderly Gentleman are not the more 'complete' human beings, with lives richer and better rounded . . . . : they are Shavian super-prigs who say the cutting and dampening things which the people have always said in Shaw's plays but who have been abstracted here from the well-observed social setting in which Shaw has always hitherto presented them. And the beings of the later epoch are young people playing in an Arcadia and ancients immersed in cogitations, alike—both cogitations and Arcadia—of the bleakest and most desolating description. There is in *Back to Methuselah* nothing burning or touching, and there is nothing genuinely thrilling except the cry of the Elderly Gentleman; and that, for all the pretense of revelation, is answered by a simple extinction.

In the *Tragedy of an Elderly Gentleman,* the Elderly Gentleman is frightened, but his tragedy is not a real tragedy. *Saint Joan* . . . is an even more frightened play, and, softened though it is by the historical perspective into which Shaw manages to throw it through his epilogue, it was the first genuine tragedy that Shaw had written. The horror of *Back to Methuselah* is a lunar horror; the horror of *Saint Joan* is human. The saint is suppressed by the practical man; and even when she comes back to earth, though all those who exploited or destroyed her are now obliged to acknowledge her holiness, none wants her to remain among them: each would do the same thing again. Only the soldier who had handed her the cross at the stake is willing to accept her now, but he is only a poor helpless clown condemned to the dungeon of the flesh. (pp. 188-89)

Heartbreak House has the same sort of setting and more or less the same form as such Shavian conversations as *Getting Married* and *Misalliance;* but it is really something new for Shaw. There is no diagram of social relations, no tying-up of threads at the end. . . . Heartbreak House, built like a ship, with its old drunken and half-crazy master, the retired adventurer Captain Shotover, is cultured and leisured England; but the characters are no longer pinned down and examined as social specimens: in an atmosphere heavily charged, through a progression of contacts and collisions, they give out thunder and lightning like storm-clouds. Brooding frustrations and disillusions, childlike hurts and furious resentments, which have dropped the old Shavian masks, rush suddenly into an utterance which for the moment has burst out of the old rationalistic wit. For once, where Bernard Shaw has so often reduced historical myths to the sharp focus of contemporary satire, he now raises contemporary figures to the heroic proportions of myth.—An air-raid brings down the final curtain: Heartbreak House has at last been split wide. The capitalist Mangan gets killed, and there is a suggestion that they may all be the better for it. (pp. 189-90)

Too True to Be Good [is] a curious 'political extravaganza,' in which he turns back upon and criticizes his own career. Here the theme of the bourgeois radical of the eighties, disillusioned with himself under stress of the disasters of the twentieth century, is treated in the same vein, with the same kind of idealist poetry, now grown frankly elegiac and despairing, which Shaw had opened in *Heartbreak House* and which had made the real beauty of *The Apple Cart.* (p. 191)

Shaw's most recent pieces are [weak]. *The Simpleton of the Unexpected Isles* . . . is the only play of the author's which has ever struck me as silly. In it, the Day of Judgment comes to the British Empire, and the privilege of surviving on earth is made to depend upon social utility. But, by setting up a purely theocratic tribunal, Shaw deprives this scene of social point: the principle of selection is so general that it might be applied by the fascists as readily as by the socialists, at the same time that the policy of wholesale extinction seems inspired by an admiration for the repressive tactics of both. The play ends with a salute to the unknown future, which, like the vision of infinity of *Back to Methuselah,* seems perfectly directionless. *The Millionairess* . . . makes a farce out of the notion that a natural boss, deprived of adventitious authority, will inevitably gravitate again to a position where he can bully and control people, and sounds as if it had been suggested by the later phases of Stalin.

Here it cannot be denied that Bernard Shaw begins to show signs of old age. As the pace of his mind slackens and the texture of his work grows looser, the contradictory impulses and principles which have hitherto provided him with drama begin to show gaping rifts. In his *Preface on Bosses* to *The Millionairess,* he talks about 'beginning a Reformation well to the left of Russia,' but composes [a] panegyric on Mussolini, with . . . respectful compliments to Hitler. . . . (pp. 195-96)

Yet the openings—the prologue to *The Simpleton,* with its skit on the decay of the British Empire and the knockabout domestic agonies of the first act or two of *The Millionairess*—still explode their comic situations with something of the old energy and wit; and the one-acter, *The Six of Calais,* though it does not crackle quite with the old spark, is not so very far inferior to such an earlier trifle as *How He Lied to Her Husband.* It is interesting to note—what bears out the idea that Shaw is at his best as an artist—that the last thing he is to lose, apparently, is his gift for pure comic invention, which has survived, not much dimmed, though we may tire of it, since the days of *You Never Can Tell.* (p. 196)

Edmund Wilson, "Bernard Shaw at Eighty (1948)," in his *The Triple Thinkers: Twelve Essays on Literary Subjects,* revised edition, Oxford University Press, 1948, pp. 165-96.

JORGE LUIS BORGES
(essay date 1951)

[In the following excerpt from a 1951 essay, Borges praises Shaw as a liberator of the human spirit and as a pre-eminent creator of characters.]

Can an author create characters that are superior to himself ? I would reply that he cannot, and my negation would apply to the intellectual as well as the moral levels. I believe that creatures who are more lucid or more noble than our best moments will not issue from us. On that opinion I base my conviction of the pre-eminence of Shaw. The problems about labor unions and municipalities of his early works will cease to be interesting, or else have already done so; the jokes of the Pleasant Plays bid fair to being, some day, no less awkward than Shakespeare's (humor, I suspect, is an oral genre, a sudden spark in conversation, not a written thing); the ideas expressed by the prologues and the eloquent tirades will be sought in Schopenhauer and in Samuel Butler; but Lavinia, Blanco Posnet, Keegan, Shotover, Richard Dudgeon, and, above all, Julius Caesar, surpass any character imagined by the art of our time. To think of Monsieur Teste or the histrionic Zarathustra of Nietzsche alongside them is to apprehend, with surprise or even astonishment, the primacy of Shaw. In 1911 Albert Soergel was able to write, repeating a commonplace of the time, "Bernard Shaw is an annihilator of the heroic concept, a killer of heroes" . . . ; he did not understand that the heroic was completely independent from the romantic and was embodied in Captain Bluntschli of *Arms and the Man,* not in Sergius Saranoff.

The biography of Bernard Shaw by Frank Harris contains an admirable letter written by Shaw, in which he says: "I understand everything and everyone, and am nobody and nothing." . . . From that nothingness (so comparable to the nothingness of God before He created the world, so comparable to the primordial divinity that another Irishman, Johannes Scotus Erigena, called *Nihil*), Bernard Shaw educed almost innumerable persons, or dramatis personae: the most ephemeral, I suspect, is G.B.S., who represented him to the public and who supplied such a wealth of easy witticisms for newspaper columns.

Shaw's basic subjects are philosophy and ethics: it is natural and inevitable that he is not esteemed in Argentina, or that he is remembered in that country only for a few epigrams. The Argentine feels that the universe is nothing but a manifestation of chance, the fortuitous combination of atoms conceived by Democritus; philosophy does not interest him. Nor does ethics: for him, social problems are nothing but a conflict of individuals or classes or nations, in which everything is licit—except ridicule or defeat.

Man's character and its variations constitute the essential theme of the novel of our time; the lyric is the complacent magnification of amorous fortunes or misfortunes; the philosophies of Heidegger or Jaspers transform each one of us into the interesting interlocutor of a secret and continuous dialogue with nothingness or with divinity; these disciplines, which may be formally admirable, foster the illusion of the self that Vedanta condemns as a capital error. They may play at desperation and anguish, but at bottom they flatter the vanity; in that sense, they are immoral. Shaw's work, on the other hand, leaves an aftertaste of liberation. The taste of the doctrines of Zeno's Porch and the taste of the sagas. (pp. 165-66)

Jorge Luis Borges, "For Bernard Shaw," in his *Other Inquisitions: 1937-1952,* translated by Ruth L. C. Simms, University of Texas Press, 1964, pp. 163-66.

ANGUS WILSON

(essay date 1956)

[In the following excerpt, Wilson comments on Shaw's contributions to English drama.]

I think that one of Shaw's greatest contributions to the English theatre is his creation of characters who express themselves through ideas as well as emotions, who have heads as well as hearts. This view in itself runs counter to the opinion of many, particularly people in the theatre itself. They are never tired of reiterating that drama is a vehicle of emotion and passion not of ideas, that ideas are not 'theatrical'. . . . At his worst, Shaw tended to smother his very real thinking, feeling people beneath his own ideas, to drown the formal truth of his work beneath the Truth about Life shouted at the top of his own voice, to kill the wonderful vitality of his creation with his own pantomime of high spirits. In his best work—in most of the pre-1914 plays, in *Heartbreak House* and in part of *Saint Joan*—his own voice is only an accompaniment, powerful to contemporary audiences, but growing fainter and less important beside the total music of the plays as the years passed. (p. 55)

[Many of the modern critics of Shaw] cannot forget that he was one of the pioneers of the modern Welfare State and they read into his work all that they dis-

like in that society. It is peculiar because they . . . accompany their declaration that the plays are unreadable by great eulogy of his 'art', yet they do not seem to find that art powerful enough to overcome these immediate reactions. . . . If the attacks on brothels and slum landlordism savour too much of Socialism for these critics, then they should logically extend their dislike to Dickens and to Fielding. In fact, as many other critics have pointed out, Shaw was well aware that the remedying of material evils was only a preliminary, though an essential preliminary, to an ideal society; he was essentially religious. . . . For Shaw [evil and pain] always remained removables like poverty, to be divested of the sickly halo which Victorian sentimentalism and romanticism had placed around them and labelled pretty crimes in good Erewhon fashion. But the reality of pain and evil have been foremost in the post-Hitler ordinary man's search for religion, and he is not likely to find satisfaction in a 'philosophy' that ignores it. The 'preaching' of Shaw, then, appears to be something of a bogy. In Shaw's best plays, it is largely irrelevant; in his later plays, after *Saint Joan,* which are his worst, it is unlikely to attract. Only *Man and Superman* is ruined by it.

In *Man and Superman,* however, Shaw's philosophy is shown from a different angle—the Life Force at work in the relations of the sexes. The conquest of Jack Tanner by Anne Whitefield, the natural selection of man by woman to fulfil her function, is a far more serious matter than the empty 'high thinking' of the ancients, for the theme runs through a great many of Shaw's good plays and makes some part even of the best almost intolerable, I think, to modern audiences. The treatment of the relations of the sexes is an even greater defect in Shaw's work than his treatment of art and the artist. Marchbanks and Dubedat talk foolish and embarrassing nonsense when they talk about art, but it is nothing to the embarrassment of the serious folly that almost any Shavian young man and woman talk to each other. The sexual qualities of most writers have both beneficial and maleficent effects on their work. It is possible that Shaw's energies, as he would have us believe, were the greater for other purposes by his dismissal of sex, though the Don Juan scene is as unconvincing as it is tedious. If Shaw had been able so summarily to dismiss sex as he wished, all might have been well, but it plays an essential part in his neo-Darwinian scheme of things. It seems evident, whatever the number of affairs he is said to have had between his twenty-ninth year and his marriage, that Shaw had deep inhibitions about sex. He seems to have found the preliminaries deeply exciting and any physical expression distasteful. The chase was the thing, and the hunter in good Life Force manner—the woman. The result is a painful series of Benedict and Beatrice situations, arch, artificial—a kind of elderly male virgin's sex-teasing dream. Flirtatious sex-teasing women have clearly a place in comedy, but as the sole representatives of young women they strike an unpleasantly prurient note. . . . It is, I believe, this sexual aspect of Shaw's work—half naïveté, half prudish prurience, with which, of course, are bound to his total failure to appreciate the meaning of cruelty and his occasional straight childish vulgarities—that is most likely to prevent a modern audience from appreciating his plays. (pp. 56-7)

His inhuman detachment and his sexual naïveté combine to make him a writer who is seldom 'moving', in the sense that that word is usually employed now to mean 'moving to pity'. In *The Devil's Disciple* he achieves this effect, in the second act of *Major Barbara* and in parts of *Saint Joan*, but this is a less important defect than we may think, for Shaw is essentially a great comedian and above all, a man who understands the comic nature of language. . . .

[He] puts upon the stage characters who live on many planes and makes them speak in a language that is formally delightful without being artificial. He knew and really understood that people lived in their ideas and their words as much as in their emotions, that every character that an actor or actress has to play is himself acting a part that is quite as integral to him as his 'real self', that 'humours' and 'grotesques' and 'caricatures' are simply the social cloaks which men assume to protect their loneliness and that these cloaks 'are' them as much as the isolated creatures hidden beneath. His masters in this were Dickens and Ibsen. It would be absurd to compare the merits of the three, but Shaw at his best was the equal of his masters. Like them he had a superb eye for the 'new' types in society and his best plays are full of people who had never yet been brought on the stage. He had equally an eye for the type that was out of date and did not know it. Some of his most comic effects are achieved in this way. It is only in his later years when he had ceased to observe so brilliantly that his art lost its magic. It is from this modernity, this power of putting real people on the stage instead of worn out stereotypes that the dramatists of today can learn most from him; from that and his passion for language, his spoken prose which is far more theatrically powerful than any revival of verse drama can be. (p. 58)

Angus Wilson, "The Living Dead: Bernard Shaw," in *London Magazine,* Vol. 3, No. 12, December, 1956, pp. 53-8.

ARCHIBALD HENDERSON
(essay date 1956)

[Henderson was a noted American mathematician, literary biographer, critic, essayist, and historian who became known as the foremost American expert on the life and works of Bernard Shaw. In the following excerpt, he contends that *Man and Superman* marked a new phase in Shaw's career as a writer and thinker.]

With *Man and Superman,* Shaw enters upon a new phase as writer and thinker. Up to this time, none of his plays reflects any conscious philosophy. The new play, with the subtitle *A Comedy and a Philosophy,* dramatizes the view of Creative Evolution reached by Shaw and Bergson after neo-Darwinism had been purged out of it by Butler. A brief study of this book shows that the comedy actually comprises only acts one, two and four; and is played as such. Act three, *Don Juan in Hell,* is a sort of philosophical interlude which is not at all necessary to the full comprehension of the society comedy, although it throws a flood of light upon Shaw's neo-Vitalist diathesis. The essence of his philosophy as embodied in this third act, together with "The Revolutionist's Handbook," a collection of aphorisms, is the most profound and impressive of any of his dramatic writings of the same compass. It is literature, philosophy and religion. Indeed, it is the first chapter in that book of modern religion which Shaw elaborated and completed in *Back to Methuselah.*

The book is dedicated to his friend and former colleague on the *Star,* then drama critic of the *Times,* the classical student and French scholar, Arthur Bingham Walkley. He was quite incapable of understanding Shaw in his higher philosophical flights and was constantly taking him to task, in a vein of witty, amusing banter, for his explanatory habit, his predilection for dialectic, and his disregard of the "rules of the game." Yet he always delighted in Shaw's plays and dealt with them at length, apparently never taking them seriously as drama but always recognizing Shaw as a "man who can give us a refined intellectual pleasure, or a pleasure of moral nature or of social sympathy, or else a pleasure which arises from being given an unexpected or wider outlook upon life." (p. 578)

Man and Superman is Shaw's fulfillment of Walkley's mischievous request of the Irish Puritan to write a Don Juan play. Shaw had repeatedly railed against plays which dealt with sex, but were devoid of sexual interest—"senseless evasions" of the real sex problem. Walkley's challenge was a poser; for Shaw was the avowed foe of romance with a profound distaste for the "mephitic atmosphere" of love and sex. The theme of Don Juan as literature had served the purposes of Molière, Mozart and Byron; and Goethe, with Don Juan's spiritual cousin, Faust, was almost a century out of date. There remained only to present Don Juan in the philosophic sense, imbued with all the advanced ideas of the age, "concerned for the future of the race instead of for the freedom of his own instincts." From this point on, in his career, Shaw appears as a race-futurist, a philosopher definitely engaged, in a manner cognate with that of his fellow Fabian and meliorist, H. G. Wells, with social and economic previsions and anticipations of a better race and a higher life. In *Man and Superman* Shaw for the first time reveals himself in prophetic, Messianic character.

At the time of the play's appearance, it was generally regarded as audaciously novel and original, for reversing the conventional idea expressed in the phrase: "Man is the hunter, woman the game." Yet it had often been employed as an effective theme in drama and fiction, from Shakespeare and Beaumont and Fletcher to Henry James and Anne Douglas Sedgwick. In the novels *Love Among the Artists* and *An Unsocial Socialist,* in the plays *Widowers' Houses* and *The Philanderer,* Shaw had already made effective use of the idea. "At no time," says Leonard Charteris [in *The Philanderer*], "have I taken the initiative and pursued women with my advances as women have persecuted me." In *Man and Superman,* Shaw denominates the driving power behind or of the universe—God, evolution, Vital Urge—the Life Force (after Bergson's *élan vital*). In woman he discerns the life force incarnate, the prime vital agency in the fulfillment of Nature's purposes and laws. He finds a superb motive for comedy in the doctrine that "woman is the pursuer and contriver, man the pursued and disposed of."

The society comedy was a mad success in the theater, with almost unbroken outbursts of merriment from the audience throughout. The epigrams and aphorisms, sallies and jests, hurtle at you like a continuous flight of arrows. Ann Whitefield, viewed by Shaw as Everywoman, makes of the comedy a modern "morality." Shaw has delineated her in strokes so bold as almost to seem crude. Ann is undoubtedly "an unscrupulous user of her personal fascination to make men give her what she wants"; but her methods are more virile than feline. The pursuit is not conducted with those obscure allurements and refined subtleties peculiar to woman; it is chiefly manifested through the comical loquacity of the pursued and fleeing man. Inability to portray sexual passion convincingly is a limitation of Shaw's art: he is no flesh painter. Yet we must not forget that, in an allegory, universal attributes require broad and sweeping treatment. Shaw himself attributes the play's popularity to its complete preoccupation with sex, and describes it as "the only play on the subject of sex ever written." (pp. 579-80)

The Dream in Hell—Act III—was largely ignored by the general public because it was almost always omitted in the stage production. The impact of Shaw's philosophy on the public was so slight as to be negligible; and there was no general understanding of his religion, which is briefly but clearly sketched in the Dream in Hell, until the appearance of *Back to Methuselah* eighteen years later.

In search for a religion, free from the Oriental legends and superstitions which inform the Christian religion, Shaw hit upon the idea which has influenced and possessed many modern thinkers: an imperfect God. He was driven to this belief by the effort to explain the problem of sin and suffering, unexplainable under Christianity. He is a confirmed mystic, rejecting entirely the notion of a personal God, but discerning a great force driving the universe. This Life Force drives steadily but experimentally towards the achievement of greater and greater power over circumstances and completer and completer intelligence; and to this end it creates organs of power and intelligence of which Man is only the last and most highly evolved in the long series of experiments which began with the amoeba and has progressed as far as Einstein. The last, be it noted, *as far:* Shaw has repeatedly warned us that we shall be scrapped for some new attempt if we persist in our present inadequacy. Thus the Life Force is God in the act of creating Himself; and we, as His instruments and helpers, can take heart and courage from this great opportunity and responsibility. It is humiliating, of course, to look in the glass, remember what you did last week, and realize that God has been able to produce nothing better! The thrust of the Life Force is onward and upward, striving ever to create higher and better forms. The crux of Shaw's philosophy is expressed in these words of Don Juan: "I tell you that as long as I can conceive something better than myself I cannot be easy unless I am striving to bring it into existence or clearing the way for it. This is the law of my life. That is the working within me of Life's incessant aspiration to higher organization, wider, deeper, intenser self-consciousness, and clearer self-understanding." Evolution, or the Life Force, may very well not stop at Man: it may go on to the Superman, the Super-Superman, the Angel, the Archangel, and finally omnipotent God. (pp. 580-81)

Archibald Henderson, in his *George Bernard Shaw: Man of the Century,* Appleton-Century-Crofts, Inc., 1956, 969 p.

TREVOR WHITTOCK

(essay date 1978)

[In the following excerpt, Whittock interprets *Major Barbara* as a "divine comedy of creative evolution."]

Shakespeare and Shaw are still the great figures in English comic drama. With Shakespeare comedy was only one facet of the universal genius. With Shaw it was the quintessential achievement of a lively and provocative man: music critic, drama critic, Fabian socialist, debater and propagandist, philosopher, wit, self-proclaimed professor of natural scientific history, and dramatist. In his best comedies all his talents meet and compound, and for us still explode in scintillating entertainment. The best of Shaw's best includes *Major Barbara.* Not only is it a delightful play, it is a great one. (p. 1)

The arguments of the play are presented by means of two interrelated plots which form the basis of the play's action. The first plot, derived from conventional melodrama, is the search for an heir to Undershaft's armament industry. (With typical effrontery Shaw inverts the convention: the heir will turn out to be not a foundling who must prove the legitimacy of his birth but a legitimate child who must prove he was really a foundling.) The second plot turns on Barbara's challenge that she may convert Undershaft to the Salvation Army, and his counter-challenge to her. . . . What connects the two plots is that Cusins too must be 'converted' before he will accept his true inheritance, and Barbara does not declare herself until he has chosen.

Shaw portrays Barbara as a truly religious person. Rejecting the meaninglessness of her secure and pampered existence at Wilton Crescent, Barbara seeks to serve a cause greater than herself, and thinks she has found it in the Salvation Army where she can bring spiritual enlightenment and practical help to the needy poor. Cusins, on the other hand, is a humanist—intellectual and sceptical—though as a scholar he is extremely well-read in the history of religions. His profession, Professor of Greek, allies him to the great, rational civilisations of Greece and Rome. He combines the best learning of the past with contemporary aspirations for justice and equality. (The character is acknowledgedly based on that of Gilbert Murray.) Behind Cusins' mild demeanour lies a strong and determined man; his pursuit of Barbara is one indication of this. To ensure that Barbara and Cusins are fitting opponents for the struggle with Undershaft, Shaw is careful in the first and second acts to show their strength:

Barbara's vitality and fervour, Cusins' determination and intelligence. (pp. 6-7)

Undershaft breaks Barbara's faith when he demonstrates that the Salvation Army can, like any other organisation of that nature, be bought. By his cheque to the Army he proves that the pipers who call the tune are Undershaft and Bodger. The full implications of this emerge gradually. One implication is that Barbara's faith rested on shaky foundations because it assumed that spiritual welfare could be separated from the material circumstances of life. Man does not live by bread alone: but without bread he may not live at all. No faith can be sustained which ignores the basic conditions of existence. Furthermore, however the Salvation Army may wish to alleviate the misery of the poor, it is incapable of abolishing the circumstances that create poverty and hardship. Should it attempt to change these circumstances it would be squashed by people whose wealth depends on their existence, and indeed it is only tolerated by the power-holders because it conditions the poor to accept their lot and thus prevents them rising in revolt for a better deal. Nor can people who are starving and scraping be brought to spiritual enlightenment: they can only be bribed by charity to pay lip-service to religious doctrines. . . . True religion is only possible when people have the energy and the freedom from want to pursue it. Undershaft argues that material prosperity must be given priority, and only when people are paid and productive, and can afford homes and food and clothing, only then can the works of the spirit really begin. The lives his employees lead at his factory prove his point: they have security and dignity, and they worship at a multitude of churches. (pp. 7-9)

Undershaft's strength of feeling about the evils of poverty springs from his own sufferings and hardships as a youth. It was in that period he became resolved to be a full-fed free man at all costs, even if he had to kill to do it. Here Shaw provides another contrast: that between Peter Shirley and Andrew Undershaft. Peter is a humble and honest man; though he is not a professing Christian he does live the life of a Christian. And where does it get him? He is sacked and forgotten. In the harsh capitalist world of competition and exploitation the Christian virtues are not only irrelevant: they are actually a handicap. The price of survival is to scrap them. Undershaft chooses to be the exploiter rather than the exploited, and flourishes.

Undershaft's creed is a capitalist one, but Undershaft speaks as a capitalist who knows what his wealth has delivered him from (and delivered his family from); he knows the benefits he can obtain for himself and his employees, the benefits of material security. This knowledge gives authority to his arguments. Now the question arises, how far is Shaw the socialist endorsing the argument of Undershaft the capitalist? To answer this we must consider another question and a much more important one. Why does Shaw make Undershaft a manufacturer of cannons, a merchant of death and destruction? The answers to this question will take us to the very heart of the play.

If Shaw had wished he could have given Undershaft some more socially approved occupation: he could have made him a capitalist of a more benevolent kind—a ship builder, a clothing magnate, or even an oil baron. But by making him an armaments manufacturer, Shaw is able to emphasize an aspect of capitalism that might otherwise be played down, namely, its ruthlessness. Undershaft, Lazarus and their employees are secure and comfortable because the goods they make murder and maim countless other people. This serves as a metaphor to describe all capitalism. Though capitalism may abolish pockets of poverty and exploitation, it will not abolish poverty and exploitation themselves: indeed its own success depends on their existence. Thus Shaw the socialist is only endorsing the gospel of Undershaft to a qualified extent. Something more adequate must be sought. This brings us to the choices that face Barbara and Cusins.

Their dilemma is greater than the one Undershaft faced as a young man; for him it was starvation or a full belly; for them the course they adopt must satisfy the demands of their consciences which tell them they must serve the spiritual and material welfare, not only of themselves or a select group, but of all men. Without this hope they cannot be reconciled to accepting the inheritance awaiting them. Earlier I said Undershaft had to convert them, but what he does is not strictly speaking a 'conversion' at all. They don't accept the capitalist aspect of his creed; rather they take from him the challenge and the pointer to how mankind may move beyond capitalism. Undershaft rallies Barbara with the challenge: 'Try your hand on my men: their souls are hungry because their bellies are full'; and Cusins he recruits with, 'Dare you make war on war?' They accept their inheritance: Barbara so that she may do God's work for its own sake when material prosperity has rendered bribes unnecessary; Cusins so that he can use the armaments works to give weapons to the poor that they may through force and revolution create a society where the necessities of life will be guaranteed to all. Undershaft's ruthless capitalism, which has demonstrated the importance of material security, points the way to socialist revolution and spiritual evolution.

At several points in the play itself Undershaft is associated with the ancient Greek god, Dionysus. Cusins calls him Dionysus several times, and also quotes lines from the Greek dramatist Euripides whose play, *The Bacchae,* was about the Dionysian religion. (pp. 9–10)

Shaw not only makes reference to Euripides' great tragedy: his own play actually echoes it. Undershaft/Dionysus comes to the Salvation Army, possesses the women (Mrs. Baines, Jenny Hill and their like)

by means of his 'charity' and leads them triumphantly in religious procession (Undershaft blowing a trombone), having torn Barbara/Pentheus to pieces—figuratively only, of course—by rending apart her religious assumptions. Through this analogy between Undershaft and Dionysus, and the parallels in the action of the two plays, Shaw emphasises how, when a form of belief arises, its assault on the old assumptions will seem savage and cruel. In the arrival of the new will be apprehended fear, cruelty, madness, destruction, as well as exhilaration, joy and release. But the spirit of life is remorseless, and bears down any opposition. 'Blood and fire' is as appropriate a motto for the Dionysian force as it is for the maker of cannons.

Cusins, the Euripidean scholar, naturally spots the analogy and, expressing it, he gives vent to his own alarm before the challenging figure of Undershaft. Cusins again, and Shaw through him, makes further use of literary mythology when he associates Undershaft with another legendary figure, that of the Prince of Darkness. Certainly the reference to Mephistophilis conjures up the story of the scholar Faust who was tempted to sell his soul to the devil, and reveals how the scholar Cusins initially responds to Undershaft's challenge to forget the pursuit of a dead language and seize the power of life and death. But the Mephistophelean portrait Shaw sketches of Undershaft owes less to the dramatists Marlowe and Goethe than it does to the poet William Blake. For Blake, particularly in *The Marriage of Heaven and Hell,* presented a new way of conceiving the devil which enormously fascinated and influenced Shaw. Briefly and oversimply, Blake envisaged life as a progression created through the clash of contraries, in particular the contraries of Reason and Energy. His Satanic figure is not a force of evil, but rather of rebellious energy denounced by the sour Jehovah of intellect and repression whom Blake sometimes called Urizen (Your reason). Blake's devil then is a force of life, of instinct, trying to break the bonds established by arid intellect and established morality. Like Blake's devil, Undershaft comes with the gifts of energy and liberation. His so-called immoral doctrines assault conventional pieties; his vitality breeds enthusiasm and commitment; even his trade testifies to his destroying in order to liberate. As Blake puts it in one of his proverbs of Hell, 'The tygers of wrath are wiser than the horses of instruction.' (Some of Undershaft's aphorisms are almost straight from Blake: for example. 'There is only one true morality for every man; but every man has not the same true morality,' is implied in Blake's, 'One Law for the Lion and Ox is Oppression.')

By bringing in these associations of godhead, Shaw gives a greater substance to the effect of Undershaft. But how does he present Undershaft's own picture of himself ? In Act I he makes Undershaft describe himself as a 'mystic': this remark is not explained until the following exchange in Act III:

> UNDERSHAFT. From the moment when you became Andrew Undershaft, you will never do as you please again. Don't come here lusting for power, young man.
>
> CUSINS. If power were my aim I should not come here for it. You have no power.
>
> UNDERSHAFT. None of my own, certainly.
>
> CUSINS. I have more power than you, more will. You do not drive this place: it drives you. And what drives the place?
>
> UNDERSHAFT. (*enigmatically*) A will of which I am a part.

The will of which Undershaft is merely a part is the will of Creative Evolution—life striving ever upward in its drive to greater comprehension. The vital spirits in each generation pass the task on to those who succeed them: so Undershaft's handing on of the inheritance is really a handing on of the creative destiny. The 'blood and fire' Barbara and Cusins choose to serve is the life and energy of godhead using its human creatures in the evolutionary surge. Hence the speeches of Barbara and Cusins, very near the end, are life-celebratory. In particular, Major Barbara who thought her soul had died in West Ham finds it resurrected in Perivale St. Andrews. She recovers her pride, and recovers her joy—the joy of submission to a Purpose, to a Life Force. (pp. 11-13)

Here is the real affirmation of the play. Now too is it possible to see how the comedy is at one with the meaning, the structure of the play with the argument. Shaw once defined comedy as 'nothing less than the destruction of old-fashioned morals.' The play begins with people set in their complacent beliefs and established illusions, as Lady Britomart is described in the first stage direction ('limited in the oddest way with domestic and class limitations, conceiving the universe exactly as if it were a large house in Wilton Crescent . . . '). Till life comes along in the shape of Dionysus Mephistophilis Undershaft to kick that little world to pieces about them. But despite the pain of loss they must welcome the actions of life because it pushes mankind forward. Life shatters and destroys, only to rebuild and re-create; at first the destructive element terrifies, later with liberation the energy and power are celebrated. Hence the anser to the question posed earlier, why did Shaw make Undershaft a manufacturer of explosives? As the agent of the Life Force he comes to demolish so that reconstruction can begin. . . . The newer and better religion, morality, political constitution, whatever, must fit the facts: that is, accept the conditions life lays down. The political level of the play—the arguments that Christian morality and liberal humanism are no longer adequate to cope with the world of the twentieth century, that the achievements of technology and capitalism must give way to social equality—these arguments are only an illustration of the more fundamental issue: that men must move forward with the movement of life itself, serving with their creative energy that ultimate Creative Energy which makes what will be. Shaw's play does more than preach this doctrine: it enacts it. In the very structure and unfolding of the play the audience is made to *experience* that movement of life within and through the mode of comedy: the dismay, the disillusion, the challenge, the doubt, the celebration. Just as Shakespeare's comedies move to a glimpse and promise of the divine harmony, so *Major Barbara* may be described as a divine comedy of creative evolution. (pp. 13-14)

Trevor Whittock, " 'Major Barbara': Comic Masterpiece," in *Theoria*, Pietermaritzburg, Vol. LI, October, 1978, pp. 1-14.

COLIN WILSON
(essay date 1979)

[A major Shaw scholar, Wilson offers the following discussion of Shaw as a life-affirming promoter of "sanity and optimism."]

[Although] I had read every Shaw play by the time I was seventeen and most of the novels and prefaces, I never became a 'complete Shavian'. I felt that after *Man and Superman*, Shaw had made no real effort to analyse the central problem of *what human beings are supposed to do with their lives*. Don Juan could speak about the need to 'help life in its struggle upward', about 'Life's incessant aspiration to higher organisation, wider, deeper intenser self-consciousness and clearer self-understanding' but how does the individual actually go about it? Shaw's political solutions always aroused my deepest scepticism. Shaw once remarked that Jesus's miracles were irrelevant because it would be absurd to say: 'You should love your enemies; and to convince you of this, I will now proceed to cure this gentleman of a cataract.' It seemed to me equally irrelevant when Shaw said: 'Life aims at deeper self awareness, therefore we must abolish capitalism.' Then, as now, Shaw's socialist dogmas struck me as largely fallacious. Similarly, the intellectual content of most of the major plays seemed to me oddly disappointing. I wanted him to talk about ultimate problems of philosophy, and he insisted on talking about politics and education and marriage and the iniquities of the medical profession (another matter on which I felt he was mildly cranky). The result was that in my first book on Shaw (*The Quintessence of Shavianism*, written at sixteen) I remained more than a little critical, and ended by implying that I would one day do better.

But then, the moment I actually opened a volume of Shaw, this hypercritical attitude vanished; I found it impossible not to keep on reading with a kind of excited approval, like a spectator at a boxing match who has to shout his enthusiasm. . . . Within a few lines, I was chuckling, then shouting with laughter—not so much because I found it funny as because it was so exhilirating. It made no difference whether I opened the *Collected Plays* at *Widowers' Houses* or *Farfetched Fables;* the effect was always the same: a sense of revitalization, of excitement, like setting out on a holiday.

Oddly enough, it never struck me to try and analyse the source of this effect until I was asked to write the present essay. And then I found it fairly easy to track down. It is the fact that, embedded in its very syntax, Shaw's prose has an irresistibly *optimistic* forward movement.

Then there was my Uncle William, a most amiable man, with great natural dignity. In early manhood he was not only an inveterate smoker, but so insistent a toper that a man who made a bet that he would produce Barney Shaw sober, and knocked him up at six in the morning with that object, lost his bet. But this might have happened to any common drunkard. What gave the peculiar Shaw finish and humour to the case was that my uncle suddenly and instantly gave up smoking and drinking at one blow, and devoted himself to the accomplishment of playing the ophicleide. . . .

As I now read these words, I find myself beginning to smile halfway through the first sentence: 'a most amiable man, with great natural dignity'—for I know this is going to be the prelude to some anticlimactic absurdity. And then there is an element in the prose which in a comedian like Groucho Marx would be called perfect timing. If Shaw had written: 'my uncle suddenly gave up smoking and drinking, and devoted himself . . . ' etc., it would not be funny; to say: "suddenly and instantly gave up smoking and drinking at one blow' produces a kind of shock effect, like a clown walking into a custard pie.

All Shaw's prose produces an effect of determined clarity, and it is this clarity that causes our ears to prick up: he is obviously saying something important or he wouldn't be making such an effort. And the air of optimism is a consequence of the directness. Inability to express ourselves makes us feel depressed and defeated—a gloomy conviction that the world is too complicated for our limited powers of assimilation. Kafka's effects of nightmare are produced by piling up dreamlike ambiguities and complications until the mind is hypnotized into a sense of helplessness. Shaw's clarity produces exactly the opposite effect, for it is obviously inspired by a conviction that any problem will yield to

a combination of reason, courage and determination. 'The brain will not fail when the will is in earnest.' No matter what Shaw happens to be saying—whether he is talking about human evolution or municipal trading—it is this underlying tone of sanity and optimism that produces the exhilarating effect. (pp. 226-27)

And what about Shaw as a thinker? Shaw liked to regard himself as an artist-philosopher. Most of us will concede that he was an artist, but we have our doubts about the philosopher. Again that could be due to our lack of perspective. We think of a list of typical philosophers—Plato, Spinoza, Locke, Hegel, Whitehead—ask if Shaw belongs on it, and decide he doesn't fit. But philosophers cannot be judged simply as abstract thinkers; what is equally important is their place in the history of ideas. And here Shaw undoubtedly qualifies. He was born in the middle of the Romantic era, the century of pessimism. . . . When Shaw came on the literary scene, in the early 1880s, the romantics had decided that mankind can be split into two groups: the stupid go-getters and the sensitive world-rejectors. You were either a shallow-minded optimist or an intelligent pessimist. (Thomas Mann made this antimony the basis of all his work.)

Shaw's revolt was instinctive. If he was a romantic, it was not of the self-pitying variety that regards the universe as cruel and meaningless because it refuses to treat them as exceptions. And it was Shaw's intuitive intelligence that made him aware that no healthy civilization can embrace a philosophy of pessimism. In *Man and Superman* he points out that man is the only animal who can be nerved to bravery by putting an *idea* into his head: that is to say, that man's inner strength depends on his beliefs; in *Back to Methuselah* he shows the other side of the coin when Pygmalion's two human creations lie down and die when they feel discouraged. It follows that a civilization that believes that Darwin and Freud are right about human nature is going to deflate like a tyre with a slow puncture. Shaw was not capable of analysing the history of philosophy since Descartes, the history of science since Newton, the history of religion since Luther, the history of romanticism since Rousseau and writing his own *Decline of the West*, yet he recognized that all have converged into the conviction that made Sartre write: 'Man is a useless passion.' He knew only one thing: *that somehow, sooner or later, the trend will have to be reversed.* His own age was not ready for that insight, and a younger generation of writers—Proust, Eliot, Joyce *et al*—continued the tradition of romantic pessimism as if Shaw had never existed. Most of them took the opportunity to denounce Shaw for failing to recognize the seriousness of the situation. Yet as this century of confusion and anxiety enters its last decades, it becomes clear that Shaw's instinct was correct. Somehow, whether we like it or not, we have to start believing in the future, and in man's power to transform it. At the end of *Too True to be Good,* the rascally clergyman declares: 'We have outgrown our religion, outgrown our political system, outgrown our own strength of mind and character. . . . But what next? Is NO enough? For a boy, yes: for a man, never. Are we any the less obsessed with a belief when we are denying it than when we are affirming it? No, I must have affirmations to preach. . . .'

The affirmations are still in the painful process of being born. When it finally happens, we shall recognize that Shaw did more than any other man to bring them into being. (pp. 228-29)

Colin Wilson, "A Personal View," in *The Genius of Shaw: A Symposium,* edited by Michael Holroyd, Holt, Rinehart and Winston, 1979, pp. 223-29.

SOURCES FOR FURTHER STUDY

Bentley, Eric. *Bernard Shaw.* New York: New Directions Publishing Corp., 1947, 242 p.

> A seminal analysis of Shaw's dramas which was highly regarded by Shaw himself.

Ervine, St. John. *Bernard Shaw.* New York: William Morrow and Co., 1956, 628 p.

> Biography of Shaw written by his intimate friend. Ervine's work contains many excerpts from Shaw's early diaries.

Evans, T. F., ed. *Shaw: The Critical Heritage.* London: Routledge & K. Paul, 1976, 422 p.

> Collects major criticism of Shaw's works. Includes index.

Henderson, Archibald. *George Bernard Shaw: Man of the Century.* New York: Appleton-Century-Crofts, 1956, 969 p.

> Authorized biography of Shaw, prepared over a period of fifty years with the playwright's full cooperation. Henderson's work contains memoirs written by Shaw expressly for the biography, and reprints many letters.

Nethercot, Arthur H. *Men and Superman: The Shavian Portrait Gallery.* Rev. ed. New York: Benjamin Blom, 1954, 327 p.

> Examines various of Shaw's dramatic character types with an eye to disproving the commonly accepted view, satirized by Shaw himself in *Fanny's First Play,* that "all Shaw's characters are himself: mere puppets stuck up to spout Shaw."

Whitman, Robert F. *Shaw and the Play of Ideas.* Ithaca, N.Y.: Cornell University Press, 1977, 293 p.

> Examination of the chief philosophic ideas espoused in Shaw's works.

Mary Wollstonecraft Godwin Shelley

1797-1851

English novelist, editor, critic, short story and travel writer.

INTRODUCTION

Shelley is best known for her novel *Frankenstein; or, The Modern Prometheus* (1818), which has transcended the Gothic and horror genres and is now recognized as a work of philosophical and psychological resonance. Critics agree that with the depiction of a seemingly godless universe where science and technology have gone awry, Shelley created a powerful metaphor for the modern age; indeed, the *Frankenstein* myth, which has been adapted to stage, film, and television, has pervaded modern culture. Shelley's achievement is considered remarkable, moreover, because she completed the book before her twentieth birthday. In addition to *Frankenstein,* Shelley's literary works include several novels that were mildly successful in their time but are little known today and an edition of poetry by her husband, the Romantic poet Percy Bysshe Shelley, which she issued with notes that are now regarded as indispensable. Her reputation rests, however, on what she once called her "hideous progeny," *Frankenstein.*

Shelley's personal life has sometimes overshadowed her literary work. She was the daughter of Mary Wollstonecraft, the early feminist and author of *A Vindication of the Rights of Woman*, and William Godwin, the political philosopher and novelist. Her parents' wedding, which occurred when Wollstonecraft was five months pregnant with Mary, was the marriage of two of the day's most noted freethinkers. While they both objected to the institution of matrimony, they agreed to marry to ensure their child's legitimacy. Ten days after Mary's birth, Wollstonecraft died from complications, leaving Godwin, an undemonstrative and self-absorbed intellectual, to care for both Mary and Fanny Imlay, Wollstonecraft's daughter from an earlier liaison. Mary's home life improved little with the arrival four years later of a stepmother and her two children. The new Mrs. Godwin, whom contemporaries described as petty and disagreeable, favored her own offspring over the daughters of the celebrated Wollstonecraft, and Mary was often solitary and unhappy. She was not formally educated, but absorbed the intellectual atmosphere created by her father and such visitors as Samuel Taylor Coleridge. She read a wide variety of books, notably those of her mother, whom she idolized. Young Mary's favorite retreat was Wollstonecraft's grave in the St. Pancras churchyard, where she went to read and write and eventually to meet her lover, Percy Shelley.

An admirer of Godwin, Percy Shelley visited the author's home and briefly met Mary when she was fourteen, but their attraction did not take hold until a subsequent meeting two years later. Shelley, twenty-two, was married, and his wife was expecting their second child, but he and Mary, like Godwin and Wollstonecraft, believed that ties of the heart superseded legal ones. In July 1814, one month before her seventeenth birthday, Mary eloped with Percy to the Continent, where, apart from two interludes in England, they spent the next few years traveling in Switzerland, Germany, and Italy. These years were characterized by financial difficulty and personal tragedy. Percy's father, Sir Timothy Shelley, a wealthy baronet, cut off his son's substantial allowance after his elopement. In 1816, Mary's half-sister Fanny committed suicide; just weeks later, Percy's wife, Harriet, drowned herself. Mary and Percy were married in London, in part because they hoped to gain custody of his two children by Harriet, but custody was denied. Three of their own children died in infancy, and Mary fell into a deep depression that was barely dispelled by the birth in 1819 of Percy Florence, her only surviving child. The Shelleys' marriage suffered, too, in the wake of their children's deaths, and Percy formed romantic attachments to other women. Despite these trying circumstances, both Mary and Percy maintained a schedule of rigorous study—including classical and European literature, Greek, Latin, and Italian language, music and art—and ambitious writing; during this period Mary completed *Frankenstein* and another novel, *Valperga* (1823). The two also enjoyed a coterie of stimulating friends, notably Lord Byron and Leigh Hunt. The Shelleys were settled near Lenci, Italy, on the Gulf of Spezzia in 1822 when Percy drowned during a storm while sailing to meet Leigh and Marianne Hunt. After one mournful year in Italy, Mary returned permanently to England with her son.

Shelley's life after Percy's death was marked by melancholy and hardship as she struggled to support herself and her child. Sir Timothy Shelley offered her a meager stipend, but ordered that she keep the Shelley name out of print; thus, all her works were published anonymously. In addition to producing four novels in the years after Percy's death, Mary contributed a series of biographical and critical sketches to *Chamber's Cabinet Cyclopedia,* as well as occasional short stories, which she considered potboilers, to the literary annuals of the day. The Shelleys' financial situation improved when Sir Timothy increased Percy Florence's allowance with his coming of age in 1840, which enabled mother and son to travel in Italy and Germany; their journeys are recounted in *Rambles in Germany and Italy in 1840, 1842, and 1843* (1844). Too ill in her last few years to complete her most cherished project, a biography of her husband, Shelley died at fifty-four.

Although *Frankenstein* has consistently dominated critical discussions of Shelley's oeuvre, she also composed several other novels in addition to critical and biographical writings. Her five later novels attracted little notice, and critics generally agree that they share the faults of verbosity and awkward plotting. After *Frankenstein, The Last Man* (1826) is her best-known work. This novel, in which Shelley describes the destruction of the human race in the twenty-first century, is noted as an inventive depiction of the future and an early prototype of science fiction. *Valperga* and *The Fortunes of Perkin Warbeck* (1830) are historical novels that have received scant attention from literary critics, while *Lodore* (1835) and *Falkner* (1837), thought by many to be autobiographical, are often examined for clues to the lives of the Shelleys and their circle. Shelley's stories were collected and published posthumously, as was *Mathilda,* a novella that appeared for the first time in the 1950s. The story of a father and daughter's incestuous attraction, it has been viewed as a fictional treatment—or distortion—of Shelley's relationship with Godwin. The posthumously published verse dramas, *Proserpine* and *Midas* (1922), were written to complement one of Percy Shelley's works and have garnered mild praise for their poetry. Critics also admire Shelley's non-fiction: the readable, though now dated, travel volumes, the essays for *Chamber's Cabinet Cyclopedia,* which are considered vigorous and erudite, and her illuminating notes on her husband's poetry.

Since Shelley's death, critics have devoted nearly all of their attention to *Frankenstein.* Early critics, generally with some dismay, usually relegated the novel to the Gothic genre then practiced by such popular authors as Ann Radcliffe and Matthew Gregory "Monk" Lewis. While most early Victorian reviewers reviled what they considered the sensationalist and gruesome elements in *Frankenstein,* many praised the anonymous author's imagination and powers of description. In the later nineteenth century and throughout *Frankenstein* criticism, commentators have focused on Prometheanism in the novel, an aspect that Shelley herself highlighted in the book's subtitle. This line of inquiry, which continues to engage critics, likens Dr. Frankenstein to the Greek mythic figure who wreaks his own destruction through abuse of power. Percy Shelley treated the same mythic-philosophic theme in his poetry, most notably in *Prometheus Unbound,* and critics have searched for his influence on *Frankenstein,* particularly in the expression of Romantic ideals and attitudes. Scholars have also debated the value of the additional narratives that he encouraged her to write. While some have praised the novel's resulting three-part structure, others have argued that these additions detract from and merely pad the story, although most have valued the other-worldly Arctic scenes. Commentators have also frequently noted the influence of Shelley's father, tracing strains of Godwin's humanitarian social views; in addition, some critics have found direct thematic links to his fiction, particularly to his novel, *Caleb Williams.* Other literary allusions often noted in *Frankenstein* include those to John Milton's *Paradise Lost,* the source of the book's epigraph, as well as Johann Wolfgang von Goethe's *Faust* and Coleridge's "The Rime of the Ancient Mariner."

Frankenstein criticism has proliferated since the 1950s, encompassing a wide variety of themes and approaches. The monster, who is often the focus of commentary, has been interpreted as representing issues ranging from the alienation of modern humanity to the repression of women. Many commentators have viewed the monster as Dr. Frankenstein's double, an example of the doppelgänger archetype. In a similar vein, critics have discussed Dr. Frankenstein and the monster as embodying Sigmund Freud's theory of id and ego. Students of the Gothic, supernatural horror, and science fiction novel have adopted *Frankenstein* as a venerable forebear and have approached it from a historical slant. Alternately, Shelley's life has served as a starting point for those who perceive in the novel expressions of the author's feelings toward her parents, husband, children, and friends. Recent feminist critics, in particular, have found Shelley and *Frankenstein* a rich source for study, describing it, for example, as a manifestation of the author's ambivalent feelings toward motherhood.

Leigh Hunt once characterized Shelley as "four-famed—for her parents, her lord / And the poor lone impossible monster abhorr'd." Today, she has emerged from the shadow of her parents and husband as an artist in her own right. The volume and variety of *Frankenstein* criticism attests to the endurance of her vision.

(For further information about Shelley's life and works, see *Nineteenth-Century Literature Criticism,* Vol. 14 and *Something about the Author,* Vol. 29.)

CRITICAL COMMENTARY

M. A. GOLDBERG

(essay date 1959)

[Goldberg's investigation of the themes of isolation and knowledge in Frankenstein, excerpted below, is considered one of the first comprehensive assessments of the novel and a milestone in *Frankenstein* studies.]

In the central pages of Mary Shelley's *Frankenstein or, The Modern Prometheus* the reader encounters for some six chapters a personal narrative of the monster. For the first time since his creation, he is approaching his maker who sits sad and pensive near the awful majesty of Mont Blanc. Conscious of his "duties as a creator towards his creature," Frankenstein agrees to listen to the tale of this blighted being who has developed from a *tabula rasa,* experiencing in true Lockean fashion first confused, then distinct sensations, and developing in turn social affections, then moral and intellectual judgments. Crucial to his learning, we discover, has been a leather portmanteau, found one day in the forest where he has hidden himself from the eyes of mankind, and in which are contained, together with some articles of dress, a volume of Plutarch's *Lives,* [Goethe's] *Sorrows of Werter,* and Milton's *Paradise Lost.* The latter, he explains, has had a most profound effect upon him:

> I read it [*Paradise Lost*], as I had read the other volumes which had fallen into my hands, as a true history. . . . I often referred the several situations, as their similarity struck me, to my own. Like Adam, I was apparently united by no link to any other being in existence; but his state was far different from mine in every other respect. He had come forth from the hands of God a perfect creature, happy and prosperous, guarded by the especial care of his Creator; he was allowed to converse with, and acquire knowledge from, beings of a superior nature: but I was wretched, helpless, and alone. Many times I considered Satan as the fitter emblem of my condition; for often, like him, when I viewed the bliss of my protectors, the bitter gall of envy rose within me.

This is no idle image which the creature evokes here, comparing his own situation with Satan's, and with Adam's paradisaic state in Eden. The confusion

Principal Works

apparent in his own consciousness—whether he is an Adam, destined ultimately for eternal grace, or a Satan, doomed to eternal darkness—is a motif crucial to the entire novel. It is crucial to the monster's tale, embedded as the innermost circle of the text. It is crucial to Frankenstein's narrative, which, unfolded to Captain Walton, encircles the monster's tale like the middle ring of a vast inferno. And it is crucial to Walton's letters, which hover about the outermost fringes of these depths. Indeed, these three circles—their relationship to one another and to the Miltonic motif—form the basic structure of the novel, a structure from which Mrs. Shelley has spun a moral web, with consistency and with precision. (pp. 27-8)

To examine [*Frankenstein*] for the terror it evokes, without perceiving its relationship to the moral context of early nineteenth-century England, is, in reality, to distort the essence of the tale.

We encounter the first indications of this moral context in the letters of Captain Walton, who has been inspired since early youth to satiate an ardent curiosity about the unknown regions of the earth. . . .

One major failing seems to threaten Walton's relentless pursuit: the lack of compassionate society, "intimate sympathy with a fellow mind." Significantly, Walton regards this want as "a most severe evil" and

he readily acknowledges that "a man could boast of little happiness, who did not enjoy this blessing."

Once he encounters Victor Frankenstein amid the ice floes of the north, this conflict—between his thirst for knowledge which increasingly carries him away from society and a thirst for social love which is frustrated by this pursuit of knowledge—appears happily reconciled. His newly-found friend reminds him, however, "You seek for knowledge and wisdom, as I once did," and hopes that Walton's temptation "may not be a serpent to sting you, as mine has been." In order that Walton might "deduce an apt moral" from his own experience, Frankenstein consents to disclose the secret of his life.

Frankenstein's tale, forming the middle circle of the novel, is clearly intended, then, as an *exemplum*, aimed at weaning the captain from his obsession. Just as Walton's opening letters sound this didactic note, so do his closing epistles. "Learn my miseries, and do not seek to increase your own," Walton is cautioned at the close of Frankenstein's narrative, just as he has been previously warned: "Learn from me, if not from my precepts, at least by my example, how dangerous is the acquirement of knowledge." (p. 29)

An examination of Frankenstein's central narrative reveals that this opening motif, the temptation of knowledge and the punishment of estrangement, is echoed with consistency and clarity.

From the beginning Frankenstein is "deeply smitten with the thirst for knowledge." He too is tempted by the forbidden fruit, and his earliest sensations are "curiosity, earnest research to learn the hidden laws of nature." For him "the world was . . . a secret which I desired to divine," and even in his youth his "inquiries were directed to the metaphysical, or, in its highest sense, the physical secrets of the world." (p. 30)

Like Prometheus—whom Apollodorus describes as having first created man out of clay, then instilled into his bosom a sacred spark of fire, stolen from the heavens—Frankenstein, his nineteenth-century disciple, succeeds in infusing "a spark of being into the lifeless being" that lies before him in his laboratory. . . . What is glory for the omnipotent deity of *Genesis* or the Babylonian god Bel, for the Egyptian father-of-gods Khnoumou or the Australian creator Pund-jel, is for lesser gods, like Frankenstein, the "modern Prometheus," a crime. The apple of knowledge bears within it the acrid seeds of punishment. As with Satan and Beëlzebub, this passion to usurp divine prerogatives casts the new creator into a burning cauldron of his own making. (pp. 30-1)

Like Coleridge's guilt-ridden mariner, Frankenstein has a deadly weight hanging round his neck, bowing him to the ground. . . . His father had wished him "to seek amusement in society [but] I abhorred the face of man," Frankenstein admits. "I felt that I had no right to share their intercourse." Now, he reveals only the "desire to avoid society" and fly "to solitude, from the society of every creature." . . . He is "immersed in solitude," for he perceives "an insurmountable barrier" between him and his fellow-man. "I felt as if I had committed some great crime, the consciousness of which haunted me. I was guiltless, but I had indeed drawn down a horrible curse upon my head, as mortal as that of crime," . . . he confesses. Though his inner-being longs for the compassion and sympathy that society affords, his guilt has already driven him out of love's garden. He dares not even whisper "paradisaical dreams of love and joy" to Elizabeth, for, as he readily concedes, "the apple was already eaten, and the angel's arm bared to drive me from all hope." . . . (pp. 31-2)

[In] his final hours of life, he confesses to Robert Walton the sin he shares with Milton's archangel:

> All my speculations and hopes are as nothing; and, like the archangel who aspired to omnipotence, I am chained in an eternal hell. . . . I conceived the idea and executed the creation of a man. Even now I cannot recollect without passion my reveries while the work was incomplete. I trod heaven in my thoughts, now exulting in my powers, now burning with the idea of their effects. From my infancy I was imbued with high hopes and a lofty ambition; but how am I sunk! . . .
>
> (p. 32)

Although parallels between the temptations of Frankenstein or Walton and those of Adam or Satan are clearly delineated, it would be a grave distortion to force the analogy without noting pertinent differences. Milton's is a seventeenth-century reinterpretation of the Fall described by the Jehovistic writer of *Genesis;* but Milton's narrative also parallels to no small degree the Hellenic myth of Prometheus who having usurped the powers of the higher gods, is alienated forever from both men and gods, and chained to the frozen top of the Caucasus. This is an allusion of which Mrs. Shelley was certainly conscious, since she refers to Frankenstein as a "Modern Prometheus" in her sub-title. Also, Shelley himself was obviously aware of the structural similarity between Milton's narrative and the Greek myth, for in his preface to *Prometheus Unbound* he remarks that "the only imaginary being resembling in any degree Prometheus, is Satan." Parallels for Mrs. Shelley's handling of the guilt-theme, however, can also be found in Dostoyevsky and Kafka, or in Jung who suggests that "every step towards greater consciousness is a kind of Promethean guilt: through knowledge, the gods are as it were robbed of their fire, that is, something that was the property of the unconscious powers is torn out of its natural context and subordinated to the whims of the conscious mind."

But Frankenstein's guilt is not the psychological

and mystic soul-searching of Kafka or Dostoyevsky, just as it is never completely the crime of *hubris* manifested in Aeschylus or the failure to recognize derivation which we discern in Milton. Frankenstein's crime, like Walton's, is social. Both sin against society. In syncretizing the Miltonic and Promethean motif Mrs. Shelley has clearly translated her materials into early nineteenth-century terms, just as Keats revised the myth of Endymion, and as Shelley transformed the story of Prometheus within his own contemporary framework.

Walton and Frankenstein both sin, not against self or God, but against the moral and social order. Though both begin their pursuit with benevolent intentions, each discovers his error in assuming that knowledge is a higher good than love or sympathy, and that it can be independent of the fellow-feeling afforded by a compassionate society. As a result, what had appeared initially as a benevolent intention becomes in the final analysis misguided pride, a selfish pursuit aimed at self-glory, because it evades the fulfillment of higher duties toward the social community, the brotherhood of man which forms the highest good. Understandably, then, Mrs. Shelley's book is paralleled most significantly, not by Aeschylus or Milton, but by her own contemporaries. In Byron's *Manfred,* for example, an analogous "quest of hidden knowledge" leads the hero increasingly toward a "solitude . . . peopled with the Furies." Manfred's avowed flaw ("though I wore the form, / I had no sympathy with breathing flesh") rises from the same ethical assumptions implicit in the guilt-ridden consciousness of Victor Frankenstein. Similarly, Shelley's prefatory remarks on *Alastor or, The Spirit of Solitude* indicate that "the Poet's self-centred seclusion was avenged by the furies of an irresistible passion pursuing him to speedy ruin." Shelley's supposition, that "the intellectual faculties, the imagination, the functions of sense, have their respective requisitions on the sympathy of corresponding powers in other human beings," is obviously engendered from the same general principle which has ordered the materials of *Frankenstein.*

Mrs. Shelley offers in her novel—as does Byron in *Manfred* and Shelley in *Alastor*—a theme which is clearly in the tradition of Cudworth and Price, the seventeenth-century Platonists. This is a conception inherited in the eighteenth century by Shaftesbury and Hutcheson; later, by the Scottish Common-Sense School, as represented by Adam Smith; and finally by William Godwin, who had assumed as basic to his doctrine of political justice that virtue is essentially social. Insistent that reason and free will, as developed in an enlightened society, would naturally result in the subordination of individual pleasures for the good of society as a whole, Godwin set himself in opposition to La Rochefoucauld, Hobbes, and Mandeville, for whom man was basically selfish and non-social, and to Rousseau, who had seen society as a force destructive to natural benevolence. "No being can be either virtuous, or vicious, who has no opportunity of influencing the happiness of others," Godwin had contended in his *Enquiry concerning Political Justice,* insistent that "the true solitaire cannot be considered as a moral being. . . . His conduct is vicious, because it has a tendency to render him miserable." Explaining that "virtue consists in a desire of the happiness of the species. . . . It must begin with a collective idea of the human species," Godwin argues that true knowledge is also dependent upon the social structure. "Even knowledge, and the enlargement of intellect, are poor, when unmixed with sentiments of benevolence and sympathy," he points out; " . . . and science and abstraction will soon become cold, unless they derive new attractions from ideas of society."

Similarly, Thomas Paine develops the relationship between happiness and social virtues in *The Rights of Man.* Since nature created man for social life, Paine writes, "no one man is capable, without the aid of society, of supplying his own wants; and those wants, acting upon every individual, impel the whole of them into society, as naturally as gravitation acts to a centre." Nature has gone even further than this, Paine continues. "She has implanted in him a system of social affections, which, though not necessary to his existence, are essential to his happiness. There is no period in life when this love of society ceases to act. It begins and ends with our being." (pp. 32-4)

Through Mrs. Shelley's journal entries we know that during 1816-1817, when *Frankenstein* was conceived, she and Shelley discussed the work many times. We know, too, through the *Journal,* that in these years she and Shelley both read Milton's *Paradise Lost,* and that Shelley was immersed at this same time in Godwin's *Political Justice* and Paine's *The Rights of Man,* as well as in the *Prometheus Bound* of Aeschylus. I do not mean to imply that Mary Shelley borrowed her social and moral conceptions from Paine, or from Shelley or Godwin, then deliberately embodied them within her mythological framework. It is perfectly understandable that she shared the social thought of her father and her husband, and that she wove these ideas, which were shared also by many of the enlightened English public during those decades, into an esthetic pattern of her own making.

The consistency of her social and moral theme is certainly nowhere more apparent than in the narrative of the monster, whose experience forms an essential parallel with that of Frankenstein and Walton. Like the latter, whose original intentions were directed at benevolence and sympathy, the creature initially bears the seeds of virtue. The sympathies of Walton and Frankenstein have been rendered torpid by their mono-

maniacal pursuit of knowledge which removes them increasingly from a compassionate society; similarly, the creature discovers that his sympathies are perpetually blunted by the misery of loneliness and isolation, estranged as he must be from human kind. At first, he views "crime as a distant evil; benevolence and generosity were ever present" in the persons of the DeLaceys, behind whose cottage he has hidden. "My heart yearned to be known and loved by these amiable creatures: to see their sweet looks directed towards me with affection was the utmost limit of my ambition," he confesses. His readings only reinforce this natural propensity for social love, so that before long he feels "the greatest ardour for virtue . . . and abhorrence for vice." . . . (pp. 35-6)

Like his maker, and like Captain Walton, the creature soon comes to realize that "sorrow only increased with knowledge," . . . for the more he learns about the nature of good and its dependence upon social intercourse, the more he recognizes the impossibility of immersing himself in it. . . .

Alternating between the role of Adam and Satan, hoping he might still be lifted to the glories of love and sympathy, but fearing that he might be forced into the depths of malevolence and depravity because of his isolation, the creature soon finds his fate determined, once the DeLaceys reject his friendly advances, just as all mankind has rejected him beforehand. "From that moment I declared everlasting war against the species," he admits. "I, like the arch-fiend, bore a hell within me; and, finding myself unsympathized with, wished to . . . spread havoc and destruction." . . . Natural proclivities toward virtue compel the creature to approach his maker and urge him to create a mate "with whom I can live in the interchange of those sympathies necessary for my being. . . . I am malicious because I am miserable," he explains, as he begs for the happiness which is his right. "Let me feel gratitude towards you for one benefit! Let me see that I excite the sympathy of some existing thing; do not deny me my request." . . . With an understanding strikingly analogous to that revealed in Godwin, Shelley, Byron, and Paine, the monster describes his moral state:

> If I have no ties and no affections, hatred and vice must be my portion; the love of another will destroy the cause of my crimes, and I shall become a thing of whose existence every one will be ignorant. My vices are the children of a forced solitude that I abhor; and my virtues will necessarily arise when I live in communion with an equal. I shall feel the affections of a sensitive being, and become linked to the chain of existence and events, from which I am now excluded.
>
> (p. 36)

In an 1817 review which has generally been ignored [see excerpt above], Shelley draws some interesting parallels between Godwin's *Caleb Williams* and *Frankenstein,* and summarizes thematic development in Mary Shelley's book with penetrating incisiveness:

> . . . The crimes and malevolence of the single Being, though indeed withering and tremendous, [are not] the offspring of any unaccountable propensity to evil, but flow irresistibly from certain causes fully adequate to their production. They are the children, as it were, of Necessity and Human Nature. In this the direct moral of the book consists. . . . Treat a person ill, and he will become wicked. Require affection with scorn;—let one being be selected, for whatever cause, as the refuse of his kind—divide him, a social being, from society, and you impose upon him the irresistible obligations— malevolence and selfishness. It is thus that, too often in society, those who are best qualified to be its benefactors and its ornaments, are branded by some accident with scorn, and changed, by neglect and solitude of heart, into a scourge and a curse.

The distinction which Shelley draws here between an "unaccountable propensity to evil" and that necessitated by external social forces which isolate the individual, thus causing selfishness and malevolence, points indeed to the "direct moral of the book." Although a recent biographer [Elizabeth Nitchie], noting this theme of estrangement throughout Mrs. Shelley's novels, interprets this as the author's "symbol of her own loneliness," it is apparent in any close examination of the text that "loneliness" assumes its fullest meaning relative only to the social and moral context of early nineteenth-century England. This is the context of Godwin and Paine, as well as Byron and Shelley, and certainly the context of the woman who came to be known as "the author of *Frankenstein.*" (pp. 37-8)

M. A. Goldberg, "Moral and Myth in Mrs. Shelley's 'Frankenstein'," in *Keats-Shelley Journal,* Vol. 8, Winter, 1959, pp. 27-38.

ROBERT KIELY

(essay date 1972)

[In the following excerpt, Kiely examines two dominant themes in *Frankenstein:* "the monstrous consequences of egotism" and "the virtue of friendship."]

Superiority through suffering is a major theme of [*Frankenstein*], a romantic half-tragedy in which the fall from greatness is nearly all fall or, more accurately, where greatness is defined in terms of the personal pain which results from the consciousness of loss which cannot be recalled or comprehended by other men. In

unique regret, Frankenstein discovers his true distinction: "I was seized by remorse and the sense of guilt which hurried me away to a hell of intense tortures, such as no language can describe." The failure of language, as always in romantic fiction, is meant to be a sign not of vacuity or of an imaginative limitation of the character or author, but of the singular noncommunicable nature of great experience.

It is unfortunate (though psychologically fitting) that in the popular mind the monster has assumed the name of his creator, because Mary Shelley considered it of some importance that the creature remain unnamed. As Elizabeth Nitchie points out, it was the custom in dramatic performances of *Frankenstein* to represent the monster's part on the playbill with "†." On first remarking this, Mary Shelley was pleased: "This nameless mode of naming the unnameable is rather good." If the phenomenon itself cannot be named, neither can the feelings it evokes in its maker. No one can know what it is like to be the monster or its "parent." (pp. 158-59)

Mary Shelley spends a great part of her narrative confronting her hero with images which evoke the sublimity of his mental state where ordinary words fail. Frankenstein journeys to Chamonix, where the mountain views elevate him from all "littleness of feeling" and "subdue and tranquilize" his grief though they cannot remove it. Mont Blanc provides him with a moment of "something like joy," but the Alps, though briefly impressive, are not in the end any more able than words to express or alleviate what Frankenstein feels. Trips up the Rhine, across the sea, even into the Arctic, hint at his unrest, but "imperial Nature," in all her "awful majesty," can no more provide truly adequate images of his misery than she can provide the fulfillment of his ambitious dreams.

At the end of the narrative, Frankenstein accuses himself of over-reaching, but even in doing this, he immodestly compares himself with the prince of over-reachers: "Like the archangel who aspired to omnipotence, I am chained in an eternal hell." Rather than looking back on his ambition with disgust, he remembers it with pleasure: "Even now I cannot recollect without passion my reveries while the work was incomplete. I trod heaven in my thoughts, now exulting in my powers, now burning with the idea of their effects." Despite the conventional speeches about the dangers of pride, it becomes more and more evident in the last pages of the novel that Frankenstein, though regretting the *result* of his extraordinary efforts, is not ashamed of having made the effort in the first place. He repeatedly warns Walton, who is engaged in an expedition into the Polar Sea, to content himself with modest ambitions and a quiet life. . . . In his last breath, he begins to warn Walton once more not to make the same mistake he did, but then changes his mind:

Seek happiness in tranquility and avoid ambition, even if it be only the apparently innocent one of distinguishing yourself in science and discoveries. Yet why do I say this? I have myself been blasted in these hopes, but another may succeed.

That Frankenstein does not die absolutely repentant once again raises the possibility that the monstrous result of his experiment was not the inevitable issue of pride but an accident of circumstance, the result of insufficient knowledge, or an imperfection in nature itself. If one wishes to accept Walton's reverent appraisal of his new friend, it can be said that Frankenstein has the immunity of all scientific and artistic genius from conventional morality, that he is somehow apart from and superior to material circumstances even when he himself seems to have brought them about. (pp. 159-60)

Mary learned her lessons in idealism well, and there is in her narrative a level on which her hero is above reproach. But it must be admitted that there is a mundane side to this fantastic tale. If genius can escape or withdraw from the material universe, ordinary mortals cannot. And however great their admiration for genius may be, they cannot fully separate it from the lesser objects of their perception.

Mary Shelley was a young and impetuous woman when she ran off with the poet; she was also an intelligent woman, but her journals and letters reveal that despite her efforts to form herself after her husband's image, common sense often intruded and made the task difficult. She was never intellectually disloyal to Shelley, yet she admitted that her mind could not follow his to the heights. Her novel, like almost everything else about her life, is an instance of genius observed and admired but not shared. In making her hero the creator of a monster, she does not necessarily mock idealistic ambition, but in making that monster a poor grotesque patchwork, a physical mess of seams and wrinkles, she introduces a consideration of the material universe which challenges and undermines the purity of idealism. In short, the sheer concreteness of the ugly thing which Frankenstein has created often makes his ambitions and his character—however sympathetically described—seem ridiculous and even insane. The arguments on behalf of idealism and unworldly genius are seriously presented, but the controlling perspective is that of an earthbound woman. (pp. 160-61)

Frankenstein digging about in graveyards and charnel houses, matching eyeballs and sawing bones, is not an inspiring sight. Even less so is the bungled construct of muscles, arteries, and shriveled skin which he had intended as a perfectly proportioned and beautiful being. The gap between the ideal and the real, the ambition and the accomplishment, produces a result as gruesome and absurd as any pseudo-science of the Middle Ages. Still, Mary is not criticizing exalted ambi-

tion, but the misapplication of it, the consequences of what Frankenstein himself describes as "unrelaxed and breathless eagerness," a "frantic impulse," a trance-like pursuit of one idea. Through the mouth of her hero, she raises a question which in life she could probably never bring herself to ask her husband: "Is genius forever separate from the reasonable, the reflective, and the probable?" (p. 162)

In describing the way in which Frankenstein's experiment seems most "unnatural," Mary Shelley implies a definition of the natural which is peculiarly feminine in bias. For her, Frankenstein's presumption is not in his attempt to usurp the power of the gods—she quite willingly grants him his "divine" attributes—but in his attempt to usurp the power of women. "A new species would bless me as its creator and source," says Frankenstein in the enthusiasm of his first experiments. "No father could claim the gratitude of his child so completely as I should deserve theirs." He seeks to combine the role of both parents in one, to eliminate the need for woman in the creative act, to make sex unnecessary. At least that would be the net result of his experiment if it were successful, despite the fact that he himself tends to see its consequences in grander and vaguer terms. Thus, while Mary grants her hero the nobility and even the innocence of his intentions, she cannot help but undercut them with her own womanly sense of how things are.

Stripped of rhetoric and ideological decoration, the situation presented is that of a handsome young scientist, engaged to a beautiful woman, who goes off to the mountains alone to create a new human life. When he confesses to Walton that he has "worked hard for nearly two years" to achieve his aim, we may wonder why he does not marry Elizabeth and, with her cooperation, finish the job more quickly and pleasurably. But one must be careful not to imply that Mary's irony is flippant or altogether conscious. Quite to the contrary, her reservations about her hero's presumptuous idealism are so deeply and seriously felt that they produce a symbolic nightmare far more disturbing and gruesome than the monster itself. As soon as the creature begins to show animation and Frankenstein realizes that he has made an abomination, the scientist races to his bedroom, paces feverishly about, and finally falls into a troubled sleep:

I slept indeed, but I was disturbed by the wildest dreams. I thought I saw Elizabeth, in the bloom of health, walking in the streets of Ingolstadt. Delighted and surprised, I embraced her; but as I imprinted the first kiss on her lips, they became livid with the hue of death; her features appeared to change, and I thought that I beheld the corpse of my dead mother in my arms; a shroud enveloped her form, and I saw the graveworms crawling in the folds of the flannel. I started from my sleep with horror . . . (and) beheld the wretch—the miserable monster whom I had created.

In this extraordinary rendition of an Oedipal nightmare, Mary shows, without moral comment, the regressive depths of her hero's mind. Frankenstein's crime against nature is a crime against womanhood, an attempt—however unconscious—to circumvent mature sex. For Mary, this is the supreme symbol of egotism, the ultimate turning away from human society and into the self which must result in desolation. Having moved away from family, friends, and fiancée to perform his "creative" act in isolation, Frankenstein later beholds the monster, in a grotesquely exaggerated re-enactment of his own behavior, "eliminate" his younger brother, his dearest friend, and his beloved Elizabeth.

All the crimes are sins against life in the bloom of youth and beauty, but the murder of the woman is the most effectively presented and, in a way, the most carefully prepared. Frankenstein's fears on his wedding night are presumably due to the monster's threat to pursue him even to his marriage chamber. But the immediate situation and the ambiguity of the language contribute to the impression that the young groom's dread of the monster is mixed with his fear of sexual union as a physical struggle which poses a threat to his independence, integrity, and delicacy of character. Frankenstein describes the event in the following manner:

> I had been calm during the day: but so soon as night obscured the shapes of objects, a thousand fears arose in my mind. I was anxious and watchful, while my right hand grasped a pistol which was hidden in my bosom; every sound terrified me; but I resolved that I would sell my life dearly, and not shrink from the conflict, until my own life, or that of my adversary, was extinguished.
> Elizabeth observed my agitation for some time in timid and fearful silence; but there was something in my glance which communicated terror to her, and trembling she asked, 'What is it that agitates you, my dear Victor? What is it you fear?'
> 'Oh! peace, peace, my love,' replied I; 'this night and all will be safe; but this night is dreadful, very dreadful.'
> . . . I reflected how fearful the combat which I momentarily expected would be to my wife, and I earnestly entreated her to retire, resolving not to join her until I had obtained some knowledge as to the situation of my enemy.

Frankenstein leaves the room, and it is while he is away that his bride is murdered by the monster on her untried marriage bed. The passage is filled with the language of anxiety, phallic inference, and imagery of conflict, yet it is in Frankenstein's absence—not in an eager assertion of his physical presence—that harm comes to Elizabeth. If we take the monster to be one side of Frankenstein's nature, an alter-ego, then we see his physically potent self as brutish, ugly, and destructive, completely unintegrated with his gentle spirit. To depict a radical separation of mind from sexuality is one way to explore an unsatisfactory rapport between the imagination and the natural world. But what is important in the thematic terms of the novel is not the mere existence of the separation, but the fact that physical life is made ugly (indeed, is made to wither and die prematurely) because it is inadequately tended by the mind. The problem is not abuse but neglect.

The importance of the wedding night scene lies in its sexual connotation insofar as that provides the basic and concrete context in which, once again, to exemplify the hero's withdrawal from physical and emotional contact with living human beings. There are earlier instances of his separating himself from his family and from his friend Clerval, even while protesting, as he has with Elizabeth, that he continues to love them in spirit. The outrage dramatized in this novel is not restricted to a specifically sexual offense—nor is it directed against genius or ambition or idealism. The enemy is an egotism which, when carried to the extreme, annihilates all life around it and finally destroys itself.

While the main theme of the novel is the monstrous consequences of egotism, the counter-theme is the virtue of friendship. For, as Frankenstein's crime is seen as a sin against humankind more than against the heavens, it is through human sympathy, rather than divine grace, that it might have been avoided or redeemed. In her treatment of friendship, Mary shows the Coleridgean side of herself. She sees a friend as a balancing and completing agent, one who is sufficiently alike to be able to sympathize and understand, yet sufficiently different to be able to correct, and refine. Above all, the friend, in giving ear to one's dreams and sufferings, provides not only a temporary release from them, but the immediate excuse to order them by putting them into words.

The entire narrative of *Frankenstein* is in the form of three confessions to individuals with whom the speaker has unusually close ties. First, the young explorer Robert Walton writes to his sister in England as he journeys into the Arctic. There he rescues Frankenstein from a shipwreck and listens to his tale, which, in turn, contains a long narrative spoken by the monster to its creator. (pp. 164-67)

Each narrator speaks of the importance of friendship—Walton and the monster because they feel the lack of it, Frankenstein because he has had friends and lost them. In Walton's second letter to his sister, he reports that he has hired a ship and is ready to set sail on his dangerous journey. The one thing that troubles him is that, though he has a well-trained crew, he has no soul companion:

I have one want which I have never yet been able to satisfy . . . I have no friend . . . When I am glowing with the enthusiasm of success, there will be none to participate in my joy; if I am assailed by disappointment, no one will endeavour to sustain me in dejection . . . I desire the company of a man who could sympathize with me; whose eyes would reply to mine. You may deem me romantic, my dear sister, but I bitterly feel the want of a friend. I have no one near me, gentle yet courageous, possessed of a cultivated as well as of a capacious mind, whose tastes are like my own, to approve or amend my plans. How would such a friend repair the faults of your poor brother!

(pp. 167-68)

Frankenstein condescends to poor Walton even on the subject of friendship. It is too late for him to take up any new ties in life, he explains, because no man could ever be more to him than Clerval was and no woman more than Elizabeth. (p. 168)

Mary was sufficiently her mother's daughter to assume that a woman, as easily as another man, could be the soul companion, the ideal friend, of a man. She did not regard sexual love as an impediment to ideal friendship, nor, it would seem, as a "small party" of the claims of true love. Elizabeth and Frankenstein almost always address one another as "dear friend," and she and Clerval simply complement different sides of Frankenstein's nature. If it were to come to a choice of one or the other, the novel leaves little doubt that the feminine companion is the more valuable since she can provide both spiritual sympathy and physical affection. It is a great and painful loss for Frankenstein when Clerval is killed, but the death of Elizabeth is the end of everything for him. He dedicates himself to the pursuit and destruction of the monster, follows him to "the everlasting ices of the north" where, surrounded by blankness and waste, he confronts the sterility and uselessness of his life. . . . (pp. 168-69)

An earlier scene of frozen desolation associated with isolation from human—especially feminine—companionship takes place between Frankenstein and the monster on a glacier at the base of Mont Blanc. The monster begs his maker to listen to him and proceeds to explain in detail how he has observed and imitated the ways of man, but is shunned because of his ugliness and is forced to wander over glaciers and hide in caves of ice because these are the only dwellings "man does not grudge." In other words, despite the bizarre details associated with his creation, the monster's lament is much the same as that of the physically presentable Caleb Williams: the world does not see him as he really is. His narrative is punctuated by outcries of loneliness:

Everywhere I see bliss, from which I alone am irrevocably excluded.
When I looked around, I saw and heard of none like me.

I had never yet seen a being resembling me, or who claimed any intercourse with me. What was I?
I am an unfortunate and deserted creature . . . I have no relation or friend upon earth.

The repetition of this theme, with slight variations, continues throughout the monster's narrative. However ludicrous or grotesque it may seem in the concrete, it is nonetheless in keeping with one of the central arguments of the novel that the monster should ask Frankenstein to make him a wife. (pp. 169-70)

The irony of the situation, though heavy-handed, is effective. Having removed himself from human companionship and the sexual means of procreation, Frankenstein brings into being a creature who, though not innately evil, is a torment to himself and to others precisely because he is without companionship and a sexual counterpart. In this respect the monster may well be taken as Frankenstein's alter-ego, his strange and destructive self, which finds no adequate means of communication with others, no true resemblances, no reciprocation, a repressed and hidden beast for whom all acceptable forms of human commerce are unavailable and therefore hateful. Frankenstein himself calls the unnameable creature "my own spirit let loose from the grave . . . forced to destroy all that was dear to me."

Mary saw, as did her father, the duality in human nature which is capable of bringing misery and ruin to the most gifted of beings. Her novel is not so pessimistic as *Caleb Williams* nor are the solutions implied in it so optimistic as those outlined in *Political Justice.* Neither her father's trust in system nor her husband's unworldliness seemed satisfactory to her. On the contrary, judging from the events of her novel, both alternatives were too likely to lead to that single-mindedness which, when carried to the extreme, was a kind of insanity. It would seem, in fact, that of all the romantic influences on her mind and work, Shelley's undoubtedly stimulated, but Coleridge's comforted; Shelley's provided confusion and enchantment, Coleridge's provided psychological and moral consolation. The ethereal reveries of her hero are loyal attempts to imitate Shelley, but they are among the most strained and unconvincing passages of the novel. Mary's natural inclination was toward synthesis, integration, a constant effort to find balance, relationship, correspondence, to root all ideals in natural process, and to find in nature the external signs of an ideal region. Her heart is with those, described by Coleridge, "who measuring and sounding the rivers of the vale at the feet of their furthest inaccessible falls have learned, that the sources must be far higher and far inward." Despite his supposedly scientific approach to things, Frankenstein's error is to circumvent an elementary principle of nature in trying to achieve his rather vaguely conceived ambition.

Boris Karloff as the monster in the 1931 Universal production of *Frankenstein*.

In stressing friendship, and especially heterosex-   ual love, as her "river of the vale," the natural symbol of a higher necessity, Mary presents her own concrete version of the theory of correspondence. We must give her more credit than to think that she supposed the problems of all men—including geniuses—would be solved by marriage to a good woman. What she does mean is that no being truly exists—except in an insane wilderness of its own creation—unless it finds and *accepts* a relationship of mutual dependence with another. The rapport with otherness is both the link with the objective world and the condition for self-delineation. (pp. 170-71)

Mary Shelley's definition of a monster is precisely that being to which nothing corresponds, the product of a genius who tried to exercise its will without reference to other beings. (p. 171)

Frankenstein's first act after creating a new life is to disown it. The problem is not, as in *Caleb Williams,* an ambiguous fascination leading to abuse and immediate and obsessive pursuit. As soon as his dream is realized in concrete form, Frankenstein wants nothing to do with it. Despite his claims to scientific interest, he demonstrates no wish whatever to observe and analyze the imperfect results of his experiment. When he does finally pursue the monster, it is not in order to possess, dominate, or torment it, but to annihilate it. Though there is something ludicrous in the way the monster stumbles upon books and learns to read during his lonely wandering, the thematic consistency of the episode is unmistakable. The monster is most impressed by *Paradise Lost;* he compares himself with Adam before the creation of Eve, but, like a good Romantic, he finds Satan an even "fitter emblem" of his condition. Still, neither emblems, nor words can really help or define him any more than ordinary men can. He can find parallels but no connections and he concludes his encounter with books by envying Satan like all the others, for even he "had his companions."

The two dominant themes of *Frankenstein* never truly harmonize, nor does one succeed effectively in canceling out the other. Surely, the most explicit "moral" theme of the novel—expressed by the author with genuine conviction—is that man discovers and fulfills himself through others and destroys himself alone. Yet played against this, not so much as an argument but as an assumption, is the idea that the genius, even in his failures, is unique, noble, and isolated from other men by divine right.

Frankenstein is neither a pure hymn of praise to Godwin and Shelley nor a simple repudiation of them. Mary's uncertainties are not reflected in parody or burlesque, as Beckford's and Lewis's are in *Vathek* and *The Monk.* Her prose style is solemn, inflated, and imitative, an unhappy combination of Godwin's sentence structure and Shelley's abstract vocabulary. Whatever else she may have thought, Mary obviously did not regard her father or husband as silly. Her reservations about them were deep, complex, and mixed with genuine admiration.

After Shelley's death, Mary considered how best to educate her son, and a friend advised that she teach him to think for himself. Mary is said to have answered, "Oh my God, teach him to think like other people!" If the young wife had been able to speak with the emphatic clarity of the widow, she probably would have had fewer nightmares and *Frankenstein* might never have been written. The book is a bad dream entwined with a moral essay. Like all romantic fiction, it resounds with the fascinating dissonance which usually results from intimate encounters between irrational symbols and reasonable statements. (pp. 171-73)

Robert Kiely, " 'Frankenstein': Mary Wollstonecraft Shelley," in his *The Romantic Novel in England,* Cambridge, Mass.: Harvard University Press, 1972, pp. 155-73.

JAMES RIEGER
(essay date 1974)

[In the following excerpt from his introduction to an edition of *Frankenstein*, Rieger disputes the notion that the novel is either Gothic romance or early science fiction, discussing it instead as an example of mythic fiction.]

The complexity of *Frankenstein* becomes apparent as soon as one tries to classify it. The difficulty is the author's rich eclecticism, together with the stylistic inconsistencies and narrative absurdities that are, perhaps, the inescapable converse of that eclecticism. Mary Shelley works so many veins at once that impatient readers have tended to falsify her book by filing it away as late Gothic romance, for example, or early science fiction. Before trying to determine what *Frankenstein* is, let us see what it is not. (pp. xxiv-xxv)

[Gothic romance] shares certain elements with *Frankenstein,* most noticeably an awareness of the deathly and nihilistic components of lust. The reader never learns whether Radcliffe's dark, brooding, and very sexy villains would prefer to rape her heroines or to murder them. Similarly, Frankenstein thinks he is affirming the life force by transfusing it into the stitched-together fragments of various corpses. But the disgusting and homicidal botch that results is a nightmare image, the surface manifestation of the unseen motives that underlie the scientist's "curiosity." It is symbolically appropriate that the monstrous miscreation should cancel the possibility of natural procreation, that he should "be with you on your wedding-night" . . . to break the neck of his maker's

---

Major Media Adaptations: Motion Pictures

Frankenstein, 1931. Universal. Director: Carl Laemmle, Jr. Cast: Boris Karloff, Colin Clive, Mae Clark, John Boles.

The Bride of Frankenstein, 1935. Universal. Director: Carl Laemmle, Jr. Cast: Boris Karloff, Colin Clive, Elsa Lancaster.

Son of Frankenstein, 1939. Universal. Director: Rowland V. Lee. Cast: Boris Karloff, Basil Rathbone, Bela Lugosi.

Ghost of Frankenstein, 1942. Universal. Director: Erle C. Kenton. Cast: Lon Chaney, Jr., Sir Cedric Hardwicke, Ralph Bellamy, Lionel Atwill, Bela Lugosi.

Frankenstein Meets the Wolf Man, 1943. Universal. Director: George Waggner. Cast: Bela Lugosi, Lon Chaney, Jr., Ilona Massey, Patric Knowles.

House of Frankenstein, 1944. Universal. Director: Erle C. Kenton. Cast: Boris Karloff, Lon Chaney, Jr., Glenn Strange.

Abbott and Costello Meet Frankenstein, 1948. Universal. Director: Charles T. Barton. Cast: Bud Abbott, Lou Costello, Lon Chaney, Jr., Bela Lugosi, Glenn Strange.

Young Frankenstein, 1974. TCF. Director: Mel Brooks. Cast: Gene Wilder, Marty Feldman, Madeleine Kahn.

---

bride. The Gothic and Shelleyan perception of the destructive side of sexuality has contemporary analogues in Byron's tragedies and verse romances and in the novels of de Sade.

The Gothic romancers aimed at a middle-class, Protestant, largely female audience, whose education barely extended beyond simple literacy. They exploited the prejudices of this audience against the Catholic south of Europe, which had been feared for centuries as the homeland of Macchiavelli, the Borgia Popes, and Philip of Spain—the source, then, of political trickery, ecclesiastical corruption, poison, and Armadas, together with what we now call polymorphous perversity. Mary Shelley turned this convention around. The lecherous, treacherous Italians and Spaniards depicted by Radcliffe and Lewis yield to Frankenstein's fiancée, Elizabeth Lavenza. In the third edition, Elizabeth's Italy stands for emotional warmth, and her birthplace is the destination of the aborted wedding trip. Conversely, the northward journeys of the two self-proclaimed rationalists, Walton and Frankenstein, are voyages into coldness, darkness, and delusion, though each traveler in his way expects to discover "light" and the innermost secret of life.

Finally, Frankenstein's interest in the occult and the quasi-magical powers he gains through the study of chemistry resemble the diabolical alliances contract-

ed by some Gothic villains and the energy acquired by others through their association with the mystique of Roman Catholic ritual. Lewis's Ambrosio and Radcliffe's Schedoni have taken holy orders, and Frankenstein has enrolled for a degree. The anticlericalism of *The Monk* and *The Italian* and the anti-intellectualism of *Frankenstein* both stem from earlier treatments of the Faust legend, whose central figure has degrees in everything from medicine to theology.

Despite these affinities, *Frankenstein* departs from the Gothic tradition as obviously as it follows it. As its name implies, Gothicism depends on spatial and temporal exoticism. The era is vaguely and unconvincingly medieval in most cases, and the scenery is cultivated, second-hand, "picturesque." Radcliffe's scenic effects, for instance, are explicitly painterly. Mary Shelley's Arctic wastes have a starkness rarely risked by the Gothic romancers, even when they varied picturesqueness with sublimity. And her other major landscapes were drawn from firsthand observation. The symbolism of light and coldness which permeates the description of the Arve glacier, the narrative setting of the second volume, is perhaps obtrusive. Nevertheless, the author had been there with Shelley in July 1816. The scene is concrete and clear, whatever its metaphorical tendency. Above all, it is immediate.

The realistic principle extends to the social context. The center of the novel's centrifugal action is the "republic" of Geneva during the decade of the French Revolution. The Frankensteins are enlightened bourgeois in the birthplace of Rousseau, a city no longer ruled by the theocracy of Calvin. . . . Unlike the rest of Europe in the 1790s, Geneva had neither bishops nor a king. It is upon this emancipated city and its progressive inhabitants—the Frankensteins and the Clervals—that the demonic legacy of the Middle Ages obtrudes in scientific guise. The reversal of the Gothic strategy could not be more complete.

Mary Shelley shared her husband's fascination with the natural sciences. In the 1830s, . . . she would contribute scientific biographies to Lardner's *Cabinet Cyclopedia,* and in her futuristic novel, *The Last Man,* she invented a flying machine. Still, it would be a mistake to call *Frankenstein* a pioneer work of science fiction. Its author knew something of Sir Humphry Davy's chemistry, Erasmus Darwin's botany, and, perhaps, Galvani's physics, but little of this got into her book. Frankenstein's chemistry is switched-on magic, souped-up alchemy, the electrification of Agrippa and Paracelsus. Things simply unknown or undone do not engage his attention; he wants the *forbidden* unknown and undone. He is a criminal magician who employs up-to-date tools. Moreover, the technological plausibility that is essential to science fiction is not even pretended at here. The science-fiction writer says, in effect, since x has been experimentally proven or theoretically postulated, *y* can be achieved by the following, carefully documented operation. Mary Shelley skips to the outcome and asks, if *y* had been achieved, by whatever means, what would be the moral consequences? In other words, she skips the science. The terms of her basic question (if that were her only question) would place *Frankenstein* with works that follow the same logic with regard, say, to eternal life or eternal youth: the Struldbrug episode in *Gulliver's Travels,* Godwin's *St. Leon,* Mary Shelley's own **"The Mortal Immortal"** (1834), Tennyson's "Tithonus," and Wilde's *The Picture of Dorian Gray.* (pp. xxv-xxviii)

Like Rousseau and Godwin before her, Mary stresses the role of education in the liberation or enslavement of the personality. She apparently agrees with Locke that the mind is a blank slate at birth, and with the sceptics that sensory evidence can mislead the moral judgment. But *Frankenstein* does not survive as a "novel with a thesis." Rather it comes through to us, in Northrop Frye's words, as "a precursor . . . of the existential thriller, of such a book as Camus's *L'Etranger.*" Its three concentric narrators, geographically, intellectually, and erotically cut off from the rest of mankind, deal with the world by means of a secret: the explorer's "secret of the magnet," the researcher's galvanic secret of life, and the Monster's pure embodiment of these secrets, together with his unique knowledge of what it is like to be born free of history. Each secret reflects the others, or rather, each is an aspect of what Shelley in "Mont Blanc" calls "The secret Strength of things / Which governs thought, and to the infinite dome / Of Heaven is as a law. . . ." By the same token, each narrator finds a mirror-image of himself in one of the others: Walton knows that once he could have possessed Frankenstein as "the brother of my heart," . . . and Frankenstein and the Monster know that their master-slave relationship, in which the balance of power constantly shifts, parodies the love existing between father and son. The attempt to kiss the mirror is thwarted always by the illicit possession of the secret, which withers the heart and condemns its owner to emotional isolation. As Frankenstein puts it, "If the study to which you apply yourself has a tendency to weaken your affections, and to destroy your taste for those simple pleasures in which no alloy can possibly mix, then that study is certainly unlawful, that is to say, not befitting the human mind." . . . (p. xxx)

The moral is Godwinian, as is the imaginative pattern that gives it flesh. Caleb Williams's actions are determined by a ruinous secret, and St. Leon possesses the elixir of life, which destroys him and all around him. Caleb's stricken conscience mirrors Falkland's, and St. Leon's aging mind is at war with his eternally youthful body. As well as foreshadowing the existential hero, Mary Shelley's and Godwin's characters have American cousins in the obsessed and claustrophobic heroes of Brockden Brown, Poe, Hawthorne, and Melville. Brockden Brown acknowledged his debt to Godwin, and it is not fortuitous that Melville read *Frankenstein* in 1849, two years before he published his own tale of a single-minded voyager, Ahab, chasing "round the Norway Maelstrom, and round perdition's flames" his own monstrous secret, "the monomaniac incarnation of all those malicious agencies which some deep men feel eating in them."

All such fiction is mythic, in the same sense that Blake's Prophetic Books and Shelley's *Prometheus Unbound* are myth-poetry. Blake's symbolic personages are fragments of a single, shattered psyche, and the cosmic struggle in Shelley's lyrical drama employs "imagery . . . drawn from the operation of the human mind, or from those external actions by which they are expressed." Psychomachia and theomachia are metaphors of each other, which is to say that the internecine warfare of the gods cannot be distinguished from the mental chaos of their victim and creator. Romantic myth-fiction replaces the fratricidal gods with *Frankenstein's* ambiguous, magnetic, devouring secret, as later with Melville's "intangible malignity which has been from the beginning." The whiteness of Moby Dick, like that of Mary Shelley's Mont Blanc and Arctic ice-cap, "shadows forth the heartless voids and immensities of the universe . . . a colorless, all-color of atheism from which we shrink." (pp. xxx-xxxi)

James Rieger, in an introduction to *Frankenstein; or, The Modern Prometheus: The 1818 Text* by Mary Wollstonecraft Shelley, edited by James Rieger, 1974. Reprint by The University of Chicago Press, 1982, pp. xi-xxxii.

GEORGE LEVINE

(essay date 1979)

[An American editor and critic, Levine coedited *The Endurance of "Frankenstein,"* the collection of essays from which the following excerpt is drawn. Here, he cites seven of the major implications of the Frankenstein metaphor in contemporary consciousness and outlines their sources in the novel.]

[While] *Frankenstein* is a phenomenon of popular culture, it is so because it has tapped into the center of Western feeling and imagination: we can hear echoes of it, not only in Gothic fiction, science fiction, and fantasies of all sorts, but in far more "respectable" works, written before the glut of popular cinematic distortions. *Frankenstein* has become a metaphor for our own cultural crises, and survives even yet in high literary culture whose professors may have seen Boris Karloff stumbling through the fog, hands outstretched, at least once too often.

Of course, *Frankenstein* is a "minor" novel, radically flawed by its sensationalism, by the inflexibly public and oratorical nature of even its most intimate passages. But it is, arguably, the most important minor novel in English. If we return to the text for a check on Boris Karloff, or, recently, Mel Brooks, or for some further light on Percy Shelley, invariably we find that the book is larger and richer than any of its progeny and too complex to serve as mere background. Even in our dictionaries, "Frankenstein" has become a vital metaphor, peculiarly appropriate to a culture dominated by a consumer technology, neurotically obsessed with "getting in touch" with its authentic self and frightened at what it is discovering: "a work, or agency that proves troublesomely uncontrollable, esp. to its creator." Latent in the metaphor are some of the fundamental dualisms, the social, moral, political and metaphysical crises of Western history since the French Revolution. It may well appear that the metaphorical implications are far more serious than the novel that gave birth to them, but that novel has qualities that allow it to exfoliate as creatively and endlessly as any important myth; if it threatens to lapse into banality and bathos, it yet lives through unforgettable dreamlike images. . . . (pp. 3-4)

Frankenstein's mysterious power derives from a thoroughly earthy, practical, and unideal vision of human nature and possibility. Its modernity lies in its transformation of fantasy and traditional Christian and pagan myths into unremitting secularity, into the myth of mankind as it must work within the limits of the visible, physical world. The novel echoes, for example, with the language and the narrative of *Paradise Lost,* but it is *Paradise Lost* without angels, or devils, or God. . . . The whole narrative of *Frankenstein* is, indeed, acted out in the absence of God. The grand gestures of *Frankenstein* may suggest a world of fantasy that has acquired a profound escapist appeal in modern culture, but they take place in a framework that necessarily makes an ironic commentary on them, even while our sympathies are drawn to dreams of the more than human the narrative will not allow.

This characteristic tension between an impinging, conditional, and time-bound world and a dream of something freer and better makes the central subject matter and form of the nineteenth-century novel and, ironically, of nineteenth-century science as well. The old myths enter nineteenth-century fiction, but they do so in the mode of realism. . . . [Though] it would be absurd to claim Mary Shelley as a direct "influence" on the dominant literary and scientific forms of the century, we can see that in her secularization of the creation myth she invented a metaphor that was irresistible to the culture as a whole. As George Eliot turned to Feuer-

bach to allow her to transform Christianity into a humanism with all the emotional power of religion, so the novel itself, as a genre, put its faith in a material world of fact that, as Matthew Arnold pointed out, had failed us. In writers as central and various as Feuerbach, Comte, Darwin, Marx, Frazer, and Freud we can find Victor Frankenstein's activity: the attempt to discover in matter what we had previously attributed to spirit, the bestowing *on* matter (or history, or society, or nature) the values once given to God.

This argument puts Mary Shelley in some rather remarkable company, but, of course, the point is not to equate the achievement of her little "ghost story" with that of the great thinkers named. The claim is simply that Mary Shelley did, indeed, create an image, with the authenticity of dream vision, that became prophetic; that the image articulates powerfully the dominant currents of her culture and ours; and that it is for these reasons that *Frankenstein* has survived its own adolescent clumsiness and its later distortions.

The pervasiveness of the Frankenstein metaphor in modern consciousness testifies to the richness and variousness of its implications. The dictionary definition focuses only on the uncontrollable nature of the thing created; but the image of the created Monster, emerging from the isolated workshop of the obsessed but otherwise gentle scientist, unfolds into more possibilities than I can describe. . . . At the risk of arbitrary exclusions and of belaboring what may seem obvious, I want to outline some of the major implications of the Frankenstein metaphor in contemporary consciousness, and as they have their sources in the novel proper.

1. *Birth and Creation.* In *Frankenstein* we are confronted immediately by the displacement of God and woman from the acts of conception and birth. Where Victor imagines himself embarked on the creation of a new race that would bless him, he behaves, even before his creation proves a monster, as though he is engaged in unnatural, shameful activity. Neither of the two attitudes is entirely undercut by the narrative, even though the dream of the new race is, of course, exploded. The image of Frankenstein in his laboratory is not only of an unnatural act, but also one of an heroic dream, and the novel's insistence, even through Walton and the Monster, on Victor's heroic nature, implies that the creation without God, without woman, need not be taken as an unequivocal evil.

The displacement of woman obviously reflects a fear of birth and Mary Shelley's own ambivalence about childbearing . . . ; the Monster's presence on the wedding night becomes a permanent image of the horror of sexuality as opposed to the ideal and nonsexual love of the cousins, Victor and Elizabeth. The image of the Monster lurking ominously in the background, with Elizabeth sprawled on the bed, is one of the dominant icons of the film versions. Obviously, the image is profoundly phallic and profoundly violent, an unacceptable alternative to and consequence of the act of conception in the laboratory. Indeed, in the novel itself . . . the two scenes precisely echo each other. In both cases, there is an association that runs as constant ground-motif through the novel.

Sexuality and birth, imagination and creation are, in this heavily material world, reverse images of death and destruction. Frankenstein and his creature come to represent, in part, an alternative to the violence of sexuality, on the one hand, and to the sheer spirituality of divine creation, on the other. (pp. 6-9)

2. *The Overreacher.* The aspiration to divine creative activity (akin to Romantic notions of the poet) places Victor Frankenstein in the tradition of Faustian overreachers. Frankenstein the creator is also Frankenstein the modern Prometheus, full of the great Romantic dream—concretized for a moment in the French Revolution—of a rebirth of mankind. True, Victor is seeking a kind of immortality, but, as Ellen Moers points out [in her essay "Female Gothic: The Monster's Mother," *The New York Review of Books,* 21 March 1974], Mary Shelley works the Faust tradition in an unusual (and, I might again add, secularizing) way by having Victor seek immortality not directly for himself but in the creation of offspring. If we detect the stirrings of selfishness in Victor's desire to have a whole species that would bless him, the text still insists on the profundity of his moral character and the conscious morality of all of his choices save the fatal one. Indeed . . . , Frankenstein is removed from direct personal responsibility even for his own ambitions: for the most part he is described as passively consumed by energies larger than himself or as quite literally unconscious and ill when his being conscious might have changed the course of the narrative.

The theme of the overreacher is largely complicated by the evidence that Victor's worst sin is not the creation of the Monster but his refusal to take responsibility for it. It is as though God had withdrawn from his creation. Characteristically, in the secularizing myth, Mary Shelley has imagined the responsibilities of God shifted to mankind. The burden is too great to allow us an easy moral placing of Victor. The theme of the overreacher in this context brings us to the kind of impasse that *Frankenstein* itself reaches in the mutual destruction of creator and created. That is, we see that the ambition is heroic and admirable, yet deadly because humans are incapable of fulfilling their dreams in material reality, or, paradoxically, of bearing the responsibility for them should they succeed. (pp. 9-10)

3. *Rebellion and Moral Isolation.* Obviously, these aspects of the myth are related to "overreaching." Yet it is important to note that they apply not only to Victor but to the Monster as well, whose ambition is really limited to the longing for domestic affection. Victor

himself is not quite imagined as a rebel, except perhaps in his pursuit of alchemical knowledge after his father ridicules him for reading Paracelsus. In any case, unlike the Monster, he does not consciously rebel against authority. Yet, "animated by an almost supernatural enthusiasm," Victor takes up an intellectual pursuit (whence did the "principle of life proceed") that places him outside the traditional Christian world, and that ought to make him, like Adam eating the apple, a rebel against God. The context, however, is quietly unChristian. Victor speaks in a scientific or at least naturalistic language that assumes a natural material answer to what was once a religious and metaphysical question. (pp. 10-11)

The moral isolation into which Victor sinks is, in effect, chosen for him by his obsession. Like Raskolnikov plotting murder, like Dimmesdale guilty of adultery, Victor lives with a secret that we understand, without explanation, must be kept from public knowledge. Here the residue of metaphysical shame works its effects, but social and psychological explanations offer themselves immediately. In any case, the activity separates Victor from normal life as fully as a direct act of murder would. (p. 11)

The Monster's isolation derives not so much from his actions as from his hideousness. Where Victor moves from domestic bliss to the garret, the Monster leaves the garret to seek that bliss. Victor's revolutionary action causes his isolation; the Monster's isolation causes his revolutionary action. "Believe me, Frankenstein," he says, "I was benevolent; my soul glowed with love and humanity; but am I not alone, miserably alone?" (pp. 11-12)

Despite the apparent moral simplicity of most modern versions of *Frankenstein,* the Frankenstein metaphor implies great ambiguity about where the burden of good and evil rests. Both Victor and the Monster imply resistance to the established order. . . . In early Romantic literature, of course, rebellion is more likely to be a virtue than a sin, and the Monster makes a strong case against social injustice. Even Walton, though warned by Victor, is instinctively convinced of the justice of the Monster's arguments.

The constantly shifting moral perspective of the narrative results from the fact that each of its major figures—Walton, Victor, the Monster—is at once victimizer and victim; and this tradition is even continued in modern movie versions. In novel and films, any singularity is punished by the community, either by forcing isolation or by literal imprisonment. The three major figures and Felix De Lacey variously challenge the established order and acquire dignity by virtue of the challenge and of the punishment that ensues. Thus the novel, which might be taken as a parable of the necessity of limits in an entirely secular world, may also be taken as a parable of the necessity for revolutionary reprisal (at whatever cost) because of the social and political limits that frustrate the noblest elements of the human spirit.

4. *The Unjust Society.* After the execution of the innocent Justine, Elizabeth Lavenza, the vessel of domestic purity, tells Victor that "men appear to me as monsters thirsting for each other's blood." . . . Even if she retracts immediately ("Yet I am certainly unjust"), the notion that the world of men is itself "monstrous" is a constant motif of the novel. Even in the most conventional of the modern Frankenstein films, the motif emerges when, in the obligatory misty night, the villagers turn out as a maddened lynch mob and transform Frankenstein and the Monster into victims of an overwhelming attack on the castle. In almost every film, the townspeople are almost comically banal, the burgomeisters and gendarmerie officious and totally without sensibility. Absurd though these figures may be . . . , they echo the essentially shallow ambitions and dreams of security that fill the background of the novel.

There the motif is handled subtly enough to make the monstrous problematic. Elizabeth's sense that "men are monsters" recurs in the monster's ingenious hectoring of Victor in a fine Godwinian rational discourse. Moreover, the De Lacey story is a continuing narrative of injustice, on all sides. And in his last speech to Walton, the Monster makes clear once more that his own monstrousness is not really different from that of the

world that condemns him. . . . The novel has taught us to distrust the evenhandedness of the law that Victor's father praises before Justine is executed; we understand with the Monster that greed is a commonplace of social activity. Not even the family unit—Frankenstein's and the Monster's ideal—escapes the contamination that almost makes rebellion necessary and that makes Victor's escape to his laboratory from Geneva seem psychologically and socially explicable.

5. *The Defects of Domesticity.* The theme of the overreacher and the rebel—the Promethean theme—is the other side of the theme of ideal domesticity. . . . Mary Shelley treats "domestic affection" in such a way as to make it possible to read *Frankenstein* as an attack on the very traditions of bourgeois society it purports to be celebrating. Certainly, as we have seen, "the amiableness of domestic affection" does nothing to satisfy Victor Frankenstein's ambitions, or to prevent the monstrous creation; nor, in the tale of the Monster's wanderings, does it extend to anything outside itself to allow for the domestication of the Monster's loving energies. "Domestic affection" is, in a way, defined by its exclusion of energy and by its resistance to the larger community. The Monster instinctively believes in the rhetoric of domesticity and the need for community; it is psychologically and dramatically appropriate that he should exhaust himself in the total destruction of ostensibly ideal domesticity when he discovers that he is excluded from it, and that the ideal is false. (pp. 13-14)

Scene from *Young Frankenstein,* starring (left to right) Gene Wilder, Teri Garr, Marty Feldman, and Cloris Leachman.

6. *The Double.* Almost every critic of *Frankenstein* has noted that Victor and his Monster are doubles. The doubleness even enters some of the popular versions and is un-self-consciously accepted by everyone who casually calls the Monster "Frankenstein." The motif of the *Doppelgänger* was certainly in Mary's mind during the writing, as it was a part of the Gothic tradition in which she wrote; moreover, it is one with which she would have been intimately connected through Shelley himself, as in "Alastor" and "Epipsychidion," So pervasive has been the recognition that the Monster and Frankenstein are two aspects of the same being that the writers in this volume assume rather than argue it. The narrative requires us to see that the doubling extends beyond the two major narrators: Walton is obviously another aspect of Frankenstein, and Clerval yet another; Elizabeth can be paired with Victor's mother, with Justine, and with the unfinished "bride" of the Monster. . . . Such doublings and triplings, with reverberations in and out of the novel in Mary Shelley's own life and in modern psychological theory, suggest again the instability and ambivalence of the book's "meanings."

They point centrally to the way "Frankenstein" as a modern metaphor implies a conception of the divided self, the creator and his work at odds. The civilized man or woman contains within the self a monstrous, destructive, and self-destructive energy. The angel in the house entails a demon outside it, the Monster leering through the window at the horrified Victor and the murdered Elizabeth. Here, in particular, we can watch the specially secularized versions of traditional mythology. The devil and the angel of the morality play are replaced by a modern pre-Freudian psychology that removes the moral issue from the metaphysical context—the traditional concepts of good and evil—and places it entirely within the self. Morality is, as it were, replaced by schizophrenia. Frankenstein's longing for domesticity is echoed in the Monster's (and in Walton's expression of loneliness in the opening pages); Frankenstein's obsession with science is echoed in the Monster's obsession with destruction. The two characters haunt and hunt each other through the novel, each evoking from us sympathy for their sufferings, revulsion from their cruelties.

The echoes force themselves on us with a persistence and intensity that override the mere narrative and even enter into popular versions that are not intrinsically concerned with doubling. The book creates a psychomachia, an internal war that has its own authenticity despite the grotesqueness of the external action. If the characters seem shallow as novelistic figures within the conventions of realism we have come to assume are natural to nineteenth-century fiction, it is partly because they are imagined from the start as incomplete. . . . They can be seen, indeed, as fragments of a mind in conflict with itself, extremes unreconciled,

striving to make themselves whole. Ambition and passivity, hate and love, the need to procreate and the need to destroy are seen, in *Frankenstein,* as symbiotic: the destruction of one is, through various narrative strategies, the destruction of the other.

7. *Technology, Entropy, and the Monstrous.* Perhaps the most obvious and continuing application of the word "Frankenstein" in modern society is to technological advances. This is altogether appropriate to Mary Shelley's original conception of the novel since Victor's discovery of the secret of life is fundamentally scientific; and he talks of his "animation" of the Monster's body as a mere trick of technology. Modern science fiction and modern industry are full of such "animated" beings, the products of computer technology; with the discovery of DNA, biologists even seem on the verge of simulating the natural process of creation of life. But both of these developments are part of the same imagination as Mary Shelley gives us with her Monster: that life is not "spirit" but matter imbued with energy, itself another form of matter.

Martin Tropp has noted that "when Mary Shelley gave her intended 'ghost story' a scientific context, she linked the Gothic concept of the double with technology." Her fears of the creation of life by mere mechanisms, Tropp notes, resulted from her awareness that "technology can never be more than a magnified image of the self." . . . And when that self is engaged in a psychomachia, the result can only be large-scale disaster. In a psychic world of the divided self, in a social world in which domesticity and ambition are seen as incompatible poles, the self expressed in technology can only be what our original dictionary definition tells us, "troublesomely uncontrollable, esp. to its creator," i.e., monstrous. The nightmare quality of the novel depends on this projection of the self into an objectively existing, independent reality over which one necessarily loses control as it acts out one's own monstrous passions. Here all the battery of Freudian equipment comes neatly or, perhaps, explosively into play. All the elements of moral isolation, the grubbing in filthy flesh, the obsessed and inhuman energies that went into the creation of the Monster, can be seen acting themselves out in the destruction they really imply—in the incestuous destructiveness of Victor's ostensibly ideal relation to Elizabeth, in the fraternal hostility buried in his love for poor William, in the hatred of his mother implied in his failure to save Justine (who has adopted Mrs. Frankenstein's very way of life). Such implications are explored in a great deal of criticism of the novel. But the point here is that technology becomes the means by which these buried aspects of the self are enacted. The "work or agency" does not rebel against the creator but actually accomplishes what the creator wants. . . . The uncontrolled technological creation is particularly frightening and obsessively attractive to modern consciousness because it forces a confrontation with our buried selves. It promises to reveal to us our deepest and most powerful desires, and to enact them. The Monster demands our sympathetic engagement while our social consciousness must by an act of will—almost like Walton's when he finds himself irresistibly attracted by the Monster's talk—reject him.

The duality of our relationship to creator and creature is an echo of our relationship to the technology that we worship even as we recognize that it is close to destroying us. Another way to express the duality, in technological terms, is through the idea of entropy. Victor's overreaching is an attempt to create *new* life. He fails to recognize the necessary secular-scientific myth of entropy: that in any closed system, the new energy generated will be less than the energy expended in its creation, and that ultimately the system will run down. It took a great deal of death to make the new life; the making of the Monster is at the expense of all of Victor's immediate world—brother, father, bride, friend. The world of mere matter is both finite and corrupted. Without the incalculable presence of divine spirit, creation can only entail destruction larger than itself. It is, ultimately, this nightmare image that the Monster represents to our culture. (pp. 15-17)

George Levine, "The Ambiguous Heritage of 'Frankenstein'," in *The Endurance of Frankenstein: Essays on Mary Shelley's Novel,* edited by George Levine and U. C. Knoepflmacher, University of California Press, 1979, pp. 3-30.

SOURCES FOR FURTHER STUDY

Bloom, Harold. "Frankenstein; or, The New Prometheus." *Partisan Review* XXXII, No. 4 (Fall 1965): 611-18.

Suggests that "what makes *Frankenstein* an important book, though it is only a strong, flawed, frequently clumsy novel, is that it vividly projects a version of the Romantic mythology of the self."

Gilbert, Sandra M., and Gubar, Susan. "Horror's Twin: Mary Shelley's Monstrous Eve." In their *The Madwoman in the Attic: The Woman Writer and the Nineteenth-Century Literary Imagination,* pp. 213-47. New Haven: Yale University Press, 1979.

A noted feminist analysis of *Frankenstein.* The critics stress the literary and sexual bases of the novel, which they term a "version of the misogynist story implied in *Paradise Lost.*"

Levine, George, and Knoepflmacher, U. C., eds. *The Endurance of "Frankenstein": Essays on Mary Shelley's Novel.* Berkeley and Los Angeles: University of California Press, 1974, 341 p.

A collection of essays by twelve contemporary critics covering various aspects of *Frankenstein,* including its literary and biographical sources, language, and adaptations for the theater and cinema. Also included are a brief chronology of Shelley's life, a select bibliography, illustrations, and an introduction by the editors attesting to *Frankenstein*'s growing critical importance.

Neumann, Bonnie Rayford. *The Lonely Muse: A Critical Biography of Mary Wollstonecraft Shelley.* Salzburg Studies in English Literature: Romantic Reassessment, edited by James Hogg, vol. 85. Salzburg: Universität Salzburg, 1979, 283 p.

A critical biography emphasizing Shelley's sense of personal alienation and tracing that theme in her work. Neumann argues for greater critical recognition of *The Last Man,* which she considers Shelley's "second outstanding work" after *Frankenstein.*

Spark, Muriel. *Child of Light: A Reassessment of Mary Wollstonecraft Shelley.* Hadleigh, Essex: Tower Bridge Publications, 1951, 235 p.

A biographical-critical study. In this, the first serious full-length consideration of Shelley's work, Spark focuses on *Frankenstein, The Last Man,* and *Perkin Warbeck,* as well as on Shelley's criticism.

Walling, William. *Mary Shelley.* Boston: Twayne Publishers, 1972, 173 p.

Critical survey of Shelley's writings in which the critic argues that Shelley's first three novels—*Frankenstein, Valperga,* and *The Last Man*—"ought to have earned for Mary a higher place in the literature about the fiction of the period than she currently holds."

Percy Bysshe Shelley

1792-1822

(Also wrote under pseudonyms Victor and The Hermit of Marlow) English poet, essayist, dramatist, translator, and novelist.

INTRODUCTION

Shelley is known as a major English Romantic poet. His foremost works, including *The Revolt of Islam* (1818), *Prometheus Unbound* (1820), *Adonais* (1821), and *The Triumph of Life* (1824), are recognized as leading expressions of radical thought written during the Romantic age, while his odes and shorter lyrics are often considered among the greatest in the English language. In addition, his essay *A Defence of Poetry* (1840) is highly valued as a statement of the role of the poet in society. Thus, although Shelley was one of the early nineteenth century's most controversial literary figures, his importance to English literature is today widely acknowledged.

Shelley's brief life was colorful. The eldest son of Sir Timothy and Elizabeth Shelley, landed aristocrats living in Horsham, Sussex, he was educated first at Syon House Academy, then Eton, and finally University College, Oxford. His idiosyncratic, sensitive nature and refusal to conform to tradition earned him the name "Mad Shelley," but during his years as a student he enjoyed several close friendships and pursued a wide range of interests in addition to his prescribed studies; he experimented in physical science, studied medicine and philosophy, and wrote novels and poetry. Before the age of twenty he had published two wildly improbable Gothic novels, *Zastrozzi* (1810) and *St. Irvyne* (1811), and two collections of verse. *Original Poetry by Victor and Cazire* (1810), written with his sister, continued in the Gothic mode, while *Posthumous Fragments of Margaret Nicholson* (1810), coauthored with his Oxford friend Thomas Jefferson Hogg, was a collection of treasonous and erotic poetry disguised as the ravings of a mad washerwoman who had attempted to stab King George III. In 1811, during his second term at Oxford, Shelley turned to philosophical concerns with his *The Necessity of Atheism,* a pamphlet challenging theological proofs for the existence of God. Assisted by Hogg, he published the tract, distributed it to the clergymen and deans of Oxford, and invited a debate. Instead, he and Hogg were expelled, an event that estranged him from his family and left him without financial means. Nonetheless, later that year he eloped to Scotland with Harriet Westbrook, a sixteen-year-old schoolmate of his sisters. The three years they spent together were marked by financial difficulties and frequent moves to avoid creditors. Despite these pressures, Shelley was actively involved in political and social reform in Ireland and Wales, writing radical pamphlets in which he set forth his views on liberty, equality, and justice. He and Harriet enthusiastically distributed these tracts among the working classes, but with little effect.

The year 1814 was a pivotal one in Shelley's personal life. Although their marriage was faltering, he remarried Harriet in England to ensure the legality of their union and the legitimacy of their children. Weeks later, however, he fell in love with Mary Godwin, the sixteen-year-old daughter of the radical English philosopher William Godwin and his first wife, the feminist author Mary Wollstonecraft. Shelley and Mary eloped and, accompanied by Mary's stepsister, Jane (Claire) Clairmont, spent six weeks in Europe. On their return, Shelley entered into a financial agreement with his family that ensured him a regular income. When Harriet declined to join his household as a "sister," he provided for her and their two children, but continued to live with Mary.

In the summer of 1816, Shelley, Mary, and Claire traveled to Lake Geneva to meet with Lord Byron, with whom Claire had begun an affair. Though Byron's interest in Claire was fleeting, he developed an enduring friendship with Shelley that proved an important influence on the works of both men. Shortly after Shelley's return to England in the fall, Harriet drowned herself in Hyde Park. Shelley thereupon legalized his relationship with Mary and sought custody of his children, but the Westbrook family successfully blocked him in a lengthy lawsuit. Citing his poem *Queen Mab* (1813), in which he denounced established society and religion in favor of free love and atheism, the Westbrooks convinced the court that Shelley was morally unfit for guardianship. Although Shelley was distressed by his separation from his daughter and infant son, he enjoyed the stimulating society of Leigh Hunt, Thomas Love Peacock, John Keats, and other literary figures during his residence at Marlow in 1817. The following year, however, motivated by ill health, financial worries, and the fear of losing custody of his and Mary's two children, Shelley relocated his family in Italy. There, they moved frequently, spending time in Leghorn, Venice, Naples, Rome, Florence, Pisa, and Lerici. Shelley hastened to renew his relationship with Byron, who was also living in Italy, and the two poets became the nucleus of a circle of expatriots that became known as the "Satanic School" because of their defiance of English social and religious conventions and promotion of radical ideas in their works. The years in Italy were predominantly happy and productive for Shelley despite the deaths of his and Mary's children Clara and William and the increasing disharmony of their marriage. Shortly before his thirtieth birthday, Shelley and his companion, Edward Williams, drowned when their boat capsized in a squall off the coast of Lerici. Shelley's body, identified by the works of Keats and Sophocles in his pockets, was cremated on the beach in a ceremony conducted by his friends Byron, Hunt, and Edward John Trelawny. His ashes, except for his heart, which Byron plucked from the fire, were buried in the Protestant cemetery in Rome.

Much of Shelley's writing reflects the events and concerns of his life. His passionate beliefs in reform, the equality of the sexes, and the powers of love and imagination are frequently expressed in his poetry. Shelley's first mature work, *Queen Mab,* was printed in 1813, but not distributed due to its inflammatory subject matter. It was not until 1816, with the appearance of *Alastor; or, The Spirit of Solitude, and Other Poems,* that he earned recognition as a serious poet. In *Alastor,* a visionary and sometimes autobiographical poem, Shelley describes the experiences of the Poet who, rejecting human sympathy and domestic life, is pursued by the demon Solitude. Shelley also used a visionary approach in his next lengthy work, *Laon and Cythna; or, The Revolution of the Golden City* (1818), written in friendly competition with Keats. An imaginative account of a bloodless revolution led by a brother and sister, the poem deals with the positive power of love, the complexities of good and evil, and ultimately, spiritual victory through martyrdom. *Laon and Cythna* was immediately suppressed by the printer because of its controversial content, and Shelley subsequently revised the work as *The Revolt of Islam,* minimizing its elements of incest and political revolution.

In 1819 Shelley wrote two of his most ambitious works, the verse dramas *Prometheus Unbound* and *The Cenci* (1819). Usually regarded as his masterpiece, *Prometheus Unbound* combines myth, political allegory, psychology, and theology. Shelley transformed the Aeschylean myth of Prometheus, the firegiver, into an allegory on the origins of evil and the possibility of regenerating nature and humanity through love. The variety of verse forms Shelley employed exhibits his poetic virtuosity and makes it one of his most challenging works. *The Cenci* differs markedly from *Prometheus Unbound* in tone and setting. Shelley based this tragedy on the history of a sixteenth-century Italian noble family. The evil Count Cenci rapes his daughter, Beatrice; she determines to murder him, seeing no other means of escape from continued violation, and is executed for parricide. Although Shelley hoped for a popular success on the English stage, his controversial treatment of the subject of incest outraged critics, preventing the play from being produced.

One of Shelley's best-known works, *Adonais: An Elegy on the Death of John Keats,* was written in 1821. Drawing on the formal tradition of elegiac verse, Shelley laments Keats's early death and, while rejecting the Christian view of resurrection, describes his return to the eternal beauty of the universe. In the same year, Shelley wrote *Epipsychidion,* in which he chronicles his search for ideal beauty through his relationships with women—Harriet, Mary, Claire, and finally Emilia Viviani, an Italian girl he and Mary befriended and to whom the poem is addressed. Although Shelley's interest in Emilia soon diminished, the work she inspired is considered one of his most revealing and technically accomplished poems. Shelley's last work, *The Triumph of Life,* left unfinished at his death, describes the relentless march of life that has destroyed the aspirations of all but the sacred few who refused to compromise to worldly pressures. Despite its fragmentary state, many critics consider *The Triumph of Life* a potential masterpiece and evidence of a pessimistic shift in Shelley's thought.

Throughout his career Shelley wrote numerous short lyrics that have proved to be among his most popular works. Characterized by a simple, personal tone, his minor poems frequently touch on themes central to his more ambitious works: the "Hymn to Intellectual Beauty" and "Mont Blanc" focus on his belief in an animating spirit, while "Ode to the West Wind" examines opposing forces in nature. In other lyrics, including "Lines Written among the Euganean Hills," "Stanzas Written in Dejection, Near Naples," and "Lines Written in the Bay of Lerici," Shelley explores his own experiences and emotions. Political themes also inspired several of his most famous short poems, among them "Ode to Liberty," "Sonnet: England in 1819," and *The Masque of Anarchy* (composed 1819; published 1832). Shelley's shorter lyrics, praised for their urbane wit and polished style, have established him as a preeminent poet of nature, ideal love, and beauty.

Mary Shelley took on the challenge of editing and annotating Shelley's unpublished manuscripts after his death. Her 1840 collection included Shelley's greatest prose work, *A Defence of Poetry.* Writing in response to *The Four Ages of Poetry* (1820), an essay by his friend Peacock, Shelley detailed his belief in the moral importance of poetry, calling poets "the unacknowledged legislators of the world." In addition to several other philosophical essays and translations from the Greek, Shelley's posthumous works include the highly personal odes addressed to Edward Williams's wife,

Jane. "To Jane: The Invitation," "To Jane: The Recollection," and "With a Guitar: To Jane" are considered some of his best love poems. At once a celebration of his friends' happy union and an intimate record of his own attraction to Jane, these lyrics are admired for their delicacy and refined style.

The history of Shelley's critical reputation has been characterized by radical shifts. During his lifetime he was generally regarded as a misguided or even depraved genius; critics frequently praised portions of his poetry in passing and deplored at length his atheism and unorthodox philosophy. Serious study of his works was hindered by widespread rumors about his personal life, particularly those concerning his desertion of Harriet and his supposed involvement in an incestuous love triangle with Mary and Claire. In addition, because of their limited publication and the scant critical attention given his works, he found only a small audience. Those few critics who voiced their admiration of his talents, particularly Hunt, who defended him vigorously in the *Examiner,* were ironically responsible for further inhibiting his success by causing him to be associated in the public mind with the despised "Cockney School" of poets belittled by John Gibson Lockhart and others in *Blackwood's Magazine.* Nevertheless, Shelley was known and admired by his great contemporaries: Byron, Keats, William Wordsworth, Samuel Taylor Coleridge, and Robert Southey regarded his works with varying degrees of sympathy and approval.

After his death, Shelley's reputation was greatly influenced by the efforts of his widow and friends to portray him as an angelic visionary. Biographies by Trelawny, Peacock, and Hogg, though frequently self-serving, inaccurate, and sensationalized, succeeded in directing interest toward Shelley's life and character and away from the controversial beliefs expressed in his works. Critics in the second half of the nineteenth century for the most part ignored Shelley's radical politics, celebrating instead the spiritual and aesthetic qualities of his poetry. In the Victorian age he was highly regarded as the poet of ideal love, and the Victorian notion of the poet as a sensitive, misunderstood genius was largely modeled after Shelley.

Shelley's works, however, fell into disfavor around the turn of the century. Many critics, influenced by Matthew Arnold's assessment of Shelley as an "ineffectual angel," objected to his seemingly vague imagery, nebulous philosophy, careless technique, and, most of all, his apparent intellectual and emotional immaturity. In the late 1930s Shelley's reputation began to revive: as scholars came to recognize the complexity of his philosophical idealism, serious study was devoted to the doctrines that informed his thought. Since that time, Shelley scholarship has covered a wide array of topics, including his style, philosophy, and major themes. In examining his style commentators have generally focused on his imagery, use of language, and technical achievements. The importance of neo-platonism, the occult, the Bible, the French Revolution, and Gothicism, as well as the works of individual philosophers—Wollstonecraft, Jean-Jacques Rousseau, and Godwin—to Shelley's thought and writings has been explored by other critics. Attention has also been devoted to recurring themes in Shelley's work. His doctrines of free love and sexual equality have particularly attracted commentary on the poet as an early proponent of feminism. Recent criticism of Shelley's works is generally marked by increasing respect for his abilities as a poet and his surprisingly modern philosophy. In addition, the details of his personal life continue to fascinate students of English literature, inspiring numerous biographies and peripheral studies about his life and friends.

(For further information about Shelley's life and works, see *Dictionary of Literary Biography*, Vol. 96: *British Romantic Poets, 1789-1832* and *Nineteenth-Century Literature Criticism*, Vol. 18.)

CRITICAL COMMENTARY

MARY W. SHELLEY

(essay date 1839)

[Mary Shelley, best known for her novel *Franken-stein; or, The Modern Prometheus*, also wrote criticism, short stories, and travel essays. In this excerpt from her preface to a collection of Shelley's poems, she describes her husband's character and summarizes the central themes of his poetry.]

The qualities that struck any one newly introduced to Shelley, were, first, a gentle and cordial goodness that animated his intercourse with warm affection, and helpful sympathy. The other, the eagerness and ardour with which he was attached to the cause of human happiness and improvement; and the fervent eloquence with which he discussed such subjects. His conversation was marked by its happy abundance, and the beautiful language in which he clothed his poetic ideas and philosophical notions. To defecate life of its misery and its evil, was the ruling passion of his soul: he dedicated to it every power of his mind, every pulsation of his heart. He looked on political freedom as the direct agent to effect the happiness of mankind; and thus any new-sprung hope of liberty inspired a joy and an exultation more intense and wild than he could have felt for any personal advantage. Those who have never experienced the workings of passion on general and unselfish subjects cannot understand this; and it must be difficult of comprehension to the younger generation rising around, since they cannot remember the scorn and hatred with which the partisans of reform were regarded some few years ago, nor the persecutions to which they were exposed. He had been from youth the victim of the state of feeling inspired by the reaction of the French Revolution; and believing firmly in the justice and excellence of his view, it cannot be wondered that a nature as sensitive, as impetuous, and as generous as his, should put its whole force into the attempt to alleviate for others the evils of those systems from which he had himself suffered. Many advantages attended his birth; he spurned them all when balanced with what he considered his duties. He was generous to imprudence, devoted to heroism.

These characteristics breathe throughout his poetry. The struggle for human weal; the resolution firm to martyrdom; the impetuous pursuit; the glad triumph in good; the determination not to despair. Such were the features that marked those of his works which he regarded with most complacency, as sustained by a lofty subject and useful aim.

In addition to these, his poems may be divided into two classes,—the purely imaginative, and those which sprung from the emotions of his heart. Among the former may be classed **"The Witch of Atlas,"** *Adonais,* and his latest composition, left imperfect, *The Triumph of Life.* In the first of these particularly, he gave the reins to his fancy, and luxuriated in every idea as it rose; in all, there is that sense of mystery which formed an essential portion of his perception of life—a clinging to the subtler inner spirit, rather than to the outward form—a curious and metaphysical anatomy of human passion and perception.

The second class is, of course, the more popular, as appealing at once to emotions common to us all; some of these rest on the passion of love; others on grief and despondency; others on the sentiments inspired by natural objects. Shelley's conception of love was exalted, absorbing, allied to all that is purest and noblest in our nature, and warmed by earnest passion; such it appears when he gave it a voice in verse. Yet he was usually averse to expressing these feelings, except when highly idealised; and many of his more beautiful effusions he had cast aside, unfinished, and they were never

Principal Works

Original Poetry by Victor and Cazire [as Victor, with Elizabeth Shelley] (poetry) 1810

Posthumous Fragments of Margaret Nicholson [with Thomas Jefferson Hogg] (poetry) 1810

Zastrozzi (novel) 1810

The Necessity of Atheism (essay) 1811

St. Irvyne; or, The Rosicrucian (novel) 1811

An Address to the Irish People (essay) 1812

A Declaration of Rights (essay) 1812

Queen Mab (poetry) 1813

A Refutation of Deism (dialogue) 1814

Alastor; or, The Spirit of Solitude, and Other Poems (poetry) 1816

An Address to the People on the Death of Princess Charlotte [as The Hermit of Marlow] (essay) 1817

"Hymn to Intellectual Beauty" (poetry) 1817; published in periodical The Examiner

A Proposal for Putting Reform to the Vote [as The Hermit of Marlow] (essay) 1817

Laon and Cythna; or, The Revolution of the Golden City: A Vision of the Nineteenth Century (poetry) 1818; also published in revised form as The Revolt of Islam, 1818

The Cenci [first publication] (verse drama) 1819

Rosalind and Helen: A Modern Eclogue, with Other Poems (poetry) 1819

Prometheus Unbound, with Other Poems (verse drama and poetry) 1820

Adonais: An Elegy on the Death of John Keats (poetry) 1821

Epipsychidion (poetry) 1821

Hellas [first publication] (verse drama) 1822

"Julian and Maddalo" (poetry) 1824; published in Posthumous Poems of Percy Bysshe Shelley

Posthumous Poems of Percy Bysshe Shelley (poetry and verse drama) 1824

The Triumph of Life (unfinished poetry) 1824; published in Posthumous Poems of Percy Bysshe Shelley

"The Witch of Atlas" (poetry) 1824; published in Posthumous Poems of Percy Bysshe Shelley

*The Masque of Anarchy (poetry) 1832

†A Defence of Poetry (essay) 1840; published in Essays, Letters from Abroad, Translations, and Fragments by Percy Bysshe Shelley

Essays, Letters from Abroad, Translations, and Fragments by Percy Bysshe Shelley. 2 vols. (essays, letters, translations, and prose) 1840

The Works of Percy Bysshe Shelley (poetry, verse dramas, and essays) 1847

The Complete Works of Percy Bysshe Shelley. 10 vols. (poetry, verse dramas, essays, and translations) 1924-30

The Letters. 2 vols. (letters) 1964

*This work was written in 1819.

†This work was written in 1821.

---

seen by me till after I had lost him. Others, as for instance, **"Rosalind and Helen,"** and **"Lines written among the Euganean Hills,"** I found among his papers by chance; and with some difficulty urged him to complete them. There are others, such as the **"Ode to the Sky Lark,"** and **"The Cloud,"** which, in the opinion of many critics, bear a purer poetical stamp than any other of his productions. They were written as his mind prompted, listening to the carolling of the bird, aloft in the azure sky of Italy; or marking the cloud as it sped across the heavens, while he floated in his boat on the Thames.

No poet was ever warmed by a more genuine and unforced inspiration. His extreme sensibility gave the intensity of passion to his intellectual pursuits; and rendered his mind keenly alive to every perception of outward objects, as well as to his internal sensations. Such a gift is, among the sad vicissitudes of human life, the disappointments we meet, and the galling sense of our own mistakes and errors, fraught with pain; to escape from such, he delivered up his soul to poetry, and

felt happy when he sheltered himself from the influence of human sympathies, in the wildest regions of fancy. His imagination has been termed too brilliant, his thoughts too subtle. He loved to idealise reality; and this is a taste shared by few. We are willing to have our passing whims exalted into passions, for this gratifies our vanity; but few of us understand or sympathise with the endeavour to ally the love of abstract beauty, and adoration of abstract good, . . . with our sympathies with our kind. In this Shelley resembled Plato; both taking more delight in the abstract and the ideal, than in the special and tangible. This did not result from imitation; for it was not till Shelley resided in Italy that he made Plato his study; he then translated his *Symposium* and his *Ion;* and the English language boasts of no more brilliant composition, than Plato's "Praise of Love," translated by Shelley. To return to his own poetry. The luxury of imagination, which sought nothing beyond itself, as a child burthens itself with spring flowers, thinking of no use beyond the enjoyment of gathering them, often showed itself in his verses: they will be only appreciated by minds which have resemblance to his own; and the mystic subtlety of many of his thoughts will share the same fate. The metaphysical strain that characterises much of what he has written, was, indeed, the portion of his works to which, apart from those whose scope was to awaken mankind to aspirations for what he considered the true and good, he was himself particularly attached. There is much, however, that speaks to the many. When he would consent to dismiss these huntings after the obscure, which, entwined with his nature as they were, he did with difficulty, no poet ever expressed in sweeter, more heart-reaching or more passionate verse, the gentler or more forcible emotions of the soul.

A wise friend once wrote to Shelley "You are still very young, and in certain essential respects you do not yet sufficiently perceive that you are so." It is seldom that the young know what youth is, till they have got beyond its period; and time was not given him to attain this knowledge. It must be remembered that there is the stamp of such inexperience on all he wrote; he had not completed his nine-and-twentieth year when he died. The calm of middle life did not add the seal of the virtues which adorn maturity to those generated by the vehement spirit of youth. Through life also he was a martyr to ill health, and constant pain wound up his nerves to a pitch of susceptibility that rendered his views of life different from those of a man in the enjoyment of healthy sensations. Perfectly gentle and forbearing in manner, he suffered a good deal of internal irritability, or rather excitement, and his fortitude to bear was almost always on the stretch; and thus, during a short life, had gone through more experience of sensation, than many whose existence is protracted. "If I die to-morrow," he said, on the eve of his unanticipated death, "I have lived to be older than my father." The weight of thought and feeling burdened him heavily; you read his sufferings in his attentuated frame, while you perceived the mastery he held over them in his animated countenance and brilliant eyes.

He died, and the world showed no outward sign; but his influence over mankind, though slow in growth, is fast augmenting, and in the ameliorations that have taken place in the political state of his country, we may trace in part the operation of his arduous struggles. His spirit gathers peace in its new state from the sense that, though late, his exertions were not made in vain, and in the progress of the liberty he so fondly loved. (pp. xi-xiv)

Mary W. Shelley, "Mrs. Shelley's Preface to the Collected Poems, 1839," in *The Complete Works of Percy Bysshe Shelley: Poems, Vol. I* by Percy Bysshe Shelley, edited by Roger Ingpen and Walter E. Peck, 1926. Reprint by Gordian Press, 1965, pp. ix-xv.

W. B. YEATS
(essay date 1900)

[Yeats was an Irish poet, playwright, and essayist. In the following excerpt from an essay dated 1900, he stresses the importance of understanding Shelley's system of belief, concluding that the author approached a mystical, revolutionary faith.]

When I was a boy in Dublin I was one of a group who rented a room in a mean street to discuss philosophy. My fellow-students got more and more interested in certain modern schools of mystical belief, and I never found anybody to share my one unshakable belief. I thought that whatever of philosophy has been made poetry is alone permanent, and that one should begin to arrange it in some regular order, rejecting nothing as the make-believe of the poets. I thought, so far as I can recollect my thoughts after so many years, that if a powerful and benevolent spirit has shaped the destiny of this world, we can better discover that destiny from the words that have gathered up the heart's desire of the world, than from historical records, or from speculation, wherein the heart withers. Since then I have observed dreams and visions very carefully, and am now certain that the imagination has some way of lighting on the truth that the reason has not, and that its commandments, delivered when the body is still and the reason silent, are the most binding we can ever know. I have re-read *Prometheus Unbound,* which I had hoped my fellow-students would have studied as a sacred book, and it seems to me to have an even more certain place than I had thought among the sacred books of the world. I remember going to a learned scholar to ask about its deep meanings, which I felt more than understood, and his telling me that it was Godwin's *Political Justice* put into rhyme, and that Shelley was a crude revolutionist, and believed that the overturning of kings and priests would regenerate mankind. I quoted the lines which tell how the halcyons ceased to prey on fish, and how poisonous leaves became good for food, to show that he foresaw more than any political regeneration, but was too timid to push the argument. I still believe that one cannot help believing him, as this scholar I know believes him, a vague thinker, who mixed occasional great poetry with a fantastic rhetoric, unless one compares such passages, and above all such passages as describe the liberty he praised, till one has discovered the system of belief that lay behind them. It should seem natural to find his thought full of subtlety, for Mrs. Shelley has told how he hesitated whether he should be a metaphysician or a poet, and has spoken of his 'huntings after the obscure' with regret, and said of the *Prometheus Unbound,* which so many for three generations have thought *Political Justice* put into rhyme,

It requires a mind as subtle and penetrating as his own to understand the mystic meanings scattered throughout the poem. They elude the ordinary reader by their abstraction and delicacy of distinction, but they are far from vague. It was his design to write prose metaphysical essays on the nature of Man, which would have served to explain much of what is obscure in his poetry; a few scattered fragments of observations and remarks alone remain. He considered these philosophical views of Mind and Nature to be instinct with the intensest spirit of poetry.

From these scattered fragments and observations, and from many passages read in their light, one soon comes to understand that his liberty was so much more than the liberty of *Political Justice* that it was one with Intellectual Beauty, and that the regeneration he foresaw was so much more than the regeneration many political dreamers have foreseen, that it could not come in its perfection till the Hours bore 'Time to his tomb in eternity.' In *A Defence of Poetry,* he will have it that the poet and the lawgiver hold their station by the right of the same faculty, the one uttering in words and the other in the forms of society his vision of the divine order, the Intellectual Beauty.

Poets, according to the circumstances of the age and nation in which they appeared, were called in the earliest epoch of the world legislators or prophets, and a poet essentially comprises and unites both these characters. For he not only beholds intensely the present as it is, and discovers those laws according to which present things are to be ordained, but he beholds the future in the present, and his thoughts are the germs of the flowers and the fruit of latest time.

Language, colour, form, and religious and civil habits of action are all the instruments and materials of poetry.

Poetry is

the creation of actions according to the unchangeable process of human nature as existing in the mind of the creator, which is itself the image of all other minds.

Poets have been challenged to resign the civic crown to reasoners and merchants. . . . It is admitted that the exercise of the imagination is the most delightful, but it is alleged that that of reason is the more useful. . . . Whilst the mechanist abridges and the political economist combines labour, let them be sure that their speculations, for want of correspondence with those first principles which belong to the imagination, do not tend, as they have in modern

England, to exasperate at once the extremes of luxury and want. . . . The rich have become richer, the poor have become poorer, . . . such are the effects which must ever flow from an unmitigated exercise of the calculating faculty.

The speaker of these things might almost be Blake, who held that the Reason not only created Ugliness, but all other evils. The books of all wisdom are hidden in the cave of the Witch of Atlas, who is one of his personifications of beauty, and when she moves over the enchanted river that is an image of all life, the priests cast aside their deceits, and the king crowns an ape to mock his own sovereignty, and the soldiers gather about the anvils to beat their swords to ploughshares, and lovers cast away their timidity, and friends are united; while the power which, in *Laon and Cythna,* awakens the mind of the reformer to contend, and itself contends, against the tyrannies of the world, is first seen as the star of love or beauty. And at the end of the **"Ode to Naples,"** he cries out to 'the spirit of beauty' to overturn the tyrannies of the world, or to fill them with its 'harmonising ardours.' He calls the spirit of beauty liberty, because despotism, and perhaps, as 'the man of virtuous soul commands not, nor obeys,' all authority, pluck virtue from her path towards beauty, and because it leads us by that love whose service is perfect freedom. It leads all things by love, for he cries again and again that love is the perception of beauty in thought and things, and it orders all things by love, for it is love that impels the soul to its expressions in thought and in action, by making us 'seek to awaken in all things that are, a community with what we experience within ourselves.' 'We are born into the world, and there is something within us which, from the instant that we live, more and more thirsts after its likeness.' We have 'a soul within our soul that describes a circle around its proper paradise which pain and sorrow and evil dare not overleap,' and we labour to see this soul in many mirrors, that we may possess it the more abundantly. He would hardly seek the progress of the world by any less gentle labour, and would hardly have us resist evil itself. He bids the reformers in [*A Philosophical View of Reform*] receive 'the onset of the cavalry,' if it be sent to disperse their meetings, 'with folded arms,' and 'not because active resistence is not justifiable, but because temperance and courage would produce greater advantages than the most decisive victory'; and he gives them like advice in *The Masque of Anarchy,* for liberty, the poems cries, 'is love,' and can make the rich man kiss its feet, and, like those who followed Christ, give away his goods and follow it throughout the world.

He does not believe that the reformation of society can bring this beauty, this divine order, among men without the regeneration of the hearts of men. Even in *Queen Mab,* which was written before he had found his deepest thought, or rather perhaps before he had found words to utter it, for I do not think men change much in their deepest thought, he is less anxious to change men's beliefs, as I think, than to cry out against that serpent more subtle than any beast of the field, 'the cause and effect of tyranny.' He affirms again and again that the virtuous, those who have 'pure desire and universal love,' are happy in the midst of tyranny, and he foresees a day when the 'Spirit of Nature,' the Spirit of Beauty of his later poems, who has her 'throne of power unappealable' in every human heart, shall have made men so virtuous that 'kingly glare will lose its power to dazzle,' and 'silently pass by,' and, as it seems, commerce, 'the venal interchange of all that human art or nature yield; which wealth should purchase not,' come as silently to an end.

He was always, indeed in chief, a witness for that 'power unappealable.' Maddalo, in **"Julian and Maddalo,"** says that the soul is powerless, and can only, like a 'dreary bell hung in a heaven-illumined tower, toll our thoughts and our desires to meet below round the rent heart and pray'; but Julian, who is Shelley himself, replies, as the makers of all religions have replied:—

> Where is the love, beauty, and truth we seek
> But in our mind? And if we were not weak,
> Should we be less in deed than in desire?

while **"Mont Blanc"** is an intricate analogy to affirm that the soul has its sources in 'the secret strength of things which governs thoughts, and to the infinite dome of heaven is as a law.' He even thought that men might be immortal were they sinless, and his Cythna bids the sailors be without remorse, for all that live are stained as they are. It is thus, she says, that time marks men and their thoughts for the tomb. And the 'Red Comet,' the image of evil in *Laon and Cythna,* when it began its war with the star of beauty, brought not only 'Fear, Hatred, Fraud and Tyranny,' but 'Death, Decay, Earthquake, and Blight and Madness pale.'

When the Red Comet is conquered, when Jupiter is overthrown by Demogorgon, when the prophecy of Queen Mab is fulfilled, visible Nature will put on perfection again. Shelley declares, in one of the notes to *Queen Mab,* that 'there is no great extravagance in presuming . . . that there should be a perfect identity between the moral and physical improvement of the human species,' and thinks it 'certain that wisdom is not compatible with disease, and that, in the present state of the climates of the earth, health, in the true and comprehensive sense of the word, is out of the reach of civilised man.' In *Prometheus Unbound* he sees, as in the ecstasy of a saint, the ships moving among the seas of the world without fear of danger—

> by the light
> Of wave-reflected flowers, and floating
> odours,
> And music soft,

and poison dying out of the green things, and cruelty out of all living things, and even the toads and efts becoming beautiful, and at last Time being borne 'to his tomb in eternity.'

This beauty, this divine order, whereof all things shall become a part in a kind of resurrection of the body, is already visible to the dead and to souls in ecstasy, for ecstasy is a kind of death. The dying Lionel hears the song of the nightingale, and cries:—

> Heardst thou not sweet words among
> That heaven-resounding minstrelsy?
> Heardst thou not, that those who die
> Awake in a world of ecstasy?
> That love, when limbs are interwoven,
> And sleep, when the night of life is cloven,
> And thought, to the world's dim boundaries clinging,
> And music, when one beloved is singing,
> Is death? Let us drain right joyously
> The cup which the sweet bird fills for me.

And in the most famous passage in all his poetry he sings of Death as of a mistress. 'Life, like a dome of many-coloured glass, stains the white radiance of Eternity.' 'Die, if thou wouldst be with that which thou dost seek'; and he sees his own soon-coming death in a rapture of prophecy, for 'the fire for which all thirst' beams upon him, 'consuming the last clouds of cold mortality.' When he is dead he will still influence the living, for though Adonais has fled 'to the burning fountain whence he came,' and 'is a portion of the Eternal which must glow through time and change, unquenchably the same,' and has 'awakened from the dream of life,' he has not gone from the 'young Dawn,' or the caverns and the forests, or the 'faint flowers and fountains.' He has been 'made one with Nature,' and his voice is 'heard in all her music,' and his presence is felt wherever 'that Power may move which has withdrawn his being to its own,' and he bears 'his part' when it is compelling mortal things to their appointed forms, and he overshadows men's minds at their supreme moments, for—

> when lofty thought
> Lifts a young heart above its mortal lair,
> And love and life contend in it for what
> Shall be its earthly doom, the dead live there,
> And move like winds of light on dark and stormy air.

'Of his speculations as to what will befall this inestimable spirit when we appear to die,' Mrs. Shelley has written,

a mystic ideality tinged these speculations in Shelley's mind; certain stanzas in the poem of *The Sensitive Plant* express, in some degree, the almost inexpressible idea, not that we die into another state, when this state is no longer, from some reason, un-apparent as well as apparent, accordant with our being—but that those who rise above the ordinary nature of man, fade from before our imperfect organs; they remain in their "love, beauty, and delight," in a world congenial to them, and we, clogged by "error, ignorance, and strife," see them not till we are fitted by purification and improvement to their higher state.

Not merely happy souls, but all beautiful places and movements and gestures and events, when we think they have ceased to be, have become portions of the Eternal.

> In this life
> Of error, ignorance and strife,
> Where nothing is, but all things seem,
> And we the shadows of the dream,
>
> It is a modest creed, and yet
> Pleasant, if one considers it,
> To own that death itself must be,
> Like all the rest, a mockery.
>
> That garden sweet, that lady fair,
> And all sweet shapes and odours there,
> In truth have never past away;
> 'Tis we, 'tis ours, are changed, not they.
>
> For love, and beauty, and delight
> There is no death nor change; their might
> Exceeds our organs, which endure
> No light, being themselves obscure.

He seems in his speculations to have lit on that memory of Nature the visionaries claim for the foundation of their knowledge; but I do not know whether he thought, as they do, that all things good and evil remain for ever, 'thinking the thought and doing the deed,' though not, it may be, self-conscious; or only thought that 'love and beauty and delight' remain for ever. The passage where Queen Mab awakes 'all knowledge of the past,' and the good and evil 'events of old and wondrous times,' was no more doubtless than a part of the machinery of the poem, but all the machineries of poetry are parts of the convictions of antiquity, and readily become again convictions in minds that brood over them with visionary intensity.

Intellectual Beauty has not only the happy dead to do her will, but ministering spirits who correspond to the Devas of the East, and the Elemental Spirits of mediaeval Europe, and the Sidhe of ancient Ireland, and whose too constant presence, and perhaps Shelley's ignorance of their more traditional forms, give some of his poetry an air of rootless fantasy. They change continually in his poetry, as they do in the visions of the mystics everywhere and of the common people in Ireland, and the forms of these changes display, in an especial sense, the flowing forms of his mind when freed from all impulse not out of itself or out of supersensual power. These are 'gleams of a remoter world which visit us in sleep,' spiritual essences whose shadows are the delights of all the senses, sounds 'folded in cells of crystal silence,' 'visions swift, and sweet, and quaint,' which lie waiting their moment 'each in its thin sheath, like a chrysalis,' 'odours' among 'ever-blooming Eden-trees,' 'liquors' that can give 'happy sleep,' or can make tears 'all wonder and delight'; 'the golden genii who spoke to the poets of Greece in dreams'; 'the phantoms' which become the forms of the arts when 'the mind, arising bright from the embrace of beauty,' 'casts on them the gathered rays which are reality'; 'the guardians' who move in 'the atmosphere of human thought,' as 'the birds within the wind, or the fish within the wave,' or man's thought itself through all things; and who join the throng of the happy Hours when Time is passing away—

> As the flying-fish leap
> From the Indian deep,
> And mix with the sea-birds half asleep.

It is these powers which lead Asia and Panthea, as they would lead all the affections of humanity, by words written upon leaves, by faint songs, by eddies of echoes that draw 'all spirits on that secret way,' by the 'dying odours' of flowers and by 'the sunlight of the spherèd dew,' beyond the gates of birth and death to awake Demogorgon, eternity, that 'the painted veil called life' may be 'torn aside.'

There are also ministers of ugliness and all evil, like those that came to Prometheus:—

> As from the rose which the pale priestess kneels
> To gather for her festal crown of flowers
> The aërial crimson falls, flushing her cheek,
> So from our victim's destined agony
> The shade which is our form invests us round;
> Else we are shapeless as our mother Night.

Or like those whose shapes the poet sees in *The Triumph of Life,* coming from the procession that follows the car of life, as 'hope' changes to 'desire,' shadows 'numerous as the dead leaves blown in autumn evening from a poplar-tree'; and resembling those they come from, until, if I understand an obscure phrase aright, they are 'wrapt' round 'all the busy phantoms that were there as the sun shapes the clouds.' Some to sit 'chattering like restless apes,' and some like 'old anatomies' 'hatching their bare broods under the shade of demon wings,' laughing 'to reassume the delegated power' they had given to the tyrants of the earth, and some 'like small gnats and flies' to throng 'about the brow of lawyers, statesmen, priest and theorist,' and some 'like discoloured flakes of snow' to fall 'on fairest bosoms and the sunniest hair,' to be 'melted by the youthful glow which they extinguished,' and many to 'fling shadows of shadows, yet unlike themselves,' shadows that are shaped into new forms by that 'creative ray' in which all move like motes.

These ministers of beauty and ugliness were certainly more than metaphors or picturesque phrases to one who believed the 'thoughts which are called real or external objects' differed but in regularity of recurrence from 'hallucinations, dreams, and the ideas of madness,' and lessened this difference by telling how he had dreamed 'three several times, between intervals of two or more years, the same precise dream,' and who had seen images with the mind's eye that left his nerves shaken for days together. Shadows that were—

> as when there hovers
> A flock of vampire-bats before the glare
> Of the tropic sun, bringing, ere evening,
> Strange night upon some Indian isle,

could not but have had more than a metaphorical and picturesque being to one who had spoken in terror with an image of himself, and who had fainted at the apparition of a woman with eyes in her breasts, and who had tried to burn down a wood, if we can trust Mrs. Williams' account, because he believed a devil, who had first tried to kill him, had sought refuge there.

It seems to me, indeed, that Shelley had reawakened in himself the age of faith, though there were times when he would doubt, as even the saints have doubted, and that he was a revolutionist, because he had heard the commandment, 'If ye know these things, happy are ye if ye do them.' I have re-read his *Prometheus Unbound* for the first time for many years, in the woods of Drim-na-Rod, among the Echtge hills, and sometimes I have looked towards Slieve ná nOg where the country people say the last battle of the world shall be fought till the third day, when a priest shall lift a chalice, and the thousand years of peace begin. And I think this mysterious song utters a faith as simple and as ancient as the faith of those country people, in a form suited to a new age, that will understand with Blake that the Holy Spirit is 'an intellectual fountain,' and that the kinds and degrees of beauty are the images of its authority. (pp. 65-78)

W. B. Yeats, "The Philosophy of Shelley's Poetry," in his *Essays and Introductions,* The Macmillan Company, 1961, pp. 65-95.

HERBERT READ
(essay date 1936)

[Read was a prolific English poet, critic, and novelist. In the following excerpt, he investigates the "particular quality" of Shelley's poetry.]

The particular quality of Shelley's poetry still remains to be defined. It is a quality directly related to the nature of his personality. . . . Understanding the personality, we may more easily, more openly, appreciate the poetry.

Byron, who was a very honest critic, even of his friends, was the first to be aware of Shelley's *particular* quality. "You know my high opinion of your own poetry," he wrote to Shelley, and added the reason: "—because it is of *no* school." To Byron all the rest of his contemporaries seemed "secondhand" imitators of antique models or doctrinaire exponents of a mannerism. Shelley alone could not be so simply classified; his verse was too honestly original, too independently thought and wrought, to be accepted as "fashionable literature." For there are always these two types of originality: originality that responds like the Aeolian harp to every gust of contemporary feeling, pleasing by its anticipation of what is but half-formed in the public consciousness; and originality that is not influenced by anything outside the poet's own consciousness, but is the direct product of his individual mind and independent feeling. The latter type is always long in winning recognition, and since Shelley's originality was essentially of this type, we need not be surprised that only a few of his contemporaries appreciated his poetry for its proper qualities.

The reaction of Keats is the most interesting, for he had perhaps a profounder understanding of the nature of poetry than any man of that age—profounder, I would say, than Bryon and even profounder than Coleridge. We only discern this from the occasional statements made in his letters—there is unfortunately no formal essay to compare with Shelley's. Nor did Keats live to write poetry with which he was personally satisfied; we must not, that is to say, treat the poetry of Keats as an exemplification of his poetic ideals. A detailed comparison of the poetry of Keats and Shelley would not therefore be of great value. But Keats's reaction to Shelley's poetry, expressed in a letter to Shelley, is most definitely critical:

> . . . You might curb your magnanimity and be more of an artist, and load every rift of your subject with ore. The thought of such discipline must fall

like cold chains upon you, who perhaps never sat with your wings furled for six months together.

We cannot doubt the force of the impact which Shelley's poetry had made on Keats. The poetry had been felt, but felt as something strange or inadequate. And actually we can see that what is involved is a clash of personalities. There is no need to describe Keats's personality at length; but it was in no way parallel to Shelley's. Keats was not, of course, a normal type—no genius is; but compared with Shelley he was far more fully adjusted to his environment; physically more masculine and heterosexual; and though a sick man ("when I shook him by the hand there was death"), not a morbid one. . . . Now though much of Keats's poetry is anything but definite and objective, he was very conscious of an intolerable hiatus between his personality and the poetic diction he had derived from traditional models and current fashions; and his whole effort, as expressed in his short but intense poetic development, is towards objective virtues.

The whole tendency of Shelley, on the contrary, is towards a clarification and abstraction of thought—away from the personal and the particular towards the general and the universal. Between the transcendental intellectualism of Shelley and the concrete sensualism of Keats there could be, and was no contact.

The highest beauties of Keats's poetry are enumerative: a positive evocation of the tone and texture of physical objects. Even when describing an abstract conception like Melancholy, the imagery of physical sensation is dominant:

Ay, in the very temple of Delight
    Veil'd Melancholy has her sovran shrine,
        Though seen of none save him whose strenuous tongue
Can burst Joy's grape against his palate fine . . .

But the highest beauties of Shelley's poetry are evanescent and imponderable—thought so tenuous and intuitive, that it has no visual equivalent; no positive impact:

Life of Life! thy lips enkindle
    With their love the breath between them;
And thy smiles before they dwindle
    Make the cold air fire; then screen them
In those looks, where whoso gazes
Faints, entangled in their mazes.

Child of Light! thy limbs are burning
    Through the vest which seems to hide them;
As the radiant lines of morning
    Through the clouds ere they divide them;
And this atmosphere divinest
Shrouds thee wheresoe'er thou shinest.

Fair are others; none beholds thee,
    But thy voice sounds low and tender

Like the fairest, for it folds thee
    From the sight, that liquid splendour,
And all feel, yet see thee never,
As I feel now, lost for ever!

Lamp of Earth! where'er thou movest
    Its dim shapes are clad with brightness,
And the souls of whom thou lovest
    Walk upon the winds with lightness,
Till they fail, as I am failing,
Dizzy, lost, yet unbewailing!

In such a poem—and it is the supreme type of Shelley's poetic utterance—every image fades into air, every outline is dissolved in fire. The idea conveyed—the notional content—is almost negligible; the poetry exists in the suspension of meaning, in the avoidance of actuality.

In other words, such poetry has no precision, and the process of its unfolding is not logical. It does not answer to a general definition of any kind. It is vain to apply to it that method of criticism which assumes that the ardour of a verse can be analysed into separate vocables, and that poetry is a function of sound. Poetry is mainly a function of language—the exploitation of a medium, a vocal and mental material, in the interests of a personal mood or emotion, or of the thoughts evoked by such moods and emotions. I do not think we can say much more about it; according to our sensitivity we recognise its success. The rest of our reasoning about it is either mere prejudice, ethical anxiety, or academic pride.

Among his contemporaries, Shelley was perhaps nearest in poetic quality to Landor, whose *Gebir* was a lasting joy to him. A critical justification for this attraction would not be far to seek. The next nearest analogies are with Schiller and Goethe, both of whom Shelley read with enthusiasm; the influence of *Faust* has been traced in *The Triumph of Life*, but between Goethe and Shelley there is a general sympathy of poetic outlook which is not explained by direct contacts. Other analogies . . . are remoter: "the gentle seriousness, the delicate sensibility, the calm and sustained energy" of Ariosto; and above all "the first awakener of entranced Europe . . . the congregator of those great spirits who presided over the resurrection of learning; the Lucifer of that starry flock which in the thirteenth century shone forth from republican Italy as from a heaven, into the darkness of the benighted world"—Dante. All great poetry, said Shelley in the same reference to Dante, is *infinite*; and that is the final quality of his own poetry, the quality which lifts it into regions beyond the detractions of moralists and sciolists.

Shelley is of no school; that is to say, Shelley is above all schools, universal in the mode of his expression and the passion of his mind. That passion, the force that urged him to abundant voice, was simple, almost single, in its aim. "I knew Shelley more intimately than any man," wrote Hogg, "but I never could discern in him any more than two fixed principles. The first was a strong, irrepressible love of liberty; of liberty in the abstract, and somewhat after the pattern of the ancient republics, without reference to the English constitution, respecting which he knew little and cared nothing, heeding it not at all. The second was an equally ardent love of toleration of all opinions, but more especially of religious opinions; of toleration, complete, entire, universal, unlimited; and, as a deduction and corollary from which latter principle, he felt an intense abhorrence of persecution of every kind, public or private." Liberty and toleration—these words have a tortured history, and are often perverted for a moral purpose. But that was not Shelley's intention. "The highest moral purpose aimed at in the highest species of the drama, is the teaching the human heart, through its sympathies and antipathies, the knowledge of itself; in proportion to the possession of which knowledge, every human being is wise, just, sincere, tolerant and kind." Inasmuch as the final quality of Shelley's poetry is infinitude, so the final quality of his mind is sympathy. Sympathy and infinitude—these are expansive virtues, not avowed in the dry air of disillusion, awaiting a world of peace and justice for their due recognition. (pp. 80-86)

Herbert Read, "In Defence of Shelley," in his *In Defence of Shelley and Other Essays,* William Heinemann Ltd., 1936, pp. 1-86.

HAROLD BLOOM

(essay date 1965)

[Bloom, an American critic and editor, is best known as the formulator of "revisionism," a controversial literary theory based on the concept that all poets are subject to the influence of earlier poets and that, to develop individual voices, they attempt to overcome this influence through a deliberate process of "creative correction," which Bloom calls "misreading." In the following excerpt from an essay first published in 1965, he provides a general introduction to Shelley's poetry.]

Percy Bysshe Shelley, one of the greatest lyrical poets in Western tradition, has been dead for more than a hundred and forty years, and critics have abounded, from his own day to ours, to insist that his poetry died with him. Until recently, it was fashionable to apologize for Shelley's poetry, if one liked it at all. Each reader of poetry, however vain, can speak only for himself, and there will be only description and praise in this introduction, for after many years of reading Shelley's poems, I find nothing in them that needs apology. Shel-

ley is a unique poet, one of the most original in the language, and he is in many ways *the* poet proper, as much so as any in the language. His poetry is autonomous, finely wrought, in the highest degree imaginative, and has the spiritual form of vision stripped of all veils and ideological coverings, the vision many readers justly seek in poetry, despite the admonitions of a multitude of churchwardenly critics. (p. 87)

The urbane lyricism of the **"Hymn of Apollo,"** and the harshly self-conscious, internalized dramatic quality of *The Triumph of Life* are both central to Shelley. Most central is the prophetic intensity, as much a result of displaced Protestantism as it is in Blake or in Wordsworth, but seeming more an Orphic than Hebraic phenomenon when it appears in Shelley. Religious poet as he primarily was, what Shelley prophesied was one restored Man who transcended men, gods, the natural world, and even the poetic faculty. Shelley chants the apotheosis, not of the poet, but of desire itself:

Man, oh, not men! a chain of linkèd thought,
  Of love and might to be divided not,
Compelling the elements with adamantine stress;
  As the sun rules, even with a tyrant's gaze,
  The unquiet republic of the maze
Of planets, struggling fierce towards heaven's free
  wilderness.
Man, one harmonious soul of many a soul,
  Whose nature is its own divine control,
Where all things flow to all, as rivers to the sea. . . .

The rhapsodic intensity, the cumulative drive and yet firm control of those last three lines in particular, as the high song of humanistic celebration approaches its goal—that seems to me what is crucial in Shelley, and its presence throughout much of his work constitutes his special excellence as a poet.

Lyrical poetry at its most intense frequently moves toward direct address between one human consciousness and another, in which the "I" of the poet directly invokes the personal "Thou" of the reader. Shelley is an intense lyricist as Alexander Pope is an intense satirist; even as Pope assimilates every literary form he touches to satire, so Shelley converts forms as diverse as drama, prose essay, romance, satire, epyllion, into lyric. To an extent he himself scarcely realized, Shelley's genius desired a transformation of all experience, natural and literary, into the condition of lyric. More than all other poets, Shelley's compulsion is to present life as a direct confrontation of equal realities. This compulsion seeks absolute intensity, and courts straining and breaking in consequence. When expressed as love, it must manifest itself as mutual destruction:

In one another's substance finding food,
Like flames too pure and light and unimbued
To nourish their bright lives with baser prey,
Which point to Heaven and cannot pass away:

One Heaven, one Hell, one immortality,
And one annihilation.

Shelley is the poet of these flames, and he is equally the poet of a particular shadow, which falls perpetually between all such flames, a shadow of ruin that tracks every imaginative flight of fire:

O, Thou, who plumed with strong desire
    Wouldst float above the earth, beware!
A Shadow tracks thy flight of fire—
    Night is coming!

By the time Shelley had reached his final phase, of which the great monuments are *Adonais* and *The Triumph of Life,* he had become altogether the poet of this shadow of ruin, and had ceased to celebrate the possibilities of imaginative relationship. In giving himself, at last, over to the dark side of his own vision, he resolved (or perhaps merely evaded, judgment being so difficult here) a conflict within his self and poetry that had been present from the start. Though it has become a commonplace of recent criticism and scholarship to affirm otherwise, I do not think that Shelley changed very much, as a poet, during the last (and most important) six years of his life, from the summer of 1816 until the summer of 1822. The two poems of self-discovery, of mature poetic incarnation, written in 1816, **"Mont Blanc"** and the **"Hymn to Intellectual Beauty,"** reveal the two contrary aspects of Shelley's vision that his entire sequence of major poems reveals. The head and the heart, each totally honest in encountering reality, yield rival reports as to the name and nature of reality. The head, in **"Mont Blanc,"** learns, like Blake, that there is no natural religion. There is a Power, a secret strength of things, but it hides its true shape or its shapelessness behind or beneath a dread mountain, and it shows itself only as an indifference, or even pragmatically a malevolence, toward the well-being of men. But the Power speaks forth, through a poet's act of confrontation with it that is the very act of writing his poem, and the Power, rightly interpreted, can be used to repeal the large code of fraud, institutional and historical Christianity, and the equally massive code of woe, the laws of the nation-states of Europe in the age of Castlereagh and Metternich. In the **"Hymn to Intellectual Beauty"** a very different Power is invoked, but with a deliberate and even austere tenuousness. A shadow, itself invisible, of an unseen Power, sweeps through our dull dense world, momentarily awakening both nature and man to a sense of love and beauty, a sense just beyond the normal range of apprehension. But the shadow departs, for all its benevolence and despite the poet's prayers for its more habitual sway. The heart's responses have not failed, but the shadow that is antithetically a radiance will not come to stay. The mind, searching for what would suffice, encountered an icy remoteness, but dared to affirm the triumph of its imaginings over the

solitude and vacancy of an inadvertent nature. The emotions, visited by delight, felt the desolation of powerlessness, but dared to hope for a fuller visitation. Both odes suffer from the evident straining of their creator to reach a finality, but both survive in their creator's tough honesty and gathering sense of form. (pp. 88-90)

Shelley was anything but a born poet, as even a brief glance at his apprentice work will demonstrate. Blake at fourteen was a great lyric poet; Shelley at twenty-two was still a bad one. He found himself, as a stylist, in the autumn of 1815, when he composed the astonishing **"Alastor,"** a blank verse rhapsodic narrative of a destructive and subjective quest. **"Alastor,"** though it has been out of fashion for a long time, is nevertheless a great and appalling work, at once a dead end, and a prophecy that Shelley finally could not evade. (p. 91)

The poem is an extremely subtle internalization of the quest-theme of romance, and the price demanded for the internalization is first, the death-in-life of what Yeats called "enforced self-realization," and at last, death itself. The Alastor or avenging demon of the title is the dark double of the poet-hero, the spirit of solitude that shadows him even as he quests after his emanative portion, the soul out of his soul that Shelley later called the epipsyche. Shelley's poet longs to realize a vision, and this intense and overconstant yearning destroys natural existence, for nature cannot contain the infinite energy demanded by the vision. Wordsworthian nature, and not the poet-hero, is the equivocal element in **"Alastor,"** the problem the reader needs to, but cannot, resolve. (p. 92)

Prometheus Unbound is a remarkably subtle and difficult poem. That a work of such length needs to be read with all the care and concentration a trained reader brings to a difficult and condensed lyric is perhaps unfortunate, yet Shelley himself affirmed that his major poem had been written only for highly adept readers, and that he hoped for only a few of these. *Prometheus Unbound* is not as obviously difficult as Blake's *The Four Zoas,* but it presents problems comparable to that work. Blake has the advantage of having made a commonplace understanding of his major poems impossible, while Shelley retains familiar (and largely misleading) mythological names like Prometheus and Jupiter. The problems of interpretation in Shelley's lyrical drama are as formidable as English poetry affords, and are perhaps finally quite unresolvable. (p. 96)

Published with *Prometheus Unbound* in 1820 were a group of Shelley's major odes, including **"Ode to the West Wind," "To a Skylark,"** and **"Ode to Liberty."** These poems show Shelley as a lyricist deliberately seeking to extend the sublime mode, and are among his finest achievements.

Wallace Stevens, in one of the marvelous lyrics of his old age, hears the cry of the leaves and knows, "it is the cry of leaves that do not transcend themselves," knows that the cry means no more than can be found "in the final finding of the ear, in the thing / Itself." From this it follows, with massive but terrible dignity, that "at last, the cry concerns no one at all." This is Stevens' modern reality of *decreation,* and this is the fate that Shelley's magnificent **"Ode to the West Wind"** seeks to avert. Shelley hears a cry of leaves that do transcend themselves, and he deliberately seeks a further transcendence that will metamorphosize "the thing itself " into human form, so that at last the cry will concern all men. But in Shelley's **"Ode,"** as in Stevens's "there is a conflict, there is a resistance involved; / And being part is an exertion that declines." Shelley too feels the frightening strength of the *given,* "the life of that which gives life as it is," but here as elsewhere Shelley does not accept the merely "as it is." The function of his **"Ode"** is apocalyptic, and the controlled fury of his spirit is felt throughout this perfectly modulated "trumpet of a prophecy."

What is most crucial to an understanding of the **"Ode"** is the realization that its fourth and fifth stanzas bear a wholly antithetical relation to one another. The triple invocation to the elements of earth, air, and water occupies the first three stanzas of the poem, and the poet himself does not enter those stanzas; in them he is only a voice imploring the elements to hear. In the fourth stanza, the poet's ego enters the poem, but in the guise only of a battered Job, seeking to lose his own humanity. From this nadir, the extraordinary and poignantly "broken" music of the last stanza rises up, into the poet's own element of fire, to affirm again the human dignity of the prophet's vocation, and to suggest a mode of imaginative renovation that goes beyond the cyclic limitations of nature. Rarely in the history of poetry have seventy lines done so much so well.

Shelley's other major odes are out of critical favor in our time, but this is due as much to actual misinterpretations as to any qualities inherent in these poems. **"To a Skylark"** strikes readers as silly when they visualize the poet staring at the bird and hailing it as nonexistent, but these readers have begun with such gross inaccuracy that their experience of what they take to be the poem may simply be dismissed. The ode's whole point turns on the lark's being out of sight from the start; the poet *hears* an evanescent song, but can see nothing, even as Keats in the "Ode to a Nightingale" never actually sees the bird. Flying too high almost to be heard, the lark is crucially compared by Shelley to his central symbol, the morning star fading into the dawn of an unwelcome day. What can barely be heard, and not seen at all, is still discovered to be a basis upon which to rejoice, and indeed becomes an inescapable motive for metaphor, a dark justification for celebrating

the light of uncommon day. In the great revolutionary **"Ode to Liberty,"** Shelley successfully adapts the English Pindaric to an abstract political theme, mostly by means of making the poem radically its own subject, as he does on a larger scale in **"The Witch of Atlas"** and *Epipsychidion.*

In the last two years of his life, Shelley subtly modified his lyrical art, making the best of his shorter poems the means by which his experimental intellectual temper and his more traditional social urbanity could be reconciled. The best of these lyrics would include **"Hymn of Apollo," "The Two Spirits: An Allegory," "To Night," "Lines . . . on . . . the Death of Napoleon,"** and the final group addressed to Jane Williams, or resulting from the poet's love for her, including **"When the lamp is shattered," "To Jane: The Invitation," "The Recollection," "With a Guitar, to Jane,"** and the last completed lyric, the immensely moving **"Lines Written in the Bay of Lerici."** Here are nine lyrics as varied and masterful as the language affords. Take these together with Shelley's achievements in the sublime ode, with the best of his earlier lyrics, and with the double handful of magnificent interspersed lyrics contained in *Prometheus Unbound* and *Hellas,* and it will not seem as if Swinburne was excessive in claiming for Shelley a rank as one of the two or three major lyrical poets in English tradition down to Swinburne's own time.

The best admonition to address to a reader of Shelley's lyrics, as of his longer poems, is to slow down and read very closely, so as to learn what Wordsworth could have meant when he reluctantly conceded that "Shelley is one of the best *artists* of us all: I mean in workmanship of style."

The Cenci occupies a curious place in Shelley's canon, one that is overtly apart from the sequence of his major works that goes from *Prometheus Unbound* to *The Triumph of Life.* Unlike the pseudo-Elizabethan tragedies of Shelley's disciple Beddoes, *The Cenci* is in no obvious way a visionary poem. Yet it is a tragedy only in a very peculiar sense, and has little in common with the stageplays it ostensibly seeks to emulate. Its true companions, and descendants, are Browning's giant progression of dramatic monologues, *The Ring and the Book,* and certain works of Hardy that share its oddly effective quality of what might be termed dramatic solipsism, to have recourse to a desperate oxymoron. Giant incongruities clash in *Prometheus Unbound* as they do in Blake's major poems, but the clashes are resolved by both poets in the realms of a self-generated mythology. When parallel incongruities meet violently in *The Cenci,* in a context that excludes myth, the reader is asked to accept as human characters beings whose states of mind are too radically and intensely pure to be altogether human. Blake courts a similar problem whenever he is only at the borderline of his own mythical world, as in *Visions of the Daughters of Albion* and *The French Revolution.* Shelley's Beatrice and Blake's Oothoon are either too human or not human enough; the reader is uncomfortable in not knowing whether he encounters a Titaness or one of his own kind.

Yet this discomfort need not wreck the experience of reading *The Cenci,* which is clearly a work that excels in character rather than in plot, and more in the potential of character than in its realization. At the heart of *The Cenci* is Shelley's very original conception of tragedy. Tragedy is not a congenial form for apocalyptic writers, who tend to have a severe grudge against it, as Blake and D. H. Lawrence did. Shelley's morality was an apocalyptic one, and the implicit standard for *The Cenci* is set in *The Mask of Anarchy,* which advocates a nonviolent resistance to evil. Beatrice is tragic because she does *not* meet this high standard, though she is clearly superior to every other person in her world. Life triumphs over Beatrice because she does take violent revenge upon an intolerable oppressor. The tragedy Shelley develops is one of a heroic character "violently thwarted from her nature" by circumstances she ought to have defied. This allies Beatrice with a large group of Romantic heroes, ranging from the Cain of Byron's

drama to the pathetic daemon of Mary Shelley's *Frankenstein* and, on the cosmic level, embracing Shelley's own Prometheus and the erring Zoas or demigods of Blake's myth. (pp. 103-04)

The aesthetic power of *The Cenci* lies in the perfection with which it both sets forth Beatrice's intolerable dilemma, and presents the reader with a parallel dilemma. The natural man in the reader exults at Beatrice's metamorphosis into a relentless avenger, and approves even her untruthful denial of responsibility for her father's murder. The imaginative man in the reader is appalled at the degeneration of an all-but-angelic intelligence into a skilled intriguer and murderess. This fundamental dichotomy *in the reader* is the theater where the true anguish of *The Cenci* is enacted. The overt theme becomes the universal triumph of life over integrity, which is to say of death-in-life over life. (p. 105)

In the spring of 1820, at Pisa, Shelley wrote *The Sensitive Plant,* a remarkably original poem, and a permanently valuable one, though it is little admired in recent years. As a parable of imaginative failure, the poem is another of the many Romantic versions of the

Casa Magni, Shelley's last home, on the Bay of San Terenzo, near Lerici.

Miltonic Eden's transformation into a wasteland, but the limitations it explores are not the Miltonic ones of human irresolution and disobedience. Like all of Shelley's major poems, *The Sensitive Plant* is a skeptical work, the skepticism here manifesting itself as a precariously posed suspension of judgment on the human capacity to perceive whether or not natural *or* imaginative values survive the cyclic necessities of change and decay. (pp. 105-06)

The tone of *The Sensitive Plant* is a deliberate exquisitiveness, of a more-than-Spenserian kind. . . .

The dark melancholy of *The Sensitive Plant* is not Spenserian, but everything else in the poem to some extent is. Like many poems in this tradition, the lament is for mutability itself, for change seen as loss. What is lost is innocence, natural harmony, the mutual interpenetrations of a merely given condition that is nevertheless whole and beyond the need of justification. The new state, experiential life as seen in Part III of the poem, is the world without imagination, a tract of weeds. When Shelley, in the noblest quatrains he ever wrote, broods on this conclusion he offers no consolation beyond the most urbane of his skepticisms. The light that puts out our eyes is a darkness to us, yet remains light, and death may be a mockery of our inadequate imaginations. The myth of the poem—its garden, lady, and plant—may have prevailed, while we, the poem's readers, may be too decayed in our perceptions to know this. Implicit in Shelley's poem is a passionate refutation of time, but the passion is a desperation unless the mind's imaginings can cleanse perception of its obscurities. Nothing in the poem proper testifies to the mind's mastery of outward sense. The "Conclusion" hints at what Shelley beautifully calls "a modest creed," but the poet is too urbane and skeptical to urge it upon either us or himself. The creed appears again in **"The Witch of Atlas,"** but with a playful and amiable disinterestedness that removes it almost entirely from the anguish of human desire.

"The Witch of Atlas" is Shelley's most inventive poem, and is by any just standards a triumph. In kind, it goes back to the English Renaissance epyllion, the Ovidian erotic-mythological brief epic, but in tone and procedure it is a new departure, except that for Shelley it had been prophesied by his own rendition of the Homeric **"Hymn to Mercury."** Both poems are in *ottava rima*, both have a Byronic touch, and both have been characterized accurately as possessing a tone of visionary cynicism. Hermes and the Witch of Atlas qualify the divine grandeurs among which they move, and remind us that imagination unconfined respects no orders of being, however traditional or natural. (pp. 106-07)

"The Witch of Atlas," as Shelley says in the poem's highly ironic dedicatory stanzas to his wife, tells no story, false or true, but is "a visionary rhyme." If the Witch is to be translated at all into terms not her own, then she can only be the mythopoeic impulse or inventive faculty itself, one of whose manifestations is the Hermaphrodite, which we can translate as a poem, or any work of art. The Witch's boat is the emblem of her creative desire, and like the Hermaphrodite it works against nature. The Hermaphrodite is both a convenience for the Witch, helping her to go beyond natural limitations, and a companion of sorts, but a highly inadequate one, being little more than a robot. The limitations of art are involved here, for the Witch has rejected the love of every mortal being, and has chosen instead an automation of her own creation. In the poignant stanzas in which she rejects the suit of the nymphs, Shelley attains one of the immense triumphs of his art, but the implications of the triumph, and of the entire poem, are as deliberately chilling as the Byzantine vision of the aging Yeats.

Though the Witch turns her playful and antinomian spirit to the labor of upsetting church and state, in the poem's final stanzas, and subverts even the tired conventions of mortality as well as of morality, the ultimate impression she makes upon us is one of remoteness. The fierce aspirations of *Prometheus Unbound* were highly qualified by a consciously manipulated prophetic irony, yet they retained their force, and aesthetic immediacy, as the substance of what Shelley passionately desired. The ruin that shadows love in *Prometheus Unbound,* the *amphisbaena* or two-headed serpent that could move downward and outward to destruction again, the warning made explicit in the closing stanzas spoken by Demogorgon; it is these antithetical hints that survived in Shelley longer than the vehement hope of his lyrical drama. *The Sensitive Plant* and **"The Witch of Atlas"** manifest a subtle movement away from that hope. *Epipsychidion,* the most exalted of Shelley's poems, seeks desperately to renovate that hope by placing it in the context of heterosexual love, and with the deliberate and thematic self-combustion of the close of *Epipsychidion* Shelley appears to have put all hope aside, and to have prepared himself for his magnificent but despairing last phase, of which the enduring monuments are *Adonais* and *The Triumph of Life.* (pp. 107-08)

Except for Blake's *Visions of the Daughters of Albion,* which it in some respects resembles, *Epipsychidion* is the most outspoken and eloquent appeal for free love in the language. Though this appeal is at the heart of the poem, and dominates its most famous passage (lines 147-54), it is only one aspect of a bewilderingly problematical work. *Epipsychidion* was intended by Shelley to be his *Vita Nuova,* celebrating the discovery of his Beatrice in Emilia Viviani. It proved however to be a climactic and not an initiatory poem, for in it Shelley culminates the quest begun in **"Alastor,"** only to find after culmination that the quest remains unfulfilled and unfulfillable. The desire of Shelley remains infinite, and the only emblem adequate to that desire is the morning and evening star, Venus, at whose sphere the shadow cast by earth into the heavens reaches its limits. After *Epipsychidion*, in *Adonais* and *The Triumph of Life*, only the star of Venus abides as an image of the good. It is not Emilia Viviani but her image that proves inadequate in *Epipsychidion*, a poem whose most turbulent and valuable element is its struggle to record the process of imagemaking. Of all Shelley's major poems, *Epipsychidion* most directly concerns itself with the mind in creation. **"Mont Blanc"** has the same position among Shelley's shorter poems, and has the advantage of its relative discursiveness, as the poet meditates upon the awesome spectacle before him. *Epipsychidion* is continuous rhapsody, and sustains its lyrical intensity of a lovers' confrontation for six hundred lines. The mind in creation, here and in *A Defense of Poetry,* is as a fading coal, and much of Shelley's art in the poem is devoted to the fading phenomenon, as image after image recedes and the poet-lover feels more fearfully the double burden of his love's inexpressibility and its necessary refusal to accept even natural, let alone societal limitations.

There is, in Shelley's development as a poet, a continuous effort to subvert the poetic image, so as to arrive at a more radical kind of verbal figure, which Shelley never altogether achieved. Tenor and vehicle are imported into one another, and the choice of natural images increasingly favors those already on the point of vanishing, just within the ken of eye and ear. The world is skeptically taken up into the mind, and there are suggestions and overtones that all of reality is a phantasmagoria. Shelley becomes an idealist totally skeptical of the metaphysical foundations of idealism, while he continues to entertain a skeptical materialism, or rather he becomes a fantasist pragmatically given to some materialist hypotheses that his imagination regards as absurd. This is not necessarily a self-contradiction, but it is a kind of psychic split, and it is exposed very powerfully in *Epipsychidion*. Who wins a triumph in the poem, the gambler with the limits of poetry and of human relationship, or the inexorable limits? Space, time, loneliness, mortality, wrong—all these are put aside by vision, yet vision darkens perpetually in the poem. "The world, unfortunately, is real; I, unfortunately, am Borges," is the ironic reflection of a great contemporary seer of phantasmagorias, as he brings his refutation of time to an unrefuting close. Shelley too is swept along by what destroys him and is inescapable, the reality that will not yield to the most relentless of imaginings. In that knowledge, he turns to elegy and away from celebration.

Adonais, Shelley's formal elegy for Keats, is a great monument in the history of the English elegy, and yet hardly an elegy at all. Nearly five hundred lines long, it exceeds in scope and imaginative ambition its major English ancestors. . . .

Like [Yeats's] *Byzantium* poems (which bear a close relation to it) *Adonais* is a high song of poetic self-recognition in the presence of foreshadowing death, and also a description of poetic existence, even of a poem's state of being.

Whether Shelley holds together the elegiac and visionary aspects of his poem is disputable; it is difficult to see the full continuity that takes the poet from his hopeless opening to his more than triumphant close, from:

I weep for Adonais—he is dead!
O, weep for Adonais! though our tears
Thaw not the frost which binds so dear a head!

to:

I am borne darkly, fearfully, afar;
Whilst, burning through the inmost veil of Heaven,
The soul of Adonais, like a star,
Beacons from the abode where the Eternal are.

From frost to fire as a mode of renewal for the self: that is an archetypal Romantic pattern, familiar to us from *The Ancient Mariner* and the *Intimations* Ode. . . . But *Adonais* breaks this pattern, for the soul of Shelley's Keats burns through the final barrier to revelation only by means of an energy that is set against nature, and the frost that no poetic tears can thaw yields only to "the fire for which all thirst," but which no natural man can drink, for no living man can drink of the whole wine of the burning fountain. As much as Yeats's "All Souls' Night," *Adonais* reaches out to a reality of ghostly intensities, yet Shelley as well as Yeats is reluctant to leave behind the living man who blindly drinks his drop, and *Adonais* is finally a *Dialogue of Self and Soul,* in which the Soul wins a costly victory, as costly as the Self 's triumph in Yeats's "Dialogue." The Shelley who cries out, in rapture and dismay, "The massy earth and spherèd skies are riven!" is a poet who has given himself freely to the tempest of creative destruction, to a reality beyond the natural, yet who movingly looks back upon the shore and upon the throng he has forsaken. The close of *Adonais* is a triumph of character over personality, to use a Yeatsian dialectic, but the personality of the lyric poet is nevertheless the dominant aesthetic element in the poem's dark and fearful apotheosis. (pp. 108-11)

Though *Adonais* has been extensively Platonized and Neoplatonized by a troop of interpreters, it is in a clear sense a materialist's poem, written out of a materialist's despair at his own deepest convictions, and finally a poem soaring above those convictions into a mystery that leaves a pragmatic materialism quite undisturbed. Whatever supernal apprehension it is that Shelley attains in the final third of *Adonais*, it is not in any ordinary sense a religious faith, for the only attitude toward natural existence it fosters in the poet is one of unqualified rejection, and indeed its pragmatic postulate is simply suicide. Nothing could be more different in spirit from Demogorgon's closing lines in *Prometheus Unbound* than the final stanzas of *Adonais,* and the ruthlessly skeptical Shelley must have known this.

He knew also though that we do not judge poems by pragmatic tests, and the splendor of the resolution to *Adonais* is not impaired by its implications of human defeat. Whether Keats lives again is unknown to Shelley; poets are among "the enduring dead," and Keats "wakes *or* sleeps" with them. The endurance is not then necessarily a mode of survival, and what flows back to the burning fountain is not necessarily the *human* soul, though it is "pure spirit." Or if it is the soul of Keats as well as "the soul of Adonais," then the accidents of individual personality have abandoned it, making this cold comfort indeed. Still, Shelley is not offering us (or himself) comfort; his elegy has no parallel to Milton's consolation in *Lycidas:*

> There entertain him all the Saints above,
> In solemn troops, and sweet Societies
> That sing, and singing in their glory move,
> And wipe the tears forever from his eyes.

To Milton, as a Christian poet, death is somehow unnatural. To Shelley, for all his religious temperament, death is wholly natural, and if death is dead, then nature must be dead also. The final third of *Adonais* is desperately apocalyptic in a way that *Prometheus Unbound,* Act IV, was not. For *Prometheus Unbound* ends in a Saturnalia, though there are darker implications also, but *Adonais* soars beyond the shadow that the earth casts into the heavens. Shelley was ready for a purgatorial vision of earth, and no longer could sustain even an ironic hope. (pp. 111-12)

There are elements in *The Triumph of Life,* Shelley's last poem, that mark it as an advance over all the poetry he had written previously. The bitter eloquence and dramatic condensation of the style are new; so is a ruthless pruning of invention. The mythic figures are few, being confined to the "Shape all light," the charioteer, and Life itself, while the two principal figures, Shelley and Rousseau, appear in their proper persons, though in the perspective of eternity, as befits a vision of judgment. The tone of Shelley's last poem is derived from Dante's *Purgatorio,* even as much in *Epipsychidion* comes from Dante's *Vita Nuova,* but the events and atmosphere of *The Triumph of Life* have more in common with the *Inferno.* Still, the poem is a purgatorial work, for all the unrelieved horror of its vision, and perhaps Shelley might have found some gradations in his last vision, so as to climb out of the poems' impasse, if he had lived to finish it, though I incline to doubt this. As

it stands, the poem is in hell, and Shelley is there, one of the apparently condemned, as all men are, he says, save for "the sacred few" of Athens and Jerusalem, martyrs to vision like Socrates, Jesus, and a chosen handful, with whom on the basis of *Adonais* we can place Keats, as he too had touched the world with his living flame, and then fled back up to his native noon.

The highest act of Shelley's imagination in the poem, perhaps in all of his poetry, is in the magnificent appropriateness of Rousseau's presence, from his first entrance to his last speech before the fragment breaks off. Rousseau is Virgil to Shelley's Dante, in the sense of being his imaginative ancestor, his guide in creation, and also in prophesying the dilemma the disciple would face at the point of crisis in his life. Shelley, sadly enough, was hardly in the middle of the journey, but at twenty-nine he had only days to live, and the imagination in him felt compelled to face the last things. Without Rousseau, Shelley would not have written the **"Hymn to Intellectual Beauty"** and perhaps not **"Mont Blanc"** either. . . . Shelley knew that the spirit of Rousseau was what had moved him most in the spirit of the age, and temperamentally (which counts for most in a poet) it makes more sense to name Shelley the disciple and heir of Rousseau than of Godwin, or Wordsworth, or any of the later French theorists of Revolution. Rousseau and Hume make an odd formula of heart and head in Shelley, but they are the closest parallels to be found to him on the emotional and intellectual sides respectively.

Chastened and knowing, almost beyond knowledge, Rousseau enters the poem, speaking not to save his disciple, but to show him that he cannot be saved, and to teach him a style fit for his despair. The imaginative lesson of *The Triumph of Life* is wholly present in the poem's title: life always triumphs, for life our life is after all what the Preface to **"Alastor"** called it, a "lasting misery and loneliness." One Power only, the Imagination, is capable of redeeming life, "but that Power which strikes the luminaries of the world with sudden darkness and extinction, by awakening them to too exquisite a perception of its influences, dooms to a slow and poisonous decay those meaner spirits that dare to abjure its dominion." In *The Triumph of Life,* the world's luminaries are still the poets, stars of evening and morning, "heaven's living eyes," but they fade into a double light, the light of nature or the sun, and the harsher and more blinding light of Life, the destructive chariot of the poem's vision. The chariot of Life, like the apocalyptic chariots of Act IV, *Prometheus Unbound,* goes back to the visions of Ezekiel and Revelation for its sources, as the chariots of Dante and Milton did, but now Shelley gives a demonic parody of his sources, possibly following the example of Spenser's chariot of Lucifera. Rousseau is betrayed to the light of Life because he began by yielding his imagination's light to the lesser but seductive light of nature, represented in the poem by the "Shape all light" who offers him the waters of natural experience to drink. He drinks, he begins to forget everything in the mind's desire that had transcended nature, and so he falls victim to Life's destruction, and fails to become one of "the sacred few." There is small reason to doubt that Shelley, at the end, saw himself as having shared in Rousseau's fate. The poem, fragment as it is, survives its own despair, and stands with Keats's *The Fall of Hyperion* as a marvelously eloquent imaginative testament, fit relic of an achievement broken off too soon to rival Blake's or Wordsworth's, but superior to everything else in its own age. (pp. 112-14)

Harold Bloom, "The Unpastured Sea: An Introduction to Shelley," in his *The Ringers in the Tower: Studies in Romantic Tradition*, The University of Chicago Press, 1971, pp. 87-116.

SOURCES FOR FURTHER STUDY

Allott, Miriam, ed. *Essays on Shelley.* Totowa, N.J.: Barnes & Noble Books, 1982, 282 p.

> Contains discussions of both individual works and such general topics as Shelley's critical reputation and his Gothicism.

Cronin, Richard. *Shelley's Poetic Thoughts.* London: Macmillan Press, 1981, 263 p.

> A highly regarded discussion of Shelley's use of language and poetic forms.

Ridenour, George M., ed. *Shelley: A Collection of Critical Essays.* Twentieth Century Views, edited by Maynard Mack. Englewood Cliffs, N.J.: Prentice-Hall, A Spectrum Book, 1965, 182 p.

> Reprints essays by such critics as Humphry House, Carlos Baker, Earl R. Wasserman, G. M. Matthews, G. Wilson Knight, and Harold Bloom.

Sperry, Stuart M. *Shelley's Major Verse: The Narrative and Dramatic Poetry.* Cambridge, Mass.: Harvard University Press, 1988, 231 p.

> Study of Shelley's poetry that seeks to "present Shelley above all as an idealist and to study the life forces that nourished and directed the power of his visionary impulse."

Wasserman, Earl. R. *Shelley: A Critical Reading.* Baltimore: Johns Hopkins Press, 1971, 507 p.

> Respected study of Shelley's major poems.

White, Newman Ivey. *Shelley.* 2 vols. New York: Alfred A. Knopf, 1940.

> Considered the definitive biography.

Richard Brinsley Sheridan

1751-1816

(Born Thomas Brinsley Sheridan) Irish dramatist, librettist, and poet.

INTRODUCTION

Sheridan is best known for his contribution to the revival of the English Restoration comedy of manners, which depicts the amorous intrigues of wealthy society. His most popular comedies, *The Rivals* (1775) and *The School for Scandal* (1777), display his talent for sparkling dialogue and farce. Like his Restoration predecessors William Congreve and William Wycherley, Sheridan satirized society, but his dramas reflect gentle morality and sentimentality. Critics often note a lack of incisiveness and psychological depth beneath the highly-polished surface of Sheridan's plays. However, they are considered by most to be the work of an outstanding theatrical craftsman.

Sheridan, the son of a prominent actor and a noted author, was born in Dublin. When he was eight, the family moved to London, where he attended Harrow School. Though he disliked school, he proved to be an excellent student and began writing poetry at an early age. After composing dramatic sketches with friends, Sheridan considered becoming a playwright. His father, however, intended him to study law, and he began an informal program of legal studies after leaving the Harrow School in 1768. When the Sheridans moved to Bath in 1770, Richard met Elizabeth Linley, an outstanding singer and famed beauty, with whom he eloped three years later. Shortly after their marriage, Sheridan abandoned his legal studies in order to devote himself to writing.

The initial performance of his first play, *The Rivals,* failed because of miscasting and the play's excessive length. Undaunted by the poor reception, Sheridan recast several roles, abbreviated sections of the play, and reopened it ten days later to unanimously positive response. The success of *The Rivals* derives from one of comedy's oldest devices: satirizing manners. Its humor is pointed, but never cruel; critics consider *The Rivals* to be the least scathing of Sheridan's satires. In the twentieth century, *The Rivals* is praised for its fine characterization. Of special interest is Mrs. Malaprop, a character infamous for her humorously inappropriate word usage, and from whose name the word "malapropism" is derived.

Sheridan's next work was *The Duenna; or, The Double Elopement* (1775), an opera for which his father-in-law, Thomas Linley, composed the music. While *The Duenna* was initially praised for its humorous libretto and amusing characters, the opera is now judged a minor effort. Some maintain that Sheridan's satirical talents were simply not suited to musical form. However, *The Duenna,* in addition to *The Rivals* and a minor comedy that was produced soon afterward—*St. Patrick's Day; or, The Scheming Lieutenant* (1775)—established Sheridan as a prominent dramatist. When David Garrick retired as owner of the Drury Lane Theatre, Sheridan purchased the theater and became its manager. In the next two years, he revived a number of Restoration comedies and wrote and produced his most successful comedy, *The School for Scandal.*

The School for Scandal is both the most popular of Sheridan's comedies and the most strongly reminiscent of the Restoration period. This attack on a gossip-loving society provides Sheridan's most brilliant display of wit, though its sharp indictment of scandal differs strongly from the gentler tone and approach in *The Rivals.* The play is also noted for its double plot lines, as well as for its superb command of language and its technical refinement. The play's continuous and numerous performances throughout the world attest to its reputation as one of England's best-loved and most enduring comedies.

In 1779 Sheridan produced his last successful work, *The Critic; or, Tragedy Rehearsed.* Strongly influenced by the Duke of Buckingham's *The Rehearsal,* the play provides a satirical look at the theatrical world and is a burlesque of the vanity of artists and critics. Though *The Critic* never achieved the popularity of *The Rivals* or *The School for Scandal,* many commentators consider it to be Sheridan's most intellectual work. He later stated that he had hoped to sum up in this piece all that previous comic poets had achieved in the satirization of tragedy. His last play was *Pizarro* (1799), an adaptation of August von Kotzebue's *Die Spanier in Peru oder Rollas Tod.* A historical drama, *Pizarro* met with popular acclaim but was soon forgotten. Critics today consider it a disappointing conclusion to Sheridan's theatrical career.

In 1780 Sheridan was elected to the House of Commons, where he excelled as an orator. His speeches are considered brilliant; in particular, the four-hour oration denouncing his fellow statesman Warren Hastings is regarded as a masterpiece of persuasion and verbal command. During this time Sheridan's interest in politics kept him from his theatrical endeavors and his management of Drury Lane became haphazard. In addition, His personal relationships began to suffer from his excessive drinking and spending habits. In an attempt to beautify the aging theater, he rebuilt the interior, but it burned down shortly thereafter. Left without resources, Sheridan was unable to finance another Parliamentary campaign. His last years were spent in poverty and disgrace. Nevertheless, when he died in 1816, he was mourned widely and was buried in the Poet's Corner of Westminster Abbey.

While *The Rivals* and *The School for Scandal* have always been popular, some recent critics charge that Sheridan was neither responsible for an English revival of comedy nor particularly innovative. Others fault his refusal to develop emotional subtleties in his characters, and find his dialogue witty, but lacking depth. They contend that the deliberate staginess of his works detracts from their artistic value. Sheridan's defenders argue, however, that the playwright chose to exaggerate and vary the traditional comedy of manners in order to heighten the play's theatricality, an aspect that he maintained intensified the audience's enjoyment. Despite controversy, his works continue to be performed. Alan Downer explained the enduring appeal of Sheridan's plays. "Sheridan is making us laugh at our own dreams, our own small follies. If we can laugh at our dreams, we may be less disappointed when they fail to materialize; if we laugh at our own follies, we may develop a tolerance for the follies of others."

(For further information about Sheridan's life and works, see *Drama Criticism,* Vol. 1 and *Nineteenth-Century Literature Criticism,* Vol. 5.)

CRITICAL COMMENTARY

MRS. OLIPHANT
(essay date 1883)

[Margaret Oliphant was a prolific Victorian novelist and critic. In her 1883 biographical and critical study of Sheridan, from which the following excerpt is drawn, she depicted the playwright as a gifted man who squandered his talents. Here, she surveys his dramas, which she praises for their vigor.]

Scarcely ever was play so full of liveliness and interest constructed upon a slighter machinery [than in *The Rivals*]. . . . [The] whole action of the piece turns upon a mystification, which affords some delightfully comic scenes, but few of those occasions of suspense and uncertainty which give interest to the drama. This we find in the brisk and delightful movement of the piece, in the broad but most amusing sketches of character, and the unfailing wit and sparkle of the dialogue. (pp. 51-2)

Mrs. Malaprop's ingenious "derangement of epitaphs" is her chief distinction to the popular critic; and even though such a great competitor as Dogberry has occupied the ground before her, these delightful absurdities have never been surpassed [from Shakespeare's *Much Ado about Nothing*]. But justice has hardly been done to the individual character of this admirable if broad sketch of a personage quite familiar in such scenes as that which Bath presented a century ago, the plausible, well-bred woman, with a great deal of vanity, and no small share of good-nature, whose inversion of phrases is quite representative of the blurred realisation she has of surrounding circumstances, and who is quite sincerely puzzled by the discovery that she is not so well qualified to enact the character of Delia as her niece would be. Mrs. Malaprop has none of the harshness of Mrs. Hardcastle, in *She Stoops to Conquer,* and we take it unkind of Captain Absolute to call her "a weatherbeaten she-dragon." The complacent nod of her head, the smirk on her face, her delightful self-satisfaction and confidence in her "parts of speech," have nothing repulsive in them. (pp. 52-3)

The other characters, though full of brilliant talk, cleverness, and folly, have less originality. The country hobbledehoy [Bob Acres], matured into a dandy and braggart by his entrance into the intoxicating excitement of Bath society, is comical in the highest degree; but he is not characteristically human. While Mrs. Malaprop can hold her ground with Dogberry, Bob Acres is not fit to be mentioned in the same breath with

the "exquisite reasons" of that delightful knight, Sir Andrew Aguecheek [from Shakespeare's *Twelfth Night*]. And thus it becomes at once apparent that Sheridan's eye for a situation, and the details that make up a striking combination on the stage, was far more remarkable than his insight into human motives and action. There is no scene on the stage which retains its power of amusing an ordinary audience more brilliantly than that of the proposed duel [between Bob Acres and Sir Lucius]. . . . The two men are little more than symbols of the slightest description, but their dialogue is instinct with wit, and that fun, the most English of qualities, which does not reach the height of humour, yet overwhelms even gravity itself with a laughter in which there is no sting or bitterness. Molière sometimes attains this effect, but rarely, having too much meaning in him; but with Shakspeare it is frequent amongst higher things. And in Sheridan this gift of innocent ridicule and quick embodiment of the ludicrous without malice or *arrière-pensée* reaches to such heights of excellence as have given his nonsense a sort of immortality.

It is, however, difficult to go far in discussion or analysis of a literary production which attempts no deeper investigation into human nature than this. Sheridan's art, from its very beginning, was theatrical, if we may use the word, rather than dramatic. It aimed at strong situations and highly effective scenes rather than at a finely constructed story, or the working out of either plot or passion. . . . The art [of the *Rivals*] is charming, the figures full of vivacity, the touch that sets them before us exquisite: except, indeed, in the Faulkland scenes, probably intended as a foil for the brilliancy of the others, in which Julia's magnificent phrases are too much for us, and make us deeply grateful to Sheridan for the discrimination which kept him . . . from the serious drama. But there are no depths to be sounded, and no suggestions to be carried out. (pp. 53-5)

[The] farce called *St. Patrick's Day; or, the Scheming Lieutenant* [is] a very slight production. . . . (p. 57)

[It] still keeps its ground among Sheridan's works, bound up between the *Rivals* and the *School for Scandal,* a position in which one cannot help feeling it must be much astonished to find itself. (p. 58)

The story of [the *Duenna*] belongs to the same

Principal Works

The Rivals (drama) 1775

The Duenna; or, The Double Elopement (libretto) 1775

St. Patrick's Day; or, The Scheming Lieutenant (drama) 1775

The School for Scandal (drama) 1777

A Trip to Scarborough [adaptor; from the drama The Relapse by John Vanbrugh] (drama) 1777

The Critic; or, Tragedy Rehearsed (drama) 1779

Pizarro [adaptor; from the drama Die Spanier in Peru oder Rollas Tod by August von Kotzebue] (drama) 1799

The Works of the Late Right Honourable Richard Brinsley Sheridan (drama) 1821

The Plays and Poems of Richard Brinsley Sheridan (drama and poetry) 1928

The Letters of Richard Brinsley Sheridan (letters) 1966

The Dramatic Works of Richard Brinsley Sheridan (drama) 1973

---

easy, artificial inspiration which dictated the trivial plot of *St. Patrick's Day.* . . . (p. 59)

There is very little character attempted, save in Isaac, who is a sort of rudimentary sketch of a too cunning knave or artful simpleton caught in his own toils; and the dialogue, if sometimes clever enough, never for a moment reaches the sparkle of the *Rivals.* (p. 61)

Posterity, which has so thoroughly carried out the judgment of contemporaries in respect to the *Rivals,* has not extended its favour to the *Duenna.* Perhaps the attempt to conjoin spoken dialogue to any great extent with music is never a very successful attempt: for English opera does not seem to last. (p. 63)

The highly polished diction of the *School for Scandal,* and the high-pressure of its keen and trenchant wit, does not look much like the excited work of the small hours inspired by port; but a man who is fully launched in the tide of society, and sought on all hands to give brilliancy to the parties of his patrons, must needs "steal a few hours from the night." "It was the fate of Sheridan through life," Moore says, "and in a great degree his policy, to gain credit for excessive indolence and carelessness." It seems very likely that he has here hit the mark, and furnished an explanation for many of the apparently headlong feats of composition by which many authors are believed to have distinguished themselves. (pp. 74-5)

The *Rivals* sprang into being without much thought, with that instinctive and unerring perception of the right points to recollect and record, which makes observation the unconscious instrument of genius, and is so immensely and indescribably different from mere

imitation. But the *School for Scandal*—a more elaborate performance in every way—required a different handling. It seems to have floated in the writer's mind from the moment when he discovered his own powers, stimulating his invention and his memory at once, and prompting half a dozen beginnings before the right path was discovered. Now it is one story, now another, that attracts his fancy. He will enlist those gossiping circles which he feels by instinct to be so serviceable for the stage, to serve the purpose of a scheming woman and separate a pair of lovers. Anon, departing from that idea, he will employ them to bring about the catastrophe of a loveless marriage, in which an old husband and a young wife, the very commonplaces of comedy, shall take a new and original development. Two distinct stories rise in his mind, like two butterflies circling about each other, keeping him for a long time undecided which is the best for his purpose. The first plot is one which the spectator has now a little difficulty in tracing through the brilliant scenes which were originally intended to carry it out, though it is distinctly stated in the first scene, between Lady Sneerwell and Snake, which still opens the comedy. As it now stands this intimation of her ladyship's purpose is far too important for anything that follows, and is apt to mystify the spectator, who finds little in the after scenes to justify it. . . . But while the author is playing with this plot, and designing fragmentary scenes in which to carry it out, the other is tugging at his fancy—an entirely distinct idea, with a group of new and individual characters: the old man and his wife, the two contrasted brothers, one of whom is to have the reputation of being her lover, while the other is the real villain. (pp. 75-7)

How it was that Sheridan was led to amalgamate . . . two plays into one we are left altogether without information. (pp. 81-2)

The scandalous scenes . . . are almost entirely without connexion with the plot. They can be detached and enjoyed separately without any sensible loss in the reader's (or even spectator's) mind. In themselves the management of all the details is inimitable. The eager interchange takes away our breath: there is no break or possibility of pause in it. The malign suggestion, the candid astonishment, the spite which assails, and the malicious good-nature which excuses, are all balanced to perfection, with a spirit which never flags for a moment. And when the veterans in the art are joined by a brilliant and mischievous recruit in the shape of Lady Teazle, rushing in amongst them in pure *gaité du coeur* [gaiety of heart], the energy of her young onslaught outdoes them all. The talk has never been so brilliant, never so pitiless, as when she joins them. She adds the gift of mimicry to all their malice, and produces a genuine laugh even from those murderers of their neighbours' reputations. This is one of the side-lights, perhaps unintentional, which keen insight throws upon human nature, showing how mere headlong imitation and high spirits, and the determination to do whatever other people do, and a little more, go further than the most mischievous intention. Perhaps the author falls into his usual fault of giving too much wit and point to the utterances of the young wife, who is not intended to be clever; but her sudden dash into the midst of the dowagers, and unexpected victory over them in their own line, is full of nature. (pp. 83-4)

Apart from these scenes, the construction of the play shows once more Sheridan's astonishing instinct for a striking situation. Two such will immediately occur to the mind of the reader—the great screen scene, and that in which Sir Charles Surface sells his family portraits. The first is incomparably the greater of the two, and one which has rarely been equalled on the stage. The succession of interviews, one after another, has not a word too much; nor could the most impatient audience find any sameness or repetition in the successive arrivals. . . . [The] most matter-of-fact spectator can scarcely repress, even when carried along by the interest of the story, a sensation of admiring wonder at the skill with which all [the] combinations are effected. It is less tragic than Tartuffe, insomuch as Orgon's profound belief, and the darker guilt of the domestic traitor, move us more deeply and it is not terrible, like the unveiling of Iago; but neither is it trivial, as the ordinary discoveries of deceitful wives and friends to which we are accustomed on the stage so generally are; and the fine art with which Sir Peter—something of an old curmudgeon in the earlier scenes—is made unexpectedly to reveal his better nature, and thus prepare the way, unawares, for the re-establishment of his own happiness at the moment when it seems entirely shattered, is worthy of the highest praise. . . . There remains for the comedy of the future (or the tragedy, which, wherever the deeper chords of life are touched, comes to very much the same thing) a still greater achievement—that of inventing an Iago who shall deceive the audience as well as the Othello upon whom he plays, and be found out only by us and our hero at the same moment. Probably, could such a thing be done, the effect would be too great, and the indignation and horror of the crowd, thus skilfully excited, produce a sensation beyond that which is permissible to fiction. But Sheridan does not deal with any tragical powers. Nothing deeper is within his reach than the momentary touch of real feeling with which Lady Teazle vindicates herself, and proves her capacity for better things. . . . The scene is in itself a succinct drama, quite comprehensible even when detached from its context, and of the highest effectiveness. (pp. 84-6)

The other great scene, that in which Charles Surface sells his pictures, has qualities of a different kind. It is less perfect and more suggestive than most of Sher-

idan's work. We have to accept the favourite type of the stage hero—the reckless, thoughtless, warm-hearted, impressionable spendthrift, as willing to give as he is averse to pay, scattering his wild oats by handfuls, wasting his life and his means in riotous living, yet easily touched and full of kind impulses—before we can do justice to it. . . . Charles Surface is the light-hearted prodigal whose easy vices have brought him to the point of destruction. Whatever grave thoughts on the subject he may have within, he is resolute in carrying out his gay career to the end, and ready to laugh in the face of ruin. A more severe taste might consider his light-heartedness swagger and his generosity prodigality; but we are expected on the stage to consider such characteristics as far more frequently conjoined with a good heart than sobriety and decency. . . . As the prodigal rattles on, with almost too much swing and "way" upon him in the tragi-comedy of fate, we are hurried along in the stream of his wild gaiety with sympathy which he has no right to. The audience is all on his side from the first word. (pp. 86-8)

It is a curious particular in the excellence of the piece, however, and scarcely a commendation, we fear, in the point of view of art, that these very striking scenes, as well as those in which the scandalmongers hold their amusing conclave, may all be detached from the setting with the greatest ease and without any perceptible loss of interest. Never was there a drama which it was so easy to take to pieces. The screen scene in itself forms, as we have already pointed out, a succinct and brilliant little performance which the simple audience could understand; and though the others might require a word or two of preface, they are each sufficiently perfect in themselves to admit of separation from the context. It says a great deal for the power of the writer that this should be consistent with the general interest of the comedy, and that we are scarcely conscious, in the acting, of the looseness with which it hangs together, or the independence of the different parts. Sheridan, who was not a playwright by science, but rather by accident, did not in all likelihood, in the exuberance of his strength, trouble himself with any study of the laws that regulate dramatic composition. The unities of time and place he preserves, indeed, because it suits him to do so; the incidents of his pieces might all happen in a few hours, for anything we know, and with singularly little change of scene; but the close composition and interweaving of one part with another, which all dramatists ought, but so very few do, study, evidently cost him little thought. He has the quickest eye for a situation, and knows that nothing pleases the playgoing public so much as a strong combination and climax; but he does not take the trouble to rivet the links of his chain or fit them very closely into each other. (pp. 88-9)

The Critic is, of all Sheridan's plays, the one which has least claim to originality. Although it is no copy, nor can be accused of plagiarism, it is the climax of a series of attempts descending downwards from the Elizabethan era. . . . But what his predecessors had tried with different degrees of success—or failure—Sheridan accomplished triumphantly. . . . In the *School for Scandal* Sheridan had held his audience in delighted suspense in scene after scene which had merely the faintest link of connexion with the plot of his play, and did little more than interrupt its action. But in [*The Critic*] he held the stage for nearly half the progress of the piece by the mere power of pointed and pungent remarks, the keen interchanges of witty talk, the personality of three or four individuals not sufficiently developed to be considered as impersonations of character, and with nothing to do but to deliver their comments upon matters of literary interest. Rarely has a greater feat been performed on the stage. . . . *The Critic* is as delightful as ever, and we listen to the gentlemen talking with as much relish as our grandfathers did. Nay, the simplest-minded audience, innocent of literature, and perhaps not very sure what it all means, will still answer to the touch and laugh till they cry over the poor author's wounded vanity and the woes of Tilburina. . . . When he has turned the author outside in, and exposed all his little weaknesses (not without a sharper touch here, for it is Mr. Puff, the inventor of the art of advertising as it was in those undeveloped days, and not any better man, who fills the place of the successful dramatist), he turns to the play itself with the same delightful perception of its absurdities. (pp. 95-8)

In *The Critic* [Sheridan] is at the height of his powers; his keen sense of the ridiculous might have, though we do not claim it for him, a moral aim, and be directed to the reformation of the theatre; but his first inspiration came from his own enjoyment of the humours of the stage and perception of its whimsical incongruities. (p. 100)

Sheridan's view of life was not a profound one. It was but a vulgar sort of drama, a problem without any depths—to be solved by plenty of money and wine and pleasure, by youth and high spirits, and an easy lavishness which was called liberality, or even generosity as occasion served. But to Sheridan there was nothing to find out in it, any more than there is anything to find out in the characters of his plays. He had nothing to say further. Lady Teazle's easy penitence, her husband's pardon, achieved by the elegant turn of her head seen through the open door, and the entry of Charles Surface into all the good things of this life, in recompense for an insolent sort of condescending gratitude to his egotistical old uncle, were all he knew on this great subject. And when that was said he had turned round upon the stage, the audience, the actors, and the writers who catered for them, and made fun of them all with the broadest mirth, and easy indifference to what

might come after. What was there more for him to say? *The Critic,* so far as the impulse of creative energy, or what, for want of a better word, we call genius, was concerned, was Sheridan's last word. (pp. 107-08)

Mrs. Oliphant, in her *Sheridan,* 1883. Reprint by Harper & Brothers, 1887, 199 p.

ROSE SNIDER
(essay date 1937)

[In the following excerpt, Snider identifies the sentimental and satiric aspects of Sheridan's dramas.]

[In his dramas,] Sheridan managed to recapture the spirit of the previous century in his presentation of heartless women, scheming men, and, in general, a cold and worldly-wise society; he tempered this, however, with a genuine warmth of tone decidedly lacking in the more formal plays of Congreve. To satisfy the tastes of an audience not yet recovered from the verbal lashing administered at the close of the previous century by the vehement Jeremy Collier, and to appease his own desire to follow the dictates of society, Sheridan frequently seasoned his comedy with sentimentality, that quality in which Georgians were wont to revel. Aware of the hypocrisy of exaggerated sentimentality, he attacked it through the medium of satire. The fact that comedy was deteriorating through the continued use of this same sentimentality stimulated the young Sheridan to call attention to the regrettable situation. As early as the **"Prologue"** to *The Rivals,* Sheridan's intentions in this direction are indicated, particularly when he laments that "the goddess of the woful countenance—the sentimental Muse" threatens to displace the Muse of comedy.

Unlike Congreve, who in his five acts found innumerable opportunities for satire, Sheridan lavishly utilized an entire play for satirizing one quality or institution or person. Thus, *The Rivals* is almost entirely given over to an exposé of hypocritical sentimentality; *The School for Scandal* is a thorough-going criticism of malicious scandal-mongering and of sentimentality; and *The Critic* is a final belittling of not only the so-called "genteel comedy" but also true comedy with a moral purpose. (p. 42)

In literary wit Congreve is easily the superior of the two, but in simple, infectious gayety Sheridan surpasses his predecessor. Unlike Congreve, Sheridan had but one ambition, that of being a gentleman. Whatever he did was directed toward this end. (p. 43)

The dramatic output of the second half of the eighteenth century was predominantly of the sentimental variety. Though occassionally plays appeared bearing resemblance to the earlier "manners" school, such examples were few and far between. . . . By the time Sheridan appeared on the Georgian theatrical scene, the sentimentality of the period was no longer novel; it was taken for granted, not only by those who continued to indulge in it, but by those who criticized it as well. This was a fortunate thing for Sheridan, who chose to be a member of the critical faction.

The words "sentiment" and "sentimentality," although they are constantly being confused, are not synonymous. Sentiment is nothing more than the truthful expression of the feelings of a sensitive person; it is sincere and unaffected. Sentimentality is a self-conscious indulgence in feeling, having for its aim either the approval of one's self as a virtuous person (moral sentimentality) or the mere pleasure in the feeling (romantic sentimentality). (pp. 43-4)

In Sheridan's plays the characters most easily remembered for their indulgence in sentimentality are Lydia Languish, Julia, and Faulkland, in *The Rivals;* and Joseph Surface and Maria, in *The School for Scandal.* Faulkland and Surface are obvious satires on the affected, virtuous strain. Julia and Maria, however, must have awed many a female of a generation brought up on that "genteel comedy" which Goldsmith derided and sought to remedy. (p. 44)

In dealing first with the romantic aspect of sentimentality, we shall need to glance at one of Sheridan's dramatic devices. In introducing the important characters, Sheridan again and again makes use of that ancient and well-worn device of putting the descriptions into the mouths of minor players. Congreve's technique of introduction, though similar, is not quite so obvious. Since the audience never anticipate the subtler artistry of Congreve, they can the more readily forgive Sheridan's undisguised methods. Sheridan is too much preoccupied with the matter of getting on with the plot to bother with such trivialities, and, accordingly, takes advantage of the easiest method of presentation. Thus, the conversation of the servants introduces us to the first of his satirical characterizations, Lydia Languish (whose surname Sheridan lifted from Congreve's *The Way of the World*). . . . When we actually come face to face with Lydia, we derive an immediate clue to her character from her literary tastes, which incline to such current fiction as *The Delicate Distress, Peregrine Pickle, Humphrey Clinker,* and *A Sentimental Journey.* (pp. 44-5)

Lydia Languish is a lively and likeable person even though she illustrates the eighteenth-century flair for sentimentality carried to the extreme. . . . From her surreptitious reading Lydia has conjured up an impossible world of romance in which she and her loved one are the only inhabitants of any importance. She has given her imagination free rein, and the result is a curious combination of sentiment, vanity, love, and sheer

caprice. She has no ulterior motive in carrying on these fanciful notions other than the mere pleasure she derives from doing so. The conventional mode of life is not for her, and in her craving for adventure she is so completely carried away by her romantic ideas that the result is a highly amusing caricature of a young woman of the eighteenth century. (p. 45)

The sentimentality exhibited by Lydia Languish is in keeping with the general taste for the romantic both in character and situation; and in Lydia, then, is to be found Sheridan's criticism of that harmless but ridiculous phase of sentimentality consisting in an excessive reveling in the romantic.

Julia, in the same play, represents the second phase of sentimentality noticed above, a variation consisting of an exaggerated promenading of one's virtues. . . . In Sheridan's hands, [Julia], for all her seriousness of mien, and no doubt because of it, is a subject for caricature, and no one can fail to detect the humor in Sheridan's mock-serious treatment of her. (p. 47)

Had he made the other characters in the play of a piece with Julia, Sheridan might have been warmly embraced by the advocates of the true "genteel" comedy, but his disinclination to be in their ranks is shown by his presenting Julia as the sole specimen of her kind in a play possessing a different manner, subject matter, and tempo. This contrast, more than anything else, gives the clue to Sheridan's motive in creating such a character as opposed to others who act and speak more naturally.

As an example of the type of speech considered "genteel" by Sheridan's contemporaries, Julia's words to Faulkland, on one of the numerous occasions when he is testing her love for him, are excellent:

> My soul is oppressed with sorrow at the nature of your misfortune: had these adverse circumstances arisen from a less fatal cause, I should have felt strong comfort in the thought that I could now chase from your bosom every doubt of the warm sincerity of my love. My heart has long known no other guardian—I now entrust my person to your honor— we will fly together. . . .

Such a speech as the one quoted above may have called forth sympathetic tears from an audience which, because of the change in moral outlook, was taking even its comedy seriously; but, appearing amid the amusing notions of Lydia Languish and the "ingeniously misapplied" verbiage of Mrs. Malaprop, it should produce the opposite effect. (pp. 48-9)

Had Sheridan created for Maria a role calling for more than four entrances which almost at once resolve into as many exits, he would have given the audience another Julia. Maria is obviously included as additional satire on the genteel-comedy heroine of the day when it was customary for writers to exhibit the virtues of society rather than its vices. Like Julia, Maria possesses a high sense of duty and loyalty as well as the usual docility and seriousness of purpose. Like all the sentimental ladies, she conveys the impression of having been mistreated.

Her virtues are even more apparent in contrast to the follies of the heterogeneous company in which she finds herself. It is not that Maria is unnecessarily decorous or irreproachable; it is merely that her general make-up is too sensible and restricted for a world where nonsense and carefree actions are in order. Amongst characters whose idiosyncrasies might well have given them a place in a Jonsonian comedy, Maria's sober virtue is noticeably out of place. (p. 49)

In regard to Faulkland, the sentimentality finds expression in a kind of self-torture which, though obviously of serious consequence to himself and the suffering Julia, is ludicrous and contemptible in the eyes of others. . . . He explains to Julia his theory of behavior for lovers as follows:

For such is my temper, Julia, that I should regard every mirthful moment in your absence as a treason to constancy. The mutual tear that steals down the cheek of parting lovers is a compact, that no smile shall live there till they meet again.

The foregoing, then, is love on the genteel plan which permitted words to speak louder than actions, and catered to false delicacy rather than to sincerity. The drama of sensibility was not an imitation of contemporary life, but a completely artificial set-up, which in turn invited imitation by its observers. True sentiment had given way to sentimentality, and even Sheridan and Goldsmith were not influential enough to restore the comic drama to normality.

Not content with a general satire on the sentimentality prevalent in the contemporary theatre, Sheridan selected the most conspicuous aspect of it—hypocrisy—for further attention. Both audience and playwrights were gradually becoming aware that sentimentality carried to excess was in itself a literary sin. Nothing, however, deserved ridicule so much as this same sentimentality when hypocrisy was its distinguishing feature. Sheridan concentrated upon this particular social fault in the character of his arch-hypocrite, Joseph Surface. (pp. 49-51)

As usual, Sheridan's dramatic technique calls for discussion of a character by those already assembled on the stage before the actual introduction of the character in question. Thus, early in the first act there takes place the following confidential interlude . . . :

Lady Sneer. . . . I know him to be artful, selfish, and malicious—in short, a sentimental knave; while with Sir Peter, and indeed with all his acquaintance,

he passes for a youthful miracle of prudence, good sense, and benevolence.

Snake. Yes; yet Sir Peter vows he has not his equal in England; and, above all, he praises him as a man of sentiment. . . .

In this way Sheridan invariably informs the audience of the proper attitude to hold in regard to the character introduced. There is no attempt, therefore, to conceal the true nature of Joseph Surface, who is himself so proficient in the art of dissembling that very few of his acquaintances ever suspect it. He is obliged to minimize his duplicity when in the company of Lady Sneerwell since they know each other too well. (pp. 51-2)

There is another rather unexpected aspect to this type of drama, for the more noble, morally, the character considers himself, the more satisfied with himself is he likely to become. In this way egotism links itself up with moralizing, since the individual indulges in it because he approves of himself as being a moral person. . . . In regard to Mr. Surface the satire is rendered greater in proportion to his own duplicity. (pp. 52-3)

Having acquainted the audience with Joseph's character, Sheridan wastes no time in developing the satire. Every moral speech assigned to this character, therefore, is a single pencil-stroke of criticism, as it were, in the outline to be completed at the close of the play. Even when in the company of his back-biting friends, Joseph can not throw off the cloak of genteel respectability which he has found so convenient to don on every other occasion, although his insincerity is so evident that his utterances always reflect the contrary intent of his mind. His winning card is the suave manner in which he poses as the exponent of the attributes of brotherly love. (p. 53)

Lydia Languish, Julia, Maria, Faulkland, and Joseph Surface afforded ample opportunity for Sheridan to develop his satire on the various phases of sentimentality. Although he expended his greatest efforts in this endeavor in *The Rivals,* which he deliberately utilized for this purpose, he introduced satirical bits throughout his dramatic composition.

That notable farce *The Critic,* for example, served more than one purpose. It brought up to date the outmoded line of critical pieces which included such successes as Beaumont and Fletcher's *The Knight of the Burning Pestle,* a satire on the currently popular plays based upon medieval romances; Buckingham's *The Rehearsal,* a burlesque directed at the heroic drama then holding sway; Gay's *The Beggar's Opera,* a farce satirizing contemporary politics and the trend of English opera in imitation of the Italian; and finally Fielding's *Tom Thumb,* a burlesque attacking the stereotyped contemporary tragedies. *The Critic* surpassed all these in its frank criticism of the current fashion in drama. The mock-serious lashing it administered to sentimental literature was one of the most effective single triumphs so far achieved among the various attempts to ameliorate the situation into which the drama, in particular, and all literature, in general, had fallen. The prologue itself is one of the most significant features of the play, and illustrates Sheridan's views on genteel comedy. It is here that his impatience with the affectations of the drama of sensibility is most conspicuous. (p. 55)

As for women, Sheridan did not have Congreve's idealistic conception of woman as a superior creature for whom must be reserved the most beautiful and most eloquent passages. For Sheridan there could be no such partiality. In his plays charming men appear as frequently as do charming women; and the less admirable characters are equally distributed between the sexes. . . . Like Congreve, Sheridan had a first-hand knowledge of women, but he chose to make other use of it. Instead of selecting women whose admirable qualities would attract attention by their rarity and beauty, he preferred more ordinary portraits which would prove attractive in spite of certain less commendable attributes. Indeed, Sheridan seems to have chosen his outstanding female characters more for their idiosyncrasies than for any intrinsically poetic values they might possess.

Female pretensions to education are satirized in Mrs. Malaprop. . . . The good-natured humor underlying each situation occupies the audience so completely that such matters as the frequency or monotony of Mrs. Malaprop's utterances are lightly passed over. Although the contrivance Sheridan employs in presenting Mrs. Malaprop's "select words so ingeniously misapplied, without being mispronounced" becomes obviously mechanical at times, it does not deserve much criticism on this score. It is merely another instance of Sheridan's insight into the commonplace methods of procuring laughter from the audience. The more sensitive the auditor is to shades of meaning in his vocabulary, the more readily does he respond to each cue offered by Mrs. Malaprop. The resulting laughter is not the intellectual mirth inspired by high comedy; it is closer in spirit to the ready laugh at each turn and tumble of the clown, but is elevated by the use of verbal rather than physical acrobatics.

Mrs. Malaprop exhibits two outstanding foibles: one of these consists in her pretensions to youth; the other, to education. There is nothing in her make-up to suggest the "superannuated frippery" of Congreve's Lady Wishfort, but there are several characteristics shared by the two. Both are conceited women who fancy that theirs has been a superior education, although in reality neither one has much to offer along that line. As *femmes savantes* [knowledgeable women] they rate ridiculously low, but they achieve distinction of a different type by means of their unusual vocabularies. Beside the disreputable language of Lady Wishfort, that of Mrs. Malaprop has an air of refinement. (pp. 56-8)

Sheridan was not merely satirizing the follies represented in Mrs. Malaprop; he was utilizing her as a laugh-provoker as well. . . . Sheridan found much to criticize in contemporary society, but whether or not his criticisms were taken seriously by this society was not to him a matter of vital concern. Above all he liked to please, and if he pleased by the humor of a situation rather than by the satire therein, he was satisfied. In creating the character of Mrs. Malaprop, Sheridan was satirizing all those old women who have a mistaken idea of their own importance and who enjoy upsetting the course of true love. To complete the caricature, Sheridan has her make use of all the verbal blunders he can invent. The inappropriateness of her words contrasts strikingly with her seriousness of mien, and this misuse of words distorts ludicrously each statement she proffers, placing her entirely at the mercy of the audience and the other characters in the play. (pp. 58-9)

Sheridan did not always strive for the clear, cold wit of high comedy, of Congreve or of Molière; he enjoyed the rich, generous laughter awakened by direct humor, whether of character or situation. The profusion of humorless sentimentality had so weakened eighteenth-century comedy that the metallic tinkle produced by the clash of wits in the Congrevean comedy was entirely lacking. Mrs. Malaprop, however, is an indication of the return to true comedy as illustrated in the plays of Goldsmith and Sheridan. (pp. 59-60)

Beneath the general satire there is to be found constantly Sheridan's good-natured humor. The audience is not asked to look upon and despise Mrs. Malaprop for her idiosyncrasies; it is, on the contrary, invited to witness and laugh at her follies. Sheridan was fond of exposing the weaknesses of his characters, but he never designed to rout these foibles; he aimed to please, and found the art of satire most suited to his métier. In only one respect does Sheridan fall short of the prescribed formula for eighteenth-century comedies: there is no happy ending in store for Mrs. Malaprop. . . . [Having] set herself up as an authority on language and love, she is now relegated to a position of minor importance; and there is no indication that she will profit by her experience.

In *The School for Scandal* Sheridan continues his practice of depicting various phases of eighteenth-century society. This play is one of the finest examples there are of the comedy of manners, and as such, it presents a highly realistic picture of the artificial society of that day. Here once again the spirit is that of Molière and Congreve, of *Le Misanthrope* and *The Way of the World*. (pp. 61-2)

Although Lady Sneerwell is obviously the motivating force in the "school for scandal," she is not so adept in the art as Mrs. Candour. The latter best illustrates the type of person who indulges in scandal-mongering for her own amusement. There is no subtlety in her procedure; she merely retails each idle rumor she has heard in her travels about the town and pounces on anything that remotely suggests a scandal. An important feature in Mrs. Candour's reportorial technique is the method of insinuation which contrasts ironically with her affected innocence of intention. The implication of each piece of gossip she relates is exactly the opposite of its accompanying apologetic remark. (p. 62)

Lady Sneerwell, on the other hand, is not so amiable a character. She represents the type who gossip for the sole purpose of defaming others, regardless of whether or not the victims deserve such ill-treatment. . . .

As a third example in this category of female gossips may be included Lady Teazle, the country girl whom Sir Peter married and took back with him to London. She joins the "scandalous college" because it is apparently the fashion of fine society to gossip and she wishes to acquire the mark of sophistication which membership in that society seems to imply. (p. 63)

To assist the "daughters of calumny" in culling and distributing the current bits of slander, Sheridan has provided four males: Joseph Surface, Snake, Sir Benjamin Backbite, and his uncle Crabtree.

The first one may be summarily dismissed. A hypocrite by nature, he can not even be consistent in his attitude to the malicious members of his society. He represents the male counterpart of Lady Sneerwell, for both take part in this slanderous reciprocity primarily for selfish reasons rather than for any light amusement they may derive. He is not a true gossip like Mrs. Candour, whose manner of tale-bearing is so diverting to her observers; he merely contributes to the school by participating in and furthering Lady Sneerwell's projects when there is a chance for individual gain on his part.

Snake is a caricature of the social sycophant. Everything about him suggests exaggeration, even his opinion of himself. His duties as a club-member are menial ones, such as carrying out Lady Sneerwell's orders, forging letters, starting rumors on their way, or perhaps inserting certain paragraphs in the papers. Even Joseph Surface's admonitions do not arouse her suspicions about Snake; and because she believes Snake to be sincere, she entrusts him with her most secret plans. It is not until the close of the play, when Snake sells his services to a higher bidder, that Lady Sneerwell realizes the extent of his perfidy. (pp. 64-5)

The real rivals of Mrs. Candour are two other notable male slanderers, Sir Benjamin Backbite and his uncle Crabtree. They are very much alike, except for the fact that Sir Benjamin poses as a wit and a poet, whereas both men bear greater resemblance to the "wittols" of Congreve than to the true wits. They work as a team, one generally acting as the chorus while the other takes charge of the narration. (p. 65)

Sheridan may have found that his ridicule of the "school for scandal" was of too brief duration for an evening's entertainment at the theatre; he may, also, have desired to follow the practice of earlier and contemporary dramatists in creating intricate plots in which to entangle the characters. Whatever his reason may have been, the complications in this play are on a par with those of almost any of the Restoration comedies of manners, with the exception, perhaps, of *The Way of the World,* a masterpiece of plot complexity. There is, in addition to the portions aimed at the gossips and scandal-mongers which give the play its title, a second plot consisting of a satirical portrait of the old bachelor who takes unto himself a young wife and is not sure he can keep her. The same plot served Wycherley for an entire play, *The Country Wife,* but for Sheridan, who used it in its expurgated form, it merely supplements the "scandal" episodes and introduces some real sentiment into the comedy. Both Sir Peter and Lady Teazle are contributions to the sentimental school of the day, and both have genuine appeal. (p. 67)

Sheridan makes of Sir Peter Teazle a far pleasanter person than the earlier prototypes, Wycherley's Pinchwife and even Congreve's Fondlewife. Although Sir Peter finds himself in a similar predicament, also having married a girl from the country, he reacts in a more gentlemanly fashion than Pinchwife or Fondlewife. Sir Peter is a man of much common sense except in regard to his wife. Like Pinchwife, he was very circumspect in making his marital choice and selected a quiet, unpresuming young lady. (p. 68)

Sheridan frequently employs that made-to-order repartee that was often resorted to by Congreve. It is a kind of wit usually ascribed to the "wittols"; at times, however, even the true wits can not resist making use of it. The audience knows exactly what to expect and yet laughs heartily each time it appears. Sheridan employs this artificial humor in connection with Sir Peter. . . . Sheridan's method of opening the way for wit is all too obvious, but the humor of the situation brings forth the ready response of the audience, nevertheless.

That Sir Peter Teazle is no fool is indicated in his public denunciation of the "school for scandal," in which he maintains that he would have Parliament enact a law against gossip, permitting only "qualified old maids and disappointed widows" to indulge. His protests are of no avail, however, and he becomes a victim of the "school's" persecution. He has his revenge when his wife resigns from the society to become a dutiful and loving wife. (pp. 69-70)

Sheridan's attitude toward the country class was one of tolerant amusement. He satirized them, but did not suggest changes in their mode of life. He portrayed them as he saw them, and he saw them as interesting material for the scrutiny of the artificial London audiences to which he was obliged to cater. . . . Sheridan's country folk . . . are satirized solely for the humor such treatment always imparts to comic drama.

"Fighting Bob" Acres, a minor rival of Captain Absolute for the hand of Lydia Languish [in *The Rivals*], is typical of Sheridan's method in regard to the country fellow and his awkward attempts to cut a fine figure in London society. . . . Acres' delicacy in the choice of oaths is characteristic of the sentimental school, but whether or not it produces the desired effect is doubtful. The reflection upon the language of the genteel comedy is obvious, however, Sheridan could not resist an opportunity which invited comment on this highly affected type of drama. Although Acres' oaths seem to be decidedly lacking in the vituperative strength generally associated with swearing, they can not be criticized in respect to variety. (pp. 70-1)

Through the character of Acres, also, Sheridan makes sport of that popular eighteenth-century pastime—duelling. Ridicule of this business of maintaining one's honor was certainly not original with our playwright. The Restoration, all too obviously influenced by the French in thought, manners, and costumes, mimicked as well the French gallantry which almost invariably resulted in duelling. . . . Sheridan, not so intent upon improving society as upon deriding the system in general, portrayed the clearly unheroic aspects of the duel by having the cowardly Bob Acres as the challenger and the smug, senile Sir Lucius as the manager who instructs Bob in the fine points of duelling, proving that a duel can be fought on no greater provocation than that of a rival's falling in love with one's own beloved. (pp. 71-2)

Through the character of Bob Acres [Sheridan] has emphasized the impossibility of disguising the earmarks of the country by mere imitation of city fashions; through his treatment of duelling he has held up for ridicule one of the most outstanding foibles of his social class. (pp. 72-3)

Rose Snider, "Richard B. Sheridan," in her *Satire in the Comedies of Congreve, Sheridan, Wilde, and Coward,* 1937. Reprint by Phaeton Press, 1972, pp. 41-73.

LOUIS KRONENBERGER
(essay date 1969)

[Kronenberger was a distinguished historian, literary critic, and author highly regarded for his expertise in eighteenth-century English history and literature. In the excerpt below, he discusses *The School for Scandal* as Sheridan's finest work.]

The Rivals is only marginally in the tradition of the comedy of manners; it is with *The School for Scandal,* that Sheridan takes his true place there, and displays his true talents. *The School for Scandal* is indeed—whether in public fame or theatrical popularity—the most famous comedy of manners in the language. Here the man of the world in Sheridan fulfills himself, here he indeed restores to the stage the wit and polish of the Restoration. Moreover, as a work for the theater, as something that deftly mingles plot and theme, characterization and background, it offers, I think, a surer hand, a stronger theatrical instinct, than any that the Restoration itself can provide. Equally for verbal polish and theatrical craftsmanship, equally for colloquial ease and theatrical canniness, it deserves its great popular fame. (p. 75)

[The scenes of the scandalmongers] constitute the play's thematic whalebone; they are at once an illustration of manners and a comment on society. They give the play spice; they can also give it a suggestion of glitter. And the theme of scandal does something further: it goes far toward solving a difficulty born of a genteel age. Scandal provides Sheridan with the *sense* of naughtiness, with the atmosphere of sinfulness, which Restoration comedy achieved through sin itself. Of sin itself there is absolutely nothing in the *action* of Sheridan's play; there is only the imputation of sinning. . . . By making scandal the theme of his play, Sheridan could thus brilliantly capitalize on the appearance without the reality. (pp. 76-7)

[But not] for being more strait-laced, is Sheridan's audience any less worldly: it is, if anything, more so, in the sense that hypocrisy is more worldly than frankness.

There is also a kind of aesthetic consideration: Sheridan is writing in an age when "taste" is not a matter of how you deal with things, but rather of what things you may deal with. And just because, in *The School for Scandal,* no one sexually sins, sin now becomes much wickeder and more important than it once was. Restoration comedy is a tedious succession of ladies and gentlemen being thrust behind screens,

---

Thomas Moore on the merits and defects of
The School for Scandal:

The beauties of [*The School for Scandal*] are so universally known and felt, that criticism may be spared the trouble of dwelling upon them very minutely. With but little interest in the plot, with no very profound or ingenious development of character, and with a group of personages, not one of whom has any legitimate claims upon either our affection or esteem, it yet, by the admirable skill with which its materials are managed,—the happy contrivance of the situations, at once both natural and striking,—the fine feeling of the ridiculous that smiles throughout, and that perpetual play of wit which never tires, but seems, like running water, to be kept fresh by its own flow,—by all this general animation and effect, combined with a finish of the details almost faultless, it unites the suffrages, at once, of the refined and the simple, and is not less successful in ministering to the natural enjoyment of the latter, than in satisfying and delighting the most fastidious tastes among the former. . . .

The defects of *The School for Scandal,* if they can be allowed to amount to defects, are, in a great measure, traceable to [an] amalgamation of two distinct plots, out of which . . . the piece was formed. From this cause,—like an accumulation of wealth from the union of two rich families,—has devolved that excessive opulence of wit, with which, as some critics think, the dialogue is overloaded; and which, Mr. Sheridan himself used often to mention, as a fault of which he was conscious in his work. That he had no such scruple, however, in writing it, appears evident from the pains which he took to string upon his new plot every bright thought and fancy which he had brought together for the two others; and it is not a little curious, in turning over his manuscript, to see how the out-standing jokes are kept in recollection upon the margin, till he can find some opportunity of funding them to advantage in the text. The consequence of all this is, that the dialogue, from beginning to end, is a continued sparkling of polish and point: and the whole of the Dramatis Personae might be comprised under one common designation of Wits. Even Trip, the servant, is as pointed and shining as the rest, and has his master's wit, as he has his birth-day clothes, "with the gloss on."

Thomas Moore, in his *Memoirs of the Life of the Right Honourable Richard Brinsley Sheridan*, third edition, 1825.

---

pushed into closets, hidden under beds, flung down back stairways; such scrambling for cover gets to be as commonplace and routine as closing a window or opening a door. But *here,* in *The School for Scandal,* we have Lady Teazle hiding behind a screen in what, without question, is the most famous scene in all English social comedy, just as the moment when the screen is knocked over constitutes the most climactic moment in all English social comedy. Some of this is clearly due to Sheridan's expertness as a playwright, to his building up the scene to get the utmost from it. But some of it is due to its being, as similar scenes a century earlier never were, so zealously, so breathlessly, scandalous. We are back in an age when sex takes on glamour through being illicit.

Impropriety is thus the very essence of what goes on; except that nothing goes on. The story itself is a good one to the extent that we regard it as merely a story; and it is worked out by someone completely at home in his medium. But, of itself, the story is almost obstreperously fictional: the key point about Sheridan here is not his high comedy but his strong theater sense, the way he can give, even to his scandalmongers, not the sheen of wit alone, but the deviousness of spiders; the way he can plot; the specific way he can unravel, or expose, or turn the tables. There is about it all the conciseness of an adroit theater mind. (pp. 78-9)

We must not undervalue the adroitness of the storytelling and all the graces that go with it—the play has a certain verbal polish and drawing room *ton;* has even a genuine *air* of worldliness. (p. 81)

But when we pass beyond manner to actual substance, we find that sound plotting and brisk movement are only had at a very steep price; that the story belongs wholly to the stage, with no overtones of real life. What I mean by this has nothing to do with surface realism. The comedy of manners has no use for surface realism; being, indeed, concerned with the shams and pretenses of human beings, it has every need of artifice. But since its very orbit is a world of masks, what it must always be moving toward is a general unmasking, so that we see at last the true faces that lurk beneath. . . . [Since] the real dramatis personae of the comedy of manners are the practices of society, the way of the world itself, we see in what fashion they alter and contaminate and corrupt; and though wickedness certainly need not triumph, a sense, at least, of man's dark, divided nature must somehow obtrude. Artifice, when expertly applied, can be a great short cut to truth.

But between artifice and the mere staginess that we encounter at times in *The School for Scandal* there is a crucial difference. Sheridan, we feel, heightens certain of his scenes not in the service of revelation but for the sake of effect. Partly from being too stagy and partly from being too sentimental, his is a real "fiction" plot where, rather than the audience finding out the truth in human nature, the characters find out, for fictional ends, the truth about one another. Even where Sheridan digs a little deeper, as with Lady Teazle's inclination toward sin, we are shown—and expected to be-lieve—that she is now thoroughly sick of social pre-tense; there is not a hint that this may only be tempo-rary repentance born of sheer fright, and that a month hence this blooming young wife of a man twice her age will be tempted once more. (pp. 82-3)

The trouble with this whole side of the play is not that it is artificial but that it is tame, is not that it snaps its fingers at realistic truth but that it clicks its heels be-fore conventional morality. . . . What Sheridan . . . wrote in *The School for Scandal* was one of the most brilliant box-office comedies in the language. He too was too worldly in his own calculations to become one of the great delineators of worldliness.

Thus we are in a world of set rewards and punish-ments, of old-fashioned—or perennial—heroes and heroines, of rich uncles who are won over and wicked brothers who are shown up. As popular theater, there may be nothing wrong with this; but there is something wrong with a man of Sheridan's gifts acquiescing in popular theater. Sheridan satirizes, here, almost noth-ing that the world in general does not condemn; he no-where boldly challenges fashionable opinion or as-saults fashionable complacency. A Wycherley may not have shocked his own generation, but he can still shock us. A Shaw may not shock us, but he did shock our grandparents. But Sheridan, if at times delightfully im-pudent, is never at all subversive. Nor, to be fair to the *man,* is this altogether calculating on his part; much of it, I suspect, he half believed in. There was a good deal of the pure romantic in the Sheridan who himself fought duels, himself eloped, himself was overdazzled by the great world. The gentility of his age clearly did him harm, but something beyond conformity enters in; actually, he often did not so much conform as concur. Sheridan's wit always tends to face south and toward the sun; in his portrayal of venom there is nothing per-sonally venomous; he had worldly tastes but not, like Congreve or Molière or La Rochefoucauld, an inviola-bly worldly mind. His scandalmongers constitute a kind of Greek chorus in a play that Sheridan never really got round to writing on their terms. Their air of iniquity is a false front for the play's essential innocu-ousness. Indeed, in terms of Sheridan's mastery of his trade, perhaps the most brilliant thing about *The School for Scandal* is not the actual glitter of its dialogue but the seeming wickedness of its plot. (pp. 83-4)

Louis Kronenberger, "The School for Scandal," in his *The Pol-ished Surface: Essays in the Literature of Worldliness,* Alfred A. Knopf, 1969, pp. 73-84.

MARK S. AUBURN
(essay date 1977)

[In the excerpt below, Auburn surveys Sheridan's lesser-known works: *St. Patrick's Day, The Duenna, A Trip to Scarborough,* and *The Critic.*]

St. Patrick's Day revolves around a typical farcical ac-tion, the boy-gets-girl-in-spite-of-parents formula. Lieutenant O'Connor wants to wed Lauretta but Justice and Bridget Credulous object to the marriage. . . .

With a line of action so broadly typical, to distin-guish Sheridan's exact debt to a farcical tradition is dif-ficult. Many of Samuel Foote's and Charles Macklin's dark satiric farces use this sort of comic frame upon which to build their potent attacks on contemporary society. Garrick's *Miss in Her Teens* and Colman's *Polly Honeycombe,* both of which have been named as sources of *The Rivals,* are as similar to this piece as to Sheri-dan's first comedy. There is less originality here, in the use of the old device of a disguised lover attempting to circumvent parents, than in *The Rivals,* where Sheri-dan added the wrinkle of tricking the daughter as well. (p. 62)

Much of the structure and content of *The Rivals* appears to have been in Sheridan's mind when he wrote [*St. Patrick's Day*]. Lauretta, like Lydia, is a spirited girl who can argue amusingly with her equally temper-amental mother and who thinks a military man the height of fashion; she is rather more like the harsh Polly Honeycombe than the sprightly Lydia, but she retains an attractiveness necessary to effect the amiable denouement. Dr. Rosy, like Mrs. Malaprop, is charac-terized largely by a verbal tic—in this case, a propensity to spout three- and four-word moral phrases of the most prosaic kind (anticipatory, perhaps, of the pomp-ously phrased sentiments of Joseph Surface)—and like Mrs. Malaprop's his "humour" has little to do with the conduct of the plot; it exists merely to embellish his playing character. Some of the comic situations arise as they do in *The Rivals* through the careful preparation of mistaken identity and misunderstanding. In both plays, for instance, the opening scenes establish the ini-tial situation through exposition but also characterize peripheral agents in order to set up further local display of them later. . . . The central scene of *The Rivals* oc-curs when Jack arrives at Mrs. Malaprop's and tricks her into admitting him to see Lydia; in *St. Patrick's Day,* there is a similar scene when O'Connor, disguised as Humphrey Hum, reveals himself to Lauretta. Sheri-dan again uses the technique of removing the parent

(Justice Credulous) from the scene so that the lovers may come to understand one another, then returning him at the crucial moment in order to discomfit them just as success seems at hand. The compressed scope of *St. Patrick's Day* forces the discomfiture to be more immediate than that of *The Rivals,* where Jack does not receive his comeuppance until four scenes later.

As in *The Rivals,* and indeed in all of Sheridan's original dramatic work before *The School for Scandal,* the tone of *St. Patrick's Day* is distinctly amiable. Lieutenant O'Connor is immediately characterized as an essentially honorable fellow. (pp. 63-4)

Little [in *St. Patrick's Day*] points to Sheridan's talent beyond the general compactness of the short piece and a few fine *bon mots.* Among these are Justice Credulous's replies to his wife's preference to follow him to the grave rather than have a quack attempt to cure him ("I'm sensible of your affection, Dearest—and believe me nothing consoles me in my present melancholy situation, so much as the thought of leaving you behind, my Angel" . . . and to her assertion that dying is quick ("Ay, but it leaves a numbness behind, that lasts for a plaguy long time." . . . But there is much in

Sheridan's Drury Lane Theatre.

St. Patrick's Day that points to a deep and growing familiarity with what will immediately please upon the stage. First, the farce is designed for a hero whose specialty is not comedy. Though his is the title role, Lieutenant O'Connor carries little of the real humor of the piece: a handsome exterior, a slight ability to mimic theatrically obvious types like a country bumpkin or the quasi-Dutch, and the soberness of a straight man to the self-exposures of Dr. Rosy and Serjeant Trounce are all that is necessary for success in the role. Since Clinch [the actor who was to play the role] specialized in tragedy, Sheridan designed for his benefit farce a character that required only enough comic talent to gain success through contrast with his accustomed roles. Second, theatrical coterie jokes abound. Rosy calls O'Connor "my Alexander," setting up a pleasant laugh for the audience which had just seen Clinch perform Alexander the Great in Nathaniel Lee's heroic *The Rival Queens,* his choice for the mainpiece of his benefit night. (pp. 64-5)

Like *The Rivals* and *St. Patrick's Day, The Duenna* is both distinctively original and slavishly derivative. Set in the never-never land that Spain was for eighteenth-century comedy, the plot of *The Duenna* is even more involved than that of *The Rivals.* As in the earlier comedy, *domnées* of character are added to multiple disguises to develop amusing and amiable comedy of situation, complicated and recomplicated, dependent on chance. Where before there was one strict father, now there are two; where before there was one couple whose happiness depended upon circumventing their elders, now there are two; but where before it was character that interested us primarily, now farcical character is subordinated much more completely to plot, so that the tangled imbroglio is constantly before our eyes. As in *The Rivals,* the crusty old father—here, Don Jerome—is hoist with the petard he thought he had so successfully laid; but now all fortifications are blown up together, and the vain Jew Isaac is exploded by his own charge just as Don Jerome's bomb clears the way for Donna Louisa to marry the impecunious Antonio, her jealous brother Ferdinand to marry the slightly sober Donna Clara, and Margaret, the old and ugly duenna who has taken Louisa's place, to make her fortune from her marriage to Isaac.

The action of *The Duenna* has much in common with such mixtures of intrigue and farce popular in Sheridan's time as Susanna Centlivre's *The Wonder: A Woman Keeps a Secret.* (pp. 66-7)

The Duenna and *The Wonder* are like one another more in tone than in any specifics of action or character. . . . [In these] pseudo-Iberian comedies, the marks of the intrigue—external obstacles rather than internal flaws, heightened but more artificial concern, frequent reversal of situation, concealed truth producing multilayered comic dramatic irony—combine with an amiability bred of basically good-natured characters and a middle-class moral view to produce comedies typical of the Georgian era.

Analogues to *The Duenna* abound, though no single source leaps forth. A comic plot similar to one principal situation of *The Duenna*—a daughter turned out of doors while the maid passes as the mistress—is found in an Italian comic opera, Carlo Goldoni's *Il Filosopho di Campagna.* (pp. 67-8)

As there are similarities to other plots, so there are to other characters. We can point from the two best playing characters of Sheridan's comic opera—Isaac the Jew and Margaret the ugly duenna—to similar roles already established and long popular on the Georgian stage, and to the actors who created them. One of the most successful comic operas written in the period before *The Duenna* is Isaac Bickerstaff 's *The Padlock.* . . . Like *The Duenna, The Padlock* combines a farcical Spanish intrigue plot with original songs. (p. 68)

The Duenna has a remarkably complicated but compact libretto, . . . is highly amusing, and . . . represents an important step in Sheridan's development.

The plot of *The Duenna* is both the most highly complex and the most highly unified, if not the most probable, of all the plots Sheridan created. The frame, of course, is provided by the four young lovers. Donna Louisa, by virtue of her sprightly grace, impish assurance, and clever trickery, is the most entertaining of these. She is matched with the handsome Antonio, whose artificial introduction with two contrasting love songs at the beginning of the opera may seem absurd and whose love and bravery are assigned, not fully developed, comic characteristics. Contrasted slightly with these two are the sober Clara and the jealous Ferdinand, yet neither is Clara so sober nor Ferdinand so jealous as to lose our interest. Sheridan may have used as lovers characters very similar to those of *The Rivals,* but he was not about to make again the aesthetic mistakes he made there. . . . [These four lovers] are portrayed as clever enough to get their own ways in spite of strict fathers but are never made particularly witty or given complex personalities with serious internal flaws to be removed. Indeed, only Ferdinand among them has anything like a comic flaw—his jealousy. Interest in the four lovers is important. But the real pleasure in the plot, taken as a whole, comes from the complications provided by three other characters: Don Jerome, Margaret the Duenna, and Isaac the Jew; their physical and psychological idiosyncrasies conflict to create the situations most skillfully designed to evoke laughter. (pp. 72-3)

Of these three idiosyncratic characters, Margaret the Duenna is the least comic. She is an ugly old woman whom Don Jerome has hired to protect his daughter's chastity. . . . Margaret is not funny for her

own foibles—she never believes, for instance, when she is pretending to be the young and beautiful Louisa, that she really is young and beautiful—but for her clever manipulation of others to expose their idiosyncrasies. (p. 73)

The most fun of the whole opera is that which is funniest about Margaret—the ongoing sight gag she represents. This technique, common to farce and the basis of a great deal of enjoyment in characters like Bob Acres, sets up a whole series of misunderstood exchanges between Don Jerome and Isaac concerning her beauty. . . .

The tradition out of which Don Jerome springs is clear; he has little to differentiate him from hundreds of other strict fathers, including Sir Anthony Absolute and Justice Credulous. Like most old fathers, he is crusty, testy, and financially motivated. His cynical realism opposes the idealism and love of his children, and of course they eventually turn the tables on him, pitting flexibility against rigidity and asserting the power of clever youth to take over and create the new social order. He is never really a serious threat to the happiness of the young people. . . . Like Sheridan's other old fathers, and like those of late eighteenth-century amiable comedy, even when over-reached he proves good-natured. (p. 74)

The Duenna is not a comedy of wit, and Don Jerome is not basically a witty character.

The one character around whom this comic opera may be said to revolve is Isaac, the conceited, covetous Jew who seeks to marry Louisa. The audience sees him compounding his egotism and avarice while they know all the while that eventually he will discover his mistakes and receive the come-uppance he so richly deserves. He is a comic villain, but never clever or strong enough to represent a real threat; his faults blind him too completely to allow him to damage the sympathetic characters. (p. 76)

All these characters are somewhat interesting and Isaac especially amusing, but none of them are particularly striking, original, or clever, and none are drawn with sufficient psychological or comic depth to stay in our minds beyond the setting in which they appear. Perhaps not surprisingly in a comic opera, they are primarily types, flat place-holders who provide vehicles for the display of mostly stock comic situations. And the most frequently employed technique of the comic opera is comedy of situation. As it was used in *The Rivals* and *St. Patrick's Day,* this technique of concealing vital information from one or more of the characters is frequently used in *The Duenna,* though never with the same multilayered effect obtained in *The Rivals.* (p. 77)

The Duenna is a one-joke comedy. But then, so are many great comedies. Sheridan's brilliant stroke was to exploit this one joke to its fullest possible extent. And his favorite technique here—allowing Isaac multiple asides in which he praises himself and his cleverness, explains his intended actions, weighs his possible alternatives, and never recognizes the cleverness, action, or alternatives as precisely the things which guarantee his downfall—intensifies the comic dramatic irony. (p. 79)

The frivolity of *The Duenna* is matched by the characteristic amiability of the denouement. But for Sheridan first the frivolity, then to a lesser extent the amiability would disappear, and its disappearance would coincide . . . with Sheridan's own growth. . . . Henceforth, Sheridan would show more concern with carefully structured plot (as he is doing in *The Duenna* in comparison to *The Rivals* and *St. Patrick's Day*), more concern with wit, more concern with satire. However entertaining his later works may be, none of them are merely frivolous. (p. 80)

The changes Sheridan made in *The Relapse* when he adapted it as *A Trip to Scarborough* indicate his awareness of its beauties and of its weaknesses. He simplified [its] Foppington-Fashion plot and redesigned the Amanda-Loveless plot. He invented ties between the two groups of people that make the Amanda-Loveless entrance into the Foppington-Fashion affair probable and necessary, and the entrance of the Foppington-Fashion group into the Amanda-Loveless affair probable, though not necessary. In removing the licentiousness of dialogue and motivation, he destroyed much of the wit, and his redesign of the moral world indicates his own and his time's tastes. In effect, he attempted to make a witty "genteel" comedy of manners with a "low" subplot. (p. 91)

Sheridan makes several other changes in the Foppington-Fashion plot necessary to accommodate the squeamish tastes of his age and typical of the comedies popular in his time. He removes, for instance, the homosexual Coupler and replaces him with the matronly Mrs. Coupler; dramatically she functions identically with her brighter original, but she lacks the spark that every character of a truly great comedy must have, that all the characters of *The Rivals* or *The Duenna* possess. Sheridan also generally cleans up the language and the more blasphemous references. Thus, Foppington refers to his watching the ladies rather than the entertainment at the opera; in *The Relapse* he ogled the women at church. (pp. 93-4)

Another change typical of Sheridan's own style in his original plays is the general emphasis on expectation rather than surprise as the main basis for comedy. . . . [Clearly] as a creator of comic situations Sheridan generally preferred to raise the expectations of the audience for comic conflict rather than surprise them with a totally unexpected reversal. Thus, in *The Relapse*, Foppington's arrival just after Tom had married Hoy-

den was unexpected; he was not supposed to come down to Tunbelly's for a fortnight, but came early instead on a whim. In *A Trip to Scarborough* he is readying himself to go to his future father-in-law's even when Tom comes to request aid for the second time. Tom does not know that Foppington plans to go so soon, but the audience does, and that knowledge heightens anxiety; Tom's marriage is awaited with the comic analogue of fear. When Tom is finally married, anxiety is allayed, and at the expected arrival of Foppington the emphasis is on the lord's discomfiture. As Sheridan does in *The Rivals* when he announces the identity of Ensign Beverley in the first scene and outlines Sir Anthony's plans for his son in the second, or in *The Duenna* when he makes clear Margaret's imposture and allows Isaac to disclose all his foolish plans, so here he stresses anticipation of situation and discomfiture of the characters over comic surprise of the auditors. (pp. 94-5)

The integration of the [Foppington-Fashion and Amanda-Loveless plots] alleviated one potentially unsatisfactory element in Vanbrugh's design and made Sheridan's adaptation, if not a more artistic work, certainly a more unified creation. The simplification of the Foppington-Fashion plot removed the difficulties of bigamy and amorality represented in Hoyden's decision to conceal her prior marriage to Fashion and also caused the omission of what some delicate-minded auditors would have found unacceptable criticism of ecclesiastics in the character of the Chaplain. Making Sir Tunbelly into an amiable character instead of the beastly country squire Vanbrugh paints was another result of Sheridan's simplification of the Foppington-Fashion dénouement. (p. 96)

While Sheridan's adaptation of the Foppington-Fashion line of action is typical both of his skills as a dramatist and his acceptance of his period's morality, the most extensive changes to *The Relapse* were in the adaptation of the Amanda-Loveless plot. (pp. 97-8)

No human heart is exposed in [the Amanda-Loveless] plot of *A Trip to Scarborough;* no truth about human nature is revealed through artistic exploration of the soul. In the elegant dance-like structure of the verbal sparring of Loveless and Berinthia in *The Relapse,* the selfishness that is the center of their existence is comically shown. In Sheridan's adaptation there is embarrassment, not comic exposure; mild flirtation, not fully achieved fornication. It is unsatisfying because the stakes are so small; the characters become mildly discomfited, not by their own natures, but by misunderstanding, by situations.

Clearly, the Sheridan who two months later oversaw production of the brilliant screen scene of *The School for Scandal* was capable of utilizing these materials for a comically satisfying and almost licentious effect. But in the Amanda-Loveless plot of *A Trip to*

Scarborough, Sheridan was either unwilling or unable to lavish the care necessary to create a masterly or even a tolerably farcical recognition scene, largely because he could not adapt either the intellectual or the moral qualities of Vanbrugh's world to the tastes and suppositions of the Georgian stage and audience. (p. 101)

What Sheridan created in adapting *The Relapse* as *A Trip to Scarborough,* then, was a simplified playing piece, typical of much comedy popular in his time. The more unified action it achieves and the softening of tone make it a complete if rather "genteel" performance. He saw the failure of *The Relapse* to coalesce as a single action, or at least, as two actions mutually dependent on one another in some important way. . . . But he failed to realize that the beauty of Vanbrugh's play lay in its very licentiousness, for that licentiousness was the heart of the comic criticism, its exposure of the selfishness that is in most souls (or at least is seen to be in a time not highly influenced by the doctrine of sentimentalism); and in tidying up the plot, he substituted, for brilliant comic discussion of adultery and virtuous conversions, innocuous situation comedy with little artistic power, mild comic embarrassment for comic revelation of human nature. (p. 103)

Measured against the comic works of Congreve, Vanbrugh, Farquhar, Steele, and Goldsmith, Sheridan's comedies still stand tall in the estimation of audiences, who have supported their frequent revival, and should stand taller in the estimation of critics.

For Sheridan was certainly the finest comic playwright after Congreve and before Shaw. As a writer of theatrical burlesque, Sheridan achieved more than any predecessor or successor in this comic line. As a writer of comedy of manners, his achievement is not so unique but just as enduring. Eschewing the didactic, the melodramatic, the coldly cynical, and the violently satiric, Sheridan charted a middle course dependent upon original characterization, tight construction, and brilliant dialogue. While he never reached the poetic unity or intellectual penetration of Congreve, he wrote in a wider variety of styles, creating a distinctive humane comedy that improved upon the fresh boisterousness of Farquhar while avoiding the cynicism of Vanbrugh, the lachrymosity of the later Steele, and the improbabilities of Goldsmith.

For his subject matter Sheridan turned to his own experience largely; he chose the problems of young love and mature affection, the battle of the sexes, and the natural rebellion of youth against age. What he knew of these subjects and what he learned as he matured are revealed indirectly, not as flashes of insight into distinctly individualized, human characters but as general observations about people in society. Like all comic writers, he was concerned with deception and trickery; but he dealt with self-deception as well, particularly in his later comedies.

He began by structuring his plots according to the bifurcated forms most frequently used by his contemporaries, then moved increasingly toward the fuller unification which achieves most dramatic force in a single comic catastrophe. From first to last he showed extraordinary skill in utilizing for his original work *coups de théâtre:* no one who has seen or read them forgets the letters of *The Rivals, St. Patrick's Day,* and *The Duenna* or the famous scenes of concealment of these and *The School for Scandal.* As he developed in his construction of plot, he became less dependent upon purely physical circumstances—duels and elopements—and more capable of using the full scene for a total theatrical effect dependent upon the movement of the actor's spirit, not upon his legs and arms; an auction scene or a screen scene call for this display of the soul more completely than Jack tricking his father or Margaret imposing upon Isaac. Excepting *The Critic,* the structures of Sheridan's plots move from those which display character for its own sake in his early works to those which enact character for the story's sake in his later comedies.

The forms Sheridan's plots took were always distinctly comic. . . . Beneath all his comic excoriations of folly flows a good-natured tolerance: he fails to be morally serious because he chooses not to scourge vice but rather to expose foibles—a course which will alienate none though it improves few. Despite his insight in his last two major comic works, into what most would call reality—a demonstration that vice is as much a part of human nature as virtue—his evident faith in well-intentioned men and benevolent providence to expel the vicious from society seems unrealistic. He was a sentimentalist.

For his characters Sheridan first chose stage types to which the audience and the actors were long accustomed. Capitalizing upon familiarity from the one and skill from the other, Sheridan molded these type characters into surprisingly original amalgams that live in audiences' minds beyond the frameworks in which they appear. As he became more familiar with his craft and with the actors who gave his plays life, Sheridan ventured to complicate his characters further, but never so far that psychological depth overwhelmed comic effect.

His dialogue was designed primarily to give life to these characters. It was "characteristic," his contemporaries would have said. Only for isolated speeches in the scandal scenes or in *The Critic* would a person reasonably familiar with Sheridan's comedies not be able to identify the speaker. The dialogue is amusing usually because it reveals character and complicates situation, though on occasion it is also manifestly absurd or witty. It is brilliant not because it is especially witty in the epigrammatic manner of a Congreve but because it is so consistently true to character without depending merely upon simple dialect or idiosyncratic tags. When Sheridan did choose to use tags, he created new ones quite beyond the grasp of an ordinary comic playwright—malapropisms, "oaths referential," or Joseph's sentiments. (pp. 178-80)

Throughout his comic work, both manners and burlesque, Sheridan's practice was to take the audience into his confidence, to share with them as much of the events yet to come as would pique their expectations concerning the complex situations unfolding before them. Surprise, when it came, arose from probable consequences joyously anticipated; but neither the expectations nor the surprises were allowed to linger long and thereby lose their force. In this manner, Sheridan managed to invent comedies of situation more delicately balanced between anticipation and astonishment than any of his eighteenth-century contemporaries were capable of creating.

In sum, Sheridan's achievement among writers of English comedy springs from his complex, fast-moving, amiably comic plots peopled by probable yet theatrical characters; from a verbal brilliance dependent not upon wit in the high Restoration comic sense but upon a full consonance of expression to character; and from a careful poise of expectation and surprise in situational comedy. (pp. 180-81)

Mark S. Auburn, in his *Sheridan's Comedies: Their Contexts and Achievements,* University of Nebraska, 1977, 221 p.

SOURCES FOR FURTHER STUDY

Bingham, Madeleine. *Sheridan: The Track of a Comet.* New York: St. Martin's Press, 1972, 383 p.

    A detailed biography. Bingham maintains that Sheridan, in both his theatrical and political careers, wished to be accepted primarily as a gentleman rather than as an artist or orator.

Brooks, Cleanth, and Heilman, Robert B. "Part Three: Sheridan, *The School for Scandal.*" In their *Understanding Drama: Twelve Plays,* pp. 194-255. New York: Henry Holt and Co., 1945.

    A study guide that interprets *The School for Scandal* as sentimental and melodramatic. Brooks observes that "Sheridan comes very close to stating outright that he does not believe in intelligence."

Colum, Padraic. "Revaluing Sheridan." *Commonweal* XXII, No. 10 (5 July 1935): 261-63.

    Surveys Sheridan's plays, noting their relationship to the works of other playwrights, including William Congreve, John Millington Synge, and Oscar Wilde.

Hare, Arnold. *Richard Brinsley Sheridan.* Writers and Their Work, edited by Ian Scott-Kilvert. Windsor, England: Profile Books, 1981, 45 p.

    An appreciation of Sheridan's plays. Hare examines them in the context of eighteenth-century theatrical history, and provides a brief analysis of Sheridan's political career.

Loftis, John. *Sheridan and the Drama of Georgian England.* Cambridge: Harvard University Press, 1977, 174 p.

    Maintains that while Sheridan was strongly influenced by his Restoration predecessors, he surpassed them by virtue of his "sensitivity to prose dialogue and . . . his capacity to give familiar dramatic situations intensified force by his mastery of the techniques of burlesque."

Nettleton, George Henry. Introduction to *The Major Dramas of Richard Brinsley Sheridan: "The Rivals," "The School for Scandal," "The Critic,"* by Richard Brinsley Sheridan, edited by George Henry Nettleton, pp. xv-cxvii. Boston: Ginn and Co., 1906.

    A discussion of Sheridan's life and his relation to Elizabethan, Restoration, and sentimental drama. Nettleton, a prominent Sheridan scholar, identifies the sources of Sheridan's major plays. He finds Sheridan's strongest influences to be Ben Jonson and William Congreve, but maintains that Sheridan's work is original.

Upton Sinclair

1878-1968

(Full name Upton Beall Sinclair, Jr.; also wrote under pseudonyms Clarke Fitch, Frederick Garrison, and Arthur Stirling) American novelist, nonfiction writer, dramatist, autobiographer, and editor.

INTRODUCTION

Best known for his controversial novel *The Jungle* (1906), Sinclair is generally regarded as the most prominent of the "muckrakers," a group of early twentieth-century American journalists and writers who sought to initiate social and political reforms by illuminating their country's worst excesses and abuses. Sinclair saw no discrepancy between fictional form and polemical intent, which he often conveyed through arbitrary plots and characters who function as ciphers for his messages. Although he has been variously labeled a romantic idealist and propagandist due to his attacks on wealth and corruption and his espousal of such liberal causes as socialism, world peace, teetotalism, and women's rights, Sinclair also has been often praised for his acute conscience, meticulous research, and historical accuracy. Alfred Kazin commented: "[What] Sinclair had to give to modern American literature was not any leading ideas as such, but an energy of personal and intellectual revolt that broke barriers down wherever he passed. At a time when all the pioneer realists seemed to be aiming at their own liberation, Sinclair actually helped toward a liberation greater than his own by making a romantic epic out of the spirit of revolt."

Born in Baltimore into an upper-class family that had become suddenly impoverished, Sinclair was raised primarily in Baltimore and New York City. He was the son of an alcoholic liquor salesman and an Episcopalian mother from a wealthy Baltimore family, and he grew up in alternate wealth and poverty. To finance his undergraduate education at the City College of New York, he became a hack writer of jokes, stories, and juvenile dime novels. Inspired by the Romantic poets of the nineteenth century, particularly Percy Bysse Shelley, Sinclair turned to writing serious literature in his twenties. While living in near destitution with his wife and child, he published three sentimental novels, which brought him scant critical or popular attention. To prepare for his next work, *Manassas: A Story of the War* (1904), Sinclair built a cabin on a small property outside Princeton University, where he purportedly read or scanned over a thousand books on the American Civil War. Although the book that resulted failed financially, *Manassas* attracted the attention of American socialists and later came to be regarded as a persuasive account of the growth of hostilities between North and South. While studying philosophy and other disciplines at Princeton, Sinclair became interested in the socialist cause and began contributing articles to socialist publications.

Sinclair's next work, *The Jungle,* established him as a leading social critic. This work is generally regarded as the most powerful and convincing muckraking novel of its era. At the request of Isaac Marcosson, a reformative editor and publisher, Sinclair spent seven weeks investigating the Packingtown district of Chicago, where he observed the unsanitary living and working conditions of the meat-packing industry and the squalid living conditions of the workers, talking intimately with them about both. His goal was to write a tract for socialism as well as a romantic exposé of the betrayal of the American dream by focusing on the character Jurgis, a worker who tolerates squalid conditions to support his family. After becoming injured and attacking his supervisor for sexually harassing his wife, Jurgis loses his job and watches his family die as a result of health-related disorders. He becomes alternately a vagabond and a strike-breaker in the meat-packing plant strike of 1904, before discovering in the socialist cause "brothers in affliction, and allies." While some reviewers have faulted the novel's conclusion, in which Jurgis is captivated by the ideological doctrine of radical intellectuals, as didactic, simplistic, or unconvincing, the book garnered widespread praise from reviewers of all political persuasions for its candid exposure of social realities. Jack London commented: "[What] *Uncle Tom's Cabin* did for black slaves, *The Jungle* has a large chance to do for the wage-slaves of today." Ironically, however, the book's exposure of poverty prompted little controversy compared to a brief passage describing contaminated meat, which led to the establishment of the Meat Inspection and Pure Food and Drug Acts but resulted in scant improvement of workers' conditions. Sinclair commented: "I aimed at the public's heart, and by accident I hit it in the stomach."

Following the success of *The Jungle,* Sinclair used his royalty checks to organize Helicon Hall, a communal living experiment in New Jersey which was destroyed by fire in 1907. Afterwards he wrote many full-length nonfiction works in which he argued for the humane institution of socialism as conceived by many optimists and early twentieth century idealists. Wealth,

corruption, and immorality are the targets of Sinclair's next two novels, *The Metropolis* (1908) and *The Moneychangers* (1908), both of which feature Alan Montague, the protagonist of *Manassas.* These works respectively attack the bourgeois strata of New York society and the world of high finance as personified by a figure reminiscent of financier J. P. Morgan, and are generally regarded as unsuccessful combinations of propaganda and fiction. Several other novels followed. To prepare for writing *King Coal* (1917), Sinclair traveled to Colorado to research the coal miners' strike of 1913-1914, in the same manner that he had investigated the meat-packing industry before writing *The Jungle. King Coal* did not attain the popular and critical status of *The Jungle,* though Sinclair insisted that the "book gives a true picture of conditions and events. . . . Practically all the characters are real persons, and every incident which has social significance is not merely a true incident, but a typical one. The life portrayed in *King Coal* is the life that is lived today by hundreds of thousands of men, women and children in this 'land of the free.' "

In 1917, Sinclair broke with the American Socialist Party on the grounds that the group opposed American intervention in World War I, which Sinclair supported due to Germany's military occupation of France. In 1918, Sinclair also became critical of American attempts to intervene in the Bolshevik revolution in Russia. These concerns inform his next book, *Jimmie Higgins* (1919), in which a member of the Socialist Party is driven insane after opposing party opposition to the war and publicly criticizing American military suppression of the Bolsheviks. The novel's protagonist was deemed unconvincing by many reviewers, yet the novel is often considered to reflect realities of American socialism during World War I. During and after the war, Sinclair completed several controversial nonfiction works, including *The Brass Check: A Study of American Journalism* (1920), in which he denies the integrity and objectivity of the journalistic profession; *The Goose-Step: A Study of American Education* (1923) and *The Goslings: A Study of the American Schools* (1924), exposés of the control of education by the wealthy class and the resulting mediocrity of college and high school curricula. And in *Mammonart: A Study in Economic Interpretation* (1925) and *Money Writes!* (1927), Sinclair denounces the writing of literature for profit. Sinclair's next major novel, *Oil!* (1927), recounts the story of the son of a wealthy oil magnate who becomes involved in radicalism at a conservative college and who finances a group of American socialists, eventually becoming active in the cause himself. While the novel's protagonist is often faulted by critics as only partially believable, some have contended that *Oil!* represents a considerable advance over the propagandistic thrust of Sinclair's earlier works in its sympathetic portrayal of wealthy individuals. Sinclair attained considerable success with *Boston: A Documentary Novel of the Sacco-Vanzetti Case* (1928), in which he used his reportorial skills to create a factual historical account of the case of Nicola Sacco and Bartolomeo Vanzetti, immigrant anarchists who were charged with murdering a paymaster and guard while robbing a shoe factory in Boston in 1920. Although the novel was faulted for unbelievable characters and forced religious parallels, and for its unsuccessful blend of poetic and documentary realism, *Boston* drew praise for its accurate reportage and genuine pathos. Upon reading the book, Sir Arthur Conan Doyle called Sinclair "one of the greatest novelists in the world," and in 1988 R. N. Mookerjee summed up the critical consensus: "The abiding appeal of *Boston* remains undiminished to this day. No matter what our political views, the novel stands out as an epic document and will outlast even the memory of Sacco and Vanzetti."

During the 1930s, Sinclair wrote less fiction as he became more directly involved in politics. In 1933, he ran for governor of California, proposing a plan to End Poverty in California (EPIC). This plan, in which he proposed instituting reforms that would have included greater taxation of the state's film industry, resulted in a Stop Sinclair campaign led by the Metro-Goldwyn-Mayer movie studio, which helped defeat his hopes of victory. Following the entrance of the United States into World War II, Sinclair became convinced of the need for American radicals to support their nation during times of national crisis. As a result, he initiated a series of novels chronicling the period from 1913 to 1949 and featuring Lanny Budd, a self-proclaimed schizophrenic who feels compelled by national necessity to defend traditional institutions, despite his liberal leanings. By posing as an art dealer and fascist sympathizer in Europe, Lanny pirates classified information from elite individuals and returns to America periodically to report his findings and to advise President Franklin Roosevelt. Despite the popularity of the series, the Lanny Budd novels were viewed by many liberal critics as a refutation of Sinclair's liberal idealism, and have not attained the critical stature of his earlier works. However, the series remains highly popular and re-

ceives continuing critical assessment. Sinclair regarded his Lanny Budd novels, known collectively as the "World's End" series, as "the most important part of my literary performance," and received the Pulitzer Prize for the third volume of the series, *Dragon's Teeth* (1942). Sinclair spent the last two decades of his life working on various literary projects, publishing his autobiography in 1962. Five years later, he was invited by President Lyndon Johnson to witness the signing of the Wholesome Meat Act, which was enacted to complete the work begun by the Meat Inspection and Pure Food and Drugs Act many years earlier, after the publication of *The Jungle.* Sinclair died in 1968.

Sinclair's works have been translated into many languages and are read worldwide. For years such works as *The Jungle* and *King Coal* were circulated throughout the communist world, where they were declared faithful depictions of the inherent oppressiveness of the capitalist system in the United States. While many Western critics have not gone so far as to see the works as tools to topple capitalism, they have praised them as significant, if flawed, indictments of the excesses of the free market. Other critics have scorned Sinclair's books as the occasionally shrill agit-prop of a man who held a naive view of human nature and the nature of statism. Today, with the vast majority of his works no longer read, Sinclair is widely deemed a figure typical of late-nineteenth-century, pre-World-War-I America: where his role as a muckraker was greatly needed, where the concept of illimitable industrial and economic progress was in serious question, and where simplistic literary depictions of good and evil were more readily embraced than they are at present.

(For further information about Sinclair's life and works, see *Concise Dictionary of Literary Biography, 1929-1941; Contemporary Authors,* Vols. 5-8, 25-28; *Contemporary Authors New Revision Series,* Vol. 7; *Contemporary Literary Criticism,* Vols. 1, 11, 15; *Dictionary of Literary Biography,* Vol. 9: *American Novelists, 1910-1945; Major 20th-Century Writers;* and *Something about the Author,* Vol. 9.)

CRITICAL COMMENTARY

ALFRED KAZIN
(essay date 1942)

[A highly respected American literary critic, Kazin is best known for his essay collections *The Inmost Leaf* (1955), *Contemporaries* (1962), and *On Native Grounds* (1942). In the following excerpt from the latter work, he assesses Sinclair's position in American literature and comments on his works up to 1942.]

If Sinclair lives to survive all the bright young novelists of today and to publish a thousand books (and he may yet), he will remain a touching and curious symbol of a certain old-fashioned idealism and quaint personal romanticism that have vanished from American writing forever. Something more than a "mere" writer and something less than a serious novelist, he must always seem one of the original missionaries of the modern spirit in America, one of the last ties we have with that halcyon day when Marxists still sounded like Methodists and a leading Socialist like Eugene V. Debs believed in "the spirit of love."

Sinclair burst into fame with the most powerful of all the muckraking novels, *The Jungle,* and he has been an irritant to American complacency ever since. His life, with its scandals and its headline excitements, its political excursions and alarums, its extraordinary purity and melodrama, is the story of a religious mission written, often in tabloid screamers, across the pages of contemporary history. As a novelist, he has suffered for his adventures, but it is doubtful if he would have been a novelist without them. The spirit of crusading idealism that gave Sinclair his chance inevitably made him a perennial crusader as well, and if his books and career have become hopelessly entangled in most people's minds, they have been entangled in his own from the day he leaped to invest his royalties from *The Jungle* in the single-tax colony of Helicon Hall. That confusion has always given his critics the opportunity to analyze his works by reciting the adventures of his life, and it is inevitable that they should. For what Sinclair had to give to modern American literature was not any leading ideas as such, but an energy of personal and intellectual revolt that broke barriers down wherever he passed. At a time when all the pioneer realists seemed to be aiming at their own liberation, Sinclair actually helped toward a liberation greater than his own by making a romantic epic out of the spirit of revolt. From the first he was less a writer than an

example, a fresh current of air pouring through the stale rooms of the past. Impulsive and erratic as he may have been, often startlingly crude for all his intransigence, he yet represented in modern American literature what William Jennings Bryan represented in modern American politics—a provincialism that leaped ahead to militancy and came into leadership over all those who were too confused or too proud or too afraid to seize leadership and fight for it.

Sinclair's importance to the prewar literature is that he took his revolt seriously, he took himself seriously—how seriously we may guess from his statement that the three greatest influences on his thought were Jesus, Hamlet, and Shelley. A more ambitious writer as such would never have been able to indulge in so many heroics; but Sinclair seems to have felt from the first the kind of personal indignation against society which could be quickly channeled into a general criticism of society, and that capacity for indignation gave him his sense of mission. The impoverished son of a prominent Baltimore family, he thought of himself from his youth as a rebel against the disintegration of the South after the Civil War, and he was determined to recite the argosy of his early tribulations for all the world to hear. Even after forty years he wrote with special bitterness, in an autobiography otherwise distinguished only by its immense cheerfulness, of those early days when he had dined with his aristocratic grandmother in great state on dried herring and stale bread, of his father's shambling efforts to peddle the liquor that he drank more often than he sold, of the flight to New York, his life on the East Side, and the unhappy years when he worked his way through college as a hack writer of jokes and stories. In those first years Sinclair was a foreshadowing of the kind of titanic Weltschmerz which Thomas Wolfe was to personify all his life, and like Wolfe he became such a flood of words that he began to write romantic epics around himself. His subject was the young Upton Sinclair and his world young Upton Sinclair's enthusiasms. He had many enthusiasms—he was intermittently enthusiastic about chastity, for example—and in that early period before he turned to Socialism, he gave full vent to his insurgence in lyrical early books like *Springtime and Harvest* (later republished as *King Midas*) and *The Journal of Arthur Stirling.*

These books were Sinclair's *Sorrows of Werther.* Living in great poverty with his wife and young child, hu-

Principal Works

Springtime and Harvest: A Romance (novel) 1901; also published as King Midas: A Romance, 1901

Manassas: A Novel of the War (novel) 1904; also published as Theirs Be the Guilt: A Novel of the War Between the States [revised edition], 1959

The Jungle (novel) 1906

The Metropolis (novel) 1908

The Moneychangers (novel) 1908

King Coal (novel) 1917

Jimmie Higgins (novel) 1919

The Brass Check: A Study of American Journalism (nonfiction) 1920

The Goose-Step: A Study of American Education (nonfiction) 1923

The Goslings: A Study of the American Schools (nonfiction) 1924

Mammonart: A Study in Economic Interpretation (nonfiction) 1925

Money Writes! (nonfiction) 1927

Oil! (novel) 1927

Boston: A Documentary Novel of the Sacco-Vanzetti Case 2 vols. (novel) 1928; published in Great Britain as Boston: A Novel, 1929; also published as August 22 [abridged edition], 1965

American Outpost: A Book of Reminiscences (memoirs) 1932; published in Great Britain as Candid Reminiscences: My First Thirty Years, 1932

The Flivver King: A Story of Ford-America (nonfiction) 1937; published in Great Britain as The Flivver King: A Novel of Ford-America, 1938

*World's End (novel) 1940

*Between Two Worlds (novel) 1941

*Dragon's Teeth (novel) 1942

*Wide Is the Gate (novel) 1943

*Presidential Agent (novel) 1944

*Dragon Harvest (novel) 1945

*A World to Win, 1940-1942 (novel) 1946

*Presidential Mission (novel) 1947

*One Clear Call (novel) 1948

*O Shepherd, Speak! (novel) 1949

*The Return of Lanny Budd (novel) 1953

My Lifetime in Letters (letters) 1960

Affectionately, Eve (novel) 1961

The Autobiography of Upton Sinclair (autobiography) 1962

The Coal War: A Sequel to King Coal (novel) 1976

*These novels form Sinclair's "World's End" series.

---

miliated by his obscurity, he wrote out the story of his own struggles in *The Journal of Arthur Stirling,* the furious romantic confession of a starving young poet who was supposed to have taken his own life at twenty-two. When it was disclosed that the book was a "hoax" and that Sinclair himself was Stirling, the sensation was over; but the book was more authentic than anyone at the moment could possibly know. "The world which I see about me at the present moment," he wrote there in the character of Arthur Stirling, "the world of politics, of business, of society, seems to me a thing demoniac in its hideousness; a world gone made with pride and selfish lust; a world of wild beasts writhing and grappling in a pit." Like the imaginary dead poet who had learned Greek while working on the horsecars and written a frenzied poetic drama, *The Captive,* at the point of death, Sinclair was full of grandiose projects, and when his early romantic novels failed he planned an ambitious epic trilogy of the Civil War that would record his family's failure and make him rich and famous. He took his family to a tent outside of Princeton, where he did the research for the first volume, *Manassas,* and supported himself by more hack work. But when even his historical novel, a work which he had written with all the furious energy that was to distinguish him after-

wards, fell on a dead market, he found himself in the very situation that he had portrayed with such anguish in the story of Arthur Stirling, the epic of the romantic genius who had stormed the heights and failed.

The Jungle saved him. Tiring of romantic novels which no one would read, he had turned to the investigation of social conditions, and in his article on **"Our Bourgeois Literature,"** in *Collier's,* 1904, he exclaimed significantly: "So long as we are without heart, so long as we are without conscience, so long as we are without even a mind—pray, in the name of heaven, why should anyone think it worthwhile to be troubled because we are without a literature?" Although he still thought of himself as a romantic rebel against "convention," he had come to identify his own painful gropings with the revolutionary forces in society, and when he received a chance to study conditions in the stockyards at Chicago, he found himself like St. Paul on the road to Damascus. Yet into the story of the immigrant couple, Jurgis and Ona, he poured all the disappointment of his own apprenticeship to life, all his humiliation and profound ambition. *The Jungle* attracted attention because it was obviously the most authentic and most powerful of the muckraking novels, but Sinclair wrote it as the great romantic document of struggle and hardship he had wanted to write all his life. In his own mind it was above all the story of the betrayal of youth by the America it had greeted so eagerly, and Sinclair recited with joyous savagery every last detail of its tribulations. The romantic indignation of the book gave it its fierce honesty, but the facts in it gave Sinclair his reputation, for he had suddenly given an unprecedented social importance to muckraking. The sales of meat dropped, the Germans cited the book as an argument for higher import duties on American meat, Sinclair became a leading exponent of the muckraking spirit to thousands in America and Europe, and met with the President. No one could doubt it, the evidence was overwhelming: Here in *The Jungle* was the great news story of a decade written out in letters of fire. Unwittingly or not, Sinclair had proved himself one of the great reporters of the Progressive era, and the world now began to look up to him as such.

Characteristically, however, Sinclair spent the small fortune he had received from the book on Helicon Hall, that latter-day Brook Farm for young rebels at which Sinclair Lewis is reported to have been so indifferent a janitor. In his own mind Upton Sinclair had become something more than a reporter; he was a crusader, and after joining with Jack London to found the Intercollegiate Socialist Society, a leading Socialist. "Really, Mr. Sinclair, you *must* keep your head," Theodore Roosevelt wrote to him when he insisted after the publication of *The Jungle* on immediate legislative action. But Sinclair would not wait. If society would not come to him, he would come to society and teach it by his books. With the same impulsive directness that he had converted Jurgis into a Socialist in the last awkward chapter of *The Jungle,* he jumped ahead to make himself a "social detective," a pamphleteer-novelist whose books would be a call to action. In *The Metropolis,* an attack on "the reign of gilt" which Phillips and Robert Herrick had already made familiar, Sinclair took the son of his Civil War hero in *Manassas,* Allan Montague, and made him a spectator of the glittering world of Wall Street finance. In *The Moneychangers* he depicted the panic of 1907; in *King Coal,* the Colorado strike; in *100%*, the activities of a labor spy. Yet he remained at the same time a busy exponent of the "new freedom" in morals, wrote the candid story of his own marriage in *Love's Pilgrimage,* "novelized" Brieux's famous shocker of the early nineteen-hundreds, *Damaged Goods,* and between pamphlets, fantasy plays, and famous anthologies like *The Cry for Justice* ("an anthology of the literature of social protest . . . selected from twenty-five languages covering a period of five thousand years") wrote stories of "the new woman" in *Sylvia* and *Sylvia's Marriage.*

Wherever it was that Sinclair had learned to write millions of words with the greatest of ease—probably in the days when he produced hundreds of potboilers—

he now wrote them in an unceasing torrent on every subject that interested him. Like Bronson Alcott and William Jennings Bryan, he had an extraordinary garrulity, and his tireless and ubiquitous intelligence led him to expose the outrages of existence everywhere. He used his books for "social purposes" not because he had a self-conscious esthetic about "art and social purpose," but because his purposes actually were social. Few writers seemed to write less for the sake of literature, and no writer ever seemed to humiliate the vanity of literature so deeply by his many excursions around it. First things came first; the follies of capitalism, the dangers of drinking, the iniquities of wealthy newspapers and universities came first. "Why should anyone think it worthwhile to be troubled because we are without a literature?" His great talent, as everyone was quick to point out, was a talent for facts, a really prodigious capacity for social research; and as he continued to give America after the war the facts about labor in *Jimmie Higgins,* the petroleum industry in *Oil!,* the Sacco-Vanzetti case in *Boston,* Prohibition in *The Wet Parade,* it mattered less and less that he repeated himself endlessly, or that he could write on one page with great power, on another with astonishing self-indulgence and sentimental melodrama. He had become one of the great social historians of the modern era. Van Wyck Brooks might complain that "the only writers who can possibly aid in the liberation of humanity are those whose sole responsibility is to themselves as artists," but in a sense it was pointless to damn Sinclair as a "mere" propagandist. What would he have been without the motor power of his propaganda, his driving passion to convert the world to an understanding of the problems of labor, the virtues of the single tax, the promise of Socialism, the need of Prohibition, a credence in "mental radio," an appreciation of the sufferings of William Fox, the necessity of the "Epic" movement, and so much else? In a day when the insurgent spirit had become obsessed with the facts of contemporary society, and newspapermen could write their social novels in the city room, Sinclair proved himself one of the great contemporary reporters, a profound educative force. He was a hero in Europe, and one of the forces leading to the modern spirit in America; it seemed almost glory enough. (pp. 116-21)

Alfred Kazin, "Progressivism: The Superman and the Muckrake," in his *On Native Grounds: An Interpretation of Modern American Prose Literature,* Reynal & Hitchcock, 1942, pp. 91-126.

WALTER B. RIDEOUT
(essay date 1956)

[In the excerpt below, Rideout examines Sinclair's early writing career and measures the achievement of his novel *The Jungle*.]

Lincoln Steffens tells in his *Autobiography* of receiving a call during the early years of muckraking from an earnest and as yet little-known young writer.

One day Upton Sinclair called on me at the office of *McClure's* and remonstrated.

"What you report," he said, "is enough to make a complete picture of the system, but you seem not to see it. Don't you see it? Don't you see what you are showing?"

Having just been converted to Socialism, Sinclair was sure he "saw it," and in the late autumn of 1905 his friend Jack London was writing to the Socialist weekly *The Appeal to Reason* in praise of a new book which it was serializing.

Here it is at last! The book we have been waiting for these many years! The *Uncle Tom's Cabin* of wage slavery! Comrade Sinclair's book, *The Jungle!* and what *Uncle Tom's Cabin* did for black slaves, *The Jungle* has a large chance to do for the wage-slaves of today.

When *The Jungle* appeared in book form the following year, even the conservative literary critics agreed, with certain reservations, that at last an American was painting a picture "of those sunk in the innermost depths of the modern *Inferno*." Part of the novel's abrupt success among the public at large may have resulted, as Sinclair himself was to lament, from the unintended relevance of a brief muckraking passage on filthy meat; but no novel is read because of half a dozen pages, and this one was read internationally. The extent of the young writer's popularity is suggested by the remark of George Brandes, on his visit to the United States eight years later, that the three modern American novelists he found worth reading were Frank Norris, Jack London, and Upton Sinclair. (pp. 30-1)

The author of *The Jungle* was born in Baltimore in 1878 of a father and mother impoverished by the economic dislocations of the postbellum South, yet proud in their family ancestries. . . . Sinclair's father, a liquor salesman, was one of his own best, or worst, customers, was unable to support his family, and slowly and terribly drank himself to death. Sinclair later ex-plained in his book of reminiscences, *American Outpost,* that one of his reasons for becoming a social rebel was his psychology as a "poor relation."

Readers of my novels know that I have one favorite theme, the contrast of the social classes; there are characters from both worlds, the rich and the poor, and the plot is contrived to carry you from one to the other. The explanation of this literary phenomenon is that, from the first days I can remember, my life was a series of Cinderella transformations; one night sleeping on a vermin-ridden sofa in a lodging-house, and the next night under silken coverlets in a fashionable home. It was always a question of one thing—whether my father had the money for that week's board. If he didn't, my mother paid a visit to her father, the railroad official.

A second influence that assisted in guiding him ultimately to revolt was, Sinclair maintains, the Protestant Episcopal Church, since he "took the words of Jesus seriously," envisioning himself as a follower of "the rebel carpenter, the friend of the poor and lowly, the symbol of human brotherhood." Although he early lost faith in Christianity as anything more than a code of ethics, Sinclair has characteristically continued to hold Jesus as one of his heroes. In his own battle for Truth against Evil, he has made his life one long saga of St. George and the Dragon. An intense, sensitive boy, he was shocked into an ascetic denial of all indulgences by the decline and death of his father, whom he stood by loyally and through whose sufferings he discovered an important social fact, that behind the saloon-keeper loomed the politicians and Big Business. Disgusted with the ugliness of the world, he turned for escape to literature, where he found his spirit of revolt so strengthened that he came to suppose that literature made life. Like his character Thyrsis in the semiautobiographical *Love's Pilgrimage,* he read *Don Quixote* and *Les Misérables;* he loved George Eliot and was thrilled by the social protest of Dickens; he admired Thackeray most of all, for Thackeray saw the human corruption which lay at the heart of the world that he described. Significantly, the boy's favorite poets were the blind Milton and the revolutionary Shelley.

Two elements in the education of this social rebel still remained to take effect. The first was a prolonged acquaintance with what he later called "the economic screw." He supported himself for a year of graduate work at Columbia by hack writing, producing thousands of words of boys' stories each week. Then he broke away to write the Great American Novel, married the adoring Meta Fuller, and endured with her several years of drudging poverty. . . . In the autumn of 1902 he was rescued from this marginal existence by the kindness of George D. Herron, a gentle-minded Socialist writer and lecturer, who gave him financial support and, equally important in Sinclair's development, helped him to discover Socialism. Reading *Wilshire's* completed the conversion. Sinclair had more years of the economic screw to endure, but now he could gird himself for the fight with the whole armor of an economic and political philosophy.

> It was like the falling down of prison walls about my mind; the most amazing discovery, after all these years—that I did not have to carry the whole burden of humanity's future upon my two frail shoulders! There were actually others who understood; who saw what had gradually become clear to me, that the heart and centre of the evil lay in leaving the social treasure, which nature had created, and which every man has to have in order to live, to become the object of a scramble in the market-place, a delirium of speculation. The principal fact which the Socialists had to teach me, was the fact that they themselves existed.

Moving his family to a tent, later a shack on the outskirts of Princeton, New Jersey, he started work on *Manassas,* the first volume of a projected trilogy based on the Civil War, while the family's poverty continued and his unhappy wife passed through long periods of black melancholy. *Manassas,* though superior to his previous novels, sold scarcely better; but it was read by the editor of *The Appeal to Reason,* who enthusiastically wrote Sinclair that, since he had described the struggle against chattel slavery in America, he should now do the same for wage slavery. With an advance payment on the new novel, Sinclair spent seven weeks in the autumn of 1904 in the Packingtown district of Chicago, where the stockyard workers had just lost a strike. Horrified by the wretched conditions under which the inhabitants of Packingtown lived and labored, he collected his evidence with the zeal and care of any muckraking reporter. He returned to Princeton, worked incessantly for three months, began serializing the novel in *The Appeal,* and finally, in February, 1906, succeeded in having it brought out by Doubleday, Page and Company, a nonradical publishing house, after an investigating lawyer sent by the company had submitted a report substantiating Sinclair's findings against the practices of the meat-packers.

The Jungle is dedicated "To the Workingmen of America." Into it had gone Sinclair's heartsick discovery of the filth, disease, degradation, and helplessness of the packing workers' lives. But any muckraker could have put this much into a book; the fire of the novel came from Sinclair's whole passionate, rebellious past, from the insight into the pattern of capitalist oppression shown him by Socialist theory, and from the immediate extension into the characters' lives of his own and his wife's struggle against hunger, illness, and fear. It was the summation of his life and experience into a manifesto. The title of the book itself represented a feat of imaginative compression, for the world in which the Lithuanian immigrant Jurgis and his family find themselves is an Africa of unintelligibility, of suffering and terror, where the strong beasts devour the weak, who are dignified, if at all, only by their agony.

After their pathetically happy marriage, the descent of Jurgis and Ona into the social pit is steady. They are spiritually and, in the case of Ona, physically slaughtered, more slowly but quite as surely as the cattle in the packing plant. Disease spread by filthy working and living conditions attacks them, they endure cold in winter and clouds of flies in summer, bad food weakens their bodies, and seasonal layoffs leave them always facing starvation. When illness destroys Jurgis's great strength, he realizes that he has become a physical cast-off, one of the waste products of the plant, and must take the vilest job of all in the packing company's fertilizer plant. The forced seduction of his wife by her boss leads him to an assault on the man and thirty days in jail. Released without money, he returns to his family evicted from their home and Ona dying in childbirth. After being laid off from a dangerous job in a steel plant, Jurgis becomes successively a tramp, the henchman of a crooked politician, a strikebreaker in the packing plant strike of 1904, and finally a bum. Having reached the bottom of the social pit, he wanders into a political meeting to keep warm and hears for the first time, though at first unaware that he is listening to a Socialist, an explanation of the capitalist jungle in which he has been hunted. The sudden realization of truth is as overwhelming to Jurgis as it had been to Jurgis's creator. He at once undertakes to learn more about Socialism, is given a job in a hotel owned by a Socialist, and is eventually taken to a meeting of radical intellectuals where he hears all the arguments for the Industrial Republic which Sinclair wants his readers to know. Jurgis throws himself into the political campaign of 1904, the one in which the Party actually made such astonishing gains, and the book concludes exultantly with a speech first given by Sinclair himself, proclaiming the coming victory of the Socialists, at which time Chicago will belong to the people.

The "conversion" pattern of *The Jungle* has been attacked as permitting too easy a dramatic solution; however, aside from the recognized fact that many conversions have occurred before and since Paul saw the light on the road to Damascus, it should be noted that in *The Jungle* Sinclair carefully prepares such an outcome by conducting Jurgis through all the circles of the workers' inferno and by attempting to show that no other savior except Socialism exists. Perhaps a more valid objection to the book is Sinclair's failure to realize his characters as "living" persons, a charge which, incidentally, may be brought against many nonconversion novels. Jurgis is admittedly a composite figure who was given a heaping share of the troubles of some twenty or thirty packing workers with whom Sinclair had talked, and the author's psychology of character is indeed a simple one. Although in the introductory wedding scene Jurgis and the other major characters are sharply sketched as they had appeared to the writer at an actual wedding feast in Packingtown, during the remainder of the book they gradually lose their individuality, becoming instead any group of immigrants destroyed by the Beef Trust. Yet paradoxically, the force and passion of the book are such that this group of lay figures with Jurgis at their head, these mere capacities for infinite suffering, finally do come to stand for the masses themselves, for all the faceless ones to whom things are done. Hardly individuals, they nevertheless collectively achieve symbolic status.

Sinclair's success in creating this jungle world emphasizes by contrast what is actually the book's key defect. Jurgis's conversion is probable enough, the Socialist explanation might well flash upon him with the blinding illumination of a religious experience; but practically from that point onward to the conclusion of his novel Sinclair turns from fiction to another kind of statement. Where the capitalist damnation, the destruction of the immigrants, has been proved almost upon the reader's pulses, the Socialist salvation, after its initial impact, is intellectualized. The reader cannot exist imaginatively in Jurgis's converted state even if willing, for Jurgis hardly exists himself. What it means to be a Socialist is given, not through the rich disorder of felt experience, but in such arbitrarily codified forms as political speeches, an essay on Party personalities, or the long conversation in monologues about the Coöperative Commonwealth which comprises most of the book's final chapter. *The Jungle* begins and lives as fiction; it ends as a political miscellany.

The fact that Jurgis's militant acceptance of Socialism is far less creatively realized than his previous victimization is indicative of how Sinclair's outraged moral idealism is attracted more to the pathos than the power of the poor, and suggests his real affinity for the mid-Victorian English reform novelists. More specifically, *The Jungle* is reminiscent of the work of the humanitarian Dickens, whose social protest had "thrilled" the young rebel. There are frequent resemblances between the two writers in narrative method, in presentation of character, in the tendency of both to intrude themselves with bubbling delight or horrified indignation into the scene described. Whole paragraphs on the wedding feast of Jurgis Rudkus and Ona recall, except for the Lithuanian, the manner of Dickens with the Cratchits' Christmas dinner, and Madame Haupt, fat, drunken, and filthy, might have been a mid-wife in Oliver Twist's London. Finally, the temper of Sinclair's protest is curiously like that of Dickens. Where the latter urges only the literal practice of Christianity as a remedy for the cruelties he describes, Sinclair, to be sure, demands the complete transformation of the

existing order of things by the Socialist revolution; yet the revolution that the orator so apocalyptically envisages at the conclusion to *The Jungle* is to be accomplished by the ballot and not by the bullet. Sinclair's spirit is not one of blood and barricades, but of humanitarianism and brotherly love. (pp. 31-6)

Walter B. Rideout, "Realism and Revolution," in his *The Radical Novel in the United States, 1900-1954: Some Interrelations of Literature and Society,* Cambridge, Mass.: Harvard University Press, 1956, pp. 19-46.

L. S. DEMBO
(essay date 1980)

[In the following excerpt, Dembo evaluates Sinclair's fusion of literary and propagandist elements in his "proletarian novels" and major works.]

In *The Radical Novel in the United States* Walter Rideout defended the long, didactic conclusion of Upton Sinclair's *The Jungle* by maintaining that the turn of the hero, Jurgis Rudkus, to socialism was carefully prepared for: Sinclair conducted Jurgis "through all the circles of the workers' inferno" and attempted to "show that no other savior except socialism exists" [see excerpt above]. The point is worth elaborating for it is crucial to an understanding of what Sinclair achieved in *The Jungle* and what he failed to achieve in most of his other novels.

Now, without the specifically socialist conclusion, Jurgis' story would be that of a naturalist man in a naturalist world. His repeated insights into the harsh terms of life in Packertown are never in themselves enough to free him. He arrives in America, for instance, with a naive faith in the ways of the world and a pride in his own powers; in reaching the inevitably disastrous decision to buy a house, he reasons: "Others might have failed at it, but he was not the failing kind—he would show them how to do it. He would work all day, and all night, too, if need be; he would never rest until the house was paid for and his people had a home." He eventually gains an understanding of his situation: "He had learned the ways of things about him now. It was a war of each against all, and the devil take the hindmost. . . . You went about with your soul full of suspicion and hatred; you understood that you were environed by hostile powers that were trying to get your money and who used all the virtues to bait their traps with."

This disillusionment does not make a socialist out of Jurgis. Quite the contrary, he accepts the state of affairs around him as a permanent reality, a given to which he must adapt himself. It is the naturalist, not the socialist, who declares the world a hopeless jungle. Thus Jurgis, still confident in his powers, goes no farther than determining on personal survival and the protection of his immediate family. His encounter with unionism teaches him that he has "brothers in affliction, and allies. Their one chance for life was in union, and so the struggle became a kind of crusade." But this sentiment, embryonic to begin with, does not withstand the despair that overtakes him as he lies convalescing from an injured ankle.

It is in the misery of his imprisonment for assaulting his wife's seducer, however, that the vision of the world as a jungle in which all that matters is personal survival overwhelms Jurgis. Sinclair makes it explicit that frustration and rage, not social consciousness, underlie Jurgis' "rebellion." . . . This response is as far as Jurgis can go; on the death of his son, the last member of his immediate family, he can feel only the same kind of rage: "There should be no more tears and no more tenderness; he had had enough of them—they had sold him into slavery! Now he was going to be free, to tear off his shackles, to rise up and fight . . . he was going to think of himself, he was going to fight for himself, against the world that had baffled him and tortured him!"

Thoroughly disillusioned but still unenlightened—trapped by ignorance as well as rage—Jurgis gains a temporary respite by fleeing to the countryside, but returns to a life of street crime and, when the opportunity presents itself, political corruption. Nor is he averse to strikebreaking, an activity that earns for him, for the first time in the novel, Sinclair's sarcasm.

Regarded from a socialist point of view, Jurgis is the very man who, because of his sufferings, can appreciate the truth once it is made known to him. His conversion is explained in the same oration that illuminates him:

> there will be some one man whom pain and suffering have made desperate. . . . And to him my words will come like a sudden flash of lightning to one who travels in darkness. . . . The scales will fall from his eyes, the shackles will be torn from his limbs—he will leap up with a cry of thankfulness, he will stride forth a free man at last! A man delivered from his self-created slavery! A man who will never more be trapped—whom no blandishments will cajole, whom no threats will frighten; who from to-night on will move forward, and not backward, who will study and understand, who will gird on his sword and take his place in the army of his comrades and brothers.

An important point is easily overlooked in the flow of the rhetoric: revelation is only the first step in a socialist education; it must be followed by hard study and experience. The conclusion of *The Jungle* is opti-mistic not simply because it envisions a socialist victory at the polls, but because it marks the socialization of a man who without the doctrine would be wholly lost.

Never committing himself to a specific social theory, Zola emphasizes the baffling multiplicity of socialist solutions and at the end of *Germinal* he sends his hero, Lantier, off to Paris still uncertain of the path he should follow. Nothing is clear but the grim possibility of anarchic and apocalyptic uprising—the one sure means of ushering in a new world. Committed to socialism, Sinclair is anxious to show the diversity in socialist thought only to indicate that, contrary to the stereotype, socialists have no "cut-and-dried program for the future of civilization." And he does go on to list the fundamental principles on which all socialists agree. For Zola, "heredity" was as crucial an influence on character as environment: that fact was expressed in the belief that there existed a jungle within as well as without. Sinclair believed there was no jungle within except that created by the jungle without, that there was a specific criterion for enlightenment, and that socially conscious men, using rational means, could bring about change.

Unfortunately, the men and women who Sinclair believed met these standards—his heroes and heroines—frequently turn out to be not proletarians or foreigners but upper-class Americans. The implications of this preference are startlingly evident even in *King Coal* (1917), an account of conditions in the unorganized coal industry that was intended to be another muckraking bombshell. The trouble with this novel is not that it insists on presenting socialist propaganda in the guise of literature; to the contrary, it is socialist merely by inference. Its real failure lies in its focussing upon the experiences of an upper-class hero (Hal Warner, a mine owner's son who decides to spend a summer, disguised, in a mining camp not owned by his father, and soon finds himself championing the miners' causes). As he was to do in many of his succeeding novels, Sinclair, though intent on exposing the oppression of the working class by an avaricious and tyrannical capitalism, chooses as his means of narration the romantic clichés of popular fiction. The education of Hal is so simplistically and obviously rendered that *King Coal* cannot be justified by one's calling it a *Bildungsroman.* Although it is probably that Sinclair felt he could better enlist the sympathies of the bourgeois reader by presenting the story as he did—and in 1917 he may indeed have been right—an account of the heroic adventures and the noble, self-sacrificing behavior of a clear-eyed, red-blooded, rich young American among a group of down-trodden, confused, often inarticulate, and impotent foreigners not only appeals to the worst kind of sentimentality but confirms more prejudices than it dispels.

"The book," comments Sinclair,

gives a true picture of conditions and events. . . . Practically all the characters are real persons, and every incident which has social significance is not merely a true incident, but a typical one. The life portrayed in *King Coal* is the life that is lived today by hundreds of thousands of men, women and children in "this land of the free."

This description may be accurate enough from a journalistic point of view but only from that point of view. Unlike the characterization in *Germinal,* or even in *The Jungle,* for that matter, that in *King Coal* is superficial and stereotypical. We are presented with a "representative" old Slovak, an Italian anarchist, a fiery Irish maid with an alcoholic father, and others—all of whom emerge precisely in their typicality, just as do the municipal and mine officials and their police.

We see these characters mostly through the eyes of a twenty-year-old youth, who is sensitive but inexperienced and still limited by many of the prejudices of his class. . . .

> Here was a separate race of creatures, subterranean gnomes, pent up by a society for purposes of its own. . . . Coal would go to the ends of the earth, to places the miner never heard of, turning the wheels of industry whose products the miner would never see. It would make precious silks for fine ladies, it would cut precious jewels for their adornment, it would carry long trains of softly upholstered cars across deserts and mountains; it would drive palatial steamships out of the wintry tempests into gleaming tropic seas. And the fine ladies in their precious silks and jewels would eat and sleep and laugh and lie at ease—and would know no more of the stunted creatures of the dark than the stunted creatures knew of them. Hal reflected upon this, and subdued his Anglo-Saxon pride, finding forgiveness for what was repulsive in these people—their barbarous jabbering speech, their vermin-ridden homes, their bare-bottomed babies.

The speciousness of this passage is apparent in almost every line. The mine-owner's son finds "forgiveness" for the people whose exploitation has made him the "superior" person he is! It is easy enough for him to deride the "fine ladies" on "palatial steamships," quite another for him to realize that he is no less implicated. All of Hal's fine heroics on behalf of the poor—including his imprisonment in his bid to become checkweighman (a representative of the miners who makes certain that each man is credited by the company with the proper weight of coal he has dug)—are, without this knowledge, little more than adolescent adventures.

What is more, this lack makes Hal's heroism dangerously misleading. Because he is "educated" and "American," he is chosen as a leader and spokesman, and we are led to believe that he alone, acting on his own initiative, has the consciousness and capability to take effective action. Even the organizer from the miners' union is relegated to a passive role. As for most of the miners, we learn, "it was impossible to work so hard and keep . . . mental alertness . . . eagerness . . . and sensitiveness." This may well be true, but the activities of a Hal Warner, disguised as Joe Smith, are, from any social perspective that goes beyond romantic sentimentalism, irrelevant.

Hal persuades his college classmate, Paul Harrigan, son of the owner of the mine in which he is working, to order the superintendent to expedite rescue operations after an explosion (the mine had been sealed to prevent further property damage) and eventually, on the advice of union representatives, convinces his fellow-workers not to go ahead with their planned strike. After these exploits, he decides to return to his normal life and to marry the spoiled girl to whom he had been engaged; even from the beginning he had spurned the love of the Irish working-class girl whom he now leaves, as he leaves all his summer working-class friends, "with more than a trace of moisture in his eyes."

Sinclair means all this quite seriously; throughout the entire novel Hal's idealism and nobility are contrasted with the insensitivity and avarice of his relatives, friends, and the institutions they control. But because it lacks the sophistication and insight to develop the full implications of class relations, the work fails in social vision. Because it creates a stereotyped hero and not a character who undergoes an authentic moral development, it fails as a novel and remains at best a piece of muckraking journalism, at worst a sentimental tale.

A decade after he published *King Coal,* Sinclair wrote an exposure of the oil industry (*Oil!,* 1927) and once again chose to tell the story of an upper-class boy, this time Bunny Ross, the son of an oil magnate, who is torn between a devotion to his father and to a working-class friend, Paul Watkins, who perpetually is victimized by and reveals the horrors of the capitalist system in America. Bunny lives a dual life: captivated by the romance of oil exploration and eventually involved with a movie star, he remains partly true to his class; still he engages in radical activities at the conservative college he attends and befriends and gives financial aid to a group of socialists. After his father dies, he gives himself over more fully to the radical cause by founding a labor college and offering marriage to a Jewish socialist girl.

Unlike *King Coal,* which centers upon the tyranny exercised over an isolated mining camp, *Oil!* is a sweeping novel that, covering Bunny's life from boyhood in the 1900's through his youth in the 1920's, includes as part of its background the First World War and the Allied invasion of Russia in 1919, as well as the election of Harding and the subsequent oil scandals. Sinclair also comments on religious superstition in capitalist America through the story of Paul Watkins' brother, Eli (modelled on Billy Sunday), "Prophet of the Third Revelation," who rises to wealth and power. As always, Sinclair can be effective in describing social injustice, but he is still heavy-handed and unconvincing in creating a hero.

Bunny, it is true, is portrayed as an ambivalent figure—and as such is neither an outright hero or villain. Sinclair is explicit about Bunny's deficiencies: his extreme dependence on his father, his inclination to "lean on others," and his general fecklessness. On the other hand, he supposedly possesses the same "nobility" as Hal Warner in *King Coal;* he is depicted as being one of the rare men of compassion of his class and this quality is meant to redeem him. But unlike George Orwell, for example, Sinclair is interested in declassment not as a psychological, social, and ethical phenomenon but rather as a device for revealing the manners and conduct of the two classes through sensitive eyes. Bunny is chiefly an observer and sympathizer. Although he undergoes something of a socialist education, he is never made to experience the hardships of an oil worker. And like Hal, even when participating in radical activities, he holds the trump card of his identity as the son of a member of the ruling class; although occasionally baited by the press, he is never really brutalized.

That Sinclair is himself aware of these weaknesses in the position of his upper-class heroes is evident in *Boston* (1928), at once an account of the Sacco-Vanzetti case and a novel about the social and moral education of a Brahmin woman, Cornelia Thornwell, who, upon the death of her wealthy and powerful husband, renounces her family (and all it stands for) and attempts to transform herself into a working-class woman. This so-called runaway grandmother does, in fact, undergo all the hardships that an unskilled worker in a New England cordage factory in 1917 would, but it is still not enough, as she learns in an argument with a French socialist:

"Understand me, Comrade Thornwell, it is good of rich and cultured ladies to take an interest in the exploited workers; but you suffer always from the fact that you can't possibly realize how they actually feel."

"Don't forget, Comrade Leon, I worked for a year and a half in a cordage plant, and lived on the wages."

"I know. . . . and I never heard anything like it.

But all the same, if you will pardon me, it wasn't practically real, because if you had been ill or out of a job, you'd have gone back to your family; it wasn't psychologically real, because you always knew you

could, and you had the moral support of knowing you were a lady. No worker has that. . . . "

This revelation does not prevent Cornelia from committing herself to a socialist view of the world, nor does it in any way detract from Sinclair's obvious admiration for his heroine and her real-life models. What helps make her a sympathetic figure, not only to Sinclair but, insofar as she is credible at all, to his readers, is precisely what is lacking or at least unemphasized in the other heroes: a strength of character that perhaps goes deeper than politics or doctrine, and manifests itself in her desire to see and act upon the truth as it reveals itself, a quality that goes against the grain of her entire Brahmin upbringing in which decorum, maintained by repression and hypocrisy, is the chief value in social conduct, especially among women. Her education through the long ordeal that begins with her flight and culminates in the execution of Sacco and Vanzetti is intended to be that of the reader as well. *Boston* is Sinclair's *Vérité*, Sacco and Vanzetti, his Dreyfus. Like Zola, he argues for "objectivity" and historical accuracy in the reconstruction of the circumstances. "An honest effort," he tells us, "has here been made to portray a complex community exactly as it is. The story has no hero but the truth." (pp. 164-71)

[For all Sinclair's prodigious research, however, *Boston*] is impelled not by detachment but moral outrage. One can concede, I suppose, that Sinclair does explore certain morally ambiguous areas—as, for example, the dilemma into which Lee Swenson, the experienced, tough, radical lawyer, leads Cornelia when he informs her that she (and she alone) has the power to destroy the prosecution's case against Sacco and Vanzetti if she'll commit perjury; the implications and ramifications of this problem occupy Sinclair for several pages. Nonetheless, we neither expect nor find any sympathy whatsoever for those who have brought Sacco and Vanzetti to trial (the "rulers" of the Commonwealth of Massachusetts) or any hostility toward those who would defend them. By a "complex community," then, Sinclair in no way means one toward which, or in which, moral neutrality can have any place. What he does mean is a society divided into the oppressors and their henchmen and the oppressed; the former contains frequently antagonistic groups, such as the Back Bay aristocracy and the wealthy and politically potent Irish, but their commercial, legal, political, and social interactions are reducible to the common motives of avarice and lust for power. The latter are the poor, chiefly Italian, who are invariably portrayed in a favorable light; they are not Zola's Parisian poor (*L'Assommoir*) or his land-hungry peasants (*La Terre*). Whereas in Zola, family life on all social levels is dominated by envy and greed and therefore is in a state of disintegration, in Sinclair, Italian family life stands in ideal contrast to that of the Brahmins. Tolerance, generosity, kindness—an openness to life—characterize the relationships of the Brinis, with whom, as a broader, Cornelia finds more than adequate compensation for the hardships she must endure as the laborer.

If Sinclair has presented an oversimplified image of the Italian family, it is not necessarily out of sentimentality that he has done so. Such an image logically underscores the view that, along with self-interest, an almost psychopathic paranoia marked the "American" attitude toward the Italians, all of whom it held to be potential bombthrowing anarchists. Accordingly, Bartolomeo Vanzetti, whom Sinclair describes as a man of words rather than action, emerges as the perfect Italian hero, a saintly man incapable of taking any life, to say nothing of gunning down the paymaster of a shoe factory.

What is ironic in all this is that the socialist view of the anarchists—that is, the one expressed by Pierre Leon in his argument with Cornelia—actually justifies the anxieties of the capitalists who wish to jail, deport, or execute the "whole lot of them." . . . That Vanzetti as a dedicated anarchist could have committed the crime with which he has been charged is a possibility that Cornelia cannot accept—nor, in a sense, can Sinclair himself, since the effectiveness of his attack on the Commonwealth—the capitalist state—depends on Vanzetti's innocence, not only as a bandit but as a bomber. Equally important is that such innocence—carrying with it an inability to act—reaffirms the notion, ubiquitous in Sinclair's work, that the oppressed cannot save themselves—that somehow their salvation, if attainable at all, requires the appearance of enlightened American aristocrats who renounce or rebel against their class.

The wealthy, clean-cut American, sympathetic to the socialist cause but accustomed to privilege and material comfort, was to remain Sinclair's favorite hero to the end. Not only does he reappear in the simple propaganda piece about the Spanish Civil War, *No Pasaran,* but he is elaborated throughout the eleven-volume Lanny Budd series, Sinclair's epic and chronicle of the period 1913-1949. Written between 1940 and 1953, these novels can scarcely be called proletarian literature since they deal mostly with the haute bourgeoisie, the aristocracy, high government officials and leaders and with the diplomatic and political history of the West. Fascism, Nazism, and finally world communism emerge as the central evils; capitalism is attacked for generating these forms of tyranny or, at least, making it possible for them to flourish. Except for one episode concerning the slums of pre-World War I London, there is no attempt to delineate consistently the conditions that inspired the muckraking novels.

From the start Sinclair's reviewers were sensitive to the aesthetic weaknesses of the series. Pedantry, sentimentality, and an irritating facetiousness permeate the entire work. Wholly unaffected by the stylistic innovations of the twentieth century, Sinclair writes in what is often the worst rhetoric of another age. His treatment of personal relations, including Lanny's pallid romances, is superficial and contrived and the dialogue of his characters often banal and awkward. He is repetitious to the point of distraction, not only in his recitation of facts or his use of epithets for his characters, but in the plotting itself. (Lanny's adventures fall into basic types that appear cyclically: the interviews with political leaders, the rescue of prisoners or victims of the fascists, the participation in seances, art agent dealings, dealings with socialists. The many visits to Hitler or Roosevelt are identical in form, if not in actual subjects discussed, as are the other adventures within their categories.) Yet all these weaknesses conceded, there is no denying that Sinclair does have a genius for recreating historical events and portraying a seemingly endless variety of actual public figures. These portraits are not the ironic or idealized sketches that one finds in Dos Passos but convincing if limited life studies. In addition to Hitler and Roosevelt, Lanny Budd, playboy, art agent, and presidential spy, has protracted or numerous dealings with most of the major and many minor Nazi officials, Harry Hopkins, Hearst, Truman, Churchill, Laval, Petain; he has illuminating encounters with hundreds of others, including English, French, German, Italian, and Spanish aristocrats, industrialists, generals, scientists, and politicians. This plethora and scope led one reviewer to argue that Lanny was "an all-seeing eye, not a dramatic hero." From the viewpoint of technique Lanny is perhaps a device, but that does not mean we can avoid judging his character or considering his development as a socialist sympathizer and its actual significance.

The illegitimate son of Robbie Budd, an American munitions maker, and his first love, Mabel Blackless (called Beauty), whose marriage had been prevented by the Budd family, Lanny is born and raised on the Riviera by his socialite mother. He comes under the sway of his father, who visits him often and exposes him to his Darwinian views of society in the hope that Lanny will eventually take his place in the family business. Thus, justifying his trade, Robbie plants the seeds of a capitalist philosophy: " 'Men hate each other. . . . They insist upon fighting, and there's nothing you can do about it, except learn to defend yourself. No nation would survive for a year unless it kept itself in readiness to repel attacks from greedy and jealous rivals . . . ' " He sees the First World War as a "war of profits," in which the steel men were "selling to both sides, and getting the whole world into their debt" and international industrialists in general "had taken charge of the war so far as their own properties were concerned."

But Lanny finally is convinced no more by his father's conclusions than by those of his uncle, Jesse Blackless, the spokesman for violent world revolution. . . . Repudiating them both, Lanny sees himself at the age of eighteen, after his experiences at the peace conference, as "the man who loved art and beauty, reason and fair play, and pleaded for these things and got brushed aside. It wasn't his world! It had no use for him! When the fighting started, he'd be caught between the lines and mowed down." (pp. 171-74)

Content to roll through life "in a well-cushioned limousine," Lanny is confronted in the years 1933-1937 with the accession to power of the Nazis and the advent of the war in Spain. Through his boyhood friend, Kurt Meissner, pianist, composer, Prussian aristocrat, and Beauty Budd's former lover, he had come to know and love pre-Hitler Germany; he is fluent in the language and seems to be as much at home in upper-class German society as he is in French and English. In aiding another long-time friend, the Jewish speculator Johannes Robin, one of whose sons has married Lanny's stepsister, to escape, Lanny is given a direct insight into the realities of the new regime, and the fate of another son, Freddi, only increases Lanny's horror.

His commitment now takes the form of financial aid to a Socialist underground, whose representative, Trudi Schultz, a dedicated young Socialist and art student, Lanny makes several trips to Berlin to meet. Irma, who has grown less and less tolerant of his leftist activities, unsuspectingly accompanies him on one of his trips, and though she consents, in an emergency, to help smuggle Trudi, threatened by the Gestapo, out of the country, she has had enough. Characteristic of Lanny's double life is that part of the escape plan includes a prearranged visit to Hitler at Berchtesgaden, and here Irma's voluntary declaration of her admiration for the Nazis precipitates Lanny's final decision to divorce her.

What is thematically important in all this is that it signals the first real moral crisis in Lanny's life, and this crisis is accentuated when it becomes apparent that not only Irma, but most of Lanny's friends and acquaintances—the aristocracy and the ruling classes of western Europe, along with powerful groups in the United States, see in fascism and Nazism only a bulwark against the "Bolshevik menace." In *Wide Is the Gate* (vol. 4) ("Wide is the gate, and broad is the way, that leads to destruction") this thesis is dramatized repeatedly and offered as the basic reason that the Nazis were unchecked in the thirties. Whether talking to French industrialists, Spanish landowners, or highborn persons in the British Foreign Service, Lanny, when he is later gathering political information, knows just what politics will ingratiate him most quickly. But when he is sincere, as he must be with his father, now building aircraft, when after his experiences in Spain he comes to argue for a pursuit plane for the loyalist gov-

ernment, he finds himself in a hopeless deadlock with his own family. Robbie's intransigence, his bitter opposition to the Republican forces is a graphic enough demonstration of the chasm that has opened between Lanny and his class.

Whatever the depth of his commitment, Lanny, as it turns out, finds himself in a position that requires his continued existence as one of the privileged. As a "presidential agent," charged by Roosevelt with learning the intentions of the rich and powerful of Europe, he poses as a Nazi sympathizer pursuing his trade as an art agent. . . . [His primary] connection with the movement is through his continued relationship with Trudi Schultz, who refuses to give up hope that her husband, though captured by the Gestapo, is still alive, and, from Paris, slavishly devotes herself to composing anti-Nazi propaganda to be smuggled to German workers. Lanny, after a less than romantic courtship, marries her, admires her, and, when she is kidnapped by Gestapo agents in France, moves heaven and earth to locate and rescue her, until he is given confirmation of her death in Dachau.

With the exception of Rick (Eric Pomeroy-Nielson), another boyhood friend, who was crippled while flying for the R.A.F. during World War I and has become a liberal journalist and playwright, there are few members of the aristocracy with whom Lanny can express his real feelings. As he is to reflect after the Nazis are defeated. "He had been living in the enemy's country, not merely physically but ideologically; he had been living capitalism and luxury, while cherishing democracy as a secret dream." The fact remains, however, that despite some mental anguish and the personal risks involved in espionage, Lanny is never called upon to make any real sacrifices, never suffers unduly, and never abandons the habits, instincts, and outlook of the man of privilege. He tells Trudi that the force of property is "so overwhelming that only a small fraction of mankind has any chance of resisting it. I am not sure if I myself am among this number; I feel myself struggling in a net, and just when I think I am out of it I discover that another fold has been cast over my head and I am as helplessly entangled as ever." This is a genuine insight, but its implications are not pursued. To Sinclair, Lanny is a wholly creditable hero whose essential high-mindedness is seriously presented: "No, he was not a Socialist, he didn't know enough to say what he was, but he knew human decency when he met it, and he had learned what it was for a modern state to be seized by gangsters and used by them to pervert the mind and moral sense of mankind." Lanny always speaks for "human decency," for the sound mind and moral sense of mankind. Thus, even though Sinclair has created a dichotomous position for his character, one that invites further inquiry into his motives and behavior, the subtleties involved have no part in Sinclair's design.

For example, it is of no thematic consequence that Lanny is a man who lives to ingratiate himself with others and that deception and manipulation are second-nature to him; that he is sanctimonious, condescending, and passionless; that his charm, his "famous smile," his ready wad of cash, his inside knowledge, his possession of credentials with intimidating signatures are his chief means of getting along in the world. Perhaps affected most by Trudi's kidnapping, and then not because he loved her but because he felt guilty for not having loved her enough (again the Moral Hero), he emerges physically and emotionally unaltered from every perilous adventure he has had, including torture by the Russians after the war. It is true he has risked much in helping relatives, friends, and allies escape from Germany, but he is wholly capable of turning down an appeal by strangers without much more than apt reflection on the sadness of the situation and perhaps a "tear in his eye."

The lack of psychological dimension in Lanny's character is no mere technical failing; it is a reflection of Sinclair's view of the world, which to its core is rationalistic and moralistic. . . . "Think more clearly, and so to organize and cooperate," "sufficient intelligence to persuade others"—these ideals are clearly the inspiration for the kind of liberal socialism that Sinclair espouses. They assume a simple human psychology and ethos in which reason and passion, intelligence and stupidity, are easily distinguishable from one another, as are good and evil, and they are founded on the hope that men can change themselves and the world by rational decision. (pp. 175-77)

Although, whatever its relation to capitalism, fascism presented its own forms of oppression and required a shift in perspective, it made a Manichean view even more credible. With the emergence of the Nazis, dragons appeared on the earth and dragon-slayers would have to be called upon to eradicate them:

> It was Lanny's fond dream that the whole people were wiser than any self-appointed leaders; that if they could once get power and keep it, they and the products of their toil would no longer be at the mercy of evil creatures spewed up from the cesspools of society. So long as such existed, so long as they could seize the wealth of great nations and turn them to fanaticism and aggression, they had to be fought . . .

Elsewhere, Lanny reasons, "It was really not the German people who were perpetrating (the atrocities of Nazism), but a band of fanatics who had seized a nation and were perverting its youth and turning them into murderers and psychopaths. Germans would awaken someday as from a nightmare and contemplate with loathing and dismay the crimes that had been committed in their name." In this view, "evil" is not in the normal order of things and certainly not within oneself; it cannot belong to a whole people but only to the fanatics among them or to specific "creatures" who can be so designated. Wholly "other," it can be isolated and fought by the forces of reason and the men of "human decency."

These sentiments are perhaps more adequate as a call to action than as an explanation of the Nazi phenomenon. They are, in fact, too simplistic even for Sinclair's own portrayals of Nazi officials. In his dealings with these figures Lanny is so often caught up with them as personalities, that he must remind himself that they are perpetrators of atrocity. They come from all walks of life, represent a variety of temperaments, and more often than not are "typical" Germans. Ironically, one of the most fanatical of them is Lanny's old friend, Kurt Meissner.

The defeat of the Nazis did not, of course, satisfy Sinclair's moral sense; after bringing the series to a conclusion with *O Shepherd, Speak* (vol. 10) in 1949, he added a new volume in 1953, *The Return of Lanny Budd*, a work permeated with the attitudes of the Cold War. The Shepherd to whom Sinclair is referring is Roosevelt, whom Lanny has adulated and whose death he sees as leaving the world without strong moral leadership.

Having for over a decade regarded the idea of "the Bolshevik Peril" as a Nazi-propagated illusion, Lanny, after a flirtation with pacifism, now embraces it as a religious truth. The moral conflict that engages him is not between socialism and capitalism but between democratic socialism and revolutionary socialism, which Sinclair translates into a holy war between democracy and tyranny. Thus, explaining his view of the world situation to Truman, Lanny begins with what appears to be a straightforward socialist critique (Truman has asked what the U.S. has done to alienate the Soviet Union):

> "What we have done . . . is to be a bourgeois nation, the biggest and richest in the world. Our affairs are run by immensely wealthy capitalists who choose dummy legislators and tell them what to do. The capitalists are automatically driven by the forces of an expanding economy to reach out to every corner of the earth for raw materials and markets. We take these by purchase where possible, but where we encounter resistance we are ready to use force. By this means we reduce all colonial peoples to the status of peons and we keep them there." . . .

After more of this palaver in which Lanny draws a picture of hate-filled hordes using every possible means to bring about the destruction of the United States, Truman concludes that the country will have to rearm, but that having a large army will not be incompatible with social progress. Lanny goes away happy.

That the ideal of social progress per se is uppermost neither in Sinclair's mind nor his hero's at this time becomes all the more obvious when it is expressed by another sympathetic character, Professor Charles T. Alston, New Dealer, foreign policy expert, and general insider. Speaking on the radio program sponsored by Lanny and Laurel's "Peace Foundation"—now sounding the alert on World Communism—he argues, "The only possible chance of defeating Communist dictatorship is by setting up industrial democracy by constitutional methods in which our political freedoms would be retained. That is one way we can gain and keep the support of the masses and bring the Red dictatorships to defeat."

Lanny's half-sister, Bessie, always strong in her views, becomes in this volume one of the Communist "fanatics" against whom Lanny supposedly scores point after point in bitter debates (though she is too far gone to realize it), whom he sorrowfully denounces to the FBI as an espionage suspect, and whose long-suffering husband, Hansi, he not only sets free but provides with a more suitable mate. In his arguments with Bessie, Lanny seems never really to answer her charges but rather presents counter-charges about Communist methods that are meant to be unanswerable. He has, in short, ceased being merely a bore and has himself become a zealot whose anti-Communist preaching fills several hundred pages. The conclusion of the Lanny Budd series in a grand peroration brings Sinclair's career full circle, a story of the triumph of moral ardor over the art of fiction. (pp. 178-80)

L. S. Dembo, "The Socialist and the Socialite Heroes of Upton Sinclair," in Toward a New American Literary History: Essays in Honor of Arlin Turner, Louis J. Budd, Edwin H. Cady, Carl L. Anderson, eds., Duke University Press, 1980, pp. 164-80

CHRISTOPHER P. WILSON

(essay date 1985)

[In the excerpt below, Wilson provides a detailed account of the biographical and historical circumstances surrounding Sinclair's novel The Jungle.]

As a rebel, lover of life, and devoted literary professional, Sinclair bore a striking resemblance to London, an author he admired, emulated, and eventually befriended. Of course, there were the obvious similarities of literary approach and style. Both men were intellectual Darwinists, popular naturalists, and internationally renowed socialists. Sinclair, in fact, remembered

being thrilled by the discovery of London's People of the Abyss (1903) and its example of literary celebrity, and London—along with David Graham Phillips and Lincoln Steffens—soon became one of Sinclair's earliest supporters. Even more strikingly, there were similarities in how the two men first approached their vocation. Both had been driven to the literary life by an abiding fear of poverty. Raised mainly in a world where it was (as he later said) cheaper to move than pay rent, surrounded by bedbugs, street danger, and personal degradation, Sinclair had first tried to escape by devoting himself to reading. By adolescence, reading had become compulsive for him, as it had for London: "I read while I was eating, lying down, sitting, standing, and walking; I read everywhere I went—and I went nowhere except to the park to read on sunshiny days." Like London, Sinclair also employed the bootstrap of college—and had more success at it—and even went on to graduate work at Columbia; also like London, he found the college curriculum too slow for his omnivorous ambition and energies. Such similarities in social background, finally, interlocked with a remarkable likeness in temperament. Like London, Sinclair was prone to fits of enthusiasm and despondency, was an activist and yet a maverick, a compulsive workaholic who mastered the marketplace and yet also repeatedly muckraked it. Sinclair's literary output was equally remarkable. In a nineteen-year span, London would produce a half-hundred books, many articles, and a sizable correspondence; in the same period, Sinclair would write over a million words worth of dime novels, twenty-four books, and perhaps more articles—all only the start of a sixty-year career. Yet even more than Jack London, Sinclair seemed to epitomize the new political power bestowed upon authorship by the new marketplace. In 1906, with the hardcover publication of The Jungle, suddenly the modern author—and notably, a socialist one—commanded an unprecedented amount of American attention. More than any of his contemporaries, Sinclair seemed to turn ideas to praxis, to put the word at the service of politics. Moreover, his career exposed the paradoxical uses to which the new language of the marketplace could be put: he became a lifelong advocate of the workingman by mastering the skills of the modern cultural entrepreneur.

And yet, this new power was riddled with compromises and veiled ironies. At the very moment the marketplace vaulted American authors to the political platform, their own appearance signaled a change in politics itself: away from the partisan "armies" of the nineteenth century and into the managed media politics of the twentieth. Needless to say, the Progressive era is a far cry from our world of televised debates, packaged candidates, and pseudo-events in which literary celebrities mingle with political life—and where, in extreme cases, they even run for high office. But the early 1900s were in fact the years in which these possibilities, and their contradictions, were first entertained in the new limelight created by the advent of mass print media. We might momentarily consider that Jack London, once an anonymous street figure, ran twice for mayor of Oakland—and that, a few decades hence, Sinclair himself would become the first (alas, not the last) celebrity to run for the governorship of California. (pp. 114-15)

Although *The Jungle* is by now a fixture in the historiography of American Progressivism, its position has always been somewhat paradoxical. Literary critics commonly discredit the novel's formal characteristics—usually attributing its failings to Sinclair's political ideology—while historians usually credit external events, especially the political context, for the novel's popularity. In either argument, the novel comes out a loser—as it were, a kind of bridesmaid who gets neither the groom nor the bouquet. Yet neither attack, it might be pointed out, accounts sufficiently for the obviously dramatic response the book generated in its readers—nor, as well, why that reading might have led to misinterpretation. Alternatively, by viewing this book from a vocational standpoint—as an expression of Sinclair's synthesis of poet and dime novelist—we may recover a better sense of why the book had such a paradoxical impact. As with Jack London, we can trace the impact of Sinclair's vocational strategy within his style.

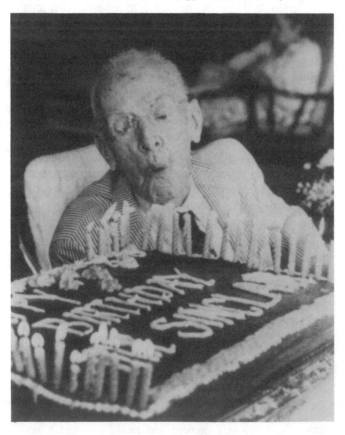

Sinclair celebrating his eighty-ninth birthday.

Sinclair himself seems to have conceived his book as a mix of popular media and political discourse, and frequently compared it to Harriet Beecher Stowe's *Uncle Tom's Cabin.* For instance, in his fourth novel, *Manassas,* the story of a Southerner turned antislavery advocate, Sinclair praises *Uncle Tom's Cabin,* calling it one of those books "which make their way into the world of literature from below, and are classics before the *literati* have discovered them." As if anticipating his own critics, he goes on to say:

In truth, its literary faults are evident enough, its skeleton sticks through its very joints, but he who can read a hundred pages of it for the first or the twentieth time, with dry eyes, is not an enviable person. It was, when it appeared, and it has remained to this day, the most unquestionable piece of inspiration in American fiction.

(The breathlessness of dictation is visible even here.) In a typed outline that he gave to George Brett in 1904, Sinclair described his own plan as "to set forth the breaking of human hearts by a system which exploits the labor of men and women for profits," yet also to make "a definite attempt to write something popular." Later he said he had wanted to "portray how modern industrial conditions . . . were driving the workingman into socialism" and to make the book "as authoritative as if it were a statistical compilation."

Despite this naturalistic-sounding rhetoric, the more significant element in Sinclair's praise of Stowe was his high-lighting of the grammar of self-projection practiced in both his poet and his cadet novels. In *Manassas* he wrote that the power of Stowe's depiction derived from her own sense of oppression as wife and mother. "Probably nowhere in the literature of all the world," Sinclair wrote with characteristic hyperbole, "is there a book more packed and charged with the agony and heartbreak of *woman.*" Describing his hero's reaction to the novel, he said it "is a mother's book, every line seemed to bring [his Southern protagonist] face to face with the very mother-soul. . . . a mother's passionate tenderness, a mother's frantic claspingness, a mother's terror at *destruction,* at cruelty and wounds and death." In sum, Sinclair now consciously believed that projection was not only a feasible technique but also a major source of literary power. (pp. 128-29)

[In preparation for *Manassas,* Sinclair] traveled north to Boston to interview abolitionists and their descendants, and spent months rummaging through Princeton's Civil War collection. This historical emphasis, in turn, had both tempered the narcissism of his earlier works and expanded the imaginative playground by giving it a larger and more topical canvas. Sinclair's surrogate in the novel, Allan Montague, acts out his personal conversion to abolitionist sympathy among figures like Abraham Lincoln and Frederick

Douglass. The author's original plan for *The Jungle* was much the same: initially, Sinclair conceived it as the story of a well-born young man who "sinks" into the proletariat. Returning to the rhetoric of his dime novels, he formulated a style of activism first by exploring it imaginatively.

This pattern, however, subtly changed during the preparation of *The Jungle.* He arrived in Chicago in September of 1904; in fact, he later made a point of the fact that he arrived on his birthday, as if the date presaged another tale of conversion. How long he had planned to stay is unknown, but he wasted little time in settling in. Almost immediately, he arranged to take his meals at the University Settlement House (thereby spending much of his time with the reformer Jane Addams). On his very first night in the yards, he sat in the kitchen of a Lithuanian cattle butcher who had spent twenty-five years in Packingtown. This conversation apparently established Sinclair's decision to focus in on the Lithuanian community—an interesting decision since, as the novel explains, at the time these were the immigrants being displaced by the newer Slovak work force. Later, near the end of his seven-week stay, Sinclair witnessed a wedding celebration or *veselija*—and there found the family for his novel, as well as the setting for its famous first chapter. . . . [However], Sinclair did not put pen to paper immediately; he kept some notebooks, but again composed mostly in his head. Speaking of his younger self in the third person, he later wrote: "From four o'clock until nearly midnight he sat, making note of every detail and composing in his mind the opening chapter. . . . By ten years of practice he had learned to go over a scene and fix it verbatim in his mind. This opening chapter was not put on paper until the following Christmas, but it varied little from the mentally recorded vision." The actual text was written when he returned to his home-built cabin in Princeton.

During his Packingtown stay, Sinclair discovered that he could travel freely in the yards, much as he had at the military academies. The difference, however, was that now he had to wear old clothes and disguise himself by carrying a workingman's dinner pail. Sadly, as a poor and struggling author, he had worn old clothes because they were all he possessed. Apparently, what began to happen was that once again while composing, Sinclair began to parallel his own situation with that of his subject—here, that of the workingman. Consequently, when Sinclair returned to write in Princeton— burdened down with personal problems that included a declining marriage and meager income—he followed the dime-novel pattern and self-consciously projected himself into the novel. In fact, in describing the book's composition only months after its release, he made reference to the method, citing the pressures put upon his own youthful "delicate sensibilities" by the "commer-

cial inferno" and "pit" of poverty. Looking back on the writing of the book, he said: "For three months I wrote incessantly; I wrote with tears and anguish, pouring into the pages all the pain that life had meant to me. Externally, the story had to do with a family of stockyard workers, but internally it was the story of my own family." This was the flip side of the term "proletarian author": Sinclair not only wrote about laborers, but now thought of himself as a brain worker. Even the speech of the socialist at the end of the book—which critics unanimously decry as needlessly tacked on—is actually a lecture Sinclair himself, once a college orator, gave at the end of his stay in Chicago. (In the 1914 film version of the novel, he played the role himself.)

Moreover, as if adopting Stowe's reputed method, Sinclair said that his identification with Jurgis's family was the source of the book's power. He called *The Jungle* an attempt to "put the content of Shelley into the form of Zola"—which might have been a synopsis of his own vocation. He said the "middle-class realists" worked with "infinite skill" and were "expert psychologists; but it is not part of their programme to live the life which they portray, and they do not feel obliged to share in the emotions of their characters. They do their work from the outside, and they resemble a doctor who is too much absorbed in the study of the case to sympathize with the patient's desire to escape from his agony." Thus, Sinclair's emphasis on "heart" meant putting his own on the line.

Sinclair's sublimation of personal and poetic desire into his exploration of the American workingman created moments of brilliance as well as lapses. In its dramatic force, execution, and empathy, *The Jungle* was clearly Sinclair's finest work so far in his career. Even as he laid claim to realistic subject matter, his prose retained the heightened tones of his earlier allegories. The commonplace socialist division of capitalist society into two classes with "an unbridged chasm between them" neatly fit the dramatic polarity of his Nibelung parables. The allegorical motive, admittedly, created moments that may strike modern readers as artificial: Jurgis seems, at points, something of an Everyman in a nightmare, encountering an unrelieved stream of tragedies that were historically possible but perhaps not entirely credible as a narrative depiction of a single individual. On the other hand, Sinclair's poetic sensibility allowed him to capture the melancholy of an immigrant worker's wedding which only straps the newlyweds financially, to depict the anguish of encroaching destitution, to demonstrate the limbo of the tramp—in short, to vivify the lived experience of oppression. Dissecting the Behemoth with an unflinching gaze, Sinclair spoke openly in the narrative about having discovered sights and "words . . . not admitted into the vocabulary of poets"; but the hard-boiled exterior of "facts" is underwritten by that neo-Romantic concern for the soul. Capitalism is exposed as a system both of exploitation and of corruption: society as a whole is debased, degraded, infested. "I have known what it is to dare and aspire," the speaker at the socialist rally cries, "to dream mighty dreams and to see them perish—to see all the fair flowers of my spirit trampled into the mire by the wild beast powers of life."

Sinclair's mode of projection and preparation, however, did not always have positive consequences. First of all, many critics—including contemporary reviewers—complain that Sinclair's socialist politics led him to polemicize almost at will. But to be precise, Sinclair's digressive style, more an opening for polemical ideas than their by-product, was well in place before his conversion to socialism. More than anything else, the episodic character of the novel reflects Sinclair's vocational apprenticeship: specifically, the fact that the text is a relatively unreworked version of Sinclair's preparation—his visit to Packingtown. Robert Cantwell once said, and I think correctly, that Sinclair's plots are a little like land-grant railroads—they meander around, trying to encompass the social whole. But this is only because of his anticipatory strategy: he tended to reconstruct his novels after a preparatory visit, compose on the spot, and write later. In the text, however, it is apparent that Sinclair, reflecting the planned quality of his book, is often jumping the gun on his research. As if he is still holding in his head those on-the-spot compositions, in all too many instances we leap ahead of the narrative to a broader thesis. This is because Sinclair's dictation method opened him up not only to rhetorical flourishes but also to expounding in ways that fragment his narrative. For instance, he writes:

> They were common enough, [Tamoszius] said, such cases of petty graft. It was simply some boss who proposed to add a little to his income. After Jurgis had been there awhile he would know that the plants were simply honeycombed with rottenness of that sort. . . . Warming to the subject, Tamoszius went on to explain the situation.

> Jurgis would find out these things for himself, if he stayed there long enough; it was the men who had to do all the dirty jobs, and so there was no deceiving them . . . he would soon find out his error—for nobody rose in Packingtown by doing good work. . . .

Here it is as if Sinclair's dictation method has led him not only to digress but to telegraph the punch of his narrative. Time is practically suspended in these passages—at worst, we lose the narrative frame altogether. Nor are we sure whose wisdom we are hearing: Sinclair's, Tamoszius's, or Jurgis's own. Sinclair rushes to his case repeatedly, and the sum effect is that the flow of the narrative is recurrently interrupted. Here we feel a tangible consequence of the market's premium on anticipation.

Of course, this might seem mere sloppiness on Sinclair's part—and some of it was. In several places it seems that we are simply rehashing Sinclair's own initial reactions to industrial life upon coming to Packingtown. Even this effect, moreover, was fundamentally a by-product of his projection technique. Sinclair's conscious decision to graft his own visit onto the Lithuanians' initiation, in other words, also had direct textual consequences. In fact, within the novel Sinclair draws an explicit parallel between the introduction of the Rudkis family to Packingtown and the initiation of an unnamed "visitor" referred to by the narrator. However, this tactic automatically gives the text a rather elliptical quality, derived from two different narrative positions: one of empathy, and yet one—not surprisingly—like an excursion. For instance, we encounter passages like the following:

> Those [streets] through which Jurgis and Ona were walking resembled streets less than they did a miniature topographical map. . . . In these pools the children played, and rolled about in the mud. . . . One wondered about this, as also about the swarms of flies which hung about the scene, literally blackening the air, and the strange, fetid odor which assailed one's nostrils, a ghastly odor. . . . It impelled the visitor to questions. . . . Was it not unhealthful? the stranger would ask, and the residents would answer, "Perhaps, but there is no telling."

> One stood and watched, and little by little caught the drift of the tide, as it set in the direction of the packing houses. . . . Our friends were not poetical, and the sight suggested to them no metaphors of human destiny; they thought only of the wonderful efficiency of it all. . . .

Valiant as the attempt may be, this "visitor" undercuts Sinclair's goal of empathy. As a literary vestige both of the originally conceived well-bred youth and of Sinclair himself, the visitor is an intelligence who is affected by Packington (smells, cattle slaughter, billboards) in a way we cannot be sure Jurgis and his co-workers are. Sinclair hoped to make his own initiation contiguous with Jurgis's, but in fact the visitor is either too far ahead of his subjects ideologically or too far behind them experientially. His projection never fully integrates into workers' emotive lives; despite Sinclair's professed intentions, this is not a novel written entirely from the "inside."

Furthermore, these passages about the visitor resonate with the dominant imagery of the novel, having the cumulative effect of reaffirming the lines of kinship between visitor and narrator. Inevitably, then, the novel's primary case is shifted to the visitor's perspective, not the workers'. One can be easily misled by the narrative camouflage which insists, consistent with Sinclair's vocational mythology, that "poetic" consciousness has been eliminated by his own rite of passage. But in fact, as the presence of the visitor attests, the text is riddled with metaphorical and analogical passages and sequences. The visitor's poetic consciousness dominates the balance of the narrative's expository images: "flowers" trod under the feet of capital, cattle prepared for slaughter, souls denied their spiritual "blossoming." The end result is inconsistency. For instance, in the opening depiction of the marriage *veselija*, Sinclair's visitor is absent, as the scene foreshadows the plot by attending to the changing music of the wedding celebration. The Lithuanian musicians play frenetically, answering the desperate pleas of the older immigrants; but soon the older tunes are shouldered out by a crass, exploitative American ragtime. The ominous mood this particular movement generates is quite effective, because here Sinclair's empathy is truly remarkable: it is one pure scene where he witnessed well. But quite a different thing occurs when the visitor reappears to compare, in his own mind, the fate of slaughtered cattle to that of the workers:

> One could not stand and watch very long without becoming philosophical, without beginning to deal in symbols and similes, and to hear the hog-squeal of the universe. . . . Each one of these hogs was a separate creature. . . . And each of them had an individuality of his own, a will of his own, a hope and a heart's desire; each was full of self-confidence, of self-importance, and a sense of dignity. And trusting and strong in faith he had gone about his business, the while a black shadow hung over him and a horrid Fate waited in his pathway. . . . Perhaps some glimpse of all this was in the thoughts of our humble-minded Jurgis, as he turned to go on with the rest of the party, and muttered: "*Diève*—but I'm glad I'm not a hog!"

Not only is this a form of telegraphing; more important, it is in passages like these that the competing consciousnesses of the novel fail to mesh. Although elsewhere (as cited earlier) Sinclair admits that Jurigs and his cohorts are not likely to wax philosophically, here he hopes that they do.

The splintering of the text, moreover, is partly why the conclusion of the novel seems literally forced. Many critics have rightly emphasized the parablelike or "morality play" quality to the plot: Jurgis is led, again like a modern Everyman, through a series of earthly tragedies before finding salvation in socialism. Indeed, the closing sections—in which, in a disturbing echo of the cadet novels, Jurgis is eyed by a beautiful young lady waiting in the wings—are the novel's weakest. But again, this wishfulness is not entirely a matter of Sinclair's naiveté. As Michael Folsom has shown, Sinclair actually also wrote a more pessimistic resolution. Nor is the pat solution merely the result of his "ideological" cast of mind. Rather, it resulted primarily from his conscious strategy of projection. The

choice of the Lithuanians was indicative: grafting on his own fears of déclassé status, Sinclair had chosen an immigrant community itself experiencing declension and humiliation. Thus, when Jurgis has his own moment of socialist vocation, it echoes Sinclair's own: "in one awful convulsion . . . there was a falling in of all the pillars of his soul, the sky seemed to split above him—he stood there . . . gasping, and whispering hoarsely to himself: 'By God! By God! By God!'" Clearly, moments like this were bred in the politics of culture, and not the other way around. Despite his claims to narrative empathy, the residual presence of Sinclair's literary practice often deflected the novel away from the day-to-day thoughts of workers.

In fact, it may have been his poetic imagery, rather than his realism, that opened the book up to misinterpretation. The dominance of Sinclair's own analogical thinking had the effect of placing the degradation of meat in the figurative center of the novel. His metaphorical musings, in sociological terms, compared producers to products, workers to slaughtered cattle. Sinclair presented his case not just in terms of exploitation but in metaphors of declension, corruption, and infestation: the workers' degradation seems, in fact, to stem from the poisonous world they inhabit. Ultimately, this metaphorical dimension, when combined with the essentially elliptical quality of the narrative, may explain why contemporary readers could find so much vicarious power in the text and yet finally misread its motives. As with earlier writers like Charles Dickens and Jacob Riis, part of Sinclair's effectiveness may have derived from the way his anonymous visitor orchestrated the reactions of more timid readers. But by the same token, middle-class readers may have interpreted the worker's embrace of revolution as a warning to implement liberal reforms before it was too late—as had been the intention of both [Dickens's] *Hard Times* and [Riis's] *How the Other Half Lives.* My point here, again, is that it may not have been simply a revulsion from the realism of the text that explains contemporary misreadings; if that were the case, one has the popularity of the novel to explain. Rather, it may have been that readers were carried along quite powerfully, but only from the guarded position of the visitor. In short, Sinclair's readers may have heard more of his heart than he suspected: at some level, they may have responded only to the echoes of his own vocation.

Perhaps Sinclair's mistake is not an uncommon one among American intellectuals, who have habitually seen the masses responding to matters of head and heart rather than to more tangible daily needs. But in this instance it was clearly also symptomatic of Sinclair projecting his own needs onto the worker. Most of all, Jurgis's soul, more than his stomach, needs answering; socialism becomes a form of belonging. Sinclair's dedication to social justice is not to be taken lightly, nor is the genuine empathy of his mind. But there is a utopian strand in his political imagination that was itself partly a by-product of his vocational strategy. The socialist solution loomed out in front of him as a promise of respite from the regimen he had chosen—an end to the hard life of the crusader, the sweat and strain of his professional devotion. For both Sinclair and Jack London, who turned briefly back to politics after *Martin Eden*, a socialist future offset the isolation and wear of professional literary dedication.

The Jungle's public career, of course, was what earned Sinclair his continuing fame and ignominy; here was where his bridesmaid status really took hold. Once again, however, viewing the novel in relation to the literary marketplace can explain more of its paradoxical history. The novel had been designed as a weapon: the immediate stimulus for the book, in fact, had come from Fred Warren, one of Sinclair's new socialist comrades and editor of the *Appeal to Reason*. But when the book skyrocketed to best-seller status, it seemed to be co-opted by the campaign to upgrade the sanitary conditions surrounding the packaging of meat—a cause Sinclair himself did not think helped workers at all. (Any close look at the novel reveals that Sinclair thought federal inspection a sham.) By our standard accounts, Progressive readers apparently took literally the symbolic degradation of meat, which Sinclair had probably employed primarily to emphasize the degradation of labor. Under the direction of Roosevelt and Senator Albert Beveridge, *The Jungle* was mobilized for both the Meat Inspection and Pure Food and Drug Acts, which, some historians have suggested, may have actually strengthened the market position of large packers. Sinclair's apt summary, because it is so often taken at face value, is also often quoted: "I aimed at the public's heart, and by accident I hit it in the stomach."

Sinclair's own socialist standard of value, of course, reflected the purism of his earlier romanticism; certainly, the lives of even workers themselves had been bettered by the new legislation. Nonetheless, to speculate about the meanings received by his audience, as Sinclair himself did, is naturally to invite the perils of "affective" criticism. Literally speaking, we cannot know precisely how Progressive-era readers actually responded. Unfortunately, reviews from the era are not much help either. Although it does seem that earlier reviews understood Sinclair's socialist intentions better than later commentary, this reflected only that the public controversy followed close upon the book's release, thereby shaping the content of the reviews. For this reason, reviews hardly provide a pure or unmediated sampling of contemporary reading. But we can know about the ways in which *The Jungle* was packaged for readers. To use the language of modern merchandising, we can discover what "bundles of attributes" were attached to the novel as it was promoted.

This promotional dimension was itself an intrinsic part of Sinclair's vocational strategy—again, part of his decision to fight the world with its own weapons. In fact, conceiving the novel itself as a weapon was an implicit, if paradoxical, acknowledgment that popular impact—and by implication, adaptation of the modern bestseller system itself—was an indispensable component of even the most "proletarian" literary practice.

The Jungle campaign was the brainchild of Isaac Marcosson, one of the new progressive editors and publishers of the era. . . . In his memoir *Adventures in Interviewing*, Marcosson spoke proudly about having used *The Jungle* to take the book industry from the antiquated conventions of the Gilded Age into modern merchandising. Although in his own privately printed account Frank Doubleday himself said that he had actually found *The Jungle* quite revolting and its author something of a crank, he claimed that the firm had proceeded with the book in order to assert its independence under pressure from threats by Armour to withdraw advertising from the house periodical *World's Work*. But apparently what really happened was that prior to the novel's hardcover publication—as if alerted by Armour's threats—the publishing house decided to take its own steps to protect its investment and take advantage of the coming controversy. What Marcosson did, well prior to publication, was to investigate Sinclair's more serious allegations. Lest we lapse into conspiracy theory here, the important point is that Marcosson really felt he was supporting his author. In the language of the military campaign that was so common to merchandisers in these years, he later called it "bulwarking," or "fortifying" Sinclair's position.

Obviously fearful of legal repercussions, Marcosson himself—and Doubleday lawyer Thomas McKee, also involved in the *Sister Carrie* episode—traveled to Packingtown to do their own work. Intriguingly, Marcosson's investigations paralleled the visit of Sinclair, with an important twist. The promoter also disguised himself to enter the factories, but this time not as a worker but as a meat inspector. Subsequently, he interviewed Dr. W. K. Jaques, formerly city bacteriologist and head of meat inspection in the stockyards, and Dr. Caroline Hedger, a physician. Obviously, what Doubleday was most interested in were the book's charges about sanitation, not labor.

From this point on, Marcosson followed through with a trend-setting promotional effort. He sent advance page proofs of the novel to the editors of major papers (and hence to reviewers), to the UPI, and to the AP. He later claimed that one Chicago paper devoted two full pages to the book's charges. He also sent advance proof to Theodore Roosevelt, who invited Sinclair down to the White House, carried on a correspondence with the author about the book, and followed through with backing of the relevant bills. Sinclair himself was channeled easily into the promotion effort, keeping the issue alive by writing follow-up letters to newspapers and backup articles in *Everybody's.* In a June 1906 interview in the *Arena,* moreover, Sinclair admitted that he had gone over the manuscript with McKee after the lawyer returned from his own investigation, and cut out every line or phrase which McKee considered an exaggeration. Marcosson, meanwhile, again invoking the military metaphor—to which the former cadet novelist must have responded—said he kept Sinclair "shoulder to shoulder" in the "front lines of publicity," down in the "trenches" with other "allies" like T. R., and Doubleday as a whole, it should be pointed out, was hardly concerned with *heading off* controversy. On the contrary, using a practice that really took hold in the Progressive era, Doubleday ads consciously fanned the flames of debate by using presolicited reactions pro and con. (Marcosson proudly said he had done the same thing for Thomas Dixon's *Clansman*). In fact, Doubleday used its own verification scheme as a hint that the book's charges were sensational. Commentary in the house periodical likewise emphasized the sanitation charges.

My point here is not the oft-repeated one that T. R. and the Progressives appropriated the novel for their own ends, though that was certainly the case. T. R. and Doubleday, for instance, actually conferred about the book, hoping some of the socialist material could be removed from the serialized version (which had appeared in *Appeal to Reason*) before going to hardcover. (As Robert Crunden has recently shown, neither Doubleday nor Roosevelt had much affection for Sinclair personally, or for his socialism, but early efforts to edit the book fell short of their plans.) Marcosson clearly recruited allies that Sinclair might not have on his own. But the more essential point here is that Marcosson's own attempts at "bulwarking" had set the terms of public debate about the book—and hence, for much of its reception. In other words, his own attempts to "fortify" the author had actually resulted in encircling a more narrow meaning in the text, an effect which only contributed to the book's public distortion. Because Doubleday's fears were themselves more middle-class; because the firm feared Armour's retaliation, and Armour was more concerned about consumer confidence, and because legal anxieties caused Marcosson to center his own investigations around what were to him the most sensationalistic aspects of the text—because of all this, the public misfire of the book was understandable. As one more bit of evidence, we might note that when Doubleday translated the novel into French, the new title they created was *Les Empoisonneurs de Chicago.* Perhaps

not too surprisingly, then, there is even the intimation throughout Marcosson's account that he felt he had *improved* upon the case of his author. Marcosson notes proudly that even a meatpacker admitted that the book had resulted in greater consumer confidence. Whatever Sinclair's "proletarian" intentions, Marcosson felt more comfortable—and compatible—with the interests of his own class.

Here, then, was the outcome of Sinclair's decision to use the weapons of the modern literary marketplace for his own ends. Lured to topicality and popularity, he found his book channeled into what publicity men, the press, and politicians construed as his real message. One recalls a vivid message in *Martin Eden:* London lamented how, upon the death of that would-be singer Brissenden, the identity of a "famous writer" could be like a vapor created by the public mind, and then injected back into the real man. This analogy typified a recurring theme in a celebrity-conscious society: the persistent fear in the celebrity himself that he is imprisoned by his image—and, moreover, that his political identity is but a shadow cast by the steady glare of promotion. To paraphrase a recent critic of the media-made New Left, it is the problem of trying to make politics with mirrors. Along with the divided consciousness of its narrative text, the promotion of *The Jungle* illustrated the considerable cultural "meanings" bearing upon Sinclair's literary vocation—and hence, upon the reception of his novel. Sinclair's own projection into his story, the narrative splintering of the text, and his public packaging only crowded the text with voices: proletarian, poet, visitor, promoter.

To Sinclair's credit, he himself recognized much of this. We often overlook the vocational confession at the core of his famous quote: thinking that a book could be a weapon that could be "aimed," he failed to account for matters—within the text and without over which he really had little control. Likewise, even when he spoke most proudly of his new literary program, we will mistake his hard-boiled hubris if we do not hear, at least partly, a lament as well. We might, in other words, hear an echo of Martin Eden's quest for knowledge. When Sinclair spoke of the "well-springs of joy and beauty" being dried up, or becoming "like a soldier upon a hard campaign"—Sinclair seemed to be acknowledging a price to the path he had chosen. (pp. 130-40)

Christopher P. Wilson, "Would-Be Singer: Upton Sinclair," in his *The Labor of Words: Literary Professionalism in the Progressive Era,* The University of Georgia Press, 1985, pp. 113-40.

SOURCES FOR FURTHER STUDY

Bloodworth, William A., Jr. *Upton Sinclair.* Boston: Twayne Publishers, 1977, 178 p.

Analysis of Sinclair's works as they reflect his stance as muckraker, propagandist, and political figure, particularly focusing on his theme of "idealistic opposition to an unjust society."

Gottesman, Ronald. *Upton Sinclair: An Annotated Checklist.* Ohio: Kent State University Press, 1973, 544 p.

Detailed bibliography of Sinclair's works in both English and foreign-language editions. Includes additional bibliographical sources and an itemized list of secondary sources, as well as notes on unpublished material.

Grenier, Judson A. "Muckraking the Muckrakers: Upton Sinclair and His Peers." In *Reform and Reformers in the Progressive Era,* edited by David R. Colburn and George E. Pozzetta, pp. 71-92. Westport, Conn.: Greenwood Press, 1983.

Examination of Sinclair's ambivalent relationship to the muckraking journalists of the Progressive era.

Harris, Leon. *Upton Sinclair: American Rebel.* New York: Crowell, 1975, 435 p.

Extensively researched biography of Sinclair.

Mookerjee, R. N. *Art for Social Justice: The Major Novels of Upton Sinclair.* Metuchen, N.J.: Scarecrow Press, 1988, 151 p.

Critical explication of representative major works from Sinclair's long career.

Yoder, Jon A. *Upton Sinclair.* New York: Ungar, 1975, 134 p.

Brief investigation of Sinclair's life and works in which the author's socialist tendencies are viewed as a justified response to the social and political conditions of his era.

Isaac Bashevis Singer

1904-1991

(Born Icek-Hersz Zynger; also transliterated as Isak, Isaak, Yitskhok; has also written under pseudonyms Isaac Tse, Isaac Bashevis, and Isaac Warshofsky; also transliterated as Varshavski, Warshavski, Warshawsky, and Warshovsky) Polish-born American novelist, short story writer, author of children's books, memoirist, playwright, journalist, editor, and translator.

INTRODUCTION

An internationally renowned figure, Singer is widely considered the foremost Yiddish writer of the twentieth century. Although he moved to the United States in 1935, Singer wrote almost exclusively in Yiddish in an attempt to preserve what he considered a rapidly disappearing language. Read primarily in translation, Singer's fiction frequently evokes the history and culture of the Polish-Jewish village or *shtetl.* Singer's themes, nonetheless, extend far beyond ethnic or provincial concerns; his work emphasizes faith, doubt, corruption, and sexuality, and expresses a profound, if often sardonic, interest in the irrational and the supernatural. In 1978, Singer was awarded the Nobel Prize in Literature for his "impassioned narrative art which, with roots in a Polish-Jewish cultural tradition, brings universal human conditions to life."

Singer was born in the Polish *shtetl* of Leoncin, near Warsaw, to parents of devout rabbinical families who intended him to become a religious scholar. Singer's interests lay elsewhere, and early in his life he began reading secular literature. This dual exposure to strict religious training and nonecclesiastical ideas is demonstrated in Singer's fiction, where faith, mysticism, and skepticism regularly conflict. In 1908, Singer and his family moved to Warsaw, where he spent most of his youth. In 1917, he and his mother moved to his grandparents' *shtetl* in Bilgoray, and, upon his return to Warsaw in 1921, Singer enrolled in a rabbinical seminary. Singer left school in 1923, began proofreading for *Literarishe Bletter*, a Yiddish literary magazine, and later worked as a translator. In 1927, Singer published his first piece of short fiction in *Literarishe Bletter*, and seven years later his first long work, *Shoten an Goray* (1935; *Satan in Goray*), an experimental piece drawing upon his experiences in Bilgoray, appeared in serial form in the Yiddish periodical *Globus*. Singer emigrated from Poland in 1935, leaving behind his illegitimate son in order to follow his older brother Israel Joshua, who later achieved prominence as a Yiddish novelist. Singer settled in New York City where he married and became a regular staff member on the *Jewish Daily Forward.* The death of Israel Joshua in 1944 had a profound if ambivalent effect upon Singer. While he has acknowledged his brother as his "spiritual father and master," Singer often felt overshadowed by Israel's achievements, which inhibited his own creativity, and he has admitted, in this context, to feelings of both grief and liberation. Throughout the 1940s, Singer's fiction was serialized in the *Forward,* and his reputation among Yiddish-speaking readers grew steadily. In 1950, *Die Familie Mushkat* (*The Family Moskat*) appeared in translation, the first of Singer's novels to be published in English, and in 1953 "Gimpel the Fool," Singer's classic tale of innocence and faith, appeared in *Partisan Review,* translated by Saul Bellow. Through the efforts of such admirers as Bellow and Irving Howe, through translations of his fiction, and through cinematic and dramatic adaptations of several of his works, Singer was introduced to the American public and in the 1950s garnered an international audience. After winning the Nobel Prize in Literature, Singer continued to publish new material until his death in 1991.

Singer's short fiction draws upon elements of Polish-Jewish folklore, fables, and history, and, as Alexandra Johnson observed, his stories "compress intricate dramas into a few single pages." Frequently torn between their faith in God and earthly temptations, Singer's characters are tormented by demons, ghosts, and *dybbuks*—wandering souls that according to Jewish folklore, inhabit humans and control their actions. In a review of *The Collected Stories of Isaac Bashevis Singer* (1982), Michael Levin noted that Singer depicts people as "defenceless, unprotected, and worse still, unable to protect [themselves] before powerful, callous or malevolent forces" that exist inside and outside the individual. The protagonist of the well-known title story from *Gimpel Tam un andere Dertseylungen* (1957; *Gimpel the Fool and Other Stories*) typifies one reaction to this worldly situation. As the victim of the town's jokes, Gimpel remains a "divine fool" and "the common man." Gimpel's naïveté, nevertheless, provides humor and also combats evil by conveying a simple goodness for which he is eventually rewarded. Singer has published many short fiction collections, among them *The Spinoza of Market Street* (1961), *Short Friday, and Other Stories* (1964), *A Crown of Feathers, and Other Stories* (1973), *Passions, and Other Stories* (1975), and *The Death of Methusaleh, and Other Stories* (1988). Although accused of repetition, Singer's stories are generally considered to evidence his exceptional narrative skills. Howe noted that Singer "plays the same tune over and over again" but

added that "if [he] moves along predictable lines, they are clearly his own, and no one can accomplish his kind of story so well as he."

While placing greater emphasis on a realistic, straightforward style than his short stories, Singer's novels similarly explore the themes of community, faith, violence, and identity within the scope of Polish-Jewish history. The novel *Satan in Goray,* widely considered Singer's best long work, is set in Poland after the Cossack raids of 1638 and 1649 and is often described as an expansive parable. This book explores the conflicts of religious law, faith, and skepticism among the Eastern European Jews who considered Sabbatai Zevi their Messiah. Singer's next major novel, *Der Knekht* (1962; *The Slave*), takes place in Poland in the same era. The book revolves around Joseph's marriage to Wanda, also known as Sarah, whose conversion to Judaism sets her apart from other Jews in the community. Because it was against the law for a Gentile to convert to Judaism in the seventeenth century, Wanda/Sarah's newly acquired religious identity and training jeopardize her life but also enable her to grow spiritually as she follows the spirit of the laws set forth in the Torah. *The Slave* also incorporates several stories from the Old Testament, including that of Joseph's bondage in Egypt, and focuses on the problem of being Jewish in a country where religion denotes social status.

With *The Manor* (1967) and *The Estate* (1969), Singer began writing about events and trends of Polish-Jewish history in the 1800s. These books, originally published as one volume in Yiddish, are detailed epic narratives written in the expansive mode of much nineteenth-century fiction. Singer's focus on the absence of spiritual unity that stems from loss of religious identity evolves as the members of the Jacoby, Mendel, and Jampolski families either accept, modify, or reject their parents' theological and political beliefs. Although *The Family Moskat* takes place during the twentieth century and ends with Nazi Germany's invasion of Poland, this book is often studied along with *The Manor* and *The Estate.* Critics have cited that *The Family Moskat* portrays not only the uprooting of one Jewish family but also the collapse of the Polish-Jewish community.

Although *Sonim, di Geschichte fun a Liebe* (1966; *Enemies: A Love Story*), *Der Baltshuve* (1974; *The Penitent*), and *Shosha* (1978) are all set in the twentieth century, Singer still emphasizes humanity's search for spirituality in a corrupt, violent, and passion-driven world. In *Enemies,* which was adapted for film in 1990, Herman Broder, a survivor of the Holocaust who lost his wife in the war, has left his homeland, remarried, and is now working as a ghostwriter for a rabbi in New York. He knowingly commits bigamy by marrying Masha, who was also the target of Nazi persecution during World War II. More complications arise when

Herman discovers that his first wife also survived the war and has since emigrated to New York. Unable and unwilling to resolve his predicament, yet driven by lust, Herman maintains relations with all three wives. Eventually Herman flees New York, realizing that the Holocaust has robbed him of his religion, philosophy, and faith in humanity. The moralistic tone of Singer's work appears again in *The Penitent,* in which Joseph Shapiro, a Jew who also settled in New York after World War II, travels to Israel in search of a pure life. Critics noted that Joseph's strongest belief is, paradoxically, his inability to believe. More didactic than most of Singer's work, this novel has been faulted for lacking the ironic perspective and multidimensional depth of his earlier fiction. *Shosha,* often considered a novelized version of his memoir *A Young Man in Search of Love* (1978), takes place in Warsaw during the 1930s. The title character, a young woman whose intellectual development has been arrested, is one of Singer's innocents who symbolize a return to the uncomplicated world of childhood, while the narrator, who succumbs to material pleasures, represents the moral disintegration of modern life.

The novels published in the years shortly before Singer's death also address Jewish themes but prominently reflect his belief that the history of the Jews is the history of humankind. Despite occasional historical discrepancies, *The King of the Fields* (1988) describes Poland as it might have been when cave and forest dwellers, or *lesniks,* were beginning to make the transition to an agrarian lifestyle. An educated Jew, Ben Dosa, enters this community and becomes its spiritual advisor until a Christian missionary arrives preaching anti-Semitism. Critics have contended that the novel explores that moment when Polish-Jewish anthropology became Polish-Jewish history; Singer, however, touted the volume as an attempt to prove that humanity's corruption and predilection for violence are universal and have always existed. In his last novel, *Scum* (1991), Singer returned to the *shtetl* of his childhood. In *Scum,* Max Barabander, an Argentinian businessman, leaves his wife, travels around Europe, and settles in his hometown, Warsaw, in 1906. Max surrounds himself with the thieves and con artists of Krochmalna Street, attempts to marry the rabbi's daughter, and, allowing what Singer intimates are base impulses to rule his conscience, engages in numerous sexual encounters. Before the rabbi will bless the marriage, the unrepentant Max is ordered to follow the traditions and rituals of orthodox Judaism but fails. Faulted for combating Jewish stereotypes with such a morally depraved protagonist, Singer countered that since Max is not a devout Jew nor even a real member of the Warsaw *shtetl,* his moral deficiencies are not those of the Jewish community but those shared by the entire world.

Although Singer has garnered additional praise for his work as a dramatist, memoirist, and children's author, he has been denounced by some Yiddish writers and members of the Jewish community for refusing to render a sentimental portrait of a minority culture that has traditionally been the target of persecution. Despite such criticism, Singer is regarded as a consummate storyteller, capable of blending folklore, dialect, and traditional modes of plot and characterization with a modernist sensibility.

(For further information about Singer's life and works, see *Children's Literature Review,* Vol. 1; *Concise Dictionary of American Literary Biography, 1941-1968; Contemporary Authors,* Vol. 1-4; *Contemporary Authors New Revision Series,* Vol. 1; *Contemporary Literary Criticism,* Vols. 1, 3, 6, 9, 11, 15, 23, 38, 69; *Dictionary of Literary Biography,* Vols. 6, 28, 52; *Major 20th-Century Writers; Short Story Criticism,* Vol. 3, and *Something About the Author,* Vols. 3, 27.)

CRITICAL COMMENTARY

J. A. EISENBERG

(essay date 1962)

[In the following excerpt, Eisenberg examines major themes in Singer's work, arguing that Singer does not allow himself to be "affected by [Judaism's] parochialisms which limit the writings of other Yiddish writers."]

Isaac Bashevis Singer is the only contemporary Yiddish writer to have achieved international recognition. Somehow he has succeeded in breaking out of the closed circle of Yiddish literature and in attracting widespread interest to his wild and imaginative novels and stories. This is especially remarkable because Singer writes in a language frequently condemned to imminent extinction, about a bizarre group which has all but disappeared from the face of the earth and which

Principal Works

Shoten an Goray (novel) 1935
  [Satan in Goray, 1955]
Di Familie Mushkat (novel) 1950
  [The Family Moskat, 1950]
Mayn Tatn's bes-din Shtub [as Isaac Warshawsky] (memoirs) 1956; published in the Jewish Daily Forward
  [In My Father's Court, 1966]
Gimpel Tam un andere Dertseylungen (short stories) 1957
  [Gimpel the Fool, and Other Stories, 1957]
*Shadows on the Hudson (novel) 1957
*A Ship to America (novel) 1958
Kunstmakher fun Lublin (novel) 1960
  [The Magician of Lublin, 1960]
The Spinoza of Market Street (short stories) 1961
Der Knekht (novel) 1962
  [The Slave, 1962]
Short Friday, and Other Stories (short stories) 1964
Selected Short Stories of Isaac Bashevis Singer (short stories) 1966
Sonim, di Geschichte fun a Liebe (novel) 1966; published in the Jewish Daily Forward
  [Enemies: A Love Story, 1972]
Zlateh the Goat, and Other Stories (juvenile) 1966
The Manor (novel) 1967
The Séance and Other Stories (short stories) 1968
A Day of Pleasure: Stories of a Boy Growing Up in Warsaw (juvenile) 1969
The Estate (novel) 1969
A Friend of Kafka, and Other Stories (short stories) 1970
An Isaac Bashevis Singer Reader (short stories) 1971
A Crown of Feathers, and Other Stories (short stories) 1973

The Mirror (drama) 1973
Der Bal-tshuve (novel) 1974
  [The Penitent, 1984]
Yentl [with Leah Napolin] (drama) 1974
Passions, and Other Stories (short stories) 1975
Der Shpigl un andere Dertseylungen (short stories) 1975
A Little Boy in Search of God: Mysticism in a Personal Light (memoirs) 1976
*Yarme and Kayle (novel) 1976
Shosha (novel) 1978
A Young Man in Search of Love (memoirs) 1978
Nobel Lecture (essay) 1979
Old Love (short stories) 1979
Lost in America (memoirs) 1981
The Collected Stories of Isaac Bashevis Singer (short stories) 1982
Love and Exile (memoirs) 1984
Remembrances of a Rabbi's Son (memoirs) 1984
Teibele and Her Demon [with Eve Friedman] (drama) 1984
The Image and Other Stories (short stories) 1985
*The Way Home (novel) 1985
The Death of Methusaleh, and Other Stories (short stories) 1988
The King of the Fields (novel) 1988
Scum (novel) 1991

*These works have only appeared in serial form in the Jewish Daily Forward.

---

evokes sympathy and understanding from few of the living. (p. 345)

With few exceptions, Singer writes about Eastern European Jewry as it existed between the mid-seventeenth century and the beginning of the Second World War. More specifically, he tends to concentrate on the Polish Hasidic element, the fanatically Orthodox mystics, as we think of them today: Against this seemingly staid background Singer has created incredible tales of fantastic and lusty happenings. Out of situations in which modesty and control dominate there develop situations in which intemperance and insanity run wild. A strange world is made stranger by the incongruous and the unexpected. Nevertheless, the reader, for his part, is fascinated. The action and its developments are intriguing. The characters come to life with amazing vigor. And in spite of its strangeness and

oddities, the world of Singer's creation comes through vividly, making itself felt in all its fullness. But what is felt with clarity is not always clearly understood.

From the very beginning the reader is beset by very perplexing problems of interpretation. Singer does not appear to be at all consistent. He seems to hop from view to view, from position to position; he never asserts a view firmly or directly. Rather, he infuses a tension of mystery into his stories by means of this apparent ambivalence. (pp. 345-46)

Probably the oddest aspects of Singer's works are his themes. An inordinate stress, certainly for a Yiddish writer, is placed on sex—on evocative scenes of passionate sensualism. Astonishingly, the participants are often old-fashioned pious Jews with earlocks and beards, or devout, bewigged matrons. No combination seems incredible to Singer. Not even the aged and malformed are excluded from his lusty erotic imagination. Adultery is prevalent, orgies crown sequences of intemperate behavior, and shutters are insidiously closed in the middle of the day. The reader, conditioned to expect a more conventional version of the pre-modern world of the Hasidim, may well wonder, what ever happened to the Torah! (pp. 346-47)

In the writings of Singer a number of revealing themes and attitudes constantly recur. Prominent are the greed, lustfulness and sensuality of man. Man repeatedly descends lower and lower, to deeper states of corruption, till he is reduced to complete bestiality. Frequently, the totally innocent are forced into compromising situations by external forces and act as humans would be expected to act. Each small weakness is soon magnified into a major flaw, and the innocent gradually become hopelessly diseased. Ultimately, all suffer horribly for a state of affairs which does not seem of their making, and in which they are the slaves of their senses, not their own masters. A frightening injustice seems to dominate man's existence. On the one hand he is irresistibly attracted by the pleasures of the senses; on the other, he is cruelly punished for submitting to the temptation.

Because of this, Singer often displays both horror and contempt of the physical world. The world he recoils from is the world of the market place, of human passions, of vain ambitions, of misguided aspirations, and of all the human relationships which result from them. (p. 348)

As a moralist, Singer follows a Judaic puritanical tradition. He advocates piety, restraint, wisdom and a spiritual involvement with humans. But these are values which are widely accepted and are not the monopoly of Judaism. In his writings, Singer rises above the values which are peculiarly Jewish. The sensuous Kabbalists, a particular kind of (ghettoish) gluttony, and the foolish seeking a Messiah on their own terms as the chosen people—these have no role in Singer's vision of good.

Thus, Singer is able to exploit the universal values of Judaism without becoming affected by its parochialisms which limit the writings of other Yiddish writers. (p. 356)

J. A. Eisenberg, "Isaac Bashevis Singer: Passionate Primitive or Pious Puritan?" in *Judaism*, Vol. 11, No. 4, Fall, 1962, pp. 345-56.

IRVING HOWE
(essay date 1966)

[Howe is one of America's most highly respected literary critics and social historians. He is associated with the "New York Intellectuals" and is widely praised for what F. R. Dulles has termed his "knowledgeable understanding, critical acumen and forthright candor." In the following excerpt from his introduction to *Selected Short Stories of Isaac Bashevis Singer*, he conducts a broad survey of Singer's work in the context of both modernist and Yiddish literature.]

No other living writer has yielded himself so completely and recklessly as has Isaac Bashevis Singer to the claims of the human imagination. Singer writes in Yiddish, a language that no amount of energy or affection seems likely to save from extinction. He writes about a world that is gone, destroyed with a brutality beyond historical comparison. He writes within a culture, the remnant of Yiddish in the Western world, that is more than a little dubious about his purpose and stress. He seems to take entirely for granted his role as a traditional storyteller speaking to an audience attuned to his every hint and nuance, an audience that values storytelling both in its own right and as a binding communal action—but also, as it happens, an audience that keeps fading week by week, shrinking day by day. And he does all this without a sigh or apology, without so much as a Jewish groan. It strikes one as a kind of inspired madness: here is a man living in New York City, a sophisticated and clever writer, who composes stories about Frampol, Bilgoray, Kreshev *as if they were still there.* His work is shot through with the bravado of a performer who enjoys making his listeners gasp, weep, laugh and yearn for more. Above and beyond everything else he is a great performer, in ways that remind one of Twain, Dickens, Sholom Aleichem. (p. vi)

Singer's stories claim attention through their vivacity and strangeness of surface. He is devoted to the grotesque, the demonic, the erotic, the quasi-mystical. He populates his alien subworld with imps, devils, whores, fanatics, charlatans, spirits in seizure, disciples of false messiahs. A young girl is captured by the spirit of a dead woman and goes to live with the mourning husband as if she were actually his wife; a town is courted and then shattered by a lavish stranger who turns out to be the devil; an ancient Jew suffering unspeakable deprivations during the First World War, crawls back to his village of Bilgoray and fathers a son whom, with marvelous aplomb, he names Isaac. Sometimes the action in Singer's stories follows the moral curve of traditional folk tales, with a charming, lightly-phrased "lesson" at the end; sometimes, the spiral of a quizzical modern awareness; at best, the complicated motions of the old and the contemporary yoked together, a kind of narrative double-stop.

Orgiastic lapses from the moral order, pacts with the devil, ascetic self-punishments, distraught sexuality occupy the foreground of Singer's stories. Yet behind this expressionist clamor there is glimpsed the world of the *shtetl*, or East European Jewish village, as it stumbled and slept through the last few centuries. Though Singer seldom portrays it full-face, one must always keep this world in mind while reading his stories: it forms the base from which he wanders, the norm from which he deviates but which controls his deviation. (p. vii)

Isaac Bashevis Singer is the only living Yiddish writer whose translated work has caught the imagination of the American literary public. Though the settings of his stories are frequently strange, the contemporary reader—for whom the determination not to be shocked has become a point of honor—is likely to feel closer to Singer than to most other Yiddish writers. Offhand this may be surprising, for Singer's subjects are decidedly remote and exotic: in *Satan in Goray* the orgiastic consequences of the false messianism of seventeenth-century East European Jewish life; in *The Magician of Lublin* a portrait of a Jewish magician-Don Juan in late-nineteenth-century Poland who exhausts himself in sensuality and ends as a penitent ascetic; in his stories a range of demonic, apocalyptic and perversely sacred moments of *shtetl* life. Yet one feels that, unlike many of the Yiddish writers who treat more familiar and up-to-date subjects, Singer commands a distinctly "modern" sensibility.

Now this is partly true—in the sense that Singer has cut himself off from some of the traditional styles and assumptions of Yiddish writing. But it is also not true—in the sense that any effort to assimilate Singer to literary "modernism" without fully registering his involvement with Jewish faith and history, is almost certain to distort his meanings.

Those meanings, one might as well admit, are often enigmatic and hard to come by. It must be a common experience among Singer's readers to find a quick pleasure in the caustic surfaces of his prose, the nervous tokens of his virtuosity, but then to acknowledge themselves baffled as to his point and purpose. That his fiction does have an insistent point and stringent purpose no one can doubt: Singer is too ruthlessly single-minded a writer to content himself with mere slices of representation or displays of the bizarre. His grotesquerie must be taken seriously, perhaps as a recoil from his perception of how ugly—how irremediably and gratuitously ugly—human life can be. He is a writer completely absorbed by the demands of his vision, a vision gnomic and compulsive but with moments of high exaltation; so that while reading his stories one feels as if one were overhearing bits and snatches of monologue, the impact of which is both notable and disturbing, but the meaning withheld.

Now these are precisely the qualities that the sophisticated reader, trained to docility before the exactions of "modernism," has come to applaud. Singer's stories work, or prey, upon the nerves. They leave one unsettled and anxious, the way a rationalist might feel if, waking at night in the woods, he suddenly found himself surrounded by a swarm of bats. Unlike most Yiddish fiction, Singer's stories neither round out the cycle of their intentions nor posit a coherent and ordered universe. They can be seen as paradigms of the arbitrariness, the grating injustice, at the heart of life. They offer instances of pointless suffering, dead-end exhaustion, inexplicable grace. And sometimes, as in Singer's masterpiece, **"Gimpel the Fool,"** they turn about, refusing to rest with the familiar discomforts of the problematic, and drive toward a prospect of salvation on the other side of despair, beyond soiling by error or will. This prospect does not depend on any belief in the comeliness or lawfulness of the universe; whether God is there or not, He is surely no protector. ("He had worked out his own religion," writes Singer about one of his characters. "There was a Creator, but He revealed himself to no one, gave no indications of what was permitted or forbidden.") Things happen, the probable bad and improbable good, both of them subject to the whim of the fortuitous—and the sacred fools like Gimpel, perhaps they alone, learn to roll with the punch, finding the value of their life in a total passivity and credulousness, a complete openness to suffering.

Singer's stories trace the characteristic motions of human destiny: a heavy climb upward (**"The Old Man"**), a rapid tumble downward (**"The East"**). Life forms a journeying to heaven and hell, mostly hell. What determines the direction a man will take? Sometimes the delicate maneuvers between his will and desire, sometimes the heat of his vanity, sometimes the blessing of innocence. But more often than not, it is all a mystery which Singer chooses to present rather than explain. As his figures move upward and downward, aflame with the passion of their ineluctable destiny, they stop for a moment in the *shtetl* world. Singer is not content with the limitations of materiality, yet not at all indifferent to the charms and powers of the phenomenal universe. In his calculus of destiny, however, the world is a resting-place and what happens within it, even within the social enclave of the Jews, is not of lasting significance. Thick, substantial and attractive as it comes to seem in Singer's representation, the world is finally but lure and appearance, a locale between heaven and hell, the shadow of larger possibilities.

In most Yiddish fiction the stress is quite different. There the central "character" is the collective destiny of the Jews in *galut,* or exile; the central theme, the survival of a nation deprived of nationhood; the central ethic, the humane education of men stripped of worldly power yet sustained by the memory of chosenness and the promise of redemption. In Singer the norm of collective life is still present, but mostly in the background, as a tacit assumption; his central actions break away from the limits of the *shtetl* ethic, what has come to be known as *Yiddishkeit,* and then move either backward to the abandon of false messianism or forward to the doubt of modern sensibility. (There is an interesting exception, the story called **"Short Friday,"** which in its stress upon family affection, ritual proprieties and collective faith, approaches rather closely the tones of traditional Yiddish fiction.)

The historical settings of East European Jewish life are richly presented in Singer's stories, often not as orderly sequences in time but as simultaneous perceptions jumbled together in the consciousness of figures for whom Abraham's sacrifice, Chmielnicki's pogroms, the rise and fall of Hasidism and the stirrings of the modern world are all felt with equal force. Yet Singer's ultimate concern is not with the collective experience of a chosen martyred people but with the enigmas of personal fate. Given the slant of his vision, this leads him to place a heavy reliance upon the grotesque as a mode of narration, even as an avenue toward knowledge. But the grotesque carries with it a number of literary and moral dangers, not the least being the temptation for Singer to make it into an end in itself, which is to say, something facile and sensationalistic. In his second-rank stories he falls back a little too comfortably upon the devices of which he is absolute master, like a magician supremely confident his tricks will continue to work. But mainly the grotesque succeeds in Singer's stories because it comes to symbolize meaningful digressions from a cultural norm. An uninstructed reader may absorb Singer's grotesquerie somewhat too easily into the assumptions of modern literature; the reader who grasps the ambivalence of Singer's relation to Yiddish literature will see the grotesquerie as a cultural sign by means of which Singer defines himself against his own past.

It is hardly a secret that in the Yiddish literary world Singer is regarded with a certain suspicion. His powers of evocation, his resources as a stylist are acknowledged, yet many Yiddish literary people, including the serious ones, seem uneasy about him. One reason is that "modernism"—which, as these people regard Singer, signifies a heavy stress upon sexuality, a concern for the irrational, expressionist distortions of character and a seeming indifference to the humane ethic of Yiddishism—has never won so strong a hold in Jewish culture as it has in the cultures of most Western countries. For Yiddish writers, "modernism" has been at best an adornment of manner upon a subject inescapably traditional.

The truly "modern" writer, however, is not quite trustworthy in relation to his culture. He is a shifty character by choice and need, unable to settle into that solid representativeness which would allow him to act as a cultural "spokesman." And to the extent that Singer does share in the modernist outlook he must be regarded with distrust by Yiddish readers brought up on such literary "spokesmen" as Peretz, Abraham Reisen and H. Leivick. There is no lack of admiration among Yiddish readers for Singer's work: anyone with half an ear for the cadence and idiom of that marvelous language must respond to his prose. Still, it is a qualified, a troubled admiration. Singer's moral outlook, which seems to move with equal readiness toward the sensational and the ascetic, is hardly calculated to put Yiddish readers at their ease. So they continue to read him, with pleasure and anxiety.

And as it seems to me, they are not altogether wrong. Their admiring resistance to Singer's work may constitute a more attentive and serious response to his iconoclasm than the gleeful applause of those who read him in English translation and take him to be another writer of "black comedy," or, heaven help us, a mid-twentieth century "swinger." (pp. xii-xvi)

Anyone with even a smattering of Yiddish should try to read Singer's stories in the original. . . . Singer has left behind him the oratorical sententiousness to which Yiddish literature is prone, has abandoned its leisurely meandering pace, what might be called the *shtetl* rhythm, and has developed a style that is both swift and dense, nervous and thick. His sentences are short and abrupt; his rhythms coiled, intense, short-breathed. The impression his prose creates is not of a smooth and equable flow of language but rather a series of staccato advances and withdrawals, with sharp breaks between sentences. Singer seldom qualifies, wanders or circles back; his method is to keep darting forward, impression upon impression, through a series of jabbing declarative sentences. His prose is free of "literary" effects, a frequent weakness among Yiddish writers who wish to display their elegance and cultivation. And at the base of his prose is the oral idiom of Yiddish, seeded with ironic proverbs and apothegms ("Shoulders are from God, and burdens too"); but a speech that has been clipped, wrenched, syncopated.

What is most remarkable about Singer's prose is his ability to combine rich detail with fiercely compressed rhythms. (p. xvii)

By its very nature, pace cannot be illustrated, but the richness of Singer's detail can. As in this characteristic passage from **"The Old Man":**

His son had died long before, and Reb Moshe Ber said the memorial prayer, *kaddish,* for him. Now alone in the apartment, he had to feed his stove with paper and wood shavings from garbage cans. In the ashes he baked rotten potatoes, which he carried in his scarf, and in an iron pot, he brewed chicory. He kept house, made his own candles by kneading bits of wax and suet around wicks, laundered his shirt beneath the kitchen faucet, and hung it to dry on a piece of string. He set the mousetraps each night and drowned the mice each morning. When he went out he never forgot to fasten the heavy padlock on the door. No one had to pay rent in Warsaw at that time. . . .

The winter was difficult. There was no coal, and since several tiles were missing from the stove, the apartment was filled with thick black smoke each time the old man made a fire. A crust of blue ice and snow covered the window panes by November, making the rooms constantly dark or dusky. Overnight, the water on his night table froze in the pot. No matter how many clothes he piled over him in bed, he never felt warm; his feet remained stiff, and as soon as he began to doze, the entire pile of clothes would fall off, and he would have to climb out naked to make his bed once more. There was no kerosene, even matches were at a premium. Although he recited chapter upon chapter of the Psalms, he could not fall asleep. The wind, freely roaming about the rooms, banged the doors; even the mice left. . . .

Or, grotesquely, from **"Blood":**

Frequently she sang for hours in Yiddish and in Polish. Her voice was harsh and cracked and she invented the songs as she went along, repeating meaningless phrases, uttering sounds that resembled the cackling of fowl, the grunting of pigs, the death-rattles of oxen. . . . At night in her dreams, phantoms tormented her: bulls gored her with their horns; pigs shoved their snouts into her face and bit her; roosters cut her flesh to ribbons with their spurs.

(pp. xviii-xix)

Those of Singer's stories which speed downward into hell are often told by devils and imps, sometimes by Satan himself, marveling at the vanity and paltriness of the human creature. Singer's arch-devil is a figure not so much of evil as of skepticism, a thoroughly modern voice to whose corrosive questions Singer imparts notable force. . . . (p. xx)

Using demons and imps as narrators proves to be a wonderful device for structural economy: they replace the need to enter the "inner life" of the characters, the whole plaguing business of the psychology of motives, for they serve as symbolic equivalents and coordinates to human conduct, what Singer calls a "spiritual stenography." In those stories, however, where Singer celebrates the power of human endurance, as in

"The Little Shoemakers" and **"The Old Man,"** he uses third person narrative in the closet he comes to a "high style," so that the rhetorical elevation will help to create an effect of "epical" sweep.

Within his limits Singer is a genius. He has total command of his imagined world; he is original in his use both of traditional Jewish materials and in his modernist attitude toward them; he provides a serious if enigmatic moral perspective; and he is a master of Yiddish prose. Yet there are times when Singer seems to be mired in his own originality, stories in which he displays a weakness for self-imitation that is disconcerting. Second-rate writers imitate others, first-rate writers themselves, and it is not always clear which is the more dangerous.

Having gone this far, we must now turn again. If Singer's work can be grasped only on the assumption that he is crucially a "modernist" writer, one must add that in other ways he remains profoundly subject to the Jewish tradition. And if the Yiddish reader is inclined to slight the "modernist" side of his work, the American reader is likely to underestimate the traditional side.

One of the elements in the Jewish past that has most fascinated Singer is the recurrent tendency to break loose from the burden of the Mosaic law and, through the urging of will and ecstasy, declare an end to the *galut.* Historically, this has taken the form of a series of messianic movements, one led in the seventeenth century by Sabbatai Zevi and another in the eighteenth by Jacob Frank. The movement of Sabbatai Zevi appeared after the East European Jewish community had been shattered by the rebellion-pogrom of the Cossack chieftain, Chmielnicki. Many of the survivors, caught up in a strange ecstasy that derived all too clearly from their total desperation, began to summon apocalytic fantasies and to indulge themselves in long-repressed religious emotions which, perversely, were stimulated by the pressures of cabalistic asceticism. As if in response to their yearnings, Sabbatai, a pretender rising in the Middle East, offered to release them of everything that rabbinical Judaism had confined or suppressed. He spoke for the tempting doctrine that faith is sufficient for salvation; for the wish to evade the limits of mundane life by forcing a religious transcendence; for the union of erotic with mystical appetites; for the lure of a demonism which the very hopelessness of the Jewish situation rendered plausible. In 1665-66 Sabbatianism came to orgiastic climax, whole communities, out of a conviction that the Messiah was in sight, discarding the moral inhibitions of exile. Their hopes were soon brutally disappointed, for Sabbatai, persecuted by the Turkish Sultan, converted to Mohammedanism. His followers were thrown into confusion and despair, and a resurgent rabbinism again took control over Jewish life. Nevertheless, Sabbatianism continued to lead an underground existence among the East European Jews—even, I have been told by *shtetl* survivors, into the late nineteenth and early twentieth century. It became a secret heretical cult celebrating Sabbatai as the apostate savior who had been required to descend to the depths of the world to achieve the heights of salvation.

To this buried strand of Jewish experience Singer has been drawn in fascination and repulsion, portraying its manifestations with great vividness and its consequences with stern judgment. It is a kind of experience that rarely figures in traditional Yiddish writing, yet is a significant aspect of the Jewish past. Bringing this material to contemporary readers, Singer writes *in* Yiddish but often quite apart from the Yiddish tradition; indeed, he is one of the few Yiddish writers whose relation to the Jewish past is not determined or screened by that body of values we call Yiddishism.

Singer is a writer of both the pre-Enlightenment and the post-Enlightenment: he would be equally at home with a congregation of Medieval Jews and a gathering of twentieth-century intellectuals, perhaps more so than at a meeting of the Yiddish P.E.N. club. He has a strong sense of the mystical and antique, but also a cool awareness of psychoanalytic disenchantment. He has evaded both the religious pieties and the humane rationalism of nineteenth-century East European Judaism. He has skipped over the ideas of the historical epoch which gave rise to Yiddishism, for the truth is, I suppose, that Yiddish literature, in both its writers of acceptance and writers of skepticism, is thoroughly caught up with the Enlightenment. Singer is not. He shares very little in the collective sensibility or the *folkstimlichkeit* of the Yiddish masters; he does not unambiguously celebrate *dos kleine menshele* (the common man) as a paragon of goodness; he is impatient with the sensual deprivations implicit in the values of *edelkeit* (refinement, nobility); and above all he moves away from a central assumption of both Yiddish literature in particular and the nineteenth century in general, the assumption of an immanent fate or end in human existence (what in Yiddish is called *tachlis*).

But again qualifications are needed. It is one thing to decide to break from a tradition in which one has been raised, quite another to make the break completely. For Singer has his ties—slender, subterranean but strong—with the very Yiddish writers from whom he has turned away.

At the center of Yiddish fiction stands the archetypal figures of *dos kleine menshele*. It is he, long-suffering, persistent, lovingly ironic, whom the Yiddish writers celebrate. This poor but proud householder trying to maintain his status in the *shtetl* world even as he keeps sinking deeper and deeper into poverty, appeals to the Yiddish imagination far more than mighty figures like Aeneas or Ahab. And from this representative man of

the *shtetl* there emerges a number of significant variations. One extreme variation is the ecstatic wanderer, hopeless in this world because profoundly committed to the other. An equally extreme variation is the wise or sainted fool who has given up the struggle for status and thereby acquired the wry perspective of an outsider. Standing somewhere between *dos kleine menshele* and these offshoots is Peretz's Bontsha Schweig, whose intolerable humbleness makes even the angels in heaven feel guilty and embarrassed. Singer's Gimpel is a literary grandson (perhaps only on one side) of Peretz's Bontsha; and as Gimpel, with the piling up of his foolishness, acquires a halo of comic sadness and comes to seem an epitome of pure spirit, one must keep balancing in one's mind the ways in which he is akin to, yet different from Bontsha.

The Yiddish critic Shlomo Bickel has perceptively remarked that Singer's dominating principle is an "anti-Prometheanism," a disbelief in the efficacy of striving defiance and pride, a doubt as to the sufficiency of knowledge or even wisdom. This seems true, but only if one remembers that in a good many of Singer's fictions the central action does constitute a kind of Promethean ordeal or striving. Singer makes it abundantly clear that his characters have no choice: they must live out their desires, their orgiastic yearnings, their apocalyptic expectations. "Anti-Prometheanism" thus comes to rest upon a belief in the unavoidable recurrence of the Promethean urge.

What finally concerns Singer most is the possibilities for life that remain after the exhaustion of human effort, after failure and despair have come and gone. Singer watches his stricken figures from a certain distance, with enigmatic intent and no great outpouring of sympathy, almost as if to say that before such collapse neither judgment nor sympathy matters very much. Yet in all of his fictions the Promethean effort recurs, obsessional, churning with new energy and delusion. In the knowledge that it will, that it must recur, there may also lie hidden a kind of pity, for that too we would expect, and learn to find, in the writer who created Gimpel. (pp. xx-xxiv)

Irving Howe, in an introduction to *Selected Short Stories of Isaac Bashevis Singer*, edited by Irving Howe, The Modern Library, 1966, pp. v-xxiv.

CYNTHIA OZICK

(essay date 1982)

[In the following review of *The Collected Stories of Isaac Bashevis Singer*, Ozick discusses supernatural elements in Singer's short fiction.]

On one flank Singer is a trickster, a prankster, a Loki, a Puck. His themes are lust, greed, pride, obsession, misfortune, unreason, the oceanic surprises of the mind's underside, the fiery caldron of the self, the assaults of time and place. His stories offer no "epiphanies" and no pious resolutions; no linguistic circumscriptions or Hemingwayesque self-deprivations. Their plentitudes chiefly serve undefended curiosity, the gossip's lure of what comes next. Singer's stories have plots that unravel not because they are "old-fashioned"—they are mostly originals and have few recognizable modes other than their own—but because they contain the whole human world of affliction, error, quagmire, pain, calamity, catastrophe, woe. Things happen; life is an ambush, a snare; one's fate can never be predicted. His driven mercurial processions of predicaments and transmogrifications are limitless, often stupendous. There are whole fistfuls of masterpieces in [*The Collected Stories of Isaac Bashevis Singer*]: a cornucopia of invention.

Because he cracks open decorum to find lust, because he peers through convention into the pit of fear, Singer has in the past been condemned by other Yiddish writers outraged by his seemingly pagan matter, his superstitious villagers, his daring leaps into gnostic furies. The moral grain of Jewish feeling that irradiates the mainstream aspirations of Yiddish literature has always been a kind of organic extension of Talmudic ethical ideals: family devotion, community probity, *derekh erets*—self-respect and respect for others—the stringent expectations of high public civility and indefatigable integrity, the dream of messianic betterment. In Singer, much of this seems absent or overlooked or simply mocked; it is as if he has willed the crashing down of traditional Jewish sanity and sensibility. As a result, in Yiddish literary circles he is sometimes viewed as—it is the title of one of these stories—**"The Betrayer of Israel."**

In fact, he betrays nothing and no one, least of all Jewish idealism. That is the meaning of his imps and demons: that human character, left to itself, is drawn to cleanliness of heart; that human motivation, on its own, is attracted to clarity and valor. Here is Singer's other flank, and it is the broader one. The goblin cun-

ning leads straight to this; Singer is a moralist. He tells us that it is natural to be good, and unholy to go astray. It is only when Lilith creeps in, or Samael, or Ketev Mriri, or the sons of Asmodeus, that evil and impurity are kindled. It is the inhuman, the antihuman, forces that are to blame for harms and sorrows. Surely these imps must be believed in; they may have the telltale feet of geese, like Satan their sire, but their difficult, shaming, lubricious urges are terrestrially familiar. Yet however lamentably known they are, Singer's demons are intruders, invaders, no true or welcome part of ourselves. They are "psychology"; and history; and terror; above all, obsessive will. If he believes in them, so, unwillingly but genuinely, do we.

And to understand Singer's imps is to correct another misapprehension: that he is the recorder of a lost world, the preserver of a vanished sociology. Singer is an artist and transcendent inventor, not a curator. His tales—though dense with the dailiness of a God-covenanted culture, its folkways, its rounded sufficiency, especially the rich intensities of the yeshiva and its bottomless studies—are in no way documents. The Jewish townlets that truly were are only seeds for his febrile conflagrations: Where, outside of peevish imagination, can one come on the protagonist of **"Henne Fire,"** a living firebrand, a spitfire burning up with spite, who ultimately, through the spontaneous combustion of pure fury, collapses into "one piece of coal"? Though every doorstep might be described, and every feature of a head catalogued (and Singer's portraits are brilliantly particularized), parables and fables are no more tied to real places and faces than Aesop's beasts are beasts.

This is not to say that Singer's stories do not mourn those murdered Jewish townlets of Poland, every single one of which, with nearly every inhabitant, was destroyed by the lords and drones of the Nazi Gehenna. This volume includes a masterly memorial to that destruction, the brokenhearted testimony of **"The Last Demon."** . . .

[Singer's] tenderness for ordinary folk, their superstitions, their folly, their plainness, their lapses, is a classical thread of Yiddish fiction, as well as the tree trunk of Singer's own Hasidic legacy—love and reverence for the down-to-earth. **"The Little Shoemakers"** bountifully celebrates the Fifth Commandment with leather and awl; the hero of **"Gimpel the Fool,"** a humble baker, is endlessly duped and stubbornly drenched in permanent grace; the beautiful story **"Short Friday"** ennobles a childless old couple who, despite privation and barrenness, turn their unscholarly piety into comeliness and virtue. Shmul-Leibele's immaculate happiness in prayer, Shoshe's meticulous Sabbath meal, shine with saintliness; Singer recounts the menu, "chicken soup with noodles and tiny circlets of fat . . . like golden ducats," as if even soup can enter holiness.

Through a freakish accident—snow covers their little house, and they are asphyxiated—the loving pair ascend in death together to Paradise. When the demons are stilled, human yearning aspires toward goodness and joy. (Singer fails to note, however, whether God or Samael sent the pure but deadly snow.)

In Singer the demons are rarely stilled, and the luminous serenity of **"Short Friday"** is an anomaly. Otherwise pride furiously rules, and wildhearted imps dispose of human destiny. In **"The Unseen,"** a prosperous and decent husband runs off with a lusty maidservant at the urging of a demon; he ends in destitution, a hidden beggar tended by his remarried wife. **"The Gentleman From Cracow"** corrupts a whole town with gold; he turns out to be Ketev Mriri, Satan himself. In **"The Destruction of Kreshev,"** a scholar who is a secret Sabbatean and devil worshiper induces his wife to commit adultery with a Panlike coachman. Elsewhere, excessive intellectual passion destroys genius. An accomplished young woman is instructed by a demon to go to the priest, convert, and abandon her community; the demon assumes the voice of the girl's grandmother, herself the child of a Sabbatean. A rabbi is "plagued by something new and terrifying: wrath against the Creator," and struggles to fashion himself into an atheist. Character and motive are turned inside out at the bidding of imps who shove, snarl, seduce, bribe, cajole. Allure ends in rot; lure becomes punishment.

This phantasmagorical universe of ordeal and mutation and shock is, finally, as intimately persuasive as logic itself. There is no fantasy in it. It is the true world we know, where we have come to expect anguish as the consequence of our own inspirations, where we crash up against the very circumstance from which we had always imagined we were exempt. In this true world, suffering is endemic and few are forgiven. Yet it may be that for Singer the concrete presence of the unholy attests the hovering redemptive holy, whose incandescence can scatter demons. (pp. 14-16)

Not all the stories in this collection emerge from that true world, however. The eerie authority of **"The Cabalist of East Broadway"** is a gripping exception, but in general the narratives set in the American environment are, by contrast, too thin. Even when intentionally spare—as in the marvelous **"Vanvild Kava,"** with its glorious opening: "If a Nobel Prize existed for writing little, Vanvild Kava would have gotten it"—the European settings have a way of turning luxuriantly, thickly coherent. Presumably some of these American locales were undertaken in a period when the fertile seed of the townlets had begun to be exhausted; or else it is the fault of America itself, lacking the centripetal density and identity of a yeshiva society, the idea of community as an emanation of God's gaze. Or perhaps it is because many of these American stories center on Singer as writer and celebrity, or on someone like him.

It is as if the predicaments that fly into his hands nowadays arrive because he is himself the centripetal force, the controlling imp. And an imp, to have efficacy, as Singer's genius has shown, must be a kind of dybbuk, moving in powerfully from outside; whereas the American narratives are mainly inside jobs, about the unusual "encounters" a famous writer meets up with.

[Singer's translators] cannot reach the deep mine and wine of Singer's mother tongue, thronged (so it was once explained to me by a Tel Aviv poet accomplished in Hebrew, Yiddish and English) with that unrenderable Hebrew erudition and burnished complexity of which we readers in English have not an inkling, and are permanently deprived. Deprived? Perhaps. *The Collected Stories*, when all is said and done, is an American master's "Book of Creation." (p. 17)

Cynthia Ozick, "Fistfuls of Masterpieces," in *The New York Times Book Review,* March 21, 1982, pp. 1, 14-17.

JOSEPH EPSTEIN
(essay date 1991)

[Epstein is an American editor, critic, essayist, and short story writer. In the following excerpt, he examines Singer's portrayal of spirituality in his fiction.]

Singer made the world of East European Jewry come alive for me like no one else; . . . [his] portrayals of life among Jews in backwater shtetls and in cities like Warsaw, Lublin, and Lodz had a vividness that surpassed—not that there needs to be a competition about this—anyone else I had read. Isaac Bashevis Singer wrote about Warsaw the way Theodore Dreiser wrote about Chicago. When you read him you felt you had been there, walked the city's streets, "come into possession of it," as Henry James might have said. And what one came into possession of was a world much richer than one had hitherto imagined.

If part of Isaac Bashevis Singer's success derived from his putting many of his readers in touch with a past that had hitherto been closed off to them, perhaps a larger part was owing to his sheer powers of storytelling. In interviews, lectures, public statements, Singer insisted over and over that writers must, on some level, give their readers pleasure. For him this pleasure was to be had through narrative. In his Nobel Lecture in Stockholm, after reading a paragraph in Yiddish about how the honor bestowed upon him was also a recognition of the Yiddish language in which he wrote, Singer said:

The storyteller and poet of our time, as in any other time, must be an entertainer of the spirit in the full sense of the word, not just a preacher of social or political ideals. There is no paradise for bored readers and no excuse for tedious literature that does not intrigue the reader, uplift his spirit, give him the joy and escape that true art always grants.

Singer not only wrote entertainingly but did so for a wider audience than most serious writers any longer even hope for. The distinction between high or sophisticated and popular art was wiped out in his work. He won the acclaim of critics and the devotion of true though not necessarily university-educated readers. Many years ago a cousin of mine, a very intelligent woman then in her early forties, who had never gone to college and who had no particular literary interests, mentioned that she and her husband were off for a week-long holiday in Bermuda and asked if I had anything in the apartment that she might take to read on the beach. Much that was in my personal library—poetry, criticism, history, philosophy—seemed inappropriate. What I eventually offered her was Isaac Bashevis Singer's novel, *The Slave.* She loved it. "A marvelous book," she reported to me upon her return. "By the way, this Singer, in what century did he live?"

Embedded in that question, I thought, was a fine compliment—a compliment with a touch of unconscious critical wisdom behind it. For not the least attraction of Singer's fiction is its timelessness. He could write about the Upper West Side of Manhattan in its current state of sad decay and ring just the right note of contemporaneity; he could also drop back a lengthy fifty or seventy years, as in *The Family Moskat,* or a full century, as in *The Manor,* or three full centuries, as in *Satan in Goray.* He could write outside time, as in his famous story, **"Gimpel the Fool,"** which has the feel of a tale passed down from generation to generation in the manner of pure folk art. No modern writer in any literature that I know is so adept at setting his stories anywhere he wishes temporally. This ability sets much of Singer's writing finally beyond time, which is of course where everyone who thinks himself an artist wishes to be. (p. 32)

Life, it seems, conspires to supply great artists with the material they require. But what is impressive about Singer is how early he knew what kind of writer he wanted to be. He quickly determined that the literature of political and social concern, a vein that his already famous brother had been working, was not for him. He knew straightaway that the delimitations of modernism in literature—with its difficulties, its determination not to worry about any audience but that of fellow artists, its concentration on the problems of art quite as much as if not more than those presented by life—were not for him. "One Kafka in a century," he would later say, "is enough." If Singer was in any way

aesthetically radical, it was in the sensuality of his stories and in the use he made in his fiction of the celestial and nether worlds of the occult, the world of spirits.

Although Singer attempted briefly to write his stories in Hebrew, nothing he did in that language pleased him. Neither, at first, did his writing in Yiddish. But it was not long before he hit his stride and his prose caught its correct and confident cadence. He published his first stories, in Warsaw journals, in his early twenties. After he emigrated to America in 1935, Singer stopped writing fiction for a period of five years or so, in despair about both the future of Yiddish and his own then-uprooted life. But once he resumed, he never looked back, and his flow of work—novels, stories, autobiographies, children's tales—ceased only with his death earlier this year.

Paul Kresh, in his biography of Singer, quotes a Yiddish journalist, Samuel L. Shneiderman, who worked on the same Warsaw journal, *Literary Pages,* with the young Isaac Bashevis Singer and who recalled his early mastery:

> His style—ah that style. From the beginning it was the envy of other Yiddish writers. His mastery of transition, for example—how gracefully he glides from description to dialogue, from the ambience of a place to the action happening there. What a storyteller! The literary world of Warsaw saw it right away—the richness of the language, the imaginative blending of the absolutely real and the totally fantastic—all absolutely new in Yiddish writing.

There are no Mozarts in literature, no true child prodigies, but Singer was apparently as much a natural as a writer can hope to be. As an artist he seems to have come into the world fully formed, so good at his craft so young, so able to vary his style from realistic family chronicle to novels and stories nearly surreal in their dalliance with mysticism to fiction strongly folkloric in its feeling. One does not have the sense of development in Singer's work. He started strong and stayed strong, except for a tailing off toward the end, when his fiction began to lose its imaginative energy and turned very dark. It is much to the point that so knowledgeable a critic as Ruth R. Wisse considers *Satan in Goray,* Singer's first novel, also his greatest.

Singer's work, though not all of the same quality, is bound together by his central concerns, which are at their heart religious. Other modern writers may talk in their fiction about man's soul and his relation to God, but they cannot keep their minds on the subject the way that Singer did throughout an entire career. He could never stop thinking of it. It is what his books, however sexy, charming, or strange they may separately be, are always and finally about.

Yet what exactly do Singer's many novels and stories mean? "I find myself full of faith and full of doubt," he once said. A lifelong student of Spinoza, Kant, and Schopenhauer, a ceaseless reader in the literature of the occult, more than a browser in the wisdom literature of Judaism, Singer always possessed the literary appetite of the quester after ultimate meanings. Did he, it seems fair to ask, find any?

It is easy to ignore this question because Singer's stories and novels provide so many subsidiary rewards. He recreated—or, perhaps better, reimagined—a world, that of East European Jewry, razed by the monstrousness of history; and the death of that world, as many have commented, seems to make Singer's recreation of it all the more potent in its magic. Within it, he found an almost endless number of stories to tell, stories of piety and impiety, tradition and the flouting of tradition, stories of derring-do, comedy, sadness, horror, and love—always and endlessly love.

Over and over again Singer insisted that at the heart of all good novels is a love story. "All stories," he said, "are love stories." And all Singer's love stories dealt with sex, for he was a writer who gave ample credit to sex as a drive, a source of human pleasure and trouble, and (most useful for a teller of tales) complication. Some of Singer's more old-fashioned readers used to complain about the sex in his fiction, but most of this sex, it must be stressed, is described with fine economy. Singer is never pornographic but instead powerfully suggestive. In *Scum,* his last, also very sex-ridden, novel, how this works is nicely on display early in the book when Singer notes merely about his forty-seven-year-old hero, Max Barabander: "What he could do with women no one, except the women involved, would believe." La Rochefoucauld said that a filthy mind never sleeps, and here, surely, is a sentence for it to consider in the late night hours.

Over the years critics have argued a fair amount about which are Singer's greatest strengths and which his greatest weaknesses. Many are ready to jettison his two ample family-chronicle novels, *The Family Moskat* and *The Manor.* Neither of these books, it is true, is nearly so well-shaped or powerful as I. J. Singer's *The Brothers Ashkenazi,* a great novel at whose center is perhaps the most extraordinary villain in all of literature, the entire country, no less, of Poland, which, I. J. Singer concludes, deserves all that it has suffered because of its horrendous treatment of the Jews. True enough, Isaac Bashevis Singer did not have his brother's powers of construction, and *The Family Moskat* and *The Manor* are sometimes cumbersome, often creaky—both were written, as were all of Singer's novels with the exception of *Satan in Goray,* for serialization in the *Jewish Daily Forward.* But both nevertheless contain magnificent things: characters, cityscapes, the sense of a destiny spun out of control, the feeling of life becoming unmoored without the anchor of tradition.

Others think Singer at his best in the mid-length novel—in such books as *The Slave, The Magician of Lublin,* or *Enemies: A Love Story.* Singer himself claimed to prefer the short story over all other forms, since in the short story "a writer can reach for perfection—more than in a novel." Though there seems to be no critical unanimity on which are Singer's best novels, there is general agreement on which are his best stories. A collection of the latter would include **"Gimpel the Fool," "The Gentleman from Cracow," "Yentl the Yeshiva Boy"** and **"Teibele and Her Demon" "The Little Shoemakers," "The Spinoza of Market Street,"** perhaps **"The Slaughterer"** and **"A Friend of Kafka."** Few of these stories, it is worth noting, have directly to do with the spirits from the nether world that are sometimes a strong element in his fiction.

Many readers identify Singer with, and they think the less of him for, those novels and stories where this element, what Dan Jacobson once nicely termed "the brimstone area," prevails. By the brimstone area, Jacobson means those supernatural elements—dybbuks, demons, imps, on occasion the devil himself—that usually are evoked by Singer to symbolize the power of evil. An admirer of Singer though he is, Jacobson's is easily the best criticism of this element in Singer's fiction. He argues that

> readers who do not share his predispositions are entitled to find that the "symbolization" to which he refers is sometimes too easily brought about, too lovingly and lengthily dwelt upon, insufficiently used or explained in any subsequent action, and insufficiently distinguished from other symbols of the same kind in many other stories.

Did Singer truly believe in such spirits? He often claimed that he did. At the same time, knowing how the world regards such beliefs, he was not above making fun of them, as when he told his biographer that demons were unlikely to flourish in Israel: "They like overcast skies, old houses. I have looked for demons in the Jewish state, but I have found very few." Elsewhere he said that he would pay half a year's income actually to see a ghost. Yet Singer, a man who distrusted and did not often use metaphors, was quite ready to avail himself of these most extravagant of all metaphors, creatures whom few but the mad have ever seen. He must have been agnostic yet hopeful on the subject. More important, he felt them useful to his fiction. "In a way demons express the human subconscious," he told an interviewer. "But to me the demons also symbolize a life without any faith altogether."

What Singer did believe in, without any question, was God. But to believe in God is not to claim to understand Him. Critics for whom the question of God is not, so to say, a lively one, attribute Singer's power to other factors, from modernist technique to the glory of his storytelling. Still others hold that behind and beyond all the talk of God there is something else in Singer's work that makes it appeal to the modern reader, suffused as that work is, as one critic has it, "with the prevailing contemporary sense of isolation, disintegration, alienation, and dread." But what makes both the technique and the storytelling possible, why Singer is able to seem at once modern and traditional, is his interest in the endless question of what God has in mind, both for us and for the universe.

The persistent attention to this question gives Singer his right to be considered a major artist. Dan Jacobson touches on this point, in a somewhat skeptical way, when considering the absence of "place" in Yiddish writers:

> Theirs is the literature of a people without power (and all its accompanying evils and guilts), without the possession of land, without statehood or political organization, without the freedom to pursue a wide variety of occupations—the literature of a society that was in many immensely important respects maimed and deprived.

All this is quite true and to the point. Yet if your subject is the ways of God toward man, as it indubitably was Isaac Bashevis Singer's, then the Jews of Eastern Eu-

Singer receiving the Nobel Prize in Literature from King Carl XVI Gustaf of Sweden.

rope, for all the reasons Jacobson mentions, are unquestionably your people. After a history of almost unremitting disenfranchisement and persecution, punctuated by pogroms and ending cataclysmically with Nazism, the Jews, above all people, have earned the right to ask certain fundamental questions of God.

Many people in Singer's stories and novels do ask. Asking itself, however, comes near to constituting a transgression. Asa Heshel Bannet, the central character in *The Family Moskat,* is a freethinker who, it turns out, is not very free after all. This same Asa Heshel, toward the end of the novel, reflects bitterly of God: "He creates easily and destroys easily. He has his own laboratory." All Singer's characters have free will—"without free will what is the difference between the throne of glory and the depths of the nether world?" asks a rabbi in the same novel. (Singer himself, during the question-and-answer sessions of his many lectures and readings, used to reply to the question of whether he himself believed in free will by answering: "Of course I believe in free will. What choice have I?") Of Asa Heshel, his first wife observes: "He was one of those who must serve God or die. He had forsaken God, and because of this he was dead—a living body with a dead soul." The simple if devastating point of *The Family Moskat* is that, without God, all of the novel's characters are dead souls, walking corpses. The unforgettable last line of the novel, delivered by a subsidiary character, himself a freethinker, as he awaits the entry of the Nazis into Warsaw, is: "Death is the Messiah. That's the real truth."

Free will, in an Isaac Bashevis Singer novel, usually comes down to little more than the freedom to choose God's way—or to perish. Modern thought will avail a man nothing. As Rabbi Dan Katzenellenbogen tells his grandson Asa Heshel apropos of modern thinking, "The sum and substance of it is that any sin is permitted. That is the root of the matter." Men—and less often women—in Singer's novels and stories are tossed about by their doubts, dreams, desires. Singer's characters suffer from Pascalian restlessness; they cannot sit, alone, quietly in a room for even an hour. "The main thing," says Max Barabander in *Scum,* "was not to remain passive." Singer himself once said: "We run away from boredom into wickedness, and there is almost nothing in between." Well, there is one thing in between—subjects for the novelist.

Singer made nearly limitless use of the material that issues from this spiritual restlessness. As he told an interviewer in the *Saturday Review* as long ago as 1968:

> To me, in my work, the religious question and the eternal question—why do we live, why do we exist?—are identical. I am not completely a religious writer, but neither am I secular. In my writing religion is always there—even when I write sexy.

To another interviewer he said:

> The supernatural is always in my writing and some-how I always wanted to say to the reader that even though life looks to us chaotic, it is not as chaotic as we think. There is a scheme and design behind it.

What was the scheme, which the design?

Singer was never certain enough to say. In *The Penitent,* the narrator is told by the chief character whose story is at the center of the novel: "If you took one step farther, you'd become a full-fledged Jew." To which he adds: "You also know all the good traits of the real Jew." To this the narrator, clearly speaking for Singer, answers: "That's not enough either. For this you must have faith that everything stated in the holy books was given to Moses on Mount Sinai. Unfortu-nately, I don't have this faith." One can only conjecture in so profound a realm, but my own guess is that Singer wanted this full faith, wanted it ardently, and never found it.

He looked for God, in whom he believed, every-where. God is in the details, a famous remark has it, and so He lurks in many passages in Singer's novels and stories. In a passage late in *The Family Moskat,* a spy is hung from a tree. "His bare feet dangled above the ditch. A butterfly danced about the fur shako." Birds and cats go about their business in Singer's pages as stars twinkle and the moon cleaves its way through clouds, and the heavens remain eternally the same as people struggle to get through their lives, writhe in their sleep under the burden of their small—though not small to them—worries. There must be a plan behind all this. As Singer writes in *The Penitent,* echoing an old philosophical staple:

> If someone found a watch on an island and said it had been made by itself or that it developed through evolution, he would be considered a lunatic. But ac-cording to modern science, the universe evolved all on its own. Is the universe less complicated than a watch?

Because Singer was always interested in the larger design, he was for the most part dismissive, even con-temptuous, of politics, especially utopian left-wing politics. In one of his stories, **"Guests on a Winter Night,"** he remarks that, of anarchists and radical stu-dents, his mother told him, "these sinful creatures had lost both their world and the world to come." Abram Shapiro, the licentious, contradictory, and finally most winning character in *The Family Moskat,* asked his opinion of who is to blame for the crisis of the Jews in Poland with Hitler at the borders, replies:

> Human nature. You can call a man capitalist, Bol-shevik, Jew, *goy,* Tartar, Turk, anything you want, but the real truth is that man is a stinker. If you beat him, he yells. And if the other fellow is beaten, then

he develops a theory. Maybe it'll be better in the next world.

As for this world, Singer, from the outset, has al-ways seemed to favor the modest, the traditional, the pious among his characters. Men and women who have accepted life in the full harshness of its terms, who go about their business, their prayers, their unquestioning routines—these Singer admires above all. "It's these lit-tle nobodies who for two thousand years have carried all of Jewry on their backs," says Asa Heshel in *The Family Moskat,* "as well as all of Christendom. It is they who have always turned the other cheeck." Where things go wrong for characters in a Singer story or novel is precisely at the point where they desert the faith and ways of their fathers, be it in the shtetl of Frampol, in Warsaw, in New York, Israel, or Buenos Aires. That way lies Gehenna.

That way, too, lies some superior fiction. Singer unlooses his magicians, his yeshiva boys rattled by en-lightened ideas, his women swept away by vanity, and the games begin. Almost always they are sex games. Because the possibility of redemption must be present in his fiction, Singer works best with philanderers. Breaking the seventh commandment makes for better fiction anyway than breaking the sixth: redemption from murder seems distinctly less convincing than re-demption from adultery. Besides, adultery, as in the bad old joke about incest, is a game the entire family can play. It is perhaps the most human of sins. As a writer, Singer played a great many variations upon it. Only toward the close did the game begin to run down.

A dark vein had always run through Singer's writing ("man is a stinker," etc.). But for the better part of his career he was best thought of as a tragicomedian. Comedy is possible even on the road to perdition, and Singer was adept at wringing high-spirited laughter from his depictions of characters as various as Gimpel the Fool and Yasha Mazur, his magician from Lublin. But in his later years the laughter was not even hollow; in fact, it was not there. Singer claimed not to be inter-ested in preaching or sending messages, but reading the flat stories in *The Death of Methuselah* one could con-clude only that its author's view of human beings ended with the observation that men are animals and women whores—case closed. In his last published novel, *Scum,* the redemption of Max Barabander is not even considered. "Oh, Mama, I'm sinking into filth up to my neck," he cries toward the close of the novel. Singer just lets him go under.

How account for this? What could have hap-pened to make Singer, in his last years, so dark—and, one must add, so much less interesting—a writer? For the last twenty years of his life, the world treated him as a great man, showering every sort of pleasing atten-tion upon him, ending with the Nobel Prize, which he won in 1978. He had money, critical acclaim, adoring readers, longevity, every reason to feel a sense of impressive achievement. Yet however playful he may have been at lectures, or with interviewers, or among friends, his late work reveals a writer who found people more disgusting than interesting. Why had his skies become so clouded? Critics used to complain that Singer often had problems with his endings: there is a problem with the ending of his own career.

The inclement Isaac Bashevis Singer is nowhere more evident than in *The Penitent,* a brief novel of 1983. That book, which tells the story of Joseph Shapiro, turns out to be an unrelieved philippic against modernity. Modern culture, Joseph Shapiro claims, is good for breeding only "cynics and whores." Modern philosophy, he avers, has a single theme: "We don't know anything and we cannot know anything." Newspapers pay "tribute to every idolatry and spit at the truth." Crime is on the loose and it is the job of lawyers to see that criminals go free. Animals, God's creatures, are slaughtered in the most hideous ways; when it comes to animals, says Joseph, "every man is a Nazi." The sum total of psychoanalysis is always "that someone else was guilty." And Jews, at least Jews without faith, are no better than anyone else. "Every few months they find a new idol, a new illusion, a new vogue, a new madness. They revere all kinds of murderers, whores, false prophets, clowns. They go wild over every little scribbler, every ham actor, every harlot." But enough.

In an author's note at the end of this novel, Singer makes plain that it was not possible for him to share Joseph Shapiro's belief in "a final escape from the human dilemma, a permanent rescue for all time" where Joseph finds it: in a "return to Jewishness, and not merely to some modern arbitrary Jewishness, but to the Jew-

ishness of my grandfathers and great-grandfathers." But it is plain enough that Singer did share much of his character's unrelenting diagnosis of the hideousness of modern life. At one point in this novel, recounting a relapse into sin after his pledge to return to purity, Joseph says to the narrator, "That's how it is with adultery, with theft, with murder, with a craze for honors or for revenge. There is always a letdown. I don't have to tell *you* about that."

Did life let Singer down in some fundamental way that turned him so against it at the close? He insisted that one could be religious and rebellious simultaneously, believing in God and arguing with Him at the same time: "Those who dedicate their lives to serving God have often dared to question His justice, and to rebel against His seeming neutrality in man's struggle between good and evil."

In the end, it was the prevalence of evil that Singer found overwhelming. He was too good—which is to say, too honest—a writer to report things other than precisely as he found them. Why this dark and troubled truth, coming from a powerful writer at the end of his career, should make for not very interesting art is another question.

What is not in question is that Singer's stories and novels figure to have as long a life as those of any other writer of the past 50 years. He was one of the last living links with the Jewish past in Poland. He wrote in a language that had been given up for dead almost from the time he began to use it and into which he pumped impressive new life. That he survived, endured, triumphed, is as astonishing, even miraculous, a story as any he himself could have written. (pp. 33-7)

Joseph Epstein, "Our Debt to I. B. Singer," in *Commentary,* Vol. 92, No. 5, November, 1991, pp. 31-7.

SOURCES FOR FURTHER STUDY

Alexander, Edward. *Isaac Bashevis Singer.* Boston: Twayne Publishers, 1980, 161 p.

> General biographical and critical study of Singer and his works.

Buchen, Irving H. *Isaac Bashevis Singer and the Eternal Past.* New York: New York University Press, 1968, 239 p.

> Studies the relationship between demons, history, and religion in Singer's early work.

Kresh, Paul. *Isaac Bashevis Singer: The Magician of West 86th Street.* New York: The Dial Press, 1979, 441 p.

> Biography of Singer.

Malin, Irving. *Isaac Bashevis Singer.* New York: Frederick Ungar, 1972, 126 p.

> Introduction to recurring themes, characters, and symbols in Singer's work.

——, ed. *Critical Views of Isaac Bashevis Singer.* New York: New York University Press, 1969, 268 p.

> Reprints several significant essays on Singer's work, as well as two interviews with him and a bibliography of primary and secondary sources.

Rosenblatt, Paul, and Koppel, Gene. *Isaac Bashevis Singer on Literature and Life.* Tucson: University of Arizona Press, 1971, 40 p.

Interviews with Singer on "the art of the novel, symbolism, dogma in religion, the literary audience, the child, pantheism, 'the establishment of the non-talent,' and other matters."

Aleksandr Solzhenitsyn

1918-

(Full name Aleksandr Isayevich Solzhenitsyn) Russian novelist, short story writer, poet, dramatist, journalist, essayist, and critic.

INTRODUCTION

Best known as the author of *Odin den' Ivana Denisovicha* (1962; *One Day in the Life of Ivan Denisovich*) and *Arkhipelag GULag, 1918-1956: Op' bit khudozhestvennopo issledovaniia* (1973-75; *The Gulag Archipelago, 1918-1956: An Experiment in Literary Investigation*), Solzhenitsyn confronts through writing the oppressive actions of the former Soviet Union as well as the political and moral problems of the West. Rejecting the precepts of socialist realism, he writes from a Christian point of view, depicting the suffering of the innocent in a world where good and evil vie for the human soul. In this he is thematically linked to such nineteenth-century Russian writers as Leo Tolstoy and Anton Chekov. Although Soviet authorities frequently banned his works, Solzhenitsyn received the 1970 Nobel Prize for what the Nobel committee termed "the ethical force with which he has pursued the indispensible traditions of Russian literature."

Born in 1918 in Kislovodsk, Russia, Solzhenitsyn never knew his father, who died in a hunting accident before Solzhenitsyn was born. Solzhenitsyn's mother, daughter of a wealthy landowner, was denied sufficient employment by the Soviet government, and they thus lived in relative squalor from 1924 to 1936. Solzhenitsyn had some sense of his literary ambition by the age of nine, and before he was eighteen he resolved to write a major novel about the Revolution. After earning degrees in philology and mathematics and physics, Solzhenitsyn began teaching physics in 1941. In 1945, while serving as the commander of a Soviet Army artillery battery, counter-intelligence agents discovered letters in which Solzhenitsyn had criticized Stalinism. Found guilty of conspiring against the state, he was confined for over a decade to numerous institutions, including a labor camp at Ekibastuz, Kazakhstan, and Marfino Prison, a *sharashka,* or government-run prison and research institute. It was while in Moscow's Luby-anka prison that he read otherwise unobtainable works by such authors as Yevgeny Zamyatin, the great Soviet prose writer of the 1920s, and American novelist John Dos Passos, whose expressionist style later influenced Solzhenitsyn's own writing. During his imprisonment, Solzhenitsyn was diagnosed with cancer, underwent surgery, and began radiation therapy. In 1953 he was released from prison and exiled to Kok-Terek in Central Asia. There, he taught mathematics and physics in a secondary school and began writing poems and plays as well as taking notes for a novel.

Freed from exile in 1956, Solzhenitsyn returned to central Russia where friends encouraged him to submit his writings to the Russian periodical *Novy Mir* which published *One Day in the Life of Ivan Denisovich* in 1962. Appearing during a period of openness fostered by Soviet leader Nikita Khrushchev, the novel proved a considerable success. However, with the fall of Khrushchev and the rise of much less tolerant regimes, Solzhenitsyn quickly fell from official favor and was closely monitored by security forces. When he was granted the Nobel Prize for Literature, he was unable to attend the awards ceremony because the Soviet government would not guarantee his reentry into Russia. The French publication of *The Gulag Archipelago* led to his arrest, and in 1974 he was expelled from his homeland and eventually settled in the United States.

Set in Stalinist Russia, *One Day in the Life of Ivan Denisovich* focuses on a simple prisoner who wants only to serve out his sentence with a certain integrity. In the novel Solzhenitsyn strove to reverse the usual procedure of Socialist Realism, which imposed thoughts and feelings on its readers. Therefore, he rendered his tale in an ironic, understated, elliptical manner intended to elicit spontaneous feelings unrelated to official propaganda. Despite the popular success of *One Day in the Life of Ivan Denisovich,* most critics consider *Vkruge pervom* (1968; *The First Circle*) and *Rakovyĭ korpus* (1968; *The Cancer Ward*) to be Solzhenitsyn's principal achievements of the 1960s. Both works are set in institutions cut off from society, feature characters with diverse backgrounds and philosophies, and incorporate Solzhenitsyn's experiences as a prisoner and cancer patient.

Although *The First Circle* is set in a prison, the novel begins in the outside world as Innokenty Volodin, an idealistic young diplomat makes a telephone call to the American embassy that results in his arrest and imprisonment in a *sharashka*. The principal prisoners whom he meets are Lev Rubin, a Jew and a dedicated Communist; Dmitry Sologdin, an engineer and idiosyncratic spiritual teacher; and Gleb Nerzhin, a scientist and aspiring writer. At the end of the novel, Nerzhin is taken away to a far more difficult camp, Sologdin is about to gain a pardon, and Rubin is kept behind. With

The First Circle Solzhenitsyn countered stifling Socialist Realism by relating his work to both Russian classics and Western culture. The principal characters, for example, each correspond to the siblings of Fyodor Dostoyevsky's *Brothers Karamazov,* while the *sharashka*—and the title itself—recall the first circle of hell in Dante's *Inferno.*

Like *The First Circle, The Cancer Ward* presents an isolated environment. Drawing a parallel between the hospital where Solzhenitsyn was treated for cancer and Soviet society, *The Cancer Ward* thus constitutes another meditation on the human condition. The work's principal protagonists present two extremes; Pavel Rusanov, a bureaucrat with connections to the secret police, expects special treatment and deference, while Oleg Kostoglotov, a former camp inmate, tolerates no elitism. Both benefit from their treatment, but each leaves the hospital with unchanged attitudes.

Solzhenitsyn's most important work of nonfiction is unquestionably *The Gulag Archipelago,* a detailed account of Stalinist repression. The book is predicated on the fact that arrest and torture were everyday practices in the Soviet Union. Solzhenitsyn proceeds as a scientist might, creating a taxonomy of arrests and tortures. In one passage, he even invites readers to participate with him in deciding which forms of torture belong in which categories. Solzhenitsyn makes his narrative vivid and direct as he speaks of his own experiences, such as his arrest and confinement in different prisons and concentration camps. He also includes many personal narratives, replete with horrifying detail from other victims of arbitrary violence. In *The Gulag Archipelago* Solzhenitsyn finds all Russians—including himself—accountable for the horrors of Stalinism. "We didn't love freedom enough," he writes. "We purely and simply deserved everything that happened afterward." He also observes that "the line dividing good and evil cuts through the heart of every human being."

Avgust chetyrnadtsatogo (1971; *August 1914*) is the first volume in *Krasnoe koleso: Povestvovane'e v otmerennykh srokakh,* better known as *The Red Wheel,* the series that Solzhenitsyn considers his life work. *August 1914* centers on the World War I battle of Tannenberg as witnessed by Colonel Georgy Vorotyntsev, a graduate of the Russian equivalent of West Point, and Arseny Blagodaryov, an enlisted man whom Vorotyntsev befriends. Vorotyntsev and Blagodaryov see various kinds of action, ultimately serving with a group of Russian soldiers who are surrounded by advancing German troops and who succeed in breaking through enemy lines. Like Solzhenitsyn's other major works, *August 1914* is polyphonic in its technique. This remarkably diverse novel consists of fifty-eight fictional chapters, two newspaper sections, five film segments (passages written in a cryptic style designed to have a cinematic quality), four historical surveys of troop movements, one interpretive historical essay, and six collections of contemporary documents. Both the film segments and the selections of newspaper clippings show the continuing influence of Dos Passos.

The second *Red Wheel* volume, *Oktyabr' shestnadtsatogo* (1984; *October 1916*) is approximately twice as long as *August 1914* and contains proportionately more characters. *October 1916* presents very little military action but emphasizes the effect of the war on the home front. Among the various storylines is one involving Vorotyntsev, a married man who falls in love with a woman professor at Petrograd University.

The publication of *March 1917* in 1986 and 1987 marked another major change in the emphasis of *The Red Wheel*. In this extraordinarily long volume, historical figures effectively replace fictional characters as the narrative shifts away from World War I and toward the communist revolution. As events unfold, politicians such as Pavel Milyukov and Vasily Maklakov connive and deal; generals consult each other; and members of the imperial family convey their uncertainty and anxiety. Solzhenitsyn minutely details various episodes, describing weather and clothing as well as actions and emotions. He therefore allows his readers to experience what happens when a society slowly but inexorably falls apart. In his fiction and nonfiction, Solzhenitsyn continues to assert the indomitableness of the human spirit and the responsibility of the writer. The task of the writer, he believes, is "to treat universal and eternal themes: the mysteries of the heart and conscience, the collision between life and death, [and] the triumph over spiritual anguish." Citing these objectives, critics agree that Solzhenitsyn's perceptive analysis of the human condition elevates his fiction above the political and places him among Russia's greatest novelists. They assert that throughout his canon, from *One Day in the Life of Ivan Denisovich* through *The Red Wheel*, Solzhenitsyn's great theme is not the effect of the revolution—for no revolution or reformation in the Marxist-Leninist sense actually occurred in Russia—but the dissolution of an anachronistic, deeply divided society under the stress of great events and the response of individuals to that dissolution.

(For further information about Solzhenitsyn's life and works, see *Contemporary Authors*, Vols. 69-72; *Contemporary Literary Criticism*, Vols. 1, 2, 4, 7, 9, 10, 18, 26, 34; and *Major 20th-Century Writers*.)

CRITICAL COMMENTARY

SERGEI LEVITZKY

(essay date 1971)

[Levitzky was a Latvian-born American educator and author. In the following excerpt, he contends that Solzhenitsyn's fiction focuses on moral rather than political issues.]

While following in his own incomparable way the naturalistic traditions in the description of the way of life in the concentration camp in *One Day in the Life of Ivan Denisovich,* Solzhenitsyn also knows how to compel us to see that the soul of his unsophisticated hero lives not by bread alone. Apart from the tremendously vital stamina of Ivan Denisovich and his good-natured, peasant cunning, we feel in him a man of goodwill whose spirit is not filled with bitterness, despite the crying injustice of his punishment and despite, too, the inhuman conditions of life in the so-called corrective labor camp. On the contrary, his soul is radiated by his belief in humanity, by the ease with which he establishes human contacts. (p. 208)

Solzhenitsyn's best works really do convey the impression of being literary miracles, achieved through a rare combination of naturalness, deep insights, and incomparability of artistic talent—talent denied in a tone of aggressive hypocrisy by those in power in the Soviet Union. Indeed, the phenomenon of Solzhenitsyn is not only a literary miracle but also a spiritual miracle.

The ethical element appears in an especially dramatic way in two main novels by Solzhenitsyn, *Cancer Ward* and *The First Circle*. The ethical aspect of these novels can be considered under three headings: Solzhenitsyn's exposition of the negative ethical essence of some of his heroes, his skill in detecting the sparks of goodness even in the souls of his negative (though not hopelessly so) heroes, and his ethical views, expressed when the author speaks through his positive heroes or in the form of author's remarks. (p. 209)

[Without] a single word of the external condemnation of a tyrant, Solzhenitsyn makes us feel the inner nemesis of the mania of total power. This nemesis is the absolute solitude, aggravated by the inner foreboding of a close, inevitable end. Men who commit evil deeds but whose conscience is still alive usually feel remorse. No trace of this is to be found in Stalin, however, as presented through the magic prism of Solzhenitsyn's art. There is not a trace of the prick of conscience, be-

Principal Works

Odin den' Ivana Denisovicha (novel) 1962
  [One Day in the Life of Ivan Denisovich, 1963]
Dlia pol'zy dela (novel) 1963
  [For the Good of the Cause, 1964]
Slucha na stantsii Krechetovka [i] Matrenin dvor (novels) 1963
  [We Never Make Mistakes, 1963]
Sochineniia (selected works) 1966
V kruge pervom (novel) 1968
  [The First Circle, 1968]
Rakovyĭ korpus (novel) 1968
  [The Cancer Ward, 1968]
Olen'i shalashovka (play) 1968
  [The Love Girl and the Innocent, 1969]
Svecha na vetru (play) 1968
  [Candle in the Wind, 1973]
*Avgust chetyrnadtsatogo (novel) 1971
  [August 1914, 1972]
Stories and Prose Poems by Aleksandr Solzhenitsyn (short stories and poetry) 1971
Nobelevskaia lektsiia po literature 1970 goda (essay) 1972
  [Nobel Lecture by Aleksandr Solzhenitsyn, 1972]
Arkhipelag GULag, 1918-1956: Op' bit khudozhestvennopo issledovaniia (nonfiction) 1973-75

[The Gulag Archipelago, 1918-1956: An Experiment in Literary Investigation, Vol. I, Parts 1 and 2, 1974; Vol. II, Parts 3 and 4, 1976; Vol. 3, 1979]
Prusskie nochi: pozma napisappaja v lagere v 1950 (poetry) 1974
  [Prussian Nights: A Poem, 1977]
Pis'mo vozhdiam Sovetskogo Soĭuza (essay) 1974
  [Letter to the Soviet Leaders, 1974]
Bodalsia telenok s dubom (autobiography) 1975
  [The Oak and the Calf, 1975]
Amerikanski rechi (essays) 1975
From under the Rubble [with others] (essays) 1975; also published as From Under the Ruins, 1975
Détente: Prospects for Democracy and Dictatorship [with others] (essays) 1976
Warning to the West (essays) 1976
Victory Celebrations: A Comedy in Four Acts [and] Prisoners: A Tragedy (plays) 1983
*Oktyabr' shestnadtsatogo (novel) 1984
*March 1917 (novel) 1986-87
*Part of the Krasnoe koleso: Povestvovane'e v otmerennykh srokakh (The Red Wheel) series.

---

cause leaders like Hitler and Stalin are full of the evil will with which they identify themselves. They strangle their own conscience. Indeed, how could they feel any pricks of an already dead conscience?

It is claimed that the essence of *The First Circle* lies in the unmasking of the evils of Stalinism. This claim is, of course, true, but to see this as the central meaning of the novel would mean a gross politicizing of Solzhenitsyn's creativity. The very idea of *The First Circle* does indeed have an intrinsically political aspect, but Solzhenitsyn is primarily concerned with denouncing the spiritual evil of Stalinism: the lives mutilated by a regime of terror, the bleeding wounds of human souls—in short, the external triumph of evil. (p. 211)

On the basis of . . . the overall impression of Solzhenitsyn's creativity, there can be no doubt about the presence of a deep ethical pathos in the writer and that his moral intuition borders on ethical clairvoyance. In our time it is often the fashion to discredit moral values, and the very word "morality" is often placed in quotation marks. Against this negative background, it is to Solzhenitsyn's great merit that, by his literary works, in which he so boldly denounces an externally triumphant immorality, he has contributed greatly to

the rehabilitation of ethics. There is a deep and urgent need for this rehabilitation today. Solzhenitsyn reminds his readers of that which makes men human: of their ethical essence, of the Eternal in man. (pp. 213-14)

Sergei Levitzky "Alexander Solzhenitsyn," in *The Politics of Twentieth-Century Novelists,* edited by George Panichas, Hawthorn Books, Inc., Publishers, 1971, pp. 207-14.

JOSEPH FRANK
(essay date 1976)

[An American educator and critic, Frank is widely known for his multi-volume work on Fyodor Dostoyevski. In the following excerpt, he favorably compares Solzhenitsyn to the tradition of nineteenth-century Russian literature.]

Solzhenitsyn is the first great voice to have come to maturity totally in the postrevolutionary period, and to have known no other physical or spiritual reality. As a result he is "the first *national* writer of the Soviet period of Russian literature." . . .

His books, impressive and compelling as they are, nonetheless inevitably seem old-fashioned to tastes schooled on Joyce, Proust, and Kafka. . . .

Solzhenitsyn came to maturity in a world dominated by the theory of "socialist realism" (a codification of the achievements of nineteenth-century Russian literature), and he still creates within its conventions. But Solzhenitsyn had been taught that realism demands the truth, and it was truth that became the hero of his works—to paraphrase what Tolstoy once said. (p. 331)

It would be a mistake, however, to attribute the old-fashioned quality of Solzhenitsyn's novels only to an external factor such as enforced cultural isolation. Such a view implicitly assumes that if Solzhenitsyn had had the opportunity, he would have utilized the experiments of modernism; but this seems to me very doubtful. Technique, after all, when it is not just arbitrarily adopted to keep up with fashion, always translates a vision of the world; and Solzhenitsyn's "vision" is diametrically opposed to that of most modern literature. . . . Solzhenitsyn's fundamental theme is precisely the *affirmation* of character, the ability to survive in a nightmare world where moral character is the only safeguard of human dignity and the very conception of humanity itself is something precious and valuable. To a western world that sees its image reflected in the wistful nihilism of Beckett's metaphysical clowns and basket cases, Solzhenitsyn is indeed old-fashioned; but literature, after all, is not (or should not conceive itself to be) in competition with haute couture, and Solzhenitsyn's technique renders a "vision" that one hopes transcends the modes of the moment. (It is instructive that when Solzhenitsyn experiments with modernism in *August 1914,* in which he uses some of Dos Passos's techniques in *USA,* he does so precisely to translate delusory mass consciousness and experiences of confusion, defeat, and despair.) (pp. 331-32)

The survivor in Solzhenitsyn . . . always feels himself in total opposition to the trivial workaday world of "the others"—those who live in abasement and subjection to the powers that be. This opposition is dramatized in *Candle in the Wind,* not a very good play but interesting for what it reveals about the author. Here a survivor (a returned prisoner) finds himself living in the midst of a materialistic and hedonistic future world resembling that of *A Clockwork Orange* (without the sadism)—a world which has lost all sense of moral value in the frantic scramble for pleasure and power. For someone who has learned to what depths of degradation men can sink if they aim only to satisfy their physical and material needs, such a world is intolerable. . . . Solzhenitsyn's ideas . . . very much resemble (in tenor if not in detail) those the southern

Agrarians used to propound in this country. (pp. 332-33)

Solzhenitsyn's works, in the words of the German novelist and fellow Nobel prize-winner Heinrich Böll, have "the sweep of Tolstoy and the spirit of Dostoevsky, thus synthesizing the two minds which were thought to be antithetical both in the nineteenth century and in present-day literary criticism." The very fact that such comparisons can be made without a sense of incongruity (what other contemporary novelist anywhere could bear their weight?) indicates Solzhenitsyn's stature, which has only increased with the recent publication of his explosive *Gulag Archipelago.* Russia has once again produced, even against its will, a writer who truly fulfills the Belinskian requirement that literature be *both* a free creation of the spirit and a powerful expression of the life of its society. (p. 333)

Joseph Frank, "From Gogol to Gulag Archipelago," in *The Sewanee Review,* Vol. LXXXIV, No. 2, Spring, 1976, pp. 314-33.

LUELLEN LUCID

(essay date 1977)

[In the following excerpt, Lucid explores the relationship of Solzhenitsyn's works to the Soviet literary tradition.]

Western critics have been quick to analyze Aleksandr Solzhenitsyn's humanitarian concerns and brilliant development of the metaphorical novel. What has been lacking in discussions of Solzhenitsyn's works is an understanding of their relationship to Soviet literary tradition; his writings need to be placed in the context not only of the dissident movement but of Soviet literature as a whole. Solzhenitsyn's writings are neither simply an anachronistic return to critical realism with no relation to the Soviet literary experience . . . nor are they a natural development of "socialist realism." . . . (p. 498)

[The] Soviet literary experience of the thirties, forties, and fifties . . . had a profound, if negative, influence on Solzhenitsyn. Stalin's aesthetic doctrine of socialist realism, as established in 1932, embodies on a literary plane the social and political facets of Soviet life to which Solzhenitsyn is responding in his own fiction. A full appreciation of Solzhenitsyn must, therefore, take his reaction to the literary aspect of Soviet socialism into account. Moreover, it can be demonstrated that Solzhenitsyn's works evidence a strong concern with technical innovation; they constitute not only a "spiritual revolution" but also a rhetorical one. . . . [His] novels are a conscious reaction to Soviet literary doctrine, which they self-consciously subvert, satirize, and parody stylistically, structurally, and thematically.

Solzhenitsyn's rejection of totalitarian values and policies is conveyed in his novels not only by their explicit concern with the repressive nature of Soviet society and its "gulag archipelago" of prison camps but by a crucial displacement of the literary norms and conventions of socialist realism. . . . Estrangement from established literary form lies at the core of Solzhenitsyn's works, as his fiction depicts the conflict between the Soviet state and the political rebel through a stylistic examination of the literary conflict between socialist realism and critical realism.

The literary displacement accomplished by Solzhenitsyn is not a simple abandonment of the canons of socialist realism but rather a transformation of those principles. (pp. 498-99)

Socialist realism itself began as a rhetorical revolution designed to meet the needs of a socialist society. It displaced nineteenth-century realist literature and transformed Russian folk themes into a functional mythology that would further the ends of the revolutionary government. (p. 499)

Solzhenitsyn has achieved a revitalization of Russian literature by not only incorporating socializing modes of expression but baring them to show the tension which exists between the nineteenth-century novel and the montage techniques of twentieth-century fiction. He displaces the doctrine of socialist realism by "baring the device" which socialist realism has covertly employed, turning it against the Soviet regime stylistically and thematically. Through parody and contrast, he has exposed the totalitarian quality of its dicta and reversed its thematic content. While Solzhenitsyn's works follow the canons of socialist realism in their public intent and political subject matter, they effect a fundamental disruption of those canons in their thematic and stylistic reexamination of Soviet reality.

Socialist realist doctrine finds its counterpart in Solzhenitsyn's fiction, but crucially transformed. . . . Solzhenitsyn shares a sense of engagement in history with the exponents of socialist realism, but his works constitute an aesthetically expressed rebellion against their basic values. His art has the avowed intention of awakening the Soviet public to the truth about its reality rather than upholding the official version of social life. . . . Whereas socialist realism attempts to reduce complexity to simple-minded formulas and calls such art "proletarian literature," Solzhenitsyn deals with the complex issues of social life by depicting a microcosm of everyday Soviet existence. (p. 500)

The metaphorical quality of Solzhenitsyn's fiction resembles the mythologized portrayals of reality in works of socialist realism in its intention of drawing a personal response from the reader. (p. 501)

In order to address the social realities and political issues of his time, Solzhenitsyn utilizes literary forms associated with political action, but in contrast to socialist realism, Solzhenitsyn's objective is to negate the automatized conventions upheld by Soviet officialdom. His novels contain journalistic reportage, political statement, intellectual debate, and political satire, and the biting polemical and satirical style of his fiction lies at the core of Solzhenitsyn's rhetorical revolution against the Soviet state. Solzhenitsyn displaces a canon of socialist realism by reversing its intention. In place of the "Party line" type of political polemic offered by socialist realism, Solzhenitsyn provides a wide-ranging spectrum of political and philosophical positions, including the "Party line" itself.

The "positive heroes" of Solzhenitsyn's works are Russia's writers, who throughout its history have provided the Russian people with an "alternative government." . . . [The] writer-hero of Solzhenitsyn's works is depicted as an iconoclast, prophet, and truth-teller; he is the ultimate and independent protector of human values and freedom. (pp. 501-02)

Although Solzhenitsyn's works have ideological concerns in common with those of socialist realism, they do not identify the author with any single character or point of view. This authorial estrangement from the characters and situations represents a displacement of socialist realism's mode of characterization and plot structure. The identification of author and hero that is made complete in socialist realism is reversed by Solzhenitsyn through a polyphonic structure which gives equal weight to each character as he appears rather than focusing on one particular character as "hero." The reader is forced to identify with a synthesis of the characters and hence with the author himself, who transcends them. In place of the "uplifting" plot of socialist realism with its "blank-faced optimism, decreed by officialdom," Solzhenitsyn's works are based on a dynamic of intellectual contestation where no easy answers or neat endings are provided for complacent readers. (p. 502)

Solzhenitsyn's revolt against the totalitarian nature of the Soviet state takes place on a linguistic level through his displacement of its slogans, clichés, and formulaic language. . . . For Solzhenitsyn, language that identifies truth with established truth and disavows its critical function is no longer capable of creating a literature. (pp. 502-03)

The German critic Theodor W. Adorno points out in *The Jargon of Authenticity* that "jargon reproduces on the level of the mind the curse which bureaucracy exercises in reality. It could be described as an ideological replica of the paralyzing quality of official functions." The "jargon" of socialist realism takes on exactly this symbolic role in Solzhenitsyn's works, linguistically expressing the repressive nature of Soviet society. . . .

The writer is particularly suited to the task of exposing Stalinist totalitarianism precisely because of the crucial role language has played in its perpetuation. . . . Solzhenitsyn defies the official discourse by using colloquial speech forms and depicting government policies in concrete human terms. (p. 503)

Solzhenitsyn's first novel, *One Day in the Life of Ivan Denisovich,* deals in an allegorical manner with the reversal of the individual from citizen to political prisoner. The Soviet prison camp serves as a microcosm of the society at large and metaphorically represents the repressive atmosphere which characterizes Soviet governance. All the features inherent in the automatization of Soviet life become explicit and obvious in the prison camp. The microcosm of the prison camp also demonstrates the ultimate similarity between "home" and "institution" in a society that has itself been turned into a prisonlike "total institution." Solzhenitsyn takes the socialist mythology of the "typical worker" and displaces it with the "typical prisoner" Ivan Denisovich, who at once typifies and exemplifies the characteristics of the Russian people. The reader is able to identify with the experiences of Ivan Denisovich whether or not he has himself been imprisoned, for the nonsensational, hour-by-hour description of the character's day suggests the institutionalized life of all Soviet citizens. . . .

The novel's portrayal of one "good" day in the life of a "typical" prisoner constitutes a reversal of socialist realism, which Solzhenitsyn underscores stylistically by referring to the prisoners familiarly through the consciousness of Ivan Denisovich while regarding the prison personnel and government officials impersonally as "they." By this stylistic device, Solzhenitsyn incorporates the reader into the world of the prisoners and alienates him from that of the officials. (p. 504)

Solzhenitsyn's use of prison slang also serves to estrange the reader from the established social order. Slang owes its origin and use to "the desire to break away from the commonplace, the stiff, or stuffy, the drab or trite, as imposed on us by the conventional community." It is the prisoners' symbolic protest against the status quo and the means for uniting themselves in their communal estrangement from the "normal" world. The language serves as a barrier between the prison-camp world and the "outside" world, and it puts a demand on the reader to enter into the prisoners' world on a linguistic level to share their dissociation from the "outside." Solzhenitsyn plunges the reader into the prison environment through this linguistic device and provides a contrast between the creative expressiveness of the prisoners and the formulaic language of the officials. Linguistically as well as themati-

cally, the author has transformed the prison camp into an allegorical presentation of Soviet society and has provided a symbolic model of opposition to its dictates. (pp. 504-05)

As in *One Day in the Life of Ivan Denisovich,* Solzhenitsyn makes use of the folk idiom in *The First Circle* by presenting his moral opposition to Stalinism in the form of peasant wisdom. The peasant Spiridon possesses the most self-assured sense of individual conscience and communicates his instinctive ethical stance to the less self-confident intellectual Nerzhin, a fellow prisoner at the scientific institute. . . . Just as the simple-minded figure of Ivan Denisovich becomes elevated to the status of a Russian Everyman, Spiridon assumes the role of moral spokesman by providing the homely answer to Nerzhin's prolonged spiritual quest to comprehend and cope with Stalinism: the cannibal or "people-eater" who kills his own people indiscriminately is wrong, whereas the wolfhound who kills only what is wantonly destructive (the wolf) is right. Solzhenitsyn uses the word "people-eater" instead of using the normal Russian word for cannibal, which would only connote "eater-of-one's-own-kind," in order to emphasize the peculiarly inhuman nature of Stalinism. The peasant proverb thus displaces the "folk sayings" of socialist realism and provides a philosophy that justifies moral opposition to Stalinism. (pp. 505-06)

Solzhenitsyn introduces into [*The First Circle*] actual historical personalities, including that of Stalin himself, transforming the remoteness of history and public life into an accessible reality for the reader. To do this, Solzhenitsyn employs modes of political satire and parody, reenacting the mentality of the bureaucrats in their language and thereby exposing the falsity of their attitudes. Solzhenitsyn reproduces Stalin's manner of expression in which every sentence contradicts the next. . . . In a chapter entitled "Language Is a Tool of Production," Solzhenitsyn attacks the rhetorical fraudulence of Stalinism most explicitly by imitating Stalin's thought processes in a journalistic manner. He assumes that the evilness of Stalin's "ideas" is revealed by the rhetoric he employs to express them, so that the author need only "report" them factually for the truth to become apparent. (p. 506)

In *The First Circle,* a character states that "a great writer . . . is, so to speak, a second government." . . . The figure of the writer enters this novel as a crucial moral force that sustains the prisoners in their convictions and lends others the courage to listen to the voice of conscience. . . . The artist is a prototype of the two possible reactions to Stalinism and their consequences; acquiescence is shown to lead to loss of creative freedom and talent, while rejection brings loss of physical freedom but preservation of conscience and imagination. (p. 507)

Cancer Ward, even more than Solzhenitsyn's other novels, presents the everyday reality of Soviet life in a metaphorical setting with which the reader can easily identify himself. The characters, ex-prisoner and official, face the common enemy of illness, which behaves as a social leveler and unites those with divergent backgrounds and politics in a common struggle. The setting of the cancer ward, while it should not be construed as simply a metaphor for Soviet society, does supply the symbolic basis for a novel concerned with the political and spiritual "health" of a society that has recently undergone the grave "illness" of Stalinism. . . . The cancer ward functions symbolically as the tuberculosis sanatorium does in Thomas Mann's novel, *The Magic Mountain,* where the political inference is to Europe's "health" as it is about to plunge into the senseless conflict of the First World War. (pp. 508-09)

As in the previous novels, the artist functions as a positive moral force in *Cancer Ward.* A work of literature is shown to exercise a profound effect on the patients, particularly the terminal ones. The epicurean Podduyev finds the means for accepting his impending death in Tolstoy's *What Men Live By,* although previously he had been unable to "see the use of books in his everyday life.". . . Solzhenitsyn satirizes the "socialist realists" and contrasts the irrelevance of their "message" to people's real needs with the impact of Tolstoy's work on even the unliterary Podduyev. When a writer fails to relate his work to his reader's reality, it becomes a meaningless jumble of words. (p. 509)

Solzhenitsyn mimics the formulaic approach of the socialist realist in his portrayal of the writer Aviette. Aviette announces her main literary objective to be avoidance of any "ideological mistakes.". . . Solzhenitsyn's satire of socialist realism, while stylistically farcical and journalistic, is nonetheless composed of the very slogans and clichés mouthed by the Stalinists. . . . In his mimicry of socialist realism, Solzhenitsyn adopts its rhetorical style, just as he reproduced Stalin's rhetoric in *The First Circle* to expose the ruler's mentality. He has displaced its conventions simply by repeating them in a satirical context.

The socialist realist convention of the "positive hero" is undercut in *Cancer Ward* by Solzhenitsyn's creation of an "anti-hero," who provides a parallel to the characteristics of the Soviet hero. The character Kostoglotov serves as the embodiment of the aftereffects of Stalinism; his submissive attitude brought about by years of imprisonment and harsh treatment poses an ironic counterpart to the socialist realist ideal. (pp. 509-10)

The "uplifting" ending of socialist realism is displaced in *Cancer Ward* by its circular plot structure. Just as there is no resolution to the problems posed in Solzhenitsyn's other novels, *Cancer Ward* ends without having the "anti-hero" overcome his submissive state of mind. (p. 510)

As a documentary presentation of the effects of Stalinism, *Gulag Archipelago* contributes a new dimension to Solzhenitsyn's writings, but, like his fiction, it constitutes a displacement of the canons of socialist realism, in this instance, those applying specifically to nonfiction or "documentary" writing. . . . The thematic ambiguity of the fictional works and the complexity contained within their polyphonic form is missing from the tendentious tone of this documentary on the Soviet prison-camp system. . . .

Gulag Archipelago is a crucial displacement of the Literature of Fact ("literatura fakta") literary movement as practiced under socialist realism, which considers nonfiction writing, particularly the diary, autobiography, memoir, and journalism, to be a high literary form. The purpose of such nonfiction writing is to provide a "collective" history of the revolution and the progress of socialism; documentary writing has a duty to advocate a specific cause and organize the "facts" for a specific social purpose. The Literature of Fact movement initiated in the twenties emphasizes the importance of daily events as opposed to the "fanciful" and subjective concoctions of the artist. (p. 511)

In *Gulag Archipelago,* Solzhenitsyn makes reference to *The White Sea Canal,* written by thirty-six Soviet writers including Gorky, which is an example of the journalistic sketch of Soviet progress. Its aim is to glorify the use of slave prisoner labor in large construction projects and the "social rehabilitation" and "moral reformation" which the prison system exercised upon political prisoners and criminals alike. . . . Nonfiction socialist realism, like its fictional counterpart, is given the task of laying out the "objective" facts of the great social tasks of the day, and the result is a romanticized and polemical description of Soviet society.

Gulag Archipelago is not only a rebuttal of the Soviet documentary but makes use of its techniques and tone by turning prison memoirs and journalistic history into an exposé of the Soviet regime. In its use of memoirs and journalism, in its emphasis on the collective nature of the history, and in its polemical counter-documentation and argumentation, *Gulag Archipelago* clearly displaces the Literature of Fact movement much as Solzhenitsyn's novels displace socialist realism. (pp. 511-12)

Solzhenitsyn's documentary writing constitutes an extension of the historical basis of his previous works of fiction. He alternates between a "bird's-eye view" of his country's recent history, providing an extensive survey of how Soviet law developed, and an autobiographical "worm's-eye view" that authenticates the impersonal history with intimate testimony from himself and other prisoners. As in his fictional works, Solzhenitsyn organizes his historical material metaphorically, thereby personalizing it and making it more accessible to his reader. The book is unified by the image of the "archipelago," a series of "islands" strung out across Russia whose inhabitants are drawn—often arbitrarily—from all segments of Soviet society. . . . Throughout *Gulag Archipelago,* Solzhenitsyn emphasizes the image of the latrine bucket, "the symbol of prison, a symbol of humiliation, of stink." . . . Unlike the unifying metaphor of *Cancer Ward,* with its Mannian overtones, and that of *The First Circle,* with its Dantesque aura, the pervasive use of the latrine metaphor undercuts in a caustic and naturalistic, almost brutal, manner the grandiose pretentions of the Soviet state.

As he does in his fiction, Solzhenitsyn stresses the collective nature of the history in order to incorporate the reader into the situation he is depicting and force him to assume moral responsibility for what happened. Solzhenitsyn offers his own personality through autobiographical references, making himself a surrogate for his entire generation. . . . Solzhenitsyn introduces his own memoirs as a typical example of the mass experience which his history documents, in contrast to the idealized abstraction of the "typical" worker in the socialist realist tract. The attention to personal pronouns takes on painful intensity in *Gulag Archipelago,* as "you" is not only directed at the contemporary Soviet reader but is also used rhetorically to fuse the reader and the victim being described. The pronoun "we" emerges with genuine force in joining the reader and writer in their mutual responsibility for shared guilt and moral duty; it is no longer acceptable simply to blame "them."

An ironic tension is maintained throughout the work by alternating between the "official" point of view and Solzhenitsyn's personally authenticated experience. . . . Solzhenitsyn resorts here to the rhetorical device of exaggeration in his contrast of Soviet and tsarist prisons, much as he did in *The First Circle.* Once again, his own account provides the rhetorical reverse image of the socialist realist perspective. (pp. 513-14)

Solzhenitsyn has transformed each of the canons of socialist realism through the themes, style, and structure of his writings. He accepts the socialist realist premise that art is a social act but posits a critical rather than conformist social function for it. In his use of folk themes and in the metaphorical quality of his works, he attempts to reach the Russian public with images and situations sufficiently limited and familiar to make a personal impact on the reader and spur him to a critical social consciousness. The premise that art should instill in the reader a sense of social interconnectedness is also implicit in Solzhenitsyn's works, as he explores both the negative and positive effects of this sense of community. On the one hand, he portrays the complic-

Solzhenitsyn during his years of imprisonment.

ity of an entire society in the policies perpetrated in its name, and on the other hand, the necessity for communal acknowledgment of this complicity and acceptance of individual responsibility as the basis for a more honest and open political system.

As in the works of socialist realism, Solzhenitsyn achieves his social purpose by utilizing socializing modes of expression, and his writings share the polemical orientation of socialist realism. In place of the "positive hero" who mindlessly upholds the Soviet state, Solzhenitsyn provides the writer-hero whose role is to exemplify an ethical and independent outlook. He also creates an "anti-hero" who serves as an ironic parallel to the acquiescent "positive hero" of socialist realism. In contrast to the "uplifting" plot structure of socialist realism, the inconclusiveness of Solzhenitsyn's novels demonstrates the problematical nature of opposition to the regime. In both his nonfiction and his fiction, Solzhenitsyn maintains the values of truth, sincerity, and completeness in opposition to the standards set by socialist realism. On a linguistic level, Solzhenitsyn attacks the totalitarian quality of Soviet society through mimicry and parody of its literary and political discourse. The profound displacement which may at any time overtake the ordinary citizen and suddenly transform him into a political exile—a reversal Solzhenitsyn knows through personal experience—is conveyed through this displacement of Soviet literary norms and values to give us the world seen anew through that reversal. (p. 515)

Luellen Lucid, "Solzhenitsyn's Rhetorical Revolution," in *Twentieth Century Literature,* Vol. 23, No. 4, December, 1977, pp. 498-517.

EDWARD E. ERICSON, JR.
(essay date 1980)

[In the excerpt below, Ericson examines Solzhenitsyn's Nobel lecture as a statement of the author's writing objectives.]

Much of the confusion about Solzhenitsyn would be eliminated if his theory of art were understood. He took the occasion of his winning the Nobel Prize in Literature in 1970 to enunciate that theory. Although he did not go to Stockholm to receive the prize in person, because the Soviet authorities would not guarantee him reentry into his homeland, he did follow the standard practice of preparing a speech for the occasion. As its final sentence summarizes, this *Nobel Lecture* both calls the writers of the world to a high sense of mission and provides the basis for understanding the author's own work. The latter is the primary concern of this [essay], which will analyze the lecture in detail, section by section.

The first section is the most important one, for in it Solzhenitsyn establishes the religious basis for his literary work. True art, he explains, is premised on two fundamental concepts: that truth is absolute and that reality is objective. Both ideas grow organically from Solzhenitsyn's belief that there is a personal God who created and sustains the world. Art, then, is a gift from God; it entails the exercising of a God-given ability. Artists may misuse this gift, "but Art is not profaned by our attempts, does not because of them lose touch with its source." Thus, art is grounded in the objective reality of God's created order, not in an individual's subjectivity; and this fact is so whether or not a given artist acknowledges it.

Solzhenitsyn elaborates this point by contrasting two kinds of artists. One kind "imagines himself the creator of an independent spiritual world. . . . " This attempt is doomed to failure, because man is not an autonomous being, in art or in any other realm. "Just as man, who once declared himself the center of existence, has not been able to create a stable spiritual system," so neither can the artist successfully create his own reality. A novel must conform to the same moral laws that govern ordinary human life.

This point Solzhenitsyn's second kind of artist understands. He "acknowledges a higher power above him and joyfully works as a common apprentice under God's heaven. . . . " And the acknowledgment of his creatureliness serves to enhance his sense of responsibility, for he is answerable to the one who created and gives direction to the world. This artist works in "a world about whose foundations he has no doubt." His task is "to sense more keenly than others the harmony of the world, the beauty and the outrage of what man has done to it, and poignantly to let people know."

"The harmony of the world" refers to the orderliness of God's original creation. "The beauty and the outrage of what man has done to it" refers to the effects of the Fall; man remains capable of both good ("beauty") and evil ("outrage"). And "poignantly to let people know" refers to the artist's calling to tell the truth about this dual nature of man. These universal matters, best explicated in the Christian schema of Creation and Fall, are the artist's primary subject. As Solzhenitsyn said elsewhere,

. . . it is not the task of the writer to defend or criticize one or another mode of distributing the social product, or to defend or criticize one or another form of government organization. The task of the writer is to select more universal and eternal questions, the secrets of the human heart and conscience, the confrontation of life with death, the triumph over spiritual sorrow, the laws of the history of mankind that were born in the depths of time immemorial and that will cease to exist only when the sun ceases to shine.

In later sections of the *Nobel Lecture,* Solzhenitsyn makes certain pronouncements on social and political matters. Yet he has denied that such subjects are the primary material of art. There is no contradiction here. The "universal and eternal questions" are played out by finite man in his daily activities, not excluding his social and political activities. A religious outlook, far from precluding one's commenting on social and political matters, demands that he do so. For the religious mind sees life as indivisible: it sees the eternal and the temporal as inextricably intertwined, and it does not abandon the affairs of this world. In Solzhenitsyn's words, "The transference of values is entirely natural to the religious cast of mind: human society cannot be exempted from the laws and demands which constitute the aim and meaning of individual human lives." Furthermore, this "transference of values" is simply a human thing to do; all men bring their whole selves to bear on any matter under consideration.

But even without a religious foundation, this sort of transference is readily and naturally made. It is very human to apply even to the biggest social events or human organizations, including the whole state and the United Nations, our spiritual values: noble, base, courageous, cowardly, hypocritical, false, cruel, magnanimous, just, unjust, and so on. Indeed everybody writes this way, even the most extreme economic materialists, since they remain after all human beings.

The relationship for Solzhenitsyn between the eternal and the temporal, or, more specifically, the religious and the political, is a crucial one, since much commentary has viewed him through political eyes. *The Gulag Archipelago* provides an illuminating case study. In a book thick with political detail, he asserts early, "So let the reader who expects this book to be a political exposé slam its covers shut right now." He proceeds immediately to set the terms in which this book, and all of his works, should be read:

If only there were evil people somewhere insidiously committing evil deeds, and it were necessary only to separate them from the rest of us and destroy them. But the line dividing good and evil cuts through the heart of every human being. . . . During the life of any heart this line keeps changing place; sometimes it is squeezed one way by exuberant evil and sometimes it shifts to allow enough space for good to flourish. One and the same human being is, at various ages, under various circumstances, a totally different human being. At times he is close to being a devil, at times to sainthood. But his name doesn't change, and to that name we ascribe the whole lot, good and evil.

(pp. 6-9)

The second section of the *Nobel Lecture* offers a not insignificant tribute to Dostoevsky, a writer with "the gift of seeing much, a man wondrously filled with light." Dostoevsky had once said that beauty would save the world. This notion initially puzzled Solzhenitsyn. But now he thinks he understands. In a world inured to the abstract claims of Truth and Goodness, in a world in which lies and evil often have their way, perhaps that beauty resident in the concretions of art will have its effect. There is a kind of art whose "artificial, strained concepts do not withstand the test of being turned into images; they fall to pieces, turn out to be sickly and pale, convince no one." But there is also a kind of art which carries a conviction which "is absolute and subdues even a resistant heart." Such a work of art "contains its verification in itself. . . . " So perhaps the beauty of genuine art can be an effective antidote to ideology and prejudice and, "in fact, help the modern world."

The third section opens with a passage reminiscent of the public prayer Solzhenitsyn circulated two years later, in 1972. . . . The passage reads as follows:

To reach this chair from which the Nobel Lecture is delivered—a chair by no means offered to every writer and offered only once in a lifetime—I have mounted not three or four temporary steps but hun-

dreds or even thousands, fixed, steep, covered with ice, out of the dark and the cold where I was fated to survive, but others, perhaps more talented, stronger than I, perished.

The prayer reads as follows:

How easy it is to live with You, O Lord.
How easy to believe in You.
When my spirit is overwhelmed within me,
When even the keenest see no further than the
   night,
And know not what to do tomorrow,
You bestow on me the certitude
That You exist and are mindful of me,
That all the paths of righteousness are not barred.

As I ascend into the hill of earthly glory,
I turn back and gaze, astonished, on the road
That led me here beyond despair,
Where I too may reflect Your radiance upon man-
   kind.
All that I may reflect, You shall accord me,
And appoint others where I shall fail.

Here Solzhenitsyn acknowledges both his creatureliness—his subservience (even as an artist) to divine providence, and his representativeness, as he seeks to speak for those "mute inglorious Miltons" who shared his hard fate in the Soviet concentration camps and from whom the world has heard nothing: "A whole national literature is there, buried without a coffin. . . . " He catalogues the dismay of his fellow prisoners when the outside world seems to invert all proper human values. No reckoning of Solzhenitsyn can divorce his art from his *zek* (prisoner) experience, for it was in the camps that he came to his settled, mature views on life. However, he always sees his role as representative voice of the zeks as synchronous with his calling to speak the truth in a world in which all men, including himself, are subordinate to God's ultimate sovereignty over human affairs. He speaks always on behalf of fellow human beings, not merely on behalf of fellow zeks. (pp. 9-11)

In a world created by God, each individual creature is duty bound to develop a global consciousness; this subject, which dominates the second half of the *Nobel Lecture,* is introduced in section four. Solzhenitsyn introduces here, then elaborates later, two foci: individuality and community. Both are important to him.

First, he calls on us to judge for ourselves and not to accept blindly others' (even leaders') standards of judgment. "As the Russian proverb puts it, 'Don't trust your brother, trust your own bad eye.' "

This is dangerous advice, and Solzhenitsyn knows it; the eye is bad. We could easily become provincial and "confidently judge the whole world according to our own domestic values." Also, what is close to home affects us more directly than what is far away, thereby shaping our perceptions. "What in one country seems a dream of improbable prosperity in another arouses indignation as savage exploitation. . . . "

The problem here is one of differing scales of value. Sixty-six million died in the Gulag Archipelago; yet some Westerners who read Solzhenitsyn's account of this unspeakable horror claim to find it dull and boring, not gripping and chilling. "The heart is especially at ease with regard to that exotic land about which nothing is known. . . . " What would be the outcry if a quarter of America's population were liquidated? Is there not a gross difference in the scale of values which we apply to the pains of the world?

Solzhenitsyn's obvious answer to this ethnocentrism is to call for one scale of moral values to be applied worldwide. (His answer is obvious unless, that is, one takes seriously the charges by certain Westerners that Solzhenitsyn is a Russophile chauvinist.) The Christian doctrine of creation insists upon the unity of mankind, and this teaching underlies the thought here: "Given six, four, or even two scales of values, there cannot be one world, one single humanity: the difference in rhythms, in oscillations, will tear mankind asunder. We will not survive together on one Earth, just as a man with two hearts is not meant for this world." (pp. 11-12)

Section five extends and refines the call for global consciousness. Humanity is divided into nations. What agency can surmount national boundaries to coordinate separate scales of value? "Who will give mankind one single system for reading its instruments . . . ?"

Solzhenitsyn's answer is art (meaning, always, primarily literature). Literature, even that clearly colored by a given national experience, has "the marvelous capacity of transmitting from one nation to another—despite differences in language, customs, and social structure—practical experience, the harsh national experience of many decades never tasted by the other nation." But, just as the unity of mankind extends across time as well as space, literature can speak from generation to generation as well as from nation to nation. It "thus becomes the living memory of a nation."

Here Solzhenitsyn takes an unpopular stance. In the very passages in which he advocates global consciousness, he praises national distinctives. As nations comprise different individuals, so the world comprises different nations, and this is as it should be. Rejecting the notion of "various peoples disappearing into the melting pot of contemporary civilization," he trumpets instead: "Nations are the wealth of humanity, its generalized personalities. The least among them harbors within itself a special aspect of God's design." Global consciousness and national loyalty are not, he holds, inherently mutually exclusive, but can and should be naturally related and mutually reinforcing. (pp. 12-13)

The focus of section six turns to the writer, not the writer in a vacuum—he or she is never in a vacuum—but rather, the writer in the world of modern social reality. Solzhenitsyn depicts a fearsome world in which the writer must move. Yet, he insists, the writer cannot escape a social responsibility. He must not, of course, be a servile mouthpiece for any regnant ideology; he must be a truth-teller. Solzhenitsyn places himself squarely in the Russian literary tradition, in which is "ingrained" the "notion that a writer can do much among his own people—and that he must." Such a writer can become, in the words of Shelley, an "unacknowledged legislator of the world." (pp. 13-14)

The seventh and final section pulls together all the preceding themes, especially the call for global consciousness and a mystical reverence for the power of the word. The section opens with a statement of optimism—this, from a writer frequently charged with pessimism. Solzhenitsyn announces that he is "encouraged by a keen sense of WORLD LITERATURE as the one great heart that beats for the cares and misfortunes of our world. . . . " He insists (doubtless to the surprise of many) that the idea of a world literature is not today "an abstraction or a generalized concept invented by literary critics, but a common body and common spirit, a living heartfelt unity reflecting the growing spiritual unity of mankind." Again optimistically, Solzhenitsyn sees world literature in a salutary role: "I think that world literature has the power in these frightening times to help mankind see itself accurately despite what is advocated by partisans and by parties." (p. 15)

This final section, focusing as it does on the writers and artists of the world, . . . concludes on the same note of the absoluteness of truth with which the lecture opened. It is the very note which Solzhenitsyn sounded before he was exiled, in his parting statement, "Live Not by Lies!" But the world's writers and artists can do more: ". . . they can VANQUISH LIES! In the struggle against lies, art has always won and always will. . . . Lies can stand up against much in the world, but not against art." So he concludes with the clarion call, for all men, but especially writers: "ONE WORD OF TRUTH OUTWEIGHS THE WORLD." (p. 16)

Edward E. Ericson, Jr., in his *Solzhenitsyn: The Moral Vision,* William B. Eerdmans Publishing Company, 1980, 239 p.

AILEEN KELLY

(essay date 1984)

[In the following excerpt, Kelly explores Solzhenitsyn's political views and theory of art.]

A century and a half ago the Russian thinker Piotr Chaadayev, reflecting on the contrast between his backward, despotic country and the flourishing cultures of its European neighbors, suggested that the entire purpose of Russian history might be to provide the world with some important lesson yet to be deciphered. Since then, successive generations of messianically inclined Russian thinkers and writers have discovered compensating virtues in their country's anomalous development; but Western Europe has had far too many messiahs of its own to be impressed by the claims of Russian Christianity or Russian socialism to be the future inspiration for mankind. Yet when Alexander Solzhenitsyn arrived in Europe in 1974 with a new version of the lessons of Russian history, he was greeted with rapt attention: his apocalyptic tone expressed the spirit of the times. Homegrown messiahs were scarce, and none had Solzhenitsyn's combination of artistic genius and moral stature. For these and other less honorable reasons the press and television throughout Europe and North America seized on his message of repentance with uncharacteristic reverence, and without inquiring too closely into its sources.

The pendulum soon swung the other way: it became obvious, even to his more devoted admirers, that Solzhenitsyn's diagnosis of the diseases of modern societies was short on facts and strong on denunciation, and that his knowledge of politics and history was weak. There is now increasing agreement among the European and American intelligentsia that his preaching has done his reputation great harm and that he would be better advised to devote his energies to the one field in which he is incontestably a master—literature. We may need prophets, but we like them to have a reassuring grasp of complex problems: we are extremely wary of being taken in by cranks.

Unfortunately for Solzhenitsyn, the kinds of specialists we recognize do not include the variety to which he belongs, which has a respectable tradition behind it in Russia: the artist as preacher. Had Dostoevsky arrived in the West with his diagnosis of the malaise of modern culture, the advice currently being offered to Solzhenitsyn would no doubt have been offered to him. But Dostoevsky was writing for an audience which, in the absence of a free press or any other public forum for the discussion of social issues, believed that it was the duty of the artist to comment on the state of society and provide moral guidance for the future. While the social and political ideas expressed in his novels and in *Diary of a Writer* were often denounced, his critics never argued that he had exceeded his brief as a writer, or that his personal political views disqualified him from his role as a moralist.

Solzhenitsyn's involuntary exile has provided him with an audience that, after its initial adulation, has made it clear that it regards what he sees as his central function as peripheral, superfluous, or even irreconcilable with his art. At a historical remove, Dostoevsky's achievement in explaining modern European man to himself is not questioned; but if Solzhenitsyn's gloomier predictions are right, there will be no distant future to judge him. Angered and frustrated by his reception, Solzhenitsyn is clearly not going to adapt his message to European or American sensibilities. If the present dialogue of the deaf is to be replaced by something more constructive, it is the intelligentsia of the West who will have to make the first move: to approach Solzhenitsyn with a greater understanding of the tradition of thought and writing, as well as the personal experiences, which gave him his sense of mission and his claim to moral authority. Michael Scammell's biography [*Solzhenitsyn: A Biography*]—the first work on Solzhenitsyn likely to reach substantially beyond the tiny minority of Russian specialists—is perhaps a first sign of a more general tendency in that direction.

Numerous biographical fragments on Solzhenitsyn have appeared since his arrival in the West, but their intention has been polemical rather than informative. His own memoir *The Oak and the Calf*, dealing with his battles with the Soviet authorities over the decade preceding his expulsion, was conceived partly as a counterblast to official attempts to discredit him, partly to provide a model of action for his compatriots, and presents an idealized hero whose cunning, courage, and foresight in dealing with his opponents are contrasted with the ideological and personal deficiencies of his allies among the intelligentsia. Not surprisingly it has been followed by a stream of countermemoirs which have painted a picture of Solzhenitsyn with a distinct resemblance to the hero of his *Lenin in Zurich*; inflexible and self-centered, with a supreme contempt for feelings and aspirations which he does not share. The debate about Solzhenitsyn's personality and ideas is also a debate about the nature and origins of the Soviet regime, and, as sectarian squabbles proliferate, stereotypes are reinforced and reality is increasingly overlaid by myth.

In the preface to his biography, Scammell predicts that his book will antagonize all parties in the debate through its demythologizing approach, whose emphasis is on explanation rather than judgment. He appears to have alienated his subject at an early stage: he reports without comment that he had Solzhenitsyn's collaboration and support only on those chapters dealing with his early life. But this has no obvious negative effects on the later part of the work, which draws heavily on Solzhenitsyn's documentation, in *The Gulag Archipelago*, of the crucial events in his life. The absence of Solzhenitsyn's guiding hand contributes to the book's main strength—the multiplicity of perspectives which are brought to bear on his personality (p. 13)

As Scammell observes, the story of the publication of *Ivan Denisovich* has acquired new embellishments with each retelling. Scammell's attempt to disentangle fact from fiction in these events, and their even more extraordinary sequel ending with Solzhenitsyn's expulsion twelve years later, is scrupulously detailed and takes up more than half of this very long book; but it was well worth the effort. His lucid account places Solzhenitsyn's personal duel with the Soviet regime in its essential context: the seesawing fortunes of writers and intelligentsia in the era which began with the euphoria after Khrushchev's celebrated speech in 1956 and was finally buried with the invasion of Czechoslovakia. Solzhenitsyn's own story of his battle of wits with the authorities has some of the features of a protean myth. Scammell shows the interdependence of the turns in his fortunes and such processes and events as the struggle between conservatives and liberalizing factions in the government, the emergence of what became known as the "democratic" or Human Rights movement, and the halt to de-Stalinization that reversed the process of liberalization in the arts and was marked by the show trial of Sinyavsky and Daniel in 1966 and the mass roundups of dissidents that followed.

Scammell shows, too, that Solzhenitsyn's fate was dependent to a far greater degree than he has ever cared to admit on people who were not always in sympathy with his views or his methods of action, notably Tvardovsky, the editor of *Novy Mir* and the hero of many of these pages, a member of the Soviet establishment whose instinct for literary excellence and uncompromisingly high editorial standards had made him a master of the technique of getting work past the censor. Convinced that *Ivan Denisovich* was a masterpiece, Tvardovsky arranged that it should find its way directly to Khrushchev's desk, on the correct assumption that he would seize on it as a weapon against the Stalinists. Tvardovsky continued to struggle for publication of Solzhenitsyn's works even after some of them were in the hands of the KGB and his protégé had compromised him by allowing others to circulate in *samizdat*.

Scammell's sensitive portrayal of this complex and enormously attractive personality is a necessary corrective to Solzhenitsyn's patronizing presentation of him in *The Oak and the Calf* as a Party loyalist at the mercy of his superiors. It reminds us that moral courage takes many different forms in the Soviet Union and that Solzhenitsyn's form of heroism was not the only way in which decent human beings could express their opposition to tyranny.

However, in its symbolic power, Solzhenitsyn's personal stand against the Soviet government had an effect on Soviet society which surpassed even that of *Ivan Denisovich,* after whose publication, in the words of one critic, "We shall never again be able to write as we wrote before." As Solzhenitsyn was informed by thousands of letters from former prisoners, the integrity of his peasant hero had returned to them the conviction of their own human worth. Solzhenitsyn's actions were to provide them with an even more potent image of integrity. His work on the history of the camps had become part of a wider strategy: to expose the workings at every level of private and public life of the "obligatory ideological lie" to which every Russian had to pay his dues; to demonstrate with a Tolstoyan simplicity that the lie could not exist without the active complicity of those whom it oppressed, and that they could bring it crashing down by following his example and withholding their dues.

The extraordinary immunity that Solzhenitsyn enjoyed for so long in the Soviet Union owed much to the fact that for a few months after the publication of *Ivan Denisovich* he became an establishment figure. Taking their cue from Khrushchev, the critics declared that Solzhenitsyn's portrayal of the iniquities of Stalinism showed him to be "a true helper of the Party in a sacred and vital cause." The bureaucracy opened its doors to him: he was invited to address a group of members of the Soviet supreme Military Tribunal (under whose auspices he had been sentenced) and was consulted by a commission engaged in reforming the corrective labor code.

Some critics deplored the fact that *Ivan Denisovich* did not have a happier ending. Meanwhile Solzhenitsyn was using his fragile immunity to gain time as he prepared his answer to them: two novels and a vast history of the camps—a clandestine operation on an epic scale, compiled from the testimony of hundreds of informants and documents from obscure libraries. These were all designed to show that Stalin's excesses were not an aberration but an expression of the essential nature of the Soviet system.

This double life ended in September 1965 when a police raid on the apartment of a friend in Moscow uncovered Solzhenitsyn's archive, including the only copy of his novel *The First Circle.* As Solzhenitsyn comments in *The Gulag Archipelago,* the natural reaction of a Soviet citizen to such a blow would have been despair and a passive acceptance of disaster, a state of mind immensely facilitating the task of the police. Solzhenitsyn's reaction (after an initial panic) was one calculated to catch them off balance: he put up a pugnacious verbal resistance and combined this with a shrewd exploitation of public opinion to expose the illegality of the police procedures even by the relaxed standards of the Soviet constitution. He fired off letters to Brezhnev, Mikhail Suslov, and Andropov (then head of the KGB) protesting against the confiscation of his archive, and began the systematic use of *samizdat* to promote the circulation and discussion of works (including the novel *Cancer Ward*) which *Novy Mir* could not now hope to print. In interviews with foreign journalists broadcast back to the Soviet Union, he proclaimed his belief in the artist's duty to fight for justice and the strengthening of spiritual values in his compatriots, and drew the world's attention to the growing campaign of harassment and defamation designed to silence him.

His major coups were planned with enormous care and precision to produce the greatest possible embarrassment for the government and the most publicity for himself. (pp. 14-15)

Every move by the authorities against him was answered by a show of strength on the grounds that "they understand that language and no other." . . . (p. 15)

The publicity generated by Solzhenitsyn's activity contributed to the growing revulsion in the West against the treatment of Russian dissidents. Writers, artists, and academics bombarded the press and Soviet embassies with protests, and a substantial body of public opinion questioned the policy of détente and called for sanctions against the Soviet government. Solzhenitsyn contributed all that he could to its embarrassment, describing in detail to Western correspondents all the incidents of harassment against him, the slanders being circulated about his acrimonious divorce and remarriage, and the anonymous threats made against his family and himself, and announcing that, if he were to be killed, they could safely conclude that it was through the agency of the KGB.

The last of Solzhenitsyn's blows was more than the Soviet regime could take. In December 1973, the first volume of *The Gulag Archipelago* was published in Paris, creating shock waves throughout the Communist parties of Europe. Summoned to appear before the public prosecutor, Solzhenitsyn fired his last shot, refusing to recognize the legality of the summons: "Before requiring citizens to obey the law, you must learn to carry it out yourselves." Two days later he was deported.

The tactics Solzhenitsyn used in his duel with the Soviet government were not regarded with unqualified admiration by other dissidents. Tvardovsky and the liberals grouped around *Novy Mir* believed that his refusal to compromise on any issue was damaging to their journal and the cause of Soviet literature, while the dissident movement as a whole resented his refusal to involve himself in public demonstrations and the signing of petitions, and condemned the ruthlessness, self-righteousness, and duplicity he displayed even toward those who helped and trusted him. Scammell points out in his defense that, given the nature of the enemy, these ambiguous elements in his character were essential to his survival, and that his tactics were dictated by his dedication to the overriding purpose of his life. His epic history of the camps was a solitary, secret, and

dangerous undertaking, and he could not afford to divert his energies to battles which others could fight; while his refusal to compromise, based on the realistic calculation that there was an unbridgeable chasm between what he stood for and what the regime would allow, was his greatest asset, making him a symbol of freedom and moral purity even for those whom his works would never reach.

Behind the arguments about tactics there were much more important differences of principle. The goals of the human rights movement—the "democratization" of society, the decentralization of the economy, and the observance of basic human rights—need no explaining to a Western audience, but Solzhenitsyn's do. Rooted in a tradition of thought that has no direct analogue in the West, they are open to a wide variety of misinterpretations. Unfortunately, the sympathy and balance of Scammell's approach to Solzhenitsyn's personality is not matched in his treatment of his ideas, which are conveyed by means of brief summaries which seem calculated to reinforce all the prejudices of liberal-minded readers whose information about Solzhenitsyn over the last ten years has mainly come from the press and television.

The moral discoveries that Solzhenitsyn made in prison were, as Scammell mentions, shaped into a coherent vision with the help of the symposium *Landmarks,* published in 1909, which he came across in 1969. Its seven authors (all ex-Marxists) accused the intelligentsia of uncritically applying the ideas of the Enlightenment in their nineteenth-century forms—materialism, positivism, and scientific socialism—to Russian problems, in the expectation that a social miracle would result from the destruction of the external forms of society. The contributors to *Landmarks* argued that the primary condition for the nation's social and political health was the regeneration of the inner life of the individual with the aid of traditional cultural and religious values. Solzhenitsyn drew heavily on the ideas of *Landmarks* in a response to Sakharov's memorandum *Progress, Co-existence, and Intellectual Freedom,* a response that was published with two other essays, after Solzhenitsyn's arrival in the West, in a symposium entitled *From Under the Rubble.*

As some of Solzhenitsyn's most considered statements of his ideological position, these essays deserve close analysis. Instead, Scammell gives only a bald enumeration of what he considers their "most interesting" points, including Solzhenitsyn's criticism of Sakharov's belief in intellectual freedom and the multi-party system, on the grounds that neither of these has done much for the West, which is spiritually racked and dejected; and the proposal that both Soviet socialism and Western democracy be rejected in favor of a form of authoritarian rule founded on national and religious traditions, suspicious of modern technology and working on the principle that small is beautiful. Any residual doubts the reader may have about where to place Solzhenitsyn on the political spectrum will vanish when he learns from Scammell that Solzhenitsyn shared his repugnance for the West and nostalgia for Russian village life and culture with the officially sponsored nationalism represented by such Soviet figures as Victor Chalmayev, whose ideas were strongly reminiscent of those of the pre-Revolutionary Black Hundreds, "Ku Klux Klan-type societies" specializing in pogroms.

Scammell does not attempt to identify Solzhenitsyn's outlook with this line of thought (he points out that charges of anti-Semitism leveled at him have never been made to stick). But he fails to make it clear that Solzhenitsyn's nationalism draws on a tradition fundamentally distinct from the type favored by the czarist and Soviet governments, whose primary function was (and is) justification of the political status quo. The romantic conservatism of the Slavophiles with which Solzhenitsyn has close affinities is distinctly subversive in its criticism of the social-atomization and spiritual disintegration of modern societies held together by formalized, coercive bonds, its ideal of a human community bound "internally" by freely shared moral convictions, and its belief that political forms are of relative and conditional value. What mattered for the Slavophiles was the quality of social relations: a view shared by Solzhenitsyn.

The central theme of his three essays (and of most of his other polemical writing) is not a discussion of political forms but an attempt to transpose the debate about the future of Russia from what he describes as "the inexpressive language of politics" to the plane of ethics. Defining the goal of society as the "triumph of inwardness over outwardness," he argues that a society as polluted as the Soviet Union cannot be redeemed by a multi-party system which, as the vehicle for the battle of sectional interests, has served no discernible moral function in the West. Privilege and corruption have never been eliminated by decree: they will cease only when society as a whole finds them repulsive. To achieve this is a moral, not a political, task.

Soviet society must pass through the spiritual filter of personal sacrifice by means of individual decisions, made in "chilling isolation," to follow the dictates of conscience at whatever personal cost and refuse every demand to support the ideological lie. The form of revolution produced by an aggregate of such acts could not be predicted: moral revolutions of this sort had no historical precedent, but Soviet society in Solzhenitsyn's ideal future would acknowledge culpability for its historical crimes, renounce its external conquests, and cease to participate in the drive for political and economic expansion which threatens the survival of mankind. It would adopt instead a policy of "self-limitation" based on the Christian ethic of love.

The political system under which this revolution would be accomplished was of secondary importance to Solzhenitsyn: its main function would be to ensure continuity and stability. In his view the brief and disastrous history of Russian constitutional democracy did not commend it for this role; hence his notorious recommendation, at least for the immediate transitional period, of a form of authoritarianism founded on national religious and cultural tradition.

Like the Slavophiles, who were a constant irritation to the czars, Solzhenitsyn cannot be located easily on any political spectrum. He has often argued that he does not oppose democratic freedoms, but only the use that is currently made of them, and has refuted attempts to identify some of his ideas with tendencies to messianic nationalism within the Soviet establishment, pointing out that the results of a policy of Russian "self-limitation" and repudiation of empire would surpass the wildest dreams of Western proponents of détente. Nor does he share the cultural messianism of the official nationalists. As he remarks in *From Under the Rubble,* the Russian people are not traversing the heavens in a blaze of glory, but sitting forlornly on a heap of spiritual cinders. His belief is that only the specific minority that escapes the general moral catastrophe by renewing contact with traditional spiritual values can offer a lesson in survival to the West.

Solzhenitsyn is not a political thinker, but a Russian moralist in the utopian tradition of Tolstoy and Dostoevsky, whose longing for a kingdom of God on earth led them to use the precept "live not by lies" as an absolute measure for judging political systems and social relations. But Scammell has chosen to approach his ideas from the narrow and distorting perspective of the political debate among Russian dissidents about the direction of future reforms. When the "democratic" dissidents and their sympathizers in the West found that Solzhenitsyn was not with them, he was declared to be against them. The parallels that Sakharov (in an essay published in *The New York Review* in June 1974) drew between Solzhenitsyn's views and those of official Russian nationalism helped to confirm a hostility to Solzhenitsyn's ideas which, for all its intended objectivity, Scammell's book will increase.

Of course, Solzhenitsyn bears much of the responsibility for the fact that his desire to alert the Western democracies to the holes in their moral armor has been received as a statement of a political position. In a country where the "moral majority" is synonymous with the political right wing, the one-sidedness of Solzhenitsyn's moral message, his apparent insensitivity to right-wing manifestations of the political "lie" and to the role of established churches (in particular, the Russian) in supporting them in the past, and his hawkish attitude to détente, seem to indicate a clear-cut political alignment. But Solzhenitsyn has never become identified with any political party and right-wing political groups have found him an unreliable ally.

The inconsistencies and the wild generalizations in his judgments on current affairs indicate not the political fanatic but the visionary for whom the political dimension is of secondary importance.

However, as Scammell's wide-ranging survey of the reactions to Solzhenitsyn's speeches, statements, and publications shows, there is still a general determination to place him unambiguously within the political spectrum; he is only occasionally accused of preaching theocracy, but there is general agreement that, as one magazine said in a headline, his main allegiance is "not to democracy but to God and Mother Russia."

Scammell notes that Solzhenitsyn has frequently denied the charges of political extremism, and points to the way in which the press has distorted his statements to reinforce the stereotype that they have created; when, for example, on a visit to Franco's Spain he warned the Spanish reformists of the dangers of going too fast, he was reported as having exalted fascism. Despite these caveats, Scammell's conclusion echoes the consensus: though he is still listened to out of respect for the magnitude of his past achievement, Solzhenitsyn's polemical writing, like a fatal addiction, is slowly killing his reputation, and it is a personal disaster that he has chosen not to appear before his Western public "only as a writer."

Solzhenitsyn's reply to his Western critics is to be found in his Nobel Prize lecture, written while he was still in the Soviet Union. He reaffirms his allegiance to the tradition of Russian literature and its demand that the writer be an active moral force in the fight against cruelty and violence and criticize his country's leaders whenever necessary. By communicating the distilled experience of a people across national barriers "so that we no longer see double," he can help to provide that common scale for distinguishing the endurable from the unendurable without which mankind is devoid of hope.

Solzhenitsyn himself has the misfortune to be a victim of our double vision. When his epic struggle with the Soviet version of the ideological lie became known in the West, his belief in his destiny and his faith in his mission were viewed with unquestioning respect, and romantic images of the poet as seer and tribune of his people were used frequently with regard to him. Yet when, after his expulsion from the Soviet Union, he turned his attention to the spiritual state of Western man, his fate was to be told firmly that he had overreached himself by making unjustified pronouncements on matters on which he was not properly informed.

He is not the first Russian writer to have addressed himself to a spiritual malaise of Western culture: Alexander Herzen's critique of the idolatry of progress and the worship of political forms in nineteenth-century Europe, Dostoevsky's Underground Man, and Tolstoy's reflections about the role of violence in maintaining social institutions all questioned fundamental assumptions on which Western democracies operate. Like Solzhenitsyn's criticism, they were based on an imperfect understanding of European history, a naively simplistic view of how societies work, and an overly general ideal of how men should live. And yet at a historical remove these defects strike us much less than the kind of holy innocence with which they pointed to the Emperor's lack of clothes. Like Dostoevsky's, Solzhenitsyn's view of essentials was formed by firsthand experience which has no need of innocence to protect it: "Life behind bars has given us a new measure for men and things, wiped from our eyes the grimy film of habit which always clogs the vision of the man who has escaped shocks."

Solzhenitsyn's confrontation with Sakharov is a twentieth-century version of those same writers' encounters with the faith of the West (and of Russian westernizers) in science, representative institutions, and material progress. With the hindsight provided by these examples and an understanding of the way in which time has filtered out some of the shortcomings in their arguments, we are better placed to look for the essentials of his case. With regard to Sakharov, we have no difficulty in seeing the essentials: his luminous personality, his decency and bravery in the face of his tormentors make him the most formidable representative to date of the tradition of the westernizers. It is therefore tempting to believe (as he does) that his vision of the convergence of communist and capitalist systems is a sober new view of a way out for humanity; yet its ultimate goal—a mankind that has outgrown nationalism and formed itself into a single demographic unit, regulating politics, the economy, education, the arts, and international affairs by "scientific methodology and a democratic spirit"—is surely quite as utopian as Solzhenitsyn's vision of mankind after a period of moral revolution and repentance. The difference is that Sakharov is using the familiar currency of everyday Western political discourse, while Solzhenitsyn is not.

The choice between these two utopias is the choice between one that attempts to solve twentieth-century problems in the language of nineteenth-century optimism, where the inbuilt defects of this optimism have helped create many of the problems themselves, and one that proposes a direction which, for all its apparent negative associations, is largely unknown in our present situation. To indicate a direction, as Solzhenitsyn has done, is not to argue that the destination is certain. He says as much in his Nobel lecture, stressing that his goal is not to be stated in political language: "It is like that small looking-glass in the fairy stories:

you glance into it and . . . you see the Inaccessible. You will never be able to ride there or fly there. But the soul cries out for it."

For the present it is enough to appreciate that the direction he believes in can itself produce unpredictable but positive results. Who, when Solzhenitsyn began to advocate it publicly after 1962, would have given anything for his chances of survival? (pp. 15-17)

Aileen Kelly, "The Path of a Prophet," in *The New York Review of Books,* Vol. XXXI, No. 15, October 11, 1984, pp. 13-17.

SOURCES FOR FURTHER STUDY

Burg, David, and Feifer, George. *Solzhenitsyn.* New York: Stein and Day, 1972, 371 p.

> First full-length biography of Solzhenitsyn.

Dunlop, John B.; Haugh, Richard; and Klimoff, Alexis. *Aleksandr Solzhenitsyn: Critical Essays and Documentary Materials.* Belmont, MA: Nordland Publishing Company, 1973, 569 p.

> Critical essays about Solzhenitsyn's works, including a bibliography of works by and about him.

Kodjak, Andrej. *Alexander Solzhenitsyn.* Boston: Twayne Publishers, 1978, 170 p.

> Study of Solzhenitsyn's major novels, plays, and short stories.

Moody, Christopher. *Solzhenitsyn.* New York: Barnes and Noble Books, 1976, 206 p.

> Overview of Solzhenitsyn's major works, including a chapter on his prose style.

Reshetovskaya, Natalya A. *Sanya: My Life with Aleksandr Solzhenitsyn.* Indianapolis: The Bobbs-Merrill Company, 1975, 284 p.

> Memoirs of Solzhenitsyn's first wife.

Scammell, Michael. *Solzhenitsyn: A Biography.* New York: W. W. Norton and Company, 1984, 1051 p.

> General biographical and critical study of Solzhenitsyn.

Wole Soyinka

1934-

(Full name Akinwande Oluwole Soyinka) Nigerian dramatist, poet, novelist, critic, translator, editor, autobiographer, and short story writer.

INTRODUCTION

Recipient of the 1986 Nobel Prize for Literature, Soyinka has been called Africa's finest writer. The Nigerian playwright's unique style blends traditional Yoruban folk-drama with European dramatic form to provide both spectacle and penetrating satire. Soyinka stated that in the African cultural tradition, the artist "has always functioned as the record of the mores and experience of his society." His plays, novels, and poetry all reflect that philosophy: they serve as a record of twentieth-century Africa's political turmoil and struggle to reconcile tradition with modernization. Eldred Jones stated in his book *Wole Soyinka* that the author's work touches on universal themes as well as addressing specifically African concerns: "The essential ideas which emerge from a reading of Soyinka's work are not specially African ideas, although his characters and their mannerisms are African. His concern is with man on earth. Man is dressed for the nonce in African dress and lives in the sun and tropical forest, but he represents the whole race."

As a young child, Soyinka was comfortable with the conflicting cultures in his world, but as he grew older he became increasingly aware of the pull between African tradition and Western modernization. Aké, his village, was mainly populated with people from the Yoruba tribe and was presided over by the *ogboni*, or tribal elders. Soyinka's grandfather introduced him to the pantheon of Yoruba gods and to other tribal folklore. His parents, however, were representatives of colonial influences: his mother was a devout Christian convert and his father was a headmaster for the village school established by the British. When Soyinka's father began urging Wole to leave Aké to attend the government school in Ibadan, the boy was spirited away by his grandfather, who administered a scarification rite of manhood. Soyinka was also consecrated to the god

Ogun, an explorer, artisan, and hunter in Yoruban folklore. Ogun is a recurring figure in Soyinka's work and has been named by the author as his muse.

Soyinka published some poems and short stories in *Black Orpheus,* a Nigerian literary magazine, before leaving Africa to attend the University of Leeds in England. There his first play was produced. *The Invention* (1955) is a comic satire about an incident that causes South Africa's native population to lose their black skin color. Unable to distinguish blacks from whites and thus enforce its apartheid policies, the government is thrown into chaos. "The play is Soyinka's sole direct treatment of the political situation in Africa," noted Thomas Hayes. Soyinka returned to Nigeria in 1960, shortly after independence from colonial rule had been declared. He began to research Yoruban folklore and drama in depth and incorporated elements of both into the play *A Dance of the Forests* (1960).

A Dance of the Forests was commissioned as part of Nigeria's independence celebrations. In the play, Soyinka warned the newly independent Nigerians that the end of colonial rule did not mean an end to their country's problems. It shows a bickering group of mortals who summon up the *egungun* (spirits of the dead, revered by the Yoruba people) for a festival. They have presumed the *egungun* to be noble and wise, but they discover that their ancestors are as petty and spiteful as any living people. "The whole concept ridicules the African viewpoint that glorifies the past at the expense of the present," suggested John F. Povey in *Tri-Quarterly*. "The sentimentalized glamor of the past is exposed so that the same absurdities may not be reenacted in the future. This constitutes a bold assertion to an audience awaiting an easy appeal to racial heroics."

While Soyinka warned against living in nostalgia for Africa's past in *A Dance of the Forests,* he lampooned the indiscriminate embrace of Western modernization in *The Lion and the Jewel* (1959). A *Times Literary Supplement* reviewer called this play a "richly ribald comedy" that combines poetry and prose "with a marvellous lightness in the treatment of both." The plot revolves around Sidi, the village beauty, and the rivalry between her two suitors. Baroka is the village chief, an old man with many wives; Lakunle is the enthusiastically Westernized schoolteacher who dreams of molding Sidi into a "civilized" woman. In *Introduction to Nigerian Literature,* Jones commented that *The Lion and the Jewel* is "a play which is so easily (and erroneously) interpreted as a clash between progress and reaction, with the play coming down surprisingly in favour of reaction. The real clash is not between old and new, or between real progress and reaction. It is a clash between the genuine and the false; between the well-done and the half-baked. Lakunle the school teacher would have been a poor symbol of any desirable kind

of progress. . . . He is a man of totally confused values. [Baroka's worth lies in] the traditional values of which he is so confident and in which he so completely outmaneouvres Lakunle who really has no values at all."

Soyinka was well established as Nigeria's premier playwright when in 1965 he published his first novel, *The Interpreters.* The novel allowed him to expand on themes already expressed in his stage dramas and to present a sweeping view of Nigerian life in the years immediately following independence. Essentially plotless, *The Interpreters* is loosely structured around the informal discussions between five young Nigerian intellectuals. Each has been educated in a foreign country and has returned hoping to shape Nigeria's destiny. They are hampered by their own confused values, however, as well as by the corruption they encounter everywhere. Some reviewers likened Soyinka's writing style in *The Interpreters* to that of James Joyce and William Faulkner. Others took exception to the formless quality of the novel. Nevertheless, Neil McEwan pointed out that for all its flaws, *The Interpreters* is "among the liveliest of recent novels in English. It is bright satire full of good sense and good humour which are African and contemporary. . . ." He further observed that although *The Interpreters* does not have a rigidly structured plot, "there is unity in the warmth and sharpness of its comic vision. There are moments which sadden or anger; but they do not diminish the fun."

The year 1965 also marked Soyinka's first arrest by the Nigerian police. He was accused of using a gun to force a radio announcer to broadcast incorrect election results. No evidence was ever produced, however, and the PEN writers' organization launched a protest campaign, headed by William Styron and Norman Mailer. Soyinka was released after three months. He was next arrested two years later, during Nigeria's civil war. Soyinka was completely opposed to the conflict, especially to the Nigerian government's brutal policies toward the Ibo people who were attempting to form their own country, Biafra. He traveled to Biafra to establish a peace commission composed of leading intellectuals from both sides; when he returned, the Nigerian police accused him of helping the Biafrans buy jet fighters. Once again he was imprisoned. This time Soyinka was held for more than two years, although he was never formally charged with any crime. Most of that time he was kept in solitary confinement. When all of his fellow prisoners were vaccinated against meningitis, Soyinka was passed by; when he developed serious vision problems, he was again ignored by his jailers. He was denied reading and writing materials, but he manufactured his own ink and began to keep a prison diary, writing on toilet paper, cigarette packages, and in between the lines of the few books he secretly obtained. Each poem or fragment of journal he managed to smuggle to the outside world became a literary event and a reassurance to his supporters that Soyinka still lived, despite rumors to the contrary. Published as *The Man Died: Prison Notes of Wole Soyinka* (1972), the author's diary constitutes "the most important work that has been written about the Biafran war," according to Charles R. Larson. He wrote: "*The Man Died* is not so much the story of Wole Soyinka's own temporary death during the Nigerian Civil War but a personified account of Nigeria's fall from sanity, documented by one of the country's leading intellectuals." Soyinka was released in 1969 and left Nigeria soon after, not returning until a change of power took place in 1975.

Many literary commentators sense that Soyinka's work changed profoundly after his prison term. His work now focused on the war and its aftermath and was darker in tone. For example, Soyinka's second novel, *Season of Anomy* (1973), expresses almost no hope for Africa's future. According to John Mellors in *London Magazine*: "Wole Soyinka appears to have written much of *Season of Anomy* in a blazing fury, angry beyond complete control of words at the abuses of power and the outbreaks of both considered and spontaneous violence. . . . The plot charges along, dragging the reader (not because he doesn't want to go, but because he finds it hard to keep up) through forest, mortuary and prison camp in nightmare visions of tyranny, torture, slaughter and putrefaction. The book reeks of pain. . . . Soyinka hammers at the point that the liberal has to deal with violence in the world however much he would wish he could ignore it; the scenes of murder and mutilation, while sickeningly explicit, are justified by . . . the author's anger and compassion and insistence that bad will not become better by our refusal to examine it."

Like *Season of Anomy*, Soyinka's postwar plays are considered more brooding than his earlier work. *Madmen and Specialists* (1970) is called "grim" by Martin Banham and Clive Wake in *African Theatre Today*. In the play, a doctor—who is trained as a specialist in torture—returns home from the war and uses his new skills on his father. The play's major themes are "the loss of faith and rituals" and "the break-up of the family unit which traditionally in Africa has been the foundation of society," according to Larson. Names and events in the play are fictionalized to avoid censorship, but Soyinka has clearly "leveled a wholesale criti-

cism of life in Nigeria since the Civil War: a police state in which only madmen and spies can survive, in which the losers are mad and the winners are paranoid about the possibility of another rebellion. The prewar corruption and crime have returned, supported by the more sophisticated acts of terrorism and espionage introduced during the war." Larson concluded: "In large part *Madmen and Specialists* is a product of those months Soyinka spent in prison, in solitary confinement, as a political prisoner. It is, not surprisingly, the most brutal piece of social criticism he has published." In a similar tone, *A Play of Giants* (1984) presents four African leaders—thinly disguised versions of Jean Bedel Bokassa, Sese Seko Mobutu, Macias Ngeuma, and Idi Amin—meeting at the United Nations building, where "their conversation reflects the corruption and cruelty of their regimes and the casual, brutal flavor of their rule," disclosed Hayes.

Soyinka's work is frequently described as demanding but rewarding reading. Although his plays are widely praised, they are seldom performed, especially outside of Africa. The dancing and choric speech often found in them are unfamiliar and difficult for non-African actors to master. Most recently, Soyinka has published two books: *Mandela's Earth, and Other Poems* (1988) and *Isarà: A Voyage around Essay* (1989). He is currently the chairman of the editorial board of *Transition*, a literary magazine revived in 1991 for the purpose of "exchanging opinions and ideas, with Africa at its center." Along with Henry Louis Gates, Jr., and Kuame Anthony Appiah, Soyinka published the first new issue in May 1991. Critics are already calling *Transition* an important forum for black writers. Yet, as Hayes summarized, Soyinka's importance and influence lie elsewhere: "[Soyinka's] drama and fiction have challenged the West to broaden its aesthetic and accept African standards of art and literature. His personal and political life have challenged Africa to embrace the truly democratic values of the African tribe and reject the tyranny of power practiced on the continent by its colonizers and by many of its modern rulers."

(For further information about Soyinka's life and works, see *Black Literature Criticism; Black Writers; Contemporary Authors*, Vols. 13-16; *Contemporary Literary Criticism*, Vols. 3, 5, 14, 36, 44; *Drama Criticism*, Vol. 2; *Dictionary of Literary Biography Yearbook: 1986;* and *Major 20th-Century Writers*.)

CRITICAL COMMENTARY

ADRIAN A. ROSCOE
(essay date 1971)

[Roscoe, an English critic and professor of African literature, is the author of *Mother Is Gold: A Study in West African Literature* (1971). In the following excerpt from this work, he examines the contrasts between traditional African culture and Western influences in Soyinka's poetry and drama.]

Soyinka is a poet of twilight zones, be they between night and day or day and night, life and death, or death and life. They are areas of transition for which he has an abiding fascination; for they are those areas in which he can most fully explore certain basic facts about life and death. *The Road* alone is enough to suggest that no other poet or dramatist in the English language has explored so extensively, and with such rapt fascination, that shrouded middle passage between death, fleshly dissolution, and arrival in the other world.

Grey, then, is a dominant colour. Soyinka calls a whole section of *Idanre and Other Poems* grey seasons; but the colour, in fact, pervades his work as a whole. In **'I think it Rains'**, a poem whose tension springs from its subtle opposition of wet and dry, fruit and sterility, we find the stanza:

I saw it raise
The sudden cloud, from ashes. Settling
They joined in a ring of grey; within
The circling spirit. . . .

One can see, too, that the ideas implied by [the] choice of colour are borne also by words like 'wisps', 'smoke', 'febrile', and 'ashes'. In **'Season'**, we find 'wood-smoke', 'shadows from the dusk' and 'the wilted corn plume'. **'In Memory of Segun Awolowo'** ends with the lines

Grey presences of head and hands
Who wander still
Adrift from understanding.

(pp. 49-50)

Soyinka, who would agree with Pound's dictum about loading the language of verse with as much meaning as it can bear, is often a difficult poet. He dictates the terms on which a reader must approach him; and, apart from an occasional explanatory note, no concessions are offered. To complicate matters further, Soyinka is a poet for whom the traditional Yoruba cosmology is a potent fact in his imaginative life, and,

thus, in the art he creates. Without a working knowledge of the Yoruba background, his work cannot fully be understood; and this presents a handicap even to non-Yoruba Nigerians. The Yoruba cosmology, embodied in Ifa, the traditional religious system of his people, constantly underlies his work and has provided growth points for his artistic development. An essential point about Soyinka, then, and one which firmly marks him off from his fellow West African poets, is that *he is still working within a traditional system;* a system which allows him to explore the problems of creation and existence from a philosophical home base. He has not felt obliged to cast off traditional thinking and dress himself in the tattered remnants of alien philosophies. Not for Soyinka the myth-building problems of Yeats or Blake's desperate cry, 'I must create a system or be enslaved by another man's.' And this, perhaps, is why his scorn of negritude has always sounded so confident. Its disciples' prideful strutting was, in any case, a natural target for his satiric mind; a mind that seems always to have been convinced of man's absurdity, his innate imperfection, and the futility of his grandiose assertions. There was something further. More acutely than anyone else, Soyinka seemed to detect an element of the spurious in negritude's professed objective of reaching back for cultural roots. Christian and westernised, its disciples were, in effect, reaching back for what was no longer there. There was a celebration of convenient symbols and trophies from the past—the external *bric à brac* that could easily be appealed to—but not the *essence* of the past, its systems of thought, which had been discarded for ever. Where they hoped to assert their African-ness by praise poems for the mask or in verse sung to African instrumental accompaniment, Soyinka has worked with the essence itself. He has never renounced it; his appeal to it is spontaneous and natural. Nor is this mere lip service, for he is imaginatively engaged with a tradition that still happens to be alive. He is the only West African poet who, in this philosophical sense, can be said to do so. Hence his complete lack of nostalgia, his lack of that melancholy recollection of a dying world that marks so much West African verse. One cannot wax nostalgic about current affairs. With Soyinka there is no problem of authenticity.

This is not to say that he rejects the modern world with its new insights and its expanding scientific knowledge. His education in Nigeria and England has enabled him to absorb much that is modern; he is learned in the modern disciplines, and his style itself—

Principal Works

The Invention (drama) 1955

The Lion and the Jewel (drama) 1959

A Dance of the Forests (drama) 1960

The Trials of Brother Jero (drama) 1960

Three Plays (dramas) 1962

Five Plays (dramas) 1964

The Strong Breed (drama) 1964

Camwood on the Leaves (radio play) 1965

The Interpreters (novel) 1965

Kongi's Harvest (drama) 1965

The Road (drama) 1965

Idanre, and Other Poems (poetry) 1967

Poems from Prison (poetry) 1969; also published as A Shuttle in the Crypt [enlarged edition], 1972

Three Short Plays (dramas) 1969

Madmen and Specialists (drama) 1970

Plays from the Third World: An Anthology [editor] (dramas) 1971

The Man Died: Prison Notes of Wole Soyinka (prose) 1972

The Bacchae of Euripides: A Communion Rite (drama) 1973

The Jero Plays (dramas) 1973

Season of Anomy (novel) 1973

Collected Plays. 2 vols. (dramas) 1973-74

Poems of Black Africa [editor] (poetry) 1975

Death and the King's Horseman (drama) 1976

Myth, Literature, and the African World (essays) 1976

Ogun Abibiman (poetry) 1976

Opera Wonyosi (drama) 1977

Aké: The Years of Childhood (autobiography) 1981

Requiem for a Futurologist (drama) 1983

A Play of Giants (drama) 1984

Six Plays (drama) 1984

Mandela's Earth, and Other Poems (poetry) 1988

Isarà: A Voyage around Essay (prose) 1989

---

recognisably modern—is evidence of absorption and adaptation. A modern grafting has been performed on a vigorous traditional plant. Or, to state it in his own way, he has achieved 'the ideal fusion—to preserve the original uniqueness and yet absorb another essence'. It means that Soyinka's work can be both strongly local and excitingly universal. (pp. 50-1)

There is an attractive human-ness about Ifa, for its gods lived among men, and usually shared man's foibles. It also offers a convincing reading of the universe, especially in its insistence on a divine balance of forces, which, as a rule, ensures harmony, but which results in chaos when the balance is disturbed. Ifa has not only survived; it has become modernised. Such is its flexibility that Sango, the god of thunder and lightning, has, with perfect ease, become also the god of electricity. Ogun, a god of prodigious power and responsibility, the deity associated with iron and metals generally, with war, exploration, artisans, and creativity, is now also the god of the roads and the god of workers. He would preside as naturally over Ibadan's Department of Metallurgy as Jeremy Bentham over the London School of Economics. There is, then, in Ifa, besides its humanness, an open-ness and flexibility which have allowed it to survive into the modern world. It also enjoys what Sowande calls 'a Diversified Unity, and not a Unified Diversity likely to come apart at the seams'. (pp. 51-2)

'Idanre', Soyinka's account of Ogun's creation pilgrimage to the earth, is, to date, by far his most extensive and ambitious poem. Firmly based in the traditional Ifa system and containing within itself those main lines of thought that have marked Soyinka's verse throughout his career, this is a darkly powerful piece of work that in parts has a strong flavour of the mythopoeic about it. (p. 56)

Ogun is the rather satanic hero of the poem. Since he is 'the septuple one', the god who carries seven gourds with him into battle, it is not unfitting that the poem should be divided into seven sections. The first is *deluge* . . . , a scene of violent primeval activity, where, in a raging storm and Cimmerian darkness torn only by lightning flashes, earth is in the process of creation. . . . In the fury of this storm, the first of the actual season (Ogun's season) in Nigeria, and, for the poet's purpose, seen as the first storm of creation, Ogun is beginning his pilgrimage to earth. He is the god of the creative essence—the rain he brings promises new life. He is also of course the god of war who tempers his promise of life abundant with the threat of death. It is a sort of bloody conferring of life and death together. (pp. 56-7)

There is violence in the first section; but it is violence fraught with the promise of life. In the second section, . . . *and after,* the promise, in keeping with the strangely dual nature of Ogun, is not completely fulfilled; or at least, it is fulfilled and then instantly blighted. The threat of doom hangs over a scene that appeared to be growing increasing 'blissful'. We thus find stanzas celebrating the joy of Ogun's coming balanced, inevitably, by stanzas insisting on the bloody side of his mission. The wine girl, for example, who, Soyinka tells us, is a representational fusion of Sango and Ogun, first appears in a scene of relaxed, sunny happiness. . . . But this rich serenity is shattered in an instant when, in the very next stanza, the girl appears as the dead victim of a hideous car smash. The lovely wine girl becomes 'a greying skull / On blooded highways', her lone face filled with sadness. Only moments before, Ogun, as the god of creation and of the harvest, had smiled his peace upon her; now, as the god of the road, as the god of war, he greedily slaughters her. . . . After some fine surrealistic writing, in which the poet describes some childhood fantasies, the section ends with Ogun bringing order to the world. He makes harmony out of dissonance, imposes a pattern on chaos, teaches the whole of creation to dance and sing. . . . (pp. 57-9)

Ogun's path, . . . his pilgrimage to earth, is an annual event, 'one loop of time'. The same point is made more firmly in the third section, *pilgrimage.* The journey Ogun is making is both his first pilgrimage and the annual pilgrimage he has been making ever since. This is how the Yoruba account for the seasons, and for the strange flow of human existence which is marked by waves of joy and waves of sadness, waves of plenty and waves of drought, waves of life and waves of death—all following, one after another, in an endless cyclical motion. (p. 59)

After section four, which describes Ogun and the gods settling down to an earthly existence, we reach section five, *the battle.* As its name suggests, it is given over to the bloodier side of Ogun's life on earth. As the poet explains, Ogun, having reluctantly been made king of Ira, gets drunk while leading his men into battle. Instead of destroying the enemy, he turns on his own warriors and wreaks appalling carnage among them. His men shout to try and bring him to his senses; but all to no avail. . . . He is called a murderer, a cannibal; but the cries fall on deaf ears. 'His being incarnate', says the poet, 'Bathes in carnage, anoints godhead/In Carnage.' To the cries of help, Esu, the troublesome god of fate, who also happens to be present, will not listen either. . . . Eventually, the drunken god grows sober; he realises his mistake: 'Passion slowly yielded to remorse'. . . . Aside from its mythic basis, its attempt to explain a universal pattern, this section clearly has a contemporary relevance. (pp. 59-60)

Section six, *recessional,* is an important stage in the poem's development, and one in which the more personal statement, the conclusions drawn from the night's experience, are emphasised. It recounts the return journey, the poet coming home from his night spent in the woods and rain. The night is ending; so, too, its furious cataclysmic upheavals. Dawn approaches. One central reflection seems to emerge from the night's events. While the previous sections of the poem have been insisting on the cyclic pattern of Ogun's pilgrimage, its eternal inevitability, Soyinka now seems to

ask: Are we, in fact, slaves to this pattern? Is it really so inevitable? Can it, indeed, be broken? In a sense, the Yoruba system within which Soyinka is working, itself provides one answer. For, as Soyinka reminds us, the Yoruba believe that Atunda, slave to the first deity, 'Either from pique or revolutionary ideas . . . rolled a rock down on his unsuspecting master, smashing him to bits, and creating the multiple godhead.' The significance of this is that Atunda's action created diversity. Hence, Ogun, though a monstrously powerful god is, after all, only one god among many; his annual visitation, and the mixed blessings associated with it, represents but one pattern, though, of course, an important one. But Atunda brings a promise of diversity, variety of patterns; and he is praised heartily for it. The section becomes not only a celebration of diversity, but a vigorous plea for it. It is only a short step now to an *apologia* for the artist's independence, for the importance of uniqueness, of individuality. There is a plea for boldness, new directions, unfettered private growth and exploration—a plea, above all, for freedom in myriad forms.

Incredibly, we find that Ogun, who seems to be all things to all men, can help here: is he not a bold innovating character himself ? Is he not, after all, the god of adventurers and explorers? (p. 61)

The emphasis in section seven, *harvest,* returns to the promise of peace and plenty. Parts here read like a magnificent fulfillment of J. P. Clark's poem 'The Year's First Rain', which ended with an image of the earth 'Swollen already with the life to break at day'. Ogun withdraws into the forests, there is 'A dawn of bright processions', and then . . . :

The first fruits rose from subterranean hoards
First in our vision, corn sheaves rose over hill
Long before the bearers, domes of eggs and flesh
Of palm fruit, red, oil black, froth flew in sun bubbles
Burst over throngs of golden gourds.

This is writing of a rare sensuous quality, unequalled by any other West African poet. Soyinka is describing the promise fulfilled, the promise heralded by the storm and the bloodshed. Reflecting on his country's sad contemporary history, which has paralleled Ogun's bloody pilgrimage, he laments that it is this and 'the brief sunled promise of earth's forgiveness' that are awaited to round out, to complete, the cycle. Yet even in this final section, Ogun's dual nature as creator and killer, and the doom of repetition that he symbolises, are insisted on; for the closing stanza of this dark poem states that the golden harvest is already, in its egregious ripeness, moving towards decay, towards 'resorption in His alloy essence'. The cycle must go on.

The poem, then, with its dark backcloth and its epic resonances, provides convincing testimony not only to Soyinka's stature as a poet, but also to his ability to work within the traditional Ifa system. That there was something both timely and timeless about its inspiration is suggested in Soyinka's Preface . . . :

> *Idanre* lost its mystification early enough. As events gathered pace and unreason around me I recognised it as part of a pattern of awareness which began when I wrote *A Dance of the Forests*. In detail, in the human context of my society, *Idanre* has made abundant sense. (The town of Idanre itself was the first to cut its bridge, its only link with the rest of the region during the uprising of October '65.) And since then, the bloody origin of Ogun's pilgrimage has been, in true cyclic manner most bloodily reenacted.

> (p. 63)

Wole Soyinka is West Africa's finest dramatist. Here is a man richly endowed with literary skill, whose work, which has poured forth abundantly in a career still in its early stages, bears the marks of a refined sensibility, stringent critical standards, and, above all, great creative energy. . . . As we have seen, by temperament a satirist, he moves about the West African scene like some marvellously gifted Malcontent, fiercely thrusting at the corruption, intrigue, and vaulting ambition which he witnesses on every side. And his blows strike home, for on two occasions he has been sent to prison.

His education and training, in Africa and the United Kingdom, partly account for his position as the West African dramatist in whom the theatrical traditions of Europe and the homeland are most successfully synthesised (though perhaps symbiosis is a more appropriate word, since both traditions are strongly alive in him). London critics have said that his roots go deep into western traditions and that he is following at a distance in the footsteps of men like Jonson and Webster. While they are right in believing that Soyinka has been receptive to such influences, it must be emphasised at the same time that his work is essentially African in material and inspiration. As our discussion of his verse revealed, Soyinka is a Yoruba who acknowledges his roots and clings to them; he is not, in any sense of the word, *déraciné*. (p. 219)

The following examination of Soyinka's works is divided into three sections. The first will discuss Soyinka as a satirist and take *Dance of the Forests* and *The Road* for special treatment; the second treats of Soyinka's interest in language as an instrument of satire; and the third offers a detailed examination of the plays' synthesis of features African and western.

'Satire in the theatre', Soyinka observed in 1965, 'is a weapon not yet fully exploited among the contemporary dramatists of Nigeria, fertile though the social and political scene is for well-aimed barbs by the sharp, observant eye.' . . . But Soyinka's interest in satire

does not stem from that *annus horribilis,* 1965. One of his early poems, **'Telephone Conversation'**, published in 1962, was a memorable sally into this field, drawing applause from many sides, and especially from the South African critic Ezekiel Mphahlele. Even earlier, however, came *A Dance of the Forests,* written for Nigeria's Independence Celebrations, and performed by The 1960 Masks, Soyinka's own company; it is the most complex satirical play which the author has so far written. Here indeed was a stroke of bold imagination that pointed up the breadth, depth and sincerity of Soyinka's vision; for in a play offered to a nation on the euphoric occasion of its Independence, the immediate victim of the satire is that nation itself; in a play ostensibly celebrating a country's birth, the talk is all of death, delusion, and betrayal. Indeed, flying in the face of all the cherished teachings of negritude, Soyinka has chosen to de-romanticise his people and their history with a boldness scarcely paralleled since the days of Synge and O'Casey. (p. 220)

We learn at once that Soyinka's vision ranges far beyond the present, even if this is his immediate concern; his theme is a large one, his frame of reference nothing less than the past, present, and ongoing stream of human existence. There is to be, then, a great gathering of the tribes at a momentous time in their history. It is a fitting occasion for the nation to show its medals and resurrect its trophies—a time to recall historic heroism of the sort that will provide inspiration for future endeavour. 'The accumulated heritage—that is what we are celebrating', declares Council Orator Adenebi. . . . Such is the spirit of the occasion; such the pride and hope of a nation at a great turning point in its history. But Soyinka possesses the satirist's passionate, almost pathological, obsession for the truth. Those heady with the excitement of the present must be bullied into setting their experience within the framework of historical fact; they must be allowed to glimpse some of the abiding truths of the human condition. Those who stand in the present and drug themselves with memories of former glories, like Orator Adenebi, whose absurd musings spiral ever further away from reality, must be faced with the grim reality behind their dreams.

The living, then, are anxious to call up from the dead a host of mighty heroes, celebrate the Gathering of the Tribes with a vision of past splendour; and in an empty clearing in the forest (with a startling piece of stagecraft), the soil breaks and there arise from the dead two pathetic human figures—a sorry link indeed 'for the season of rejoicing'. The Dead Man has behind him a wretched history of misery, thwarted hopes, and betrayal; The Dead Woman, his wife, sorrowful, and pregnant 'for a hundred generations', has an equally miserable past, and is soon to be delivered of a half-child, her baby who symbolises the future.

Soyinka allows us to see the details of their past in a Faustian recreation of the Court of Mata Kharibu, a mythical king who represents the 'glorious' history to which the living look back with nostalgia. Soyinka's purpose here is clear, for, as he observes elsewhere, the past 'clarifies the present and explains the future'. As Soyinka sees it, Africa's past is a sadly inglorious one. Thus, here in this shrine of historic magnificence, in this reign to which living Africans look back with pride, we find a whore as queen, and a king unrivalled in barbaric ferocity; a king who will brook no opposition to his every whim, who fears, like all tyrants, the independent mind, and will sell into slavery even his most devoted subjects. Dead Man is one of them, sold for a cask of rum because he dared to think for himself and suggest that he and the king's warriors should only go to war in a just cause. A figure of mutating significance, Dead Man is here representative of ordinary, thinking, reasonable mankind. (pp. 221-22)

Dead Man's history also includes involvement with the slave-trade, Africa's most traumatic historical experience. Soyinka gives his audience the brutal truth that the Kharibus of Africa's past had as much blood on their hands as the white slavers. At this point in a play notable for its Janus-like viewpoint, we begin to find Africa's inglorious past pointing a finger towards the present and the future. . . . There is a strong hint that Africa too easily accepts its chains, be they inflicted by strangers or brothers. More startling, however, is the clear implication that the chains are, and always have been, a permanent feature of the landscape. The 'new' ship in which Kharibu and all his ancestors would be proud to ride suggests modern forms of slavery that the author's fellow Africans are blindly accepting. It is as though Soyinka sees the whole of African history in the crushingly powerful image of a great slave galley sailing down the straits of time, from the dim past down to the present and on towards the horizon of the future. (pp. 223-24)

And what of the present? 'The pattern is unchanged,' says Dead Man, who was 'one of those who journeyed in the marketships of blood', and who is now visiting the modern world of the living. It is a lesson in disillusionment, for, as he is at one point reminded, 'Your wise men, casting bones of oracle/Promised peace and profit/New knowledge, new beginnings after toil . . . ' Treated abominably in the past, he and his wife are abominably treated in the present. The bearers of bitter truth about an inglorious history, they are given at the Gathering of the Tribes the cold welcome of beggars at a feast. . . . It is a measure of the subtlety of Soyinka's art that the satire here works on two levels; for this shocking treatment of guests, and, furthermore, guests from the dead (we have stressed their importance often enough), is immediately recognised as a flagrant violation of rules of conduct upon which African societies pride themselves. At a more profound level, we are meant to witness in this behavior not only a wilful blindness to the truth about the past, but also an arrogant rejection of that past as it is enshrined in these two representative figures. . . .

The experience of Dead Man and his wife is clear enough. It is a case of *plus ça change*. Men treated each other appallingly in the past; they treat each other appallingly in the present; they will treat each other appallingly in the future. (p. 224)

Such, then, is Soyinka's message for the happy occasion of Nigeria's Independence Celebrations—a sobering reminder of some basic, and abiding, truths about mankind in general and about Africans and their history in particular. Events since 1960 have proved with a vengeance the accuracy of at least that part of his vision which dealt with the future. But in addition, *A Dance of the Forests* supplies proof, if proof is needed, that Soyinka saw the need for national self-criticism six years before Achebe raised the subject as a matter of urgency in the pages of *Présence Africaine*. Soyinka's satiric vision is a curious affair—partly Swift's savage indignation, partly the Conradian 'horror', and partly the Wordsworthian lament over 'what man has made of man'. It informs every part of this difficult but remarkable play.

An equally difficult and powerful piece of satire is Soyinka's *The Road* published in 1965. From the very title of the play (a work that stands in relation to pieces such as *The Lion and the Jewel* like *Hamlet* to *Twelfth Night*), one realises that here is a further exploration of a subject which has fascinated Soyinka throughout his literary career. [The] road here is a fertile central motif. At one level it is any Nigerian road beside which the main scenes of the play are acted or danced. At another level, it is the proverbial road of life, along which all men must travel, individually or collectively as nations. Closely associated with this is the idea of the road of progress, a notion lightly ridiculed in Soyinka's poem **'Death in the Dawn'**. Above all, however, it is the road between life and death which runs precisely through that hazy landscape between this world and the next that so fascinates Soyinka. Along this highway the dead must travel.

Watching over the road, lurking behind all the events of the play, is Ogun, the greedy god who feeds on the butchery that the roads daily provide. Ogun lives on death and needs feeding regularly. The lorry drivers in the play are his devotees, their festival is his festival. Significantly, during their masquerade in his honour, they carry a dog tied to a stake as a sacrificial offering. Ogun's driver followers are notorious killers of dogs that stray onto the road. . . . But Ogun shows little care for his own (one recalls the manner in which he slew his warriors when king of Ira). Hence so many of the road's 'heroes' in the play—Zorro, Akanni the lizard, Sigidi Ope, Sapele Joe, Saidu-Say, Indian Charlie, Humphrey Bogart, Cimmarron Kid, Muftau, and Sergeant Burma—are dead. Hence so many of the play's central figures are probing towards death, or are actually dead and undergoing decomposition, their voices ghosting forth from this twilight zone in a most unnerving manner. . . .

[Soyinka chooses] a middle ground, a sort of no-man's land belonging neither to the world of the flesh nor the spirit. . . . (p. 228)

This dark middle area, reminiscent of many of Soyinka's poems, effortlessly grows suggestive of ideas other than those of death and dissolution. It suggests, for example, the overall position of Africa, caught, in Mabel Segun's memorable words, 'hanging in the middle way'. Soyinka portrays a hideous mingling of cultures that he finds in this middle state, though he does so with a complexity, a subtlety, and a revulsion, unparralleled in those innumerable publications that exhibit the cultural clash through stale commonplaces.

Professor himself is the best illustration of this. With his Victorian outfit of top hat and tails, all threadbare, with his academic title, earned through prowess in forgery, with his past connection with the Christian church, and his clear leanings towards Ifa, he is a sort of amphibious creature, neither right African nor right European; neither wholly spiritually oriented nor wholly materialistic. We have mentioned already the psychological problems of modern Africa: there are definite suggestions of schizophrenia or mere lunacy in Professor, and Soyinka wants us to notice them. A veritable aura of symbolism surrounds this weird scoundrel. It is no mere chance that he is dressed in Victorian garb. In part, presumably, Soyinka is making the common joke that Africa follows absurdly, at a distance, the fashions of Europe, and never actually catches up. Similar jibes are found in Achebe and Nicol. But he is also hinting that Professor represents the first real nineteenth-century encounter with the West, and furthermore, the subsequent history of that encounter. Hence, almost everything about this creature is betwixt and between. He is partly a genuine seeker after the Word, which means here knowledge of the essence of death, and partly a genuine criminal, bold, selfish, and rapacious. It is the sort of contradiction that suggests the familiar Afro-European dichotomy. . . . (p. 229)

If Professor is an unpleasant mingling of Africa and Europe, so, too, are the play's drivers and thugs. They are men with names inspired by American crime and western films, men like Say Tokyo Kid who can affect a tough Chicago gangster's drawl ('I don give a damn for that crazy guy and he know it') yet sing traditional Yoruba praise songs and worship Ogun. With his tough talk, his alleged scorn for Professor's spiritualism (belied by his belief that there are 'a hundred spirits in every guy of timber' he carries), Say Tokyo represents

an ugly fusion of the traditionally African and the hard-headed materialism of an alien culture. (p. 230)

The play is also a bitter attack on Nigerian society as a whole: here is a scathing criticism of *A Dance of the Forests* in a wormier form. It is as though Soyinka, in his deliberate choice of the Agemo idea, is trying to say that he sees the whole of his contemporary society dissolving into the rottenness and stench of death. Apart from Murano, who is deaf, dumb, dead (and therefore, impotent), there is not a single undiseased figure in the play. The whole dark scene is pervaded by vice and greed in all its forms. The sun never seems to rise in this play. It is a picture of unrelieved gloom and decadence, where a dog-eat-dog morality rules supreme. . . . To complete this revolting picture, Soyinka ensures that a representative of all ranks of society is included: his country must be seen to be corrupt from top to bottom. The law, as represented by Particulars Joe, is corrupt in the most blatant manner; the Church stands as an empty shell behind the entire play, irrelevant and powerless. Chief-in-Town, a modern version of the traditional Oba, is a political representative who keeps a gang of thugs in hire and distributes opium. The common people, like Samson and Kotonu, prey on one another like hyenas.

The Road is Soyinka's writing on the nation's wall. He draws a society that is on the road to death and dissolution, a society for which there seems no hope. Perhaps, like Professor, who speaks of death as 'the moment of our rehabilitation', this society will have to die before it learns the truth. Rebirth is only possible after the descent from life is complete. This movement itself is foreshadowed by the mask at the end of the play which sinks slowly until 'it appears to be nothing beyond a heap of cloth and raffia.'

In *A Dance of the Forests* and *The Road,* a whole nation was under attack. In other plays, too, the satirical element has figured strongly; but there it is not a whole society but particular members of it who come in for abuse. Soyinka particularly loathes those who possess power and use it dishonestly, those whose selfishness drives them to keep the people in a state of ignorance and subservience.

In *The Swamp Dwellers,* Kadiye is the target, a fat village priest who remains 'smooth and well-preserved' even in time of drought by exploiting the simple piety of those whom he represents before the local god. He lies upon the land and 'choke(s) it in the folds of a serpent'. In *The Trials of Brother Jero,* Jeroboam himself is under attack, an eloquent fraud working as a Beach Prophet and striding the boards like some strange character from mediaeval times. He cuts a striking figure with his heavily-bearded face, his rod of office, long flowing hair, white gown and fine velvet cape—all of them aids to deceit. The West African scene is alive with weird scoundrels of this sort. In a lighter vein, *The*

Lion and the Jewel focuses its attack on Lakunle, a westernised schoolteacher who appears ridiculous with his modicum of book learning, his complete vacuity of wisdom and his preposterous arrogance; he is a man who feels elevated enough to call his people 'a race of savages' and sees himself as the prophet of a new order. Despising ancestral ways, he is determined to drag his community into the vulgar daylight of the modern world. Soyinka would probably call *The Lion and the Jewel* a recreational piece. But *Kongi's Harvest* appeared during the years of Nigeria's gathering storm and strikes a more urgent and 'engaged' note. At the heart of his country's afflictions he sees politicians with their lust for power and their illiberal vision. He has stated elsewhere that it is not the continent's writers but its politicians who have shaped 'the present philosophy, the present direction of modern Africa', and he asked, 'is this not a contradiction to a society whose great declaration of uniqueness to the outside world is that of a superabundant humanism? Hence *Kongi's Harvest*, theatrically a rather dull play, is a fierce onslaught on West Africa's modern breed of politicians, and especially on Kongi himself, the President of Isma and a modern version of Mata Kharibu complete with all the image-making paraphernalia of the twentieth century. . . . After the more general satire of *A Dance of the Forests* these, then, are some of the individual victims chosen as targets in the plays that have followed. (pp. 231-33)

Reaping the harvest of a past dominated by the spoken word, Soyinka is deeply interested in the rhetorical arts. Hence no doubt his special penchant for the dramatic form and the appearance in each of his plays of at least one outstanding orator. We usually find, too, a carefully ordered range of linguistic styles, which not only affords Soyinka a necessary variety of voices, but constitutes a basic item in his satirical armour as well. . . .

As a satirist vitally concerned about language and style, Soyinka stands in line with distinguished predecessors. It is enough to recall the names of Skelton, Swift, Pope, and Sterne to establish how consistently the great satiric tradition of English letters has opposed itself to the abuse of language. (p. 234)

Where historically the abuse of language has been decried mainly in its literary manifestations, satire in the modern world has attacked its debasement by propagandists and political machinery. George Orwell, the twentieth century's Swift, provides a useful example. In Orwell's view, the decline of a language 'must ultimately have political and economic causes'; bad politics encourage the abuse of language, and the slovenliness of our language leads to woolly thinking. (p. 235)

Now, Orwell and Soyinka can be taken as kindred spirits. . . . We have already cited Soyinka's complaint that 'the present philosophy, the present direction of modern Africa was created by politicians' (including men who felt it necessary on two occasions to strip him of his freedom). It is not surprising, therefore, that politicians and their abuse of language should become a theme of his plays.

Kongi's Harvest offers perhaps the best example. Here traditional African politics, which placed the power of ruling in the hands of local chieftains, is being ousted by the politics of Kongi with his passion for dictatorship in the modern style. It is a familiar case of the traditional ways in conflict with the forces of change. The old order is represented by Oba Danlola and his followers, whose choice of language sharply marks them off from Kongi's party of modernists. Their style has a concreteness of metaphor and imagery which recalls the traditional Yoruba verse. . . . (p. 236)

The difference between the era which Danlola represents and Kongi's new dispensation is seen in the play as largely one of language. Having dismissed Danlola and his followers as 'a backward superstitious lot', Kongi is firmly committed to building a political machine that is recognisably modern and recognisably western. Hence, the linguistic style which Soyinka gives to the tyrant and his minions is fraught, not with the metaphor and proverbial wisdom of Old Africa, but with the 'washer words' and politico-scientific jargon of the modern world. (p. 237)

Thus, Kongi's harvest is to be 'a harvest of words', and Soyinka will shape his satire accordingly. Kongi has decided that there must be a deliberate break with the past—essentially a political break of course, but involving a cultural and linguistic break as well. . . . The effort is hard to sustain, and of course Soyinka's point is that their new style is a gross affectation; but on the whole, they succeed and we hear the familiar jargon that a man like Orwell loathed so passionately. 'Progressive forces', 'a step has already been taken in that direction', 'contemporary situation', 'reactionary', 'positive stamp', 'scientific image', 'positive scientificism', 'so-called wise ones', 'clean break'—the cliches pour forth, and one half expects to hear 'consensus', 'escalation', 'dialogue', 'credibility gap', and 'all-time highs' thrown in for good measure. (pp. 238-39)

The whole movement of the play is towards the great Festival of the New Yam, traditionally the responsibility of Danlola; Kongi plans to 'secularise' this event, ceremonially ring out the old order, and assert his supremacy as the fountainhead of all meaningful power in the country. . . . In the event, the show is a fiasco, and the play ends in the style of Danlola, though he is on his way into exile when the curtain falls. (p. 240)

Lakunle's style in *The Lion and the Jewel* is a clear window through which we see his worthless values. This is a much less serious play than *Kongi's Harvest,*

Soyinka directing a scene from *Death and the King's Horseman* in 1979.

but nevertheless the style given to Lakunle represents a deliberate attempt to reflect the encroachment of western values upon African mores.

Lakunle, the torch-bearer of modernity in his community, is in love with Sidi, an unlettered village nymph; but the foxy old Bale of the village, Baroka, wants her too, and the play becomes an amusing struggle between these rivals, who represent, once again, the old order and the new. Lakunle is a fervent disciple of romantic love (that recent western import into West African society) and a champion of all those freedoms for which the feminists have struggled. He sketches for his beloved the splendid life that will be hers if only she will consent to marry him without his paying the traditional bride price. . . . Sidi of course is disgusted with this 'strange unhealthy mouthing' and retreats, leaving Lakunle to complain wearily and comically. . . . This is all light satire, but it has its point. The conflict is between the champions of two worlds, and Baroka, the spokesman of tradition, wins the fight; the modern, westernised representative not only loses but is the laughing stock of the play. It is as if Soyinka, even in this gay comedy, cannot resist taking sides; as if he, in company with satirists in general, is on the side of con-

servatism, seeing in tradition a bedrock of sanity that will defy the swirling torrents of change and revolution. But it is not as simple as this, for Soyinka's very achievement consists in his own coming to terms, artistically, with the modern world. A clue to his real position probably lies in the fact that it is largely the trivia, that superficies of western life that Lakunle espouses— western life observed at one remove in the streets of Lagos. Thus, Soyinka is no doubt saying to his people, 'Don't throw away your heritage (which still has much to offer you) for the glossy manifestations of western life. Look at Lakunle and see how absurd it would be.' (pp. 240-42)

The Trials of Brother Jero is dominated by the personality and style of the holy fraud himself, whose oratory is cultivated to deceive, whose rhetoric serves duplicity rather than divinity. . . . As usual, the play uses two contrasting styles. Jero's is one, and the second belongs to the plain folk who are his victims. Their language is as humble as their status, and in moments of deepest sincerity it becomes mainly West African pidgin. In the . . . scene on the beach, an emotional prayer session is in progress under the direction of Chume, the assistant prophet whose wife Jero has seduced. The petitions are frankly materialistic but, coming from the poor, touchingly human for all that. They are punctuated regularly with Amens, and the whole effort builds to a tremendous climax as these humble people whip up their emotional fervour. . . . (pp. 243-44)

Thus we can understand Soyinka's fundamental interest in language. Language as a key to man's inner being; language as a mirror of social standing; language as an instrument of deceit and oppression; language as a device for sheer entertainment; language as a vehicle for man's deepest utterances; language as a source of comedy; language as an instrument of satire—Soyinka is keenly aware of all these facets and explores them energetically in his plays.

Although Soyinka's work reveals a definite blending of African and western elements, the basic material out of which the plays are fashioned is overwhelmingly indigenous. The elements of African pre-drama, for instance, are here in force, as a brief survey of the plays will reveal.

Soyinka's first play was called, significantly, *A Dance of the Forests,* and its opening words indicate that it is meant to partake of the nature of a dance. The resurrected ancestors were rejected by the living 'So I took them under my wing', says Aroni. 'They became my guests and the Forests consented to dance for them.' And the dance, thus, is a common feature throughout the play. The villagers dance around the totem carved for the festivities, there is the dance of the Half-Child, offspring of the Dead Woman, and a dance by the god Eshuoro and his jester, called the Dance of the Unwilling Sacrifice. Ritual is added to dance at one point when a dancer is followed by a young girl acting as an acolyte who sprinkles the dancing area as she goes. This itself is followed shortly by a solemn recitation by a dirgeman, urging everyone to stand back and 'Leave the dead/Some room to dance', and then by Agboreko's oracular consultation. At the climax of the play we find the ceremonial masking of the three 'earthly protagonists', who, ridden and possessed by the various spirits which the Interpreter calls up, 'chorus' the future in the manner of the religious masks of Egungun and Voodoo.

The Lion and the Jewel is a lively combination of dancing, singing, and drumming. A particularly memorable feature is the Dance of the Lost Traveller, a reenactment in mime form of an important event occurring prior to the time period of the play, and about which the audience must be informed. It was the unexpected visit of a Lagos photographer whose car broke down as it passed near the village. Sidi chooses villagers to dance the different parts of 'devil horse' (car) and python; and persuades Lakunle (warmly African beneath his western veneer) to dance the part of the stranger. . . . The stranger's arrival and short stay in the village are then mimed, and, to simulate the car wheels, four dancers

roll the upper halves of their bodies to the accompaniment of throbbing drums.

In the same play, Baroka wins Sidi by spreading abroad a rumour that he is impotent—a rumour that leads to the performance and a frankly sexual 'dance of virility', carried out exclusively by the ladies. It is a wild triumphant affair in which the Bale's sexual life from his days of great potency to his final 'defeat', is acted out with enormous gusto. Sadiku, his eldest wife, leads a dancing group of younger women in pursuit of a male, who rushes about, dancing in tortured movements as defeat draws near, and is finally 'scotched', to the unbounded delight of the ladies. It is a bold piece of theatre (made nicely ironic by having the dancers burst on stage at precisely the moment of Sidi's seduction) which not even Aristophanes could have bettered.

In the other plays, too, traditional elements feature strongly. *Kongi's Harvest,* for example, reaches a grand climax at the Yam Festival, which is a veritable orgy of feasting, dancing, chanting, and parading, all to the frenzied accompaniment of dozens of pounding pestles. As we have seen in *The Road,* Soyinka's note *For the Producer* with its reference to the mask idiom, is evidence enough of the tradition in which he is working.

A play replete with dirge and praise singing, and which contains a festival in honour of Ogun, god of iron, it serves to indicate how deeply the roots of Soyinka's art are sunk in African traditional practice.

But the most interesting example of how Soyinka uses pre-dramatic material can be found in *The Strong Breed,* a dark, powerfully moving play built around the scapegoat idea, one of the most ancient conventions devised by social man for the easing of his collective conscience. In the village of the play, there is a New Year's Eve ritual in which the evil of the old year is cleansed away for the beginning of the new. The theme is introduced by a sick girl, who appears dragging an effigy or 'carrier' that is to be beaten, hanged, and burnt so that it will carry away her illness. . . . It is a clear example of pre-drama at the heart of a most moving play.

Traditional material, then, features strongly. What of those elements borrowed from the West? Some of these are extremely simple, yet fundamental. For instance, the plays have a text, and, therefore, a fixed form, which in itself is a basic departure from traditional practice. The improvisation of the early Yoruba troupes would be unthinkable in any of the Soyinka plays which we have discussed. Again, the texts are in English and the plays are designed for western stages rather than for the traditional open square.

There are, too, several techniques learnt from European practice that give Soyinka's art a flexibility and freedom it would otherwise lack. A day in the life of Brother Jero, introduced to the audience by the Prophet himself, and then acted out by him, represents a device more likely to have been learnt from Brecht or Pirandello than from Africa. The flashback technique, for which Soyinka has been criticised by Martin Esslin, is likewise a western borrowing. . . . A divided stage is used in the first section of *Kongi's Harvest,* for the play alternates between two scenes; it is a device used memorably in the Isherwood-Auden play *On the Frontier,* and, of course, it is common in films and in television plays. Soyinka might have borrowed it from any one of these sources; there is no evidence of it in the dramatic tradition inherited from his forefathers. His plots, too, reveal an ingenuity inspired more perhaps by Ben Jonson than by indigenous models. Certainly there is no plot in Yoruba Folk Opera to match the complexity of *The Lion and the Jewel* or *A Dance of the Forests.*

Western influence emerges, too, in the matter of characterisation. Soyinka's figures have a degree of psychological depth and complexity which vernacular drama has never achieved. Professor, in *The Road,* to take but one illustration, is a distinctly African personality in a distinctly African play, but the bewildering complexity of his character, the shadows of the past that enshroud it, its aura of insanity, its weird admixture of the criminal and spiritual—all this is felt to have been made possible only by Soyinka's knowledge and imitation of western dramatists.

Soyinka has rapidly emerged as West Africa's most distinguished dramatist, and indeed he is beginning to claim attention as one of the foremost English-speaking playwrights of our time. As a satirist he is certainly in the front rank. As a poetic dramatist, he has few equals. (pp. 244-48)

Adrian A. Roscoe, " 'Drama' and 'Progress in Verse'," in his *Mother Is Gold: A Study in West African Literature,* Cambridge at the University Press, 1971, pp. 13-70, 176-248.

JAMES OLNEY

(essay date 1982)

[In the following excerpt, Olney praises *Aké,* declaring that the book "is destined to become a classic of African autobiography."]

[*Aké*] is destined to become a classic of African autobiography, indeed a classic of childhood memoirs wherever and whenever produced.

What Mr. Soyinka makes most vividly present is the living landscape of Aké, the Nigerian village where he grew up on a parsonage compound. . . . It is from the wonderfully colorful, agitated, aroma-laden markets, the likes of which one finds all across West Africa,

that Mr. Soyinka distills the essence of the Aké of his memories. . . .

In one of the finest chapters of *Aké,* Mr. Soyinka eulogizes the markets of his childhood. His memory is remarkable; he still seems able to hear the sounds, taste the flavors and smell the aromas of 35 and 40 years ago. Every sound and smell blended together in the evenings of Mr. Soyinka's childhood to form "part of the invisible network of Aké's extended persona." They are gone now, but once he could be sure of "Ibarapa's sumptuous resurrection of flavours every evening." . . .

Throughout his previous work, Wole Soyinka has insisted on the dual nature of the role performed by the African artist. The artist "has always functioned in African society . . . as the record of the mores and experience of his society *and* as the voice of vision in his own time." In *Aké* Mr. Soyinka rehearses his own vision even as he traces its roots in the experiences and people of his African childhood. The world that Mr. Soyinka recalls in *Aké,* that he creates or re-creates from memories of the past (for it is sadly different now), is a world of pervasive, indwelling spiritual presences.

A sense of these presences is felt as Mr. Soyinka recalls the people among whom he grew up: his mother and father . . . ; his paternal grandfather, who was crucially important to Mr. Soyinka's education in Yoruba traditions. . . . But the importance of the spiritual world is seen more obviously in the descriptions of the *egúngún,* ancestral spirits who return in all their power and vitality when their masks are danced in festive procession and who represent the extended being of parents, grandparents and elders. Indeed, the *egúngún* even assert their presence through the organ in the Christian church. . . . (p. 7)

There is more than a little method in this mingling of African ancestors and the Christian deity. Mr. Soyinka sees this and other ritual performances as more or less successful attempts (Yoruba more successful, Christian less) at restoring to a condition of unity and cosmic balance the three interpenetrating, interdependent worlds of his traditional Yoruba (and more generally African) belief: the ancestors, the yet unborn and the living.

In addition to these three realms Mr. Soyinka distinguishes a "Fourth Stage," and throughout his work we find symbolic figures, spirits and objects that have an especially intimate tie to the stage that he calls "the numinous area of transition." The *egúngún,* who make the transition and bind the worlds of the living and the dead together with the dancing of their masks, belong to this Fourth Stage. But in *Aké* there are other examples: There is the girl named Bukola, who is an *àbikú* ("a child which is born, dies, is born again and dies in a repetitive cycle"); there are the wood spirits around the parsonage compound; there is Mr. Soyinka's little sister, whose death, on her first birthday, makes him expect some sort of universal cataclysm; there is the guava tree that Mr. Soyinka imagines to be *his* tree, inhabited by spirits that he can command. . . . Such symbolic figures and incidents in *Aké* perform the function of ordering and vitalizing the cosmos that they do in Mr. Soyinka's other work, whatever the mode. (pp. 7, 18)

For all its seriousness, *Aké* is not at all a solemn book. On the contrary, it is full of high good humor and a lyric grace. The book's structure is largely one of strung-together sketches and anecdotes. . . . But even these sketches and anecdotes are used to describe and realize a world to which Mr. Soyinka's mature understanding and his dozen or so volumes of fiction, drama and poetry are deeply committed. . . .

Through recollection, restoration and re-creation, he conveys a personal vision that was formed by the childhood world that he now returns to evoke and exalt in his autobiography. This is the ideal circle of autobiography at its best. It is what makes *Aké,* in addition to its other great virtues, the best available introduction to the work of one of the liveliest, most exciting writers in the world today. (p. 18)

James Olney, "The Spirits and the African Boy," in *The New York Times Book Review,* October 10, 1982, pp. 7, 18.

WOLE SOYINKA WITH ANTHONY APPIAH

(interview date 1986-87)

[The following interview was conducted in late 1986 or early 1987, soon after Soyinka had won the Nobel Prize for Literature. Here, Soyinka talks with Anthony Appiah about receiving the Nobel Prize and discusses his play *Death and the King's Horseman*. A variant form of this interview first appeared in 1987 in *The New Theater Review* under the title "Easing the Transition."]

[Appiah]: *Now that you've had three months or so to think about it, can you tell us what you think the significance is of the award of the Nobel Prize, first of all to you and then to you as an African?*

[Soyinka]: To me, it's been hell. (Laughter). On one level, yes. I understand what Bernard Shaw meant when he was given the Prize and he said he could forgive the man who invented dynamite, but it took the mind of a devil to invent the Nobel Prize for literature. I share some of this feeling, but only to a certain extent. The other side of the coin, of course, is that it increases one's literary family, increases one's awareness of the

need of many activities, many paths, many concerns of the common Earth we inhabit. It increases an awareness of the need of people to fasten onto a voice, a representative, and that refers to your question about Africa in particular. So, it's of great importance, I think, not so much to me as to the literary craftsmen of my continent, to those who share the longing for a brotherhood/sisterhood which transcends the African continent and reaches out into the diaspora. The way in which the Prize has been received by people all over the world, particularly the African diaspora—in the West Indies, in the United States, and across the various language boundaries—has reinforced my insistent conviction that the African world is not limited by the African continent.

I noticed that when you gave your Nobel lecture, you chose to discuss apartheid and southern Africa. Did you feel that that was a particularly important thing to do at that moment?

A lot of my writing has been concerned with injustice, with inhumanity, with racism, inside and outside of my immediate environment, which is Nigeria. This is a world platform, and I could not think of any more appropriate moment for voicing this particular level of my literary concerns. I thought it was most appropriate, yes.

How does it enhance or change your position when you're speaking within Nigeria?

I've always insisted that I do not accept any kind of double standards. I do not accept a distinction, excuses on behalf of either our own black oppressors or the white oppressors of our race. In other words, the more one emphasizes the oppression which we receive from outside, the more we obtain the moral strength and the moral authority to criticize our own black oppressors. So this is equally important. Many African heads of state sent messages, personal telegrams, telexes, etc., and for me this means they have already accepted the imperative of the moralities which guide my work. So now it becomes a little bit more difficult for many of them to say, "Oh, you are criticizing us to the outside world!" when they understand that a kind of moral authority attaches to events of this kind and they have identified themselves with it. Otherwise, I'll tell them, "Take back your congratulatory telegrams." (Laughter.)

I wonder if this wouldn't be a good moment to go back a bit in time and ask you to comment on **Aké,** *your book about your early childhood. Could you say something about the process of writing about your early life?*

You know, one recaptures certain aspects of some elements of smells and sounds, either by actually smelling and hearing them or by suddenly missing them, because something triggers off the memory. You suddenly realize that a certain slice of your life is disappearing, and you get a feeling that you want to set it down in one form or another. This period of my childhood belongs to that sudden realization of a lost period, a lost ambience, a lost environment. I don't like autobiographies, because they're mostly lies, but there's a period of innocence in which one can write down things quite frankly. Even *Aké* is not totally truthful. (Laughs.) You have to expunge some things. You are embarrassed by some things, so you leave them out. But this is obviously more truthful because of the lack of inhibition than many other things I write about my life. It's not lying—you don't tell untruths, you just do not tell all the truth. It's part and parcel of the protection of human dignity. I've always been repelled by the general Euro-American habit of telling all, revealing all the dirty secrets of human relationships, even without asking permission of those who share this personal relationship with you. (Laughter, applause.)

So the childhood is one period in which there is really nothing much to hide, and I'd always wanted to set it down. I spoke to my publisher, he gave me a small advance, and I spent it. It took three years after that before I could enter the frame of mind to recapture this particular life in the way I wanted to set it down.

Aké was very successful in this country—it's a widely read book—, and that success makes plain how intelligible you have made the world of your childhood to those of us who in different ways didn't share it, because we lived either in other parts of Africa or in other parts of the world. There presumably are, however, problems in presenting your work, especially as a dramatist, because of the different traditions of interpretation of theater and performance in Nigeria, in West Africa, in Africa, and in the rest of the world. Could you reflect a little while on some of the ways in which these problems affect the production that you're now engaged in, **Death and the King's Horseman***?*

It's interesting that you ask that question apropos of *Aké,* because in one of the sessions with the company, some of the cast expressed their difficulty in finding a sort of corresponding experience in their own lives with the content, theme, and characters in *Death and the King's Horseman.* I have to confess that I was very impatient about this kind of difficulty. But, remarkably, one of the actresses—and a white one at that—said to the others, "Well, why don't you read *Aké*?" At least one portion is, in fact, very significant in terms of the position of the women in *Death and the King's Horseman.*

But, as I said and admit freely, I have a very impatient attitude towards this. I grew up, as many of us did, on the fare of European literature. Even in school we didn't have too much problem understanding the worlds of William Shakespeare, Bernard Shaw, Galsworthy, Moliere, and Ibsen, and, frankly, I'm irritated when people from outside my world say they find it difficult to enter my world. It's laziness, it's intellectual laziness . . . especially today when communication is a matter of course. There are economic relations between all the nations of the world. I see in Nigeria millionaires, multi-corporations, a constant exchange of films, video tapes, radio, music; Fela comes here with his music. I find no difficulty at all in entering into Chinese literature, Japanese literature, Russian literature, and this has always been so. I think the barrier is self-induced. "This is a world of the exotic, we can not enter it." The barrier is self-created. By now it has to be a two-way traffic. There can be no concessions at all; the effort simply has to be made.

But at the same time the work of a director principally involves responsibility towards the audience. He must always find idioms, whether in the field of music, poetry, or scenography, to interpret what might be abstruse elements. The director must bring out images in concrete terms which are merely in verbal terms within the book. When he moves a play from one area to another, the director seeks certain symbols, certain representational images in order to facilitate—because you're encapsulating a history of a people within a couple of hours. If you take *Coriolanus* to Africa, it's the responsibility of the director to try to transmit the metaphors within that particular language, the visual images, in terms which cannot be too remote. But then again I believe that the audience must not be overindulged, and once as a director I feel I have satisfied myself, that I've eased the transition, the rest is up to the audience. They can take it or leave it. (Applause.)

I take it that part of the passion of your remarks is in response to some of the ways in which your work has been received in the United States and in Europe, perhaps more in the United States.

I have to say Europeans are a little bit—if one can make comparisons—more receptive. Americans are very insular. I suppose that's because you have so many cultures in America, and Americans don't feel they have to go outside what is already here. But there's a great deal of insularity in America, and that applies not merely to culture, but to politics. Americans don't even make an attempt to understand the politics of outside nations. They think they do, but they do not. And I mean this on all levels. I speak not merely of the taxi driver who asked me, "Yea, what's happening, man. You're from Neegeria. Is that in Eer*an*?" (Laughter.) I find the same attitude even among university lecturers. Not so long ago there was a professional, very intelligent, highly trained, and I happened to remark that one of my ways of relaxing is just to go into the bush and do some hunting. And he said, "Oh, what do you use for hunting?" What he was asking was, "Is it clubs? Or bows and arrows?" I mean we've been fighting wars with cannons and guns in Africa for I don't know how long. I said, "No, it's catapult." (Laughter.) So, it's the same thing with culture. Americans are far more insular.

I'd like to talk a little more about **Death and the King's Horseman.** *Is this a political play, or would you rather read it* *as relatively apolitical, by contrast, for example, to* **A Play of Giants***?*

Of course there's politics in *Death and the King's Horseman.* There's the politics of colonization, but for me it's very peripheral. The action, the tragedy of *Death and the King's Horseman* could have been triggered off by circumstances which have nothing to do with the colonial factor—that's very important to emphasize. So it's political in a very peripheral sense. The colonial factor, as I insist, is merely a catalytic event. But the tragedy of a man who fails to fulfill an undertaking is a universal tragedy. I regard it as being far, far, far less political than *A Play of Giants,* yes.

You've said that **Horseman** *is fundamentally a metaphysical play. That might invite the speculation that it is a difficult play, since* metaphysical *is a word—I know this as a philosopher— which invites difficulties. Is there something you want to say, in advance of people's seeing it, about the metaphysical issues, the issues of death and transition, which the play addresses?*

All his life, the principal character, the Elesin Oba—the Horseman of the King—, has enjoyed certain unique privileges for a certain function. At the critical moment he fails to fulfill that function, so he's doomed. That's straightforward. But then, one asks, how is it that, in the first place, such a function was the norm for a community of people? We can ask that from this distance. And that's not so long ago. In fact, societies like this still exist.

I've given my company current examples from India, for instance, of human sacrifice and so on to the goddess Kali, which were in the newspapers quite recently. So one must begin by understanding what is the spiritual context of a people for whom this is not an aberration, not an abnormality, and one finds it in the world view, the metaphysical beliefs of the Yoruba people.

We believe that there are various areas of existence, all of which interact, interlock in a pattern of continuity: the world of the ancestor, the world of the living, and the world of the unborn. The process of transition among these various worlds is a continuing one and one which is totally ameliorated. For instance, the function of ritual, of sacrifice—whether it's a ram or a chicken—, the function of seasonal ceremonies, is in fact allied to the ease of transition among these various worlds.

So, in effect, death does not mean for such a society what it means for other societies. And it's only if one establishes this kind of context, through whatever symbolic means, that one can begin—distanced as you and I are from this particular kind of society, even if we are part of the world. It's only by exposing this world as a hermetic, self-regulating universe of its own that a tragedy of a character like Elesin can have absolute

validity. So within that context, this is what enables him. For him it's not death.

At the same time, even journeying from New York to Boston is an activity of loss. You leave something behind. It involves a pain. How much you want to live in this world which you know very well, which is concrete, which one can only relate to in symbolic terms. And so for Elesin the difficulty does exist as a human being within this world. But he's been brought up to believe, and his whole community believes, in the existence of these various worlds which are secure and even concrete in their own terms. And his failure to make that transfer from one to the other, *that* really is the tragedy of Elesin.

You spoke just now of **Horseman** *as a tragedy, which of course it is. I think the concept of tragedy tends to get used in our culture very much and in a debased form and with very little sense of classical tragedy. You chose, very deliberately I think, to frame* **Horseman** *as a classical tragedy. Is that not a difficulty, turning once again to the problems of production? Is it not difficult to produce a tragedy for a contemporary American audience? Not because it's alien or exotic or African, but because the concept of tragedy required to enter this world is a distant one to many people?*

Yes. But that's only if one begins by accepting the European definition of tragedy. I remember my shock as a student of literature and drama when I read that drama originated in Greece. What is this? I couldn't quite deal with it. What are they talking about? I never heard my grandfather talk about Greeks invading Yorubaland. I couldn't understand. I've lived from childhood with drama. I read at the time that tragedy evolved as a result of the rites of Dionysus. Now we all went through this damn thing, so I think the presence of eradication had better begin. It doesn't matter what form it takes. (Applause.)

Nevertheless, whatever their origins, tragedy does have a specific, formal . . .

But I've never made a claim that I'm presenting tragedy in European terms. *Tragedy*—quite apart from the misuse of the word which we know about— whether we translate it in Yoruba or Tre or Ewe, I think we'll find a correlative somewhere in which we're all talking about the same thing. Just as the equivalent of the word *tragedy* in Yoruba can be debased in Africa, so it can be debased in Europe. But ultimately there is a certain passage of the human being, a certain development or undevelopment of the human character, a certain result in the processes of certain events which affects the human being which has that common definition of tragedy in no matter what culture. And it is to that kind of linguistic bag, that symbolic bag, which audiences in theater must attune themselves, whether it is Japanese tragedy or Chinese tragedy.

There may be difficulties, but I think they're very superficial. As I explained to some of my company,

"You say you have difficulty looking for some parallel experience in America. But what do you call what happened to Richard Nixon? If ever there was a tragic character, that is it. Begin from there." (Laughter.) Just begin from there. We all have these experiences; it's universal. It's only in the details we differ. What happens to a man psychologically in terms of his valuation within the community in which he resides, the fall from—to use a cliché—grace to grass, that's the element of tragedy.

Wole Soyinka and Anthony Appiah, in an interview in *Black American Literature Forum,* Vol. 22, No. 4, Winter, 1988, pp. 777-85.

JONATHAN COE

(essay date 1990)

[In the following essay, Coe favorably reviews Soyinka's most recent works: *Isarà: A Voyage around Essay* and *Mandela's Earth, and Other Poems.*]

Nothing speaks louder about British insularity than the fact that we tend to be impressed by Booker rather than Nobel prizewinners. *Isarà* is Soyinka's first major prose work since he won the Nobel prize in 1986, and while it would be idle to expect it to make the bestseller lists, it certainly ought to win a few more admirers for this most accessible of African writers—particularly as it is being issued in tandem with a paperback of his newly-topical poems inspired by Nelson Mandela.

In truth the most exhilarating aspect of reading Soyinka is the contact it affords, not with a different culture, but with a different attitude towards language. One of his poems in *Mandela's Earth* describes the experience of arriving in New York and being confronted by a poster:

> This film star / space star /
>   mayor or porn queen
> Toothsomely pledges: "New
>   York loves you!"
> Forgive my innocence, does
>   New York know me?
> The word has turned mere
>   gesture in N.Y.

This disdain for a use of language which can turn words into "mere gestures" informs Soyinka's prose as much as his verse. In *Aké,* his childhood memoir (published in 1981), he recalled a visit made when he was a young boy to the market outside Ibara, and his awe and excitement at the profusion of items on display: "it did not seem possible that there was so much thing in the world!"

The whole book was infused with this sense of raw physicality, made feasible by an unflinching respect for words which required that economy be prized over sentimental "gestures." *Isarà* is in some ways a sequel to *Aké,* which introduced us to his mother, Wild Christian, and his father, the schoolmaster nicknamed Essay. Soyinka himself does not appear; however the book describes events which took place before he was born—and the perspective is not that of a child but of an impersonal narrator. Intended as "a tribute to 'Essay' and his friends and times," Isara observes the shifting preoccupations of a group of contemporaries, all of them (in Soyinka's punning phrase) "Ex-Ilés" from their native town, over a period of 15 years.

Its starting point, apparently, was a tin box in which Soyinka found some of his father's documents: "a handful of letters, old journals with marked pages and annotations, notebook jottings, tax and other levy receipts, minutes of meetings and school reports, programme notes of special events, and so on." Around these he has constructed a series of semi-fictional (and often very funny) episodes foregrounding some of the political, intellectual and financial concerns which would have been current in Western Nigeria before and after the Second World War.

Its central characters are the schoolmaster, Soditan Akinyode, and a college drop-out called Sipe who has since gone on to become an energetic and erratically successful entrepreneur. Sipe sets up a benevolent fund for his friends but finds his ambitious schemes constantly thwarted by their unworldliness: a plan to invest in Belgian bonds comes to nothing when Soditan starts agonising over the moral objections ("trust the teacher to run into a reference to an ancient instrument by a British knight who had uncovered unspeakable cruelties by the Belgians in the Congo!"). Although specific in period and location, this account of the compromises of liberal capitalism coming up against the wobbly dictates of idealism is handled with a boisterous subtlety which preserves its relevance intact.

Throughout the book, Soyinka feelingly evokes a society whose very cultural identity has been called into question by colonialists. Sometimes this is brought home by large-scale comic incidents—such as the much hyped recital of Western classical music which reduces its entire audience to a torpor—and sometimes by telling turns of phrase, as when one of Soditan's former pupils admits "I can bomb the English language worse than Hitler and no one will complain." At such moments you realise that, for these people, violence done to property and violence done to language are two sides of the same coin.

There are critics on the left in Nigeria who accuse Soyinka of failing to take an explicit political position, but from a British perspective this claim seems hard to understand. Soditan expresses irritation at one point with the coyness of the British—"they had this tendency towards apologetic, even tentative, language in straightforward matters."

The issues treated in *Isarà* are rarely straightforward, and its language is never tentative or apologetic. Instead of offering a merely wistful or elegiac portrait of a lost father-figure, it pays him an even more handsome tribute: it celebrates the life of the mind, and nails down a moment in history, with a wit, accuracy and intelligence which our own writers would do well to emulate.

Jonathan Coe, "Riches in a Box," in *Manchester Guardian Weekly,* April 8, 1990, p. 26.

SOURCES FOR FURTHER STUDY

Gibbs, James, ed. *Critical Perspectives on Wole Soyinka.* Washington, D. C.: Three Continents Press, 1980, 274 p.

> Collection of twenty-eight critical essays on Soyinka's works.

———; Katrak, Ketu H.; and Gates, Henry Louis, Jr., eds. *Wole Soyinka: A Bibliography of Primary and Secondary Sources.* Westport, Conn.: Greenwood Press, 1986, 107 p.

> Primary and secondary bibliography of Soyinka.

Jones, Eldred Durosimi. *The Writing of Wole Soyinka.* Portsmouth, N.H.: Heinemann Educational Books & Twayne, 1988, 191 p.

> Detailed study of Soyinka and his works. The critic devotes majority of the book to discussing Soyinka's plays and poetry.

Maduakor, Obi. *Wole Soyinka: An Introduction to His Writings.* New York: Garland Publishing, 1987, 339 p.

> Comprehensive discussion of Soyinka's works, evaluating Soyinka as a poet, novelist, dramatist, and critic.

Moore, Gerald. *Wole Soyinka.* New York: Africana Publishing Corporation, 1971, 114 p.

> Overview of Soyinka's literary accomplishments, interspersed with biographical commentary.

Peters, Jonathan A. "Wole Soyinka." In his *A Dance of Masks: Senghor, Achebe, Soyinka,* pp. 161-221. Washington, D. C.: Three Continents Press, 1978.

> Examines African themes and images in Soyinka's works.

Edmund Spenser

1552?-1599

English poet and essayist.

INTRODUCTION

Spenser is known as "the poet's poet" for his delight in the pure artistry of his craft: the pictorial imagery, sensuous description, and linguistic richness of his verse combine to establish him as one of the greatest of English poets. His work has inspired the approbation and respect of some of the most illustrious names in poetry: John Milton spoke of "our sage and serious poet, Spencer"; John Dryden acknowledged him as his "master" in poetry; James Thomson named him "Fancy's pleasing son"; John Keats characterized him as "Elfin Poet"; and William Wordsworth envisioned "Sweet Spenser, moving through his clouded heaven / With the moon's beauty and the moon's soft pace. . . ." Such praise is due principally to Spenser's epic allegorical poem *The Faerie Queene* (1590-96), which, though unfinished, is indisputably a masterwork of English literature. In this poem of chivalric romance and fantasy, Spenser created a mythic world which has captured the imaginations of centuries of readers.

Spenser was born into a tailor's household in London. His early schooling took place at the Merchant Taylors' Free School, where he received an education considered quite progressive by the standards of the day. He studied under the tutelage of Richard Mulcaster, a humanist educator who included in his curriculum the study of English language and literature, which at the time was an unusual innovation. In 1569 Spenser entered Pembroke College, Cambridge, receiving his bachelor's degree in 1573 and his master's in 1576. Beyond a few external facts, little is known of the remainder of Spenser's life. In 1578 he was in London, employed as secretary to Dr. John Young, Bishop of Rochester. The following year he entered the household of the Earl of Leicester, whose nephew, Sir Philip Sidney, became Spenser's friend. It is thought that Spenser married his first wife at about this time, but little is known of the woman or the circumstances. In 1580 Spenser became secretary to Lord Grey de Wilton, lord deputy of Ireland, and in that capacity made his residence in Ireland. It is surmised that Spenser began writing *The Faerie Queene* at this time, though the first books were not published until ten years later, when, at the urging of his friend Sir Walter Raleigh, Spenser journeyed to London for that purpose. When Grey was recalled to England in 1582, Spenser remained in Ireland serving in various governmental capacities, including clerk to the Munster Council and Sheriff of Cork. In 1594 Spenser, whose first wife had died, married Elizabeth Boyle; their courtship and marriage are immortalized in Spenser's sonnet sequence the *Amoretti* (1595) and his wedding ode, the "Epithalamion." Four years later, political unrest in Ireland forced Spenser and his family to flee the country; his Irish estate, Kilcolman Castle, was destroyed in Tyrone's Rebellion. (The long-standing rumor that Spenser's youngest son died in the uprising has been dismissed by modern biographers.) Spenser and his family arrived in London where he died within months. He was buried in Poets' Corner, Westminster Abbey; at his burial the leading poets of the day gathered to ceremoniously toss commendatory verses into his tomb.

Any discussion of Spenser's work must be dominated by *The Faerie Queene,* a narrative epic of legends and romance, purportedly medieval in conception but actually more closely related to the sixteenth-century Italian romantic epic, particularly Ludovico Ariosto's *Orlando furioso* (1532) and Torquato Tasso's *Gerusalemme liberata* (1581). Like these works, *The Faerie Queene* is a series of chivalric adventures, replete with tales of knightly honor, damsels in distress, and evil forces to be conquered. Spenser conceived of *The Faerie Queene* on an ambitious scale, outlining his design in a letter to Raleigh which appeared as a prefix to the first three published books of the poem. His intent was to write twelve books, each featuring a central hero or heroine representing one of twelve moral virtues. Spenser died before he could complete his task; as it stands, *The Faerie Queene* consists of six books and a fragment of a seventh, commonly referred to as the Mutability Cantos. Spenser planned his poem as "a continued Allegory, or darke conceit," and indeed the pervasive allegory of *The Faerie Queene* is one of its most remarkable aspects. The allegory works principally on two levels—moral and political—although subsidiary spiritual, historical, and personal allegories have also been noted. The moral allegory is the most consistent as well as the most accessible; here Spenser usually either directly stated or unmistakably indicated his intended meaning. The political allegory is the more obscure for the modern reader, as it necessarily requires a specialized knowledge of Elizabethan England. It has, however, often been remarked that a lack

of this knowledge does not preclude enjoyment of the poem, and some critics have suggested that an understanding of the allegory is not essential to an appreciation of *The Faerie Queene.* Many have argued that the allegory is actually intrusive. Algernon Charles Swinburne has objected to "this indefinite and inevitable cloudiness of depiction rather than conception, which reduces the most tangible things to impalpable properties, resolves the solidest realities into the smoke of perfumed metaphor." Other critics, without denying the relevance of the allegory to the poem, have found it cumbersome and inconsistent. It seems clear, for example, that Gloriana, the fairy queen, is meant to represent Elizabeth I, yet Elizabeth appears to be figured just as clearly in other characters. The dual moral and political allegory becomes at times so complicated that it cannot be successfully maintained; some critics have contended that the allegory lacks a comprehensive structure. Dissenting critics respond that as the allegory on all its levels is integral to *The Faerie Queene,* to reject it is to misread the poem. A resolution to this conflict is implied in the criticism of William Hazlitt, who, noting the poem's lyrical grace and other attributes not reliant on allegory, advised readers that "If they do not meddle with the allegory, the allegory will not meddle with them."

If some commentators have minimized the importance of allegory in *The Faerie Queene,* it does not follow that they have thus condemned the poem. Many critics have based their admiration of *The Faerie Queene* solely on the beauty of Spenser's poetic art, arguing that Spenser's moral and allegorical concerns are actually secondary to his role as what William Butler Yeats has called the "poet of the delighted senses." It is commonly agreed that Spenser's work, particularly *The Faerie Queene,* is "poetical" above all else, that his greatest talent lay in his creative artistry—in the sheer aesthetic pleasure evoked by his masterly use of vivid imagery and description. Leigh Hunt has stated that Spenser wrote "as if with a brush instead of a pen," concluding firmly: "Not to like Spenser is not to like poetry." Virginia Woolf has described feeling in reading *The Faerie Queene* "that we are confined in one continuous consciousness, which is Spenser's; that he has saturated and enclosed this world, that we live in a great bubble blown from the poet's brain." However, although Spenser's success in creating such a world and enthralling readers with its beauty is widely acknowledged, the validity of his vision in terms other than the aesthetic remains in doubt. A number of critics have argued that the poem's setting, language, and characters lack authenticity: the setting, because of the conscious artificiality engendered by Spenser's rendering of a medieval epic from a Renaissance perspective; the language, because of its saturation with archaisms and Spenser's own archaic-sounding neologisms; and the characters, because, critics argue, they are little more than allegorical stick figures. However, the poem's many champions, while occasionally acknowledging such weaknesses, respond that Spenser's intent was to create a mythic romance, which thus should not be held to standards of literary verisimilitude; the quaint, mannered verse and fantastic nature of the poem, they argue, only reinforce the lushness that is one of the epic's primary attractions. *The Faerie Queene* has also been faulted as having an incoherent narrative structure. Many sections of the poem lack dramatic action, episodes are frequently and jarringly halted short of their resolution, and characters wander in and out for no apparent purpose. Other scholars, however, attribute these weaknesses to the fact that the epic was never finished. Ultimately, the enduring appeal of Spenser's creation lies in its pictorial beauty and metric innovation. The poem is composed in what has come to be known as the Spenserian stanza, consisting of eight iambic pentameters and a final Alexandrine, with the rhyme scheme ababbcbcc; critic's credit the sonorous, stately rhythm of the stanza with establishing the poem's famous dreamlike ambience.

Compared with the magnitude of his achievement in *The Faerie Queene,* all of Spenser's other work is minor, though it shows a considerable range and diversity. *The Shepheardes Calender* (1579) is a series of twelve eclogues, corresponding to each month of the year, written in the pastoral tradition. The *Calender,* like *The Faerie Queene,* is distinguished by linguistic oddities, in this case, rustic dialect. The eclogues range from political satire to the lyrical lamentations of an unrequited lover.· The enthusiastic praise accorded *The Shepheardes Calender* upon its publication has abated somewhat in recent times: the poem now occupies a decidedly minor status. Although C. S. Lewis has dismissed the *Calender* as "pretentious" and "nearly worthless," and although the poem is generally thought lacking in formal and contextual unity, many modern critics have found the *Calender* of interest for the light it sheds on Spenser's perception of his poetic vocation. In the *Calender* and in "Colin Clouts Come Home Againe," a later poem in which Spenser resurrected many of the characters and themes of the *Calender,* Spenser revealed through his persona, Colin Clout, his attitudes towards art, pastoral idealism, and the socio-political world of the Elizabethan court.

Spenser's sequence of love sonnets, the *Amoretti,* is fairly conventional in conception—an expression of the tradition of Petrarch's *Canzoniere* by way of Elizabethan sonneteers. Although critics have noted that the *Amoretti* occasionally displays the linguistic beauty that so distinguishes *The Faerie Queene,* the distinction granted the sonnets lies not so much in felicity of poetic execution as in originality of purpose. The Petrarchan sonnet sequence and its Elizabethan imitations typically conclude with either the death of the beloved or with unfulfilled longing; Spenser's ends with union. The culmination of the *Amoretti* is the "Epithalamion," a celebratory ode of marriage. The "Epithalamion," which describes a wedding day in lavish detail from the bride's awakening to the couple's retirement, is generally thought by modern critics to be Spenser's best work with the sole exception of *The Faerie Queene;* Douglas Bush in 1952 pronounced it "the finest love poem in the language." Notably, the "Epithalamion" differs from *The Faerie Queene* in its introduction of the author's personal emotion, an addition which is believed to immeasurably heighten the beauty and intensity of the poem. John Middleton Murry has surmised that, in this ode, Spenser's primary concern was not, as it usually was, "the making of a beautiful thing," but rather, "the communication of experience."

From the sixteenth century to the twentieth, Spenser's work has maintained a place of distinction in English literature. Spenser's importance and his impact on the development of English poetry have been incalculable: Murry has stated that "the tradition of English poetry is rooted in Spenser"; G. Wilson Knight has called *The Faerie Queene* "a storehouse for poets of the future." But it is the intrinsic merit of his masterpiece that accounts for his lasting attraction; Lewis, in his *Studies in Medieval and Renaissance Literature* (1966) has thus defined the unique quality of *The Faerie Queene:* "It demands of us a child's love of marvels and dread of bogies, a boy's thirst for adventures, a young man's passion for physical beauty. . . . It is of course much more than a fairy-tale, but unless we can enjoy it as a fairy-tale first of all, we shall not really care for it."

(For further information about Spenser's life and works, see *Literature Criticism from 1400 to 1800,* Vol. 5.)

CRITICAL COMMENTARY

WILLIAM HAZLITT
(lecture date 1818)

[A British critic of the first half of the nineteenth century, Hazlitt wrote what was later termed "impressionist" criticism: a deeply personal and subjective methodology that departed from eighteenth-century attempts at setting objective standards for criticism. In the following excerpt, he discusses imagination, allegory, and language in *The Faerie Queene*.]

[Spenser's] poetical temperament was as effeminate as Chaucer's was stern and masculine, was equally engaged in public affairs, and had mixed equally in the great world. So much does native disposition predominate over accidental circumstances, moulding them to its previous bent and purposes! For while Chaucer's intercourse with the busy world, and collision with the actual passions and conflicting interests of others, seemed to brace the sinews of his understanding, and gave to his writings the air of a man who describes persons and things that he had known and been intimately concerned in; the same opportunities, operating on a differently constituted frame, only served to alienate Spenser's mind the more from the "close-pent up" scenes of ordinary life, and to make him "rive their concealing continents," to give himself up to the unrestrained indulgence of "flowery tenderness."

It is not possible for any two writers to be more opposite in this respect. Spenser delighted in luxurious enjoyment; Chaucer, in severe activity of mind. As Spenser was the most romantic and visionary, Chaucer was the most practical of all the great poets, the most a man of business and the world. His poetry reads like history. Everything has a downright reality; at least in the relator's mind. A simile, or a sentiment, is as if it were given in upon evidence. (pp. 31-2)

Spenser, as well as Chaucer, was engaged in active life; but the genius of his poetry was not active: it is inspired by the love of ease, and relaxation from all the cares and business of life. Of all the poets, he is the most poetical. Though much later than Chaucer, his obligations to preceding writers were less. He has in some measure borrowed the plan of his poem (as a number of distinct narratives) from Ariosto; but he has engrafted upon it an exuberance of fancy, and an endless voluptuousness of sentiment, which are not to be found in the Italian writer. Further, Spenser is even more of an inventor in the subject-matter. There is an originality, richness, and variety in his allegorical personages and fictions, which almost vies with the splendour of the ancient mythology. If Ariosto transports us into the regions of romance, Spenser's poetry is all fairyland. In Ariosto, we walk upon the ground, in a company, gay, fantastic, and adventurous enough. In Spenser, we wander in another world, among ideal beings. The poet takes and lays us in the lap of a lovelier nature, by the sound of softer streams, among greener hills and fairer valleys. He paints nature, not as we find it, but as we expected to find it; and fulfils the delightful promise of our youth. He waves his wand of enchantment—and at once embodies airy beings, and throws a delicious veil over all actual objects. The two worlds of reality and of fiction are poised on the wings of his imagination. His ideas, indeed, seem more distinct than his perceptions. He is the painter of abstractions, and describes them with dazzling minuteness. In the Mask of Cupid he makes the God of Love "clap on high his coloured winges *twain*": and it is said of Gluttony, in the Procession of the Passions,

In green vine leaves he was right fitly clad.

At times he becomes picturesque from his intense love of beauty. . . . The love of beauty, however, and not of truth, is the moving principle of his mind; and he is guided in his fantastic delineations by no rule but the impulse of an inexhaustible imagination. He luxuriates equally in scenes of Eastern magnificence or the still solitude of a hermit's cell—in the extremes of sensuality or refinement.

In reading the *Faery Queen,* you see a little withered old man by a wood-side opening a wicket, a giant, and a dwarf lagging far behind, a damsel in a boat upon an enchanted lake, wood-nymphs, and satyrs; and all of a sudden you are transported into a lofty palace, with tapers burning, amidst knights and ladies, with dance and revelry, and song, "and mask, and antique pageantry." (pp. 52-4)

The finest things in Spenser are, the character of Una, in the first book; the House of Pride; the Cave of Mammon, and the Cave of Despair; the account of Memory . . . ; the description of Belphoebe; the story of Florimel and the Witch's son; the Gardens of Adonis, and the Bower of Bliss; the Mask of Cupid; and Colin Clout's vision, in the last book. But some people will say that all this may be very fine, but that they cannot understand it on account of the allegory. They are afraid of the allegory, as if they thought it would bite

---

Principal Works

"Epigrams" and "Sonets" [translator] (poetry) 1569; published in A Theatre for Worldlings

The Shepheardes Calender: Conteyning Twelve Aeglogues Proportionable to the Twelve Monethes (poetry) 1579

*Three Proper, and Wittie, Familiar Letters Lately Passed between Two Universitie Men: Touching the Earthquake in Aprill Last, and Our English Reformed Versifying (letters) 1580

†The Faerie Queene, Disposed into Twelve Bookes Fashioning XII Morall Vertues [Books I-III] (poetry) 1590

Complaints: Containing Sundrie Small Poemes of the Worlds Vanitie (poetry) 1591

Amoretti and Epithalamion (poetry) 1595

Colin Clouts Come Home Againe (poetry) 1595

‡The Faerie Queene, Disposed into Twelve Bookes Fashioning XII Morall Vertues: The Second Part of The Faerie Queene, Containing the Fourth, Fifth, and Sixth Bookes (poetry) 1596

Fowre Hymnes (poetry) 1596

Prothalamion; or, A Spousall Verse (poetry) 1596

§A View of the State of Ireland, Written Dialogue-wise, betweene Eudoxus and Irenaeus (essay) 1633

The Complete Works in Verse and Prose of Edmund Spenser. 10 vols. (poetry, essay, and letters) 1882-84

*This work also includes letters written by Gabriel Harvey.

†This work was not published in its entirety until 1609, when the Two Cantos of Mutabilitie were added.

‡This work includes a revision of the earlier The Faerie Queene, Disposed into Twelve Bookes Fashioning XII Morall Vertues [Books I-III].

§This work was written from 1595-97.

---

them: they look at it as a child looks at a painted dragon, and think it will strangle them in its shining folds. This is very idle. If they do not meddle with the allegory, the allegory will not meddle with them. Without minding it at all, the whole is as plain as a pikestaff. It might as well be pretended that we cannot see Poussin's pictures for the allegory, as that the allegory prevents us from understanding Spenser. For instance, when Britomart, seated amidst the young warriors, lets fall her hair and discovers her sex, is it necessary to know the part she plays in the allegory, to understand the beauty of the following stanza?

And eke that stranger knight amongst the rest
Was for like need enforc'd to disarray.
Tho when as vailed was her lofty crest,
Her golden locks that were in trammels gay
Upbounden, did themselves adown display,
And raught unto her heels like sunny beams
That in a cloud their light did long time stay;
Their vapor faded, shew their golden gleams,
And through the persant air shoot forth their azure streams.

(pp. 56-7)

[In reading such] descriptions, one can hardly avoid being reminded of Ruben's allegorical pictures; but the account of Satyrane taming the lion's whelps and lugging the bear's cubs along in his arms while yet an infant whom his mother so naturally advises to "go seek some other play-fellows," has even more of this high picturesque character. Nobody but Rubens could have painted the fancy of Spenser; and he could not have given the sentiment, the airy dream that hovers over it!

With all this, Spenser neither makes us laugh nor weep. The only jest in his poem is an allegorical play upon words, where he describes Malbecco as escaping in the herd of goats, "by the help of his fayre horns on hight." But he has been unjustly charged with a want of passion and of strength. He has both in an immense degree. He has not indeed the pathos of immediate action or suffering, which is more properly the dramatic; but he has all the pathos of sentiment and romance—all that belongs to distant objects of terror, and uncertain, imaginary distress. His strength, in like manner, is not strength of will or action, of bone and muscle, nor is it coarse and palpable—but it assumes a character of vastness and sublimity seen through the same visionary medium, and blended with the appalling associations of preternatural agency. We need only turn, in proof of this, to the Cave of Despair, or the Cave of Mammon, or to the account of the change of Malbecco into Jealousy. . . . The Cave of Despair is described with . . . gloominess and power of fancy; and the fine moral declamation of the owner of it, on the evils of life, almost makes one in love with death. In the story of Malbecco, who is haunted by jealousy, and in vain strives to run away from his own thoughts—

High over hill and over dale he flies—

the truth of human passion and the preternatural ending are equally striking,—It is not fair to compare Spenser with Shakespeare, in point of interest. A fairer comparison would be with *Comus;* and the result would not be unfavourable to Spenser. There is only one work of the same allegorical kind, which has more interest than Spenser (with scarcely less imagination): and that is the

Pilgrim's Progress. The three first books of the *Faery Queen* are very superior to the three last. One would think that Pope, who used to ask if any one had ever read the *Faery Queen* through, had only dipped into these last. The only things in them equal to the former, are the account of Talus, the Iron Man, and the delightful episode of Pastorella.

The language of Spenser is full, and copious, to overflowing: it is less pure and idiomatic than Chaucer's, and is enriched and adorned with phrases borrowed from the different languages of Europe, both ancient and modern. He was, probably, seduced into a certain licence of expression by the difficulty of filling up the moulds of his complicated rhymed stanza from the limited resources of his native language. This stanza, with alternate and repeatedly recurring rhymes, is borrowed from the Italians. It was peculiarly fitted to their language, which abounds in similar vowel terminations, and is as little adapted to ours, from the stubborn, unaccommodating resistance which the consonant endings of the northern languages make to this sort of endless sing-song.—Not that I would, on that account, part with the stanza of Spenser. We are, perhaps, indebted to this very necessity of finding out new forms of expression, and to the occasional faults to which it led, for a poetical language rich and varied and magnificent beyond all former, and almost all later example. His versification is, at once, the most smooth and the most sounding, in the language. It is a labyrinth of sweet sounds, "in many a winding bout of linked sweetness long drawn out"—that would cloy by their very sweetness, but that the ear is constantly relieved and enchanted by their continued variety of modulation—dwelling on the pauses of the action, or flowing on in a fuller tide of harmony with the movement of the sentiment. It has not the bold dramatic transitions of Shakespeare's blank verse, nor the high-raised tone of Milton's; but it is the perfection of melting harmony, dissolving the soul in pleasure, or holding it captive in the chains of suspense. Spenser was the poet of our waking dreams; and he has invented not only a language, but a music of his own for them. The undulations are infinite, like those of the waves of the sea: but the effect is still the same, lulling the senses into a deep oblivion of the jarring noises of the world from which we have no wish to be ever recalled. (pp. 61-5)

William Hazlitt, "On Chaucer and Spenser," in his *Lectures on the English Poets,* 1818. Reprint by Oxford University Press, 1924, pp. 30-65.

WILLIAM BUTLER YEATS
(essay date 1902)

[An Irish poet, dramatist, and critic, Yeats judged the works of others according to his own poetic values of passion, sincerity, and imagination. In the following excerpt from an essay written in 1902, he assesses Spenser as representative of the transitional period between medieval and modern England.]

When Spenser was buried at Westminister Abbey many poets read verses in his praise, and then threw their verses and the pens that had written them into his tomb. Like him they belonged, for all the moral zeal that was gathering like a London fog, to that indolent, demonstrative Merry England that was about to pass away. Men still wept when they were moved, still dressed themselves in joyous colours, and spoke with many gestures. Thoughts and qualities sometimes come to their perfect expression when they are about to pass away, and Merry England was dying in plays, and in poems, and in strange adventurous men. . . . His *Faerie Queene* was written in Merry England, but when Bunyan wrote in prison the other great English allegory, Modern England had been born. Bunyan's men would do right that they might come some day to the Delectable Mountain, and not at all that they might live happily in a world whose beauty was but an entanglement about their feet. Religion had denied the sacredness of an earth that commerce was about to corrupt and ravish, but when Spenser lived the earth had still its sheltering sacredness. His religion, where the paganism that is natural to proud and happy people had been strengthened by the platonism of the Renaissance, cherished the beauty of the soul and the beauty of the body with, as it seemed, an equal affection. He would have had men live well, not merely that they might win eternal happiness but that they might live splendidly among men and be celebrated in many songs. How could one live well if one had not the joy of the Creator and of the Giver of gifts? He says in his **"Hymn to Beauty"** that a beautiful soul, unless for some stubbornness in the ground, makes for itself a beautiful body, and he even denies that beautiful persons ever lived who had not souls as beautiful. They may have been tempted until they seemed evil, but that was the fault of others. And in his **"Hymn to Heavenly Beauty"** he sets a woman little known to theology, one that he names Wisdom or Beauty, above Seraphim and Cherubim and in the very bosom of God, and in the *Faerie Queene* it is pagan Venus and her lover Adonis who create the forms of all living things and send them out into the world, calling them back again to the gardens of Adonis at their lives' end to rest there, as it seems, two thousand years between life and life. He began in English poetry, despite a temperament that delighted in sensuous beauty alone with perfect delight, that worship of Intellectual Beauty which Shelley carried to a greater subtlety and applied to the whole of life.

The qualities, to each of whom he had planned to give a Knight, he had borrowed from Aristotle and partly Christianised, but not to the forgetting of their heathen birth. The chief of the Knights, who would have combined in himself the qualities of all the others, had Spenser lived to finish the *Faerie Queene,* was King Arthur, the representative of an ancient quality, Magnificence. Born at the moment of change, Spenser had indeed many Puritan thoughts. It has been recorded that he cut his hair short and half regretted his hymns to Love and Beauty. But he has himself told us that the many-headed beast overthrown and bound by Calidor, Knight of Courtesy, was Puritanism itself. Puritanism, its zeal and its narrowness, and the angry suspicion that it had in common with all movements of the ill-educated, seemed no other to him than a slanderer of all fine things. One doubts, indeed, if he could have persuaded himself that there could be any virtue at all without courtesy, perhaps without something of pageant and eloquence. He was, I think, by nature altogether a man of that old Catholic feudal nation, but, like Sidney, he wanted to justify himself to his new masters. He wrote of knights and ladies, wild creatures imagined by the aristocratic poets of the twelfth century, and perhaps chiefly by English poets who had still the French tongue; but he fastened them with allegorical nails to a big barn door of common sense, of merely practical virtue. Allegory itself had risen into general importance with the rise of the merchant class in the thirteenth and fourteenth centuries; and it was natural when that class was about for the first time to shape an age in its image, that the last epic poet of the old order should mix its art with his own long-descended, irresponsible, happy art.

Allegory and, to a much greater degree, symbolism are a natural language by which the soul when entranced, or even in ordinary sleep, communes with God and with angels. They can speak of things which cannot be spoken of in any other language, but one will always, I think, feel some sense of unreality when they are used to describe things which can be described as well in ordinary words. Dante used allegory to describe visionary things, and the first maker of *The Romance of the Rose,* for all his lighter spirits, pretends that his adventures came to him in a vision one May morning; while Bunyan, by his preoccupation with heaven and the soul, gives his simple story a visionary strangeness and intensity: he believes so little in the world, that he takes us away from all ordinary standards of probabili-

ty and makes us believe even in allegory for a while. Spenser, on the other hand, to whom allegory was not, as I think, natural at all, makes us feel again and again that it disappoints and interrupts our preoccupation with the beautiful and sensuous life he has called up before our eyes. It interrupts us most when he copies Langland, and writes in what he believes to be a mood of edification, and the least when he is not quite serious, when he sets before us some procession like a court pageant made to celebrate a wedding or a crowning. One cannot think that he should have occupied himself with moral and religious questions at all. He should have been content to be, as Emerson thought Shakespeare was, a Master of the Revels to mankind. I am certain that he never gets that visionary air which can alone make allegory real, except when he writes out of a feeling for glory and passion. He had no deep moral or religious life. He has never a line like Dante's "Thy Will is our Peace," or like Thomas à Kempis's "The Holy Spirit has liberated me from a multitude of opinions," or even like Hamlet's objection to the bare bodkin. He had been made a poet by what he had almost learnt to call his sins. If he had not felt it necessary to justify his art to some serious friend, or perhaps even to "that rugged forehead," he would have written all his life long, one thinks, of the loves of shepherdesses and shepherds, among whom there would have been perhaps the morals of the dovecot. One is persuaded that his morality is official and impersonal—a system of life which it was his duty to support—and it is perhaps a half understanding of this that has made so many generations believe that he was the first poet laureate, the first salaried moralist among the poets. His processions of deadly sins, and his houses, where the very cornices are arbitrary images of virtue, are an unconscious hypocrisy, an undelighted obedience to the "rugged forehead," for all the while he is thinking of nothing but lovers whose bodies are quivering with the memory or the hope of long embraces. When they are not together, he will indeed embroider emblems and images much as those great ladies of the courts of love embroidered them in their castles; and when these are imagined out of a thirst for magnificence and not thought out in a mood of edification, they are beautiful enough; but they are always tapestries for corridors that lead to lovers' meetings or for the walls of marriage chambers. He was not passionate, for the passionate feed their flame in wanderings and absences, when the whole being of the beloved, every little charm of body and of soul, is always present to the mind, filling it with heroical subtleties of desire. He is a poet of the delighted senses, and his song becomes most beautiful when he writes of those islands of Phaedria and Acrasia, which angered "that rugged forehead," as it seems, but gave to Keats his *Belle Dame sans Merci* and his "perilous seas in faery lands forlorn," and to William Morris his "waters of the wondrous Isle." (pp. 225-35)

William Butler Yeats, "Edmund Spenser," in his *The Cutting of an Agate,* The Macmillan Company, 1912, pp. 213-55.

C. S. LEWIS
(essay date 1936)

[An English novelist and critic, Lewis upheld conservative values in literary criticism, championing a Christian aesthetic and arguing against modern tendencies toward psychological and biographical interpretation. In the following excerpt, he analyzes each book of *The Faerie Queene*, examining elements of allegory, romance, and fantasy in the poem.]

Not everything in [*The Faerie Queene*] is equally allegorical, or even allegorical at all. We shall find that it is Spenser's method to have in each book an allegorical core, surrounded by a margin of what is called "romance of types," and relieved by episodes of pure fantasy. Like a true Platonist he shows us the Form of the virtue he is studying not only in its transcendental unity (which comes at the allegorical core of the book) but also "becoming Many in the world of phenomena." (p. 334)

The subject of the first book is Sanctification—the restoring of the soul to her lost paradisal nature by holiness. This is presented in two interlocked allegories. Una's parents, who represent *homo,* or even, if you like, Adam and Eve, after long exclusion from their native land (which of course is Eden) by the Devil, are restored to it by Holiness whom Truth brings to their aid. That is the first allegory. In the second, we trace the genesis of Holiness; that is, the human soul, guided by Truth, contends with various powers of darkness and finally attains sanctification and beats down Satan under her feet. Truth, rather than Grace, is chosen as the heroine of both actions because Spenser is writing in an age of religious doubt and controversy when the avoidance of error is a problem as pressing as, and in a sense prior to, the conquest of sin: a fact which would have rendered his story uninteresting in some centuries, but which should recommend it to us. This is why forces of illusion and deception such as Archimago and Duessa play such a part in the story; and this is why St. George and Una so easily get separated. Intellectual error, however, is inextricably mixed with moral instability, and the soul's desertion of truth (or the knight's desertion of his lady) has an element of wilful rebellion as well as of illusion. . . . The various temptations with which he contends are, for the most part, easily recognizable. The distinction between Pride and Orgoglio is the only difficulty. In the historical allegory, no doubt, Orgoglio is the dungeons of the Inquisition, but his moral signification is not so obvious. If we remember, however, that he is a blood relation to Disdain, and consider (with our imagination rather than our intellect) the character of both giants, I think we shall get an inkling. Pride and Orgoglio are both pride, but the one is pride within us, the other pride attacking us from without, whether in the form of persecution, oppression, or ridicule. The one seduces us, the other browbeats us. But the utter hopelessness with which St. George, unarmed and newly roused from the fountain of sloth, staggers forward ("Disarmd, disgraste, and inwardly dismayde"), to meet Orgoglio, is not very easily reconciled with this view, and it is by no means unlikely that the giant is a survival from some earlier version of the poem.

This is the allegorical core of the book. Una's adventures are much less allegorical. In a very general sense the lion, the satyrs, and Satyrane represent the world of unspoiled nature, which, in the words of a modern critic [Janet Spens, in her *Spenser's "Faerie Queene": An Interpretation* (1934)], "cannot hold Una: she blesses it and passes on her way." But to go further than this—to expect that Truth parted from the soul could, or should, be allegorized as fully as the soul parted from Truth—is almost certainly a mistake. Satyrane himself is the first of many characters in the poem who are types rather than personifications. He is one of Spenser's happy pictures of the "child of nature." Although he is a knight, we are told that "in vaine glorious frayes he little did delight"—which is a deliberate rejection by Spenser of that essential element of chivalry which had most clearly survived, as the *duello,* into the courtly code of his own time. (pp. 334-36)

It will be noticed that I have made no mention of Prince Arthur. The regrettable truth is that in the unfinished state of the poem we cannot interpret its hero at all. We know from the preface that he personifies Magnificence and is seeking Gloriana, or Glory. But if we consider how little we should know of Britomart from the mere statement that she is Chastity, we shall see that this tells us little about Arthur. . . . Spenser's whole method is such that we have a very dim perception of his characters until we meet them or their archetypes at the great allegorical centres of each book. Amoret, for example, would reveal nothing of her real nature if the Garden of Adonis and the Temple of Venus had been lost. Spenser must have intended a final book on Arthur and Gloriana which would have stood to the whole poem as such central or focal cantos stand to their several books. If we had it we should know what the city of Cleopolis and its tower Panthea really are; we should have the key to the tantalizing history of Elfe and Fay; and we should be much less troubled than we now are by the recollection of Queen Elizabeth throughout the poem. As things are, however, Arthur is inexplicable. . . . Here, at the very outset, we come up against an irremovable obstacle. The poem is not finished. It is a poem of a kind that loses more than most by being unfinished. Its centre, the seat of its highest life, is missing.

Book II is plain sailing. As the theme of Light and Darkness, though present throughout the poem, becomes specially prominent in Book I, so that of Life and Death or Health and Sickness dominates Book II. Its subject is the defence of Health or Nature against various dangers, and the allegoric centre of this book is to be sought in the description, and siege, of the House of Alma—the human soul ruling the healthy body. The dangers are of three kinds. In the first five cantos we meet passions which are the direct and admitted enemies of Nature and "foes to life"—passions of Wrath and Grief. These cantos are full of drought and heat, of "smouldering dust," armours that sparkle fire, blood-red horses, red hair, gnashing teeth, and burning. They contain some of the simplest, but also the most powerful allegory in *The Faerie Queene.* From these we pass on to Phaedria. Phaedria is not an enemy to nature at all. Her charming island (in sharp antithesis to the Bower of Bliss) is the work of "Natures cunning hand"; and if she excludes Guyon's Palmer she excludes Atin as well. She is mirth, rest, recreation—the relaxed will floating in the idle lake, secure against the arduous virtues and the arduous vices alike. Ethically she is evil *per accidens* ["by chance"] and in a given situation: on the natural level, she is not evil at all. From the enemies and the neutral we pass on to the false friends, to the hypertrophies and diseases of natural desires, Mammon and Acrasia. Both are created by Spenser at the height of his power and are among the most obviously poetical passages in *The Faerie Queene.* But he is well aware that the virtue he here presents to us is a dull and pedestrian one to fallen man. That is why Guyon loses his horse in the second canto. It is better that he should be without it, for he had found it difficult to restrain its pace to that of the Palmer and impossible to pull up in the presence of St. George. But Spenser continually reminds us of the weariness of his subsequent journey on foot, and the book is full of allurements to rest. Interwoven with this allegory we have the story of Mordant and Amavia, a romance of types which illustrates opposite kinds of intemperance, and things that are not allegorical at all such as the story of Braggadochio or the sonorous history of the Kings of Britain.

For the purposes of our particular study the third and fourth books of *The Faerie Queene* are by far the most important, for in them Spenser . . . becomes our collaborator and tells the final stages of the history of courtly love. (pp. 336-38)

The subjects of these two books are respectively Chastity and Friendship, but we are justified in treating them as a single book on the subject of love. Chastity,

in the person of Britomart, turns out to mean not virginity but virtuous love: and friends are found to be merely "another sort of lovers" in the Temple of Venus. The Proem to the legend of Friendship deals entirely with "lovers deare debate," and its story is equally concerned with friendship, reconciliation and marriage. In the ninth canto Spenser explicitly classifies Eros, Storgë, and Philia as "three kinds of love." Finally, his conception of love is enlarged so as to include even the harmonies of the inanimate world, and we have the wedding of Thames and Medway. For this all-embracing interpretation of love Spenser, of course, has precedent in ancient philosophy, and specially in the *Symposium.* His subject-matter in these two books is therefore extremely complex: and as, in these same books, the non-allegorical fringe becomes wider and more brilliant than ever, there is some excuse for the bewilderment of those critics (too quick despairers!) who suppose that Spenser has abandoned his original design. But those who have learned to look for the allegorical centres will not go astray. (pp. 338-39)

[The Bower of Bliss is] a place not of lawless loves or even lawless lusts, but of disease and paralysis in appetite itself. . . . [The] Bower is the home not of vicious sexuality in particular, but of vicious Pleasure in general. The poet has selected one kind of pleasure chiefly because it is the only kind that can be treated at length in serious poetry. The Bower is connected with sex at all only through the medium of Pleasure. And this is borne out by the fact—very remarkable to any one well read in previous allegory—that Cupid is never mentioned in the Bower, a clear indication that we are not yet dealing with love. The Bower is not the foe of Chastity but of Continence—of that elementary psychic integration which is presupposed even in unlawful loves. To find the real foe of Chastity, the real portrait of false love, we must turn to Malecasta and Busirane. The moment we do so, we find that Malecasta and Busirane are nothing else than the main subject of this study—Courtly Love; and that Courtly Love is in Spenser's view the chief opponent of Chastity. But Chastity for him means Britomart, married love. The story he tells is therefore part of my story: the final struggle between the romance of marriage and the romance of adultery.

Malecasta lives in Castle Joyeous amid the "courteous and comely glee" of gracious ladies and gentle knights. Somebody must be paying for it all, but one cannot find out who. The Venus in her tapestries entices Adonis "as well that art she knew": we are back in the world of the Vekke and the commandments of Love. In the rooms of the castle there is "dauncing and reveling both day and night," and "Cupid still emongst them kindles lustfull fyres." The six knights with whom Britomart contends at its gate (Gardante, Parlante, and the rest) might have stepped straight out of the

Roman de la Rose, and in the very next stanza the simile of the rose itself occurs. The place is dangerous to spirits who would have gone through the Bower of Bliss without noticing its existence. Britomart gets a flesh wound there, and Holiness himself is glad to be helped in his fight against Malecasta's champions by Britomart; by which the honest poet intends, no doubt, to let us know that even a religious man need not disdain the support which a happy marriage will give him against fashionable gallantry. For Britomart is married love.

Malecasta clearly represents the dangerous attractions of courtly love—the attractions that drew a Surrey or a Sydney. Hers is the face that it shows to us at first. But the House of Busirane is the bitter ending of it. In these vast, silent rooms, dazzling with snakelike gold, and endlessly pictured with "Cupid's warres and cruell battailes," scrawled over with "a thousand monstrous formes" of false love, where Britomart awaits her hidden enemy for a day and a night, shut in, entombed, cut off from the dawn which comes outside "calling men to their daily exercize," Spenser has painted for us an unforgettable picture not of lust but of love—love as understood by the traditional French novel or by Guillaume de Lorris—in all its heartbreaking glitter, its sterility, its suffocating monotony. And when at last the ominous door opens and the Mask of Cupid comes out, what is this but a picture of the deep human suffering which underlies such loves? . . . The Mask, in fact embodies all the sorrows of Isoud among the lepers, and Launcelot mad in the woods, of Guinevere at the stake or Guinevere made nun and penitent, of Troilus waiting on the wall, of . . . Sydney rejecting the love that reaches but to dust; or of Donne writing his fierce poems *from* the house of Busirane soon after Spenser had written *of* it. When Britomart rescues Amoret from this place of death she is ending some five centuries of human experience, predominantly painful. The only thing Spenser does not know is that Britomart is the daughter of Busirane—that his ideal of married love grew out of courtly love.

Who, then, is Amoret? She is the twin sister of Belphoebe and both were begotten by the Sun. . . . And we know that the Sun is an image of the Good for Plato, and therefore of God for Spenser. The first important event in the life of these twins was their adoption by Venus and Diana: Diana the goddess of virginity, and Venus from whose house "all the world derives the glorious features of beautie." Now the circumstances which led up to this adoption are related in one of the most medieval passages in the whole *Faerie Queene*—a *débat* between Venus and Diana; but this *débat* has two remarkable features. In the first place, the Venus who takes part in it is a Venus severed from Cupid, and Cupid, as we have already seen, is associat-

ed with courtly love. . . . We are therefore fully justified in stressing the fact that Venus finds Amoret only because she has lost Cupid, and finally adopts Amoret *instead of* Cupid. The other important novelty is that this *débat* ends with a reconciliation; Spenser is claiming to have settled the old quarrel between Venus and Diana. . . . [Amoret] was taken by Venus to be reared in the Garden of Adonis, guarded by Genius the lord of generation, among happy lovers and flowers (the two are here indistinguishable) whose fecundity never ceases to obey the Divine Command. This was her nursery: her school or university was the Temple of Venus. This is a region neither purely natural, like the Garden, nor artificial in the bad sense, like the Bower of Bliss. . . . Here Amoret no longer grows like a plant, but is committed to the care of Womanhood; the innocent sensuousness of the garden is replaced by "sober Modestie," "comely Curtesie,"

Soft Silence and submisse Obedience,

which are gifts of God and protect His saints "against their foes offence." Indeed the whole island is strongly protected, partly by Nature, and partly by such immemorial champions of maidenhead in the Rose tradition, as Doubt, Delay, and Daunger. But when the lover comes he defeats all these and plucks Amoret from her place among the modest virtues. The struggle in his own mind before he does so, his sense of "Beauty too rich for use, for earth too dear," is a beautiful gift made by the humilities of medieval love poetry to Spenser at the very moment of his victory over the medieval tradition. . . . The natural conclusion is marriage, but Busirane for centuries has stood in the way. That is why it is from the marriage feast that Busirane carries Amoret away, to pine for an indefinite period in his tomblike house. When once Britomart has rescued her thence, the two lovers become one flesh—for that is the meaning of the daring simile of the Hermaphrodite in the original conclusion of Book III. But even after this, Amoret is in danger if she strays from Britomart's side; she will then fall into a world of wild beasts where she has no comfort or guide, and may even become the victim of monsters who live on the "spoile of women."

If it is difficult to write down in prose the *significacio* of all this, the difficulty arises from the fact that the poetic version has almost too much meaning for prose to overtake. Thus, in general, it is plain that Amoret is simply love—begotten by heaven, raised to its natural perfection in the Garden and to its civil and spiritual perfections in the Temple, wrongly separated from marriage by the ideals of courtly gallantry, and at last restored to it by Chastity—as Spenser conceives chastity. (pp. 339-44)

The less allegorical parts group themselves easily enough round this core. The swashbucklers—the Paridells and Blandamours—are an almost literal picture of court life. In Book IV they are the enemies of true friendship; they are the young men, described by Aristotle, who change their friends several times in the same day. In Book III, Paridell wooing Hellenore, is a picture of courtly love in action: he is the *learned* lover and knows all the Ovidian tricks. That is why the one constant element in him is his hatred of Scudamour. Marinell is a sort of pendant to Belphoebe: she represents virginity as an ideal, while he avoids love on prudential grounds, which Spenser disapproves. His marriage with Florimel probably expresses no allegorical relation; it comes in, like the wedding of the rivers, or Arthur's reconciliation of Poeana and Amyas, to illustrate the general theme of the book, which is Reconciliation rather than what we should call Friendship. Concord is for Spenser the resolution of discord: her two sons are Hate and Love, and Hate is the elder. That is why we meet Ate, and her works, long before we meet Concord, and also why the titular heroes of the book are friends who were once foes; and the same theme of reconciliation connects Arthur's activities with the main subject.

In addition to such merely typical adventures, we have, as usual, passages that are quite free from allegory. Such are the beautiful "episode" of Timias and Belphoebe, and the prophecies of Merlin. We also have, so to speak, "islands" of pure allegory such as that of Malbecco or the House of Care, which are not closely connected with the central allegorical action. The two books, taken together, are a kind of central *massif* in *The Faerie Queene,* in which the poet's originality is at its highest and his command (for his own purposes) of the Italian art of interweaving is most perfect. It is very unfortunate that they also contain some of his worst writing; but this must not be taken as proof that he is tiring of his design. It comes mainly from the very simple cause, that in these books Spenser is facing the necessity, incumbent on a professed disciple of Ariosto, of giving us some big, set battle-pieces, and Spenser, like all the Elizabethans, does this kind of thing very badly. It is idle to seek deep spiritual causes for literary phenomena which mere incompetence can explain. (pp. 346-47)

The fifth book is the least popular in *The Faerie Queene.* This is partly the poet's fault, for he has included in it some flat and uninspired passages; but in part it results from the differences between his conception of justice and ours. The modern reader is apt to start from an egalitarian conception; to assume, in fact, that the fair way of dividing a cake between two people is to cut it into two equal pieces. But to this Aristotle, and the most reputable political thinkers between Aristotle's time and Spenser's, would have replied at once "It all depends who the two people are. If A is twice as good a man as B, then obviously justice means giving A twice as much cake as B. For justice is not equality *simpliciter* ["without reserve"] but proportional

equality." . . . The egalitarian giant in Canto II offends against subordination by believing in equality *simpliciter.* The amazon Radigund, who enslaves men and sets them to female tasks, represents another form of insubordination—the "monstrous regiment of women." Apart from its political allusions, this allegory is an attack on uxoriousness—a vice to which the way is easily left open when once we have directed the whole force of romantic passion into marriage, and which is, for Spenser, a form of injustice—a disturbance of the hierarchy of things. For we must not conceal the fact that Spenser, for all his chivalry, is in complete agreement with Milton about the right relations of the sexes, and his picture of Radigund is a good commentary on the fact that Amoret had learned "soft silence and submisse obedience" in the Temple of Venus. The doctrine is not very congenial to modern sentiment; but perhaps Spenser's delineation of the cruelty of Radigund (So hard it is to be a woman's slave), if seasoned with our recollections of Mrs. Proudie or of the Simla memsahibs in Kipling's early work, will go down palatably and profitably enough.

But these considerations do not alter the fact that Artegall is one of the most disagreeable characters in the whole poem. He alienates us from the very beginning by his vindictive ill temper at being defeated in a perfectly fair tournament, and continues to alienate us by his cruelty. And when we reflect on the judicial methods of the time, the statement that his iron page Talus "could reveale all hidden crimes" becomes abominable, for it means that Talus is the rack as well as the axe. In all this there is something I shall not attempt to excuse. Spenser was the instrument of a detestable policy in Ireland, and in his fifth book the wickedness he had shared begins to corrupt his imagination. But while it would be absurd to suggest that Spenser saw Artegall with our eyes, he has none the less made it clear that Artegall is not intended to be perfect. His motto *Salvagesse sans Finesse* ["salvage unceasingly"] warns us that, if he is Justice, he is not meant to be more than a rough justice. . . . Artegall, in fact, is to the whole virtue much as Talus is to Artegall. This fruitful idea ought to have found its full expression in the canto on Mercilla, but Spenser has allowed himself to be carried away by flattery and historical allegory (his "fatal Cleopatra") and that canto is his one great failure in this kind—a failure which paralyzes the whole book because that canto should have been its heart. The actual behaviour of his Mercilla vies with that of Tertullian's *patientia* ["resignation"] for the palm of absurdity:

So did this mightie Ladie, when she saw
Those two strange knights such homage to her
  make,
Bate somewhat of that Majestie and awe
That whylome wont to doe so many quake.

An exquisite Mercy this, that can just velvet her claws for a moment if you gorge her with cream!

The rest of the book needs little comment. It is not, and ought not to be, a favourite, but it contains some excellent passages, such as the vanishing of false Florimel, the fight with Gerioneo, and, above all, the weird scene of Malengin's capture among the mountains.

From this stony plateau—for the fifth book would have been severe even if it had been successful—the sixth leads us down into the gracious valley of Humiliation. Spenser himself seems to pause at the brow of the barren country and look down with relief at this delightful land, spacious and wide, and sprinkled with such sweet variety. The greatest mistake that can be made about this book is to suppose that Callidore's long delay among the shepherds is a pastoral truancy of Spenser's from his moral intention. On the contrary, the shepherd's country and Mount Acidale in the midst of it are the core of the book, and the key to Spenser's whole conception of Courtesy. As any one who has read *The Faerie Queene* carefully will expect, Courtesy, for the poet, has very little connexion with court. . . . Since the virtue, as Spenser saw it, is one that does not exist in the modern scheme of values at all, we have to represent it by combining those virtues we do know. We may say for the moment that it is a combination of charity and humility, in so far as these are social, not theological, virtues. But there is another important aspect of it to be noticed. According to Spenser, courtesy, in its perfect form, comes by nature; moral effort may produce a decent substitute for everyday use, which deserves praise, but it will never rival the real courtesy. . . . We are to conceive of courtesy as the poetry of conduct, an "unbought grace of life" which makes its possessor immediately loveable to all who meet him, and which is the bloom (as Aristotle would say)—the supervenient perfection—on the virtues of charity and humility.

Around this central conception we find the usual variety of allegories, romance of types, and pure fiction. The episode of Disdaine and Mirabella is remarkable for its close approximation to the oldest models. Turpine and Blandina are Aristotelian—the boor and the flatterer, representing the defect and excess which lie on either side of the virtue. The courtly life which Meliboe condemns, and the brutal life of Serena's or Pastorella's captors, are arranged according to the same scheme—the one being a sophistication of nature, in whose humilities true courtesy dwells, and the other being a lapse below nature, as nature was defined by Aristotle. The noble savage I have already referred to. He and the Hermit are in a sense opposites: one emphasizes the natural aspect of courtesy, the other its spiritual aspect—its affinity with the sterner or more awful forms of the good. The wise old man, full of true cour-

THE FAERIE QVEENE.

Difpófed into twelue books,
Fashioning
XII. Morall vertues.

LONDON
Printed for William Ponfonbie.
1 5 9 0.

Title page of the first edition of *The Faerie Queene,* 1590.

tesy without "forged shows" such as "fitter beene for courting fools," happy as "carelesse bird in cage," and gently teaching his penitents that the Blatant Beast cannot do you much permanent injury unless something is wrong within, is one of the loveliest of Spenser's religious figures. The whole book is full of sweet images of humility; Calidore and Priscilla carrying the wounded knight, Calepine looking after the baby, the Salvage man fumblingly doing his best with the harness of Serena's horse. (pp. 347-52)

The sixth book is distinguished from its predecessors by distinct traces of the influence of Malory (a welcome novelty) and by the high proportion of unallegorical, or faintly allegorical, scenes. This last feature easily gives rise to the impression that Spenser is losing grip on the original conception of his poem; and it suggests a grave structural fault in *The Faerie Queene* in so far as the poem begins with its loftiest and most solemn book and thence, after a gradual descent, sinks away into its loosest and most idyllic. But this criticism overlooks the fact that the poem is unfinished. The proportion of allegoric core to typical, or purely fictional, fringe has varied all along from book to book; and the loose texture of the sixth is a suitable relief after the very high proportion of pure allegory in the fifth. The only fragment of any succeeding book which we have proves that the poem was to rise from the valley of humiliation into allegory as vast and august as that of the first book.

In the poem as a whole our understanding is limited by the absence of the allegorical centre, the union of Arthur and Gloriana. In the Mutabilitie cantos the opposite difficulty occurs—we have there the core of a book without the fringe. The fact that this should be so is interesting because it suggests (what is likely enough *a priori*) that Spenser was in the habit of writing his "cores" first and then draping the rest round them. But we lose much by not seeing the theme of change and permanence played out on the lower levels of chivalrous adventure. It is obvious, of course, that the adventures would have illustrated the theme of constancy and inconstancy, and that the mighty opposites would have appeared in the form of Mutabilitie and the Gods only at the central allegorical gable of the book—which is the bit we have. It is obvious too, that the Titaness, despite her beauty, is an evil force. Her very name "bold Alteration," and the fact that she rises against the gods, put her at once among the enemies for any reader who understands Spenser's conceptions of health, concord, and subordination. . . . She is, in fact, Corruption, and since corruption, "subjecting the creature to vanity," came in with the Fall, Spenser practically identifies his Titaness with sin, or makes her the force behind the sin of Adam. . . . The enemies of Mutability are, first, the gods, and then *Nature.* Taken together they represent the Divine order in the universe—the concord, the health, the justice, the harmony, the Life, which, under many names, is the real heroine of the whole poem. If we take them apart, however, then the gods represent precisely what we should call "nature," the laws of the phenomenal universe. That is why the Titaness so far prevails with them—they are that world over which, even in the highest regions, she asserts some claim. But *Nature,* taken apart, is the ground of the phenomenal world. The reverence with which Spenser approaches this symbol contrasts favorably with the hardier attempts of Tasso and Milton to bring God, undisguised, upon the stage—and indeed it would be a pleasant task, if this chapter were not already too long, to show how much more religious a poem *The Faerie Queene* is than the *Paradise Lost.* (pp. 353-55)

The modern reader is tempted to inquire whether Spenser . . . equates God with Nature: to which the answer is, "Of course not. He was a Christian, not a pantheist." His procedure . . . would have been well understood by all his contemporaries: the practice of using mythological forms to hint theological truths was well established and lasted as late as the composition of *Comus.* It is, for most poets and in most poems, by far the best method of writing poetry which is religious without being devotional—that is, without being an act of worship to the reader. (pp. 355-56)

To praise this fragment seems almost an impertinence. In it all the powers of the poet are more happily united than ever before; the sublime and the ridiculous, the rarified beauties of august mythology and the homely glimpses of daily life in the procession of the months, combine to give us an unsurpassed impression of the harmonious complexity of the world. And in these cantos Spenser seems to have soared above all the usual infirmities of his style. His verse has never been more musical, his language never so strong and so sweet. Such poetry, coming at the very end of the six books, serves to remind us that the existing *Faerie Queene* is unfinished, and that the poet broke off, perhaps, with many of his greatest triumphs still ahead. Our loss is incalculable; at least as great as that we sustained by the early death of Keats. (p. 357)

People find a "likeness" or "truth" to life in Shakespeare because the persons, passions and events which we meet in his plays are like those which we meet in our own lives: he excels, in fact, in what the old critics called "nature," or the probable. When they find nothing of the sort in Spenser, they are apt to conclude that he has nothing to do with "life"—that he writes that poetry of escape or recreation which (for some reason or other) is so intensely hated at present. But they do not notice that *The Faerie Queene* is "like life" in a different sense, in a much more literal sense. When I say that it is like life, I do not mean that the places and people in it are like those which life produces. I mean precisely what I say—that it is like life itself, not like the products of life. . . . The things we read about in it are not like life, but the experience of reading it is like living. The clashing antitheses which meet and resolve themselves into higher unities, the lights streaming out from the great allegorical *foci* to turn into a hundred different colours as they reach the lower levels of complex adventure, the adventures gathering themselves together and revealing their true nature as we draw near the *foci*, the constant re-appearance of certain basic ideas, which transform themselves without end and yet ever remain the same (eterne in mutability), the unwearied variety and seamless continuity of the whole—all this is Spenser's true likeness to life. (p. 358)

C. S. Lewis, "The Faerie Queene," in his *The Allegory of Love: A Study in Medieval Tradition,* Oxford at the Clarendon Press, 1936, pp. 297-360.

VIRGINIA WOOLF
(essay date 1941?)

[A British novelist and literary critic, Woolf greatly influenced the development of modern literature through her stylistically innovative fiction, numerous critical essays in the *Times Literary Supplement,* and establishment of the literary circle known as the "Bloomsbury Group." In the following excerpt from an essay discovered and published posthumously, she examines the timeless appeal of *The Faerie Queene.*]

The Faery Queen, it is said, has never been read to the end; no one has ever wished *Paradise Lost,* it is said, a word longer; and these remarks however exaggerated probably give pleasure, like a child's laugh at a ceremony, because they express something we secretly feel and yet try to hide. Dare we then at this time of day come out with the remark that *The Faery Queen* is a great poem? So one might say early rising, cold bathing, abstention from wine and tobacco are good; and if one said it, a blank look would steal over the company as they made haste to agree and then to lower the tone of the conversation. Yet it is true. Here are some general observations made by one who has gone through the experience, and wishes to urge others, who may be hiding their yawns and their polite boredom, to the same experience.

The first essential is, of course, not to read *The Faery Queen.* Put it off as long as possible. Grind out politics; absorb science; wallow in fiction; walk about London; observe the crowds; calculate the loss of life and limb; rub shoulders with the poor in markets; buy and sell; fix the mind firmly on the financial columns of the newspapers, weather; on the crops; on the fashions. At the mere mention of chivalry shiver and snigger; detest allegory; revel in direct speech; adore all the virtues of the robust, the plain-spoken; and then, when the whole being is red and brittle as sandstone in the sun, make a dash for *The Faery Queen* and give yourself up to it.

But reading poetry is a complex art. The mind has many layers, and the greater the poem the more of these are roused and brought into action. They seem, too, to be in order. The faculty we employ upon poetry at the first reading is sensual; the eye of the mind opens. And Spenser rouses the eye softly and brilliantly with his green trees, his pearled women, his crested and plumed knights. (Then we need to use our sympathies, not the strong passions, but the simple wish to go with our knight and his lady to feel their heat and cold, and

their thirst and hunger.) And then we need movement. Their figures, as they pass along the grass track, must reach a hovel or a palace or find a man in weeds reading his book. That too is gratified. And then living thus with our eyes, with our legs and arms, with the natural quiet feelings of liking and disliking tolerantly and gently excited, we realise a more complex desire that all these emotions should combine. There must be a pervading sense of belief, or much of our emotion will be wasted. The tree must be part of the knight; the knight of the lady. All these states of mind must support one another, and the strength of the poem will come from the combination, just as it will fail if at any point the poet loses belief.

But it may be said, when a poet is dealing with Faery Land and the supernatural people who live there, belief can only be used in a special sense. We do not believe in the existence of giants and ogres, but in something that the poet himself believed them to represent. What then was Spenser's belief, when he wrote his poem? He has himself declared that the "general intention and meaning" of *The Faery Queen* was "to fashion a gentleman or noble person in vertuous and noble discipline." It would be absurd to pretend that we are more than intermittently conscious of the poet's meaning. Yet as we read, we half-consciously have the sense of some pattern hanging in the sky, so that without referring any of the words to a special place, they have that meaning which comes from their being parts of a whole design, and not an isolated fragment of unrelated loveliness. The mind is being perpetually enlarged by the power of suggestion. Much more is imagined than is stated. And it is due to this quality that the poem changes, with time, so that after four hundred years it still corresponds to something which we, who are momentarily in the flesh, feel at the moment.

The question asks itself, then, how Spenser, himself imprisoned in so many impediments of circumstance, remote from us in time, in speech, in convention, yet seems to be talking about things that are important to us too? Compare, for example, his perfect gentleman with Tennyson's Arthur. Already, much in Tennyson's pattern is unintelligible; an easy butt for satire. Among living writers again, there is none who is able to display a typical figure. Each seems limited to one room of the human dwelling. But with Spenser, though here in this department of our being, we seem able to unlock the door and walk about. We miss certain intensities and details; but on the other hand we are uncabined. We are allowed to give scope to a number of interests, delights, curiosities, and loves that find no satisfaction in the poetry of our own time. But though it would be easy to frame a reason for this and to generalize about the decay of faith, the rise of machines, the isolation of the human being, let us, however, work from the opposite point of view. In reading

The Faery Queen the first thing, we said, was that the mind has different layers. It brings one into play and then another. The desire of the eye, the desire of the body, desires for rhythm, movement, the desire for adventure—each is gratified. And this gratification depends upon the poet's own mobility. He is alive in all his parts. He scarcely seems to prefer one to another. We are reminded of the old myth of the body which has many organs, and the lesser and the obscure are as important as the kingly and important.

Here at any rate the poet's body seems all alive. A fearlessness, a simplicity that is like the movement of a naked savage possesses him. He is not merely a thinking brain; he is a feeling body, a sensitive heart. He has hands and feet, and, as he says himself, a natural chastity, so that some things are judged unfit for the pen. "My chaster muse for shame doth blush to write." In short, when we read *The Faery Queen,* we feel that the whole being is drawn upon, not merely a separate part.

To say this is to say that the conventions that Spenser uses are not enough to cut us off from the inner meaning. And the reason soon makes itself apparent. When we talk of the modern distaste for allegory, we are only saying that we prefer our qualities in another form. The novelist uses allegory; that is to say, when he wishes to expound his characters, he makes them think; Spenser impersonated his psychology. Thus if the novelist now wished to convey his hero's gloom, he would tell us his thoughts; Spenser creates a figure called Despair. He has the fullest sense of what sorrow is. But he typifies it; he creates a dwelling, an old man who comes out of the house and says I cannot tell; and then the figure of Despair with his beautiful elegy. Instead of being prisoned in one breast we are shown the outer semblance. He is working thus on a larger, freer, more depersonalized scale. By making the passions into people, he gives them an amplitude. And who shall say that this is the less natural, the less realistic? For the most exact observer has to leave much of his people's minds obscure.

Once we get him out of his private mythology, there is no mythology which can personify his actions. We wish to convey delight and have to describe an actual garden, here and now; Spenser at once calls up a picture of nymphs dancing, youth, maidens crowned. And yet it is not pictorial merely. Nothing is more refreshing, nothing serves more to sting and revive us than the spray of fresh hard words, little colloquialisms, tart green words that might have been spoken at dinner, joining in easily with the more stately tribe. But such externality is impossible to us, because we have lost our power to create symbols. Spenser's ability to use despair in person depends on his power to create a world in which such a figure draws natural breath, living breath. He has his dwelling at the centre of a universe which offers him the use of dragons, knights, magic; and all the company that exist about them; and flowers and dawn and sunset. All this was still just within his reach. He could believe in it, his public could believe in it, sufficiently to make it serviceable. It was, of course, just slipping from his grasp. That is obvious from his own words. His poem, he says, will be called the abundance of an idle brain. His language, too, oddly compounded of the high-flown and the vernacular, was just then at the turn. On the one hand we have the old smooth conventions—Tithonus, Cynthia, Phoebus, and the rest; on the other fry and rascal and losel, the common speech that was current on the lips of the women at the door. He was not asking the reader to adopt an unnatural pose; only to think poetically. And the writer's faith is still effective. We are removed four hundred years from Spenser; and the effort to think back into his mood requires some adjustment, some oblivion; but there is nothing false in what is to be done; it is easier to read Spenser than to read William Morris.

The true difficulty lies elsewhere. It lies in the fact that the poem is a meditation, not a dramatization. At no point is Spenser under the necessity of bringing his characters to the surface; they lack the final embodiment which is forced so drastically upon the playwright. They sink back into the poet's mind and thus lack definition. He is talking about them; they are not using their own words. Hence the indistinctness which leads, as undoubtedly it does lead, to monotony. The verse becomes for a time a rocking-horse; swaying up and down; a celestial rocking-horse, whose pace is always rhythmical and seemly, but lulling, soporific. It sings us to sleep; it lulls the teeth of the wind. On no other terms, however, could we be kept in being. And to compensate we have the quality of that mind; the sense that we are confined in one continuous consciousness, which is Spenser's; that he has saturated and enclosed this world, that we live in a great bubble blown from the poet's brain. Yet if it ignores our own marks, houses, chimneys, roads, the multitudinous details which serve like signposts or features to indicate to us where our emotions lie, it is not a private world of fantasy. Here are the qualities that agitate living people at the moment; spite, greed, jealousy, ugliness, poverty, pain; Spenser in his poet's castle was as acutely aware of the rubs and tumbles of life as the living, but by virtue of his poetry blew them away into the higher air. So we feel not shut in, but freed; and take our way in a world which gives expression to sensation more vigorously, more exactly than we can manage for ourselves in the flesh. It is a world of astonishing physical brilliance and intensity; sharpened, intensified as objects are in a clearer air; such as we see them, not in dreams, but when all the faculties are alert and vigorous; when the stuffing and the detail have been brushed aside; and we see the bone and the symmetry; now in a landscape, in Ireland or in Greece; and now when we think of ourselves, under the more intense ray of poetry; under its sharper, its lovelier light. (pp. 14-18)

Virginia Woolf, "The Faery Queen," in her *Collected Essays, Vol. I,* edited by Leonard Woolf, Harcourt Brace Jovanovich, 1967, pp. 14-18.

ALASTAIR FOWLER
(essay date 1977)

[In the following excerpt, Fowler surveys Spenser's non-epic poetry.]

[*The Shepherd's Calendar*] shows a high sense of control, and yet an astonishing freedom in the treatment of genre. It is far from mere imitation or combination of Theocritus, Virgil, Mantuan and Marot. Indeed, considered historically, its achievement is so considerable as to make it a watershed on any map of English verse.

Spenser enlarged the pastoral tradition in several ways. Renaissance eclogues by Mantuan and Barclay had already treated moral or religious matters: pastoral could be microcosmic and satiric rather than idyllic. Spenser took up this option and invested in it heavily. The landscape that he makes a mirror of his shepherd's plight is "barren ground, whom winter's wrath hath wasted": a land suffering from adverse weather, wolves and disease. In fact, it is real country. And he introduces many fresh images from nature (such as the oak's top "bald and wasted with worms" or the bee "working her formal rooms in waxen frame"), besides many country phrases not previously heard in serious poetry.

Most creative of all is his approach to the structure. Instead of the usual collection of independent "eclogues" (the term anciently implied separateness), Spenser has made a single work, unified by the structural principle of the natural year, and of seasons that symbolize stages in human life. As Pope noted, "the addition he has made of a calendar to his ecologues is very beautiful." The calendrical form not only holds the eclogues together, but contributes to their special character of endless variety combined with complex, elusive order. It works multifariously: in the changing weather; in seasonal customs (April's flower gathering was the occupation for that month by the conventions of visual art); explicitly astronomical imagery (Sol appears in July, the month of his own sign Leo, "making his way between the Cup, / and golden Diadem"); and even in physical proportions (May is by far the longest eclogue, since the sun was known to stay longer in Gemini than in any other sign). Spenser also achieved controlled variety by varying the metre, all the way from rough alliterative lines to the gentle, grave stateliness of November's elegy for Dido. . . . (pp. 12-13)

Inset songs and fables introduce farther variation. Then there is the alternation of three modes or categories ("plaintive," "moral" and "recreative"); and the interweaving of three large subjects: love, poetry, and religious politics. The command with which genres are deployed makes for admiration, even where this is not accompanied with understanding or enjoyment. Everything seems in scale, and orchestrated; giving a sense of various modes of life in harmony. January's love complaint gives way to February's *débat* between youth and age, which encloses (and perhaps underlies too) the fable of an episcopal oak and a Puritan briar. March offers an exploit of Cupid; April, an inset ode in praise of Elizabeth, with some delicately Skeltonic flower poetry; and May, a beast fable and more controversy.

The poetic statement made on this complex instrument is itself complex. For one thing, the shepherds enact a *roman-à-clef,* to which the key has been lost. Algrin is Grindal and Hobbinol Gabriel Harvey; but others remain unidentified, even with the help of fashionably elaborate annotation by "E. K." (himself unknown). Moreover, some of the roles are multivalent. Thus, besides being a *persona* for Spenser, Colin Clout is a highly idealized laureate (combining poetic names from Skelton and Marot). Tityrus is both Virgil and Chaucer. And Pan figures severally as Henry VIII, as the Pope, and as Christ. Nevertheless, the topical allegory is probably not intricate: Spenser seems to have tended to political simplicity as much as to intellectual subtlety. (pp. 13-14)

The *Calendar*'s second half becomes increasingly dark, the secular idyll more and more plainly illusion. Art's solace now replaces that of nature. But the mirror of art, which itself mirrors nature, brings deeper disenchantments still. October questions the use of poetry and even the possibility of literary life. Its talk of war contradicts the olive coronal of April, the matching month (with sign in opposition) of the *Calendar*'s first half. To lighten this gloom there emerges the theme of grace. In September Diggon Davie repents, in December Colin himself. Indeed, one might see the whole *Calendar* as a confession of Colin's developing religious consciousness: as his palinode or retraction from earlier secularity. But the poem is more inclusive, more Chaucerian perhaps, than this would suggest. It finds room, after all, for natural beauty, for the worldly Palinode, for the retired Hobbinol. And it is the reformer Piers who overstates his case. The *Calendar* leaves us, in the end, with a sense of manifold fictive worlds, all comprehended in Spenser's detached vision of mutability. (pp. 14-15)

"Astrophel: a Pastoral Elegy" appeared as the framing introduction to a volume of elegies on Sidney.

Certainly later than 1586, and probably later than 1590, it is a finer work than most of *The Shepherd's Calendar;* although it has not usually been valued so highly. The first part (lines 1-216) relates, under the allegory of a boar-hunt, Sidney's death from a wound received at the battle of Zutphen (1586). Astrophel is gored by one of "the brutish nation" (Spanish oppressors); mourned by his widow; and metamorphosed to a flower. This part, while always felicitous, preserves so impersonal a tone as to seem now a shade pallid, a little too consciously Bionesque. It is another matter with the Lay of Clorinda. This part, exactly half as long as the first— the proportions of harmony—purports to give the mourning song of Sidney's sister Mary, Countess of Pembroke. It is a deeply serious expression of grief, from which Milton learnt for "Lycidas." Who is the mourner to address? She can hope for comfort neither from men nor from gods ("From them comes good, from them comes also ill"); so that she addresses her complaint to herself:

> The woods, the hills, the rivers shall resound
> The mournful accent of my sorrow's ground. . . .

The resonance of *ground* ("ground-bass"; "basis") is characteristic of the Lay's self-referring style, which can be poignant—as in "The fairest flower . . . Was Astrophel; that *was,* we all may rue." The resolution in this second part is deeper and darker: Clorinda reflects that when we grieve we may be self-regarding, "Mourning in others, our own miseries." Sidney is better where he is. If this part was by Mary herself (as some have suggested), she wrote a better poem than Spenser on this occasion.

In December 1591, from Kilcolman, Spenser dedicated to Sir Walter Raleigh **"Colin Clout's Come Home Again,"** a pastoral eclogue about a recent visit to court. . . . [The poem's] engaging method is that of general conversation, with no fewer than ten shepherds and shepherdesses interrupting and questioning Colin. These familiar exchanges establish a sense of Spenser's social and literary circle. They also, by their distancing or alienating effect, allow transitions through a wide range of tones, from the strangely exalted to the quietly humorous. The humour of Colin's account of his voyage is quite broad: sea ("A world of waters heaped up on high"), ships ("Glued together with some subtle matter") and mythologized admirals (Triton and Proteus) are consistently described as they might appear to an innocent, quite unironic shepherd's eye. (pp. 16-18)

Most good eclogues are deeper than they look; and this one, probably the longest and most complex in the language, is no exception. It has an elaborate symmetrical structure to reflect its various but carefully balanced moods. There is even an inset eclogue, an account of a previous conversation with Raleigh "the Shepherd of the Ocean," in which the narrative's dou-

bly reported status expresses the remoteness of a primitive river-myth of sexual rivalry in the far past. The first half is divided between nature (the watery wilderness; wild Ireland) and art (epitomized by a catalogue of England's twelve chief poets). This passage, where Spenser authoritatively reviews his literary milieu and freely reveals his tastes, has an interest similar to that of, say, Auden's *Letter from Iceland.* Most praise goes to Daniel and Alabaster (both named), to Astrophel, to Alcyon (Sir Arthur Gorges) and to the mysterious Aetion. The second half answers with a catalogue of twelve ladies, courteously praised, and a lofty encomium of the Queen. Why then did Colin ever leave the court? His reply offsets the gallantry with a sharp attack on the court's incivility: "it is no sort of life," and all its glory is "but smoke, that fumeth soon away." Hobbinol speaks up for Leicester, giving a well-informed review of his patronage programme; but Colin responds with renewed attacks, this time on the court's immorality.

All this has been seen as Spenser's ambivalence; and so in a way it may have been, in personal terms. But the poem's effect seems not so much ambiguous as poised. Peaceful England is excellent, by comparison with disordered Ireland: the court is frivolous, by comparison with true civility. . . . For the rest, the poem glances at several of the main interests of Spenser's mature work: cosmogonic myth; a metaphysic of "Beauty the burning lamp of heaven's light"; and a passionate theology of love, with a myth of the Androgynous Venus. He condemns the court's lewdness not from a puritanical standpoint, but because it profanes the "mighty mysteries" of love, "that dread lord." The poem's range of feeling is immense: no work gives a better sense of the possibilities of eclogue. (pp. 18-19)

[In *Amoretti* and **"Epithalamion"**], Spenser lays aside the pastoral weeds of Colin Clout to sing in his own person, as the lover of Elizabeth Boyle. . . . The *Amoretti* can easily seem low pressure work, lacking the dramatic intensity of Sidney's *Astrophel and Stella.* However, interest grows when one appreciates how far Spenser's quieter virtues and more deeply poetic qualities have been missed. Take *Amoretti* 18, for example, in which the lover complains that whereas "The rolling wheel . . . The hardest steel in tract of time doth tear" and raindrops wear the "firmest flint," yet he cannot move his lady. Stock images of obduracy; but how originally and deceptively they are put to work. Is the lady really discouraging? If tears are "but water," then the proverb holds, and she will yield: only if tears contrasted with rain, would she be unmoved. Similarly when she "*turns* herself to laughter," who now is "the rolling wheel" and who "doth still remain"? Again, what association have flint and steel together, but kindled fire? The poetic indirection here is quite unlike anything in the other sonneteers of Spenser's time.

And in deeper ways too he is unlike them. Indeed, he came late enough in the vogue—after a dozen other English sonnet sequences—to have to offer something different. Shakespeare responded to a similar challenge by writing sonnets that seem to be about friendship and jealousy. But Spenser's are not about passion at all, in the ordinary sense, but about a love that ends happily, in marriage: the British romantic love, mingling friendship with sexual desire, in praise of which he wrote at greater length in *The Faerie Queen*. The lover of the *Amoretti* (partly followed by the reader) gets to know Elizabeth Boyle well, forming a full personal relation with her. And a keenly intelligent, witty person she is—an Elizabeth Bennett rather than a Penelope Rich—with a firm, unmistakeable character. Unlike the usual Petrarchist lady, who is a trigger of passion and little else, Elizabeth does not wound with Cupid's darts, but calms passion's storm and, characterized herself by "goodly temperature" frames and tempers her lover's feelings too. Even after they are mutually committed, in 84, we hear of her "too constant stiffness." This intense but tender courtship of a young girl by a middle aged lover has the air of reality. . . . Their love is deep, but too serious, too responsible, for passion.

Nevertheless, Elizabeth must receive every tribute usually paid to a slavishly worshipped sonneteer's goddess. In performing this contract Spenser shows an astonishing capacity to fulfil the forms of love complaint, and yet all the time to be free from them, above them—not so much through irony or travesty (although these are sometimes not far away) as through the direct, open refusal of conventional literary attitudes. To the latter, he prefers the more complex human comedy. Sometimes, it is true, he carries the Petrarchist commonplaces far enough towards absurdity to expose their false logic; as in 32: "What then remains but I to ashes burn . . . ?" But more often the commonplaces—the fire and ice, the tyrant and captive, the storm and cruel tigress—are taken up with just a hint of distancing humour, a bantering tone or self-deprecating smile, to remind us that they belong to only one of the ways of wooing. The lover knows Elizabeth too well to think that she is really a tigress (in that way, at least). Not that the pains of love are merely acted, in a sense that would make them unreal. Indeed, where the idea of acting becomes most explicit, in the theatrical conceit of 54, the lady—who as unmoved spectator does not act—sits admonished: she is less than alive: "a senseless stone." Alternatively, the commonplaces may be taken up seriously but transformed. . . . There is a tenderness and reciprocity of feeling here that would be impossible to match anywhere else in the Renaissance sonnet. (pp. 19-22)

Amoretti may fascinate as an interesting departure from the usual sequence, or as a shorter treatment of themes developed in *The Faerie Queen*. But "Epithalamion" is unique. Nothing shows Spenser's creativity better than this poem, which most agree to be the finest major ode in English, and to be surpassed in ancient literature, if at all, only by Pindar. Classical comparisons are inevitable, because Spenser here invented for English literature the humanist ceremonial mode that was to be so important for Drayton, Herrick and others—and carried it at once to its greatest height. Like Catullus' *Carmina* 61, Spenser's poem moves in festal exaltation through the events of a wedding day. But its structure is very different; rising as it does through a crescendo of gathering voices and sounds and excitement to the roaring organs and public affirmation of the marriage service at the altar, in the central two stanzas or strophes; before the feasting, the public "bedding" of the bride, consummation and soft recession into the silence and darkness of the night. Each stage is due and accepted. . . . Throughout, mythological imagery mingles with real, external with psychological. Indeed, the comprehensiveness takes in even negative feelings, such as dread of an "affray," and sexual fears of "Medusa's mazeful head." Spenser's robust yet sensitive personal address is unflinchingly inclusive, as he faces both day and unconscious night in the ritual of love. His ceremony remains reverent; yet it affirms nature and finds authenticity in the role of Jupiter, spouse of Night. These and other deep archetypes and powers are recognized and profoundly composed: the *Horae*, the *Gratiae*, the *amorini* of passion, Cynthia the chaste destroyer yet patroness of childbirth, and, in the one stanza, Juno foundress of marriage and female genius, together with Genius himself, god of pleasure and generation. As Spenser invokes them in turn, or turns from one wedding scene to another, he dwells on each in such a way that the stanzas acquire their own characters and modalities. They are like the dances of a suite. Now all is private communing with the "learned sisters"; now expectant bachelors wait for Hymen's torchlit masque to move off; now pristine garlanded "nymphs" make final arrangements. One stanza will be a blazon of Elizabeth's beauties admired by all ("lips like cherries charming men to bite"): the next a mysterious praise of her chaste inner character. The poem's movement through this variety is fluid but calm and firm and sure. It is as if everything had its inevitable place.

And so, in numerological terms, it had. The spatial disposition of **"Epithalamion"** mimes with extraordinary precision the astronomical events of the day it celebrates. Thus the 24 stanzas represent its 24 hours, with night falling at the right point for St Barnabas' Day, the summer solstice, "the longest day in all the year." Then, after Stanza 16, the refrain changes from positive to negative: "The woods no more shall answer, nor your echo ring." And the *canzone*-like stanzas consist of pentameters and occasional trimeters, with the long lines numbering just 365 to represent the days of the year, during which the sun completes his journey round the 24 sidereal hours. The ceremony of time has never been realized so fully as in this most musical of Spenser's poems. It is indeed an "endless monument" to the poignantly short time of his day. Yet before the end it has carried the torches of its masque up to join the "thousand torches flaming bright" in the temple of the gods. It aspires to commemorate an anticipated cosmic event, addition to the communion of saints, eventual "stellification." (pp. 23-5)

["**Prothalamion,**"] written for an aristocratic betrothal, has similar ceremonial qualities and a form almost as highly wrought. It too is a masterpiece of occasional art in the grand mannerist style. But, in spite of autobiographical references to "old woes," it is more public, more philosophical and harder at first to warm to. Only after prolonged consideration and the effort of attending to its closely overdetermined images does its profundity emerge. It not only sums up the whole river

epithalamium genre, but sings the mutability of the height of life. Spenser wrote other short works, notably the medievalizing satire "**Mother Hubberd's Tale**" and the lofty Christian-Platonic *Hymns*. The former is not dull; but neither does it show Spenser to have been a great satirist. As for the *Hymns*, they challenge more attention, as a vastly ambitious undertaking, a poetic theology of love and generation. Their extreme difficulty (and the correspondingly glorious opportunity they offer to the commentator) is not their only interest for Spenserians. They cast much cloudy light on Spenser's unexpected, syncretistic thinking. But this is not enough to make them great poems. Whether their metaphysical puzzles yield to solution or remain attributed to blunders, the *Hymns* must be counted noble failures. When all is said and done (and much has still to be said, for the love poems particularly), the work in which Spenser chiefly lives is *The Faerie Queen*. (p. 25)

Alastair Fowler, in his *Edmund Spenser,* edited by Ian Scott-Kilvert, The British Council, 1977, 57 p.

SOURCES FOR FURTHER STUDY

Berger, Harry, Jr., ed. *Spenser: A Collection of Critical Essays.* Englewood Cliffs, N.J.: Prentice-Hall, 1968, 182 p.

Collection of ten critical views of Spenser. The work is divided into two sections: the minor poems and *The Faerie Queene.*

Giamatti, A. Bartlett. *Play of Double Senses: Spenser's "Faerie Queene."* Englewood Cliffs, N.J.: Prentice-Hall, 1975, 140 p.

Critical study of Spenser, divided into two sections: the first illuminates the contexts framing Spenser's epic poem—including biographical data, the epic genre and Spenser's relation to Geoffrey Chaucer; the second discusses *The Faerie Queene* itself—its structure, allegory, and the quality Giamatti calls "the play of double senses," i.e., duality and ambiguity within the poem.

Lewis, C. S. *Studies in Medieval and Renaissance Literature.* Edited by Walter Hooper. Cambridge: Cambridge University Press, 1966, 195 p.

Reprints five essays on Spenser: an address and refutation of three common charges leveled against *The Faerie Queene;* a subjective account of the pleasure the poem afforded Lewis; a discussion of neo-Platonic ideas expressed in the poem; Spenser's portrayal of the character of Cupid; and his treatment of the figure of Genius.

Rathbone, Isabel E. *The Meaning of Spenser's Fairyland.* New York: Russell & Russell, 1965, 275 p.

Reprints a 1937 examination of Spenser's "fairy mythology."

Spenser Studies: A Renaissance Poetry Annual I– (1980–).

Annual publication containing scholarly articles on Spenser's life and works.

Whitaker, Virgil K. *The Religious Basis of Spenser's Thought.* New York: Gordian Press, 1966, 70 p.

Reprints a 1950 examination of Spenser's religious thought.

Gertrude Stein

1874-1946

American novelist, poet, essayist, autobiographer, and dramatist.

INTRODUCTION

A controversial figure during her lifetime, Stein is now regarded as a major literary Modernist and one of the most influential writers of the twentieth century. Working against the naturalistic conventions of nineteenth-century fiction, she developed an abstract manner of expression that was a counterpart in language to the work of the Post-Impressionists and Cubists in the visual arts. Stein wrote prolifically in many genres, composing novels, poetry, plays, and literary portraits. Her radical approach to these forms was admired and emulated by other writers of her era, including Ernest Hemingway, Thornton Wilder, and Sherwood Anderson, and has served as a key inspiration for such Postmodernist writers as the French New Novelists and William H. Gass.

The youngest daughter of a wealthy Jewish-American family, Stein spent most of her childhood in Oakland, California. Biographers describe her mother as a weak, ineffectual woman, and her father as an irrational tyrant; a few have inferred that this family situation is the origin of Stein's lifelong aversion to patriarchal cultural values. Lacking a satisfactory relationship with her parents, she grew very close to her brother Leo. When Leo went to Harvard in 1892, she enrolled in the all-female Harvard Annex—soon to become Radcliffe—the following year. Radcliffe, and in particular her favorite professor there, the psychologist William James, proved a decisive influence on her intellectual development. Many of James's teachings, including his theories of perception and personality types, would inspire her own theories of literary aesthetics. With James's encouragement, Stein decided to become a psychologist, and began medical studies at Johns Hopkins University as part of her training. However, in 1902, after several years of study, she grew disaffected with medicine and left the university without completing her degree. In the months that followed, Stein devoted herself to the study of literary classics. Inspired by her reading, particularly the works of Gustave Flaubert and Henry James, she began to write her first novels.

In 1903, after travels in Europe and Africa, she and Leo settled in Paris, where they began to collect work by the new Modernist painters and became personally acquainted with many of them, including Paul Cézanne, Henri Matisse, and Pablo Picasso. The Steins' apartment at 27 rue de Fleurus became a salon where numerous artists and literary figures, such as Guillaume Apollinaire, Marie Laurencin, and Max Jacob, met regularly. Stein particularly enjoyed the company of Picasso, who in 1906 painted a portrait of her that would become one of his best-known works, and she greatly admired his artistic style, as well as that of such other painters as Cézanne and Juan Gris, who experimented in their works with ways of conveying a more profound and truthful vision of reality than that allowed by the naturalistic techniques of the nineteenth century. The Cubist painters broke a subject down to its essential geometric forms, then reassembled those forms in ways that offer the viewer startling new perceptions of the subject. This revolution in the visual arts encouraged Stein to formulate a literary aesthetic that would, similarly, violate existing formal conventions in order to allow the reader to experience language and ideas in provocative new ways. Leo, however, who was not enthusiastic about Cubist painting, responded to his sister's work with scorn, causing her anxiety and self-doubt. Stein found a much more appreciative audience in her friend Alice Toklas, a young woman from California who was staying in Paris. In 1909 Stein invited Toklas to live with her, and the women developed a close and affectionate relationship that Stein referred to as a marriage; they remained together for the rest of their lives. Toklas was not only Stein's devoted friend and lover but a vital part of her literary work, helping her to prepare manuscripts and providing her with much-needed encouragement. Because commercial publishers initially rejected her work, Stein was forced to subsidize the printing of her first books. However, many of her distinguished and influential friends, most notably art patron Mabel Dodge, critic Carl Van Vechten, and poet Edith Sitwell, admired and promoted her writings, and by the outbreak of World War I she was regarded as a central figure in the Modernist movement.

Stein remained in Paris for most of the war, winning commendation for her volunteer work as a medical supply driver and befriending many American servicemen. After the war, she became the friend and mentor of a number of young writers from the United States, notably Ernest Hemingway. She encouraged his early attempts at writing fiction; he, in turn, was instrumental in arranging for the publication of Stein's epic novel *The Making of Americans* (1925). As an epigraph to his 1926 novel *The Sun Also Rises,* Hemingway quoted Stein's remark, "You are all a lost generation," which came to refer to Hemingway, F. Scott Fitzgerald, and other young American writers gathered in Paris during the 1920s. At this time Stein was as well known for her many friendships with talented, wealthy, and famous persons as for her innovative literary work. At a publisher's urging, she wrote a memoir, *The Autobiography of Alice B. Toklas* (1933), which became a bestseller and made her an international celebrity. Stein at first feared that personal notoriety might spoil her as an artist. As it happened, however, she used the publicity to her advantage, especially in a series of lectures she delivered at American universities in 1934. Explaining her literary theories not only increased her confidence in and understanding of her own methods, but also provided readers and scholars with valuable keys for interpreting her work.

During World War II, Stein and Toklas remained in Nazi-occupied France. As Jews, both women were at risk of being deported to concentration camps, but they were protected from the Nazis by collaborationist friends such as the French scholar Bernard Faÿ. After the liberation of Paris, Stein was once again visited by many admiring American soldiers. She maintained an active social and literary life until her death, in 1946, from cancer. In a famous anecdote from her autobiography *What Is Remembered,* Toklas recalled a conversation she had with Stein just before her death. "She said to me early in the afternoon, What is the answer? I was silent. In that case, she said, what is the question?"

Some commentators, including Stein herself, divide her career into three phases: early, middle, and late. Her early works, according to critics, are among her most accessible. Her first novel, *Q.E.D.,* written in 1903, is an apparently autobiographical study of a young woman's unhappy relationship with a fickle female lover. Because of its taboo subject matter, the novel was not published until after Stein's death. Her next major work, *Three Lives* (1909), consists of three novella-length stories concerning the lives of ordinary women: "The Good Anna" and "The Gentle Lena," about two German-American servants, and "Melanctha," which, commentators note, is essentially a reworking of the love story in *Q.E.D.,* this time presenting it as a heterosexual affair between two black characters. Although critics now recognize "Melanctha" as an inaccurate, stereotyped depiction of black American life, it was virtually unprecedented as a serious attempt by a white author to portray realistic black characters. Both *Q.E.D.* and *Three Lives,* although relatively conventional, contain some traces of Stein's later, experimental style, such as minimal punctuation, lack of emphasis on plot, and the depiction of characters as psychological types rather than as unique individuals.

Stein regarded *The Making of Americans,* the 925-page epic novel that initiated the next phase in her career, as her masterpiece, a revolutionary work on the scale of James Joyce's *Ulysses* (1922) or Marcel Proust's *À la recherche du temps perdu* (1913-27; *Remembrance of Things Past*). Stein's approach to the psychology of her characters became even more abstract and clinical in this novel, which she intended to illustrate personality types, revealing the "bottom nature," or essential type, of individuals by depicting their patterns of behavior. In addition to its psychological plan, *The Making of Americans* is an autobiographical work which chronicles the lives of three generations of the Herslands, a German-American family modeled after the Steins. The text also contains numerous digressions in which Stein records her thoughts, often anxious and doubtful, about the process of writing *The Making of Americans.* In other works, such as her literary portraits of Picasso and Mabel Dodge, she further developed her characteristic middle style: long sentences made up of simple words and repeated phrases, stripped of subordinate clauses and of all punctuation except periods. Because many of Stein's prose works of this period are written in this dense, ruminative style, with little conventional narrative continuity to sustain reader interest, many critics have pronounced them virtually unreadable.

Stein developed her avant-garde style one step further in *Tender Buttons* (1914), a collection of prose poems. Presented in three sections, "Objects," "Food," and "Rooms," the poems are written in language not meant to evoke emotional or intellectual associations in readers, but to focus their attention on the things described and on the language of the poem itself. While many supporters of Modernism hailed *Tender Buttons* as a brilliant achievement, others derided it as incomprehensible. Some critics compared the hermetic style of these poems to the deliberate absurdities of the Dadaists or to the experiments in automatic writing conducted by the Surrealists. In fact, Stein disliked the deliberate irrationality of Dadaism; although her writings are often frustratingly complex or obscure, they are never purely nonsensical. Stein used psychological theory as a basis for her writings, as did the Surrealists, but she was interested in the dynamics of the conscious mind, not the subconscious. The writings of her middle period reflect theories of consciousness that she learned from William James at Radcliffe. According to James, the individual perceives the world not in discrete temporal segments of past, present, and future, but as a continuous awareness of the moment being presently lived. In her long, static narratives, Stein sought to evoke this atemporal sense of a continuous present. In her *Geographical History of America*

(1936), she explains this concept in detail. She divides the conscious self into two parts: human nature and human mind. Human nature governs spoken language, identity, memory, and awareness of time; "I am I because my little dog knows me" is an attitude of human nature. Human mind, conversely, embodies the essential nature of the individual, the awareness of the continuous present.

Throughout the 1920s, Stein continued to develop and implement her theories. Her writings became less accessible to readers, not only because of the increasingly complex intellectual plans behind their composition but also because Stein used so many words and phrases that had meanings only she or close friends could understand. Her poem "Lifting Belly," for instance, while not at all explicit, has been interpreted as an erotic love poem filled with private references to her relationship with Toklas. By this time, the anxiety expressed in Stein's early writings had given way to a mood of serenity, good humor, and confidence. Many of her writings of this era, such as *Lucy Church Amiably* (1930), reflect the pleasant domestic life she shared with Toklas. Stein characterized *Lucy Church Amiably* as a "landscape"; while this particular work is, literally, a description of the scenic area in southern France where she and Toklas spent their summers, she also used the term metaphorically to refer to some of her plays, such as *Four Saints in Three Acts* (1934). Stein's landscape plays, like the prose of her middle period, depict the relations between static elements in a static situation, rather than focusing on plot progression or character development. Composer Virgil Thomson, intrigued by the nonrepresentational, musical quality of Stein's language, adapted *Four Saints* as a successful opera. Stein later collaborated with Thomson on *The Mother of Us All* (1947), an opera based on the life of feminist Susan B. Anthony.

With *The Autobiography of Alice B. Toklas,* Stein proved to her critics that she was capable of writing a relatively conventional, commercially successful work. While most reviewers were charmed by the autobiography's wit and engaging conversational style, not all were pleased. A group of Stein's friends from the art world, including Tristan Tzara and Henri Matisse, published "Testimony against Gertrude Stein," in which they condemned the *Autobiography* as a shallow, distorted portrayal of their lives and work. "Miss Stein understood nothing of what went on around her," protested painter Georges Braque. Stein nevertheless followed the popular success of the *Autobiography* with other memoirs, *Everybody's Autobiography* (1937) and *Wars I Have Seen* (1945). She also published her *Lectures in America* (1935) and *Narration* (1935), theoretical writings which have proved invaluable to students of her work in explaining her often esoteric style. While she continued to write avant-garde narratives, her last works reflect an awareness of current social and political realities absent from the introspective writings of her early and middle period. For example, *Brewsie and Willie* (1946), a set of fictional dialogues between American soldiers and nurses, deals with the atomic bomb and other issues relevant to the post-World War II era.

From the time she started to publish her writings, Stein has proved a challenge to critics. Because much of her work violates basic formal and thematic conventions, certain interpretative methods, such as the close textual analysis practiced by the New Critics, are of no use in approaching her writings. It is partly for this reason that much of the commentary on Stein from 1910 through the 1950s is evaluative rather than interpretative, either arguing her merits, as does Carl Van Vechten, or deriding her, in the case of Wyndham Lewis and B. L. Reid. The linguistically based critical methods of structuralism and deconstruction that emerged in the 1960s and 1970s offered readers of Stein a critical method better suited to understanding her work as she had conceived it. Feminist critics have also provided a fresh perspective on Stein, discussing such issues as Stein's treatment of sexuality and her defiance of patriarchal literary traditions. An additional topic often raised by commentators is Stein's relation to the Post-

Impressionists and Cubists. As with other Modernists, such as Cézanne and Picasso, Stein was at first attacked by those who did not accept the validity of her artistic methods. However, as her innovations became institutionalized by succeeding generations of writers, such attacks have given way to more temperate discussions of her work. Although critics acknowledge her as one of the leading literary Modernists, her often cryptic style has made her works less accessible than those of her contemporaries Joyce and Virginia Woolf; her true worth as an artist, many commentators note, has been felt more strongly in her influence on other writers than in the appreciation of her works for their own sake. "I think it can be said," observed Thornton Wilder, "that the fundamental occupation of Miss Stein's life was not the work of art but the shaping of a theory of knowledge, a theory of time, and a theory of the passions."

(For further information about Stein's life and works, see *Concise Dictionary of American Literary Biography, 1917-1929; Contemporary Authors,* Vols. 104, 132; *Dictionary of Literary Biography,* Vols. 4, 54, 86; *Major 20th-Century Writers;* and *Twentieth-Century Literary Criticism,* Vols. 1, 6, 28.)

CRITICAL COMMENTARY

LAURA RIDING AND ROBERT GRAVES
(essay date 1927)

[Riding is an American critic, essayist, novelist, and poet. Graves was a prolific English man of letters who is considered one of the most accomplished minor poets of the twentieth century. Riding and Graves together ran the Seizin Press, which in 1926 published Stein's *An Acquaintance with Description;* they are also the co-authors of *A Survey of Modernist Poetry.* In the following excerpt from the conclusion to that work, Riding and Graves comment on what they consider Stein's literary "barbarism."]

The modernist poet . . . has an exaggerated preoccupation with criticism. He has a professional conscience forced on him by the encroachments and pressure of new period activities; and this is understandable. When the prestige of any organization is curtailed—the army or navy for example—a greater internal discipline, morality and study of tactics results, a greater sophistication and up-to-date-ness. In poetry this discipline

means the avoidance of all the wrongly-conceived habits and tactics of the past: poetry becomes so sophisticated that it seems to know at last how it should be written and written at the very moment. The more definitely activities like religion, science, psychology and philosophy, which once existed in poetry as loose sentiment, are specialized and confined to their proper departmental technique, the more pure and sharp the technique of poetry itself seems bound to become. It ceases to be civilized in the sense of becoming more and more cultured with loose sentiment; everything in it is particular and strict. It is, indeed, as if poetry were beginning as at the beginning; using all its civilized sophistications to inaugurate a carefully calculated, censored primitiveness. (pp. 262-63)

Gertrude Stein is perhaps the only artisan of language who has ever succeeded in practising scientific barbarism literally. Her words are primitive in the sense that they are bare, immobile, mathematically placed, abstract: so primitive indeed that the theorists of the new barbarism have repudiated her work as a romantic

---

Principal Works

Three Lives (novellas) 1909

Tender Buttons (poetry) 1914

Geography and Plays (dramas and prose) 1922

*The Making of Americans: Being a History of a Family's Progress (novel) 1925; also published as The Making of Americans: The Hersland Family [abridged edition], 1934

Composition as Explanation (essay) 1926

Lucy Church Amiably (prose) 1930

How to Write (prose) 1931

Operas and Plays (dramas) 1932

The Autobiography of Alice B. Toklas (autobiography) 1933

Matisse, Picasso, and Gertrude Stein with Two Shorter Stories (portraits) 1933

Four Saints in Three Acts (drama) 1934

Lectures in America (lectures) 1935

Narration (lectures) 1935

The Geographical History of America; or, The Relation of Human Nature to the Human Mind (prose) 1936

Everybody's Autobiography (autobiography) 1937

Ida (novel) 1941

Wars I Have Seen (prose) 1945

Brewsie and Willie (prose) 1946

Four in America (prose) 1947

The Mother of Us All (libretto) 1947

Last Operas and Plays (prose, dramas, and librettos) 1949

†Things as They Are (novel) 1950; also published as Q.E.D., 1971

The Yale Edition of the Unpublished Writings of Gertrude Stein. 8 vols. (novels, poetry, and novellas) 1951-58

*This work was written between 1903 and 1911.

†This work was written in 1903.

---

vulgar barbarism, expressing the personal crudeness of a mechanical age rather than a refined historical effort to restore a lost absolute to a community of co-ordinated poets. Mr. Eliot has said of her work that "it is not improving, it is not amusing, it is not interesting, it is not good for one's mind. But its rhythms have a peculiar hypnotic power not met with before. It has a kinship with the saxophone. If this is the future then the future is, as it very likely is, of the barbarians. But this is the future in which we ought not to be interested." Mr. Eliot was for the moment speaking for civilization. He was obliged to do this because it seemed suddenly impossible to reconcile the philosophy of the new barbarism with the historical state of the poetic mind and with the professional dignity of poetry which the new barbarism was invented to restore: a sincere attempt to do so was at once crude and obscure like the work of Miss Stein. Except for such whole-hog literalness as hers, professional modernist poetry has lacked the co-ordination which professional modernist criticism implies: and this contradiction between criticism and workmanship makes it incoherent. It has been too busy being civilized, varied, intellectual—too socially and poetically energetic—to take advantage of the privileged consistency of the new barbarism. (pp. 274-75)

[While] a philosophical tangle was forcing modernist poets into an unwitting romanticism, Gertrude Stein went on—and kept going on for twenty years—quietly, patiently and successfully practising an authentic barbarism; quite by herself and without encouragement. Her only fault, from the practical point of view, was that she took primitiveness too literally, so literally that she made herself incomprehensible to the exponents of primitivism—to everyone for that matter. She exercised perfect discipline over her creative faculties and she was able to do this because she was completely without originality. Everybody being unable to understand her thought that this was because she was too original or was trying hard to be original. But she was only divinely inspired in ordinariness: her creative originality, that is, was original only because it was so grossly, so humanly, all-inclusively ordinary. She used language automatically to record pure ultimate obviousness. She made it capable of direct communication not by caricaturing contemporary language—attacking decadence with decadence—but by purging it completely of its false experiences. None of the words Miss Stein uses ever had experience. They are no older than the use she makes of them, and she has been herself no older than her age conceived barbarically.

> Put it there in there where they have it
> Put it there in there there and they halve it
> Put it there in there there and they have it
> Put it there in there there and they halve it

These words have had no history, and the design that Miss Stein has made of them is literally "abstract" and mathematical because they are commonplace words without any hidden etymology; they are mechanical and not eccentric. If they possess originality it is that of mass-automatism.

Miss Stein in her *Composition as Explanation* has written:

> Nothing changes from generation to generation except the thing seen, and that makes a composition.

Her admission that there are generations does not contradict her belief in an unvarying first principle. Time does not vary, only the sense of time.

Automatically with the acceptance of the time-sense comes the recognition of the beauty, and once the beauty is accepted the beauty never fails anyone.

Beauty has no history, according to Miss Stein, nor has time: only the time-sense has history. When the time-sense acclaims a beauty that was not at first recognized, the finality of this beauty is at once established; it is as though it had never been denied. All beauty is equally final. The reason why the time-sense if realized reveals the finality or classicalness of beauty, is that it is the feeling of beginning, of primitiveness and freshness which is each age's or each generation's version of time.

Beginning again and again and again explaining composition and time is a natural thing. It is understood by this time that everything is the same except composition and time, composition and the time of the composition and the time in the composition.

Originality of vision, then, is invented, she holds, not by the artist but by the collective time-sense. The artist does not see things "as no one else sees them." He sees those objective "things" by which the age repeatedly verifies and represents the absolute. He sees concretely and expressibly what everyone else possessed of the time-sense has an unexpressed intuition of: the time-sense may not be generally and particularly universal; but this does not mean that the artist's vision, even his originality of vision, is less collective or less universal.

The composition is the thing seen by everyone living in the living they are doing, they are the composing of the composition that at the time they are living is the composition of the time in which they are living. It is that that makes living a thing they are doing. Nothing else is different, of that almost anyone can be certain. The time when and the time of and the time in that composition is the natural phenomena of that composition and of that perhaps everyone can be certain.

All this Gertrude Stein has understood and executed logically because of the perfect simplicity of her mind. Believing implicitly in an absolute, she has not been bothered to doubt the bodily presence of a first principle in her own time. Since she is alive and everybody around her seems to be alive, of course there is an acting first principle, there is composition. This first principle provides a theme for composition because there is time, and everybody, and the beginning again and again and again, and composition. In her primitive good-humour she has not found it necessary to trouble about defining the theme. The theme is to be inferred

from the composition. The composition is clear because the language means nothing but what it means through her using of it. The composition is final because it is "a more and more continuous present including more and more using of everything and continuing more and more beginning and beginning and beginning." She creates this atmosphere of continuousness principally by her progressive use of the tenses of verbs, by intense and unflagging repetitiousness and an artificially assumed and regulated child-mentality: the child's time-sense is so vivid that an occurrence is always consecutive to itself, it goes on and on, it has been going on and on, it will be going on and on (a child does perhaps feel the passage of time, does to a certain extent feel itself older than it was yesterday because yesterday was already to-morrow even while it was yesterday). (pp. 280-84)

Repetition has the effect of breaking down the possible historical senses still inherent in the words. So has the infantile jingle of rhyme and assonance. So has the tense-changing of verbs, because restoring to them their significance as a verbal mathematics of motion. Miss Stein's persistence in her own continuousness is astonishing: this is how she wrote in 1926, and in 1906. She has achieved a continuous present by always beginning again, for this keeps everything different and everything the same. It creates duration but makes it absolute by preventing anything from happening in the duration.

And after that what changes what changes after that, after that what changes and what changes after that and after that and what changes and after that and what changes after that.

The composition has a theme because it has no theme. The words are a self-pursuing, tail-swallowing series and are thus thoroughly abstract. They achieve what Hulme called but could not properly envisage—not being acquainted, it seems, with Miss Stein's work—a "perpendicular," an escape from the human horizontal plane. They contain no reference; no meaning, no caricatures, no jokes, no despairs. They are ideally automatic, creating one another. The only possible explanation of lines like the following is that one word or combination of words creates the next.

Anyhow means furls furls with a chance chance with a change change with as strong strong with as will will with as sign sign with as west west with as most most with as in in with as by by with as change change with as reason reason to be lest lest they did when when they did for they did there and then. Then does not celebrate the there and then.

This is repetition and continuousness and beginning again and again and again.

Nothing that we have said here should be understood as disrespectful to Gertrude Stein. She has had courage, clarity, sincerity, simplicity. She has created a human mean in language, a mathematical equation of ordinariness which leaves one with a tender respect for that changing and unchanging slowness that is humanity and Gertrude Stein. (pp. 285-87)

Laura Riding and Robert Graves, in a conclusion to their *A Survey of Modernist Poetry,* William Heinemann Ltd., 1927, pp. 258-91.

WILLIAM CARLOS WILLIAMS
(essay date 1931)

[Williams was one of America's most renowned poets of the twentieth century. Rejecting as overly academic the Modernist poetic style established by T. S. Eliot, he sought a more natural poetic expression, endeavoring to replicate the idiomatic cadences of American speech. Perhaps Williams's greatest accomplishment is *Paterson* (1946), a collection of poems depicting urban America. He is best known, however, for such individual poems as "The Red Wheelbarrow," "To Waken an Old Lady," and "Danse Russe." In the following excerpt from an essay originally published in 1931, he examines the nature of Stein's artistic achievement.]

Let it be granted that whatever is new in literature the germ of it will be found somewhere in the writings of other times; only the modern emphasis gives work a present distinction.

The necessity for this modern focus and the meaning of the changes involved are, however, another matter, the everlasting stumbling block to criticism. Here is a theme worth development in the case of Gertrude Stein—yet signally neglected. (p. 113)

Did my father, mother, uncle, aunt, brothers or sisters, ever see a white bear? What would they give? . . . How would they behave? How would the white bear have behaved? Is he wild? Tame? Terrible? Rough? Smooth?

Note the play upon *rough* and *smooth* (though it is not certain that this was intended), *rough* seeming to apply to the bear's deportment, *smooth* to surface, presumably the bear's coat. In any case the effect is that of a comparison relating primarily not to any qualities of the bear himself but to the words rough and smooth. . . .

Is the white bear worth seeing?

Is there any sin in it?

Is it better than a black one?

In this manner ends Chapter 43 of [Laurence Sterne's] *The Life and Opinions of Tristram Shandy.* The handling of the words and to some extent the imaginative quality of the sentence is a direct forerunner of that which Gertrude Stein has woven today into a synthesis of its own. It will be plain, in fact, on close attention, that Sterne exercises not only the play (or music) of sight, sense and sound contrast among the words themselves which Stein uses, but their grammatical play also. . . . It would not be too much to say that Stein's development over a lifetime is anticipated completely with regard to subject matter, sense and grammar—in Sterne.

Starting from scratch we get, possibly, thatch; just as they have always done in poetry.

Then they would try to connect it up by something like—The mice scratch, beneath the thatch.

Miss Stein does away with all that. The free-versists on the contrary used nothing else. They saved—The mice, under the . . .,

It is simply the skeleton, the "formal" parts of writing, those that make form, that she has to do with, apart from the "burden" which they carry. The skeleton, important to acknowledge where confusion of all knowledge of the "soft parts" reigns as at the present day in all intellectual fields.

Stein's theme is writing. But in such a way as to be writing envisioned as the first concern of the moment, dragging behind it a dead weight of logical burdens, among them a dead criticism which broken through might be a gap by which endless other enterprises of the understanding should issue—for refreshment.

It is a revolution of some proportions that is contemplated, the exact nature of which may be no more than sketched here but whose basis is humanity in a relationship with literature hitherto little contemplated.

And at the same time it is a general attack on the scholastic viewpoint, that medieval remnant with whose effects from generation to generation literature has been infested to its lasting detriment. It is a breakaway from that paralyzing vulgarity of logic for which the habits of science and philosophy coming over into literature (where they do not belong) are to blame.

It is this logicality as a basis for literary action which in Stein's case, for better or worse, has been wholly transcended.

She explains her own development in connection with *Tender Buttons.* "It was my first conscious struggle with the problem of correlating sight, sound and sense, and eliminating rhythm;—now I am trying grammar and eliminating sight and sound." Having taken the words to her choice, to emphasize further what she has in mind she has completely unlinked them (in her most recent work) from their former relationships in the sentence. This was absolutely essential and unescapable. Each under the new arrangement has a quality of its own, but not conjoined to carry the burden science, philosophy and every higgledy-piggledy figment of law and order have been laying upon them in the past. They are like a crowd at Coney Island, let us say, seen from an airplane.

Whatever the value of Miss Stein's work may turn out finally to be, she has at least accomplished her purpose of getting down on paper this much that is decipherable. She has placed writing on a plane where it may deal unhampered with its own affairs, unburdened with scientific and philosophic lumber.

For after all, science and philosophy are today, in their effect upon the mind, little more than fetishes of unspeakable abhorrence. And it is through a subversion of the art of writing that their grip upon us has assumed its steel-like temper.

What are philosophers, scientists, religionists, they that have filled up literature with their pap? Writers, of a kind. Stein simply erases their stories, turns them off and does without them, their logic (founded merely on the limits of the perceptions) which is supposed to transcend the words, along with them. Stein denies it. The words, in writing, she discloses, transcend everything. (pp. 114-17)

There remains to be explained the bewildering volume of what Miss Stein has written, the quantity of her work, its very apparent repetitiousness, its iteration, what I prefer to call its extension, the final clue to her meaning.

It is, of course, a progression (not a progress) beginning, conveniently, with **"Melanctha"** from *Three Lives,* and coming up to today.

How in a democracy, such as the United States, can writing which has to compete with excellence elsewhere and in other times remain in the field and be at once objective (true to fact) intellectually searching, subtle and instinct with powerful additions to our lives? It is impossible, without invention of some sort, for the very good reason that observation about us engenders the very opposite of what we seek: triviality, crassness and intellectual bankruptcy. And yet what we do see can in no way be excluded. Satire and flight are two possibilities but Miss Stein has chosen otherwise.

But if one remain in a place and reject satire, what then? To be democratic, local (in the sense of being attached with integrity to actual experience) Stein, or any other artist, must for subtlety ascend to a plane of almost abstract design to keep alive. To writing, then, as an art in itself. Yet what actually impinges on the senses must be rendered as it appears, by use of which,

only, and under which, untouched, the significance has to be disclosed. It is one of the major problems of the artist.

"Melanctha" is a thrilling clinical record of the life of a colored woman in the present-day United States, told with directness and truth. It is without question one of the best bits of characterization produced in America. It is universally admired. This is where Stein began. But for Stein to tell a story of that sort, even with the utmost genius, was not enough under the conditions in which we live, since by the very nature of its composition such a story does violence to the larger scene which would be portrayed.

True, a certain way of delineating the scene is to take an individual like Melanctha and draw her carefully. But this is what happens. The more carefully the drawing is made, the greater the genius involved and the greater the interest that attaches, therefore, to the character as an individual, the more exceptional that character becomes in the mind of the reader and the less typical of the scene.

It was no use for Stein to go on with *Three Lives.* There that phase of the work had to end. See *Useful Knowledge,* the parts on the U.S.A.

Stein's pages have become like the United States viewed from an airplane—the same senseless repetitions, the endless multiplications of toneless words, with these she had to work.

No use for Stein to fly to Paris and forget it. The thing, the United States, the unmitigated stupidity, the drab tediousness of the democracy, the overwhelming number of the offensively ignorant, the dull nerve—is there in the artist's mind and cannot be escaped by taking a ship. She must resolve it if she can, if she is to be.

That must be the artist's articulation with existence.

Truly, the world is full of emotion—more or less—but it is caught in bewilderment to a far more important degree. And the purpose of art, so far as it has any, is not at least to copy that, but lies in the resolution of difficulties to its own comprehensive organization of materials. And by so doing, in this case, rather than by copying, it takes its place as most human.

To deal with Melanctha, with characters of whomever it may be, the modern Dickens, is not therefore human. To write like that is not in the artist, to be human at all, since nothing is resolved, nothing is done to resolve the bewilderment which makes of emotion an inanity: That, is to overlook the gross instigation and with all subtlety to examine the object minutely for "the truth"—which if there is anything more commonly practiced or more stupid, I have yet to come upon it.

To be most useful to humanity, or to anything

else for that matter, an art, writing, must stay art, not seeking to be science, philosophy, history, the humanities, or anything else it has been made to carry in the past. It is this enforcement which underlies Gertrude Stein's extension and progression to date. (pp. 118-20)

William Carlos Williams, "The Works of Gertrude Stein," in his *Selected Essays of William Carlos Williams,* Random House, 1954, pp. 113-20.

TONY TANNER
(essay date 1965)

[In the following excerpt, Tanner analyzes Stein's attempt to express a fresh vision of reality through stylistic innovations.]

After Mark Twain, the naive vernacular narrator reappears constantly in American fiction, from the crude and derivative efforts of Don Marquis (*Danny's Own Story*) and Edgar Lee Masters (*Mitch Miller*), up to the sophisticated successes of J. D. Salinger (*Catcher in the Rye*) and Saul Bellow (*Adventures of Augie March*). But a more interesting line of development leads from Twain to Hemingway and it is a development which depends for its success on the separation of the vernacular from the young narrator. The naive vernacular ceases to be an adopted voice and develops into an achieved style; instead of appearing to be spontaneous unarranged talk it is subjected to a rigorous and careful stylization. In this line of development Gertrude Stein played the part of the indispensable provoking theorist. (p. 187)

Few people these days are greatly moved by much of Stein's work, and yet in her time she attracted a reverence and respect which at least attest to an unusually original and stimulating mind. . . . [She] had an unusually penetrating insight into the intellectual climate of her time and a gift for the clarification of ideas and novel experiment. Her ideas ventured beyond what she took from William James, just as her prose changes considerably between the felicitous Henry James imitation of her first novel (which she called *Q.E.D.* and which was [also] . . . published as *Things As They Are*) and the post-experimental clarity of *The Autobiography of Alice B. Toklas.* She is more an innovator than an imitator. One forgets, perhaps, how early she was with her ideas and experiments. Her first important experimental work, *Three Lives,* was published in 1905. *The Making of Americans* followed between 1906 and 1908: her important and understanding book on *Picasso* appeared in 1909 while her own work had achieved almost a maximum of experimentation in *Tender But-*

tons in 1910-12. For good or bad she was truly original. (pp. 188-89)

Curiously enough her little book on Picasso contains an unusually lucid statement of certain notions which, no matter how relevant they are to Picasso, are certainly very relevant to American literature. The book is based on the premise that "nothing changes in people from one generation to another except the way of seeing and being seen" and that "another vision than that of all the world is very rare. That is why geniuses are rare, to complicate things in a new way that is easy, but to see the things in a new way that is really difficult, everything prevents one, habits, schools, daily life, reason, necessities of daily life, indolence, everything prevents one, in fact there are very few geniuses in the world." That the artist awakes us out of dulled perceptual habits and offers and enforces new ways of looking at the world, new visual attitudes towards reality, seems to me an insight of perennial relevance: but in this case it is peculiarly relevant in that it leads Stein to take up a question . . . raised by earlier American writers: namely, what is the most rewarding way to look at the world, the best mode of vision. (p. 189)

She first compares his way of regarding reality with the way of the child who sees only vivid fragments (one side of its mother's face) and has not learnt to infer the whole. Picasso's struggle was difficult because "no one had ever tried to express things seen not as one knows them but as they are when one sees them without remembering having looked at them." But "he was right, one sees what one sees, the rest is a reconstruction from memory and painters have nothing to do with reconstruction, nothing to do with memory, they concern themselves only with visible things." The difference between what one can see and what one knows is there, is crucial for Stein and she sees the aim of art as an effort to capture the former: an effort continually interrupted and foiled by reminiscences of the latter. She maintains that, like Picasso, she is trying to look at things as though for the first time and for this reason she works to exclude memory and knowledge from her work.

In the beginning when Picasso wished to express heads and bodies not like every one could see them, which was the problem of other painters, but as he saw them, *as one can see when one had not the habit of knowing what one is looking at,* inevitably when he commenced he had the tendency to paint them as a mass as sculptors do or in profile as children do [my italics].

The ideas here relate to Thoreau's notion of "seeing without looking," Whitman's "first step," and the general American interest in a recovered naivety of vision. All these ideas are the result of the inquiry: how can man establish an authentic first hand relationship with existing reality? Stein too is addressing herself to the problem of how we can establish contact with the "reality of things that exist." She thought that the greatest hindrances to this contact were memories of other comparable impressions which blur the uniqueness of the present perceptual instant, and all the associations and thoughts which our minds discharge as soon as we are confronted with an object which we want to recognize and classify. What she wanted, and found in Picasso, were "things seen without association but simply as things seen" and she comments approvingly that "only the things seen are knowledge for Picasso." She wants no interpretation, no reference to other previous "things seen," no contributions from the storehouse of the mind. For Picasso, she asserts, and we feel her agreement, "remembered things are not things seen, therefore they are not things known."

More extreme than Thoreau, Stein has an ideal of what we may call seeing without remembering, without associating, without thinking. She wants the eye to open to the reality of the material world as though it had never opened before: for then we catch reality at its "realest," unfiltered through the schemata of the sophisticated eye which is dimmed from too long domestication in the world. And even though she does not develop or push the comparison she clearly cites the child's way of looking as exemplary: naivety must be cultivated in order that we may see reality as it is and not as we remember it to be. This takes us back to the problem of how a child does in fact perceive reality. More basically, whether one can in fact see anything clearly at all without the aid of memory, the subtle reawakening of innumerable past visual experiences, is open to doubt. Certainly, words are full of memories—are perhaps pure memory—and the impressions gained by the unremembering eye could never be transmitted by the unremembering voice. For without memory there is no metaphor; and without metaphor we would never have had language. Stein avoids live metaphors but to communicate at all she has to use those dead ones we all use continually in our daily speech. Her ideal properly carried out, if it did not lead to a visual confusion akin to blindness, would certainly lead to silence.

To draw these inferences is perhaps unfair. In fact what Stein wants is to purify the eye, to break old visual habits, to initiate a more vivid commerce between the senses and the real world. That Picasso himself managed to do this is indisputable: that Stein's interest in this relates her to a number of American writers from Emerson onwards is my contention. Perhaps all art ultimately contributes to an endless rediscovery of the world around us and within us. American writing in particular has shown a consistent interest in scraping the grime of old emotions from reality, in shedding complex habits of vision, in cleansing words of those

clusters of associations which may produce dullness as often as they contribute richness. To equate seeing things as though for the first time with knowledge as Stein does, is a peculiarly American idea. And having described Picasso in these terms, having dismissed memory as an aid to vision, she adds a further idea which makes us think more of Anderson and Hemingway than Picasso. "And so then always and always Picasso commenced his attempt to express not things felt, not things remembered, not established in relations but things which are there, really everything a human being can know *at each moment of his existence and not an assembling of all his experiences*" (my italics). A preference for a moment-by-moment notation of impressions is clearly discernible in Anderson and Hemingway: the "assembling" of experience reveals itself in generalizations and abstractions, just as an interest in the "relations" between things tends to produce a complex syntax: and it is precisely these two things which their prose attempts to avoid. And of course the naive eye which refuses to remember anything can ill afford to pass by anything: hence the detailed inclusiveness of this way of writing, its moment-by-moment quality. Needless to say a more or less subtle sense of selection must be at work, but the close itemizing contact with the concrete world and the predominantly paratactic syntax which we have remarked in much American writing must be related to this preferred mode of seeing, a mode which separates sensations out rather than assembling them together.

Stein's attack on memory and her related preference for a moment-by-moment notation of experience is also in evidence in her *Lectures in America,* particularly in the one entitled **"Portraits and Repetition."** She discusses what she had attempted in some of her prose portraits and revealingly she turns to the cinema to explain how she managed to make portraits of people "as they are existing" without having recourse to "remembering":

> Funnily enough the cinema has offered a solution of this thing. By a continuously moving picture of any one there is no memory of any other thing and there is that thing existing. . . . I was doing what the cinema was doing, I was making a continuous succession of the statement of what that person was until I had not many things but one thing.

Just as life never repeats itself, and the cinema doesn't quite repeat itself, so her prose, she claims, does not really repeat itself: rather there is a series of small additions and modifications in her prose, just as there are minute differences in each successive picture flashed on a cinema screen. "As I told you in comparing it to a cinema picture one second was never the same as the second before or after." She maintains that "existing as a human being . . . is never repetition" and goes on to say that "remembering is the only repetition" just as "remembering is the only confusion." The confusion comes from allowing the past to get mixed up with the present, presumably a sullying intrusion which mars the accuracy of our perception of what is actually there in the present. Her ideal is a continuously developing present—complete and actual at any given moment—which is yet a whole, just as an existing thing is a whole or even as a single frame of a film is a whole, although both are made up of many minute parts. What she is against is "letting remembering mix itself with looking": what she is in favour of is "moment to moment emphasizing." As before, the two go together. In a later lecture she makes a simple remark which succinctly hints at her whole theory of prose. "After all the natural way to count is not that one and one make two but to go on counting by one and one. . . . One and one and one and one and one. That is the natural way to go on counting." Applied to prose this would mean no "assembling," no complex "relating," no accumulation, no interpretation, no comparison, no increasing density of significance. It would mean a prose that, literally, was not additive. Rather language would have to adapt itself to registering the "complete and actual present" again and again and again: now and now and now—one and one and one. If we hold on to the cinema for an analogy we can see that this will mean a series of still pictures: reading her prose is at times like holding a strip of movie film and looking at each frame separately. Understandably Stein sometimes uses the idea of the still life to explain her intentions and this whole relation between movement and stillness, and their relation in turn to the twin ideas of rejection of memory and the refusal of assembling, must now be looked at rather carefully.

In her lectures on narration Stein took up a very clear hostile attitude towards traditional narrative habits. (pp. 189-94)

[Stein takes] issue with narrative which concerns itself with giving an account of purposive action, narrative like a chain of causes and effects leading to a final crisis, narrative which deals with successive things and not existing things. It seems to me that she fails to demonstrate that the existence of a thing cannot be revealed by showing it in action but her intention in making these into mutually exclusive alternatives is fairly clear. It is part of the modern rebellion against conventional plot—it is in Anderson as well—which, it was felt, slighted reality by its habit of erecting a spurious superstructure of eventfulness. Old narrative, so the argument would run, forces the attention to inquire, what has happened, what will happen next, to what resolution does all this tend: it never concentrates on the more basic miracle of what *is*. It ignores the man standing still. Stein's dislike of "successive" action is not a distrust of all movement: "it is something strictly American to conceive a space that is filled with moving,

a space of time that is filled always filled with moving" she asserts. Movement is inherent in the existing thing, even in its stillness: but in successive narrative, reality is wrenched, suppressed and ignored to fit the traditional arc of beginning, middle and end. Stein is against narrative which fosters a causal time sense, which forces us to ask of the material in front of us—what is happening and why? Better, she would maintain, to develop an art which makes us ponder what is existing, now and for itself. The present participle—the standing man. Memory deflects our attention into the past and thence to the future. Better to seize the moment—in its fullness and in its stillness, a stillness throbbing with latent movement. Her fondness for art is relevant here and it is worth noting that *Lucy Church Amiably* is subtitled "A Novel of Romantic beauty and nature and which Looks Like an Engraving." More to the point we should recall that she wrote *Three Lives,* so she tells us, "looking and looking" at a Cézanne portrait of a woman. Cézanne would indeed seem to exemplify the attitude to reality which Stein spent so much time and care trying to define.

In turning away from academic and classical subjects and preferring the challenge of still-life painting he spoke revealingly of "the heroism of the real" and went on to formulate his magnificent phrase about "the immensity, the torrent of the world in a little bit of matter." This perfectly explains why his still lives are not still. He needs no reference to heroic actions to convey a dynamic sense of movement and charged reality. Presumably Stein had something like this in mind when she wrote in favour of a style of writing which could catch and hold the existing thing and exclude the successive thing. She wanted a writing that would give, not the thing in history, but the thing-in-itself. It is perhaps illustrative of this strain in her thinking that she could write in one of her lectures: "I wonder now if it is necessary to stand still to live if it is not necessary to stand still to live, and if it is if that is not perhaps to be a new way to write a novel."

It is when we come to Stein's specific ideas about writing that we see not only what she was really getting at, but also perhaps why it was that she never really managed to write a work that came up to her ideals. She once wrote "description is explanation"—a phrase very relevant to Hemingway—but in her later lectures, particularly **"Poetry and Grammar,"** she redefines description in a way which separates it from the activity as we might understand it. In **"Portraits and Repetition"** she tells of looking at something and then trying to find words that looked like the thing under observation:

I became more and more excited about how words which were the words that made whatever I looked at look like itself were not the words that had in them any quality of description. . . . And the thing that excited me so very much at that time and still does is that the words or words that make what I looked at be itself were always words that to me very exactly related themselves to that thing the thing at which I was looking, but as often as not had as I say nothing whatever to do with what any words would do that described that thing.

The idea here—if I understand it correctly—is that if you want to convey a sense of reality, catch the very quality of the thing seen, it is not sufficient to name the object and list its properties. Recreation is not description. Her portraits seem to me for the most part idiosyncratic and unintelligible—too arcane, too subjective, or merely too full of private jokes to communicate any recognizable reality. Similarly the prose studies of "Objects: food: rooms" which make up *Tender Buttons* resist most attempts to find any conventional meaning in them. What is clear is that Stein is not interested in conventional ways of transmitting sense and impressions: rather she seems to want to try and find out how she can manipulate the patterning of the sounds of words to create a verbal still-life so that we may receive the proferred thing itself and not the thing summed up. This example has some novel quality:

> A table means does it not my dear it means a whole steadiness. Is it likely that a change.

> A table means more than a glass even a looking glass is tall. A table means necessary places and a revision a revision of a little thing it means it does mean that there has been a stand, a stand where it did shake.

However, some recognizable statements are discernible there. In the following example we have mere word play (though it may be fair to say that by playing, literally, with words, writers often discover forgotten properties in them which are later available for more serious employment).

> Go red go red laugh white. Suppose a collapse in rubbed purr, in rubbed purr get. Little sales ladies little sales ladies little saddles of mutton. Little sales of leather and such beautiful, beautiful, beautiful.

These attempts are obviously too private in their associations and too arbitrary in their procedure: but it seems that a new and careful look is being taken at words themselves, even at the cost of all communicated meaning. And had Gertrude Stein's work matured into real significance she would not have been the first modern artist who had to descend into apparent meaninglessness to emerge with new meanings. Certainly it is worth considering the motivating ideas behind these attempts.

These emerge more clearly in **"Poetry and Grammar."** Her first, and most significant, attack, is on the use of nouns. And here she both makes a valid point and overstates it:

A noun is a name of anything, why after a thing is named write about it. . . . Nouns are the names of anything and just naming names is alright when you want to call a roll but is it any good for anything else. . . . As I say a noun is the name of a thing, and therefore slowly if you feel what is inside that thing you do not call it by the name by which it is known. Everybody knows that by the way they do when they are in love and a writer should always have that intensity of emotion about whatever is the object about which he writes. And therefore and I say it again more and more one does not use nouns.

Adjectives, since their job is to affect nouns, are also "not really and truly interesting." From this extreme point of view nouns, with all their qualifying adjuncts, appear as barriers which interpose themselves between the passionate perceiver and the thing perceived. This is valid only if you are considering that crude use of nouns which makes them opaque; mere utilitarian gestures uninhabited by reality. As in a roll call or inventory. There are indeed ways of naming and describing which inhibit, even prohibit, awareness and discourage all sensitivity of response. But to hypothesize an ideal of prose unfurnished with any nouns and adjectives is to recommend a banishment of reality from language which language could not survive. Stein's aim is, however, not so fantastic as that. This is how she phrases her problem: "Was there not a way of naming things that would not invent names, but mean names without naming them." She is here lamenting a common phenomenon whereby once we have named a thing (and as always in Stein's use of the word "thing" she means emotions as well as objects), we tend to forget the reality which lurks or dances beyond the name. Of course there is a way of naming things which embraces and discloses and celebrates that reality—poetry, says Stein. "So I say poetry is essentially the discovery, the love, the passion for the name of anything." But—so her arguement trends—as the names become dull, common, and opaque, new ways of access to the reality of things must be sought. "After all one had known its name anything's name for so long, and so the name was not new but the thing being alive was always new." In face of a continually self-renewing reality we must retain an ever renewed sense of wonder. Look at things as for the first time. Here nouns impede us, they have been around too long. So Stein tries "looking at anything until something that was not the name of that thing but was in a way that actual thing would come to be written." Her point is that the name of a thing (the conventional, accredited name) and the actual thing are inevitably separate and different; the former an impoverished substitute for the latter. After looking at something she tries "creating it without naming it" and so she "struggled desperately with the recreation and the avoidance of nouns as nouns." Walt Whitman is singled out for praise—"He wanted really wanted to express the thing and not call it by its name"—and Stein finishes her lecture with her clear conviction that "the noun must be replaced by the thing in itself." To answer that words never are nor ever can be things is of course too crude and unsympathetic to Stein's point. We could recall Emerson's distinction between language which is heavy with the bullion of nature and language which has become a false paper currency. Stein's ambition is a manifestation of that compelling reality-hunger which we have seen to be a motivating power in many American writers. Stein wants to create verbal models or constructs which do not point to reality but somehow simulate it and evoke the sheer quality of existing things. It is her method, her idea of banishing the noun, which is open to question. Consider language as a reticulated transparent screen through which we look at the world: the reticulations provide relatively stable shapes—names, notions, species, etc.—which help us to bring into focus and thereby recognize a relatively unstable reality continually in flux. The screen is not reality, but without it reality remains undifferentiated and, to that extent, unseen. Without language we would suffer reality: it would beset us. To perceive the thing we need the word. The word is not the thing, but the word lasts longer than the thing. Stein's idea would seem to be to remove much of this reticulated screen, this patchwork of old names, and to substitute an improvised vocabulary which communicates the present feel of reality without identifying it by recourse to accepted nomenclature. Because names, by virtue of their very acceptance, refer back to the past: and Stein would like to get the past out of language, cleanse words of their dark history, cut them off from those roots which anchor and nourish. Ideally she wants the impossible. (pp. 194-200)

Tony Tanner, "Gertrude Stein and the Complete Actual Present," in his *The Reign of Wonder: Naivety and Reality in American Literature,* Cambridge at the University Press, 1965, pp. 187-204.

BRUCE F. KAWIN

(essay date 1972)

[In the following excerpt, Kawin examines the function of repetition in Stein's attempt to reproduce human perception of time.]

"Gertrude Stein," she wrote of herself, "has always been possessed by the intellectual passion for exactitude in the description of inner and outer reality." Yet her descriptions seem totally unrelated to their objects. We naturally ask, what does the description of Oranges

in *Tender Buttons,* "Build is all right," have to do with oranges? Gertrude Stein rejected ordinary speech—which is full of irrelevant associations, connotations, and evocations—in favor of what she considered an accurate, directed, and consistent language, both objective and abstract, whose words and movements would be in her absolute control, and which would not refer obliquely to the associations of old poetry. Stein's manner of recording exactly what she sees—or the movements of her consciousness in relation to its object of attention—in a language that means only what it means *now,* is a discipline of objectivity that her audience has tended to receive as incomprehensibly subjective, if not decadent. For Stein, experience itself "was objective to the point of being indistinguishable from reality."

It is not enough to reinvent language; the act of recording itself must be clear and alive. Gertrude Stein attempted, through simultaneously observing and recording, and by beginning again with each new instant of observing and recording, to make her carefully, consciously chosen individual and nonevocative words record what she actually saw. In her "portraits" particularly, it was important to see each thing, each person, in its or his uniqueness, apart from any resemblance to other things or persons. The success of these observations depended on her being able to see only the present, to write only in the present, to educate her audience to read only in the present.

The effect of Stein's unfamiliar syntax on our spoken-language-oriented ears is to make us consider each word in the relations which it imposes on the words around it. Every mental observation has its own syntax, or manner of organization. Language changes with its object and subject. As we pay attention to each word, our idealized concentration reveals the exact image these exact words here generate; to what else *can* we relate them but to their simple meaning in their immediate context? Another way of putting this is to say that these words do not "remember" how they have been used before, that their author puts them down as if this were the first time she had ever seen them, as if their present context—since the present is the only existing time, and this syntax defies relation to ordinary syntax or to earlier moments in its own world—were the only context that could ever be important for these words. Each word begins its history in this particular usage.

Her mind free of old associations, literal or otherwise, Stein lets words come together in new ways, as they are appropriate and forceful and interesting, in the spontaneous and deliberate act of writing.

There is nothing that anyone creating needs more than that there is no time sense inside them no past present or future.

The author must allow her work to take shape in front of her, with all her concentration. She must move with the progress of the work, keeping not the past or future of the work in mind, but only its present; not the past usages of her words, but her words; not what she remembers the subject looks like, but how it looks. If she concentrates completely in the moment of writing she must also concentrate completely in the simultaneous moment of observation, seeing the object for what it exactly is, not what it has been compared to or considered. If the grass under the pigeons becomes shorter then longer then yellow, she can see it and write it. . . . She must see in the present, and see the present completely. What is "recollected in tranquility" is falsified.

In the overfamous line "A rose is a rose is a rose . . . ," for example, we find what looks very like repetition playing an important part in making a dead word ("rose") real again, removing the word from its "history," and insisting on its existence in advancing time. The difficulty of writing poetry in a "late age," as

Stein in 1937, singing her favorite song, "On the Trail of the Lonesome Pine." Photograph by W.G. Rogers, Yale Collection of American Literature, The Beinecke Rare Book and Manuscript Library, Yale University.

she explains, is precisely that of giving words life, in the face of all their remembering. . . . Nevertheless Stein denied that repetition had anything to do with the success of that line. She insisted in fact that her writing contained no repetitions.

In her verbal portraits Stein was reproached with being repetitious, and her defense of her method, the lecture **"Portraits and Repetition"**—informed perhaps even on her part by a confusion between "repetitive" and "repetitious"—makes quite clear her belief that where there is life, there is no repetition. Her use of the term is strict; for her it means identical recurrence with no increase in force, with none of the slight differences in composition that constitute life. Something that is being taught (a piece of knowledge with the excitement of discovery taken out of it) can be repeated in drill; an artwork that simply copies another work can be said to be a repetition; but in her writing there is no repetition. We can see what she means from those portraits.

If we do not pay complete attention to the person before us, we cannot write an accurate portrait of that exact person. To produce these abstract verbalizations of her experience of her subjects, Gertrude Stein trained herself to observe people without caring whom else they were like, and to write with that same concentration, faithful to the integrity of her subject. Each of us is unique, and each of our instants is unique. No matter how many times something happens to us, it is real each time. And each ideal Steinian statement— each new instant of writing synchronized with the subject's fresh movement of consciousness—is unique, and real each time.

Stein preferred to call her near-repetitions "insistence." In this succession of simultaneously observed and recorded instants she felt progress; remaining in phase with her subject, she believed she accurately experienced and transcribed its identity, its assurance, its "excitingness of pure being."

> Exciting as a human being, that is being listening and hearing is never repetition. It is not repetition if it is that which you are actually doing because naturally each time the emphasis is different just as the cinema has each time a slightly different thing to make it all be moving.

In comparing the slight differentiation between the successive frames of a motion picture to the differences among her statements and observations— asserting that the differences keep both images moving, just as they constitute the life of the subject—Gertrude Stein makes clear one reason why it is so futile to skim her writing and clarifies her definition of repetition. A motion picture in which each frame was identical would not move. The near-repetition of similar frames, when properly projected, communicates life. If you take a yard of film out of the can and just look at it, you cannot see the movement although you might possibly infer it; the frames look identical. You certainly cannot see how the slight changes act on each other, or feel the movement they produce. Scanning the frames is like skimming Stein; it isn't possible to feel her work without putting yourself in its present. Like each frame of a film, each Steinian statement fills the reader's ideal attention, excluding (by baffling) memory, until the object of her attention is insisted into complex and coherent existence:

> Funnily enough the cinema has offered a solution of this thing. By a continuously moving picture of any one there is no memory of any other thing and there is that thing existing. . . . I was doing what the cinema was doing, I was making a continuous succession of the statement of what that person was until I had not many things but one thing.

It appears to be the act of saying what something is that divides the perception into instants: observe and record, then begin observing again without any memory of the earlier observation that might obscure or misdirect this observation. In a process not of emphasis but of beginning again and again, she describes what something is, and what it is now, and what it is now, until it is.

Just as the primitive kept his world new by yearly returning to the moment of the creation, and by making his life the repetition of archetypal actions gave himself the feeling that time was not irreversibly accumulating, Gertrude Stein's beginnings again keep her writing in its continuous present, keep it alive. She was interested in history, but she resisted "remembering," and felt that "the first time" was "of no importance." While the primitive believed in unbuilding time by returning to Time Zero every year, Gertrude Stein returns to the time of the beginning with each statement, so that there is never any accumulation of building time but an abstract, objective, and jerky continuing.

Implicit in this method of capturing the instant is the assumption that the instant could be looked at hard and precisely. If we hold to the simile of the sequence of motion picture frames, we must see Miss Stein's "film" as like Chris Marker's *La Jetée* (1962), which with one exception is a sequence of tableaux, and there is time to take a good look at each frame—or like the progressing freeze-frames which show one character's memory of the assassination in Costa-Gavras' Z. Twenty-four frames a second (normal projection speed) is too fast for precise apprehension of each image. Stein's attention slows time: her attention is her time. In reaction to William James's "flow" or "stream" of consciousness, Frederick Hoffman notes,

> Miss Stein was much more interested in the fact of an *arrested* consciousness, apparently static and fixed and sacrificing motion or flow to precision. . . . She

did not ignore "flow," but found it very difficult to attend to, and dangerous as well, for attention to it ran the risk of losing the integrity and precision of the word-object nexus.

There is progress in Gertrude Stein's narration, but it is slow; and plot, of course ("What Happened"), is not very important. The progress is among the instants, toward complete expression, not, as Reid has put it, toward "the collapse of the artist's attention to his subject." A lecture is over when its audience has experienced its meaning, a portrait when its image is complete, a life when the subject has reached the present or has died. Here are some endings:

> Now that is all.
>
> ["**Composition as Explanation**"]
>
> Through to you.
>
> [*Four in America*]
>
> And now it is today.
>
> [*Everybody's Autobiography*]
>
> And she has and this is it.
>
> [*The Autobiography of Alice B. Toklas*]
> (pp. 117-28)

Bruce F. Kawin, "The Continuous Present," in his *Telling It Again and Again: Repetition in Literature and Film,* Cornell University Press, 1972, pp. 108-64.

JAYNE L. WALKER
(essay date 1984)

[Walker is the author of *The Making of a Modernist: Gertrude Stein from "Three Lives" to "Tender Buttons."* In the following excerpt from that work, she comments on the theoretical bases of the innovative narrative techniques developed by Stein in her early works.]

From *Three Lives* to *Tender Buttons,* Gertrude Stein created a series of texts that engage, early and radically, what we have come to recognize as the most crucial issue of modernist art—the problem of representation. *Three Lives* was her first major assault on the conventions governing literary representation in the nineteenth century. This text, in which the halting, repetitive uncertainties of colloquial speech supplant the authoritative voice of conventional narrative discourse, gradually came to be regarded as a central force in reshaping the tradition of American fiction in the twentieth century. Long before *Three Lives* received that belated recognition, however, Stein had gone on to invent far more radical ways of manipulating language to create ever-closer approximations of "reality" as she defined and redefined it. By 1912 her uncompromising efforts to embody her sense of reality in language culminated in *Tender Buttons,* the iconoclastic text in which "real is only, only excreate, only excreate a no since."

Tender Buttons is both a manifesto and a demonstration of the new mode of writing that it announces. "Act so that there is no use in a center"—this imperative produces a text that enacts the principles of fragmentation and difference and celebrates the freeplay of writing as a combinative game limited only by the systemic laws of language. If these principles seem to echo the post-structuralist characterizations of the modernist text that have already become clichés of contemporary literary criticism, it is no less remarkable to find them so explicity thematized and so rigorously enacted in Stein's 1912 text. By the time she wrote *Tender Buttons,* she had already embraced the major premises that would shape most of her subsequent work: the epistemological model of present-tense vision, unmediated by memory or habitual associations, and the literary strategy of subverting, defying, or simply denying the normal discursive order of language. Although she continued to write prolifically for more than thirty years, inventing countless ways to "excreate a no since," no subsequent period of her work exhibits either the range of formal invention or the intense reexamination of fundamental aesthetic principles that impelled the extreme and rapid stylistic changes in her work from *Three Lives* to *Tender Buttons.*

Precisely how and why did this writer who set a new standard for colloquial realism in *Three Lives* come to flaunt the radical iconoclasm of *Tender Buttons* only a few years later? Surely this is the single most compelling question posed by Stein's career as a modernist writer. In her later theoretical writings, Stein herself always claimed that everything she wrote was equally motivated by an "intellectual passion for exactitude in the description of inner and outer reality." But she was equally adamant in her insistence that "reality" is a dynamic configuration that changes from one century—and one generation—to the next: "One must never forget that the reality of the twentieth century is not the reality of the nineteenth century, not at all."

This is the kind of polemical appeal to the "real" that has characterized avant-garde art since the mid-nineteenth century, as successive assaults on artistic conventions have been launched in the name of the uncoded "reality" that lies outside *vraisemblance.* Both challenged and reassured by these claims, the viewing public long ago learned to recognize the images that Cézanne, Picasso, and other painters created as new ways of seeing and rendering the world. In the case of Stein's writings, however, readers who encounter so little in the texts she wrote after *Three Lives* that they can *recognize* as realistic find it extremely difficult to understand what "realities" her increasingly unconventional texts engage and how they do it.

The more radically a literary text departs from familiar conventions, the more actively the reader must struggle to determine how to read it. How does it "work"? What are the theoretical premises that shape its formal strategies? Nowhere is the question of artistic intention, in this sense, such a pressing concern as in the encounter with a new artistic work that systematically refuses to conform to traditional expectations. Faced with the extreme unconventionality of Stein's texts, many readers have simply declared them "meaningless." The more intrepid have generally sought the keys to their significance elsewhere—in Stein's later theoretical writings or, even more frequently, in cubist painting or Jamesian psychology.

Both the retrospective theoretical statements that Stein began to issue in the twenties and the everpopular legend of her intimate involvement with modernist painting and Jamesian psychology have frequently been mined for evidence of the "influences" that shaped her work during the early years of her career. No study of her literary production fails to acknowledge these affinities or to suggest that, somehow, one or another of these extrinsic models will explain the difficulties of her enigmatic texts. As early as 1912, Alfred Stieglitz, who published Stein's portraits of Picasso and Matisse in his influential magazine *Camera Work,* suggested that her texts proffered a "Rosetta stone of comparison; a decipherable clew to that intellectual and esthetic attitude which underlies and inspires the [modernist] movement." Instead of approaching Stein's texts in this way, as "decipherable clews" that could elucidate the premises of modernism, Stein's critics have generally employed the opposite procedure, turning to modernist painting and Jamesian psychology for clues to the intentions that inform Stein's texts. This procedure, which has dominated the history of reception of Stein's writings, has given rise to strikingly different—and sometimes mutually contradictory—accounts of her intentions, all of which equally short-circuit any serious effort to decipher her texts in their own terms.

Until recently, many of Stein's critics simply ignored her professed commitment to "reality" in favor of the assumption that she was emulating the premises and methods of "abstract," nonobjective painting. This historically untenable assumption, which went virtually unchallenged until a few years ago, long served as the most serious impediment to deciphering Stein's difficult texts. The opposite approach has long been to endorse Stein's claims to "realism" by regarding her most unconventional texts as direct notations—or faithful re-creations—of the Jamesian stream of consciousness. Although Jamesian psychology can help to clarify the epistemological assumptions that Stein's writings explore, it has evident limitations as an interpretative model. Purporting to offer a global explanation of her writings, it tends to discourage interpretation as effectively as the model of nonobjective painting. While the one assumes that the language of the text is totally opaque, the other posits the ideal transparency of pure naturalism. But that assumed transparency is equally uninterpretable, because this model locates the meaning of these surface manifestations in the irrecoverable private associations of the moment—and the mind— that created it. Even when Stein's writings are regarded as more general demonstrations of the operations of consciousness, this psychological approach tends toward the conclusion that they belong to the "phenomenology of mind, not to literature," as Allegra Stewart asserts in her Jungian analysis of Stein's works.

Stein's later theoretical writings, with their relentless emphasis on composition as a present-tense process liberated from the preconceptions of memory, lend some support to this account of her texts as naturalistic renderings of the movements of consciousness. But in her equally strong insistence that "[l]anguage as a real thing is not imitation either of sound or colors or emotions it is an intellectual recreation and there is no possible doubt about it," she clearly acknowledges that her commitment to the reality of immediate experience was always matched by—if not mastered by—her intense awareness of the separate but equal reality of language.

The lectures and other theoretical works Stein began to write in the late twenties have been among the most popular and influential of her literary productions. Many critics have used them as shortcuts to understanding her more difficult texts, which allow them to be read as demonstrations of the theories of composition and time that the essays present in a relatively straightforward style. This approach, too, has its pitfalls, especially as a way of dealing with the texts that preceded Stein's wholehearted embrace of present-tense composition in *Tender Buttons*. These later writings, which have more polemical force than theoretical precision, systematically refuse to acknowledge how fundamentally both her conception of reality and her evaluation of the powers and limitations of language changed during the early years of her career. For this reason, they tend more to obscure than to clarify the terms of her exploration of the problem of representation from *Three Lives* to *Tender Buttons*.

In these essays, Stein attempted to provide a unifying theoretical framework for all of her writings by reinterpreting her early texts as a steady progress toward the theory and practice of present-tense composi-

tion that dominated her writings beginning in 1912. The first essay, **"Composition as Explanation,"** inaugurates this strategy by claiming that as early as *Three Lives* she had "naturally" created a "prolonged present" that prefigures the "continuous present" of *The Making of Americans* and all her subsequent writings. Denying that the seismic changes in her work between *The Making of Americans* and *Tender Buttons* have any particular significance, Stein declares that both are equally "natural" consequences of this uniform immersion in present-tense experience: "if it is all so alike it must be simply different and everything simply different was the natural way of creating it then." In **Portraits and Repetition"** and **"The Gradual Making of** *The Making of Americans,"* she presents a more detailed account of the premises that guided her efforts to render the essential qualities of personality in these early works; but again she refuses to provide an adequate explanation for the radical reversal of these premises by the time she wrote *Tender Buttons.* The latter essay proffers a series of six quotations from *A Long Gay Book,* one of the transitional texts that spans these two phases of her writing, in order to "show how it changed, changed from *Making of Americans* to *Tender Buttons.*" But even while asserting that this was a "necessary change," she again evades the question of why it was necessary, with a flippant refusal to acknowledge the magnitude of the issues that were at stake. Why after years of struggling to render the underlying mechanisms of human character in terms of a totalizing unity did she come to celebrate the principle of pure difference? And what considerations led her to abandon her efforts to make language embody essential truths of human experience for the systematic subversion of sense in *Tender Buttons* and the texts that followed?

It is the evident failure of her later essays to explain this fundamental reorientation that has encouraged so many critics to conclude that it must have been the result of her imitation of modernist painting. . . . [The] most common explanation of Stein's literary evolution . . . regards the modernism of *Tender Buttons* and other texts as at best derivative, dependent upon innovation in another medium, and at worst a failure, predicated upon a naïve or perverse refusal to acknowledge the inherent differences between the resources of painting and those of literature.

Interestingly, one of the few challenges to this negative assessment comes from an art historian. In a little-known 1974 essay David Antin argues that Gertrude Stein was the only thoroughly modernist writer in English, because she was the only one who rigorously practiced what art historians recognize as the central axiom of modernism: "that it is necessary to begin from a radical act of definition or redefinition of the domain of the elements and the operations of the art or of art itself." From this perspective, *Tender Buttons* is not derivative from painting but a logical product of Stein's parallel investigation of the same fundamental issue that preoccupied first Cézanne and then Picasso and Braque: the problem of representation, redefined in terms of the distinctive resources of their medium. (pp. xi-xvii)

Stein's unpublished notebooks, which record her extensive commentaries on the painters whose work interested her most, amply confirm the crucial role of modernist art as a catalyst for her own investigations of the problem of representation in language. But they reveal that scholarly studies of the impact of painting on her work, which have always focused primarily, if not exclusively, on Picasso's cubism, have been somewhat misdirected. . . . Stein's own notebooks provide persuasive evidence that it was Cézanne's legendary dedication to "realizing" his sensations that served as the seminal model not only for *Three Lives* but for all her subsequent work as well. Even during the years of Stein's greatest intimacy with Picasso, she continued to regard Cézanne as the "great master," while what she admired most in Picasso's work was the extent of his adherence to the aesthetic principles of Cézanne. (pp. xvii-xviii)

The most compelling evidence of the enormous impact of Cézanne's painting on Stein's work is the transformation of her writing from *Q.E.D.* to *Three Lives.* Begun a year after her initial confrontation with Cézanne, *Three Lives* is the first of many texts that resulted from Stein's resolve to reinvent literary realism on new foundations, grounded in "direct" experience and embodied in the material patterning of language. During the next few years this project entailed both a continuing revaluation of the semiotic resources of language and a series of redefinitions of those aspects of language that could be "figured" in language.

By 1912 Stein's relentless pursuit of reality in and through language had led her, with its own inexorable logic, to *Tender Buttons,* her brilliantly subversive demonstration of the unbreachable gulf that separates the chaotic plenitude of the sensory world from the arbitrary order of language. In the same year Picasso's exploration of the conditions and limitations of pictorial representation had reached a similar culmination in cubist *collage,* with its provocative explorations of how far the iconography and syntax of painting can depart from the order of natural appearances and still signify elements of external reality. But the powerful internal coherence of Stein's writings from *Three Lives* to *Tender Buttons* suggests that these similarities cannot be explained merely as Stein's imitations or translations of Picasso's most recent work. They must be understood, instead, as parallel derivations from Cézanne, their common point of departure.

Between 1905 and 1912 Stein was engaged in a monumental struggle with the problem of realism, in which she worked through successive revaluations of the issue of representation that parallel the course of modernist painting from Cézanne to cubist *collage.* In painting, E. H. Gombrich has argued, it was the ideal of the "innocent eye"—the demand for ever-greater fidelity to immediate sensory data—that led, inevitably, to the breakdown of the long tradition of illusionistic painting. Cézanne was the crucial pivotal point in this historical process; it was his techniques of activating the surface patterning of the canvas to encode the multiple and contradictory signs of visual perception that laid the groundwork for the cubists' deliberate attenuation of the connection between pictorial signs and perceptual reality. Unlike Picasso, Stein wholeheartedly embraced Cézanne's legendary ideal of "realizing" his sensations in terms of the material resources of the medium. Far from merely following Picasso's lead during these years, she struggled desperately to retain her faith that language could be manipulated to embody the structures and rhythms of reality. By the time she wrote *Tender Buttons,* she had accepted the inevitable defeat of this ideal and gone on to create a new art from the ruins of this Cézannesque dream of capturing reality in the lineaments of language. As the terms of her successes and her failures are better understood, the trajectory of Stein's writings from *Three Lives* to *Tender Buttons* should come to be regarded as a crucial episode in the history of representation. (pp. xviii-xix)

Jayne L. Walker, in her *The Making of a Modernist: Gertrude Stein from "Three Lives" to "Tender Buttons,"* The University of Massachusetts Press, 1984, 167 p.

SOURCES FOR FURTHER STUDY

Bridgman, Richard. *Gertrude Stein in Pieces.* London: Oxford University Press, 1970, 411 p.

Highly regarded critical study.

Copeland, Carolyn Faunce. *Language and Time and Gertrude Stein.* Iowa City: University of Iowa Press, 1975, 183 p.

Considers Stein's career in three periods: her early years which include her ties with nineteenth-century literature and her initial experiments; her middle years which include her experiments with the nonrepresentational use of language; and her later years marked by a return to narrative form and a closer examination of time.

Mellow, James R. *Charmed Circle: Gertrude Stein and Company.* New York: Praeger, 1974, 528 p.

Biography focusing on Stein as literary celebrity, including many anecdotes about her friendships with Hemingway, F. Scott Fitzgerald, Picasso, and others.

Miller, Rosalind S. *Gertrude Stein: Form and Intelligibility.* New York: Exposition Press, 1949, 162 p.

General introduction to Stein's works which includes several previously unpublished compositions written by Stein as a student at Radcliffe.

Neuman, S. C. *Gertrude Stein: Autobiography and the Problem of Narration.* Victoria, B.C., Canada: University of Victoria, 1979, 88 p.

Examines Stein's innovative approach to autobiography in *The Autobiography of Alice B. Toklas, Everybody's Autobiography, Paris France,* and *Wars I Have Seen.*

Steiner, Wendy. *Exact Resemblance to Exact Resemblance: The Literary Portraiture of Gertrude Stein.* New Haven, Conn.: Yale University Press, 1978, 225 p.

Theoretical analysis of Stein's literary portraiture.

John Steinbeck

1902-1968

American novelist, short story writer, dramatist, non-fiction writer, scriptwriter, journalist, and poet.

INTRODUCTION

Best known for his controversial Pulitzer Prize-winning novel, *The Grapes of Wrath* (1939), Steinbeck is considered among the most significant American novelists of the twentieth century. When he was honored in 1962 with the Nobel Prize in literature, the awards committee cited Steinbeck's "sympathetic humor and sociological perception" and his "instinct for what is genuinely American, be it good or bad." In his fiction, Steinbeck professed both sympathy and anger toward American society. An active opponent of social exploitation, puritanism, and materialistic values, Steinbeck is noted for his sharp, forceful writing style, his wry humor, and his profound compassion for the poor, the inarticulate, and the politically maligned.

Early in his career, as a result of his study of biology at Stanford University during the 1920s, Steinbeck developed a "biological" view of humanity. He insisted that such evolutionary concepts as adaptation and natural selection apply to human society and that more profound observations could be gleaned from examining people in groups than as individuals. Steinbeck's characters usually live in harmony with nature until such malevolent political or natural forces as progress, scarcity, or drought upset that balance. Through mutual cooperation, the will to adapt, and a mystical religious faith in the power of the just individual, Steinbeck's characters are usually able to survive destructive circumstances.

Many of Steinbeck's novels and stories are set in and around the Salinas Valley in California, where he was born and where he held a variety of jobs prior to his writing career. He often used this setting to stress his theme of the importance of the "relationship between man and his environment," Peter Shaw claimed. "The features of the valley at once determined the physical fate of his characters and made symbolic comment on them." Moreover, while Steinbeck dwelled on the beauty and "fruitfulness" of the valley, he "did not make it a fanciful Eden," Shaw commented. "The river brought destructive floods as well as fertility, and the summer wind could blow hot for months without let-up." Thus, "Man struggled within a closed system that both formed and limited him; there he was responsible for his acts and yet unable to control the larger forces."

Steinbeck achieved popular acclaim with his fourth novel, *Tortilla Flat* (1935), a colorful and sentimental treatment of the idle, anti-materialistic existence of a group of *paisanos*—California natives of mixed Spanish, Indian, and Anglo-Saxon descent—in Monterey, California. Writing in a modernized epic style and influenced by Thomas Malory's *Le morte d'Arthur,* Steinbeck characterizes the *paisanos* as "whores, pimps, gamblers, and sons of bitches" and also as "saints and angels and martyrs and holy men." The novel ends somberly, with Steinbeck's assertion that the *paisanos* lack the material selfishness necessary to modern survival. A grim clash of interests is again evident in his next novel, *In Dubious Battle* (1936), which depicts a strike of migrant fruit pickers and the conflict which results between union organizers and California apple growers. In this book, Steinbeck questions whether humanity is capable of postponing individual differences to work for the greater benefit of the group. Steinbeck's examination of political and social concerns throughout *In Dubious Battle* prompted critical reassessment of his reputation as an author of light social commentary.

Steinbeck gained national recognition with *Of Mice and Men* (1937), a pastoral novel which addresses such themes as the conflict between idealism and reality and the loneliness which divides people of all classes. This work centers on two itinerant ranch hands—Lennie, a strong retarded man, and George, who looks after Lennie and dreams of owning a small farm. After Lennie accidentally kills the conniving wife of his employer's son, George mercifully kills Lennie to spare him a crueler death by a lynch mob. Steinbeck adapted the novel for the Broadway stage in 1937 to great popular and critical acclaim. The drama, for which Steinbeck received a New York Drama Critics Circle Award, was described by Stark Young as an "absorbing work of theater art," by Brooks Atkinson as "a masterpiece," and by John Mason Brown as "one of the finest, most pungent, and most poignant realistic productions."

From 1937 to 1939, Steinbeck studied the problems of a large group of migrant workers during their trek from Oklahoma to California. *The Grapes of Wrath* is his attempt to understand and authenticate this experience. Considered Steinbeck's masterpiece and a landmark in American literature, the novel presents both a biological and political view of the role played by economic conditions in upsetting the delicate balance between humanity and nature. The inability of farmers to seasonally rotate their crops due to market demands, together with drought and the depressed American economy, culminate in *The Grapes of Wrath* in the loss of once-productive farms and the displacement of many rural Oklahoma families. One such family, the Joads, is lured to California by promises of high-paying jobs from large landowners who seek to ensure cheap labor by creating a massive supply of jobless people competing for a limited number of employment opportunities. The Joads discover brutal, systematized migrant labor camps where low wages and the threat of starvation make the workers increasingly dependent upon their employers. *The Grapes of Wrath* is a work of contrasts dramatized in alternately humorous and horrifying episodes: the hopeful westward migration of the Joads is ironically compared to that of the original Western settlers, and the family's dreams of a "land of milk and honey" contrast sharply with descriptions of California farm corporations which destroy crops to maintain high market prices. *The Grapes of Wrath* provoked heated controversy. Community, agricultural, and political interest groups charged Steinbeck with exaggerating conditions in Oklahoma and California, and according to Daniel Aaron, the coalition Spokesmen for the Association farmers "accused Steinbeck of writing a brief for Communism." However, the novel won international acclaim as a powerful depiction of the common person's vulnerability to social and natural forces. Peter Lisça summarized the novel's importance: "*The Grapes of Wrath* was a phenomenon on the scale of a national event. It was publicly banned and burned by citizens; it was debated on national radio hook-ups; but above all it was read."

Steinbeck's critical favor began to decline during the 1940s, and many of his later works received mixed reviews. *The Moon Is Down* (1942), a war novel set in an unspecified country which many critics assumed to be Norway during the German Occupation, was often interpreted as an antiwar statement. Although some reviewers praised Steinbeck for attempting an unsensationalized portrayal of both oppressors and oppressed, many charged that he failed to fully examine the evil of his Nazi characters. John S. Kennedy explained: "His Nazi characters emerged as something like human beings, by no means admirable, but by no means demoniac either. For not making them intrinsically and uniformly monstrous, at a time when some of our most celebrated writers were trying to whip Americans up to a frenzy of indiscriminate hatred, Steinbeck was pilloried." Steinbeck adapted the novel for the theater in 1942. *Cannery Row* (1945), his next novel, centers upon a group of indolent Monterey vagrants and their bumbling adventures with a sympathetic biologist. According to F. W. Watt, *Cannery Row* satirizes "contemporary American life with its commercialized values, its ruthless creed of property and status, and its relentlessly accelerated pace." Although highly popular, the book was generally regarded by critics as light entertainment. In *Sweet Thursday* (1954), a sequel to *Cannery Row* written as the basis for a musical comedy, Steinbeck bids farewell to the disappearing way of life of carefree American vagabonds.

Steinbeck regarded *East of Eden* (1952) as the culmination of his career. Written as a family epic ranging from the Civil War to World War I, this novel is a parable of the fall of man focusing primarily on the Trask family. Paralleling the biblical story of Cain and Abel, two generations of brothers must resolve disputes between one another; in each conflict, evil results from the inexplicable rejection of one child's gift to his father. Steinbeck maintained: "The greatest terror a child can have is that he is not loved. . . . And with rejection comes anger, and with anger, some kind of revenge for rejection, and with the crime, guilt—and there is the story of mankind." The novel centers on Adam, who attempts to create his Eden in the Salinas Valley with Cathy, his beautiful but remote wife. Cathy, who was sexually involved with Adam's brother, Charles, is a figure of evil and destruction reminiscent of the biblical serpent. She gives birth to the twins Caleb and Aron before deserting Adam to assume a new identity as Kate, a vicious and sadistic prostitute. Caleb, the son whose gift Adam rejects, believes his desire for revenge to be preordained, and he exposes Aron to the truth about their mother. Although Aron is eventually destroyed by this revelation, Caleb is offered the possibility of salvation through understanding the meaning of *timshel,* a Hebrew word indicating humanity's power to choose between good and evil. Although *East of Eden* initially drew positive reviews, its overt symbolism and allegorical structure has resulted in critical controversy, and the book has not attained the stature of *The Grapes of Wrath.*

Steinbeck's last novel, *The Winter of Our Discontent* (1961), concerns the disintegration of American moral values. Set in the fictional Long Island community of New Bay, the book depicts a member of a prestigious New England family who succumbs to materialism and the enticements of success. Steinbeck's last major work, *Travels with Charley: In Search of America* (1962), describes his reflections on American values and society during a tour of forty states with Charley, his pet poodle. Steinbeck's other nonfiction works include *A Russian Journal* (1948), a heavily illustrated collection of pieces based on his travels in the Soviet Union, and *The Acts of King Arthur and His Noble Knights* (1976), a modern rendition of Arthurian legends. Many of Steinbeck's works have been adapted for television, film, and the theater.

In addition to his novels and nonfiction, Steinbeck produced several volumes of short fiction during his early career. Although his achievement in this genre is less highly regarded than that of such contemporaries as William Faulkner and F. Scott Fitzgerald, several of Steinbeck's novellas and short stories are considered significant accomplishments. *The Pastures of Heaven* (1932), one of Steinbeck's earliest works to use Eden as a symbol and metaphor, is a loosely related collection set in California's Corral de Tierra Valley. These stories concern a group of "unfinished children of nature" who fail in their attempt to establish an idyllic farming community free from restrictive urban pressures. The novella *The Red Pony* (1937; revised, 1945) showcases Steinbeck's descriptive talents by detailing a boy's maturation and his acceptance of death when he loses his colt to pneumonia. *The Long Valley* (1938), Steinbeck's first collection to achieve wide critical acclaim, contains *The Red Pony* and the light novella *Saint Katy and the Virgin* (1936). The volume also includes the widely anthologized stories "The Chrysanthemums" and "Flight." "The Chrysanthemums" involves a woman who seeks love but is manipulated by a crafty vagrant, while "Flight" chronicles the destruction of a headstrong young Mexican who dies in the mountains after killing a man. *The Pearl* (1947), Steinbeck's last attempt at short fiction, is a lyrical parable about a poor Mexican fisherman's discovery of a giant pearl which brings evil to his household.

In 1962, Steinbeck was awarded the Nobel Prize, an honor that many believed "had been earned by his early work," noted a critic writting in the London *Times,* rather than for his later efforts. Several reviewers, however, thought this attitude was unjust. F. W. Watt, for example, offered this assessment: "Like America itself, his work is a vast, fascinating, paradoxical universe: a brash experiment in democracy; a naive quest for understanding at the level of the common man; a celebration of goodness and innocence; a display of chaos, violence, corruption and decadence. It is no neatly-shaped and carefully-cultivated garden of artistic perfections, but a sprawling continent of discordant extremes." Peter Shaw was seemingly in agreement when he wrote: "When one begins to talk about the shape of a career rather than about single books, one is talking about a major writer. Steinbeck used to complain that reviewers said each new book of his showed a falling-off from his previous one, yet they never specified the height from which his apparently steady decline had begun. What he was noticing was the special kind of concern for a grand design that readers feel when they pick up the book of a writer whose career seems in itself to be a comment on the times."

(For further information about Steinbeck's life

and works, see *Concise Dictionary of American Literary Biography, 1929-1941; Contemporary Authors,* Vols. 1-4, 25-28 [obituary]; *Contemporary Authors New Revision Series,* Vols. 1, 35; *Contemporary Literary Criticism,* Vols. 1, 5, 9, 13, 21, 34, 45; *Dictionary of Literary Biography,* Vols. 7, 9; *Dictionary of Literary Biography Documentary Series,* Vol. 2; *Major 20th-Century Writers;* and *Something about the Author,* Vol. 9.)

CRITICAL COMMENTARY

JOSEPH WARREN BEACH
(essay date 1941)

[In the following excerpt, Beach examines *The Grapes of Wrath* as a proletarian novel encompassing universal themes.]

The Grapes of Wrath is perhaps the finest example we have so far produced in the United States of the proletarian novel. This is a somewhat loose term to designate the type of novel that deals primarily with the life of the working classes or with any social or industrial problem from the point of view of labor. There is likely to be a considerable element of propaganda in any novel with such a theme and such a point of view. And it often happens that the spirit of propaganda does not carry with it the philosophical breadth, the imaginative power, or the mere skill in narrative which are so important for the production of a work of art. Upton Sinclair is an example of a man of earnest feeling and admirable gifts for propaganda who has not the mental reach of a great artist nor the artist's power of telling a plausible story and creating a world of vivid and convincing people. (p. 327)

With Steinbeck, it is the other way round. He has been interested in people from the beginning, from long before he had any theory to account for their ways. What is more, he is positively fond of people, more obviously drawn to them than any other of our group of writers. More especially he has shown himself fond of men who work for bread in the open air, on a background of fields and mountains. They have always appealed to him as individuals, and for something in them that speaks to his esthetic sense. He sees them large and simple, with a luster round them like the figures in Rockwell Kent's engravings. He likes them strong and lusty, ready to fight and ready to make love. He likes to see the women nursing their babies. He likes to see people enjoying their food, however coarse, and sharing it with others, what there is of it. And when they are in distress. . . .

When people are in distress, you want to help them. If the distress is so widespread that anyone's help is a mere drop in the bucket, you begin to reflect on the causes. You develop theories. The people in distress themselves begin to ponder causes, the rights and wrongs of the case, and they develop theories. Their theories may not be scientific, but they have the merit of growing out of a real experience. The best of social philosophies, so far as fiction is concerned, is that which comes spontaneously to the lips of people trying to figure out a way through life's labyrinth. The best sort of story from the point of view of sociology is one that by the very nature of its incidents sets you pondering the most fundamental human problems. (pp. 327-28)

[The final episode of *The Grapes of Wrath,* in which Rosasharn nurses a starving man with the milk intended for her child,] is symbolic in its way of what is, I should say, the leading theme of the book. It is a type of the life-instinct, the vital persistence of the common people who are represented by the Joads. Their sufferings and humiliations are overwhelming; but these people are never entirely overwhelmed. They have something in them that is more than stoical endurance. It is the will to live, and the faith in life. The one who gives voice to this is Ma. When they are driven out of their Hooverville and Tom is with difficulty restrained from violent words and acts against the deputies, it is Ma who explains to him what we might call the philosophy of the proletariat.

"Easy," she said. "You got to have patience. Why, Tom—us people will go on livin' when all them people is gone. Why, Tom, we're the people that live. They ain't gonna wipe us out. Why, we're the people—we go on."

"We take a beatin' all the time."

"I know," Ma chuckled. "Maybe that makes us tough. Rich fellas come up an' they die, an' their kids ain't no good, an' they die out. But, Tom, we keep a comin'. Don' you fret none, Tom. A different time's comin'."

"How do you know?"

"I don' know how."

That is, you will recognize, the philosophy of Sandburg in *The People, Yes*—the mystical faith of the poet in the persistence and the final triumph of the plain people. Sandburg knows no better than Ma how he knows. He feels it in his bones. And that feeling is, I suppose, with Ma the very mark of the will to live.

Rosaharn's gesture in the barn is not the only symbol of this will to live. Very early in the book the author devotes a whole chapter—a short one—to the picture of a turtle crossing the highway. It is an act of heroic obstinacy and persistence against heavy odds.

This is a gem of minute description, of natural history close-up, such as would delight the reader of Thoreau or John Burroughs. There are things like this in Thomas Hardy's Wessex novels. And as in Hardy, so here—it is not a mere piece of gratuitous realism. It may be enjoyed as such. But it inevitably carries the mind by suggestion to the kindred heroisms of men and women. It sets the note for the story that is to follow.

This chapter is an instance of a technical device by which the author gives his narrative a wider reference and representative character. The story of the Joads is faithfully told as a series of particular incidents in their stirring adventure. We hang with concern and suspense over each turn of their fortunes. But the author is not content with that. He wishes to give us a sense of the hordes of mortals who are involved with the Joads in the epic events of the migration; and along with the material events he wishes us to see the social forces at play and the sure and steady weaving of new social patterns for a people and a nation. And so, to every chapter dealing with the Joads, he adds a shorter, more general, but often not less powerful chapter on the general situation.

There is, to begin with, an account of the dust storm over the gray lands and the red lands of Oklahoma—a formidable example of exact and poetic description matched by few things in fiction. Like Hardy with Egdon Heath, Steinbeck begins with physical nature and comes by slow degrees to humanity. The chapter ends with an account of the reactions of the men, women and children in the face of this catastrophe. The conception is large and noble. Humanity has been stripped of all that is adventitious and accidental, leaving the naked will and thought of man. Under the stress of desperate calamity the children watch their elders to see if they will break. The women watch the men to see if this time they will fail. It is a question of going soft or going hard; and when the men go hard the others know that all is not lost. The corn is lost, but something more important remains. And we are left with the picture of the men on whom they all depend. It is man reduced to the simplest terms—man pitted against the brute forces of nature—man with the enduring will that gives him power to use his brains for the conquering of nature. Man's thinking is an extension of his powers of action—he thinks with his hands. (pp. 332-34)

Most of these intercalary chapters have more particular themes. There is the theme of buying cheap and selling dear—the wonderful chapter of the second-hand automobile dealers. There is the theme of social forms coming into being as occasion requires. In the roadside camps the separate families are quickly assembled into one community; and community spontaneously develops its own laws out of its own obvious needs. There is the theme of large-scale production for economy and profit—the land syndicates in California who ruin the small owners. There is the theme of spring in California—its beauty, the scent of fruit, with the cherries and prunes and pears and grapes rotting on the ground to keep up the price. There are hungry men come for miles to take the superfluous oranges; but men with hoses squirt kerosene on the fruit. "A million people hungry, needing the fruit—and kerosene sprayed over the golden mountains." And there is the theme of the blindness of property in its anonymous forms. . . .

There is the theme of a common interest as opposed to a private and exclusive. "Not my land, but ours." "All work together for our own thing—all farm our own lan'." And finally we have the theme of man who has lost his soul and finds it again in devotion to the common cause.

Some of these themes are expressed in the spontaneous utterance of the Okies; some of them in the more abstract and theoretical language of the author. In general we may say that he is most effective when he puts his views in the mouths of the characters. For this is fiction; and fiction has small tolerance for the abstractions of an author. Still, there are cases where the theme is too broad and too complicated to find adequate expression in the words of a single man on a particular occasion. This is a great challenge to the ingenuity of a writer, and Steinbeck has found a number of ingenious and effective means of dramatizing the thought of a whole group of people faced with a difficult problem in economics. There is one remarkable chapter in which he shows us the debate between the tenant farmers and the agents of the banking syndicates come to put them off the land. It is a debate which recurs over and over again with each unfortunate family; and Steinbeck has presented it in a form that is at the same time generalized and yet not too abstract and theoretical. We are shown the farmers squatting on their heels while the owner men sit in their cars and explain the peculiar nature of the institution which they represent. It is a kind of impersonal monster that does not live on side-meat like men, but on profits. It has to have profits all the time, and ever more profits or it will die. And now that the land is poor, the banks cannot afford to leave it in the hands of men who cannot even pay their taxes. (pp. 334-36)

[In] a kind of parable, with allegorical figures, and with Biblical simplifications, our author has managed to give in summary, in essence, what must have gone on a million times all over the world, when the two groups were confronted—two groups that represent two opposed and natural interests, and both of them caught in an intricate web of forces so great and so automatic in their working that they are helpless to combat them or even to understand them. This is not an individual scene of drama; but many of the remarks must have been made a thousand times in individual cases.

It is not an economic treatise; but the substance of many such a treatise is presented in simplified form suited to the apprehensions of the men who speak. There is enough local color to make it appropriate to this story of the Okies; and sufficient differentiation of the manner of the two groups to give it a properly fictional cast. The apologetic tone of the one party, their patience and firmness; the bewilderment and indignation of the other party; the reasonableness on both sides—are admirably rendered. In each case the speaker is like a chorus in ancient tragedy, embodying the collective sentiments of a large group. Anyone who has tried to write will understand the number of difficulties which have been overcome in the application of this literary device. Anyone, at least, who has tried to write fiction, and who has tried in fiction to present a general view of things without cutting loose from the concrete and particular. This is but one of many instances in *The Grapes of Wrath* of Steinbeck's resourcefulness in meeting his main problem—to reconcile the interests of theory with those of imaginative art—to render the abstractions of thought in the concrete terms of fiction. (pp. 337-38)

The narrative method in these chapters is thus an extremely flexible medium, in which many different modes of statement are composed in a consistent whole diversified in coloring as a Persian carpet. What really needs stressing is the virtuosity of the performance, a virtuosity fully as great as—say—Thornton Wilder's, though it is likely to be passed over because of the homeliness of the subject matter, because Steinbeck is supposed to be simply rendering the plain reactions of plain people. And so he is, and much concerned not to introduce any foreign element of preciousness or affectation. But he is rendering them, the reactions of plain people, with tenderness, insight, and artistic detachment, and with the power of modulating freely round the dominant key. He is like an actor capable of doing things with his voice, varying his tone with the changing rôle and emotion. He has more than usual of the storyteller's ventriloquism.

He is one who feels strongly on the subject of man's essential dignity of spirit and his unexhausted possibilities for modification and improvement. It is natural that at times he should slip into a prophetic tone not unlike that of our midwestern poet.

For man, unlike any other thing organic or inorganic in the universe, grows beyond his work, walks up the stairs of his concepts, emerges ahead of his accomplishments. . . . Having stepped forward, he may slip back, but only half a step, never the full step back. This you may say and know it and know it. . . . And this you can know—fear the time when Manself will not suffer and die for a concept, for this one quality is the foundation of Manself, and this one quality is man, distinctive in the universe.

Here let me lay my cards on the table. About such a passage as this I have a divided feeling, as I do about some of the quietly eloquent sayings of Tom to his mother when he leaves her to take up the cause of labor. These statements of Tom about his mission, these statements of Steinbeck about Manself, do not seem to me among the best things in the book, considered as literary art; and yet I do not see how we could dispense with them. I would not wish them away. For they are important clues to the author's feeling—to his hope and faith in humanity. But they do not seem to me altogether successful as imaginative shapings of the stuff of life in keeping with the most rigorous demands of fictional art.

The passage about Manself and dying for a concept is considerably longer than what I have quoted. It is in substance highly creditable to the author's feeling about man's nature and destiny. But there is something a trifle stiff about it, a trifle abstract, "talky," and magniloquent. It is as if at this point Steinbeck's art, generally so flexible and sure, had weakened—as if he was hurried or tired, and had for the moment allowed mere words to take the place of images or the dramatic evocations which are his most effective medium. In the case of Tom's remarks to his mother when he is setting out on his career as a labor organizer (Chapter Twenty-eight), they are cast, like all the dialogue, in the familiar language of the Okie, the untutored man of the people. Perhaps for that very reason, however, there is something just a bit questionable in the high seriousness, the wistful Christlikeness, of the sentiments he expresses. One does not so much question his harboring these sentiments, along with others less exalted in tone; what one questions is whether he could have brought himself to utter just these sentiments in just this tone. One asks whether the author has not a little too obviously manipulated his material here in order to point the moral of his tale. (pp. 339-41)

If I were asked to say just exactly what are the economic theories of John Steinbeck, and how he proposes to apply them in terms of political action, I should have to answer: I do not know. The book offers no specific answer to these questions. It reminds us of what we all do know: that our system of production and finance involves innumerable instances of cruel hardship and injustice; that it needs constant adjustment and control by the conscience and authority of the sovereign people. This author is concerned with what has been called the forgotten man; it is clear that he holds the community responsible for the man without work, home, or food. He seems to intimate that what cannot be cured by individual effort must needs be met by collective measures. It is highly important that our people should be made aware of the social problems which remain to be solved within the system which is so good to so many of us. And there is no more

effective way of bringing this about than to have actual instances presented vividly to our imaginations by means of fiction. For this reason I regard *The Grapes of Wrath* as a social document of great educational value.

Considering it simply as literary art, I would say that it gains greatly by dealing with social problems so urgent that they cannot be ignored. It gains thereby in emotional power. But it is a notable work of fiction by virtue of the fact that all social problems are so effectively dramatized in individual situations and characters—racy, colorful, pitiful, farcical, disorderly, well meaning, shrewd, brave, ignorant, loyal, anxious, obstinate, insuppressible, cockeyed . . . mortals. I have never lived among these Okies nor heard them talk. But I would swear that this is their language, these their thoughts, and these the very hardships and dangers which they encountered. They represent a level, material and social, on which the reader has never existed even for a day. They have lived for generations completely deprived of luxuries and refinements which in the life he has known are taken for granted as primary conditions of civilization.

And yet they are not savages. They are self-respecting men and women with a traditional set of standards and proprieties and rules of conduct which they never think of violating. Beset with innumerable difficulties, cut off from their familiar moorings, they are confronted with situations of great delicacy, with nice problems in ethics and family policy to be resolved. Decisions are taken after informal discussion in the family council organized on ancient tribal lines. Grampa was a rather flighty and childish old fellow. He was still the titular head of the tribe, but his position was honorary and a matter of custom. He had the right of first comment; but actual decision was made by the strong and wise, by Pa and Tom, and above all by Ma. Pa was the representative of practical prudence; Ma the voice of right feeling and generous impulse and the traditional code of decent conduct. It was she who decided that they should take Casy with them although they were already overcrowded. (pp. 345-46)

And so the Joads and the Okies take their place with Don Quixote, with Dr. Faustus, with Galsworthy's Forsytes and Lewis' Babbitt, in the world's gallery of symbolic characters, the representative tapestry of the creative imagination. Will the colors hold? That is a large question, which only time can answer. It depends on whether the dyes are synthetic aniline or the true vegetable product. And who at the present moment can make sure of that?

I will put the question in another way. Is the subject too special for this book to have continuing artistic appeal? Are the issues fundamental enough in human nature to give it what is called universality? Perhaps the best theme is a combination of a particular and local subject with one more general and lasting. The particular subject here is the Oklahoma farmer and an over-supply of labor in the California orchards. The general subject is hunger; the general subject is man pitted against the forces of nature. There is much to remind one of *Robinson Crusoe.* Steinbeck will certainly do well if he can last as long and be as widely read as Daniel Defoe. (p. 347)

Joseph Warren Beach, "John Steinbeck: Art and Propaganda," in his *American Fiction: 1920-1940,* The Macmillan Company, 1941, pp. 327-47.

JOSEPH FONTENROSE
(essay date 1964)

[Fontenrose was an American educator and critic. In the following excerpt, he discusses Steinbeck's biblical allusions and portrayal of good and evil in *East of Eden.*]

In the forties Steinbeck was clearly turning his principal interest from biology and sociology to individual ethics. He was one of several writers whom the Second World War and its aftermath made aware of the "problem of evil." . . . [In *East of Eden,* Steinbeck] completed the transition; it is a lengthy treatment of man's capacity for both good and evil. In it Steinbeck "plainly announces . . . that it is as a moralist that he wants to be taken," as Joseph Wood Krutch expressed it [in "John Steinbeck's Dramatic Tale of Three Generations"]. (p. 118)

[In 1947, Steinbeck] started work upon a book that he called "Salinas Valley," which would be the story of the Hamiltons, his mother's family. Early in the drafting he introduced a fictitious second family, the Trasks, whose role expanded to the point of taking over the novel; and in 1951 the title was changed to *East of Eden.* The finished novel is still two stories, the Trasks and the Hamiltons, or rather three: the story of Cathy Ames is really a separate strand that becomes entwined with the central Trask story in one phase only; thereafter it goes its own way, a parallel strand that comes occasionally into important contact with the Trask strand. The Hamilton story is a subordinate and independent strand that barely touches the other two: the Hamiltons have almost nothing to do with Cathy and little to do with the Trasks. The Trask story needs Cathy Ames, but not the Hamiltons, who can be dropped out without affecting the Trask story at all.

[*East of Eden*] has four Parts. In the first (1862-1900) the three stories are begun, and the Trask and Cathy stories are developed until Adam Trask marries Cathy. Part Two (1900-1902) brings the Trasks and

Hamiltons together in the Salinas Valley, ending with the naming of Cathy's twins, after she has abandoned them and her husband and become a whore (called Kate) in Salinas; and her story is carried to the point where by devious means she acquired ownership of the brothel in which she worked. In Part Three (1911-12) the Hamilton story moves forward on its own from the last days of Samuel Hamilton to its conclusion in the deaths of Dessie and Tom Hamilton, while the Trask story marks time (Adam Trask becomes half alive after ten years of spiritual coma), and Cathy is all but absent. Part Four (1812-18) is the story of Adam Trask and his sons after they had moved from the Trask ranch to Salinas; the parallel Cathy-Kate story ends with her suicide; and the Hamilton story is touched upon only in Will Hamilton's role as Cal Trask's partner in a bean brokerage. The central narrative throughout is the fictional biography of Adam Trask from his birth in the second year of the Civil War until his death in the last year of World War I. . . . The design and magnitude of *East of Eden,* and Steinbeck's own remarks about it, indicate that it was meant to be a climactic work, his greatest achievement, for which every earlier book was practice. But few Steinbeck readers will place it higher than *The Grapes of Wrath;* the majority may see it as a second peak in his career, but not nearly so high as the first. (pp. 118-19)

After ten years in the army and more years wandering across the country, Adam was living with Charles on the Trask farm when Cathy Ames crawled to their door, terribly beaten by the whoremaster Edwards. Adam fell in love with her while nursing her, and married her, obstinately refusing to inquire into her past. Cathy was the sort of person who would put sleeping medicine in Adam's tea on her wedding night so that she could enter Charles's bed; and she appears to have been impregnated by both brothers, for she bore nonidentical twins, one of whom (Caleb) looked like Charles and was like Charles in nature. Contrary to the Biblical story, it was Adam (Abel), not Charles (Cain), who left the family land and went west to California, where the twins were born and Cathy deserted him. There he became the first Adam who lost his Eden (a happy life with Cathy and his children on excellent farm land in the Salinas Valley) and was father of Cain (Caleb) and Abel (Aaron). Adam preferred his son Aaron (later spelled Aron), who in boyhood raised Belgian hares (the herdsman role); the less likeable Caleb (Cal) wanted to be a farmer. When he was seventeen, Cal, in partnership with Will Hamilton, contracted for bean crops to sell to the British Purchasing Agency; he made $15,000 and gave it to his father, who had suffered severe losses in a business venture. Adam cruelly refused Cal's gift on the ground that the money was war profit, unfairly gained, and invidiously compared it to Aron's success in entering Stanford one year early. . . . Cal got revenge by taking Aron to watch the "circus" at Kate's whorehouse and revealing to him that Kate was their mother (Cal had discovered this some time before). Aron, a pure boy who had intended to enter the Episcopal ministry, was profoundly shocked, as Cal had expected, since the knowledge shattered Aron's unreal image of an angelic mother who had died in his infancy. The very next morning Aron enlisted in the army, soon was sent to France, and died in action. (p. 121)

Steinbeck, of course, puts more into the story than can be found in Genesis 4, which says nothing about either brother's attitude towards Adam. The irony of the father's partiality in *East of Eden* is that neither Adam nor Aron loved his father, whereas Charles loved [his father] Cyrus and Cal loved Adam, and each tried hard to please his father. Again, Steinbeck introduces rivalry over a woman into both generations of brothers, more obscurely in the first, since Charles disliked Cathy; but he did admit her to his bed and left her half his fortune when he died. In the next generation Abra, Aron's boyhood sweetheart, transferred her love to Cal after Aron's enlistment. Steinbeck read a good deal about Genesis while writing *East of Eden* and probably came upon a later Jewish legend (current before 300 A.D.) which elaborates the brief and bare scriptural narrative; both Cain and Abel had a twin sister, each intended to become her twin's wife and so ensure the survival of mankind. Abel's twin sister was so beautiful that Cain wanted her; therefore he picked a quarrel with Abel, killed him, and married Abel's twin, that mysterious wife of Cain who bore his son Enoch in the land of Nod (Genesis 4:17).

Furthermore, Steinbeck had to fuse Adam and Jehovah in one person, Cyrus Trask in the first generation, Adam Trask in the second. Cathy is a fusion of Eve, the Eden serpent, and Cain's wife—the beating which the whoremaster gave her had left a scar on her forehead. Steinbeck emphasizes her serpent nature by giving her a heartshaped face, an abnormally small mouth, a little pointed tongue that sometimes flicked around her lips, small sharp teeth with the canine teeth longer and more pointed than the others, tiny ears without lobes and pressed close to her head, unblinking eyes, narrow hips. (p. 122)

The story of Cain and Abel, Lee said to Adam and Sam, "is the symbol story of the human soul," "the best-known story in the world because it is everybody's story." The three men found the story perplexing when they first discussed it. Ten years later, when they had gathered for the last time, Lee had cleared up the difficulties with the help of four aged Chinese sages, who had studied Hebrew for just this purpose.

Dust jacket of Steinbeck's 1939 novel.

They solved the problem of Genesis 4:7, as given in the King James version, "And unto thee shall be his desire, and thou shalt rule over him," by translating the verb form *timshol* (not *timshel* as Steinbeck has it) "thou mayest rule" instead of "thou shalt rule"; and they took "sin" as antecedent of the masculine pronouns. This, Lee said in triumph, "was the gold from our mining": the translation "thou shalt rule" implies predestination; "do thou rule," as in the American Standard version, orders a man to master sin; but "thou mayest rule" gives a man a choice: he can master sin if he wants to. " 'Thou mayest,' " Lee said, "might be the most important word in the world," for "that makes a man great, . . . for in his weakness and his filth and his murder of his brother he has still the great choice."

This, then, is the message of *East of Eden,* a message that many can accept, even though those who "love true things" must reject Lee's interpretation of Genesis 4:7. That verse has an obviously corrupt text, and the sentence at issue appears to be out of place. For one thing, the masculine pronouns cannot refer to "sin," which translates a Hebrew feminine noun. And *timshol* will not bear the meaning which Steinbeck puts upon it. He apparently read or was told that the Hebrew imperfect tense, which indicates incomplete action at any time, is used where English employs either the vivid future tense (*will, shall*) or the potential (*would, should, may, might*); in either case the action is unfulfilled. If a translation as potential suited this verse, it would be simply "you would rule"; it cannot be a permissive "may." Steinbeck, furthermore, constantly translates *timshol* "thou mayest," dropping "rule," as if the Hebrew form were simply an auxiliary. Many a sermon, however, has drawn a fine meaning from a faulty translation of a corrupt text.

According to Lee, the story of Cain and Abel is important because it is a story of rejection, from which all evil flows, since "with rejection comes anger, and with anger some kind of crime in revenge for the rejection, and with the crime guilt—and there is the story of mankind." Or as the author states it in a moralizing chapter . . . , "most of . . . [men's] vices are attempted short cuts to love." . . . As Krutch has pointed out, for Steinbeck as moralist good and evil are absolute and objective. We have come a long way, it seems, from Jim Casy's doctrine in *The Grapes of Wrath* that "There ain't no sin and there ain't no virtue. There's just stuff people do," and from Doc Burton's refusal in *In Dubious Battle* "to put on the blinders of 'good' and 'bad,' " because they would limit his vision and destroy his objectivity. And it seems to me that Steinbeck has limited his vision in *East of Eden.*

The reader is never clear about the relation of good to evil in this novel, for it is presented in four inconsistent ways. (1) Good is opposed to evil. . . . Charles, Cathy, and Cal have bad traits opposed to the good traits of Adam and Aron. In the "thou mayest" doctrine, evil can be rejected and good chosen. (2) Good and evil are complementary. Lee thought that they might be so balanced that if a man went too far either way an automatic slide restored the balance. Good and evil are symbolized by the church and the whorehouse, which "arrived in the Far West simultaneously," and each "intended to accomplish the same thing: . . . [to take] a man out of his bleakness for a time." (3) Evil is the source of good and may even be necessary to good. The evil Cathy, quite without intending it, "set off the glory in Adam." The wealth which Cyrus Trask acquired dishonestly was inherited by Adam Trask, an honest man who used the money to rear and educate his sons. . . . (4) Good and evil are relative terms. Lee said to Adam in that same speech, "What your wife is doing is neither good nor bad," although she was operating the most perverted and depraved brothel in California. This seems to hark back to Casy's doctrine: Kate's activities were simply not nice.

Good is identified both with admirable individual qualities (philanthropy, kindness, generosity, self-respect, courage, creativity) and with conventional moral goodness (sexual purity, abstinence from carnal pleasures of any kind). Evil is identified with ignoble individual qualities (meanness, cruelty, violent temper, avarice, hatefulness, selfishness), with criminal acts (murder, arson, theft, embezzlement), and with carnal pleasures, particularly sex acts; and not only with prostitution and perversions, but with sexual satisfaction in general. That is, the author appears to accept Cal's label of "bad" for his adolescent desires and impulses, and of "good" for Aron's self-indulgent purity and abstinence, and to accept Abra's use of "good" and "bad" when she says that Aron is too good for her, that she herself is not good, and that she loves Cal because he isn't good. Of course, this is the way that young people talk. But Cal and Abra are never allowed to reach a more enlightened view of "good" and "bad"; Steinbeck is using them to illustrate his thesis: that there is good and bad in everyone, and that some bad is necessary (that is, it is good to be bad); and he is understanding good and bad in their terms.

We should notice that in contrast to Steinbeck's treatment of sex in earlier novels, there is no good or healthy or lusty sexual intercourse in *East of Eden.* It is always sordid, joyless, depraved, or mercenary. . . . This is not at all like the old Steinbeck who celebrated sexuality. It turns out that Steinbeck's view of good and evil is that of his mythical source: it is the Mosaic view, which is to say a legal view; particular acts are good or bad, regardless of circumstances. The earlier Steinbeck saw acts in context and evaluated them accordingly, if he evaluated them at all, dismissing the religious conception of "sin" entirely. For a novel on good and evil, *East of Eden* strangely lacks ethical insight. It is true, as I have pointed out, that its author evaluates qualities as well as acts, but they remain abstract. Adam is honest and kind, we are told; but these are negative virtues in him. In truth, virtue seems to be a function of lack of energy: pernicious anemia may account for George Hamilton's sinless life, and Adam Trask was passive, inert, non-resistant. The positive behavior of the "good" characters is at best unpleasant. Aron is selfish, inconsiderate, unloving. Adam neglects his boys for twelve years, never loves anybody except Cathy, and loves her blindly. His rejection of Cal's gift was brutal, unfeeling, and this after he had begun a cordial relationship with his son. Did Steinbeck, perhaps, intend to show that these "good" persons were not what others thought them to be? Hardly. Lee, his spokesman, said about Adam, "I think in him kindness and conscience are so large that they are almost faults. They trip him up and hinder him." Like Aron, he is too good; a man needs a little "bad" in him; you can be good if you don't have to be perfect, said Lee. We come back to moral confusion, since "good," "bad," and "perfect" are given conventional definitions, never questioned. If Steinbeck had delved into a father's ambivalent feelings for his sons, his awareness of favoring one son over the other, his fairness or unfairness to either son, and the moral and spiritual problems arising from his relation to his sons, then *East of Eden* might have been a great novel. As it is, we do not understand Adam's actions; in this novel we cannot resort to saying that they just happened. (pp. 123-26)

Joseph Wood Krutch's favorable review ended with the questions: "Does the fable really carry the thesis; is the moral implicit in or merely imposed upon the story; has the author recreated a myth or merely moralized a tale?" He did not answer the questions. Our answer must be, "No. The moral is imposed upon the story, which is not a recreated myth." A reader can enjoy *East of Eden* for its many fine passages of description and many pages of skillful narrative; but the myth invoked does not adequately interpret the narrated events. (pp. 126-27)

Joseph Fontenrose, in his *John Steinbeck: An Introduction and Interpretation*, Barnes & Noble, Inc., 1964, 150 p.

MARK SPILKA

(essay date 1974)

[Spilka is an American literary critic. In the following excerpt, he addresses Steinbeck's concept of "sweet violence," or pleasure derived from destruction, in *Of Mice and Men*.]

A minor classic of proletarian conflict, *Of Mice and Men* was written in 1937, first as a novel, then as a play. . . .

The sycamore grove by the Salinas River, so lovingly described in the opening lines, is more than scene-setting: it is an attempt to evoke the sense of freedom in nature which, for a moment only, the protagonists will enjoy. By a path worn hard by boys and hobos two migrant laborers appear. The first man is mouse-like. . . . He is the planner from the poem by Robert Burns: as with other mice and men, his best arrangements will often go astray. (p. 170)

The nearest town is Soledad, which means "lonely place" in Spanish; the town where they last worked, digging a cesspool, was Weed. Their friendship is thus quickly placed as a creative defense against rank loneliness; it will be reinforced, thematically, by the hostility and guardedness of bunkhouse life, and by the apparent advance of their dream toward realization. But the secluded grove, the site of natural freedom, provides the only substantiation their dream will ever receive; and when our mouse-like planner tells his friend to return there in case of trouble, we sense that the dream will end where it essentially begins, in this substantiating site.

The second man to appear is "opposite" to the first. . . . This bear-like man becomes equine when they reach the grove: flinging himself down, he drinks from the pool there, "snorting into the water like a horse." (pp. 170-71)

These animal actions and his childish speech place him for us quickly as an idiot. What the first man plans for, the second already has. Like other Steinbeck idiots—Tularecito in *The Pastures of Heaven* (1932), Johnny Bear in *The Long Valley* (1938)—he participates in natural life freely, has access to its powers, and his attraction for Steinbeck is his freedom to use those powers without blame or censure. (p. 171)

In his pocket the idiot carries an actual mouse, dead from too much handling. Later he kills a puppy with playful buffeting. A child fondling "lesser" creatures, he is Steinbeck's example of senseless killing in nature. He is also part of an ascending hierarchy of power. His name is Lennie *Small*, by which Steinbeck means subhuman, animal, childlike, without power to judge or master social fate. His friend's name, George Milton, puts him by literary allusion near the godhead, above subhuman creatures, able to judge whether they should live or die. . . . [In] a later set-up scene . . . old Candy, the lowly bunkhouse sweeper, says that he should have shot his own decrepit dog—should not have let a stranger do it for him. George too will decide that he must shoot Lennie, like a mad rather than a decrepit dog, for the unplanned murder of another man's wife; that he cannot allow strangers to destroy him.

Both shootings have been sanctioned by the jerkline skinner, Slim, "prince of the ranch," who moves "with a majesty achieved only by royalty" and looks with "calm, God-like eyes" upon his bunkhouse world. Since his word is "law" for the migrant farmhands, and since Milton, a rational farmhand, can recognize and accept such godlike laws, he must choose to shoot his friend. By *East of Eden* Steinbeck would conclude that it is choice which separates men from animals, a belief which supports one critic's view of George's decision as "mature." But it is not his "ordinariness" which George will accept, in destroying Lennie and the comforting dream they share, as this critic holds: it is his *humanness*, his responsibility for actions which the animal Lennie, for all his vital strength, cannot comprehend.

And yet George will be diminished—made "ordinary"—by his choice. As many critics insist, he uses Lennie selfishly, draws from him a sense of power, of superiority, which he sorely needs. If he is sensitive to Lennie's feelings—cares for and about him in demonstrable ways—he also "lords" it over him almost vengefully. . . . [Lennie] will always feed this satisfaction, will always do, in effect, what George desires—which means that George himself invites the troubles ahead, makes things go astray, uses Lennie to provoke and settle his own quarrel with a hostile world. (pp. 171-72)

This is to move from social into psychological conflict: but Steinbeck, in taking a boss's son and his wife as sources of privileged pressure on migrant farmhands, has moved there before us. He has chosen aggressive sexuality as the force, in migrant life, which undermines the friendship dream. This variation on the Garden of Eden theme is, to say the least, peculiar. (p. 172)

In *Of Mice and Men* Lennie first pets Curley's wife, then breaks her neck, without any awareness that she provokes both reactions. His conscious desires are simple: to stroke something furry, and to stop the furry thing from yelling so George won't be mad at him. But George has predicted this episode, has called Curley's wife a rat-trap, a bitch, a piece of jail-bait; and he has roundly expressed disgust at Curley's glove full of vaseline, which softens the hand that strokes his wife's genitals. Lennie has obligingly crushed that hand for George, and now he obligingly breaks the rat-trap for him, that snare for mice and men which catches both in its furry toils. (p. 173)

[A] frightening capacity for violence is what Lennie brings into the unsuspecting bunkhouse world: he carries within him, intact from childhood, that low threshold between rage and pleasure which we all carry within us into adulthood. But by adulthood we have all learned to take precautions which an idiot never learns to take. The force and readiness of our feelings continues: but through diversions and disguises, through civilized controls, we raise the threshold of reaction. This is the only real difference, emotionally, between Lennie and ourselves.

A great deal of Steinbeck's power as a writer comes, then, from his ability to bring into ordinary scenes of social conflict the psychological forcefulness of infantile reactions: his creation of Lennie in *Of Mice and Men* is a brilliant instance of that ability—so brilliant, in fact, that the social conflict in this compact tale tends to dissolve into the dramatic urgencies of Lennie's "fate." In his next novel, *The Grapes of Wrath* (1939), Steinbeck would find a situation commensurate with his own low threshold for idiot rage. . . . With Lennie's pathetic fate in mind, the meaning of Rose of Sharon's mysterious smile as she breastfeeds a starving middleaged man is not hard to fathom: she has found in the adult world what Lennie has never been able to find—an adequate way to satisfy inchoate longings, a way to nurture helpless creatures, perform useful tasks, indulge innocent pleasures, without arousing self-destructive anger. Steinbeck has called *Of Mice and Men* "a study of the dreams and pleasures of everyone in the world" and has said that Lennie especially represents "the inarticulate and powerful yearning of all men," their "earth longings" for land of their own, for innocent-pleasure farms. In a profoundly psychological way he was right about the pleasures, though strangely neglectful of the rages which, in his world at least, accompany them. Tom Joad's confident smile, his flaunting of homicide to a truckdriver as *The Grapes of Wrath* begins, and Rose of Sharon's mysterious satisfaction as it closes, suggest that fuller accommodation of universal urges which gives his greatest novel much of its extraordinary power.

Of Mice and Men helped him to release that power by making murder seem as natural and innocent as love. . . . There are natural killings too in *The Red Pony,* where the little boy, Jody, cuts up the bird he has stoned and hides the pieces out of deference to adults: "He didn't care about the bird, or its life, but he knew what older people would say if they had seen him kill it; he was ashamed because of their potential opinion." Jody is too small to push these primitive sentiments very far; but Lennie, a more sizeable child, is better able to amplify their meaning. After killing Curley's wife he flees to the grove near the Salinas River, as George has told him to. Back in his own element, he moves "as silently as a creeping bear," drinks like a wary animal, and thinks of living in caves if George doesn't want him any more. Then out of his head come two figures: his aunt Clara and (seven years before Mary Chase's *Harvey*) a giant rabbit. These figments of adult opinion bring all of George's petty righteousness to bear against him, shame him unmercifully, and threaten him with the only thing that matters: the loss of his beloved bun-

Major Media Adaptations: Motion Pictures and Television

Of Mice and Men, 1939. United Artists. Director: Lewis Milestone. Cast: Burgess Meredith, Lon Chaney, Jr., Noah Beery, Jr.

The Grapes of Wrath, 1940. Twentieth Century-Fox. Director: John Ford. Cast: Henry Fonda, Jane Darwell, John Carradine.

Tortilla Flat, 1942. Metro-Goldwyn-Mayer. Director: Victor Fleming. Cast: Spencer Tracy, Hedy Lamarr, John Garfield.

The Moon Is Down, 1943. Twentieth Century-Fox. Director: Irving Pichel. Cast: Henry Travers, Sir Cedric Hardwicke, Lee J. Cobb.

The Red Pony, 1949. Republic. Director: Lewis Milestone. Cast: Myrna Loy, Robert Mitchum, Peter Miles, Margaret Hamilton.

East of Eden, 1954. Warner Brothers. Director: Elia Kazan. Cast: James Dean, Raymond Massey, Julie Harris.

The Wayward Bus, 1957. Twentieth Century-Fox. Director: Victor Vicas. Cast: Dan Dailey, Jayne Mansfield, Joan Collins.

The Red Pony, 1976. National Broadcasting Company. Director: Robert Totten. Cast: Henry Ronda, Maureen O'Hara, Jack Elom.

East of Eden, 1980. American Broadcasting Company. Director: Harvey Hart. Cast: Jane Seymour, Timothy Bottoms, Bruce Boxleitner, Lloyd Bridges.

Cannery Row, 1982. Metro-Goldwyn-Mayer. Director: David S. Ward. Cast: Nick Nolte, Debra Winger.

nies. Then out of the brush, like a third figment of Miltonic pettiness, comes George himself, as if to punish him once more for "being bad." But for Lennie as for Jody, badness is a matter of opinions and taboos, not of consequences and responsibilities. He doesn't care about Curley's wife, who exists for him now only as another lifeless animal. Nor does Steinbeck care about her except as she arrives at natural innocence; but he does care about that, and through Lennie, who possesses it in abundance, he is able to affirm his belief in the causeless, blameless animality of murder. Of course, he also believes in the responsibility of those who grasp the consequences of animal passion, and it is one of several paradoxes on which this novel ends that George comes humbly now to accept responsibility for such passions, comes not to punish Lennie, then, but to put him mercifully away, to let him die in full enjoyment of their common dream. (pp. 176–77)

What makes this ending scary and painful and perplexing is the weight given to all that Lennie represents: if contradictory values are affirmed—blameless animality, responsible humanity; innocent longing, grim awareness—it is Lennie's peculiar mixture of human dreams and animal passions which matters most. George's newfound maturity is paradoxically an empty triumph: without Lennie he seems more like a horseless rider than a responsible adult. "The two together were one glorious individual," says Steinbeck of the boy Jody and his imagined pony, Black Demon, the best roping team at the Rodeo. Without such demonic vitality, by which any kind of meaningful life proceeds, George is indeed friendless and alone. With it, needless to say, he is prone to destructive rages. On the horns of that adolescent dilemma—that inability to take us beyond the perplexities of sexual rage—Steinbeck hangs his readers. Impales them, rather, since the rich tensions of this poignant perplex, however unresolved, are honestly and powerfully presented. (p. 178)

In *Tortilla Flat,* an otherwise comic novel, [Steinbeck shows] . . . how Danny tires of the chivalric life and reverts to the "sweet violence" of outlawry. "Sweet violence" means something more here than the joys of boyish rebellion: it means delight in pulling the house down on one's own and other people's heads, which is what Danny does when the friendship dream proves insubstantial, and he pays with his life—and later, with his friends' help, with his house—for the pleasure of destroying it. Lennie too pays with his life for the pleasure of destructive rages; but he serves in this respect as an extension of his friend's desires: he is George Milton's idiot Samson, his blind avenger for the distastefulness of aggressive sexuality. Which may be why their friendship seems impossible from the first, why the pathos of their dream, and of its inevitable defeat, seems less important than the turbulence it rouses. Once more "sweet violence" is the force which moves these characters, and which moves us to contemplate their puzzling fate.

By *East of Eden* Steinbeck would learn that rages generally follow from rejected love, that parental coldness or aloofness breeds violence in youthful hearts; and he would come also to accept sexuality as a vulnerable condition, a blind helplessness by which men and women may be "tricked and trapped and enslaved and tortured," but without which they would not be human. . . . But by accepting sex now as a human need, he would redeem his Lennie's and Danny's from outlawry and animality, and he would finally repair the ravages of sweet violence. *Of Mice and Men* remains his most compelling tribute to the force behind those ravages, "the most disturbing impulse humans have," as it moves a selfish master and his dancing bear to idiot rages. And once more it must be said to move us too. For however contradictory it seems, our sympathy for these characters, indeed their love for each other, is founded more deeply in the humanness of that impulse than in its humanitarian disguises. (pp. 178-79)

Mark Spilka, "Of George and Lennie and Curley's Wife: Sweet Violence in Steinbeck's Eden," in *Modern Fiction Studies,* Vol. 20, No. 2, Summer, 1974, pp. 169-79.

PAUL MCCARTHY

(essay date 1980)

[McCarthy is an American educator and critic. In the excerpt below, he provides an introduction to Steinbeck's works.]

Like William Faulkner and Willa Cather, John Steinbeck wrote his best fiction about the region in which he grew up and the people he knew from boyhood. . . .

Far more extensive than Faulkner's county or Cather's homeland, the Steinbeck territory covers thousands of square miles in central California, particularly in the Long Valley, which extends south of Salinas, Steinbeck's hometown, for over one hundred miles and lies between the Gabilan Mountains on the east and the Santa Lucia Mountains along the Pacific coast. (p. 23)

In the territory appear Mexicans, Spanish, and Chinese, as well as German, Irish, and English; not only ranchers and farmers but also migrant workers, community leaders, assorted whores and bums, as well as fishermen, bartenders, schoolteachers, and radicals. The characters include the wealthy, poor, and economically in-between; the able, bigoted, mature, puritanic, psychotic, and happy. The vast territory is a factor also in shaping dominant themes in the fiction, including man's relationships with the land, the attractions of the simple life, the conflicts of the haves and have-nots, the failures or dangers of middle-class existence. (p. 24)

[*The Red Pony*] examines the relationship of man and the land. (p. 30)

Unlike the luckless Pepé in "**Flight,**" Jody grows up on good, fertile land, benefits from a secure family life, and survives his encounters with death and unpredictable nature. Steinbeck's accounts of Jody's life and survival show a similarly graceful and detailed realism. We gain a firm impression of the outward boy, his playing with Doubletree Mutt, deference to his parents, and a close relationship with Buck. The sensitive language and point of view create a sense also of the inner Jody, of his daydreams about armies marching down the country road behind him, of the large colt next to Nellie. . . . Descriptions of farm activities, the countryside, and other people are inseparable from de-

scriptions of a boy growing up. The descriptions, point of view, concentration on the farm scenes and activities and on Jody in particular unify the four parts of the novel. (pp. 31-2)

Learning from experience like Hemingway's young Nick Adams, but more soundly prepared by farm life and his elders, Jody Tiflin learns that dying is natural and living requires sacrifices. Like Nick he learns also that forces in nature can be unpredictable and dangerous. The closing scenes of *The Red Pony* dramatize Jody's maturing tolerance for others and indicate that eventually he will outgrow his teachers. (p. 32)

In portraying dreams, friendships, and grim necessities, Steinbeck wrote his best novel to date [*Of Mice and Men*]. A more sensitive and perceptive work than *Tortilla Flat* or *In Dubious Battle, Of Mice and Men* compares favorably with the best short novels of the decade. It is also the first and best of Steinbeck's experiments with the novel-play form, which combines qualities of each genre. . . . The individual chapters or scenes contain few descriptions of place, character, or action. The unities in *Of Mice and Men* are based on drastic limitations. Action is restricted usually to the bunkhouse. The restriction of time to three days—sunset Thursday to sunset Sunday—intensifies suspense and drama. With place and time compressed, the action is necessarily simple and dramatic; the superfluous and complex have been eliminated. There are no scenes of travel or of work and few of the past. Foreshadowing is obvious and suspenseful. Lennie's rough play with mice and the shooting of Candy's old dog foretell subsequent violence. Future action is more or less anticipated by what is said. And the characters themselves make for simplicity of action.

To create such effects, Steinbeck's craftsmanship was at its best. All aspects of the novel are finely done. A few techniques can be noted. A general technique, as the above would suggest, is a highly restricted focus. With the emphasis upon the scenic, a skillfully managed third-person point of view is also essential. To create a sense of the impersonal and objective, Steinbeck concentrates, with exceptions, on exteriors: a river bank, a bunkhouse, a character's appearance, card players at a table. The setting is not panoramic, as in the description of a valley scene in *In Dubious Battle;* it is, figuratively speaking, only as wide as a stage. The focus is also upon the present: what can be seen or heard. Thoughts, recollections, and fantasies are directly expressed by the characters involved, except in the case of Lennie's Aunt Clara and the giant rabbit in chapter 6. This interlude of fantasy may or may not violate the objectivity of the third-person narration. Generally, however, the point of view remains objective and exterior.

The prose style—particularly the rhythms and

diction—possess greater sensitivity and naturalness than in *In Dubious Battle.* The language is generally more realistic and precise. Descriptions of the bunkhouse interior—walls, bunks, scanty possessions, stove and table, George's things—and of sights and sounds in Crooks's room and the barn, create a sense of the workaday world and its crudities. Hanging in the harness room, where Crooks stays, are "pieces of harness, a split collar with the horsehair stuffing sticking out, a broken hame, and a trace chain with its leather covering split." The precision is notable. Although there are no work scenes, references to bucking barley eleven hours daily, to workers who put in a month and leave, to evenings of card games and pulp magazines underline the weary monotony. The physical bareness of the bunkhouse, the mechanical neatness of bunks and wooden boxes, suggest a bareness of spirit as well. Yet, appearing throughout the novel, often in ironic contrast, are sensitive, sometimes poetic descriptions of the pleasant, secure, or beautiful: the pastoral scene at the beginning; the warm, sunlit scene in the barn on early Sunday afternoon; the late afternoon scene at the "green pool of the Salinas River" at the end.

The symbolism, which does not include the pervasive mythical materials of *In Dubious Battle,* is convincingly part of the talk, places, and incidents of the time. The river bank scene is at least suggestive of life-in-nature, a level Lennie is not too far above. The river bank is reassuringly peaceful until George fires the luger and destroys friend and dream. The ranch provides another kind of security and also a place for dreams, but for the Lennies and the Georges of the world it remains essentially unfulfilling.

The river bank and the ranch provide on one level the idyllic and real boundaries of their world. The centrally placed bunkhouse and barn, offering only physical security and a minimum of that, symbolize the essential emptiness and impersonality of that world. The fundamental symbol is the dream itself—"a little house and a couple of acres an' a cow and some pigs and . . . "—which keeps the two men together, stimulates hope for two others, and very likely expresses the hopes of still others. (The "little house" symbol reappears under more difficult circumstances in *The Grapes of Wrath.*) The action traced in *Of Mice and Men,* possessing a parable-like simplicity and theme, reminds one of journeys of other figures in American fiction, Wellingborough Redburn, Huck Finn, and Henry Fleming, who with others also search for ever-elusive goals.

Another mark of excellence appears in the variety and depth of characterization. . . . The superb dialogue gives life to all the characters.

In the last analysis, George and Lennie symbolize something of the enduring and hopeful as well as the meaningless. They manage—if only for a brief time—

to rise above circumstances and to convince others as well as themselves that dreams are part of the territory, that all they have to do is keep working and hoping and some day they will have their own place. If they could only somehow control their own weaknesses and keep a little ahead of circumstances. But they cannot. These and other matters are examined by Steinbeck in more complex terms and with greater range and authority in *The Grapes of Wrath.* (pp. 60-4)

Appearing in a decade that saw the publication also of *As I Lay Dying* and *Absalom, Absalom!* by William Faulkner and the trilogy *USA* by John Dos Passos, *The Grapes of Wrath* is one of the period's brilliant, innovative works. It combines a long, eventful narrative and many passages of exposition, broadens the narrative level with several important structural patterns, and demonstrates, among other things, the writer's imaginative techniques and craftsmanship. (p. 67)

To create a work of such scope and depth, Steinbeck relied upon a number of techniques. The most general one pertains to the language itself, which, in order to serve various functions, had to be supple and figurative, yet often plain. The novel has in fact several languages. . . . These various levels of language, both written and spoken, show affinities with the free verse of [Walt] Whitman and [Carl] Sandburg, the ironic simplicity of Hemingway, and the distinctive rhythm and phrasing of biblical passages. The most characteristic qualities of the written language are precision, natural and sometimes biblical rhythms, and imagery customarily based on elements of the land or daily life.

Craftsmanship in *The Grapes of Wrath* is generally excellent in other respects as well. While customarily narrated in the third-person voice, the novel's point of view varies dramatically in tone, purpose, and method, providing an elevated panoramic view, as in most intercalary chapters, or a close dramatic one, as in narrative chapters. The point of view within a chapter, moreover, may shift from the personal to the impersonal, from the objective to the ironic. (pp. 69-70)

The principal focus in early and later chapters . . . is not so much on the land as on the farmers themselves and their families. In a general sense *The Grapes of Wrath* is a book about families. These include the many anonymous families appearing throughout the novel, usually in intercalary chapters; the individual families, particularly the Joads and a few others; and, in a general or thematic sense, the family of men. (p. 72)

The views and feelings of dispossessed families are particularized in accounts of the Joads, Steinbeck's most significant family and as noteworthy in modern American fiction as Cather's Bergsons and Faulkner's Bundrens. (p. 73)

The Joads are impressively drawn: a down-to-earth farm family unexceptional in most respects but determined to survive and keep their identities intact. (p. 74)

The Grapes of Wrath can be read not only as fiction but as a social document of the time: a record of drought conditions, economic problems, the sharecropping life. Not separate from the fictional, this level or record is a vital aspect of it. The document clarifies the nature of family and small farm life and also of underlying concepts. One of the most important is the traditional agrarian idea of the simple rural life based on principles of natural rights. Those who live and work on the land, who pay for it with their blood, sweat, and toil, own the land. Muley Graves believes this, and up to a point so do the Joads. This way of life is seriously threatened by nature and, more ominously, by another tradition, a largely modern one that has reappeared in recent years: the combination of big farms and financial establishments. (p. 76)

The migration of hundreds of thousands of people westward was a major cultural phenomenon of the 1930s. Steinbeck's portrayal of that phenomenon is another example of *The Grapes of Wrath* as a form of social document. (p. 78)

The four novels appearing between 1947 and 1952 show the continued importance of western materials and a preoccupation with two familiar staples of his fiction, allegory and realism. Steinbeck's interest in allegory had appeared first in his boyhood love of *Morte d'Arthur,* a little later in characters and actions of a Stanford story, **"The Gifts of Iban,"** and then in *Cup of Gold* (1929) and *To a God Unknown* (1933). Characters and actions representing ideas or attitudes, archetypal patterns, and a strong ethical focus—all qualities of allegory, and particularly of parable—appeared most noticeably in *Tortilla Flat* (1935).

Although such qualities are less vital in the realistic Depression novels, portrayals of Joy and Jim and of the strike confrontations in *In Dubious Battle* (1936) include an allegorical level stressing ideas or qualities. That emphasis appears also in the two-dimensional figures and specialized situations and patterns of *The Grapes of Wrath* (1939). *Cannery Row* (1945) may be regarded as primarily a parable. . . . (p. 106)

Important though allegory and parable are in the postwar fiction, they are no more so than another long-standing Steinbeckian predilection, the realistic, which goes back almost as far as his interest in allegory, appearing, for example, in **"The Chrysanthemums"** and **"Flight"** in the 1930s and also in the Depression novels. In fact, as we shall see, novels of the late 1940s and early 1950s reveal a weakening of the allegorical emphasis and a strengthening of Steinbeck's disposition toward both realism and the romantic, a blending of

which is evident also in his earlier works, including *The Grapes of Wrath.* (p. 107)

To regard *East of Eden* as a romance, or as significantly romantic, is to make the same kind of critical realignment that appears necessary for a reevaluation of *The Wayward Bus.* Both novels rely upon allegorical materials, with the important general difference that realism is the central shaping influence and mode in *The Wayward Bus* and romanticism provides that influence and mode in *East of Eden.* The romanticism of *East of Eden* differs from that of *Cannery Row* in being more complex, pervasive, and affirmative. In its confident treatment of many topics and various aspects of the national identity, and in its expansiveness and variety of remarkable characters and actions, *East of Eden* resembles [Herman Melville's] nineteenth-century romance *Moby-Dick.* (p. 118)

Although [inconsistencies in his treatment of the biblical motif] and other flaws provide ample evidence that Steinbeck's hopes for another major work were not to be realized, *East of Eden* remains impressive. It shows a largeness of vision and treatment evident previously only in *The Grapes of Wrath.* If the insights into good and evil reveal no unusual depths or subtlety, they do show a complexity seldom evident in Steinbeck's earlier works. The problem of evil— oversimplified in earlier works, sometimes avoided, or often expressed in largely political terms—is examined in the discussions between Sam, Lee, and Adam, and in the motivations and fates of several figures, principally Cathy-Kate, Charles, and Caleb Trask. Affirmations of the good are effectively dramatized through Sam and Lee, the former an inventive dreamer, and the latter a humanist who never loses faith in human dignity and reason; and through the persistence of Adam and Cal, who, despite odds, manage to illustrate that faith.

Although the novel's language lacks the vitality and richness of prose found in *The Grapes of Wrath,* it is usually equal to the demands the author places on it. *East of Eden,* despite failures, not only deals with a wealth of diverse materials but does so primarily through the elusive and challenging forms of romance. (pp. 123-24)

Literary historians may have difficulty in placing John Steinbeck and his work because neither belongs convincingly with a recognized trend or group. Developing as a writer about the same time as Fitzgerald, Dos Passos, Faulkner, and Hemingway—all born around the turn of the century—he appears separate from them in various ways. Unlike these writers, Steinbeck was not powerfully influenced by World War I; and unlike them and others he was not among the expatriates writing from Paris in the 1920s about the predicaments of Americans in Europe and at home.

Along with such writers as John Dos Passos and James T. Farrell, Steinbeck has been considered a social-protest writer of the 1930s. *In Dubious Battle, Of Mice and Men,* and *The Grapes of Wrath* strongly criticize economic injustices and particularly the plight of the have-nots. Yet the generic hallmarks of social-protest fiction—a revolutionary message, and characters and actions designed to express that message—rarely appear. The 1930s fiction and other works by Steinbeck have been described also as realistic or naturalistic, familiar terms for dominant literary trends or groups in those years. However, Steinbeck's fiction resists such categories, for in *The Grapes of Wrath* the realism is enriched by a poetic language and by concerns with the mystical aspects of the biological. The naturalistic emphases, which are sometimes as severe as those of Dos Passos, are moderated in that novel and in *Of Mice and Men* by down-to-earth humor and compassion. The man and his work may be regarded as western—possibly the most apt of these descriptions—until one thinks of various fictions and nonfictions that are not western and of others like *Tortilla Flat* and *Cannery Row* that appear to be western, but do not deal with such primary concerns as space, the land and nature, and man's place in them.

The nature and direction of Steinbeck's fiction may be understood more clearly if approached through characteristic symbols and themes, such as the tide-pool image. . . . The family is another important symbol, often at the center of the dramatic forces of a story or novel and illustrating human strengths and weaknesses. (pp. 139-40)

Territory and social protest are two other identifying marks of the fiction. Central California—most memorably Monterey and several valleys—and the area near Sallisaw, Oklahoma, may appear less familiar to readers than Frenchman's Bend, Jefferson, and the farms of Faulkner's Yoknapatawpha county, yet the Steinbeck treatment of land is nonetheless remarkable for its acute and graphic portrayal of environment and of the effects of nature on man. It is remarkable as well for an early and brilliant study of the predicaments of the small farmer and migrant worker confronted by the powerful alignment of big farmers and finance—a confrontation that persists into the 1970s. Social protest, a *sine qua non* in many of Steinbeck's novels, figures significantly in the satiric realism of *The Wayward Bus* and in a more subtle form in *The Winter of our Discontent,* as well as in the tougher-grained novels of the 1930s.

Instrumental in shaping such elements and the fictions themselves is Steinbeck's moral vision which has been variously described, interpreted, praised, and questioned through the years. Steinbeck's pervasive compassion for human beings appears most characteristically in portrayals of the most vulnerable: the naive, handicapped, and disenfranchised—the Maltbys, Danny and the paisanos, George and Lennie—who rarely find the promised land, at least not as they dream of it. Tolerance and sympathy are evident also in the complicated predicaments of Elisa, Doc of *Cannery Row,* Juan Chicoy, and Adam Trask. The fundamentally affirmative quality of the vision, however, tends on the one hand to minimize complexities and shadings of modern life, particularly in ethical values or choices, and on the other hand, to reveal more of group characteristics and ideas than of an individual's heart and mind. This is in keeping with the strong idealistic and intuitive elements in the vision. Major characters such as Danny, Jim Nolan, Tom Joad, and Sam Hamilton, whose feelings and motives are rarely probed in psychological depth, tend to lose concreteness as the novel's end approaches; they gradually become vague embodiments of social and economic views.

The literary craftsmanship and skill with which the themes, symbols, and moral vision are expressed would seem to identify most definitely Steinbeck's fiction and ensure his place with the best writers of his generation. With them he shared a ceaseless dedication to mastering the art of fiction. **"The Chrysanthemums," "Flight,"** and *Of Mice and Men* are distinguished for precision, clarity, and sensitivity of language and for economy and proportion of form. Characters in these and other works illustrate a versatility of execution from the minutely realistic Jody Tiflin, to a variety of allegorical figures in many of the fictions, to the symbolic realism of Ma Joad and Juan Chicoy, to the complicated and introspective narrator, Ethan Allen Hawley. No less effectively at times than Fitzgerald and Hemingway, Steinbeck experimented with nuances of dialogue and prose style and with varieties of point of view; and in diversity of works if not in richness he may have equalled Faulkner, creating not only stories and novels but also parables, plays, novel-plays, and nonfiction, among the latter being the superb *Sea of Cortez,* written with Ed Ricketts. (pp. 140-42)

Steinbeck's best works brilliantly expose mankind's "grievous faults and failures," alert us to social and economic dangers, and remind us of our forgotten commitments and dreams. Steinbeck's strongest convictions and passions appear in his fundamental belief in humanity, in his expectation that man will endure, and that the creative forces of the human spirit will prevail. (p. 143)

Paul McCarthy, in his *John Steinbeck,* F. Ungar, 1980, 163 p.

SOURCES FOR FURTHER STUDY

Benson, Jackson J. *The True Adventures of John Steinbeck, Writer.* New York: The Viking Press, 1984, 1116 p.

Well-documented biography.

————, ed. *The Short Novels of John Steinbeck: Critical Essays with a Checklist to Steinbeck Criticism.* Durham: Duke University Press, 1990, 349 p.

Collects criticism on Steinbeck's short novels. Includes bibliographical survey of Steinbeck criticism.

Kiernan, Thomas. *The Intricate Music: A Biography of John Steinbeck.* Boston: Little, Brown, 1979, 331 p.

Biography.

Moore, Harry T. *The Novels of John Steinbeck.* 2d ed. Port Washington, N.Y.: Kennikat Press, 1968, 106 p.

Critical assessment of Steinbeck's novels.

Timmerman, John H. *John Steinbeck's Fiction: The Aesthetic of the Road Taken.* Norman: University of Oklahoma Press, 1986, 314 p.

Thorough critical examination of Steinbeck's novels and short fiction.

————. *The Dramatic Landscape of Steinbeck's Short Stories.* Norman: University of Oklahoma Press, 1990, 333 p.

Detailed critique of Steinbeck's short fiction.

Stendhal

1783-1842

(Pseudonym of Marie-Henri Beyle; also wrote under pseudonyms Louis-Alexandre-César Bombet, Henri Brulard, and M. B. A. A., among others) French novelist, autobiographer, travel writer, essayist, critic, and novella writer.

INTRODUCTION

*T*he quintessential egoist, Stendhal depicted the individual's lifelong quest for self-knowledge and perpetual search for love in writings admired as early and incisive examples of modern psychological realism. In a spare, understated prose style, his two principal works, the novels *Le rouge et le noir* (1831; *The Red and the Black*) and *La chartreuse de Parme* (1839; *The Charterhouse of Parma*), describe his characters' examinations of their mental and emotional states. Stendhal's introspective fictional characters mirror their author, whose indefatigable self-analysis is recorded in such autobiographical works as *Vie de Henri Brulard* (1890; *The Life of Henri Brulard*) and *Souvenirs d'égotisme* (1892; *Memoirs of an Egotist*). Virtually ignored by his contemporaries, Stendhal—who predicted himself that he would be recognized only after his lifetime—became the object of literary hero worship in the 1880s and is today regarded as one of the greatest authors of nineteenth-century France.

Born Marie-Henri Beyle in Grenoble, Stendhal adored his mother, and her death when he was seven was the first misfortune of his lonely and embittered childhood. He was left thereafter in the care of people he detested: his father, a prosperous middle-class lawyer to whom he always referred as "the bastard," his Aunt Séraphie, and his tutor, Abbé Raillane—all, to Stendhal's mind, conservative, bourgeois, pious hypocrites. Grenoble, too, he found stultifying and provincial. In reaction to this environment, Stendhal adopted a liberal political stance and became an atheist. Stendhal was finally able to escape his family and Grenoble at the age of nineteen, when, because of his remarkable proficiency in mathematics, he was sent to Paris to enroll at the École Polytechnique. Stendhal quickly lost interest, however, and never matriculated. Nonetheless, many biographers link his early skill in mathematics to his enduring attraction to logic and precision. In 1800 Stendhal obtained a commission in the French army and was stationed in Milan, the city he came to love above all others. The rest of Stendhal's life was divided between France and Italy; he supported himself with a series of minor government posts.

An understanding of Stendhal's emotional and intellectual life, scholars stress, is essential to an appreciation of his work. Stendhal's absorbing interests were always himself, love, and writing. The love affairs of the never-married Stendhal, which were many, passionate, and generally short-lived, have received much attention from biographers and literary critics. Perpetually in love, Stendhal considered the emotion a transcendent experience. He maintained a contradictory attitude toward women, as revealed in his many autobiographical writings: inclined to idealize the objects of his affections, at the same time Stendhal fancied himself a conquering, cynical seducer. Of related importance in Stendhal's life was his longing for social success. An admitted egoist, yet often painfully shy and self-conscious, Stendhal, was acutely sensitive to the impression he made upon others and frequently adopted the persona of the satirical wit to amuse companions and hide his own insecurity. Always partial to mystery and disguise (he employed over two hundred pseudonyms in his published works and correspondence), Stendhal became increasingly secretive, almost paranoid, in later years. For all his romances, Stendhal was ultimately a solitary man; toward the end of his life, he wrote that he was "sad to have nothing to love." Stendhal died at the age of 59, hours after collapsing in a Paris street following a stroke. Only three people attended his funeral. In accordance with his wishes, on his tombstone was inscribed *"Arrigo Beyle, Milanese. Visse, scrisse, amo"* ("Henri Beyle, Milanese. He lived, he wrote, he loved").

The themes of Stendhal's work are those of his life: the quest for self-knowledge and for love. Indeed, the titles of two of his minor works, *Memoirs of an Egotist* and *De l'amour* (1822; *On Love*), could stand as descriptive designations of his entire oeuvre. Many scholars agree that each of Stendhal's heroes is, in some sense and to varying degrees, Stendhal himself, a "reconstituted Beyle," according to Albert Thibaudet. Stendhal's preoccupation with the psychology of self and the task of attaining self-knowledge is shared by his protagonists, who endlessly analyze their own actions, motivations, perceptions, and emotions. Further, they, like their author, are impelled, willingly or unwillingly, by love. His characters are thus ruled, in Stendhal's terms, by two principles that at times conflict: *la logique,* rational, precise, scientific thought, and *espagnolisme,* a tendency toward impulsive, passionate, and occasionally violent behavior.

Stendhal began his literary career inauspiciously, publishing biographies, criticism, and travel essays. These early pieces, derivative and often plagiaristic, contain traces of his trademark introspection, and critics agree that personal remarks and allusions constitute their primary interest. Stendhal's essay *Racine et Shakespeare* (*Racine and Shakespeare*), a comparative analysis in which he expresses his preference for the "Romantic" dramas of William Shakespeare over the neoclassical works of Jean Racine, is of some interest to scholars insofar as it reveals his primary concern with the emotions. However, Stendhal diverged from his contemporaries in the Romantic Movement not only in his psychological realism but in his forging of a different stylistic ideal: clear, concise, dispassionate writing. In *On Love,* an analytical treatise augmented by personal reflection and allusion, Stendhal defined seven varieties of love, declared his preference for *amour-passion* ("passionate love"), and catalogued the phases of the experience. This work contains his well-known theory of "crystallization," a metaphor—drawn from the scientific phenomenon of a tree branch becoming covered with crystals when left in a salt mine—describing the initial phases of love. Stendhal was in his mid-forties before he published his first novel, *Armance,* a psychological study of two highly sensitive and morally scrupulous young people in love.

The Red and the Black attracted little attention when it appeared in 1831 but is now considered one of Stendhal's masterpieces. The novel boasts one of the most memorable and compelling protagonists in French literature—Julien Sorel. Stendhal himself usually referred to *The Red and the Black* simply as "Julien," and critics agree that the character dominates the novel, forming the central enigma of what has long been acknowledged as a mystifying book. The very title of *The Red and the Black* was a puzzle to early readers, though it is now generally recognized that the colors represent the two main avenues of social mobility in nineteenth-century France: red refers to the army, black to the church. The son of working-class parents, Julien is ambitious, calculating, and morbidly sensitive. Because he comes of age too late to participate in the military glory of France under Napoleon (his hero and Stendhal's own), he looks to the church for the social and economic advancement he desires. Consciously modeling himself on Tartuffe, the arch-hypocrite of Molière's 1664 play of the same name, Julien is on the threshold of his desired success, achieved through a combination of intelligence, charm, and seduction, when he destroys it all by an impetuous, emotional act of violence. Stendhal culled the basic plot of *The Red and the Black* from newspaper accounts of Antoine Berthet, a seminary student who, employed as a tutor in two successive households, seduced the wife of his first employer and the daughter of his second. Later, believing that his first lover was responsible for his blighted career, Berthet shot her, for which crime he was executed. The melodramatic action is typical, critics note, of the Romantic tendency of the period, but they add that Stendhal was not interested, as were other Romantic novelists, in dramatic effect for its own sake. Indeed, in this work as in Stendhal's others, he avoided sensational description. The interest of Stendhal's novel thus lies in his exploration of his characters' psychological states, his depiction of the emotional duress that precipitates the melodrama.

During the 1830s Stendhal began several autobiographies and two novels, *Lucien Leuwen* and *Lamiel,* all of which remained unfinished and were not published until years after his death; he also composed several novella-length tales of intrigue, set in Renaissance Italy. Then, after several years of literary frustration, Stendhal wrote *The Charterhouse of Parma* in only seven weeks. Today, the novel is ranked with *The Red and the Black* as one of his greatest works. Comparing the two classics, Howard Clewes wrote: "*Le Rouge* is a young man's anguish—a shout of rage and defiance; *La Chartreuse* is the ironic daydream of one who, if not content, is at least mollified." Urbane irony pervades *The Charterhouse of Parma,* a novel of political intrigue set in Italy. The ostensible main character of the book, Fabrizio (or Fabrice) del Dongo, is generally accounted uninteresting in comparison with the complex, fiery Julien Sorel. From the novel's beginning, with its famous description of Fabrizio's confusion in the chaotic battle of Waterloo, to its conclusion, when he withdraws to the monastery of the title, Fabrizio is a passive rather than active character. Even in his consuming love for Clélia, he reacts more often than he acts. In this novel, unlike *The Red and the Black,* it is not the young idealist who draws the reader's attention but the mature, worldly, even cynical characters. Fabrizio and Clélia's love is set in apposition to that of Gina, Duchess of Sansévérina, and Count Mosca, the former beautiful, intelligent, self-assured, and ruthless in the cause of her unrequited love for her nephew Fabrizio, and the latter, Gina's lover, a wily, Machiavellian statesman with a heart. A knowing and satirical analysis of politics and a penetrating exploration of love, *The Charterhouse of Parma* is a panoramic, complex book, dedicated, as Stendhal wrote, "To the Happy Few."

As his dedication indicates, Stendhal believed that he wrote only for a select few capable of appreciating his work. Indeed, his writings were almost entirely neglected by his contemporaries. *On Love* sold only seventeen copies in eleven years, and the novels were similarly ignored. In a lengthy, laudatory review of *The Charterhouse of Parma,* the great French novelist Honoré de Balzac praised Stendhal's depiction of the subtle intrigues of court life, but added that most readers—

unacquainted with the corridors of power—would not recognize its genius. This prediction proved true of Stendhal's canon as a whole. Stendhal, then, was a literary nonentity during his lifetime and for forty-odd years after his death. "Je serais célèbre vers 1880" ("I will be famous around 1880"), Stendhal once remarked, and his prediction proved true. In the late 1880s Stendhal's works began to attract widespread attention, and over the next few years, as his autobiographies and *Lamiel* and *Lucien Leuwen* were published for the first time, a cult of admirers—known as Stendhalians, or Beylists—formed. Within a very short time, Stendhal had attained national recognition as one of France's greatest novelists and a significant precursor of psychological realism in fiction. "Beylism"—a rather vaguely defined philosophy encompassing, among other elements, intense concern with self, uncompromising individualism, preoccupation with romantic love, and an energetic, idealistic devotion to the *chasse au bonheur* ("pursuit of happiness")—became highly fashionable in France. English-speaking readers were somewhat less enthusiastic; while admitting the power and fascination of Stendhal's writing, many were disturbed by what George Saintsbury described as its "disagreeable" tone. The perceived immorality of such characters as Julien Sorel, Gina Sansévérina, and Mosca created a barrier to a full appreciation of Stendhal.

Gradually, however, these moral objections lost their force, and since the mid-twentieth century British and American critics have agreed with their French counterparts in designating Stendhal one of the most significant and influential writers of nineteenth-century France. Recent critics, while echoing earlier commentators in their assessment of Stendhal's psychological insight, compelling characterization, and realistic method, have discovered new aspects of modernity in his work. Frequently discussed, for example, is the theme of the individual in conflict with society. Paradoxically, as criticism of the author's work explores a broader spectrum of themes and issues, Stendhal remains as elusive to readers as he was to himself—and as fascinating a subject for study. As Warner Berthoff wrote in 1986: "It is as if, no matter how many good and true things have been said about his rendering of human experience . . . [Stendhal] retains a power to surprise the next round of readers and to convince them that something essential to the whole performance remains critically undefined."

(For further information about Stendhal's life and works, see *Nineteenth-Century Literature Criticism,* Vol. 23.)

CRITICAL COMMENTARY

HONORÉ DE BALZAC
(essay date 1840)

[Widely recognized as one of the greatest French authors of all time, Balzac considered his *Comédie humaine*, a sequence of 91 novels and stories, to be a definitive chronicle of the social, political, and moral life of the nineteenth century. In the following excerpt from a review that first appeared in the *Revue Parisienne* in September 1840, he champions *The Charterhouse of Parma*, a work that was not well received in its own time.]

If I have so long delayed, in spite of its importance, in speaking of [*La Chartreuse de Parme*], you must understand that it was difficult for me to acquire a sort of impartiality. Even now I am not certain that I can retain it, so extraordinary, after a third, leisurely and thoughtful reading, do I find this work.

I can imagine all the mockery which my admiration for it will provoke. There will be an outcry, of course, at my infatuation, when I am simply still filled with enthusiasm after the point at which enthusiasm should have died. Men of imagination, it will be said, conceive as promptly as they forget their affection for certain works of which the common herd arrogantly and ironically protest that they can understand nothing. Simple-minded, or even intelligent persons who with their proud gaze sweep the surface of things, will say that I amuse myself with paradox, that I have, like M. Sainte-Beuve, my *chers inconnus.* I am incapable of compromise with the truth, that is all.

M. Beyle has written a book in which sublimity glows from chapter after chapter. He has produced, at an age when men rarely *find* monumental subjects and after having written a score of extremely intelligent volumes, a work which can be appreciated only by minds and men that are truly superior. In short, he has written *The Prince up to date,* the novel that Machiavelli would write if he were living banished from Italy in the nineteenth century.

And so the chief obstacle to the renown which M. Beyle deserves lies in the fact that *La Chartreuse de Parme* can find readers fitted to enjoy it only among diplomats, ministers, observers, the leaders of society, the most distinguished artists; in a word, among the twelve or fifteen hundred persons who are at the head of things in Europe. Do not be surprised, therefore, if, in the ten months since this surprising work was pub-lished, there has not been a single journalist who has either read, or understood, or studied it, who has announced, analysed and praised it, who has even alluded to it. I, who, I think, have some understanding of the matter, I have read it for the third time in the last few days: I have found the book finer even than before, and have felt in my heart the kind of happiness that comes from the opportunity of doing a good action.

Is it not doing a good action to try to do justice to a man of immense talent, who will appear to have genius only in the eyes of a few privileged beings and whom the transcendency of his ideas deprives of that immediate but fleeting popularity which the courtiers of the public seek and which great souls despise? If the mediocre knew that they had a chance of raising themselves to the level of the sublime by understanding them, *La Chartreuse de Parme* would have as many readers as *Clarissa Harlowe* had on its first appearance.

There are in admiration that is made legitimate by conscience ineffable delights. Therefore all that I am going to say here I address to the pure and noble hearts which, in spite of certain pessimistic declamations, exist in every country, like undiscovered pleiads, among the families of minds devoted to the worship of art. Has not humanity, from generation to generation, has it not here below its constellations of souls, its heaven, its angels, to use the favourite expression of the great Swedish prophet, Swedenborg, a chosen people for whom true artists work and whose judgments make them ready to accept privation, the insolence of upstarts and the indifference of governments? (pp. 85-6)

This is what happened to me. At the first reading, which took me quite by surprise, I found faults in the book. On my reading it again, the *longueurs* vanished, I saw the necessity for the detail which, at first, had seemed to me too long or too diffuse. To give you a good account of it, I ran through the book once more. Captivated then by the execution, I spent more time than I had intended in the contemplation of this fine book, and everything struck me as most harmonious, connected naturally or by artifice but concordantly.

Here, however, are the errors which I pick out, not so much from the point of view of art as in view of the sacrifices which every author must learn to make to the majority.

If I found confusion on first reading the book, my impression will be that of the public, and therefore evidently this book is lacking in method. M. Beyle has in-

Principal Works

De l'amour (essay) 1822
  [On Love, 1915]
Racine et Shakespeare (criticism) 1823
  ["Racine and Shakespeare" published in Racine and
  Shakespeare, 1962]
Racine et Shakespeare no. II (criticism) 1825
  ["Racine and Shakespeare II" published in Racine and
  Shakespeare, 1962]
Armance; ou, Quelques scènes d'un salon de Paris en
  1827 (novel) 1827
  [Armance published in The Abbess of Castro, and Other
  Tales, 1926]
Le rouge et le noir: Chronique du dix-neuvième siècle
  (novel) 1831
  [Red and Black: A Chronicle of the Nineteenth Century,
  1898; also published as The Red and the Black, 1914]
La chartreuse de Parme (novel) 1839
  [The Charterhouse of Parma, 1902]
Journal de Stendhal . . . , 1801-1814 (journal) 1888
*Lamiel (unfinished novel) 1889

[Lamiel; or, The Ways of the Heart, 1929]
†Vie de Henri Brulard (unfinished autobiography) 1890
  [The Life of Henri Brulard, 1925]
‡Souvenirs d'égotisme (unfinished autobiography) 1892
  [Memoirs of an Egotist, 1949]
§Lucien Leuwen (unfinished novel) 1901
  [Lucien Leuwen, 1951]
Stendhal. 79 vols. (novels, unfinished novels, unfinished
  autobiographies, journal, novellas, essays, biogra-
  phies, criticism, and letters) 1927-37
To the Happy Few: Selected Letters of Stendhal (letters)
  1952
The Private Diaries of Stendhal (journal) 1954

*This work was primarily written in 1839.
†This work was written between 1835 and 1836.
‡This work was written in 1832.
§This work was written between 1834 and 1835.

deed disposed the events as they happened, or as they ought to have happened; but he has committed, in his arrangement of the facts, a mistake which many authors commit, by taking a subject true in nature which is not true in art. When he sees a landscape, a great painter takes care not to copy it slavishly, he has to give us not so much its letter as its spirit. So, in his simple, artless and unstudied manner of telling his story, M. Beyle has run the risk of appearing confused. Merit which requires to be studied is in danger of remaining unperceived. And so I could wish, in the interest of the book, that the author had begun with his magnificent sketch of the battle of Waterloo, that he had reduced everything which precedes it to some account given by Fabrizio or about Fabrizio while he is lying in the village in Flanders where he arrives wounded. Certainly, the work would gain in lightness. The del Dongo father and son, the details about Milan, all these things are not part of the book: the drama is at Parma, the principal characters are the Prince and his son, Mosca, Rassi, the Duchessa, Ferrante Palla, Lodovico, Clelia, her father, the Raversi, Giletti, Marietta. Skilled advisers or friends endowed with simple common sense might have procured the development of certain portions which the author has not supposed to be as interesting as they are, and would have called for the excision of several details, superfluous in spite of their fineness. For instance, the work would lose nothing if the Priore Blanès were to disappear entirely.

I will go farther, and will make no compromise, in favour of this fine work, over the true principles of art. The law which governs everything is that of unity in composition; whether you place this unity in the central idea or in the plan of the book, without it there can be only confusion. So, in spite of its title, the work is ended when Conte and Contessa Mosca return to Parma and Fabrizio is Archbishop. The great comedy of the court is finished. (pp. 128-30)

If, beneath the Roman purple and with a mitre on his head, Fabrizio loves Clelia, become Marchesa Crescenzi, and if you were telling us about it, you would then wish to make the life of this young man the subject of your book. But if you wished to describe the whole of Fabrizio's life, you ought, being a man of such sagacity, to call your book *Fabrizio, or the Italian in the Nineteenth Century.* In launching himself upon such a career, Fabrizio ought not to have found himself outshone by figures so typical, so poetical as are those of the two Princes, the Sanseverina, Mosca, Ferrante Palla. Fabrizio ought to have represented the young Italian of to-day. In making this young man the principal figure of the drama, the author was under an obligation to give him a large mind, to endow him with a feeling which would make him superior to the men of genius who surround him, and which he lacks. Feeling, in short, is equivalent to talent. *To feel* is the rival of *to understand* as *to act* is the opposite of *to think.* The friend of a man of genius can raise himself to his level by affection, by understanding. In matters of the heart, an inferior man may prevail over the greatest artist. There lies the justification of those women who fall in love with imbeciles. So, in a drama, one of the most ingenious resources of the artist is (in the case in which we suppose M. Beyle to be) to make a hero superior by his feeling when he cannot by genius compete with the people among whom he is placed. In this respect, Fabrizio's part requires recasting. The genius of Catholicism ought to urge him with its divine hand towards the Charterhouse of Parma, and that genius ought from time to time to overwhelm him with the tidings of heavenly grace. But then the Priore Blanès could not perform this part, for it is impossible to cultivate judicial astrology and to be a saint according to the Church. The book ought therefore to be either shorter or longer.

Possibly the slowness of the beginning, possibly that ending which begins a new book and in which the subject is abruptly strangled, will damage its success, possibly they have already damaged it. M. Beyle has moreover allowed himself certain repetitions, perceptible only to those who know his earlier books; but such readers themselves are necessarily connoisseurs, and so fastidious. M. Beyle, keeping in mind that great principle: "Unlucky in love, as in the arts, who says too much!" ought not to repeat himself, he, always concise and leaving much to be guessed. In spite of his sphinx-like habit, he is less enigmatic here than in his other works, and his true friends will congratulate him on this.

The portraits are brief. A few words are enough for M. Beyle, who paints his characters both by action and by dialogue; he does not weary one with descriptions, he hastens to the drama and arrives at it by a word, by a thought. His landscapes, traced with a somewhat dry touch which, however, is suited to the country, are lightly done. He takes his stand by a tree, on the spot where he happens to be; he shews you the lines of the Alps which on all sides enclose the scene of action, and the landscape is complete. The book is particularly valuable to travellers who have strolled by the Lake of Como, over the Brianza, who have passed under the outer-most bastions of the Alps and crossed the plains of Lombardy. The spirit of those scenes is finely revealed, their beauty is well felt. One can see them.

The weak part of this book is the style, in so far as the arrangement of the words goes, for the thought, which is eminently French, sustains the sentences. The mistakes that M. Beyle makes are purely grammatical; he is careless, incorrect, after the manner of seventeenth-century writers. . . . In one place, a discord of tenses between verbs, sometimes the absence of a verb; here, again, sequences of *c'est*, of *ce que*, of *que*, which weary the reader, and have the effect on his mind of a journey in a badly hung carriage over a French road. These quite glaring faults indicate a scamping of work. But, if the French language is a varnish spread over

thought, we ought to be as indulgent towards those in whom it covers fine paintings as we are severe to those who shew nothing but the varnish. If, in M. Beyle, this varnish is a little yellow in places and inclined to scale off in others, he does at least let us see a sequence of thoughts which are derived from one another according to the laws of logic. His long sentence is ill constructed, his short sentence lacks polish. He writes more or less in the style of Diderot, who was not a writer; but the conception is great and strong; the thought is original, and often well rendered. This system is not one to be imitated. It would be too dangerous to allow authors to imagine themselves to be profound thinkers.

M. Beyle is saved by the deep feeling that animates his thought. All those to whom Italy is dear, who have studied or understood her, will read *La Chartreuse de Parme* with delight. The spirit, the genius, the customs, the soul of that beautiful country live in this long drama that is always engaging, in this vast fresco so well painted, so strongly coloured, which moves the heart profoundly and satisfies the most difficult, the most exacting mind. The Sanseverina is the Italian woman, a figure as happily portrayed as Carlo Dolci's famous head of *Poetry*, Allori's *Judith*, or Guercino's *Sibyl* in the Manfredini gallery. In Mosca he paints the man of genius in politics at grips with love. It is indeed love without speech (the speeches are the weak point in *Clarisse*), active love, always true to its own type, love stronger than the call of duty, love, such as women dream of, such as gives an additional interest to the least things in life. Fabrizio is quite the young Italian of to-day at grips with the distinctly clumsy despotism which suppresses the imagination of that fine country; but . . . the dominant thought or the feeling which urges him to lay aside his dignities and to end his life in a Charterhouse needs development. This book is admirably expressive of love as it is felt in the South. Obviously, the North does not love in this way. All these characters have a heat, a fever of the blood, a vivacity of hand, a rapidity of mind which is not to be found in the English nor in the Germans nor in the Russians, who arrive at the same results only by processes of revery, by the reasonings of a smitten heart, by the slow rising of their sap. M. Beyle has in this respect given this book the profound meaning, the feeling which guarantees the survival of a literary conception. But unfortunately it is almost a secret doctrine, which requires laborious study. *La Chartreuse de Parme* is placed at such a height, it requires in the reader so perfect a knowledge of the court, the place, the people that I am by no means astonished at the absolute silence with which such a book has been greeted. That is the lot that awaits all books in which there is nothing vulgar. The secret ballot in which vote one by one and slowly the superior minds who make the name of such works, is not counted until long afterwards. (pp. 130-33)

After the courage to criticise comes the courage to praise. Certainly it is time someone did justice to M. Beyle's merit. Our age owes him much: was it not he who first revealed to us Rossini, the finest genius in music? He has pleaded constantly for that glory which France had not the intelligence to make her own. Let us in turn plead for the writer who knows Italy best, who avenges her for the calumnies of her conquerors, who has so well explained her spirit and her genius. (p. 133)

M. Beyle is one of the superior men of our time. It is difficult to explain how this observer of the first order, this profound diplomat who, whether in his writings or in his speech, has furnished so many proofs of the loftiness of his ideas and the extent of his practical knowledge should find himself nothing more than Consul at Civita-vecchia. No one could be better qualified to represent France at Rome. M. Mérimée knew M. Beyle early and takes after him; but the master is more elegant and has more ease. M. Beyle's works are many in number and are remarkable for fineness of observation and for the abundance of their ideas. Almost all of them deal with Italy. He was the first to give us exact information about the terrible case of the Cenci; but he has not sufficiently explained the causes of the execution, which was independent of the trial, and due to factional clamour, to the demands of avarice. His book *De l'amour* is superior to M. de Sénancour's, he shews affinity to the great doctrines of Cabanis and the School of Paris; but he fails by the lack of method which, as I have already said, spoils *La Chartreuse de Parme.* (pp. 134-35)

M. de Chateaubriand said, in a preface to the eleventh edition of *Atala,* that his book in no way resembled the previous editions, so thoroughly had he revised it. M. le Comte de Maistre admits having rewritten *Le Lépreux de la vallée d'Aoste* seventeen times. I hope that M. Beyle also will set to work going over, polishing *La Chartreuse de Parme,* and will stamp it with the imprint of perfection, the emblem of irreproachable beauty which MM. de Chateaubriand and de Maistre have given to their precious books. (p. 135)

Honoré de Balzac, "Stendhal," in *Novelists on Novelists: An Anthology,* edited by Louis Kronenberger, Doubleday & Company, Inc., 1962, pp. 85-136.

LYTTON STRACHEY
(essay date 1914)

[In the following excerpt from an essay written in 1914, Strachey explores Stendhal's simultaneous use of rigorous logic and emotional intensity in his work.]

It was as a novelist that Beyle first gained his celebrity, and it is still as a novelist—or rather as the author of *Le Rouge et Le Noir* and *La Chartreuse de Parme* (for an earlier work, *Armance,* some short stories, and some later posthumous fragments may be left out of account) that he is most widely known to-day. These two remarkable works lose none of their significance if we consider the time at which they were composed. It was in the full flood of the Romantic revival, that marvellous hour in the history of French literature when the tyranny of two centuries was shattered for ever, and a boundless wealth of inspirations, possibilities, and beauties before undreamt-of suddenly burst upon the view. It was the hour of Hugo, Vigny, Musset, Gautier, Balzac, with their new sonorities and golden cadences, their new lyric passion and dramatic stress, their new virtuosities, their new impulse towards the strange and the magnificent, their new desire for diversity and the manifold comprehension of life. But, if we turn to the contemporaneous pages of Stendhal, what do we find? We find a succession of colourless, unemphatic sentences; we find cold reasoning and exact narrative; we find polite irony and dry wit. The spirit of the eighteenth century is everywhere. . . . It is true that Beyle joined the ranks of the Romantics for a moment with a *brochure* attacking Racine at the expense of Shakespeare; but this was merely one of those contradictory changes of front which were inherent in his nature; and in reality the whole Romantic movement meant nothing to him. . . . To him the whole apparatus of "fine writing"—the emphatic phrase, the picturesque epithet, the rounded rhythm—was anathema. The charm that such ornaments might bring was in reality only a cloak for loose thinking and feeble observation. Even the style of the eighteenth century was not quite his ideal; it was too elegant; there was an artificial neatness about the form which imposed itself upon the substance, and degraded it. No, there was only one example of the perfect style, and that was the *Code Napoléon;* for there alone everything was subordinated to the exact and complete expression of what was to be said. A statement of law can have no place for irrelevant beauties, or the vagueness of personal feeling; by its very nature, it must resemble a sheet of plate glass through which every object may be seen with absolute distinctness, in its true shape. (pp. 275-77)

This attempt to reach the exactitude and the detachment of an official document was not limited to Beyle's style; it runs through the whole tissue of his work. He wished to present life dispassionately and intellectually, and if he could have reduced his novels to a series of mathematical symbols, he would have been charmed. The contrast between his method and that of Balzac is remarkable. That wonderful art of materialisation, of the sensuous evocation of the forms, the qualities, the very stuff and substance of things, which was perhaps Balzac's greatest discovery, Beyle neither possessed nor wished to possess. Such matters were to him of the most subordinate importance, which it was no small part of the novelist's duty to keep very severely in their place. In the earlier chapters of *Le Rouge et Le Noir,* for instance, he is concerned with almost the same subject as Balzac in the opening of *Les Illusions Perdues*—the position of a young man in a provincial town, brought suddenly from the humblest surroundings into the midst of the leading society of the place through his intimate relations with a woman of refinement. But while in Balzac's pages what emerges is the concrete vision of provincial life down to the last pimple on the nose of the lowest footman, Beyle concentrates his whole attention on the personal problem, hints in a few rapid strokes at what Balzac has spent all his genius in describing, and reveals to us instead, with the precision of a surgeon at an operation, the inmost fibres of his hero's mind. In fact, Beyle's method is the classical method—the method of selection, of omission, of unification, with the object of creating a central impression of supreme reality. Zola criticises him for disregarding "le milieu." . . . Zola, with his statistical conception of art, could not understand that you could tell a story properly unless you described in detail every contingent fact. He could not see that Beyle was able, by simply using the symbol "nuit," to suggest the "milieu" at once to the reader's imagination. Everybody knows all about the night's accessories—"ses odeurs, ses voix, ses voluptés molles"; and what a relief it is to be spared, for once in a way, an elaborate expatiation upon them! And Beyle is perpetually evoking the gratitude of his readers in this way. "Comme il insiste peu!" as M. Gide exclaims. Perhaps the best test of a man's intelligence is his capacity for making a summary. Beyle knew this, and his novels are full of passages which read like nothing so much as extraordinarily able summaries of some enormous original narrative which has been lost.

It was not that he was lacking in observation, that he had no eye for detail, or no power of expressing it; on the contrary, his vision was of the sharpest, and his pen could call up pictorial images of startling vividness, when he wished. But he very rarely did wish: it was apt to involve a tiresome insistence. In his narratives he is like a brilliant talker in a sympathetic circle, skimming swiftly from point to point, taking for granted the intelligence of his audience, not afraid here and there to throw out a vague "etc." when the rest of the sentence is too obvious to state; always plain of speech, never self-assertive, and taking care above all things never to force the note. His famous description of the Battle of Waterloo in *La Chartreuse de Parme* is certainly the finest example of this side of his art. Here he produces an indelible impression by a series of light touches applied with unerring skill. Unlike Zola, unlike Tolstoi, he shows us neither the loathsomeness nor the devastation of a battlefield, but its insignificance, its irrelevant detail, its unmeaning grotesquenesses and indignities, its incoherence, and its empty weariness. Remembering his own experience at Bautzen, he has made his hero—a young Italian impelled by Napoleonic enthusiasm to join the French army as a volunteer on the eve of the battle—go through the great day in such a state of vague perplexity that in the end he can never feel quite certain that he really *was* at Waterloo. He experiences a succession of trivial and unpleasant incidents, culminating in his being hoisted off his horse by two of his comrades, in order that a general, who has had his own shot from under him, might be supplied with a mount; for the rest, he crosses and recrosses some fields, comes upon a dead body in a ditch, drinks brandy with a *vivandière,* gallops over a field covered with dying men, has an indefinite skirmish in a wood—and it is over. (pp. 278-81)

It is . . . in his psychological studies that the detached and intellectual nature of Beyle's method is most clearly seen. When he is describing, for instance, the development of Julien Sorel's mind in *Le Rouge et Le Noir,* when he shows us the soul of the young peasant with its ignorance, its ambition, its pride, going step by step into the whirling vortex of life—then we seem to be witnessing not so much the presentment of a fiction as the unfolding of some scientific fact. The procedure is almost mathematical: a proposition is established, the inference is drawn, the next proposition follows, and so on until the demonstration is complete. Here the influence of the eighteenth century is very strongly marked. Beyle had drunk deeply of that fountain of syllogism and analysis that flows through the now forgotten pages of Helvétius and Condillac; he was an ardent votary of logic in its austerest form—"la logique" he used to call it, dividing the syllables in a kind of awe-inspired emphasis; and he considered the ratiocinative style of Montesquieu almost as good as that of the *Code Civil.*

If this had been all, if we could sum him up simply as an acute and brilliant writer who displays the scientific and prosaic sides of the French genius in an extreme degree, Beyle's position in literature would present very little difficulty. He would take his place at once as a late—an abnormally late—product of the eighteenth century. But he was not that. In his blood there was a virus which had never tingled in the veins of Voltaire. It was the virus of modern life—that new sensibility, that new passionateness, which Rousseau had first made known to the world, and which had won its way over Europe behind the thunder of Napoleon's artillery. Beyle had passed his youth within earshot of that mighty roar, and his inmost spirit could never lose the echo of it. It was in vain that he studied Condillac and modelled his style on the Code; in vain that he sang the praises of *la Lo-gique,* shrugged his shoulders at the Romantics, and turned the cold eye of a scientific investigator upon the phenomena of life; he remained essentially a man of feeling. . . . In short, as he himself admitted, he never could resist "le Beau" in whatever form he found it. *Le Beau!* The phrase is characteristic of the peculiar species of ingenuous sensibility which so oddly agitated this sceptical man of the world. His whole vision of life was coloured by it. His sense of values was impregnated with what he called his "espagnolisme"—his immense admiration for the noble and the high-resounding in speech or act or character—an admiration which landed him often enough in hysterics and absurdity. Yet this was the soil in which a temperament of caustic reasonableness had somehow implanted itself. The contrast is surprising, because it is so extreme. Other men have been by turns sensible and enthusiastic: but who before or since has combined the emotionalism of a schoolgirl with the cold penetration of a judge on the bench? . . . Such were the contradictions of his double nature, in which the elements, instead of being mixed, came together, as it were, in layers, like superimposed strata of chalk and flint.

In his novels this cohabitation of opposites is responsible both for what is best and what is worst. When the two forces work in unison the result is sometimes of extraordinary value—a product of a kind which it would be difficult to parallel in any other author. An eye of icy gaze is turned upon the tumultuous secrets of passion, and the pangs of love are recorded in the language of Euclid. The image of the surgeon inevitably suggests itself—the hand with the iron nerve and the swift knife laying bare the trembling mysteries within. It is the intensity of Beyle's observation, joined with such an exactitude of exposition, that makes his dry pages sometimes more thrilling than the wildest tale of adventure or all the marvels of high romance. The passage in *La Chartreuse de Parme* describing Count Mosca's jealousy has this quality, which appears even more clearly in the chapters of *Le Rouge et Le Noir* concerning Julien Sorel and Mathilde de la Mole. Here Beyle has a subject after his own heart. The loves of the peasant youth and the aristocratic girl, traversed and agitated by their overweening pride, and triumphing at last rather over themselves than over each other—these

things make up a gladiatorial combat of "espagnolismes," which is displayed to the reader with a supreme incisiveness. The climax is reached when Mathilde at last gives way to her passion, and throws herself into the arms of Julien, who forces himself to make no response. . . . (pp. 282-85)

[This scene] contains the concentrated essence of Beyle's genius, and . . . , in its combination of high passion, intellectual intensity and dramatic force, may claim comparison with the great dialogues of Corneille. (p. 286)

At times his desire for dryness becomes a mannerism and fills whole pages with tedious and obscure argumentation. And, at other times, his sensibility gets the upper hand, throws off all control, and revels in an orgy of melodrama and "espagnolisme." Do what he will, he cannot keep up a consistently critical attitude towards the creatures of his imagination: he depreciates his heroes with extreme care, but in the end they get the better of him and sweep him off his feet. When, in *La Chartreuse de Parme,* Fabrice kills a man in a duel, his first action is to rush to a looking-glass to see whether his beauty has been injured by a cut in the face; and Beyle does not laugh at this; he is impressed by it. In the same book he lavishes all his art on the creation of the brilliant, worldly, sceptical Duchesse de Sanseverina, and then, not quite satisfied, he makes her concoct and carry out the murder of the reigning Prince in order to satisfy a desire for amorous revenge. This really makes her perfect. But the most striking example of Beyle's inability to resist the temptation of sacrificing his head to his heart is in the conclusion of *Le Rouge et Le Noir,* where Julien, to be revenged on a former mistress who defames him, deliberately goes down into the country, buys a pistol, and shoots the lady in church. Not only is Beyle entranced by the *bravura* of this senseless piece of brutality, but he destroys at a blow the whole atmosphere of impartial observation which fills the rest of the book, lavishes upon his hero the blindest admiration, and at last, at the moment of Julien's execution, even forgets himself so far as to write a sentence in the romantic style: "Jamais cette tête n'avait été aussi poétique qu'au moment où elle allait tomber." Just as Beyle, in his contrary mood, carries to an extreme the French love of logical precision, so in these rhapsodies he expresses in an exaggerated form a very different but an equally characteristic quality of his compatriots—their instinctive responsiveness to fine poses. (pp. 286-87)

Lytton Strachey, "Henri Beyle," in his *Books and Characters: French & English,* Harcourt Brace Jovanovich, 1922, pp. 267-93.

JOSEPH WOOD KRUTCH
(essay date 1930)

[In the following excerpt, Krutch examines Stendhal's protagonists, characterizing them as extensions of the author's personality and philosophy.]

Always the desire to be great in some respect had been with Stendhal more definite and more constant than the desire for greatness of any particular kind. He had abandoned one career after another and he had put off until his youth was past even those literary efforts which, since childhood, he had planned to make. He had been a soldier, business man, diplomat and lover without finding satisfaction in any capacity. His whole life had been a search for a role which he could play whole-heartedly. And now when he came to write novels he began to multiply his personalities—to give himself a multiplicity of lives with which to experiment—not only because the pleasure of watching himself live was the only one he had ever had, but also because in novels he could set according to his own will the conditions of the game. In life, unfortunately, these conditions had been set for him. (p. 234)

Of these *alter egos* who lived for him, Julien Sorel, hero of *The Red and the Black,* may be taken as typical and in him may be discovered Stendhal's dream of himself. Julien is of humble birth, son of a coarse-grained father whom he hates and, because of humiliations, fired with a double ambition—to succeed and to be loved. The external circumstances of his life are quite different from those of his creator but his character and his methods are the same. Like Stendhal he formulates a Machiavellian plan (in which conscious hypocrisy plays a large part) for the cultivation of his personality, and like Stendhal he is not wholly aware of the incompatibility between the ideals of the Saint Preux and the Don Juan. His character is purged of all that Stendhal recognized as potentially ridiculous in himself and his schemes are made more successful than Stendhal was ever able to make his own, but he remains essentially an *alter ego,* merely more perfectly Stendhalian than Stendhal himself.

And what may be said of Julien Sorel may, in general, be said also of the heroes of *The Charter House of Parma* and *Lucien Leuwen.* Both the settings and all the circumstances under which the characters make their *débuts* are varied, but the central figure is in each case the same romantic egotist seeking the same satisfactions through the same means. Stendhal did not care how completely the accident of birth varied the details of the problem to be solved—probably indeed he preferred to set it each time anew—and he even consented to give Lucien Leuwen an admirable father, but the problem must be always the same—how a young man, at once romantic and clear-sighted, may go about to win a knowledge of the human heart and through that knowledge achieve the kind of success which consists in the realization of self.

Moreover, his heroes are, again like himself, victims of a not wholly comprehended bitterness. They feel themselves invested with a certain right to move in a moral universe beyond good and evil, because something—unusual sensibilities and unusual, hardly defined, wrongs—sets them apart. The world is their oyster and they will open it ruthlessly, yet the pearl which they are always hoping to find is a delicate jewel—some great love or the opportunity for some dazzling ultimate heroism. And so it is that they too go about dishonourably in search of honour, and attempt to attain an ideal love by seducing and abandoning the wives or daughters of those who befriend them. Aristocratically disdainful of the vulgar, they are nevertheless champions of the people against their oppressor and this paradox is related to all the others. For at bottom their perversities are masquerading as the protests of a man who finds the world not good enough for him. Just as Stendhal himself felt relieved of any loyalty to the aims of Napoleon because the soldiers of Napoleon did not fulfil his idea of what military chivalry demanded, so his heroes abandon their mistresses because the latter are not quite worthy, and act the hypocrite because the world is too low to deserve honest treatment.

Thus whether "Beylism" be studied in the person of its creator or in that of one of his characters, it is not, as he supposed, a logical philosophy of life, but rather a complex of ideas, desires and quasi-ethical principles which attain such unity as they have, not because of any necessary relation of one to another, but because they found themselves together in the personality of Stendhal and were by him transferred to his characters. To be a Beylist one must believe (1) in romantic love, (2) in the cult of the ego, (3) in the morality of the superman, (4) in military glory and (5) in political liberalism. One need not act always in the direction which all of these beliefs would seem to recommend. The egotist may momentarily be lost in the lover; the cult of self and the morality of the superman may interfere with the lover of political justice. But one must at different times be aware of all these impulses and one must think of them not as essentially contradictory but as somehow fusible into a philosophy never quite grasped. (pp. 235-37)

Now in the case of Stendhal himself the psychological determinants in this *mélange* of warring elements are clearer than they ever are in the case of the characters to whom he transfers them. His own mental life may be explained in terms of a reaction to his earlier experiences, as an effort to divest himself of the fixations of his childhood and, while purging his hatreds away, to salve his wounds with the triumphal successes imagined during the period of his intensest humiliations. The death of the too well beloved mother had burdened him with a romantic longing which no actual person could satisfy, and the hatred of his father had generated in him that fixed delusion of persecution which seemed to justify an amoral struggle against an inimical world. Sheer negativism had made him a Jacobin in the midst of a conservative family, but he had, nevertheless, all those feelings of aristocratic superiority which are commonly cherished by morbidly sensitive souls who compensate by imagining themselves endowed with some capacity or some fineness of feeling belonging exclusively to those whom Stendhal loved to call "the happy few."

But however clear the psychology of Beylism may be when it is thought of as an attribute of Henri Beyle, it is less so when it is thought of in connection with the characters of his novels considered as persons entirely separate from him, and it is less clear for the simple reason that though Stendhal attributes to them all that he recognized as significant in himself he could not, because he himself did not thoroughly understand, explain their personalities on the basis of the factors which determined his own. Hence they appear as Beylists without having gone through the experiences which, in the case of its creator, generated that philosophy.

When a novelist draws his material, as Stendhal did, from himself, when he creates characters in his own image in order to put them through adventures emotionally satisfying to himself, he must, before his novels attain the full validity of art, detach them from their psychological origins and make them something capable of an existence independent of himself and of the purely individual needs they were created to fulfil. So long as their interest or their significance is understandable only in relation to the author, they are documents (perhaps highly interesting ones) for the study of his personality, but they are not in any complete sense works of art and it must be confessed that the novels of Stendhal are, in this respect, inferior to those of other masters no more renowned than he. Nor is it merely that the virtue of the heroes (exaggerated by way of compensation for Stendhal's own bungling efforts) is often too remarkable for the taste of the reader. The fact is that the novels are too perfectly fitted to gratify the emotional needs of their creator to be wholly satisfying to anybody else and that the secret of the personality of the characters can never be unlocked with any key furnished by the works in which they are found. The key is Stendhal himself.

And yet, though these novels may not be wholly

satisfactory as art, they have exercised a fascination over many minds and an influence upon novel writing which may be attributed in part to the interest of the man who half reveals himself in them and in part to the fact that, whether through accident or not, they furnish a sort of bridge between the romantic literature of his epoch and the psychological realism that was to follow. Perhaps a nature as unstable and chaotic as his, is not likely to produce perfect art, but its restless, rebellious eccentricity is very likely, on the other hand, to throw off hints and to discover new modes of sensibility. It is in minds like his that intellectual or emotional "sports" destined to play important roles take their rise, and so it was in his case. In the very heart of romanticism something antiromantic was born.

As to the romantic elements they are so obvious that it is hardly worth while to insist upon them. Not only is his tendency to revolve around the ideas of Love and Glory typically romantic but so too is that whole conception of the "storminess" of the superior character. And yet the ideal of analysis tends to replace that of ecstasy so that Beylism differs from, let us say, the philosophy of Rousseau by the presence of a certain cynical dryness, by the abstraction of all that is genuinely transcendental and the introduction of utilitarian principles which lead him to consider even the pleasures of romantic love as the result of an agreeable delusion—which a rational man may permit himself to use as he uses alcohol—rather than as a mysterious gift of God. (pp. 238-40)

And however inharmonious or unstable the particular combination of discordant elements which Stendhal called Beylism may be, his variations from the romantic were variations in the direction in which the temper of Europe was moving. Not only is there present in him that conflict between rationalism and romantic sensibility which was to destroy the latter but there is also clearly foreshadowed that moral nihilism into which the nineteenth century was unwillingly driven. His heroes were very imperfect supermen struggling desperately against their romantic impulse in the effort to achieve a Nietzschean morality and coming near enough to it to make Nietzsche one of the most enthusiastic of Stendhal's admirers. The experiences of the latter's infancy plus the literature upon which he nourished his morbid sensibilities fixed certain romantic conceptions indelibly upon him, but if one can imagine him with certain of the delusions to which he recurrently fell victim stripped away, he would be very nearly a contemporary man looking at the contemporary man's bleak world and wondering what may be found to take the place of all that we have outgrown.

In the course of some very brief remarks upon the novels of Stendhal, Croce let fall the phrase "unconscious irony," and it is, perhaps, the most pregnant one ever applied in an effort to describe these works. No writer since Stendhal has ever succeeded in completely resolving the conflicts which form the moral substance of his fiction. Romantic love persists in spite of all possible disillusion with it and the typical contemporary hero is one who, like Julien Sorel, gropes his way toward new standards and new ethics while he is still emotionally controlled by the world in which he half believes. But man, more and more convinced of his littleness, is more and more inclined to regard his predicament with bitter irony. The last delusion of grandeur gone, he is haunted by the suspicion that the play in which he is the protagonist is not tragedy but farce and so he finds in the heroes of Stendhal who still trail the remnants of the romantic robes an unconscious irony which the author never makes explicit because he never, except in flashes, perceived it. (pp. 241-42)

To say that *The Life of Henri Brulard* is Stendhal's best book, that the posterity to whom its author looked must find its direct revelations more completely satisfying than any of his imaginative treatments of his ego, is, of course, to say that in a measure he failed as a novelist. Yet the fact is hardly to be doubted. The reality which emerges from the pages of *Brulard* is more continuously fascinating than any fantasies he was able to create, the man more intriguing than any of the roles he allowed himself in imagination to play. He had never quite succeeded in transforming the personal into the universal, and while the amoral heroics of his characters seemed shocking to his contemporaries, they sometimes strike us as a little theatrical and forced. But *Henri Brulard* takes its place with the great confessions; it is a book as searching and honest as any a troubled man ever succeeded in writing about himself. (pp. 247-48)

Joseph Wood Krutch, "Stendhal," in his *Five Masters: A Study in the Mutations of the Novel,* Jonathan Cape & Harrison Smith, 1930, pp. 175-249.

SIMONE DE BEAUVOIR

(essay date 1949)

[A French essayist and novelist, Beauvoir was a prominent figure in the establishment of existentialism and feminism as major movements of the twentieth century. Her *Le deuxieme sexe* (1949; *The Second Sex*) is considered a seminal text. In the following excerpt from this work, she contends that Stendhal evinced a progressive sense of sympathy with and identification toward his female characters.]

Stendhal loved women sensually from childhood. . . .

Women inspire his books, feminine figures people them; the fact is that he writes for them in large part. "I take my chance of being read in 1900 by the souls I love, the Mme Rolands, the Mélanie Guilberts. . . ." They were the very substance of his life. How did they come to have that preferment?

This tender friend of women does not believe in the feminine mystery, precisely because he loves them as they really are; no essence defines woman once for all; to him the idea of "the eternal feminine" seems pedantic and ridiculous. . . . The differences to be noted between men and women reflect the difference in their situations. (pp. 147-48)

The worst handicap [women] have is the besotting education imposed upon them; the oppressor always strives to dwarf the oppressed; man intentionally deprives women of their opportunities. . . . A great many women are doomed to idleness, when there is no happiness apart from work. This state of affairs makes Stendhal indignant, and he sees in it the source of all the faults for which women are reproached. They are not angels, nor demons, nor sphinxes: merely human beings reduced to semislavery by the imbecile ways of society.

It is precisely because they are oppressed that the best of them avoid the defects that disfigure their oppressors; they are in themselves neither inferior nor superior to man; but by a curious reversal their unhappy situation favors them. It is well known how Stendhal hated serious-mindedness: money, honors, rank, power seemed to him the most melancholy of idols; the vast majority of men sell themselves for profit; the pedant, the man of consequence, the bourgeois, the husband—all smother within them every spark of life and truth; larded with ready-made ideas and acquired sentiments and conformable to social routines, their personalities contain nothing but emptiness; a world peopled by these soulless creatures is a desert of ennui. There are many women, unfortunately, who wallow in the same dismal swamps; these are dolls with "narrow and Parisian ideas," or often hypocritical devotees. Stendhal experiences "a mortal disgust for respectable women and their indispensable hypocrisy"; they bring to their frivolous occupations the same seriousness that makes their husbands stiff with affectation; stupid from bad education, envious, vain, gossipy, worthless through idleness, cold, dry, pretentious, malicious, they populate Paris and the provinces; we see them swarming behind the noble figure of a Mme de Rênal, a Mme de Chasteller. The one Stendhal has painted with the most malevolent care is without doubt Mme Grandet, in whom he has set forth the exact negative of a Mme Roland, a Métilde. Beautiful but expressionless, scornful and without charm, she is formidable in her "celebrated virtue" but knows not the true modesty that comes from the soul; filled with admiration for herself, puffed up with her own importance, she can only copy the outer semblance of grandeur; fundamentally she is vulgar and base; "she has no character . . . she bores me," thinks M. Leuwen. "Perfectly reasonable, careful for the success of her plans," her whole ambition is to make her husband a cabinet minister; "her spirit is arid"; prudent, a conformist, she has always kept away from love, she is incapable of a generous act; when passion breaks out in that dry soul, there is burning but no illumination.

This picture need only be reversed to show clearly what Stendhal asks of women: it is first of all not to permit themselves to be caught in the snares of seriousness; and because of the fact that the things supposed to be of importance are out of their range, women run less risk than men of getting lost in them; they have better chances of preserving that naturalness, that naïveté, that generosity which Stendhal puts above all other merit. What he likes in them is what today we call their authenticity: that is the common trait in all the women he loved or lovingly invented; all are free and true beings. Some of them flaunt their freedom most conspicuously: Angela Pietragrua, "strumpet sublime, in the Italian manner, *à la* Lucretia Borgia," and Mme Azur, "strumpet *à la* Du Barry . . . one of the least vain and frivolous Frenchwomen I have met," scoff openly at social conventions. Lamiel laughs at customs, mores, laws; the Sanseverina joins ardently in intrigue and does not hesitate at crime. Others are raised above the vulgar by their vigor of spirit: such is Menta, and another is Mathilde de La Mole, who criticizes, disparages, and scorns the society around her and wants to be distinguished from it. With others, again, liberty assumes a quite negative aspect; the remarkable thing in Mme de Chasteller is her attitude of detachment from everything secondary; submissive to the will of her father and even to his opinions, she none the less disputes bourgeois values by the indifference which she is reproached for as childishness and which is the source of her insouciant gaiety. Clélia Conti also is distinguished for her reserve; balls and other usual amusements of young girls leave her cold; she always seems distant "whether through scorn for what is around her, or through regret for some absent chimera"; she passes judgment on the world, she is indignant at its baseness.

But it is in Mme de Rênal that independence of soul is most deeply hidden; she is herself unaware that she is not fully resigned to her lot; it is her extreme delicacy, her lively sensitivity, that show her repugnance for the vulgarity of the people around her; she is without hypocrisy; she has preserved a generous heart, capable of violent emotions, and she has a flair for happiness. The heat of this fire which is smoldering within her can hardly be felt from outside, but a breath would be enough to set her all ablaze.

These women are, quite simply, *alive;* they know that the source of true values is not in external things but in human hearts. This gives its charm to the world they live in: they banish ennui by the simple fact of their presence, with their dreams, their desires, their pleasures, their emotions, their ingenuities. The Sanseverina, that "active soul," dreads ennui more than death. To stagnate in ennui "is to keep from dying, she said, not to live"; she is "always impassioned over something, always in action, and gay, too." Thoughtless, childish or profound, gay or grave, daring or secretive, they all reject the heavy sleep in which humanity is mired. And these women who have been able to maintain their liberty—empty as it has been—will rise through passion to heroism once they find an objective worthy of them; their spiritual power, their energy, suggest the fierce purity of total dedication.

But liberty alone could hardly give them so many romantic attributes: pure liberty gives rise rather to esteem than to emotion; what touches the feelings is the effort to reach liberty through the obstructive forces that beat it down. It is the more moving in women in that the struggle is more difficult. Victory over mere external coercion is enough to delight Stendhal; in his *Chroniques italiennes* he immures his heroines deep within convents, he shuts them up in the palaces of jealous husbands. Thus they have to invent a thousand ruses to rejoin their lovers; secret doors, rope ladders, bloodstained chests, abductions, seclusions, assassinations, outbursts of passion and disobedience are treated with the most intelligent ingenuity; death and impending tortures add excitement to the audacities of the mad souls he depicts for us. Even in his maturer work Stendhal remains sensitive to this obvious romanticism: it is the outward manifestation of what springs from the heart; they can be no more distinguished from each other than a mouth can be separated from its smile. Clélia invents love anew when she invents the alphabet that enables her to correspond with Fabrice. The Sanseverina is described for us as "an always sincere soul who never acted with prudence, who abandoned herself wholly to the impression of the moment"; it is when she plots, when she poisons the prince, and when she floods Parma that this soul is revealed to us: she is herself no more than the sublime and mad escapade she has chosen to live. The ladder that Mathilde de La Mole sets against her windowsill is no mere theatrical prop: it is, in tangible form, her proud imprudence, her taste for the extraordinary, her provocative courage. The qualities of these souls would not be displayed were they not surrounded by such inimical powers as prison walls, a ruler's will, a family's severity.

But the most difficult constraints to overcome are those which each person encounters within himself: here the adventure of liberty is most dubious, most poignant, most pungent. Clearly Stendhal's sympathy for his heroines is the greater the more closely they are confined. To be sure, he likes the strumpets, sublime or not, who have trampled upon the conventions once for all; but he cherishes Métilde more tenderly, held back as she is by her scruples and her modesty. Lucien Leuwen enjoys being with that free spirit Mme de Hocquincourt; but he passionately loves the chaste, reserved, and hesitant Mme de Chasteller; he admires the headstrong soul of the Sanseverina, who flinches at nothing; but he prefers Clélia to her, and it is the young girl who wins Fabrice's heart. And Mme de Rênal, fettered by her pride, her prejudices, and her ignorance, is of all the women created by Stendhal perhaps the one who most astounds him. He frequently locates his heroines in a provincial, limited environment, under the control of a husband or an imbecile father; he is pleased to make them uncultured and even full of false notions. Mme de Rênal and Mme de Chasteller are both obstinately legitimist; the former is timid and without experience; the latter has a brilliant intelligence but does not appreciate its value; thus they are not responsible for their mistakes, but rather they are as much the victims of them as of institutions and the mores; and it is from error that the romantic blossoms forth, as poetry from frustration.

A clear-headed person who decides upon his acts in full knowledge of the situation is to be curtly approved or blamed; whereas one admires with fear, pity, irony, love, the courage and the stratagems of a generous heart trying to make its way in the shadows. It is because women are baffled that we see flourishing in them such useless and charming virtues as their modesty, their pride, their extreme delicacy; in a sense these are faults, for they give rise to deception, oversensitiveness, fits of anger; but they are sufficiently accounted for by the situation in which women are placed. Women are led to take pride in little things or at least in "things of merely sentimental value" because all the things "regarded as important" are out of their reach. Their modesty results from their dependent condition: because they are forbidden to show their capabilities in action, they call in question their very being. It seems to them that the perception of others, especially that of their lover, reveals them truly as they are: they fear this and try to escape from it. A real regard for value is expressed in their flights, their hesitations, their revolts, and even in their lies; and this is what makes them worthy of respect; but it is expressed awkwardly, even in bad faith; and this is what makes them touching and even mildly comic. It is when liberty is taken in its own snares and cheats against itself that it is most deeply human and therefore to Stendhal most engaging.

Stendhal's women are touching when their hearts set them unforeseen problems: no law, no recipe, no reasoning, no example from without can any longer guide them; they have to decide for themselves, alone.

This forlornness is the high point of freedom. Clélia was brought up in an atmosphere of liberal ideas, she is lucid and reasonable; but opinions acquired from others, true or false, are of no avail in a moral conflict. Mme de Rênal loves Julien in spite of her morality, and Clélia saves Fabrice against her better judgment: there is in the two cases the same going beyond all recognized values. This hardihood is what arouses Stendhal's enthusiasm; but it is the more moving in that it scarcely dares to avow itself, and on this account it is more natural, more spontaneous, more authentic. In Mme de Rênal audacity is hidden under innocence: not knowing about love, she is unable to recognize it and so yields to it without resistance; it would seem that because of having lived in the dark she is defenseless against the flashing light of passion; she receives it, dazzled, whether it is against heaven and hell or not. When this flame dies down, she falls back into the shadows where husbands and priests are in control. She has no confidence in her own judgment, but whatever is clearly present overwhelms her; as soon as she finds Julien again, she gives him her soul once more. Her remorse and the letter that her confessor wrests from her show to what lengths this ardent and sincere soul had to go in order to escape from the prison where society shut her away and attain to the heaven of happiness.

In Clélia the conflict is more clearly conscious; she hesitates between her loyalty to her father and her amorous pity; she tries to think of arguments. The triumph of the values Stendhal believes in seems to him the more magnificent in that it is regarded as a defeat by the victims of a hypocritical civilization; and he is delighted to see them using trickery and bad faith to make the truth of passion and happiness prevail over the lies they believe in. Thus Clélia is at once laughable and deeply affecting when she promises the Madonna not to *see* Fabrice any more and then for two years accepts his kisses and embraces on condition that she keep her eyes shut!

With the same tender irony Stendhal considers Mme de Chasteller's hesitancies and Mathilde de La Mole's incoherencies; so many detours, reversals, scruples, hidden victories and defeats in order to arrive at certain simple and legitimate ends! All this is for him the most ravishing of comedies. There is drollery in these dramas because the actress is at once judge and culprit, because she is her own dupe, because she imposes roundabout ways upon herself when she need only decree that the Gordian knot be cut. But nevertheless these inner struggles reveal all the most worthy solicitude that could torture a noble soul: the actress wants to retain her self-respect; she puts her approbation of herself above that of others and thus becomes herself an absolute. These echoless, solitary debates are graver than a cabinet crisis; when Mme de Chasteller asks herself whether she is or is not going to respond to Lucien Leuwen's love, she is making a decision concerning herself and also the world. Can one, she asks, have confidence in others? Can one rely on one's own heart? What is the worth of love and human pledges? Is it foolish or generous to believe and to love?

Such interrogations put in question the very meaning of life, the life of each and of all. The so-called serious man is really futile, because he accepts ready-made justifications for his life; whereas a passionate and profound woman revises established values from moment to moment. She knows the constant tension of unsupported freedom; it puts her in constant danger: she can win or lose all in an instant. It is the anxious assumption of this risk that gives her story the colors of a heroic adventure. And the stakes are the highest there are: the very meaning of existence, this existence which is each one's portion, his only portion. Mina de Vanghel's escapade can in a sense seem absurd; but it involves a whole scheme of ethics. "Was her life a miscalculation? Her happiness had lasted eight months. Hers was a soul too ardent to be contented with the reality of life." Mathilde de La Mole is less sincere than Clélia or Mme de Chasteller; she regulates her actions according to the idea of herself which she has built up, not according to the clear actuality of love, of happiness: would it be more haughty and grand to save oneself than to be lost, to humiliate oneself before one's beloved than to resist him? She also is alone in the midst of her doubts, and she is risking that self-respect which means more to her than life. It is the ardent quest for valid reasons for living, the search through the darkness of ignorance, of prejudices, of frauds, in the shifting and feverish light of passion, it is the infinite risk of happiness or death, of grandeur or shame, that gives glory to these women's lives.

Woman is of course unaware of the seductiveness she spreads around her; to contemplate herself, to act the personage, is always an inauthentic attitude; Mme Grandet, comparing herself with Mme Roland, proves by the act that she is not like her. If Mathilde de La Mole remains engaging, it is because she gets herself involved in her comedies and because she is frequently the prey of her heart just when she thinks she is in control of it; she touches our feelings to the degree that she escapes her own will. But the purest heroines are quite unselfconscious. Mme de Rênal is unaware of her elegance, as Mme de Chasteller is of her intelligence. In this lies one of the deep joys of the lover, with whom both reader and author identify themselves; he is the witness through whom these secret riches come to light; he is alone in admiring that vivacity which Mme de Rênal's glances spread abroad, that "lively, mercurial, profound spirit" which Mme de Chasteller's entourage fails to appreciate; and even if others appreciate the Sanseverina's mind, he is the one who penetrates farthest into her soul.

Before woman, man tastes the pleasure of contemplation; he is enraptured with her as with a landscape or a painting; she sings in his heart and tints the sky. This revelation reveals him to himself: it is impossible to comprehend the delicacy of women, their sensitiveness, their ardor, without becoming a delicate, sensitive, and ardent soul; feminine sentiments create a world of nuances, of requirements the discovery of which enriches the lover: in the company of Mme de Rênal, Julien becomes a different person from that ambitious man he had resolved to be, he makes a new choice. If a man has only a superficial desire for a woman, he will find it amusing to seduce her. But true love really transfigures his life. "Love such as Werther's opens the soul . . . to sentiment and to the enjoyment of the *beautiful* under whatever form it presents itself, however ill-clothed. It brings happiness even without wealth. . . . " "It is a new aim in life to which everything is related and which changes the face of everything. Love-passion flings all nature with its sublimities before a man's eyes like a novelty just invented yesterday." Love breaks the everyday routine, drives ennui away, the ennui in which Stendhal sees such deep evil because it is the lack of any reason for living or dying; the lover has an aim and that is enough to turn each day into an adventure: what a pleasure for Stendhal to spend three days hidden in Menta's cave! Rope ladders, bloodstained caskets, and the like express in his novels this taste for the extraordinary. Love—that is to say, woman—makes apparent the true ends of existence: beauty, happiness, fresh sensations, and a new world. It tears out a man's soul and thereby gives him possession of it; the lover feels the same tension, knows the same risks as his mistress, and proves himself more authentically than in his professional career. When Julien hesitates at the foot of a ladder placed by Mathilde, he puts in question his entire destiny: in that moment his true measure is taken. It is through women, under their influence, in reaction to their behavior, that Julien, Fabrice, Lucien work out their apprenticeship in dealing with the world and themselves. Test, reward, judge, friend—woman truly is in Stendhal what Hegel was for a moment tempted to make of her: that other consciousness which in reciprocal recognition gives to the other subject the same truth that she receives from him. Two who know each other in love make a happy couple, defying time and the universe; such a couple is sufficient unto itself, it realizes the absolute.

But all this presupposes that woman is not pure alterity: she is subject in her own right. Stendhal never limits himself to describing his heroines as functions of his heroes: he gives them a destiny of their own. He has attempted a still rarer enterprise, one that I believe no novelist has before undertaken: he has projected himself into a female character. He does not hover over Lamiel like Marivaux over Marianne or Richardson over Clarissa Harlowe; he assumes her destiny just as he had assumed Julien's. On this account Lamiel's outline remains somewhat speculative, but it is singularly significant. Stendhal has raised all imaginable obstacles about the young girl: she is a poor peasant, ignorant, coarsely raised by people imbued with all the prejudices; but she clears from her path all moral barriers once she understands the full meaning of the little words: "that's silly." Her new freedom of mind allows her in her own fashion to act upon all the impulses of her curiosity, her ambition, her gaiety. Before so stout a heart, material obstacles could not but be smoothed away, and her only problem will be to shape a destiny worthy of her in a mediocre world. She must find fulfillment in crime and death; but this is also Julien's lot. There is no place for great souls in society as it exists. And men and women are in the same boat.

It is noteworthy that Stendhal should be at once so deeply romantic and so decidedly feministic; usually feminists are rational minds who in all matters take a universal point of view; but Stendhal demands woman's emancipation not only in the name of liberty in general but also in the name of individual happiness. Love, he believes, will have nothing to lose; on the contrary, it will be the more true as woman, being man's equal, is able to understand him the more completely. No doubt certain qualities admired in women will disappear; but their worth comes from the freedom they express. This will be manifested under other forms, and the romantic will not vanish from the world. Two separate beings, in different circumstances, face to face in freedom and seeking justification of their existence through one another, will always live an adventure full of risk and promise. Stendhal puts his trust in truth. To depart from it means a living death; but where it shines forth, there shine forth also beauty, happiness, love, and a joy that carries its own justification. That is why he rejects the mystifications of the serious, as he rejects the false poetry of the myths. Human reality suffices him. Woman according to him is simply a human being: nor could any shape of dreams be more enrapturing. (pp. 148-56)

Simone de Beauvoir, "Stendhal or the Romantic of Reality," in *Stendhal: A Collection of Critical Essays,* edited by Victor Brombert, Prentice-Hall, Inc., 1962, pp. 147-56.

WALLACE FOWLIE

(essay date 1969)

[In the following excerpt, Fowlie surveys Stendhal's autobiographical writings.]

In his art as novelist, Stendhal never uses directly the activities and adventures of his own life and never draws directly upon his personal suffering. The tone of self-complacency and the habit of the unabashed self-confession of the typical romantic writer are totally absent in Stendhal's novels. By means of the style and the plots of his books, he created a distance between himself and his readers. If in a fundamentally psychic sense he identifies himself with his heroes; his heroes are not recognizably Stendhal in any exterior sense. He separated his personal writings from his novels. His autobiography is to be found in two books: *Souvenirs d'égotisme* of 1832 and *Vie de Henry Brulard* of 1836.

The first of these writings, the *Souvenirs,* is a scrupulous self-analysis. With no desire to idealize his features or exalt his traits, Stendhal quite resolutely wrote about himself for the purpose of reaching some degree of self-knowledge. He had just begun his consulate service in Città Vecchia and had considerable leisure ahead of him, when he announced his intention of using this leisure (*pour employer mes loisirs*) in that foreign land for the purpose of writing out what happened to him during his Paris years of 1821 to 1830. Did he do all within his power to reach happiness at the time of the minor and major events in his life during those nine years? What kind of man had he become? What was the quality of his mind? His self-evaluation had varied so much from day to day, from month to month, that he now distrusted his judgments. He was struck by the fact that his judgments had varied as much as his disposition had fluctuated. . . . With these opening questions, Stendhal announced the frankness with which he hoped to write about himself and the rigorous tone reminiscent of a La Rochefoucauld with which he planned to consign his observations to paper.

This tone of honesty and scrupulosity with respect to difficult personal problems we have come to associate with the personal journal of the twentieth century, with André Gide, for example, and Julien Green. There is no reason to believe that Stendhal ever planned to publish his *Souvenirs d'égotisme,* but he did plan to leave it with his papers for the use of posterity.

The word *égotisme,* as used by Stendhal, has often been given a Nietzschean-like meaning, equivalent to a superman's drive to reach happiness at any cost. The worship of oneself, the cult of self-development, is a concept not applicable to Stendhal. The cult of the self, as found in such a romantic work as Musset's *Confession d'un enfant du siècle* and much later in the writings of Maurice Barrès, is not what Stendhal meant by egotism. Stendhal exhibits an interest in himself because of a greater interest in analysis itself, because of his belief that analysis is a therapeutic exercise by means of which a man's disposition can be understood and improved. Stendhal is not self-admiring, as Rousseau is, in his *Confessions.* He is not presenting himself as an exceptional human being whose sensitivity sets him apart from mankind, in the manner Chateaubriand develops in his autobiography *Mémoires d'outretombe.*

The two texts *Egotisme* and *Henry Brulard* are self-appraisals which have the value of documents, first, and of a literary art, second. As he wrote them, he had probably very little sense of the value they were to possess today, and yet they are the texts in which Stendhal's mind is the sharpest, in which his powers of observation are the most developed. In these two books, as well as in his letters and other personal writings, Stendhal appears the moralist, in the manner of a Montaigne and a Gide—a man inhabiting a moral world, who is determined to analyze his conduct in that world in terms of the prevalent moral conventions and in terms of the hypocrisy by which moral conventions are sustained. We see Stendhal play a social role and participate in the game of society, and at the same time we see him trying to preserve in himself and express his most spontaneous feelings and his noblest impulses. There is peril, obviously, in these two ways of behavior, both moral and social peril. Precisely these forms of peril are the substance of *Souvenirs d'égotisme* and *Vie de Henry Brulard.* Henri Beyle is the lonely hero of these two books, and he is actually far more lonely than his lonely heroes, Julien Sorel and Octave and Fabrice del Dongo. (pp. 141-43)

Vie de Henry Brulard is the story of his life through adolescence. It is the third of Stendhal's books to rally an impressive number of admirers who are anxious to announce the outstanding book: Is it *Le Rouge et le Noir* or *La Chartreuse de Parme* or *Vie de Henry Brulard?* Those who give first place to *Vie de Henry Brulard* base their claims on the boldness with which Stendhal explored his past and sought to recover time that had been lost. About to turn fifty (*je vais avoir cinquante ans*), Stendhal declared it was time to know himself, or to know the boy and the man he was. What was to count the most for him was simplicity and honesty in the narration. The determination to speak the truth explains why he took pen in hand. (p. 144)

He never rewrote or reworked any of the passages in the manuscript because of his belief that the first draft of such writing would be the most accurate, the most truthful. The portraits he gives of his childhood and adolescence are precious commentaries for an understanding of his work. The genesis and the development of his sensibility and his thought are carefully described and annotated.

Stendhal succeeds in resurrecting moments of his past and giving them a freshness as if they had been lived the day before he wrote, rather than thirty-five or forty years earlier. The facts of chronological time do not count as much as the power of the writer's memory which is able, on the most striking pages of *Vie de*

Henry Brulard to reinstate the past within the present. . . .

Such a meticulous scholar as Paul Arbalet who has written extensively on the early years of Stendhal's life (*La Jeunesse de Stendhal*) has discovered errors in facts and dates in *Vie de Henry Brulard,* and he has proved quite conclusively that the portraits of the father, Chérubin Beyle and the priest Abbé Raillane, represented them as more sinister than they actually were. But such points, made in the name of historical truth, do not alter the veracity Stendhal records of the effect of such figures on the young boy Henri Beyle. The writer is concerned with relating the truthfulness of his reactions to people and events and to the city of Grenoble.

He yearned for affection and did not receive it. When, in the country setting of Les Echelles, he experienced happiness by simply being in close proximity to young women in beautiful dresses, the transport he felt was of such a nature that it was impossible to analyze. In narrating his life, Stendhal moves back and forth between sentiments of suspicion and despair, and sentiments of elation and daydreaming. The man is already in the child. The entire book is an explicit document on the explanation and the analysis of a temperament that was fully formed at a very early age. The memory of a sensation leads him to a very concrete scene he is able to recall. He trusts the sensation. He distrusts the judgments of others and his own judgments. Scrupulously he moves into his past and tries not to alter or embroider his memories. What happened to Henri Beyle we see happening at the moment when we are reading the text.

Souvenirs d'égotisme begins, in 1832, with the end of Stendhal's great love for Métilde Dembowska. But he is too close to that suffering to write about it. Throughout the book there are a large number of portraits. The meditations about himself are grouped especially at the beginning. The rest of the work is concerned with episodes and anecdotes.

The portraits undoubtedly suffer from a lack of rewriting. Those portraits that seem the best are based on models from whom Stendhal was the most detached emotionally. The proprietor of the Hôtel de Bruxelles, M. Petit, is a good example of a portrait Stendhal struck off that is successful because of an absence of any emotional involvement. Mérimée is clearly described in certain salon scenes, but the reason for his friendship with Beyle is not clear. Destutt de Tracy is given a fuller portrait, especially in his physical appearance and in the casualness of his conversation. Métilde Dembowska and her cousin Madame Traversi are only vaguely sketched.

The personal meditations, of which there are many, follow a similar pattern. They start up because of a need to write, and they proceed without plan, without organization. The themes are repetitive. The questions asked by the writer are numerous, but the answers given are few. The kind of writing, so obviously improvised in *Souvenirs,* does not permit Stendhal to judge himself, to judge the events of his past and to measure their importance. He oscillates too much from theme to theme, and without the necessary details, to reach any conclusions about the relative importance of events and thoughts.

Stendhal is more intriguing, more successful, in the purely narrative sections of *Souvenirs d'égotisme.* For the story of an event, he chooses details that are both important and vivid. These parts of the work do not need rewriting. His remarkable memory serves him well, as well as his power of imagination and his ability to imagine the circumstances of the scenes. Whenever his heart is involved, as with the appearance of Countess Curial in his life, he avoids any real analysis. This kind of commentary is reserved for the novels. The writing of *Souvenirs* was interrupted by Stendhal's activities in Città Vecchia, but even if he had continued, he would probably not have written any real analyses of his loves and of his temptations to love. That part of his life remained within his memory, to be recast in his novels. The telling portraits he is able to write out so swiftly, the dream or meditation sequences and the constant check he makes on his mental attitudes—all of this is announced in *Souvenirs d'égotisme* and will be pursued in the writing of *Vie de Henry Brulard.*

Stendhal had no intention of making *Vie de Henry Brulard* correspond to a given technique of writing, or even, for that matter, to a given genre. The book is both an effort to recall the past and a struggle, as the sentences are being consigned to paper, to be sincere and truthful. Whenever he digresses from the narrative, he indulges in that kind of meditation and revery for which he has a marked predilection: *Je vois que la rêverie a été ce que j'ai préféré à tout, même à passer pour homme d'esprit.* In recomposing his memories, Stendhal tends to alter the accuracy of facts in order to write a story that will appear logical and likely. It is paradoxical that the writer's sincerity in both Rousseau and Stendhal tended to deform accuracy. The tone of sincerity is reached at the expense of historical truth.

On turning fifty, Stendhal seems suddenly aware that most of his life is behind him. The past is a treasure house, out of which he can call up the memory of his loves and try to pass judgment on them. As he writes, the past comes back and he ceases worrying about whether he will forget essential episodes. The scenes are fragments from a life rather than a continuous narrative of a childhood. Their power comes from the imperious sense of truthfulness with which Stendhal endows them (even if factual accuracy is sometimes sacrificed). A close reader seldom has the impression that

such and such an episode is invented. Stendhal convinces us of his veracity, to such a degree that we recognize the bareness and the cruelty of certain childhood experiences.

What is Stendhal's method of writing in the *Vie de Henry Brulard?* He says that by writing about an event, he sees it more clearly. His childhood memories, as memories in his mind, are amorphous and covered over by a strange light whose source seems to be the acuteness of the original sensations that accompanied the experiences. In writing of them he instinctively employs a scientific method by which he will see friends and members of his family and other acquaintances as *genres.* He tends to classify human beings as a botanist classifies plants. His mind still holds the pictures of the physical traits of these characters thirty or forty years later, but he begins to understand the traits only when he begins writing about them. Some of the characters whom he observed as a child have disappeared from his memory. The fresco of his past is incomplete.

Stendhal's method is a mental investigation of the past. An image comes to his mind and he begins describing it, and thereupon many details rush into his mind and he realizes he understands and sees the past thanks to this exercise of writing it down. As the writing of a given scene continues everything comes to life: furniture in a room, the design of the room, human features, gestures and activities. They are scenes that have been preserved in his memory because of some deeply felt emotion: anger, for example, or sorrow. When his emotion returns clear to him, he is then able to analyze it and to understand it more fully than he had when it was originally experienced. Stendhal is very much bent on exploring the significance of a given scene. The intensity of the emotion that accompanied the scene is a clue and guide for this research. Within the scenes where Stendhal is describing members of his family, the sense of an autobiography gives way to the sense of a novel, as Henry Brulard takes on the proportions of a protagonist. (pp. 144-49)

Emotionally Stendhal separated himself from his family, and intellectually he separated himself from the bourgeoisie. But he confessed that he could not have lived with the proletariat. He was a new kind of aristocrat, always out of place socially and intellectually, and that is why he founded, in his mind, a tiny community of the "happy few." What Baudelaire was to call *dandysme* corresponded quite closely to Stendhal's attitude. It was a form of isolation, on many levels: artistic, social, intellectual. *Vie de Henry Brulard* is a lengthy explanation and rationalization of this position. It is the demonstration of how a man's life turned into the enactment of a drama of excessive solitude. He himself became the characters in his life. His abundant use of pseudonyms is a proof of the need he felt to multiply his personality. It is significant that throughout *Henry*

Brulard, Henri Beyle never tries to solve the dilemma of his life and of his character. He is quite content with reasoning about it and elucidating it. He learned to live with the drama of the many selves, and in his fiction, always depicted the same situation of the hero unable to fit into whatever society and whatever situation were his. (p. 155)

Wallace Fowlie, in his *Stendhal,* The Macmillan Company, 1969, 240 p.

SOURCES FOR FURTHER STUDY

Day, James T. *Stendhal's Paper Mirror: Patterns of Self-Consciousness in His Novels.* American University Studies, Series II: Romance Languages and Literature, vol. 20. New York: Peter Lang, 1987, 236 p.
An analysis of reflexive and self-conscious narrative in Stendhal's fiction.

Goldberger, Avriel H., ed. *The Stendhal Bicentennial Papers.* Contributions to the Study of World Literature, no. 19. New York: Greenwood Press, 1987, 111 p.
Eleven essays on Stendhal.

Mitchell, John. *Stendhal: "Le Rouge et le Noir."* London: Edward Arnold, 1973, 64 p.
In-depth analysis of *The Red and the Black.*

Richardson, Joanna. *Stendhal.* New York: Coward, McCann & Geoghegan, 1974, 344 p.
Biography of Stendhal that describes the evolution and current status of critical opinion on the author.

Strickland, Geoffrey. *Stendhal: The Education of a Novelist.* Cambridge: Cambridge University Press, 1974, 302 p.
Details Stendhal's intellectual development over his lifetime.

Tillet, Margaret. *Stendhal: The Background to the Novels.* London: Oxford University Press, 1971, 157 p.
Considers Stendhal's nonfiction works in an effort to isolate his conception of the ideal human being.

Laurence Sterne

1713-1768

(Also wrote under pseudonym Mr. Yorick) Irish-born English novelist, essayist, diarist, and sermonist.

INTRODUCTION

Sterne is the author of *The Life and Opinions of Tristram Shandy, Gentleman* (1759-67) and *A Sentimental Journey through France and Italy* (1768), two of the most eccentric and influential works in Western literature. *Tristram Shandy*'s uniqueness brought about its wide success during the 1760s; and the novel's universal appeal has enabled the work to overcome the disparagement of such important eighteenth-century authors as Samuel Johnson, whose comment on Sterne's novel was that "nothing odd will do long," and to survive the outright loathing of such nineteenth-century figures as William Makepeace Thackeray. The primary object of this critical scorn was the innovative style in which *Tristram Shandy* was composed, comprising an array of idiosyncratic narrative devices which, as examinations of Sterne's life have revealed, form an artistic counterpart to his personal idiosyncracies: parallel to the high-spirited prose style and often scabrous incidents of the work were the author's undisguised love of amusement and penchant for scandalous liaisons during his life.

Sterne was born in Clonmel, in County Tipperary, Ireland. His English father made a poor living as an ensign in the army; his mother, a woman of Irish and French ancestry, was of a lower class than her husband, who apparently married her to settle a debt with her father. Sterne spent much of his childhood moving with his family from one army barracks to another throughout England and Ireland, and his recollections of the military surroundings in which he grew up formed the basis for the characters of Uncle Toby and Corporal Trim in *Tristram Shandy.* In 1723, Sterne began attending a school in Halifax, Yorkshire; however, when his father died penniless in 1731, he was forced to discontinue his education and live with relatives in Elvington, Yorkshire. Two years later his cousin arranged for him to enter Jesus College, Cambridge, as a sizar, which allowed Sterne to defray his university expenses by working as a servant to other students. At Cambridge he met John Hall-Stevenson, a rich and reckless young man whose home—Skelton Castle, renamed "Crazy Castle"—has figured prominently in the Sterne legend as the site of boisterous drinking parties and of a library containing a notable collection of curiosa and erotic literature.

After receiving his bachelors degree from Cambridge, Sterne was influenced by his uncle Jacques, a prominent churchman active in Whig politics, to enter the clergy. Sterne's decision to follow an ecclesiastic career resulted from his need to earn a living rather than from any sense of spiritual calling. He was ordained a deacon in 1736, a priest in 1738, and afterward received various appointments in Yorkshire. In 1741 Sterne was married to Elizabeth Lumley, who is described by Sterne's biographers as an unpleasant woman whose instability—she eventually became insane—was not improved by her husband's incessant philandering. However, despite his lack of faithfulness, Sterne was not the cruel husband and parent once portrayed by his detractors. After his marriage was effectively dissolved in separation, which was actually initiated by Elizabeth rather than Sterne, he continued to provide for his wife and daughter. Likewise, there is reason to believe that his reputedly vicious treatment of his mother and sister derives largely from the machinations of his uncle Jacques, with whom Sterne had had a falling out, rather than being the outcome of a pathological insensitivity on Sterne's part.

From the time of his marriage until the publication of *Tristram Shandy* in 1759, Sterne lived for the most part the life of an average Yorkshire clergyman, although some of his activities—his extramarital affairs, his frequenting the society of Hall-Stevenson's "Demoniacs" at Crazy Castle, his lawful but self-serving acquisition of his parishioners' property, and his casual attitude toward the theological doctrines of his church—would by subsequent generations be considered extraordinary conduct, however common it was in Sterne's time. Prior to the composition of his masterpiece, Sterne's only works were the sermons in which he preached an abstract rather than specifically Christian morality, articles of political propaganda written at the instigation of his uncle Jacques, and *A Political Romance* (1759), a satirical allegory concerned with local church politics which indicates some of the humor and narrative flair of Sterne's major work.

Sterne was forty-six when the initial volumes of *Tristram Shandy* were published, in which his fictional alter-ego Tristram vowed to produce two additional volumes each year for the remainder of his life. Although the novel received mixed reviews, readers of the time elevated both the book and its author to a phenomenal status of celebrity. A short while after the publication of *Tristram Shandy,* Sterne happened to be in London and found himself the center of a following that included aristocrats, members of fashionable society, and leading figures in the arts. His lively, amusing manner made him well liked, and his attendance at social affairs was eagerly sought. However, upon the discovery that the author of *Tristram Shandy* was a clergyman, Sterne was attacked in the English press. The complaint of journalists was that the slyly erotic and scatological humor of Sterne's novel was unacceptable coming from a man of the cloth. Nevertheless, with the appearance of subsequent volumes of his novel, Sterne retained much of his popularity, not only in England but on the Continent as well. The social successes of London were repeated when Sterne visited Paris in 1762. A second visit to continental Europe in 1765 served as the material for *A Sentimental Journey,* a work which in its extreme subjectivity, emotionalism, and narrative verve is as striking a contrast to the literary travelogue as *Tristram Shandy* is to the realistic novel. During his few remaining years, Sterne continued to compose installments of *Tristram Shandy* and wrote *The Journal to Eliza* (1904), a self-conscious record of his romance with a woman named Eliza Draper. Having suffered poor health since his youth, when the first signs of tuberculosis probably appeared, Sterne died in London a few weeks after the publication of *A Sentimental Journey.*

Sterne's *Tristram Shandy* is an unusual work by the literary standards of any period, but it particularly stands out in the century that saw the birth and early development of the realistic novel. While such novels as Daniel Defoe's *Moll Flanders,* Samuel Richardson's *Pamela,* and Henry Fielding's *Tom Jones* display their authors' attempts to make prose fiction a means for depicting contemporary life, *Tristram Shandy* demonstrates aspirations of an entirely different kind. Its characters, although profoundly human, are also profoundly odd and do not have the significant connections with their society held by characters in the great realistic novels of the time; its style is one of cultivated spontaneity and unpredictability, a series of digressions as opposed to the progressive movement of events common in the works of Sterne's contemporaries; and, perhaps most conspicuously, its narrator is concerned with relating his "Life and Opinions" rather than the more usual "Life and Adventures" of the eighteenth-century *bildungsroman,* making the novel largely a plotless discourse on an encyclopedic array of subjects.

Unlike many authors whose works are discussed in relative isolation from their lives, Sterne is closely identified with his narrator Tristram Shandy. Especially in the eighteenth and nineteenth centuries, Sterne was often judged by the narrator's opinions and liberties of taste; inverting this approach, an appraisal of Sterne's work became inseparable from an appraisal of his life, either to demonstrate a reprehensible similarity between the two or a paradoxical contrast. The issue of the often salacious humor in *Tristram Shandy* pervaded Victorian commentary, both positive and negative, on Sterne's work. In the twentieth century, critics have emphasized the remarkable likenesses between Sterne's narrative techniques in *Tristram Shandy* and the formal experimentation of modern literature, particularly in Sterne's unorthodox punctuation, his use of nonverbal devices like drawings, his disregard for sequence, and his self-conscious dwelling on his manner of composition. Despite the evidence presented by John Ferriar and others that Sterne borrowed heavily and blatantly from a number of sources, including Robert Burton's *Anatomy of Melancholy* and Rabelais's *Gargantua and Pantagruel,* few critics have questioned the success with which he adapted these borrowings to his own purposes, and transformed old materials into one of the most original and important works in literature.

Sterne's other major work, *A Sentimental Journey,* is important as a nonfictional memoir that conveys much the same sensibility as the fictional *Tristram Shandy.* An account of Sterne's travels in France and Italy, this memoir has as its central concern the subjective side of the author's experiences rather than the objective rendering of people and places, which is the more usual concern of the travel writer. V. S. Pritchett has written that "Sterne displays the egotist's universe: life is a personal dream," an observation that is exampled by the minute and self-conscious attention that Sterne pays to his own feelings in *A Sentimental Journey.* Sterne's preoccupation with feelings, especially those of tender pathos, led to his establishing the word "sentiment" as it is presently understood, giving connotations of heightened, somewhat artificial emotion to a term which previously had denoted "thought" and "moral reflection." The deliberate courting and elaborate description of feeling in *A Sentimental Journey*

also appears in Sterne's letters and his *Journal to Eliza,* provoking a major controversy in criticism of Sterne—the sincerity or pretense of both his personal writings and those written for a reading audience. As the issue of sincerity by its nature is restricted to the realm of individual opinion, critics have tended to praise or condemn Sterne to the extent that they believe in the truth of the feelings he describes. Modern critics have generally treated the question of Sterne's sincerity as a more subtle and complex matter than had been previously realized, attributing to him a facility for taking an ironic view of his most intense feelings or, as in Ernest Nevin Dilworth's *The Unsentimental Journey of Lawrence Sterne,* finding in his work a satirical mockery of sentiment.

Perhaps the most important factor contributing to the ambiguities in Sterne's work, as well as to the controversies surrounding it, is his provocative and persuasive humor. Some critics have seen this quality of Sterne's writing as an end in itself, a viewpoint represented by Wilbur L. Cross, who contends that Sterne "was a humorist pure and simple, and nothing else." Other critics, including those of the English Romantic movement and most modern commentators, perceive more profound motives underlying these works, with a number of recent studies contending that Sterne's humor derives from an acute awareness of the ultimate evil and suffering of human existence and that each farcical antic is an allusion to a grim truth. Whether or not it is justified to place Sterne in the philosophical company of modernists who blend comedy and despair in their works, critics are now largely in agreement that Sterne is an exceptional case of an eighteenth-century writer whose works are particularly sympathetic with the concerns and temperament of twentieth-century readers.

(For further information about Sterne's life and works, see *Concise Dictionary of British Literary Biography,* Vol. 2; *Dictionary of Literary Biography,* Vol. 39: *British Novelists, 1660–1800;* and *Literature Criticism from 1400 to 1800,* Vol. 2.)

CRITICAL COMMENTARY

WILLIAM MAKEPEACE THACKERAY
(lecture date 1851)

[Thackeray was one of the most important English novelists of the nineteenth century. The following is an excerpt from his famous attack on what he views as the immorality and insincerity of Sterne and his

works. This text was first delivered as a lecture in 1851.]

A perilous trade, indeed, is that of a man who has to bring his tears and laughter, his recollections, his personal griefs and joys, his private thoughts and feelings to market, to write them on paper, and sell them for money. Does [Sterne] exaggerate his grief, so as to get

---

Principal Works

A Political Romance (satire) 1759

The Life and Opinions of Tristram Shandy, Gentleman. 9 vols. (novel) 1759-67

The Sermons of Mr. Yorick. 7 vols. (sermons) 1760-69

A Sentimental Journey through France and Italy (travel essay) 1768

Letters from Yorick to Eliza (letters) 1773

Sterne's Letters to His Friends on Various Occasions (letters) 1775

*The Journal to Eliza and Various Letters (journal and letters) 1904; published in *The Life and Works of Laurence Sterne*

The Life and Works of Laurence Sterne. 12 vols. (novel, sermons, travel essay, satire, journal, and letters) 1904

*This work was written in 1768.

---

his reader's pity for a false sensibility? feign indignation, so as to establish a character for virtue? elaborate repartees, so that he may pass for a wit? steal from other authors, and put down the theft to the credit side of his own reputation for ingenuity and learning? feign originality? affect benevolence or misanthropy? appeal to the gallery gods with claptraps and vulgar baits to catch applause?

How much of the paint and emphasis is necessary for the fair business of the stage, and how much of the rant and rouge is put on for the vanity of the actor. His audience trusts him: can he trust himself ? How much was deliberate calculation and imposture—how much was false sensibility—and how much true feeling? Where did the lie begin, and did he know where? and where did the truth end in the art and scheme of this man of genius, this actor, this quack? Some time since, I was in the company of a French actor, who began after dinner, and at his own request, to sing French songs of the sort called *des chansons grivoises* ["bawdy songs"], and which he performed admirably, and to the dissatisfaction of most persons present. Having finished these, he commenced a sentimental ballad—it was so charmingly sung that it touched all persons present, and especially the singer himself, whose voice trembled, whose eyes filled with emotion, and who was snivelling and weeping quite genuine tears by the time his own ditty was over. I suppose Sterne had this artistical sensibility; he used to blubber perpetually in his study, and finding his tears infectious, and that they brought him a great popularity, he exercised the lucrative gift of weeping; he utilised it, and cried on every occasion. I own that I don't value or respect much the cheap dribble of those fountains. He fatigues me with his perpetual disquiet

and his uneasy appeals to my risible or sentimental faculties. He is always looking in my face, watching his effect, uncertain whether I think him an impostor or not; posture-making, coaxing, and imploring me. "See what sensibility I have—own now that I'm very clever—do cry now, you can't resist this." The humour of Swift and Rabelais, whom he pretended to succeed, poured from them as naturally as song does from a bird; they lose no manly dignity with it, but laugh their hearty great laugh out of their broad chests as nature bade them. But this man—who can make you laugh, who can make you cry, too—never lets his reader alone, or will permit his audience repose: when you are quiet, he fancies he must rouse you, and turns over head and heels, or sidles up and whispers a nasty story. The man is a great jester, not a great humourist. He goes to work systematically and of cold blood; paints his face, puts on his ruff and motley clothes, and lays down his carpet and tumbles on it.

For instance, take the *Sentimental Journey,* and see in the writer the deliberate propensity to make points and seek applause. He gets to Dessein's Hotel, he wants a carriage to travel to Paris, he goes to the inn-yard, and begins what the actors call "business" at once. There is that little carriage the *désobligeant.* "Four months had elapsed since it had finished its career of Europe in the corner of Monsieur Dessein's courtyard, and having sallied out thence but a vamped-up business at first, though it had been twice taken to pieces on Mount Sennis, it had not profited much by its adventures, but by none so little as the standing so many months unpitied in the corner of Monsieur Dessein's coachyard. Much, indeed, was not to be said for it—but something might—and when a few words will rescue misery out of her distress, I hate the man who can be a churl of them."

Le tour est fait! ["The journey is completed!"] Pail-lasse has tumbled! Paillasse has jumped over the *désobligeant,* cleared it, hood and all, and bows to the noble company. Does anybody believe that this is a real Sentiment? that this luxury of generosity, this gallant rescue of Misery—out of an old cab, is genuine feeling? (pp. 300-04)

Our friend purchases the carriage—after turning that notorious old monk to good account, and effecting (like a soft and good-natured Paillasse as he was, and very free with his money when he had it,) an exchange of snuff-boxes with the old Franciscan, jogs out of Calais; sets down in immense figures on the credit side of his account the sous he gives away to the Montreuil beggars; and, at Nampont, gets out of the chaise and whimpers over that famous dead donkey, for which any sentimentalist may cry who will. It is agreeably and skilfully done—that dead jackass; like M. de Soubise's cook, on the campaign, Sterne dresses it, and serves it up quite tender and with a very piquante sauce. But tears, and fine feelings, and a white pocket-handkerchief, and a funeral sermon, and horses and feathers, and a procession of mutes, and a hearse with a dead donkey inside! Psha! Mountebank! I'll not give thee one penny more for that trick, donkey and all! (p. 304)

There is not a page in Sterne's writing but has something that were better away, a latent corruption—a hint, as of an impure presence.

Some of that dreary *double entendre* may be attributed to freer times and manners than ours, but not all. The foul Satyr's eyes leer out of the leaves constantly: the last words the famous author wrote were bad and wicked—the last lines the poor stricken wretch penned were for pity and pardon. I think of these past writers and of one who lives amongst us now, and am grateful for the innocent laughter and the sweet and unsullied page which the author of "David Copperfield" gives to my children. (pp. 309-10)

William Makepeace Thackeray, "Sterne and Goldsmith," in his *The English Humourists of the Eighteenth Century,* Smith, Elder, and Co., 1858, pp. 286-341.

LESLIE STEPHEN

(essay date 1880)

[Stephen was one of the most important English literary critics of the Victorian age. In the following excerpt from an essay that first appeared in *The Cornhill Magazine* in 1880, he contrasts the artistry of Sterne's work, along with his creation of a profound human character in Uncle Toby, with what he sees as Sterne's essentially shallow and hypocritical personality.]

"Love me, love my book" is a version of a familiar proverb which one might be slow to accept. There are, as one need hardly say, many admirable persons for whose sake one would gladly make any sacrifice of personal comfort short of that implied in a study of their works. . . . I may by an intellectual effort perceive the greatness of a writer whose character is essentially antagonistic to my own; but I cannot feel it as it must be felt for genuine enjoyment. (pp. 53-4)

If this be true in some degree of all imaginative writers, it is especially true of humourists. (p. 54)

We love the humour in short so far as we love the character from which it flows. Everybody can love the spirit which shows itself in the *Essays of Elia*; but you can hardly love the *Tale of a Tub* or *Gulliver* unless you have a sympathy with the genuine Swift which overpowers your occasional disgust at his misanthropy. But to this

general rule there is one marked exception in our literature. It is impossible for any one with the remotest taste for literary excellence to read *Tristram Shandy* or the *Sentimental Journey* without a sense of wondering admiration. One can hardly read the familiar passages without admitting that Sterne was perhaps the greatest artist in the language. No one at least shows more inimitable felicity in producing a pungent effect by a few touches of exquisite precision. He gives the impression that the thing has been done once for all; he has hit the bull's eye round which inspiring marksmen go on blundering indefinitely without any satisfying success. Two or three of the scenes in which Uncle Toby expresses his sentiments are as perfect in their way as the half-dozen lines in which Mrs. Quickly describes the end of Falstaff, and convince us that three strokes from a man of genius may be worth more than the life's labour of the cleverest of skilled literary workmen. And it may further be said that Uncle Toby, like his kinsmen in the world of humour, is an incarnation of most lovable qualities. In going over the list—a short list in any case—of the immortal characters in fiction, there is hardly any one in our literature who would be entitled to take precedence of him. To find a distinctly superior type, we must go back to Cervantes, whom Sterne idolised and professed to take for his model. But to speak of a character as in some sort comparable to Don Quixote, though without any thought of placing him on the same level, is to admit that he is a triumph of art. Indeed, if we take the other creator of types, of whom it is only permitted to speak with bated breath, we must agree that it would be difficult to find a figure even in the Shakespearean gallery more admirable in its way. Of course, the creation of a Hamlet, an Iago, or a Falstaff implies an intellectual intensity and reach of imaginative sympathy altogether different from anything which his warmest admirers would attribute to Sterne. I only say that there is no single character in Shakespeare whom we see more vividly and love more heartily than Mr. Shandy's uncle.

It should follow, according to the doctrine just set forth, that we ought to love Uncle Toby's creator. But here I fancy that everybody will be sensible of a considerable difficulty. The judgment pronounced upon Sterne by Thackeray seems to me to be substantially unimpeachable. The more I know of the man, for my part, the less I like him. It is impossible to write his biography (from the admiring point of view) without making it a continuous apology. His faults may be extenuated by the customary devices; but there is a terrible lack of any positive merits to set against them. He seems to have been fond of his daughter and tolerant of his wife. The nearest approach to a good action recorded of him is that when they preferred remaining in France to following him to England, he took care that they should have the income which he had promised. The liberality was nothing very wonderful. He knew that his wife was severely economical, as she had good reason to be; inasmuch as his own health was most precarious, and he was spending his income with a generous freedom which left her in destitution at his death. Still we are glad to give him all credit for not being a grudging paymaster. Some better men have been less good-natured. The rest of his panegyric consists of excuses for his short-comings. We know the regular formulae. He had bad companions, it is said, in his youth. Men who show a want of principle in later life have a knack of picking up bad companions at their outset. We are reminded as usual that the morals of the time were corrupt. (pp. 56-9)

But, in any case, such apologies rather explain how a man came to be bad, than prove that he was not bad. They would show at most that we were making an erroneous inference if we inferred badness of heart from conduct which was not condemned by the standard of his own day. This argument, however, is really inapplicable. Sterne's faults were of a kind for which if anything there was less excuse then than now. The faults of his best-known contemporaries, of men like Fielding, Smollett, or Churchill, were the faults of robust temperament with an excess of animal passions. Their coarseness has left a stain upon their pages as it injured their lives. But, however much we may lament or condemn, we do not feel that such men were corrupt at heart. And that, unfortunately, is just what we are tempted to feel about Sterne. When the huge, brawny parson, Churchill, felt his unfitness for clerical life, he pitched his cassock to the dogs and blossomed out in purple and gold. He set the respectabilities at defiance, took up with Wilkes and the reprobates, and roared out full-mouthed abuse against bishops and ministers. He could still be faithful to his friends, observe his own code of honour, and do his best to make some atonement to the victims of his misconduct. Sterne, one feels, differs from Churchill not really as being more virtuous, but in not having the courage to be so openly vicious. Unlike Churchill, he could be a consummate sneak. He was quite as ready to flatter Wilkes or to be on intimate terms with atheists and libertines, with Holbach and Crébillon, when his bishop and his parishioners could not see him. His most intimate friend from early days was John Hall Stevenson—the country squire whose pride it was to ape in the provinces the orgies of the monks of Medmenham Abbey, and once notorious as the author of a grossly indecent book. The dog-Latin letter in which Sterne informs this chosen companion that he is weary of his life contains other remarks sufficiently significant of the nature of their intimacy. The age was not very nice; but it was quite acute enough to see the objections to a close alliance between a married ecclesiastic of forty-five and the rustic Don Juan of the district. But his cynicism becomes doubly disgusting when we remember that Sterne was all the time as eager as any patronage hunter to ingratiate himself into the good graces of bishops. (pp. 60-2)

I do not, however, wish to preach a sermon upon Sterne's iniquities, or to draw any edifying conclusions upon the present occasion. We have only to deal with the failings of the man so far as they are reflected in the author. Time enables us to abstract and distinguish. A man's hateful qualities may not be of the essence of his character, or they may be only hateful in certain specific relations which do not now affect us. Moreover, there is some kind of immorality—spite and uncharitableness, for example—which is not without its charm. (p. 66)

But the case is different when the sentiment itself is offensive, and offensive by reason of insincerity. When the very thing by which we are supposed to be attracted is the goodness of a man's heart, a suspicion that he was a mere Tartufe cannot enter our minds without injuring our enjoyment. We may continue to admire the writer's technical skill, but he cannot fascinate us unless he persuades us of his sincerity. (pp. 67-8)

Of the literary skill there cannot be a moment's question; but if we for a moment yield to the enchantment, we feel ashamed, at the next moment, of our weakness. We have been moved on false pretences; and we seem to see the sham Yorick with that unpleasant leer upon his too expressive face, chuckling quietly at his successful imposition. It is no wonder if many of his readers have revolted, and even been provoked to an excessive reaction of feeling. The criticism was too obvious to be missed. (pp. 68-9)

The Sentimental Journey is a book of simply marvellous cleverness, to which one can find no nearer parallel than Heine's *Reisebilder*. But one often closes it with a mixture of disgust and regret. The disgust needs no explanation; the regret is caused by our feeling that something has been missed which ought to have been in the writer's power. He has so keen an eye for picturesque effects; he is so sensitive to a thousand little incidents which your ordinary traveller passes with eyes riveted to his guidebook, or which "Smelfungus" Smollett disregarded in his surly British pomposity; he is so quick at appreciating some delicate courtesy in humble life or some pathetic touch of commonplace suffering, that one grows angry when he spoils a graceful scene by some prurient double meaning, and wastes whole pages in telling a story fit only for John Hall Stevenson. . . . A man of Sterne's admirable delicacy of genius, writing always with an eye to the canons of taste approved in Crazy Castle, must necessarily produce painful discords, and throw away admirable workmanship upon contemptible ribaldry. But the very feeling proves that there was really a finer element in him. Had he been thoroughly steeped in the noxious element, there would have been no discord. We might simply have set him down as a very clever reprobate. But, with some exceptions, we can generally recognise something so amiable and attractive as to excite our regret for the waste of genius even in his more questionable passages. (pp. 70-1)

Sterne has been called the English Rabelais, and was apparently more ambitious himself of being considered as an English Cervantes. To a modern English reader he is certainly far more amusing than Rabelais, and he can be appreciated with less effort than Cervantes. But it is impossible to mention these great names without seeing the direction in which Sterne falls short of the highest excellence. We know that, on clearing away the vast masses of buffoonery and ribaldry under which Rabelais was forced, or chose, to hide himself we come to the profound thinker and powerful satirist. Sterne represents a comparatively shallow vein of thought. He is the mouthpiece of a sentiment which had certainly its importance in so far as it was significant of a vague discontent with things in general, and a desire for more exciting intellectual food. He was so far ready to fool the age to the top of its bent; and in the course of his ramblings he strikes some hard blows at various types of hide-bound pedantry. But he is too systematic a trifler to be reckoned with any plausibility amongst the spiritual leaders of any intellectual movement. In that sense, *Tristram Shandy* is a curious symptom of the existing currents of emotion, but cannot, like the *Emile* or the *Nouvelle Héloïse,* be reckoned as one of the efficient causes. This complete and characteristic want of purpose may indeed be reckoned as a literary merit, so far as it prevented *Tristram Shandy* from degenerating into a mere tract. But the want of intellectual seriousness has another aspect, which comes out when we compare Tristram Shandy, for example, with Don Quixote. The resemblance, which has been often pointed out (as indeed Sterne is fond of hinting at it himself) consists in this, that in both cases we see lovable characters through a veil of the ludicrous. As Don Quixote is a true hero, though he is under a constant hallucination, so Uncle Toby is full of the milk of human kindness, though his simplicity makes him ridiculous to the piercing eyes of common-sense. In both cases, it is inferred, the humourist is discharging this true function of showing the lovable qualities which may be associated with a ludicrous outside. (pp. 90-1)

The imaginative force of Cervantes is proved by the fact that Don Quixote and his followers have become the accepted symbols of the most profoundly tragic element in human life—of the contrast between the lofty idealism of the mere enthusiast and the sturdy common-sense of ordinary human beings—between the utilitarian and the romantic types of character; and as neither aspect of the truth can be said to be exhaustive, we are rightly left with our sympathies equally

balanced. The book may be a sad one to those who prefer to be blind; but in proportion as we can appreciate a penetrative insight into the genuine facts of life, we are impressed by this most powerful presentation of the never-ending problem. It is impossible to find in *Tristram Shandy* any central conception of this breadth and depth. If Trim had been as shrewd as Sancho, Uncle Toby would appear like a mere simpleton. Like a child, he requires a thoroughly sympathetic audience who will not bring his playthings to the brutal test of actual facts. The high and earnest enthusiasm of the Don can stand the contrast of common-sense, though at the price of passing into insanity. But Trim is forced to be Uncle Toby's accomplice, or his Commander would never be able to play at soldiers. If Don Quixote had simply amused himself at a mock tournament, and had never been in danger of mistaking a puppet-show for a reality, he would certainly have been more credible, but in the same proportion he would have been commonplace. The whole tragic element which makes the humour impressive would have disappeared. Sterne seldom ventures to the limit of the tragic. (pp. 92-4)

He takes things too easily. He shows us the farce of life, and feels that there is a tragical background to it all; but somehow he is not usually much disposed to cry over it, and he is obviously proud of the tears which he manages to produce. The thought of human folly and suffering does not usually torment and perplex him. The highest humourist should be the laughing and weeping philosopher in one; and in Sterne the weeping philosopher is always a bit of a humbug. The pedantry of the elder Shandy is a simple whim, not a misguided aspiration; and Sterne is so amused with his oddities that he even allows him to be obtrusively heartless. Uncle Toby undoubtedly comes much nearer to complete success; but he wants just that touch of genuine pathos which he would have received from the hands of the greatest writers. But the performance is so admirable in the best passages, where Sterne can drop his buffoonery and his indecency, that even a criticism which sets him below the highest place seems almost unfair. (pp. 96-7)

We may wish, if we please, that Sterne had always been in his best, and that his tears flowed from a deeper source. But so long as he really speaks from his heart—and he does so in all the finer parts of the Toby drama—why should we remember that the heart was rather flighty, and regarded with too much conscious complacency by its proprietor? The Shandyism upon which he prided himself was not a very exalted form of mind, nor one which offered a very deep or lasting satisfaction. Happily we can dismiss an author when we please; give him a cold shoulder in our more virtuous moods, and have a quiet chat with him when we are graciously pleased to relax. In those times we may admit Sterne as the best of jesters, though it may remain an open question whether the jester is on the whole an estimable institution. (p. 101)

Leslie Stephen, "Sterne," in his *Hours in a Library, Vol. IV,* revised edition, The Putnam Publishing Group, 1904, pp. 53-101.

ERNEST NEVIN DILWORTH
(essay date 1948)

[In the excerpt below, Dilworth views Sterne as a thoroughly comic writer who had an exclusively ironic interest in human pathos.]

"Everything in this world, *said my father,* is big with jest,—and has wit in it, and instruction too,—if we can but find it out." This is not the only hint Sterne gives us of what we lose by a literal and incurious habit of mind. When, with the publication of the first two volumes of *Tristram Shandy,* at the beginning of 1760, he first walked in among his countrymen and made himself known and at home, it was as a whimsical wit and humorist. Nobody doubted. But all writing makes serious demands upon a reader—the chief one being that the reader read what is written; sooner or later the eyes glaze, a cue is missed, then another, until the dreaming brain begins to make its own book, and the writer had better have spent his time hoeing a garden. In the light of his later reputation it is discouraging to remember that Sterne did his best, without spoiling his joke, to remind the reader that his purpose was to amuse.

—Certainly, if there is any dependence upon Logic, and that I am not blinded by self-love, there must be something of true genius about me, merely upon this symptom of it, that I do not know what envy is: for never do I hit upon any invention or device which tendeth to the furtherance of good writing, but I instantly make it public; willing that all mankind should write as well as myself.

—Which they certainly will, when they think as little.

What does the literal mind do when confronted by a passage like this one? Does it notice that the last sentence is not an anticlimax? Does it take warning when warning is given with an almost flatfooted bluntness? Or does it simply decide to believe when it wants to believe?

In Sterne's use of the trimmings and commonplaces of the sentimental style, are all the keys we need to the character of the feelings advertised. There is no mystery, nor was there any intended.

Tristram Shandy introduces us to the histrionic powers of our man of feeling, to the hand over the heart, the bended knee, the hand clapped to the head, and the passionate outcry. The book is full of apostrophes and invocations—to Heaven, to Slawkenbergius, to the stars and the critics and Mrs. Wadman—and, like the O's and *Alas's,* they are all comic. Sterne is not disposed to enjoy them all to himself; he jogs the laggard reader. "Unhappy Mrs. Wadman!" he cries, "—For nothing can make this chapter go off with spirit but an apostrophe to thee—." (pp. 10-11)

In the references to his dear, dear Jenny he plays somewhat roughly with the fashionable sentiment of platonic love. There is nothing unnatural or extravagant, he says, in the supposition that his dear Jenny may be his friend.

Surely, Madam, a friendship between the two sexes may subsist, and be supported without—Fy! Mr. *Shandy:*—Without anything, Madam, but that tender and delicious sentiment, which ever mixes in friendship, where there is a difference of sex. Let me intreat you to study the pure and sentimental parts of the best *French* Romances;—it will really, Madam, astonish you to see with what a variety of chaste expressions this delicious sentiment, which I have the honour to speak of, is dress'd out.

This amiably leering emphasis on tender and delicious sentiments and on chastity and purity goes all through the works and letters of Sterne. The tone of voice is struck once for all at the outset, and he who has no ear for it is only to be pitied. As for Jenny, let us not be such unmannerly detectives as to declare that she was in actual life Miss Catherine Fourmantel. (pp. 12-13)

Who can say, however, that the sentimental is not treated, in *Tristram Shandy* at least, with the respect that it deserves? It is even elevated to a branch of physics or metaphysics—I am not certain which. Slawkenbergius opens to the world an untranslatable view of "the involutions of the heart of woman," in a tale the moral of which must have a new word invented for it—"exquisitiveness."

What can he mean by the lambent pupilability of slow, low, dry chat, five notes below the natural tone—which you know, Madam, is little more than a whisper? The moment I pronounced the words, I could perceive an attempt towards a vibration in the strings, about the region of the heart.—The brain made no acknowledgement.—There's often no good understanding betwixt 'em—I felt as if I understood it.—I had no ideas.—The movement could not be without cause.—I'm lost. I can make nothing of it—unless, may it please your worships, the voice, in that case being little more than a whisper, unavoidably forces the eyes to approach not only within six inches of each other—but to look into the pupils—is not that dangerous?—But it can't be avoided—for to look up to the ceiling, in that case the two chins un-avoidably meet—and to look down into each other's lap, the foreheads come to immediate contact, which at once puts an end to the conference—I mean to the sentimental part of it.—What is left, madam, is not worth stooping for.

Sterne knows as much as any Slawkenbergius about the convolutions of the heart, and about the verbal threads and bodily contortions that are supposed to be the means of perambulating that warm labyrinth. It cannot be said, though, that he treats these mysteries with reverence. See with what diddle-diddle of the fiddle, what prut-trut-krish-krash-krush he leads up to the affecting powers of music, of the music of him who "fiddles to be felt,—who inspires me with his joys and hopes, and puts the most hidden springs of my heart into motion"; that's the time to borrow money of me, Sir, he says; that's the time to get your bill paid. The Eye of Pity must submit to even worse indignities than the Hidden Springs of the Heart. When Walter Shandy—in despair over the winding of the clock, the use of his jackboots as imitation mortars, and now the crushing of his child's nose—flings himself across his bed in "the most lamentable attitude of a man borne down with sorrows, that ever the eye of pity dropp'd a tear for," his arm hangs over the side, and his knuckles recline upon the handle of the chamberpot. The picture is a fine one, anyhow, and Sterne is probably right when he says (calling us "madam," as always when he is most mischievous), that a horizontal position is best for pain and—for aught he knows—pleasure too. (pp. 14-15)

It is not likely that the Shandean habit of confronting the grave with the gay, and the soulful with the prurient, was either an accident of Sterne's sinful nature or the horrid result of an incapacity to make his pen behave like a little gentleman—long enough, that is, to finish such courtesies as the sentimental reader thought it had begun. We know by *Tristram Shandy* that Sterne was able to keep in mind what he had written; and so we must suppose that he was aware of constantly dousing the head of the so-called Elevated in the horse-pond of the so-called Low, and that if the Elevated emerged looking as if it had been in a horse-pond, that was the effect intended. Only the fatuous would ask *why?*—with the portrait in their heads of some strenuous Yorick mapping out a program for the belligerent disposal of his infinite jest. But if *why?* is not the question, at least *why not?* is the answer.

In the tale of the Ass of Lyons there is no lachrymose corporal whose voice grows hoarse with philanthropic emotion, and who, in order to resume his relation of agreeable obscentities, must clear his throat and "aid nature" by striking an attitude "with his left arm akimbo on one side, and with his right a little extended, supporting her on the other." This Lyons episode is at the other extreme of good nature, simple, careless, and all on the surface. It has been approved as an expression of sentiment, but it deserves more praise as a caprice. In the first place, an ass is not only a disarming animal with a countenance that begs pity from the idle onlooker, but it makes even a humorless person think of man. And in the second place, Sterne—as good-natured as any of us—was not interested in parading his humane impulses, but was intent on drawing the ass's picture, and letting it invite whatever nimble extravaganza might choose to come. The difference between Sterne's approach to the animal and that of any of our own contemporaries is clear at a glance; if Sterne talks to an animal or professes to interpret for it, he does so with none of our animal-story sentimentalism, but with an adult humor that springs from an essential preoccupation with man.

I have ever something civil to say to him [an ass] on my part; and as one word begets another (if he has as little to do as I)—I generally fall into conversation with him; and surely never is my imagination so busy as in framing his responses from the etchings of his countenance—and where those carry me not deep enough—in flying from my own heart into his, and seeing what is natural for an ass to think—as well as a man, upon the occasion. In truth, it is the only creature of all the classes of beings below me, with whom I can do this: for parrots, jackdaws, &c.—I never exchange a word with them—nor with the apes, &c., for pretty near the same reason; they act by rote, as the others speak by it, and equally make me silent: nay my dog and my cat, though I value them both—(and for my dog he would speak if he could)—yet somehow or other, they neither of them possess the talents for conversation—I can make nothing of a discourse with them, beyond the *proposition,* the *reply,* and *rejoinder,* which terminated my father's and my mother's conversations, in his beds of justice—and those utter'd—there's an end of the dialogue—

—But with an ass, I can commune for ever.

There is the same deftly inconsistent treatment of small or common things as if they were large or uncommon ones, and the same murmur of parody, which we hear in the orchestration of all his humor. While being communed with, the ass is eating, with obvious distaste, the stem of an artichoke, and Tristram declaims in tragic style on the bitter lot of Jack. "Thou hast not a friend perhaps in all this world, that will give thee a macaroon"; upon which, like magic, Tristram pulls a paper of macaroons from his pocket and gives him one. The last words of the conversation finish, to perfection, the portrait of the jackass. The halter breaks short in Tristram's hand. The beast looks up "pensive" in his face—" 'Don't thrash me with it—but if you will, you may'—If I do, said I, I'll be d—d." At this, some one comes in and beats the ass, the pannier in rushing by tears Tristram's breeches "in the most disastrous direction you can imagine," and after an equivoque the curtain falls with elaborate delicacy. (pp. 29-31)

The man who looks morally down his nose at Sterne is invited, before he passes judgment, to explore the cesspool of his own self-interest. The egotistical affectations of Sterne were as harmless and open as the grimaces of a clown; he changed costume before the eyes of his audience; he frankly enjoyed himself as the good Lord made him, and the Lord had not made him serious.

Frivolity was his mainspring. The *Journal to Eliza* was a mere affair of flimflam gallantry; if it fails to tick, that is because passion does not go by main force of trifling—and so much the worse for it. In the two works by which Sterne is known, his frivolity and he together exist as art. *Tristram Shandy* is the fruit of all that he found laugh-at-able in his way; now comes the final fling, the *Sentimental Journey,* in which he takes a family of jokes from *Tristram Shandy* (modish ideas which by other people were courted and pursued in earnest) and writes a book about them—not as a satirist, but as a jester capitalising on things of the moment, and having his fun.

The young fellow [Yorick's new valet, La Fleur], said the landlord, is beloved by all the town, and there is scarce a corner in Montriul, where the want of him will not be felt: he has but one misfortune in the world, continued he, "He is always in love." I am heartily glad of it, said I; 'twill save me the trouble every night of putting my breeches under my head. In saying this, I was making not so much La Fleur's eloge, as my own, having been in love, with one princess or other, almost all my life, and I hope I shall go on so till I die, being firmly persuaded, that if ever I do a mean action, it must be in some interval betwixt one passion and another: whilst this interregnum lasts, I always perceive my heart locked up, I can scarce find in it to give Misery a sixpence; and therefore I always get out of it as fast as I can, and the moment I am rekindled, I am all generosity and good-will again; and would do anything in the world, either for or with any one, if they will but satisfy me there is no sin in it.

But in saying this, sure I am commending the passion, not myself.

It was a pleasant conceit to make philandering the parent of philanthropy; heat expands the heart, by anybody's law of physics, but the effects—we are glad to learn—are likely to be subtle: under these combined influences he would do anything in the world, not only for, but with anyone—provided there was no sin in it. Who was thinking of the possibility of sin? And now notice the undulant grace with which he slithers away into another corner: he is commending the passion, not himself. Sterne's is a slippery wit, and the reader must be quick to catch every word as it glides by him. Did the word "misfortune," for example, pass unrecognized, riding the circus-horse of Love?

Critics and scholars are as apt to bolt their literary meals as are those boorish common readers for whom, in matters of taste, they legislate. How else than by gross feeding can a man fail to notice the humorous flavor of the very first course in the *Sentimental Journey?* The values of the finer feelings as opposed to and ineffably beyond the reach of a selfish, dry philosophy of materialism—such lights and shades are going to be played with, to the edification of all who are capable of enjoying the show. (pp. 80-1)

There are men who shy away from the superficial as there are men who shrink from the profound; and there are some to whom one or the other is simply unknown. Both are a fabric of words. All of us cover the hide of the brute with the clothes of art; those precious jewels, our complicated high-toned states of mind, we owe to literature. The savage cannot yawn without pedantry, and civilised man, naked for bed or for war, is plastered with the leaves of an infinite book. Some of those leaves, Sterne, like millions who wear them, could not read; but since he could not read the rest without laughing, he gathered all together and kept the unknown with the known as a wardrobe of words for his amusement. The difference between Sterne and other shallow men is that he made comic art of what is called a disability. He is a master, and of a species that is unwanted. The giants of the world become its oxen; the small slippery fellows are feared like the first in Eden, and are hunted down. In impishly putting on any face that for the moment pleases him, Sterne shivers the worm-eaten timbers of a world whose lies are serious.

Double meanings are occasionally useful; they may allow a jester to save his life and an unsmiling listener to keep his sanity. The organic irreverence of Sterne has goaded the graver members of his audience to such prodigies of labored misapprehension, that they have not only conceived but borne him anew, a black sheep, but somehow in the image of themselves and their special cravings. It may be that none but the young, the unlicked and callow, the pure in heart, the irretrievably debauched, can afford to look at him as he is. Who knows?

He is not a nice man, but he is worth reading all the same. He is not cruel, unless it is cruelty to make a joke of kindness; and the joke is often a good one. Though he cares for little beyond himself, he makes fun of all self-indulgence; and though he is always an actor, he is no pretender. He is the humorist of appearances; what men choose to call realities can neither be liked nor laughed at until they have been cut away from their roots of feeling. Saintsbury said that Sterne does not laugh but sniggers; what he does is rather to keep himself in a state of crackling amusement—kindling nonsense, and malice, and the humors of his workmanship, with the spark of impropriety. His literary technique is no more artfully unconventional than his wit. But his sense of humor is not unique. In his use of the equivoque he is close kin to Shakespeare, most of whose jollier puns—lucky for him—are no longer understood. Sterne lived with language as all poets do, and the poet who has no obscenity in him is an impostor.

To the sentimentalist of yesterday, today, and tomorrow, as to the plain honest man, something is sacred; to Sterne everything is words, the immaterial substance out of which appear the clothes, the rattle, and the handspring of a jester. The proof of his craft in words lies open to us, phrase after phrase; and the small world he made gesticulates and bows and fibs and listens at keyholes, all to the motion of his hand. The jester sets the pace and every word follows. Only look at his style, the fleet shadow of his mind. Try to put your finger on it. It slides along swiftly, easily, to right and to left—not zigzag, but in a continuous stream, it curls back upon itself like smoke, and away.

The show goes on between the covers of a book. It is a long time since the man died. God rest his bones, but there is little doubt that the dust they have become is still dancing. (pp. 108-10)

Ernest Nevin Dilworth, in his *The Unsentimental Journey of Laurence Sterne,* King's Crown Press, 1948, 115 p.

JOHN TRAUGOTT

(essay date 1954)

[Traugott is an American critic and educator. In the following excerpt, he views *Tristram Shandy* as a work in which philosophical and rhetorical forms are used ironically in order to demonstrate that passion, not reason, is the basis of human behavior.]

Sterne was not unwilling that his readers should make themselves uneasy while at his book; to this end he left, as he tells us, "so many openings for equivocal strictures." He has had his way. In nearly every opening some critic has taken a stand, but, usually, with nicely averted eyes. Nineteenth-century horror has given way to twentieth-century indulgence; Sterne survives both, and, indeed, in his perverse way takes increase from both. Yet many appreciative readers have understood *Tristram Shandy* as a comedy that is one vast rhetorical trap for the unwary. For it is a book that beckons us—is it with a sensible smile or a civil leer?—into indulgence in all the marginal vices: sentiment, affectation, pre-

sumption, pedantry, puerility, pruriency, and so on through the category of our human blemishes. What a piece of work is Man! Stern says,—so equivocally compounded. But if Sterne's wit encourages the reader to a dallying with unscrupulous or dubious ideas and affections, including the love of fools and madmen, it also insists upon the reader's catching himself at his lapse. Once awakened, of course, one is already convicted of participation in certain impurities. As a later ironic rhetorician, Shaw, was to set logical traps for his reader's instruction, so Sterne plotted rhetorical snares which engage and reveal the affections. That his rhetoric remains vital though it is concerned ostensibly with such antique interests as Locke's philosophy, rhetorical forms, and odd scraps of recondite lore, only suggests to us what the eighteenth-century reader was willing to take on faith: the proposition that there are common springs of behavior that work men. Abnormal psychology was not an eighteenth-century interest.

Though some readers are easily arrided by the self-knowledge (albeit of a very mundane sort) so discovered, others have never forgiven Sterne and have had a sort of revenge: on the one hand he is a foul satyr, a disgrace to his collar, a whining hypocrite, a presumptuous and really unlearned (someone is always discovering a Sterne "borrowing") pedant; and on the other, a whimsical sentimentalist or, at best, a whimsical humorist. A nineteenth-century edition of *Tristram Shandy* was retitled *My Uncle Toby,* and *The Beauties of Sterne* is in the libraries. And his sensible heart, his Shandy humor, have in our day been enough commended. Whether Sterne is to be censured or felicitated for his literary and real characters is a question vastly uninteresting today. Once honestly read, *Tristram* fascinates us not merely for its Toby but for its ironic relation of Toby to Walter, to ourselves, and to all the world. It is a book of relations, revealed through a rhetorical wit of paradox and dialectical ingenuity. Like Walter a rhetorician, Sterne could find the mainsprings of our reactions, and he wrote his book, toward the end of his life, because mere social carping and scoffing and flouting—and understanding—were not enough for him. He was an artist, and for all his Augustan satire of system builders he could see the masks and coloring of personality in the system of relations that is the Shandy world. (pp. xi-xii)

[Sterne] was a rhetorician and not a "novelist." A critic looking at Sterne as a chapter in his history of the novel will find him a sad case of arrested development: neither the characters, though they are as "real" as any in literature, nor the action, though it is indeed sufficiently complicated, develops as other than an argumentative device of the opinionative Tristram. What does develop is a history of the reader's mind. The *argumentum ad hominem* was Sterne's device for revealing his perceptions. He argued to his readers, using their own responses as his illustrations. Just as he argued the cause of a worldly morality to his parishioners by exciting their sentiments, vexing them, and then pointing to their motives for those sentiments, so Tristram speaks as a preacher, arguing not for sentiment or cynicism or whimsicality, those supposedly Shandean touchstones, but for the recognition of their real influences in our pharisaical rationales. Writing, properly managed, our author seems to say, is warfare with the reader.

In every way, Sterne's rhetoric in *Tristram* sets the affections at war, and the forms of his rhetoric are a map of that conflict. My Uncle Toby is no more important than My Father, and My Father's systems are mad only north-north-west. Possibly every one of the Shandys is mad in some direction (except My Mother, and she is a universal blank), but they are mad because everyone, including My Mother, does service as a "voice" in Tristram's crisscrossed rhetorical demonstration of the history of the mind. Tobys and Walters understand one another when they understand the human need of organizing one's own associations and symbols into some meaningful pattern. Toby is not deluded by his scheme, for he knows that it is his scheme alone and he knows also his own fallibility. Ultimately, Walter too sees himself as a figure in his own drama, and though it is part of that drama to be elaborately at odds with the world, he too, in Sterne's words, rides his Hobby-Horse on the King's Highway. Evil for Sterne is not the wearing of a mask, but the assumption that Your Worship alone of all men is not wearing a mask. Sterne enjoyed pulling down masks, but only so that the wearer might not forget the accouterment. There is no disputing about Hobby-Horses, but there is disputing when one assumes that he is himself the only knight errant pricking on the plain. There is, says Sterne, a fair field of folk. Tristram makes plain that the schemes of men, from the Sorbonne doctors' disputation *in utero* to the Lockean rationale, may be seen in one vast scheme as necessary orderings of human experience according to a standard human nature.

Such is the argument of Sterne's rhetoric, that rhetoric which is the real form of *Tristram.* . . . Though *Tristram Shandy* is a medley of vividly characterized "voices" colliding in fractured plot-sequences, of interrogations of the reader, of learned wit-play, and of seemingly vagrant associations, it has the consistent pattern of demonstrating by stratagems of apparent paradox and contrast probable human reactions to certain archetypal situations. It is argument, just as the sermons of Mr. Yorick are argument, and the stratagems through which probable reactions are displayed when overtly called into the reader's consciousness (as they always are) become a map of the actions of the mind. The forms of rhetorical argument as Sterne uses them, his ingenious with which can turn any side of an argument, are ultimately important not as logical de-

velopment, but as symbols of our thinking processes. Sterne's end is discovered in his technique. . . . Both as a pulpit rhetorician and a profane one he was always concerned with form and its possibilities for statement. (pp. xiii-xiv)

[Sterne achieved a peculiar significance] by warping certain traditional materials: the philosophy of John Locke and the standard schemes, available in countless manuals, for rhetorical invention. Both materials served his invention, and he developed from both a formalization for his witty drama of warring affections or conceptions.

It was Locke's scheme in the *Essay concerning Human Understanding* to invade "that sanctuary of vanity and ignorance" the use of "vague and insignificant forms of speech"; this scheme Sterne perverts to a rhetorical formula for the invention of dramatic situations (which are always symbols of mental gymnastics) in *Tristram.* . . . Whereas Locke would resolutely analyze all ideas and exactly determine the significations of words in order to reconcile necessarily isolated minds (necessarily, because mind is substance and therefore unknowable), Sterne's purpose is to demonstrate and describe the constant frustration of such analysis, the impossibility of determining meaning apart from a context of human situations. Using Locke's terminology and logic with a solemn mock-devotion, Sterne sets up an interplay of characters, in which his readers are implicated by traps of sentiment and logic, as a test of the philosopher's method. Exploiting Locke's own skepticism to a point where, as analytical method, even his limited rationalism is undermined, Tristram-Sterne invents the dramatic situations implicit in these conflicts of personal apprehension. Every invention tightens the knot for the reader. By such implicit opposition to Locke's rationalism, and by explicit ridicule, too, Sterne maintains the case for wit, rather than rational analysis, in discovering and communicating human motives. If, philosophically considered, wit is a kind of *discordia concors* (an occult association of ideas), it is the most comprehensive technique for establishing relations: if communication depends upon establishing the most comprehensive relations (since it cannot depend upon rationalistic determination of ideas), wit is its most effective technique. Such was Sterne's logic. By burlesquing and subverting the philosophical assumptions of Locke, who believed wit to be a positive evil, Sterne protests the moral value of wit. (pp. xiv-xv)

Since [Sterne] insists upon the efficacy of rhetorical wit in exploring human motives, the inventions on any topic examine dialectically, by verbal forms of paradox and contrast, probable reactions. Moreover, by the agency of various techniques, often by being enticed into an unsavory train of logic, the reader is forced to participate in the rhetorical proofs. Having spread his lime and with the bird in hand, Tristram then examines the reader's motives in accepting those proofs. Rhetoric becomes the subject of rhetoric, and the ironic view so created is one method of contrast among many which Sterne's rhetoric develops as the defining form of his persuasion. Thus does Sterne write a history of the mind. The forms of rhetoric are themselves the demonstrations of that history. This rhetorical play with philosophical and rhetorical forms—this play which reveals motives and measures one affection against another in various situations—is Sterne's pathetic comedy. By it he demonstrates that, though they will not analyze ideas, Tobys and Walters may communicate; that the ultimate fact of moral philosophy is human nature itself; that the "true" shibboleths and "objective" definitions by which we live mirror unaccountably our passions; and (perhaps most important) that such moral antitheses as "delicacy" and "concupiscence" are, indeed and alas, sometimes one affection. (pp. xv-xvi)

John Traugott, in an introduction to his *Tristram Shandy's World: Sterne's Philosophical Rhetoric,* University of California Press, 1954, pp. xi-xvi.

ARTHUR HILL CASH
(essay date 1966)

[Cash is an American critic and educator and a noted authority on Sterne. In the following excerpt, he outlines differences of tone, theme, and viewpoint between *The Journal to Eliza* and *A Sentimental Journey.*]

Laurence Sterne experimented with one work of fullblown emotionalism, independent of rational restraints—the day-book to Eliza Draper which is now called *The Journal to Eliza.* (p. 133)

The view popularized by Wilbur Cross, that the document reveals "the pathological state of the emotions—long suspected but never quite known to a certainty—whence springs the *Sentimental Journey,*" was exploded by Rufus Putney's series of articles. . . . I cannot subscribe to Putney's view of Sterne's sentimentalism as a "hoax," but his opinion that Sterne "mocked in the *Sentimental Journey* the foolish figure he had cut with Eliza Draper" cannot be doubted. Sterne was not deeply in love with Mrs. Draper, but was consciously toying with the experiences and the literature of the heart.

All parties admit that *The Journal to Eliza* was written as a public, not private, epistle. Cross reports, "As if designed for publication, the manuscript contains numerous blots and interlineations for better phrases, in addition to the introductory note, which was clearly framed to mystify the general reader." Flattered by the interest of a young, handsome woman, Sterne must have enjoyed concocting a literary chronicle which he fancied as a complement to the experience. (pp. 133-34)

In my opinion, Sterne realized, as do most readers today, that the daybook was an inferior work. Wilbur Cross and those who shared his view were led astray by an assumption that [*Sentimental Journey* and *The Journal to Eliza*] emanated from the same sentimental animus. What strikes me is the remarkable difference between the two, the loose irrationality of the epistle to Eliza contrasting with the moral rationality which underpins the novel. In *The Journal to Eliza,* Sterne seems to forget or invert all the values which support the *Sentimental Journey.* The emphasis in the love letters is upon feeling alone, quite aside from the actions which give rise to them or result from them. Sterne writes about his loving regard for Eliza, his misery at their separation, his anticipation of their eventual reunion and marriage. The writing is maudlin and tasteless. He flaunts the account of his diseased genitals . . . , and blatantly wishes for the deaths of Daniel Draper and Mrs. Sterne. . . . His craving for sentiments, which in the *Sentimental Journey* is comically set over against his duty, is here excused by a neurotic hedonism: "[I] begin to feel a pleasure in this kind of resigned misery arising from this situation, of heart unsupported by ought but its own tenderness." . . . In the novel, Yorick too wants the pleasure of feeling "the movements which rise" out of desire, but he knows he must "govern them" as a good man. . . . Mr. Yorick is constantly tortured by self-doubt, but not so Sterne in *The Journal to Eliza:* "I trust all I have to it [love]—as I trust Heaven, which *cannot leave me, without a fault, to perish.*" . . . (pp. 135-36)

Furthermore, there is no opposition between the head and the heart in the *Journal.* "Thou hast only turned the tide of my passions a new way," writes Sterne; "they flow, Eliza, to thee—and ebb from every other object in this world—and reason tells me they do right." . . . "Thou art mistress, Eliza, of all the powers he [Sterne] has to soothe and protect thee—for thou art mistress of his heart; his affections; and his reason." . . . In the published novel, Yorick never gives up his reason to his sentiments, least of all when women evoke the affection: when he is embarrassed at holding the hand of Madame de L***, the lady herself remarks on the conflict of heart and head—"the heart knew it [Yorick's wish], and was satisfied; and who but an English philosopher would have sent notice of it to the brain to reverse the judgment?" . . .

The references to God in the two works show a remarkable contrast. In the *Sentimental Journey* Yorick's prayers, comic though they be, are prayers for moral strength (the one exception is immediately corrected by Yorick . . .) or for the welfare of others. Yorick may feel sexual desire for Maria at one moment and call upon God to protect her at the next . . . , but he is taking leave of the maid, and we cannot doubt his altruism. In *The Journal to Eliza,* Sterne's prayers are selfish and petty. He may ask Jesus for a "recompense for the sorrows and disappointments" Eliza has suffered, but he also wants himself to be "the instrument." . . . His ill-founded confidence that God will protect his and Eliza's interests, he guilelessly describes as a "religious elixir." . . . (p. 136)

The *Journal to Eliza* is not a rationalistic work. It is not, for that matter, a moral work, for it sets aside all moral standards.

The document should be taken as evidence for the kind of weakness at which Sterne laughed in the *Sentimental Journey.* No doubt, Sterne himself had the weakness. To the *Journal* can be added the fragmentary evidences of numerous sentimental dalliances. (p. 137)

Of course Sterne wrote autobiographically. How can a writer do otherwise? He drew from his abundant experience as a flirt when writing both the *Journal* and the *Journey,* but the results differ. In *The Journal to Eliza* Sterne's amorous sentimentality is regarded as an end in itself. In the *Sentimental Journey* it is laughed at. Had Sterne been completely captivated by his love for Eliza Draper, had he thought that an effusion of emotions without the control of reason had any value, he would have abandoned the novel in order to complete *The Journal to Eliza.* Instead, he chose to be the humorist, to laugh at himself along with the rest of the world, to turn his own folly into a comedy of moral sentiments. (p. 139)

Arthur Hill Cash, in his *Sterne's Comedy of Moral Sentiments: The Ethical Dimension of the "Journey,"* Duquesne University Press, 1966, 152 p.

RICHARD A. LANHAM
(essay date 1973)

[In the following excerpt, Lanham discusses Sterne's use of comedy in *Tristram Shandy,* emphasizing the absence of a reassuringly affirmative vision of life in the work.]

Each comedy defines comedy in a new way. And no book, surely, teaches us the vanity of comic dogmatizing better than *Tristram Shandy.* Nothing reminds us more often that definitions are hazardous. For the book seems almost a sampler of comic effect. If it defines its own kind of comedy, it is one composed of many simples. Comedy may perhaps be a serious thing. Sterne's kind, however, so changeable as it is in its theoretical basis, seems calculated to deny this seriousness by denying us a single comic perspective. We laugh first from incongruity, then from sudden glorious superiority, then from relief. (p. 151)

Comedy, Bergson tells us, is half in life and half out of it. So with Sterne. We can never decide who speaks when and in what mask. Sterne manages to make us think of him and his work as a single body. Although we split off one part for analysis, in the end we must come to terms with the rest. Yorick the clown leads sooner or later to Yorick the preacher. Sterne insists on an unbroken continuum from the most artificial literary patterning to the most spontaneous gesture in life—a broad, uninterrupted reach from style to life style. He argues for the coherence of life and art directly counter to the Victorians' split, yet paradoxically in agreement with it. Lamb divided life and art to save the delicious artificiality of drawing-room comedy. The Victorian mentality would not. Sterne does both, saves the artificiality by calling attention to the artificiality in life.

Bergson's theory of comedy remains, with all its perceptiveness and modifications, romantic humor theory. There is a real self. There is a pattern of behavior natural to it. The natural pattern varies spontaneously. The enemy is mindless repetition. Conventional and affected behavior is inherently unnatural. So wit "consists, for the most part, in seeing things *sub specie theatri.*" "It is comic to wander out of one's own self. It is comic to fall into a ready-made category." "The comic expresses, above all else, a special lack of adaptability to society." . . . Such a theory, suggestive as it is for *Tristram Shandy,* follows it only part way. Bergson sees that "the comic comes into being just when society and the individual, freed from the worry of self-preservation, begin to regard themselves as works of art." But he does not carry the implications of this self-consciousness to the end. Dramatic perspective attained, we lose our reference point. No norm remains. Every action is an acting. Spontaneity becomes, the more one reaches for it, the more affected. You end up, like Castiglione's Courtier, *affecting* nonchalant spontaneity. Comic correctives evaporate. Comic transcendence becomes problematic.

In sum, the comic frame should enable people *to be observers of themselves, while acting.* Its ultimate would not be *passiveness,* but *maximum consciousness.* One would "transcend" himself by noting his own foibles. He would provide a rationale for locating the irrational and the nonrational. [Kenneth Burke, *Attitudes Toward History*]

Unless we greatly mistake it, *Tristram Shandy*

---

destroys such a rationale. It includes and illustrates too many kinds of comedy. Bergson puts his finger on Sterne's basic comic strategy clearly enough. "A situation is invariably comic when it belongs simultaneously to two altogether independent series of events and is capable of being interpreted in two entirely different meanings at the same time." But neither Tristram nor Sterne tells us which meaning is the reference one, which comic theory is to be applied. We can build a comic theory on the postulate of spontaneity, as Bergson did. We can, perhaps more convincingly, build one on repetition, as Kierkegaard does. But what kind of theory will account for a document that builds its comic effects first on one postulate, then on the other? "We have no deeper interest than our integrity," Emerson tells us with his characteristic sobriety, "and that we should be made aware by joke and by stroke of any lie we entertain. Besides, a perception of the Comic seems to be a balance-wheel in our metaphysical structure. It appears to be an essential element in a fine character." But *Tristram Shandy* can be accounted for by no theory of comedy like this, or like Hazlitt's which sees comedy as dramatic ego reducer ("A man cannot be a very great egotist, who every day, sees himself rep-

resented on the stage"). *Tristram Shandy* seems to abolish the ego altogether. It does not see comedy as essential to fine character; it eliminates character. The comic therapy may indeed be relief that we need not take seriously something we feared we should have to. . . . But the seriousness *Tristram Shandy* diminishes is the seriousness of the self.

The self persists, if by it we mean Freud's tireless seeker after pleasure. But, under a conception of comedy as dramatic self-consciousness at least, it does not renew its ties to society. . . . *Tristram Shandy* shows us defending ourselves against the pressures of culture and of instinct by converting them to pleasure. It does not satirize this conversion. Sterne stands it as the center of mortal life. We accept it. We use it. The book begins, after all, by conceiving laughter as defensive gesture.

> Never poor Wight of a Dedicator had less hopes from his Dedication, than I have from this of mine; for it is written in a bye corner of the kingdom, and in a retired thatch'd house, where I live in a constant endeavour to fence against the infirmities of ill health, and other evils of life, by mirth; being firmly persuaded that every time a man smiles,—but much more so, when he laughs, that it adds something to this Fragment of Life.

Tristram Shandy remains rhetorical in this sense: it preserves from the beginning an extraliterary purpose—to keep the spirits up.

I cannot, then, accept the current conception of *Tristram Shandy* as absurdist comedy with sentimental light at the end of the tunnel. Such a view is serious, essentially philosophical. And *Tristram Shandy* is essentially rhetorical, comic. The seriousness the Victorians missed and that the moderns find is tragic seriousness, and it requires a tragic self. . . . The tragic self and its seriousness *Tristram Shandy* takes pains to deny. They are present on the stage. They form subject, *theme* if you will. But they are denied, not affirmed. *Tristram Shandy* from its pattern-book illustration of comic types does precipitate out a theory, but not one that yields Arnoldian seriousness. It tells us what goes on in the redemptive green world. We change selves. Kinds of self. In dealing with the process of changing selves, or in the conflict between the two kinds of self, Sterne goes beyond comedy. He discusses the relation of tragedy and comedy, writes—it is as close as we will allow the word—a "philosophy" of comedy. In thus dealing with this relationship of the two he resumes the ancient quarrel between philosophy and rhetoric. His narrative, like its predecessors in the older tradition of rhetorical narrative, deals with the tradition's central theme, the clash of two fundamentally opposed conceptions of self. How to type such a work, or this long succession of works, perplexes in the extreme. Without arguing about its previous meaning, I am going to appropriate "tragicomedy." Let it refer to the kind of poesy, play, poem, or novel, which takes as artistic subject the relationship between the tragic and comic views of man. This kind of work will both invite us to be serious, as Rabelais does, and Cervantes and Sterne, and mock us for it. It will depict the comic view prevailing, but prevailing by authorial first. The author, like Shakespeare at the end of *Measure for Measure,* insists on it by visible, contorted irresolution. Such works will often be didactic: although they show a struggle between the two views, they both show and tell us that the comic should prevail. They are always pushing, as if they were not quite sure the comic view will stick. The struggle against seriousness must never be relaxed. *Tristram Shandy* does not struggle so. Tristram sets up the "Life and Times" format as symbolic of the integral, serious personality, and then never tires—as sometimes we do—of tearing it apart. But Sterne contents himself with showing how the comic does, rather than ought to, prevail. (pp. 154-60)

[We cannot] finally separate the two sides of Sterne's literary production or either side from his clerical self. . . . Sterne's religious faith stands, I take it, unquestioned and unquestionable. However he postures to Eliza about his sermons coming "all hot from the heart," and however [Lansing Van der Heyden Hammond's *Laurence Sterne's Sermons*] shows them all hot from the library, still they were produced by an extraordinary clergyman with ordinary religious opinions. They, or at least the first four volumes, share several techniques with the two novels, but are less remarkable for this than for their time of appearance, their concomitant publication with *Tristram Shandy.* We have our choice. We may think of Sterne's saying essentially the same thing, but in two different ways, in the two publications. . . . *Tristram Shandy* becomes, in this view, a kind of extended, freewheeling sermon on the text: "the principal spirit in the Universe is one of joy" [W.B. Watkins, *The Perilous Balance*]. Thinking Sterne a philosopher of the sentimental absurd essentially extends this view. Critical respectability comes with a much closer analysis of the novel as a verbal structure, but the philosophical arena of the novel—and its conception of the human heart—remains that of the *Sermons* minus God. The cure for our problems remains in fellow-feeling, in sentiment rightly construed and bravely applauded.

Another interpretation offers itself. We may think of the two statements, sermon and novel, as fundamentally different in kind and intention. Here is Sterne himself on preaching:

> Preaching (you must know) is a theologic flap upon the heart, as the dunning for a promise is a political flap upon the memory:—both the one and the other is useless where men have *wit enough* to be honest.

Surely *Tristram Shandy*'s *paideia* of the reader's imagination premises that man has wit enough to be honest. (In the sermons, however, Sterne preaches to the gluttons of sensual delight.) The book declares Sterne's independence from the need to write sermons. He allows himself a secular mode, and this mode, this pagan *consolatio,* has its own rules and implications. In the sermons, Sterne presents himself again and again as literary critic of the sacred text. In *Tristram Shandy,* the text has become a secular, even a profane, one. The *Sermons* tell us repeatedly that the path of righteousness is the path of joy: "good is that which can only give the mind pleasure and comfort—and . . . evil is that, which must necessarily be attended sooner or later with shame and sorrow." Religion is calculated to make us happy in this life, as in the next. God bids us enjoy life. And the path of truth and knowledge leads to joy too:

> There is nothing generally in which our happiness and honour are more nearly concerned, than in forming true notions both of men and things.

Here, in the *Sermons,* we can find the dependable center of Laurence Sterne's optimism. But we cannot automatically transfer it to the novel because so much in the novel seems to recall these passages in the *Sermons,* so many of the techniques seem to be the same. True notions of men *sub specie aeternitatis* are not those of man *sub specie ludi.* Sterne's *Sermons* do betray remarkable optimism and faith. The novel deliberately does without both. Coming to it from reading the *Sermons* is like plunging into a cold bath. The reassurance is gone. The comfortable, traditional conception of moral identity, so reassuring in the *Sermons,* vanishes. We have instead the chilly paganism Bagehot noticed, the Stoicism of Hamlet and Horatio. Moralizing is everywhere, but no moral anywhere. Instead of the firm conviction that reason and feeling go on together, and that both jump with the humor of God, we have feeling ironically qualified, sentiment scrutinized, reason attacked. In the novel, Sterne may be ventilating the many doubts that a lifetime of sermonizing reassurance in others had created in himself. But however our biographical guesswork runs, he certainly tests all the sermons' assumptions by secular experience. He supplies not a complementary—or a complimentary—but a counter statement.

The only way out of the novel's radical skepticism lies through religious belief, and we are as free to take it as Sterne was. [In his *Homo Ludens,* J. Huizinga] puts the relation of the two domains in the most general terms:

> The human mind can only disengage itself from the magic circle of play by turning towards the ultimate. Logical thinking does not go far enough. Surveying all the treasures of the mind and all the splendours

of its achievements we shall still find, at the bottom of every serious judgement, something problematical left. In our heart of hearts we know that none of our pronouncements is absolutely conclusive. At that point, where our judgement begins to waver, the feeling that the world is serious after all wavers with it. Instead of the old saw: "All is vanity," the more positive conclusion forces itself upon us that "all is play."

We are free to break out of the magic circle in *Tristram Shandy,* and if we choose to do so, a very different reading will result. But nothing in the novel invites us to break out or shows us a way to. *We* must supply both the inclination and the direction. The form of the fiction works not to favor such an inclination but to discourage it. It is Eros that supplies the obvious link between the two selves, opens the circle, and precisely this Sterne chose to leave out of his book. *Tristram Shandy* does not create a universe suffused with grinning existential despair, but full of tireless pleasure-seekers and inexhaustible sources of pleasure. About this search, Sterne says nothing. (Tristram is, of course, all for it.) He simply reports it. He is far less intrusive a moralist than Freud, for example, far less a champion of reason. In disposing of the enemies of reason, Freud finally comes not to passion but the conscience as the last and greatest enemy. Sterne simply, via the sermon, throws conscience on the banquet table of pleasure along with everything else, and observes the feast.

If there is an unexposed root assumption in the novel, it is not that the principle of the universe is one of joy, "Tochter aus Elisium," but rather that consciousness is good. Awareness is more likely to make people good than bad. Sterne, unlike Shakespeare, seems to have had no nightmares about this assumption. He dreamed no Iagos. Historically, such an assumption can hardly be sustained; but in the sphere of the private life, perhaps. One is continually tempted by the great suggestiveness of the form of *Tristram Shandy* to force from it statements about the public life. It makes none. It is tempting, for example, to argue that all the novel's play with formal rhetorical theory satirizes the public life that rhetorical theory so nicely symbolizes. But finally the satire is so mild it may not be there at all. Sterne simply introduces all that theory into the domain of private life and watches his characters sport with it. Its character, nature, whatever, in the public sphere is plainly irrelevant. A strong strand of

"Yorkshire Epic" commentary runs through Sterne criticism. Can we take over this strand and make of the novel an epic treatment of the narrowest and yet the broadest locale of all, the private life? Surely it is not Yorkshire, or Shandy Hall Sterne talks of but Home and Garden. The uniqueness, singularity of Shandy Hall which he is forever pointing to stands for the uniqueness of home to each of us. Which of us, faced with the need to explain *our* family, would not fall back on Tristram's clichés of singularity?

If we read the novel in this way, we go some distance toward bringing together those who find the Sterne of the *Sermons* in *Tristram Shandy* and those who might follow this essay's argument. Sterne explores the resources of pleasure to be found in the private life. The novel analyzes the private life. But it does not say this is all of human experience. Nor does it offer advice on what to do once we have anatomized the private life in this way. It is a closed system. It is violently reductive of human motive. It is full of implications. But, as the history of Sterne criticism amply proves, each will pursue the implications of his choice. Each will grab his own handle. This is a matter of supreme indifference—no, perhaps, of amused indifference—to Sterne. It confirms his point. The boundary of his ambition was a book where ambition was irrelevant. He aimed to measure not accomplishment but contentment. It is the *nature* of the private life to seek pleasure. This is Sterne's point and the novel's. What ethical or passionate cathedrals the reader chooses to build on this rock are his own business. He can reproach with the Victorians, philosophize with the moderns, believe with the pious, laugh his own laughter.

The novel thus philosophizes the relation of humor to wit, and of both to satisfaction. It provides a pleasure equation of mutual tolerance for the private life. But it philosophizes little else. It does not tell us that, if we ponder role-playing long enough, we shall find a role that is really us. It does not find motive unfathomable. It supplies pleasure at the bottom and proves its valence. It does not tell us how to endure time and chance but how to play games with them, capitalize on them, make them our own. (pp. 161-67)

Richard A. Lanham, in his *"Tristram Shandy": The Games of Pleasure,* University of California Press, 1973, 174 p.

SOURCES FOR FURTHER STUDY

Cash, Arthur H. *Laurence Sterne: The Early & Middle Years.* London: Methuen and Co., 1975, 333 p.

Sterne's life from birth through the publication of the first two volumes of *Tristram Shandy.* This is the first of a multi-volume biography of Sterne, the second volume being *Laurence Sterne: The Later Years* (1986).

Conrad, Peter. *Shandyism: The Character of Romantic Irony.* New York: Harper & Row, Barnes & Noble, 1978, 190 p.

Relates *Tristram Shandy* to the artistic milieu of its period.

Fluchère, Henri. *Laurence Sterne: From Tristram to Yorick, an Interpretation of "Tristram Shandy".* London: Oxford University Press, 1965, 459 p.

Detailed study of the structure, themes, characters, and style of *Tristram Shandy.*

Hammond, Lansing Van der Heyden. *Laurence Sterne's "Sermons of Mr. Yorick."* New Haven: Yale University Press, 1948, 195 p.

Detailed study of *The Sermons of Mr. Yorick.*

Thomson, David. *Wild Excursions: The Life and Fiction of Laurence Sterne.* London: Weidenfeld & Nicolson, 1972, 325 p.

Biographical and critical study of Sterne.

Traugott, John, ed. *Laurence Sterne: A Collection of Critical Essays.* Englewood Cliffs, N.J.: Prentice-Hall, 1968, 183 p.

Includes studies by Benjamin Lehman, Alan Dugald McKillop, D. W. Jefferson, and W. B. C. Watkins.

Wallace Stevens

1879-1955

American poet, essayist, and dramatist.

INTRODUCTION

Stevens is one of the most important poets of the twentieth century. Integrating such European influences as Symbolism, Imagism, and Romanticism into his distinctly American idiom, he created a poetic language that has been praised for its originality, intricacy, and vibrancy. Throughout his works, Stevens sought to discover the interconnectedness of life and art and in such poems as "Sunday Morning," *Notes toward a Supreme Fiction* (1942), and "An Ordinary Evening in New Haven," he succeeded, seamlessly combining comic irony and epistemological skepticism with traditional forms and meters to reflect the complex concerns of modernity.

Stevens was born in Reading, Pennsylvania, to an upper-middle-class family of Dutch origin. His father, a prominent attorney, and his mother, a schoolteacher by training, encouraged their son's early interest in literature. As a student in the classical curriculum at Reading Boys High School, Stevens studied several languages and national literatures. In 1897 he enrolled as a special student at Harvard University, where he attended the lectures of the philosopher George Santayana and began writing lyric poetry in the style of the English Romantics. These early poems, which critics generally perceive as formally advanced and thematically derivative, were published in the *Harvard Advocate,* a student magazine that numbered Stevens as a staff member. In 1900 Stevens left Cambridge for New York City, where he pursued a career in journalism, eventually writing for the New York *Tribune.* The urging of his father persuaded Stevens to enroll at the New York Law School in 1901. He was admitted to the New York bar in 1904 and practiced law with several firms in New York City until 1908, when he accepted a position as an attorney with an insurance company. The following year Stevens married, wrote poetry and dramas when time permitted, and was in contact with the literary and artistic milieu of Greenwich Village. His New York poems were published in Harriet Monroe's *Poetry* magazine and in *Trend* in 1914. The next two years were a particularly fecund period of Stevens's poetic career; he published several poems in "little magazines," including "Sunday Morning," which appeared in *Poetry* in 1915.

Stevens moved to Hartford, Connecticut, in 1916, having accepted a position with the Hartford Accident and Indemnity Company. Although puzzling to some commentators, Stevens's career in business not only ensured him the comfortable life-style that he desired but, as he once stated, gave "a man character as a poet to have this daily contact with a job." Writing in the evenings, on weekends, and while traveling on business in Florida and throughout the southern United States, Stevens published his New York poems, along with several more recent endeavors, as *Harmonium* in 1923. The imagistic and sensuous descriptions, orientalism, and exotic language of the volume were perceived by most reviewers as the work of a literary hedonist who ignored the "wasteland crisis" of modern society. After the publication of *Harmonium* and the birth of his daughter Holly in 1924, Stevens ceased writing poetry for the next six years. His next book, *Ideas of Order* (1935), was not published until 1935 and was followed by *Owl's Clover,* which appeared in 1936. Stevens received some critical and popular recognition for the poems collected in *Ideas of Order* although he noted that *"Harmonium* was a better book than *Ideas of Order* notwithstanding the fact that *Ideas of Order* probably contains a small group of poems better than anything in *Harmonium."* *Owl's Clover* (1936) departed more radically from Stevens's earlier poetry and he called the unstructured and prosaic work a complete failure. In *The Man with the Blue Guitar, and Other Poems* (1937), Stevens reexamined his poetic style and returned to thematic and formal unity and a metered verse structure, traits that he had modified in *Owl's Clover.* In 1942 he published *Parts of a World* and what many consider his greatest poetic and theoretical statement, *Notes toward a Supreme Fiction.* The late 1940s and early 1950s brought further recognition of Stevens's poetic achievements and the continued success of his career in business. The recipient of many awards and honorary degrees, he delivered several lectures on poetic theory and aesthetics, which were collected in *The Necessary Angel: Essays on Reality and the Imagination* (1951). His *Collected Poems* were published in 1954 and he was offered the Charles Eliot Norton chair of poetry at Harvard University in 1955, which he refused, remaining with the Hartford Indemnity Company until his death that same year.

As a poet, Stevens sought to bridge the distance between consciousness and the physical world—that is, between imagination and reality—in order to regain a sense of human necessity in an apparently meaningless universe. Influenced by the secular humanism of Ralph Waldo Emerson and the aesthetic philosophy of Santayana, Stevens sought to counter the godlessness and skepticism of the modern age with a faith in art. In such early poems as "Sunday Morning," Stevens illustrated his proposition that "after one has abandoned a belief in god, poetry is that essence which takes its place as life's redemption." The stylized and evocative language of "Sunday Morning" describes the withering away of accepted religious rituals and icons—the Sabbath, the crown of thorns, the cross—and proposes new symbols and metaphors, which are now derived from secular artistic creations, as replacements for the old myths. Stevens further explores the role of art in the modern age in "Anecdote of the Jar in Tennessee," which Helen Vendler has deemed as important to the structuring of the American poetic imagination as John Keats's "Ode on a Grecian Urn" was to the English Romantic tradition. The speaker in "Anecdote of the Jar in Tennessee" discovers that order and meaning in nature must be derived from aesthetic form. Throughout Stevens's poetry his theoretical interests are balanced by a fascination with language. His interest in the sound, appearance, and etymologies of words is particularly evident in such poems as "The Comedian as the Letter C" and "Le Monocle de Mon Oncle."

Throughout the 1940s Stevens's theoretical and poetic investigations are centered on what he termed the "Supreme Fiction." Stevens introduced the phrase in his 1942 poem *Notes toward a Supreme Fiction.* That work comprises thirty short poems, a prologue, and coda, and is considered by many to encapsulate the traits of Stevens's strongest poetry: colorful concrete images, a range of poetic diction, thematic unity, and playful language. According to Stevens, the "Supreme Fiction" or "Grand Poem" is an ideal fusion of reality and the imagination. In *Notes toward a Supreme Fiction,* which was written during World War II, Stevens illustrates this fusion by conflating the terms of war and artistic creation: "Soldier, there is a war between the mind / And sky, between thought and day and night. It is / For that the poet is always in the sun, / Patches the moon together in his room / To his Virgilian cadences, up down, / Up down. It is a war that never ends." Stevens's mature works, such as *Esthétique du Mal* (1945) and *The Auroras of Autumn* (1950) reiterate and refine the aesthetic philosophies that he had evolved in his earlier works. In the mature poem "An Ordinary Evening in New Haven," Stevens outlines his understanding of the relationship between art, life, and language: "the theory / Of poetry is the theory of life, / As it is, in the intricate evasions of as, / In things seen and unseen, created from nothingness, / The heavens, the hells, the worlds, the longed-for lands."

Some critics have found Stevens's solution to twentieth-century metaphysical uncertainties to be rarefied and impersonal, frequently derogating his poetry for its abstraction and paucity of recognizably human characters and situations. However, Stevens insisted that his interest was not in individual personalities or social issues, but in humanism, art, and epistemology. Believing that his poetry addressed the general human condition by asking that "men turn to a fundamental glory of their own and from that create a style of bearing themselves in reality," Stevens never perceived his poetry as existing simply in the realm of aesthetics. His theoretical acumen and poetic skill have appealed to a wide range of critical schools. Harold Bloom has called Stevens the heir to the Romantic tradition in America, while poststructuralist and deconstructivist critics have praised Stevens's investigations of pure poetry and language. The diverse influences in Stevens's work are united by his unique style and his ambition to define the role of art in an age of anxiety and skepticism. The poetry that grew out of this quest represents one of the major accomplishments in modern literature.

(For further information about Stevens's life and works, see *Concise Dictionary of American Literary Biography, 1929-1941; Contemporary Authors*, Vols. 104, 124; *Dictionary of Literary Biography*, Vol. 54: *American Poets, 1880-1945*; and *Twentieth-Century Literary Criticism*, Vols. 5, 12.)

CRITICAL COMMENTARY

GORHAM B. MUNSON

(essay date 1928)

[In the following excerpt, Munson praises the "impeccable form" of the poetry in *Harmonium*.]

Until the advent of Wallace Stevens American literature had lacked the dandy. Of swaggering and nonchalant macaronis there had been a-plenty, but . . . these artists are not impeccable, and impeccability is the sine qua non of the true dandy.

The impeccability of the dandy, when reflected upon, resolves into two elements: correctness and elegance. (p. 78)

Certainly as a poetic craftsman, Wallace Stevens is eminently correct—notwithstanding the probable testimony of professorial versifiers to the contrary. For they confuse the pale correctness of the copyist who adds nothing, with the fresh correctness of the creating poet who extends the range of the existing poetic order or refines upon it. But Stevens' knowledge of verbal music is profound: he has presumably absorbed the teachings of the academy: at any rate he can trust himself to make departures and yet obey the underlying laws. (pp. 78-9)

Wallace Stevens takes all the musical risks of poetry (alliteration, free irregular rhyming, irregular stanzaic forms, and vers libre) and can be counted on to overcome them because for one thing he is so cognizant of dangers. Nor is his musical range limited. It touches at one extreme the light measures of **"The Apostrophe to Vincentine"** and at the other the deep organ-tones of **"To the One of Fictive Music"** with most of the intervening tonalities perfectly under control. (p. 80)

Wallace Stevens gains elegance in large measure by his fastidiously chosen vocabulary and by the surprising aplomb and blandness of his images. . . . The whole tendency of his vocabulary is, in fact, toward the lightness and coolness and transparency of French, into which tongue he sometimes glides with cultivated ease. As for his images, they are frequently surprising in themselves, yet they always produce the effect of naturalness by virtue of their consistency with the design and the flowing motion that Stevens imparts to them. (p. 81)

The safeguards that Stevens employs to keep "the torments of confusion" from rumpling his attitude are three: wit, speculation and reticence. . . . [By] wit and mockery one maintains one's perfect poise. (pp. 82-3)

[Stevens' discipline] is the discipline of the connoisseur of the senses and the emotions. His imagination comes to rest upon them, it is at their service, it veils them in splendor. It is clearly not in the service of the mind which is philosophical and constructed for the plumbing of life in the large, and consequently in the final analysis Wallace Stevens is a temperate romanticist. The integration he achieves is exclusively one of feeling.

But Stevens has a quality that is very rarely associated with romanticism, a quality that his illustrious predecessor, Baudelaire, lacked, . . . [for] tranquillity enfolds and inheres in all of Stevens' production. (p. 85)

Because of this tranquillity, this well-fed and

Principal Works

Harmonium (poetry) 1923

Ideas of Order (poetry) 1935

Owl's Clover (poetry) 1936

The Man with the Blue Guitar, and Other Poems (poetry) 1937

Notes toward a Supreme Fiction (poetry) 1942

Parts of a World (poetry) 1942

Esthétique du mal (poetry) 1945

Transport to Summer (poetry) 1947

The Auroras of Autumn (poetry) 1950

The Necessary Angel: Essays on Reality and the Imagination (essays) 1951

Collected Poems (poetry) 1954

Opus Posthumous (poetry, dramas, and essays) 1957

Letters (letters) 1966

The Palm at the End of the Mind (poetry and drama) 1971

---

is more skillful in arranging his music, his figures and his design. None else, monocled and gloved, can cut so faultless a figure standing in his box at the circus of life.

There are, as A. R. Orage once observed, masters of art and art-masters. The virtue of the former is wisdom, and the virtue of the latter is impeccable form. Nowhere has Wallace Stevens been more canny and more definite than in distinguishing between major and minor, than in observing to the letter the restrictions of the art-master. (pp. 88-9)

Gorham B. Munson, "The Dandyism of Wallace Stevens," in his *Destinations: A Canvass of American Literature Since 1900,* Sears, 1928, pp. 75-89.

---

well-booted dandyism of contentment, Stevens has been called Chinese. Undeniably, he has been influenced by Chinese verse as he has been by French verse, but one must not force the comparison too strongly. For Chinese poetry as a whole rests upon great humanistic and religious traditions: its quiet strength and peace are often simply by-products of a profound understanding, and its epicureanism is less of an end and more of a function in a wider pattern of living than Stevens expresses. To this critic, at least, Stevens' tranquillity is decidedly American. (pp. 86-7)

Growing more reckless, we might say that if Dr. Jung is correct in asserting that in American psychology there is a unique alliance of wildness and restraint, then Stevens would seem to have another general tie with his country. I do not discover in him the ferocity that some critics have remarked upon, but there is at least a flair for bright savagery, for "that tuft of jungle feathers, that animal eye, that savage fire": he has at least an appreciative eye for "raspberry tanagers in palms, high up in orange air." With some romanticists such symbols would betray insatiable longings, the desire for a nature that never existed. But in the case of Stevens they are purely spectacular. He has achieved the restraint of a spectator, but he prefers to view the wildness of the tropical. The Old World romantic, restless amid the stratifications of his culture, yearns for the untamed: the New World romantic, a participant in the unsettled, prefers to assume the easy posture of an audience. (pp. 87-8)

No American poet excels him in the sensory delights that a spick-and-span craft can stimulate: none

---

ELIZABETH JENNINGS
(essay date 1961)

[In the following excerpt, Jennings examines Stevens's treatment of poetry as serving a metaphysical function similar to that of religion.]

Wallace Stevens is a poet without faith in the religious sense, nor does he affirm in the familiar humanist sense. He would have agreed only with the second half of Keats' dictum about 'the holiness of the heart's affections and the truth of imagination.' But he pursued truth *through* imagination with as much rigour and passion as mystics seek God or philosophers seek meaning. Every poem he wrote is fundamentally about the same thing—the search for reality by means of imagination. His poetry enacts his philosophy; one cannot extract the thought, the content, the meaning, without emptying out, as it were, the whole poem. Yet there is nothing purely abstract in his work. Indeed, a superficial reading might persuade the reader that Stevens is a hedonist, a self-indulgent pleasure-seeker. His poems abound in scents, sounds and tangible objects. Often his images arise from paintings or *objets d'art.* Anything which appeals to the senses may, in fact, be the springboard to his inquiries. But these things are present for their significances not merely for their sensuousness. (p. 201)

In a poem called **"Of Modern Poetry"** [Stevens] speaks of 'the poem of the act of the mind'. This is metaphysics in the strictly philosophical sense, but with Stevens it is also something more. The poem which is 'the act of the mind' is created by the imagination working on the findings of the senses, and working on them not to elaborate them but to elucidate them. If Stevens's attitude is agnostic, if his answers are often negative, his poems are, nevertheless, a repudiation of chaos, a gesture against disorder. And where the mystics make contact with God through their wills and their intellects, Stevens makes contact with reality through his own poetic imagination. All poets do this, of course, but not all poets make this very search the prevailing subject-matter of their verse. In this sense, Stevens is a poet in the pure state, constantly reiterating and calling in question what most poets take for granted. And this search has its own torments since so much intrudes between the poet and his vision. (p. 202)

It would be easy, too easy, to lay great stress on Stevens's use . . . of religious or ritual terms such as 'sacrament'. In fact, he appropriates such terminology for purely secular and utilitarian purposes. His tone, his personal voice, is created by an extraordinarily rich vocabulary. He draws his language from art, philosophy, poetry, nature and many other things. But he impresses these words not so much with his own personality (he is, in most ways, a remarkably impersonal poet) as with the colour and light of his own vision of the world. The vision is, as it were, trapped in this highly idiosyncratic yet extremely decorous language.

"Sunday Morning" is a poem about a world without faith yet it is neither a negative poem nor a despairing one. As with his language, so with his imagery—Stevens draws upon every resource of language to express his ideas. In this poem he uses the articles of Christian faith (the doctrine of the Resurrection in particular) to lend colour to his verse, to intensify his vision. . . . (pp. 203-04)

Stevens's final rejection of God is a melancholy one and yet, because he must have order, he makes the measure of his verse impose order even upon what he feels is without design or meaning. . . . (p. 204)

Stevens's view of the universe is not entirely unlike Rilke's. Both poets seek for reality by means of the imagination but where Rilke, at the end of the *Duino Elegies,* is prepared to admit a transcendent vision, Stevens remains content simply with the relation between the mind and the objective world. He needs no mediator but his own imagination and this limitation perhaps accounts for the repetitiveness (even though it is an exquisite and compelling repetitiveness) of his poems. His mind never rests but must always be teasing at his one great theme. He knows nothing of 'negative capability' or serene receptiveness. In a sense, Stevens is to his poetry what the God he himself cannot believe in is to the world of the Christian visionary. Yet Stevens's vision is quite without pride or megalomania; he celebrates only what he can affirm. The tension in his verse, that tension which is the life of all important poetry, resides in the struggle for something which he feels his intellect cannot accept. So he transfers the idea of divinity to the realm of art. . . . (p. 205)

The poet, by means of his poetry, makes contact with reality and tries to maintain that contact. It is in this attempt at adherence, at unity, that Stevens's conception of the poet approximates to the Christian idea of the mystic. At the beginning of **"Notes toward a Supreme Fiction"**, he makes poetry the embodiment of reality, the apex of truth. It is a lofty vision and also a supreme act of faith by a man who in all other ways would have regarded himself as an agnostic. Indeed, it may very well be that there is something at the heart of poetry which forbids the total gesture of agnosticism. Simply to write is, after all, some kind of affirmation, but to lay upon poetry, as Stevens does, all those things which other men have assigned to religion and philosophy, is a kind of enthronement of credence itself. (p. 207)

Stevens's world is, on the whole, an impersonal world. The people in it tend to be merely figures in a landscape or images to which the poet can attach his own meanings. They are, in short, his raw material and no more and no less august or important than the *objets d'art* or natural phenomena which he also incorporates into his verse. It is the *being* of his men and women, their mere existence, that Stevens is concerned with, not their emotions or conflicts—still less, his own. Paradoxically, Stevens's fastidious care for particulars is, in fact, only an exquisite mask over a passion for generalities. His work is highly sophisticated, yes, but it lacks the supreme sophistication of the great humanist poets (Chaucer, Shakespeare, Yeats) who are concerned not so much with meaning as with feeling. If there is tragedy in Stevens's work it is a tragedy not of individual emotions and sufferings but of a vision of the world as a place which can only be illuminated by the fitful insights of the individual imagination. Thus a poem entitled **"God is Good. It is a Beautiful Night,"** turns out not to be the celebration of a moment of human awe and reverence, but simply one more examination of order. . . . (pp. 208-09)

[Stevens] is a poet of *being* yet his doctrine of existence is closer to Plato's timeless essences than to modern existentialism. His infinite caution in proposing absolutes sometimes conceals not only a concern for but also an unawakened belief in absolutes. In other words, his poems sometimes go further than his severe beliefs would lead us to expect. It may be indeed, as I have suggested already, that poetry is of its nature antagonistic to complete incredulity or negation; a 'willing suspension of disbelief ' is, perhaps, at the heart of poetry as well as at the heart of the perfect reading of poetry. Certainly, with Stevens, his poems appear sometimes to catch him off guard and amaze him with an affirmation. . . . For Stevens, the imaginative faculty is august and autonomous and also, as Coleridge has said, 'the living power and prime agent of all human perception'. The senses supply it with material from which it shapes images and then gropes towards order.

Crowded with *objets d'art,* fastidiously selective, uncompromisingly honest, quick to detect error— Stevens's art is all these things. On the surface it appears, in his own words, 'less and less human', but this is only because he takes things at their source; he is concerned with perception, feeling, desire in their pure state, before they have become involved in passion or personal conflict. Yet his verse takes its tension from a battle between disinterestedness and self-expression, since all poems are made with feelings as well as with thought. Stevens's passion is a controlled passion but it is a passion nonetheless. (pp. 211-12)

Elizabeth Jennings, "Vision without Belief: A Note on the Poetry of Wallace Stevens," in her *Every Changing Shape,* Andre Deutsch, 1961, pp. 201-12.

JOHN J. ENCK
(essay date 1964)

[In the following excerpt, Enck discusses the underlying philosophical system of Stevens's work.]

[Stevens's] fully evolved outlook does have a coherence. Its validity hardly matters outside his poetic universe; within it, it seems to have supplied him a system of faculties. He rarely indulges in the philosophic method: generalization, logic, fullness, and universality. Rather, he resembles the essayist who sketches his opinions graciously as personal preferences. This manner excuses him from rectifying inconsistencies, which worry him little, and tolerates manipulating subtlely his preferred, granted rather simple and old-fashioned, opposites from the anecdotes to the late poems. For him, then, man's non-physical faculties constitute one side and the physical world, including man's body, the other. Such a scheme does not terminate in a vicious dualism. One might arrange these two areas on a scale which implies degrees of evolution but not necessarily values. (The terms are not always Stevens'.)

[Logic]

Thinking	Order
Imaginative	Things
Practical	Quotidian
Subhuman	Rock

[Skeleton]

Communication between these areas varies, and sometimes, it seems, messages get through to the wrong level. Also, he arrived at such a division gradually; although the full diagram should apply to **"The Rock,"** only a segment describes *Harmonium.* Ideally, it works in the following way.

The column on the right causes slight difficulty. The rock consists of matter, nearly undifferentiated, intractable, almost unformed, a needed base, a blank substance which subsumes the rest. It may correspond with similar materials in the philosophies of Plato and Plotinum, although Stevens imposes no moral judgments upon it. The quotidian consists of items handled daily for commerce or secondary pleasures or just to keep one alive. It covers red cherry pie in a restaurant, birds and animals, an insurance policy, or an exploding bomb. The quotidian substances have no intrinsic value, although excessive prices may be put upon fashionable ones because they can symbolize nearly anything. In the social world they are prized for what they will accomplish, and this condition extends to people when treated as anything other than ends. Many of these very items can escape from use and exist by themselves or in a proper company of their species. They may then become things and exhibit truly poetic characteristics. Things range from a blackbird across (not up or down) to the fictive hero, from a dead soldier to an idea. Order belongs to the laws, not quite empirical, upon which the continuation of the rest depends: the construct behind the theory of the atom from Heraclitus to Hiroshima. None of this partakes of anything divine nor, particularly, human. The principle is not man's contrivance and exists independent of him, whether he has discovered it or not, whether he has employed it or not. Corruption of uses may disrupt any area, the quotidian being especially susceptible, but such violations cannot destroy any true essence. Stevens' consciousness of man's skill in perverting ends accounts for the dual aspect throughout all his values, particularly for the exalted ones, until he has worked out their full implications. Freedom from a dedicated belief means that nothing dare be taken on faith. "Truth"—whatever it is—belongs to no single category nor, it would seem, the sum total. These four areas impress themselves upon men differently, and here the trouble in most theory and all practice begins. The imperfect communication represents no original sin nor fall of man. The Garden of Eden, had there been any, would have had to endure the same kinds, if probably not degrees, of confusions which afflict the present.

One may as well start with the practical, to move to the column on the left. . . . Stevens holds nothing against it, really, as long as it keeps its place, not a very elevated but regrettably an important one. The practical handles the quotidian. It tends orchards, bakes, sells, and, with most people, eats red cherry pie. It cannot formulate very much and need not have gone beyond the eighth grade in school, although it may have persisted to an LL.B. or Ph.D., and that pomposity causes part of the trouble. It fails to recognize that things in themselves—properly *by* themselves—exist and that from them the imagination can contrive valid artifacts. Apparently every man should have all four faculties, although no one has them developed in the same proportions. From an exaggerated sense of its powers, the practical supplies public statues of generals, as well as most generals, to say nothing of advertising campaigns, amplified music, organized sports, and all charlatans. Although suffering from delusions of adequacy, it possesses a pride and thus probably scorns the rock or, perhaps, finds that, having no practical value, the rock lacks existence. The subhuman it dismisses as childish or uncivilized. Its attitude toward the imaginative and things ranges from ignorance to hate, and it mismanages order, which it can barely comprehend except when applied by science as inventions. The scorn for intellect, thinking, reflects its engrained prejudices. Most traits of personality, and the more prevalent emotions, arise from this area, and consequently, in Stevens' terms, poetry can do little with character and daily desires. Indeed, poetry makes little of practical manifestations except for satire. Otherwise, it simply recoils in disinterested boredom. However one judges Stevens' attitude toward the practical, it does not rest merely on fastidiousness but shows a genuine concern for the welfare of the imaginative.

The imaginative has so many guises that no one can exhaust them; all the poems themselves cannot do that. Apparently it alone encompasses by intuition the other three areas on the left as well as, of course, all those on the right. Often it appears that the subhuman, the practical, and thinking abandon their proper functions and charter a triumvirate to overthrow the imaginative, but they have no greater chance of prevailing than do Caliban, sailors, and noblemen against Prospero. From the imaginative come all the arts and, for this discussion, particularly, poetry. Basically poetry is the imaginative treating things, and Stevens' fondness for Imagism may derive from such an outlook. The imaginative sees and enhances things nearly in defiance of their quotidian aspects, and as a result Stevens' poetry borders on surrealism, a result comparable with Max Ernst's appropriating catalogues. Likewise, his poetry must prize words because principally through vocabulary can one separate things from their quotidian bondage. For such a reason, too, poetry is "abstract"; it treats not specific daily configurations but discrete entities freed of impure functions and adjuncts. It seeks to get at an essential nature devested of its stable garb and clothed in a new magnificence. The imaginative aspires to encompass order which always eludes it because no individual objects can survive there and because it offers static paradigms while poetry requires the constant change of interplay among things. (Music, it would seem, may almost annex order, and Stevens always stresses this component of verse.) As for the rock, it challenges the imaginative; neither one can wrest all advantages from the other and banish it. Poetry, and all the arts, do not directly communicate things (nor order, nor the quotidian, nor the rock) but attributes which reveal themselves in no other fashion: a poem, or a piece of music, has no single meaning. On the other hand, the imaginative must have things and order, at least, to work with, and if it seeks independence, if it makes its muse fictive music, it betrays itself by aspiring beyond its station. Stevens always insists that the imaginative depends upon reality and that it does reach limits. Finally, the imaginative may observe the interchange between thinking, the practical, and subhuman with the outside, although such a commerce, to him, lacks poetry and belongs, perhaps, to drama and novels.

Thinking, likewise, has limits; because it deals in conceptual matters, it can make little of the rock. Ideally it would arrange values for the quotidian, like a superior parent with a child. It reassures when it becomes scientific but may veer toward sentimentality when it promises goods beyond its powers. In treating things, thinking grows philosophic or theological. The damage it may do things, in light of the imaginative, arises from its addiction to first causes and a hankering for a neat teleology. In this drive it may impose a system where none exists for a violent order and prevent the imaginative from functioning freely. Between thinking and order there can be no direct communication. Could there be, man would walk in unbearable clarity; his habits grace, his gestures art, his sounds music, his deeds charity. Through logic thinking may attempt such a direct assault on order, but it must fail as a satanic enterprise. Thinking must approach order through the imaginative, and in this view Stevens can see logic as illogical, the longest way round as the shortest way home, disorder as order, and an evening's thought as a day of clear weather. If thinking and the imaginative ever could join forces, they might abridge logic, but, so far, they agree like Darby and Joan, at best. When it regards literature, thinking clumsily insists upon moral allegory. As with all the other instances of rivalry between faculties, which should bolster each other, Stevens accepts the condition and does not rail against it. Together they might compose that central diamond, but it cannot become a habitation. The imaginative, thus, cannot work miracles, cannot redeem the supposed evils contrived by other faculties, cannot practice metamorphosis, but it provides the sole refuge from many ills.

The subhuman comes and goes in these poems, and one can make only limited guesses about it. Its force would seem largely negative. Like thinking, it can never encompass order. Intimations about order lead to superstitions, to the worship of false deities: Ananke in Africa or the imago of modern Europe. It may preach an impossible order based on fundamentalist phantasies about an unknowable heaven or hell; it cannot understand the rock, either. Linked to the material world by a skeleton, it would deny any human life if joined with the bones. Because they help compose man, something human may cling to them, so far can the imaginative extend. When the subhuman observes the quotidian, it unleashes the vulgarities of primitive desire corrupted by industrialization, but its lack of restraints may have a pathos which the more genteel practical lacks. If it joins with the imaginative to grasp things, the results provide an antidote to prevailing complacency through valid poems, such as **"Domination of Black"** or **"Like Decorations in a Nigger Cemetery."** Such bizarre pieces may express an essential violence understandable in no other way. The subhuman does not match the Freudian concept of the Id, although they share some affinities, nor does it quite perpetuate Jung's postulate of a racial memory. It has little more than any other faculty to do with the emotions. For Stevens, emotions may reside anywhere as an accompaniment of communications between faculties, although pleasure, particularly, belongs to the noting of resemblances and from this pursuit composes poems. (pp. 235-40)

Far from being a withdrawn connoisseur, Stevens stands in his landscape through all weathers to record its constancy within changes. In this world the ordinary light and what it connects give his imagination all he needs except, of course, the necessary darkness. Ultimately he appears one of the least specialized and most consistent poets. The multiple pleasures which spring from these abstracted things and shifting resemblances order his whole poetic: native and cosmopolitan, vigorous and aloof, uncompromising and witty, primordial and elegant, idiomatic and stylized. (pp. 244-45)

John J. Enck, in his *Wallace Stevens: Images and Judgments,* Southern Illinois University Press, 1964, 258 p.

HELEN HENNESSY VENDLER
(essay date 1969)

[In the following excerpt, Vendler discusses Stevens's long poetry.]

Stevens, like Keats, believed in writing long poems, and defended the practice to Harriet Monroe in 1922: "The desire to write a long poem or two is not obsequiousness to the judgment of people. On the contrary, I find that prolonged attention to a single subject has the same result that prolonged attention to a senora has, according to the authorities. All manner of favors drop

from it. Only it requires a skill in the varying of the serenade that occasionally makes me feel like a Guatemalan when one particularly wants to feel like an Italian." . . . For the rest of Stevens' life, long poems alternated with short ones, and while it may be that Stevens will be forever anthologized as the poet of **"The Snow Man,"** his own sense of balance required verse on a large scale. (p. 1)

Though Stevens never wrote anything approaching the length of *The Faerie Queene* . . . , his own long poems can have the same naturalizing power, and in fact they do. We become most acclimated to Stevens in reading them, and they form the illumined large to which the lyrics, volume by volume, attach themselves. In each period of Stevens' life as a poet, they are characteristic, and to read them in sequence is one way, if not the only way, of tracing both his states of feeling and his enterprises and inventions. It is also true that his greatest poems, by almost any judgment, are the longer ones, whether one agrees with Yvor Winters' preference for **"Sunday Morning,"** Harold Bloom's for **"Notes toward a Supreme Fiction,"** Daniel Fuchs' for **"Esthetique du Mal,"** or yet choose, as I am sometimes inclined to do, **"The Auroras of Autumn."**

Through the long poems Stevens discovered his own strengths. It was, for instance, not until 1942, in *Notes* that he settled on his final metrical form. Even then, he deserted that form to write **"Esthetique du Mal"** in 1944, and returned to it only in 1948, with **"The Auroras of Autumn."** Those triads, as everyone has recognized, somehow organize his mind in its long stretches better than any other alternative, and yet to reach them he had to experiment with blank verse, couplets, ballads, terza rima, sonnetlike forms, and so on. This is the most obvious instance of Stevens' patient experimentation toward his own voice, but others come to light in reading the long poems. They are all directed toward a proper mode for his austere temperament, which is as different as can be from the temperament of Whitman or Wordsworth or Keats or Tennyson, those poets from whom he learned and to whom he is often compared. Neither is his sense of the world that of the French poets, however much he learned from them in his Harvard years. His manner was slow in evolving, and it evolved through his sense of himself and through a search for his own style. . . . (pp. 2-3)

Most criticism of Stevens has been concerned, understandably, with his "choice of subject"—variously defined. Some readers have seen his subject as an epistemological one, and have written about his views on the imagination and its uneasy rapport with reality. Others have seen his subject as a moral one, a justification of an aesthetic hedonism. Still others have seen his subject as a native humanist one, the quest of the American Adam for a Paradise in the wilderness. Stevens of course offers justification for all these views, and it is perhaps partial, in view of his many letters and essays on reality and the imagination, to prefer one of his more wayward statements, as usual objectively put, of what his own subject was, and how it developed through his life. Nevertheless, this brief summation seems closest in spirit to the Stevens one finds in the greatest poems: "One's cry of O Jerusalem becomes little by little a cry to something a little nearer and nearer until at last one cries out to a living name, a living place, a living thing, and in crying out confesses openly all the bitter secretions of experience." . . . This confession needs to be completed by the third stage of that repeated cry: after O Jerusalem, after the cry to something near, comes that final unseeking cry of the very late poems, notably **"The Course of a Particular."** A year or so earlier, Stevens had written that the poem was the "cry of its occasion, / Part of the res itself and not about it," but he could not rest in this partial identification of cry and creation. At last [in **"The Course of a Particular"**] the cry is entirely simple. . . . This is, of Stevens, "the text he should be born that he might write," to paraphrase his own line in **"Description without Place."** One can hardly doubt that the leaves, as well as being leaves, are Stevens too, and that he has gone beyond crying out to Jerusalem, beyond crying out even to a living name or place or thing, beyond all directed cries at all. Utterance is utterance, and the exertion to make it something more has disappeared. Stevens recapitulates in this poem all his previous efforts—his efforts to be part of the universe, his efforts to create divinities, heroes, and human beings, all his fantasia—and dismisses those attempts at self-transcendence in the presence of this pure sound. This is "the authentic and fluent speech" he told Harriet Monroe . . . he hoped eventually to perfect for himself, a syllable intoning "its single emptiness." . . . (pp. 3-5)

But before the authentic came many trials of the less and the more authentic, and before the fluent came episodes of the halting and the borrowed, times when Stevens wanted to feel like an Italian and felt instead like a Guatemalan, as he wryly said. All these "trials of device" are recorded in his major poems, and underneath them all is the fatal stratum he will at last discover in **"The Auroras of Autumn,"** that blank which Harold Bloom rightly traces back to Emerson's *Nature:* "The ruin or the blank that we see when we look at nature, is in our own eye." . . . If we find, in reading Stevens, that he tries and discards mode after mode, genre after genre, form after form, voice after voice, model after model, topic after topic, we also find a marvelous sureness mysteriously shaping his experiments. The story does not have an entirely happy ending: **"An Ordinary Evening in New Haven"** represents a decline from **"Notes toward a Supreme Fiction"** and **"The Auroras of Autumn,"** as even Stevens himself seems

to have recognized when he called it "this endlessly elaborating poem" and wished that it could have been written by "a more severe, more harassing master" who could propose "subtler, more urgent proof " than he could himself. . . . On the other hand, there are short pieces written in Stevens' last years which are the equal of anything he ever wrote, and, some would say, the best poems he ever wrote. Each poem is of course autonomous: "We never arrive intellectually," as Stevens said, "but emotionally we arrive constantly (as in poetry, happiness, high mountains, vistas)." . . . But each is also a stage in a sequence of development.

We keep, in reading Stevens, a double attitude, seeing the major poems both as things in themselves and as steps in a long progress toward his most complete incarnations of his sense of the world: "What is the poet's subject? It is his sense of the world. For him, it is inevitable and inexhaustible. If he departs from it he becomes artificial and laborious and while his artifice may be skillful and his labor perceptive no one knows better than he that what he is doing, under such circumstances, is not essential to him." . . . This is Stevens speaking, no doubt, of his own writing, and if we call him at times artificial and laborious we may be forgiven since he was there before us. There was no way for him to leap over those artifices; he had to go on by way of them: "The truth is that a man's sense of the world dictates his subjects to him and that this sense is derived from his personality, his temperament, over which he has little control and possibly none, except superficially. It is not a literary problem. It is the problem of his mind and nerves. These sayings are another form of the saying that poets are born not made." . . . The long poems give us very clearly Stevens' world, and naturalize us in it, so that we may be forgiven also if we say he invites this, he avoids that, he shrinks from this, he is shocked by this, he is indifferent to something else, he is consoled by these things. This is not censure, it is classification in the human world. (pp. 5-7)

After **"Notes toward a Supreme Fiction,"** Stevens discovers no new forms for long poems, and **"An Ordinary Evening in New Haven"** may seem only an extension implicit in the earlier poems, though with its episodic looseness, its lack of forward motion, and its ruminativeness, it enacts old age contemplating itself in sporadic proliferations, in "long and sluggish lines," as Stevens heavily described them. Sometimes this November voice in Stevens cannot even articulate itself into verse, and must content itself with those feelings, deep but inchoate, which the pine trees intimate in **"The Region November,"** or which the leaves express in **"The Course of a Particular."** As Stevens speaks in the voice of extreme old age, he and the interior paramour are finally stripped to the total lifelessness foretold by the total leaflessness. . . . This is a version, conceived in wretchedness, of the plain sense of things, "a theorem proposed" about life in this brutally geometric end of reductive memory. If Stevens had ended only with this naked style, we would see it as the fitting gasp of the final poverty, the victory of Madame La Fleurie.

But if, as Stevens said, a change of style is a change of subject, so perhaps a change of subject may be regarded as a change of style. Though there are no more "long" poems after **"An Ordinary Evening in New Haven,"** certain late poems, taken together, make up what we may call Stevens' poem of infancy, as his west touches his east. He had begun his poetic life as a "marvellous sophomore," already armored with well-traveled sophistication, knowing all the languages and poetries of the world. Now after his summer credences and his autumnal littering leaves, he has come to the "inhalations of original cold, and of original earliness" . . . which, though they lie in mid-winter, are yet intimations of the pristine. On the threshold of heaven, Stevens rediscovers earth, and writes a sublime poetry of inception.

The work which best shows the progress from the bitter geometry of age into an unbidden perception of the new is a poem which has gone, in the calendar of Stevens' year, beyond the deaths of October, November, December, and January, into the tenuous midwinter spring of February, with its hint of budding in magnolia and forsythia, its "wakefulness inside a sleep." Stevens begins in the toneless naked language of tedium. . . . Old age, seemingly prehistoric in its survival, is in fact inhabiting a pre-history, as the soul, not yet born, waits to be reincarnated. One morning in March it will wake to find not ideas about the thing, that intellectuality of old age, but the youthful thing itself. At that moment, in the first scrawny cry of the first returning bird, the poet's tentative infancy of perception will sense a signal of the approach of the colossal sun. Though this "bubbling before the sun" is as yet "too far / For daylight and too near for sleep," . . . Stevens is not daunted from imagining a possible for its possibleness, even in the leaden misery of winter.

In the great late poem **"A Discovery of Thought"** the perfect ideal is realized—the self is reincarnated as a child who, though newborn, remembers his previous existence and can speak his infant language, not in the rowdy summer syllables of ohoyo, but with "the true tone of the metal of winter in what it says." This extraordinary creature, Stevens' last mythical invention, is the child one becomes in second childhood, in that sickness where the eyes dim, where the body is a chill weight, and the old winning fairy tales of bearded deities become irrelevant. The wintry habitat of the man in second childhood is superbly real. . . . But in the midst of February's deathly wind and mist, there is a tinkling of hard ice and a trickling of melting ice which

co-exist, as a continual metamorphosis thwarts finality. . . . And though the scene is populated with "blue men that are lead within" holding leaden loaves in their hands, nevertheless "when the houses of New England catch the first sun" we think that "the sprawling of winter" (like the wilderness commanded by the jar) "might suddenly stand erect." . . . In the strict ending of the poem, which gathers itself together after the great freedom of the sprawling lines of description, Stevens defines in three ways, with verse of metaphysical density, that speech of the antipodal creature:

> The accent of deviation of the living thing
> That is its life preserved, the effort to be born
> Surviving being born, the event of life. . . .

The remembered continuity between past life and present life accounts for the deviation in the accent of this miraculous creature who remembers his previous incarnation; he remembers the trauma of being born and has no infantile amnesia; his life, like the life of the pines in **"An Ordinary Evening in New Haven,"** is "a coming on and a coming-forth," an event, and he does not forget its prehistoric origins. Knowing everything, this infant creature is everything, and he represents Stevens' final image of perfection, one step beyond the naked majesty of poverty in which he had left the old philosopher in Rome. If the high stoic elegies of Stevens' plain sense of things make a fitting close to his withering into the truth, these short late poems, equally truthful, are those liquid lingerings into which the angel of reality transforms, for a moment, the bleak continuo of life's tragic drone. (pp. 309-14)

Helen Hennessy Vendler, in her *On Extended Wings: Wallace Stevens' Longer Poems,* Cambridge Mass.: Harvard University Press, 1969, 334 p.

ALFRED CORN

(essay date 1982)

[In the following excerpt, Corn discusses Stevens's concept of a "Supreme Fiction" that would achieve a unity of imagination and reality.]

Wittgenstein enjoins us not to speak of those things that do not belong to discourse: "Whereof we cannot speak, we must remain silent." And yet wonderfully often speakers or writers manage to find ways of talking approximately or indirectly about experience that they actually hold to be outside or above the reach of words. Ways of overcoming the obstacles to speech vary; they are part of the set of stylistic and contextual qualities that confer identity and identifiability on a writer. Of course the unsayable or "ineffable" itself is not the same category for all potential speakers (few of whom, in any case, will be writers). In certain religious faiths, it is accounted a sin to make any mention of the name of God, or of the divine; thereof, the righteous will keep silent. In other instances, both religious and secular, verbal expression is not held to be sinful or contaminating but merely inadequate and paltry, compared to some areas of private experience. This group includes most of the writers thought of as being concerned with the ineffable. It includes, for example, the later Stevens; but the early Stevens is often best understood as belonging to yet another contingent. This third group includes the temperaments who find imaginative writing (in a nontrivial sense) impossible: because they see no transcendent sanctions that could be drawn on to form truthful statements in literature. For them, the universe is silent, and thus silence is truer than any utterance. To invent is to fabricate, to fabricate is base or invalid, and so there is truly nothing to write.

It is tempting to call this last obstacle to speech "negative ineffability"; and it is one that determines much of Stevens's early poetry. The negative mythological figure for the world of *Harmonium* is the Snow Man, who perceives "Nothing that is not there, and the nothing that is." If there had been no other figures in the pantheon Stevens invented for his poetry, he could not have written many more poems. But Stevens began to imagine other altars, engaging in an extended poetic pilgrimage and entertaining many ideas on the nature of truth, of the imagination, and the philosophical status of poetic utterance. Why Stevens didn't from the start understand poems as "fictions," and statements in them as hypothetical, has to do both with his own skeptic's temperament . . . and with modernist developments in American poetry during the first two decades of this century. . . . In any case, the notion that the poet "nothing affirmeth and therefore never lieth," clearly failed to satisfy Stevens: poems must be true, otherwise they are of no importance.

Poems must be true because, with the death of God, the arts must come to replace religion. In a letter to Barbara Church (which is dated August 12, 1947, but reflects beliefs he developed during his student days at Harvard fifty years earlier) Stevens said, "As scepticism becomes both complete and profound, we face either a true civilization or a blank; and literature ought to be one of the factors to determine the choice. Certainly, if civilization is to consist only of man himself, and it is, the arts must take the place of divinity, at least as a stage in whatever general principle or progress is involved." What did living in a universe empty of deity mean for Stevens? The blankness, cold, and misery mentioned in **"The Snow Man"** are metaphoric ways of conveying it, and a more succinct formulation is found in his *Adagia:* "Reality is a vacuum." Against human mortality, suffering, and meaninglessness, Ste-

vens proposes the imagination as a redemptive force, to push back (here he inverts the metaphor) against the "pressure of reality." The imagination is also the psychological faculty that allows poems to be written; indeed, the proportional equation "silence is to speech as death is to life" stands at the center of Stevens's poetic vocation. If one can write poems, one may find a sanction for human existence, and so may live.

Stevens's view of the "imagination as value," a conviction he repeats in many prose contexts and draws on as the emotional substance for so many poems, could be seen as absolute, no less comprehensive than a belief in the divine. Just as frequently, however, he expressed an opposing view: "The ultimate value is reality." When poetry fails to reflect reality, it presents merely a "dead romantic," a "falsification." Stevens is never clear and precise as to how the false imagination is to be distinguished from the true, the dead romanticism from the live; but, in general, he seems to look for a marriage, a mystic union between the imagination and reality, without explaining how wedlock is to be effected. (Readers will recall, in this connection, the fable of the "mystic marriage" between the captain and the maiden Bawda in **"Notes toward a Supreme Fiction."**)

It is apparent that, although Stevens was drawn to philosophical issues and discourse, he did not demand of himself the development of a system organized and expressed with philosophical rigor: "What you don't allow for," he said, "is the fact that one moves in many directions at once. No man of imagination is prim: the thing is a contradiction in terms." This is as much a program as a description: Stevens wishes to *postpone* the hasty formulation of a system, to forestall final conclusions. He wishes to rest neither in the imagination nor in reality because rest is undesirable; is hard to distinguish from philosophical or psychological stasis or perhaps paralysis; and life is supremely a question of movement and change. In a letter to Sister Bernetta Quinn (April 7, 1948) he says: "however, I don't want to turn to stone under your very eyes by saying 'This is the centre that I seek and this alone.' Your mind is too much like my own for it to seem to be an evasion on my part to say merely that I do seek a centre and expect to go on seeking it. I don't say that I do not expect to find it. It is the great necessity even without specific identification."

Even if philosophical or religious finality were attainable, Stevens recognizes that the "never-resting mind" would not accept any such finality: "Again, it would be the merest improvisation to say of any image of the world, even though it was an image with which a vast accumulation of imaginations had been content, that it was the chief image. The imagination itself would not remain content with it nor allow us to do so. It is the irrepressible revolutionist." The view of truth (and life) that emerges from these statements is one shared by many modern philosophers of mind: truth is not a set of propositions but is a psychological process. For Stevens, there is (and should be) a constant oscillation between the categories reason/fact and imagination/fable. A poetry or a life content with either of these opposing terms will not constitute fulfillment. Poets (considered exemplary for all of us) will always be seeking, voyaging, and questing, so long as they are alive.

This summary of philosophic and poetic ideas, though it is partial and perhaps supererogatory for the Stevens scholar, may retrace for nonspecialists the steps taken during Stevens's long career. In early Stevens, the ground is, generally, bare reality, the wintry landscape of nothingness seen by the Snow Man; the *figure* is the imagination that comes to free the mind from its subjection to reality. In the later Stevens it is more often the imagination that is the ground, all-pervasive and easily available. Reality then comes to seem the figure brought in as a contrast, a "refreshment," a cleansing away of the dull fictional film habitually covering our view of things. The emblematic figure typically summoned by Stevens in 1922 is the **"One of Fictive Music";** for the later Stevens, it is the **"Necessary Angel"** of reality. But, more and more often, Stevens begins to call for a fusion of reality and imagination into one entity, variously referred to as the Grand Poem, the Supreme Fiction, the Central Mind, or the Central Imagination. This hypothetical category comes to seem in some sense possible to Stevens, even though it always remains a projection. There is a constant future-tenseness to Stevens's visionary insight; he gives notes *toward* the Supreme Fiction, *prologues* "to what is possible." A title Stevens considered for his first book was *The Grand Poem: Preliminary Minutiae;* and the early Stevens could say, "The book of moonlight is not written yet nor half begun," and, "Music is not yet written but is to be."

The implication is that Stevens believes the great book can be written and that he will do it. By 1943 and the writing of **"Notes,"** it is apparent that the projective character of his vision has crystallized as doctrine. In an essay composed that same year he says, "The incredible is not a part of poetic truth. On the contrary, what concerns us in poetry, as in everything else, is the belief of credible people in credible things. It follows that poetic truth is the truth of credible things, not so much that it is actually so, as that it might be so." (pp. 225-29)

Although Stevens's *summum bonum* belongs to futurity, his adumbrations of it remind one of other poets' efforts to recount mystic experiences actually undergone, remembered wordlessly, and termed ineffable in the usual sense. Here it will be useful to consider some of Stevens's reflections on ultimate value, which, in this instance, he terms "nobility":

> I mean that nobility which is our spiritual height and depth; and while I know how difficult it is to express it, nevertheless I am bound to give a sense of it. Nothing could be more evasive and inaccessible. Nothing distorts itself and seeks disguise more quickly. There is a shame of disclosing it and in its definite presentations, a horror of it. But there it is. The fact that it is there is what makes it possible to invite to the reading and writing of poetry men of intelligence and desire for life. I am not thinking of the ethical or the sonorous or at all of the manner of it. The manner of it is, in fact, its difficulty, which each man must feel each day differently for himself. I am not thinking of the solemn, the portentous or demoded. On the other hand, I am evading a definition. If it is defined, it will be fixed and it must not be fixed. As in the case of an external thing, nobility resolves itself into an enormous number of vibrations, movements, changes. To fix it is to put an end to it. [**"The Noble Rider and the Sound of Words,"** in *The Necessary Angel*]

"Vibrations, movements, changes": much of Stevens's poetic style is covered by these terms, and they constitute part of the difficulty of his "manner." The whole passage, with its strenuous effort to get at the inexpressible, suggests that Stevens's first intuitions concerning the nature of a supreme and always future fiction may have come to him out of his struggle with style and expression itself. The title of the essay from which this passage is drawn refers not only to nobility, but also to "the sound of words." Consider then another passage from the same essay in *The Necessary Angel,* one where Stevens discusses our feeling for words themselves.

> The deepening need for words to express our thoughts and feelings which, we are sure, are all the truth that we shall ever experience, having no illusions, makes us listen to words when we hear them, loving them and feeling them, makes us search the sound of them, for a finality, a perfection, an unalterable vibration, which it is only within the power of the acutest poet to give them.

A paradox present in this apologia for words and their sounds, words at their most *physical,* in short, is that the principal result is immaterial and nonverbal. Stevens says as much in another essay (**"Effects of Analogy"**): "There is always an analogy between nature and the imagination, and possibly poetry is merely the strange rhetoric of that parallel: a rhetoric in which the feeling of one man is communicated to another in words of the exquisite appositeness that takes away all their verbality."

The inference, then, is that our surest clue, our only available insight, into the nature of the "central imagination" are words and their sound. Unlike most poets of mystic insight, Stevens does not deplore the inadequacies of his medium; he celebrates it and becomes its hierophant. Is it appropriate to call this a "verbal sublime"? There is at least one major precedent for it in literature—the poetry of Mallarmé. Other affinities between the two poets have been noted: the view of the poet as a sacramental figure; the recourse to music as the best analogy for poetry; and the belief (Mallarmé's belief) in a final Book that the world was meant to become, a Book not yet written. (This must be one of the sources of Stevens's Supreme Fiction.) In actual fact, the French poet Stevens most often mentions is not Mallarmé, but Paul Valéry, who, however, belongs to the same tradition. . . . This view of the sacramental role of the poet, whose poems may be considered incantations or prayers, is not foreign to Valéry's own poetics and fits well with something he once said about prayer and unknown tongues (his prototype, obviously, was Roman Catholic liturgical Latin): . . . "That is why one should pray only in unknown words. Return the enigma to the enigma, enigma for enigma. Lift up what is mystery in you to what is mystery in itself. There is in you something equal to what goes beyond you" ["Comme le temps est calme," translation mine]. . . . For his part, Stevens said (in the *Adagia*), "Poetry is a search for the inexplicable," and "It is necessary to propose an enigma to the mind." Although he did not write his poems in Latin, no small number of the incantations Stevens proposed to his mind (and ours) employ French words; and much of his vocabulary (in the poems) is composed of archaism, coinages, and sound-words either onomatopoetic in nature, or modeled on Elizabethan singing syllables ("hey-derry-derry-down," etc.), or similar to scat-singing in jazz ("shoo-shoo-shoo," and "ric-a-nic," for example). The point is, no doubt, to invent that "imagination's Latin" Stevens speaks of in **"Notes toward a Supreme Fiction."** It is in this sense, perhaps, that he wished to be understood when he said, "Personally, I like words to sound wrong." An overstatement; but it is certainly true that Stevens has one of the most noticeable styles in our poetry; and it could be said that he wrote an English that often sounds as if it were another language. How is the poet to overcome universal silence? One way is to make a joyful noise.

In view of his high claims for poetry, it appears that nothing can be more serious than poetic style. In his essay **"Two or Three Ideas,"** he proposes that, as poems and their style are one, so men and their style are one; the same may be said of "the gods." Then why not interchange *all* the terms? The style of men, and their poems, and their gods, are one; thus, style is an index of the divine. The task, as Stevens saw it, was to discover and compose a style that would serve as just such an index. Already noted is Stevens's reliance on

a special diction to give the effect of "otherness," of enigmatic mystery, an effect appropriate to a supreme, future fulfillment. Beyond that, the poet must include in his repertoire accents of grandeur and nobility. Stevens draws on several sources for these. Anyone who has heard him read, or has heard recordings of his reading, will have immediately noted the resemblance of his elocutionary style to that of the Protestant minister—the intonations of prayer, the accents of exhortation. By the same token, the language of Stevens's poems is often Christian in flavor: "Sister and mother, and diviner love. . . ." Stevens is like other Romantic poets in adapting Christian rhetoric to his purposes, and, of course, he borrows directly from Wordsworth, Shelley, Keats, and Whitman themselves. More surprising, however, is his enormous reliance on Shakespeare, and not merely for personae like Peter Quince and Marina. He tends to draw on Shakespeare's high rhetoric for certain moments of large, visionary utterance. When, in **"Final Soliloquy of the Interior Paramour,"** he writes, "We say God and the imagination are one . . . / How high that highest candle lights the dark," It is impossible not to think of Portia's lines in Act V of *The Merchant of Venice:* "How far that little candle throws his beams! / So shines a good deed in a naughty world." Stevens's recasting is no disgrace to its source; and part of the power of these lines lies in the connection the reader makes between the sense of Shakespeare's greatness and the philosophical amplitude of the issues being treated in this poem.

Stevens has come so far from "the nothing that is" as to speak of deity, God, with a capital letter. The gradual pilgrimage from Nothing to Something recapitulated in his career as a poet is a process enacted constantly (though on a much smaller scale) in his later poems. The typical embodiment of the change is metaphor, which he describes variously as "metamorphosis," "transformation," "transmutation," and even "apotheosis." Metaphor is the agency by which a real but empty thing is imaginatively transformed into something "unreal" and fulfilling. The poem as a whole is to be taken as an extended metaphor. (pp. 229-32)

The metaphor of the passage from winter to spring as representing the shift from one ontology to another is very frequent in Stevens, and, in fact, is the basis for . . . **"Not Ideas About the Thing, But the Thing Itself."** Recalling that "metaphor," by its etymology, can suggest the notion of "transport" (itself a term with several possible meanings), one is given a clue to part of the intention in a volume like *Transport to Summer* . . . , which may be understood as a book-length embodiment of the central doctrine of metaphysical transformation. The volume opens with a summer poem, **"God Is Good. It Is A Beautiful Summer Night"** (to be read, "God=Good=Summer"), but, not resting with that, goes on to include poems oscillating back and forth between summer and winter settings, and ends with **"Notes,"** which includes the same constant pendulum swing, beginning with autumn and ending with the "Fat girl, terrestrial, my summer, my night." If it is desirable to isolate a central controlling "structure" in the Stevensian imagination, no doubt it is the idea of metaphoric transformation that must be proposed. At the lower end of the scale, this provides the endless variety of tropes invented by Stevens in the poems; at the next level, it presents the poem under the aspect of transfiguration or apotheosis; and then, the *volume* of poems as a change from the wintry mind to the *summum bonum* of summer. It is fair to say, too, that Stevens's long poetic career moves generally from a predominantly "wintry" metaphysics to a more positive and reassurring stance. And, if seasonal change is the most frequent *temporal* metaphor for revelation in Stevens, the most frequent *spatial* one is **"Pilgrimage."** . . . (p. 233)

The metaphorical transformation of reality, then, was actually a kind of religious pilgrimage for Stevens. And its completion he viewed as an apotheosis, but one that must be undertaken again and again—it is never final. The exact nature of deity is not to be stated; Stevens is content with formulae such as the "central imagination" or the "central poem." The act of writing offers the only clue Stevens has to the nature of the divine, and the intuitions of poetry all have to do with a directional transformation, from thing to figure, from fact to fable. A poem such as **"A Primitive Like an Orb,"** which touches on all these ideas, can be read almost as a catechism for Stevens's beliefs about poetry and its relationship to the divine. (p. 234)

The universal vacancy so apparent to Stevens in the first phase of his career has come to be replaced by a sense and a rhetoric of fullness. A primary source of his conviction as to the certitude of that fullness is the feeling emanating from that very rhetoric, in poems lesser than the "essential poem." The obstacle to utterance is removed, for Stevens, by the transforming power and cosmic harmony manifest in *poesis* itself. (p. 235)

Alfred Corn, "Wallace Stevens: Pilgrim in Metaphor," in *The Yale Review,* Vol. 71, No. 2, Winter, 1982, pp. 225-35.

SOURCES FOR FURTHER STUDY

Bloom, Harold. *Wallace Stevens: The Poems of Our Climate.* Ithaca, N.Y.: Cornell University Press, 1976, 413 p.
> Thorough study of Stevens's work.

Burney, William. *Wallace Stevens.* New York: Twayne Publishers, 1968, 190 p.
> In-depth study that examines Stevens's poetry, prose, and drama.

Buttel, Robert. *Wallace Stevens: The Making of "Harmonium."* Princeton: Princeton University Press, 1967, 169 p.
> Examination of Stevens's writings through the publication of *Harmonium.*

Litz, A. Walton. *Introspective Voyager: The Poetic Development of Wallace Stevens.* New York: Oxford University Press, 1972, 326 p.
> Study of Stevens's work through 1937.

Morris, Adalaide Kirby. *Wallace Stevens: Imagination and Faith.* Princeton: Princeton University Press, 1974, 205 p.
> Contends that Stevens sought to invest art with many of the attributes of religion.

Morse, Samuel French. *Wallace Stevens: Poetry as Life.* New York: Pegeasus, 1970, 232 p.
> Critical biography.

Robert Louis Stevenson

1850-1894

(Full name Robert Louis Balfour Stevenson) Scottish novelist, short story writer, poet, essayist, and dramatist.

INTRODUCTION

An inventive prose stylist, Stevenson has been a favorite of both children and adults from his lifetime through the present for his colorful tales of adventure. Just as his famous stories of piracy and horror have placed him at the forefront of writers of romances, his unusual life and personality have made him one of literature's most intriguing individuals, to the extent that his biography has often overshadowed his literary reputation, even among scholars. Critics credit the appeal of his romances, including *Treasure Island* (1883), *Kidnapped: Being Memoirs of the Adventures of David Balfour in the Year 1751* (1886), and *Strange Case of Dr. Jekyll and Mr. Hyde* (1886), to their fast-paced action, intricate plots, and well-drawn characters. Stevenson is also esteemed for his fecund imagination and affinity for the psychology of children, as displayed most notably in his early "boys' novels" and his poetry collection *A Child's Garden of Verses* (1885). Although his present critical standing does not equal that accorded him by his contemporaries, his mass popularity continues, and his novels and stories are still considered seminal in the development of adventure and romance literature.

Stevenson was a sickly, fragile child and suffered from severe respiratory ailments that frequently interrupted his schooling. His relations with his parents became increasingly difficult as he reached adolescence. His father, a civil engineer, expected him to train for the family profession of lighthouse-building. Stevenson refused, and though he agreed to study law, he rarely attended classes and never practiced the profession, preferring the study of literature instead. He decided to teach himself to write by "playing the sedulous ape to Hazlitt, to Lamb, to Wordsworth, to Sir Thomas Browne, to Defoe, to Hawthorne, to Montaigne, to Baudelaire, and to Obermann." Indeed, critics of Stevenson's work often note the influence of these authors, particularly Defoe and Montaigne, as well as George Meredith.

Motivated by his love for adventure and his need for a climate congenial to his health, Stevenson traveled extensively throughout his life. His journeys to France in the 1870s provided much of the material for his early travel books, *An Inland Voyage* (1878) and *Travels with a Donkey in the Cévennes* (1879). In 1876, while in France, Stevenson met Mrs. Fanny Osbourne, an American woman eleven years his senior. When Osbourne returned to California two years later to arrange a divorce, Stevenson followed. The newly married couple stayed in America for almost a year and then returned to Europe with Lloyd Osbourne, Fanny's son.

In the 1880s, despite his continuing poor health, Stevenson wrote many of his best-known works, including *Treasure Island.* Originally begun as a game for his stepson, the novel was published serially in a children's magazine under the title "The Sea-Cook" and became Stevenson's first popular and critical success. The works that followed, including *A Child's Garden of Verses, Dr. Jekyll and Mr. Hyde,* and *Kidnapped,* strengthened his growing reputation. In 1887, the Stevensons returned to America. From California, they sailed to Samoa, where they settled, Stevenson finding the climate congenial to his respiratory condition. His life on the island consisted of dabbling in local politics, managing his plantation, and writing several works, including collaborations with Lloyd Osbourne. He died unexpectedly at forty-four from a cerebral hemorrhage.

Critics frequently praise Stevenson for what Margaret Oliphant called "that fine, transparent, marvellously lucid style," though some claim that Stevenson substituted style for ideas. Most commentators agree that, in their emphasis on exciting plots, rather than analysis or character, Stevenson's fictional works are derived from the tradition of prose romance. His works in genres other than the novel have received mixed reactions. His dramas, written in collaboration with William Ernest Henley, are considered unsuccessful, a judgment attributed to Stevenson's ignorance of dramatic technique and over-reliance on dialogue. His essays and travel sketches have been praised for their humor, perception, grace, and charm. Response to his poetry for adults, in contrast, has been almost uniformly negative. Edmund Gosse criticized the subjectivity of the collection *Underwoods,* noting that Stevenson "enters with great minuteness, and in a very confidential manner, into the theories and moods of the writer himself."

A Child's Garden of Verses has enjoyed a far more favorable reception. Although written for children, these poems appeal to adults through their simplicity, tenderness, and ability to entice the reader into the child's world. *Treasure Island* and *Kidnapped* also reflect his sympathy for and understanding of youth. Both rely heavily on plot to sustain interest, and both contain Stevenson's first credible characters. Yet critics appreciate these books for varying reasons. *Treasure Island* is considered a brilliantly constructed adventure story, while critics praise *Kidnapped* for its authenticity, which strengthens its appeal for adults. Stevenson himself wrote that, in his fiction, he sought to fulfill the desire, ingrained in humanity from childhood, to see one's surroundings transcend mundanity; the romance writer's role, as he saw it, is to will the world into the sphere of the fantastic.

Stevenson's short stories and novels for adults include the works most often cited by modern critics as his best: *The Merry Men and Other Tales and Fables* (1887), *Island Nights' Entertainments* (1893), *Dr. Jekyll and Mr. Hyde, The Master of Ballantrae: A Winter's Tale* (1889), and *Weir of Hermiston: An Unfinished Romance* (1896). Unlike his earlier works, these novels and stories examine moral dilemmas presented in an atmosphere imbued with mystery and horror. Modern commentators note certain recurring themes, such as those of the divided self and the nature of evil. His longer narratives are often criticized for their faulty and abrupt endings. *Weir of Hermiston,* the novel that Stevenson was at work upon when he died, is considered by many his best work for its forceful style and for its psychologically and morally complex characters. Although critics question whether he would have been able to sustain the novel's dramatic interest, *Weir of Hermiston* has fueled conjecture about how Stevenson might have developed artistically had he lived longer.

Explanations vary for the critical fascination with Stevenson's personality rather than his work. His stoic optimism in the face of serious illness, his move to the South Seas, and the personal nature of many of his essays and poems have been much discussed. This fascination resulted in essays, many of them by friends and family, that are now considered eulogistic rather than critical. Although several critics, notably Arthur Symons, have warned readers against this approach, the content of Stevenson criticism did not change until 1914, when Frank Swinnerton published his *R. L. Stevenson: A Critical Study.* Considered by modern critics the most important challenger to the Stevenson myth, Swinnerton rejected the uncritical adoration of early readers and inspired a change in the critical approach to Stevenson, which had previously focused on personal rather than literary aspects. Many commentators underrated Stevenson by assuming that a children's writer has nothing to say to adults. Although critics are still fascinated by his life and reputation, they now respond to his work more often with serious analysis and acclaim. Opinion is still divided over the value of his oeuvre, yet his children's poetry, adventure stories, and adult romances continue to attract readers who appreciate fine writing and exciting adventure.

(For further information about Stevenson's life and works, see *Children's Literature Review*, Vols. 10, 11; *Dictionary of Literary Biography*, Vols. 18, 57; *Nineteenth-Century Literature Criticism*, Vols. 5, 14; and *Yesterday's Authors of Books for Children;* Vol. 2.)

CRITICAL COMMENTARY

ROBERT LOUIS STEVENSON
(essay date 1882)

[In the following excerpt from an essay that first appeared in *Longman's Magazine* in 1882, Stevenson expounds his theory of romantic literature: that such fiction fulfills a deep-seated desire for excitement prompted by the places and objects of the real world.]

In anything fit to be called by the name of reading, the process itself should be absorbing and voluptuous; we should gloat over a book, be rapt clean out of ourselves; and rise from the perusal, our mind filled with the busiest, kaleidoscopic dance of images, incapable of sleep or of continuous thought. The words, if the book be eloquent, should run thenceforward in our ears like the noise of breakers, and the story, if it be a story, repeat itself in a thousand coloured pictures to the eye. It was for this last pleasure that we read so closely, and loved our books so dearly, in the bright, troubled period of boyhood. Eloquence and thought, character and conversation, were but obstacles to brush aside as we dug blithely after a certain sort of incident, like a pig for truffles. For my part, I liked a story to begin with an old wayside inn where, "towards the close of the year 17—," several gentlemen in three-cocked hats were playing bowls. . . . Give me a highwayman and I was full to the brim; a Jacobite would do, but the highwayman was my favourite dish. I can still hear that merry clatter of the hoofs along the moonlit lane. . . . [We] read storybooks in childhood, not for eloquence or character or thought, but for some quality of the brute incident. That quality was not mere bloodshed or wonder. Although each of these was welcome in its place, the charm for the sake of which we read depended on something different from either. . . . [All my] early favourites have a common note—they have all a touch of the romantic.

Drama is the poetry of conduct, romance the poetry of circumstance. The pleasure that we take in life is of two sorts—the active and the passive. Now we are conscious of a great command over our destiny; anon we are lifted up by circumstance, as by a breaking wave, and dashed we know not how into the future. Now we are pleased by our conduct, anon merely pleased by our surroundings. It would be hard to say which of these modes of satisfaction is the more effective, but the latter is surely the more constant. Conduct is three parts of life, they say; but I think they put it high. There is a vast deal in life and letters both which is not immoral, but simply a-moral; which either does not regard the human will at all, or deals with it in obvious and healthy relations; where the interest turns, not upon what a man shall choose to do, but on how he manages to do it; not on the passionate slips and hesitations of the conscience, but on the problems of the body and of the practical intelligence, in clean, open-air adventure, the shock of arms or the diplomacy of life. With such material as this it is impossible to build a play, for the serious theatre exists solely on moral grounds, and is a standing proof of the dissemination of the human conscience. But it is possible to build, upon this ground, the most joyous of verses, and the most lively, beautiful, and buoyant tales.

One thing in life calls for another; there is a fitness in events and places. The sight of a pleasant arbour puts it in our mind to sit there. One place suggests work, another idleness, a third early rising and long rambles in the dew. . . . Some places speak distinctly. Certain dank gardens cry aloud for a murder; certain old houses demand to be haunted; certain coasts are set apart for shipwreck. Other spots again seem to abide their destiny, suggestive and impenetrable. . . . The inn at Burford Bridge, with its arbours and green garden and silent, eddying river—though it is known already as the place where Keats wrote some of his *Endymion* and Nelson parted from his Emma—still seems to wait the coming of the appropriate legend. Within these ivied walls, behind these old green shutters, some further business smoulders, waiting for its hour. The old Hawes Inn at the Queen's Ferry makes a similar call upon my fancy. There it stands, apart from the town,

Principal Works

The Pentland Rising: A Page of History, 1666 (essay) 1866

An Inland Voyage (travel sketches) 1878

Travels with a Donkey in the Cévennes (travel sketches) 1879

Virginibus Puerisque and Other Papers (essays) 1881

Deacon Brodie; or, The Double Life: A Melodrama Founded on Facts [with William Ernest Henley] (drama) 1882

Familiar Studies of Men and Books (essays) 1882

New Arabian Nights (short stories) 1882

Treasure Island (novel) 1883

A Child's Garden of Verses (poetry) 1885

Kidnapped: Being Memoirs of the Adventures of David Balfour in the Year 1751 (novel) 1886

Strange Case of Dr. Jekyll and Mr. Hyde (novel) 1886

Memories and Portraits (essays) 1887

The Merry Men and Other Tales and Fables (short stories) 1887

Underwoods (poetry) 1887

The Black Arrow: A Tale of the Two Roses (novel) 1888

The Master of Ballantrae: A Winter's Tale (novel) 1889

Catriona, a Sequel to "Kidnapped": Being Memoirs of the Further Adventures of David Balfour at Home and Abroad (novel) 1893; also published as David Balfour: Being Memoirs of His Adventures at Home and Abroad, 1893

Island Nights' Entertainments (short stories) 1893

The Ebb-Tide: A Trio and Quartette [with Lloyd Osbourne] (novel) 1894

The Works of R. L. Stevenson. 28 vols. (novels, unfinished novels, short stories, travel sketches, poetry, essays, drama, letters, and prayers) 1894-98

Weir of Hermiston (unfinished novel) 1896

---

beside the pier, in a climate of its own, half inland, half marine—in front, the ferry bubbling with the tide and the guardship swinging to her anchor; behind, the old garden with the trees. Americans seek it already for the sake of Lovel and Oldbuck, who dined there at the beginning of the *Antiquary*. But you need not tell me—that is not all; there is some story, unrecorded or not yet complete, which must express the meaning of that inn more fully. So it is with names and faces; so it is with incidents that are idle and inconclusive in themselves, and yet seem like the beginning of some quaint romance, which the all-careless author leaves untold. . . . I have lived both at the Hawes and Burford in a perpetual flutter, on the heels, as it seemed, of some adventure that should justify the place; but though the feeling had me to bed at night and called me again at morning in one unbroken round of pleasure and suspense, nothing befell me in either worth remark. The man or the hour had not yet come; but some day, I think, a boat shall put off from the Queen's Ferry, fraught with a dear cargo, and some frosty night a horseman, on a tragic errand, rattle with his whip upon the green shutters of the inn at Burford.

Now, this is one of the natural appetites with which any lively literature has to count. The desire for knowledge, I had almost added the desire for meat, is not more deeply seated than this demand for fit and striking incident. . . . The right kind of thing should fall out in the right kind of place; the right kind of thing should follow; and not only the characters talk aptly and think naturally, but all the circumstances in a tale

answer one to another like notes in music. The threads of a story come from time to time together and make a picture in the web; the characters fall from time to time into some attitude to each other or to nature, which stamps the story home like an illustration. Crusoe recoiling from the footprint, Achilles shouting over against the Trojans, Ulysses bending the great bow, Christian running with his fingers in his ears, these are each culminating moments in the legend, and each has been printed on the mind's eye for ever. Other things we may forget; we may forget the words, although they are beautiful; we may forget the author's comment, although perhaps it was ingenious and true; but these epoch-making scenes, which put the last mark of truth upon a story and fill up, at one blow, our capacity for sympathetic pleasure, we so adopt into the very bosom of our mind that neither time nor tide can efface or weaken the impression. This, then, is the plastic part of literature: to embody character, thought, or emotion in some act or attitude that shall be remarkably striking to the mind's eye. . . . Compared with this, all other purposes in literature, except the purely lyrical or the purely philosophic, are bastard in nature, facile of execution, and feeble in result. It is one thing to write about the inn at Burford, or to describe scenery with the word-painters; it is quite another to seize on the heart of the suggestion and make a country famous with a legend. It is one thing to remark and to dissect, with the most cutting logic, the complications of life, and of the human spirit; it is quite another to give them body and blood in the story of Ajax or of Hamlet. The first is literature, but the second is something besides, for it is likewise art. (pp. 229-38)

[Nothing] can more strongly illustrate the necessity for marking incident than to compare the living fame of [Defoe's] *Robinson Crusoe* with the discredit of [Richardson's] *Clarissa Harlowe. Clarissa* is a book of a far more startling import, worked out, on a great canvas, with inimitable courage and unflagging art. It contains wit, character, passion, plot, conversations full of spirit and insight, [and] letters sparkling with unstrained humanity. . . . And yet a little story of a shipwrecked sailor, with not a tenth part of the style nor a thousandth part of the wisdom, exploring none of the arcana of humanity and deprived of the perennial interest of love, goes on from edition to edition, ever young, while *Clarissa* lies upon the shelves unread. . . . *Clarissa* has every quality that can be shown in prose, one alone excepted—pictorial or picture-making romance. While *Robinson* depends, for the most part and with the overwhelming majority of its readers, on the charm of circumstance.

In the highest achievements of the art of words, the dramatic and the pictorial, the moral and romantic interest, rise and fall together by a common and organic law. Situation is animated with passion, passion clothed upon with situation. Neither exists for itself, but each inheres indissolubly with the other. This is high art; and not only the highest art possible in words, but the highest art of all, since it combines the greatest mass and diversity of the elements of truth and pleasure. Such are epics, and the few prose tales that have the epic weight. But as from a school of works, aping the creative, incident and romance are ruthlessly discarded, so may character and drama be omitted or subordinated to romance. (pp. 240-42)

True romantic art . . . makes a romance of all things. It reaches into the highest abstraction of the ideal; it does not refuse the most pedestrian realism. *Robinson Crusoe* is as realistic as it is romantic: both qualities are pushed to an extreme, and neither suffers. Nor does romance depend upon the material importance of the incidents. To deal with strong and deadly elements, banditti, pirates, war and murder, is to conjure with great names, and, in the event of failure, to double the disgrace. (pp. 244-45)

[In romance, something] happens as we desire to have it happen to ourselves; some situation, that we have long dallied with in fancy, is realised in the story with enticing and appropriate details. Then we forget the characters; then we push the hero aside; then we plunge into the tale in our own person and bathe in fresh experience; and then, and then only, do we say we have been reading a romance. It is not only pleasurable things that we imagine in our day-dreams; there are lights in which we are willing to contemplate even the idea of our own death; ways in which it seems as

if it would amuse us to be cheated, wounded, or calumniated. It is thus possible to construct a story, even of tragic import, in which every incident, detail, and trick of circumstance shall be welcome to the reader's thoughts. Fiction is to the grown man what play is to the child; it is there that he changes the atmosphere and tenor of his life; and when the game so chimes with his fancy that he can join in it with all his heart, when it pleases him with every turn, when he loves to recall it and dwells upon its recollection with entire delight, fiction is called romance. (p. 248)

Robert Louis Stevenson, "A Gossip on Romance," in his *Memories and Portraits,* Charles Scribner's Sons, 1910, pp. 229-53.

HENRY JAMES
(essay date 1888)

[One of the most important novelists and critics of his day, James has been lauded for his contributions to psychological realism and for exposing minutiae of thought and character through a subtle, mannered prose style. He was a close friend of Stevenson and a critic and admirer of his work. In the following excerpt, he surveys most of Stevenson's major fiction, extolling his evocation of excitement and sense of childlike wonderment.]

There are writers who present themselves before the critic with just the amount of drapery that is necessary for decency; but Mr. Stevenson is not one of these—he makes his appearance in an amplitude of costume. His costume is part of [his] character . . . , it never occurs to us to ask how he would look without it. Before all things he is a writer with a style—a model with a complexity of curious and picturesque garments. It is by the cut and the colour of this rich and becoming frippery—I use the term endearingly, as a painter might—that he arrests the eye and solicits the brush.

That is, frankly, half the charm he has for us, that he wears a dress and wears it with courage, with a certain cock of the hat and tinkle of the supererogatory sword; or in other words that he is curious of expression and regards the literary form not simply as a code of signals, but as the key-board of a piano, and as so much plastic material. He has that voice deplored, if we mistake not, by Mr. Herbert Spencer, a manner—a manner for manner's sake it may sometimes doubtless be said. He is as different as possible from the sort of writer who regards words as numbers and a page as the mere addition of them; much more, to carry out our image, the dictionary stands for him as a wardrobe, and a proposition as a button for his coat. Mr. William Archer, in an article so gracefully and ingeniously turned that the writer may almost be accused of imitating even while he deprecates speaks of him as a votary of "lightness of touch," at any cost, and remarks that "he is not only philosophically content but deliberately resolved, that his readers shall look first to his manner, and only in the second place to his matter." I shall not attempt to gainsay this; I cite it rather, for the present because it carries out our own sense. Mr. Stevenson delights in a style, and his own has nothing accidental or diffident; it is eminently conscious of its responsibilities, and meets them with a kind of gallantry—as if language were a pretty woman, and a person who proposes to handle it had of necessity to be something of a Don Juan. This bravery of gesture is a noticeable part of his nature, and it is rather odd that at the same time a striking feature of that nature should be an absence of care for things feminine. His books are for the most part books without women, and it is not women who fall most in love with them. But Mr. Stevenson does not need, as we may say, a petticoat to inflame him: a happy collocation of words will serve the purpose, or a singular image, or the bright eye of a passing conceit, and he will carry off a pretty paradox without so much as a scuffle. The tone of letters is in him. . . . (pp. 139-41)

[It is] because he has no speciality that Mr. Stevenson is an individual, and because his curiosity is the only receipt by which he produces. Each of his books is an independent effort—a window opened to a different view. *Doctor Jekyll and Mr. Hyde* is as dissimilar as possible from *Treasure Island; Virginibus Puerisque* has nothing in common with *The New Arabian Nights,* and I should never have supposed *A Child's Garden of Verses* to be from the hand of the author of *Prince Otto.*

Though Mr. Stevenson cares greatly for his phrase, as every writer should who respects himself and his art, it takes no very attentive reading of his volumes to show that it is not what he cares for most, and that he regards an expressive style only, after all, as a means. It seems to me the fault of Mr. Archer's interesting paper, that it suggests too much that the author of these volumes considers the art of expression as an end—an ingenious game of words. He finds that Mr. Stevenson is not serious, that he neglects a whole side of life, that he has no perception, and no consciousness, of suffering, that he speaks as a happy but heartless pagan, living only in his senses (which the critic admits to be exquisitely fine), and that in a world full of heaviness he is not sufficiently aware of the philosophic limitations of mere technical skill. . . . He is not the first reader, and he will not be the last, who shall have been irritated by Mr. Stevenson's jauntiness. That jauntiness is an essential part of his genius; but to my sense it ceases to be irritating—it indeed becomes positively touching and constitutes an appeal to sympathy and even to tenderness—when once one has perceived what lies beneath the dancing-tune to which he mostly moves. Much as he cares for his phrase, he cares more for life, and for a certain transcendently lovable part of it. He feels, as it seems to us, and that is not given to every one. This constitutes a philosophy which Mr. Archer fails to read between his lines—the respectable, desirable moral which many a reader doubtless finds that he neglects to point. He does not feel everything equally, by any manner of means, but his feelings are always his reasons. He regards them, whatever they may be, as sufficiently honourable, does not disguise them in other names or colours, and looks at whatever he meets in the brilliant candle-light that they shed. (pp. 142-44)

The part of life which he cares for most is youth, and the direct expression of the love of youth is the beginning and the end of his message. his appreciation of this delightful period amounts to a passion, and a passion, in the age in which we live, strikes us on the whole as a sufficient philosophy. . . . Mingled with this almost equal love of a literary surface, it represents a real originality. This combination is the keynote of Mr. Stevenson's faculty and the explanation of his perversities. The feeling of one's teens, and even of an earlier period (for the delights of crawling, and almost of the rattle, are embodied in *A Child's Garden of Verses*), and the feeling for happy turns—these, in the last analysis (and his sense of a happy turn is of the subtlest), are the corresponding halves of his character. . . .

What makes him so [rare] is the singular maturity of the expression that he has given to young sentiments: he judges them, measures them, sees them from the outside, as well as entertains them. He describes credulity with all the resources of experience, and represents a crude stage with infinite ripeness. In a word, he is an artist accomplished even to sophistication, whose constant theme is the unsophisticated. Sometimes, as in *Kidnapped,* the art is so ripe that it lifts even the subject into the general air: the execution is so serious that the idea (the idea of a boy's romantic adventures), becomes a matter of universal relations. What he prizes most in the boy's ideal is the imaginative side of it, the capacity for successful make-believe. The general freshness in which this is a part of the gloss seems to him the divinest thing in life; considerably more divine, for instance, than the passion usually regarded as the supremely tender one. The idea of making believe appeals to him much more than the idea of making love. That delightful little book of rhymes, the *Child's Garden,* commemorates from beginning to end the picturing, personifying, dramatising faculty of infancy—the view of life from the level of the nursery-fender. The volume is a wonder for the extraordinary vividness with which it reproduces early impressions:

a child might have written it if a child could see child-hood from the outside, for it would seem that only a child is really near enough to the nursery floor. . . . [He] doesn't speak as a parent, or an uncle, or an educator—he speaks as a contemporary absorbed in his own game. That game is almost always a vision of dangers and triumphs, and if emotion, with him, infallibly resolves itself into memory, so memory is an evocation of throbs and thrills and suspense. He has given to the world the romance of boyhood, as others have produced that of the peerage and the police and the medical profession.

This amounts to saying that what he is most curious of in life is heroism—personal gallantry, if need be with a manner, or a banner, though he is also abundantly capable of enjoying it when it is artless. . . . The love of brave words as well as brave deeds . . . is simply Mr. Stevenson's essential love of style. . . . Alan Breck, in *Kidnapped,* is a wonderful picture of the union of courage and swagger; the little Jacobite adventurer, a figure worthy of Scott at his best, and representing the highest point that Mr. Stevenson's talent has reached, shows us that a marked taste for tawdry finery—tarnished and tattered, some of it indeed, by ticklish occasions—is quite compatible with a perfectly high mettle. Alan Breck is at bottom a study of the love of glory, carried out with extreme psychological truth. . . . Mr. Stevenson's kindness for adventurers extends even to the humblest of all, the mountebank and the strolling player, or even the pedlar whom he declares that in his foreign travels he is habitually taken for. . . . The hungry conjurer, the gymnast whose *maillot* is loose, have something of the glamour of the hero, inasmuch as they too pay with their person. "To be even one of the outskirters of art leaves a fine stamp on a man's countenance. . . . That is the kind of thing that reconciles me to life: a ragged, tippling, incompetent old rogue, with the manners of a gentleman and the vanity of an artist, to keep up his self-respect!" What reconciles Mr. Stevenson to life is the idea that in the first place it offers the widest field that we know of for odd doings, and that in the second these odd doings are the best of pegs to hang a sketch in three lines or a paradox in three pages.

As it is not odd, but extremely usual, to marry, he deprecates that course in *Virginibus Puerisque,* the collection of short essays which is most a record of his opinions—that is, largely, of his likes and dislikes. It all comes back to his sympathy with the juvenile and that feeling about life which leads him to regard women as so many superfluous girls in a boy's game. They are almost wholly absent from his pages (the main exception is *Prince Otto,* though there is a Clara apiece in *The Rajah's Diamond* and *The Pavilion on the Links*), for they don't like ships and pistols and fights, they encumber the decks and require separate apartments, and,

almost worst of all, have not the highest literary standard. Why should a person marry when he might be swinging a cutlass or looking for a buried treasure? Why should he waste at the nuptial altar precious hours in which he might be polishing periods?

(pp. 144-49)

• • • • •

[The] colour of Scotland has entered into [Stevenson] altogether, and though, oddly enough, he has written but little about his native country, his happiest work shows, I think, that she has the best of his ability, the best of his ambition. *Kidnapped* (whose inadequate title I may deplore in passing) breathes in every line the feeling of moor and loch, and is the finest of his longer stories, and *Thrawn Janet,* a masterpiece in thirteen pages (lately republished in the volume of *The Merry Men*), is, among the shorter, the strongest in execution. . . . If it be a good fortune for a genius to have had such a country as Scotland for its primary stuff, this is doubly the case when there has been a certain process of detachment, of extreme secularisation. Mr. Stevenson has been emancipated: he is, as we may say, a Scotchman of the world. (pp. 154-55)

The novelist who leaves the extraordinary out of his account is liable to awkward confrontations, as we are compelled to reflect in this age of newspapers and of universal publicity. . . . Mr. Stevenson leaves so wide a margin for the wonderful—it impinges with easy assurance upon the text—that he escapes the danger of being brought up by cases he has not allowed for. When he allows for Mr. Hyde he allows for everything, and one feels moreover that even if he did not wave so gallantly the flag of the imaginative and contend that the improbable is what has most character, he would still insist that we ought to make believe. He would say we ought to make believe that the extraordinary is the best part of life even if it were not, and to do so because the finest feelings—suspense, daring, decision, passion, curiosity, gallantry, eloquence, friendship—are involved in it, and it is of infinite importance that the tradition of these precious things should not perish. He would prefer, in a word, any day in the week, Alexandre Dumas to Honoré de Balzac, and it is indeed my impression that he prefers the author of *The Three Musketeers* to any novelist except Mr. George Meredith. . . . He makes us say, Let the tradition live, by all means, since it was delightful; but at the same time he is the cause of our perceiving afresh that a tradition is kept alive only by something being added to it. In this particular case—in *Doctor Jekyll* and *Kidnapped*—Mr. Stevenson has added psychology.

The New Arabian Nights offer us, as the title indicates, the wonderful in the frankest, most delectable form. Partly extravagant and partly very specious, they are the result of a very happy idea, that of placing a series of adventures which are pure adventures in the setting of contemporary English life, and relating them in the placidly ingenuous tone of Scheherezade. This device is carried to perfection in *The Dynamiter,* where the manner takes on more of a kind of high-flown serenity in proportion as the incidents are more "steep." In this line *The Suicide Club* is Mr. Stevenson's greatest success. . . . [Mr. Stevenson's most brilliant stroke] is the opening episode of *Treasure Island,* the arrival of the brown old seaman with the sabre-cut at the "Admiral Benbow," and the advent, not long after, of the blind sailor, with a green shade over his eyes, who comes tapping down the road, in quest of him, with his stick. *Treasure Island* is a "boy's book" in the sense that it embodies a boy's vision of the extraordinary, but it is unique in this, and calculated to fascinate the weary mind of experience, that what we see in it is not only the ideal fable but, as part and parcel of that, as it were, the young reader himself and his state of mind: we seem to read it over his shoulder, with an arm around his neck. It is all as perfect as a well-played boy's game, and nothing can exceed the spirit and skill, the humour and the open-air feeling with which the thing is kept at the palpitating pitch. It is not only a record of queer chances, but a study of young feelings: there is a moral side in it, and the figures are not puppets with vague faces. If Jim Hawkins illustrates successful daring, he does so with a delightful rosy good-boyishness and a conscious, modest liability to error. His luck is tremendous, but it does not make him proud, and his manner is refreshingly provincial and human. So is that, even more, of the admirable John Silver, one of the most picturesque and indeed in every way most genially presented villains in the whole literature of romance. He has a singularly distinct and expressive countenance, which of course turns out to be a grimacing mask. Never was a mask more knowingly, vividly painted. *Treasure Island* will surely become—it must already have become and will remain—in its way a classic: thanks to this indescribable mixture of the prodigious and the human, of surprising coincidences and familiar feelings. The language in which Mr. Stevenson has chosen to tell his story is an admirable vehicle for these feelings: with its humorous braveries and quaintnesses, its echoes of old ballads and yarns, it touches all kinds of sympathetic chords.

Is *Doctor Jekyll and Mr. Hyde* a work of high philosophic intention, or simply the most ingenious and irresponsible of fictions? It has the stamp of a really imaginative production, that we may take it in different ways; but I suppose it would generally be called the most serious of the author's tales. It deals with the relation of the baser parts of man to his nobler, of the capacity for evil that exists in the most generous natures; and it expresses these things in a fable which is a wonderfully happy invention. The subject is endlessly interesting, and rich in all sorts of provocation, and Mr.

Stevenson is to be congratulated on having touched the core of it. I may do him injustice, but it is, however, here, not the profundity of the idea which strikes me so much as the art of the presentation—the extremely successful form. There is a genuine feeling for the perpetual moral question, a fresh sense of the difficulty of being good and the brutishness of being bad; but what there is above all is a singular ability in holding the interest. I confess that that, to my sense, is the most edifying thing in the short, rapid, concentrated story, which is really a masterpiece of concision. There is something almost impertinent in the way, as I have noticed, in which Mr. Stevenson achieves his best effects without the aid of the ladies, and *Doctor Jekyll* is a capital example of his heartless independence. . . . The gruesome tone of the tale is, no doubt, deepened by their absence: it is like the late afternoon light of a foggy winter Sunday, when even inanimate objects have a kind of wicked look. (pp. 165-70)

I have left Mr. Stevenson's best book to the last. . . . [There] are parts of [*Kidnapped*] so fine as to suggest that the author's talent has taken a fresh start, various as have been the impulses in which it had already indulged, and serious the hindrances among which it is condemned to exert itself. There would have been a kind of perverse humility in his keeping up the fiction that a production so literary as *Kidnapped* is addressed to immature minds, and, though it was originally given to the world, I believe, in a "boy's paper," the story embraces every occasion that it meets to satisfy the higher criticism. . . . [The] history stops without ending, as it were; but I think I may add that this accident speaks for itself. Mr. Stevenson has often to lay down his pen for reasons that have nothing to do with the failure of inspiration, and the last page of David Balfour's adventures is an honourable plea for indulgence. The remaining five-sixths of the book deserve to stand by *Henry Esmond* as a fictive autobiography in archaic form. The author's sense of the English idiom of the last century, and still more of the Scotch, has enabled him to give a gallant companion to Thackeray's *tour de force.* The life, the humour, the colour of the central portions of *Kidnapped* have a singular pictorial virtue: these passages read like a series of inspired footnotes on some historic page. . . . There could be no better instance of the author's talent for seeing the familiar in the heroic, and reducing the extravagant to plausible detail, than the description of Alan Breck's defence in the cabin of the ship and the really magnificent chapters of "The Flight in the Heather." Mr. Stevenson has in a high degree (and doubtless for good reasons of his own) what may be called the imagination of physical states, and this has enabled him to arrive at a wonderfully exact translation of the miseries of his panting Lowland hero, dragged for days and nights over hill and dale, through bog and thicket, without meat or drink or rest, at the tail of an Homeric High-lander. The great superiority of the book resides to my mind, however, in the fact that it puts two characters on their feet with admirable rectitude. I have paid my tribute to Alan Breck, and I can only repeat that he is a masterpiece. It is interesting to observe that though the man is extravagant, the author's touch exaggerates nothing: it is throughout of the most truthful, genial, ironical kind; full of penetration, but with none of the grossness of moralising satire. The figure is a genuine study, and nothing can be more charming than the way Mr. Stevenson both sees through it and admires it. Shall I say that he sees through David Balfour? This would be perhaps to underestimate the density of that medium. Beautiful, at any rate, is the expression which this unfortunate though circumspect youth gives to those qualities which combine to excite our respect and our objurgation in the Scottish character. Such a scene as the episode of the quarrel of the two men on the mountainside is a real stroke of genius, and has the very logic and rhythm of life: a quarrel which we feel to be inevitable, though it is about nothing, or almost nothing, and which springs from exasperated nerves and the simple shock of temperaments. The author's vision of it has a profundity which goes deeper, I think, than *Doctor Jekyll.* I know of few better examples of the way genius has ever a surprise in its pocket—keeps an ace, as it were, up its sleeve. And in this case it endears itself to us by making us reflect that such a passage as the one I speak of is in fact a signal proof of what the novel can do at its best, and what nothing else can do so well. In the presence of this sort of success we perceive its immense value. It is capable of a rare transparency—it can illustrate human affairs in cases so delicate and complicated that any other vehicle would be clumsy. To those who love the art that Mr. Stevenson practises he will appear, in pointing this incidental moral, not only to have won a particular triumph, but to have given a delightful pledge. (pp. 171-74)

Henry James, "Robert Louis Stevenson," in his *Partial Portraits,* Macmillan and Co., 1888, pp. 137-74.

VLADIMIR NABOKOV

(lecture date 1941-59)

[A Russian-born American novelist and critic, Nabokov is widely held to be one of the twentieth century's premier writers. In the following excerpt from a series of lectures delivered between 1941 and 1959, he examines the character of the protagonist Dr. Jekyll.]

Dr. Jekyll and Mr. Hyde was written in bed, at Bourne-mouth on the English Channel, in 1885 in between hemorrhages from the lungs. It was published in January 1886. Dr. Jekyll is a fat, benevolent physician, not without human frailties, who at times by means of a potion projects himself into, or concentrates or precipitates, an evil person of brutal and animal nature taking the name of Hyde, in which character he leads a patchy criminal life of sorts. For a time he is able to revert to his Jekyll personality—there is a down-to-Hyde drug and a back-to-Jekyll drug—but gradually his better nature weakens and finally the back-to-Jekyll potion fails, and he poisons himself when on the verge of exposure. This is the bald plot of the story.

First of all, if you have the Pocket Books edition I have, you will veil the monstrous, abominable, atrocious, criminal, foul, vile, youth-depraving jacket—or better say straitjacket. You will ignore the fact that ham actors under the direction of pork packers have acted in a parody of the book, which parody was then photographed on a film and showed in places called theatres; it seems to me that to call a movie house a theatre is the same as to call an undertaker a mortician.

And now comes my main injunction. Please completely forget, disremember, obliterate, unlearn, consign to oblivion any notion you may have had that *Jekyll and Hyde* is some kind of a mystery story, a detective story, or movie. It is of course quite true that Stevenson's short novel, written in 1885, is one of the ancestors of the modern mystery story. But today's mystery story is the very negation of style, being, at the best, conventional literature. Frankly, I am not one of those college professors who coyly boasts of enjoying detective stories—they are too badly written for my taste and bore me to death. Whereas Stevenson's story is—God bless his pure soul—lame as a detective story. Neither is it a parable nor an allegory, for it would be tasteless as either. It has, however, its own special enchantment if we regard it as a phenomenon of style. It is not only a good "bogey story," as Stevenson exclaimed when awakening from a dream in which he had visualized it much in the same way I suppose as magic cerebration had granted Coleridge the vision of the most famous of unfinished poems. It is also, and more importantly, "a fable that lies nearer to poetry than to ordinary prose fiction" [according to Stephen Gwynn] and therefore belongs to the same order of art as, for instance, *Madame Bovary* or *Dead Souls.*

There is a delightful winey taste about this book; in fact, a good deal of old mellow wine is drunk in the story: one recalls the wine that Utterson so comfortably sips. This sparkling and comforting draft is very different from the icy pangs caused by the chameleon liquor, the magic reagent that Jekyll brews in his dusty laboratory. Everything is very appetizingly put. Gabriel John Utterson of Gaunt Street mouths his words most roundly; there is an appetizing tang about the chill morning in London, and there is even a certain richness of tone in the description of the horrible sensations Jekyll undergoes during his *hydizations.* Stevenson had to rely on style very much in order to perform the trick, in order to master the two main difficultues confronting him: (1) to make the magic potion a plausible drug based on a chemist's ingredients and (2) to make Jekyll's evil side before and after the hydization a believable evil. (pp. 179-80)

The names Jekyll and Hyde are of Scandinavian origin, and I suspect that Stevenson chose them from the same page of an old book on surnames where I looked them up myself. Hyde comes from the Anglo-Saxon *hyd,* which is the Danish *hide,* "a haven." And Jekyll comes from the Danish name *Jökulle,* which means "an icicle." Not knowing these simple derivations one would be apt to find all kinds of symbolic meanings, especially in Hyde, the most obvious being that Hyde is a kind of hiding place for Dr. Jekyll, in whom the jocular doctor and the killer are combined.

Three important points are completely obliterated by the popular notions about this seldom read book:

1. Is Jekyll good? No, he is a composite being, a mixture of good and bad, a preparation consisting of a ninety-nine percent solution of Jekyllite and one percent of Hyde (or *hydatid* from the Greek "water" which in zoology is a tiny pouch within the body of man and other animals, a pouch containing a limpid fluid with larval tapeworms in it—a delightful arrangement, for the little tapeworms at least. Thus in a sense, Mr. Hyde is Dr. Jekyll's parasite—but I must warn that Stevenson knew nothing of this when he chose the name.) Jekyll's morals are poor from the Victorian point of view. He is a hypocritical creature carefully concealing his little sins. He is vindictive, never forgiving Dr. Lanyon with whom he disagrees in scientific matters. He is foolhardy. Hyde is mingled with him, within him. In this mixture of good and bad in Dr. Jekyll, the bad can be separated as Hyde, who is a precipitate of pure evil, a precipitation in the chemical sense since something of the composite Jekyll remains behind to wonder in horror at Hyde while Hyde is in action.

2. Jekyll is not really transformed into Hyde but projects a concentrate of pure evil that becomes Hyde, who is smaller than Jekyll, a big man, to indicate the larger amount of good that Jekyll possesses.

3. There are really three personalities—Jekyll, Hyde, and a third, the Jekyll residue when Hyde takes over. (pp. 182-83)

Stevenson has set himself a difficult artistic problem, and we wonder very much if he is strong enough to solve it. Let us break it up into the following points:

1. In order to make the fantasy plausible he wishes to have it pass through the minds of matter-of-fact persons, Utterson and Enfield, who even for all their commonplace logic must be affected by something bizarre and nightmarish in Hyde.

2. These two stolid souls must convey to the reader something of the horror of Hyde, but at the same time they, being neither artists nor scientists, unlike Dr. Lanyon, cannot be allowed by the author to notice details.

3. Now if Stevenson makes Enfield and Utterson too commonplace and too plain, they will not be able to express even the vague discomfort Hyde causes them. On the other hand, the reader is curious not only about their reactions but he wishes also to see Hyde's face for himself.

4. But the author himself does not see Hyde's face clearly enough, and could only have it described by Enfield or Utterson in some oblique, imaginative, suggestive way, which, however, would not be a likely manner of expression on the part of these stolid souls.

I suggest that given the situation and the characters, the only way to solve the problem is to have the aspect of Hyde cause in Enfield and Utterson not only a shudder of repulsion but also something else. I suggest that the shock of Hyde's presence brings out the hidden artist in Enfield and the hidden artist in Utterson. Otherwise the bright perceptions that illumine Enfield's story of his journey through the lighted, empty streets before he witnessed Mr. Hyde's assault on the child, and the colorful imaginings of Utterson's dreams after he has heard the story can only be explained by the abrupt intrusion of the author with his own set of artistic values and his own diction and intonation. A curious problem indeed.

There is a further problem. Stevenson gives us the specific, lifelike description of events by humdrum London gentlemen, but contrasting with this are the unspecified, vague, but ominous allusions to pleasures and dreadful vices somewhere behind the scenes. On the one side there is "reality"; on the other, "a nightmare world." If the author really means there to be a sharp contrast between the two, then the story could strike us as a little disappointing. If we are really being told "never mind what the evil was—just believe it was something very bad," then we might feel ourselves cheated and bullied. We could feel cheated by vagueness in the most interesting part of the story just because its setting is so matter of fact and realistic. The question that must be asked of the work is whether Utterson and the fog and the cabs and the pale butler are more "real" than the weird experiments and unmentionable adventures of Jekyll and Hyde. (pp. 192-93)

Vladimir Nabokov, "Robert Louis Stevenson: 'The Strange Case of Dr. Jekyll and Mr. Hyde,'" in his *Lectures on Literature,* edited by Fredson Bowers, Harcourt Brace Jovanovich, 1980, pp. 179-204.

V. S. PRITCHETT

(essay date 1946)

[A prolific British author, Pritchett is admired as a master of the short story form and as a particularly lucid and engaging literary critic. In the following excerpt, he examines the development of themes in Stevenson's fiction, culminating in the unfinished novel *Weir of Hermiston*.]

To the hardworking British reader of the late 19th century, bent on his practical purposes, Stevenson proposed an opposite ideal. He spoke of the rewards of idleness and art, of the Bohemian and vagrant life which has freed itself of middle-class convention and has replaced this by the sensible notion of doing as one pleases. Or rather of doing what one pleases with an air. The attack upon the standards of the commercial middle class had proceeded since the early years of middle-class power after the French Revolution. . . . Stevenson brought his own moral, practical, genteel and very Scottish contribution to this general movement. He was not prepared in fact to say with Rabelais, "Do what you will." He was not prepared to preach the unthinking sensuality of Burns, the vagrant brotherhood of Whitman or the hard-living, passionate, criminal and medieval vagrancy of Villon. The dualism and caution of his Calvinist heritage soon extinguished the impulse of real rebellion in Stevenson. What he did propose was the safe, respectable and harmless indulgence of having the Bohemian air, if not the Bohemian heart. He proposed a form of personal dandyism which would relieve the drabness of commercial life. He established an egoism, a declaration of personal independence from established religions, creeds and codes which unconsciously reflected the self-regarding, not to say swashbuckling, philosophy of economic life. He proposed to dress up. (pp. vii-viii)

[In Stevenson, preacher] and actor change clothes. By temperament he has the virtues and defects of youth. He is a writer of brilliant beginnings. He catches the sensation of being athletically alive, which is especially the gift of youth. In *Treasure Island* and in *Kidnapped* this sense of physical action is wonderful and youth's dominant preoccupation with its own fear and courage plays naturally upon it. The timidity, the pride, the caution, the heady excitement of youth, its day dreams and admirations, are wonderfully rendered by Stevenson in these two books. They have been dismissed as boys' books; but *Kidnapped* is far more than a boys' book. It is about the hunter and the hunted in man, and it is criss-crossed by the comedy of youthful

vanity. When we complain of Stevenson's mannerisms and of his artificiality, we ought to distinguish between the purely mannered, and that ingrained love of the devious and elaborate which comes naturally from the rich and compressed scruples of the Scottish character and from the tribal ironies of Scottish religious history. The Scottish character in all its tribal varieties is an onion with many skins; it is given to strife, to infinitely drawn-out arguments; it cultivates evasion; it jumps from the wanton to the secretive. A consuming conceit is relieved by a fantastic and racy vanity. The vanity of Alan Breck and the conceit of David Balfour in *Kidnapped* issue from the deeper places of Scottish character; and so does the acuteness with which they see through each other. But the story of their relationship contains a universal statement about the loyalties and uncertainties of youth.

In *Kidnapped* we see Stevenson writing within his range. He knows youth. He knows fear. He knows courage. And, to clinch his judgment, he writes of the Scottish scene. It can be said without any doubt at all that Stevenson is at his best only when he sticks to the scene he knew from his childhood. *The Master of Ballantrae* is a second argument for this view and once more Stevenson is writing out of his very bones. This book has been criticised for two undoubtedly serious defects. The woman in the story is a complete failure. The story turns on her behaviour and, because she is wooden, it never turns, but simply lengthens. The second criticism seems far less serious now than it did to the critics who looked for an exciting last act to the dramatic story. The Master wilts at the end. But neither of these criticisms affects the fine indigenous quality of the story which is well-rooted in a peculiar and important layer of the Scottish mind—I mean the Calvinist conscience and in that part of it that plays with the conception of pure evil. . . . Can we imagine a character formed by the doctrine of Predestination, that is to say, a man absolutely evil and certainly damned? This theme of the damned soul is one to which Stevenson often returns. The Master is precisely such a character. His graceful and inexhaustively wicked figure breaks through the mannered cloak and dagger convention in which the story is written. He is an evil spirit but not a romantic one. One feels he is some animal atom of elemental energy. There is nothing more frightening than his courage, frightening because it is not selfless courage; but courage with a brain to restrain it at the last minute but one. He is a master mind driving others to the wicked or fatal act. He is thinking of the last trick, not the last stand; and when he dies, Stevenson thinks of a brilliant twist of fate for him. He dies not because of his defiance, but because of a miscalculation.

This story contains a theme recurrent in Stevenson's work. It appears in *Jekyll and Hyde,* in an earlier story called *Markheim* on a similar theme; in a story called *Olalla* [in *The Merry Men and Other Tales and Fables*]; I am not referring to the theme of pure evil or the division of good and evil in a single nature; but to a more personal theme that lies inside it. Stevenson was intensely preoccupied with cruelty and especially with the relation of torturer and tortured. He was a puritan who saw his problems in black and white. He saw the fulfilled man oppressing the frustrated, the graceful man oppressing the graceless, the man of wilful energy punishing the stoic. We can imagine that as an invalid Stevenson was far more preoccupied with the unheroic, the degrading and injurious power of pain than he usually cared to admit among the brave gestures of his essays. . . . And so in *The Master of Ballantrae* we see in the portrait of the Master's unjustly treated brother, an unsparing condemnation of the weak. Too much injustice, too much suffering, too much submission to a bad fate and of what cannot be cured poisons his character. Robbed, he becomes a miser, betrayed in his love, he eats his heart out until he has no heart, outraged he is enslaved by the desire for revenge. It is one of the masterly psychological perceptions of this story that the persecuted character is enfeebled when he acts against his own nature and puts his vengeance into action. Our sympathies change. We begin to admire the devil of the story. To the end he is in full possession of his diabolical faculties and refreshingly free from Calvinist introspection.

Stevenson presented this tale of persecution and disloyalty with the spaciousness and ingenuity of the great and measured storyteller. The scenes are precise. The incident of the duel by candlelight and the removal of the body by smugglers, has vivid physical life. The choice of detail is in our highest dramatic tradition. Long after putting the book down we see Alison's hand fly open when by accident she touches the blood on the sword. We still see that scene in the American wilderness when the Master, failing to trick the men hired to murder him, turns over on his side by the camp fire. They can stab him now his back is turned, but neither fear nor recklessness has made him turn. He turns with the hopelessness that the intellectual man feels when he finds that he has got to start his brain working it all out again with painful cunning once more. Stevenson was a subtle and mature psychologist in these narrow dramas of calculation and conscience. The dreams of the Master's brother are what the modern psychoanalyst would predict. Stevenson's intuitions in the province of illness and self-inflicted pain are never off the mark. (pp. viii-xi)

Weir of Hermiston has all the air of being the complete, the unanswerably great Scottish novel. Could Stevenson have sustained the quality of those sixty thousand words? With him, the brilliant beginner, the question must always be doubtful; but in *Weir* he at last wrote a book in which he throws off the coat

of a youthfulness grown threadbare and merely professional and enters upon maturity. One thing we notice at once. His marriage has at last taught Stevenson one thing: it has taught him to draw a woman. The character of the younger Kirstie in *Weir of Hermiston* suggests that Stevenson's instinct has become warm and normal. He is no longer frozen by what he has so often called "the ambiguity" of female nature. The younger Kirstie is the beginning of a real woman, coquettish, variable, passionate, unabashed by her sexual instincts, powerful in her feeling and undisturbed by her quite conscious desire for power which, we are told by Chaucer, is the chief wish of her sex. And the young Kirstie is matched by old Kirstie, her aunt, who is a woman in the mould of Juliet's nurse. How far both these women are from the wooden heroines of the early novels.

I suppose that within his artificial conventions, Stevenson's distinctive quality is his sense of space. A man so preoccupied with attitude has an eye for placing attitude where it can be most effectively seen, and so he places his scenes at a fitting distance from each other, with an unflurried order and particularity, so that we do not blunder into them but are quietly brought to the point where the view is best. This leisurely expertness of direction makes him a master of narrative, and we are always engaged at once by it. We enjoy it as we enjoy the performance, the clean, cunningly varied speeds and trained movements of an athlete on a long run. In *Weir of Hermiston* Stevenson has extended the application of this sense of space to character. In the portrait of the appalling hanging judge, the Lord Justice Clerk, full to the neck with port, bubbling obscenities, pursuing the wretches in the dock with inhuman witticisms, and sitting up all night on his cases, Stevenson drew one of those three-dimensional and majestic figures which reconcile us to the shocking exigencies of human nature. There is more than a hint of Sheridan Le Fanu's Mr. Justice Harbottle in this portrait, and remarkable as Le Fanu's story is, we must grant that Stevenson's is greater. For if Lord Hermiston is soaked in port and brutality he is also transfigured by authority. He is a good deal more like Justice than the detached and insipid lady with the scales. . . . [*Weir of Hermiston*] has come out of the roots of Stevenson's life, and though the Lord Justice Clerk is a grotesque and heightened creation of the romantic mind, we can hear the accent of Stevenson's own father, in Hermiston's bitter words to his son: "Na, there's no room for splairgers (people who splash about) under the fower quarters of John Calvin."

Stevenson has stopped "splairging"; he has reached the richest moment of life, the moment of power and judgment. He has ceased to act or to romance away from Calvinism. (pp. xii-xiii)

If we ask whether Stevenson could have sustained the imposing architectural plan of *Weir* we are

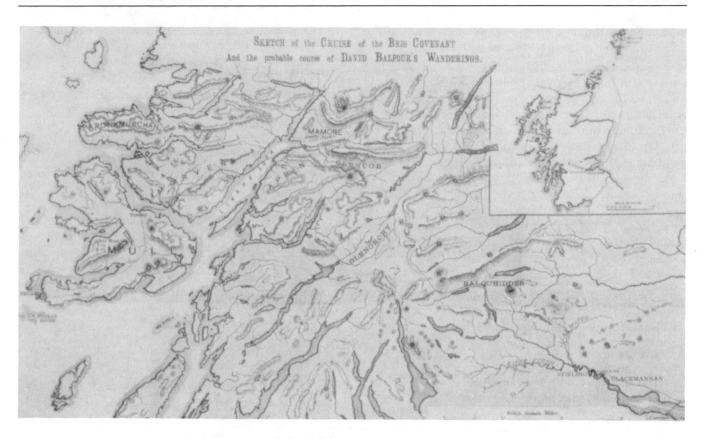

Map from the first edition of *Kidnapped.*

obliged to admit to ourselves that the answer is in doubt. His versatility stands against him. His addiction to words for their own sake has not gone. *Weir,* like *The Master of Ballantrae,* is a mannered book; one can only say that *Weir* has a better manner. And then we cannot forget the narrowness of his range. With Stevenson it is either all youth, or all conscience. His unmistakable contribution to the English novel is a small one, though, when he was writing, it was very important. I repeat, it is his gift of narrative. That is a quality which his plainer successors in our time especially value. His men with a conscience or an air are the fathers of those modern heroes, the tough or the Byronic, who are all air and no conscience. His *Letters,* so many of which were written with one eye on the reading public, are filled with small, exciting examples of the narrator's art and throughout his work he uses the first person singular with a flexibility which our contemporaries must admire. His "I" is something more than the reporter's "I," that is to say, it is not neutral, timeless and uttered in a void, but has some ascertainable human complexity in it. It is an "I" with a background, with a past as well as a present. It has the seductive art of impersonation. (p. xiv)

V. S. Pritchett, in an introduction to *Novels & Stories* by Robert Louis Stevenson, edited by V. S. Pritchett, The Pilot Press, Inc., 1946, pp. vii-xv.

DAVID DAICHES
(essay date 1947)

[In the following excerpt from his influential critical study *Robert Louis Stevenson*, Daiches examines the principal themes and techniques of Stevenson's collection of children's poetry, *A Child's Garden of Verses.*]

The poems of *A Child's Garden of Verses* are almost all attempts to capture some particular and clearly remembered childhood mood or scene, and their effectiveness depends on the extent to which they succeed in doing this. The idea was suggested by Kate Greenaway's *Birthday Book for Children,* but Stevenson's essentially autobiographical poems draw their real inspiration from his own memories. The childhood moods expressed in the poems are fairly limited in number; the same ones recur frequently, establishing principal *motifs* which run through the collection. And the scenes familiar to his childhood similarly recur, though not mentioned by name—the garden of his grandfather's manse at Colinton, his parents' house at 17 Heriot Row, and the cottage at Swanston; and all the sights and sounds of the Edinburgh of the late 1850's and early 1860's.

Stevenson was a sickly child, and as he lay in bed with one of his numerous childhood illnesses he would be forced to depend largely on his imagination for his entertainment. **"The Land of Counterpane"** was all too familiar to him, and the imaginative qualities which this familiarity helped him to cultivate stood him in good stead throughout his childhood and beyond. All his daily activities as a small boy were transmuted into significant and exciting episodes. Travel was a theme that haunted him continually: the river flowing on through unvisited regions to the sea; the road winding away into the unknown—these are recurring symbols, so that even his bed becomes a boat in which to sail away to foreign parts. . . . (pp. 174-75)

This travel theme is found again and again in *A Child's Garden of Verses.* We see it in one of its more elemental forms in **"Foreign Lands":**

Up into the cherry tree
Who should climb but little me?
I held the trunk with both my hands
And looked abroad on foreign lands. . . .

I saw the dimpling river pass
And be the sky's blue looking-glass;
The dusty roads go up and down
With people tramping into town.

And then the child's ambition:

If I could find a higher tree
Farther and farther I should see,
To where the grown-up river slips
Into the sea among the ships. . . .

The simple metrical scheme and the straightforward, concrete imagery convey with great purity the child's view of the world and its activities. We see it again when he writes of sailing paper boats down the stream. . . . (p. 176)

The sense of the world's diversity, the exciting realization of the fact that at any given moment all sorts of different things are happening in all sorts of different places, was continually impressing [Stevenson] as a child. . . . (p. 177)

The idea of a map as the symbol of travel and adventure, which Stevenson used so effectively in *Treasure Island,* underlies many of these poems. The countryside as seen from a treetop, the thin line of the river winding its way through ever further off places into the distant sea, is a favourite image: we hardly need Stevenson's use of the balloon in *St. Ives* to remind us that had he lived in the age of aviation he would have delighted in the idea of the countryside as viewed from an airplane. (pp. 177-78)

The theme of adventure is naturally closely linked to that of travel:

Where shall we adventure, to-day that we're afloat,
Wary of the weather and sterring by a star?
Will it be to Africa, a-steering of the boat,
To Providence, or Babylon, or off to Malabar?

Occasionally a note of adult sophistication creeps into the travel poems:

I should like to rise and go
Where the golden apples grow. . . .

but more often the childhood attitude is remembered and captured:

We built a ship upon the stairs
All made of the back-bedroom chairs,
And filled it full of sofa pillows
To go a-sailing on the billows.

We took a saw and several nails,
And water in the nursery pails;
And Tom said, "Let us also take
An apple and a slice of cake;"—
Which was enough for Tom and me
To go a-sailing on, till tea.

To be at home and yet to enjoy the thrill of travel—this was one of the ideals of Stevenson's childhood. . . . **"From a Railway Carriage,"** describing an experience which neatly combines comfort with adventure, is thus a poem of particular interest. The child sits still and is carried through the map. (pp. 178-79)

Throughout these poems can be found the sights and sounds of the Edinburgh of Stevenson's childhood, as they impinged on the mind of a child. In the summer time, it is the trees and flowers of Colinton Manse and the long light evenings when "I have to go to bed by day." In the winter, it is the warm fireside interior contrasted with the chill dark outside; the lamplighter going on his rounds as the early dusk descends; the indistinct sound of grown-ups talking by the lamplight as the child lies in bed upstairs or hunts imaginary wild animals behind the sofa; the howling wind racing round the city on a stormy night. Stevenson was very sensitive to the changes the different seasons brought to his native city: the two extremes were the sunny "garden days" of mid-summer and the cosy winter interiors:

Sing a song of seasons!
Something bright in all!
Flowers in the summer,
Fires in the fall!

The poems of the *Garden* show an equal lingering over the garden days of summer and the "happy chimney-corner days" of winter: there is "something bright in all" the seasons, and always in describing them he emphasizes specific images drawn from his own childhood memories:

The lamps now glitter down the street;

Faintly sound the falling feet;
And the blue even slowly falls
About the garden trees and walls.

Now in the falling of the gloom
The red fire paints the empty room:
And warmly on the roof it looks,
And flickers on the backs of books.

This is in the true Scottish poetic tradition: Henryson, Dunbar, Fergusson and Burns all excelled in the painting of interiors, and though Stevenson has not the technical skill or the intense poetic imagination of his predecessors, confining himself as he does to the deliberately restricted area of childhood reminiscence, it is impossible not to be struck by this general resemblance. . . . Family resemblance that runs through all these Scottish poets, so different though they are in so many fundamental respects, must be attributed, perhaps, to the northern climate, which emphasizes the difference between the comfortable fireside within and the bleak weather outside. Like Stevenson's, theirs is the poetry of people who live indoors most of the year, and in whose life the contrast between interiors and exteriors is constantly being driven home. Only Steven-

son, whose Colinton days gave him the opportunity to enjoy to the full the brief but memorable outdoor life that a Scottish summer makes possible, adds to these traditional themes that of the wild Edinburgh garden, with all its opportunities for childhood adventure. Later, the moorland and the seacoast were to provide very different open-air experiences, which left their mark on much of his fiction.

The *Child's Garden* thus represents a deliberate attempt on Stevenson's part to recapture the sights, sounds and emotions of his childhood, made at the time when the peace he had finally achieved with his family sent him back to explore those recollections which hitherto he had, in some degree, been forced to suppress. The atmosphere of his early home life, the affectionate care of his nurse Alison Cunningham, . . . and above all the essential quality of the city in which he grew up, are all to be found here. Stevenson was perfectly conscious of the nature of his achievement in these poems. They were written, as he said in the "envoy" addressed to his mother, "for love of unforgotten times." And behind all the poems lies the poignant sense of days of innocence for ever over:

But do not think you can at all,
By knocking on the window, call
That child to hear you. He intent
Is all on his play-business bent.
He does not hear; he will not look,
Nor yet be lured out of this book.
For long ago, the truth to say,
He has grown up and gone away,
And it is but a child of air
That lingers in the garden there.

(pp. 179-82)

The morality of these poems is the somewhat prim morality a child will adopt in those rare moments when, self-satisfied and at peace with his environment, he indulges in a complacent feeling of virtue. Stevenson, affectionately reconciled with his family after a long series of unhappy crises, sees himself as the little boy who has decided to be good. There is thus a "goody-goody" note in many of these poems which sounds hypocritical, but which in fact represents fairly accurately, though in a deliberately simplified form, Stevenson's mood when he began working on the collection:

It is very nice to think
The world is full of meat and drink,
With little children saying grace
In every Christian kind of place.

And yet the underlying emotion of these verses is an adult one, deriving from adult reminiscence. Anyone who compares the *Garden* with its twentieth century English counterpart—A. A. Milne's *When We Were Very Young* and *Now We Are Six*—will notice this at once. Except for the occasional intrusion of a sophisticated note when dealing with the world of nature. . . . Milne's poems seem to derive almost entirely from interested observation of a child's behavior and moods, not, as with Stevenson, from passionately retained personal recollection.

The versification in the *Child's Garden* is technically quite accomplished, though on a fairly simple level. Short, simply constructed stanzas, alternating or couplet rhymes, lines varying in length to correspond in a fairly direct way with the nature of the subject— these features enable Stevenson to cope adequately with his subject-matter and at the same time keep all the poetic devices on a level at which they can be readily appreciated by a young reader. The book is, in fact, first-rate children's poetry—that is, poetry which uses the devices of the poet naively, not sentimentally or corruptly. Good children's poetry is distinguished from bad by the avoidance of sentimental clichés which so many writers of children's verses seem to consider essential to this species of writing, and is distinguished from adult poetry by its use on a lower or simpler level of the techniques employed with greater subtlety in "full-grown" literature. The underlying emotion which we have noted in Stevenson's poems of childhood is not noticeable as an adult sophistication depriving the poems of their simplicity; it acts as a sort of cohesive agent, giving form and unity to the individual poems and to the collection as a whole, and thus adds to, rather than detracts from, the effective presentation of the theme. (pp. 182-84)

David Daiches, in his *Robert Louis Stevenson,* New Directions Books, 1947, 196 p.

ROBERT KIELY

(essay date 1964)

[In the following excerpt, Kiely examines elements of unreality and escape in *Treasure Island*, focusing on the novel's boy hero, Jim Hawkins, and pirate Long John Silver.]

Treasure Island is one of the most satisfying adventure stories ever told primarily because it is the most unhampered. The great pleasure in reading the first few chapters depends not only on the gathering mystery, but on the exhilarating sense of *casting off* which Stevenson gives us. I mean casting off both in the nautical sense of leaving port and in the conventional sense of leaving port and in the conventional sense of throwing off encumbrances. It is the perennial thrill of the schoolboy tossing away his books on the last day of the term or the youth flinging off his sticky clothes for the first swim of the season. What this amounts to is a temporary change of roles, a peeling down to what seems for the moment our least complicated and perhaps our most essential self.

Stevenson begins the process in *Treasure Island* with shameless dispatch by getting rid first of geographical place and time present and all the demands that go with them. We are relieved of place in the first sentence when Jim Hawkins explains that he will keep "nothing back but the bearings of the island, and that only because there is treasure not yet lifted." He then speaks of taking up his pen to write the story "in the year 17—," but, like other "historical romanticists," fails to fill in the last two numbers or to say how long before 17— the adventure actually occurred. He says at the beginning of the second paragraph, in introducing Billy Bones, "I remember him as if it were yesterday," and here we have another notch in our release from time. Not only are we well removed historically, but we are offered as our only authority the imperfect memory of a boy who assures us casually that he recalls past events as though they had all happened the previous day.

We become aware almost at once that Jim Hawkins' memory is anything but flawless. He recalls his first impression of Bones upon his arrival at the Admiral Benbow:

> . . . a tall, strong, heavy, nut-brown man; his tarry pigtail falling over the shoulders of his soiled blue coat; his hands ragged and scarred, with black, broken nails; and the saber cut across one cheek, a dirty, livid white.

And, of course, the stranger immediately breaks into a chorus of "Fifteen men on the dead man's chest." There seem to be a great number of details here, but they would hardly help distinguish Bones, tanned, scarred, and pigtailed, from the general run of disreputable seamen, especially as conceived in the mind of a child who has never seen one. "Character to the boy is a sealed book," Stevenson wrote in **"A Humble Remonstrance."** "For him a pirate is a beard, a pair of wide trousers, and a liberal complement of pistols." Here then is the next item dismissed from the book. We are early relieved of personality except as a costume or disguise which may be put on and off at will.

Before the *Hispaniola* can sail in search of the treasure, the characters must all shed their old selves, determined up until then only by the faintly vocational fact that one is an innkeeper's boy, one a doctor, one a squire, and so forth, and assume the new roles required by the nature of the adventure. As in any game, the assumed roles should and do have some connection with the original talents or inclinations of the character. Just as a strong arm and a straight eye make the best "pitcher" and the smallest boy the best "cox," so the characters of *Treasure Island* are assigned roles which best fit their previously if sketchily established selves. Even the selecting is accomplished, as in a boy's game, by a self-appointed leader who achieves the desired transformation merely by stating it;

"Livesey," said the squire (to the doctor), "you will give up this wretched practice at once . . . we'll have the best ship, sir, and the choicest crew in England. Hawkins shall come as cabin-boy. You'll make a famous cabin-boy, Hawkins. You, Livesey, are ship's doctor; I am admiral."

Only Long John Silver takes on a role not befitting his preestablished character as buccaneer. When he becomes sea-cook aboard the *Hispaniola,* the first ominous rumblings begin which threaten to spoil the game, but really make it interesting.

Perhaps a corollary to the dismissal from the novel of historically measurable time and the complexity of human personality is Stevenson's cavalier casting off of the serious consequences of mortality. It is not that people do not die in *Treasure Island.* They drop on all sides throughout most of the book. There are, of course, the expected casualties among the pirates and the loyal but minor members of the crew, once the fighting gets under way on the island. But the fatalities before that are rather different and particularly indicative of the efficient purpose death serves in the story. The first demise, which takes place in Chapter III, is that of Jim's sick father, who we know is ailing somewhere in an upstairs bedroom, but whom we never meet face to face. Jim's account of the event is characteristically matter-of-fact and inaccurate. "But as things fell out, my poor father died quite suddenly that evening, which put all other matters on one side."

Actually, the death of Jim's father puts nothing aside at all. He is buried in the next paragraph and not mentioned again, while the incidents of the mystery continue to accumulate at the same headlong rate which had been established while he was still alive and ailing. The only thing the death of Jim's father puts aside is Jim's father. Critics are forever trying to read something of Stevenson's youthful difficulties with his own father into the recurring theme of filial isolation in his fiction. (pp. 68-71)

[We] need not reach very far into an author's private relationships to recognize the universal truth that boyish adventures, especially games involving danger, are possible only when the limiting authority symbolized by the male parent is absent. . . . A mother may be overridden, convinced, left temporarily behind. But the father must give way altogether so that his place may be taken by a kind of romantic opposite, dusky and disreputable, a Nigger Jim, a Queequeg, a Long John Silver.

The next two deaths, occurring in fairly rapid

succession before Treasure Island is reached and the main part of the story begins, efficiently eliminate characters who had served as narrative and psychological preliminaries to Long John Silver. Billy Bones and Blind Pew are the first to intrude seriously on the life of the inn at Black Hill Cove as representatives and messengers from a vast and mysterious other world where terror prevails; they also introduce separately the two apparently contradictory aspects of personality combined in Long John Silver.

One role we first see played by Billy Bones, the browned and burly pirate, lusty, loud, and frightening to behold, but basically good-natured and kind. His strong exterior hides not only a kind heart, but a weak one, which is the eventual cause of his death by apoplexy when he receives the black spot. This is the bogieman who turns out to be less of a threat than he had seemed, both kinder *and weaker* than he looked. When Bones dies of a stroke he has served the narrative purpose of bearing the sea chest containing the chart of Treasure Island into the story and the psychological purpose of presenting Jim and the reader with half of what we can expect from Long John Silver. Jim dispenses with Bones quickly, and interestingly enough associates his tearful reaction to his death with leftover emotion from the death of his father.

The other half of Long John Silver and the next character to threaten the order of the Admiral Benbow Inn from a faraway renegade world is Blind Pew. He is the nightmare of every child, and perhaps of every adult—the deformed stranger, apparently harmless, even feeble, offering friendship and requesting help, and suddenly demonstrating unexpected reserves of cruel strength. (pp. 72-3)

When Blind Pew has delivered the black spot, a warning of doom, to Bones, he too has served his narrative purpose and may die. He is stamped to death by horses, but the scene is too swift to be gory. . . . (pp. 73-4)

Death in *Treasure Island* is quick, clean, and above all, efficient for the rapid advancement of the plot. It never provokes a sense of real pathos even in the case of Jim's father, and it is not an impediment in the lives of the surviving characters. On the contrary, especially in the early part of the book, removal of characters by natural or "accidental" means is another step in the process of casting off the potential obstacles to free movement in the adventure to come. Bones and Pew could perhaps have wandered off, run away, disappeared from the plot without dying, when their respective missions were completed. But they would then have lurked in the background of the rest of the story, complicating its essential simplicity with minor but unanswered questions. It is appropriate anyway that these two advance guards from the pirate world, these two preludes to the character of Long John Silver, should die before that legendary and duplex buccaneer is born into the novel twenty pages later.

Long John Silver is the kind of character critics like to give hyphenated names to: villain-as-hero, devil-as-angel, and so forth. Certainly the duplicity of the man justifies these labels even if it does not seem adequately explained by the clichés they have become. Silver appears to be physically weak because of the loss of one of his legs, yet Jim repeatedly notes what a husky man he is and how well he maneuvers even aboard ship. He is capable of being generous, kind, and reasonable, as he demonstrates on the voyage out and at the end of the story when his position on the island is weakened. But he is also capable of uncomplicated cruelty. In both moods he holds a kind of parental sway over Jim. In the early chapters Jim attaches himself to Silver and obeys him for much the same reasons he obeyed Billy Bones, partly out of curiosity, partly out of admiration, and partly out of pity for his physical disability. As for Long John, there is no doubt that he regards Jim Hawkins with paternal affection. " 'Come away, Hawkins,' he would say; 'come and have a yarn with John. Nobody more welcome than yourself, my son.' " And much later, on the island, Silver offers Jim a kind of partnership in piracy in words not unlike those of a self-made man inviting his son to join the family business: "I've always liked you, I have, for a lad of spirit, and the pitcher of my own self when I was young and handsome. I always wanted you to jine and take your share.". . . (pp. 74-5)

But Jim has also seen Silver, like Pew, reveal startling physical power in spite of his debility, and brutality, in spite of his previous kindness. Jim is watching when Tom Morgan, a loyal member of the crew, refuses Silver's invitation to mutiny. The sailor stretches his hand out to Long John: " 'Hands off,' cried Silver, leaping back a yard, as it seemed to me, with the speed and security of the trained gymnast." And when the sailor turns his back and begins to walk away,

> John seized the branch of a tree, whipped the crutch out of his armpit, and sent that uncouth missile hurtling through the air . . . Silver, agile as a monkey, even without leg or crutch, was on top of him next moment, and had twice buried his knife up to the hilt in that defenceless body.

At moments like this it is obviously fear mixed with awe at the athleticism of this supposed cripple that compels Jim. (pp. 75-6)

What, finally, are we to make of Long John Silver? Is he after all the heroic villain or the angelic devil? In a general way he is both. But this anxious reaching out for a permanent judgment overemphasizes the moral dimension of Silver's character and of the whole novel. David Daiches, in an excellent essay, "Stevenson and the Art of Fiction," suggests that

all of Stevenson's novels have a highly sensitive moral pattern . . . Consider even *Treasure Island,* that admirable adventure story . . . What we admire is not always what we approve of . . . That Stevenson was here consciously exploring the desperate ambiguity of man as a moral animal is perhaps too much to say.

I would agree that the structural design of Stevenson's later moral tales is visible in *Treasure Island,* but the "desperate ambiguity of man" seems to me to have been left deliberately—and successfully—unexplored. We should take Stevenson at his word when he explains to Henry James that the luxury in reading a good adventure novel, *Treasure Island* in particular, "is to lay by our judgment, to be submerged by the tale as by a billow."

Silver is a player with two faces, that of the blustering buccaneer with a good heart (like Bones) and that of the cripple with a vicious heart and almost superhuman strength (like Pew). For us to ask which is the "real" Silver, to push aside the whiskers and try to see which of the two roles is better suited to the countenance is unfair, irrelevant to the spirit of the novel, and not worth the trouble because it is impossible to do. It is also unconvincing to attempt integrating Bones and Pew in order to show Silver's double nature as springing from a single psychological source. The contradictory tendencies are not presented as part of a complex personality fraught with tension and paradox. Such a union of traits is not impossible for a novelist to achieve in a seadog. Melville and Conrad both accomplish it. But Stevenson does not do it in *Treasure Island.* And that is another reason for questioning the value of the hyphenated labels. Not only do they stress moral issues where they barely exist, but they imply an integration of Silver's dual roles whereas Stevenson seems to have taken some pains to keep them apart.

One of the pleasures in reading *Treasure Island* is in observing Long John Silver making his repeated "quick changes," alternating rather than growing or developing, bounding back and forth between "Bones" and "Pew." Stevenson again and again allows him to assume his most Pew-like part, unctuous and perfidious, only to be defied and shattered by a verbal barrage from a loyal member of the crew which transforms him into "Bones," a roaring but impotent husk. One of the best examples of Silver's capacity for rapid change is when Captain Smollett replies to his treacherous offer of "protection" if the pirates are given the treasure chart:

> "You can't find the treasure," (said Smollett). "You can't sail the ship—there's not a man among you fit to sail the ship. You can't fight us—Gray, there, got away from five of you. Your ship's in irons, Master Silver . . . and they're the last good words you'll get from me; for, in the name of heaven, I'll put a bullet

in your back when next I meet you. Tramp, my lad. Bundle out of this, please, hand over hand, and double quick."

Smollett speaks to Silver as though he were a bad boy, not only naughty, but bungling in his attempts at villainy. And at once, the fearsome and oleaginous enemy becomes a comic, almost pathetic, buffoon, bellowing hollow threats. Retreating without dignity, he literally "crawled along the sand" to safety.

Jim, too, gets in his verbal "licks" against the pirate chief when he falls into the enemy's hands and things are looking blackest for him. He pelts the Pew-disguise with a furious tirade and concludes by shouting: "I no more fear you than I fear a fly."

What self-respecting pirate would take this kind of talk from a child? None at all, of course, but then as we have pointed out, Silver is given no self to respect. There is no basic personality from which he may derive strength when challenged or to which the reader may assign responsibility when Silver himself is doing the threatening. He is a weed that flourishes in ideal conditions but shrivels without resistance at the first sign of opposition. The point of the story as well as the pleasure in reading it is in the active conflict, not in its cause or even its final result. To try to speak seriously of good or evil in *Treasure Island* is almost as irrelevant as attempting to assign moral value in a baseball game, even though a presumable requisite to enjoying the contest involves a temporary if arbitrary preference for one side or the other.

The fuss that some critics have made over Silver's escape with a small part of the treasure at the end of the book as a sign of Stevenson's moral softness or of his "liberation" from strict Calvinist dogma seems rather foolish. Silver has murdered, robbed, and lied, but he has also been a good cook, a remarkable physical specimen in spite of his lost leg, and a rather affectionate if irresponsible replacement for Jim's dead father. Above all, he has been entertaining, and in a timeless, placeless, nearly conscienceless world, Stevenson seems justified in paying him off and sending him packing. To have killed him would have implied a punishment, a moral judgment Stevenson apparently did not want to make in this book. By the same token, to have rewarded him too generously or to have brought about his conversion would also have introduced a

moral element not anticipated by anything earlier in the novel and therefore hardly appropriate at the conclusion. (pp. 76-9)

Later on, most obviously in *Dr. Jekyll and Mr. Hyde* and in *The Master of Ballantrae,* Stevenson returns to the theme of the double personality and tries with varying success to raise in the midst of melodrama serious moral and psychological questions. But it is important to see that his first impulse is to play a game and to teach us nothing more or less than how to play it with him. *Treasure Island* belongs not in the ironic mold of *Huckleberry Finn,* in which the adult world is seen through the eyes of a boy for what it really is. Without the transcendental overtones, it follows more closely in the tradition of Blake's *Songs of Innocence* and Wordsworth's "We Are Seven." The child is isolated from the adult world, protected from it by his own lack of experience, and does not really see it at all except in imperfect and distorted glimpses. We learn precious little about the psychology of evil from Long John Silver and nothing of real consequence about nineteenth-century morality from reading *Treasure Island.*

William Golding's *Lord of the Flies,* as a serious variation on the theme of boys' adventure, may make twentieth-century readers suspicious of the ingenuousness of a *Treasure Island* or a *Swiss Family Robinson.* In fact, it must have been intended, in part, as an antiromantic antidote to that "escapist" genre. But it ought to be remembered that, unlike *Treasure Island* and despite its popularity among adolescents, *Lord of the Flies* depends almost entirely on adult assumptions for its effectiveness as a novel. Moreover, one of the ironies of the book is that, for any of the youngest participants, the whole ghastly episode might have been regarded, even to the end, as little more than an exciting (if bewildering) romp on a desert island. It is this limited attitude toward reality, without benefit of adult insinuation, which Stevenson sought to capture in *Treasure Island.* His extraordinary success depended largely on his early conviction that, with respect to certain areas of experience, the child's amoral view was perfectly valid. (pp. 79-80)

Robert Kiely, in his *Robert Louis Stevenson and the Fiction of Adventure,* Cambridge, Mass.: Harvard University Press, 1964, 285 p.

SOURCES FOR FURTHER STUDY

Balfour, Graham. *The Life of Robert Louis Stevenson.* Rev. ed. New York: Charles Scribner's Sons, 1915, 364 p.

> Biography, approved by Stevenson's family, that was chief among the many works following upon the author's death that sought to polish Stevenson's public image. Many scholars hold that works such as this contributed to the critical backlash against Stevenson that began in the 1920s.

Chesterton, G. K. *Robert Louis Stevenson.* New York: Dodd, Mead & Co., 1928, 211 p.

> Critical biography that defends Stevenson against early hostile criticisms, and that, unlike earlier Stevenson criticism, approaches the study of the author by focusing on his work rather than details of his personal life.

Furnas, J. C. *Voyage to Windward: The Life of Robert Louis Stevenson.* New York: William Sloane Associates, 1951, 566 p.

> A comprehensive and balanced biography that makes use of much previously unavailable material on the author.

Maixner, Paul, ed. *Robert Louis Stevenson.* The Critical Heritage Series, edited by B. C. Southam. London: Routledge & Kegan Paul, 1981, 532 p.

> Collection of critical writings on Stevenson, primarily from the nineteenth century.

Osbourne, Lloyd. *An Intimate Portrait of R. L. S.* New York: Charles Scribner's Sons, 1924, 155 p.

> A personal reminiscence of Stevenson by his stepson.

Steuart, J. A. *Robert Louis Stevenson: Man and Writer.* London: Sampson Low, Marston & Co., 1924, 655 p.

> A biography written largely as a reaction against early accounts of Stevenson's life, such as the one by Graham Balfour (see above) that sought to lionize the writer. Steuart's intent, he writes, is to "make [Stevenson] out a living, breathing human being."

ISBN 0-8103-8366-7